Lecture Notes in Computer Science 16768

The series Lecture Notes in Computer Science (LNCS), including its subseries Lecture Notes in Artificial Intelligence (LNAI) and Lecture Notes in Bioinformatics (LNBI), has established itself as a medium for the publication of new developments in computer science and information technology research, teaching, and education.

LNCS enjoys close cooperation with the computer science R & D community, the series counts many renowned academics among its volume editors and paper authors, and collaborates with prestigious societies. Its mission is to serve this international community by providing an invaluable service, mainly focused on the publication of conference and workshop proceedings and postproceedings. LNCS commenced publication in 1973.

Osvaldo Gervasi · Beniamino Murgante ·
Chiara Garau · Ana Maria A.C. Rocha ·
M. Noelia Faginas Lago · David Taniar ·
Yeliz Karaca
Editors

Computational Science and Its Applications – ICCSA 2026

26th International Conference
Braga, Portugal, June 30 – July 3, 2026
Proceedings, Part II

Springer

Editors
Osvaldo Gervasi
University of Perugia
Perugia, Italy

Chiara Garau
University of Cagliari
Cagliari, Italy

M. Noelia Faginas Lago
University of Perugia
Perugia, Italy

Yeliz Karaca
University of Massachusetts
Amherst, MA, USA

Beniamino Murgante
University of Basilicata
Potenza, Italy

Ana Maria A.C. Rocha
University of Minho
Braga, Portugal

David Taniar
Monash University
Melbourne, VIC, Australia

ISSN 0302-9743 ISSN 1611-3349 (electronic)
Lecture Notes in Computer Science
ISBN 978-3-032-30487-2 ISBN 978-3-032-30488-9 (eBook)
https://doi.org/10.1007/978-3-032-30488-9

This Springer imprint is published by the registered company Springer Nature Switzerland AG
The registered company address is: Gewerbestrasse 11, 6330 Cham, Switzerland

Preface

These 3 volumes (LNCS volumes 16767–16769) comprise the peer-reviewed papers from the 6 tracks of the 2026 International Conference on Computational Science and Its Applications (ICCSA 2026), held between June 30 and July 3, 2026, in Braga (Portugal). The peer-reviewed papers from the 57 Workshops are published in a separate set of 9 volumes (LNCS 16758–16766).

The conference was held in a hybrid format, with the vast majority of participants attending in person, hosted by the University of Minho in Braga, Portugal. We enabled virtual participation for those who did not attend the event in person due to logistical, political, or economic constraints by adopting a technological infrastructure based on open-source software (Jitsi + Riot) and a commercial Cloud infrastructure. ICCSA 2026 was organized by the University of Minho (Portugal), the University of Perugia (Italy), the University of Basilicata (Italy), the University of Cagliari (Italy), Monash University (Australia), and Kyushu Sangyo University (Japan).

With the 2026 edition, ICCSA celebrated its 26th anniversary, marking a new chapter in its longstanding history after its memorable 25th anniversary celebrated in Istanbul, Türkiye. Hosted in Braga, Portugal, the conference found a particularly meaningful setting in one of Europe's oldest and most vibrant academic cities, a place where historical depth, cultural continuity, and contemporary scientific exchange meet. Braga offers an inspiring European context for renewing the international and intercultural dialogue that has always characterized ICCSA, while giving new visibility to the role of computational science in addressing the complex challenges of cities, territories, technologies, and societies.

ICCSA 2026 marked another fruitful and thought-provoking academic event in the International Conferences on Computational Science and Its Applications (ICCSA) conference series, previously held in Istanbul, Türkiye (2025), Hanoi, Vietnam (2024), Athens, Greece (2023), Málaga, Spain (2022), Cagliari, Italy (hybrid with few participants in presence in 2021 and completely online in 2020), whilst earlier editions took place in Saint Petersburg, Russia (2019), Melbourne, Australia (2018), Trieste, Italy (2017), Beijing, China (2016), Banff, Canada (2015), Guimarães, Portugal (2014), Ho Chi Minh City, Vietnam (2013), Salvador, Brazil (2012), Santander, Spain (2011), Fukuoka, Japan (2010), Suwon, South Korea (2009), Perugia, Italy (2008), Kuala Lumpur, Malaysia (2007), Glasgow, UK (2006), Singapore (2005), Assisi, Italy (2004), Montreal, Canada (2003), and (as ICCS) Amsterdam, the Netherlands (2002) and San Francisco, USA (2001).

Computational Science constitutes the main pillar of most present research, industrial and commercial applications, and plays a unique role in exploiting innovative ICT technologies, and the ICCSA conference series has, accordingly, provided ample opportunities to researchers and industry practitioners to discuss new ideas, to share complex problems and their solutions, and to shape new trends in Computational Science. As the conference mirrors society from a scientific point of view, this year's undoubtedly dominant theme was large language models, machine learning, and Artificial Intelligence (AI), and their applications across the most diverse technological, economic, and industrial fields, amongst others.

The ICCSA 2026 conference was structured into six general tracks covering computational science and its applications: Computational Methods, Algorithms and Scientific Applications; High-Performance Computing and Networks; Geometric Modelling, Graphics and Visualisation; Advanced and Emerging Applications; Information Systems and Technologies; and Urban and Regional Planning. In addition, the conference included 57 workshops, focusing on topical issues of utmost importance to science, technology, and society: from new computational approaches for earth science, to mathematical methods for image processing, new statistical and optimisation methods, several Artificial Intelligence approaches, sustainability issues, smart cities and related technologies, to name some.

In the Main Conference Proceedings, we accepted 119 full papers, 3 short papers and 2 Ph.D. Showcase papers on 405 submissions to the General Tracks of the Conference (with an acceptance rate of 29.9%). Reviews were single blind, and submissions received 2.6 reviews each, on average. In the Workshops proceedings, we accepted 321 full papers, 23 short papers and 3 Ph.D. Showcase papers from a total of 1184 submissions (Acceptance rate 29.9%). We would like to convey our sincere appreciation to the workshop chairs and co-chairs, and program committee members, for their diligent work, commitment, and dedication.

The success and consistent maintenance of the ICCSA conference series in general, and of ICCSA 2026 in particular, rely upon the support of many people: authors, presenters, participants, keynote speakers, workshop chairs, session chairs, Organizing Committee members, student volunteers, Program Committee members, Advisory Committee members, International Liaison chairs, reviewers, and other individuals in various roles. Thus, we take this opportunity to wholeheartedly thank each and every one.

We also wish to thank the publisher, Springer, for accepting the proceedings, for sponsoring part of the best paper awards, and for their kind assistance and cooperation during the editing process. We would cordially like to invite you to refer to the ICCSA website https://iccsa.org, where you can find the relevant details regarding this academic endeavour and our event.

June 2026

Chiara Garau
Ana Maria A. C. Rocha
Osvaldo Gervasi
Beniamino Murgante

Welcome Message from the Organizers

On behalf of the Local Organizing Committee of ICCSA 2026, it is our great pleasure to welcome you to the 26th International Conference on Computational Science and Its Applications, held from June 30 to July 3, 2026, at the University of Minho in Braga, Portugal.

We are deeply honoured by the trust placed in us by the ICCSA General Chairs in organizing another edition of this successful conference series. We hope that ICCSA 2026 provided an inspiring environment for scientific exchange, collaboration, and discussion among researchers from all over the world.

The conference took place at the University of Minho, one of the most prestigious higher education institutions in Portugal. Founded in 1973, the University of Minho has campuses in Braga and Guimarães and is widely recognized for its academic excellence, research activity, and strong international outlook.

Braga, one of the oldest cities in Portugal, is renowned for its historical heritage, cultural vitality, and welcoming atmosphere. Located in the heart of the Minho region, the city combines tradition with modernity, offering visitors renowned gastronomy, beautiful landscapes, and the unique character of *Vinho Verde* wine.

The scientific program of ICCSA 2026 included plenary lectures delivered by distinguished scientists, together with a broad range of workshops covering several areas of Computational Science and its Applications. We believe that the conference provided excellent opportunities to share ideas, discuss emerging challenges, and foster new collaborations.

In addition to the scientific sessions, participants had the opportunity to enjoy a rich social program. Planned activities included a Welcome Reception at Largo do Paço, the Rectorate of the University of Minho, located in the former Archbishop's Palace - one of the most emblematic historical buildings in the city center; a *Vinho Verde* wine tasting experience at Quinta d'Amares, where you can discover the art of winemaking; and a guided visit to the coastal city of Viana do Castelo, renowned for its maritime heritage, traditional architecture, and beautiful Atlantic scenery. The conference gala dinner took place at Colunata Eventos, located within the Bom Jesus do Monte sanctuary, a UNESCO World Heritage Site, where ICCSA participants enjoyed delicious recipes and a wonderful view over the city of Braga.

The success of ICCSA 2026 would not have been possible without the dedication and enthusiasm of many collaborators and volunteers, whose hard work and commitment greatly contributed to the organization of the conference. On behalf of the Local Organizing Committee, it was our honour to warmly welcome you to the beautiful city of Braga and we hope you had an enjoyable and productive conference.

Sincerely yours,

On behalf of the Local Organizing Committee

Ana Maria A. C. Rocha

Organization

Honorary General Chairs

Bernady O. Apduhan	Kyushu Sangyo University, Japan
Kenneth C. J. Tan	Sardina Systems, UK

General Chairs

Ana Maria A. C. Rocha	University of Minho, Portugal
David Taniar	Monash University, Australia
Osvaldo Gervasi	University of Perugia, Italy

Program Committee Chairs

Beniamino Murgante	University of Basilicata, Italy
Chiara Garau	University of Cagliari, Italy

International Advisory Committee

Jemal Abawajy	Deakin University, Australia
Dharma P. Agarwal	University of Cincinnati, USA
Jagannath Aryal	University of Melbourne, Australia
Rajkumar Buyya	University of Melbourne, Australia
Claudia Bauzer Medeiros	University of Campinas, Brazil
Carl K. Chang	Iowa State University, USA
Elizabeth Chang	University of the Sunshine Coast, Australia
Manfred M. Fisher	Vienna University of Economics and Business, Austria
Pierre Frankhauser	University of Franche-Comté/CNRS, France
Marina L. Gavrilova	University of Calgary, Canada
Sumi Helal	University of Florida, USA & Lancaster University, UK
Bin Jiang	University of Gävle, Sweden
Yee Leung	Chinese University of Hong Kong, China
Biswajeet Pradhan	University of Technology Sydney, Australia
My Thai	University of Florida, USA

International Liaison Chairs

Giuseppe Borruso	University of Trieste, Italy
Elise De Donker	Western Michigan University, USA
Maria Noelia Faginas Lago	University of Perugia, Italy
Maria Irene Falcão	University of Minho, Portugal
Robert C. H. Hsu	Chung Hua University, Taiwan
Yeliz Karaca	UMass Chan Medical School, USA
Tae-Hoon Kim	Zhejiang University of Science and Technology, China
Vladimir Korkhov	Saint Petersburg University, Russia
Takashi Naka	Kyushu Sangyo University, Japan
Rafael D. C. Santos	National Institute for Space Research, Brazil
Maribel Yasmina Santos	University of Minho, Portugal
Anastasia Stratigea	National Technical University of Athens, Greece
Nguyen Canh Thai	Thuyloi University, Vietnam
Kh Md Nahiduzzaman	Mohammed VI Polytechnic University, Rabat, Morocco

Workshop and Session Organizing Chairs

Beniamino Murgante	University of Basilicata, Italy
Chiara Garau	University of Cagliari, Italy

Award Chair

Wenny Rahayu	La Trobe University, Australia

Publicity Committee Chairs

Elmer Dadios	De La Salle University, Philippines
Nataliia Kulabukhova	Saint Petersburg University, Russia
Daisuke Takahashi	Tsukuba University, Japan
Doan Quang Tu	Academy of Military Science and Technology, Vietnam
Shangwang Wang	Beijing University of Posts and Telecommunications, China

Local Organizing Committee Chairs

Maria Irene Falcão	University of Minho, Portugal
Ana Cristina Braga	University of Minho, Portugal
Rui José	University of Minho, Portugal
José Manuel Machado	University of Minho, Portugal
Jorge G. Rocha	University of Minho, Portugal

Technology Chair

Damiano Perri	University of Perugia, Italy

Program Committee

Vera Afreixo	University of Aveiro, Portugal
Vladimir Alarcon	Northern Gulf Institute, USA
Filipe Alvelos	University of Minho, Portugal
Debora Anelli	Polytechnic University of Bari, Italy
Muhammad Waqas Arshad	University of Bologna, Italy
Vittorio Astarita	University of Calabria, Italy
Hartmut Asche	Hasso-Plattner-Institut für Digital Engineering Ggmbh, Germany
Nizamettin Aydın	İstanbul Technical University, Türkiye
Ginevra Balletto	University of Cagliari, Italy
Nadia Balucani	University of Perugia, Italy
Socrates Basbas	Aristotle University of Thessaloniki, Greece
David Berti	ART SpA, Italy
Sandro Bimonte	CEMAGREF, TSCF, France
Ana Cristina Braga	University of Minho, Portugal
Tiziana Campisi	University of Enna KORE, Italy
Alessandra Capolupo	Polytechnic of Bari, Italy
Leocadio G. Casado	University of Almeria, Spain
Ilaria Catapano	National Research Council, IREA, Italy
Maria Cerreta	University of Naples Federico II, Italy
Rachel Chien-Sing Lee	Sunway University, Malaysia
Birol Ciloglugil	Ege University, Turkey
Florbela Maria da Cruz Domingues Correia	Polytechnic Institute of Viana do Castelo, Portugal
Alessandro Costantini	INFN, Italy
Roberto De Lotto	University of Pavia, Italy
Luiza De Macedo Mourelle	State University of Rio De Janeiro, Brazil

Marcelo De Paiva Guimaraes	Federal University of São Paulo, Brazil
Marco De Santis	University of Salerno, Italy
Frank Devai	London South Bank University, UK
Joana Matos Dias	University of Coimbra, Portugal
Aziz Dursun	Virginia Tech University, USA
Laila El Ghandour	Heriot Watt University, UK
Maria Irene Falcão	University of Minho, Portugal
Florbela P. Fernandes	Polytechnic Institute of Bragança, Portugal
Paula Odete Fernandes	Polytechnic Institute of Bragança, Portugal
Adelaide de Fátima Baptista Valente Freitas	University of Aveiro, Portugal
Andreas Fricke	University of Potsdam, Germany
Raffaele Garrisi	Centro Operativo per la Sicurezza Cibernetica, Italy
Ivan Gerace	University of Perugia, Italy
Maria Giaoutzi:	National Technical University of Athens, Greece
Salvatore Giuffrida	University of Catania, Italy
Teresa Guarda	Universidad Estatal Península de Santa Elena, Ecuador
Gabriel Guerrero Contreras	University of Cádiz, Spain
Malgorzata Hanzl	Technical University of Lodz, Poland
Maulana Adhinugraha Kiki	Telkom University, Indonesia
JungYoon Kim	Gachon University, South Korea
Clement Ho Cheung Leung	Chinese University of Hong Kong, China
Andrea Lombardi	University of Perugia, Italy
Marcos Mandado Alonso	University of Vigo, Spain
Ernesto Marcheggiani	Katholieke Universiteit Leuven, Belgium
Barbara Martelli	INFN, Italy
Antonino Marvuglia	Luxembourg Institute of Science and Technology, Luxembourg
Michele Mastroianni	University of Salerno, Italy
Hideo Matsufuru	High Energy Accelerator Research Organization, Japan
Fernando Miranda	Universidade do Minho, Portugal
Giuseppe Modica	University of Reggio Calabria, Italy
Majaz Moonis	UMass Chan Medical School, USA
Leila Moradi	University of Salerno, Italy
Nadia Nedjah	State University of Rio de Janeiro, Brazil
Paolo Nesi	University of Florence, Italy
Suzan Obaiys	University of Malaya, Malaysia
Marcin Paprzycki	Polish Academy of Sciences, Poland
Eric Pardede	La Trobe University, Australia

Ana Isabel Pereira	Polytechnic Institute of Bragança, Portugal
Damiano Perri	University of Perugia, Italy
Massimiliano Petri	University of Pisa, Italy
Telmo Pinto	University of Coimbra, Portugal
Maurizio Pollino	ENEA, Italy
Marcos Quiles	Federal University of São Paulo, Brazil
Nguyen Huu Quynh	Thuyloi University, Vietnam
Albert Rimola	Universitat Autònoma de Barcelona, Spain
Humberto Rocha	University of Coimbra, Portugal
Marzio Rosi	University of Perugia, Italy
Lucia Saganeiti	University of L'Aquila, Italy
Francesco Scorza	University of Basilicata, Italy
Marco Paulo Seabra dos Reis	University of Coimbra, Portugal
Jie Shen	University of Michigan, USA
Bruno Sousa	University of Coimbra, Portugal
Francesco Tajani	Sapienza University of Rome, Italy
Daniela Tavano	University of Calabria, Italy
Ho Sy Tam	Thuyloi University, Vietnam
Deodato Tapete	Italian Space Agency ASI, Italy
Rodrigo Tapia-McClung	Centro de Investigación en Ciencias de Información Geoespacial, Mexico
Tarek Teba	University of Portsmouth, UK
Ana Paula Teixeira	Universidade do Minho, Portugal
Luis Teodoro	University of Oslo, Norway
Yiota Theodora	National Technical University of Athens, Greece
Elena Todella	Polytechnic University of Turin, Italy
Graca Tomaz	Instituto Politécnico da Guarda, Portugal
Anna Tonazzini	National Research Council, Italy
Francesca Torrieri	Polytechnic University of Milan, Italy
Vincenza Torrisi	University of Catania, Italy
Vincenzo Totaro	Polytechnic University of Bari, Italy
Arianna Travaglini	University of Basilicata, Italy
Stefanos Tsigdinos	National Technical University of Athens, Greece
Aime Tsinda	University of Rwanda, Rwanda
Elen Twrdy	University of Ljubljana, Slovenia
Doan Quang Tu	Academy of Military Science and Technology, Vietnam
Le Quang Tuan	Thuyloi University, Vietnam
Toshihiro Uchibayashi	Kyushu University, Japan
Fukuko Yuasa	High Energy Accelerator Research Organization, Japan
Ljiljana Zivkovic	Republic Geodetic Authority, Serbia

General Tracks

1. Computational Methods, Algorithms and Scientific Applications

Computational Biology
Computational Combustion
Computational Chemistry
Computational Fluid Dynamics
Computational Physics
Computational Geometry
Computational Mathematics
Computational Mechanics
Computational Electro-magnetics
Numerical Methods and Algorithms

2. Track: High Performance Computing and Networks

Parallel and Distributed Computing
Cluster Computing
Supercomputing
Cloud Computing
Autonomic Computing
P2P Computing
Mobile Computing
Edge Computing
Workflow Design and Practice
Computer and Network Architecture

3. Track: Geometric Modeling, Graphics and Visualization

Scientific Visualization
Computer Graphics
Geometric Modeling
Pattern Recognition
Image Processing
CAD/CAM
Web3D, Virtual and Augmented Reality

4. Track: Advanced and Emerging Applications

Biochemistry
Bioinformatics
Astrophysics

Biometric Modeling
Environmental, Climate and Weather Modeling
Geology and Geophysics
Nuclear Physics
Financial and Economical Modeling
Computational Journalism

5. Track: Information Systems and Technologies

Information Retrieval
Scientific Databases
Security Engineering
Risk Analysis
Reliability Engineering
Software Engineering
Data Mining
Artificial Intelligence
Machine Learning
Learning Technologies
Web Based Computing
Web 2.0
Blockchain

6. Track: Urban and Regional Planning

Urban and regional growth
Sustainable urban and regional development
Socio-ecological systems
Open Data- Big Data
Cultural Heritage
Smart and Sustainable Cities
Mobility and Intelligent Transport Systems
Geographical Information Systems
Decision Support Systems
Complexity assessment and mapping
Logistics

Workshops

Workshop on Advancements in Applied Machine-Learning and Data Analytics (AAMDA 2026)

Workshop Organizers:

Alessandro Costantini	INFN, Italy
Elisabetta Ronchieri	INFN CNAF, Italy

Artificial Intelligence Tools In Managing Future Communities (AiMFutCOM 2026)

Workshop Organizers:

Marco Vona	University of Basilicata, Italy
Francesco Scorza	University of Basilicata, Italy
Donatello Cardone	University of Basilicata, Italy
Maurizio Pollino	ENEA, Italy
Gregorio DAgostino	ENEA, Italy

Advanced and Innovative Web Apps 2026 (AIWA 2026)

Workshop Organizers:

Damiano Perri	University of Perugia, Italy
Osvaldo Gervasi	University of Perugia, Italy
Luciano Alessandro Ipsaro Palesi	University of Florence, Italy

Advanced Mathematics and Computing Models in Complex Data-Intensive Computational Systems (AMCM 2026)

Workshop Organizers:

Yeliz Karaca	UMass Chan Medical School and Massachusetts Institute of Technology, USA
Dumitru Baleanu	Lebanese American University, Lebanon
Osvaldo Gervasi	University of Perugia, Italy
Yudong Zhang	University of Leicester, UK
Majaz Moonis	UMass Chan Medical School, USA

Advanced Numerical Approaches for Assessment and Design of No-Tension Masonry Structures (ANAMS 2026)

Workshop Organizers:

Antonino Iannuzzo	Universitá degli studi del Sannio, Italy
Natalia Pingaro	Politecnico di Milano, Italy
Andrea Montanino	International Centre for Numerical Methods in Engineering, Spain
Elham Mousavian	University of Edinburgh, UK
Stefano Galassi	University of Florence, Italy

Artificialization of land, Urban Transformation, and Territorial Resilience in a Changing Climate (AUTTREC 2026)

Workshop Organizers:

Celestina Fazia	Università di Enna Kore, Italy
Kh Md Nahiduzzaman	Mohammed VI Polytechnic University, Morocco
Hassan Radoine	Mohammed VI Polytechnic University, Morocco
Cezar Morar	University of Oradea, Romania
Antonio García Martínez	Universidad de Sevilla, Spain
Clara Stella Vicari Aversa	Università degli Studi Mediterranea di Reggio Calabria, Italy

Blockchain and Distributed Ledgers: Technologies and Applications (BDLTA 2026)

Workshop Organizers:

Vladimir Korkhov	Saint Petersburg State University, Russia
Elena Stankova	Saint Petersburg State University, Russia
Nataliia Kulabukhova	AutoTech, Russia

Bio and Neuro inspired Computing and Applications (BIONCA 2026)

Workshop Organizers:

Nadia Nedjah	State University of Rio de Janeiro, Brazil
Luiza de Macedo Mourelle	State University de Rio de Janeiro, Brazil

Computational and Applied Mathematics (CAM 2026)

Workshop Organizers:

Maria Irene Falcao	University of Minho, Portugal
Fernando Miranda	Universidade do Minho, Portugal

Computational and Applied Statistics for Data and AI (CAS 2026)

Workshop Organizers:

Ana Cristina Braga	University of Minho, Portugal
Ines Sena	University of Minho, Portugal
Joao Mendes	Polytechnic Institute of Bragança, Portugal

Circular Economy and Territorial Competitiveness (CETC 2026)

Workshop Organizers:

Gerardo Carpentieri	University of Naples Federico II, Italy
Carmen Guida	Università degli Studi di Napoli Federico II, Italy
Floriana Zucaro	University of Naples Federico II, Italy
Zhadyra Konurbaeva	D. Serikbayev East Kazakhstan Technical University, Kazakhstan
Saule Kumargazhanova	D.Serikbayev East Kazakhstan Technical University, Kazakhstan

Circular Ecological Heritage Communities: Regeneration and Evaluation Strategies for Historic Villages, Landscapes and Rural Territories (CHEC 2026)

Workshop Organizers:

Mariarosaria Angrisano	Pegaso University, Italy
Antonia Gravagnuolo	CNR Institute of Heritage Science, Italy
Francesca Buglione	CNR ISPC, Italy
Piera Della Morte	Pegaso Telematic University, Italy

Cyber Intelligence and Applications (CIA 2026)

Workshop Organizers:

Gianni DAngelo	University of Salerno, Italy
Francesco Palmieri	University of Salerno, Italy
Massimo Ficco	University of Salerno, Italy

Computational Methods, Statistics and Industrial Mathematics (CMSIM 2026)

Workshop Organizers:

Maria Filomena Teodoro	CINAV, Escola Naval, Instituto Universitário Militar, Portugal
Paula Simões	Academia Militar, Portugal
Teresa A. Oliveira	University of Lisbon and Universidade Aberta, Portugal

Computational Optimization and Applications (COA 2026)

Workshop Organizers:

Ana Maria A. C. Rocha	University of Minho, Portugal
Humberto Rocha	University of Coimbra, Portugal

Computational Methods in Advanced Networking Technologies (CoMANT 2026)

Workshop Organizers:

Eslam Farsimadan	University of Salerno, Italy
Leila Moradi	University of Salerno, Italy
Francesco Palmieri	University of Salerno, Italy

Computational Astrochemistry 2026 (CompAstro 2026)

Workshop Organizers:

Marzio Rosi	University of Perugia, Italy
Daniela Ascenzi	Università degli Studi di Trento, Italy
Nadia Balucani	University of Perugia, Italy
Stefano Falcinelli	University of Perugia, Italy

Computational Methods for Porous Materials (CompPor 2026)

Workshop Organizers:

Vadim Lisitsa	Institute of Petroleum Geology and Geophysics SB RAS, Russia
Evgeniy Romenski	Sobolev Institute of Mathematics, Russia

Workshop on Computational Science and HPC (CSHPC 2026)

Workshop Organizers:

Elise de Doncker	Western Michigan University, USA
Hideo Matsufuru	High Energy Accelerator Research Organization, Japan
Robert Makin	Western Michigan University, USA

Cities, Technologies and Planning (CTP 2026)

Workshop Organizers:

Giuseppe Borruso	University of Trieste, Italy
Beniamino Murgante	University of Basilicata, Italy
Malgorzata Hanzl	Lodz University of Technology, Poland
Anastasia Stratigea	National Technical University of Athens, Greece
Ljiljana Zivkovic	Republic Geodetic Authority, Serbia
Ginevra Balletto	University of Cagliari, Italy

Evaluating Inner Areas Potentials (EIAP 2026)

Workshop Organizers:

Diana Rolando	Politecnico di Torino, Italy
Manuela Rebaudengo	Politecnico di Torino, Italy
Alice Barreca	Politecnico di Torino, Italy
Giorgia Malavasi	Politecnico di Torino, Italy

sustainablE mobiLity and Last mIle lOgisTic in Urban Context (ELLIOT 2026)

Workshop Organizers:

Tiziana Campisi	University of Enna Kore, Italy
Socrates Basbas	Aristotle University of Thessaloniki, Greece
Florin Rusca	National University of Science and Technology Politehnica Bucharest, Romania
Grigorios Fountas	Aristotle University of Thessaloniki, Greece
Aleksandra Deluka-Tibljas	University of Rijeka, Croatia

Econometrics and Multidimensional Evaluation in Urban Environment (EMEUE 2026)

Workshop Organizers:

Maria Cerreta	University of Naples Federico II, Italy
Giuseppe Ciciriello	University of Naples Federico II, Italy
Simona Panaro	University of Sussex Business School, UK
Piero Zizzania	Università of Naples Federico II, Italy
Pierluigi Morano	Polytechnic University of Bari, Italy
F rancesco Tajani	Sapienza University of Rome, Italy

Ecosystem Services in Spacial Planning for Climate Neutral Urban and Rural Areas (ESSP 2026)

Workshop Organizers:

Sabrina Lai	University of Cagliari. Italy
Carmela Gargiulo	Università Federico II di Napoli, Italy
Beniamino Murgante	University of Basilicata, Italy
Francesco Scorza	University of Basilicata, Italy
Corrado Zoppi	University of Cagliari, Italy
Floriana Zucaro	University of Naples Federico II, Italy

The 16th International Workshop on Future Information System Technologies and Applications (FiSTA 2026)

Workshop Organizers:

Bernady O. Apduhan	Kyushu Sangyo University, Japan
Rafael Santos	National Institute for Space Research (INPE), Brazil

Geographical Analysis, Urban Modeling, Spatial Statistics (Geog-And-Mod 2026)

Workshop Organizers:

Giuseppe Borruso	University of Trieste, Italy
Beniamino Murgante	University of Basilicata, Italy
Hartmut Asche	Hasso Plattner Institute for Digital Engineering, Germany
Rodrigo Tapia McClung	Centro de Investigación en Ciencias de Información Geoespacial, Mexico
Andreas Fricke	Hasso Plattner Institute for Digital Engineering, University of Potsdam, Germany

Generative and Neuro-Symbolic Artificial Intelligence for Real-World Systems (GNS-AI 2026)

Workshop Organizers:

Hugo Peixoto	University of Minho, Portugal
Manuel Rodrigues	University of Minho, Portugal
Regina Sousa	University of Minho, Portugal

Geomatics for Resource Monitoring and Management (GRMM 2026)

Workshop Organizers:

Alberico Sonnessa	Politecnico di Bari, Italy
Eufemia Tarantino	Politecnico di Bari, Italy
Marco Locurcio	Polytechnic University of Bari, Italy

International Workshop on Information and Knowledge in the Internet of Things (IKIT 2026)

Workshop Organizers:

Teresa Guarda	Universidad Estatal Península de Santa Elena, Ecuador

Intelligent Sustainable Development: from Models to Real-World Impact (ISD 2026)

Workshop Organizers:

Diego Brandão	Federal Center for Technological Education of Rio de Janeiro, Brazil
Angela Ferreira	Polytechnic University of Bragança, Portugal
Eduardo Bezerra	Federal Center for Technological Education of Rio de Janeiro, Brazil
Raphael Guerra	Universidade Federal Fluminense, Brazil
Douglas Cardoso	University of Coimbra, Portugal
Rui Pedro Lopes	Polytechnic Institute of Bragança, Portugal

Multidimensional Evolutionary Evaluations for Transformative Approaches (MEETA 2026)

Workshop Organizers:

Maria Cerreta	University of Naples Federico II, Italy
Giuliano Poli	Università Federico II di Napoli, Italy
Gaia Daldanise	CNR Institute for Research on Innovation and Services for Development, Italy
Ludovica La Rocca	University of Federico II of Naples, Italy
Maria Somma	University of Naples Federico II, Italy
Sabrina Sacco	University of Naples Federico II, Italy

Building Multi-dimensional Models for Assessing Complex Environmental Systems (MES 2026)

Workshop Organizers:

Vanessa Assumma	University of Bologna, Italy
Caterina Caprioli	Politecnico di Torino, Italy
Giulia Datola	Politecnico di Milano, Italy

Federico DellAnna	Politecnico di Torino, Italy
Marta DellOvo	Politecnico di Milano, Italy
Marco Rossitti	Politecnico di Milano, Italy

Computational Mechanics, Intelligence, and Data (MIND 2026)

Workshop Organizers:

Lelio Campanile	Università degli Studi della Campania Luigi Vanvitelli, Italy
Renato Zona	Università della Campania Vanvitelli, Italy

Modelling Liveable Cities: Techniques, Methods, Challenges, and Perspectives Behind the X-Minute City (MLC 2026)

Workshop Organizers:

Federico Mara	University of Pisa, Italy
Valerio Cutini	University of Pisa, Italy

Mathematical Methods for Image Processing and Understanding 2026 (MMIPU 2026)

Workshop Organizers:

Ivan Gerace	Università degli Studi di Perugia, Italy
Gianluca Vinti	Università degli Studi di Perugia, Italy
Arianna Travaglini	Lucian Blaga University of Sibiu, Romania

MOdels and Indicators for Assessing and Measuring the Urban Settlement deVElopment in the View of NET ZERO by 2050 (MOVEto0 2026)

Workshop Organizers:

Lorena Fiorini	University of L'Aquila, Italy
Lucia Saganeiti	Institute of Methodologies for Environmental Analysis (IMAA) CNR, Italy
Angela Pilogallo	Institute of Methodologies for Environmental Analysis (IMAA), Italy
Francesco Zullo	University of L'Aquila, Italy
Alessandro Marucci	University of L'Aquila, Italy

Numerical Aspects in Machine Learning for Dynamical Systems (NAMLYS 2026)

Workshop Organizers:

Pasquale De Luca	Parthenope University of Naples, Italy
Livia Marcellino	University of Naples Parthenope, Italy
Valeria Mele	University of Naples Federico II, Italy

Numerical Methods and Machine Learning in Science and Engineering (NMLSE 2026)

Workshop Organizers:

Cecília Coelho	Helmut Schmidt University, Germany
M. Fernanda P. Costa	University of Minho, Portugal
Luís Ferrás	University of Minho, Portugal
Eliana Costa e Silva	Polytechnic of Porto, Portugal

6th Workshop on Privacy in the Cloud/Edge/IoT World 2026 (PCEIoT 2026)

Workshop Organizers:

Lelio Campanile	Università degli Studi della Campania Luigi Vanvitelli, Italy
Mauro Iacono	Università degli Studi della Campania Luigi Vanvitelli, Italy
Michele Mastroianni	University of Foggia, Italy

Preserving Our Past: Spatial and Remote Sensing Technologies for Cultural Heritage in a Changing Climate (POP 2026)

Workshop Organizers:

Maria Danese	Institute of Heritage Science of the National Research Council of Italy (CNR ISPC), Italy
Rosa Lasaponara	Institute of Methodologies for Environmental Analysis (CNR IMAA), Italy
Nicola Masini	Institute of Heritage Science of the National Research Council of Italy (CNR ISPC), Italy

Scientific Computing Infrastructure (SCI 2026)

Workshop Organizers:

Vladimir Korkhov	Saint Petersburg State University, Russia
Elena Stankova	Saint Petersburg State University, Russia

Socio-Economic and Environmental Models for Land Use Management (SEMLUM 2026)

Workshop Organizers:

Debora Anelli	Sapienza University of Rome, Italy
Pierluigi Morano	Polytechnic University of Bari, Italy
Francesco Tajani	Sapienza University of Rome, Italy
Felicia Di Liddo	Polytechnic University of Bari, Italy

Ports and Logistics of the Future - Smartness and Sustainability (SmartPorts 2026)

Workshop Organizers:

Andrea Gallo	Università degli Studi di Trieste, Italy
Giuseppe Borruso	University of Trieste, Italy
Gianfranco Fancello	University of Cagliari, Italy
Veronica Camerada	Università degli studi di Sassari, Italy
Clara Di Fazio	University of Trieste, Italy

Sustainable Evolution of Long-Distance frEight and paSsenger Transport (SOLIDEST 2026)

Workshop Organizers:

Antonio Russo	University of Enna Kore, Italy
Giuseppe Musolino	Università Mediterranea di Reggio Calabria, Italy
Socrates Basbas	Aristotle University of Thessaloniki, Greece
Oana Dinu	National University of Science and Technology Politehnica Bucharest, Romania
Sanja Šurdonja	University of Rijeka, Croatia
Elen Twrdy	University of Ljubljana, Slovenia

Sustainability Performance Assessment: Models, Approaches, and Applications Toward Interdisciplinary and Integrated Solutions. (SPA 2026)

Workshop Organizers:

Francesco Scorza	University of Basilicata, Italy
Sabrina Lai	University of Cagliari, Italy
Jolanta Dvarioniene	Kaunas University of Technology, Lithuania
Michele Campagna	University of Cagliari, Italy

Specifics of Smart Cities Development in Europe (SPEED 2026)

Workshop Organizers:

Chiara Garau	University of Cagliari, Italy
Katarína Vitálišová	Matej Bel University, Slovak Republic
Marco Fanfani	University of Florence, Italy
Anna Vaňová	Matej Bel University, Slovak Republic
Kamila Borsekova	Matej Bel University, Slovak Republic
Paola Zamperlin	University of Pisa, Italy

Smart, Safe, and Health Cities (SSHC 2026)

Workshop Organizers:

Chiara Garau	University of Cagliari, Italy
Gerardo Carpentieri	University of Naples Federico II, Italy
Carmen Guida	Università degli Studi di Napoli Federico II, Italy
Martina Carra	University of Brescia, Italy
Vincenza Torrisi	University of Catania, Italy
Silvia Rossetti	Università degli Studi di Parma, Italy

Smart and Sustainable Island Communities (SSIC 2026)

Workshop Organizers:

Chiara Garau	University of Cagliari, Italy
Anastasia Stratigea	National Technical University of Athens, Greece
Yiota Theodora	National Technical University of Athens, Greece
Giovanna Concu	University of Cagliari, Italy
Tiziana Campisi	University of Enna Kore, Italy
Tanja Congiu	University of Sassari, Italy

Sustainable Tourism Economy, Silk Road, Reuse and Enhancement of Cultural Heritage (STESilkRoad 2026)

Workshop Organizers:

Celestina Fazia	Università di Enna Kore, Italy
Alexandru Ilies	University of Oradea, Romania
Dorina Camelia Ilies	University of Oradea, Romania
Cristina Natoli	Ministero dell'Ambiente e della Sicurezza Energetica, Italy
Bahodirhon Safarov	Samarkand Branch of Tashkent State University of Economics, Uzbekistan
Clara Stella Vicari Aversa	Università degli Studi Mediterranea di Reggio Calabria, Italy

Theoretical and Computational Chemistry and its Applications (TCCM 2026)

Workshop Organizers:

Noelia Faginas Lago	Università di Perugia, Italy
Andrea Lombardi	Università di Perugia, Italy
Marcos Mandado Alonso	University of Vigo, Spain

Transport Infrastructures for Smart Cities (TISC 2026)

Workshop Organizers:

Francesca Maltinti	University of Cagliari, Italy
Mauro Coni	University of Cagliari, Italy
Chiara Garau	University of Cagliari, Italy
Benedetto Barabino	University of Brescia, Italy
Nicoletta Rassu	Università di Cagliari, Italy
James Rombi	University of Cagliari, Italy

Transforming Urban Analytics: The Impact of Crowdsourced Mapping and Advanced AI Techniques on Future Cities (Tr-UrbAna 2026)

Workshop Organizers:

Ayse Giz Gulnerman Gengec	Ankara Hacı Bayram Veli University, Turkey
Müslüm Hacar	Yildiz Technical University, Turkey

From Structural to TRAnsformative-Change of City Environment: Challenges and Solutions and Perspectives (TRACE 2026)

Workshop Organizers:

Maria Rosaria Guarini	Sapienza University of Rome, Italy
Pierluigi Morano	Polytechnic University of Bari, Italy
Francesco Sica	Sapienza University of Rome, Italy
Alejandro Segura	Universidad Politécnica de Madrid, Spain
Yilsy María Nuñez Guerrero	Universidad Politécnica de Madrid, Spain

Urban Artificial Intelligence for Modelling, Analysis and Planning (Urban plAnnIng 2026)

Workshop Organizers:

Chiara Garau	University of Cagliari, Italy
Romano Fistola	University of Naples Federico II, Italy
Beniamino Murgante	University of Basilicata, Italy
Dessislava Petrova Antonova	Sofia University, GATE Institute, Bulgaria
Gianni Pantaleo	University of Florence, Italy
Rosa Anna La Rocca	University of Naples Federico II, Italy

Urban Space Accessibility and Mobilities (USAM 2026)

Workshop Organizers:

Chiara Garau	University of Cagliari, Italy
Alessandro Plaisant	University of Sassari, Italy
Barbara Caselli	Università degli Studi di Parma, Italy
Mauro D. Apuzzo	University of Cassino and Southern Lazio, Italy
Francesco Pinna	University of Cagliari, Italy
Silvio Nocera	IUAV University of Venice, Italy

Virtual Reality, Augmented Reality and Applications (VRA 2026)

Workshop Organizers:

Damiano Perri	University of Perugia, Italy
Osvaldo Gervasi	University of Perugia, Italy
Paolo Nesi	University of Florence, Italy

Workshop on Advanced and Computational Methods for Earth Science Applications (WACM4ES 2026)

Workshop Organizers:

Luca Piroddi	University of Cagliari, Italy
Patrizia Capizzi	University of Palermo, Italy
Marilena Cozzolino	Università del Molise, Italy
Giuseppina Vacca	University of Cagliari, Italy
Luigi Capozzoli	Hydrogeosite Laboratory of CNR-IMAA, Italy
Nikos Papadopoulos	Foundation for Research and Technology Hellas, Greece

Sponsoring Organizations

ICCSA 2026 would not have been possible without the tremendous support of many organizations and institutions, for which all organizers and participants of ICCSA 2026 express their sincere gratitude:

Universidade do Minho Escola de Engenharia	University of Minho, Portugal (https://www.uminho.pt/)

(*continued*)

(*continued*)

	University of Perugia, Italy (https://www.unipg.it)
	University of Basilicata, Italy (http://www.unibas.it)
	University of Cagliari, Italy (https://unica.it/)
	Monash University, Australia (https://www.monash.edu/)
	Kyushu Sangyo University, Japan (https://www.kyusan-u.ac.jp/)

Venue

ICCSA 2026 took place at:

the University of Minho campus:
Campus de Gualtar
4710-057 Braga
Portugal

Plenary Lectures

Digital Twins for Cities – The Rise of the Socio-Technical System

Claudia van der Laag

Professor of Urban Analytics, Department of Built Environment, Oslo Metropolitan University, Oslo

Abstract. Cities are entering a new era in which digital twins are no longer simply technical replicas of urban systems, but evolving socio-technical infrastructures that shape how cities are planned, governed, and experienced. Across the world, urban digital twins are being adopted to address some of the most pressing challenges of our time—climate adaptation, urban resilience, mobility transitions, decarbonisation, infrastructure management, and inclusive governance. Yet as these technologies become increasingly sophisticated, a fundamental question emerges: can digital twins truly support more democratic and human-centred cities, or will they reinforce existing structures of power and expertise? In this keynote, Claudia van der Laag, explores the transformation of urban digital twins from data-driven modelling tools into collaborative platforms for urban decision-making and societal change. It argues that the future of digital twins lies not only in advances in artificial intelligence, real-time data integration, simulation, and predictive analytics, but equally in the ability to connect technological innovation with governance, participation, and human agency. Drawing on emerging international research and practical case studies, the keynote examines the complex ecosystem surrounding urban digital twins, bringing together planners, policy-makers, researchers, technologists, and communities. It highlights how digital twins increasingly function as meeting points between multiple forms of knowledge—technical, political, social, and experiential—and why interdisciplinary collaboration is essential for their success. The talk will critically reflect on the tensions between technological ambition and civic inclusion, exploring themes such as transparency, interoperability, participation, and trust. It will also discuss how digital twins can become powerful environments for scenario exploration, urban experimentation, and collective learning, enabling cities to better navigate uncertainty and complexity in an age of rapid urban transformation. Ultimately, this keynote presents a vision of digital twins not as neutral technological systems, but as living socio-technical infrastructures capable of reshaping urban governance itself. The challenge ahead is therefore not only how accurately cities can be modelled, but how inclusively they can be imagined, negotiated, and governed through these emerging digital environments.

Short Bio – Claudia van der Laag (also known as Claudia Yamu) is Professor of Urban Analytics at Oslo Metropolitan University. Her work advances urban analytics and spatial modelling through an integrated multi-method approach, informing sustainable urban planning and policy. She is widely recognised for bridging theory and practice and received the prestigious Michael Breheny Prize for her contributions to multi-scale modelling. Van der Laag is co-author of the widely recognised textbook 'Introduction to Space Syntax in Urban Studies'. She also serves on the editorial advisory board of Springer's The Urban Book Series and the journal Environment and Planning B: Urban Analytics and City Science.

Prescriptive AI in Practice: Bridging Optimisation, Generative AI and Agentic Decision-Making

Bernardo Almada-Lobo

Universidade do Porto, Faculdade de Engenharia, INESC TEC, Portugal

Abstract. Prescriptive AI, viewed through the lens of mathematical optimisation and operations research, addresses complex business decision-making problems involving limited resources, multiple decision options and competing objectives. This talk considers the full decision pipeline: problem framing, model formulation, computational solution, implementation, monitoring and organisational adoption. The practical success of prescriptive AI depends less on algorithmic sophistication alone than on the quality of the translation between real-world decision contexts and formal optimisation models. In practice, this translation remains a major bottleneck. Objectives are often ambiguous, constraints are incomplete or tacit, data may be fragmented, and the operational consequences of a recommendation may be poorly understood. As a result, optimisation projects can fail even when the underlying mathematical model is technically sound. The talk will address the persistent gap between optimisation theory and deployment practice. While optimisation has generated substantial value in domains such as supply chain planning, logistics, production, revenue management, workforce planning and inventory control, many initiatives still face a significant risk of under-delivery. Common failure modes include incorrect problem framing, weak data readiness, brittle assumptions, infeasible or non-actionable recommendations, limited explainability, insufficient ownership by business users and inadequate post-deployment monitoring. Crossing this gap requires moving from one-off model building to an operational lifecycle in which models are stress-tested, embedded in workflows, monitored for drift and revised as the business environment changes. Recent developments in generative and agentic AI create new opportunities to reduce these barriers. Generative AI can support the elicitation of decision-maker preferences, the structuring of unstructured operational knowledge, the drafting of candidate formulations and the explanation of model outputs in business language. Agentic AI can extend this role by orchestrating multi-step workflows that involve model formulation, solver-code generation, execution, debugging, infeasibility diagnosis, sensitivity analysis and human review. However, these capabilities should not be interpreted as replacing optimisation expertise. Rather, they create a new interface between human judgement, analytical modelling and computational decision support. This talk will discuss a cross-fertilisation agenda between optimisation, generative AI and agentic AI, with a focus on how these technologies should be calibrated to the decision at hand.

Short Bio – Full Professor of Industrial Engineering and Management at the Faculty of Engineering of University of Porto (FEUP). Co-founder and Partner at LTPlabs, a Business AI company. Member of the Board of Trustees of the Belmiro de Azevedo

Foundation. Member of the Academy of Engineering. Former Board Member of INESC TEC and Researcher at the MIT Sloan School of Management. Holds a BEng, PhD and Habilitation in Industrial Engineering and Management from FEUP. Completed the Advanced Management Programme at INSEAD, and the Mergers and Acquisitions at London Business School. Certified Analytics Professional (CAP) by INFORMS. His area of activity is Business Analytics and Artificial Intelligence. He researches, develops and implements analytical models and methods to support decision-making, solving management problems across various domains—manufacturing, consumer goods, retail and transport—with a particular focus on Operations Management and the Operations–Marketing interface. He has coordinated and participated in more than 300 development, consultancy and research projects funded by private organisations, science agencies from several countries, the European Commission and regional bodies. He has published more than 100 scientific articles and is co-author of the book Analytics Sandwich: Bringing People and Artificial Intelligence Together to Unlock Business Value. He has supervised more than 20 doctoral theses.

Net-Zero Communities Through Life Cycle Thinking: Canadian Lessons and Global Implications

Kasun Hewage

Professor of Engineering, School of Engineering (Okanagan Campus), The University of British Columbia (UBC), Canada, FortisBC Smart Energy Chair, Associate Director, Clean Energy Research Centre (CERC)

Abstract. This keynote presentation discusses how life cycle thinking supports the transformation of communities toward sustainable, resilient, and net-zero futures. Drawing on Canadian research, practice, and policy experience, the presentation highlights how integrated life cycle approaches can move beyond conventional carbon accounting to inform practical decision-making across buildings, infrastructure, energy systems, waste management, water systems, and industrial processes [1-8]. The keynote features research conducted at the Life Cycle Management Laboratory (LCML) at the University of British Columbia, Canada, an internationally recognized research hub led by Prof. Kasun Hewage. LCML brings together engineers, scientists, policy researchers, postdoctoral fellows, visiting scholars, and graduate researchers to translate data-intensive sustainability research into actionable climate solutions. The laboratory's work is organized around six interconnected research themes: energy systems, urban development, water systems, waste management, construction and asset management, and industrial processes and products. Together, these themes provide an integrated platform for advancing life cycle–based pathways to net-zero communities. Supported by strong partnerships with government, industry, and community stakeholders, LCML has contributed to a substantial body of applied sustainability research, including more than 400 journal articles, 100 conference papers, and numerous technical reports that have informed real-world planning and implementation. This keynote presentation highlights selected success stories that demonstrate how life cycle thinking can be translated into practical strategies for reducing environmental impacts while strengthening community resilience. These insights are especially relevant to the interdisciplinary focus of ICCSA 2026, which will be held in collaboration with the University of Minho in Braga, Portugal, from June 30 to July 3, 2026.

References

1. Weerasinghe, O., Hewage, K., Razi, F., Fatmi, M., Sadiq, R.: Applicability of land use models for sustainable urban planning: a review. J. Urban Plann. Dev. ASCE (2025). Accepted 3 Marc 2025

2. Sultana, S.R., et al.: Looking beyond energy efficiency targets: life cycle sustainability of mechanical and water heating equipment in Canadian homes. J. Clean. Prod. **473**, 143469 (2024). https://doi.org/10.1016/j.jclepro.2024.143469
3. Liyanage D.R., Hewage K., Hussain S.H., Razi F., Sadiq R.: Climate adaptation of existing buildings: a critical review on planning energy retrofit strategies for future climate. Renew. Sustain. Energy Rev. **199**, 114476 (2024). https://doi.org/10.1016/j.rser.2024.114476
4. Liyanage D.R., Hewage K., Karunathilake H., Sadiq R.: Feasibility of carbon-capturing in building heating systems: a life cycle thinking-based approach. Int. J. Greenhouse Gas Control **132** (2023). https://doi.org/10.1016/j.ijggc.2023.104056
5. Moudgil, V., Sadiq, R., Bakhtavar, E., Paudel, A., Hewage, K.: A cloud-oriented data-analysis framework to analyze peak demand dynamics in institutional building clusters. Sustain. Cities Soc. **111**, 105553 (2024). https://doi.org/10.1016/j.scs.2024.105553
6. Liyanage D.R., Hewage K., Ghobadi M., Sadiq R.: Thermal resiliency of single-family housing stock under extreme hot and cold conditions. Energy Build. **323**, 114809 (2024). https://doi.org/10.1016/j.enbuild.2024.114809
7. Wijayasekera S.C., et al.: Sustainability of waste-to-hydrogen conversion pathways: a life cycle thinking-based assessment. Energy Convers. Manage. **270** (2022). https://doi.org/10.1016/j.enconman.2022.116218
8. Jayasena A., Hewage K., Siddiqui O., Sadiq R.: Socio-economic and environmental cost-benefit analysis of passive houses: a life cycle perspective. J. Clean. Prod. **373** (2022). https://doi.org/10.1016/j.jclepro.2022.133718

Short Bio – Prof. Kasun Hewage is a Full Professor and FortisBC Smart Energy Chair in the School of Engineering at the University of British Columbia. He also serves as Associate Director of UBC's Clean Energy Research Centre and Director of the Life Cycle Management Laboratory. Prof. Hewage brings extensive multidisciplinary industrial experience in Canada and internationally. Prior to joining UBC in 2008, he worked as a business management cost specialist in the oil and gas sector and as a civil engineer on hydropower and infrastructure development projects. His research focuses on integrating life-cycle thinking into urban development, energy policy, and infrastructure planning. A distinctive feature of his work is its whole-system perspective, extending beyond conventional assessment methods to evaluate products, processes, and built assets from material extraction through end-of-life. Through this approach, Prof. Hewage and his research team have supported governments, infrastructure developers, and communities in advancing low-impact and net-zero development strategies for both existing and planned communities. Prof. Hewage currently leads many collaborative research projects on life-cycle management of built assets, green construction, smart energy systems, and sustainable community planning. His contributions have helped establish important benchmarks, decision-support methods, and implementation pathways for advancing sustainability in the Canadian and global construction sectors. He has authored or co-authored more than 300 peer-reviewed journal publications, in addition to numerous book chapters and conference papers presented at national and international forums. Prof. Hewage is registered as a Professional Engineer in British Columbia, Canada. He is a Fellow of the Canadian Society for Civil Engineering, the Canadian Society of Senior Engineers, and the Engineering Institute of Canada.

Machine Learning Based Methodologies for Grape and Wine Production

Pedro Melo-Pinto

University of Trás-os-Montes and Alto Douro, Engineering Department, Centre for the Research and Technology of Agro-Environmental and Biological Sciences, Portugal

Abstract. Wine production is a major area in Portuguese economy. The sector accounts for approximately 2.6% of Portugal's GDP, and is crucial to the development of inland regions. Wine quality depends on grape quality, which is a result of different factors such as harvesting at the optimal point of maturity, or selecting the grapes according to quality features. The growing importance of precision agriculture, demands novel methods to make the most out of the data generated. Machine learning approaches are particularly suitable for complex processes' modelling, where too many arguments are involved. Many of the agricultural processes such as yield estimation or ripening, fall into this category. However, several challenges may arise: even if models are available for particular cases, general models are difficult to come by, largely due to the high variability involved; with such models, there is a need for huge amounts of data, in a way which will not always be easy to obtain. This is particularly true in the case of grape production and the wine industry, where the number of grape varieties, climate, soil, etc., introduce a degree of variability that is uncommon in other sectors. One way of obtaining more information in such cases has been the use of images, whether RGB, multi-spectral or hyperspectral. The use of images introduces additional challenges, such as data size and lighting conditions, which underscores the need for data-driven modelling methodologies. The use of machine learning (ML) techniques combined with images has been establishing itself as a viable alternative predicting yields or quality parameters in grapes, and assist on harvesting critical decisions. Several ML approaches have been proposed to handle such data characteristics, but selecting a suitable methodology that best address the problem under study and make sure it generalizes well, is, most of the times, a cumbersome task. We will address three wine and grape production problems, yield estimation, grape quality assessment and illness detection, presenting different difficulties. Yield estimation is a major aspect in the wine production industry. The number of berries is one of the most relevant yield aspects, and can be estimated using computer vision, namely image segmentation algorithms. Lighting is one of the key factors in computer vision approaches, and occlusions—which are common in this problem—can be minimized, but require estimation models to achieve reliable results. Illness early detection is, of course, of the utmost importance, with an impact on production and quality. Detecting early symptoms and distinguishing them from other conditions is a difficult task, which makes the use of machine learning algorithms advisable, using automatic visual inspection of the leaves, addressed as a pixel-based classification problem. However, the available datasets are limited and complex to compile, as different diseases typically require very specific timeframes and locations. The use of generative models to overcome this obstacle, in conjunction with robust classification models, lead to models that are intended to be as general as possible. The evaluation of the grape's maturation profile based on the evolution of their oenological parameters over time is one of the most important aspects for ensuring wine quality, playing a decisive role in the definition of the optimal time for harvesting. The use hyperspectral imaging combined with learning algorithms represents a faster and non-destructive grape ripeness assessment method. We focus in two fundamental aspects to address the resulting data variability: a possible wavelength bands selection (with the purpose of reducing the dimensionality of data without losing predictive power) and the generalization ability of the ML model under such demanding conditions.

Short Bio – Pedro Melo-Pinto graduated from Univ. do Porto in 1984 and received a Ph.D. in Computer Science from the Univ. de Trás-os-Montes e Alto Douro (UTAD) in 1998. He is a Full Professor at UTAD where he served as Pro-Rector, as Director and Vice-Director of R&D units, and as member of UTAD's General Council. He also served as a member of The Portuguese Strategic Infrastructures (for the Digital Areas) Monitoring Committee and usually serves as a member (or co-chair) of the evaluation panel for different Portuguese and international R&D projects and grants competitions. He is currently Associate Editor of Computers and Electronics in Agriculture journal. He was Chair of the EuroFuse 2011 conference and the NATO 2001 Advanced Research Workshop, and served as member of the organization committee for more than 40 international conferences/workshops/special sessions. He is the head of the Image-Based Systems Lab from the Centre for the Research and Technology of Agro-Environmental and Biological Sciences.

His scientific interests include Computer Vision (CV) and Machine Learning (ML) and, in the last 15 years, their applications to the Agro-forestry area, namely to grape oenological parameters assessment. He authored/co-authored more than 100 scientific papers. He participated in many Portuguese and international R&D projects, predominantly in the areas mentioned above.

Contents

General Track 5: Information Systems and Technologies

LLM-Based Applications for Healthcare: A Systematic Mapping Study

Ramon Santos Malaquias(✉), Itamir de Morais Barroca Filho, Jean Mário Moreira de Lima, André Morais Gurgel, and Bruna A. O. de Brito

Digital Metropolis Institute, Federal University of Rio Grande do Norte, Natal 59078970, Brazil
{malaquias,itamir.filho,jean.lima}@imd.ufrn.br, andre.gurgel@ufrn.br, bruna.oliveira.124@ufrn.edu.br

Abstract. Large Language Models (LLMs) have been increasingly incorporated into real-world applications, including systems in the healthcare domain. In this context, these models have been applied to tasks such as clinical documentation, information extraction, medical record summarization, and clinical decision support. Despite the rapid growth of the literature on this topic, existing studies often focus on specific applications or techniques, with limited consolidation regarding the characteristics of these systems, the architectural approaches adopted, and the challenges associated with their development. This paper presents a systematic mapping study aimed at identifying the main characteristics of LLM-based healthcare applications, the architectures, patterns, and architectural styles employed in their development, as well as the challenges reported in the literature. The analysis considers recent studies describing LLM applications in healthcare contexts. The results reveal architectural approaches, including multi-stage processing pipelines, knowledge retrieval mechanisms, and integrations with external data sources, as well as common challenges related to hallucinations, data quality, privacy, and computational costs.

Keywords: Large Language Models · LLM · Software Architecture · Literature Review · Healthcare

1 Introduction

Large Language Models (LLMs) have been increasingly incorporated into real-world applications across multiple domains due to their ability to process and generate natural language at scale. Recent surveys report a rapid growth of systems integrating LLMs as core software components, highlighting their adoption in a wide range of application contexts [15,26,48].

In the healthcare domain, this trend has intensified in recent years. Studies report the use of LLMs in tasks such as clinical documentation, information

O. Gervasi et al. (Eds.): ICCSA 2026, LNCS 16768, pp. 3–19, 2027.
https://doi.org/10.1007/978-3-032-30488-9_1

extraction from electronic health records, medical record summarization, and clinical decision support [23,44]. However, deploying these technologies in clinical environments introduces strict requirements related to patient safety, data privacy, reliability, and regulatory compliance.

In this context, the way LLMs are integrated into system architectures becomes a critical concern. Unlike traditional components, LLMs introduce probabilistic behavior, external dependencies, and challenges related to hallucination mitigation, cost control, and lifecycle governance. Recent studies show that LLM-based applications frequently rely on multi-component architectures that combine retrieval mechanisms, processing pipelines, and validation layers [11,32].

Despite the growing body of research on LLM applications in healthcare, architectural knowledge in this area remains fragmented. Most studies focus on specific applications or techniques, while systematic analyses that consolidate application characteristics, architectural approaches, and development challenges remain limited.

To address this gap, this paper presents a systematic mapping study on LLM-based healthcare applications. Based on the analysis of 43 primary studies from recent literature, the study identifies key characteristics of these applications, the architectures and architectural patterns adopted in their development, and the challenges reported in the literature.

The remainder of this paper is organized as follows. Section 2 describes the research methodology adopted in this study, including the research questions, search strategy, inclusion and exclusion criteria, and the study selection process. Section 3 presents the results of the systematic mapping, discussing the main characteristics of LLM-based healthcare applications, the architectural approaches identified in the literature, and the challenges reported in the analyzed studies. Section 4 discusses the research gaps identified from the analysis of the literature. Finally, Sect. 5 concludes the paper and outlines directions for future research.

2 Methodology

This study was conducted as a Systematic Mapping Study (SMS), following the guidelines proposed by Kitchenham et al. [21]. The goal is to identify and organize evidence on LLM-based applications in healthcare, focusing on their characteristics, architectural approaches, and development challenges.

2.1 Research Questions

The study is guided by the following research questions:

- **RQ1:** What are the main characteristics of LLM-based applications in healthcare?
- **RQ2:** What architectures, patterns, and architectural styles are used in healthcare LLM-based applications?
- **RQ3:** What are the main challenges related to the development of LLM-based applications in healthcare?

2.2 Search Process

The search was conducted in the Scopus database [5], considering titles, abstracts, and keywords. Scopus indexes the main scientific literature databases in the field of Computer Science, such as the ACM Digital Library [28], IEEE Xplore [10], ScienceDirect [38], and SpringerLink [39]. For this reason, it was selected as the primary database to execute the search string defined in the review protocol and to collect the relevant studies.

The following search string was used:

("large language model" OR LLM) AND ("application" OR "case study") AND ("healthcare" OR "health")

2.3 Inclusion and Exclusion Criteria

Studies written in English describing LLM applications in healthcare were considered. The following exclusion criteria were applied:

- **EC1:** Duplicate studies;
- **EC2:** Studies without full-text access;
- **EC3:** Studies without an abstract;
- **EC4:** Studies not addressing any research question;
- **EC5:** Studies not describing LLM applications in healthcare;

2.4 Quality Assessment

The selected studies were evaluated using five quality assessment questions, as follows:

- **QA1:** Is the paper based on research (or is it merely a "lessons learned" report based on expert opinion)?
- **QA2:** Does the paper present a clear statement of the research objectives?
- **QA3:** Does the paper clearly describe the context in which the research was conducted?
- **QA4:** Are the development challenges clearly described?
- **QA5:** Is there a clear statement of the study limitations and conclusions?

Each criterion was scored as 0 (not satisfied), 0.5 (partially satisfied), or 1 (fully satisfied).

2.5 Extraction, Analysis and Study Selection

The selection process consisted of three phases:

- (i) execution of the search string in Scopus, resulting in 3,226 studies;
- (ii) title and abstract screening using the defined criteria, resulting in 206 studies;
- and (iii) quality assessment and full-text analysis, resulting in 43 primary studies.

Figure 1 illustrates the study selection process and the number of studies retained at each stage.

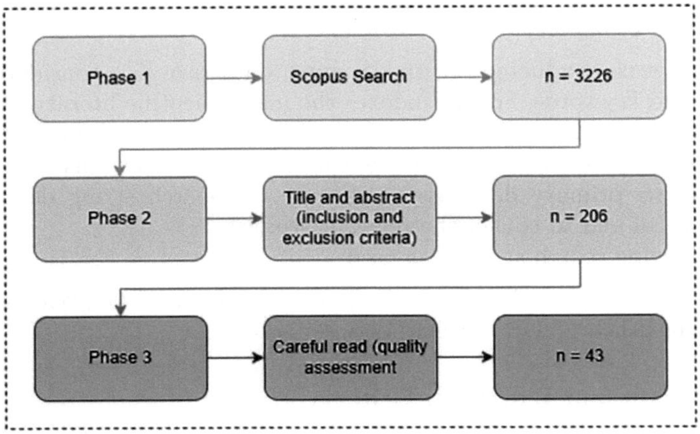

Fig. 1. Study extraction, analysis and selection process.

3 Review Results

Phase 3 of the selection process resulted in 43 primary studies, listed in Table 1. These studies were analyzed in detail to identify evidence related to the research questions defined in the protocol. To support analysis and evidence traceability, an online spreadsheet was used and is available at this link.

Table 1. Studies included in the review and their publication year.

ID	Title	Year
A01	A Multiagent Summarization and Auto-Evaluation Framework for Medical Text: Development and Evaluation Study [7]	2025
A02	A personal health large language model for sleep and fitness coaching [20]	2025
A03	A Smart System for Continuous Sitting Posture Monitoring, Assessment, and Personalized Feedback [35]	2025
A04	Advancing entity recognition in biomedicine via instruction tuning of large language models [19]	2024
A05	AI driven cardiovascular risk prediction using NLP and Large Language Models for personalized medicine in athletes [24]	2025
A06	An innovative X-RAG technique combined with GPT-4o for summarizing medical information from EHR and EMR to assist doctors in clinical decision-making effectively and efficiently [46]	2025
A07	Application of Generative Artificial Intelligence Models for Accurate Prescription Label Identification and Information Retrieval for the Elderly in Northern East of Thailand [43]	2025
A08	Application of generative language models to orthopaedic practice [6]	2024
A09	Benchmarking Large Language Models on Communicative Medical Coaching: A Dataset and a Novel System [16]	2024
A10	CARE-AD: a multi-agent large language model framework for Alzheimer's disease prediction using longitudinal clinical notes [27]	2025

(*continued*)

Table 1. (*continued*)

ID	Title	Year
A11	ChatDiet: Empowering personalized nutrition-oriented food recommender chatbots through an LLM-augmented framework [50]	2024
A12	ChatENT: Augmented Large Language Model for Expert Knowledge Retrieval in Otolaryngology–Head and Neck Surgery [30]	2024
A13	Chat-ePRO: Development and pilot study of an electronic patient-reported outcomes system based on ChatGPT [8]	2024
A14	ChatGPT provides inconsistent risk-stratification of patients with atraumatic chest pain [14]	2024
A15	Clinical risk prediction using language models: Benefits and considerations [1]	2024
A16	ClinicalAgent: Clinical Trial Multi-Agent System with Large Language Model-based Reasoning [53]	2024
A17	Critical care studies using large language models based on electronic healthcare records: A technical note [55]	2025
A18	DALK: Dynamic Co-Augmentation of LLMs and KG to answer Alzheimer's Disease Questions with Scientific Literature [25]	2024
A19	Development and evaluation of a large language model of ophthalmology in Chinese [56]	2024
A20	Development and Evaluation of a Retrieval-Augmented Large Language Model Framework for Ophthalmology [33]	2024
A21	Effectiveness of the Medical Chatbot PROSCA to Inform Patients About Prostate Cancer: Results of a Randomized Controlled Trial [3]	2024
A22	Efficient and Personalized Mobile Health Event Prediction via Small Language Models [47]	2024
A23	Efficient Inference Offloading for Mixture-of-Experts Large Language Models in Internet of Medical Things [52]	2024
A24	Empowering large language models for automated clinical assessment with generation-augmented retrieval and hierarchical chain-of-thought [13]	2025
A25	Enhancing Large Language Model Reliability: Minimizing Hallucinations with Dual Retrieval-Augmented Generation Based on the Latest Diabetes Guidelines [22]	2024
A26	Genomics-Enhanced Cancer Risk Prediction for Personalized LLM-Driven Healthcare Recommender Systems [31]	2025
A27	Identifying signs and symptoms of urinary tract infection from emergency department clinical notes using large language models [17]	2024
A28	Large language models forecast patient health trajectories enabling digital twins [37]	2025
A29	Leveraging long context in retrieval augmented language models for medical question answering [54]	2025
A30	Leveraging Medical Knowledge Graphs Into Large Language Models for Diagnosis Prediction: Design and Application Study [12]	2025
A31	LlamaMTS: Optimizing Metastasis Detection with Llama Instruction Tuning and BERT-Based Ensemble in Italian Clinical Reports [29]	2024
A32	Mental-LLM: Leveraging Large Language Models for Mental Health Prediction via Online Text Data [49]	2024
A33	Multimodal AI and Large Language Models for Orthopantomography Radiology Report Generation and Q&A [9]	2025
A34	PharmaLLM: A Medicine Prescriber Chatbot Exploiting Open-Source Large Language Models [2]	2024
A35	Retrieval-augmented generation elevates local LLM quality in radiology contrast media consultation [45]	2025
A36	Scaffolding Empathy: Training Counselors with Simulated Patients and Utterance-level Performance Visualizations [41]	2025
A37	Systematic Analysis of Retrieval-Augmented Generation-Based LLMs for Medical Chatbot Applications [4]	2024
A38	Systematic evaluation of common natural language processing techniques to codify clinical notes [42]	2024
A39	Talk2Care: An LLM-based Voice Assistant for Communication between Healthcare Providers and Older Adults [51]	2024
A40	Trustworthy AI Psychotherapy: Multi-Agent LLM Workflow for Counseling and Explainable Mental Disorder Diagnosis [36]	2025
A41	Using the Retrieval-Augmented Generation to Improve the Question-Answering System in Human Health Risk Assessment: The Development and Application [34]	2025
A42	Virtual Agents for Alcohol Use Counseling: Exploring LLM-Powered Motivational Interviewing [40]	2024
A43	ZebraMap: A Multimodal Rare Disease Knowledge Map with Automated Data Aggregation & LLM-Enriched Information Extraction Pipeline [18]	2026

3.1 Publication Year Distribution

Figure 2 shows the distribution of the 3,226 studies identified in the initial search. Between 2019 and 2022, the number of publications is minimal, with only one study per year. From 2023 onward, there is a significant increase, with 173 studies, followed by sharp growth in 2024 (886) and 2025 (1,845). Although 2026 was still incomplete at the time of data collection, 318 studies had already been identified.

This increase may be associated with technological and ecosystem shifts in the LLM landscape. In particular, the public release of conversational foundation models such as ChatGPT in late 2022 significantly increased awareness and accessibility of LLM capabilities among researchers and practitioners. At the same time, the availability of commercial LLM APIs (e.g., GPT-based services) enabled rapid prototyping and integration of language models into software systems without requiring extensive machine learning infrastructure.

Another relevant factor is the emergence of open-source foundation models, such as the LLaMA family and other community-driven models, which lowered the barrier for experimentation and allowed researchers to fine-tune models for domain-specific tasks, including biomedical and clinical applications. In parallel, the research community has introduced several medical and biomedical benchmarks designed to evaluate LLM performance in clinical reasoning, question answering, and medical knowledge tasks.

Together, these developments have accelerated the exploration of LLM-based systems in healthcare, contributing to the rapid growth of publications observed from 2023 onward.

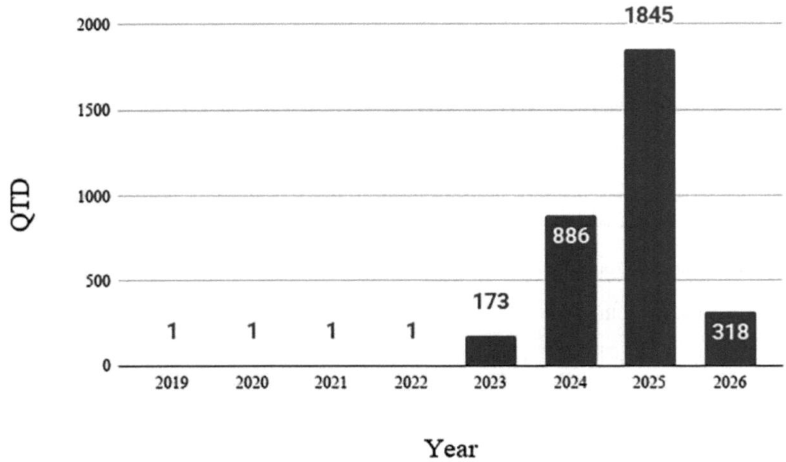

Fig. 2. Distribution of publications per year.

3.2 Application Types

Figure 3 presents the distribution of the selected studies by application type. Question Answering is the most frequent category (19 studies), followed by Information Extraction (13). Other categories include Prediction (8), Conversational Assistant (6), Summary and Recommendation (4 each), as well as Educational Training (3), NER and Clinical Assessment (2 each).

3.3 Model Family Distribution

Figure 4 presents the distribution of model families used in the analyzed studies. The GPT family (OpenAI) is the most frequent (26 studies), followed by LLaMA (16). Other relevant families include Mistral/Mixtral (8), Qwen (6), and both Gemini and biomedical variants of BERT (4 each). Several other model families appear less frequently, indicating the diversity of models used in the analyzed applications.

3.4 Research Question Analysis

This section presents the analysis of the selected studies based on the research questions defined in this systematic mapping. For each question, the extracted data were organized and analyzed to identify patterns, recurring characteristics, and trends in healthcare applications based on LLMs.

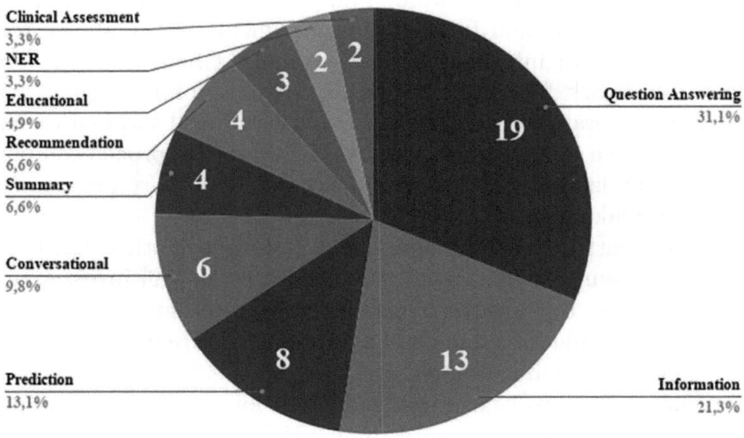

Fig. 3. Distribution of studies by application type.

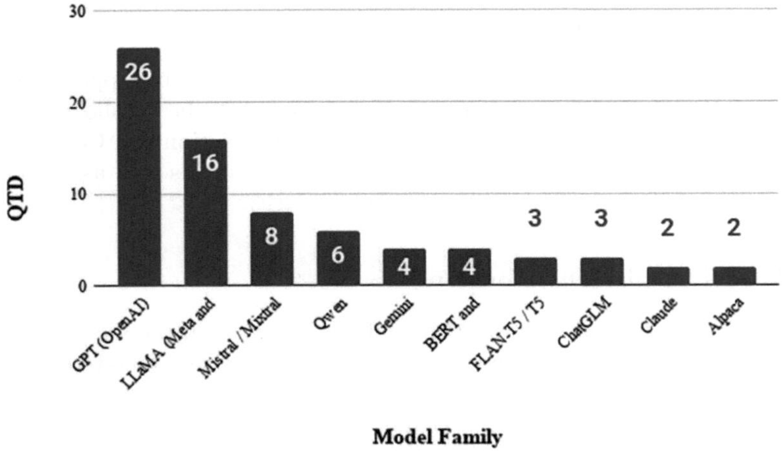

Fig. 4. Distribution of Top 10 model families used in the analyzed studies.

RQ1: What are the main characteristics of LLM-based applications in healthcare?

The analysis of the selected studies suggests a recurring set of functional and non-functional requirements among the analyzed healthcare LLM applications. In general, functional requirements are mainly associated with the processing and interpretation of clinical data, while non-functional requirements focus on response quality, data security, and integration with clinical systems.

One of the most common functional requirements is the ability to process and summarize clinical information. For example, Chen et al. [7] propose a multi-agent framework for automatic medical text summarization, where different agents collaborate to generate and evaluate clinical summaries. Similarly, Wang et al. [46] use a Retrieval-Augmented Generation approach combined with GPT-4o to synthesize information from electronic health records and support clinical decision-making.

Another frequently identified requirement is the automatic extraction of clinical information from unstructured texts. Keloth et al. [19] investigate the use of instruction tuning to improve biomedical entity recognition, while Iscoe et al. [17] use LLMs to identify signs and symptoms of urinary tract infections in emergency department clinical notes.

Applications related to health risk and condition prediction also appear frequently. Acharya et al. [1] investigate clinical risk prediction using medical textual data, while Xu et al. [49] propose Mental-LLM, a model designed to predict mental health conditions from online text data. Similarly, Li et al. [27] introduce the CARE-AD multi-agent framework for predicting Alzheimer's disease using longitudinal clinical notes.

Another group of applications involves conversational interaction with users. Baumgärtner et al. [3] present the PROSCA medical chatbot to provide information about prostate cancer, while Yang et al. [51] propose Talk2Care, an LLM-based voice assistant to support communication between healthcare professionals and older adults. Azam et al. [2] introduce PharmaLLM, a clinical chatbot designed to support medication prescription.

Some studies also explore personalized recommendation and health coaching. Khasentino et al. [20] present a language model designed for personalized sleep and fitness coaching, while Yang et al. [50] propose ChatDiet, a system that uses LLMs to provide personalized nutritional recommendations.

Regarding non-functional requirements, the studies emphasize aspects such as clinical accuracy, response reliability, and data security, which are critical in healthcare applications. Other frequently mentioned requirements include scalability, interpretability, hallucination mitigation, and integration with clinical systems, such as electronic health records.

Table 2 summarizes the main non-functional requirements identified and the studies that mention them and Fig. 5 presents a word cloud highlighting the most frequently cited non-functional requirements in the analyzed applications.

Fig. 5. Word cloud of non-functional requirements in healthcare LLM applications.

3.5 RQ2: What Architectures, Patterns, and Architectural Styles Are Used in Healthcare LLM-Based Applications?

The analysis of the selected studies shows that many of the analyzed healthcare LLM applications adopt modular and composite architectures in which language models are integrated with components responsible for knowledge retrieval, clinical data processing, and user interaction. Rather than relying on standalone models, most systems embed LLMs within broader software architectures designed to support clinical workflows and ensure response reliability.

Few recurring architectural patterns were identified. One of the most common is *Retrieval-Augmented Generation* (RAG), where LLMs are combined with retrieval mechanisms that access external medical sources such as scientific literature, clinical guidelines, or electronic health records. For example, Wang et al. [46] apply this approach to summarize information extracted from EHR and EMR systems to support clinical decision-making.

Another pattern is the use of *multi-agent architectures*, in which multiple LLM-based agents perform specialized roles within the system. Chen et al. [7] propose a multi-agent framework for medical text summarization, while Li et al. [27] apply a similar approach to predict Alzheimer's disease using longitudinal clinical notes. Additional architectural approaches include multimodal architectures, NLP processing pipelines, knowledge graph integration, and domain-specific fine-tuned models. Table 3 summarizes the architectural patterns identified in the analyzed studies.

The analysis also revealed a relationship between application types and the architectural approaches adopted. Table 4 summarizes the dominant architectures observed across different healthcare application categories.

These findings suggest that question answering systems predominantly rely on RAG architectures to improve factual grounding through external medical knowledge retrieval. In contrast, information extraction tasks frequently adopt structured NLP pipelines to process unstructured clinical texts. Conversational assistants typically employ multi-agent or chatbot architectures to manage interaction and dialogue, while prediction-oriented systems tend to rely on domain-specialized or fine-tuned models capable of integrating textual reasoning with structured clinical data.

Table 2. Non-functional requirements identified in healthcare LLM applications and the studies that mention them.

Non-functional requirement	Studies
Clinical accuracy	A01, A05, A06, A14, A15, A24, A28, A33, A36
Response reliability	A01, A14, A24, A25, A28, A36
Scalability	A03, A22, A23, A31
Data privacy and security	A08, A13, A21, A34
Interpretability/explainability	A15, A24, A30, A38
Hallucination mitigation	A24, A25, A28
Integration with clinical systems (EHR/EMR)	A06, A27, A32
Response personalization	A02, A11, A26
Model robustness	A24, A25, A28
Computational efficiency	A22, A23
Multimodal support	A03, A33
Interoperability	A06, A32

Table 3. Architectural patterns identified in healthcare LLM applications and the studies that adopt them.

Architectural Pattern	Studies
Retrieval-Augmented Generation (RAG)	A06, A07, A12, A20, A25, A35, A37, A41, A43
Multi-agent architecture	A01, A09, A10, A16, A36, A40, A42
Multimodal architecture	A02, A07, A33, A34, A43
NLP pipeline/text processing	A04, A14, A21, A27, A38, A43
Conversational/chatbot architecture	A13, A21, A42
Specialized/fine-tuned models	A02, A15, A19
LLM + Knowledge Graph integration	A18, A30
Mixture-of-Experts (MoE)	A23, A26

Across several analyzed studies, similar architectural compositions can be observed in which user requests are processed through input processing or prompt engineering layers, followed by retrieval mechanisms that access clinical data sources. The retrieved context is then provided to the LLM reasoning component, whose output is typically validated through guardrails or post-processing layers before producing the final clinical response.

Such architectural composition is particularly important in healthcare systems due to the critical nature of their non-functional requirements. Applications in this domain must satisfy strict requirements related to clinical accuracy, reliability, explainability, privacy, and regulatory compliance, while ensuring safe interaction with sensitive patient data and clinical workflows. Consequently, domain-specialized architectures that incorporate mechanisms such as knowledge grounding, validation layers, auditability, and human oversight are essential to mitigate risks such as hallucinations and unsafe clinical recommendations.

Table 4. Relationship between healthcare application types and dominant architectural approaches.

Application Type	Dominant Architecture
Question Answering	Retrieval-Augmented Generation (RAG) architectures combined with external medical knowledge retrieval mechanisms
Information Extraction/NER	NLP processing pipelines integrating LLM reasoning with text preprocessing, entity extraction, and classification modules
Conversational Assistants	Multi-agent or chatbot-oriented architectures combining dialogue management and LLM-based interaction modules
Prediction/Risk Assessment	Fine-tuned domain-specific models or hybrid architectures combining LLM reasoning with structured clinical data
Recommendation and Coaching	Personalized architectures integrating LLM reasoning with contextual patient data and knowledge bases
Summarization	RAG-based pipelines and multi-agent architectures responsible for generating and validating medical summaries

RQ3: What are the main challenges related to the development of LLM-based applications in healthcare?
The analysis of the selected studies revealed a recurring set of challenges associated with the development of applications based on LLMs in the healthcare domain and Fig. 6 presents this challenges. In general, these challenges are concentrated in five main dimensions: reliability of generated responses, availability and quality of clinical data, privacy and regulatory concerns, computational limitations, and difficulties related to integrating heterogeneous data and systems. Figure 6 presents a word cloud summarizing the challenges discussed in the analyzed studies.

The most frequently reported challenge concerns the reliability of model-generated outputs. Several studies report issues such as hallucinations, inconsistencies, and low accuracy in clinical tasks. Chen et al. [7], for example, highlight this issue in medical text summarization systems, while Heston and Lewis [14] observe inconsistencies in risk stratification tasks performed by ChatGPT.

Another relevant group of challenges relates to the availability and quality of clinical data. Many studies report scarcity of annotated datasets, the high cost of expert labeling, and the presence of noise or bias in clinical records. Keloth et al. [19] and Li et al. [24] show that the limited availability of high-quality biomedical datasets restricts model training and generalization.

Fig. 6. Word cloud of challenges in the development of LLM-based healthcare applications.

The literature also emphasizes challenges related to privacy, ethics, and regulatory compliance, particularly in applications that use electronic health records or other sensitive patient data [8,27,33]. In addition, issues such as computational cost, latency, and infrastructure requirements are frequently reported, along with difficulties in the integration of heterogeneous and multimodal data sources [2,22,31,47]. Finally, many studies point to limitations associated with clinical reasoning, domain adaptation, and rigorous evaluation of solutions [25,50]. Overall, these findings indicate that progress in this area depends not only on improvements in foundation models, but also on more robust architectures, better data ecosystems, and systematic mechanisms for evaluation and human oversight.

Taken together, the results of RQs 1, 2, and 3 show that LLM-based healthcare applications already cover multiple tasks and usage contexts, while adopting composite architectures that combine LLMs with retrieval mechanisms, external knowledge bases, specialized agents, and integration with clinical systems. At the same time, important challenges remain regarding response reliability, data quality and availability, privacy, regulation, computational costs, and interoperability. These findings suggest that advances in this area may depend not only on improvements in foundation models but also on the design of robust software architectures.

4 Identified Research Gaps

The analysis of the selected studies revealed several gaps in the literature on healthcare applications based on LLMs. Overall, these gaps relate to architectural aspects, engineering and evaluation practices, and challenges associated with real-world adoption.

- **Lack of reference architectures.** Most applications described in the literature adopt ad hoc architectures designed for specific tasks. Reference architectures that systematically organize recurring components such as LLMs, retrieval mechanisms, multimodal pipelines, and clinical knowledge bases are still scarce.
- **Limited discussion of architectural trade-offs.** Although quality attributes such as clinical accuracy, latency, computational cost, privacy, and explainability are frequently mentioned, few studies explicitly discuss how architectural decisions balance these competing requirements.
- **Limited architectural governance mechanisms.** Techniques such as RAG, specialized agents, and knowledge base integration are commonly used, but rarely accompanied by comprehensive architectural strategies for monitoring, auditing, fallback mechanisms, and lifecycle management of LLM components.
- **Limited integration with existing clinical systems.** Although the need for integration with electronic health records and hospital systems is frequently acknowledged, few studies propose robust architectural approaches to ensure interoperability at scale.

5 Conclusions and Future Work

This study presented a systematic mapping of the literature on healthcare applications based on LLMs, aiming to identify their main characteristics, architectural approaches, and development challenges.

The results show that LLM-based applications are being explored in several contexts, including clinical decision support, medical data analysis, interaction with patients and healthcare professionals, and processing of unstructured clinical data. These applications emphasize requirements such as clinical accuracy, reliability, personalization, and integration with multiple medical data sources.

From an architectural perspective, the analyzed studies frequently adopt retrieval mechanisms, natural language processing pipelines, and modular architectures that combine LLM reasoning with external knowledge sources and specialized processing components.

Despite recent progress, several challenges remain, including hallucinations, limited availability and quality of clinical data, privacy and security concerns, computational cost, and the need for human supervision. These challenges highlight that the adoption of LLM-based systems in healthcare requires architectures capable of ensuring reliability, explainability, and safe interaction with clinical workflows.

The results also provide relevant implications for research and practice. From a research perspective, the findings indicate the need for reference architectures for healthcare LLM systems, more standardized evaluation protocols, and architectural strategies to mitigate risks such as hallucinations, bias, and privacy concerns. From a practical perspective, the development of these systems should consider early integration with clinical infrastructures, explicit treatment of non-functional requirements, and validation in real-world healthcare environments.

As future work, we intend to investigate reference architectures for healthcare LLM systems and explore architectural strategies to mitigate issues such as hallucinations, bias, privacy, and integration with clinical systems. In addition, further studies involving validation in real clinical environments are essential to better understand the practical impact and reliability of these applications.

Acknowledgments. This study was funded by its authors.

Disclosure of Interests. The authors have no competing interests to declare that they are relevant to the content of this article.

References

1. Acharya, A., et al.: Clinical risk prediction using language models: benefits and considerations. J. Am. Med. Inf. Assoc. **31**(9), 1856–1864 (2024)
2. Azam, A., Naz, Z., Khan, M.U.G.: Pharmallm: a medicine prescriber chatbot exploiting open-source large language models. Human-Centric Intell. Syst. **4**(4), 527–544 (2024)
3. Baumgärtner, K., et al.: Effectiveness of the medical chatbot prosca to inform patients about prostate cancer: results of a randomized controlled trial. Eur. Urol. Open Sci. **69**, 80–88 (2024)
4. Bora, A., Cuayáhuitl, H.: Systematic analysis of retrieval-augmented generation-based LLMs for medical chatbot applications. Mach. Learn. Knowl. Extract. **6**(4), 2355–2374 (2024)

5. Boyle, F., Sherman, D.: Scopus^{TM}: the product and its development. Ser. Libr. **49**(3), 147–153 (2006)
6. Caterson, J., Ambler, O., Cereceda-Monteoliva, N., Horner, M., Jones, A., Poacher, A.T.: Application of generative language models to orthopaedic practice. BMJ Open **14**(3), e076484 (2024)
7. Chen, Y., Wen, B., Zulkernine, F.: A multiagent summarization and auto-evaluation framework for medical text: development and evaluation study. JMIR AI **4**, e75932 (2025)
8. Chen, Z., Wang, Q., Sun, Y., Cai, H., Lu, X.: Chat-epro: development and pilot study of an electronic patient-reported outcomes system based on chatgpt. J. Biomed. Inf. **154**, 104651 (2024)
9. Dasanayaka, C., Dandeniya, K., Dissanayake, M.B., Gunasena, C., Jayasinghe, R.: Multimodal ai and large language models for orthopantomography radiology report generation and q&a. Appl. Syst. Innov. **8**(2), 39 (2025)
10. Durniak, A.: Welcome to IEEE xplore. IEEE Power Eng. Rev. **20**(11), 12 (2000)
11. Esposito, M., et al.: Generative AI for software architecture: applications, challenges, and future directions. J. Syst. Softw. (2026). https://doi.org/10.1016/j.jss.2025.112607, https://www.sciencedirect.com/science/article/abs/pii/S0164121225002766
12. Gao, Y., et al.: Leveraging medical knowledge graphs into large language models for diagnosis prediction: design and application study. JMIR AI **4**, e58670 (2025)
13. Gu, Z., Jia, W., Piccardi, M., Yu, P.: Empowering large language models for automated clinical assessment with generation-augmented retrieval and hierarchical chain-of-thought. Artif. Intell. Med. **162**, 103078 (2025)
14. Heston, T.F., Lewis, L.M.: Chatgpt provides inconsistent risk-stratification of patients with atraumatic chest pain. PLoS ONE **19**(4), e0301854 (2024)
15. Hou, X., et al.: Large language models for software engineering: a systematic literature review. ACM Trans. Softw. Eng. Methodol. (2024). https://doi.org/10.1145/3695988. https://dl.acm.org/doi/10.1145/3695988
16. Huang, H., Wang, S., Liu, H., Wang, H., Wang, Y.: Benchmarking large language models on communicative medical coaching: a dataset and a novel system. In: Findings of the Association for Computational Linguistics: ACL 2024, pp. 1624–1637 (2024)
17. Iscoe, M., et al.: Identifying signs and symptoms of urinary tract infection from emergency department clinical notes using large language models. Acad. Emerg. Med. **31**(6), 599–610 (2024)
18. Islam, M.S., Jamal, A., Alkhathlan, A.: Zebramap: a multimodal rare disease knowledge map with automated data aggregation & LLM-enriched information extraction pipeline. Diagnostics **16**(1), 107 (2026)
19. Keloth, V.K., et al.: Advancing entity recognition in biomedicine via instruction tuning of large language models. Bioinformatics **40**(4), btae163 (2024)
20. Khasentino, J., et al.: A personal health large language model for sleep and fitness coaching. Nat. Med. **31**(10), 3394–3403 (2025)
21. Kitchenham, B., Brereton, O.P., Budgen, D., Turner, M., Bailey, J., Linkman, S.: Systematic literature reviews in software engineering-a systematic literature review. Inf. Softw. Technol. **51**(1), 7–15 (2009)
22. Lee, J., Cha, H., Hwangbo, Y., Cheon, W.: Enhancing large language model reliability: minimizing hallucinations with dual retrieval-augmented generation based on the latest diabetes guidelines. J. Pers. Med. **14**(12), 1131 (2024)

23. Leiser, F., Guse, R., Sunyaev, A.: Large language model architectures in health care: scoping review of research perspectives. J. Med. Internet Res. (2025). https://doi.org/10.2196/70315. https://www.jmir.org/2025/1/e70315
24. Li, A., Wang, Y., Chen, H.: AI driven cardiovascular risk prediction using NLP and large language models for personalized medicine in athletes. SLAS Technol. **32**, 10028 (2025)
25. Li, D., et al.: Dalk: dynamic co-augmentation of LLMs and kg to answer Alzheimer's disease questions with scientific literature. arxiv 2024. arXiv preprint arXiv:2405.04819
26. Li, J., Gao, J., et al.: Fundamental capabilities and applications of large language models: a survey. ACM Comput. Surv. (2024). https://doi.org/10.1145/3735632. https://dl.acm.org/doi/10.1145/3735632
27. Li, R., Wang, X., Berlowitz, D., Mez, J., Lin, H., Yu, H.: Care-ad: a multi-agent large language model framework for Alzheimer's disease prediction using longitudinal clinical notes. npj Dig. Med. **8**(1), 541 (2025)
28. Library, A.D.: ACM digital library home page (2021). https://dl.acm.org/
29. Lilli, L., et al.: Llamamts: optimizing metastasis detection with llama instruction tuning and bert-based ensemble in Italian clinical reports. In: Proceedings of the 6th Clinical Natural Language Processing Workshop, pp. 162–171 (2024)
30. Long, C., et al.: Chatent: augmented large language model for expert knowledge retrieval in otolaryngology-head and neck surgery. medrxiv 2023 (2023)
31. Lu, K., et al.: Genomics-enhanced cancer risk prediction for personalized LLM-driven healthcare recommender systems. ACM Trans. Inf. Syst. **43**(6), 1–30 (2025)
32. Lu, Q., Zhu, L., Xu, X., Liu, Y., Xing, Z., Whittle, J.: A taxonomy of foundation model based systems through the lens of software architecture. In: Proceedings of the IEEE/ACM International Conference on AI Engineering – Software Engineering for AI (2024). https://doi.org/10.1145/3644815.3644956. https://dl.acm.org/doi/10.1145/3644815.3644956
33. Luo, M.J., et al.: Development and evaluation of a retrieval-augmented large language model framework for ophthalmology. JAMA Ophthalmol. **142**(9), 798–805 (2024)
34. Meng, W., Li, Y., Chen, L., Dong, Z.: Using the retrieval-augmented generation to improve the question-answering system in human health risk assessment: the development and application. Electronics **14**(2), 386 (2025)
35. Odesola, D.F., Kulon, J., Verghese, S., Partlow, A., Gibson, C.: A smart system for continuous sitting posture monitoring, assessment, and personalized feedback. Sensors **25**(18), 5610 (2025)
36. Ozgun, M.C., Pei, J., Hindriks, K., Donatelli, L., Liu, Q., Wang, J.: Trustworthy AI psychotherapy: multi-agent LLM workflow for counseling and explainable mental disorder diagnosis. In: Proceedings of the 34th ACM International Conference on Information and Knowledge Management, pp. 2263–2272 (2025)
37. Rodriguez-Esteban, R., Schmich, F., Menden, M.P.: Large language models forecast patient health trajectories enabling digital twins (2025)
38. ScienceDirect: Science direct home page (2021). https://www.sciencedirect.com/
39. of Springer Nature, S.N.S.A.P.: Springer link home page (2021). https://link.springer.com/
40. Steenstra, I., Nouraei, F., Arjmand, M., Bickmore, T.: Virtual agents for alcohol use counseling: exploring LLM-powered motivational interviewing. In: Proceedings of the 24th ACM International Conference on Intelligent Virtual Agents, pp. 1–10 (2024)

41. Steenstra, I., Nouraei, F., Bickmore, T.: Scaffolding empathy: training counselors with simulated patients and utterance-level performance visualizations. In: Proceedings of the 2025 Chi Conference on Human Factors in Computing Systems, pp. 1–22 (2025)
42. Tavabi, N., Singh, M., Pruneski, J., Kiapour, A.: Systematic evaluation of common natural language processing techniques to codify clinical notes. medrxiv. Preprint posted online October **10** (2022)
43. Thetbanthad, P., Sathanarugsawait, B., Praneetpolgrang, P.: Application of generative artificial intelligence models for accurate prescription label identification and information retrieval for the elderly in northern east of thailand. J. Imaging **11**(1), 11 (2025)
44. Thirunavukarasu, A.J., Ting, D.S.J., et al.: Large language models in medicine. Nat. Med. (2023). https://doi.org/10.1038/s41591-023-02448-8. https://www.nature.com/articles/s41591-023-02448-8
45. Wada, A., et al.: Retrieval-augmented generation elevates local LLM quality in radiology contrast media consultation. NPJ Dig. Med. **8**(1), 395 (2025)
46. Wang, J.F., et al.: An innovative x-rag technique combined with gpt-4o for summarizing medical information from EHR and EMR to assist doctors in clinical decision-making effectively and efficiently. Health Inf. J. **31**(3), 14604582251381232 (2025)
47. Wang, X., Dang, T., Kostakos, V., Jia, H.: Efficient and personalized mobile health event prediction via small language models. In: Proceedings of the 30th Annual International Conference on Mobile Computing and Networking, pp. 2353–2358 (2024)
48. Xu, M., et al.: Resource-efficient algorithms and systems of large language models: a survey. ACM Comput. Surv. (2025). https://doi.org/10.1145/3706418. https://dl.acm.org/doi/10.1145/3706418
49. Xu, X., et al.: Mental-LLM: leveraging large language models for mental health prediction via online text data. Proc. ACM Interact. Mob. Wearable Ubiq. Technol. **8**(1), 1–32 (2024)
50. Yang, Z., et al.: Chatdiet: empowering personalized nutrition-oriented food recommender chatbots through an LLM-augmented framework. Smart Health **32**, 100465 (2024). https://doi.org/10.1016/j.smhl.2024.100465
51. Yang, Z., et al.: Talk2care: an LLM-based voice assistant for communication between healthcare providers and older adults. Proc. ACM Interact. Mob. Wearable Ubiq. Technol. **8**(2), 1–35 (2024)
52. Yuan, X., Kong, W., Luo, Z., Xu, M.: Efficient inference offloading for mixture-of-experts large language models in internet of medical things. Electronics **13**(11), 2077 (2024)
53. Yue, L., Xing, S., Chen, J., Fu, T.: Clinicalagent: clinical trial multi-agent system with large language model-based reasoning. In: Proceedings of the 15th ACM International Conference on Bioinformatics, Computational Biology and Health Informatics, pp. 1–10 (2024)
54. Zhang, G., et al.: Leveraging long context in retrieval augmented language models for medical question answering. npj Dig. Med. **8**(1), 239 (2025)
55. Zhang, Z., Ni, H.: Critical care studies using large language models based on electronic healthcare records: a technical note. J. Intensive Med. **5**(02), 137–150 (2025)
56. Zheng, C., et al.: Development and evaluation of a large language model of ophthalmology in Chinese. Br. J. Ophthalmol. **108**(10), 1390–1397 (2024)

GazeMIL: Attention-Based Multiple Instance Learning for Interpretable Dyslexia Detection from Multi-task Eye-Tracking Data

Jayakanth Kunhoth, Moutaz Saleh(✉), Somaya Al-Maadeed, and Younes Akbari

Department of Computer Science and Engineering, Qatar University, Doha 2713, Qatar
{j.kunhoth,moutaz.saleh,s_alali,younes.akbari}@qu.edu.qa

Abstract. Automated dyslexia detection from eye-tracking data has predominantly relied on globally aggregated oculomotor statistics or image-based representations that discard the fine-grained structure of individual fixation events. Moreover, most methods evaluate on a single reading task, overlooking complementary cognitive demands across task types, and none provides word-level localization of where dyslexic patterns emerge. In this work, we introduce GazeMIL, an attention-based multiple instance learning framework that addresses these limitations. Rather than collapsing a reading trial into a fixed-size feature vector, GazeMIL treats each trial as a bag of fixation instances encoding spatial position, duration, saccadic context, and regression behavior. Task-specific gated-attention encoders learn to assign diagnostic importance weights to individual fixations, and the resulting bag embeddings from multiple cognitively distinct reading tasks are fused for subject-level classification. Because attention weights are intrinsic to the forward pass, they map directly to word and line positions on the reading stimulus, yielding interpretable heatmaps without post-hoc attribution. Evaluated on the ETDD70 benchmark under 5-fold stratified cross-validation, the best multi-task configuration achieves 90.0% accuracy, 0.914 AUC, and 0.899 F1 score, surpassing or matching existing methods on this benchmark. Attention heatmaps reveal that dyslexic readers exhibit concentrated high-attention fixations at specific word positions, while typically developing readers show broadly distributed attention. Dyslexic readers also show significantly lower attention entropy (4.08 ± 0.65 vs. 4.61 ± 0.54, $p = 0.0005$), providing a novel biomarker of reading regularity. To our knowledge, GazeMIL is the first application of attention-based multiple instance learning to eye-tracking data for dyslexia classification.

Keywords: Dyslexia Detection · Eye-Tracking · Multiple Instance Learning · Attention Mechanism · Multi-Task Learning · Explainable AI

O. Gervasi et al. (Eds.): ICCSA 2026, LNCS 16768, pp. 20–37, 2027.
https://doi.org/10.1007/978-3-032-30488-9_2

1 Introduction

Developmental dyslexia is a prevalent neurodevelopmental condition that impairs fluent and accurate word recognition despite normal intellectual ability and adequate instructional exposure [1,2]. Delayed identification compounds the risk of academic underachievement and emotional distress [3,4], motivating the development of objective, scalable screening instruments. Eye-tracking technology offers a compelling pathway toward this goal: by recording fixation durations, saccade kinematics, and regression patterns at millisecond resolution, it captures the moment-by-moment unfolding of reading in a non-invasive manner [5,6]. Dyslexic readers consistently exhibit prolonged fixations, elevated regression rates, and reduced saccade amplitudes relative to typically developing peers [7,8], prompting a growing body of work on machine-learning-based classification from eye-tracking data [9–11].

Despite encouraging results, two key limitations persist. First, most prior methods either operate on globally aggregated feature vectors that condense an entire reading trial into summary statistics (e.g., mean fixation duration, total regression count) for traditional classifiers [7,12,13], or convert gaze data into image representations such as scanpath visualizations or fixation heatmaps for CNN-based classification [9,10]. In both paradigms, the fine-grained sequential and spatial structure of individual fixation events is lost: a single prolonged fixation on a morphologically complex word carries different diagnostic information than one caused by momentary distraction, yet neither approach preserves this distinction. Second, most studies evaluate on a single reading task or model multiple tasks independently [14,15], forfeiting the opportunity to capture both task-invariant and task-specific markers of reading difficulty across cognitively diverse contexts [16].

We address both limitations by casting eye-tracking-based dyslexia classification as a multiple instance learning (MIL) problem. Each reading trial is treated as a bag of fixation instances, each described by a compact 10-dimensional feature vector of spatial, temporal, and oculomotor attributes. Task-specific gated-attention MIL encoders learn to weight individual fixations by diagnostic relevance, and the resulting bag embeddings from three cognitively distinct reading tasks are fused for subject-level classification. Because attention weights are intrinsic to the forward pass, they map directly back to word- and line-level positions on the stimulus, yielding interpretable heatmaps without post-hoc attribution.

Our contributions are as follows:

- We introduce, to the best of our knowledge, the first MIL formulation for eye-tracking-based dyslexia detection, replacing globally aggregated features with fixation-level instance representations.
- We propose a multi-task gated-attention MIL architecture that fuses task-specific bag embeddings to capture complementary reading-difficulty markers across diverse tasks.

- We provide intrinsic explainability via attention-derived heatmaps and entropy analysis that reveal where in the text the model focuses its diagnostic attention.
- We evaluate on the ETDD70 dataset [12] and demonstrate competitive or superior classification performance relative to existing methods.

By shifting the unit of analysis from globally aggregated trial statistics to individual fixation events and by jointly modelling multiple reading tasks through learned attention, the proposed framework offers a more granular, interpretable, and generalizable approach to automated dyslexia screening. The remainder of this paper is organized as follows. Section 2 reviews prior work. Section 3 describes the dataset. Section 4 presents the proposed methodology. Section 5 reports experimental results. Section 6 provides a discussion, and Sect. 7 concludes the paper.

2 Related Work

Early work on eye-tracking-based dyslexia detection followed a common pipeline: extract oculomotor summary statistics from a single reading task, select informative features, and train a supervised classifier. Rello and Ballesteros [9] trained SVMs and decision trees on fixation and regression features from 97 Spanish-speaking participants. Nilsson Benfatto et al. [10] applied a linear SVM with recursive feature elimination to gaze data from 185 Swedish schoolchildren. Smyrnakis et al. [13] proposed the RADAR composite score combining fixation duration, saccade length, and regression rate, while Asvestopoulou et al. [11] applied LASSO-based selection to reduce the feature space. Prabha and Bhargavi [7] compared random forests, SVMs, and gradient-boosted classifiers on compact fixation and saccade features. A common limitation across these studies is the reliance on globally aggregated statistics that compress an entire reading trial into a fixed-length vector, with evaluation limited to a single cognitive task.

To reduce dependence on manual feature engineering, subsequent work applied deep learning to gaze signal representations. Nerušil et al. [14] trained a CNN on raw gaze coordinate trajectories, while Vajs et al. [17] extracted spatiotemporal features from multiple reading trials, though all trials involved the same reading activity. Svaricek et al. [18] introduced INSIGHT, converting fixation sequences into two-dimensional visualizations classified with a ResNet18 backbone and Grad-CAM explainability, evaluating across tasks and languages but modelling each task independently. Le et al. [19] proposed a time-series grid representation preserving spatial and temporal dynamics of gaze trajectories. While these methods capture richer structure than global statistics, they still operate on fixed-size representations that discard individual fixation-level information, and tasks are analysed in isolation.

Only a few studies have examined the influence of task type on classification. El Hmimdi et al. [15] evaluated four heterogeneous oculomotor tasks and observed substantial performance variation across task types, yet each task was modelled independently. Sedmidubsky et al. [12] released the ETDD70 dataset with three cognitively distinct reading tasks and provided single-task baselines using over 400 features, but did not pursue cross-task fusion. Nguyen et al. [20] explored feature learning strategies on multi-task data, though analysis remained at the level of global feature vectors. Across the surveyed literature, no prior work has proposed a unified framework that jointly models fixation-level information from multiple cognitively distinct tasks through learned attention. The present work bridges this gap by introducing an attention-based MIL framework that retains fixation-level granularity, learns task-specific attention distributions, fuses multi-task bag embeddings for subject-level classification, and provides intrinsic interpretability by mapping attention weights back to positions on the reading stimulus.

3 Dataset

We evaluate the proposed framework on the ETDD70 dataset [12], the only publicly available eye-tracking dataset explicitly designed for multi-task dyslexia screening in children. Alternative datasets considered include the Swedish dataset by Nilsson Benfatto et al. [10], which contains recordings from 185 children but is limited to a single reading task, and the CopCo dataset [21], which comprises recordings from adult participants under a single-task design. Neither dataset supports the multi-task analysis central to our framework, making ETDD70 the most suitable choice for this study.

The dataset comprises recordings from 70 participants, 35 diagnosed with developmental dyslexia and 35 typically developing controls, aged 9 to 10 years, with balanced gender distribution across both groups. Dyslexia diagnoses were established prior to data collection through cooperation with psychological counseling centers, which facilitated the recruitment of pupils formally diagnosed with dyslexia. Non-dyslexic participants showing no symptoms of dyslexia were recruited through counseling facilities of selected elementary schools. The diagnostic tasks were designed based on standardized paper-based dyslexia screening instruments used in Czechia, transferred to a controlled digital format for eye-tracking measurement. Full details of the diagnostic procedure, screening instruments, and participant recruitment are reported in the original dataset paper [12].

Three cognitively distinct reading tasks are included, each targeting a different aspect of reading ability. Syllable reading presents a 9×10 grid of syllables probing sub-word phonological decoding ability in isolation from lexical or semantic context. Meaningful text reading presents a 7-line narrative paragraph at an appropriate reading level for the age group, targeting reading fluency, word recognition, and comprehension simultaneously. Pseudo-Text reading presents artificial sentences composed of phonologically plausible but semantically meaningless words, requiring pure phonetic decoding in the absence of semantic support. Together the three tasks capture complementary cognitive dimensions of reading, making their joint analysis well-suited to a multi-task learning framework.

Eye movements were recorded using a stationary SMI RED 250 remote eye tracker at a sampling rate of 250 Hz under controlled laboratory conditions. The dataset provides four file types per subject per task: raw binocular gaze streams, fixation events, saccade events, and a pre-extracted metrics file containing over 400 globally aggregated oculomotor features. The proposed framework operates exclusively on the fixation and saccade event files, constructing per-fixation instance vectors as described in Sect. 4.

Each fixation event is annotated with area-of-interest (AOI) labels at two levels of granularity: `aoi_line`, identifying the text line number ($l \in \{1, \ldots, 7\}$) on which the fixation landed, and `aoi_subline`, identifying the specific word position within that line ($w \in \{1, \ldots, W\}$). The average number of fixations per subject per task ranges from approximately 100 to 150, confirming that each reading trial produces a bag of sufficient size for attention-based aggregation. Figure 1 shows the reading stimuli presented across the three tasks.

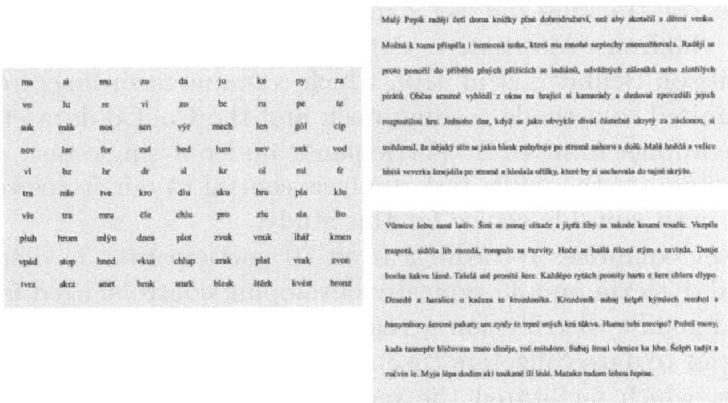

Fig. 1. Reading stimuli used in the three tasks. Left: T1 (syllable reading), a 9×10 grid of isolated syllables. Top right: T2 (meaningful text), a 7-line narrative paragraph. Bottom right: T3 (pseudo-text), a 7-line passage of phonologically plausible but semantically meaningless words.

4 Methodology

Figure 2 presents an overview of the proposed multi-task attention-based multiple instance learning framework for dyslexia classification from eye-tracking data. The framework consists of four sequential components: (1) fixation instance construction from raw eye-tracking recordings, (2) instance-level feature extraction, (3) task-specific attention-based MIL encoding, and (4) multi-task fusion and classification. An auxiliary explainability module maps learned attention weights back to word-level and line-level positions on the reading stimulus.

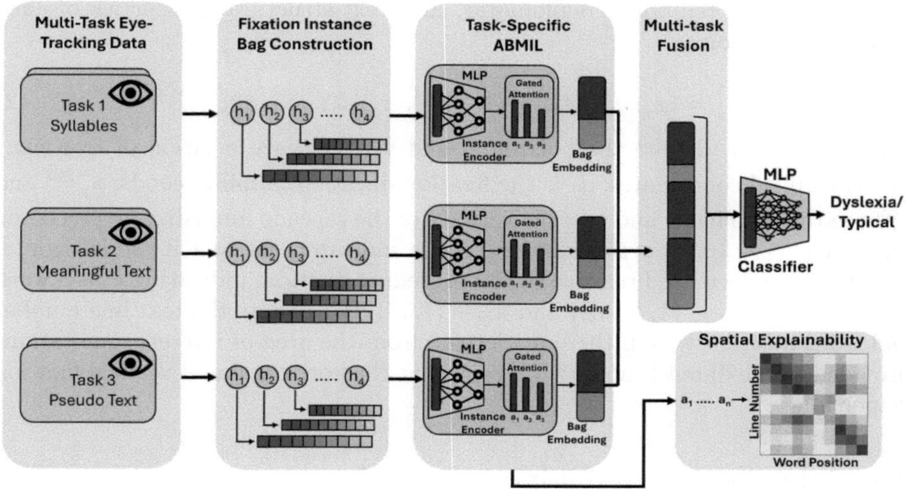

Fig. 2. Overview of the proposed GazeMIL framework. For each reading task, fixation instances are encoded by a task-specific MLP and aggregated via gated attention pooling into a fixed-size bag embedding. The task-specific bag embeddings are concatenated and passed to a classification head for binary prediction. Attention weights are mapped back to word and line positions on the reading stimulus for explainability.

4.1 Problem Formulation

Let $\mathcal{D} = \{(\mathbf{X}_i, y_i)\}_{i=1}^{N}$ denote the dataset of N subjects, where $y_i \in \{0, 1\}$ is the subject-level label (0: typically developing, 1: dyslexic). Each subject participates in T reading tasks, $\mathcal{T} = \{T_1, T_2, T_3\}$, corresponding to syllable reading, meaningful text reading, and pseudo-text reading respectively.

For subject i and task t, the reading trial is represented as a *bag* of fixation instances:

$$\mathbf{X}_i^{(t)} = \{\mathbf{h}_{i,j}^{(t)}\}_{j=1}^{N_i^{(t)}} \tag{1}$$

where $\mathbf{h}_{i,j}^{(t)} \in \mathbb{R}^d$ denotes the j-th fixation instance vector and $N_i^{(t)}$ is the total number of fixations recorded for subject i during task t. In accordance with the MIL assumption, only the bag-level label y_i is observed during training; no instance-level annotations are available or required. The classification objective is to learn a mapping $f : \{\mathbf{X}_i^{(t)}\}_{t \in \mathcal{T}} \to y_i$ from multi-task fixation bags to subject-level dyslexia labels.

4.2 Instance Feature Extraction

Each fixation instance $\mathbf{h}_{i,j}^{(t)} \in \mathbb{R}^{10}$ is constructed by merging the fixation and saccade event files for the corresponding subject and task. The feature vector encodes spatial, temporal, oculomotor, and text-structural properties of each individual fixation:

$$\mathbf{h}_{i,j}^{(t)} = \left[x_j,\ y_j,\ d_j,\ s_j^{\mathrm{ampl}},\ s_j^{\mathrm{vel}},\ r_j,\ l_j,\ w_j,\ \sigma_j^x,\ \sigma_j^y\right]^\top \tag{2}$$

where x_j and y_j denote the horizontal and vertical gaze position of fixation j in screen pixel coordinates; d_j is the fixation duration in milliseconds; s_j^{ampl} and s_j^{vel} are the amplitude and average velocity of the saccade immediately preceding fixation j; $r_j \in \{0, 1\}$ is a binary regression indicator, set to 1 if the horizontal gaze position decreased relative to the preceding fixation, indicating a backward eye movement; $l_j \in \{1, \ldots, L\}$ and $w_j \in \{1, \ldots, W\}$ denote the text line number and word position within the line, derived from the area-of-interest annotations provided in the dataset; and σ_j^x, σ_j^y represent the horizontal and vertical fixation dispersion.

4.3 Attention-Based Multiple Instance Learning

Instance Encoder. Each fixation instance $\mathbf{h}_{i,j}^{(t)}$ is independently encoded by a task-specific instance encoder $f_\theta^{(t)} : \mathbb{R}^{10} \to \mathbb{R}^E$, implemented as a two-layer multilayer perceptron (MLP) with ReLU activations and dropout regularization:

$$\mathbf{e}_{i,j}^{(t)} = f_\theta^{(t)}\left(\mathbf{h}_{i,j}^{(t)}\right) \in \mathbb{R}^E \tag{3}$$

where E denotes the embedding dimension. The set of encoded instances for subject i under task t is denoted $\mathbf{E}_i^{(t)} = \{\mathbf{e}_{i,j}^{(t)}\}_{j=1}^{N_i^{(t)}}$.

Gated Attention Pooling. To aggregate the variable-length set of instance embeddings into a fixed-size bag-level representation, we adopt the gated attention mechanism proposed by Ilse et al. [22]. For each instance embedding $\mathbf{e}_{i,j}^{(t)}$, a scalar attention weight $a_{i,j}^{(t)}$ is computed as:

$$a_{i,j}^{(t)} = \frac{\exp\left\{\mathbf{w}^\top \left(\tanh\left(\mathbf{U}\,\mathbf{e}_{i,j}^{(t)}\right) \odot \sigma\left(\mathbf{V}\,\mathbf{e}_{i,j}^{(t)}\right)\right)\right\}}{\sum_{k=1}^{N_i^{(t)}} \exp\left\{\mathbf{w}^\top \left(\tanh\left(\mathbf{U}\,\mathbf{e}_{i,k}^{(t)}\right) \odot \sigma\left(\mathbf{V}\,\mathbf{e}_{i,k}^{(t)}\right)\right)\right\}} \tag{4}$$

where $\mathbf{U}, \mathbf{V} \in \mathbb{R}^{A \times E}$ are learnable weight matrices, $\mathbf{w} \in \mathbb{R}^A$ is a learnable weight vector, A denotes the attention dimension, $\tanh(\cdot)$ and $\sigma(\cdot)$ denote the hyperbolic tangent and sigmoid activation functions, respectively, and $\odot$ denotes element-wise multiplication. The softmax normalization ensures $\sum_{j=1}^{N_i^{(t)}} a_{i,j}^{(t)} = 1$.

The bag-level embedding for subject i under task t is then computed as the attention-weighted sum of instance embeddings:

$$\mathbf{z}_i^{(t)} = \sum_{j=1}^{N_i^{(t)}} a_{i,j}^{(t)}\,\mathbf{e}_{i,j}^{(t)} \in \mathbb{R}^E \tag{5}$$

4.4 Multi-task Fusion and Classification

Independent ABMIL encoders are applied to the fixation bags from each reading task, yielding task-specific bag embeddings $\mathbf{z}_i^{(T_1)}$, $\mathbf{z}_i^{(T_2)}$, and $\mathbf{z}_i^{(T_3)}$. These embeddings are concatenated to form a unified multi-task representation:

$$\mathbf{z}_i^{\text{fused}} = \mathbf{z}_i^{(T_1)} \parallel \mathbf{z}_i^{(T_2)} \parallel \mathbf{z}_i^{(T_3)} \in \mathbb{R}^{3E} \tag{6}$$

where $\parallel$ denotes vector concatenation. The fused representation is passed to a classification network $g_\phi : \mathbb{R}^{3E} \to \mathbb{R}$, implemented as a two-layer MLP, producing a scalar logit. The predicted probability of dyslexia is:

$$\hat{p}_i = \sigma\big(g_\phi\big(\mathbf{z}_i^{\text{fused}}\big)\big) \tag{7}$$

where $\sigma(\cdot)$ denotes the sigmoid function. The model is trained end-to-end by minimizing the binary cross-entropy loss over bag-level labels:

$$\mathcal{L} = -\frac{1}{N}\sum_{i=1}^{N}\left[y_i \log \hat{p}_i + (1 - y_i)\log(1 - \hat{p}_i)\right] \tag{8}$$

4.5 Explainability via Attention Mapping

A key property of the proposed framework is that the attention weights $\{a_{i,j}^{(t)}\}$ are produced as part of the model's forward pass and carry direct interpretive meaning, unlike post-hoc approximation methods such as Grad-CAM. Since each fixation instance $\mathbf{h}_{i,j}^{(t)}$ is annotated with its text line number l_j and word position w_j, the attention weights can be directly mapped back to positions on the reading stimulus.

Attention Heatmap Construction. For a given task t and subject group $\mathcal{G} \in \{\text{dyslexic}, \text{TD}\}$, the group-averaged attention weight at text position (l, w) is defined as:

$$\bar{a}^{(t)}(l, w) = \frac{1}{|\mathcal{G}|}\sum_{i \in \mathcal{G}} \frac{\sum_{j:\, l_j = l,\, w_j = w} \tilde{a}_{i,j}^{(t)}}{|\{j : l_j = l,\ w_j = w\}|} \tag{9}$$

where $\tilde{a}_{i,j}^{(t)}$ denotes the per-subject min-max normalized attention weight:

$$\tilde{a}_{i,j}^{(t)} = \frac{a_{i,j}^{(t)} - \min_k a_{i,k}^{(t)}}{\max_k a_{i,k}^{(t)} - \min_k a_{i,k}^{(t)} + \epsilon} \tag{10}$$

with ϵ being a small constant for numerical stability. Per-subject min–max normalisation ensures that no single subject dominates the group-level heatmap due to differences in absolute attention magnitude. However, it prevents the group heatmap from reflecting between-group differences in overall attention intensity, preserving only the relative spatial distribution of attention within each subject.

Attention Entropy. To quantify the regularity of reading attention patterns at the subject level, we define the attention entropy for subject i under task t as the Shannon entropy of the attention weight distribution. Since the attention weights $a_{i,j}^{(t)}$ are produced by the softmax operation in Eq. (4), they satisfy $\sum_j a_{i,j}^{(t)} = 1$ and $a_{i,j}^{(t)} \geq 0$, forming a valid probability distribution. The entropy is therefore defined directly over these weights:

$$H_i^{(t)} = -\sum_{j=1}^{N_i^{(t)}} a_{i,j}^{(t)} \log\left(a_{i,j}^{(t)}\right) \tag{11}$$

The mean attention entropy across tasks is computed as:

$$\bar{H}_i = \frac{1}{|\mathcal{T}|} \sum_{t \in \mathcal{T}} H_i^{(t)} \tag{12}$$

Higher entropy indicates that attention is broadly and evenly distributed across fixations, reflecting smooth and systematic reading behavior. Lower entropy indicates that attention is concentrated on a small subset of fixations, reflecting erratic or struggling reading patterns. Group-level differences in $\bar{H}_i$ between dyslexic and typically developing readers are assessed using the non-parametric Mann-Whitney U test.

5 Evaluation and Results

All experiments follow a 5-fold stratified cross-validation protocol in which splits are performed at the subject level: all trials from a given subject are assigned exclusively to either the training or test fold, ensuring no subject appears in both partitions and preventing subject-level data leakage. For each fold, feature normalization is performed by fitting a `StandardScaler` on the training split and applying the learned statistics to both training and validation instances independently per task, preventing information leakage across folds.

Each task-specific instance encoder consists of a two-layer MLP mapping the 10-dimensional fixation input to a 64-dimensional hidden representation and then to a 32-dimensional embedding, with ReLU activations and dropout ($p = 0.3$) applied after the first layer. The gated attention module operates with an attention dimension of 16. The classification head maps the concatenated multi-task bag embeddings to a scalar logit through a two-layer MLP (hidden dimension 32, dropout $p = 0.3$). The model is trained end-to-end using the Adam optimizer with a learning rate of 10^{-3} and binary cross-entropy loss, for a maximum of 150 epochs with early stopping (patience = 20) based on validation loss. All experiments are implemented in PyTorch.

Classification performance is evaluated using accuracy, area under the ROC curve (AUC), F1 score, sensitivity, and specificity, each reported as mean $\pm$ standard deviation across the five folds.

5.1 Task Combination Ablation

To assess the contribution of individual reading tasks and their combinations, we evaluate all single-task and multi-task configurations. Table 1 reports the results.

Among single-task models, T2 (meaningful text) achieves the highest accuracy (78.6%) and AUC (0.902), suggesting that narrative reading, which engages lexical, syntactic, and semantic processing simultaneously, produces the most discriminative fixation patterns. T1 (syllable reading) and T3 (pseudo-text) perform comparably in accuracy but with higher variance, likely reflecting the more constrained cognitive demands of these tasks.

Multi-task fusion consistently improves performance over single-task models. The T2 + T3 combination achieves the best overall performance across all metrics (90.0% accuracy, 0.914 AUC, 0.899 F1), indicating strong complementarity between meaningful text reading and pseudo-text decoding. Notably, the full three-task combination (T1 + T2 + T3) achieves 85.7% accuracy, which, while superior to all single-task models, falls below the T2 + T3 configuration. This suggests that T1 (syllable grid reading), with its structurally different stimulus layout and more constrained reading pattern, may introduce representational noise that dilutes the discriminative signal captured by T2 and T3.

To assess whether the performance advantage of T2+T3 over T1+T2+T3 is statistically reliable, we conduct a one-sided paired Wilcoxon signed-rank test over the five fold-level scores, with the directional hypothesis that T2+T3 outperforms T1+T2+T3, motivated by the cognitive argument that T1's grid-based stimulus introduces qualitatively different scanning patterns that do not share the oculomotor signatures of continuous text reading. The test yields $W = 9.0$, $p = 0.41$ (accuracy) and $W = 6.0$, $p = 0.44$ (AUC), indicating no statistically significant difference at $\alpha = 0.05$. Given only five folds and 14 subjects per test fold, the test has inherently limited statistical power, and the observed mean difference (4.3% points in accuracy) should be interpreted as indicative. The preference for T2+T3 is further supported by its consistently lower variance (5.7 vs 6.4) and the cognitive complementarity between meaningful text and pseudo-text reading tasks.

Table 1. Ablation study over task combinations. T1: syllable reading, T2: meaningful text, T3: pseudo-text. Best result per metric is in **bold**.

Config	Acc. (%)	AUC	F1	Sens. (%)	Spec. (%)
T1 only	74.3 ± 10.7	0.869 ± 0.080	0.723 ± 0.134	71.4 ± 20.2	77.1 ± 11.4
T2 only	78.6 ± 13.6	0.902 ± 0.070	0.803 ± 0.109	82.9 ± 10.7	74.3 ± 26.2
T3 only	72.9 ± 14.6	0.829 ± 0.069	0.759 ± 0.094	80.0 ± 11.4	65.7 ± 35.7
T1 + T2	81.4 ± 7.3	0.878 ± 0.070	0.811 ± 0.079	82.9 ± 16.7	80.0 ± 14.6
T1 + T3	77.1 ± 7.0	0.869 ± 0.040	0.748 ± 0.106	71.4 ± 15.6	82.9 ± 5.7
T2 + T3	**90.0 ± 5.7**	**0.914 ± 0.062**	**0.899 ± 0.057**	**88.6 ± 5.7**	**91.4 ± 7.0**
T1 + T2 + T3	85.7 ± 6.4	0.894 ± 0.047	0.854 ± 0.068	85.7 ± 12.8	85.7 ± 9.0

Table 2. Ablation of MIL aggregation mechanisms. Classification accuracy (%) reported as mean ± std over 5-fold stratified cross-validation across all task configurations. The proposed gated attention results are reported in Table 1 for reference.

Config	Mean Pool	Max Pool	Std Attention
T1 only	72.9 ± 15.3	78.6 ± 7.8	78.6 ± 10.1
T4 only	81.4 ± 7.3	78.6 ± 10.1	81.4 ± 8.6
T5 only	77.1 ± 8.3	75.7 ± 9.7	77.1 ± 18.3
T1 + T4	81.4 ± 8.6	78.6 ± 9.0	82.9 ± 10.7
T1 + T5	68.6 ± 17.8	82.9 ± 7.3	74.3 ± 7.3
T4 + T5	74.3 ± 14.0	80.0 ± 9.5	82.9 ± 14.7
T1 + T4 + T5	81.4 ± 7.3	78.6 ± 12.8	80.0 ± 5.3

5.2 Ablation of MIL Aggregation Mechanisms

To evaluate the contribution of the proposed gated attention pooling, we compare it against three alternative MIL aggregation mechanisms: mean pooling, max pooling, and standard (non-gated) attention. In mean pooling, the bag-level embedding is computed as the arithmetic mean of all instance embeddings. Max pooling selects the maximum activation across instances. Standard attention uses a single-branch tanh mechanism without the sigmoid gate. All other components, the instance encoder, multi-task fusion, and classification head, remain identical across variants, and all experiments follow the same 5-fold stratified subject-level cross-validation protocol with identical random seeds.

Table 2 reports the classification accuracy across all task configurations for each aggregation variant. The proposed gated attention consistently achieves the highest accuracy on the best-performing T4+T5 configuration (90.0% ± 5.7), outperforming mean pooling (74.3% ± 14.0), max pooling (80.0% ± 9.5), and standard attention (82.9% ± 14.7) by margins of 15.7, 10.0, and 7.1% points respectively.

5.3 Comparison with Existing Methods

Table 3 compares the proposed GazeMIL framework against state-of-the-art methods evaluated on the ETDD70 dataset.

GazeMIL achieves 90.0% accuracy and 0.899 F1 score, surpassing or almost matching all published methods on this benchmark. The MLP baselines from Sedmidubsky et al. [12] achieve comparable accuracy on individual tasks (90.0–91.4%) but rely on 400+ globally aggregated statistical features per task and do not perform cross-task fusion. We followed same evaluation protocol as Sedmidubsky et al. [12], where all experiments employ 5-fold stratified subject-level cross-validation with random state 42.

The ResNet18-based INSIGHT method [18] and the time-series grid approach [19] both operate on single tasks with fixed-size representations. The LLM-based approach [20] performs multi-task fusion but requires 1,270 features and

Table 3. Comparison with published methods on the ETDD70 dataset. "Fusion" indicates whether multi-task information is combined.

Method	Fusion	Acc. (%)	F1
MLP (T1) [12]	No	91.43 ± 5.35	–
MLP (T2) [12]	No	90.00 ± 7.28	–
MLP (T3) [12]	No	88.57 ± 5.71	–
ResNet18 (T3) [18]	No	88.57 ± 8.57	–
TS-Grid + KNN [19]	No	85.7	0.86
LLM Few-shot [20]	Yes	80.6 ± 3.1	0.82 ± 0.06
GazeMIL (T2+T3)	Yes	$\mathbf{90.0 \pm 5.7}$	$\mathbf{0.899 \pm 0.057}$

achieves lower accuracy (80.6%). In contrast, GazeMIL operates on only 10 features per fixation instance, fuses information across tasks, and additionally provides intrinsic fixation-level interpretability that none of the compared methods offer.

5.4 Explainability Analysis

A key advantage of the proposed framework is that the learned attention weights provide intrinsic interpretability without requiring post-hoc attribution methods. In this section, we analyze the attention distributions produced by the best-performing T2 + T3 configuration through two complementary views: spatial attention heatmaps mapped to the reading stimulus, and attention entropy as a measure of reading regularity.

Attention Heatmaps. To examine where in the text the model concentrates its diagnostic attention, we visualize the group-averaged attention weights at two levels of granularity. For each task, a grid heatmap shows the mean attention weight at each line-by-word position, and a stimulus overlay maps attention-weighted fixation circles directly onto the reading stimulus. The grid heatmaps use absolute group-averaged attention values, while the stimulus overlays use per-subject min-max normalized weights to preserve relative within-subject patterns.

For the meaningful text task (Fig. 3), typically developing readers show high attention concentrated in the later lines (L5–L7) and early word positions (positions 1–3), with comparatively lower attention in the upper lines. Dyslexic readers show a different pattern: attention is elevated in the early-to-middle lines (L1–L3) with a prominent peak at specific word positions (e.g., position 7 in L3), and diminishes noticeably toward the later lines, particularly L5–L7. The stimulus overlay confirms this pattern, with TD fixation circles showing strong, uniformly sized circles in the lower portion of the text, while dyslexic fixation circles appear more variable in size across the stimulus.

For the pseudo-text task (Fig. 4), a distinct pattern emerges. TD readers show relatively uniform attention across lines, with moderate concentration in

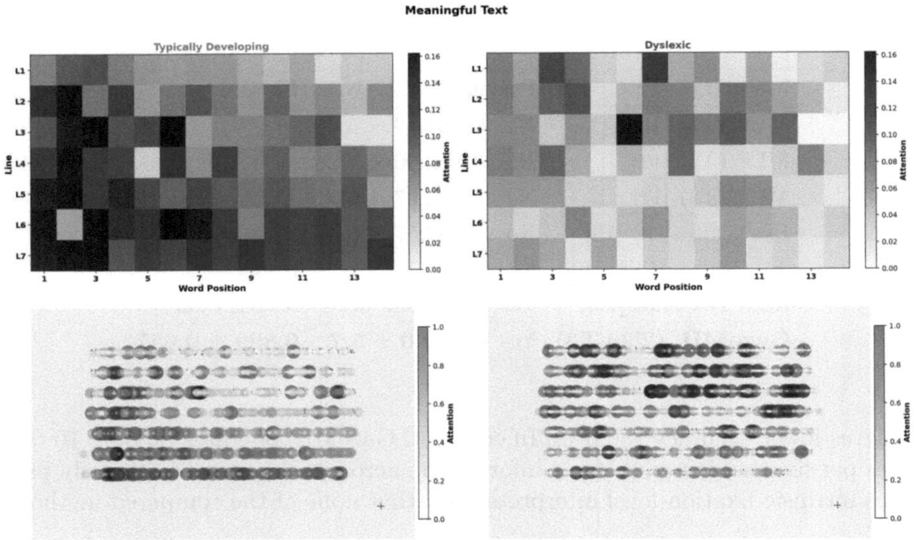

Fig. 3. Attention visualization for the meaningful text task. Top row: grid heatmap of mean attention weight per line and word position. Bottom row: attention-weighted fixation circles overlaid on the reading stimulus. Left column: typically developing readers. Right column: dyslexic readers. Grid heatmaps use absolute group-averaged values; stimulus overlays use per-subject min-max normalized weights.

the middle-to-later lines. Dyslexic readers, in contrast, exhibit markedly concentrated attention in the later lines (L5–L7), with the highest attention weights appearing in L6–L7 at both early and late word positions. The stimulus overlay for the dyslexic group shows visibly larger and darker fixation circles in the lower lines compared to the upper lines, indicating that the model identifies the strongest diagnostic signal in the later portions of the pseudo-text stimulus.

Attention Entropy. Beyond spatial localization, we quantify the overall regularity of each subject's reading attention using Shannon entropy computed over the attention weight distribution. Higher entropy indicates that attention is broadly and evenly distributed across fixations, while lower entropy indicates concentration on a smaller subset of fixations.

Figure 5 presents the distribution of mean attention entropy across subjects for both groups. Dyslexic readers show significantly lower attention entropy than typically developing peers (4.08 ± 0.65 vs. 4.61 ± 0.54, Mann-Whitney $U = 314.0$, $p = 0.0005$). The group-level separation is clearly visible in the boxplot, with minimal overlap between the two distributions. However an apparent outlier is observed in the typically developing group, likely reflecting individual variability in reading strategy or occasional lapses in sustained attention during the reading tasks.

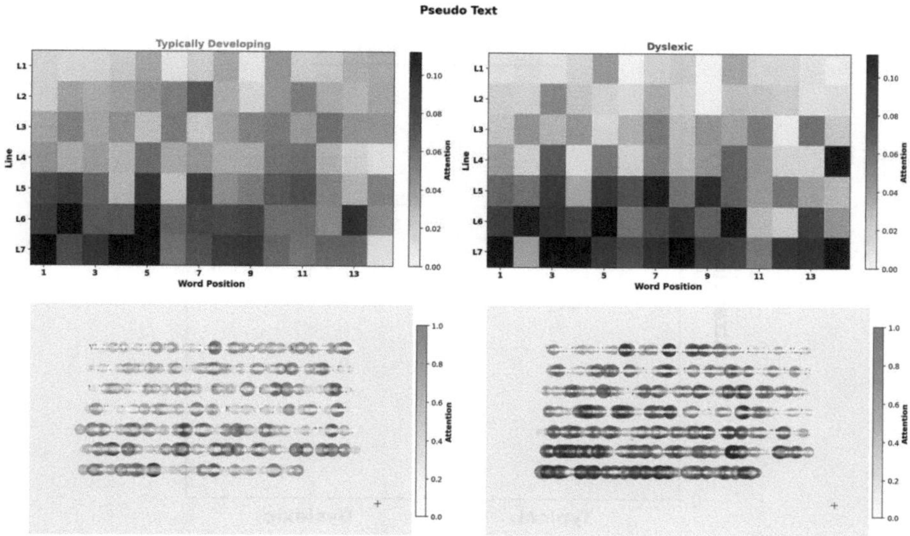

Fig. 4. Attention visualization for the pseudo-text task. Top row: grid heatmap of mean attention weight per line and word position. Bottom row: attention-weighted fixation circles overlaid on the reading stimulus. Left column: typically developing readers. Right column: dyslexic readers. Grid heatmaps use absolute group-averaged values; stimulus overlays use per-subject min-max normalized weights.

6 Discussion

The experimental results highlight several key observations regarding task complementarity, attention-based interpretability, and the trade-off between classification performance and explainability. The ablation study reveals that the combination of meaningful text (T2) and pseudo-text (T3) consistently outperforms all other configurations, including the full three-task model. This can be attributed to the complementary cognitive demands of these two tasks: meaningful text reading engages lexical access, syntactic parsing, and semantic integration simultaneously, while pseudo-text reading strips away semantic support and isolates phonological decoding ability. Together, these tasks capture both top-down language-driven processes and bottom-up decoding mechanisms, providing a richer diagnostic signal than either task alone. The inclusion of T1 (syllable grid reading) reduces performance, likely because its grid-based stimulus layout elicits qualitatively different scanning patterns that do not share the oculomotor signatures associated with reading difficulty in continuous text, introducing representational noise into the fused embedding.

The spatial attention patterns reveal qualitatively different reading strategies between groups, and these patterns vary meaningfully across tasks. In meaningful text, TD readers exhibit high attention in the later lines (L5–L7), suggesting that the model identifies sustained reading momentum as a distinguishing fea-

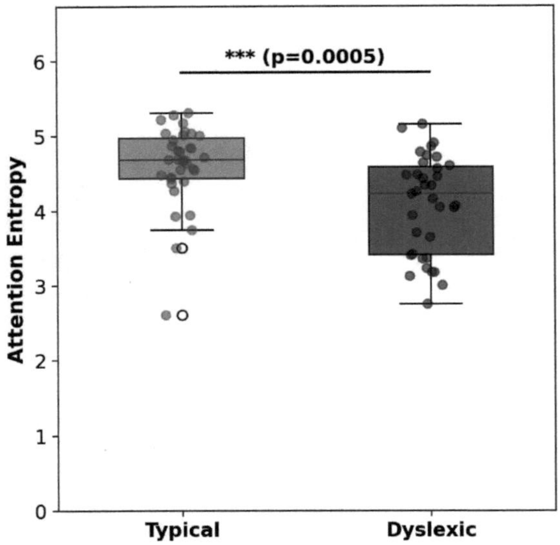

Fig. 5. Distribution of mean attention entropy for typically developing and dyslexic readers. Lower entropy reflects concentrated attention on fewer fixations. Statistical comparison via Mann-Whitney U test ($p = 0.0005$).

ture, while dyslexic readers show elevated attention in the early-to-middle lines (L1–L3) where initial decoding demands are highest. In pseudo-text, this pattern shifts: dyslexic readers show markedly concentrated attention in the later lines (L5–L7), where the absence of semantic context causes phonological decoding demands to accumulate progressively. This progressive degradation likely reflects the accumulation of phonological decoding demands in the absence of semantic support. The contrasting patterns across tasks further validate the multi-task design, as meaningful text and pseudo-text expose different aspects of reading difficulty that the model learns to exploit through task-specific attention encoders.

The significantly lower attention entropy observed in dyslexic readers ($p = 0.0005$) provides a quantitative characterization of reading regularity derived directly from the model's internal representation. High entropy indicates that many fixations contribute roughly equally to the bag-level representation, corresponding to smooth and regular reading, while low entropy indicates concentration on a small number of diagnostically salient fixations, reflecting intermittent periods of pronounced difficulty. This finding aligns with established observations that dyslexic readers produce more variable gaze patterns [7,8], but unlike conventional oculomotor statistics such as fixation duration variance, attention entropy captures this irregularity through learned diagnostic relevance, providing a complementary and potentially more sensitive measure.

A distinguishing property of the proposed framework is that its explainability is intrinsic to the model architecture. Post-hoc methods such as Grad-

CAM [18] generate attribution maps by perturbing or backpropagating through a trained model, producing explanations that approximate the decision process but are not guaranteed to reflect the model's actual internal computation. In contrast, the gated attention weights in the proposed MIL framework directly determine how individual fixation embeddings are aggregated into the bag-level representation, and in this computational sense constitute a faithful record of the aggregation process. While attention weights govern the aggregation process, we interpret them as indicators of relative fixation relevance within the model's learned representation rather than as causal explanations of diagnostic importance [23, 24]. Combined with area-of-interest annotations, these weights produce spatially grounded explanations that are interpretable to clinicians and educators. Formal faithfulness evaluation through attention permutation or erase-and-evaluate analysis remains an avenue for future work.

GazeMIL achieves 90.0% accuracy, within 1.4% points of the best single-task MLP baseline (91.43%) reported by Sedmidubsky et al. [12]. This marginal difference should be interpreted in context: the MLP baseline relies on over 400 hand-crafted statistical features per task, evaluates each task independently without cross-task fusion, and provides no mechanism for identifying which fixation events or text positions contribute to the classification decision. GazeMIL surpasses all other published methods on this benchmark, including INSIGHT [18] (88.57%), the time-series grid method [19] (85.7%), and the LLM-based approach [20] (80.6%). Among these, only INSIGHT provides any form of explainability through post-hoc Grad-CAM, whereas GazeMIL offers intrinsic, fixation-level, stimulus-grounded attention maps alongside a statistically validated entropy-based biomarker.

Several limitations should be acknowledged. The ETDD70 dataset comprises 70 participants from a single site recorded in Czech, and generalizability to other languages, age groups, and recording conditions remains to be established. The current fusion strategy uses simple concatenation; more sophisticated mechanisms such as cross-task attention or learned task weighting may further improve performance. Additionally, the present analysis does not link attention patterns to specific linguistic properties of the stimulus words such as word frequency or morphological complexity, which would provide deeper cognitive insights. Finally, the evaluation is cross-sectional; longitudinal studies examining whether attention entropy changes in response to reading interventions could establish its clinical utility as a progress monitoring tool.

7 Conclusion

We presented GazeMIL, the first application of attention-based multiple instance learning to eye-tracking data for dyslexia classification. The framework replaces globally aggregated feature representations with fixation-level instance modelling, jointly processes multiple cognitively distinct reading tasks through task-specific gated-attention encoders, and provides intrinsic stimulus-grounded explainability without relying on post-hoc attribution methods. On the ETDD70 benchmark, GazeMIL achieves 90.0% accuracy and 0.914 AUC while operating on a compact per-fixation representation, demonstrating that preserving fixation-level granularity and exploiting multi-task complementarity offers a viable alternative to heavily engineered feature pipelines. The attention entropy measure introduced in this work provides a statistically significant ($p = 0.0005$) quantitative marker distinguishing dyslexic from typically developing reading patterns. Future work will target validation across languages and datasets, explore richer fusion strategies such as cross-task attention, correlate attention patterns with linguistic properties of stimulus words, and investigate longitudinal tracking of attention entropy to assess its utility for monitoring reading intervention progress.

Acknowledgment. This publication is supported by Qatar University High Impact Grant QUHI-CENG-25/26-665. The contents of this manuscript are solely the responsibility of the authors and do not necessarily represent the official views of Qatar University.

Data Availibility Statement. The ETDD70 dataset used in this study is publicly available at https://doi.org/10.5281/zenodo.13332134 [12]. The complete source code for the proposed method is available at https://github.com/Jayakanth21/GazeMIL.

Ethics Statement. This study uses the publicly available ETDD70 dataset [12]; all ethics approvals, parental consent, and GDPR compliance for eye-tracking data of minors were established by the original dataset authors [12].

References

1. Ahire, N., Awale, R., Patnaik, S., Wagh, A.: A comprehensive review of machine learning approaches for dyslexia diagnosis. Multimedia Tools Appl. **82**, 13557–13577 (2023)
2. Valdois, S.: The visual-attention span deficit in developmental dyslexia: review of evidence for a visual-attention-based deficit. Dyslexia **28**, 397–415 (2022)
3. Haft, S.L., Greiner de Magalhães, C., Hoeft, F.: A systematic review of the consequences of stigma and stereotype threat for individuals with specific learning disabilities. J. Learn. Disabil. **56**, 193–209 (2023)
4. Kunhoth, J., Al-Maadeed, S., Kunhoth, S., Akbari, Y., Saleh, M.: Automated systems for diagnosis of dysgraphia in children: a survey and novel framework. Int. J. Doc. Anal. Recogn. (IJDAR) **27**, 707–735 (2024)
5. Liu, Z., Yang, Z., Gu, Y., Liu, H., Wang, P.: The effectiveness of eye tracking in the diagnosis of cognitive disorders: a systematic review and meta-analysis. PLoS ONE **16**, e0254059 (2021)
6. Nguyen, T.K.C., Le, D.D., Le, T.H., Nguyen, T.C.H., Ngo, T.D.: The use of eye tracking in supporting individuals with dyslexia: a review. Disabil. Rehabil. Assist. Technol. **20**, 1183–1198 (2025)
7. Prabha, A.J., Bhargavi, R.: Predictive model for dyslexia from fixations and saccadic eye movement events. Comput. Methods Programs Biomed. **195**, 105538 (2020)

8. Raatikainen, P., Hautala, J., Loberg, O., Kärkkäinen, T., Leppänen, P., Nieminen, P.: Detection of developmental dyslexia with machine learning using eye movement data. Array **12**, 100087 (2021)
9. Rello, L., Ballesteros, M.: Detecting readers with dyslexia using machine learning with eye tracking measures. In: Proceedings of 12th International Web for All Conference, pp. 1–8 (2015)
10. Benfatto, M.N., et al.: Screening for dyslexia using eye tracking during reading. PLoS ONE **11**, e0165508 (2016)
11. Asvestopoulou, T., et al.: DyslexML: screening tool for dyslexia using machine learning. arXiv preprint arXiv:1903.06274 (2019)
12. Sedmidubsky, J., Dostalova, N., Svaricek, R., Culemann, W.: ETDD70: eye-tracking dataset for classification of dyslexia using AI-based methods. In: Proceedings of International Conference on Similarity Search and Applications, pp. 34–48 (2024)
13. Smyrnakis, I., et al.: RADAR: a novel fast-screening method for reading difficulties with special focus on dyslexia. PLoS ONE **12**, e0182597 (2017)
14. Nerušil, B., Polec, J., Škunda, J., Kačur, J.: Eye tracking based dyslexia detection using a holistic approach. Sci. Rep. **11**, 15687 (2021)
15. El Hmimdi, A.E., Ward, L.M., Palpanas, T., Kapoula, Z.: Predicting dyslexia and reading speed in adolescents from eye movements in reading and non-reading tasks: a machine learning approach. Brain Sci. **11**, 1337 (2021)
16. Toki, E.I.: Using eye-tracking to assess dyslexia: a systematic review of emerging evidence. Educ. Sci. **14**, 1256 (2024)
17. Vajs, I., Ković, V., Papić, T., Savić, A.M., Janković, M.M.: Spatiotemporal eye-tracking feature set for improved recognition of dyslexic reading patterns in children. Sensors **22**, 4900 (2022)
18. Svaricek, R., Dostalova, N., Sedmidubsky, J., Cernek, A.: Insight: combining fixation visualisations and residual neural networks for dyslexia classification from eye-tracking data. Dyslexia **31**, e1801 (2025)
19. Le, L., Nguyen, Q.T., Duong-Trung, N., Williams-King, D.: Time-series grid encoding of eye-tracking data for explainable AI in dyslexia detection. In: Proceedings of Symposium on Eye Tracking Research and Applications, pp. 1–3 (2025)
20. Nguyen, Q.-T., et al.: Learning disorder detection using eye tracking: are large language models better than machine learning?. In: Proceedings of Symposium on Eye Tracking Research and Applications, pp. 1–13 (2025)
21. Hollenstein, N., Barrett, M., Björnsdóttir, M.: The Copenhagen corpus of eye tracking recordings from natural reading of Danish texts. arXiv preprint arXiv:2204.13311 (2022)
22. Ilse, M., Tomczak, J., Welling, M.: Attention-based deep multiple instance learning. In: Proceedings of International Conference on Machine Learning (ICML), pp. 2127–2136 (2018)
23. Jain, S., Wallace, B.C.: Attention is not explanation. In: Proceedings of 2019 Conference on North American Chapter of the Association for Computational Linguistics: Human Language Technologies (NAACL-HLT), pp. 3543–3556 (2019)
24. Wiegreffe, S., Pinter, Y.: Attention is not not explanation. In: Proceedings of 2019 Conference Empirical Methods in Natural Language Processing and 9th International Joint Conference on Natural Language Processing (EMNLP-IJCNLP), pp. 11–20 (2019)

Soft Routing-Inspired Specialization for Efficient Satellite Image Time Series Segmentation

Paulo Victor de Magalhães Rozatto, Saulo Moraes Villela, Luiz Maurílio da Silva Maciel, and Marcelo Bernardes Vieira(✉)

Department of Computer Science, Federal University of Juiz de Fora, Juiz de Fora, Brazil
paulo.rozatto@estudante.ufjf.br, {saulo.moraes,luiz.maciel,marcelo.bernardes}@ufjf.br

Abstract. Satellite image time series segmentation requires models that capture complex temporal patterns while remaining computationally efficient for large-scale remote sensing applications. Motivated by principles from Mixture-of-Experts (MoE) models, we introduce routing-inspired specialization into the Exchanger architecture to increase representational flexibility without substantially increasing inference cost. Rather than using sparse expert routing, the proposed approach leverages soft routing mechanisms, incorporating expert-specific transformations within the temporal processing pipeline to utilize model capacity more efficiently while maintaining linear computational complexity.

We evaluate the approach on the PASTIS and MTLCC benchmarks and compare it to a consistently trained Exchanger baseline. While absolute improvements in mean Intersection-over-Union (mIoU) are modest and within the expected cross-validation variability, certain configurations achieve baseline-level accuracy while reducing FLOPs by up to 30%, lowering latency and increasing throughput. These results provide evidence that MoE-inspired specialization can improve the efficiency and scalability of dense temporal models for satellite image segmentation.

Keywords: Satellite Image Time Series · Semantic Segmentation · Mixture of Experts · Remote Sensing

1 Introduction

Satellite Image Time Series (SITS) are sequences of satellite observations of the same geographic area acquired over time. They provide rich information for monitoring agricultural activity, vegetation cycles, and land-cover change at large scales [13]. Effectively exploiting SITS requires modeling long-term temporal contexts to capture seasonal patterns, crop phenology, and gradual land-cover dynamics.

Vision Transformers (ViTs) have recently emerged as a powerful paradigm for visual representation learning and have been successfully adapted to SITS analysis due to their ability to model long-range dependencies in time and space [16].

O. Gervasi et al. (Eds.): ICCSA 2026, LNCS 16768, pp. 38–51, 2027.
https://doi.org/10.1007/978-3-032-30488-9_3

However, their quadratic self-attention cost makes direct application to long temporal sequences computationally expensive.

Exchanger [1] addresses this limitation by replacing full self-attention with a linear-complexity token exchange mechanism based on a Collect–Update–Distribute pipeline. While this design enables efficient global information flow, the grouped representations are processed using shared transformations across all groups, leaving limited room for group-specific specialization.

In this work, we apply Mixture-of-Experts (MoE) [4] principles to the Exchanger framework to increase representational flexibility while maintaining linear computational complexity. Inspired by Soft MoE [9], we reinterpret Exchanger's collect stage as a form of soft routing, analogous to the dispatch operation, and incorporate expert-specialized transformations within the update stage. We further adapt the distribute stage to more closely resemble the combine operation in Soft MoE.

Our experiments suggest that interpreting Exchanger through the lens of soft routing specialization can lead to a more efficient utilization of model capacity on the PASTIS benchmark [13], where Exchanger already serves as a strong baseline. While the observed improvements in mean Intersection over Union (mIoU) are modest and fall within typical cross-validation variability, the proposed modifications provide a more favorable trade-off between predictive performance and computational cost. In particular, the revised combine operation allows certain configurations to achieve baseline-level accuracy while reducing FLOPs (float point operations) and latency, and improving throughput.

Contributions. The main contributions of this work are as follows:

- We reinterpret Exchanger's Collect–Update–Distribute pipeline using the perspective of soft expert routing, highlighting structural and functional similarities between token exchange and mixture-of-experts computation.
- We introduce a soft routing-inspired specialization mechanism within the Exchanger temporal encoder, where latent groups act as soft slots processed by expert-specific modules, enabling group-wise specialization while maintaining linear complexity.
- We propose a more efficient implementation of the distribute (combine) stage by reusing attention logits from the collect stage, reducing computational and memory costs without noticeably affecting predictive performance.
- We empirically show that the proposed modifications maintain comparable segmentation accuracy to the Exchanger baseline on PASTIS [13] and MTLCC [12], while providing improved efficiency and more favorable scaling behavior with sequence length.

2 Related Work

Transformer architectures have become widely used for SITS segmentation. U-TAE [13] introduced temporal attention on top of a convolutional backbone, while TSViT [16] demonstrated the effectiveness of fully transformer-based spatiotemporal modeling.

To improve scalability for long temporal sequences, Exchanger proposed a non-hierarchical Vision Transformer that replaces quadratic self-attention with a linear-complexity token exchange mechanism based on a three-stage pipeline and, to the best of our knowledge, represents the state of the art on the PASTIS dataset [13]. VistaFormer [8] later explored scalable transformer architectures for large-scale SITS segmentation through factorized spatiotemporal modeling. Our work builds directly on Exchanger and investigates how introducing routing-based specialization affects the balance between computational cost and segmentation accuracy.

Mixture-of-Experts (MoE) models increase model capacity through expert specialization, combined with routing mechanisms that assign inputs to different subnetworks [15]. MoE layers were first widely adopted to scale Transformer models in natural language processing, where sparse routing enables large parameter counts with limited per-token computation [3,5]. Similar sparse MoE strategies have recently been explored in computer vision to scale Vision Transformers while controlling computational costs [10].

More recently, soft routing has emerged as a competitive alternative in computer vision, replacing hard expert selection with continuous routing weights that enable specialization without conditional execution [9]. In Soft MoE, routing is performed by first computing token–slot affinities and then deriving normalized dispatch and combination weights that distribute information between tokens and expert-specific latent representations. We adopt this viewpoint to reinterpret the collect stage of Exchanger as an affinity-based routing mechanism and introduce expert-specialized transformations within its update stage, increasing model capacity while preserving the linear-complexity inference behavior of the original architecture.

3 Proposed Method

The Exchanger has a factorized design, which means it separates temporal and spatial modeling for satellite image time series. Given an input sequence $X \in \mathbb{R}^{T \times C \times H \times W}$, the temporal encoder processes each spatial location as an independent temporal sequence. After this processing, the features are reshaped back to the spatial grid and fed to a spatial encoder for segmentation.

In this work, we modify only the temporal encoder, keeping both the spatial encoders unchanged. We also retain Exchanger's original strategy for collapsing spatial dimensions prior to temporal modeling: each position (h, w) is treated independently across time, reshaping the input from $T \times C \times H \times W$ into $(HW) \times T \times C$. This ensures that temporal attention operates at each spatial location without altering the spatial modeling stage.

Figure 1 provides an overview of the full architecture and highlights the routing-based specialization introduced within the temporal encoder.

Building on this formulation, the remainder of this section details the proposed modifications to the Collect–Update–Distribute pipeline. We first describe the collect operation as an attention-based soft routing mechanism, then intro-

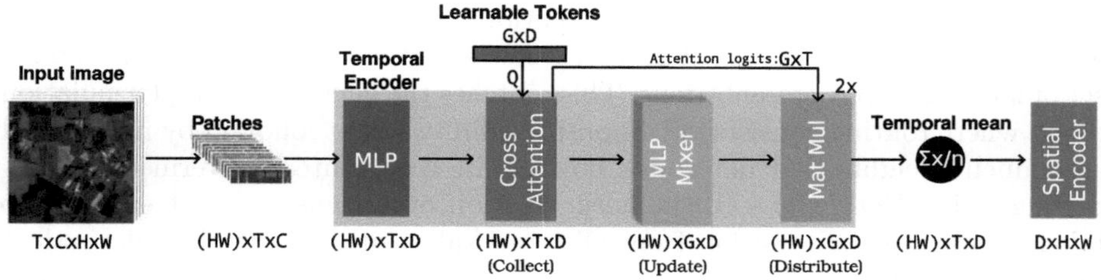

Fig. 1. Overview of the proposed architecture. The input is a satellite image time series of shape $T \times C \times H \times W$, where T denotes the number of time steps, C the number of channels, and $H \times W$ the spatial resolution. Spatial locations are processed independently over time by reshaping the input to $(HW) \times T \times C$ and projecting features to a D-dimensional embedding. Cross-attention with learnable tokens softly routes temporal features into G temporal groups. Grouped features are then updated by E MLP mixer experts. Finally, the Distribute step softly combines grouped features back into the temporal dimension. Temporal mean aggregation is applied before reshaping features to $D \times H \times W$ and passing them to a spatial encoder for pixel-wise segmentation.

duce expert-specialized transformations in the update stage, and finally present the modified distribute stage that recombines group representations using routing-derived weights.

3.1 Collect: Exchanger Group Attention as Soft Routing

Let $X \in \mathbb{R}^{T \times D}$ denote a temporal sequence of feature embeddings, where T is the number of time steps and D is the feature dimension after an MLP projection. We denote $X_t \in \mathbb{R}^D$ the embedding at time step $t \in \{1, \ldots, T\}$. The collect stage aggregates these temporal tokens into a fixed set of G latent group tokens using the group attention mechanism introduced in Exchanger. Each group is associated with a learnable query vector $q_g \in \mathbb{R}^D$, where $g \in \{1, \ldots, G\}$. Temporal tokens provide keys $k_t \in \mathbb{R}^D$ and values $v_t \in \mathbb{R}^D$, obtained through linear projections of X_t.

Formally, the attention score between group g and time step t is computed as:

$$A_{g,t} = \frac{q_g \cdot k_t}{\sqrt{d}} + B_{g,t}, \tag{1}$$

where $B_{g,t}$ denotes the positional bias defined in [1]. The attention weights are obtained via softmax over the temporal dimension:

$$a_{g,t} = \text{softmax}_t(A_{g,t}). \tag{2}$$

The resulting group token representations are given by:

$$Z_g = \sum_{t=1}^{T} a_{g,t} X_t. \tag{3}$$

From a routing perspective, the attention weights $a_{g,t}$ can be interpreted as a learned assignment matrix that distributes each temporal token across a fixed set of latent group representations. This matches the general routing formulation of [6], where routing consists of computing affinity scores followed by normalized assignment weights that determine how inputs contribute to intermediate processing units. Here, the softmax normalization over t ensures that each group token aggregates information from all temporal positions with data-dependent weights, making the collect stage a continuous, differentiable routing mechanism over the temporal dimension.

3.2 Update: Expert Specialization Within the Exchanger Block

In the original Exchanger block, the update stage processes all group tokens using the same set of shared transformations. This stage enables information exchange among groups, playing the role of global interaction in place of full self-attention.

We retain this overall structure but introduce specialization within the feature transformation applied to each group. Specifically, the update stage still consists of two steps: (1) a shared transformation that mixes information across groups and (2) a feature transformation applied within each group. In the original Exchanger, both steps use shared MLP-Mixer components. In our model, the across-group transformation remains shared, while the within-group feature transformation is replaced with expert-specific modules.

First, a shared across-group mixing module, denoted as $\text{Mix}_{\text{group}}(\cdot)$, is applied to all group tokens:

$$Z'_g = Z_g + \text{Mix}_{\text{group}}(\text{Norm}(Z_g)), \tag{4}$$

which enables information exchange across latent groups and preserves the global interaction mechanism of the Exchanger.

Subsequently, the within-group feature transformation is performed using expert-specific modules. Let E denote the number of experts, which may differ from the number of group tokens G. Each group token Z'_g is associated with an expert through a predefined mapping $e(g) \in \{1, \ldots, E\}$ and is updated as:

$$\tilde{Z}_g = Z'_g + f_{e(g)}(\text{Norm}(Z'_g)), \tag{5}$$

where $f_{e(g)}(\cdot)$ denotes the expert-specific feature transformation for the expert $e(g)$. When $E < G$, multiple groups share the same expert, enabling controlled parameter sharing and allowing us to adjust the degree of specialization without increasing the number of groups.

By introducing specialization only in the within-group transformation while keeping the across-group mixing shared, the update stage preserves the global information exchange mechanism of the Exchanger. At the same time, expert-specific transformations allow different latent groups to develop specialized representations for distinct temporal patterns.

3.3 Distribute: Combine Operation

The distribute stage maps the updated group representations back to temporal tokens by reusing the attention logits from the collect stage with a different normalization. Under the routing interpretation, this corresponds to the combine operation in Soft Mixture-of-Experts, where outputs are recombined using the same affinity scores that define dispatch.

This perspective enables a more efficient formulation of the distribute stage. In the original Exchanger, distribution is implemented as a separate cross-attention operation, where temporal tokens act as queries over group representations, requiring additional projection matrices and a full attention computation. In contrast, our method leverages the shared routing structure and directly reuses the logits $A_{g,t}$ computed during collect. The combine weights are obtained by simply changing the normalization dimension, eliminating the need for new query–key interactions or additional attention passes. As a result, routing, expert processing, and recombination are all derived from a single set of attention scores, reducing both computational cost and memory overhead.

Let $A_{g,t}$ denote the attention scores defined in Eq. (1). During the collect stage, routing (dispatch) weights are obtained via a softmax over the temporal dimension,

whereas in the distribute stage, the same scores are normalized over the group dimension:

$$c_{g,t} = \text{softmax}_g(A_{g,t}), \tag{6}$$

producing combined weights that determine how each group representation contributes to a temporal token.

The redistributed temporal features are then computed as follows:

$$\tilde{X}_t = \sum_{g=1}^{G} c_{g,t}\, \tilde{Z}_g, \tag{7}$$

where $\tilde{Z}_g$ denotes the updated group tokens from the Update stage as defined in Eq. (5).

This asymmetric normalization enables a two-way soft routing mechanism: temporal tokens are first aggregated into group representations, and group representations are then softly recombined back into the temporal domain. Unlike classical sparse MoE layers, this process involves no conditional execution; all groups contribute to every temporal token through continuous combine weights.

Following redistribution, the resulting features are integrated into the block output in the same manner as in the Exchanger. The redistributed features are concatenated with the original temporal features and linearly projected:

$$Y_t = \text{Proj}\big([X_t \,\|\, \tilde{X}_t]\big), \tag{8}$$

where $[\cdot\|\cdot]$ denotes channel-wise concatenation, and $\text{Proj}(\cdot)$ is a learned linear projection.

Finally, a feed-forward network (FFN) with a residual connection is applied:

$$X_t^{\text{out}} = Y_t + \text{FFN}(\text{Norm}(Y_t)). \tag{9}$$

This sequence of operations substitutes the standard residual self-attention and feed-forward layers of a Transformer block, following the design principles introduced in GPViT [17] and adopted in Exchanger.

3.4 Spatial Encoder

After the Collect–Update–Distribute pipeline, the resulting token sequence is averaged over the temporal dimension and reshaped to recover the original spatial grid of size $C \times H \times W$. This design choice, retained from Exchanger, allows the use of any established semantic segmentation architecture for spatial modeling and pixel-level prediction.

4 Experiments

4.1 Datasets

We evaluate our method primarily on the Panoptic Agricultural Satellite Time Series (PASTIS) dataset [13], which consists of Sentinel-2 image time series acquired over French rural areas. The dataset contains 2,433 multi-spectral Satellite Image Time Series (SITS), each covering a spatial extent of 1.28 km×1.28 km at a spatial resolution of 10 m, resulting in image patches of size 128×128 pixels and spanning from September 2018 to November 2019.

PASTIS includes 20 semantic classes: 18 crop types, a background class, and a void class. Pixels labeled as void correspond either to parcels belonging to non-annotated crop types or to parcels whose majority lies outside the patch boundaries. Following the dataset protocol, the void class is ignored during evaluation. The dataset is provided with an official 5-fold cross-validation scheme, summarized in Table 1.

Table 1. Official 5-fold cross-validation splits used for PASTIS. Each row defines one split, indicating which folds are assigned to the training, validation, and test sets.

Split	Train	Validation	Test
I	1, 2, 3	4	5
II	2, 3, 4	5	1
III	3, 4, 5	1	2
IV	4, 5, 1	2	3
V	5, 1, 2	3	4

In addition to PASTIS, we report results on the Multitemporal Land Cover Classification (MTLCC) dataset [12] to assess the applicability of the proposed method across different SITS benchmarks. MTLCC comprises 17 crop classes and consists of Sentinel-2 image time series extracted over agricultural regions in Germany, provided as small spatial tiles of size 24×24 pixels.

4.2 Training Protocol

Our training protocol is largely similar to that of Exchanger, with a small number of modifications described below. We first pre-train the temporal encoder using the pixel-set representation introduced in PASTIS-R [14], which isolates parcel-level temporal signals while discarding background pixels. This pre-training stage focuses on temporal modeling and runs for 50 epochs with a batch size of 128. We then attach a spatial encoder and fine-tune the full model end-to-end on the standard semantic segmentation split of the PASTIS dataset for 20 epochs with a batch size of 8. While Exchanger evaluates two spatial decoders, namely U-Net [11] and Mask2Former [2], we use a U-Net architecture in all experiments based on preliminary trials with our implementation.

When initializing the full model from the temporal pre-training checkpoint, we do not load all weights. Specifically, parameters associated with group token embeddings and update-stage MLP-Mixers are reinitialized, while the remaining weights are transferred from pre-training. We believe that this partial weight loading avoids forcing pretrained representations onto architectural components that differ between the temporal-only and full spatiotemporal models and provides additional regularization during fine-tuning.

During training, we divide each 128×128 image patch into a regular grid of 32×32 spatial crops and treat each crop as an independent sample. This strategy differs from the standard Exchanger training protocol, and it increases both the number of training samples and the spatial coverage of the training data. We further apply temporal dropping as data augmentation, randomly removing time steps from each temporal sequence with a drop rate of 0.3. During validation and testing, we perform inference on full-resolution 128×128 images without cropping and use the complete temporal sequences without temporal dropping.

We train all models using a standard pixel-wise cross-entropy loss for semantic segmentation, ignoring pixels belonging to the void class during loss computation. Optimization is performed with AdamW [7] using a learning rate of 2×10^{-4}, weight decay of 5×10^{-3}, and $(\beta_1, \beta_2) = (0.9, 0.999)$. We apply a polynomial learning rate schedule with linear warm-up. The warm-up phase spans 10% of the total training iterations with a warm-up factor of 10^{-3}. After warm-up, the learning rate follows a polynomial decay with power 0.9, combined with step-wise decay at 70% and 90% of the training schedule.

Unless otherwise specified, we use the same optimization settings in all experiments and follow the remaining hyperparameters of Exchanger.

4.3 Ablation Study

The ablation study examines two main architectural factors that control specialization and model capacity: the number of groups and the number of expert mixers. Grouping determines how temporal tokens are partitioned and routed, affecting both representation learning and computational cost, as attention relies on learnable group-specific queries. Varying the number of mixers is analogous to adjusting expert capacity in MoE-inspired designs. For a fair comparison, we also train the original Exchanger baseline using an identical training protocol.

The experiments are conducted exclusively on the first split of the PASTIS cross-validation protocol, using folds 1–3 for training, fold 4 for validation, and fold 5 held out. Ablation results reported in Table 2 refer to metrics on the validation set only, and no test data are used for model selection or architectural comparison.

Table 2. Ablation study on PASTIS using the first cross-validation split. Results report validation mIoU and overall accuracy (OA) for different numbers of groups and expert mixers.

Effect	Model	Groups	Mixers	mIoU	OA
Groups	Ours	2	1	68.86%	85.47%
	Ours	4	1	69.26%	85.45%
	Ours	8	1	69.25%	85.69%
	Ours	16	1	69.38%	85.68%
Experts	Ours	4	2	69.56%	85.62%
	Ours	4	4	69.51%	85.76%
	Ours	16	2	69.25%	85.44%
	Ours	16	4	69.47%	85.71%
	Ours	16	8	69.76%	85.66%
	Ours	16	16	69.37%	85.71%

Looking into the groups effect, increasing the number of groups while keeping a single mixer leads to small but consistent gains in mIoU, a trend that is less pronounced for overall accuracy. This suggests that finer-grained token partitioning improves class-wise segmentation quality, even if the impact on global accuracy remains limited. Based on these results, we select the two most promising group configurations (4 and 16 groups) to further investigate the effect of increasing the number of expert mixers.

When varying the number of mixers within these group settings, we again observe modest but generally consistent improvements as model capacity increases, followed by saturation at higher values. This behavior aligns with the intended role of expert specialization, where additional mixers provide greater representational flexibility but with diminishing returns. From this analysis, we retain two representative configurations for the main experiments: 16 groups with 8 mixers, which achieves the highest validation mIoU and represents a higher-capacity setting, and 4 groups with 2 mixers, which offers a favorable balance between performance and theoretical computational efficiency.

4.4 Main Results

Final performance on PASTIS is reported following the official 5-fold cross-validation protocol. For each fold, we retrain the best-performing configuration identified in the ablation study using the corresponding training split and evaluate it on the designated test split. Reported results are averaged across all five folds.

For MTLCC, no additional ablation is conducted. All architectural choices and hyperparameters are fixed to those selected on PASTIS. The temporal encoder is initialized with the same Pixel-Set pretraining weights obtained from the first PASTIS split and used during ablation; the full model is then fine-tuned on the MTLCC training set and evaluated on its test set.

Table 3 compares our models with the original Exchanger architecture. Because our training protocol differs from that used in [1], we report both the results from the literature and the performance of the original Exchanger architecture trained under our setup. This distinction helps separate improvements due to optimization and training strategies from those introduced by routing-based specialization. Our models are identified by the pair (G, E), where G denotes the number of groups and E the number of expert mixing modules.

Table 3. Main results on PASTIS and MTLCC in terms of mIoU, model parameters, and GFLOPs, computed using a dummy input of size $30 \times 10 \times 128 \times 128$.

Model	mIoU		Params	GFLOPs
	PASTIS	MTLCC		
Exchanger+Unet [1]	66.8%	90.7%	8.08 M	300
Exchanger+Mask2Former [1]	67.9%	90.5%	24.59 M	329
Exchanger+Unet (our training)	68.67%	91.07%	8.08 M	300
Ours (16, 8)+Unet	**68.81%**	**91.62%**	9.93 M	276
Ours (4, 2)+Unet	68.78%	91.40%	8.34 M	**210**

In order to ensure a fair comparison with prior work, FLOPs are computed following [1] using a dummy input of size $T \times C \times H \times W = 30 \times 10 \times 128 \times 128$. Under this protocol, our models achieve comparable or improved segmentation performance while reducing computational cost. In particular, the $(4, 2)$ configuration matches the performance of the re-trained Exchanger+UNet baseline on PASTIS (+0.11 mIoU) and improves results on MTLCC (+0.33 mIoU), while reducing FLOPs by approximately 30%. The $(16, 8)$ configuration provides consistent, though modest, gains in accuracy across both datasets (+0.14 mIoU on PASTIS and +0.55 mIoU on MTLCC) together with a moderate reduction in FLOPs.

While FLOPs provide a hardware-agnostic estimate of computational complexity, they do not fully capture the practical efficiency of a model. To complement this analysis, we report additional runtime metrics including inference latency and throughput (in samples/s) across varying sequence lengths T. All measurements are performed on a single NVIDIA A30 GPU (24 GB VRAM) using float32 precision. Due to memory constraints of the profiling setup, experiments are limited to sequence lengths up to $T = 40$. These results are summarized in Table 4 and illustrated in Fig. 2.

Table 4. Comparison of models across sequence lengths T. We report GFLOPs, latency (ms), and throughput (samples/s).

T	Exchanger			Model (4,2)			Model (16,8)		
	GFLOPs	Lat.	Thr.	GFLOPs	Lat.	Thr.	GFLOPs	Lat.	Thr.
10	139	98.81	10.12	92	63.50	15.75	134	99.86	10.01
20	220	155.29	6.44	161	95.56	10.46	205	158.35	6.32
30	300	209.17	4.78	230	129.89	7.70	275	197.05	5.07
40	381	291.41	3.43	298	162.75	6.14	346	232.60	4.30

The extended evaluation provides a more complete view of the computational behavior of the models. In particular, the $(4, 2)$ configuration achieves lower latency and higher throughput than the baseline across all tested sequence lengths, while maintaining comparable segmentation accuracy. In addition, its computational cost increases more gradually with T, as observed in both FLOPs and runtime measurements. The $(16, 8)$ configuration exhibits intermediate behavior, reflecting a trade-off between the baseline and the more efficient $(4, 2)$ variant.

Across all models, throughput decreases as the sequence length increases, which is expected given the growing temporal dimension. However, the rate of degradation differs: the proposed models show a slower decline in throughput, indicating improved scalability with respect to T.

A qualitative example of predicted segmentation maps is shown in Fig. 3. All three models produce spatially coherent predictions that largely respect parcel boundaries, indicating that they can capture the geometric structure of agricultural fields. While the overall predictions are similar, differences can be observed in specific regions, particularly for smaller or less distinctive parcels where class confusion occurs. For instance, the Exchanger model incorrectly classifies a road segment as spring barley, whereas the other models do not exhibit this error. Additionally, areas labeled as void are ignored during both training and evaluation. As a result, apparent misclassifications in these regions do not impact the reported performance and should not be interpreted as model errors.

Given the inherent variability of cross-validation, we do not claim statistically significant accuracy gains. Instead, the results demonstrate that the proposed architecture enables a more favorable trade-off between accuracy and efficiency. This is consistent with the design motivation of mixture-of-experts approaches, which aim to increase representational capacity while controlling computational cost through conditional computation.

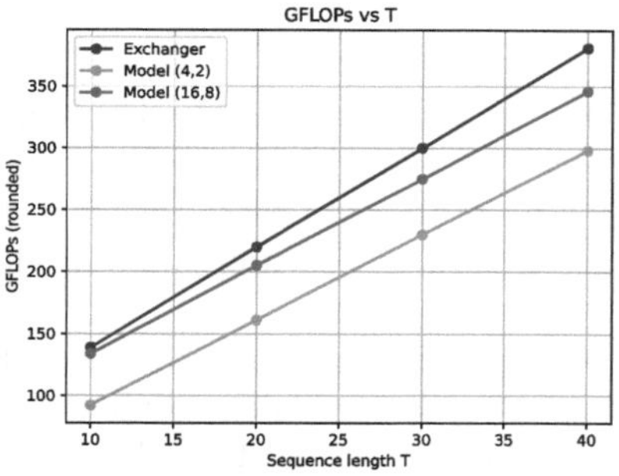

(a) GFLOPs vs Sequence length T

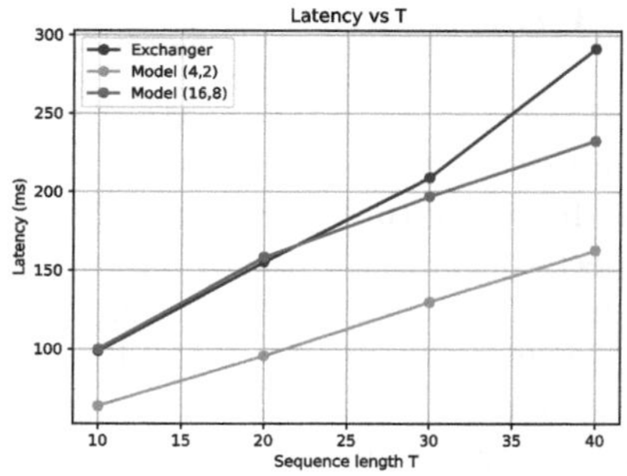

(b) Latency vs Sequence length T

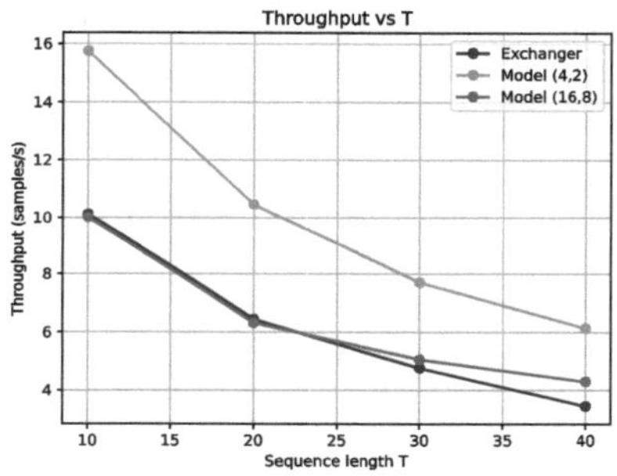

(c) Throughput vs Sequence length T

Fig. 2. Efficiency comparison across models as a function of sequence length T. We report (a) computational cost in GFLOPs, (b) inference latency (ms), and (c) throughput (samples/s).

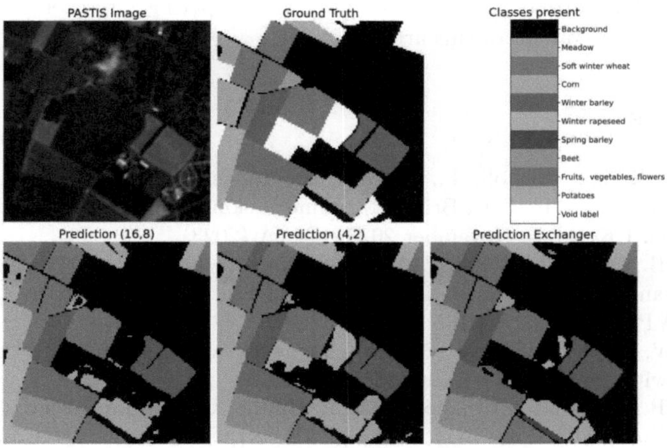

Fig. 3. Qualitative segmentation example on PASTIS. Top row (left to right): RGB composite, ground-truth labels, and the legend of classes present in the patch. Bottom row (left to right): predictions from the proposed (16,8) and (4,2) models, and the baseline Exchanger model.

5 Conclusion

In this work, we introduced routing-inspired specialization into the Exchanger architecture for satellite image time series segmentation. Motivated by principles from Mixture-of-Experts (MoE) models, the proposed design incorporates expert-specialized transformations within the temporal processing pipeline while maintaining linear computational complexity.

Evaluations on the PASTIS and MTLCC benchmarks show that the proposed modifications maintain segmentation accuracy comparable to an original Exchanger baseline while reducing computational cost. Beyond FLOPs, we analyzed practical efficiency by measuring inference latency and throughput across varying sequence lengths. Results indicate that certain configurations, such as $(4, 2)$, achieve lower latency and higher throughput than the baseline, and their efficiency degrades more gradually as sequence length increases. The $(16, 8)$ configuration exhibits intermediate behavior, providing a trade-off between baseline accuracy and efficiency.

Overall, these findings demonstrate that soft MoE-inspired specialization can improve both theoretical and practical efficiency of dense temporal models in remote sensing. Future work could explore adaptive or more explicit routing mechanisms to further enhance scalability and representation learning in large-scale satellite time series analysis.

Acknowledgments. The authors would like to thank the Minas Gerais State Research Foundation - FAPEMIG, Brazil. This study was financed in part by the Coordenação de Aperfeiçoamento de Pessoal de Nível Superior - Brasil (CAPES) - Finance Code 001. This work has been supported by UFJF's High-Speed Integrated Research Network (RePesq) https://www.repesq.ufjf.br/.

Disclosure of Interests. The authors have no competing interests to declare that are relevant to the content of this article.

References

1. Cai, X., Bi, Y., Nicholl, P., Sterritt, R.: Revisiting the encoding of satellite image time series. In: 34th British Machine Vision Conference 2023, BMVC 2023, Aberdeen, UK, 20–24 November 2023. BMVA (2023)
2. Cheng, B., Misra, I., Schwing, A.G., Kirillov, A., Girdhar, R.: Masked-attention mask transformer for universal image segmentation (2022). https://doi.org/10.1109/CVPR52688.2022.00135
3. Fedus, W., Zoph, B., Shazeer, N.: Switch transformers: scaling to trillion parameter models with simple and efficient sparsity (2022)
4. Jacobs, R.A., Jordan, M.I., Nowlan, S.J., Hinton, G.E.: Adaptive mixtures of local experts. Neural Comput. **3**(1), 79–87 (1991). https://doi.org/10.1162/neco.1991.3.1.79
5. Lepikhin, D., et al.: {GS}hard: scaling giant models with conditional computation and automatic sharding. In: International Conference on Learning Representations (2021)

6. Liu, T., Blondel, M., Ruiz, C.R., Puigcerver, J.: Routers in vision mixture of experts: an empirical study. Trans. Mach. Learn. Res. (2024). https://doi.org/10.48550/arXiv.2401.15969
7. Loshchilov, I., Hutter, F.: Decoupled weight decay regularization. In: International Conference on Learning Representations (2019). https://doi.org/10.48550/arXiv.1711.05101
8. MacDonald, E., Jacoby, D., Coady, Y.: Vistaformer: scalable vision transformers for satellite image time series segmentation. arXiv preprint arXiv:2409.08461 (2024)
9. Puigcerver, J., Ruiz, C.R., Mustafa, B., Houlsby, N.: From sparse to soft mixtures of experts. In: The Twelfth International Conference on Learning Representations (2024). https://doi.org/10.48550/arXiv.2308.00951
10. Riquelme, C., et al.: Scaling vision with sparse mixture of experts. In: Proceedings of the 35th International Conference on Neural Information Processing Systems, NIPS '21. Curran Associates Inc., Red Hook (2021)
11. Ronneberger, O., Fischer, P., Brox, T.: U-net: convolutional networks for biomedical image segmentation. CoRR arxiv:1505.04597 (2015). https://doi.org/10.48550/arXiv.1505.04597
12. Rußwurm, M., Körner, M.: Multi-temporal land cover classification with sequential recurrent encoders. ISPRS Int. J. Geo-Inf. **7**(4) (2018). https://doi.org/10.3390/ijgi7040129
13. Sainte Fare Garnot, V., Landrieu, L.: Panoptic segmentation of satellite image time series with convolutional temporal attention networks. In: ICCV (2021). https://doi.org/10.1109/ICCV48922.2021.00483
14. Sainte Fare Garnot, V., Landrieu, L., Chehata, N.: Multi-modal temporal attention models for crop mapping from satellite time series. ISPRS J. Photogram. Remote Sens. (2022). https://doi.org/10.1016/j.isprsjprs.2022.03.012
15. Shazeer, N., et al.: Outrageously large neural networks: the sparsely-gated mixture-of-experts layer. In: International Conference on Learning Representations (2017)
16. Tarasiou, M., Chavez, E., Zafeiriou, S.: Vits for sits: vision transformers for satellite image time series. In: Proceedings of the IEEE/CVF Conference on Computer Vision and Pattern Recognition (CVPR), pp. 10418–10428 (2023)
17. Yang, C., Xu, J., Mello, S.D., Crowley, E.J., Wang, X.: GPViT: a high resolution non-hierarchical vision transformer with group propagation (2023)

Ending the War Between Model Selection and Combination: A Cross-Validation Approach

Elio Zhang[1(✉)] and Craig Rolling[2]

[1] Seattle University, Seattle, WA 98112, USA
ezhang2@seattleu.edu
[2] HNTB, Kansas City, MO 64105, USA
crolling@hntb.com

Abstract. Model averaging is a powerful alternative to model selection, often yielding improved prediction accuracy by combining the strengths of multiple models. However, in high-dimensional settings, the large number of candidate models poses serious challenges: many existing averaging methods become computationally infeasible, and indiscriminate combination can lead to poor performance. Furthermore, model averaging may underperform model selection when a single well-specified model exists. To address these challenges, we propose Cross-Validated Procedure Averaging (CVPA), a data-driven method that uses cross-validation to adaptively determine both which models to include and how many to combine. A key innovation of CVPA is its ability to select the optimal number of models in the ensemble, balancing variance reduction with robustness to model misspecification. When appropriate, CVPA reduces to model selection, providing a seamless bridge between selection and averaging. We establish theoretical guarantees for CVPA in high-dimensional linear regression, including selection consistency. Empirical studies further confirm its strong predictive performance across various settings with differing signal strengths and sparsity levels. Our results highlight the importance of controlling ensemble size and demonstrate that adaptive model combination—guided by cross-validation—is essential for reliable performance in high-dimensional applications.

Keywords: model averaging · forecast combination · cross-validation · high-dimensional prediction · risk minimization

1 Introduction

High-dimensional prediction problems arise in many modern applications, including genetics, genomics, and many other fields, where the number of potential predictors can be enormous while the sample size remains limited. In such settings, analysts often face multiple plausible modeling pipelines, differing in

O. Gervasi et al. (Eds.): ICCSA 2026, LNCS 16768, pp. 52–69, 2027.
https://doi.org/10.1007/978-3-032-30488-9_4

screening rules, tuning criteria, or selection methods, and predictive performance can depend strongly on which pipeline is used. Relying on a single selected model may therefore be unstable, yet combining many candidate models indiscriminately can reduce interpretability and may harm prediction. Motivated by this practical dilemma, we focus on two fundamental challenges for high-dimensional model combination.

Challenge 1: Selection vs. *Combination.* Model combination should not be applied blindly. In many scientific applications, identifying a small set of relevant features is as important as prediction (e.g., biomarker discovery), and averaging across many models can harm interpretability. Even from a purely predictive standpoint, if one candidate model adequately captures the data-generating process, combining it with inferior alternatives cannot improve and may even degrade performance [11]. In such cases, the optimal number of models to combine is one—that is, combination should reduce to model selection. A practical high-dimensional method should therefore adaptively decide, based on the observed data, whether selection or combination is preferred.

Challenge 2: Which and How Many Models to Combine. When combination is beneficial, the size of the candidate model space typically grows exponentially with the number of features p, making exhaustive averaging infeasible even for moderately large p [9]. In practice, analysts rarely attempt to average over all conceivable models; instead, they work with a finite pool of candidates chosen using scientific judgment, interpretability requirements, or computational feasibility. Classical approaches such as Bayesian model averaging [13] and frequentist model averaging [12] are designed to combine a prespecified collection of candidate models, but direct application is still prohibitive in high-dimensional regression when even that practical pool is large. Consequently, any viable procedure must include a screening mechanism to identify a manageable subset of models to combine [2,15]. Despite long-standing recognition of the importance of "selecting forecasts prior to combination," this problem remains unresolved in the forecast combination literature [18]. A key goal is therefore to determine the number of models to combine adaptively from the data, rather than fixing it *a priori.*

Limitations of Existing Work. Relative to model selection, model combination has received limited attention in the high-dimensional regression literature [2]. Moreover, existing methods primarily target the second challenge while treating selection and combination as separate tasks. For instance, [2] trims the model space by filtering features using a correlation test with a user-chosen p-value threshold, while [15,22] averages the best m models (with m fixed *a priori*) ranked by a criterion such as AIC. Such approaches reduce computation, but rely on ad hoc thresholds and do not provide a principled mechanism to choose between selection and combination.

Our Approach: Procedure Averaging Upstream. We address both challenges with a *method-centric* strategy that combines *procedures* rather than models. Here a *procedure* refers to a modeling pipeline (algorithm and tuning/selection rule) that maps data to a fitted model—for example, CART [6], logistic regression, or penalized regression with distinct information criteria such as AIC [1] and BIC [16]. This distinction is important in practice: a model is the fitted predictive object ultimately used for prediction, while a procedure is the rule that produces such a model from the data. We use the labels "upstream" and "downstream" only as informal descriptors of *when* combination occurs in the workflow, not in the sense of abstraction layers. Conventional model averaging is performed *downstream*, meaning at the model level after a procedure has produced fitted models: a single preferred procedure is chosen first, then a collection of models produced by that procedure is averaged [2,15]. In contrast, we perform "procedure combination" *upstream*, meaning at the procedure level before the final model-level combination, by first assessing and selecting a set of qualified procedures and then combining the models they produce. Candidate procedures in this framework may include screening-based, threshold-based, or penalized-regression pipelines, so the method is compatible with common dimension-reduction practices rather than opposed to them.

Our method, Cross-Validated Procedure Averaging (CVPA), uses delete-n_v cross-validation to repeatedly select a qualified procedure from a candidate set. Here the validation set is simply the held-out portion of the data used to compare candidate procedures through an out-of-sample prediction criterion; throughout the paper, "validation" refers to this held-out predictive assessment step rather than to external outcome validation in an application-specific sense. Delete-n_v cross-validation is known to be consistent for selecting the risk-optimal procedure under suitable conditions [21,24]. Repeating the cross-validation B times yields B selected (not necessarily distinct) qualified procedures. Each selected procedure is then refit on the full dataset to produce a predictive model, and predictions for a new point are obtained by simple averaging across the resulting set of B models.

A distinctive feature of CVPA is that it adapts between selection and combination. If there exists a sufficiently dominant procedure in predictive risk, it will be selected by essentially all cross-validation repetitions, so CVPA reduces to model selection and combines a single model. When signal-to-noise is lower or misspecification is more prevalent, multiple procedures are selected across repetitions, and CVPA averages their corresponding fitted models. Thus, the number of models combined is estimated from the data rather than chosen *a priori*.

The rest of the paper is organized as follows. Section 2 develops the CVPA algorithm. Section 3 presents the theoretical properties of CVPA. Simulation results are reported in Sect. 4, and a real-data application is discussed in Sect. 5. Section 6 concludes with a discussion.

2 Proposed Method: Cross-validated Procedure Averaging (CVPA)

This section defines our high-dimensional regression framework and describes the CVPA algorithm to estimate the regression function.

2.1 Problem Setup and Definitions

Our work is done in a random-design regression setting, where

$$Y = f(\boldsymbol{X}) + \varepsilon.$$

In this framework, Y is the response, $\boldsymbol{X}$ is comprised of p features $(X_1, \cdots, X_p)$ with unknown distribution P_X having support $\mathcal{X}$, $f(\boldsymbol{X}) = E(Y|\boldsymbol{X})$ is the true regression function, and ε is the random error with $E(\varepsilon|\boldsymbol{X}) = 0$ and $E(\varepsilon^{4k}|\boldsymbol{X}) < \infty$ for a positive integer k. The data $\mathbf{Z} = (\mathbf{X}, \mathbf{Y})$ is comprised of n independent and identically distributed observations on $(X_1, \cdots, X_p, Y)$, where $\mathbf{Y}$ is an n-dimensional vector and $\mathbf{X}$ is an $n \times p$ feature matrix. For our theoretical results, we assume that $(\log p)/n \to 0$ as $n \to \infty$; in other words, p is not considered fixed but is allowed to grow with n at a controlled rate.

The true regression function f may be linear or nonlinear; however, as is typical in high-dimensional regression analysis, throughout this article only linear predictive models of the form

$$\widehat{f}(\boldsymbol{X}) = \sum_{j=1}^{p} \widehat{\beta}_j X_j \tag{1}$$

are considered as candidates. If the true regression function is linear,

$$f(\boldsymbol{X}) = E(Y|\boldsymbol{X}) = \sum_{j=1}^{p} \beta_j X_j,$$

then we define the "true model" M_0 as the set of variables whose regression coefficient $\beta_j \neq 0$. We formally define a linear modeling procedure as follows:

Definition 1. *A linear modeling procedure δ is a mapping from a sample $\mathbf{Z} = (\mathbf{X}, \mathbf{Y})$ to a p-dimensional vector $\widehat{\boldsymbol{\beta}}(\delta, \mathbf{Z}) = \left(\widehat{\beta}_1(\delta, \mathbf{Z}), \cdots, \widehat{\beta}_p(\delta, \mathbf{Z})\right)^T$, i.e., $\mathbf{Z} :\rightarrow \widehat{\boldsymbol{\beta}}(\delta, \mathbf{Z})$.*

For ease of notation, we sometimes denote $\widehat{\boldsymbol{\beta}}(\delta, \mathbf{Z})$ by $\widehat{\boldsymbol{\beta}}_\delta$. A linear modeling procedure applied to $\mathbf{Z}$ results in a predictive model, defined as follows:

Definition 2. *A predictive model is a functional relationship between a set of inputs $\boldsymbol{X} = (X_1, \cdots, X_p)$ and a predicted outcome $\widehat{f}$.*

For example, the linear modeling procedure δ applied to $\mathbf{Z}$ produces the estimates $\widehat{\boldsymbol{\beta}}_\delta$, and the predictive model estimated by this modeling procedure is

$$\widehat{f}_\delta(\mathbf{X}^0) = \sum_{j=1}^{p} \widehat{\beta}_j(\delta, \mathbf{Z}) X_j^0$$

where $\mathbf{X}^0$ is a new observation on all p features and independent of $\mathbf{Z}$.

2.2 Procedure, Model and Feature Selection

In the setting of high-dimensional regression, there are on the order of billions of candidate models, so combining all of them is obviously infeasible. A filter step, which aims to select a set of "good" models, needs to be done before combination. Thus, model selection is an indispensable step in any method of model combination for high-dimensional regression. However, confusion can occur when discussing the distinct but intertwined concepts of model selection, procedure selection and feature selection in regression [24]. In this section, we clarify the differences and connections between these concepts before introducing our method.

In the general regression setting, a predictive model (1) is a mathematical function that is able to produce a point forecast $\widehat{f}$ for a given input $\boldsymbol{X} = \{X_1, \ldots, X_p\}$. The ultimate goal of our article is to develop and combine a set of such predictive models by making use of various selection and estimation methods. As soon as a predictive model is obtained, a set of active features (those whose values affect $\widehat{f}$ in the model) are defined. In other words, feature selection is a byproduct of model selection.

While feature selection is an important goal of many academic efforts, especially where questions of causation are concerned, optimal feature selection does not guarantee optimal model selection. To illustrate this point, consider the following example. Suppose $X_1 \sim N(0,1)$, $X_2 \sim N(0,1)$ and $\epsilon \sim N(0,1)$ are mutually independent. Let $Y = X_1 + X_2 + \epsilon$ and $X_3 = X_1 + 2X_2$. Then $\rho(Y, X_1) = 1/\sqrt{3}$, $\rho(Y, X_2) = 1/\sqrt{3}$, and $\rho(Y, X_3) = \sqrt{3/5}$. Thus, the variable X_3 is more strongly correlated with Y than X_1 or X_2. However,

$$E\big(Y - (X_1 + X_2)\big)^2 = 1 \tag{2}$$

$$E(Y - (\beta X_3))^2 = 1 + (1-\beta)^2 + (1-2\beta)^2 \tag{3}$$

where $1 + (1-\beta)^2 + (1-2\beta)^2 \geq 1.2$ (when $\beta = 0.6$). Thus, the model defined by (2), which does not use the most important feature X_3 in the feature set, is preferred to any model that uses only X_3. As exhibited by the example, a feature selection approach does not necessarily perform the best in model selection when the ultimate goal is prediction.

Moreover, model selection is fundamentally different from procedure selection. A modeling procedure is a method that is able to produce (1) from a sample of data. This definition implies that a general methodology that involves one or more tuning parameters is *not* a modeling procedure. For example, LASSO [17] as formulated as

$$\|Y - \sum_j X_j \beta_j\|_2^2 + \lambda \sum_{j=1}^{p} |\beta_j|, \tag{4}$$

when λ is unknown, is not a modeling procedure because (4) cannot produce a predictive model. However, for a given $\lambda = 2$, which is either selected by cross-validation or just chosen according to personal flavor, (4) becomes a modeling procedure. In other words, LASSO (4) represents a family of modeling procedures except when λ is known.

Although a modeling procedure should be evaluated by the predictive accuracy of the model selected by it, procedure selection should not be viewed as redundant or be equated to model selection. They are fundamentally different, and there is a clear-cut border between them. In the above sample, when we make a choice between two competing models $Y = X_1 + X_2 + \epsilon$ and $Y = 0.6X_3 + \epsilon$, we have to turn to a modeling procedure or model selection criterion such as AIC [1]. However, why not BIC [16]? Obviously, procedure selection has to be done first. In summary, if we want to develop a predictive model, then two steps are necessary. The first (upstream) step is defined as procedure selection in this paper. The second (downstream) step is model selection, which is achieved by applying the procedure selected in the first step to a set of sample data.

2.3 Cross-validated Procedure Averaging (CVPA) Algorithm

The example in Sect. 2.2 illustrates the disadvantage of methods originating from feature selection such as the method of [2], which ranks the correlation of each feature with Y and selects only features above some threshold. As for model selection, a single method is not the ultimate solution because various procedures such as AIC and BIC often select different models, and there are irreconcilable differences between them [20]. Overall, methods based on feature selection or model selection have severe limitations when the ultimate goal is prediction from high dimensional data. In our view, the most useful methods of selection or combination, generally speaking, are those that select or combine candidate *procedures*, each of which produces a model when applied to the data sample $\mathbf{Z}$. Thus our approach, which we describe next, uses a procedure selection approach to combine selected promising models. The most important characteristic of our proposed method is to select a set of promising modeling procedures first and then combine the models estimated by the set of "selected" procedures, which distinguishes our method from other model combination methods. As demonstrated below, this double-selection method (procedure selection followed by model selection) has substantial advantages over competing approaches.

Although our method of Cross-Validated Procedure Averaging (CVPA) is a very general idea that could be applied to many types of procedures and models, in this article we focus on the procedures of penalized linear regression that are most common in the study and practice of high-dimensional regression. Specifically, we consider modeling procedures that minimize an objective function $\mathcal{C}_{\delta,\mathbf{Z}}(\boldsymbol{\beta})$ in the form of

$$\mathcal{C}_{\delta,\mathbf{Z}}(\boldsymbol{\beta}) \equiv \frac{1}{n}\|\mathbf{X}\boldsymbol{\beta} - \mathbf{Y}\|_2^2 + P_\delta(\boldsymbol{\beta}), \tag{5}$$

where $P_\delta(\boldsymbol{\beta})$ is a positive penalty function on $\boldsymbol{\beta}$ serving to impose sparsity. For example, the methods of LASSO [17], SCAD [10], and MCP [23] are all modeling procedures that minimize an objective function of the form (5).

As mentioned in the introduction, the inherently large set of candidate models in high-dimensional regression creates two questions for model averaging:

which and how many models to combine? To answer these questions, Cross-Validated Procedure Averaging identifies a set of promising modeling procedures and uses them to select and estimate a set of predictive models to combine. The set of utilized procedures $\widehat{\mathbf{\Delta}}^*_{\mathcal{B}} = \{\widehat{\delta}^*_b; b = 1, \cdots, B\}$ is determined by applying procedure selection (via cross-validation) B times. This is akin to conducting selection by applying CV to each member of a collection of B pseudo-samples $\mathbf{Z}^*_{\mathcal{B}} = \{\mathbf{Z}^*_b; b = 1, \cdots, B\}$, each created from the original sample data $\mathbf{Z}$ by resampling without replacement (i.e., permutation). Because modeling procedure selection, when applied to different pseudo-samples, may select the same procedure, the number of predictive models to combine is determined by the number of unique procedures in $\widehat{\mathbf{\Delta}}^*_{\mathcal{B}}$ and thus is adaptive to the data. The set of promising procedures $\widehat{\mathbf{\Delta}}^*_{\mathcal{B}}$, which may consist of only one unique procedure, select and estimate a set of promising models $\widehat{f}_{\mathcal{B}} = \{\widehat{f}_1, \cdots, \widehat{f}_B\}$, which may consist of only one unique model. As a consequence, the CVPA procedure is a model combination method that includes model selection as a special case.

In summary, given a practitioner-specified set of candidate procedures $\mathbf{\Delta} = \{\delta_1, \cdots, \delta_D\}$, the Cross-Validated Procedure Averaging (CVPA) algorithm includes three steps. In applications, $\mathbf{\Delta}$ is intended to be a finite pool of scientifically and operationally reasonable procedures rather than an exhaustive list of all possible models:

1. *Selection: Apply the delete-n_v cross-validation to $\mathbf{Z}$ to select the best procedure $\widehat{\delta}^*$. Repeat the selection B times to get B procedures $\widehat{\delta}^*_b$; $b = 1, \cdots, B$.*
2. *Estimation: Apply $\widehat{\mathbf{\Delta}}^*_{\mathcal{B}} = \{\delta^*_b; b = 1, \cdots, B\}$ to $\mathbf{Z}$ to produce B predictive models, $\{\widehat{\boldsymbol{\beta}}(\widehat{\delta}^*_b, \mathbf{Z}); b = 1, \cdots, B\}$.*
3. *Combination: Given a new observation $\mathbf{X}^0$, the forecast of Y^0 by* CVPA *is*

$$\widehat{Y}^0_{\text{CVPA}} = \frac{1}{B}\sum_{b=1}^{B}(\mathbf{X}^0)^T\widehat{\boldsymbol{\beta}}(\widehat{\delta}^*_b, \mathbf{Z}). \tag{6}$$

In words, CVPA does repeated selection of modeling procedures and ultimately averages the selected models for prediction. Although the algorithm just described is relatively simple, to the best of our knowledge it has not been proposed before now in the literature. As we will show in the following section, the CVPA algorithm possesses attractive theoretical properties with regard to variable selection.

A simple example may help illustrate the criteria and rules used in practice. Suppose an analyst specifies the candidate set $\Delta = \{$lasso with AIC, lasso with BIC, MCP with BIC, SCAD with BIC$\}$. For one delete-n_v split, each candidate procedure is fit on the training portion and evaluated on the held-out validation portion using prediction error. The procedure with the smallest validation error is the winner for that split. Repeating this comparison B times produces a sequence of selected procedures. Each selected procedure is then refit on the full dataset, and the final CVPA prediction is the simple average of the resulting fitted-model predictions. In this way, the criterion is held-out prediction error, the selection rule is "choose the procedure with the lowest validation error" within each repetition, and the combination rule is "average the predictions from the selected procedures across repetitions."

From an implementation perspective, the two main tuning choices in CVPA are the number of repetitions B and the validation size n_v in delete-n_v cross-validation. The role of B is to stabilize the empirical distribution of selected procedures: when B is too small, the final average may reflect Monte Carlo variability from only a few resamples, whereas larger B values give a clearer picture of whether the data support one dominant procedure or several competitive ones. The role of n_v is to control the bias-variance trade-off in procedure comparison. A larger validation set yields a more reliable out-of-sample comparison of candidate procedures, while a sufficiently large training set remains necessary so that each candidate procedure can still be fit well. Thus, in practice, B governs stability of the averaging step and n_v governs stability of the selection step.

It is worth noting that delete-n_v cross-validation plays an important role in our method. As shown in [24], when n_v satisfies certain conditions, delete-n_v CV is consistent for procedure selection, which in turn yields optimality properties for our proposed procedure.

The computational cost of CVPA is also transparent. If there are D candidate procedures, then each repetition requires comparing those D procedures on one training-validation split, and the final step refits the selected procedures on the full data. Hence the dominant cost is driven by B repeated procedure-selection problems, followed by B refits. This is more expensive than choosing a single procedure once, but it remains practical when the candidate collection is moderate, which is the intended regime of the method. Moreover, the B repetitions are embarrassingly parallel, so modern multicore or cluster environments can reduce wall-clock time substantially.

3 Properties of CVPA

3.1 CVPA for Prediction

The selected B procedures $\{\widehat{\delta}_1^*, \cdots, \widehat{\delta}_B^*\}$ are independent and identically distributed conditional on $\mathbf{Z}$. As a consequence,

$$E(\widehat{Y}^0_{\text{CVPA}} - Y^0)^2|\mathbf{Z} = \sigma^2 + Var\big(\widehat{Y}^0_{\text{CVPA}}|\mathbf{Z}\big) + \big(E(\widehat{Y}^0_{\text{CVPA}}|\mathbf{Z}) - \mu^0\big)^2$$

where $\mu^0 = E(Y^0)$ and $\sigma^2 = Var(Y^0)$.

$$Var\big(\widehat{Y}^0_{\text{CVPA}}|\mathbf{Z}\big) = \frac{1}{B}Var\big((\mathbf{X}^0)^T\widehat{\boldsymbol{\beta}}(\widehat{\delta}_b^*, \mathbf{Z})|\mathbf{Z}\big),$$

which indicates that CVPA accomplishes lower variance than a single selected procedure $\widehat{\delta}_b^*$. As a result, the method of Cross-Validated Procedure Averaging (CVPA) is guaranteed to have lower risk than selection. The favorable predictive performance of CVPA compared to other model selection and combination methods also is demonstrated through numerical studies in Sects. 4 and 5.

3.2 CVPA for Variable Selection

A key contribution of Cross-Validated Procedure Averaging (CVPA) is that it bridges the gap between model combination and model selection, so we focus on the selective performance of CVPA in this section. As shown by the equation (6), the prediction by CVPA typically is produced by the average of many different models. However, if one modeling procedure stands out and is selected by every pseudo-sample $\mathbf{Z}_b^*$, then $\widehat{\boldsymbol{\beta}}_b^* = \widehat{\boldsymbol{\beta}}(\widehat{\delta}_b^*, \mathbf{Z})$ will be the same for every b. In this case, the prediction $\widehat{Y}^0_{\text{CVPA}} = (\mathbf{X}^0)^T \widehat{\boldsymbol{\beta}}_1^*$ from CVPA is based on only one predictive model. In other words, model selection is performed and an active set of variables $\widehat{M}_0 \equiv \{j : \hat{\beta}_j \neq 0\}$ is identified by CVPA in this case. The following result shows that if the true regression function is linear with active set M_0, and if the best procedure among the candidates is able to consistently identify the true active set of variables, then CVPA also will perform consistent variable selection.

For a modeling procedure δ, let $\widehat{M}_\delta$ denote the active set in $\widehat{\boldsymbol{\beta}}(\delta, \mathbf{Z})$ and $\widehat{M}_{\widehat{\delta}_b^*}$ denote the active set in $\widehat{\boldsymbol{\beta}}(\widehat{\delta}_b^*, \mathbf{Z})$. Define the risk of a modeling procedure δ as

$$R_n(\delta) = E\|\mathbf{X}^0 \widehat{\boldsymbol{\beta}}(\delta, \mathbf{Z}) - Y^0\|_2^2, \tag{7}$$

where Y^0 represents a new observation on the response and the expectation is taken over the joint distribution of $\mathbf{Z}$ and $\mathbf{Z}^0 = ((\mathbf{X}^0)^T, Y^0)^T$. We use δ_0 to denote the procedure with the lowest risk $R(\delta)$ among the candidates in Δ, i.e.,

$$\delta_0 = \arg\min_{\delta \in \Delta} R_n(\delta) \tag{8}$$

For every b, a procedure is selected by delete-n_v CV [24], where n_v denotes the number used in cross-validation and n_t the number of observations used for parameter estimation with $n_v + n_t = n$. The delete-n_v CV error of a modeling procedure δ is calculated by

$$CV(\delta) = \sum_{i=1}^{n_v} E\big(\mathbf{X}_{v_i} \widehat{\boldsymbol{\beta}}(\delta, \mathbf{Z}_t) - Y_{v_i}\big)^2 = \|\mathbf{X}_v \widehat{\boldsymbol{\beta}}(\delta, \mathbf{Z}_t) - \mathbf{Y}_v\|_2^2, \tag{9}$$

where $\mathbf{Z}_t$ are the n_t observations allocated to the training set and $\{\mathbf{Z}_{v_i} : i = 1, \cdots, n_v\}$ are the n_v observations allocated to the validation set. In other words, the validation criterion used throughout is out-of-sample prediction error measured on held-out observations.

Theorem 1. *Suppose resampling without replacement and modeling procedure selection by delete-n_v CV are performed for each b and the following assumptions are satisfied:*

1. *For any $\delta \in \Delta$ such that $\delta \neq \delta_0$, $\liminf_{n\to\infty} n\big(R_n(\delta) - R_n(\delta_0)\big) \geq \xi$, where ξ is a positive constant;*
2. $\lim_{n\to\infty} n_t/n_v = 0$;
3. *The number of resamplings B satisfies $\lim_{n\to\infty} B(n_t/n_v)^k = 0$.*

Then $\lim_{n\to\infty} P\left(\cap_{b=1}^{B}\left\{\widehat{M}_{\widehat{\delta}_b^*} = \widehat{M}_{\delta_0}\right\}\right) = 1.$

Proof. First, by Bonferroni's inequality,

$$P\left(\cap_{b=1}^{B}\{\widehat{\delta}_b^* = \delta_0\}\right) \geq 1 - B\,P(\widehat{\delta}_b^* \neq \delta_0).$$

For any $\delta \neq \delta_0$, write $CV_b(\delta) = \|\mathbf{X}_v\widehat{\boldsymbol{\beta}}(\delta, \mathbf{Z}_t) - \mathbf{Y}_v\|_2^2$ and let

$$R_{n_t}(\delta) = E\big(\mathbf{X}'_{v_1}\widehat{\boldsymbol{\beta}}(\delta, \mathbf{Z}_t) - Y_{v_1}\big)^2.$$

Then, by Markov's inequality,

$$\begin{aligned}
& P(CV_b(\delta) < CV_b(\delta_0)) \\
\leq\ & \frac{E[CV_b(\delta_0) - CV_b(\delta) + n_v(R_{n_t}(\delta) - R_{n_t}(\delta_0))]^{2k}}{n_v^{2k}[R_{n_t}(\delta) - R_{n_t}(\delta_0)]^{2k}} \\
\leq\ & \frac{2E[CV_b(\delta_0) - n_v R_{n_t}(\delta_0)]^{2k} + 2E[CV_b(\delta) - n_v R_{n_t}(\delta)]^{2k}}{n_v^{2k}[R_{n_t}(\delta) - R_{n_t}(\delta_0)]^{2k}}.
\end{aligned}$$

Using the same argument as in Theorem 1 of [21] together with Whittle's inequality [19], the numerator is of order $(n_v/n_t)^k$, while Assumption 1 bounds the denominator away from zero. Hence $P(\widehat{\delta}_b^* \neq \delta_0) = O((n_t/n_v)^k)$, so

$$P\left(\cap_{b=1}^{B}\{\widehat{\delta}_b^* = \delta_0\}\right) \geq 1 - O\big(B(n_t/n_v)^k\big) \to 1$$

by Assumption 3. Therefore $P\left(\cap_{b=1}^{B}\{\widehat{M}_{\widehat{\delta}_b^*} = \widehat{M}_{\delta_0}\}\right) \to 1.$

As implied by Theorem 1, if the best procedure δ_0 is able to consistently identify the true active set (that is, $P(\widehat{M}_{\delta_0} = M_0) \to 1$), then CVPA also performs consistent variable selection when appropriate values of B, n_t and n_v are used. Notably, even if the best procedure δ_0 is not able to consistently identify the true active set, CVPA still has a chance to do so. Indeed, the probability CVPA selects the true active set is at least

$$\begin{aligned}
& P(\{\cap_{b=1}^{B}\widehat{M}_{\widehat{\delta}_b^*}\} = M_0) \\
& \geq P(\cap_{b=1}^{B}\{\widehat{M}_{\widehat{\delta}_b^*} = \widehat{M}_{\delta_0}\}; \widehat{M}_{\delta_0} = M_0) + P(\{\cap_{b=1}^{B}\widehat{M}_{\widehat{\delta}_b^*}\} = M_0; \widehat{M}_{\delta_0} \neq M_0),
\end{aligned} \tag{10}$$

where the second term may be greater than zero in some cases, as shown by [3] and [14]. Consequently, CVPA may surpass model selection by a single procedure in terms of variable selection accuracy. This is also demonstrated in the simulation results of Sect. 4.2.

Assumptions 1 and 2 are standard in delete-n_v CV theory [21,24], and Assumption 3 ensures that the number of pseudo-samples does not grow too quickly. Together they imply that, when an outstanding procedure exists in Δ, CVPA inherits its selection consistency.

3.3 CVPA for Variable Selection in Practice

For practical variable selection, let

$$\widehat{p}_j^* = \frac{1}{B}\sum_{b=1}^{B} I_{\{\widehat{\beta}_j(\widehat{\delta}_b^*,\mathbf{Z})\neq 0\}}$$

denote the selection frequency of variable X_j across the B selected procedures. Theorem 1 implies that, if the best candidate δ_0 consistently identifies M_0, then $\widehat{p}_j^* \to 1$ for active variables and $\widehat{p}_j^* \to 0$ otherwise. In practice we select variables with $\widehat{p}_j^* \geq p_0$, as in related stability-based procedures [3, 14]. The case $p_0 = 1$ is asymptotically consistent under Theorem 1, while smaller values such as 0.9 or 0.95 may be useful in finite samples. The results in Sect. 4.2 show that this approach can work well in practice.

Our proposed procedure results in two important advantages of CVPA relative to selection. First, the predictions from CVPA will have lower mean squared error than those from selection. Second, if there is an outstanding modeling procedure, CVPA will reduce to model selection.

4 Simulations

This section presents simulation studies that compare CVPA against other modeling procedures in high-dimensional linear regression settings with different degrees of sparsity and correlation between predictors.

We adopt the simulation settings of [2] and make some minor adjustments to accommodate a wider variety of patterns. Each row of the $n \times p$ design matrix $\mathbf{X} = (X_{i,j})$ is independently generated from $N(\mathbf{0}, \mathbf{\Sigma})$, where $\mathbf{0}$ denotes the p-dimensional vector of 0 and the $p \times p$ covariance matrix $\mathbf{\Sigma} = (\rho^{|j_1 - j_2|})$, where j_1 and j_2 $(j_1, j_2 = 1, \cdots, p)$ are the row and column indices, respectively. Two values of ρ (0.5 and 0.9) are examined. The responses are generated from

$$Y_i = \sum_{j=1}^{p} \beta_j X_{i,j} + \varepsilon_i; \quad i = 1, \cdots, n \tag{11}$$

where $\varepsilon_i \sim N(0, 0.2^2)$. We let $n = 100$ and $p = 2000$. Among $\boldsymbol{\beta} = (\beta_1, \cdots, \beta_p)^T$, $q = 3$, 6 or 12 randomly selected coefficients are assigned nonzero values, which are generated by $N(0, 0.5^2)$ independently. The set of candidate procedures $\mathbf{\Delta}$ consists of LASSO, MCP and SCAD with the 100 different λ values that are the default candidates in the R package `ncvreg` [4], so $|\mathbf{\Delta}| = 300$. For each setting, 200 replications (realizations of sample data) are performed.

4.1 Prediction Accuracy

The following four methods are compared by their predictive performances:

(1) The Model selection method (denoted by SEL in the following figures and tables): Using delete-n_v CV to select the optimal procedure $\widehat{\delta}$ from $\mathbf{\Delta}$. Then apply $\widehat{\delta}$ to $\mathbf{Z} = (\mathbf{X}, \mathbf{Y})$ to develop the model for prediction.
(2) CVPA: Select the best procedure from $\mathbf{\Delta}$ by delete-n_v CV and perform the CV $B = n$ times. This generates B selected procedures $\widehat{\mathbf{\Delta}}^*_{\mathcal{B}} = (\widehat{\delta}^*_1, \cdots, \widehat{\delta}^*_B)$. Apply each procedure in $\widehat{\mathbf{\Delta}}^*_{\mathcal{B}}$ to $\mathbf{Z}$ to produce B predictive models and make predictions by (6).
(3) MCV2 [2]: In this method, candidate models are least-squares fits of the response on various subsets of predictors with similar marginal correlation with the outcome. Within each predictor subset, the number of regressors is determined by cross-validation. Then the candidate models are averaged, with the weights optimized by cross-validation and without the constraint that the weights sum to unity. [2] propose three algorithms, and MCV2 has the best overall performance of these in their simulation studies.
(4) Bagging (denoted by BAGG in the following figures and tables) [5]: Obtain $\widehat{\mathbf{\Delta}}^*_{\mathcal{B}}$ by the same method as above. For each $b = 1, \cdots, B$, apply $\widehat{\delta}^*_b$ to $\mathbf{Z}^*_b$ to yield B different predictive models, and make predictions by averaging the B predictions.

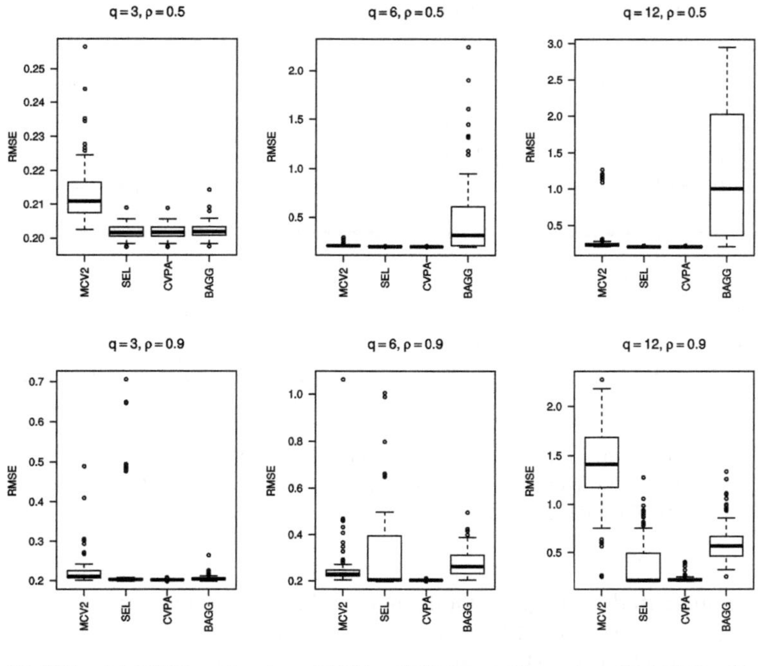

Fig. 1. RMSE of MCV2, selection (SEL), CVPA and bagging (BAGG). Simulation setting: $n = 100$, $p = 2000$; the q nonzero β_j are drawn from $N(0, 0.5^2)$. The feature matrix is generated as $N(\mathbf{0}, \mathbf{\Sigma})$ with $\mathbf{\Sigma} = \rho^{|j_1 - j_2|}$.

In this comparison, SEL, CVPA and BAGG all use delete-n_v cross-validation for tuning parameter λ selection where $n_v = n\log_{10} n/(\log_{10} n + 1)$ as suggested by [24]. The cross-validation error is calculated by (9). This choice makes the validation sample large enough to compare procedures on prediction performance while still leaving enough observations for estimation in each split. We also tried other forms of CV, such as 5-fold and 10-fold, and the relative results were similar. In MCV2, leave-one-out CV is employed to estimate the weights as suggested by [2]. For each competitor, we establish predictions $\widehat{Y}_k^0$ at 10,000 independent new observations $(\mathbf{X}_k^0, Y_k^0)$ from the same distribution as $(X_1, \cdots, X_p, Y)$ and the model (11). The RMSE $= \sqrt{\sum_{k=1}^{10000}\left(Y_k^0 - \widehat{Y}_k^0\right)^2/10000}$ for each competitor over the 200 replications is presented in Fig. 1.

As shown in Fig. 1, when the correlation among features is moderate ($\rho = 0.5$) and the true model is sparse ($q \leq 6$), CVPA and SEL outperform the other two methods in predictive accuracy. CVPA performs slightly better than SEL. As the true model size increases to $q = 12$, the advantage of CVPA over SEL becomes more pronounced due to the increased likelihood of model misidentification. The results for $q = 12$ are consistent with Figures 1–2 of [2], which show that, as the true model becomes dense, model selection methods can perform poorly by omitting important features. When the correlation among features is strong ($\rho = 0.9$), CVPA outperforms all competitors, and model selection becomes unstable even when the true model is sparse.

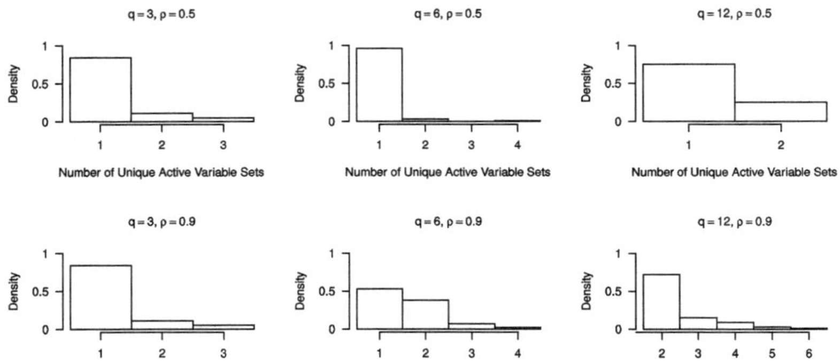

Fig. 2. Histogram of unique variable sets selected by CVPA. Simulation setting: $n = 100$, $p = 2000$. The q nonzero β_j are drawn from $N(0, 0.5^2)$, and the feature matrix is generated as $N(\mathbf{0}, \mathbf{\Sigma})$ with $\mathbf{\Sigma} = \rho^{|j_1 - j_2|}$.

As demonstrated by Fig. 2, when the correlation among features is moderate ($\rho = 0.5$) and the true model is sparse ($q = 3$), CVPA usually identifies a unique set of active variables for the regression. Moreover, as will be seen in Sect. 4.2, in this setting whenever CVPA identifies a unique active set (using $p_0 = 1$), the variables selected match those in the true model. As a consequence, CVPA and the model selection method (SEL) outperform all other methods in terms of predictive accuracy. However, when the correlation between features is strong ($\rho = 0.9$), model misspecification becomes more likely. Therefore, the number of unique active variable sets combined by CVPA goes up with q to counter the worsening negative effect caused by omission of relevant features.

4.2 Selection Accuracy

In this subsection, the data are generated under the same setting as in Sect. 4.1, except that n=200, p=1000 and all nonzero regression coefficients are set to 1. Here we examine the performance of CVPA for variable selection. Table 1 compares the selective performance of CVPA to the model selection method (denoted by SEL) using three indices: the proportion of replications where the method selects the true active set (PROP), the average number of false positives (FP), and the average number of false negatives (FN). To implement variable selection by CVPA, we test three different threshold values ($p_0 = 0.9$, 0.95 and 1). As described in Sect. 3.3, an input variable showing up among the B models with frequency above p_0 is treated as a variable selected by CVPA.

Table 1. Comparison of selection accuracy for $n = 200$, $p = 1000$, and $B = 200$. Each nonzero $\beta_j = 1$, and $\Delta = \{$LASSO, MCP, and SCAD with 100 values of $\lambda\}$. The first column lists the true model size q. The other columns report the proportion of times the true active set is selected (PROP) and the average numbers of false negatives (FN) and false positives (FP).

q	SEL			CVPA, $p_0 = 0.9$			CVPA, $p_0 = 0.95$			CVPA, $p_0 = 1$		
	PROP	FN	FP	PROP	FN	FP	PROP	FN	FP	PROP	FN	FP
$\rho = 0.5$												
3	0.86	0	0.18	0.86	0	0.19	0.91	0	0.12	1	0	0
6	0.98	0	0.02	0.98	0	0.04	0.99	0	0.01	1	0	0
12	1.00	0	0.00	1.00	0	0.00	1.00	0	0.00	1	0	0
$\rho = 0.9$												
3	0.67	0.36	0.38	0.99	0.00	0.02	0.98	0.02	0.00	0.93	0.07	0.00
6	0.84	0.20	0.26	0.98	0.03	0.04	0.94	0.08	0.04	0.69	0.42	0.02
12	0.74	0.51	1.36	0.67	0.72	0.30	0.61	0.91	0.29	0.18	2.22	0.17

When the correlation among features is moderate ($\rho = 0.5$), both SEL and CVPA are able to identify the true model with high probability. When the correlation among features increases ($\rho = 0.9$), the frequency of selecting the true model decreases, but CVPA with $p_0 = 0.95$ achieves higher selective accuracy than SEL for $q = 3$ and $q = 6$. On the surface, it seems strange that CVPA would outperform SEL in variable selection, since CVPA is implemented by applying a selected procedure to a number of pseudo-samples. However, when a selected procedure is used to do model selection, the selection uncertainty can be high in the sense that this procedure does not necessarily work well for another sample generated by the same population. CVPA averages out the selection uncertainty, which can improve both variable selection and prediction accuracy. The threshold p_0 controls how conservative this aggregation step is. Smaller values such as $p_0 = 0.9$ retain variables that appear frequently but not universally across the B selected models, which can reduce false negatives at the expense of admitting more false positives. Larger values such as $p_0 = 1$ keep only variables that appear in every selected model, which is more stringent and often preferable when a practitioner wants a highly stable final feature set. The intermediate choice $p_0 = 0.95$ balances these two goals and therefore works well in our simulations.

Overall, Cross-Validated Procedure Averaging (CVPA) outperforms other methods in terms of both prediction accuracy and variable selection and accomplishes adaptivity between selection and combination by mimicking whichever works better for the task at hand. In practice, $B = n$ repetitions of selections and $p_0 = 0.95$ are recommended for using CVPA when feature selection is a primary goal of the analysis. This recommendation is also computationally reasonable: using $B = n$ provides a stable estimate of selection frequencies without making the resampling burden excessively large for the moderate candidate sets considered here.

5 Real Data Application

The dataset `riboflavin` regarding vitamin B2 production is publicly available through the R package `hdi` [8]. The data is comprised of $N = 71$ observations on a single real-valued response variable, the logarithm of the B2 production rate, and $p = 4088$ predictors measuring the logarithm of the expression level of 4088 genes. The dataset is described in more detail in [7]. The goal of our analysis is to predict the logarithm of B2 production rate.

This dataset is a useful test bed for CVPA because it reflects the small-n, large-p regime that motivates the paper: the number of predictors is far larger than the sample size, procedure choice is consequential, and prediction is sensitive to how aggressively variables are screened or combined. In that sense, riboflavin is representative of the type of high-dimensional application in which neither pure model selection nor indiscriminate averaging is obviously satisfactory.

We evaluate and compare the performances of the same four procedures studied in Sect. 4 (SEL, CVPA, BAGG, and MCV2) in three steps. First, the $N = 71$ observations are divided into an evaluation set of size N_e ($N_e = 1, \cdots, 6$) and an estimation set of size $n = N - N_e$. Second, the four competitors each develop predictive models from the estimation set, which are used to make predictions on the evaluation set. Finally, for $N_e = 2, \cdots, 6$, we perform the above two steps 100 times, selecting the evaluation sets at random each time, and get 100 average prediction errors for each method. For $N_e = 1$, each record is used exactly once for evaluation, producing 71 prediction errors for each method. The average root mean squared error (RMSE) for each of the four procedures are displayed in Table 2. In this representative example, CVPA features the best predictive accuracy among the competitors.

Table 2. For each method, the table shows the average root mean square error (RMSE) and standard error (SE) (in parentheses). Note that the SEs reported are not the standard errors in the i.i.d. case.

Comparison of Prediction Errors for Riboflavin Data				
N_e	MCV2	SEL	CVPA	BAGG
1	0.413 (0.036)	0.538 (0.041)	0.277 (0.022)	0.399 (0.032)
2	0.552 (0.050)	0.589 (0.038)	0.342 (0.022)	0.435 (0.031)
3	0.577 (0.039)	0.584 (0.034)	0.416 (0.028)	0.533 (0.029)
4	0.666 (0.045)	0.590 (0.026)	0.429 (0.022)	0.495 (0.024)
5	0.582 (0.040)	0.665 (0.026)	0.457 (0.021)	0.538 (0.022)
6	0.672 (0.051)	0.669 (0.024)	0.451 (0.023)	0.518 (0.019)

6 Discussion

In high-dimensional regression, many models may be plausible for prediction, making model selection and model combination central parts of the analysis. Model selection can yield an interpretable model and support valid inference when the model is correctly specified, but in high dimensions it often selects the wrong model, leading to poor prediction and unreliable conclusions. Model combination can improve predictive performance, but when the true model is sparse and included among the candidates, combining models may add unnecessary complexity with little—or even negative—benefit.

Our proposed method addresses this trade-off by using the data to adaptively choose between selection and combination. When the true model is linear and sparse, it consistently recovers the active set; when the true model is unlikely to be identified by selection alone, it remains competitive for prediction. In this sense, CVPA leverages the strengths of both selection and combination while mitigating their weaknesses.

This work also broadens the role of cross-validation beyond choosing a single best model. By using cross-validation to guide adaptive combination, our method can outperform a cross-validation-selected model in a range of settings (Sect. 4) and helps clarify how cross-validation can be used more effectively for prediction.

Finally, the idea of "procedure combination" appears promising for high-dimensional problems, and a natural next step is to extend it to broader machine-learning settings, including hybrid approaches that combine methods such as trees with parametric models like logistic regression.

Disclosure of Interests. The authors have no competing interests to declare that are relevant to the content of this article.

References

1. Akaike, H.: A new look at the statistical model identification. IEEE Trans. Autom. Control **19**(6), 716–723 (1974)
2. Ando, T., Li, K.C.: A model-averaging approach for high-dimensional regression. J. Am. Stat. Assoc. **109**(505), 254–265 (2014)
3. Bach, F.R.: Bolasso: model consistent lasso estimation through the bootstrap. In: Proceedings of the 25th International Conference on Machine Learning. pp. 33–40. ACM (2008)
4. Breheny, P., Huang, J.: Coordinate descent algorithms for nonconvex penalized regression, with applications to biological feature selection. Ann. Appl. Stat. **5**(1), 232–253 (2011)
5. Breiman, L.: Bagging predictors. Mach. Learn. **24**(2), 123–140 (1996)
6. Breiman, L.: Classification and Regression Trees. Routledge, Abingdon (2017)
7. Bühlmann, P., Kalisch, M., Meier, L.: High-dimensional statistics with a view toward applications in biology. Ann. Rev. Stat. Appl. **1**, 255–278 (2014)
8. Dezeure, R., Bühlmann, P., Meier, L., Meinshausen, N.: High-dimensional inference: confidence intervals, p-values and R-software HDI. Stat. Sci. **30**(4), 533–558 (2015)
9. Donoho, D.L.: High-dimensional data analysis: the curses and blessings of dimensionality. In: AMS Math Challenges Lecture, pp. 1–32 (2000)
10. Fan, J., Li, R.: Variable selection via nonconcave penalized likelihood and its oracle properties. J. Am. Stat. Assoc. **96**(456), 1348–1360 (2001)
11. Hibon, M., Evgeniou, T.: To combine or not to combine: selecting among forecasts and their combinations. Int. J. Forecast. **21**(1), 15–24 (2005)
12. Hjort, N.L., Claeskens, G.: Frequentist model average estimators. J. Am. Stat. Assoc. **98**(464), 879–899 (2003)
13. Hoeting, J.A., Madigan, D., Raftery, A.E., Volinsky, C.T.: Bayesian model averaging: a tutorial (with comments by m. clyde, david draper and ei george, and a rejoinder by the authors. Stat. Sci. **14**(4), 382–417 (1999)
14. Meinshausen, N., Bühlmann, P.: Stability selection. J. R. Stat. Soc. Ser. B (Stat. Methodol.) **72**(4), 417–473 (2010)
15. Nan, Y., Yang, Y.: Variable selection diagnostics measures for high-dimensional regression. J. Comput. Graph. Stat. **23**(3), 636–656 (2014)
16. Schwarz, G.: Estimating the dimension of a model. Ann. Stat. **6**(2), 461–464 (1978)
17. Tibshirani, R.: Regression shrinkage and selection via the lasso. J. R. Stat. Soc. Ser. B Stat Methodol. **58**(1), 267–288 (1996)
18. Wang, X., Hyndman, R.J., Li, F., Kang, Y.: Forecast combinations: an over 50-year review. Int. J. Forecast. (2022)
19. Whittle, P.: Bounds for the moments of linear and quadratic forms in independent variables. Theory Probabil. Appl. **5**(3), 302–305 (1960)
20. Yang, Y.: Can the strengths of AIC and BIC be shared? A conflict between model identification and regression estimation. Biometrika **92**(4), 937–950 (2005)
21. Yang, Y.: Consistency of cross validation for comparing regression procedures. Ann. Stat. **35**(6), 2450–2473 (2007)

22. Yuan, Z., Yang, Y.: Combining linear regression models: when and how? J. Am. Stat. Assoc. **100**(472), 1202–1214 (2005)
23. Zhang, C.H.: Nearly unbiased variable selection under minimax concave penalty. Ann. Stat. 894–942 (2010)
24. Zhang, Y., Yang, Y.: Cross-validation for selecting a model selection procedure. J. Econometr. **187**(1), 95–112 (2015)

Misbehavior Detection in VANETs Using Tree-Based Machine Learning Techniques

Dariush Ebrahimi[1(✉)], Shreya Bandyopadhyay[2], Ankit Kundal[2], and Fadi Alzhouri[3]

[1] Department of Computer Science and Physics, Wilfrid Laurier University, 75 University Ave W, Waterloo, ON N2L 3C5, Canada
debrahimi@wlu.ca

[2] Department of Computer Science, Lakehead University, Thunder Bay, ON, Canada
{sbandyo1,akundal}@lakeheadu.ca

[3] Department of Electrical and Computer Engineering, Gulf University for Science and Technology (GUST), Mishref, Kuwait
alzhouri.f@gust.edu.kw

Abstract. The Internet of Things (IoT) is rapidly becoming an integral part of our lives. Concurrently, the new dawn of Artificial Intelligence is also witnessed by the world, hence integrating these IoT devices with the power of Machine Learning (ML) aims to elevate our standard of living in a better way. Intelligent Transport System (ITS) is one of such IoT technologies that uses modern information and telecommunications technology to provide smart transportation systems. One of the sectors of ITS is Vehicular Ad-hoc Networks (VANETs), constituting vehicles equipped with wireless devices. One of the critical messages in these networks is broadcast-authenticated periodic one-hop beacons, which are used for safety and traffic efficiency applications, like traffic jam detection and collision avoidance. In such a network environment, it is often habitual for cyber attackers to conduct intrusionsy. For example, Place spoofing, which is an intentional location deception in a vehicle-to-everything (V2X) communication, can cause traffic congestion and other safety hazardsy. The main objective of this paper is to trace such misbehavior conducted by attackers with the help of lightweight ML tree-based models, such as Decision Tree, Random Forest, and Extra Tree Ensemble algorithms, and compare the models to analyze the best approach in terms of computational cost and complexit. This will be achieved by utilizing the Dedicated Short Range Communications (DSRC) Data Set.

Keywords: Vehicular ad hoc networks (VANETs) · intelligent transport systems (ITS) · dedicated short range communications (DSRC) · machine learning · intrusion detection system · internet of things (IoT) security breach

1 Introduction

The IoT is an emerging technology that brings significant changes in various industries such as government, retail, and Wholesale, healthcare, etc. Intercon-

O. Gervasi et al. (Eds.): ICCSA 2026, LNCS 16768, pp. 70–88, 2027.
https://doi.org/10.1007/978-3-032-30488-9_5

nection of devices over the Internet provides people with immense comfort, such as smart transportation, reducing traffic jams, home automation, e-health, etc. [1,2]. One of the fundamental issues posing a serious threat to the IoT networks is a security breach. For example, remote adversaries might compromise Implantable Medical Devices (IMDs) for patients or smart vehicles, which not only cause tremendous economic damage, but are also life-threatening [3]. Due to the connectivity of IoT devices, remote attacks are feasible, and intruders can easily initiate attacks on a massive scale. In addition to the simplicity of executing efficient attacks, the magnitude and effect of the aftermath provide the attackers with ample chances to initiate further attacks.

In the automobile sector, via the use of Vehicular Ad-Hoc Networks (VANETs), developments have been made towards incorporating autonomous driving vehicles into Intelligent Transport Systems (ITS). VANET architecture consists of different components, such as On-Board Units (OBUs) and Road-Side Units (RSUs) . This type of network intends to promote reliable communication between vehicles (V2V communication) or between vehicles and infrastructure (V2I communication) to enhance the safety of the driver, prevent traffic congestion, and effectively manage transportation networks [4]. VANETs have the ability to greatly increase transportation quality. VANETs enable vehicles to connect with one another and exchange information such as vehicle dynamics and driving intentions, allowing for autonomous driving management. V2I links vehicles to infrastructure networks and even the Internet, allowing for real-time data distribution and traffic administration. Advances in data analysis and control algorithms have made the transportation network more efficient, where vehicles in the VANET can adapt and organise their driving behaviours, such as driving routes and speed [5]. Vehicle Platooning is an application of VANETs that enables vehicles to pursue a leading vehicle very closely by receiving acceleration and steering details via wireless communication [6]. One of the main safety application fields of VANETs is the traffic information system, which offers the most up-to-date obstacle data to a vehicle's satellite navigation system [7]. In the Electronic Brake Warning (EBW) feature, a vehicle sends out an event-based message to alert other vehicles about its braking operations [8]. This allows the driver to react timely manner to the other vehicles braking, even when the view of the brake lights is blocked by other vehicles.

According to the World Health Organization (WHO) [9], every year, nearly 1.35 million people's lives are cut short as a result of a car accident. Non-fatal accidents affect between 20 and 50 million more people, with many of them resulting in disability as a result of their injury. Individuals, their communities, and nations as a whole suffer significant economic damage as a result of road traffic accidents. Many countries lose 3% of their gross domestic product due to traffic accidents. Therefore, VANETs have a great impact on traffic management and avoiding road accidents. However, this path towards restricted human interference in vehicular communication implies that VANETs are vulnerable to a series of attacks, such as incorporating false information, manipulating and replicating messages, etc. [10,11]. This paper focuses on a few such attacks, particularly the jamming and spoofing attacks. These are the worst degree of Denial of Service (DOS) attacks. In these attacks, the intruder blocks the communication link, and therefore, other devices are unable to connect to the network. There are two possible cases in these types of attacks. In the first possibility, in a specific domain, high frequencies sent by an intruder jam the communication between nodes. Consequently, nodes in that network are not able to send or receive messages. Therefore, services are not accessible in that specific network. It is only possible to transmit or receive messages when a node leaves the target domain. Jamming the communication channel between the nodes and the RSU is the second scenario of attack. The scenario is that, near the RSU, the intruder executes an attack to disrupt the network, causing the network to break down. Nodes and RSUs are also noteworthy for sending or receiving messages from each other, contributing to network inaccessibility [12]. With the assistance of a tree based Machine Learning (ML) models such as Decision Trees (DT), Random Forest (RF), and Extra Tree Ensemble (ETE), this paper aims to track misconduct by attackers and compare the models to analyze the best approach in terms of computational cost and complexity. This paper attempts to leverage a comprehensive analysis of the problem and explore findings and insights to address the problem using lightweight ML tree-based models: DT, RF, and ETE. The contributions of the paper are summarized as follows:

- Exploring the findings of DT, FR, and ETE algorithms. This contribution will be made through devising the results based on two levels: hyperparameters and performance metrics.
- In pursuit of finding the best decision to maintain high-security ANETs, empirical discussions are produced to find the best algorithm in terms of computational cost and complexity.
- Providing significant insights to create more secure VANET systems and reduce potential cyber-attacks. Considering manuscript results increases VANET security.

The rest of this paper is organized as follows: Sect. 2 reviews VANETs' security literature. Section 3 illustrates the system model and defines the problem. Section 4 presents all the proposed Tree-based ML algorithms for misbehaviour detection. Section 5 reports detailed experimental results and analysis. Section 6 concludes the paper and highlights future works.

2 Literature Review

In VANETs, malicious nodes may disrupt the network performance. For example, modifying or inserting fake information in the network, which could incur life-threatening accidents. The security of VANETs is a highly important issue that has been the focus of research during the last few decades. One of the most important challenges in this regard is the existence of rogue vehicles. Several approaches have been reported in the literature to tackle this issue in VANETs. The authors of [13] and [14] have used features like Centroid Localization and the bloom filter data structure to detect attacks and examine jammers. The authors of [15] have proposed a data mining technique for a real-time detection of jamming attacks in V2V communication for platoons of vehicles. In [11], the authors have used two layers of metric combination, which comprises the physical layer and the application layer, in which the relative speed between the sender and receiver is measured. Physical layer provides the Signal to Interference plus noise Ratio (SINR), Received Signal Strength Indicator (RSSI), and PDR for detecting the jamming attacks. Also, the application layer helps in extracting Global Positioning System (GPS) coordinates for location tracking.

Many studies have provided several approaches to address the security threats in VANETS. These approaches are generally divided into three categories: 1) Confidence or reputation-based system, 2) data-centric detection system for misbehaviour, and 3) Intrusion Detection System (IDS). In [16–18], a decentralized confidence-based infrastructure scheme has been implemented. The authors have built a reputation management mechanism for each vehicle that facilitates rapid adjustment to changing local circumstances and establishes confidence relationships with other vehicles. A centralized framework (an attack-resistant confidence management scheme) has been proposed by [19], which not only identifies and deals with cyber attacks, but also determines the reliability of information and vehicles. The method of data-centred misbehaviour detection has been suggested in [20, 21]. It has been used to enhance the reliability of VANETs in shared data.

In [11], the effect of the density of vehicles on network efficiency is defined in order to achieve accurate identification, followed by analysis of jamming effectiveness, based on various mobility patterns and attitudes. In [6], the authors introduced a two-step intrusion detection algorithm that detects both spoofing and jamming attacks in a Connected Autonomous Vehicle (CAV) environment. The proposed method reduces the risk of cyber attacks that cause traffic disruptions and accidents. The identification mechanism of the proposed IDS is centered on the RF, k-Nearest Neighbour (KNN), and One-Class Support Vector Machine (OCSVM) approaches, as well as cross-layer data fusion methods. Specifically, the paper has focused on analysing the effect of jamming based on the behaviour of jammers and mobility trends. The effect of the distribution of vehicles on network efficiency is first established in order to accomplish trustworthy identification. The efficacy of jamming is then analysed by the following various mobility patterns (fixed, irregular, or attacking) and behaviours (steady, arbitrary, and responsive). Their approach demonstrates promising results in IEEE802.11p networks to reliably detect various types of jammers.

It is worth mentioning in this context to recall the debate about the Federated Learning (FL) approach. Recently, many new applications have been seen utilizing FL to improve the quality and privacy of data-driven applications, especially in IoT applications. The unbalanced distribution of samples across local nodes in FL poses a critical issue in terms of varying performance among the local nodes. For more information about the FL, we direct the reader to [22]. It may be unjust to discuss security matters in any area without any reference to the most widely known technique, namely, blockchain technology. The technology's popularity has soared with the advent of Bitcoin. In building a secure system, it's important to consider security at all layers of the technology, for example, secure communication, data privacy, and whether it is a public or private system. In fact, we can implement blockchain in certain layers to strengthen security, but this technique works well in a high density of clients and data. While our environment assumes hundreds of connected vehicles in a given area, which is very small compared to other applications. For more information about the pros and cons of blockchain security, we forward readers to read [23–25].

The authors in [26] adopted machine learning techniques, Random Forest, on the VeReMi dataset to detect the misbehavior. However, our paper poses tree-based ML algorithms like DT, RF, and ETE approaches to create an IDS. To the best of our knowledge, the ETE approach has not been used in this regard. Although it is better than the other two algorithms in terms of computational cost and complexity. The study compares the approaches and explains how the ETE approach surpasses the other approaches and will give better results.

3 System Model and Problem Definition

An IDS is an integral part of a defense mechanism that helps in detecting attacks or proof of unusual activity in a vehicular communication system. In the network security and intrusion prevention domains, various ML techniques have been extensively used. An ML-IDS is focused on models that help to classify gathered information. The use of ML techniques, especially the tree-based approaches, has shown precision of IDS in the field of network security. In this paper, three tree-based ML methods are collectively compared and tried to determine the best of them. In Fig. 1, a visual representation of the flow of the proposed system is created. When these algorithms are applied independently, each of the proposed classification algorithms provides consistent results. The mixture of these algorithms will therefore lead to an overall efficient IDS. Algorithms such as RF, ETE, and DT are assessed to determine attacks in communication. VANETs use vehicles as mobile nodes to communicate between neighboring vehicles and between vehicles and nearby roadside units; however, due to their characteristics, they tend to be different from other networks. Primarily, while traveling, the nodes(vehicles) are restricted to road topology; therefore, if the road information is available, a vehicle's future location can be predicted. In addition, vehicles can manage critical computation, communication, and sensing capabilities and have persistent transmission power to support these functions independently. Nonetheless, VANETs have some challenging features as well, such as being potentially large-scale networks and having high mobility. As shown in Table 1, VANETs consist of various components such as On Board Units (OBUs), Road Side Units (RSUs), Application Units (AUs), and Trusted Authorities (TAs) [27].

Communications in VANETs are concentrated on Vehicle-to-Everything (V2X), which plays a key role in the ITS by providing actual and exceptionally accurate information such as accident alerts, road bottlenecks information,

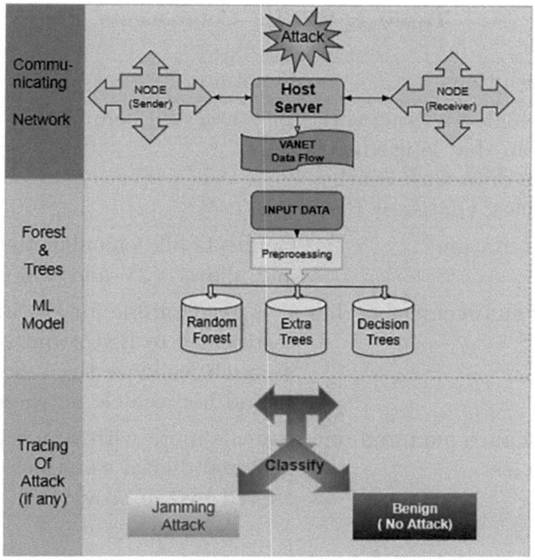

Fig. 1. System Flow Diagram

traffic congestion warnings, emergencies, and other transportation services to enhance traffic quality, traffic protection, and driving experiences. Some of specific important terms in V2X communication are [28]:

- *V2V Group Communications:* Only vehicles that share some of the same characteristics shall engage in this communication, such as vehicles with the same brand or vehicles sharing the same location over time.
- *Vehicle Beacons:* In this method, the vehicle regularly sends beacon messages to all nearby vehicles and RSUs. These messages provide the speed, coordinates, velocity, and acceleration of being sent.
- *Vehicle Warning Infrastructure:* In order to improve the flow of traffic and road safety, warning signals are transmitted from the infrastructure through RSUs to all vehicles in the vicinity of an area, where potential accidents or collisions are detected, in particular at curves, intersections, or narrow roads.

3.1 Attacks in Focus

Our model addresses two kinds of attacks: Jamming and Spoofing attacks.

Spoofing Attacks: To warn neighbouring vehicles of their presence, all the vehicles in a platoon broadcast beacon messages. Each beacon message consists of various fields such as Time Instance, Identifier Node, Mac Address, and Vehicle Current Position. The intruder will change any of these. In order to transmit false GPS position coordinates inside the cameras or sensors, the intruder exploits these fields, misdirecting the platoon of linked vehicles to an incorrect spot. As

Table 1. VANET Components

Components	Description	Function
On Board Units (OBU)	A vehicle-fixed network system that is used to share data with nearby vehicles, OBUs, or RSUs	V2V and V2I communication
Road Side Units (RSU)	Base Station	Connects all vehicular nodes to the Internet and allows V2V and V2I communication
Trusted Authorities (TA)	Law enforcement bodies	It is accountable for the issuing of digital certificates to RSUs and vehicles that uniquely validate the vehicle and RSU in the ad hoc vehicle network
Application Units (AU)	Appliance mounted on vehicles	It deals more with security applications and personal digital assistance (PDA) services offered by the provider

a consequence of wireless communication between transmitter (Tx) and receiver (Rx), this has to shift to a different stage (to the observed RSSI values [6]) to indicate the spoofing attack. The level of the RSSI values changes drastically when the location of the transmitter, which is the spoofer during the spoofing attack, is somewhat different from the legitimate position. The spoofing attack can be indicated by this fact, also demonstrating that the RSSI can be a critical metric for detecting a spoofing attack using an ML approach.

Jamming Attacks: A jammer is a system that does not comply with valid MAC protocols and attempts to interfere with the transmitter or receiver to disrupt communications. Various jammers can be categorized as shown in Table 2.

3.2 System Model

The System model consists of a troop of vehicles fitted with embedded Cooperative Adaptive Cruise Control (CACC) technology, which is a more sophisticated version of Adaptive Cruise Control (ACC). Vehicles in CACC systems can interact with the vehicle in front of them using V2V communication. We have considered the concept of vehicle platooning (or road trains), which is basically a collection of vehicles or nodes in which one leading vehicle, which is manually driven, has following vehicles that are automatically controlled by the leading vehicle. Figure 2 depicts four vehicles moving on a highway. We assume that the first two vehicles, V1 and V2, are forming a platoon, with V1 being the leading vehicle followed by V2, and consequently, they can share information by using V2V communication, and the other two vehicles, V3 and V4, are out of the platoon. Let us also assume that V1 and V2 have local sensors and are installed with computing devices in order to avoid longitudinal instability while forming a platoon. Connected nodes will broadcast beacon or basic safety messages (BSMs)

Table 2. Jamming Techniques

Jamming Techniques	Properties	Merits from the standpoint of the intruder
Constant	It generates a signal made up of random bits. No MAC protocol rules are observed by the signal generator	It will still keep the media occupied
Deceptive	It generates packets where the header is useful, but the payload is of no use	Legitimate nodes will sense a busy channel and hence withdraw themselves due to permanently being in the listening mode
Random	There are two modes: 1) Jammer keeps the channel busy at random time periods; 2) Jammer turns off its transmitter for a random time period	
Reactive	Targets the receiver. It uses enough noise to change as many bits as possible, because the modification of the bits requires only a minimal amount of power. If a checksum is executed at the receiving end of a packet, it is listed as invalid and discarded	It jams communications when it detects one, so that it does not waste energy

over the 5.9 GHz Dedicated Short Range Communication channel (around one kilometer range). These messages contain information such as GPS coordinates, location, speed, velocity, and warnings related to accidents or collisions, in addition to information related to vehicles' route changes. The intruder, which is not a part of the platoon, would use vehicles out of the platoon, like vehicles V3 and V4, to execute jamming and spoofing attacks, respectively (see Fig. 2). The attacker may jam the communication by interfering with any BSMs longitudinally and block communication between vehicle V1 and V2 by transmitting in a reactive manner. The vehicles forming the platoon, i.e., V1 and V2, are connected to the Remote Cloud and Management Center (RCMC) that manages all the real-time statistical data containing values like transmission power, received power, PDR, RSSI, and so on, which have also been collected from other nodes in the area (such as V3 and V4). Each node is directly connected to the internet through LTE technology for sending real-time statistical data to a cloud or server. The RCMC, by using the statistical data received from all nodes, can detect whether there is a jamming attack on nodes in the platoon or not. On the other hand, the RCMC can also detect a also beenspoofing attack by using and monitoring the BSM data sent in V2V communication. Hence, this data can be used for misbehavior detection.

As shown in Fig. 2, the data flow is managed by the cloud when a sender node/vehicle is sending data to a receiver node/vehicle via a host server (i.e., when vehicles are connected in a platoon through V2V communication). The

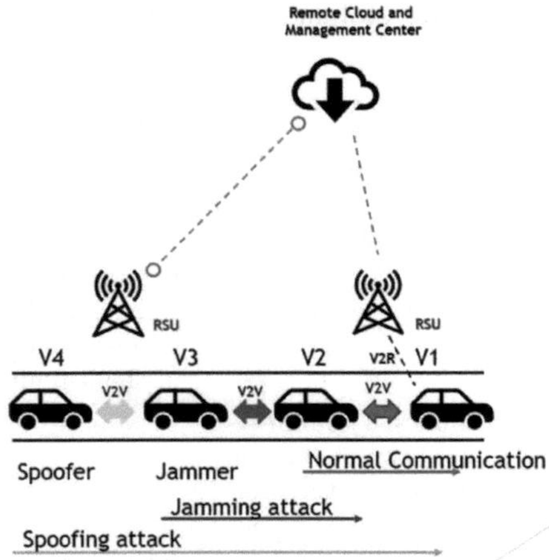

Fig. 2. VANET System Model

received data in the platoon, which contains information like PDR ratio, transmission power, and other values, is preprocessed before being fed into machine learning algorithms to classify whether it is malicious or benign, and eventually predict whether a jamming attack has occurred.

3.3 Jamming and Spoofing Detection System Framework

The purpose of an IDS is to detect evidence of attacks and suspicious operations. In intrusion detection and enhancing the security of the VANET network, various ML approaches can be beneficial. With each day, the use of ML methods in VANETs is gaining more popularity. ML for Jamming and Spoofing Detection Framework is essentially focused on classification models that help to identify the information analyzed with enhanced precision. Using feature extraction and data classification, three of the most effective models that will help distinguish the type of attack are incorporated.

3.4 Dedicated Short Range Communications Data Set

The used dataset for our IDS consists of information regarding Dedicated Short Range Communications (DSRC) [29] between vehicles and roadside units [11]. The two separate sets of normal scenario and attack scenario are combined into one set for the experimental analysis. For running vehicular network simulation, Veins [30] has been used here. The communications in the dataset were set up based on IEEE 802.11p standards at 5.9 Ghz, 10 BSM (Basic Service messages) per second, and are using Control Channel (Ch172), a 10 Mhz channel. The dataset consists of 390 simulations in a normal scenario as well as in the presence of an attacker. The key attributes are Transmitted node ID number, Received

Node Id number, Received Signal Strength in dbm, Packet Error Rate, Received Signal Strength Indicator, Signal to noise ratio, and the Target value, indicating whether the scenario is normal or in the presence of a jammer.

4 Tree-Based Algorithms and Frameworks

The ML-based IDS is focused on categories for classifying the analyzed data. In ML, the most popular and most often used supervised learning approaches are tree-based learning algorithms. They are diversified, easy to understand, and can be extended to a number of cases. This paper proposes three well known Tree-based ML algorithms for misbehaviour detection in vehicle communication.

These proposed algorithms are categorized under the supervised learning technique, and they are DT, RF, and ETE. A DT is a decision-making mechanism that uses a tree-like decision model. It is one way of displaying an algorithm consisting only of conditional statements. DTs are widely used classification techniques, but they are also a prominent means of ML in organizational analysis, especially for evaluating decisions. It is the building block of all tree models, including RF and ETE.

The structure of the RF algorithm is shown in Fig. 3, and it is a supervised learning algorithm focused on decision-tree models that partitions the data with the majority of votes in the groups of individual trees by a subset of training. The training algorithm applies the general technique of bootstrap aggregation, known as bagging. This method of bootstrapping boosts model efficiency as it lowers model variance without increasing the bias. This implies that, while for a single tree, predictions are extremely noise sensitive, the average of several trees is stable as long as trees are not correlated. RF is generally favored over others due to several reasons: Firstly, it has considerably higher precision for both classification and regression tasks. Secondly, it does not allow unnecessary trees in the model if there are more trees. It has the ability to manage a massive, multidimensional data set. Finally, the RF classifier manages the missing values and leaves a significant proportion of the data accurate.

Adding another randomization stage results in extremely random trees, or Extra Trees. While they are an aggregation of individual trees, they are comparable to ordinary random forests, as two key distinctions exist. First, each tree is trained using the whole sample of information and learning (rather than a bootstrap sample), and second, the top-down division of a tree learner is randomized. The random cutoff-point for any feature is chosen instead of determining the local optimum cutoff (based on Information gain or Gini impurity). This value is chosen from a uniform distribution within the analytical spectrum of the feature (in the tree training set). The division that gives the highest score is then chosen to divide the node with all randomly generated splits. The random number of features to be taken into account at any node can be defined, equivalent to ordinary random forests. Thus, it makes the ETE algorithm have less computational cost as compared to RF. The structure of the ETE method is shown in Fig. 4.

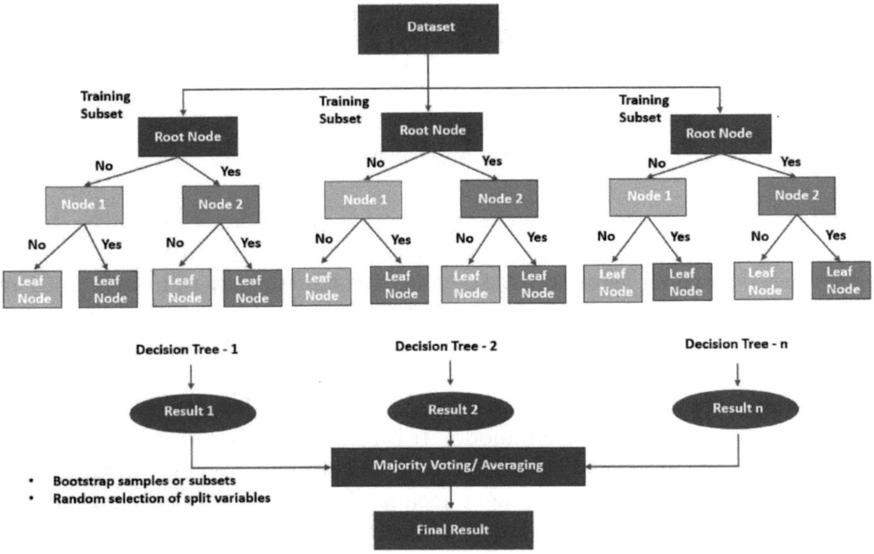

Fig. 3. Structure of Random Forest

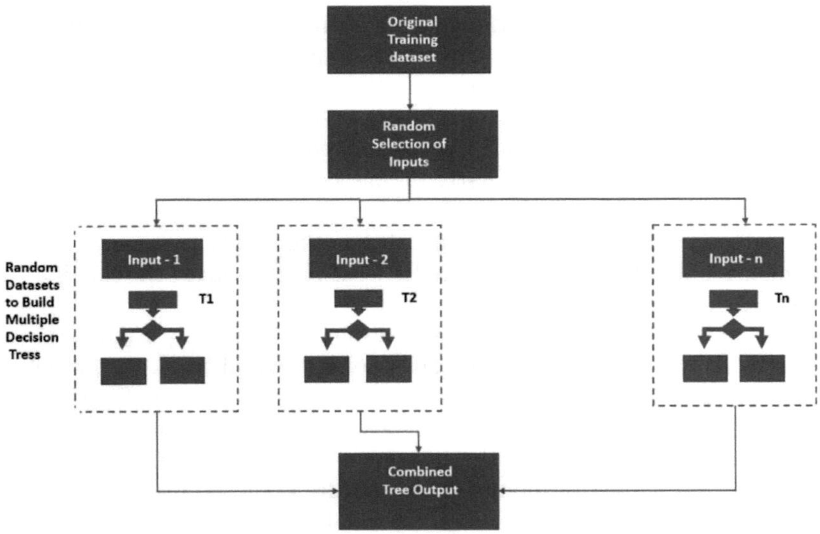

Fig. 4. Structure of Extra Tree

Table 3. Key Notations

Notation	Description
r	Pearson's Correlation Coefficient
x_i	values of the x-feature
$\bar{x}$	mean of the values of the x-feature
y_i	values of the y-feature
$\bar{y}$	mean of the values of the y-feature
AUC	the Area Under the Curve. It is used to measure the ability of a classifier to distinguish between classes
ROC	a graph showing the performance of a classification model across all rating thresholds

5 Experimental Analysis and Results

An ML approach has some principal steps that are applied in any kind of problem-solving scenario. These steps include data accumulation, data preprocessing, training, hyperparameter tuning, and prediction. For ML technique implementation, Jupyter Notebook is used. In addition, we will use Table 3 notation for the rest of the paper.

5.1 Data Preprocessing

The first and foremost step in any ML process is data preprocessing. The outlier features have been removed using the standard deviation. Standard Deviation is a measure that determines how often individual data points deviate from the mean. The features with zero Standard Deviation imply that they do not have any predictive capability. Hence, including such features may lead to overfitting, the scenario where the model gives good performance while training, but fails to perform well with new data.

Data can be available in various formats such as text files, audio files, video files, images, etc. In our case, the DSRC dataset is an Excel table with various numeric values in each feature (Table 4 shows the features of our dataset), the target has two classes: Benign (for normal scenario) and Malign (in the presence of an attacker). A machine cannot read such data since it can only understand binary information. Data Preprocessing is a step in which data is cleaned and encoded so that it can be easily interpreted by the machine. The target values are encoded, '1' representing the malignant data and '0' representing benign data.

To get a meaningful outcome from the experiment, it is important to understand the data as much as possible. The concept of correlation has been used here, and a Pearson's correlation matrix for each feature has been plotted. Correlation is a statistical measure that determines the dependency of features on

Table 4. Features used for modeling

Model Features Used	Description
RSU-BTx-Car	Roadside unit to car bidirectional transmission
RSU-PSR (%)	Road Side unit- soft routing protocol in percentage
Car P-Received	Number of packets received by car
Car-PDR (%)	Car packet delivery ratio in percentage
RSU PDSR (%)	Roadside unit - Packet Delivery / send ratio in percentage
Car Received power (dBm)(%)	The received power for a car in decibel milliwatts
Car-Btx-RSU	Car to Road Side Unit bidirectional transmission
RSU P-Received	Roadside unit packets received
RSU-PDR (%)	Roadside unit packet Delivery ratio in percentage
RSU Received power (dBm)	Power received by Roadside unit in decibel milliwatts
OBU	Type of On-Board units: 1OBU, 10OBU, 20OBU, 40OBU, 60OBU, 80OBU, 100OBU

each other. In other words, it tells us how much one feature is different from another. When a dependent variable and an independent variable have a high correlation value, it implies that the independent variable is very important in deciding the output. It is important to identify correlations among features and discard irrelevant ones to build a high-precision model.

Figure 5 shows the correlation matrix of features of our dataset. The Pearson's correlation coefficient is computed as:

$$\mathrm{r} = \frac{\sum_{i=1}^{n}(x_i - \overline{x})(y_i - \overline{y})}{\sqrt{\sum_{i=1}^{n}(x_i - \overline{x})^2(y_i - \overline{y})^2}} \tag{1}$$

5.2 Hyperparameter Tuning

Hyperparameters are parameters that cannot be learnt from the data and need to be defined before training. They indicate the ability of a model to train data and the complexity of the model. Hyperparameter tuning is the adjustment of the value of hyperparameters by the trial-and-error method, such that the model obtains an optimal solution. In DT, the maximum depth of the tree is the hyperparameter. In RF and ETE, the maximum depth and number of features considered by each tree while splitting are the hyperparameters. The Area Under

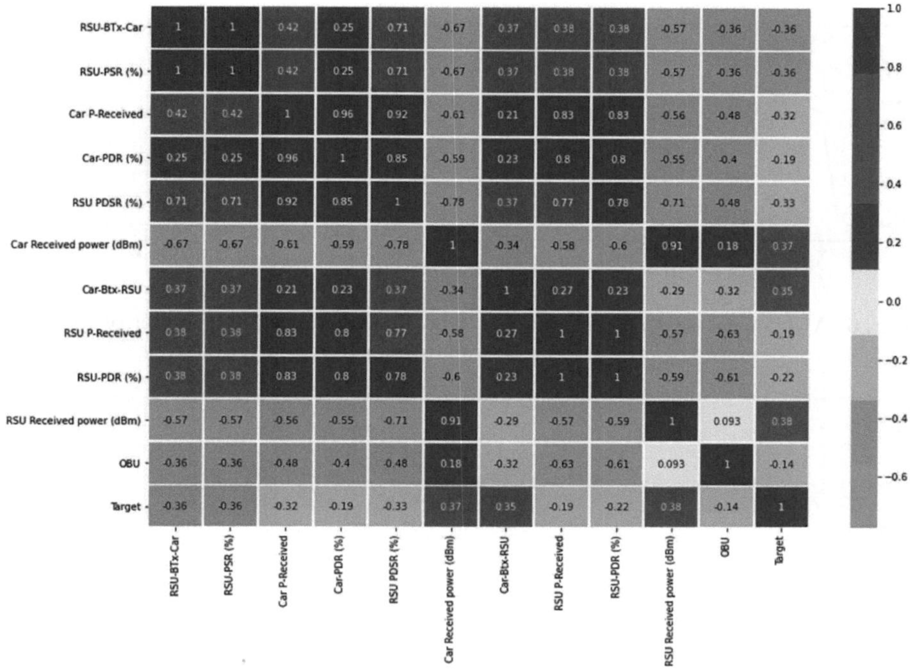

Fig. 5. Correlation Matrix of DSRC Dataset features

the Curve (AUC) graph for the RF model is plotted between AUC scores and the number of Estimators, and for other models, it is plotted between AUC scores and maximum depth. The AUC graph indicates the capacity of a model to distinguish between classes, in our data, malign and benign. If the AUC score is 1, this indicates that the model perfectly classifies positive and negative values, whereas when the AUC score is 0, it implies that the model incorrectly predicts positive values as negative and vice versa.

In DT, the graph becomes constant at the maximum depth of 20, implying that the optimal value of maximum depth for DT is 20. Figure 6 shows the AUC curve for DT, where Fig. 7 shows the AUC curve for the number of estimators. Even though the train AUC (blue line) becomes constant at 20 estimators, the test AUC is still varying. We decided to take 100 as the optimal number of estimators because increasing the number of estimators further will make the model more complex, resulting in poor performance. Figure 8 shows the AUC curve for maximum depth for Random Forest. For the ETE model, shown in Fig. 9, although the AUC curve becomes steady for some time starting at a maximum depth of 6 to 9, there has been a slight increase at the maximum depth of 10, implying that the optimal value of maximum depth for ETE is 10.

Furthermore, to prevent overfitting, we have applied Stratified K-Fold Cross Validation on RF and ETE classifiers, keeping the value of K as 10. In cross-

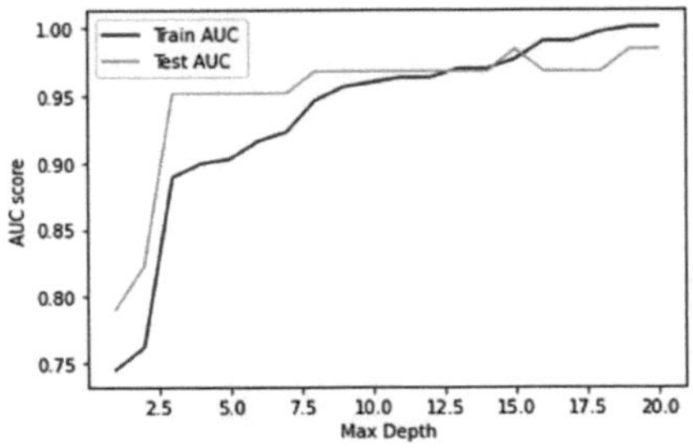

Fig. 6. AUC curve for Decision Tree

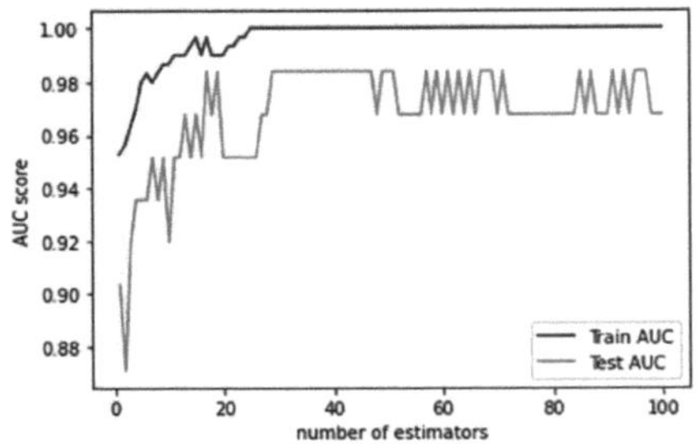

Fig. 7. AUC curve for Number of Estimators in Random Forest

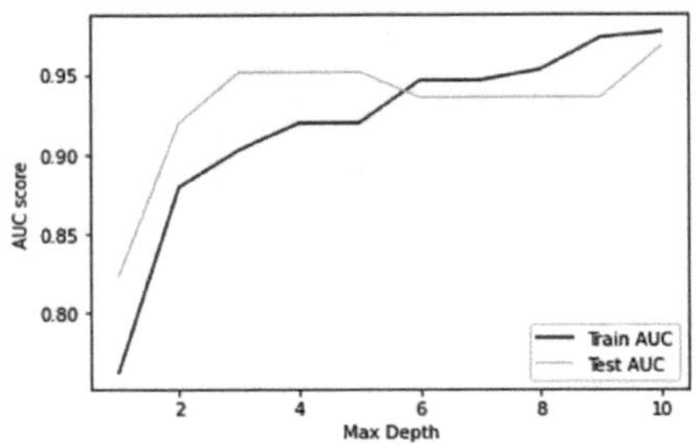

Fig. 8. AUC curve for Maximum Depth in Random Forest

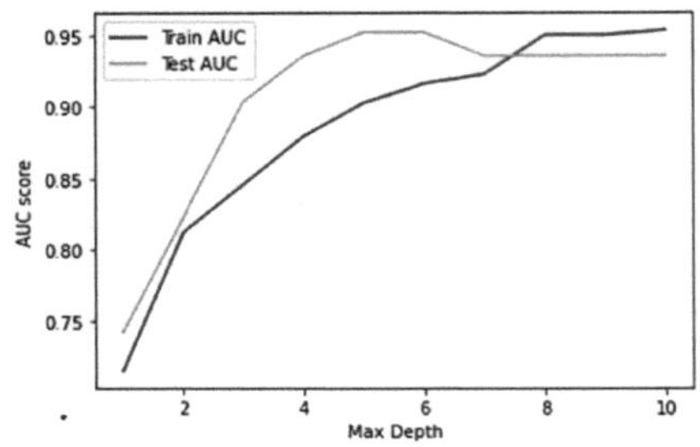

Fig. 9. AUC curve for Maximum Depth in Extra Tree Classifier

validation, data is split into K equal samples and the model is fit K times, with K-1 folds for training data and the Kth fold for validation data. The validation fold keeps changing with each iteration, implying that by the end of the evaluation, the entire data is utilized. The divisions are chosen in stratified K-fold cross-validation such that the average solution value is exactly proportional across all divisions.

5.3 Performance Metrics

To assess the performance of the ML algorithms, we employ Precision, Recall, Accuracy, and F1 Score. DT, RF, and ETE models are used to assess the efficiency of the established IDS. To validate our approach, we have to conduct the three targeted ML algorithms, including DT, on the same data set based on the same features. Then we compare the results of each algorithm under an identical experimental setup. Table 5 shows comparisons of the performance metrics results of the tree-based ML algorithms. It is evident that DT has 97% better test accuracy performance compared to 94% for RF and ETE, the reason being that our dataset is really small, having 390 instances and 15 features, and DT performs well with simpler data. Moreover, RF and ETE give 89% accuracy in 10 fold Cross Validation compared to 87% for DT, which implies that, overall,

Table 5. Results of the three models

Model	Test Accuracy %	Train Accuracy %	10 Fold Cross Validation Accuracy %	Test AUC	Train AUC	Precision	Recall	F1-Score
Extra Trees	94	95	89	0.93	0.94	1.0	0.87	0.93
Random Forest	94	95	89	0.93	0.94	1.0	0.87	0.93
Decision Tree	97	95	87	0.96	0.94	1.0	0.93	0.96

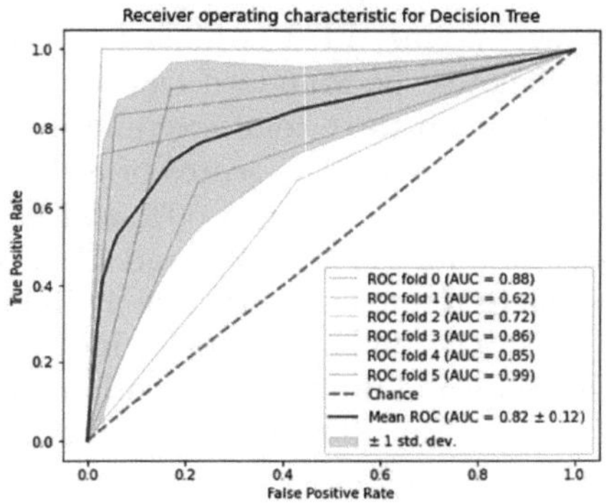

Fig. 10. ROC Curve for Decision Tree. (Color figure online)

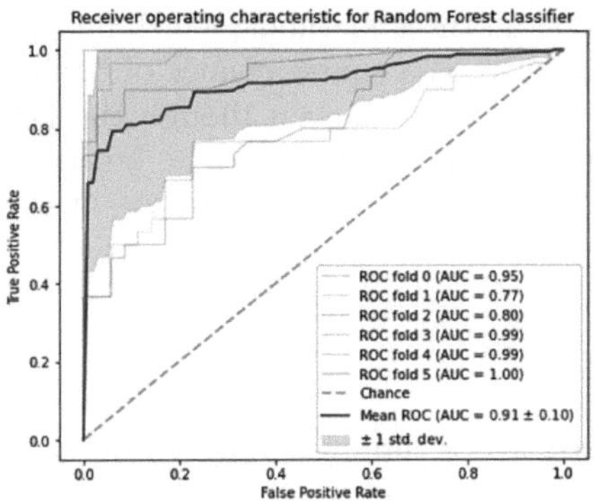

Fig. 11. ROC Curve for Random Forest

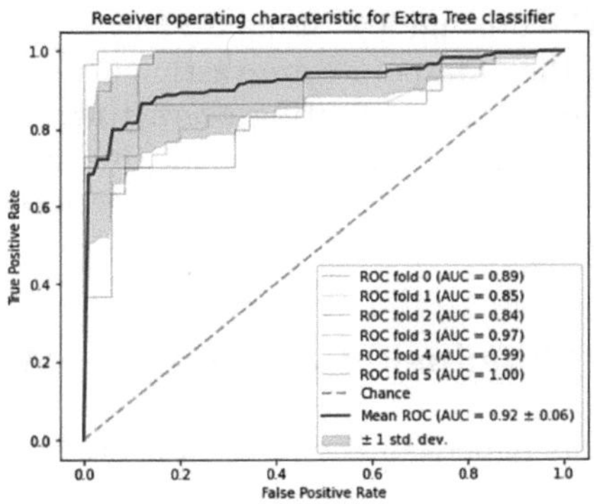

Fig. 12. ROC Curve for Extra Tree

RF and ETE are performing better than DT. In the future, when more data is added to this dataset or a more complex dataset is used, ETE shall surpass RF and DT in performance as it is computationally inexpensive due to random splitting of features at each node.

The results have been plotted on Receiver Operating Characteristic (ROC) plots individually for the three ML techniques. The ROC graph shows how well the classification model is performing by comparing the TPR (Recall) and FPR. An AUC curve is basically a synopsis of the ROC curve. We have plotted an ROC curve for each of the three ML approaches over a 6-fold Stratified Cross Validation data split.

Figure 10 shows the ROC curve for DT. The red dotted line represents the decision boundary or the chance line, and any point on that line will represent equal TPR and FPR. If the curve is above the red line, it denotes a higher TPR. The more the curve is bent above the red line, the better the model performs. If the curve is bent below the line, FPR is high, i.e., the model is performing poorly. The gray region denotes the Standard Deviation (measures how spread out the data points are) between the 6-foldlower and upper true positive rates. The individual 6 folds for DT have AUC scores of 88%, 62%, 72%, 86%, 85%, 95%, which means the scores range between 60% and 95%. The average ROC score and Standard Deviation for DT are 82% and 12%, respectively.

Figure 11 illustrates the ROC curve for RF. The individual 6-fold AUC scores for RF are 95%, 77%, 80%, 99%, 99%, and 100%, indicating a range of 75% to 100%. The average ROC score and Standard Deviation for RF are 91% and 10% respectively. Figure 12 depicts the ROC curve for ETE. The individual 6-fold ETE AUC scores are 95%, 77%, 80%, 99%, 99%, and 100%, indicating a range of 75% to 100%. The average ROC score and Standard Deviation for ETE are 92% and 0.06%, respectively.

From the three ROC graphs, it is clear that ETE has a higher mean AUC-ROC score and low Standard Deviation among all three methods, which implies that the data points are vastly clustered and there is a sparse chance of having outliers, thus preventing overfitting. This concludes that even though the DT model is performing better for the current dataset, ETE shall surpass both DT and RF when experiments are performed with more complex datasets in the future.

6 Conclusion and Future Work

In this paper, an IDS system using tree-based ML techniques, namely, decision tree, random forest, and extra tree ensemble algorithms, for detecting both spoofing and jamming attacks in a VANET network is proposed. The three techniques have been compared to analyze the best approach in terms of computational cost and complexity. For analysis purposes, the dedicated short-range communication DSRC dataset has been used. The simulation results showed that the decision tree in terms of test accuracy outperforms the other two approaches; however, in terms of cross-validation, it scores lower than them. The extra tree ensemble approach shall exceed the other two when tests are conducted with larger and more complex datasets. In future work, we will extend our approach to augmenting features extracted from the behavioral history of each vehicle in the platoon, as well as experiments on a wide range of different datasets.

References

1. Rocha Filho, G.P., et al.: Enhancing intelligence in traffic management systems to aid in vehicle traffic congestion problems in smart cities. Ad Hoc Networks **107** (2020)
2. Brennand, C.A.R.L., Filho, G.P.R., Maia, G., Cunha, F., Guidoni, D.L., Villas, L.A.: Towards a fog-enabled intelligent transportation system to reduce traffic jam. Sensors **19** (2019)
3. Zhou, W., Jia, Y., Peng, A., Zhang, Y., Liu, P.: The effect of iot new features on security and privacy: New threats, existing solutions, and challenges yet to be solved. IEEE Internet Things J. **6**(2), 1606–1616 (2018)
4. Mihai, S., Dokuz, N., Ali, M.S., Shah, P., Trestian, R.: Security aspects of communications in vanets. In: 2020 13th International Conference on Communications (COMM), pp. 277–282. IEEE, 2020
5. Englund, C., Chen, L., Vinel, A., Lin, S.Y.: Future applications of VANETs. In: Campolo, C., Molinaro, A., Scopigno, R. (eds.) Vehicular ad hoc Networks, LNCS, pp. 525–544. Springer, Cham (2015). https://doi.org/10.1007/978-3-319-15497-8_18
6. Kosmanos, D., et al.: Intrusion detection system for platooning connected autonomous vehicles. In: 2019 4th South-East Europe Design Automation, Computer Engineering, Computer Networks and Social Media Conference (SEEDA-CECNSM), pp. 1–9. IEEE, 2019
7. Sommer, C., Tonguz, O.K., Dressler, F.: Traffic information systems: efficient message dissemination via adaptive beaconing. IEEE Commun. Mag. **49**(5), 173–179 (2011)
8. Mousannif, H., Khalil, I., Al Moatassime, H.: Cooperation as a service in vanets. J. UCS **17**(8), 1202–1218 (2011)
9. W. H. O. (WHO), "Road Traffic Injuries", 2021. https://www.who.int/news-room/fact-sheets/detail/road-traffic-injuries. Accessed 21 June 2021
10. Vijayabharathi, V., Malarchelvi, P.S.K.: Implementing hmac in expedite message authentication protocol for vanet. In: International Conference on Information Communication and Embedded Systems (ICICES2014), pp. 1–5. IEEE, 2014
11. Malebary, S., Huang, C.: Jamming mobility in 802.11 p networks: modeling, evaluation, and detection. In: 2016 IEEE 35th International Performance Computing and Communications Conference (IPCCC), pp. 1–7. IEEE, 2016
12. Raghuwanshi, V., Jain, S.: Denial of service attack in vanet: a survey. Int. J. Eng. Trends Technol. **28**(1), 15–20 (2015)
13. Murshed, M., Wickramasurendra, N., Jubaida, A., De Grande, R.E., Carvalho, G.H.: Novel rf-jamming ids for vehicular networks: Lstm, xgboost, and meta-models approaches. Int. J. Crit. Infrastruct. Prot. 100830 (2026)
14. Alam, M.S., Oluoch, J., Kim, J.: A mechanism to localize, detect, and prevent jamming in connected and autonomous vehicles (cavs). IEEE Trans. Intell. Transp. Syst. **25**(2), 1215–1224 (2023)
15. Ahmad, J., et al.: Machine learning and blockchain technologies for cybersecurity in connected vehicles. Wiley Interdiscip. Rev. Data Min. Knowl. Discovery **14**(1), e1515 (2024)
16. Awan, K.A., Din, I., Syed, T., Cengiz, K., Almogren, A.: Trustworthy clustering for wireless energy sharing in vehicular systems for consumer applications. IEEE Trans. Consum. Electron. **71**(4), 12 236–12 243 (2025)

17. Boutahala, R., Fouchal, H., Ayaida, M., Mao, S.: Trust verification in connected vehicles using unsupervised variational autoencoder. In: 2025 12th International Conference on Wireless Networks and Mobile Communications (WINCOM), pp. 1–6. IEEE, 2025
18. Cheong, C., Song, Y., Cao, Y., Zhang, Y., Cai, B., Ni, Q.: Multidimensional trust evidence fusion and path-backtracking mechanism for trust management in vanets. IEEE Internet Things J. **11**(10), 18 619–18 634 (2024)
19. Sun, Y., et al.: PPDR: a privacy-preserving dual reputation management scheme in vehicle platoon. IEEE Trans. Dependable Secure Comput. (2025)
20. Xu, X., Wang, Y., Wang, P.: Comprehensive review on misbehavior detection for vehicular ad hoc networks. J. Adv. Transp. **2022**(1), 4725805 (2022)
21. Nobahari, A., Bakhshayeshi Avval, D., Akhbari, A., Nobahary, S.: Investigation of different mechanisms to detect misbehaving nodes in vehicle ad-hoc networks (vanets). Secur. Commun. Netw. **2023**(1), 4020275
22. Banabilah, S., Aloqaily, M., Alsayed, E., Malik, N., Jararweh, Y.: Federated learning review: fundamentals, enabling technologies, and future applications. Inf. Process. Manag. **59**(6) (2022)
23. Berdik, D., Otoum, S., Schmidt, N., Porter, D., Jararweh, Y.: A survey on blockchain for information systems management and security. Inf. Process. Manag. **58**(1) (2021)
24. Ridhawi, I.A., Aloqaily, M., Karray, F.: Intelligent blockchain-enabled communication and services: solutions for moving internet of things devices. IEEE Robot. Autom. Mag. **29**(2), 10–20 (2022)
25. Makani, S., Pittala, R., Alsayed, E., Aloqaily, M., Jararweh, Y.: A survey of blockchain applications in sustainable and smart cities. Clust. Comput. **25**(6), 3915–3936 (2022)
26. Singh, P.K., Gupta, S., Vashistha, R., Nandi, S.K., Nandi, S.: Machine learning based approach to detect position falsification attack in VANETs. In: Nandi, S., Jinwala, D., Singh, V., Laxmi, V., Gaur, M., Faruki, P. (eds.) Security and Privacy. ISEA-ISAP 2019. CCIS, vol. 939, pp. 166–178. Springer, Singapore (2019). https://doi.org/10.1007/978-981-13-7561-3_13
27. Zaidi, T., Faisal, S.: An overview: various attacks in vanet. In: 2018 4th International Conference on Computing Communication and Automation (ICCCA), pp. 1–6. IEEE, 2018
28. Sheikh, M.S., Liang, J.: A comprehensive survey on vanet security services in traffic management system. Wirel. Commun. Mob. Comput. **2019** (2019)
29. Malebary, S.: Dsrc vehicle communications dataset, center for machine learning and intelligent systems, 2017 https://archive.ics.uci.edu/ml/datasets/DSRC+Vehicle+Communications
30. Sommer, C., German, R., Dressler, F.: Bidirectionally coupled network and road traffic simulation for improved ivc analysis. IEEE Trans. Mob. Comput. **10**(1), 3–15 (2010)

Systematic Review of PPCP Models, Artificial Intelligence, and Optimization Applied to the Small-Scale Textile Industry

Gabriel R. B. da Silva(✉), Itamir de M. B. Filho, André M. Gurgel, Lhayana V. de Macedo, Débora N. de A. Valentim, Ramon S. Malaquias, Dinorah de F. Chagas, Yasmim A. Lopes, and Jean M. M. Lima

Digital Metropolis Institute (IMD), Federal University of Rio Grande do Norte (UFRN), Natal, Brazil
{gabriel.ribeiro.099,dinorah.farias.080,yasmim.araujo.709}@ufrn.edu.br, {itamir.filho,jean.lima}@imd.ufrn.br, andre.gurgel@ufrn.br, lhayana11@gmail.com, ramon@nutit.com.br
https://www.metropoledigital.ufrn.br/portal/

Abstract. The textile industry, vital to the global economy, is dominated by Micro and Small Enterprises (MSEs) struggling with digitalization and resource limitations in volatile markets. The adoption of Production Planning, Scheduling, and Control (PPCP) models enhanced by Artificial Intelligence (AI) and optimization is a key strategy for improving their operational efficiency. This paper presents a Systematic Literature Review (SLR) investigating the application of these advanced solutions in textile MSEs. The findings show that hybrid models, such as Genetic Algorithms combined with other heuristics, and process optimization frameworks like Lean Six Sigma, are highly effective, leading to significant gains such as productivity increases of up to 55%. However, a clear gap was identified in the literature regarding the use of Large Language Models (LLMs), presenting a clear opportunity for future research. Integrating specialized AI and optimization techniques is crucial for the digital transformation of textile MSEs, enabling flexible and robust production management.

Keywords: PPCP · textile industry · micro and small enterprises · workload balancing · optimization algorithms · artificial intelligence

1 Introduction

The textile industry is projected to reach a market size of US$295.87 billion by 2025 [28]. Despite this significant volume, the sector relies heavily on Micro and Small Enterprises (MSEs) for both raw material production and apparel manufacturing. This pattern is global: in the European Union (EU), the Organization

O. Gervasi et al. (Eds.): ICCSA 2026, LNCS 16768, pp. 89–106, 2027.
https://doi.org/10.1007/978-3-032-30488-9_6

for Economic Co-operation and Development (OECD) [23] classifies the textile industry as reliant on MSEs, which account for 77% of its workforce. In Asia, according to SEED [25], this predominance is even more pronounced, with 99.6% of the firms in the sector qualifying as MSEs.

Industrial MSEs struggle to adapt to digitalization and modern manufacturing methods. According to Hulla et al. [15], key challenges include inefficient production processes, the need for agility to respond to a volatile market, and difficulties in maintaining a competitive edge. This gap is particularly evident in Asia, where two-thirds of the sector's large corporations report investing in innovation, whereas this figure drops to just 40% for small companies, highlighting the challenge they face in keeping pace with the competition.

Thus, the implementation of Production Planning and Control Processes (PPCP) is crucial. PPCP is a management system that translates market demands into operational plans by organizing materials, labor and capacity. Integrating Artificial Intelligence (AI) and Optimization into PPCP is a promising path for textile MSEs to boost productivity, reduce idle time, and lower costs, enhancing their competitiveness by improving existing processes.

However, according to the authors' analysis, the volume of scientific publications on AI between 2000 and 2024 has not kept pace with the growth of academic output involving PPCP. This finding is based on searches conducted on the Scopus platform, using the following strings:

- **AI:**

```
    ALL("optimization algorithm*" OR "deep learning" OR "
genetic algorithm*" OR "metaheuristic*" OR "machine learning"
OR "LLM" OR "large language model*" OR "generative AI" )
```

- **AI e PPCP**

```
    ALL(("production planning" OR "PPCP" OR "PCP" OR "
scheduling" OR "job shop scheduling") AND ("workload balancing"
 OR "line balancing" OR "resource allocation" OR "production
optimization") AND ("small enterprise*" OR "small business*" OR
 "small companies" OR "SME") AND ("optimization algorithm*" OR
"deep learning" OR "genetic algorithm*" OR "metaheuristic*" OR
"machine learning" OR "LLM" OR "large language model*" OR "
generative AI"))
```

- **PPCP**

```
    ALL(("production planning" OR "PPCP" OR "PCP" OR "
scheduling" OR "job shop scheduling") AND ("workload balancing"
 OR "line balancing" OR "resource allocation" OR "production
optimization") AND ("small enterprise*" OR "small business*" OR
 "small companies" OR "SME"))
```

The results were then normalized using the formula $\frac{\text{Current Year}}{\text{Base Year}}/100$, with 2000 as the base year, which produced the graph shown in Figure 1:

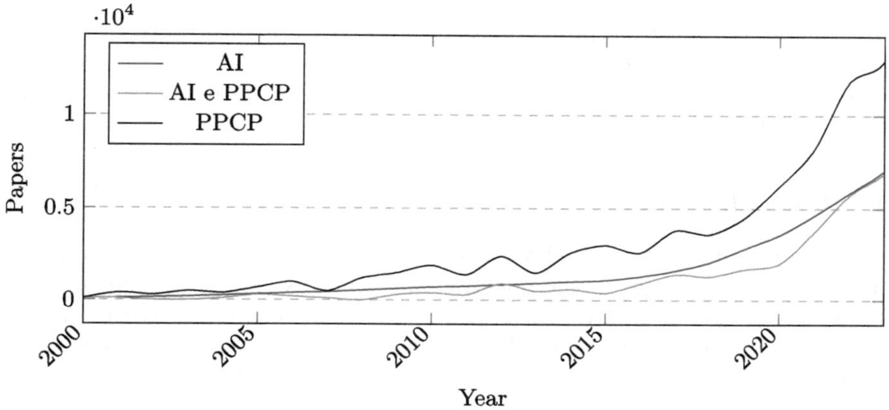

Fig. 1. Normalized growth in the volume of publications for AI, AI and PPCP, and PPCP between 2000 and 2024.

Analysis of the graph reveals that despite the sharp increase in the volume of publications addressing PPCP, the number of publications involving both PPCP and AI has not mirrored this growth. This indicates a gap between the volume of scientific publications on the intersection of PPCP and AI and those focusing solely on PPCP. Such a discrepancy suggests a clear research opportunity to explore these two fields by applying advances from one to the domain of the other.

Ultimately, this work aims to analyze, through a systematic review, the application of models that integrate Artificial Intelligence (AI) and Optimization in textile MSEs—covering both raw material production and apparel manufacturing—to identify the research opportunities the field presents.

Previous reviews, such as Giri et al. [13] and Bi et al. [9], discuss specific technologies within the textile industry. However, the key differentiator of this systematic review lies in its evaluation of diverse technologies within the context of PPCP applied to the textile and similar sectors. The authors begin from an agnostic standpoint and identify which approaches emerge as most promising. This heterogeneous lens reduces bias and strengthens confidence in the findings.

The article is organized as follows: Methodology (planning, objectives, and research questions); Results (selected studies); Discussion (interpretation against the research questions); and Conclusion (key insights and future work).

2 Methodology

The methodology adopted in this Systematic Literature Review (SLR) follows the guidelines proposed by Kitchenham et al. [16], aiming to identify, evaluate, and synthesize scientific evidence on models and techniques for workload balancing applicable to textile Micro and Small Enterprises (MSEs). The methodological process was structured into three main phases: review planning, execution of the search and selection protocol, and data extraction and synthesis. Each of these phases was conducted rigorously, using explicit inclusion, exclusion, and quality assessment criteria for the studies to ensure reproducibility and reduce bias in the analysis.

2.1 Research Planning

The Systematic Literature Review begins with a methodological planning phase to reduce errors and bias in the selection and analysis of studies. This planning defines the research objective, the research questions, the search string, and the inclusion and exclusion criteria. These elements are essential for the subsequent conduction phase.

Research Objective and Research Questions

- **Research Objectives**:
  - To identify existing models and algorithms for workload balancing in the textile sector or similar industrial contexts, aiming to optimize the utilization of available human resources;
  - To analyze optimization approaches applied to PPCP problems in similar industries, with the goal of mitigating the impact of these challenges;
  - To evaluate modern artificial intelligence techniques (e.g., deep learning, genetic algorithms, LLMs) for solving NP-Hard problems—which are difficult to solve but easy to verify—in industrial contexts;
  - To identify strategies for simplifying order entry and allocation processes within production systems;
  - To map stochastic demand forecasting solutions that address the challenges of the textile industry, such as high volatility and short product lifecycles.

To ensure all established objectives are addressed, the research questions were formulated to guide the investigation. These are divided into a primary question and secondary questions. The primary question (PQ) is: "**What are the most effective models and techniques for workload balancing in textile Micro and Small Enterprises (MSEs) or companies in similar contexts?**". The secondary questions are as follows:

- **Secondary Questions (SQ)**:
  - SQ1: Which optimization algorithms perform best regarding computational time and solution quality for PPCP problems within the textile context or similar companies?
  - SQ2: How have deep learning, genetic algorithm, and LLM approaches been applied to solve job shop scheduling problems in industries with characteristics similar to the textile sector?
  - SQ3: What strategies for data entry simplification and process automation have been utilized in PPCP systems for MSEs?

- SQ4: Which demand forecasting models are most suitable for the context of order variability in the textile sector or companies in similar contexts?
- SQ5: What are the key factors affecting production line balancing in textile companies?
- SQ6: What are the types of applications and scenarios utilized in the reviewed models?

Search Engine, Inclusion and Exclusion Criteria. The search strategy was designed to identify studies involving production planning, optimization techniques, and artificial intelligence, with a focus on the textile industry and Micro and Small Enterprises (MSEs).

The initial string was developed for the Scopus database [5] and adapted for other databases, such as: IEEE Xplore [3], ACM Digital Library [1], Web of Science [7], Science Direct [4], Springer Link [6], and arXiv [2]. The primary search string is as follows:

```
ALL(("production planning" OR "PPCP" OR "PCP" OR "scheduling" OR
"job shop scheduling") AND
("workload balancing" OR "line balancing" OR "resource allocation"
OR "production optimization") AND
("small enterprise*" OR "small business*" OR "small companies" OR
"SME") AND
("optimization algorithm*" OR "deep learning" OR "genetic
algorithm*" OR "metaheuristic*" OR
"machine learning" OR "LLM" OR "large language model*" OR
"generative AI"))
```

The inclusion and exclusion criteria, which determine which studies are to be included in or excluded from the systematic review, were established as follows:

- **Inclusion Criteria**:
  - Studies that address workload balancing techniques in the textile sector or in similar contexts;
  - Studies that apply optimization algorithms to PPCP problems;
  - Studies that utilize deep learning, genetic algorithms, or large language models (LLMs) for PPCP;
  - Studies that propose demand forecasting models applicable to the textile industry or to sectors with similar characteristics;
  - Studies that discuss process simplification in PPCP systems;
  - Studies published in English;
  - Full papers published in peer-reviewed scientific journals or conference proceedings;
  - Studies published from 2019 onwards.

- **Exclusion Criteria**:

- Studies lacking practical application or empirical validation;
- Studies focused exclusively on large enterprises, without applicability to MSEs;
- Studies that do not detail the methodology or the algorithms used;
- Literature reviews, editorials, conference abstracts, and other types of gray literature;
- Duplicate studies (with only the most complete version being considered);
- Studies with unavailable full text;
- Studies published before 2019.

2.2 Execution

The review's execution followed a protocol structured into two main phases: preliminary selection and final selection. Table 1 presents the number of studies included and excluded in each phase.

Table 1. Works included and excluded at each phase

	Input	Removed	Remaining
Initial Screening	379	353	26
Final Selection	26	3	23

During the preliminary selection phase, a search was conducted across the previously selected databases using the search strings defined in the methodology. After retrieving the results, duplicates were removed. Subsequently, the titles and abstracts of the remaining studies were screened against the established inclusion and exclusion criteria.

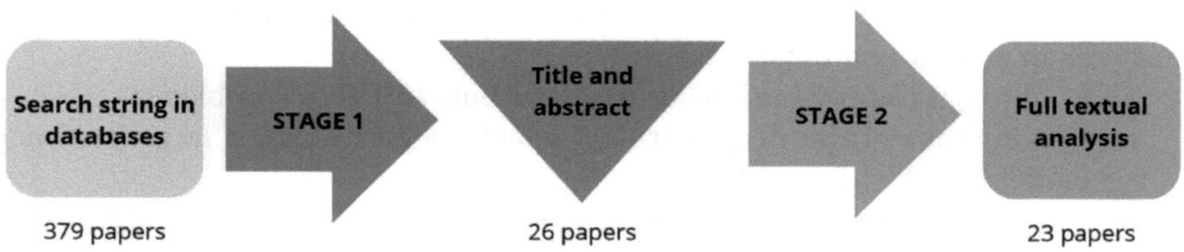

Fig. 2. Review steps

As illustrated in Fig. 2, preliminary screening excluded 353 out of 379 studies that did not meet the inclusion criteria or met the exclusion criteria. The remaining 26 studies were deemed relevant and thus advanced to the full-text review stage.

In the final selection, the articles underwent a complete reading, with strict application of the inclusion and exclusion criteria, resulting in the exclusion of 3 of the 26 articles, ensuring the final set aligned with the research objectives and questions.

In cases of disagreement between reviewers, decisions were reached through consensus.

3 Results

3.1 Overview of the Papers

Table 2 lists all the articles remaining after the final selection.

Table 2. Overview of all papers

Id	Authors	Year	Document Type
[27]	Singh et al.	2025	Article
[19]	Li et al.	2025	Article
[18]	Le et al.	2024	Article
[26]	Shahin et al.	2024	Article
[33]	Wang	2024	Conference paper
[24]	Qaffas et al.	2023	Article
[21]	Marín et al.	2023	Article
[29]	Stavropoulos et al.	2023	Review
[20]	Li et al.	2023	Article
[11]	De Oliveira et al.	2023	Article
[22]	Nedra et al.	2022	Article
[10]	Darmian et al.	2022	Article
[17]	Kulka et al.	2022	Article
[31]	Wan et al.	2022	Article
[37]	Zhang et al.	2021	Article
[14]	Guo et al.	2021	Article
[32]	Wang et al.	2021	Article
[30]	Teerasoponpong et al.	2021	Article
[8]	Bai et al.	2021	Article
[35]	Wang et al.	2021	Article
[36]	Zennaro et al.	2020	Article
[34]	Wang et al.	2020	Article
[12]	Eccher et al.	2020	Review

Most of the selected studies were published in 2021 (n = 6) and 2023 (n = 5). The remainder of the publications were from 2022 (n = 4), 2020 (n = 3),

2024 (n = 3), and 2025 (n = 2). No studies from 2019 were selected. Figure 3 shows a chart with the distribution of the studies by year.

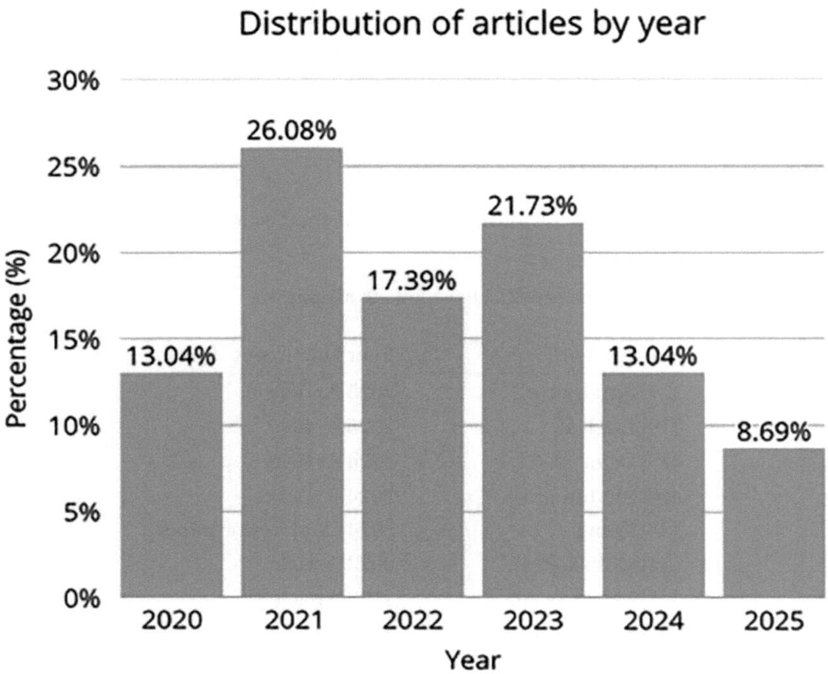

Fig. 3. Distribution of articles by year.

Furthermore, to aid in the thematic analysis, a word cloud was generated from the abstracts of the articles approved in the final phase (Fig. 4). To prevent visual clutter, numbers and common stop words were excluded.

Fig. 4. Word cloud of the abstracts of the selected articles

4 Discussion

This section addresses the primary research question (PQ) and the secondary questions (SQ).

4.1 PQ: What Are the Most Effective Models and Techniques for Workload Balancing in Textile Micro and Small Enterprises (MSEs) or Companies in Similar Contexts?

Several studies indicate that the most effective models and techniques for workload balancing in textile Micro and Small Enterprises (MSEs), or in similar industrial contexts, are those that combine hybrid and adaptive approaches capable of handling the production variability and resource constraints characteristic of these organizations [14,19,22,27,30,33,35,37]. Notable among these are models that integrate Lean Six Sigma with discrete-event simulation [22], providing significant gains in operational efficiency; hybrid genetic algorithms applied to the optimized allocation of human resources and production tasks [33]; and approaches based on Dynamic Takt Time (dTT), which adjust the production pace in real-time, reducing idle time by up to 46% [37]. Other relevant strategies include the use of Intelligent Machine Monitoring System (IMMS) [27], digital twins combined with GRAFCET [14], flexible cellular manufacturing, and models that logically separate assembly and line-feeding tasks to optimize labor utilization [19]. Techniques such as Shojinka [35] and models based on neural networks combined with evolutionary algorithms [30] also prove effective, especially in environments with highly variable demand.

Table 3. Models

Model	Refs
Lean Six Sigma	[22]
Hybrid Genetic Algorithms	[33]
Semi-Supervised Explainable k-means	[24]
Digital Maturity Level	[21]
Iterative Two-step heuristic based on Local Search	[10]
XGBoost Stacked Model	[31]
Analytic Hierarchy Process	[11]
Smart Machine Monitoring System	[27]
AC-Ptr	[19]
Convolutional Neural Network	[26]
Monte Carlo Tree Search	[34]
Bee Colony	[37]
Artificial Neural Network	[30]
Recommended Cleaning Scheduling	[12]

4.2 SQ1: Which Optimization Algorithms Exhibit the Best Performance in Terms of Computational Time and Solution Quality for PPCP Problems in the Textile Sector or Similar Industrial Settings?

Analysis of the literature reveals a divergence of opinion among various authors regarding which optimization algorithm exhibits the best performance [10,11, 19,22,27,30,33–35].

Nedra et al. [22] propose the use of Lean Six Sigma (LSS), which resulted in a 5% reduction in process time compared to the original baseline. It is worth noting that Lean methods combined with a cellular layout can be highly effective in terms of solution quality and implementation simplicity, especially when computational resources are constrained [35].

Similarly, Wang [33] and Teerasoponpong et al. [30] address the use of genetic algorithms (GA). While Teerasoponpong et al. [30] highlight the robust and effective search capabilities of GA, Wang [33] utilizes a combination of GA with tabu search, a type of Hybrid GA, aiming to increase calculation accuracy. The proposed algorithm demonstrates better performance in human resource allocation, resulting in an optimized utilization of at least 92%, whereas other algorithms, such as Ant Colony and cyclic neural network, could not exceed 80% utilization. Furthermore, the Hybrid GA required 40 iterations, compared to 240 for the other algorithms, demonstrating faster convergence.

Finally, some authors propose their own custom models. Darmin et al. [10] developed a two-stage iterative heuristic based on local search (ITbLS), which showed superior performance to CPLEX with a gap of less than 2.4%. Singh et al. [27] propose an algorithm named Intelligent Machine Monitoring System

(IMMS), which increased productivity by 55% compared to a conventional ERP. The AC-Ptr algorithm, proposed by Li et al. [19], has a worse computational time compared to Actor-Critic, Proximal Policy Optimization, and Approximation algorithms; however, in terms of revenue, it results in an increase of 7.23% to 37.44% compared to the other algorithms. Wang et al. [34] compare Monte Carlo Tree Search (MCTS) with the value iteration (VI) algorithm, concluding that MCTS provides an optimal solution with a 0 to 1% gap and a lower computational time than VI, thus being a solution with better overall performance. In contrast, De Oliveira et al. [11] propose algorithms but do not present performance metrics or comparisons with other algorithms.

In conclusion, different optimization approaches perform well on PPCP problems, highlighting the trade-off between computational time and solution quality. Methods such as the Hybrid Genetic Algorithm (GA), Monte Carlo Tree Search (MCTS), and Lean Six Sigma (LSS) achieved satisfactory results along with a reduction in computational time.

4.3 SQ2: How Have Deep Learning, Genetic Algorithm, and LLM Approaches Been Applied to Solve Job Shop Scheduling Problems in Industries with Characteristics Similar to the Textile Sector?

Job Shop Scheduling (JSS) is the process of determining the sequence in which different tasks must be performed on each machine, with the objective of minimizing the total production time (makespan). In this context, Teerasoponpong et al. [30] propose the use of Artificial Neural Networks (ANN) and Genetic Algorithms (GA), where the ANN is trained to simulate the production process, and the GA utilizes the ANN to evaluate each proposed solution in search of the optimal one. However, the paper in question does not use a Job Shop model, but rather a Flow Shop model, as there is a predefined flow of tasks, which is not the case in JSS. Nevertheless, the way the simulation/optimization methods are employed is noteworthy due to its flexibility.

Ultimately, only Eccher et al. [12] mentions JSS. In it, the authors advocate for their own solution, called Recommended Cleaning Scheduling (RCS). The solution uses mathematical operations and concepts, such as summations and objective functions, to determine the decision-making process. However, despite discussing the disadvantages of other solutions, no concrete metrics are presented comparing other algorithms, such as genetic algorithms, with RCS.

Therefore, after analyzing the articles, it is not possible to specify how the application of technologies like deep learning, genetic algorithms, and LLMs can directly affect Job Shop Scheduling. This becomes problematic, since JSS is NP-Hard and MSEs don't have the computational capacity for exhaustive search (brute force and back tracking) of solutions, so the question of performance under such circumstances becomes interesting for them. It can be stated, however, that GA, ANN, and Deep Learning can be used for simulation and optimization within the industrial context [30].

4.4 SQ3: What Strategies for Data Entry Simplification and Process Automation Have Been Utilized in PPCP Systems for Micro and Small Enterprises (MSEs)?

Analysis of the reviewed literature indicates that to simplify data entry and system setup, object-oriented modeling is utilized to create virtual factory models, often in conjunction with direct data importation from ERP and MES systems. This approach reduces the manual workload of data entry and maintenance for planners [32]. The same study notes that the use of package diagrams also enhances modeling efficiency and data stability. Additionally, for MSEs with fragmented data, observational and empirical data are employed as an alternative, which minimizes collection costs and operational disruptions without the need for complex ERPs [30].

In the context of process automation, prominent solutions include Cloud-based Advanced Planning and Scheduling (C-APS) systems, which provide cost-effective, practical solutions featuring 'on-demand self-service' and rapid adaptation to new products or processes [32]. Additionally, Digital Twins (DTs) enable continuous simulation and optimization of production lines, allowing for fast adjustments to layout and processes [14]. They also support micro smart factories in intelligent data collection, control, and maintenance, including blockchain integration for authenticity and traceability [8]. For specific task automation, RFID is used for material tracking, AGVs for flexible movement, and MES for scheduling and resource optimization logic [8].

In terms of operations, the active and idle assembly islands (AII) strategy optimizes operator time and parts feeding for large, customized products by allowing for parallel preparation and avoiding non-value-added activities. Finally, modeling and simulation using Lean Six Sigma (LSS) and BPMN help to identify waste and bottlenecks, thereby facilitating future automations [22].

4.5 SQ4: Which Demand Forecasting Models Are Most Suitable for the Context of Order Variability in the Textile Sector or Companies in Similar Contexts?

A review of the literature indicates that to manage the typical order variability in micro and small enterprises (MSEs) in the textile sector, the most suitable models are those that capture non-stationary and stochastic demand. This characteristic is common in products with short life cycles and production variable demand patterns [30,34].

Models based on Markov Decision Processes (MDP), combined with algorithms such as Monte Carlo Tree Search (MCTS), demonstrate efficiency in considering demand dynamics and lead times, while also offering good computational scalability [34].

Furthermore, simulation-optimization approaches are recommended for environments with incomplete data and uncertainty, which are typical of MSEs [30]. The integration of Artificial Neural Networks (ANNs) and Genetic Algorithms (GAs) into simulation frameworks allows for learning patterns from observational data, thereby overcoming collection limitations and producing optimal solutions for various production targets [30].

4.6 SQ5: What Are the Key Factors Affecting Production Line Balancing in Textile Companies?

Based on the analysis of the reviewed studies, the key factors affecting production line balancing in textile companies involve both operational and structural aspects. Among the operational factors, notable issues include: demand variability [30,32,35]; the sequencing of operations and sequence-dependent setup times [32]; and labor variability, along with the need for flexibility to handle different product types and volumes [30].

Regarding structural aspects, Guo et al. [14] highlights elements such as inadequate layouts and unbalanced process capacity, while task precedence constraints and finite machine capacity directly influence line efficiency, as evidenced by Eccher et al. [12]. Other critical factors include: bottlenecks at specific workstations, noted by Nedra et al. [22]; the use of buffers, according to Bai et al. [8]; as well as Cleaning-In-Place (CIP) times, equipment failures (MTBF), and imprecise logistics, which are also pointed out by Guo et al. [14].

Additionally, the digital maturity of companies, as discussed by Stavropoulos et al. [29], as well as technological integration and human-machine collaboration, are crucial for achieving an efficient balance. This is especially true when these are combined with intelligent systems like Manufacturing Execution Systems (MES) and real-time control technologies such as RFID. When not managed in an integrated manner, these factors can compromise the production flow and make it difficult to achieve a consistent work pace (takt time) [37].

4.7 SQ6: What Are the Types of Applications and Scenarios Utilized in the Reviewed Models?

The models examined in the literature have been applied across a broad spectrum of industrial scenarios and operational contexts. There is a notable emphasis on micro, small, and medium-sized enterprises (MMSEs) in diverse sectors, including textile, automotive, electronics, and chemicals. These applications also extend to custom assembly and high-mix production industries [37].

Applications range from production line balancing [14]; dynamic worker allocation [19,33]; adaptive production capacity planning [30,34]; and multi-criteria inventory classification [24]; to more specific scenarios such as predictive maintenance [26]; quality control; industrial cybersecurity; and logistics during health crises [10].

Studies featuring simulations of real production lines were identified, with applications including trouser manufacturing in the textile sector [22], and the production of air conditioners, printed circuit boards and automotive seals [8, 32]. The tools utilized in these simulations include digital twins, reinforcement learning models (e.g., MDP and MCTS), and discrete-event simulation [35].

The models have also been applied to companies in emerging economies [18]. These applications focus on areas such as supply chain resilience; digital transformation [20,21]; and operational flexibility. This demonstrates the versatility and adaptability of these solutions across different industrial environments.

4.8 Comparative Analysis

Due to space constraints, a comprehensive comparison of the models detailing their respective inputs, evaluation metrics, datasets, and limitations is provided as external supplementary material[1]. An analysis of the data presented in this comparison reveals a pattern: the proposed models operate on a large input space comprising multiple variables, yet their performance is evaluated against a narrow, set of metrics. This suggests that problem complexity resides not in the outputs, but in the intricate relationships between the various inputs.

Furthermore, no pattern emerges regarding dataset usage, as the reviewed studies utilize a wide variety of real-world, synthetic, public, and private datasets of varying sizes.

Finally, the identified limitations can be categorized into two groups: low external validity and low practical applicability. For models with low external validity, the most recurrent limitations were the assumption that dynamic factors are constant and the failure to consider influential process factors. As for models with low applicability, the primary limitations revolved around a lack of flexibility, high cost, and significant operational time.

4.9 Broader Implications

The findings of these studies can benefit Micro and Small Enterprises (MSEs) in several ways. Notably human resource optimization [19,33], and increased operational efficiency, whether through faster process execution or cost reduction [12,22,30].

From an organizational perspective, the evaluated models not only simplifly routine tasks but also aids in the holistic assessment of processes. Implementing these models enables an organization to optimize staff allocation, forecast demand, and minimize idle time. For instance, a manager can utilize these models to assign an employee to tasks where they excel and for which demand is forecasted, thereby optimizing the production process.

From a theoretical perspective, this review identifies a clear trend in PPCP: a shift from monolithic models to more flexible approaches. Recent literature shows growth in hybrid algorithms [30,33], and of models with well-defined functionalities [14,27]. Accordingly, modern PPCP system should not be confined to a single algorithm but should integrate the complementary strengths across models. The feasibility of collaboration between these models, observed in the analysis, reinforces the potential for the development of modular, multi-model PPCP systems.

[1] The complete comparison table is available at: https://drive.google.com/file/d/1X02QxtRvIZ0ZDHm8HyWUja9duyOdSKSN/view?usp=sharing.

4.10 Limitations of the Review

The review process revealed several limitations. Notably, identifying studies that met the inclusion criteria was difficult, especially those demonstrating practical applications of PPCP algorithms. A further limitation was finding multiple articles covering the same technologies. As demonstrated in Table 3, each paper proposes a different model, making it more complex to compare the various lines of thought and impeding a straightforward interpretation.

Another limitation concerns the differences within the final set of studies. We searched for studies that offered solutions for textile SMEs or other sectors with similar characteristics (e.g. high demand variability, labour-intensive, limited resources). Consequently, the last group of studies includes various industries. The findings may not be very generalizable to textiles are in line with the intent of identifying approaches that may be transferable.

5 Conclusion and Future Work

The studies reveal a pattern in the use of genetic algorithms (GAs) combined with other technologies, such as Tabu Search or Artificial Neural Networks (ANNs). These combinations aim to enhance the GA's performance, which is notable for its capabilities in load balancing, as well as the optimization and simulation of resources and environments.

Solutions involving Lean Six Sigma (LSS) are effective for load optimization and balancing by their ability to identify waste and bottlenecks. Other approaches, such as Monte Carlo Tree Search (MCTS), focus on load balancing and demand forecasting, while Intelligent Machine Monitoring Systems (IMMS) focus on load balancing and resource optimization.

No study included in this review has explicitly addressed the use of LLMs within PPCP systems, which indicates a clear gap in the current literature. This lack of research makes itself apparent when considering that SMEs usually lack structured data and generally run on undocumented knowledge. LLMs might address this shortage of structured data by providing a human - like interface that allows for easy order submission or decision-making support, thus bypassing the need for extensive computer knowledge from those running the business. Moreover, while Eccher et al. [12] covers Job Shop Scheduling (JSS), the paper does not provide concrete metrics to demonstrate the proposed algorithm's performance against genetic and deep learning algorithms.

For future work, the authors plan to investigate the application of JSS to process planning within MSEs, with the goal of enhancing productivity and lowering costs. Additionally, a PPCP system focused on the textile industry's MSEs will be developed. Furthermore, the potential of applying intelligent models optimized for this specific context will be explored to increase productivity, reduce costs, and shorten idle periods. The proposed model will be designed to understand natural language, generate context-aware responses, and support decision-making processes.

Acknowledgments. This study was supported by the CNPq, National Council for Scientific and Technological Development - Brazil (grant number 443723/2024-9).

Disclosure of Interests. The authors have no competing interests to declare that are relevant to the content of this article.

References

1. Acm digital library (2025). https://dl.acm.org/. Accessed 4 July 2025
2. arxiv e-print archive (2025). https://arxiv.org/. Accessed 4 July 2025
3. Ieee xplore digital library (2025). https://ieeexplore.ieee.org/. Accessed 4 July 2025
4. Sciencedirect (2025). https://www.sciencedirect.com/. Accessed 4 July 2025
5. Scopus (2025). https://www.scopus.com/. Accessed 4 July 2025
6. Springer link (2025). https://link.springer.com/. Accessed 4 July 2025
7. Web of science (2025). https://www.webofscience.com/. Accessed 4 July 2025
8. Bai, Y., You, J.B., Lee, I.K.: Design and optimization of smart factory control system based on digital twin system model. Math. Probl. Eng. **2021**(1), 2596946 (2021)
9. Bi, Y., Pan, L., Cao, L.: Research status and development trends of digital twin technology in apparelproduction: a review. J. Text. Inst. (2025)
10. Darmian, S.M., Farughi, H.: An optimization-based approach for managing downstream logistic operations: a real application in pandemic outbreak conditions. Comput. Ind. Eng. **171**, 108495 (2022)
11. De Oliveira, U.R., de Souza, H.A.D., Menezes, C.A.G., Rocha, H.M.: Straightening machine preventive maintenance intervention plan based on ahp: a case study in a steel company in brazil. Oper. Manag. Res. **16**, 1577–1593 (2023)
12. Eccher, C., Geraghty, J.: Incorporating sustainable criteria in a dynamic multi-objective recommendation planning tool for a continuous manufacturing process: a dairy case study. J. Manuf. Syst. **55**, 159–170 (2020)
13. Giri, C., Jain, S., Zeng, X., Bruniaux, P.: A detailed review of artificial intelligence applied in the fashion and apparel industry. IEEE Access **7**, 95376–95396 (2019)
14. Guo, H., Chen, M., Mohamed, K., Qu, T., Wang, S., Li, J.: A digital twin-based flexible cellular manufacturing for optimization of air conditioner line. J. Manuf. Syst. **58**, 65–78 (2021)
15. Hulla, M., Herstätter, P., Wolf, M., Ramsauer, C.: Towards digitalization in production in smes – a qualitative study of challenges, competencies and requirements for trainings. Procedia CIRP **104**(1), 887–892 (2021)
16. Kitchenham, B., Brereton, O.P., Budgen, D., Turner, M., Bailey, J., Linkman, S.: Systematic literature reviews in software engineering-a systematic literature review. Inf. Softw. Technol. **51**(1), 7–15 (2009)
17. Kulka, J., Mantic, M., Onofrejova, D., Siman, M.: Case study of production optimization using the enumerative method. MM Sci. J. **June | 2022**, 5656–5661 (2022)
18. Le, T.T., Behl, A.: Linking artificial intelligence and supply chain resilience: roles of dynamic capabilities mediator and open innovation moderator. IEEE Trans. Eng. Manag. **71**, 8577–8590 (2023)

19. Li, D., Jin, H., Zhang, Y.: Dynamic worker allocation in seru production systems with actor-critic and pointer networks. Eur. J. Oper. Res. **324**(1), 62–74 (2025)
20. Li, L., Xu, S.X., Ning, Y., Liu, Y., Yang, S.: How should companies deploy their digital supply chain platforms to gain competitive advantages? An asset orchestration perspective. Inf. Manag. **60**(6), 103842 (2023)
21. Marín Díaz, G., Galdón Salvador, J.L.: Group decision-making model based on 2-tuple fuzzy linguistic model and ahp applied to measuring digital maturity level of organizations. Systems **11**(7), 341 (2023)
22. Nedra, A., Néjib, S., Boubaker, J., Morched, C.: An integrated lean six sigma approach to modeling and simulation: a case study from clothing sme. Autex Res. J. **22**(3), 305–311 (2022)
23. OECD: Introductory paper on smes and responsible business conduct in the garment and footwear sector. Website (2018). https://mneguidelines.oecd.org/Introductory-paper-on-smes-and-responsible-business-conduct-in-the-garment-and-footwear-sector.pdf. Accessed 5 July 2025
24. Qaffas, A.A., Hajkacem, M.A.B., Ncir, C.E.B., Nasraoui, O.: Interpretable multi-criteria abc analysis based on semi-supervised clustering and explainable artificial intelligence. IEEE Access **11**, 43778–43792 (2023)
25. SEED: Asia future lab for innovation and policy background note: Textile and fashion in asia. Website (2022). https://www.switch-asia.eu/site/assets/files/3488/asia_future_lab_background_note.pdf. Accessed 5 July 2025
26. Shahin, M., Maghanaki, M., Hosseinzadeh, A., Chen, F.F.: Improving operations through a lean ai paradigm: a view to an ai-aided lean manufacturing via versatile convolutional neural network. Int. J. Adv. Manuf. Technol. **133**(11), 5343–5419 (2024)
27. Singh, J., Singh, A., Singh, H., Doyon-Poulin, P.: Implementation and evaluation of a smart machine monitoring system under industry 4.0 concept. J. Ind. Inf. Integr. **43**, 100746 (2025)
28. Statista: Textiles - worldwide. Website (2025). https://www.statista.com/outlook/io/manufacturing/material-products/textiles/worldwide. Accessed 5 July 2025
29. Stavropoulos, P., Papacharalampopoulos, A., Sabatakakis, K., Mourtzis, D.: Metamodelling of manufacturing processes and automation workflows towards designing and operating digital twins. Appl. Sci. **13**(3), 1945 (2023)
30. Teerasoponpong, S., Sopadang, A.: A simulation-optimization approach for adaptive manufacturing capacity planning in small and medium-sized enterprises. Expert Syst. Appl. **168**, 114451 (2021)
31. Wan, J.: Demand prediction and optimization of workshop manufacturing resources allocation: a new method and a case study. Adv. Prod. Eng. Manag. **17**(4), 413–424 (2022)
32. Wang, L.C., Chen, C.C., Liu, J.L., Chu, P.C.: Framework and deployment of a cloud-based advanced planning and scheduling system. Robot. Comput.-Integr. Manuf. **70**, 102088 (2021)
33. Wang, L.: Improved human resource allocation method based on genetic algorithm. In: Intelligent Computing Technology and Automation, pp. 97–104. IOS Press (2024)
34. Wang, L., Ai, W., Deng, T., Shen, Z.J.M., Hong, C.: Optimal production ramp-up in the smartphone manufacturing industry. Nav. Res. Logist. (NRL) **67**(8), 685–704 (2020)
35. Wang, P.S., Lin, C.C., Yang, T.: A study on shojinka design for automobile engine piston-rod manufacturing. Comput. Ind. Eng. **151**, 106974 (2021)

36. Zennaro, I., Finco, S., Calzavara, M., Battini, D., Persona, A.: A parts feeding model for big size products: the active and idle assembly islands strategy. Int. J. Adv. Oper. Manag. **12**(3), 211–236 (2020)
37. Zhang, W., Hou, L., Jiao, R.J.: Dynamic takt time decisions for paced assembly lines balancing and sequencing considering highly mixed-model production: an improved artificial bee colony optimization approach. Comput. Ind. Eng. **161**, 107616 (2021)

DepthGate: Confidence-Gated Depth Verification for Multimodal Industrial Anomaly Detection

Soyeon Kim, Tae-Yong Kim, and Jongpil Jeong(✉)

Department of Smart Factory Convergence, Sungkyunkwan University, Suwon-si, Gyeonggi-do 16419, Republic of Korea
{kimsoyeon744,jpjeong}@skku.edu, skywin94@naver.com

Abstract. Multimodal industrial anomaly detection often combines RGB and depth, but most existing methods fuse the two modalities at every inference step regardless of whether depth actually helps. We show this is harmful: on MVTec 3D-AD, naive fusion drops mean Image-Area Under the Receiver Operating Characteristic curve (I-AUROC) by 5.2 points compared to an RGB-only baseline. We propose DepthGate, which pairs a training-free depth memory bank with EfficientAD and gates depth at two levels. A category-level gate uses a mini-AUROC check to decide whether depth is discriminative for a given object class; an unreliable class is permanently bypassed. A sample-level gate then applies a small residual depth correction only when the depth score exceeds the RGB score. Across all 10 MVTec 3D-AD categories, DepthGate improves mean I-AUROC by 3.1 points while leaving Pixel-AUROC (P-AUROC) unchanged. For geometric-defect categories such as cable_gland and cookie, gains reach 16.9 and 16.4 points. Because the depth branch needs no gradient-based training, deploying to a new product class only requires populating the memory bank with normal samples.

Keywords: Anomaly Detection · Multimodal Fusion · Confidence-based Gating · Industrial Inspection · RGB-D Fusion

1 Introduction

Industrial anomaly detection aims to identify defective products in manufacturing environments through automated visual inspection [1]. As modern production lines demand ever-higher throughput and quality standards, the ability to detect subtle defects—ranging from surface scratches and discolorations to geometric deformations and structural cracks—has become a critical requirement. With the increasing availability of 3D sensing technologies such as structured-light scanners and time-of-flight cameras [2], recent approaches have begun to exploit both RGB imagery and geometric depth information for more comprehensive defect detection [3–5]. The combination of appearance and geometry is particularly appealing because certain defect types manifest primarily in one

O. Gervasi et al. (Eds.): ICCSA 2026, LNCS 16768, pp. 107–125, 2027.
https://doi.org/10.1007/978-3-032-30488-9_7

modality: scratches, stains, and color variations are visible in RGB, while dents, warping, and surface deformations are better captured through depth measurements [4].

Current state-of-the-art multimodal methods, including M3DM [3], AST [6], and Shape-Guided [7], adopt a full-fusion strategy in which both RGB and 3D features are always processed jointly. While this approach can in principle capture complementary information from both modalities, it suffers from three fundamental limitations that restrict its practical applicability. First, these methods require training separate feature extractors for the 3D modality, typically involving pretrained point cloud encoders such as Point-MAE [8] or PointBERT [9] that must be fine-tuned on the target domain. This increases both computational cost and deployment complexity, preventing rapid adaptation to new product categories. Second, unconditional fusion means that even when depth information provides no discriminative value for a given category, it is still computed and integrated at every inference step, wasting computational resources. Third, and most critically, when the depth branch produces unreliable or near-random anomaly scores, full fusion can actively degrade detection performance below what the RGB-only baseline achieves. As we demonstrate in our experiments, unconditional fusion reduces the mean Image-AUROC (I-AUROC) by 5.2% points compared to the RGB baseline across the MVTec 3D-AD benchmark.

Recent work has begun to recognize this issue: for instance, Daci et al. [10] introduce reliability-gated mapping and confidence-weighted reconstruction to mitigate unreliable cross-modal cues, suggesting that adaptive use of depth—rather than unconditional fusion—is an emerging design principle for multimodal industrial anomaly detection. The MVTec 3D-AD benchmark [4] makes this issue easy to see. Among its 10 object categories, depth-based anomaly detection achieves strong performance for categories with predominantly geometric defects—for example, cable_gland achieves a depth-only I-AUROC of 0.99 and cookie achieves 0.80. However, for categories where defects are primarily chromatic or textural, depth performs at or near random chance: peach achieves only 0.19, tire 0.38, and foam 0.44. An ideal multimodal system should leverage depth information when it provides reliable geometric cues and gracefully ignore it when it does not, rather than blindly fusing both modalities at all times.

In this paper, we address these limitations with DepthGate. The framework has three components:

- **Training-free depth branch.** We replace learned depth encoders with a PatchCore-style [11] depth memory bank that requires no gradient-based training. Normal depth patch features are simply stored during the setup phase, and anomaly scores are computed via k-Nearest Neighbor (KNN) distance at test time. This enables instant deployment to new product categories by simply collecting normal samples and populating the memory bank, with no optimization loop required.
- **Two-level confidence gate.** We introduce a hierarchical gating mechanism operating at two complementary granularities. At the category level, a mini-AUROC validation procedure—a small-scale AUROC computed on

a held-out subset of normal and anomalous samples—automatically assesses whether the depth branch produces reliable anomaly signals for each object category. Categories where depth is unreliable (mini-AUROC below a threshold $\tau = 0.65$) have their gate permanently closed, completely bypassing all depth computation. At the sample level, within gate-open categories, depth correction is applied only when the normalized depth anomaly score exceeds the normalized RGB score.
- **Selective score fusion with map preservation.** Our fusion strategy applies depth correction exclusively at the image level through a residual score addition formula, while the pixel-level anomaly map relies solely on the RGB branch output. This asymmetric design reflects our empirical finding that the depth memory bank operates at 64×64 resolution, producing coarse anomaly maps that degrade localization accuracy by 2.5–4.7% points in Pixel-AUROC (P-AUROC) when fused with high-resolution RGB maps.

We evaluate our framework on the complete MVTec 3D-AD benchmark across all 10 object categories. The results demonstrate a mean I-AUROC improvement of +3.1% points over the EfficientAD RGB-only baseline while maintaining zero P-AUROC degradation across every category. For categories with geometric defects, improvements are substantial: cable_gland improves by +16.9 and cookie by +16.4% points. For the seven categories where depth is unreliable, the confidence gate automatically closes and preserves the RGB baseline with negligible deviation (maximum ±0.15 points). Additionally, when the gate is closed, inference throughput improves substantially compared to unconditional depth processing, as the computationally expensive k-Nearest Neighbor (KNN) memory bank queries are entirely bypassed.

The remainder of this paper is organized as follows. Section 2 reviews related work. Section 3 describes the proposed method in detail. Section 4 presents comprehensive experimental results. Section 5 concludes with a discussion of limitations and future directions.

2 Related Work

2.1 RGB-Based Anomaly Detection

Unsupervised anomaly detection methods for RGB images have evolved through several paradigms [12]. Reconstruction-based methods train autoencoders [13] or generative models [14,15] on normal data, detecting anomalies through reconstruction error. However, deep autoencoders can generalize well enough to reconstruct some anomalous patterns, limiting their discriminative power [16].

Knowledge distillation methods [17] represent a more effective paradigm. These approaches train a student network to mimic a pretrained teacher on normal samples, exploiting the observation that the student will fail to replicate the teacher's representations for anomalous inputs [18,19]. EfficientAD [20] advances this paradigm with a dual-branch architecture combining teacher-student distillation with autoencoder reconstruction. The distillation error captures semantic anomalies where the student diverges from the teacher, while the reconstruction error captures structural anomalies. Both error maps are normalized and summed to produce the final anomaly map. Critically, EfficientAD achieves inference speeds under 2 ms per image through its lightweight Patch Description Network (PDN) architecture, making it suitable for real-time industrial deployment. We adopt EfficientAD as the RGB backbone of our framework.

Memory-bank approaches, exemplified by PatchCore [11], store representative normal patch features extracted from a pretrained backbone [21] and compute anomaly scores via nearest-neighbor distance. SPADE [22] similarly leverages multi-resolution feature correspondences for anomaly localization. These methods require no gradient-based training—only forward-pass feature extraction and storage. This training-free property is central to our depth branch design, where we adapt the memory-bank paradigm to operate directly on raw depth patch statistics rather than deep network features. Normalizing flow-based methods such as CFLOW-AD [23] and FastFlow [24] model the distribution of normal features through invertible transformations, achieving competitive performance with efficient density estimation.

2.2 Multimodal 3D Anomaly Detection

The release of MVTec 3D-AD [4] catalyzed research into multimodal anomaly detection leveraging both RGB and 3D information. M3DM [3] pioneered this direction by combining RGB features from a pretrained vision transformer [25] with 3D point cloud features from Point-MAE [8] through a decision-layer fusion mechanism. While effective, both encoders require separate pretraining and the fusion operates unconditionally regardless of modality reliability.

AST [6] introduced asymmetric student-teacher networks where separate student-teacher pairs process RGB and 3D modalities with architecturally distinct networks. CPMF [26] proposed cross-modal pseudo-feature mapping to bridge the representation gap between RGB and depth. Shape-Guided [7] leveraged geometric shape priors derived from depth to guide RGB-based detection. BTF [5] demonstrated that classical 3D features such as FPFH [27] remain competitive with learned representations, suggesting that complex 3D encoders may not always be necessary.

Despite their architectural differences, many of these methods keep both modalities active during inference and rely on a dedicated trained 3D feature extractor. This unconditional fusion implicitly assumes that depth is universally beneficial—an assumption our experiments directly challenge. Our work differs from prior multimodal industrial anomaly detection methods by introducing a two-level confidence gate—operating at both category and sample granularity—for selective depth utilization with a training-free depth branch.

2.3 Confidence-Based and Adaptive Fusion

Selective modality weighting based on reliability has been explored in autonomous driving [28], where sensor fusion frameworks dynamically weight

Light Detection And Ranging (LiDAR), camera, and radar inputs based on conditions. Recent surveys also highlight the importance of adaptive multimodal fusion strategies in anomaly detection. In medical imaging, multi-modal segmentation networks employ attention mechanisms for modality-specific contribution weights [29]. In multi-task learning, Kendall et al. [30] proposed uncertainty-based weighting that adjusts loss contributions based on homoscedastic uncertainty estimates.

Our approach differs in two respects. First, our gate operates at two distinct granularities: a category-level binary gate that completely eliminates unreliable modalities before they can introduce any noise, and a sample-level binary gate that provides finer-grained control within reliable categories. This is more conservative but also more robust than soft-weighting approaches, which may still propagate noisy signals with merely reduced weight. A small but nonzero weight on a fundamentally unreliable modality can accumulate across many samples to produce measurable degradation—a problem our binary gate avoids entirely.

Second, our gate requires no learned parameters: the category-level gate uses a straightforward AUROC threshold and the sample-level gate uses direct score comparison. This parameter-free design aligns with our philosophy of a training-free depth pathway. The entire depth pipeline—from feature extraction to memory bank construction to fusion gating—is deployable without any gradient-based optimization.

3 DepthGate Framework

The proposed DepthGate framework comprises three stages operating in sequence. First, an EfficientAD-based RGB branch outputs an image-level score and a pixel-level anomaly map. Second, a depth memory bank—built without any training—gives an image-level geometric score. The fusion module then combines the two scores under a confidence gate, while the pixel map comes only from the RGB branch. Figure 1 presents the overview of DepthGate framework.

3.1 Stage 1: RGB Branch (EfficientAD)

The RGB branch is based on the EfficientAD [20] architecture, serving as both the primary detector and the baseline that the depth branch aims to improve.

In the teacher-student distillation branch, a pretrained teacher network based on the PDN-Small extracts feature maps from 256×256 RGB images.. A lightweight student network with identical architecture is trained to replicate the teacher's representations on normal samples. At test time, the element-wise squared difference yields the distillation error map St_map, highlighting regions where the student fails to mimic the teacher. The teacher's weights are frozen while the student's weights are optimized during training.

In the autoencoder reconstruction branch, a separate encoder-decoder network reconstructs the teacher's features. The reconstruction error map Ae_map

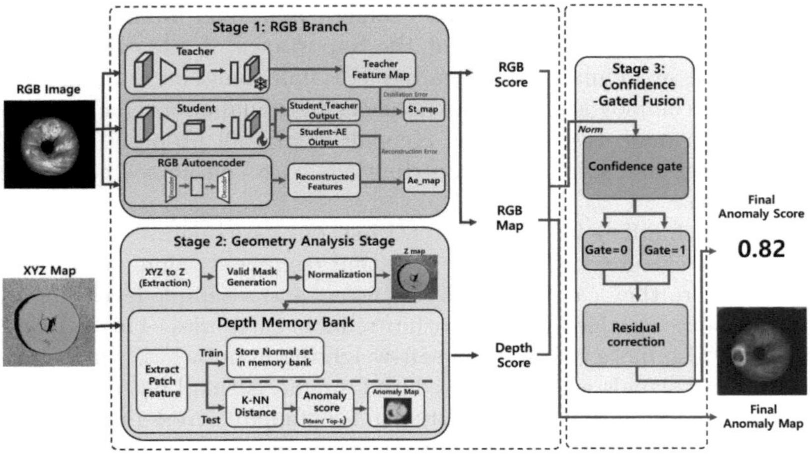

Fig. 1. Overview of DepthGate framework. The RGB branch (top, blue) uses EfficientAD with teacher-student distillation and autoencoder reconstruction to produce RGB anomaly scores and maps. The depth branch (bottom, gray/purple) uses a training-free memory bank with k-NN distance to produce depth scores. The fusion module (right, pink) applies score normalization, a confidence gate (Gate = 0 for RGB-sufficient cases, Gate = 1 for depth-assisted cases), and residual correction. The pixel-level anomaly map uses only the RGB branch output. (Color figure online)

captures structural anomalies. Both maps are normalized and combined:

$$\mathbf{M}_{\text{rgb}} = \frac{\text{St\_map}}{q_{\text{st}}} + \frac{\text{Ae\_map}}{q_{\text{ae}}} \tag{1}$$

where q_{st} and q_{ae} are the 99.5th percentile normalization factors from training.

The image-level RGB score is computed via top-k aggregation:

$$S_{\text{rgb}} = \text{mean}\left(\text{Top}_k(\text{M}_{\text{rgb}})\right), \quad k = 0.01 \times |\mathbf{M}_{\text{rgb}}| \tag{2}$$

Both S_{rgb} and Mrgb are forwarded to the fusion module.

3.2 Stage 2: Geometry Analysis Stage

Unlike existing multimodal approaches that train separate neural network encoders for depth [3,6], our depth branch requires no gradient-based optimization, following a PatchCore-inspired [11] design adapted for raw depth maps.

Given an XYZ point cloud map, we extract the Z (depth) channel. Invalid pixels (sensor noise, occlusion) are masked via validity check ($z \neq 0$), NaN values are zeroed, and the map is downscaled to 64×64 via bilinear interpolation. The validity mask is downscaled using nearest-neighbor interpolation. This pipeline is identical for training and testing.

During the training phase, each 64×64 depth map is padded and divided into overlapping $p \times p$ patches ($p = 5$) centered at each valid pixel. Per patch, we extract a feature vector comprising:

- Raw patch values: The $p^2 = 25$ pixel values flattened, capturing local surface geometry.
- Patch standard deviation: A scalar measuring local surface roughness.
- Center deviation: $|z_{\text{center}} - \bar{z}_{\text{patch}}|$, capturing local point anomalies.

This yields a $(p^2 + 2)$-dimensional feature vector. Features from normal samples are accumulated into memory bank $\mathcal{M}$ (up to 500 per image, 100 images, ≈50,000 features per category). A k-NN index is built over $\mathcal{M}$.

At test time, test features are queried against $\mathcal{M}$ using k-NN ($k = 3$) to compute an image-level geometric anomaly score S_{geom}, which quantifies how much the test sample's depth patches deviate from the normal depth distribution stored in the memory bank. Specifically, S_{geom} aggregates the top 1% highest patch distances:

$$S_{\text{geom}} = \text{mean}\left(\text{Top}_k\left(d(f_i, \mathcal{M})\right)\right), \quad i = 1, \ldots, N \tag{3}$$

where $d(f_i, \mathcal{M})$ denotes the mean k-NN distance for patch feature f_i and N is the number of valid patches. A higher S_{geom} indicates stronger geometric deviation from normal samples, i.e., a higher likelihood of an anomaly based on depth information alone.

The entire depth branch—preprocessing, memory bank construction, k-NN scoring—requires no gradient-based optimization. Deploying to a new category requires only collecting normal samples and populating the memory bank, avoiding any category-specific gradient-based optimization.

3.3 Stage 3: Confidence-Gated Fusion

The fusion module is the core contribution of our framework. It combines RGB and depth scores through a two-level gating mechanism that leverages depth when informative while protecting the RGB baseline when depth is unreliable.

Score Normalization. Since the RGB and depth scores operate on incomparable scales, both are mapped to a common normalized score $S_{\text{norm}} \in [0, 1]$ using percentile-based normalization:

$$S_{\text{norm}} = \text{clip}\left(\frac{S - P_5}{P_{95} - P_5 + \epsilon},\ 0,\ 1\right) \tag{4}$$

where P_5, P_{95} are the 5th/95th percentiles across test samples and $\epsilon = 10^{-8}$.

Category-Level Reliability Gate. Before full evaluation, we assess depth discriminability per category using a *mini-AUROC*, a lightweight validation metric defined as the AUROC of depth-only anomaly scores (S_{geom}) computed on a small held-out subset, distinct from the test set used for final evaluation. Specifically, we use 20 held-out normal samples and up to 10 samples per test subcategory. The category-level gate $G_{\text{cat}} \in \{0,1\}$ indicates whether depth is used (1) or bypassed (0) for a given category, and is defined as:

$$G_{\text{cat}} = \mathbb{1}\left[\text{AUROC}_{\text{mini}}(S_{\text{geom}}) \geq \tau\right] \tag{5}$$

where $\tau = 0.65$. When $G_{\text{cat}} = 0$, the framework defaults to RGB-only inference, providing both performance protection and substantial computational savings (Sect. 4.3). In our experiments, the mini-AUROC values show a clear separation between reliable and unreliable categories: reliable categories cluster between 0.74–1.00 while unreliable categories cluster between 0.15–0.60, making the threshold choice relatively insensitive within the 0.60–0.70 range.

Sample-Level Residual Correction. For categories with $G_{\text{cat}} = 1$, a sample-level gate $g_i \in \{0,1\}$ determines whether depth correction is applied to sample i, activating only when the depth score exceeds the RGB score:

$$g_i = \mathbb{1}\left[S_{\text{geom}}^{\text{norm}}(i) > S_{\text{rgb}}^{\text{norm}}(i)\right] \tag{6}$$

The final score combines both branches via residual correction:

$$S_{\text{final}}(i) = S_{\text{rgb}}^{\text{norm}}(i) + \alpha \cdot G_{\text{cat}} \cdot g_i \cdot S_{\text{geom}}^{\text{norm}}(i) \tag{7}$$

where $\alpha = 0.5$ controls depth contribution. When either gate closes, the product vanishes and $S_{\text{final}} = S_{\text{rgb}}^{\text{norm}}$, reducing to the normalized RGB-only score. In our experiments, the sample-level gate activates for approximately 64–66% of samples within gate-open categories.

Map Preservation Strategy. For pixel-level localization, we use only the RGB branch:

$$\text{M}_{\text{final}} = \text{M}_{\text{rgb}} \tag{8}$$

The depth memory bank operates at 64×64 resolution; upscaled depth maps introduce spatial blurring that degrades localization by 2.5–4.7 points in P-AUROC. This asymmetric strategy—score fusion with map preservation—achieves image-level improvements without sacrificing pixel-level precision.

Algorithm Summary. Algorithm 1 summarizes the inference procedure. Lines 12–14 implement early termination: when the category gate is closed, depth computation is entirely bypassed, yielding substantial runtime savings.

Algorithm 1. DepthGate Inference Procedure

Require: RGB image $\mathbf{x}_{\text{rgb}}$, XYZ map $\mathbf{x}_{\text{xyz}}$, category c
Parameters:
  $G_{\text{cat}}[c] \in \{0, 1\}$: pre-computed category gate (Eq. 5)
  $\mathcal{M}_c$: depth memory bank for category c
  $\alpha = 0.5$: depth contribution weight
Intermediate variables:
  $S_{\text{rgb}}, \text{M}_{\text{rgb}}$: RGB anomaly score and map (from EfficientAD)
  Z, F: preprocessed depth map and patch features
  S_{geom}: depth anomaly score (Eq. 3)
  $S_{\text{rgb}}^{\text{norm}}, S_{\text{geom}}^{\text{norm}}$: normalized scores (Eq. 4)
  $g \in \{0, 1\}$: sample-level gate (Eq. 6)
Ensure: Final score S_{final}, Final map M_{final}
$S_{\text{rgb}}, \text{M}_{\text{rgb}} \leftarrow \text{EfficientAD}(\mathbf{x}_{\text{rgb}})$ ▷ Stage 1
if $G_{\text{cat}}[c] = 0$ **then**
  return $\text{Normalize}(S_{\text{rgb}}), \text{M}_{\text{rgb}}$ ▷ Skip depth (gate closed)
end if
$\text{Z} \leftarrow \text{Preprocess}(\mathbf{x}_{\text{xyz}})$ ▷ Stage 2
$\text{F} \leftarrow \text{ExtractPatchFeatures}(\text{Z})$
$S_{\text{geom}} \leftarrow \text{TopKMeanDistance}(\text{F}, \mathcal{M}_c)$
$S_{\text{rgb}}^{\text{norm}} \leftarrow \text{Normalize}(S_{\text{rgb}})$ ▷ Stage 3
$S_{\text{geom}}^{\text{norm}} \leftarrow \text{Normalize}(S_{\text{geom}})$
$g \leftarrow \mathbb{1}[S_{\text{geom}}^{\text{norm}} > S_{\text{rgb}}^{\text{norm}}]$ ▷ Sample gate
$S_{\text{final}} \leftarrow S_{\text{rgb}}^{\text{norm}} + \alpha \cdot g \cdot S_{\text{geom}}^{\text{norm}}$ ▷ Residual correction
$\text{M}_{\text{final}} \leftarrow \text{M}_{\text{rgb}}$ ▷ Map preserved
return $S_{\text{final}}, \text{M}_{\text{final}}$

4 Experiments

4.1 Experimental Setup

Dataset. We evaluate on the MVTec 3D-AD benchmark [4], which contains 10 object categories (bagel, cable_gland, carrot, cookie, dowel, foam, peach, potato, rope, tire) with both RGB images and structured-light 3D scans. Each category includes normal training samples and test samples with various defect types. The dataset provides pixel-level ground truth annotations for anomaly localization.

Implementation Details. The RGB branch uses EfficientAD with a small PDN architecture (out_channels = 384) and pretrained teacher weights. The depth memory bank uses patch size $p = 5$, $k = 3$ nearest neighbors, and a downscaled resolution of 64×64. Normal features are subsampled to 500 per image with a maximum of 100 images, yielding approximately 50,000 features per category. The fusion parameters are set to $\alpha = 0.5$ and $\tau = 0.65$ unless otherwise specified. The k-NN index uses scikit-learn's NearestNeighbors with Euclidean distance and parallel computation. All experiments are conducted on a single NVIDIA GPU.

Evaluation Metrics. We report I-AUROC for anomaly detection, P-AUROC for anomaly localization, and Area Under the Per-Region Overlap curve (AU-PRO) for region-level evaluation. We additionally report the category-level gate status (OPEN/CLOSE), the mini-AUROC from depth reliability validation, and the sample-level gate activation ratio.

4.2 Results

Table 1 presents the complete evaluation results across all 10 categories of MVTec 3D-AD.

Table 1. Main results on MVTec 3D-AD. I-AUROC and P-AUROC are reported as percentages. Gate indicates category-level depth reliability status. Δ denotes improvement over the RGB-only baseline. mini-AUROC is the depth reliability score used for gating.

Category	Gate	I-RGB	I-Fused	I-Δ	P-RGB	P-Fused	P-Δ	mini-AUROC
bagel	CL	82.13	81.97	−0.15	96.69	96.69	0.00	0.545
cable_gland	OP	74.55	91.41	+16.86	98.15	98.15	0.00	1.000
carrot	CL	87.18	87.40	+0.22	99.28	99.28	0.00	0.600
cookie	OP	58.46	74.83	+16.37	93.46	93.46	0.00	0.765
dowel	OP	96.15	94.01	−2.14	99.50	99.50	0.00	0.745
foam	CL	76.19	76.19	0.00	82.49	82.49	0.00	0.473
peach	CL	71.73	71.66	−0.07	95.57	95.57	0.00	0.188
potato	CL	77.42	77.40	−0.02	98.86	98.86	0.00	0.400
rope	CL	97.64	97.64	0.00	99.51	99.51	0.00	0.433
tire	CL	64.97	65.03	+0.07	98.42	98.42	0.00	0.380
Mean	—	78.64	**81.75**	**+3.11**	96.19	**96.19**	**0.00**	—

Three key findings emerge from Table 1. First, for categories where the depth branch achieves high standalone discriminative power (cable_gland: mini-AUROC = 1.000, cookie: mini-AUROC = 0.765), the confidence gate correctly opens and substantial I-AUROC improvements are achieved (+16.86 and +16.37% points respectively). These two categories are characterized by geometric defects—surface deformations and structural irregularities—that are well captured by depth measurements but may be subtle or invisible in RGB. Second, for categories where depth is unreliable (mini-AUROC < 0.65), the gate remains closed and the RGB baseline is preserved with negligible deviation (maximum ±0.15 points). The gate handles this protection automatically—we never had to tune anything per category. Third, P-AUROC is preserved at $\Delta = 0.00$ across all categories, confirming that the map preservation strategy (Eq. 8) successfully decouples image-level score improvements from pixel-level localization (Table 2).

Table 2. Comparison on MVTec 3D-AD. Mean image-level AUROC (%). "Depth Train" indicates whether the depth branch requires training. "Selective" indicates conditional modality usage. "P-AUROC Δ" indicates pixel-level degradation from fusion. For EfficientAD, we report our own reproduction on MVTec 3D-AD, since the original paper does not report this benchmark.

Method	Depth Train	Selective	I-AUROC	P-AUROC Δ
BTF [5]	Yes	No	87.3	—
AST [6]	Yes	No	93.7	—
M3DM [3]	Yes	No	94.5	—
Shape-Guided [7]	Yes	No	94.7	—
EfficientAD (our reproduction)	—	—	78.6	—
DepthGate (Ours)	**No**	**Yes**	81.8	**0.00**

DepthGate achieves 81.8% mean I-AUROC, a +3.1 point improvement over its EfficientAD baseline. While fully-trained multimodal methods such as M3DM (94.5%) and AST (93.7%) achieve higher absolute performance on MVTec 3D-AD, they require dedicated 3D encoders and process both modalities for all categories. In contrast, DepthGate requires no depth-branch training, automatically bypasses depth for unreliable categories, and maintains zero P-AUROC degradation in our setting. To the best of our knowledge, existing methods do not combine all of these properties in a single framework. The gating mechanism is orthogonal to the fusion backbone and could potentially be applied on top of methods such as M3DM or AST to improve robustness against unreliable depth categories.

Figure 2 presents anomaly localization results of the RGB branch across representative categories from MVTec 3D-AD.

The RGB branch achieves high-quality pixel-level localization across diverse defect types, successfully identifying anomalous regions that align closely with the ground truth masks. This strong localization performance—reflected in the mean P-AUROC of 96.19% across all categories—motivates our map preservation strategy. Since the RGB branch already provides precise spatial localization, fusing depth maps (which operate at 64×64 resolution) would only introduce blurring artifacts without improving localization accuracy. Instead, depth contributes exclusively through image-level score correction, where its geometric signal is most valuable.

4.3 Ablation Study

Gate Confidence. To validate the contribution of the confidence gate, we compare three configurations: (a) RGB-only baseline (EfficientAD), (b) unconditional fusion without gating ($\tau = 0$, all categories open), and (c) the full method with confidence gating ($\tau = 0.65$). Table 3 presents results for representative categories.

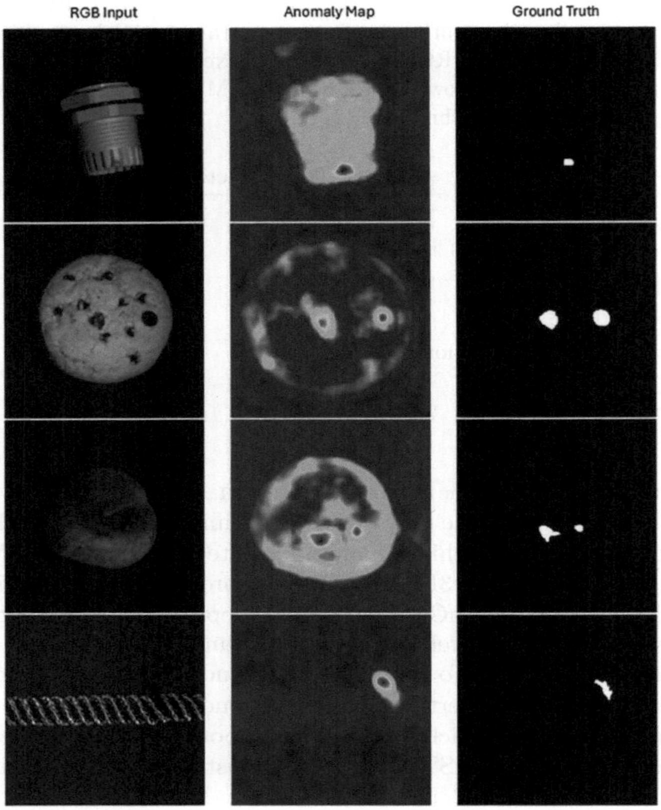

Fig. 2. Anomaly localization results of the RGB branch (EfficientAD) across representative categories. Left: RGB input. Center: predicted anomaly heatmap. Right: ground truth mask. The RGB branch provides precise pixel-level localization across diverse defect types including geometric deformations (cable_gland), textural anomalies (cookie, rope), and chromatic defects (peach). This strong localization capability motivates our map preservation strategy ($M_{final} = M_{rgb}$), where depth contributes only to image-level scoring.

Table 3. Ablation study (I-AUROC %). Configuration (b) without gating shows that unconditional fusion catastrophically degrades depth-unreliable categories, while configuration (c) with gating preserves the baseline. Mean Δ is computed across all 10 categories.

Config.	cable_gl.	cookie	carrot	foam	peach	rope	dowel	Mean Δ
(a) RGB only	74.55	58.46	87.18	76.19	71.73	97.64	96.15	—
(b) No gate	90.20	76.07	71.72	63.00	57.15	89.27	93.86	−5.23
(c) Full (ours)	91.41	74.83	87.40	76.19	71.66	97.64	94.01	+3.11

The ablation reveals the critical role of the confidence gate. Without gating (configuration b), depth fusion improves cable_gland (+15.65) and cookie (+17.61) but catastrophically degrades carrot (−15.46), peach (−14.59), foam (−13.19), and rope (−8.38), resulting in a mean Δ of −5.23 across all 10 categories. The confidence gate (configuration c) resolves this by automatically closing depth for unreliable categories, converting the −5.23 mean degradation into a +3.11 improvement—a swing of over 8% points. This demonstrates that the gate is not merely a minor refinement but the essential mechanism that makes multimodal fusion viable.

Map Fusion. We investigated whether depth anomaly maps could improve pixel-level localization by applying the same gating mechanism to maps: $\mathbf{M}_{\text{final}} = \mathbf{M}_{\text{rgb}}^{\text{norm}} + \alpha \cdot g \cdot \mathbf{M}_{\text{geom}}^{\text{norm}}$. Table 4 presents the results for gate-open categories.

Table 4. Impact of depth map fusion on P-AUROC (%) for gate-open categories. Fusing depth maps degrades localization due to resolution limitations.

Category	Map preserved	Map fused	Δ
cable_gland	98.15	95.65	−2.50
cookie	93.46	88.76	−4.70

Depth map fusion causes P-AUROC drops of 2.50 and 4.70% points for cable_gland and cookie respectively. The degradation stems from the memory bank's 64 × 64 operating resolution: the resulting depth anomaly maps, when bilinearly upscaled to 256 × 256, introduce spatial blurring that corrupts the precise localization boundaries provided by the RGB branch.

Hyperparameter Sensitivity. We analyze sensitivity to the two key hyperparameters: depth contribution weight α and reliability threshold τ.

Effect of α *(Depth Weight).* Table 5 shows the mean I-AUROC Δ across all 10 categories for varying α with fixed $\tau = 0.65$.

A clear trade-off emerges: increasing α amplifies the depth contribution, yielding larger improvements for geometric-defect categories (cable_gland, cookie) but also amplifying depth-induced degradation for dowel. The overall mean peaks at $\alpha = 0.7$ (+3.54), but the dowel degradation at this setting (−6.21) is substantially worse than at $\alpha = 0.5$ (−2.63). We retain $\alpha = 0.5$ as the default because it achieves near-optimal mean improvement (+3.09) while limiting the worst-case per-category degradation. This reflects a practical design choice: in industrial deployment, avoiding catastrophic failure in any single category is often more important than maximizing average performance.

Table 5. Sensitivity to α (depth contribution weight) with $\tau = 0.65$. I-AUROC Δ reported for gate-open categories and overall mean. Results may differ slightly from Table 1 due to differences in sampling and evaluation splits used for the sensitivity analysis.

α	0.1	0.3	0.5	0.7	1.0
cable_gland	+5.09	+11.82	+16.42	+19.70	+21.35
cookie	+4.82	+12.03	+17.06	+21.84	+23.61
dowel	+1.00	−0.15	−2.63	−6.21	−11.43
Mean (all 10)	+1.10	+2.38	+3.09	**+3.54**	+3.36

Table 6. Sensitivity to τ (reliability threshold) with $\alpha = 0.5$. "Open" indicates the number of gate-open categories. Results may differ slightly from Table 1 due to differences in sampling and evaluation splits used for the sensitivity analysis.

τ	0.50	0.60	0.65	0.70	0.75	0.80
Open cats	5	3	3	3	2	1
Mean I-Δ	+0.85	+3.20	+3.06	+3.10	**+3.40**	+1.69
cable_gland	+16.91	+17.41	+16.69	+16.48	+16.09	+16.80
cookie	+17.23	+17.30	+16.75	+17.20	+17.82	0.00
dowel	−2.22	−2.74	−2.88	−2.70	+0.07	+0.07

Effect of τ (Reliability Threshold). Table 6 shows the effect of varying τ with fixed $\alpha = 0.5$. Lower thresholds open more category gates, risking depth-induced degradation; higher thresholds are more conservative.

The results reveal an interesting pattern. At $\tau = 0.50$, the gate opens for 5 categories including bagel and carrot, whose unreliable depth causes severe degradation that offsets the gains, yielding only +0.85 mean improvement. Increasing τ to 0.60 closes these harmful categories, jumping to +3.20. Performance remains stable across $\tau \in [0.60, 0.70]$, confirming the insensitivity of the threshold within this range due to the bimodal distribution of mini-AUROC values.

At $\tau = 0.75$, the dowel gate closes (mini-AUROC$\approx$0.71), eliminating its degradation and achieving the highest mean improvement of +3.40. However, at $\tau = 0.80$, the cookie gate also closes (mini-AUROC$\approx$0.77), losing its +17 point improvement and dropping the mean to +1.69. We retain $\tau = 0.65$ as the default for its balance between improvement and robustness, though $\tau = 0.75$ represents an attractive alternative that eliminates the dowel failure case.

Per-Category Depth Reliability Analysis. To provide deeper insight into the relationship between depth reliability and defect characteristics, Table 7 presents a comprehensive per-category analysis.

Table 7. Per-category depth reliability analysis. Depth-only I-AUROC indicates standalone depth discriminability. Primary defect type explains why depth is or is not effective. Gate status: OP (open) = depth used, CL (close) = depth bypassed.

Category	Depth AUROC	Gate	Defect Type	Why Depth Helps/Fails
cable_gland	0.99	OP	Geometric	Surface deformations visible in Z
cookie	0.80	OP	Geometric	Dough deformations alter depth
dowel	0.68	OP	Mixed	Some geometric; RGB already strong
carrot	0.52	CL	Textural	Color/texture defects on flat surface
bagel	0.54	CL	Textural	Surface blemishes; consistent shape
foam	0.44	CL	Textural	Porosity variations; noisy depth
rope	0.43	CL	Textural	Fiber damage; no depth signature
potato	0.40	CL	Textural	Skin defects; organic shape variance
tire	0.38	CL	Textural	Surface marks; consistent geometry
peach	0.19	CL	Chromatic	Color defects only; no depth info

A clear pattern emerges: categories with geometric defects (cable_gland, cookie) achieve high depth-only AUROC and benefit from fusion, while categories with primarily textural or chromatic defects (peach, foam, tire) show near-random depth performance. This aligns with the physical characteristics of structured-light depth sensors, which capture surface geometry but provide no signal for color-based or texture-based anomalies. The confidence gate automatically discovers this pattern without requiring manual annotation of defect types.

Inference Speed. A key practical advantage of the confidence gate is computational savings when depth is bypassed. Table 8 compares inference throughput for gate-closed and gate-open categories.

Table 8. Inference speed comparison. Gate-closed categories skip depth computation entirely, yielding substantial speedup.

Configuration	Throughput (samples/s)	Relative
Gate CLOSE (RGB only)	∼25–57	1.0×
Gate OPEN (RGB + Depth)	∼3.0–5.2	0.06–0.21×

When the category-level gate is closed, inference throughput ranges from approximately 25 to 57 samples per second depending on the category, compared to 3.0–5.2 samples per second when depth memory bank queries are executed. Since 7 out of 10 categories have their gate closed in our experiments, the framework achieves substantial average throughput gains across the full benchmark.

Failure Case. The dowel category presents an instructive failure case. Despite a mini-AUROC of 0.745 (above $\tau = 0.65$), fusion decreases I-AUROC by 2.14% points. This occurs because the RGB baseline is already very high (96.15%), leaving minimal headroom for improvement while retaining capacity for depth-induced false alarms at the sample level.

Specifically, within dowel's gate-open inference, approximately 64.6% of samples have their sample-level gate activated. Among these, a subset of normal samples receive elevated final scores due to depth noise, pushing them above the decision boundary and increasing the false positive rate. The fundamental issue is that the category-level gate assesses depth *discriminability* (whether depth can separate normal from anomalous), but does not account for the *marginal value* of depth given an already-strong RGB baseline.

Two potential mitigations exist. First, conditioning the category gate on both depth reliability and RGB baseline performance: if the RGB baseline already exceeds a threshold (e.g., 95% I-AUROC), the gate closes regardless of depth reliability. Second, increasing τ to 0.75 would close the dowel gate (mini-AUROC = 0.745) while keeping cable_gland (1.000) and cookie (0.765) open. We leave the integration of these refinements into a unified gating criterion for future work.

5 Conclusion

A few practical lessons emerged from our experiments. Naive fusion of RGB and depth is not safe: depth gains in geometric-defect classes were wiped out by losses in classes where depth carries no useful signal, costing 5.23 points on average. A simple binary gate flips this picture, turning a 5.23-point loss into a 3.11-point gain—and the gate-closed classes incur no depth computation at all. We also found that image-level and pixel-level fusion behave very differently: depth helps the score but hurts the localization map at 64×64 resolution, which is why we keep the RGB map untouched. Finally, because the depth pathway needs no gradient-based training, adding a new product category is just a matter of populating the memory bank.

In summary, we presented DepthGate, a confidence-gated depth verification framework for multimodal industrial anomaly detection. By combining a training-free depth memory bank with a two-level gating mechanism, our approach selectively leverages depth information only when it provides reliable discriminative value. Evaluated on MVTec 3D-AD across all 10 categories, the framework achieves a mean I-AUROC improvement of +3.1% points over the EfficientAD baseline while maintaining zero P-AUROC degradation. For geometric-defect categories, improvements reach +16.9 and +16.4% points for cable_gland and cookie respectively.

Several directions remain for future work. First, the gating criterion could be extended to incorporate the RGB baseline performance, addressing failure cases where the baseline is already very strong (e.g., dowel). Second, the depth feature representation could be enriched beyond raw patch statistics, potentially using lightweight pretrained geometric encoders within the gated framework.

Third, the confidence-gated fusion paradigm could be applied to other multimodal fusion pipelines such as M3DM [3] or AST [6], potentially improving their robustness without modifying their core architectures. Finally, evaluation on additional industrial datasets with diverse sensor modalities would test the generalizability of the gating approach beyond RGB-depth fusion.

Acknowledgments. This work was supported by the Institute of Information & Communications Technology Planning & Evaluation (IITP)-ICT Creative Consilience Program grant funded by the Korea government (MSIT) (IITP-2026-RS-2020-II201821), This work was supported by the Korea Institute for Advancement of Technology (KIAT) grant funded by the Korea Government under the Industrial Innovation Talent Growth Support Project (KIAT-2026-RS-2026-25532917).

Disclosure of Interests. The authors have no competing interests to declare that are relevant to the content of this article.

References

1. Li, Z., Yan, Y., Wang, X., Ge, Y., Meng, L.: A survey of deep learning for industrial visual anomaly detection. Artif. Intell. Rev. **58**(9), 279 (2025). https://doi.org/10.1007/s10462-025-11287-7
2. Lin, Y., et al.: A survey on RGB, 3D, and multimodal approaches for unsupervised industrial image anomaly detection. Inf. Fusion **121**, 103139 (2025). https://doi.org/10.1016/j.inffus.2025.103139
3. Wang, Y., Peng, J., Zhang, J., Yi, R., Wang, Y., Wang, C.: Multimodal industrial anomaly detection via hybrid fusion. In: 2023 IEEE/CVF Conference on Computer Vision and Pattern Recognition (CVPR), pp. 8032–8041 (2023). https://doi.org/10.1109/CVPR52729.2023.00776
4. Bergmann, P., Jin, X., Sattlegger, D., Steger, C.: The MVTec 3D-AD dataset for unsupervised 3D anomaly detection and localization. In: VISAPP, pp. 202–213 (2022). https://doi.org/10.5220/0010865000003124
5. Horwitz, E., Hoshen, Y.: Back to the feature: classical 3D features are (almost) all you need for 3D anomaly detection. In: CVPR Workshops, pp. 2968–2977 (2023). https://doi.org/10.1109/CVPRW59228.2023.00298
6. Rudolph, M., Wehrbein, T., Rosenhahn, B., Wandt, B.: Asymmetric student-teacher networks for industrial anomaly detection. In: WACV, pp. 2591–2601 (2023). https://doi.org/10.1109/WACV56688.2023.00262
7. Chu, Y., Liu, C., Hsieh, T., Chen, H., Liu, T.: Shape-guided dual-memory learning for 3D anomaly detection. In: ICML. Proceedings of Machine Learning Research, vol. 202, pp. 6185–6194. PMLR (2023). https://proceedings.mlr.press/v202/chu23b.html
8. Pang, Y., Wang, W., Tay, F.E.H., Liu, W., Tian, Y., Yuan, L.: Masked autoencoders for point cloud self-supervised learning. In: Avidan, S., Brostow, G., Cissé, M., Farinella, G.M., Hassner, T. (eds.) Computer Vision – ECCV 2022. ECCV 2022. LNCS, vol. 13662, pp. 604–621. Springer, Cham (2022). https://doi.org/10.1007/978-3-031-20086-1_35
9. Yu, X., Tang, L., Rao, Y., Huang, T., Zhou, J., Lu, J.: Point-BERT: pre-training 3D point cloud transformers with masked point modeling. In: CVPR, pp. 19291–19300 (2022). https://doi.org/10.1109/CVPR52688.2022.01871

10. Daci, R., et al.: Cross-modal mapping and dual-branch reconstruction for 2D-3D multimodal industrial anomaly detection. arXiv preprint arXiv:2603.03939 (2026). https://arxiv.org/abs/2603.03939
11. Roth, K., Pemula, L., Zepeda, J., Schölkopf, B., Brox, T., Gehler, P.: Towards total recall in industrial anomaly detection. In: CVPR, pp. 14298–14308 (2022). https://doi.org/10.1109/CVPR52688.2022.01392
12. Shukla, V., Shukla, A., Surya Prakash, S.K., Shukla, S.: A systematic survey: role of deep learning-based image anomaly detection in industrial inspection contexts. Front. Robot. AI **12**, 1554196 (2025). https://doi.org/10.3389/frobt.2025.1554196
13. Bergmann, P., Löwe, S., Fauser, M., Sattlegger, D., Steger, C.: Improving unsupervised defect segmentation by applying structural similarity to autoencoders. In: VISIGRAPP, pp. 372–380 (2019). https://doi.org/10.5220/0007364503720380
14. Akcay, S., Atapour-Abarghouei, A., Breckon, T.P.: GANomaly: semi-supervised anomaly detection via adversarial training. In: Jawahar, C., Li, H., Mori, G., Schindler, K. (eds.) Computer Vision – ACCV 2018. ACCV 2018. LNCS, vol. 11363, pp. 622–637. Springer, Cham (2018). https://doi.org/10.1007/978-3-030-20893-6_39
15. Schlegl, T., Seeböck, P., Waldstein, S.M., Langs, G., Schmidt-Erfurth, U.: f-AnoGAN: fast unsupervised anomaly detection with generative adversarial networks. Med. Image Anal. **54**, 30–44 (2019). https://doi.org/10.1016/j.media.2019.01.010
16. Zavrtanik, V., Kristan, M., Skocaj, D.: DRAEM – a discriminatively trained reconstruction embedding for surface anomaly detection. In: ICCV, pp. 8310–8319 (2021). https://doi.org/10.1109/ICCV48922.2021.00822
17. Hinton, G., Vinyals, O., Dean, J.: Distilling the knowledge in a neural network. arXiv preprint arXiv:1503.02531 (2015). https://arxiv.org/abs/1503.02531
18. Bergmann, P., Fauser, M., Sattlegger, D., Steger, C.: Uninformed students: student-teacher anomaly detection with discriminative latent embeddings. In: CVPR, pp. 4182–4191 (2020). https://doi.org/10.1109/CVPR42600.2020.00424
19. Deng, H., Li, X.: Anomaly detection via reverse distillation from one-class embedding. In: CVPR, pp. 9727–9736 (2022). https://doi.org/10.1109/CVPR52688.2022.00951
20. Batzner, K., Heckler, L., König, R.: EfficientAD: accurate visual anomaly detection at millisecond-level latencies. In: WACV, pp. 127–137 (2024). https://doi.org/10.1109/WACV57701.2024.00020
21. He, K., Zhang, X., Ren, S., Sun, J.: Deep residual learning for image recognition. In: CVPR, pp. 770–778 (2016). https://doi.org/10.1109/CVPR.2016.90
22. Cohen, N., Hoshen, Y.: Sub-image anomaly detection with deep pyramid correspondences. arXiv preprint arXiv:2005.02357 (2020). https://arxiv.org/abs/2005.02357
23. Gudovskiy, D., Ishizaka, S., Kozuka, K.: CFLOW-AD: real-time unsupervised anomaly detection with localization via conditional normalizing flows. In: WACV, pp. 1819–1828 (2022). https://doi.org/10.1109/WACV51458.2022.00188
24. Yu, J., et al.: FastFlow: unsupervised anomaly detection and localization via 2D normalizing flows. arXiv preprint arXiv:2111.07677 (2021). https://arxiv.org/abs/2111.07677
25. Dosovitskiy, A., et al.: An image is worth 16 × 16 words: transformers for image recognition at scale. In: ICLR (2021). https://openreview.net/forum?id=YicbFdNTTy

26. Cao, Y., Xu, X., Shen, W.: Complementary pseudo multimodal feature for point cloud anomaly detection. Pattern Recognition **156**, 110761 (2024). https://doi.org/10.1016/j.patcog.2024.110761
27. Rusu, R.B., Blodow, N., Beetz, M.: Fast point feature histograms (FPFH) for 3D registration. In: ICRA, pp. 3212–3217 (2009). https://doi.org/10.1109/ROBOT.2009.5152473
28. Qian, H., Wang, M., Zhu, M., Wang, H.: A review of multi-sensor fusion in autonomous driving. Sensors **25**(19), 6033 (2025). https://doi.org/10.3390/s25196033
29. Zhou, T., Ruan, S., Canu, S.: A review: deep learning for medical image segmentation using multi-modality fusion. Array **3–4**, 100004 (2019). https://doi.org/10.1016/j.array.2019.100004
30. Kendall, A., Gal, Y., Cipolla, R.: Multi-task learning using uncertainty to weigh losses for scene geometry and semantics. In: CVPR, pp. 7482–7491 (2018). https://doi.org/10.1109/CVPR.2018.00781

Impact of Anatomical Positioning Markers on Breast Cancer Detection Thermography

João Augusto Pilato de Castro, Fabrício Araújo Filgueiras, Luíza Machado Costa de Nascimento, Heder Soares Bernardino(✉), and Saulo Moraes Villela

Federal University of Juiz de Fora, Juiz de Fora, MG, Brazil
pilato.joao@estudante.ufjf.br, fabricio.filgueiras@estudante.ufjf.br, luiza.machado@estudante.ufjf.br, heder.bernardino@ufjf.br, saulo.moraes@ufjf.br

Abstract. In the literature on thermographic breast image classification, methods of pre-processing are used to focus on relevant information. Segmentation of the region of interest and elimination of noise are examples widely adopted. However, such approaches can eliminate relevant contextual features used on learning process. In the datasets utilized by the majority of studies, one relevant element is a marker, often discarded by those techniques. This study investigates the influence of this marker on breast cancer identification, through combination of different aspects influenced by the marker. We studied the effects of its presence, as well as the impact of different methods of pre-processing images. Results show that the markers can improve perfomance, and its removal or displacement can impact directly on learning process. These findings suggest that the marker collaborates in the evaluation of the entire image field, focusing on discriminative features that indicates presence of cancer, demonstrating that external elements should not be treated as noise, but may contribute to interpreting spatial patterns in thermographic data.

1 Introduction

Breast cancer represents one of the major global public health concerns. According to data from the International Agency for Research on Cancer (IARC)[1], it is estimated that approximately one in every twenty women will be diagnosed with the disease over their lifetime. Projections also suggest that this scenario may worsen in the coming decades. According to Nature Medicine [1], if current trends are maintained, the annual number of new cases could reach 3.2 million by 2050, with an estimated 1.1 million deaths.

In this context, thermography has been increasingly explored as a complementary approach for breast cancer screening. As a non-invasive technique, it enables the mapping of thermal patterns associated with tumor metabolic activity without requiring physical contact [2,3]. In addition, its low operational cost,

[1] https://www.iarc.who.int.

O. Gervasi et al. (Eds.): ICCSA 2026, LNCS 16768, pp. 126–140, 2027.
https://doi.org/10.1007/978-3-032-30488-9_8

combined with the absence of ionizing radiation [4], makes it a suitable option for early detection, especially in settings with limited resources.

Despite these advantages, the clinical interpretation of thermographic images remains challenging [5], as the observed thermal patterns are often subtle and influenced by multiple physiological factors. For this reason, deep learning models have been used to identify patterns that are difficult to detect through visual inspection alone [6, 7].

Recent advances in the field have focused mainly on architectural improvements. Even so, many computational pipelines still rely on aggressive preprocessing strategies based on region of interest (ROI) segmentation to remove background noise and emphasize the relevant anatomical region [8]. In practice, this means that external visual elements are often treated as irrelevant to learning process. As a result, acquisition related artifacts and reference markers are commonly removed, discarding information that may contribute to model performance.

This assumption becomes more problematic when considering that thermographic datasets often contain structured visual patterns introduced during image acquisition. These patterns may include methodological artifacts, such as segmentation masks, as well as physical elements, such as anatomical positioning markers, which create localized thermal discontinuities. Although these elements are often discussed in the context of shortcut learning [9], where models rely on non-causal correlations, their presence does not always imply a spurious effect. In some cases, acquisition related elements may provide spatial or geometric references that interact with the region of interest.

This issue becomes even more relevant because the literature relies on a small number of public datasets, especially the Visual Lab Database [10], which has been widely used in breast thermography research [11,12]. When many studies depend on the same dataset, recurring acquisition patterns and artifacts are more likely to influence model behavior in a systematic way. This makes controlled investigations into their role in the learning process especially important.

Preliminary experiments with the Visual Lab dataset showed that models trained on original images containing the anatomical positioning marker consistently performed better than those trained on images in which the marker was removed or indirectly excluded through segmentation. This result is counterintuitive, since conventional preprocessing strategies would normally suggest that removing external elements should improve model generalization. These observations indicate that such elements may do more than introduce noise, as they can function as contextual references that affect how models interpret thermal patterns.

Based on these observations, this study investigates the role of non-physiological visual elements in deep learning models for breast cancer classification. Specifically, we analyze the impact of the anatomical positioning marker (TAG) under different preprocessing conditions, including marker removal, spatial relocation, and normalization of its physical properties. The goal is to determine whether these elements behave as spurious shortcuts or as meaningful contextual cues that contribute to model performance.

2 Related Work

The application of neural models for the classification of breast thermograms is not a new idea, recent systematic reviews indicate a wide range of studies in this area with very promising results. Looking at the methods used and the results obtained, one thing is clear CNNs (Convolutional Neural Networks) are the most prevalent models, almost always along with Transfer Learning. Although classic architectures such as VGG [13] and ResNet [14] work well yield strong results, newer models that prioritize computational efficiency, such as EfficientNet and MobileNet, appear far less frequently [15]. This suggests that the field has become stuck in what is already known and has failed to explore what is new.

Another problem lies in the fact that the overwhelming majority of the literature is dependent on a single dataset. More than 77% of studies are based solely on the Visual Lab (DMR-IR) image set from the Federal Fluminense University. This creates what some authors call "data hegemony," which, while standardizing comparisons, imposes technical and demographic biases. Since this dataset has become the standard in the field, we must ask ourselves: what works within it, does it work outside of it? What kind of variation completely changes the performance of the models? This type of analysis is lacking.

In the context of preprocessing, the literature largely focuses on basic procedures: resizing, normalizing, and augmenting data. This helps to circumvent overfitting, mainly because the dataset is small, but it is not as interesting as a case study because these techniques ignore details that come from the image acquisition itself, such as anatomical markers, relevant background regions, and non-physiological patterns.

Bringing all this information together from the literature, it becomes clear that there is a significant gap in the literature regarding the analysis of visual biases and acquisition methods that affect the performance and interpretability of CNN-based models in breast thermography. This work seeks to question this limitation and investigate, in a controlled manner, how these factors impact the ability of models to generalize to new data, comparing their reliability and the results obtained.

3 Materials and Methods

In order to systematically investigate the influence of the marker will describe the following in four parts: the dataset used and its particularities, how the preprocessing was done, the models and architectures used, and finally the experimental protocol adopted.

3.1 Dataset

This study uses the dataset Visual Lab Database [10], a public repository widely used in the literature on breast thermography research. It consists of several thermographic images captured with a fixed protocol, at five different angles, including frontal, left lateral 45°, left lateral 90°, right lateral 45°, and right lateral 90° views.

For our study, only frontal images were considered to ensure greater geometric consistency between samples and to avoid unnecessary variability from different angles. Therefore, the main dataset used contains only frontal images, all captured under controlled conditions.

An interesting detail in the images is that they have a square marker attached to the patient's chest, here called an anatomical positioning marker (TAG), which serves as a geometric reference during the image acquisition process, appearing in virtually all images and always in the same style (Fig. 1).

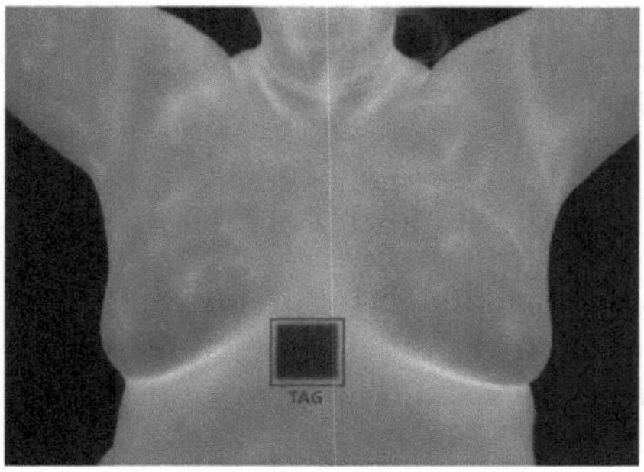

Fig. 1. Example of an image from the dataset.

3.2 Preprocessing and Data Augmentation

In the domain of machine learning applied to computer vision, preprocessing and data augmentation constitute fundamental stages for dataset preparation and enrichment [16], serving distinct methodological purposes.

The preprocessing stage encompasses a more mechanical concept, in which standardized transformations are applied to the raw image, such as resizing and normalization on the temperature scale [17], with the goal of leaving all samples in a canonical format and aligned for the model to process. In data augmentation, the idea is to synthetically generate new samples through controlled random transformations, rotating the images slightly, for example. This increases the diversity of the training set and acts as an implicit regularization [18] during network training.

3.3 Model Architectures and Training

For the main analysis architecture, VGG-16 (Visual Geometry Group) [13] was chosen, a deep convolutional network architecture created by Simonyan and Zisserman in 2014 that is characterized by systematically using small 3×3 filters and organizing the layers in a more homogeneous way. There are two more common versions, VGG-16 and VGG-19 (16 and 19 weighted layers, respectively). What is striking about this neural network is its conceptual simplicity and the proof that a critical factor in obtaining good results is the number of layers; the more layers, the better the hierarchical representations it learns.

4 Methodology

Prior to defining the formal evaluation protocol, preliminary experiments were conducted to visually assess model behavior under different preprocessing strategies.

These initial observations suggested that model performance is influenced by factors beyond the region of interest, motivating a more controlled and systematic experimental design.

4.1 Experimental Protocols and Variations

The experimental design was guided by preliminary qualitative observations of model behavior under different preprocessing strategies. In particular, models trained on original images consistently outperformed those trained on segmented regions.

To better understand this discrepancy, activation maps (EigenCAM) were analyzed, revealing that the networks frequently concentrated attention on the anatomical positioning marker (TAG) in the original images.

Comparative observations across original, segmented, and segmented-with-marker images indicated that the presence of the TAG systematically alters the model's attention patterns, as illustrated by the activation maps in Fig. 2. This effect was especially evident in correctly classified healthy cases, where no strong pathological thermal patterns are present.

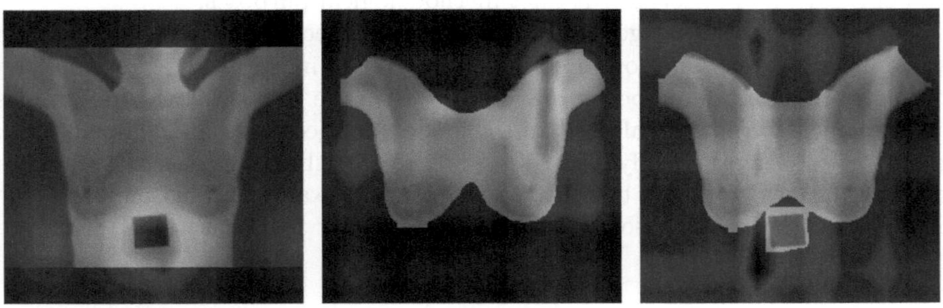

(a) Original image (with TAG) (b) Segmented image (without TAG) (c) Segmented image with preserved TAG

Fig. 2. EigenCAM activation maps.

These findings suggested that removing the marker through segmentation may eliminate not only irrelevant background information, but also a potentially useful spatial reference. To investigate this hypothesis, we designed a set of controlled experimental configurations aimed at isolating the individual contributions of segmentation and marker presence.

To systematically evaluate these effects, we defined a set of experimental configurations, described in the following subsection.

4.2 Creation of Manipulated Subsets and Justification

The Size, Position, and Temperature Normalized subsets were derived from the original dataset (ORIG). The TAG region was manually delineated using Adobe Photoshop, producing high-precision masks that ensured geometric consistency across all subsequent manipulations.

Breast-Segmented Set (SEG). The segmented subset was defined as a complementary negative control. Images were obtained through the automatic segmentation of the breast region using a previously trained YOLO-Seg model, subsequently specialized with breast images and masks from the same dataset, removing extra-mammary thoracic tissue and consequently the TAG. This subset allows for the assessment of the impact of the strict restriction on the region of interest (ROI) on model performance in a scenario where contextual information external to the breast is eliminated.

Breast-Segmented Set with Preserved TAG (SEG+TAG). In order to dissociate the effect of ROI segmentation from the effect of marker removal, a subset was created in which automatic breast segmentation was performed while explicitly preserving the region corresponding to the TAG. For this purpose, breast segmentation masks obtained by the YOLO-Seg model were combined with manual marker masks, resulting in images where only breast tissue and the TAG are retained.

This configuration allows for the evaluation of whether the performance degradation observed in segmented scenarios arises from marker removal or from the spatial restriction to the ROI itself. Thus, the SEG+TAG subset works as an intermediate control, allowing us to analyze the effect of segmentation without removing the marker.

TAG-Removed Set (WT Without TAG). In the WT. subset, the TAG was completely removed from the original images. The marker was removed using Photoshop's Healing Brush tool, which fills the region by sampling texture and temperature from the surrounding thoracic area. This subset represents an extreme scenario in which the marker is entirely eliminated, allowing assessment of the effect of its absence on the classification process.

TAG Size-Normalized Set (FS Fixed Size). To analyze the effect of marker size, a dataset was created in which the TAG size was fixed. First, the smallest marker dimension present in the original set was identified (28×28 pixels). For each image, a square region of this size was cropped from within the original TAG. Subsequently, the original marker was removed using the Healing Brush tool, and the cropped region was reinserted in the same original position. This manipulation eliminates variability in marker size, enabling the evaluation of whether TAG scale influences the model learning process.

TAG Moved Set (MV Moved). To isolate the effect of spatial marker location, the TAG was repositioned in all images to a fixed and standardized location outside the thoracic region, in the right corner of the image. For this purpose, the marker was manually cropped, the original area reconstructed using the Healing Brush tool, and the TAG pasted into the new position. This subset allows for the evaluation of whether the anatomical position of the marker influences learning, independently of its shape or thermal signature.

TAG Temperature-Normalized Set (FT Fixed Temperature). To analyze the influence of the marker's thermal signature, pixel values corresponding to the TAG region were homogenized. A single TAG was selected as a canonical reference, and the intensity value at its central point (27.87° C) was sampled using the Eyedropper tool. This value was then applied to all pixels within the TAG mask across the remaining images, replacing the original thermal signatures. This manipulation removes thermal variability within the marker, making it possible to evaluate whether the model is sensitive to its thermal pattern.

4.3 Preprocessing, Training, and Validation Protocol

To ensure that differences between experimental subsets are due only to TAG manipulations, a standardized protocol for preprocessing, training, and evaluation was adopted. The pipeline described below, illustrated in Fig. 3, was applied identically across all configurations, keeping the model architecture, training parameters, and validation criteria fixed. This allows direct comparison between the evaluated scenarios.

Data Partitioning and Normalization. The data were split into training (60%), validation (20%), and test (20%) sets, keeping patient-level separation between them. This avoids information leakage and ensures that the models are evaluated on unseen patients.

Image normalization was performed using min–max with a $[0, 1]$ range. To prevent data leakage, the minimum and maximum values used for normalization were computed exclusively from the training set and applied to the corresponding validation and test sets.

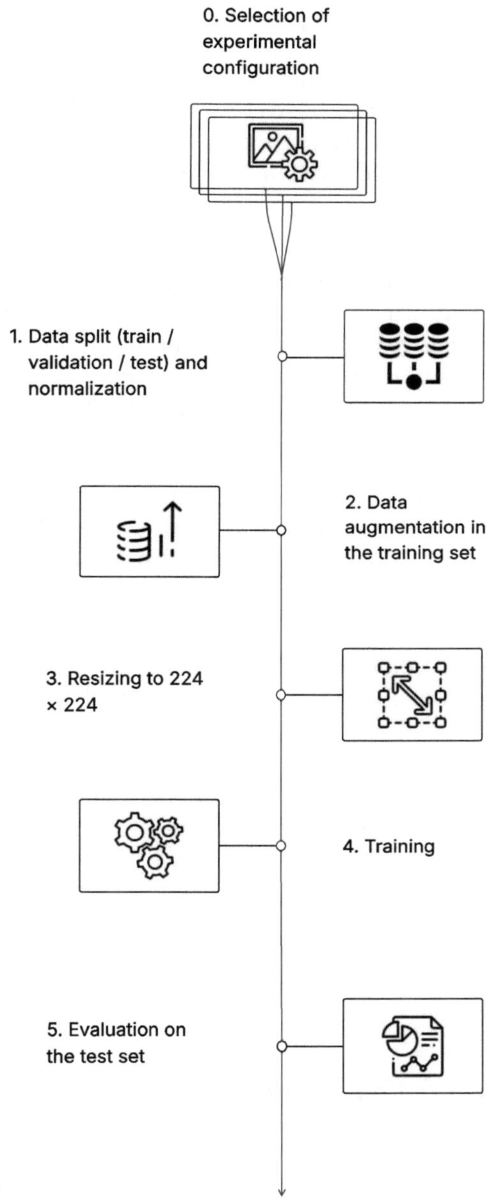

Fig. 3. Overview of the experimental pipeline.

Resizing and Data Augmentation. To standardize network input dimensions and reduce computational costs without introducing geometric distortions, all images were resized to a resolution of 224 × 224 pixels using letterbox resizing with black padding. This approach preserves the original aspect ratio, preventing deformations.

To mitigate overfitting and improve model generalization, data augmentation techniques were applied exclusively to the training set. Transformations included small-magnitude rotations, zoom, brightness variations, and horizontal flipping, which were applied with a 50% probability in conjunction with the other transformations.

Model Architecture and Training Configuration. Experiments were conducted using a VGG-16-based Convolutional Neural Network architecture, selected due to its extensive validation in the literature for medical and thermographic image classification tasks. This choice makes it easier to compare our results with previous studies and helps focus the analysis on preprocessing and marker manipulation rather than architectural changes.

The network consists of five convolutional blocks with 3×3 filters, followed by max pooling and batch normalization. The fully connected layers include two dense layers with 4096 neurons each, interleaved with dropout at a rate of 0.5 to reduce overfitting. The output layer has a single neuron with a sigmoid activation function for binary classification (healthy vs diseased).

Training and Model Selection. Training was performed using binary cross-entropy loss and the Adam optimizer, with an initial learning rate of 10^{-4}. To improve computational efficiency, experiments were conducted under a mixed precision policy and keeping the numerical stability of the loss function.

Each model was trained for up to 500 epochs, with early stopping monitoring validation loss, using a patience of 50 epochs and a minimum improvement threshold of 0.01. The model achieving the best validation performance was stored and subsequently used for evaluation on the test set.

In scenarios involving segmentation, a pre-trained YOLOv8-Seg model was previously specialized using breast images and masks for ROI segmentation and was employed to automatically segment images in the training, validation, and test sets according to the evaluated experimental configuration.

5 Computational Experiments

This section presents the computational experiments designed to evaluate, in a controlled and systematic manner, the impact of different preprocessing strategies and Anatomical Positioning Marker (TAG) manipulations on model performance. The experiments are structured to ensure direct comparability across configurations, allowing the isolation of the effects associated with each modification. We adopted multiple repetitions in each experiment to evaluate the significance of each configuration with or without the marker, which are detailed in the following subsections.

5.1 Experimental Protocol

For the purpose of comparison, initially the models were trained using the original images, without extraction of features, in other words, full images. Subsequently, the tag configurations were modified to simulate different scenarios, including the marker removed artificially or as a consequence of ROI segmentation.

The same VGG-16-based architecture was adopted, and the data partitioning, training parameters, and preprocessing steps remained the same. The goal was to observe how TAG manipulation and dataset arrangement affected the training results.

5.2 Evaluation Strategy and Repetitions

To consistently evaluate each experiment, 30 independent runs were performed for each configuration, totaling 210 executions. Distinct random seeds were adopted for both data partitioning and network weight initialization.

The evaluation metrics at the end of each run were ROC_AUC, F1-score, Recall, Precision, and Accuracy, using a fixed decision threshold of 0.5. The final results of each experiment were obtained from the model's binary predictions, using the mean of each metric. This approach was applied to reduce the influence associated with the weight initialization and data partitioning of each independent run.

5.3 Statistical Analysis Procedure

A number of independent runs were performed during the experiments. To determine whether the observed differences among the means of the experimental configurations are statistically significant, a multi-stage statistical analysis procedure was adopted. First, the normality of the metric distributions was assessed using the Shapiro–Wilk test. Results indicated that the Accuracy metric presented at least one group violating the normality assumption, whereas ROC_AUC, F1-score, Recall, and Precision satisfied this assumption across all evaluated configurations.

So, analysis of variance was applied exclusively to these four metrics, using a one-way Welch ANOVA, which is suitable for independent samples and does not require homogeneity of variances. A significance level of 5% was used.

Following the rejection of the ANOVA null hypothesis, post hoc comparisons were performed using the Games–Howell test to identify which pairs of configurations differed statistically.

6 Results and Discussion

Here, we discuss the experimental results obtained from the controlled manipulation of TAG in thermographic breast images. The analysis is conducted on two levels: (i) a global statistical assessment to verify whether the preprocessing differences significantly affect the model's performance, and (ii) a pairwise analysis to identify which specific TAG features are responsible for the observed differences.

6.1 Descriptive Performance Analysis

The means and standard deviations of the performance metrics across the 30 independent runs for each experimental setup are summarized in Table 1. A consistent performance hierarchy pattern is observed across all evaluated metrics.

Table 1. Means and standard deviations of performance metrics for different configurations. FT (TAG Temperature-Normalized Set with Fixed Temperature) and SEG+TAG (Breast-Segmented Set with Preserved TAG).

Configuration	Accuracy	Precision	Recall	F1-Score	ROC_AUC
FT	0.875 ± 0.039	0.839 ± 0.062	0.836 ± 0.097	0.833 ± 0.053	0.955 ± 0.023
Original	0.871 ± 0.045	0.823 ± 0.081	0.847 ± 0.073	0.832 ± 0.063	0.944 ± 0.024
TAG Size-Normalized	0.851 ± 0.043	0.797 ± 0.071	0.827 ± 0.087	0.807 ± 0.057	0.939 ± 0.024
SEG + TAG	0.853 ± 0.048	0.808 ± 0.077	0.806 ± 0.128	0.799 ± 0.075	0.924 ± 0.033
TAG-Moved	0.831 ± 0.039	0.780 ± 0.068	0.775 ± 0.093	0.773 ± 0.055	0.899 ± 0.039
Breast-Segmented	0.831 ± 0.053	0.791 ± 0.103	0.755 ± 0.107	0.766 ± 0.080	0.906 ± 0.040
TAG-Removed	0.825 ± 0.042	0.774 ± 0.082	0.764 ± 0.106	0.762 ± 0.060	0.905 ± 0.040

The original dataset (ORIG) and the dataset with the Fixed Temperature Marker (FT) showed the highest average values across all evaluated metrics. Conversely, the configurations in which the marker was removed (WT), spatially shifted (MV), or implicitly eliminated due to breast segmentation (SEG) consistently exhibited lower performance. Intermediate results were observed for configurations that preserve the marker under controlled conditions, such as fixed size (FS) or segmentation with marker preservation (SEG+TAG).

This initial observation suggests that the presence of TAG is positively associated with the performance of the models. However, descriptive statistics alone are not sufficient to determine whether these differences are statistically significant or if they are simply due to the inherent stochastic variability in training deep neural networks.

6.2 Global Statistical Analysis: Does the Marker Make a Difference?

To assess whether the differences between the results are statistically significant, a one-way ANOVA with Welch's correction was applied to the ROC_AUC, F1-score, Recall, and Precision values. This choice is justified by the independence of the samples and the absence of the homogeneity of variances assumption (Sect. 5).

In Table 2, the ANOVA results indicate statistically significant differences between the configurations for all four analyzed metrics ($p < 0.05$). ROC_AUC ($\eta^2 \approx 0.48$) and F1-score ($\eta^2 \approx 0.32$) show moderate to high effect sizes, suggesting a strong influence of the evaluated strategies.

Table 2. ANOVA results across the evaluated configurations.

Metric	F	df_1	df_2	p-value	η^2
ROC	13.876	6	89.687	4.25×10^{-11}	0.481
F1-Score	7.137	6	90.049	3.04×10^{-6}	0.322
Recall	4.635	6	89.930	3.79×10^{-4}	0.236
Precision	3.163	6	90.023	7.33×10^{-3}	0.174

The results indicate that the null hypothesis can be rejected, suggesting that the different configurations do not perform equally. In particular, the treatment of the TAG has a significant effect on model performance, showing that its influence cannot be explained only by random variation.

6.3 Pairwise Comparisons: Which Marker Properties Influence Performance?

Once the global null hypothesis was rejected, we conducted pairwise comparisons using the Games-Howell test. Figure 4 shows the lower triangular matrices of p-values for the F1-score and ROC_AUC metrics.

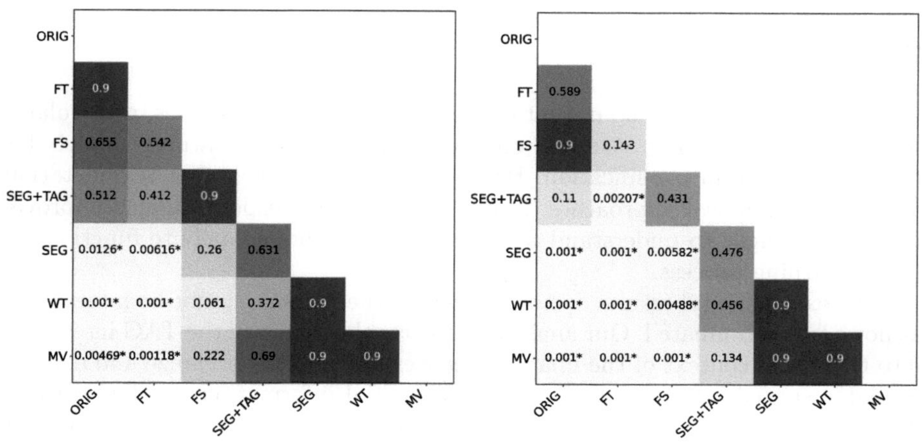

(a) F1-score.

(b) ROC_AUC.

Fig. 4. The p-values of the post hoc tests.

Presence Versus Absence of the Marker. Comparisons between configurations that preserve the TAG (ORIG, FT, FS, SEG+TAG) and those that remove or invalidate it (SEG, WT, MV) yield statistically significant differences ($p < 0.05$). By contrast, pairwise comparisons among ORIG, FT, FS, and SEG+TAG configurations rarely show statistically significant differences. This result indicates that preserving the marker is more important than maintaining its exact physical characteristics, reinforcing the idea that the TAG contributes functionally to the classification task.

Effect of Temperature and Marker Size. The lack of statistically significant differences between ORIG and FT in the metrics suggests that the specific thermal signature of the TAG is not a critical factor for the models' performance. Similarly, fixing the marker size does not result in systematic performance degradation.

These findings indicate that the model does not depend on an exact thermal pattern or a specific scale associated with the TAG, reducing concerns that the observed performance gains are due to trivial or non-physiological cues.

Effect of Marker Position: A Critical Factor. In contrast, the configurations in which the TAG was spatially displaced (MV) show statistically significant performance degradation when compared to the ORIG and FT configurations. Notably, the MV configuration often behaves similarly to the WT and SEG configurations in the pairwise analyses.

This pattern suggests that the spatial relationship between the marker and the breast anatomy plays a central role. When the marker is displaced, this relationship is lost, which reduces its usefulness as a spatial reference.

7 Conclusions

This study investigates the impact of non-physiological visual cues, particularly Anatomical Positioning Markers, on the training of deep learning models for breast thermogram classification. Based on the observation that segmentation and artifact removal approaches do not always result in performance improvements, we sought to understand whether such elements contribute functionally to the learning process.

The experimental results demonstrate that the marker cannot be interpreted as noise to be eliminated. Our analysis indicates that the way the TAG integrates into the visual context of the image influences how models organize and explore available spatial information. Particularly, spatial information was found to be more important than other physical properties, such as thermal signature or scale. Thus, the TAG's contribution relies on the geometric context of the image.

This work implies that pre-processing must be framed as a critical analytical step rather than a default filtering process. By underscoring the potential benefits of contextual elements for generalization, we extend the debate on bias, shortcut learning, and interpretability in standard benchmark datasets.

Future research aims to investigate the introduction of simplified and controlled artificial geometric references, seeking to assess whether such structural markers can replicate the effects observed with the original TAG. Future research also includes extending this analysis to other architectures and datasets to check whether these results remain consistent and to better understand how visual context affects the representations learned by the models.

Acknowledgments. This study was financed in part by the Coordenação de Aperfeiçoamento de Pessoal de Nível Superior - Brasil (CAPES) - Finance Code 001. The authors thank the financial support provided by National Council for Scientific and Technological Development – CNPq (313452/2025-3), Minas Gerais State Research Foundation – FAPEMIG, and Federal University of Juiz de Fora (UFJF). This work has been supported by High-Speed Integrated Research Network (RePesq).

Disclosure of Interests. The authors have no competing interests to declare that are relevant to the content of this article.

References

1. Webb, R.: Digital revolution: how ai is reshaping science. Nature (2025)
2. Maitra, I.K., Bandyopadhyay, S.K.: Identification of abnormal masses in digital mammogram using statistical decision making. In: Hybrid Intelligence for Image Analysis and Understanding, pp. 339–368. Wiley (2017)
3. Gonçalves, C.B., Souza, J.R., Fernandes, H.: Cnn architecture optimization using bio-inspired algorithms for breast cancer detection in infrared images. Comput. Biol. Med. **142**, 105205 (2022)
4. Saadizadeh, S.: Breast cancer detection in thermal images using glrlm algorithm. In: International Conference on Electrical, Communication, and Computer Engineering (ICECCE), pp. 1–6. Kuala Lumpur, Malaysia (2021)
5. Bandyopadhyay, S.K.: Survey on segmentation methods for locating masses in a mammogram image. Int. J. Comput. Appl. **9**(11), 25–28 (2010)
6. Salmeri, M., Mencattini, A., Rabottino, G., Accattatis, A., Lojacono, R.: Assisted breast cancer diagnosis environment: a tool for dicom mammographic images analysis. In: IEEE International Workshop on Medical Measurements and Applications, pp. 160–165 (2009) IEEE
7. Gamal, S., Atef, H., Youssef, D., Ismail, T., El-Azab, J.: Early breast cancer screening from thermography via deep pre-trained edge detection with extreme gradient boosting. In: 2023 Intelligent Methods, Systems, and Applications (IMSA), pp. 430–433 (2023)
8. Fabbrizzi, S., Papadopoulos, S., Ntoutsi, E., Kompatsiaris, I.: A survey on bias in visual datasets. Comput. Vis. Image Underst. **223**, 103552 (2022)
9. Geirhos, R., et al.: Shortcut learning in deep neural networks. Nat. Mach. Intell. **2**(11), 665–673 (2020)
10. Silva, L.F., et al.: A new database for breast research with infrared image. J. Med. Imaging Health Inform. **4**(1), 92–100 (2014)
11. Nogales, A., Pérez-Lara, F., Morales, J., García-Tejedor, Á.J.: How do thermography colors influence breast cancer diagnosis? A hybrid model of convolutional networks with a weighted average evolutionary algorithm. In: Arai, K. (ed.) Intelligent Systems and Applications. IntelliSys 2022. LNNS, vol. 543, pp. 271–281. Springer, Cham (2023). https://doi.org/10.1007/978-3-031-16078-3_17

12. Garyali, P., Ranjbar, I., Movahedi, S.: Screening of breast cancer from thermogram images by edge detection aided deep transfer learning model. In: 2022 IEEE 22nd International Conference on Bioinformatics and Bioengineering (BIBE), pp. 262–266. IEEE (2022)
13. Simonyan, K., Zisserman, A.: Very deep convolutional networks for large-scale image recognition. In: International Conference on Learning Representations (ICLR) (2015)
14. He, K., Zhang, X., Ren, S., Sun, J.: Deep residual learning for image recognition. arXiv preprint arXiv:1512.03385 (2015)
15. Zuluaga-Gomez, J.: A cnn-based methodology for breast cancer diagnosis using thermal images. Comput. Methods Biomech. Biomed. Eng.: Imaging Vis. **9**(2), 131–145 (2021)
16. Lecun, Y., Bottou, L., Bengio, Y., Haffner, P.: Gradient-based learning applied to document recognition. Proc. IEEE **86**(11), 2278–2324 (1998)
17. Shorten, C., Khoshgoftaar, T.M.: A survey on image data augmentation for deep learning. J. Big Data **6**(1), 60 (2019)
18. Lu, Y., Chen, L., Li, Y., Kim, J., Wang, Z.: Data augmentation in classification and segmentation: a survey and new strategies. J. Imaging **9**(2), 46 (2023)

Predicting Temporal Metrics in Dynamic Systems Using Machine Learning

Eduardo S. O. Marques[1], Saulo Moraes Villela[1,2](✉), Heder Soares Bernardino[1,2], and Alex Borges Vieira[1,2]

[1] Graduate Program in Computational Modeling, Federal University of Juiz de Fora, Juiz de Fora, Brazil
eduardo.santos@estudante.ufjf.br

[2] Department of Computer Science, Federal University of Juiz de Fora, Juiz de Fora, Brazil
{saulo.moraes,heder.bernardino,alex.borges}@ufjf.br

Abstract. Understanding and anticipating the behavior of dynamic systems is essential to support decision-making in complex scenarios. Time-Varying Graphs (TVGs) provide a natural representation for such systems, enabling the analysis of temporal interaction patterns. In this context, temporal centrality metrics, such as Cover Time and Time-constrained Coverage, allow the characterization of information propagation dynamics and the identification of relevant time instants. However, the computation of these metrics typically depends on the complete knowledge of future interactions, which restricts their applicability in real-time or predictive scenarios. To address this limitation, this work formulates the prediction of temporal centrality metrics as a time series forecasting problem, where past observations are used to estimate future values without requiring full knowledge of the network evolution. We evaluate four forecasting models, including Linear Regression, Elastic-Net, Multilayer Perceptron (MLP), and Temporal Convolutional Networks (TCN), using both real-world and synthetic datasets. The results show that linear models outperform neural approaches, achieving error reductions of up to 30% in terms of MAE and RMSE. These findings suggest that the temporal dynamics of the analyzed metrics can be effectively captured by low-complexity models, providing an interpretable and computationally efficient alternative for forecasting global properties in time-varying networks.

Keywords: Temporal centrality metrics · Forecasting models · Time-Varying Graphs

1 Introduction

Understanding how systems evolve over time—whether on the scale of hours, days, or years—is essential for supporting decision-making in complex scenarios such as epidemic spreading, communication networks, and human interaction

O. Gervasi et al. (Eds.): ICCSA 2026, LNCS 16768, pp. 141–156, 2027.
https://doi.org/10.1007/978-3-032-30488-9_9

systems. These systems are often characterized by emergent collective phenomena, in which global dynamics cannot be fully explained solely by the properties of individual components.

In the context of complex networks, analyzing such systems requires specialized tools, conceptual frameworks, and interpretations of quantitative results [1]. Complex systems are widely applied across domains such as biology, social sciences, and engineering, where different systems may share common structural and dynamical patterns despite their distinct nature [2].

Network metrics play a central role in this analysis, as they enable the characterization of structural and dynamical properties. In particular, metrics that incorporate the temporal dimension allow not only identifying relevant entities but also determining when interventions are most effective. For instance, in epidemiological scenarios, disease spreading depends not only on biological factors but also on the temporal organization of human contacts [3]. Therefore, understanding how the structure of contact networks evolves over time is essential to anticipate how such processes unfold.

Time-Varying Graphs (TVGs) provide a natural framework to model these systems by explicitly representing temporal interactions. Within this framework, temporal centrality metrics allow identifying not only the most relevant nodes but also critical moments in the network dynamics. In this work, we focus on two representative temporal centrality metrics: Cover Time (CT), which measures how quickly a node can reach all others, and Time-constrained Coverage (TCC), which quantifies the fraction of nodes reached within a limited time window. These metrics are particularly useful for capturing how quickly information or influence can propagate through the network [4].

However, the computation of these metrics depends on the availability of future interactions in the network. In practical scenarios, such information is inherently unavailable, making the direct application of these metrics in real-time or decision-support contexts challenging [5]. Most existing approaches address this limitation by focusing on predicting links, node states, or reconstructing the future topology of the network [6]. While effective, these strategies introduce additional complexity and often require modeling fine-grained network dynamics.

In this context, machine learning techniques—particularly time-series forecasting methods—offer a promising alternative by enabling the estimation of future values of these metrics based solely on past observations, without requiring explicit reconstruction of future network topology [7]. This perspective allows shifting the problem from predicting individual connections to forecasting aggregate structural properties.

In this work, we propose to model the temporal evolution of centrality metrics in TVGs as a time-series forecasting problem. Instead of reconstructing the network, our approach directly targets global structural metrics by predicting global metrics, such as CT and TCC, based solely on historical observations. We evaluate four forecasting models—Linear Regression, ElasticNet, Multilayer Perceptron (MLP), and Temporal Convolutional Networks (TCN)—using both a real-world dataset of hospital contact interactions and synthetic temporal networks [4,8]. The main contributions of this work are:

- The formulation of temporal centrality estimation as a time-series forecasting problem, avoiding the need for future network reconstruction;
- A comparative evaluation of four forecasting models applied to temporal centrality metrics;
- An experimental analysis using both real-world and synthetic datasets, highlighting the relationship between data characteristics and model performance;
- Evidence that low-complexity linear models can outperform deep learning approaches in this context, achieving significant reductions in prediction errors;

Experimental results show that linear models consistently outperform the neural architectures, achieving reductions of up to 30% in MAE and RMSE. These findings indicate that the temporal dynamics of the evaluated metrics can be effectively captured by low-complexity models, providing an interpretable and computationally efficient alternative for forecasting global properties of time-varying networks under partial information.

2 Background

This section introduces the fundamental concepts that underpin this study, covering the structure and dynamics of time-varying graphs, as well as temporal centrality metrics.

2.1 Time-Varying Graphs

A graph is defined as an ordered pair $G = (V, E)$, where V represents the set of vertices (nodes) and E the set of edges that connect pairs of vertices. The edges can be directed or undirected and may be weighted, representing costs, distances, or interaction intensities [9].

In many real systems, the interactions between elements do not remain constant over time. To capture this dynamic behavior, the Time-Varying Graph (TVG) model is used, in which the network topology can evolve over time. Intuitively, a TVG can be interpreted as an ordered sequence of static graphs, each representing a distinct point in time, also called a snapshot [5]. This representation allows for explicitly modeling the temporal order of interactions, a fundamental aspect for the analysis of dynamic processes in networks. Formally, a TVG can be represented as an object $H = (V, E, T)$, where V is the set of vertices, T is the set of time instants considered, and E is the set of edges that connect vertices associated with different time instants [10].

In this work, TVGs are modeled as Multi-Aspect Graphs (MAGs) [11], a general structure capable of representing multilayer, dynamic, and temporal networks. A MAG is defined as an object $H = (A, E)$, where A is a finite list of sets called aspects, and E is the set of edges. In the specific case of a TVG, two main aspects are considered: the vertices and the time instants, that is, $|A| = 2$. Thus, the model can be represented as $H = (V, E, T)$, maintaining formal equivalence with the classical definition of TVGs.

From this modeling, the concept of a temporal node is defined as an ordered pair (u, t), where $u \in V(H)$ and $t \in T(H)$. The set of all temporal nodes is given by the Cartesian product $VT(H) = V(H) \times T(H)$. This representation allows one to demonstrate that a TVG modeled as a MAG is isomorphic to a static directed graph [12]. This result enables the direct application of classical metrics and algorithms for directed graphs to the analysis of structural properties and dynamic processes in time-varying networks.

2.2 Temporal Centrality Metrics

In time-varying networks, the significance of a dynamic process depends not only on where it begins, but also on when it initiates. In various real-world scenarios—such as the spread of epidemics, the diffusion of information in social networks, or the dissemination of failures in complex systems—the specific point in time at which a process is triggered can decisively influence its speed, reach, and impact [5]. In this context, temporal centrality metrics emerge as a natural extension of traditional centrality measures used in static graphs, shifting the focus from the importance of vertices to the relative importance of moments in time.

While classical centrality metrics produce a ranking of vertices according to different structural criteria—such as degree, closeness, or betweenness—temporal centrality metrics establish a ranking of time instants that reflects the potential of each moment to influence the evolution of dynamic processes in the network [13]. Different definitions of temporal centrality, therefore, capture distinct notions of time-associated importance and are suitable for various types of applications and analytical objectives.

Temporal metrics do not depend solely on the network's state at a single point in time but also on its evolution over time. Consider a TVG $H = (V, E, T)$, as defined in Sect. 2.1, where $T(H)$ represents the set of time instants in the graph. Let $N = |T(H)|$ be the total number of time points considered and $T(H) = \{t_0, t_1, \ldots, t_{N-1}\}$ the ordered temporal sequence of these instants. For each instant $t_i \in T(H)$, temporal centrality metrics assess the potential impact of processes initiated at that moment, taking into account not only the topology of the graph at t_i but also the connections established in subsequent instants [5].

The temporal centrality metrics adopted in this work were originally proposed by [4] and are particularly suitable for characterizing both the speed and reach of diffusion processes in time-varying graphs. While Cover Time emphasizes the number of temporal steps needed to reach a predefined fraction of the network, Time-constrained Coverage evaluates the fraction of nodes reached under a fixed temporal constraint. In both cases, the metric values depend not only on the network configuration at the initial instant t_i but also on its future evolution, reflecting the dynamic diffusion potential associated with different process start times. This temporal dependence allows the metric values to be modeled as time series over the instants t_i, which are explored in the following sections for dataset construction and the evaluation of forecasting models.

The Cover Time metric (CT) measures the minimum number of time instants (or steps) required for a diffusion process to reach a given fraction of nodes in the network [4]. The metric $CT(t_i, \tau)$ returns the average number of time instants (steps) across all nodes for a diffusion, starting at instant t_i, to reach a certain fraction τ of the network, and is represented by:

$$CT(t_i, \tau) = \begin{cases} \frac{1}{|V(H))|} \sum_{u \in V(H)} d_t(t_i, u, \tau), & \text{if } \tau \text{ is reached,} \\ \infty, & \text{otherwise,} \end{cases} \tag{1}$$

where $d_t(t_i, u, \tau)$ is the number of time instants (steps) required for a diffusion, starting at node u at instant t_i, to reach a fraction τ of the nodes. If the fraction τ of nodes is not reached for a diffusion process that starts at any node at instant t_i, then $CT(t_i, \tau)$ is considered to be ∞.

It is assumed that the diffusion process follows a breadth-first search; that is, a generic node (u, t_i) starts the diffusion by sending information to all its adjacent nodes. Then, the adjacent temporal nodes retransmit information to their own adjacent nodes in the next time instant, and so on. The information is spread until the fraction τ of nodes is reached, and the time required for diffusion is recorded. This evaluation is repeated for each node $(u, t_i) \in VT(H)$. The average diffusion time is the cover time centrality of the time instant t_i.

The Time-constrained Coverage metric (TCC) evaluates the network coverage achieved by a diffusion process after a limited number of time steps [4]. For a given time instant t_i, $TCC(t_i, \Phi)$ returns the average fraction of TVG nodes reached by the diffusion process in Φ time steps, and is represented by:

$$TCC(t_i, \Phi) = \frac{1}{|V(H))|^2} \sum_{u \in V(H)} d_t(t_i, u, \Phi) \tag{2}$$

where $d_c(t_i, u, \Phi)$ is the number of nodes reached from node u after Φ time steps, when the diffusion starts at instant t_i. For this problem, the same diffusion process defined for the CT metric is considered.

3 Related Work

The modeling of complex systems using TVGs has been widely investigated in the literature as a means of representing structural dynamics that cannot be adequately captured by static graphs. Foundational works have established the theoretical basis for the analysis of temporal networks, including formal definitions, structural properties, and time-aware metrics [5,10]. In this context, several classical complex network metrics have been extended to the temporal domain, emphasizing that the order, duration, and frequency of interactions play a fundamental role in network dynamics [14,15].

Several studies explore temporal networks to analyze patterns of contact, mobility, and the diffusion of processes, especially in scenarios involving human interaction and epidemiology [16]. However, most of these approaches focus on descriptive analyses or on simulating dynamic processes over the network, devoting little attention to the predictive modeling of the temporal evolution of structural metrics derived from these representations.

Surveys such as [17] and [18] provide comprehensive overviews of methods for dynamic graph representation learning, including recurrent, attention-based, and continuous-time models. Architectures such as Temporal Graph Networks (TGN) and Temporal Graph Attention Networks (TGAT) have been proposed to model complex temporal dependencies in evolving graphs, achieving strong performance in tasks like link prediction and node classification [19,20].

In the field of dynamic network estimation and construction, methods based on regularized logistic regression with temporal smoothing were developed to infer graphs that evolve over time [21]. Later works extended this line of research to online and non-stationary scenarios, formulating the learning of TVGs as composite optimization problems that balance fidelity to observed data, structural sparsity, and temporal smoothness [22].

With the rise of machine learning techniques, particularly deep learning, a large body of work has focused on learning representations from dynamic graphs. Works have explored spatiotemporal forecasting in graph-structured data, where the goal is to predict signals associated with nodes over time. For example, models such as Dyn-GWN explicitly incorporate dynamic graph structures into time series forecasting frameworks [23]. Additionally, reinforcement learning approaches have been employed to identify optimal strategies for information diffusion in temporal networks, demonstrating the predictive potential of temporal and structural patterns [24].

Despite these advances, the majority of existing approaches focus on predicting either the graph topology (e.g., link prediction) or node-level signals. In contrast, the prediction of global structural metrics in temporal networks remains relatively underexplored. In particular, temporal centrality measures, which capture the importance of nodes considering the temporal dimension of interactions, have been widely studied from an analytical perspective but are rarely addressed in a predictive setting.

In this work, we address this gap by formulating the prediction of temporal centrality metrics as a supervised time series regression problem. Instead of reconstructing the network topology or relying on complex graph neural architectures, we model the temporal evolution of these metrics directly using lagged features. This approach enables capturing temporal dependencies in a simple, interpretable, and computationally efficient manner, while providing competitive predictive performance. By focusing on global structural properties rather than local or topological reconstruction tasks, our work complements existing literature and offers a novel perspective on forecasting in time-varying graphs.

4 Materials and Methods

This section describes the materials and methods adopted in this study, including the datasets used, the modeling of time-varying graphs, the computation of temporal centrality metrics, the transformation of data into time series, and the forecasting models employed.

Figure 1 presents an overview of the proposed methodology. The process begins with the acquisition of raw temporal interaction data, followed by its modeling as TVGs. Temporal centrality metrics are then computed at each time instant, generating time series that represent the evolution of the network dynamics. These series are transformed into a supervised learning format using lagged features, enabling the application of forecasting models. Finally, the predictions are evaluated using linear and neural models.

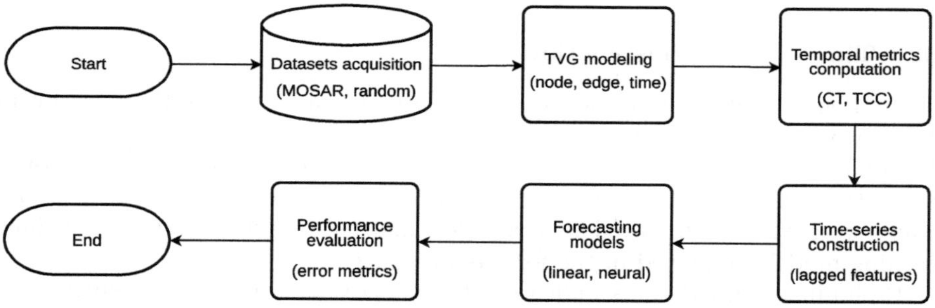

Fig. 1. Overview of the proposed methodology.

4.1 Datasets

The evaluation of temporal centrality metrics was carried out using a temporal graph (TVG) dataset collected in the context of the MOSAR project [8]. MOSAR (Mastering hOSpital Antimicrobial Resistance and its spread) is an international scientific collaboration initiative focused on analyzing the dynamics of transmission of antimicrobial-resistant bacteria in hospital environments. The dataset consists of records of face-to-face contacts between individuals—including healthcare professionals, staff, and patients—collected in a medical ward over two weeks, from July 25 to August 8, 2009.

In total, 160 volunteers participated in the study, each equipped with an RFID (Radio Frequency Identification) device capable of detecting other devices within an approximate radius of one meter. Contacts were recorded with a 30-second temporal granularity, enabling the inference of face-to-face interactions and the construction of network topology at each point in time.

The dataset was modeled as a TVG $M = (V, E, T)$, as defined in Sect. 2.1, where $V(M)$ represents the set of participants, $E(M)$ the face-to-face contacts, and $T(M)$ the discretized time instants. In this context, $|V(M)| = 160$ and $|T(M)| = 40320$. The contacts were represented by undirected edges, modeled by including a directed edge and its reciprocal.

In addition to the real TVG, the metrics were also evaluated on a random TVG $R = (V, E, T)$, used as a synthetic reference for comparison. Each time instant corresponds to an independent Erdős–Rényi graph $G(n, p)$, maintaining the same number of vertices as the MOSAR TVG ($n = 160$) and considering $|T(R)| = 800$ time instants. The probability of edge creation was defined as $p = 0.01 \times \frac{\ln n}{n}$, ensuring a level of sparsity similar to that observed in the real network and mostly disconnected graphs, according to the classical connectivity threshold in random networks [25].

For both datasets, temporal metrics were calculated at each time instant, yielding time series that were later used in the forecasting stage. In this work, the results presented focus only on the finite values of the CT metric.

4.2 Time-Series Construction

The temporal centrality metrics were calculated at each discrete time instant in the network, yielding time series for the CT and TCC metrics. For this purpose, Python code was developed to generate the TVGs and calculate the corresponding metrics at each network snapshot. Next, only the time instants and metric values were extracted, stored in `.csv` files, and used as input for the machine learning models employed in the forecasting stage.

Preliminary experiments indicated that using time alone as the explanatory variable was insufficient to capture the dynamics of the analyzed metrics. In such cases, the models tended to learn only an approximately linear average trend, resulting in low predictive power. Given this limitation, the problem was reformulated as a time-series forecasting task using lagged features. This approach transforms the problem into a supervised format, in which past values of the series itself are used as explanatory variables for forecasting future values [26]. Furthermore, this strategy allows capturing nonlinear temporal relationships without imposing explicit assumptions of stationarity or linearity, and is widely adopted in machine learning models applied to time series [27].

Formally, let $y(t)$ be the result of a temporal centrality metric at a discrete instant t. For a given window size k, an attribute vector is constructed from the k immediately preceding values of the series. The prediction problem is then formulated as:

$$y(t+1) = f\big(y(t), y(t-1), \ldots, y(t-k+1)\big), \tag{3}$$

where $f(\cdot)$ represents a machine learning model trained to map the past values of the metric to its future value. The parameter k controls the amount of historical information provided to the model and directly influences its ability to capture short- and medium-term temporal dependencies. This formulation ensures that only information available up to instant t is used to predict $y(t+1)$, thus avoiding any form of temporal data leakage, as recommended in best practices for time series predictive modeling [26].

Additionally, the separation between the training and test sets was carried out strictly in accordance with the temporal order of the data, so that the models were trained exclusively on past observations and evaluated on future instants, ensuring the validity of the evaluation process. By reformulating the problem in this way, it became possible to explicitly explore the temporal dependencies inherent to the temporal centrality metrics, resulting in significant gains in the predictive capacity of the models employed.

4.3 Datasets Parameters and Time Series Construction

The parameters used to construct the MOSAR and random datasets were defined based on previous studies to ensure methodological consistency and comparability of results [4]. For both networks, a fixed temporal window size of 30 time instants was adopted, which defines the resolution of the snapshots and the aggregation of events over time.

Not all available time instants were considered in the evaluation stage to ensure that the diffusion processes had a sufficiently wide temporal window to propagate throughout the TVGs, thereby avoiding truncation effects. For the MOSAR dataset, the parameters $\tau = 0.6$ and $\Phi = 2000$ were adopted, considering the first 33,000 time instants, although the network contains 40320 in total. Similarly, for the random dataset, the parameters $\tau = 0.6$ and $\Phi = 100$ were used, restricting the analysis to the first 660 instants out of a total of 800. The temporal centrality metrics were calculated at each time instant, yielding a time series.

To evaluate the time series using forecasting models, temporal windows of size k were used. The values were empirically set to $k = 15$ for the MOSAR and $k = 20$ for the random dataset, and were kept constant across both metrics in each network. Finally, the series was normalized to standardize the value scales and facilitate the learning process. The division between the training and test sets strictly preserved the temporal order of the data, with 80% of the initial observations used for training and the remaining 20% for testing.

4.4 Configuration and Evaluation of Prediction Models

The time series results were evaluated using different machine learning models for forecasting, including Linear Regression, Elastic Net, Multi-layer Perceptron (MLP), and Temporal Convolutional Network (TCN). All experiments were implemented in Python (version 3.12), using the Google Colab environment.

Additional models were also investigated during the exploratory phase, including ARIMA, SARIMAX, Long Short-Term Memory (LSTM) networks, Random Forest, Gradient Boosting, and Support Vector Machines (SVM). However, these approaches did not achieve satisfactory performance in the analyzed context, either due to limited predictive capability, instability in the results, or difficulty in adequately capturing the temporal dependencies of the studied metrics. Therefore, the results presented in this work focus on the models that demonstrated the best performance and greater consistency.

The quantitative evaluation of model performance was carried out using metrics widely employed in the regression and time series forecasting literature, namely: coefficient of determination (R^2), adjusted coefficient of determination (R^2_{adj}), mean absolute error (MAE), mean squared error (MSE), root mean squared error (RMSE), and mean absolute percentage error (MAPE). These metrics enable performance analysis from different perspectives, accounting for both the magnitude and variability of errors.

Hyperparameter selection aimed to balance predictive capacity, complexity control, and stability of results, guided by best practices reported in the literature and preliminary experiments. Linear Regression was used as the reference model, with intercept and tolerance set to 10^{-6}. The Elastic Net model was employed as a regularized extension of linear regression, combining ℓ_1 and ℓ_2 penalties with parameters $\alpha = 10^{-4}$ and $l_1\_ratio = 0.1$, aiming to reduce the risk of overfitting and handle possible feature correlations.

MLP was adopted to capture nonlinear relationships among temporal lags, with two fully connected hidden layers of 64 and 32 neurons, respectively, a ReLU activation function, and a linear output layer. Training was performed with the Adam optimizer, a learning rate of 10^{-3}, and an MSE loss function, and early stopping was used to mitigate overfitting. The TCN was used to explore local temporal patterns via one-dimensional causal convolutions, thereby preserving temporal causality. The architecture consists of two convolutional layers with 32 and 16 filters, respectively, each with a kernel size of 3, followed by a fully connected output layer. As with the MLP, training was performed with the Adam optimizer and the MSE loss function.

5 Results

This section presents the results obtained from applying machine learning models to forecast temporal centrality metrics. The analysis is conducted considering both the real MOSAR dataset and a synthetic random dataset.

5.1 MOSAR Dataset

Figure 2 presents the comparison between the actual values and the forecasts generated by the models for the CT metric, while Table 1 summarizes the quantitative performance. All models achieved high coefficients of determination ($R^2 > 0.9996$). The Linear model obtained the lowest MAE (1.3488) and MSE (14.0302), followed by the MLP and ElasticNet models. The TCN model presented higher error values compared to the other approaches.

For the TCC metric, the results are presented in Fig. 3 and Table 2. All models achieved high predictive performance, with R^2 values above 0.9997. The Linear model achieved the lowest error values, followed closely by the TCN model. The MLP and ElasticNet models presented slightly higher errors.

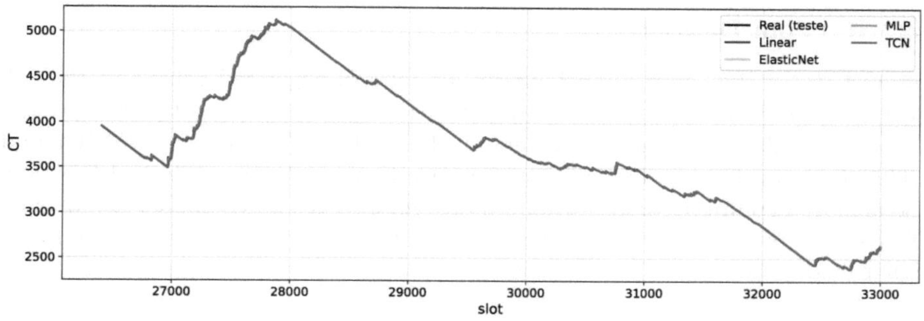

Fig. 2. Predictions from the models for the CT metric of the MOSAR dataset.

Table 1. Simulation results for the CT metric of the MOSAR dataset.

Model	R^2	MAE	MSE	R^2_{adj}	MAPE	RMSE
Linear	**0.999973**	**1.348768**	**14.030166**	**0.999973**	**0.000371**	**3.745686**
MLP	0.999917	3.698706	43.292463	0.999917	0.001015	6.579701
ElasticNet	0.999829	5.689566	89.036372	0.999829	0.001570	9.435909
TCN	0.999624	9.078452	195.793738	0.999623	0.002500	13.992632

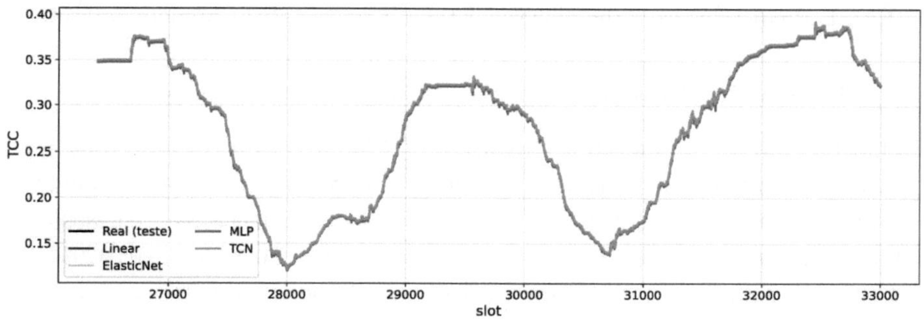

Fig. 3. Predictions from the models for the TCC metric of the MOSAR dataset.

Table 2. Simulation results for the TCC metric of the MOSAR dataset.

Model	R^2	MAE	MSE	R^2_{adj}	MAPE	RMSE
Linear	**0.999930**	**0.000270**	**4.568998e-07**	**0.999929**	**0.001150**	**0.000676**
MLP	0.999762	0.001073	1.544978e-06	0.999762	0.004080	0.001243
ElasticNet	0.999771	0.000659	1.489974e-06	0.999770	0.002782	0.001221
TCN	0.999869	0.000617	8.534101e-07	0.999868	0.002220	0.000924

5.2 Random Dataset

Figure 4 shows the comparison between actual and predicted values for the CT metric, while Table 3 presents the quantitative results. For the CT metric, the Linear and ElasticNet models achieved the highest R^2 values (0.979564 and 0.979236, respectively), along with the lowest error metrics. The MLP model also achieved competitive performance, although with slightly higher errors. The TCN model presented significantly lower performance, with $R^2 = 0.687641$ and higher error values.

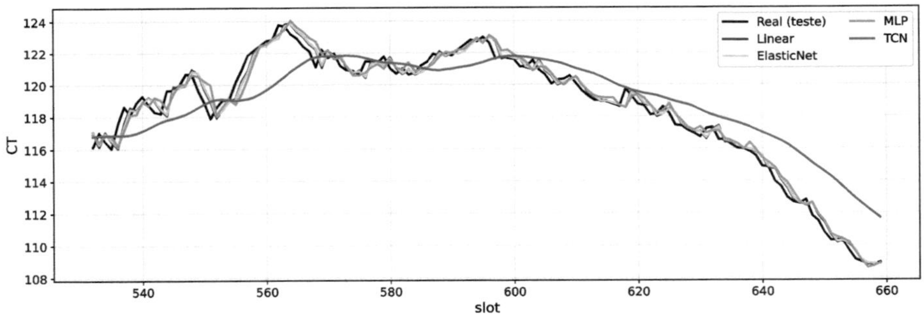

Fig. 4. Predictions from the models for the CT metric of the random dataset.

Table 3. Simulation results for the CT metric of the random dataset.

Model	R^2	MAE	MSE	R^2_{adj}	MAPE	RMSE
Linear	**0.979564**	**0.418950**	**0.284968**	**0.975745**	**0.003526**	**0.533824**
MLP	0.971709	0.493089	0.394507	0.966421	0.004158	0.628098
ElasticNet	0.979236	0.421180	0.289542	0.975355	0.003547	0.538091
TCN	0.687641	1.691775	4.355762	0.629256	0.014488	2.087046

For the TCC metric, the results are shown in Table 4 and Fig. 5. The ElasticNet model achieved the best performance, followed closely by the Linear model. The MLP and TCN models showed lower predictive accuracy, with higher error values across all evaluated metrics.

Table 4. Simulation results for the TCC metric of the random dataset.

Model	R^2	MAE	MSE	R^2_{adj}	MAPE	RMSE
Linear	0.946844	0.005697	0.000049	0.936908	0.014334	0.007029
MLP	0.886079	0.008413	0.000106	0.864785	0.021127	0.010290
ElasticNet	**0.949571**	**0.005524**	**0.000047**	**0.940145**	**0.013900**	**0.006847**
TCN	0.867562	0.009274	0.000123	0.842807	0.023401	0.011095

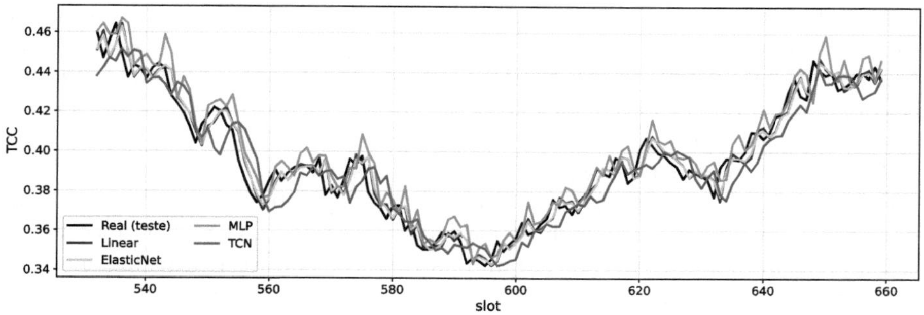

Fig. 5. Predictions from the models for the TCC metric of the random dataset.

6 Discussion

The results reveal distinct behaviors depending on the dataset characteristics and the evaluated temporal centrality metric. For the MOSAR dataset, all models achieved extremely high predictive performance, with R^2 values close to 1. This suggests that the temporal evolution of both CT and TCC metrics follows well-defined and stable patterns. In this context, linear models were sufficient to accurately capture these dynamics, outperforming more complex approaches such as MLP and TCN in terms of error minimization.

A possible explanation for this behavior lies in the structural properties of the MOSAR network, which may induce smoother and more predictable temporal relationships. As a consequence, increasing model complexity does not necessarily translate into performance gains, and may even introduce unnecessary variance.

In contrast, the random dataset exhibited a different behavior. Although linear models still achieved the best overall results, their performance was significantly lower compared to the MOSAR dataset, especially for the CT metric. This indicates that the temporal dynamics in random networks are less structured and more irregular, making them inherently more difficult to predict.

Furthermore, the poor performance of the TCN model in the random dataset suggests that deep temporal architectures are not universally suitable for this type of problem. This may be related to the absence of strong temporal dependencies or patterns that can be effectively exploited by convolutional structures.

Overall, the results highlight the importance of aligning model complexity with the underlying characteristics of the data. Simpler models not only achieved competitive or superior performance but also offer advantages in terms of interpretability and computational efficiency.

These findings have practical implications. In real-world applications where computational efficiency and interpretability are critical—such as monitoring dynamic systems or supporting decision-making—simpler models may provide a more reliable and cost-effective solution. This is particularly relevant when rapid predictions are required without access to future network information.

Despite these contributions, this study has some limitations. The analysis is restricted to two types of datasets and a specific set of temporal centrality metrics (CT and TCC). Additionally, the forecasting models were evaluated under a fixed experimental setup, which may not capture all possible configurations or parameter optimizations.

Future work may extend this approach by considering additional types of networks, including more heterogeneous and large-scale systems, as well as exploring other temporal metrics and hybrid modeling strategies. Moreover, integrating domain-specific knowledge or combining statistical and deep learning methods may further improve predictive performance in more complex scenarios.

7 Conclusion

This work investigated the feasibility of forecasting temporal centrality metrics in TVGs using machine learning models, considering both a real-world dataset (MOSAR) and a synthetic random network. The analyzed metrics (Cover Time and Time-constrained Coverage) enabled the assessment of the predictability of global dynamic properties across different temporal network structures.

The main contribution of the study lies in the formulation of temporal centrality prediction as a supervised time series forecasting problem, where lagged features are used to model temporal dependencies without requiring explicit knowledge of future network evolution. This perspective shifts the focus from predicting network topology or local interactions to forecasting global structural properties, providing a simple, interpretable, and computationally efficient alternative to more complex graph-based approaches.

Experimental results demonstrated that linear and regularized models, particularly Linear Regression and ElasticNet, consistently outperformed more complex neural architectures, achieving reductions of up to 30% in MAE and RMSE. These findings suggest that the temporal dynamics of the evaluated metrics exhibit patterns that can be effectively captured by low-complexity models, even in networks with evolving structures.

Overall, the proposed approach enables the estimation of relevant temporal network properties using only past observations, which is particularly valuable in scenarios where future interactions are inherently unknown, such as real-time monitoring of contact networks. This capability can support decision-making processes by providing timely insights into the evolution of information diffusion dynamics.

The study reinforces the importance of matching model complexity to the intrinsic characteristics of the data, showing that simpler approaches may be preferable even in dynamic and structured contexts such as temporal networks. For future work, we intend to extend the evaluation to a broader range of real-world temporal networks, incorporate additional metrics, and investigate more advanced validation strategies, such as statistical significance testing and cross-dataset generalization. Furthermore, exploring hybrid approaches that combine time series forecasting with graph-based learning methods may provide additional insights into the modeling of complex temporal systems.

Acknowledgments. This study was financed in part by the Coordenação de Aperfeiçoamento de Pessoal de Nível Superior – Brasil (CAPES) – Finance Code 001. The authors would also like to thank the Federal University of Juiz de Fora (UFJF) for the institutional and scientific support provided throughout this research.

Disclosure of Interests. The authors have no competing interests to declare that are relevant to the content of this article.

References

1. Amaral, L.A., Ottino, J.M.: Complex networks: augmenting the framework for the study of complex systems. Eur. Phys. J. B **38**(2), 147–162 (2004)
2. Ma'ayan, A.: Complex systems biology. J. R. Soc. Interface **14**(134), 20170391 (2017)
3. Salathé, M., Freifeld, C.C., Mekaru, S.R., Tomasulo, A.F., Brownstein, J.S.: Influenza a (h7n9) and the importance of digital epidemiology. N. Engl. J. Med. **369**(5), 401 (2013)
4. Costa, E.C., Vieira, A.B., Wehmuth, K., Ziviani, A., Da Silva, A.P.C.: Time centrality in dynamic complex networks. Adv. Complex Syst. **18**(07n08), 1550023 (2015)
5. Holme, P., Saramäki, J.: Temporal networks. Phys. Rep. **519**(3), 97–125 (2012)
6. Lü, L., Zhou, T.: Link prediction in complex networks: a survey. XXPhys. A **390**(6), 1150–1170 (2011)
7. Box, G.E., Jenkins, G.M., Reinsel, G.C., Ljung, G.M.: Time Series Analysis: Forecasting and Control. Wiley, Hoboken (2015)
8. Lucet, J.C., et al.: Electronic sensors for assessing interactions between healthcare workers and patients under airborne precautions. PLoS ONE **7**(5), e37893 (2012)
9. Newman, M., Barabási, A.L., Watts, D.J.: The Structure and Dynamics of Networks. Princeton University Press (2011)
10. Casteigts, A., Flocchini, P., Quattrociocchi, W., Santoro, N.: Time-varying graphs and dynamic networks. IJPEDS **27**(5), 387–408 (2012)
11. Wehmuth, K., Fleury, É., Ziviani, A.: On multiaspect graphs. Theoret. Comput. Sci. **651**, 50–61 (2016)
12. Wehmuth, K., Ziviani, A., Fleury, E.: A unifying model for representing time-varying graphs. In: Proceedings of the 2015 IEEE International Conference on Data Science and Advanced Analytics (DSAA), pp. 1–10 (2015)
13. Kim, H., Anderson, R.: Temporal node centrality in complex networks. Phys. Rev. E-Stat. Nonlinear, Soft Matter Phys. **85**(2), 026107 (2012)
14. Holme, P.: Modern temporal network theory: a colloquium. Eur. Phys. J. B **88**(9), 1–30 (2015)
15. Battiston, F., et al.: Networks beyond pairwise interactions: structure and dynamics. Phys. Rep. **874**, 1–92 (2020)
16. Isella, L., Stehlé, J., Barrat, A., Cattuto, C., Pinton, J.F., Van den Broeck, W.: What's in a crowd? analysis of face-to-face behavioral networks. J. Theor. Biol. **271**(1), 166–180 (2011)
17. Kazemi, S.M., et al.: Representation learning for dynamic graphs: a survey. J. Mach. Learn. Res. **21**(70), 1–73 (2020)
18. Khoshraftar, S., An, A.: A survey on graph representation learning methods. ACM Trans. Intell. Syst. Technol. **15**(1), 1–55 (2024)

19. Rossi, E., Chamberlain, B., Frasca, F., Eynard, D., Monti, F., Bronstein, M.: Temporal graph networks for deep learning on dynamic graphs. arXiv preprint arXiv:2006.10637 (2020)
20. Xu, D., Ruan, C., Korpeoglu, E., Kumar, S., Achan, K.: Inductive representation learning on temporal graphs. arXiv preprint arXiv:2002.07962 (2020)
21. Kolar, M., Song, L., Ahmed, A., Xing, E.P.: Estimating time-varying networks. Ann. Appl. Stat. 94–123 (2010)
22. Natali, A., Isufi, E., Coutino, M., Leus, G.: Learning time-varying graphs from online data. IEEE Open J. Signal Process. **3**, 212–228 (2022)
23. Ibrahim, S., Tell, M., Mazumder, R.: Dyn-gwn: time-series forecasting using time-varying graphs with applications to finance and traffic prediction. In: Proceedings of the Fourth ACM International Conference on AI in Finance, pp. 167–175 (2023)
24. Mendonça, M.R., Barreto, A.M., Ziviani, A.: Efficient information diffusion in time-varying graphs through deep reinforcement learning. World Wide Web **25**(6), 2535–2560 (2022)
25. Erdős, P., Rényi, A.: On the evolution of random graphs. Publ. Math. Inst. Hung. Acad. Sci. **5**, 17–61 (1960)
26. Hyndman, R.J., Athanasopoulos, G.: Forecasting: principles and practice. OTexts (2018)
27. Franklin, J.: The elements of statistical learning: data mining, inference and prediction. Math. Intell. **27**(2), 83–85 (2005)

Implementation of an Orchestrated Multi-agent System for PPCP in Textile MSMEs: A Prompt Engineering Approach

Gabriel R. B. da Silva(✉), Itamir de M. B. Filho, André M. Gurgel, Lhayana V. de Macedo, Suellen R. B. Ferraz, Beatriz S. de Moura, Ramon S. Malaquias, and Jean M. M. Lima

Digital Metropolis Institute (IMD), Federal University of Rio Grande do Norte (UFRN), Natal, Brazil
{gabriel.ribeiro.099,suellen.ferraz.113,beatriz.moura.116}@ufrn.edu.br, {itamir.filho,jean.lima}@imd.ufrn.br, andre.gurgel@ufrn.br, lhayana11@gmail.com, ramon@nutit.com.br
https://www.metropoledigital.ufrn.br/portal/

Abstract. The textile sector, especially Micro, Small and Medium Enterprises (MSMEs), faces high pressure to operate efficiently and flexibly. Conventional manufacturing setups do not allow real-time rescheduling with traditional PPCP systems. Moreover, monolithic LLM-based approaches frequently suffer from arithmetic hallucinations and high inference latency. To address this gap, the current paper proposes a multi-agent architecture orchestrated by LangGraph in order to compute a solution for dynamic PPCP. Empirical results showed that the approach can completely eliminate arithmetic hallucinations with 100% accuracy while significantly reducing inference time and token usage by 79% and 75% respectively. The software allows for flexible processing of unstructured orders, optimizes setups and uses a decision support system for dynamic reallocation of operators. The current system democratizes Industry 4.0 technology for MSMEs, unlocking smart and resilient management of manufacturing.

Keywords: Large Language Models · Textile · Production Planning and Control Processes · Multi-Agent Systems · MSMEs · Artificial Intelligence · Workload Balancing · Optimization Algorithms · Prompt Engineering

1 Introduction

The intensification of global competition and demand volatility impose on manufacturing industries the need for rigorous Production Planning and Control Processes (PPCP). In practice, PPCP operates in complex and dynamic operational scenarios, being responsible for coordinating the shop floor, optimizing work order sequencing, and managing finite resources, such as fluctuations in workforce availability and equipment failures [22,23].

O. Gervasi et al. (Eds.): ICCSA 2026, LNCS 16768, pp. 157–172, 2027.
https://doi.org/10.1007/978-3-032-30488-9_10

As analyzed by Gereffi and Frederick [8], in the textile industry, fast fashion requires the continuous launch of products in a large variety of styles and small lots, unlike traditional approach which relied on replenishment of basic items. Due to this, there occur very short lifecycles of the products and high operational volatility. As a result of this operation model and the repercussions of the financial crisis after 2008, the economic pressure on the textile sector has been exacerbated. As a result, flexibility production, and cost reduction became important conditions for the company. As per Gereffi and Frederick [8], the sector has to strategically aim at investing in advanced technologies and the adoption of flexible production systems for its long-run viability.

There's particularly significant dependence on it when we consider the sector of Micro, Small and Medium Enterprises (MSMEs) [16]. Indeed, the deployment of intelligent PPCP models which promote productivity increases and also provide greater flexibility and cost reduction constitutes more than just a competitive weapon, it represents a condition for survival, profitability and the sustainability of its activities [22]. But all these steps in that direction require tackling major difficulties. As stressed by Moeuf et al. [16], numerous internal characteristics prevent MSMEs from embracing Industry 4.0, such as the lack of technical skills, limited means to develop R&D activities, and the difficulty to manage advanced computer architectures.

According to Giri et al. [9], in the textile sector, embracing AI methods means going beyond incremental updates. This leap is essential if the industry wishes to grow profitability and stay competitive. Despite that, there's a technological discrepancy between the industry and academic circles. Modern AI methods continue to exist largely in the academic domain, while the industry is still content using traditional computational algorithms, leaving the sector vulnerable in the face of market instability that is inherent to the supply chain for fashion and apparel items.

In view of the previous statements, this article proposes an AI agent-based system that will manage production order examination, the appropriate distribution of workers and the creation of management reports according to the textile MSMEs' empirical output figures.

This solution has been devised to address and improve the PPCP in this niche to thereby increase overall worker throughput and efficiency, reduce idle time of factory resources and maximize their earnings. Section 2 of this article will cover previous research in the area. Section 3 will describe the system's structure, detailing the rationale behind the use of LLMs for managing factory resources. Section 4 will showcase the system's outputs and outcomes. Finally, section 5 of will present the challenges and unique contributions of this study.

2 Related Works

The use of AI in PPCP is a revolutionary step towards Industry 4.0, especially to textile MSMEs which should, at the same time, be operational efficient and cost efficient [16,22] to base the architectural choices of the suggested system and map the state. Therefore, a Systematic Literature Review (SLR) was chosen to review scientific articles, applying the process proposed by Kitchenham [13] to minimize researchers subjectivity and increase the credibility of the findings due to its rigid and auditable process [14]. This SLR was designed to explore, survey and aggregate scientific publications concerned with PPCP models, artificial intelligence and optimization techniques applicable to textile MSMEs.

The study was undertaken in the context of addressing the primary problem question of identifying which models were the most efficient at workload distribution in the textile sector, this was addressed through six sub-question topics ranging from the best-performing optimization algorithms, to methods of Artificial Intelligence use and automation in manufacturing, to issues within the structures that underpin textile production as a PPCP for the textile SMEs. A summary review of the resulting questions, as derived from these research questions, is below.

The results converge toward the adoption of hybrid models as the most effective approach for workload balancing in textile MSMEs [10,15,17,20,22,24,26, 29], with a predominance of dedicated heuristics and Genetic Algorithms (GA) [22,24], although a clear trade-off between computational time and solution quality persists [4,5,15,17,20,25,26].

In terms of automation, the literature mentions modeling with the support of ERP/MES systems [23], Digital Twins [10], and other technologies, like RFID and Lean Six Sigma [2,17], as approaches to minimize the overhead of manual data entry and detect operational bottlenecks. With regard to the variability of demand, which is an inherent feature of the industry, simulation-optimization methods with the usage of Artificial Neural Networks (ANNs) and GAs are distinguished by the ability to represent non-stationary and stochastic behavior [22,24]. The influencing factors on line balancing range between operational, labor variability, setup times, sequence of tasks [22,23,26], and structural ones, including poor layout and limited processing capacity [7,10].

Nevertheless, one gap was found: none of the studies included in the review mentioned the use of Large Language Models in PPCP systems, this is an uncharted area in the existing literature, which directly prompts the current work.

In short, hybrid genetic algorithms along with complementary technologies are promising in areas of load balancing, optimization of resources as well as simulation of production. However, GAs have the tendency of premature convergence to local optima, leading to inadequate accuracy in calculations in their output [24]. Moreover, their application in very dynamic production settings, like sewing workshops, is critically constrained: GAs, as mentioned by Zhang et al. [28], can solve large-scale combinatorial problems, but cannot respond to real-time changes: the computation of the rescheduling process in the case of disruptions is not computationally efficient. On constant replanning scenarios, because of sudden machine failures or absences of operators, the time taken to converge at an iterative search can make an instantaneous operational response impossible.

Here, the critical advantage that the LLMs provide in the form of speed and interpretability is a cognitive agent that can dynamically reason and interpret the production data in real-time, thus eliminating the rigidity of the traditional automation systems. These models create process plans and allocation advice in seconds using semantic instructions with reported inference latencies of 100ms to 10 s [27], which are agile enough to support operation replanning in MSMEs. In addition to this speed, the capability to convert the complex production constraints into understandable justifications in a human readable form [12] is the key to the viability of PPCP. This system allows managers to take almost instantaneous decisions and keep the production running in case of disruption, without losing the human factor as the core of the decision process. Based on this, the proposed research aims to fill this gap created by the lack of presence of the LLMs in the domain of PPCP, by deploying an LLM-based PPCP system in the textile MSMEs.

3 Architecture

In order to apply the LLM-based PPCP solution, a modular design based on the Orchestrator-Worker design pattern was chosen, in accordance with the principles presented by Adimulam et al. [1] and Yeddula et al.[1]. This framework is explained by the qualitative consistency of multi-agent orchestration compared to the single-agent systems which often generate superficial or patchy recommendations in application settings. To counter this weakness, Drammeh [6] show that deterministic behavior and predictability needed to enable production-ready environments are attained by decomposing tasks into single-objective prompts that are focused and deterministic in nature. Although multifaceted multi-objective prompts enhance the variability and ambiguity of outputs, shorter, specialized prompts (50–100 tokens) decrease the cognitive load per inference and reduce hallucinations.

Also, orchestration, as introduced by Qi et al. [18], helps the system react to demand fluctuations and environmental changes without necessarily re-initiating the process, and it mitigates the inefficiencies of the traditional planning models. Technical implementation uses the LangChain model of LLM and tool coordination, and LangGraph library of state and execution flow in the computational graph. To empower the agents, we leveraged GPT-4o-mini as our chosen LLM. The criteria for this selection were its low inference latency, affordability and ample reasoning power required for the specific domain tasks at hand, moreover, it possesses multimodal capabilities which support the computer vision infrastructure involved in the extraction of information from PDF scans.

The system architecture[2] was developed keeping in mind the flexibility and scalability. The core of the application, which is accessed through a Python

[1] Yeddula, S., Dhinakaran, A., and Chavali, S. (2025). *Orchestrator-Worker Agents: A Practical Comparison of Common Agent Frameworks*. Arize AI Blog. Available at: https://arize.com/blog/orchestrator-worker-agents-a-practical-comparison-of-common-agent-frameworks/.

[2] The image of the architecture diagram is available at: https://drive.google.com/file/d/11_lIWtNWYlXRXddyCxeLgBArUT-EmHrV/view.

API (FastAPI), communicates with a hybrid persistence layer that uses PostgreSQL for structured data storage (production orders, collaborators, etc.) and MongoDB for unstructured data storage (production logs). The submission of a natural language query triggers the workflow, and is intercepted by the Orchestrator Agent.

The Orchestrator Agent is the main routing element of the system that uses the reasoning features of the LLM to interpret the semantic intent of the query made by the user. On the basis of this analysis, it identifies-by conditional edges within the computational graph of LangGraph (the specialized workflow to be activated). The elements that make up this architecture are as follows:

- **Orchestrator Agent:** The core routing module that uses FastAPI, LangChain and LangGraph. It has the role of accepting the requests of the external system, decoding the intent of the user, and delegating the work to the respective specialized agent.
- **Production Order Registration Agent:** This is created to remove manual data entry of production order forms to reduce transcription errors and standardize data entry. It scans sewing operations and standard times and production phases off technical specification sheets in PDF format, and authenticates the extracted data using Pydantic and Guardrails AI before permitting persistence.
- **Setup Suggestion Agent:** It works during the planning stage of the production line, suggesting a smart and optimized distribution of operators prior to the initiation of production. In order to accomplish this, it uses historical information to construct a personal efficiency model of each collaborator, calculated through cross-referencing of MongoDB production logs to postgreSQL standard times and aligning the models with the needs of the new production order.
- **Operator Reallocation Agent:** It is dedicated to the dynamic management of human resources in the production process and is involved in targeted workforce changes to eliminate bottlenecks or reorganize workloads in real-time. It examines the present situation on the production floor and confirms competencies in accordance with the personal experience of collaborators on the basis of individual tasks.
- **Operation Report Agent:** The duties of the agent is to convert raw data of production to operational intelligence. It takes all logs taken by smart devices and puts them in MongoDB, compares real timestamps with standard times, stored in PostgreSQL and determines the efficiency of individual operators and the overall efficiency of production orders. The findings, such as identified productivity variations, are organized into an executive summary delivered to the outside system through API and use it to create a PDF report.
- **Response Formatter:** The role of the Response Formatter is to standardize and consolidate the output of all the specialized agents. It ensures that answers are sent to the orchestrator using a standardized data contract, and communication between the calling system and the orchestrator is consistent, despite the agent that handled the request.

The architecture has a common PDF ingestion pipeline to seamlessly incorporate the processing of attached documents. The system identifies the information on the technical specification sheet irrespective of the invoked workflow and applies the same hybrid approach: native text extraction is initially tried with PyMuPDF (`page.get_text()`); in case the document is a scanned PDF (or no text is found in the scanned document), a computer vision pipeline is turned on. Here, pages are rendered at high resolution (432 DPI), processed with OpenCV (CLAHE, bilateral filter, and adaptive binarization) and processed with GPT-4o-mini in multimodal vision mode. The production in both roads is strictly verified by Pydantic and Guardrails AI models.

This extraction pipeline is single, however, the objective of the extracted data varies fundamentally with the active agent. The operations extracted in the Production Order Registration Agent are given to make a new record in the database. Conversely, with the Setup Suggestion Agent, the extraction is a lookup key: the operations are employed to find which existing-registered production order in PostgreSQL is related to the document posted.

This manner of orchestration of specialized agents, through the LangGraph computational graph, goes beyond the mere automation of individual tasks. The suggested architecture defines a cooperative ecosystem whereby the reasoning ability of the LLM is guided to address domain-specific issues and optimize results. The scalability of the system is not only guaranteed by this approach to the possibility of adding new agents in the future, but also enables the flexibility needed to meet the variability that is inherent to the textile industry.

3.1 Prompt Optimization Strategy

The optimization strategy of the processing flow is one of the main architectural contributions of this system. The project, initially, had a monolithic approach where the LLM did all the strategic analysis and also implementation of mathematical calculations, which are part of PPCP. This involved a lot of prompts that entailed specifications on how to draw up cycle time formulations and critical path computations. But the literature suggests that prompt complexity has a detrimental effect on the quality of analysis when overdone [3], and that generative models such as GPT-4o-mini actually have limitations in their ability to solve multi-step mathematical tasks [11,21].

The following theoretical vulnerabilities proved empirically in the process of testing the monolithic version of the system. This unconstrained transfer of mathematical operations to the model led to the accuracy of calculating within a range of about 95% due to the occasional arithmetic hallucinations. In addition to the intolerable imprecision in industrial settings, the reasoning overhead of the LLM increased the average inference time to about 11 s. In order to overcome these bottlenecks, the architecture was refined to form a strict separation of deterministic operations.

In this modified design, essential measurements are computed beforehand by autonomous server-side calculator modules. This structure ensures deterministic execution, unlike generative models. To take an example, the time that each single production cycle takes is calculated directly out of the non-relational database logs as follows:

$$D_{min} = \frac{T_{actual} - T_{previous}}{60000} \tag{1}$$

where T_{actual} and $T_{previous}$ are the time-stamps of consecutive events. The final numerical results are only injected into the context prompt after the parameters like per-cell time, bottlenecks and critical path have been calculated precisely.

This disjunction of interests ensures 100% mathematical correctness of the operational measures and a decrease of 1,500 to about 350 tokens per call. Thus, the average inference time is reduced to 2.3 s, and the LLM can only work within its field of competence, which is semantic interpretation of structured information and developing adaptive strategies in natural language. Lastly, the system avoids structural non-determinism of LLMs by delegating strict calculation logic to deterministic algorithms, which is necessary to assure reproducibility and auditability in industrial manufacturing settings [19].

4 Results and Discussion

Two complementary analytical dimensions are used to describe the results of the proposed PPCP system obtained by empirical testing of the proposed system in this section. Section 4.1 compares the computational performance of the architectural refactoring with the monolithic and decoupled methods against monolithic and decoupled latency, token consumption, cost efficiency, and mathematical accuracy metrics.

Section 4.2 studies the feasibility of the solution in a practical scenario in a textile manufacturing setting where the multi-agent system is orchestrated to run a simulated case study. This design is intended to authenticate the technical stability of the timely optimization plan as well as the operational feasibility and strategic profits of the dynamic workload balancing in the MSMEs.

4.1 Performance Evaluation: Monolithic vs. Decoupled Architecture

In experimental benchmark analyses performed using the GPT-4o-mini as the base model, a comprehensive assessment comparing the two methods is detailed in Table 1. These results clearly show a significant improvement across all performance and dependability benchmarks post-decoupling. Average response latency dropped from 11.0 ± 1.5 s to 2.3 ± 0.1 s. This is aligned with literature that states that timely complexity is a predictive factor in the processing time of language models [3].

In terms of resource consumption, the chosen prompt engineering strategy allowed a significant decrease in the amount of information handled with each call. Mean token usage decreased from $1{,}250 \pm 250$ to 350 ± 50, which is more than three-quarters of the cost per call to the API. The applicability of the solution

Table 1. Performance and Reliability Comparison: Monolithic vs. Decoupled Architecture (Mean ± SD)

Metric	Monolithic Approach	Decoupled Approach
Average Latency (s)	11.0 ± 1.5	2.3 ± 0.1
Token Consumption (units)	1250 ± 250	350 ± 50
Estimated Cost (USD)	0.0035 ± 0.0015	0.00075 ± 0.00025
Calculation Accuracy (%)	95%	100%
Numerical Reproducibility	Variable	1.00

to the MSMEs requires this optimization: on the one hand, the financial savings are important, and on the other hand, a surplus of information in a prompt can overload the model, adversely affecting the accuracy and consistency of the responses [3].

And lastly with regards to integrity of PPCP operations, the decoupled method met 100% mathematical accuracy and 1.00 numerical reproducibility. Conversely, the monolithic method was 95% accurate and had arithmetic hallucinations and structural non-determinism of the LLMs. The literature suggests that the correctness of the responses produced by intelligent systems can be improved only through more specific, well-structured prompts [3]. The proposed system therefore guarantees the reliability in industrial textile manufacturing settings by isolating deterministic calculations and semantic interpretation.

4.2 Case Study: Dynamic Orchestration in a Textile MSME

This paper provides qualitative evaluation through a case study. Data was collected in a simulated shop floor setting by using real data retrieved from the textile MSME. The dataset consists of production orders (POs) in unstructured PDF, collaborator performance history and logs from production smart devices. In the authors setting, every station on the shop floor has some smart device which logs production events happening at this station in real time. First, the system receives a production order in PDF format.

In the manual process, to register such order, one has to enter more than $7{+}3N$ fields, where N is the number of production operations. Given the example PO had 12 operations, this amounts to $7 + 3 * 12 = 43$ fields to manually fill, which often results in transcription mistakes due to cognitive load and the high number of data to enter.

We show the step-by-step operation of the solution, from initial document ingestion to the final efficiency report, in Fig. 1. The detailed explanation of each phase is provided in the following subsections.

Intelligent Digitization via Production Order Registration Agent. In the simulated scenario, the technical specification sheet for the production order was given as a scanned PDF document. Since it couldn't contain native extractable text, the Production Order Registration Agent classified it as a scanned document and invoked the computer vision path. Pre-processed image representations of the technical specification sheet were fed into the GPT-4o-mini vision model. Through its object detection capabilities, it properly identified its vertical hierarchical arrangement of sewing operations within each phase by utilizing defined spatial mapping rules applied via prompt engineering.

As a consequence, 12 operations within the four defined production phases were successfully extracted without any error relative to the original document. The resulting structured information (shown below) was validated by the Pydantic/Guardrails AI layer and recorded into the database.

```
{
  "order_reference": "ABC1001",
  "target_quantity": 100,
  "extracted_phases": {
    "Phase 1 - Pre-assembly": [
      {"operation": "Coin pocket hem", "standard_time_min":
          0.06},
      {"operation": "Back pocket hem", "standard_time_min":
          0.125},
      {"operation": "Close/turn front split pocket", "
          standard_time_min": 0.155},
      {"operation": "Attach flap and facing on split pocket",
           "standard_time_min": 0.135},
      {"operation": "Topstitch pocket mouth", "
          standard_time_min": 0.23},
      {"operation": "Attach front/side pockets", "
          standard_time_min": 0.185},
      {"operation": "Attach pockets to opening", "
          standard_time_min": 0.185}
    ],
    "Phase 2 - Front": [
      {"operation": "Attach pockets", "standard_time_min":
          1.85},
      {"operation": "Final inspection", "standard_time_min":
          1.11}
    ],
    "Phase 2 - Back": [
      {"operation": "Attach and topstitch zipper", "
          standard_time_min": 0.44},
      {"operation": "Attach yoke", "standard_time_min": 0.75}
    ],
    "Phase 3 - Assembly": [
      {"operation": "Count pieces", "standard_time_min":
          0.58}
    ]
  }
}
```

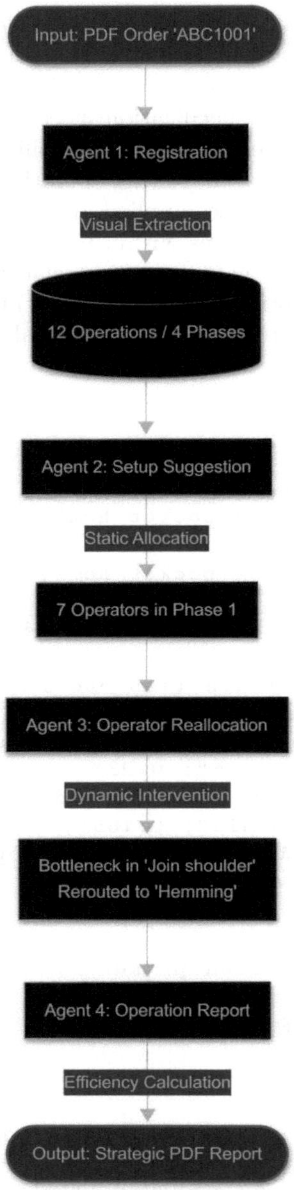

Fig. 1. Workflow of the proposed multi-agent architecture in the simulated case study.

With this Human-in-the-Loop (HITL) paradigm, the production manager checks the extracted data rather than filling the 43 fields by hand, removing the burden of the process, and preventing critical registration errors.

Setup Optimization via Setup Suggestion Agent. The structured data generated from POs is then input into the Setup Suggestion Agent. The primary function of this agent is to make a global allocation of human resources available on the production line to the available operational needs that are recorded in the database through the history of collaborator performances.

In this experiment, 7 operators were available to handle the 12 operations identified in the mapping step. The agent attempts a simultaneous assignment of all operation tasks based on the matching process that compares the operation name in the technical documentation for each operation and the history that is saved per operator, respectively. In this case, only the Phase 1 operations found matches between the operation names from the technical sheet and the histories recorded per collaborator, therefore, the 7 operators were assigned to the 7 simultaneous operations of that phase. The operator best matched for each specific operation and smart device was chosen and assigned according to their competency profile. Operations from Phases 2 and 3 (that didn't have any matched names on the operator histories) were assigned using the fallback policy, therefore, operators without any historical matches to any specific operations were allocated and noted with an asterisk () on the table showing the generation of the plan to demonstrate that no specific operator was specialized on any operation.

From the generated plan, the deterministic calculator estimated a total time required to produce 100 items of 4.43 h, identifying the operation "Attach pockets" in Phase 2 (taking 1.85 min) as the bottleneck. In addition, the idleness projected for the operations to be completed after this identified bottleneck operation illustrated the limitations that result from having a plan set up statically, just by matching historical performances, which serves as one architectural feature that allows the dynamic reallocation agent to intervene in case of unforeseen events.

Dynamic Intervention via Operator Reallocation Agent. Despite that the planner may statically assign operators to each operation, the dynamic changes on the shop floor, like early batch completions and emergent bottleneck situations, necessitate real-time adjustments to such assignments. The implemented architecture addresses this requirement through an Operator Reallocation Agent that handles the movement of operators across operations according to the PO's progress and each collaborator's past assignments.

This agent was validated with a simulated bottleneck event in which the system was tasked to identify the optimal transition of the operator currently assigned to the "Join shoulder" operation, which was identified as a bottleneck. The system looked up the PO and found three possible destination operations: "Hemming" (0.75 min), "Double stitch" (1.0 min) and "Close side seam" (0.5 min).

It is important to note that a cross-reference to the database showed that the operator didn't have experience assigned to any of the three options (`has_experience: false`). With classical rule-based systems, this usually leads to an allocation failure. The system overcomes this problem with a simple heuristic: if the operator doesn't have prior experience in any alternative option, it chooses the first operation after ordering the operations alphabetically. The recommendation is as shown in the JSON object below:


```
{
  "collaborator": "Collaborator A",
  "current_operation": "Join shoulder",
  "total_options": 3,
  "options": [
    {
      "operation": "Hemming",
      "suggested_time": 0.75,
      "has_experience": false,
      "best_option": true,
      "justification": "Best available option: operator lacks
          prior experience in alternatives. Selected based
         on suggested time balancing."
    },
    {
      "operation": "Close side seam",
      "suggested_time": 0.50,
      "has_experience": false,
      "best_option": false
    }
  ]
}
```


The system not only processes the main data used by the front-end, but it also creates a simple summary for the production manager. This summary is written in plain language and is made by the GPT-4o-mini model. It looks at the options that have already been ranked by an algorithm. In the scenario that was tested, the model found that while the "Hemming" operation would make the workload more even, moving tasks to "Close side seam" would cut production time by up to 0.5 min per unit. This would get the most work done right away.

This system gives us two things: a standardized algorithmic recommendation (`best_option`) and a semantic tactical analysis generated by the LLM, endows the system with the characteristics of a robust Decision Support System (DSS). Production management ceases to be a subjective visual inference and becomes data-driven, enabling smooth workforce redistribution in MSMEs even in the face of competency profile uncertainty.

Efficiency Analysis via Operation Report Agent. The last step of the process is to take the information we got from making things and turn it into something we can actually use. When the production order is done, the Operation Report Agent makes sure the production record in MongoDB matches the standard record in PostgreSQL. It then fixes the timestamps and figures out how well each operator did their job, compared to how long it was supposed to take. It also looks at how efficient the whole purchase order was.

In the simulated experiment, the reporting system accurately alerted the agent about this situation: the operation, designated “Close back pocket” had a expected completion time of 4 min, while its logged processing time was 0.07 min. Thus, an efficiency of 5.714% was computed. While the computation is technically correct, such high values typically reveal outdated standard times, possibly reflecting outdated technical instructions that might not incorporate recent innovations like rapid stitching processes designed to accommodate higher volumes of individual clothing items. Consequently, this should warrant a review of the relevant time standard. The resulting data is neatly organized into the analytical report payload displayed below, which is then fed into an external engine to generate the corresponding PDF report:


```
{
  "standard_piece_time_min": 9.0,
  "actual_operation_time_min": 0.07,
  "total_production_pieces": 2,
  "operator_performance_map": [
    {
      "operator": "Collaborator A",
      "operation": "Close back pocket",
      "standard_time_min": 4.0,
      "actual_time_min": 0.07,
      "efficiency_percent": 5714.3
    },
    {
      "operator": "Collaborator B",
      "operation": "Overlock fly",
      "standard_time_min": 5.0,
      "actual_time_min": 0.07,
      "efficiency_percent": 7142.9
    }
  ]
}
```


The data is put together in a clear and easy-to-understand report, and another system uses this information to create a PDF report through an interface. This makes it simple for the manager to check the report and see overall efficiency numbers, how different operations compare, and exactly how much a task has improved compared to the standard time. The report provides a straightforward way to measure and compare performance, making it easier to identify areas for improvement and track progress over time. With this information, the manager can make informed decisions and take steps to optimize operations and increase efficiency.

The system takes care of production documents from start to finish. It begins with unorganized documents, then plans and makes adjustments as needed, and finally creates strategic reports, thereby defining a valid infrastructure to modernize PPCP within textile MSMEs.

5 Conclusion and Future Work

This study put forward and confirmed a multi-agent design, managed by LangGraph and driven by LLMs, specifically engineered for the dynamic enhancement of PPCP within textile MSMEs. The core innovation of this architecture lay in separating the traditional mathematical operations from the stage of semantic interpretation. This method effectively countered the arithmetic inaccuracies often seen in generative models, guaranteeing perfect accuracy in structural computations. Simultaneously, it achieved a 79% reduction in inference time and a 75% decrease in token usage.

The real-world utility of this solution was illustrated via a simulated case study, which incorporated actual operational data from a textile MSME. The system demonstrated its capacity to manage the full production life cycle, starting with the multimodal input and semantic extraction of Production Orders directly from PDF documents, thereby eliminating the need for manual data entry, and extending to the creation of strategic efficiency reports. The Agent designed for Operator Reallocation proved especially beneficial, functioning as a DSS, it navigated the lack of historical operator data by employing a deterministic heuristic. This approach enabled the generation of tactical recommendations, delivered in natural language through an LLM.

A significant hurdle during the development process stemmed from the limited academic research specifically linking LLMs to PPCP in manufacturing settings, with an even greater deficit concerning textile MSMEs. This gap, identified during a thorough literature review, directly informed the architectural choices made for this project. Consequently, the proposed architecture aims to contribute to this developing field, showing that integrating semantic inference with deterministic calculation offers a practical and scalable pathway for modernizing production planning in smaller enterprises.

Looking ahead, the research team intends to move the architecture beyond its simulated environment and implement it in actual manufacturing settings. This will allow for a thorough evaluation of its performance under genuine shop-floor conditions. Such practical validation will generate crucial feedback, guiding the incorporation of new features and refinements specifically tailored to the unique operational demands faced by textile MSMEs.

Acknowledgments. This study was supported by the CNPq, National Council for Scientific and Technological Development - Brazil (grant number 443723/2024-9).

Disclosure of Interests. The authors have no competing interests to declare that are relevant to the content of this article.

References

1. Adimulam, A., Gupta, R., Kumar, S.: The orchestration of multi-agent systems: architectures, protocols, and enterprise adoption. arXiv preprint arXiv:2601.13671 (2026). https://arxiv.org/abs/2601.13671
2. Bai, Y., You, J.B., Lee, I.K.: Design and optimization of smart factory control system based on digital twin system model. Math. Probl. Eng. **2021**(1), 2596946 (2021)
3. Balaji, K., Lokesha, A., G., C., H. M., P.: Optimizing prompt length and specificity for enhanced ai chatbot responses. Int. J. Comput. Sci. Res. Rev. **07** (2024). https://ijcsrr.org/wp-content/uploads/2024/09/61-3009-2024.pdf
4. Darmian, S.M., Farughi, H.: An optimization-based approach for managing downstream logistic operations: a real application in pandemic outbreak conditions. Comput. Ind. Eng. **171**, 108495 (2022)
5. De Oliveira, U.R., de Souza, H.A.D., Menezes, C.A.G., Rocha, H.M.: Straightening machine preventive maintenance intervention plan based on AHP: a case study in a steel company in brazil. Oper. Manag. Res. **16**, 1577–1593 (2023)
6. Drammeh, P.: Multi-agent LLM orchestration achieves deterministic, high-quality decision support for incident response. arXiv preprint arXiv:2511.15755 (2025)
7. Eccher, C., Geraghty, J.: Incorporating sustainable criteria in a dynamic multi-objective recommendation planning tool for a continuous manufacturing process: a dairy case study. J. Manuf. Syst. **55**, 159–170 (2020)
8. Gereffi, G., Frederick, S.: The global apparel value chain, trade and the crisis: challenges and opportunities for developing countries. Policy Research Working Paper 5281, The World Bank (2010)
9. Giri, C., Jain, S., Zeng, X., Bruniaux, P.: A detailed review of artificial intelligence applied in the fashion and apparel industry. IEEE Access **7**, 95376–95396 (2019)
10. Guo, H., Chen, M., Mohamed, K., Qu, T., Wang, S., Li, J.: A digital twin-based flexible cellular manufacturing for optimization of air conditioner line. J. Manuf. Syst. **58**, 65–78 (2021)
11. Hoza, P.: Evaluating reasoning in large language models with a modified think-a-number game: case study. Acta Informatica Pragensia **14**(2), 246–260 (2025)
12. Keskin, Z., et al0.: LLM-enhanced human-machine interaction for adaptive decision making in dynamic manufacturing process environments. IEEE Access (2025)
13. Kitchenham, B.: Procedures for undertaking systematic reviews. Technical report. TR/SE-0401, Keele University and NICTA (2004)
14. Kitchenham, B., Brereton, O.P., Budgen, D., Turner, M., Bailey, J., Linkman, S.: Systematic literature reviews in software engineering-a systematic literature review. Inf. Softw. Technol. **51**(1), 7–15 (2009)
15. Li, D., Jin, H., Zhang, Y.: Dynamic worker allocation in seru production systems with actor-critic and pointer networks. Eur. J. Oper. Res. **324**(1), 62–74 (2025)
16. Moeuf, A., Pellerin, R., Lamouri, S., Tamayo-Giraldo, S., Barbaray, R.: The industrial management of SMEs in the era of industry 4.0. Int. J. Prod. Res. **56**(3) (2017)
17. Nedra, A., Néjib, S., Boubaker, J., Morched, C.: An integrated lean six sigma approach to modeling and simulation: a case study from clothing SME. Autex Res. J. **22**(3), 305–311 (2022)
18. Qi, Y., et al.: Leveraging LLM-based agents for intelligent supply chain planning. arXiv e-prints pp. arXiv–2509 (2025)
19. Semmelrock, H., et al.: Reproducibility in machine learning-based research: Overview, barriers and drivers. arXiv preprint arXiv:2406.14325 (2024). https://arxiv.org/html/2406.14325v2

20. Singh, J., Singh, A., Singh, H., Doyon-Poulin, P.: Implementation and evaluation of a smart machine monitoring system under industry 4.0 concept. J. Ind. Inf. Integr. **43**, 100746 (2025)
21. Singh, J., Nambi, A., Vineet, V.: Exposing the achilles' heel: evaluating LLMs ability to handle mistakes in mathematical reasoning. In: Proceedings of the 63rd Annual Meeting of the Association for Computational Linguistics, vol. 1, pp. 27044—-27065 (2025). https://aclanthology.org/2025.acl-long.1313.pdf
22. Teerasoponpong, S., Sopadang, A.: A simulation-optimization approach for adaptive manufacturing capacity planning in small and medium-sized enterprises. Expert Syst. Appl. **168**, 114451 (2021)
23. Wang, L.C., Chen, C.C., Liu, J.L., Chu, P.C.: Framework and deployment of a cloud-based advanced planning and scheduling system. Robot. Comput. Integr. Manuf. **70**, 102088 (2021)
24. Wang, L.: Improved human resource allocation method based on genetic algorithm. In: Intelligent Computing Technology and Automation, pp. 97–104. IOS Press (2024)
25. Wang, L., Ai, W., Deng, T., Shen, Z.J.M., Hong, C.: Optimal production ramp-up in the smartphone manufacturing industry. Naval Res. Logistics (NRL) **67**(8), 685–704 (2020)
26. Wang, P.S., Lin, C.C., Yang, T.: A study on shojinka design for automobile engine piston-rod manufacturing. Comput. Ind. Eng. **151**, 106974 (2021)
27. Xia, Y., Zhang, J., Jazdi, N., Weyrich, M.: Incorporating large language models into production systems for enhanced task automation and flexibility. arXiv preprint arXiv:2407.08550 (2024)
28. Zhang, F., Mei, Y., Nguyen, S., Zhang, M.: Survey on genetic programming and machine learning techniques for heuristic design in job shop scheduling. IEEE Trans. Evol. Comput. **28**(1), 147–167 (2023)
29. Zhang, W., Hou, L., Jiao, R.J.: Dynamic takt time decisions for paced assembly lines balancing and sequencing considering highly mixed-model production: An improved artificial bee colony optimization approach. Comput. Ind. Eng. **161**, 107616 (2021)

Adversarial Detection in EEG-Based BCIs: A Comparative Study of Classical and Neuro-Fuzzy Approaches

Beatriz Conceição da Costa[1](✉), Giancarlo Lucca[1], Lizandro de Souza Oliveira[2], Rafael Berri[1], Roger Immich[3], Eduardo Borges[1], Richard F. Pinto[1], Fabian C. Cardoso[4], and Bruno L. Dalmazo[1]

[1] Universidade Federal do Rio Grande (FURG), Rio Grande, Brazil
{beatrizdacosta1,giancarlo.lucca,rafaelberri,eduardoborges,dalmazo}@furg.br
[2] Universidade Católica de Pelotas (UCPel), Pelotas, Brazil
lizandro.oliveira@ucpel.edu.br
[3] Universidade Federal do Rio Grande do Norte (UFRN), Natal, Brazil
roger@imd.ufrn.br
[4] University of Rio Verde (UniRV), Rio Verde, Brazil
fabian@unirv.edu.br

Abstract. Brain–Computer Interfaces (BCIs) based on electroencephalography (EEG) allow users to interact with external systems through brain activity and are increasingly used beyond clinical applications. As these systems rely on machine learning and process sensitive neural data, their resilience to malicious manipulation becomes a key concern. Adversarial attacks are especially problematic, as they introduce subtle perturbations that can significantly disrupt model predictions. This paper evaluates the impact of adversarial attacks on EEG-based BCI classifiers and investigates detection strategies related to this domain. Using the BCI Competition IV 2a dataset and EEGNet as a baseline model, we emulate FGSM, PGD, and DeepFool attacks with the Foolbox framework. Results show consistent performance degradation under all attacks, confirming the vulnerability of EEG-based classification pipelines. To address this issue, we compare traditional machine learning detectors with an Adaptive Neuro-Fuzzy Inference System (ANFIS). The results indicate that detector effectiveness is related to the attack: ANFIS performs best under FGSM and PGD, while Random Forest achieves the strongest results for DeepFool in the current setup. However, due to the limited number of effective adversarial examples and the single-subject evaluation, these findings should be interpreted as preliminary evidence rather than as a general benchmark. Even when not leading in accuracy, ANFIS remained competitive in AUC-based evaluation and provided a continuous adversarial risk score, which may support uncertainty-aware decision making in safety-critical BCI systems.

Keywords: Brain-computer interfaces · adversarial attacks · EEG · cybersecurity · neuro-fuzzy systems

O. Gervasi et al. (Eds.): ICCSA 2026, LNCS 16768, pp. 173–184, 2027.
https://doi.org/10.1007/978-3-032-30488-9_11

1 Introduction

Advances in technology have allowed Brain-Computer Interfaces (BCIs) [20] to help people with motor disabilities control wheelchairs and prosthetic devices. These systems often use electroencephalography (EEG) [19], a non-invasive and low-cost method that records electrical activity from the scalp. The recorded signals are processed, converted into meaningful features, and analyzed by machine learning classifiers to determine the user's intentions.

Recently, BCIs have expanded beyond clinical and assistive applications, finding use in entertainment, cognitive enhancement, and emotion analysis, as demonstrated by Neurable[1]. As these systems become more widespread and share personal and sensitive data between different places, concerns over their security and trustworthiness become increasingly relevant.

These devices become potential targets for various cyberattacks [24], such as adversarial attacks [22], buffer overflow attacks [16], malware attacks [15] and others [4,10,13,17]. Among emerging threats to BCIs, adversarial machine learning poses a urgent challenge.

Adversarial attacks are manipulations crafted to deceive machine learning models by introducing smal perturbations that are often imperceptible to humans. These attacks can be categorized into poisoning, exploratory, and evasion attacks [21], with the latter two being especially relevant in BCI contexts. In poisoning attacks, adversaries inject manipulated data during training, while evasion attacks target the model during inference. Despite the growing awareness of cybersecurity in AI-driven applications, the specific vulnerabilities of BCI systems to adversarial perturbations remain underexplored. This gap highlights the need for targeted investigations into both the feasibility of attacks and the development of detection mechanisms tailored to EEG-based classification pipelines.

This work contributes an early experimental evaluation of adversarial attack impact and detection strategies in EEG-based BCI classification. Rather than claiming a definitive comparative benchmark, the study focuses on analyzing how different detectors behave under distinct adversarial perturbation regimes and on exploring the potential of neuro-fuzzy inference as an uncertainty-aware complement to classical machine learning detectors. To provide a structured analysis, the proposed approach is organized into three main components:

1. By using the Foolbox tool, we have applied attacks such as the Fast Gradient Sign Method (FGSM), Projected Gradient Descent (PGD), and DeepFool on EEG data to assess classifier robustness.
2. By analyzing three classical classifiers (Random Forest (RF) [6], Support Vector Machine (SVM) [8], and K-Nearest Neighbors (KNN) [9]).
3. By exploring the use of fuzzy logic as an uncertainty-aware detection mechanism. Specifically, an Adaptive Neuro-Fuzzy Inference System (ANFIS) [11] is employed to model adversarial risk as a continuous score rather than a binary decision.

[1] https://www.neurable.com//.

The remainder of this paper is organized as follows. Section 2 presents the related work. Section 3 describes the experimental setup and the proposed detection strategy. Section 4 reports the results and discussion. Finally, Sect. 5 concludes the paper.

2 Related Work

In this section, we present a literature review aimed at understanding previous studies on adversarial attacks in Brain-Computer Interfaces (BCIs), focusing on attack generation, impact analysis, and detection methods.

2.1 Search Methodology

In this study, a Systematic Literature Review was conducted to answer the following research question:

> *How are adversarial attacks applied to EEG-based brain-computer interface classifiers, and how effective are existing detection strategies in mitigating their impact on system robustness?*

For this, we used the IEEE Xplore platform to search for relevant articles that would enable an understanding of the state of the art in this topic, using the query: "Brain-Computer Interfaces AND Adversarial Attack AND detector AND fuzzy logic". IEEE Xplore is a traditional and well-established source of scientific information. We considered studies published between 2020 and 2025, excluding surveys and papers that did not address adversarial attacks.

A total of 14 papers was selected for detailed review after filtering duplicates and applying the above criteria. Table 1 compiles their results.

Table 1. Selected Studies

Results	Total
IEEE Xplore	28
Not included due to IC1, IC2	3
Excluded due to EC1, EC2	11
Selected Articles	**14**

2.2 Analysis and Discussion of Selected Works

Recent studies investigate adversarial threats to electroencephalography (EEG)-based Brain–Computer Interface (BCI) pipelines and report substantial performance degradation in commonly used deep models under small perturbations. More advanced attacks exploit structured representations, for example time–frequency features, to deceive brainprint-based systems [14]. Data poisoning has also been explored, including label-flipping in federated learning settings, showing significant drops in model accuracy [3].

Research on defenses proposes detection architectures that combine clean-signal classification with adversarial detection [1]. Federated-learning scenarios have been studied with augmented training data, including electroencephalography samples generated by Generative Adversarial Networks (GANs) and multiple classifier backbones, reporting mixed robustness depending on the model and data regime [2]. Related efforts also leverage GAN-based anomaly detection to identify deviations in EEG patterns [5].

Fuzzy-based approaches are comparatively rare. Among the selected studies, [23] proposes a hierarchical TakagiâĂŞSugenoâĂŞKang fuzzy classifier with adversarial learning for epileptic EEG classification, indicating potential benefits of fuzzy reasoning in noisy and uncertain EEG settings.

Overall, the literature concentrates on attack crafting, adversarial training, and deep learning-based detectors, while uncertainty-aware neuro-fuzzy detection remains underexplored. In particular, the use of Adaptive Neuro-Fuzzy Inference Systems (ANFIS) have not been widely investigated for adversarial detection in EEG-based BCIs. This work addresses this gap by evaluating an ANFIS-based detector using deep-model features under strong attacks (PGD, DeepFool, and FGSM).

3 Experimental Setup

This section describes the experimental configuration adopted to evaluate adversarial robustness and detection in EEG-based BCI classification. First, we present the conceptual organization of the proposed pipeline. Next, we describe the dataset, preprocessing steps, and baseline classifier, followed by the adversarial attack generation procedure and the neuro-fuzzy detection strategy used in the experiments.

3.1 Conceptual Model

The proposed pipeline follows a structured four-steps roadmap, as illustrated in Fig. 1. (i) First, a baseline EEG classifier is established to set the performance benchmark for clean signal recognition. (ii) This is followed by a stage of adversarial emulation, where signal perturbations are generated to systematically challenge the model's robustness. (iii) Subsequently, a specialized detection system is implemented to identify these adversarial inputs in real-time. (iv) Finally, the framework concludes with a performance analysis phase that quantifies both the resulting accuracy degradation of the classifier and the overall effectiveness of the detection mechanism.

To evaluate the efficacy of the proposed framework under controlled conditions, we conducted the following experimental setup.

Dataset: We utilize the BCI Competition IV 2a dataset [7], which contains recordings from 9 subjects across four motor-imagery classes (left hand, right hand, feet, and tongue) using 22 EEG channels.

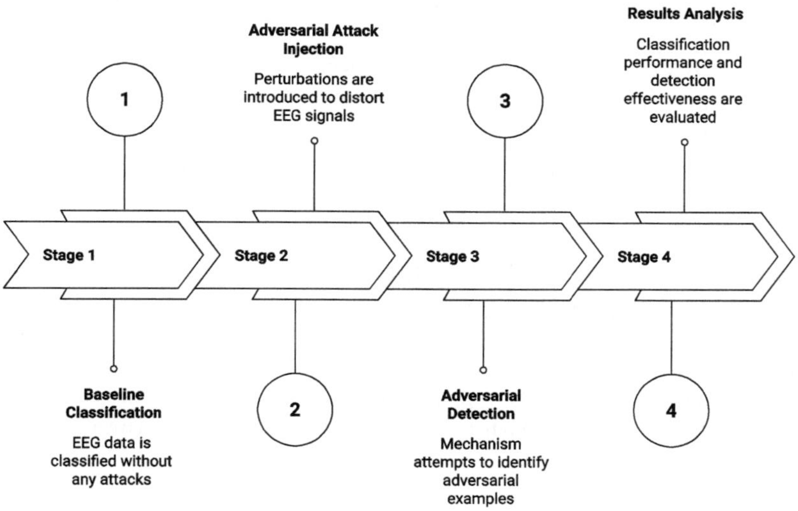

Fig. 1. Conceptual roadmap of the proposed framework

Preprocessing: The raw EEG signals are bandpass filtered (7–35 Hz) to isolate the relevant mu and beta rhythms, downsampled to 200 Hz, and cleaned using Independent Component Analysis (ICA) for artifact removal. Task-related epochs are then segmented using the MNE-Python library.

Classifier: EEGNet [12] is adopted as the baseline model because of its efficiency in extracting spatial and temporal features through depthwise and separable convolutions. Training is conducted using the Adam optimizer ($lr = 0.001$, batch size 64).

3.2 Adversarial Attack Emulation

Adversarial examples are generated using Foolbox [18]. We simulate a threat landscape by employing three standard attacks:

- **FGSM and PGD**: Gradient-based methods that introduce perturbations along the direction of the loss function's gradient.
- **DeepFool**: A geometry-based approach that calculates the minimal perturbation required to cross the decision boundary.

3.3 Adversarial Detection with Fuzzy Inference

Detection is formulated as a binary classification problem (*clean* vs. *adversarial*) using features extracted from EEGNet's output layer. While conventional detectors (SVM, RF) provide rigid boundaries, our approach utilizes an Adaptive Neuro-Fuzzy Inference System (ANFIS) [11] to explicitly represent the uncertainty inherent in perturbed BCI signals.

Table 2. Impact of adversarial attacks on EEGNet.

Attack	Clean Acc.	Adv. Acc.	Success Rate	Avg. L_2 Pert.
FGSM	0.690	0.509	0.190	4.452
PGD	0.690	0.526	0.172	4.034
DeepFool	0.690	0.509	0.181	2.601

Fuzzy models are well suited to this domain because adversarial noise is often minimal, leading to overlapping distributions where"hard" decision boundaries are unreliable. By mapping classifier outputs into linguistic concepts such as *low confidence* or *high anomaly*, ANFIS produces a continuous adversarial risk score. This is particularly relevant for safety-critical BCIs, where ambiguous cases should be flagged with calibrated confidence rather than strict binary labels.

4 Results and Discussion

This section evaluates the robustness of the EEGNet classifier under adversarial attacks and compares classical and neuro-fuzzy detectors for identifying adversarial EEG samples.

4.1 Attack Impact on EEGNet

The EEGNet baseline achieved a test accuracy of 68.97% on clean samples, providing a baseline reference point for the subsequent adversarial analysis. Under attack, performance decreased consistently across all evaluated methods, confirming the vulnerability of EEG-based BCI classification to adversarial perturbations. As shown in Table 2, FGSM and DeepFool reduced the classifier accuracy to 50.86%, while PGD resulted in 52.59%. Although the attack success rates were relatively close in this experimental setting, DeepFool produced the smallest average perturbation ($L_2 = 2.601$), suggesting that it can induce misclassification with lower overall distortion.

4.2 Detector Comparison Across Attack Families

After establishing classifier vulnerability, we evaluated four adversarial detectors: Random Forest (RF), Support Vector Machine (SVM), k-Nearest Neighbors (KNN), and ANFIS. In contrast to the previous version of this work, the current evaluation includes cross-attack detection results as well as threshold-independent metrics such as ROC-AUC and PR-AUC. Table 3 summarizes the results.

The detector comparison revealed heterogeneous behavior across attack families. For FGSM, ANFIS achieved the best overall performance, reaching 76.92% accuracy, 0.786 ROC-AUC, and 0.769 F1-score. A similar trend was observed for

PGD, where ANFIS again obtained the strongest results, with 75.00% accuracy, 0.861 ROC-AUC, and 0.877 PR-AUC. These results indicate that the neuro-fuzzy detector can be competitive under moderate attacks, especially when the perturbation induces gradual rather than sharply separable changes in the classifier outputs.

For DeepFool, however, the best performance was obtained by RF, which achieved perfect separation in the current sample. ANFIS remained competitive in AUC-based evaluation, with 0.857 ROC-AUC and 0.882 PR-AUC, but did not surpass RF in accuracy. This result suggests that adversarial EEG detection is highly attack-dependent and that no single detector consistently dominates across all perturbation regimes. In practical terms, this supports a more balanced interpretation of ANFIS: rather than universally outperforming classical methods, it should be viewed as an uncertainty-aware complementary detector that may be particularly useful when continuous risk scoring is preferred over hard binary decisions.

Table 3. Performance of adversarial detectors across attack families. Best result per attack is shown in bold.

Attack	Detector	Accuracy	Precision	Recall	F1-score	ROC-AUC	PR-AUC
FGSM	RF	0.692	0.750	0.500	0.600	0.667	0.686
	SVM	0.385	0.375	0.500	0.429	0.405	0.541
	KNN	0.538	0.500	0.500	0.500	0.560	0.632
	ANFIS	**0.769**	**0.714**	**0.833**	**0.769**	**0.786**	0.675
PGD	RF	0.500	0.500	0.500	0.500	0.500	0.549
	SVM	0.417	0.429	0.500	0.462	0.389	0.479
	KNN	0.500	0.500	0.500	0.500	0.458	0.500
	ANFIS	**0.750**	**0.714**	**0.833**	**0.769**	**0.861**	**0.877**
DeepFool	RF	**1.000**	**1.000**	**1.000**	**1.000**	**1.000**	**1.000**
	SVM	0.615	0.556	0.833	0.667	0.905	0.933
	KNN	0.615	0.556	0.833	0.667	0.667	0.562
	ANFIS	0.692	0.667	0.667	0.667	0.857	0.882

4.3 Uncertainty-Aware Analysis and Feature Relevance

The precision-recall behavior of ANFIS under DeepFool supports the usefulness of a continuous adversarial risk score. Even when it did not outperform RF in accuracy, ANFIS achieved 0.882 PR-AUC, indicating that its continuous output still captures relevant adversarial structure. This is particularly relevant in safety-critical BCI scenarios, where a graded suspicion score may be more informative than a rigid binary prediction. As shown in Fig. 2, the precision–recall curve remains in a high-performance region for a broad range of thresholds, reinforcing the ranking ability of the ANFIS score under DeepFool. In addition, Fig. 3 shows that clean and adversarial samples tend to occupy different confidence regions, although overlap is still visible. This behavior is consistent with the idea that adversarial perturbations in EEG do not always create a perfectly separable signature, but rather induce gradual shifts in uncertainty-related quantities derived from the classifier output.

To better understand the contribution of the extracted features, we also performed a simple ablation study with Random Forest on the FGSM scenario. The results in Table 4 show that the pair formed by maximum confidence and logit margin achieved the best performance, with 76.92% accuracy, 0.798 ROC-AUC, and 0.863 PR-AUC. This finding suggests that much of the detector's discriminative capacity comes from uncertainty-related quantities derived from the classifier output, particularly those associated with decision sharpness and boundary proximity. By contrast, adding all five features did not improve performance, indicating that feature relevance is uneven and that compact uncertainty-oriented subsets may be more effective than larger feature vectors.

Table 4. Feature ablation with Random Forest for FGSM detection.

Feature Set	Accuracy	ROC-AUC	PR-AUC
All features	0.692	0.667	0.686
Entropy + Confidence + Margin + Stability	0.692	0.643	0.720
Norm + Confidence + Margin + Stability	0.538	0.738	0.749
Norm + Entropy + Margin + Stability	0.692	0.667	0.686
Norm + Entropy + Confidence + Stability	0.615	0.548	0.526
Norm + Entropy + Confidence + Margin	0.692	0.690	0.710
Entropy + Confidence + Margin	0.692	0.762	0.843
Confidence + Margin	**0.769**	**0.798**	**0.863**

4.4 Limitations

Despite these promising findings, it is important to interpret the results with some caution, as they are still preliminary. One key limitation is the relatively small number of effective adversarial examples retained after filtering: only 21 for FGSM, 19 for PGD, and 21 for DeepFool. With such limited sample sizes, the evaluation becomes more sensitive to variation, which can influence performance metrics. This likely contributes to the perfect separation achieved by the Random Forest in the DeepFool scenario, a result that may not hold under larger or more diverse datasets.

In addition, the study was conducted under a very specific setting, involving a single subject, one EEG dataset, and one backbone architecture. While this is common in early-stage investigations aimed at exploring feasibility, it

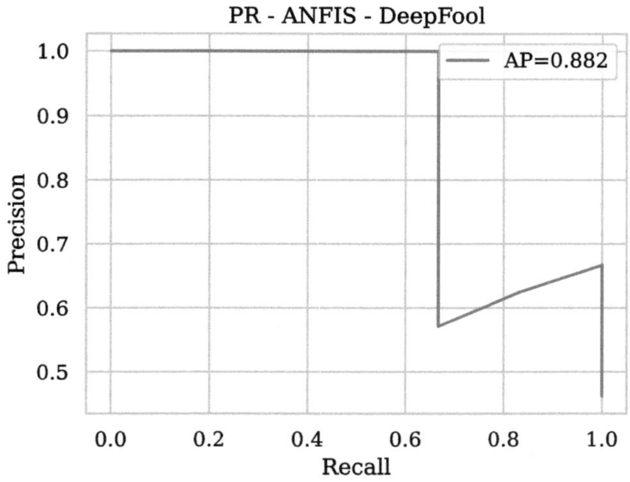

Fig. 2. Precision–recall curve of ANFIS under DeepFool, with AP = 0.882.

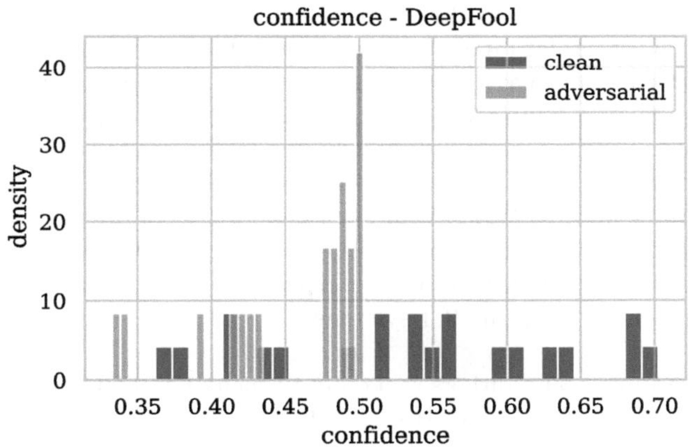

Fig. 3. Distribution of maximum confidence for clean and adversarial DeepFool samples.

restricts the ability to generalize the findings. In practical terms, it remains unclear whether the same performance would be observed across different individuals, experimental paradigms, or model architectures.

For this reason, further validation is necessary. Future work should expand the analysis to include multiple subjects, a wider range of EEG datasets, and different modeling approaches. Only with this broader evaluation will it be possible to determine whether the patterns observed here are robust and generalizable to more realistic and varied scenarios.

5 Conclusion

This paper investigated adversarial robustness in EEG-based Brain–Computer Interfaces by combining attack emulation and adversarial detection analysis. Using EEGNet as a baseline classifier, we showed that FGSM, PGD, and DeepFool consistently reduce classification accuracy, confirming the vulnerability of EEG-based pipelines to adversarial perturbations.

We then compared classical machine learning detectors with a neuro-fuzzy alternative based on ANFIS. The results showed that detector performance is strongly attack-dependent: ANFIS obtained the best results for FGSM and PGD, while Random Forest achieved the strongest performance under DeepFool in the current experimental setup. These findings reinforce the main conclusion of this study: adversarial detection in EEG-based BCIs is attack-dependent, and no single detector should be assumed to generalize across perturbation regimes without broader validation.

Beyond hard classification results, ANFIS remained competitive in AUC-based evaluation and offered an interpretable continuous adversarial risk score. This characteristic is especially relevant in safety-critical BCI scenarios, where representing uncertainty may be more useful than strict binary decisions. In addition, the feature ablation analysis indicated that confidence and logit margin are particularly informative for adversarial detection, highlighting the relevance of uncertainty-related quantities derived from classifier outputs.

The present study remains preliminary due to the limited number of effective adversarial examples and the restriction to a single subject, one EEG dataset, and one backbone architecture. Future work should therefore extend the analysis to cross-subject settings, additional EEG paradigms, and richer representation strategies, as well as further explore interpretable neuro-fuzzy mechanisms for adversarial risk estimation in BCI systems.

Acknowledgements. The authors would like to thank FAPERGS (24/2551-0001396-2, 25/2551-0002584-2), CNPq (307416/2025-9), FAPERGS/CNPq (23/2551-0000126-8) and the Fesurv-University of Rio Verde.

References

1. Aissa, N.E.H.S.B., Lakas, A., Korichi, A., Kerrache, C.A., Belkacem, A.N.: Robust detection of adversarial attacks for EEG-based motor imagery classification using hierarchical deep learning. In: 2023 15th International Conference on Innovations in Information Technology (IIT), pp. 156–161 (2023). https://doi.org/10.1109/IIT59782.2023.10366492
2. Alsereidi, M., Awadallah, A., Alkaabi, A., Yoon, S., Yeun, C.Y.: Data poisoning against federated learning: Comparative analysis under label-flipping attacks and GAN-generated EEG data. In: 2024 2nd International Conference on Cyber Resilience (ICCR), pp. 1–5 (2024). https://doi.org/10.1109/ICCR61006.2024.10533012

3. Alshebli, S., Alshehhi, M., Yeun, C.Y.: Investigating how data poising attacks can impact an EEG-based federated learning model. In: 2024 2nd International Conference on Cyber Resilience (ICCR), pp. 1–6 (2024). https://doi.org/10.1109/ICCR61006.2024.10532875
4. Bernal, S.L., Celdrán, A.H., Pérez, G.M., Barros, M.T., Balasubramaniam, S.: Security in brain-computer interfaces: state-of-the-art, opportunities, and future challenges. ACM Comput. Surv. **54**(1) (2021). https://doi.org/10.1145/3427376
5. Bidgoli, N.S., Kheradpisheh, S.R., Farahani, H.: EEG anomaly detection using generative adversarial networks (GANs). In: 2024 20th CSI International Symposium on Artificial Intelligence and Signal Processing (AISP), pp. 1–6 (2024). https://doi.org/10.1109/AISP61396.2024.10475243
6. Breiman, L.: Random forests. Mach. Learn. **45**(1), 5–32 (2001)
7. Brunner, C., Leeb, R., Müller-Putz, G.R., Schlögl, A., Pfurtscheller, G.: BCI competition 2008 graz data set a (2008). https://www.bbci.de/competition/iv/desc_2a.pdf
8. Cortes, C., Vapnik, V.: Support-vector networks. Mach. Learn. **20**(3), 273–297 (1995)
9. Cover, T., Hart, P.: Nearest neighbor pattern classification. IEEE Trans. Inf. Theory **13**(1), 21–27 (1967). https://doi.org/10.1109/TIT.1967.1053964
10. Dalmazo, B.L., Vilela, J.P., Curado, M.: Performance analysis of network traffic predictors in the cloud. J. Netw. Syst. Manage. **25**, 290–320 (2017)
11. Jang, J.S.: ANFIS: adaptive-network-based fuzzy inference system. IEEE Trans. Syst. Man Cybern. **23**(3), 665–685 (1993). https://doi.org/10.1109/21.256541
12. Lawhern, V.J., Solon, A.J., Waytowich, N.R., Gordon, S.M., Hung, C.P., Lance, B.J.: Eegnet: a compact convolutional neural network for EEG-based brain–computer interfaces. J. Neural Eng. **15**(5), 056013 (2018). https://doi.org/10.1088/1741-2552/aace8c
13. Leite, L., Santo, Y., Dalmazo, B., Riker, A.: Federated learning under attack: improving gradient inversion for batch of images. In: Anais do XXIV Simpósio Brasileiro de Segurança da Informação e de Sistemas Computacionais, pp. 794–800. SBC, Porto Alegre, RS, Brasil (2024). https://doi.org/10.5753/sbseg.2024.241680, https://sol.sbc.org.br/index.php/sbseg/article/view/30070
14. Li, Y., Yu, X., Yu, S., Chen, B.: Adversarial training for the adversarial robustness of EEG-based brain-computer interfaces. In: 2022 IEEE 32nd International Workshop on Machine Learning for Signal Processing (MLSP), pp. 1–6 (2022). https://doi.org/10.1109/MLSP55214.2022.9943479
15. Naik, N., Jenkins, P., Savage, N., Yang, L., Boongoen, T., Iam-On, N.: Fuzzy-import hashing: a malware analysis approach. In: 2020 IEEE International Conference on Fuzzy Systems (FUZZ-IEEE), pp. 1–8 (2020). https://doi.org/10.1109/FUZZ48607.2020.9177636
16. Pandey, S.K., Mustafa, K., Ahson, S.I.: A checklist based approach for the mitigation of buffer overflow attacks. In: 2007 Third International Conference on Wireless Communication and Sensor Networks, pp. 115–117 (2007). https://doi.org/10.1109/WCSN.2007.4475759
17. Quevedo, A., Ayres, D., Dimuro, G., Riker, A., Lucca, G., Dalmazo, B.L.: Optimizing big data traffic prediction using generalizations of choquet integral with adaptive weighting. In: ICC 2025 - IEEE International Conference on Communications, pp. 4872–4877 (2025). https://doi.org/10.1109/ICC52391.2025.11161751
18. Rauber, J., Zimmermann, R., Bethge, M., Brendel, W.: Foolbox native: fast adversarial attacks to benchmark the robustness of machine learning models in pytorch,

tensorflow, and jax. J. Open Source Softw. **5**(53), 2607 (2020). https://doi.org/10.21105/joss.02607
19. Sanei, S., Chambers, J.A.: Machine learning for EEG analysis, pp. 177–233 (2021). https://doi.org/10.1002/9781119386957.ch7
20. Schalk, G., McFarland, D., Hinterberger, T., Birbaumer, N., Wolpaw, J.: BCI 2000: a general-purpose brain-computer interface (BCI) system. IEEE Trans. Biomed. Eng. **51**(6), 1034–1043 (2004). https://doi.org/10.1109/TBME.2004.827072
21. Shi, Y., Sagduyu, Y., Grushin, A.: How to steal a machine learning classifier with deep learning. In: 2017 IEEE International Symposium on Technologies for Homeland Security (HST), pp. 1–5 (2017). https://doi.org/10.1109/THS.2017.7943475
22. Tan, W., et al.: Noisecam: explainable AI for the boundary between noise and adversarial attacks. In: 2023 IEEE International Conference on Fuzzy Systems (FUZZ), pp. 1–8 (2023). https://doi.org/10.1109/FUZZ52849.2023.10309766
23. Zhai, J., Song, G., Zhou, T.: Recognition of epilepsy EEG by two-view adversarial-incentived-based t-s fuzzy classifier. In: 2023 2nd International Conference on Artificial Intelligence, Human-Computer Interaction and Robotics (AIHCIR), pp. 146–153 (2023). https://doi.org/10.1109/AIHCIR61661.2023.00032
24. Zhang, H., Li, L., Qiao, L.: A control and attack detection scheme for fuzzy systems against cyber-attacks. In: 2023 IEEE International Conference on Fuzzy Systems (FUZZ), pp. 1–6 (2023). https://doi.org/10.1109/FUZZ52849.2023.10309687

DeOP-Light: Analyzing the Fine-Tuning Paradox in CLIP Visual Encoder Compression for Open-Vocabulary Semantic Segmentation

Junghun Kim and Jongpil Jeong(✉)

Department of Smart Factory Convergence, Sungkyunkwan University, Suwon-si, Gyeonggi-do 16419, Republic of Korea
{hun0919,jpjeong}@skku.edu

Abstract. Open-vocabulary semantic segmentation (OVSS) relies on contrastive language-image pre-training (CLIP) visual encoders to classify *unseen* categories at inference time. Compressing these encoders for efficient deployment is practically important, yet the impact on the critical *seen/unseen* class distinction has not been studied. We present a diagnostic empirical study rather than a new architectural proposal of CLIP visual encoder compression within the decoupled one-pass (DeOP), applying floating-point (FP)16 quantization and low-rank adaptation (LoRA) on COCO-Stuff and Pascal VOC. We uncover a consistent asymmetric degradation: fine-tuning (FT) the CLIP visual encoder recovers *seen* class performance but simultaneously degrades *unseen* class performance, emerging within the first 1,000 iterations. By comparing against an uncompressed FT baseline, we show that FT itself not compression is the primary driver of this degradation. FT-free compression best preserves *unseen* performance, and post-hoc weight restoration partially recovers it without retraining. Our findings provide practical guidelines for model compression in resource-constrained deployment and highlight the need for *seen/unseen*-aware evaluation in OVSS.

Keywords: Open-vocabulary semantic segmentation · CLIP · Model compression · Catastrophic forgetting · Zero-shot generalization · LoRA

1 Introduction

Semantic segmentation has traditionally required training with a closed set of predefined categories. Open-vocabulary semantic segmentation (OVSS) breaks this limitation by leveraging pre-trained vision-language models (VLMs) such as contrastive language-image pre-training (CLIP) [1] to classify image regions into an arbitrary set of categories including those never *seen* during training, referred to as *unseen* classes. State-of-the-art OVSS methods [2–4] decouple the

O. Gervasi et al. (Eds.): ICCSA 2026, LNCS 16768, pp. 185–201, 2027.
https://doi.org/10.1007/978-3-032-30488-9_12

mask proposal and classification streams, keeping the CLIP visual encoder frozen to preserve its zero-shot generalization capability.

Despite impressive performance, deploying CLIP-based OVSS models at scale raises practical concerns, particularly for resource-constrained environments such as edge devices, autonomous systems, and real-time data analytics pipelines where both efficiency and generalization to novel categories are critical. The large CLIP vision transformer (ViT)-B/16 [5] backbone accounts for the majority of model parameters and inference cost. Model compression methods including floating-point (FP)16 quantization and low-rank adaptation (LoRA) [6] are natural candidates for reducing this overhead. However, a critical question remains unanswered: *does compressing the CLIP visual encoder affect seen* and *unseen* class performance differently?

This question is far from trivial.OVSS performance is conventionally reported as overall mean intersection-over-union (mIoU), which aggregates *seen* and *unseen* classes. An improvement or negligible drop in mIoU could mask a catastrophic drop in *unseen* performance compensated by improved *seen* performance undermining the core value proposition of OVSS. Prior work on CLIP fine-tuning (FT) for image classification has shown that adapting the model to a specific distribution improves in-distribution accuracy while degrading robustness to distribution shifts [7]. We hypothesize an analogous phenomenon in OVSS: compression combined with FT recovers *seen* performance (the training distribution) at the cost of *unseen* generalization (an out-of-distribution (OOD) challenge).

Crucially, OVSS presents a structurally distinct challenge compared to standard image classification. In classification, *seen* and *unseen* classes are evaluated on separate datasets, and the CLIP encoder serves as a feature extractor for one task at a time. In OVSS, however, the CLIP visual encoder must simultaneously serve as a shared feature backbone for both *seen* and *unseen* classes within the same image. This shared-encoder constraint means that any feature-space distortion caused by FT asymmetrically affects the two class groups, creating a degradation pattern that cannot be detected by aggregate metrics alone. In this paper, we confirm and characterize this hypothesis through a systematic study of CLIP visual encoder compression within the decoupled one-pass (DeOP) [4]. We refer to our experimental configurations collectively as DeOP-Light to denote DeOP variants with a compressed CLIP visual encoder. We emphasize that DeOP-Light is not a new architectural proposal but a diagnostic study and design principle: a controlled experimental setting designed to isolate and analyze the effects of compression and FT on the *seen/unseen* performance gap, and to inform principled deployment choices for CLIP-based OVSS systems.

Our main contributions of this study are summarized as follows:

- We apply FP16 quantization and LoRA to the CLIP visual encoder in the DeOP, and evaluate each on COCO-Stuff and Pascal VOC with separate *seen* and *unseen* metrics. While the general phenomenon of FT degrading OOD robustness is known, no prior work has quantified this effect in the *seen/unseen* split specific to OVSS.

- We define the FT Paradox as the phenomenon where FT the CLIP visual encoder consistently recovers *seen* performance while degrading *unseen* performance an asymmetric degradation that undermines the core open-vocabulary capability. Through a FT iteration ablation (no-FT, $1k$, $5k$ and $10k$), we demonstrate that this degradation emerges within the first 1,000 iterations and does not recover with continued training.
- By comparing compressed fine-tuned models against an uncompressed fine-tuned baseline (FP32 FT), we show that FT itself not compression is the primary driver of unseen degradation. Compression plays a secondary, modulatory role.
- FT-free compression best preserves *unseen* generalization. The paradox is more pronounced on COCO-Stuff (171 classes) than Pascal VOC (20 classes), indicating that dataset complexity amplifies the effect.
- Inspired by WiSE-FT, we investigate weight-space interpolation and find that unlike the image classification setting the optimal strategy in OVSS is full restoration of the original CLIP visual encoder weights ($\alpha = 0$), providing a training-free recovery of *unseen* performance.

The remainder of this paper is organized as follows. Section 2 reviews related work; Sect. 3 describes the DeOP-Light framework; Sect. 4 presents the main experiments; Sect. 5 discusses practical guidelines and limitations; Sect. 6 outlines future directions; Sect. 7 conclude the paper.

2 Related Work

2.1 Open-Vocabulary Semantic Segmentation

OVSS aims to segment images into regions belonging to both *seen* (base) and *unseen* (novel) categories [8]. CLIP [1] is a VLM pre-trained on 400 million image-text pairs using contrastive learning, which learns to align visual and textual representations in a shared embedding space; this alignment enables zero-shot recognition of arbitrary categories described by text, making CLIP a natural backbone for OVSS. Early approaches such as ZS3Net [8] and SPNet [9] used generative or projection-based methods but were limited to simple datasets. OpenSeg [10] explored the use of ALIGN [11] for segment classification. ZegFormer [2] and SimBaseline [3] introduced the decoupled two-stream design, separating mask proposal from CLIP-based classification.

DeOP [4] our base framework further improved efficiency by enabling a single-pass through the CLIP encoder via its patch severance (PS) and classification anchor learning (CAL) modules. Subsequent methods have further advanced OVSS: SAN [12] introduced a side adapter network for efficient open-vocabulary segmentation, CAT-Seg [13] proposed cost aggregation for improved spatial alignment, and FC-CLIP [14] achieved strong performance with a single frozen CLIP backbone. More recently, training-free OVSS methods such as NACLIP [15] and ClearCLIP [16] have demonstrated that competitive dense prediction can be achieved without any FT of CLIP, which aligns with our finding that preserving the original CLIP weights is beneficial for *unseen* class performance.

2.2 CLIP Compression and Adaptation

Compressing large VLMs for efficient deployment is an active research area. Model compression approaches include quantization [17,18] and parameter-efficient FT (PEFT) such as LoRA [6] and prompt tuning [19]. TinyCLIP [20] demonstrated that CLIP can be compressed to 50% of its original size via affinity mimicking and weight inheritance while retaining much of its zero-shot accuracy. CLIP-KD [21] systematically studied various distillation losses for compressing CLIP models across different frameworks. Prompt learning methods such as CoOp [22] adapt CLIP to downstream tasks by learning continuous prompt vectors, achieving strong generalization with minimal parameter updates. Token reduction methods for ViTs [23] have demonstrated significant speedups on image classification, though their interaction with dense prediction frameworks remains underexplored. However, existing compression and adaptation methods are evaluated solely on overall accuracy, without distinguishing *seen* from unseen categories a critical distinction for OVSS.

2.3 Catastrophic Forgetting in Foundation Models

FT pre-trained models on specific tasks often leads to catastrophic forgetting of their original generalization capabilities [24]. For CLIP, Wortsman et al. showed that standard FT on ImageNet improves in-distribution accuracy but reduces out-of-distribution robustness, proposing weight-space ensembling-FT (WiSE-FT) as a mitigation [7]. Zheng et al. observed similar forgetting in continual learning of VLMs [25]. Akbarian Bafghi et al. demonstrated that selective LoRA FT reduces forgetting of zero-shot capabilities [26]. Our work extends these observations to the specific scenario of CLIP visual encoder compression in OVSS. While the general phenomenon of FT degrading OOD robustness is well established, we provide the first quantitative evidence of its asymmetric impact on *seen* versus *unseen* classes within the OVSS evaluation framework.

3 DeOP-Light Framework

DeOP-Light builds upon the DeOP [4] by applying compression exclusively to its CLIP visual encoder. This section describes the problem setting and the base framework on which all compression experiments are conducted. Figure 1 illustrates the overall pipeline of DeOP-Light. Following [3], the class set is partitioned into *seen* classes C_s (available during training) and *unseen* classes C_u (only at inference), with $C_s \cap C_u = \emptyset$. A model is trained on images annotated with C_s and evaluated on both C_s and C_u at test time. Performance is reported as *seen* IoU, *unseen* IoU, and their harmonic mean (hIoU), which equally weights both.

DeOP adopts a two-stream framework that combines a class-agnostic mask proposal network with a CLIP-based mask classification stream. The proposal stream is based on MaskFormer [27] with a ResNet-101c backbone, whereas the

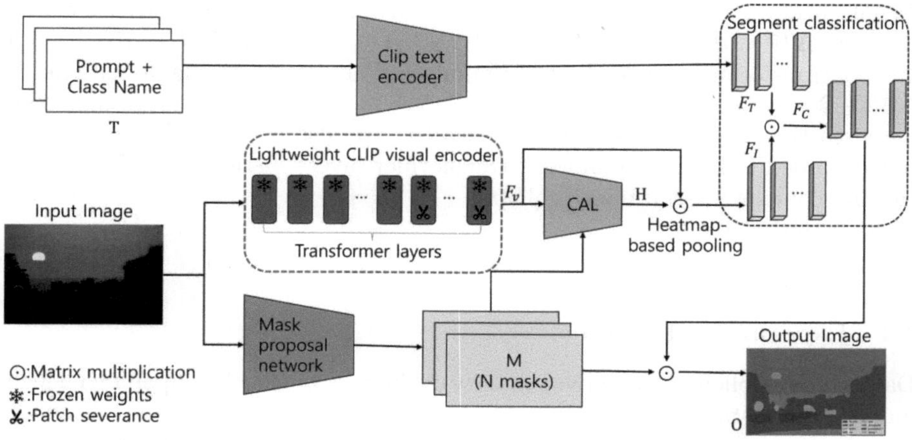

Fig. 1. Overview of the DeOP-Light framework. Compression is applied exclusively to the CLIP visual encoder (highlighted in red dashed border). All other components mask proposal network, CLIP text encoder, and CAL module remain unchanged from the original DeOP. (Color figure online)

classification stream uses a frozen CLIP ViT-B/16 visual encoder. Given an input image I, the mask proposal network generates N proposal masks M. The CLIP visual encoder equipped with PS produces a feature map F_V. The CAL module then generates heatmaps H from F_V and M, which are used for heatmap-based pooling to obtain segment embeddings $F_I = H \odot F_V$. Classification is performed by matching F_I against text embeddings F_T from the CLIP text encoder: $F_C = F_T \cdot F_I$. The final segmentation output is obtained by combining the class scores with the proposal masks: $O = F_C \cdot M$.

In DeOP-Light, the CLIP visual encoder is our sole target for compression. All other components (MaskFormer backbone, CAL module, text encoder and prompt learner) remain unchanged from the original DeOP. This design isolates the effect of visual encoder compression on the *seen/unseen* performance gap, which is the central question of this study. We apply two representative compression methods to the CLIP ViT-B/16 visual encoder within DeOP-Light. Importantly, these techniques target only the 158 parameter tensors (weights and biases) of the visual encoder, out of 308 total CLIP parameter tensors, leaving the text encoder and all other modules untouched. We convert all non-LayerNorm parameters in the CLIP visual encoder from FP32 to FP16 precision. LayerNorm parameters are kept in FP32 to maintain numerical stability. For FT variants, the model is trained with FP16 forward pass and FP32 optimizer state (standard mixed-precision training), and the checkpoint is saved in FP32 (which we then re-quantize to FP16 at evaluation time). We note that FP16 represents the most conservative form of quantization; more aggressive methods (e.g., INT8, INT4) are left for future work. We inject LoRA adapters [6] with rank $r = 4$ into the `out_proj` layers of the self-attention modules in the CLIP visual encoder. LoRA freezes the pre-trained weights W_0 and learns low-rank updates $\Delta W = BA$, where $B \in \mathbb{R}^{d \times r}$ and $A \in \mathbb{R}^{r \times d}$. With $d = 768$, $r = 4$, and 12 transformer layers, the total number of additional trainable parameters is $12 \times 2 \times r \times d = 12 \times 2 \times 4 \times 768 = 73{,}728 \approx 73.7k$, which is negligible compared to the $86M$-parameter visual encoder. We also considered layer pruning but excluded it because removing transformer layers disrupts the PS module, causing complete performance collapse.

4 Experiments

4.1 Experimental Setup

Datasets. We follow the open-vocabulary evaluation protocol of [3] on two benchmarks. COCO-Stuff-171 [28] uses 156 *seen* classes for training and 15 *unseen* (novel) classes for evaluation. We train on COCO-Stuff-164k and evaluate on the 5k validation split. For cross-dataset generalization, we evaluate models trained on COCO-Stuff on Pascal VOC 2012 [29] (15 *seen* / 5 *unseen* classes) without any FT.

All experiments are conducted on a single NVIDIA A100 80GB GPU using the official DeOP codebase with Detectron2 [30]. The baseline model uses the published DeOP checkpoint. For FT experiments, we train for 1k, 5k, and 10k iterations with batch size 8 using AdamW (learning rate $= 10^{-4}$, weight decay $= 10^{-4}$).

4.2 Performance Metrics

We evaluate all models using three metrics that separately capture *seen* and *unseen* class performance. *seen* IoU and *unseen* IoU denote the mIoU computed over *seen* classes C_s and *unseen* classes C_u, respectively. hIoU is the harmonic mean of *seen* and *unseen* IoU, defined as:

$$hIoU = \frac{2 \times seenIoU \times unseenIoU}{seenIoU + unseenIoU}, \tag{1}$$

Which equally penalizes degradation in either category and serves as the primary metric for evaluating the *seen/unseen* trade-off.Frames per second (FPS) is measured on COCO-Stuff with batch size 1 to assess inference efficiency. Note that FP16 fine-tuned models show slightly lower FPS (7.99) than FP16 no-FT (8.33) because the fine-tuned checkpoints are saved in FP32 and re-quantized to FP16 at evaluation, introducing a small overhead from the mixed-precision conversion.

Table 1. DeOP-Light results on COCO-Stuff. All methods compress only the CLIP visual encoder. "no-FT" denotes no FT after compression. FPS, V.E. Mem., and Peak GPU are measured on an A100 80 GB at 512×512 input with batch 1.

Method	FT Iter.	*seen*	*unseen*	*h*IoU	FPS	V.E. Mem(*MB*)	Peak GPU(*MB*)
DeOP (Baseline)		37.97	38.41	38.19	7.34	338.94	1808.59
DeOP-Light FP16 no-FT	0	37.00	35.12	36.03	8.33	169.55	1614.58
DeOP-Light FP16 FT	1*k*	36.31	31.08	33.49	7.99	169.55	1619.91
DeOP-Light FP16 FT	5*k*	38.23	31.83	34.74	7.99	169.55	1614.49
DeOP-Light FP16 FT	10*k*	36.53	29.80	32.82	7.99	169.55	1619.31
DeOP-Light LoRA (r=4) FT	1*k*	36.37	30.32	33.07	8.33	339.22	1811.24
DeOP-Light LoRA (r=4) FT	5*k*	38.23	32.13	34.92	8.33	339.22	1809.05
DeOP-Light LoRA (r=4) FT	10*k*	38.40	31.58	34.66	8.33	339.22	1807.75

4.3 Quantitative Analysis

Table 1 shows a clear *seen/unseen* trade-off. Fine-tuned variants recover or improve *seen* IoU (36.3–38.4) but consistently reduce *unseen* IoU (29.8–32.1) relative to the baseline (38.41), whereas FP16 no-FT preserves the highest *unseen* IoU among compressed models (35.12). LoRA 5*k* yields the best fine-tuned *h*IoU (34.92), but LoRA 10*k* already shows a decline in *unseen* IoU, indicating that longer FT further erodes zero-shot generalization.

The efficiency columns show that FP16 halves the CLIP visual encoder weight memory (338.94→169.55*MB*) and reduces peak inference memory by about 10.7%. LoRA adds only 73.7*k* adapter parameters and leaves inference memory nearly unchanged, so its main benefit is training-time parameter efficiency rather than deployment-time weight compression. To test cross-dataset generalization, we evaluate COCO-Stuff-trained models on Pascal VOC without VOC-specific FT. Table 2 shows the results. The VOC baseline *h*IoU (89.62) is higher than the original DeOP intra-dataset result because our setting follows [3]: training on COCO-Stuff and testing on VOC.

Table 2. Cross-dataset comparison on Pascal VOC. Models are trained on COCO-Stuff and evaluated on VOC without FT.

Method	FT Iter.	*seen*	*unseen*	*h*IoU
DeOP (Baseline)		90.31	88.94	89.62
DeOP-Light FP16 no-FT	0	90.31	88.93	89.61
DeOP-Light FP16 FT	5*k*	87.81	83.29	85.49
DeOP-Light LoRA (r=4) FT	5*k*	87.48	85.75	86.60

On VOC, FP16 no-FT is nearly identical to the baseline, while fine-tuned FP16 and LoRA degrade both *seen* and *unseen* IoU. The smaller drops compared with COCO-Stuff suggest that dataset complexity amplifies the *seen/unseen* trade-off. To identify when degradation begins, we train FP16 and LoRA models for different iteration counts. Table 3 and Figs. 2–3 summarize the results.

Table 3. FT iteration ablation on COCO-Stuff. FP16 and LoRA are evaluated at multiple iteration counts.

Method	FT Iter.	*seen*	*unseen*	*h*IoU
FP16	no-FT	37.00	35.12	36.03
	1*k*	36.31	31.08	33.49
	5*k*	38.23	31.83	34.74
	10*k*	36.53	29.80	32.82
LoRA	1*k*	36.37	30.32	33.07
	5*k*	38.23	32.13	34.92
	10*k*	38.40	31.58	34.66

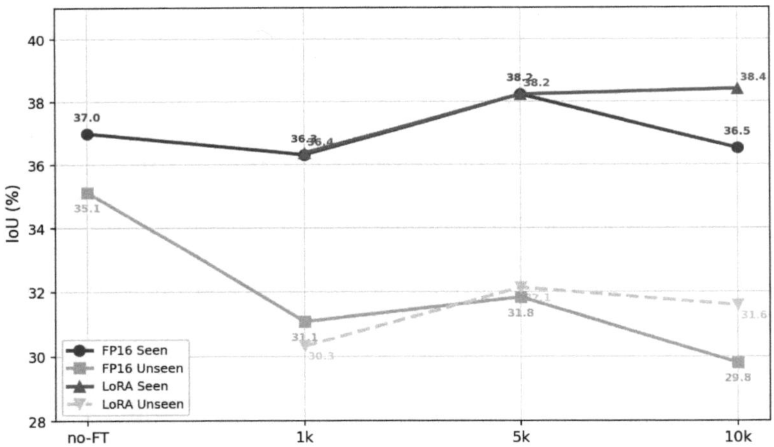

Fig. 2. *seen* and *unseen* IoU as a function of FT iterations on COCO-Stuff. *seen* IoU recovers with FT while *unseen* IoU consistently degrades for both FP16 and LoRA.

unseen degradation appears within the first 1*k* iterations: FP16 drops from 35.12 (no-FT) to 31.08, and LoRA follows the same pattern. Although LoRA is slightly more stable and peaks at 5*k*, both methods lose *unseen* performance as FT proceeds. This confirms that the phenomenon is not method-specific; as shown in Table 4, it also occurs without compression.

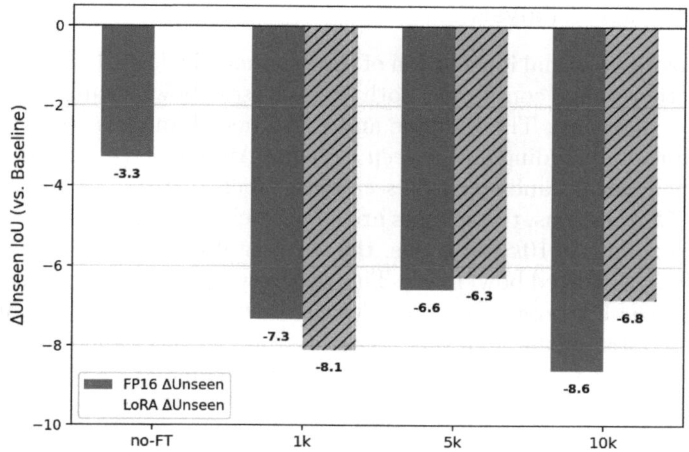

Fig. 3. *unseen* IoU degradation relative to the baseline (38.41). The drop accumulates progressively for both FP16 and LoRA across all iteration counts, confirming the method-agnostic nature of the FT Paradox.

Comparing COCO-Stuff and Pascal VOC, the degradation is stronger on the more complex COCO-Stuff benchmark. FP16 no-FT causes a −3.29 *unseen* drop on COCO-Stuff but only −0.01 on VOC, suggesting that a larger and semantically denser class space increases the risk of confusing *unseen* classes after visual-encoder adaptation. To separate the effects of compression and FT, we fine-tune the original DeOP model without compression (FP32 FT) using the same hyperparameters.

Table 4. Disentangling compression from FT on COCO-Stuff. FP32 FT applies no compression the CLIP visual encoder is fine-tuned in its original FP32 precision.

Method	FT Iter.	*seen*	*unseen*	*h*IoU
Baseline (no FT)		37.97	38.41	38.19
FP32 FT (no compression)	1*k*	36.04	31.34	33.53
FP32 FT (no compression)	5*k*	36.47	30.84	33.42
FP16 FT	1*k*	36.31	31.08	33.49
FP16 FT	5*k*	38.23	31.83	34.74

FP32 FT produces nearly the same *unseen* degradation as FP16 FT: at 1*k*, the *unseen* IoU values are 31.34 and 31.08, respectively. Thus, FT the CLIP visual encoder itself is the primary driver of *unseen* degradation, while compression plays a secondary role. This is consistent with Sect. 4.5, where fully restoring the original CLIP visual weights ($\alpha = 0$) gives the best recovery.

4.4 Qualitative Analysis

Figure 4 provides a visual illustration of the asymmetric degradation on a COCO-Stuff validation image containing both *seen* classes (bowl, dining table) and an *unseen* class (scissors). The baseline and FP16 no-FT models correctly identify all three objects, including the *unseen* scissors. After just 1k FT iterations, the scissors region shrinks and spurious *seen*-class labels (cardboard, metal) begin to appear. At 5k iterations, the scissors are completely lost, and the bowl boundary becomes irregular. At 10k iterations, the segmentation quality further degrades with a severely distorted bowl mask. This progression visually confirms the quantitative findings: FT progressively erodes the model's ability to recognize *unseen* classes while introducing spurious *seen*-class predictions, whereas compression without FT preserves the original segmentation quality.

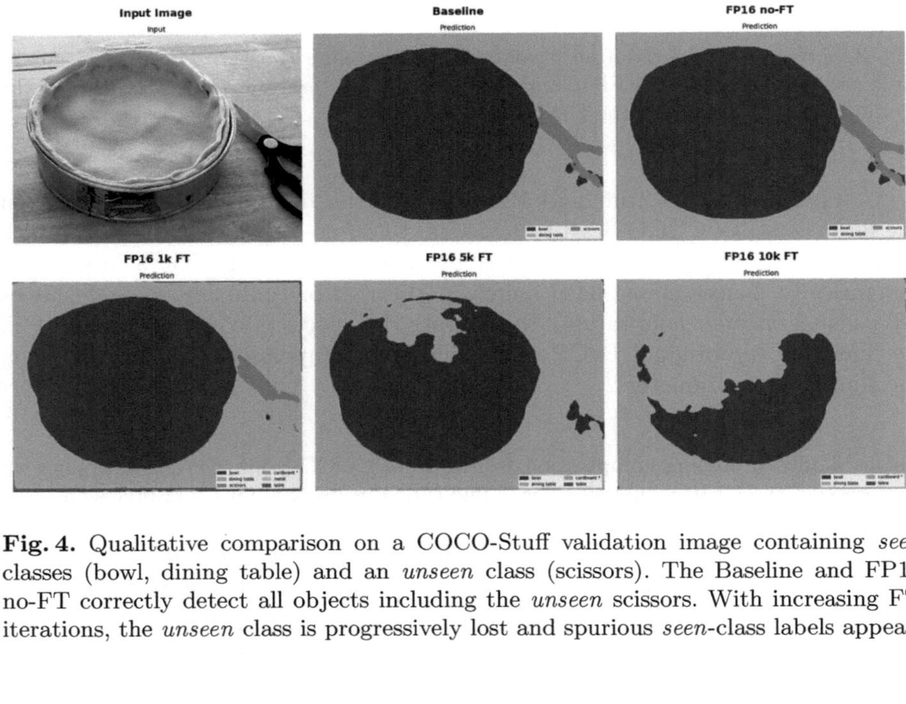

Fig. 4. Qualitative comparison on a COCO-Stuff validation image containing *seen* classes (bowl, dining table) and an *unseen* class (scissors). The Baseline and FP16 no-FT correctly detect all objects including the *unseen* scissors. With increasing FT iterations, the *unseen* class is progressively lost and spurious *seen*-class labels appear.

4.5 Post-hoc Weight Restoration

Having identified the asymmetric *seen/unseen* degradation, we investigate whether it can be mitigated without retraining. Inspired by WiSE-FT [7], we interpolate between the original zero-shot CLIP visual encoder weights W_0 and the fine-tuned compressed weights W_{ft}:

$$W_\alpha = (1 - \alpha) \cdot W_0 + \alpha \cdot W_{\text{ft}}, \tag{2}$$

where $\alpha \in [0, 1]$. At $\alpha = 0$, the model uses the original CLIP visual encoder from the DeOP checkpoint, whereas at $\alpha = 1$, it uses the fine-tuned CLIP visual encoder. The interpolation is restricted to the 158 CLIP visual encoder parameter tensors. All other modules, including the MaskFormer proposal network, CAL module, prompt learner, and CLIP text encoder, are kept fixed and identical across all α values.

Table 5. Weight interpolation comparison on COCO-Stuff (DeOP-Light FP16 5k). $\alpha =$ 0: original CLIP visual encoder weights; $\alpha = 1$: fully fine-tuned weights. Interpolation is applied only to the CLIP visual encoder.

α	*seen*	*unseen*	*h*IoU
0.0 (original)	38.77	33.04	35.68
0.3	38.65	32.58	35.35
0.5	38.57	32.38	35.20
1.0 (fine-tuned)	38.23	31.83	34.74

Table 5 shows a monotonic trend: moving from the fine-tuned weights ($\alpha = 1$) toward the original CLIP weights ($\alpha = 0$) improves both *seen* and *unseen* IoU. The best result is obtained by full restoration, which recovers 1.21 *unseen* points (31.83→33.04) and 0.54 *seen* points (38.23→38.77) over the fully fine-tuned model. This differs from WiSE-FT in image classification, where an intermediate interpolation often balances in-distribution and OOD performance. In OVSS, the CLIP visual encoder is shared by *seen* and *unseen* classes within the same dense prediction task, so any FT-induced bias toward *seen* classes can harm *unseen* recognition. The appropriate mitigation is therefore closer to weight restoration than weight interpolation. However, full restoration still remains below the original uncompressed baseline (*unseen* 38.41), indicating that the fine-tuned non-visual modules have become partially mismatched with the restored CLIP features. FP16 no-FT also preserves *unseen* IoU better than restoration (35.12 *vs.* 33.04), reinforcing our main conclusion that avoiding visual-encoder FT is the safest strategy for preserving zero-shot generalization.

4.6 Training-Time Mitigation: Feature Distillation

While post-hoc weight restoration (Sect. 4.5) provides a training-free mitigation, we also investigate whether training-time regularization can prevent the asymmetric degradation from occurring in the first place. Inspired by recent work on preserving CLIP's zero-shot capabilities through knowledge distillation [21], we add a feature-level distillation loss that encourages the compressed (student) CLIP visual encoder to remain close to the original (teacher) encoder during FT:

$$L_{\text{total}} = L_{\text{DeOP}} + \lambda \cdot L_{\text{KD}}, \quad L_{\text{KD}} = 1 - \cos(F_{\text{student}}, F_{\text{teacher}}), \tag{3}$$

where F_{student} and F_{teacher} are the spatial feature maps from the compressed and original CLIP visual encoders, respectively. The teacher is a frozen deep copy of the original CLIP visual encoder, requiring no additional training.

Table 6. Feature distillation results on COCO-Stuff. The teacher is the original frozen CLIP visual encoder. All models use FP16 compression. "None" denotes standard FT without distillation.

Mitigation	λ	*seen*	*unseen*	*h*IoU
None (FP16 FT 5*k*)	–	38.23	31.83	34.74
Feature KD (5*k*)	0.5	21.10	16.85	18.74
Feature KD (5*k*)	0.01	27.98	22.30	24.82
Feature KD (10*k*)	0.01	17.74	14.77	16.12

Table 6 reports the results. Contrary to our expectation, feature distillation degrades both *seen* and *unseen* performance compared to standard FT across all tested configurations. With $\lambda = 0.5$, the distillation loss dominates the total loss (accounting for 97% of the gradient signal), effectively preventing the model from learning the segmentation task. Reducing λ to 0.01 restores a balanced loss ratio (KD $\approx$ 54% of classification loss), but performance remains substantially below the non-distilled baseline. Moreover, continued training to 10*k* iterations worsens performance further (*h*IoU: 24.82→16.12), indicating that the distillation objective actively interferes with task learning over time.

We attribute this failure to a fundamental gradient conflict: the segmentation loss L_{DeOP} requires the visual features to adapt to the downstream task, while the distillation loss L_{KD} constrains them to remain fixed. These two objectives produce opposing gradients on the same parameters, preventing the model from satisfying either goal effectively. This conflict is particularly severe in DeOP's framework, where the PS module modifies self-attention patterns and the CAL module learns spatial heatmaps on top of the visual features both of which require feature adaptation to function properly. This negative result carries an important implication: naive feature-level distillation is not a viable strategy for preserving zero-shot generalization during OVSS compression. The success of post-hoc weight restoration (Sect. 4.5) over training-time distillation suggests that decoupling the two objectives temporally first adapting, then restoring is more effective than forcing them to coexist in a single optimization.

5 Discussion and Limitations

5.1 Practical Guidelines

Based on our analysis, we offer the following practical guidelines for compressing CLIP-based OVSS models, particularly relevant to edge deployment and resource-constrained inference pipelines. When *unseen* performance is the priority, FT-free compression is the recommended choice: DeOP-Light FP16 no-FT achieves 8.33 FPS (*vs.* 7.34 baseline) with only 3.3-point *unseen* degradation. When *seen/unseen* balance is required and FT is necessary, LoRA at rank r=4 with a limited budget (5k iterations) is preferable, achieving the best fine-tuned hIoU (34.92) and degrading *unseen* IoU less than FP16; FT beyond this point progressively erodes *unseen* generalization, so iterations should be limited and *unseen* performance monitored throughout training. When FT has already been performed, post-hoc weight restoration (Sect. 4.5) provides training-free recovery of *unseen* performance. Finally, regardless of the compression method chosen, we strongly recommend evaluating *seen* and *unseen* IoU separately (alongside their harmonic mean), as overall mIoU can mask catastrophic *unseen* degradation behind improved *seen* performance.

5.2 Limitations

Our study has several limitations that should be acknowledged. All experiments are conducted on a single OVSS framework (DeOP). While the consistency across two different compression methods and two datasets suggests generality, we cannot rule out that DeOP's specific architectural choices (PS, CAL) may amplify or attenuate the observed effects. In particular, DeOP's PS and CAL modules are tightly coupled to the CLIP visual encoder's feature space: PS modifies self-attention patterns in the last transformer layer, and CAL learns spatial heatmaps conditioned on these features. In frameworks without such tight coupling (e.g., SimBaseline [3], which uses independent mask-and-crop passes, or OVSeg [31]), the asymmetric degradation may be less severe, as the visual encoder features are consumed more independently. Validating this hypothesis on additional OVSS frameworks is an important direction for future work.

Our compression study is intentionally restricted to FP16 quantization and LoRA at rank $r = 4$ in order to isolate the FT effect under minimally perturbative compression. While this design choice is essential to our diagnostic objective, the conclusions may not directly generalize to more aggressive and practically relevant settings such as INT8/INT4 quantization, structured pruning, or higher LoRA ranks, which we treat as orthogonal axes of investigation.

All reported numbers are single-run point estimates without variance estimates across multiple training runs. While the observed effect sizes (e.g., 7–8 IoU points of *unseen* degradation under FT) are substantially larger than typical run-to-run variance reported for semantic segmentation models, formal statistical analysis with multiple seeds and confidence intervals would further strengthen the reliability of our conclusions.

6 Future Directions

We demonstrated that restoring the original CLIP visual encoder weights can partially recover *unseen* performance (Sect. 4.5), but the recovered model still underperforms the uncompressed baseline. Our feature distillation experiment (Sect. 4.6) showed that naive training-time regularization is insufficient, as the gradient conflict between task adaptation and feature preservation actively degrades performance. This suggests that future mitigation strategies should avoid forcing these two objectives to compete within a single optimization loop. Promising directions include two-stage approaches that first train non-visual modules with frozen CLIP weights and then apply compression with targeted adaptation; *seen/unseen*-aware regularization using proxy text embeddings from classes outside the training set to maintain alignment without accessing *unseen* class labels; and framework-aware distillation that accounts for the structural dependencies introduced by modules such as PS and CAL, rather than applying generic feature matching. The weight restoration results also suggest that training the non-visual modules (CAL, prompts) with original CLIP weights while deploying with compressed weights could reduce the distribution mismatch observed in our experiments.

Beyond mitigation strategies, several directions for empirical extension would strengthen the generalizability of our findings. First, multi-run experiments with variance reporting would provide a formal statistical foundation for the observed asymmetric degradation, particularly for boundary cases where the *seen/unseen* gap is small. Second, validating the FT Paradox on additional OVSS frameworks such as SimBaseline [3], OVSeg [31], SAN [12], and CAT-Seg [13] would clarify whether the effect is specific to DeOP's tightly coupled PS/CAL design or a general property of CLIP-based OVSS systems. Third, extending the compression spectrum to more aggressive methods such as INT8/INT4 quantization, structured pruning, and higher LoRA ranks would characterize the trade-off between compression aggressiveness and zero-shot preservation, which is essential for practical deployment in resource-constrained environments.

Our findings also have implications beyond static deployment. The FT Paradox observed here where adapting CLIP to *seen* classes degrades *unseen* performance closely parallels the catastrophic forgetting phenomenon studied in continual and lifelong learning of foundation models [24,25]. In a continual OVSS setting, where new categories are incrementally introduced over time, naively FT the visual encoder on each new task would compound the asymmetric degradation we observe, potentially eroding the model's open-vocabulary capability across the learning trajectory. Our weight restoration result ($\alpha = 0$ being optimal) suggests that maintaining a snapshot of the original CLIP weights and selectively adapting only the non-visual modules could serve as a principled starting point for continual OVSS an avenue we leave for future investigation.

7 Conclusion

We present DeOP-Light, a systematic study of how CLIP visual encoder compression affects *seen* and *unseen* class performance in OVSS. Across two representative compression methods (FP16, LoRA) and two datasets (COCO-Stuff, Pascal VOC), we consistently observe an asymmetric degradation pattern: FT the CLIP visual encoder recovers *seen* class performance but persistently degrades *unseen* class performance, with the degradation emerging within the first 1,000 iterations. Crucially, by comparing against an uncompressed FT baseline, we demonstrate that FT itself not compression is the primary driver of this degradation, with compression playing a secondary role. Post-hoc weight restoration partially recovers *unseen* performance, while training-time feature distillation fails due to gradient conflicts. Our key practical finding is that keeping the CLIP visual encoder frozen best preserves the zero-shot generalization that defines OVSS. We advocate for *seen/unseen*-separated evaluation as a standard practice when FT or compressing CLIP-based OVSS models.

Acknowledgments. This work was supported by the Institute of Information & Communications Technology Planning & Evaluation (IITP)-ICT Creative Consilience Program grant funded by the Korea government (MSIT) (IITP-2026-RS-2020-II201821), This work was supported by the Korea Institute for Advancement of Technology (KIAT) grant funded by the Korea Government under the Industrial Innovation Talent Growth Support Project (KIAT-2026-RS-2026-25532917).

Disclosure of Interests. The authors have no competing interests to declare that are relevant to the content of this article.

References

1. Radford, A., et al.: Learning transferable visual models from natural language supervision. In: Proceedings of the 38th International Conference on Machine Learning (ICML), pp. 8748–8763 (2021)
2. Ding, J., Xue, N., Xia, G.S., Dai, D.: Decoupling zero-shot semantic segmentation. In: Proceedings of the IEEE/CVF Conference on Computer Vision and Pattern Recognition (CVPR), pp. 11583–11592 (2022)
3. Xu, M., et al.: A simple baseline for open-vocabulary semantic segmentation with pre-trained vision-language model. In: Avidan, S., Brostow, G., Cissé, M., Farinella, G.M., Hassner, T. (eds.) Computer Vision - ECCV 2022. LNCS, vol. 13689, pp. 736–753. Springer, Cham (2022). https://doi.org/10.1007/978-3-031-19818-2_42
4. Han, C., Zhong, Y., Li, D., Han, K., Ma, L.: Open-vocabulary semantic segmentation with decoupled one-pass network. In: Proceedings of the IEEE/CVF International Conference on Computer Vision (ICCV), pp. 1086–1096 (2023)
5. Dosovitskiy, A., et al.: An image is worth 16x16 words: transformers for image recognition at scale. In: International Conference on Learning Representations (ICLR) (2021)
6. Hu, E.J., et al.: LoRA: low-rank adaptation of large language models. In: International Conference on Learning Representations (ICLR) (2022)
7. Wortsman, M., et al.: Robust fine-tuning of zero-shot models. In: Proceedings of the IEEE/CVF Conference on Computer Vision and Pattern Recognition (CVPR), pp. 7959–7971 (2022)
8. Bucher, M., Vu, T.H., Cord, M., Pérez, P.: Zero-shot semantic segmentation. In: Advances in Neural Information Processing Systems (NeurIPS), vol. 32 (2019)

9. Xian, Y., Choudhury, S., He, Y., Schiele, B., Akata, Z.: Semantic projection network for zero- and few-label semantic segmentation. In: Proceedings of the IEEE/CVF Conference on Computer Vision and Pattern Recognition (CVPR), pp. 8256–8265 (2019)
10. Ghiasi, G., Gu, X., Cui, Y., Lin, T.Y.: Scaling open-vocabulary image segmentation with image-level labels. In: Avidan, S., Brostow, G., Cissé, M., Farinella, G.M., Hassner, T. (eds.) Computer Vision - ECCV 2022. LNCS, vol. 13696, pp. 540–557. Springer, Cham (2022). https://doi.org/10.1007/978-3-031-20059-5_31
11. Jia, C., et al.: Scaling up visual and vision-language representation learning with noisy text supervision. In: Proceedings of the 38th International Conference on Machine Learning (ICML), pp. 4904–4916 (2021)
12. Xu, M., Zhang, Z., Wei, F., Hu, H., Bai, X.: Side adapter network for open-vocabulary semantic segmentation. In: Proceedings of the IEEE/CVF Conference on Computer Vision and Pattern Recognition (CVPR), pp. 2945–2954 (2023)
13. Cho, S., Shin, H., Hong, S., Arnab, A., Seo, P.H., Kim, S.: CAT-seg: cost aggregation for open-vocabulary semantic segmentation. In: Proceedings of the IEEE/CVF Conference on Computer Vision and Pattern Recognition (CVPR), pp. 4113–4123 (2024)
14. Yu, Q., He, J., Deng, X., Shen, X., Chen, L.C.: Convolutions die hard: open-vocabulary segmentation with single frozen convolutional CLIP. In: Advances in Neural Information Processing Systems (NeurIPS), vol. 36 (2023)
15. Hajimiri, S., Ben Ayed, I., Dolz, J.: Pay attention to your neighbours: training-free open-vocabulary semantic segmentation. In: Proceedings of the Winter Conference on Applications of Computer Vision (WACV), pp. 5061–5071 (2025)
16. Lan, M., Chen, C., Ke, Y., Wang, X., Feng, L., Zhang, W.: ClearCLIP: decomposing CLIP representations for dense vision-language inference. In: Leonardis, A., Ricci, E., Roth, S., Russakovsky, O., Sattler, T., Varol, G. (eds.) Computer Vision - ECCV 2024. LNCS, vol. 15105, pp. 143–160. Springer, Cham (2024). https://doi.org/10.1007/978-3-031-72970-6_9
17. Nagel, M., van Baalen, M., Blankevoort, T., Welling, M.: Data-free quantization through weight equalization and bias correction. In: Proceedings of the IEEE/CVF International Conference on Computer Vision (ICCV), pp. 1325–1334 (2019)
18. Frantar, E., Ashkboos, S., Hoefler, T., Alistarh, D.: OPTQ: accurate post-training quantization for generative pre-trained transformers. In: International Conference on Learning Representations (ICLR) (2023)
19. Jia, M., et al.: Visual prompt tuning. In: Avidan, S., Brostow, G., Cissé, M., Farinella, G.M., Hassner, T. (eds.) Computer Vision - ECCV 2022. LNCS, vol. 13693, pp. 709–727. Springer, Cham (2022). https://doi.org/10.1007/978-3-031-19827-4_41
20. Wu, K., et al.: TinyCLIP: CLIP distillation via affinity mimicking and weight inheritance. In: Proceedings of the IEEE/CVF International Conference on Computer Vision (ICCV), pp. 21970–21980 (2023)
21. Yang, C., et al.: CLIP-KD: an empirical study of CLIP model distillation. In: Proceedings of the IEEE/CVF Conference on Computer Vision and Pattern Recognition (CVPR), pp. 15952–15962 (2024)
22. Zhou, K., Yang, J., Loy, C.C., Liu, Z.: Learning to prompt for vision-language models. Int. J. Comput. Vision **130**(9), 2337–2348 (2022)
23. Rao, Y., Zhao, W., Liu, B., Lu, J., Zhou, J., Hsieh, C.J.: DynamicViT: efficient vision transformers with dynamic token sparsification. In: Advances in Neural Information Processing Systems (NeurIPS), vol. 34, pp. 13937–13949 (2021)

24. Zhai, Y., et al.: Investigating the catastrophic forgetting in multimodal large language model fine-tuning. In: Conference on Parsimony and Learning (CPAL), vol. 234, pp. 202–227. PMLR Proceedings of Machine Learning Research (2024)
25. Zheng, Z., Ma, M., Wang, K., Qin, Z., Yue, X., You, Y.: Preventing zero-shot transfer degradation in continual learning of vision-language models. In: Proceedings of the IEEE/CVF International Conference on Computer Vision (ICCV), pp. 19125–19136 (2023)
26. Bafghi, A., Bagwell, R., Ravichandran, C., Shrivastava, A., Raissi, A., M.: Fine tuning without catastrophic forgetting via selective low rank adaptation. arXiv preprint arXiv:2501.15377 (2025)
27. Cheng, B., Schwing, A.G., Kirillov, A.: Per-pixel classification is not all you need for semantic segmentation. In: Advances in Neural Information Processing Systems (NeurIPS), vol. 34, pp. 17864–17875 (2021)
28. Caesar, H., Uijlings, J., Ferrari, V.: COCO-stuff: thing and stuff classes in context. In: Proceedings of the IEEE/CVF Conference on Computer Vision and Pattern Recognition (CVPR), pp. 1209–1218 (2018)
29. Everingham, M., Van Gool, L., Williams, C.K.I., Winn, J., Zisserman, A.: The PASCAL visual object classes (VOC) challenge. Int. J. Comput. Vision **88**(2), 303–338 (2010)
30. Wu, Y., Kirillov, A., Massa, F., Lo, W.Y., Girshick, R.: Detectron2 [Computer software]. Facebook AI Research (2019). https://github.com/facebookresearch/detectron2
31. Liang, F., et al.: Open-vocabulary semantic segmentation with mask-adapted CLIP. In: Proceedings of the IEEE/CVF Conference on Computer Vision and Pattern Recognition (CVPR), pp. 7061–7070 (2023)

A Model Implementation to Detect Hate Speech Associated with Gender Violence by Natural Language Processing and Machine Learning

Genesis Calapaqui, David Guarderas, and Walter Fuertes(✉)

Department of Computer Science, Universidad de las Fuerzas Armadas ESPE, Sangolquí 171103, Ecuador
gicalapaqui@espe.edu.ec, adguarderas@espe.edu.ec, wmfuertes@espe.edu.ec

Abstract. The expression of hate speech against women on social media has become a worrying problem due to the popularity of these platforms and the reach they provide to such messages. This study addresses this problem from a technological perspective by developing an Artificial Intelligence model to detect and mitigate hate speech against women on social media, combining Natural Language Processing (NLP) and Machine Learning (ML) techniques. The process begins with an ETL process to collect and clean training data, which includes removing duplicates, null values, and special characters; transforming labels using a threshold of 0.5; and consolidating three datasets into a final corpus of 440,380 records with a balanced distribution between hate speech and non-hate speech categories. Next, both detection models are trained separately and then combined using weighting. The resulting classifier is integrated into a three-stage pipeline that incorporates Gemini Flash 1.5 for gender-specific filtering. The model is then implemented within a web prototype of a content wall, developed in Python using the Flask framework under the MVC architectural pattern and with a Firebase Firestore non-relational database to evaluate its performance in real-world environments. Finally, performance and quality tests of the system are conducted. The study demonstrates the relevance of the proposed solution, as the combination of BERT- and random forest-based models achieves 96% accuracy.

Keywords: Hate speech · Natural Language Processing · Machine Learning

1 Introduction

In recent years, hate speech has increased on social networks, seriously affecting women's lives and limiting their freedom of expression. Although much research has focused on the identification of explicit hate and violence, these problems also manifest themselves in more subtle ways, through stereotypes and normalized

O. Gervasi et al. (Eds.): ICCSA 2026, LNCS 16768, pp. 202–219, 2027.
https://doi.org/10.1007/978-3-032-30488-9_13

attitudes that, although often unnoticed, have a profound and harmful impact on women and society as a whole [26].

Social networks have facilitated the rapid spread of hate speech, exacerbated by online anonymity and the increasing number of digital hate crimes. Given the huge volume of data, manual analysis is impractical and prone to bias [23]. As a result, several researchers have developed hate speech detection models for social networks using Natural Language Processing (NLP) and Machine Learning (ML) algorithms. For example, the FAST-RRN detection model achieved one of the highest accuracy rates at 98%. This is because it is a model within the field of ML, specifically Deep Learning, that uses neural networks to predict and classify hate speech. The second model to achieve high accuracy was BERT, with 97%. This is due to its transformer-based architecture and its pre-training as an NLP model [17].

The main objective of this study was to develop a model for detecting and preventing hate speech against women, combining NLP and ML techniques. To this end, we constructed a dataset of 440,380 labeled data points and trained two models: one based on NLP using BERT, and the other using ML with Random Forest. Subsequently, a three-stage pipeline was designed: first, BERT and Random Forest classify the text in parallel; second, their outputs are combined using probability-weighted fusion to produce a binary classification; and third, Gemini Flash 1.5 filters only the texts classified as hate speech to determine if the content is specifically directed at women. In addition, Google Translate was incorporated to extend the model's coverage to publications in English and Spanish, since the models were trained in English. Finally, a functional web prototype was developed as a message board that allows users to write comments; these are automatically analyzed by the system, and if hate speech is detected, the message is blocked before its publication.

The main contribution of this article is the design of a multi-stage moderation pipeline. This architecture comprises a hybrid model combining BERT and Random Forest, integrated with a contextual validation layer based on Gemini Flash 1.5, to discern whether hate speech is implicitly or explicitly directed at women. This addresses a limitation present in previous studies that focus on general toxicity. The system is validated by a web prototype that blocks content in real time. This demonstrates the viability of a scalable approach focused on preventing gender-based violence in the digital sphere.

The remainder of the article is organized as follows: Sect. 2 describes the related work and the theories that underpin this study. Section 3 presents the methodological design to detect and prevent hate speech. Section 4 presents the evaluation of the results, along with the quality and performance tests and their respective discussion. Finally, Sect. 5 presents the conclusions and future work.

2 Related Work

Previous studies, such as [8], aim to determine the best source of training data for detection models. X (formerly Twitter) is a social network whose content is primarily text-based [10]. For this reason, several researchers extract the data necessary to train hate speech detection models from this social network using the X API [1]. Similarly, the platform's features allow developers to find relevant data, identifying hate-related content through hashtags, keywords, and search terms [19,20]. Other common sources for hate speech data include Facebook [4,15,16,24], the YouTube comments section [4,25,27,29], and others. Similarly, some researchers choose to use pre-made datasets available online [2,5,9,11,12, 21,32]. Even song lyrics can be a useful source of information, as demonstrated by [9], who collected data from songs containing offensive expressions for women.

Another aspect to consider when collecting data for training is the language of the data. English, being such a popular language globally, contains a wealth of data and datasets on various topics and biases, which contribute to the development of better artificial intelligence models, including hate speech detection models [10,16,19,20].

In recent years, several authors have focused on addressing the lack of data for other languages, which despite their large numbers of speakers worldwide, lack sufficient data for adequate detector training. Some of these languages include Arabic [4], Urdu [22], Spanish [25], and Hindi [19]. Some studies, such as [31], have gone a step further by training their models in multiple languages. In this case, models such as mBERT and XLM-R have been trained in more than a hundred languages.

According to the research community, BERT is one of the most widely used models to detect hate speech, as its transformer structure allows it to capture contextual and semantic relationships in English and other languages [27]. Studies such as [13] highlight its popularity for classifying the emotional tone within hate speech. Multiple models have also been built using traditional machine learning techniques, including Support Vector Machines (SVMs), Naive Bayes, and Random Forests. Although these models have limitations in their accuracy with complex texts, they are characterized by their efficiency in handling large amounts of data [1,2,11]. Zero-Shot Learning (ZSL) machine learning models, such as LLAMA2-13B, are also relevant in this field, as they, like BERT, utilize transformers. However, this model is distinguished by its ability to perform classification tasks in contexts that have not been previously trained, making it useful for multilingual environments [28].

Similarly, some authors consider the use of deep neural networks to detect sequential patterns and high-level features in text [10]. Examples of this include CNNs for extracting local features and LSTMs [15,20] for capturing long-term dependencies.

Other researchers, such as [30], consider the potential of large language models (LLMs), including ChatGPT and Bard. For example, they can be used to analyze sentiment, detect hate speech, and identify disinformation and propaganda campaigns. These models are continually improving and are a valuable contribution to the study and understanding of social phenomena, such as expressions of hate. Some researchers are using a combination of architectures to improve detection performance and adapt to hate speech, which in many cases can be complex [6,25].

Research shows that combining NLP algorithms with other artificial intelligence techniques improves results in classification and pattern-detection tasks. The work presented in [7], for example, combines NLP with Deep Learning (DL) to analyze website content and detect phishing attacks. Essentially, they use NLP to pre-process the input text by removing irrelevant content that generates noise and reduces analysis performance. They then evaluate different DL algorithms to determine whether a word is phishing-related, using pattern recognition and weight adjustments as text from web pages is exposed. This provides greater accuracy when performing detection tasks.

Across these lines, [3] applied text mining combined with machine learning techniques to identify cyberattack patterns and trends in cybersecurity research, demonstrating that the integration of NLP-based methods with other artificial intelligence approaches improves the analysis and detection of harmful behaviors in digital environments. Similarly, [18] implemented a hybrid architecture that combines a variant of BERT, Nor-BERT, with an LSTM to detect hate speech in bilingual environments (Norwegian and English).

The FAST-RRN detection model is one of the most effective, with an accuracy of 98% [17], along with BERT, which has an accuracy of 97%. This is because their architectures enable them to understand and detect linguistic patterns in data more deeply. They also apply learning techniques such as fine-tuning to leverage previously learned linguistic representations and adapt their knowledge to specific tasks. It should be noted that their efficiency is maximized due to the large volume of data developers use to train these models [20].

Unfortunately, the reviewed models have limitations that lead to bias in their hate-speech detection. This is the case with [14]. This study focused on the use of BERT to detect hate speech in German. However, while it showed optimal performance with offensive language that uses specific terms, its performance dropped considerably when detecting hate speech expressed with terms and expressions currently used by young people.

3 Research Design

3.1 Proposed Architecture

In this study, we implemented a system based on the client-server architecture pattern. We divided the detection and classification model developed into two separate modules: The server, on the one hand, contains and runs the model, along with the various plugins it uses to enhance its performance. Meanwhile, the client comprises a prototype web application that provides users with a platform for posting content to a wall.

As shown in Fig. 1, the system implements a three-stage pipeline. First, BERT and Random Forest classify the text in parallel using their respective representations. Second, their probabilities are combined using weighted fusion (60/40), producing a binary classification. Third, only texts classified as hate speech are sent to Gemini Flash 1.5, which determines whether the content is specifically targeted at women. This design separates general detection from gender-specific filtering.

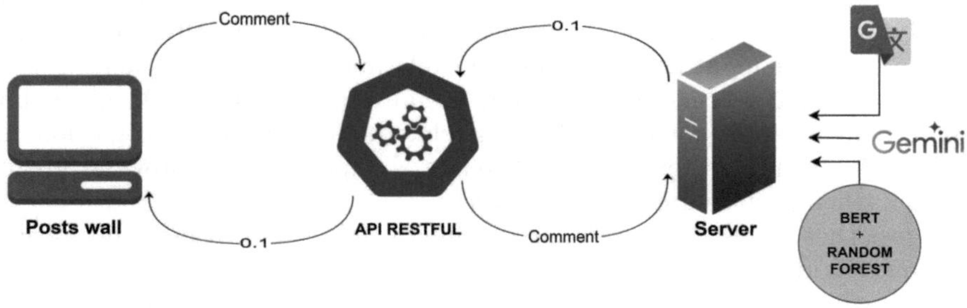

Fig. 1. System Architecture Diagram for the prototype.

3.2 Classification Models and Techniques Used

This section describes the models used for hate speech detection. We include BERT, a natural language processing model; Random Forest, a decision tree-based algorithm; and Gemini Flash, a complementary tool that improves classification efficiency and accuracy.

Dataset Construction: The data set was constructed using an Extraction, transformation and Loading (ETL) process. In the extraction phase, data was collected from Kaggle (http://www.kaggle.com/datasets, a repository of datasets on various topics for researchers, developers, and learners. Since there was no specific data set on hate speech against women in English, three more general datasets were selected, containing 24,783, 1,048,570, and 1,804,874 records, respectively, with tags such as *hate_speech*, *offensive_language*, *insult*, *sexual_explicit*, and *obscene*.

In the cleaning and transformation phase, duplicates, null values, and special characters such as usernames were removed from text extracted from social networks. Additionally, the original labels were transformed into Boolean values (i.e., 1 for hate speech and 0 otherwise), using a threshold of 0.5 to assign each text a category.

Finally, in the unification phase, the data were combined into a single file with two columns: Content (comment text) and Label (hate speech indication). After the ETL process, the final dataset was reduced to 440,380 records. Subsequently, the data set was divided into 80% for training and 20% for testing, ensuring a suitable distribution for model training.

BERT: BERT was chosen as the basis for developing the NLP model. BERT is a pretrained model developed by a group of Google researchers to improve next-generation language representation. BERT has surpassed models such as the "Generative Pretrained Transformer" (GPT) and "Embeddings from Language" (ELMo). It is characterized by its transformer-based technology, which transforms one sequence into another, eliminates recurrences, and replaces them with attention mechanisms to handle dependencies between inputs and outputs. This means that BERT analyzes all words in a sentence simultaneously, allowing it to identify the relationships between them and better understand the context. [27].

Unlike previous NLP models, which use unidirectional training, BERT employs bidirectional training, reading the entire sentence at once and analyzing the context surrounding a word to better understand its meaning. BERT also uses masking techniques, replacing parts of a sentence with tokens called masks, and then predicting those words based on the context of the unmasked words, thus optimizing the performance of the model [27].

Training BERT is computationally expensive. However, once trained, the model can be easily applied to text classification tasks [27].

BERT training was carried out as follows: upon loading the datasets, they were batched for improved data handling performance. The data were then tokenized; that is, the sentences were converted into word-level vectors, each sentence separated by a word. Subsequently, each batch was fed into the pre-trained model in a loop. Through bidirectional passing, a prediction was obtained for each data point (1 or 0), which was then compared with the actual label to calculate the loss. This value was then used for the evaluation phase. To achieve better results in terms of model accuracy, epoch training was applied, which means that the aforementioned process was repeated several times (i.e., in this case 3) (see Fig. 2).

Random Forest: The following hyper parameters were defined for training the Random Forest model:

- **Node size:** The default values were used, setting a minimum of two samples to split a node and one sample for leaf nodes, allowing the capture of specific patterns in the data.
- **Number of trees:** Training was performed over 10 epochs, increasing the number of trees by 10 in each epoch, until a total of 100 trees were reached.
- **Number of features sampled:** 5000 features were defined during text vectorization, and each tree used approximately $\sqrt{5000} \approx 71$ features.

Since machine learning models cannot directly process text, a pre-processing step was applied that converted the texts into numerical representations using the TF-IDF technique, generating a 5000-feature matrix.

Training started with 10 trees and was gradually increased to 100. Each tree made a prediction and the final result was obtained by majority vote, consolidating a robust decision based on the combination of multiple individual predictions (see Fig. 3).

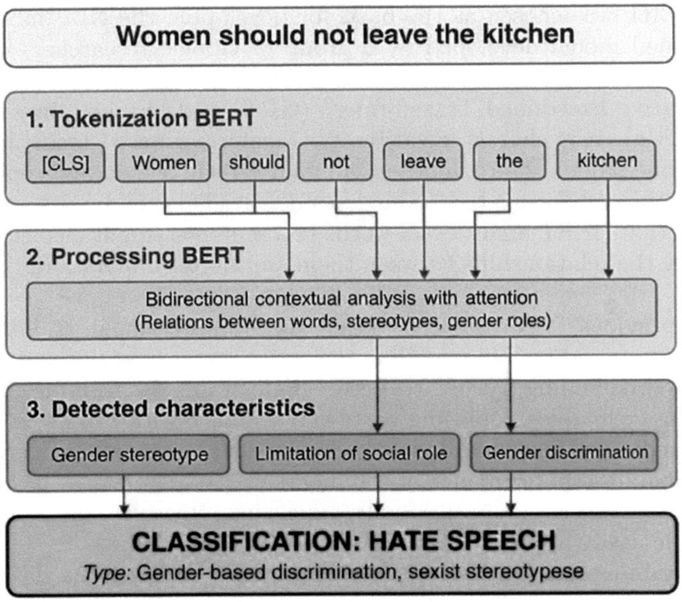

Fig. 2. BERT Training

Model Combination: To improve the accuracy of hate speech detection, the **Random Forest (RF)** and **BERT** models were combined using probability weighting. Each model was assigned a weight based on its individual performance.

- **Random Forest (RF)**: 40%
- **BERT**: 60%

The weighting was not based solely on precision (94% BERT, 93% RF), but also on theoretical foundations: BERT has consistently demonstrated a greater capacity to capture semantic context in implicit hate speech [18,27], while Random Forest is more sensitive to superficial lexical features. This asymmetry justifies the favoring BERT in the ensemble. Regarding the 0.5 threshold, it corresponds to the standard decision boundary in binary classification under balanced distributions [21], a condition that is met in the constructed corpus.

From a mathematical perspective, the weights can be approximated proportionally to the accuracy of each model as follows:

$$w_{\mathrm{BERT}} = \frac{94}{94+93} \approx 0.5027, \quad w_{\mathrm{RF}} = \frac{93}{94+93} \approx 0.4973 \tag{1}$$

However, it was decided to manually adjust the proportion to 60%-40% to reflect BERT's qualitative advantage and its greater ability to generalize to unseen data.

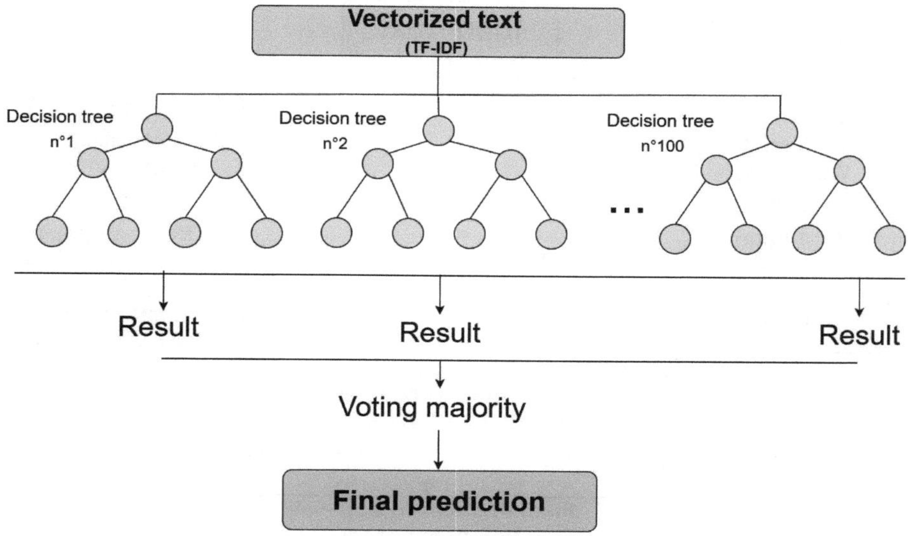

Fig. 3. Random Forest Training

Each model processes the text independently: RF uses TF-IDF vectorization, while BERT employs tokenization. Once the prediction probabilities of each model are obtained, the weighted combination is performed (see Fig. 4).

As shown, the individual probabilities of each model are multiplied by their respective weights and then summed to obtain the weighted probability. The class with the highest final probability determines the system's prediction. This combination leverages BERT's ability to understand language and RF's ability to capture specific patterns, thus improving the accuracy of the hate speech detection system.

Gemini Flash: Gemini Flash 1.5 acts as a contextual specificity filter in the third stage of the pipeline, applying exclusively to texts already classified as hate speech by the hybrid model. Its role is not the general detection of hate speech, but rather determining whether the offensive content is specifically directed at women. This separation is architecturally relevant, as general-purpose models tend to lack sensitivity to gender-specific targeting. The Gemini Flash API is queried via a structured prompt that identifies explicit references, generalizations, or stereotypes about women, returning 'yes' to block the content or 'no' otherwise. This approach does not require fine-tuning on gender-specific corpora and handles implicit expressions that rule-based filters miss.

3.3 Web Interface Implementation

We develop a web prototype of a posting wall to test the model's functionality in a near-real-world environment and evaluate it from the user's perspective. This

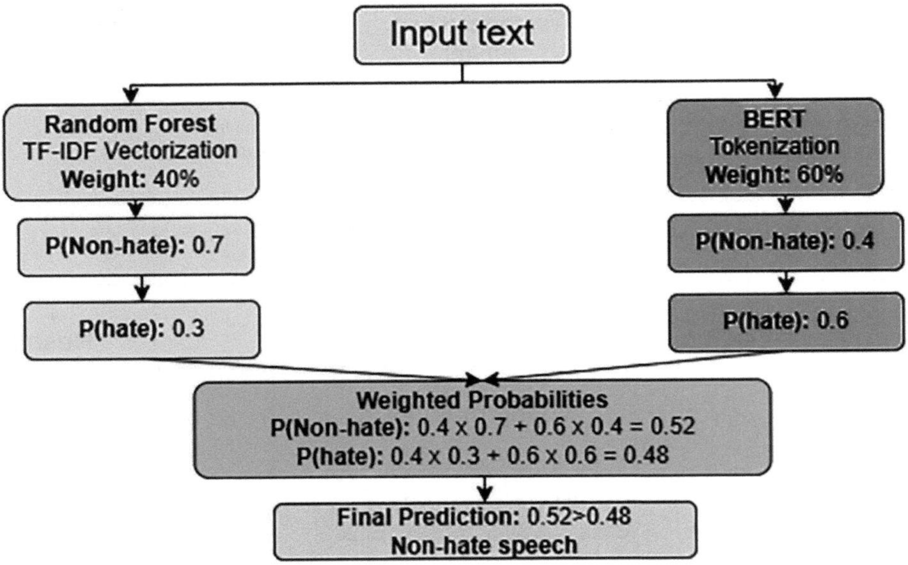

Fig. 4. Weighted scoring

application was developed using the Model-View-Controller (MVC) architectural pattern, which separates the user interface from the business logic and user interaction handling. We also used the Object-Oriented Programming (OOP) paradigm to generate more structured and understandable code by abstracting the different concepts related to the website's functionality (see Fig. 5).

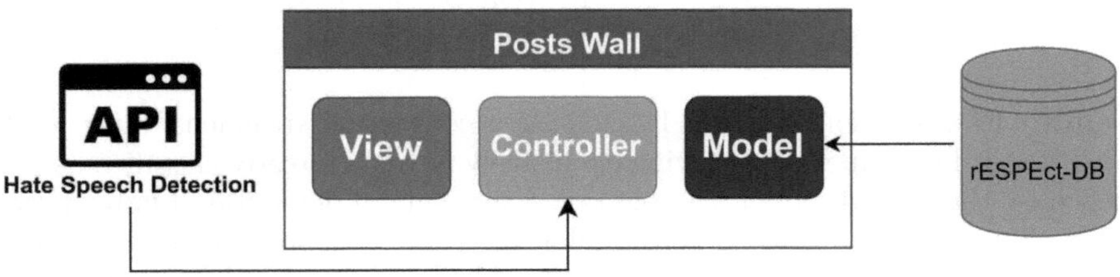

Fig. 5. Web application software architecture

We used Python as the programming language to develop the application. We used Flask, a Python framework known for its ease of use in developing web applications with minimal code. A non-relational database was chosen to store the application's data, as it enables efficient handling of the large volumes of data typically required by social media platforms. Additionally, this type of database offers structural flexibility, facilitating modifications to the business logic if needed. For this purpose, the Firebase Firestore database was used to store the data in the cloud.

The application consists of a posting wall where users can register, log in, and access the main page. There, they can post short text messages, edit, delete, read other users' posts, and like them. When a user attempts to post on the wall, the content is sent via a REST API to a developed detection model. This model identifies whether the text constitutes hate speech against women. If it is not hate speech, the post is published normally. Otherwise, the post is blocked, and the user is notified that they attempted to publish offensive text against women.

4 Results

4.1 Trained Model Results

To evaluate the performance of trained models, we use the Holdout Set method, dividing the data set into 80% for training (352,304 data points) and 20% for testing (88,076 data points). Within the test set, 44,478 comments were labeled as 0 and 43,598 as 1.

We evaluated three approaches: BERT, Random Forest, and a weighted combination of both models. The evaluation used Accuracy, Recall, and F1-score metrics to compare the performance of each model in detecting hate speech. Detailed results are presented in Table 1.

Table 1. Evaluation results of the models

Label	Model	Precision	Recall	F1-Score
0	BERT	0.94	0.95	0.94
0	Random Forest	0.95	0.91	0.93
0	Combined	0.97	0.95	0.96
1	BERT	0.93	0.91	0.93
1	Random Forest	0.95	0.97	0.93
1	Combined	0.97	0.96	0.96
Support (0)				44478
Support (1)				43598

The weighted fusion (BERT 60% and Random Forest 40%) performs better than the individual models because it combines BERT's contextual semantic understanding with Random Forest's lexical pattern detection. The standard 0.5 decision threshold is maintained in binary classification with a balanced distribution, ensuring an optimal balance between false positives and negatives and preventing overfitting. This compensates for the individual shortcomings of each model and reduces classification errors. (See Fig. 6).

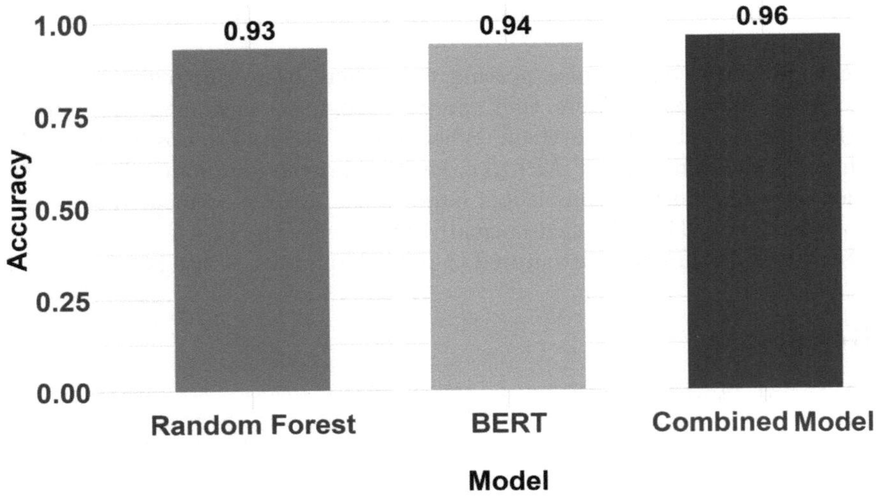

Fig. 6. Comparative chart of model accuracy.

To validate these results, we present the confusion matrix of the evaluated models (see Fig. 7), which shows the values corresponding to True Positives (TP), True Negatives (TN), False Positives (FP) and False Negatives (FN).

The comparative confusion matrix between the BERT, Random Forest and combined models is shown in Fig. 7. The combined model exhibits the best overall performance, as evidenced by the lowest number of false negatives and false positives compared to BERT and Random Forest. These results indicate that integrating both approaches improved recall and accuracy by reducing errors associated with failing to detect hate speech when it is indeed hate speech (FN) and with misclassifying non-offensive messages as hate speech (FP). Furthermore, the combined model achieved the highest values for true positives and true negatives, indicating a greater capacity to correctly distinguish between offensive and non-offensive messages.

On the other hand, Fig. 8 shows the comparative behavior between the ROC curves (Receiver Operating Characteristic) and the AUC (Area Under the Curve) of the three models evaluated. As shown in the AUC, BERT demonstrates the greatest effectiveness in discriminating between messages with and without hate speech, regardless of the applied threshold. As shown, with a difference of only 0.004, it is followed by the model that combines BERT with Random Forest, while the latter shows the lowest overall capacity among the three models, although it remains quite favorable, above 0.9.

When comparing the results from the Confusion Matrix and the ROC-AUC plot, the combined model continues to perform better. Although BERT achieved a higher AUC, the difference between its AUC and the combined model's is minimal. Furthermore, it is important to note that this graph calculates the overall performance of the models. However, under the calibration metrics used in model

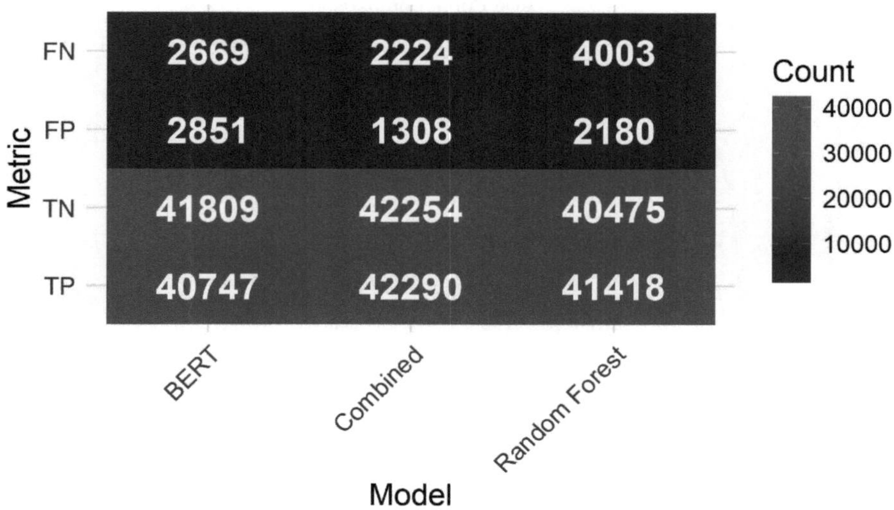

Fig. 7. Confusion matrix for evaluating model performance.

construction, specifically, the conditions of this case study, the combination of BERT and Random Forest continues to yield better results, as demonstrated by the confusion matrix. This matrix shows a clear superiority in the combined model, as it not only identifies more true positives and negatives than the other models but also produces fewer errors. Contrary to the AUC figures, the difference between the models' confusion matrices is more significant, favoring the combined model.

4.2 API Performance Evaluation

To verify the behavior of the REST API under different load levels, performance tests were conducted using JMeter. This tool allows for the simulation of multiple simultaneous users interacting with the system, facilitating the measurement of response times, error rates, and the number of requests processed per second. Such analyzes help identify potential bottlenecks and optimize the system's infrastructure.

During the tests, different load scenarios were established, varying the number of concurrent users and the request frequency to examine the API's performance under high-traffic conditions. Indicators such as average response time, latency, and CPU and memory consumption on the server, as well as system stability under a progressive increase in requests, were evaluated.

As shown in Table 2, the tests started with a concurrency of 100 users and were progressively increased to 600, at which point failures in request execution were detected.

The performance tests presented show a notable decrease in responsiveness as the number of concurrent users increases. With up to 300 users, the system

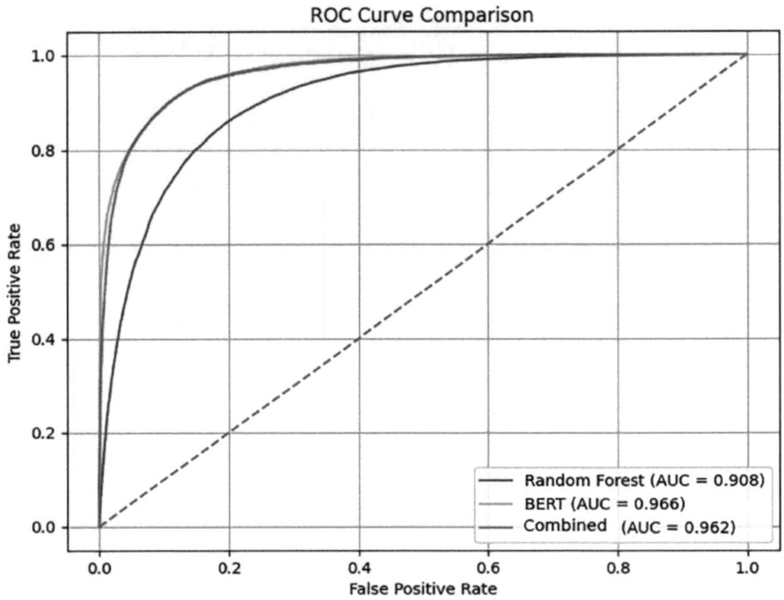

Fig. 8. ROC-AUC graph to evaluate and compare model performance.

Table 2. Performance Test Results

Users	Std. Deviation	Error (%)	Throughput (req/sec)
100	4927.90	0.00	5.5
200	9731.98	0.00	5.7
300	15191.54	0.00	5.6
400	17303.65	24.73	7.3
500	16822.24	40.40	9.3
600	16928.18	50.83	11.2
Total	16303.78	28.71	4.8

maintains a stable standard deviation and a 0% error rate, indicating reliable performance under moderate load. However, starting at 400 users, the error rate increases considerably, reaching 50.83% with 600 users, suggesting that the API struggles to handle high traffic.

4.3 Web Client Quality Assessment

Quality testing focused on the developed web client, as it was considered prudent to ensure a pleasant user experience when using the application, since this is where the user will interact with the model.

To this end, the tests were performed using Lighthouse. This is an open-source Google tool that improves the quality of web pages. Lighthouse enables auditing several essential aspects, including performance, accessibility, Progressive Web Apps (PWAs), and Search Optimization (SEO).

Performing quality tests with Lighthouse is straightforward as it is accessible through the developer tools in the Google Chrome browser. After properly configuring, Lighthouse generates a diagnostic report on the website's quality and identifies areas for improvement.

At the time of the first test, the resulting diagnostic report showed metrics that, while not entirely low, indicate a need for improvement to reach the expected quality standards. The tool suggested several steps to improve the quality and best practices of the application's development, such as replacing GIF animations with WebM, replacing PNG or JPEG images with WebP, providing accessible button names and including alternative text for images, and adding meta descriptions so search engines can find and recommend the website.

After implementing these changes, the website was re-evaluated with Lighthouse, resulting in the highest quality scores, as shown in Fig. 9.

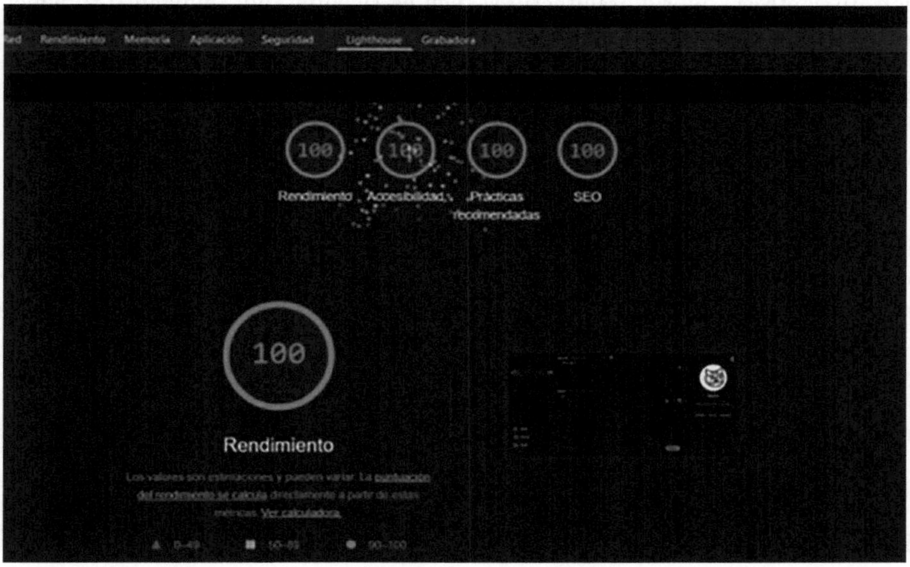

Fig. 9. Second Web Quality Lighthouse Test

4.4 Discussion

The results demonstrate the effectiveness of the hybrid architecture in detecting hate speech against women. The precision of the combined model (96%) exceeds that of BERT (94%) and Random Forest (93%) separately. BERT's contextual semantic understanding, along with Random Forest's lexical pattern detection, significantly reduces errors associated with content review and filtering costs. The combined model registered 2,224 false negatives, compared to 2,669 for BERT and 4,003 for Random Forest, for a 44.5% reduction. However, the qualitative analysis of residual errors reveals shortcomings in three areas: (i) subtle sarcasm (e.g., "it is good that women don't drive," a comment interpreted as neutral due to the lack of explicitly offensive vocabulary), (ii) contextual ambiguity (e.g., phrases from academic debates or news reports with sensitive terms that are not intended to be hostile), and (iii) cultural nuances not reflected in the training dataset. The AUC of BERT (0.966) slightly outperforms the combined model (0.962). However, it does not reflect the behavior of the model under a fixed threshold of 0.5. In this scenario, the hybrid model demonstrates superiority, as it prioritizes gender-specificity over overall toxicity.

Compared with the existing literature, the proposed model performs competitively. Reference models such as FAST-RNN (98%) and fine-tuned BERT(97%) achieve higher scores, but were trained on narrow domains and with specialized corpora, conditions that favor high metrics without guaranteeing generalization. In contrast, hybrid architectures such as Hashmi and Yayilgan [18], which combine Nor-BERT with LSTM, corroborate the trend that integrating models improves performance in complex tasks, consistent with the findings of this study. The main differentiation contribution lies in the incorporation of Gemini Flash 1.5 as a contextual specificity layer, which adds the ability to distinguish whether hate speech is specifically directed at women, a dimension that most comparable studies do not explicitly address.

However, it should be noted that the model was initially developed in English, so its application in other languages would benefit from adaptation or translation. Training exclusively in English requires translation into other languages, which introduces noise that degrades the detection of implicit or colloquial expressions [14]. Furthermore, performance tests revealed that the system remains stable only up to 300 concurrent users, with an error rate of 50.83% at 600 users, limiting its applicability on high-traffic platforms. Finally, constructing the data set from generic Kaggle sources can introduce labeling biases that affect the detection of subtle gender-based hate.

5 Conclusions and Future Work

This study developed and implemented a multi-stage moderation pipeline that detects and prevents hate speech against women by integrating natural language processing and machine learning. This hybrid architecture achieved 96% accuracy by combining BERT's semantic understanding with Random Forest's pattern-detection capabilities. This resulted in a 44.5% reduction in false negatives compared to Random Forest alone. We include Gemini Flash as a filter to improve the detection of comments targeting women provides a competitive advantage over more traditional models. This leads to the conclusion that a multi-stage approach is more effective against online violence by improving the contextualization and specificity of the processing.

In future work, we propose incorporating multilingual models such as mBERT or XLM-R to reduce the noise introduced by machine translation in input from other languages. To improve scalability, promising approaches include model distillation, asynchronous request queues, and container-based horizontal scaling. We also propose evaluating deep neural networks based on Transformers, applying fine-tuning techniques. Finally, we could explore the integration of emotion analysis to improve hate speech detection from an affective perspective.

Acknowledgements. The authors express their gratitude to the Distributed Systems, Cybersecurity, and Content Research Group (RACKLY) for the use of the High-Performance Systems Research Laboratory and its specialized software and hardware.

References

1. Alhayan, F., et al.: Detection of cyberhate speech towards female sport in the Arabic Xsphere. PeerJ Comput. Sci. **10** (2024). https://doi.org/10.7717/peerj-cs.2138
2. Ali, M., Muhammad, A., Asad, M., Sajawal, M., Alexopoulos, C., Charalabidis, Y.: Towards Perso-Arabic Urdu language hate detection using machine learning: a comparative study based on a large dataset and time-complexity. In: Proceedings of the 26th Pan-Hellenic Conference on Informatics, pp. 317–321 (2023). https://doi.org/10.1145/3575879.3576011
3. Andrade, R.O., Fuertes, W., Cazares, M., Ortiz-Garcés, I., Navas, G.: An exploratory study of cognitive sciences applied to cybersecurity. Electronics **11**(11), 1692 (2022). https://doi.org/10.3390/electronics11111692
4. Badri, N., Kboubi, F., Habacha Chaibi, A.: Abusive and hate speech classification in Arabic text using pre-trained language models and data augmentation. ACM Trans. Asian Low-Resour. Lang. Inf. Process. (2024). https://doi.org/10.1145/3679049
5. Bandyopadhyay, R., Assenmacher, D., Alonso-Moral, J.M., Wagner, C.: Sexism detection on a data diet. In: Companion Publication of the 16th ACM Web Science Conference, pp. 94–102 (2024). https://doi.org/10.1145/3630744.3663609
6. Bashar, M.A., Nayak, R., Luong, K., Balasubramaniam, T.: Progressive domain adaptation for detecting hate speech on social media with small training set and its application to COVID-19 concerned posts. Soc. Netw. Anal. Min. **11**(1), 1–18 (2021). https://doi.org/10.1007/s13278-021-00780-w
7. Benavides-Astudillo, E., Fuertes, W., Sanchez-Gordon, S., Nuñez-Agurto, D., Rodríguez-Galán, G.: A phishing-attack-detection model using natural language processing and deep learning. Appl. Sci. **13**(9), 5275 (2023)
8. Calapaqui, G., Guarderas, D., Fuertes, W., López, A., Aules, H.: Detection of hate speech on on-line social platforms using machine learning and natural language processing - a literature review. In: Rocha, A., Peñalvo, F.G., Costa, C.J., Gonçalves, R. (eds.) Proceedings of 20th Iberian Conference on Information Systems and Technologies (CISTI 2025), pp. 441–452. Springer Nature Switzerland, Cham (2026)

9. Calderon-Suarez, R., Ortega-Mendoza, R.M., Montes-Y-Gomez, M., Toxqui-Quitl, C., Marquez-Vera, M.A.: Enhancing the detection of misogynistic content in social media by transferring knowledge from song phrases. IEEE Access **11**, 13179–13190 (2023). https://doi.org/10.1109/ACCESS.2023.3242965
10. Chiril, P., Pamungkas, E.W., Benamara, F., Moriceau, V., Patti, V.: Emotionally informed hate speech detection: a multi-target perspective. Cogn. Comput. **14**(1), 322–352 (2021). https://doi.org/10.1007/s12559-021-09862-5
11. Daouadi, K.E., Boualleg, Y., Guehairia, O.: Systematic investigation of recent pre-trained language model for hate speech detection in Arabic tweets. ACM Trans. Asian Low-Resour. Lang. Inf. Process. (2024). https://doi.org/10.1145/3674970
12. Dorris, W., Hu, R.R., Vishwamitra, N., Luo, F., Costello, M.: Towards automatic detection and explanation of hate speech and offensive language. In: Proceedings of the Sixth International Workshop on Security and Privacy Analytics, pp. 23–29 (2020). https://doi.org/10.1145/3375708.3380312
13. Escobar Díaz, A., Rivadeneira, R., Fuertes, W.: Emotional tone detection in hate speech using machine learning and NLP: methods, challenges, and future directions—a systematic review. Appl. Sci. **15**(23) (2025). https://doi.org/10.3390/app152312686
14. Fillies, J., Paschke, A.: Youth language and emerging slurs: tackling bias in BERT-based hate speech detection. AI Ethics **1**(1), 1–12 (2025). https://doi.org/10.1007/s43681-025-00701-z
15. Ganfure, G.O.: Comparative analysis of deep learning based Afaan Oromo hate speech detection. J. Big Data **9**(1), 76 (2022). https://doi.org/10.1186/s40537-022-00628-w
16. Han, H., Asif, M., Awwad, E.M., Sarhan, N., Ghadi, Y.Y., Xu, B.: Innovative deep learning techniques for monitoring aggressive behavior in social media posts. J. Cloud Comput. **13**(1), 19 (2024). https://doi.org/10.1186/s13677-023-00577-6
17. Hashmi, E., Yayilgan, S.Y.: Multi-class hate speech detection in the Norwegian language using FAST-RNN and multilingual fine-tuned transformers. Complex Intell. Syst. **10**(3), 4535–4556 (2024). https://doi.org/10.1007/s40747-024-01392-5
18. Hashmi, E., Yayilgan, S.Y., Abomhara, M.: Metalinguist: enhancing hate speech detection with cross-lingual meta-learning. Complex Intell. Syst. **11**(1), 179 (2025)
19. Kapil, P., Kumari, G., Ekbal, A., Pal, S., Chatterjee, A., Vinutha, B.N.: HHSD: Hindi hate speech detection leveraging multi-task learning. IEEE Access **11**, 101460–101473 (2023). https://doi.org/10.1109/ACCESS.2023.3312993
20. Kumbale, S., Singh, S., Poornalatha, G., Singh, S.: BREE-HD: a transformer-based model to identify threats on Twitter. IEEE Access **11**, 67180–67190 (2023). https://doi.org/10.1109/ACCESS.2023.3291072
21. Marshan, A., Nizar, F.N.M., Ioannou, A., Spanaki, K.: Comparing machine learning and deep learning techniques for text analytics: detecting the severity of hate comments online. Inf. Syst. Front. (2023). https://doi.org/10.1007/s10796-023-10446-x
22. Mehmood, F., Ghafoor, H., Asim, M.N., Ghani, M.U., Mahmood, W., Dengel, A.: Passion-Net: a robust precise and explainable predictor for hate speech detection in Roman Urdu text. Neural Comput. Appl. **36**(6), 3077–3100 (2024). https://doi.org/10.1007/s00521-023-09169-6
23. Mullah, N.S., Zainon, W.M.N.W.: Advances in machine learning algorithms for hate speech detection in social media: a review. IEEE Access **9**, 88364–88376 (2021). https://doi.org/10.1109/ACCESS.2021.3089515

24. Polignano, M., Basile, P., de Gemmis, M., Semeraro, G.: Hate speech detection through ALBERTO Italian language understanding model. CEUR Workshop Proc. **2521** (2019)
25. Redondo, R.P.D., Vilas, A.F., Merino, M.R., Rodríguez, S.M.V., Guijarro, S.T., Hafez, M.M.: Anti-sexism alert system: identification of sexist comments on social media using AI techniques. Appl. Sci. (Switzerland) **13**(7) (2023). https://doi.org/10.3390/app13074341
26. Rodríguez-Sánchez, F., Carrillo-de Albornoz, J., Plaza, L.: Automatic classification of sexism in social networks: an empirical study on twitter data. IEEE Access **8**, 219563–219576 (2020). https://doi.org/10.1109/ACCESS.2020.3042604
27. Salminen, J., Hopf, M., Chowdhury, S.A., Jung, S., Almerekhi, H., Jansen, B.J.: Developing an online hate classifier for multiple social media platforms. HCIS **10**(1), 1–34 (2020). https://doi.org/10.1186/s13673-019-0205-6
28. Shaikh, S., Yayilgan, S.Y., Abomhara, M., Zoto, E.: Multilingual user perceptions analysis from twitter using zero shot learning for border control technologies. Soc. Netw. Anal. Min. **15**(19), 1–24 (2025)
29. Shanmugavadivel, K., Subramanian, M., Shri Durga, R., Srigha, S., Sree Harene, J., Yasvanth Bala, P.: KEC AI nlp@dravidianlangtech:abusive comment detection in Tamil language using machine learning techniques. In: DravidianLangTech 2023 - 3rd Workshop on Speech and Language Technologies for Dravidian Languages, Associated with 14th International Conference on Recent Advances in Natural Language Processing, RANLP 2023 - Proceedings, pp. 293–299 (2023). https://doi.org/10.26615/978-954-452-085-4_043
30. Thapa, S., et al.: Large language models (LLM) in computational social science: prospects, current state, and challenges. Soc. Netw. Anal. Min. **15**(4), 4 (2025). https://doi.org/10.1007/s13278-025-01428-9
31. Xu, Y., et al.: A survey on multilingual large language models: corpora, alignment, and bias. Front. Comput. Sci. **19**(11), 1911362 (2025). https://doi.org/10.3389/fcomp.2023.1911362. open Access at link.springer.com and journal.hep.com.cn
32. Yuan, L., Wang, T., Ferraro, G., Suominen, H., Rizoiu, M.A.: Transfer learning for hate speech detection in social media. J. Comput. Soc. Sci. **6**(2), 1081–1101 (2023). https://doi.org/10.1007/s42001-023-00224-9

Behavioral Finance in Determining the Financial Choices of Households

George Abuselidze[1](✉), Nadiia Davydenko[2], Natalia Mocanu[3], Oleh Onyshko[2], and Alina Buriak[2]

[1] Batumi Shota Rustaveli State University, 35/32, Ninoshvili/Rustaveli Street, 6010 Batumi, Georgia
george.abuselidze@gmail.com
[2] State Tax University, Universytetska, 31, Irpin 08205, Ukraine
[3] State University of Moldova, Strada Alexei Mateevici, 60, 2009 Chişinău, Moldova

Abstract. The article investigates the relationship between financial and digital literacy and household financial behavior under contemporary economic challenges. Particular attention is devoted to the role of digital inclusion in shaping economic well-being and financial decision-making processes. The findings indicate a gradual improvement in financial literacy indicators over recent years, reflecting convergence with broader regional trends in financial competence development. The study demonstrates that access to digital infrastructure, particularly Internet connectivity, exerts a significant positive influence on household income levels and overall economic resilience. Correlation analysis confirms a strong direct relationship between digital access and economic well-being. In this context, digital financial literacy is conceptualized as a multidimensional competency encompassing the ability to identify, process, critically evaluate and effectively apply financial information through modern digital technologies while adequately managing cybersecurity and digital risks. Drawing on statistical analysis and regression modelling, the research confirms that higher levels of financial and digital literacy contribute to more rational financial behavior, lower vulnerability to economic shocks and improved quality of life. The article further identifies the growing importance of fintech competencies, information management skills and cybersecurity awareness as essential components of sustainable financial inclusion. Based on the empirical findings, the study proposes a comprehensive framework of recommendations aimed at strengthening financial and digital competencies across different social and age groups through integrated educational initiatives and digital learning mechanisms. The results contribute to the broader discourse on financial resilience, digital transformation and inclusive economic development, and may serve as a practical reference for policymakers, financial institutions, educators and researchers in the field of economic behavior.

Keywords: financial literacy · digital literacy · behavioral finance · financial security · financial inclusion · financial decisions · household finance

O. Gervasi et al. (Eds.): ICCSA 2026, LNCS 16768, pp. 220–232, 2027.
https://doi.org/10.1007/978-3-032-30488-9_14

1 Introduction

The interrelationship between digital and financial literacy and their influence on household financial behavior has become increasingly significant in the context of contemporary economic instability, growing internal and external challenges and the accelerating transformation of the financial environment. This trend is largely associated with the persistently insufficient level of public awareness regarding personal finance management, household resource allocation, taxation principles and the fundamentals of lending, investment, pension systems and social and health insurance mechanisms.

At the same time, increasing accessibility to financial instruments has intensified public interest in financial markets as a potential source of income generation. However, alongside the expansion of Internet usage and digital financial services, the prevalence of high-risk and fraudulent practices has also increased, including deceptive investment schemes, pseudo-financial structures and speculative financial operations. Inadequate levels of financial literacy, combined with limited competencies in managing both personal and borrowed financial resources, adversely affect household financial stability and overall quality of life.

Under conditions of rapid digital transformation affecting virtually all spheres of socio-economic activity, particularly the financial sector, the importance of digital and financial competencies is expected to continue growing. In this context, the development of digital financial products is reflected in the modernization of payment systems aimed at enhancing the speed, accessibility and scalability of financial transactions. Simultaneously, increasing attention is being devoted to strengthening data security through the implementation of blockchain technologies, cryptographic instruments and advanced cybersecurity mechanisms, as well as through the widespread adoption of Internet banking and mobile financial services [1–4].

Alongside new opportunities, the financial system and its economic entities are faced with a number of tasks and challenges. In particular, economic entities must acquire the appropriate level of financial literacy, digital skills and competencies if they are to achieve positive financial results from the implementation of digital technologies in their activities [5, 6].

In the current socio-economic transformation, financial literacy is a subject of active research by domestic and international scholars. Given its pivotal role in the development of the financial market - encompassing banking and non-banking financial institutions - the scientific community is focusing on analysing how the financial awareness of the population impacts the behavior of households when consuming financial services. Considerable attention is also paid to developing applied mechanisms for improving financial literacy and to searching for effective forms of interaction between stakeholders in order to strengthen it. The issue of improving financial literacy is actively discussed in scientific circles and at the national level. The National Bank of Ukraine initiated a discussion on the National Strategy for the Development of Financial Literacy until 2025, which was later incorporated into the Strategy for the Development of the Financial Sector of Ukraine until 2025 [7].

In the last few years, researchers have paid close attention to financial literacy among the population. Geyenko, Rybina and Guzenko, for example, consider it to be a combination of knowledge and understanding of financial processes, as well as the ability to manage financial resources effectively and make informed financial decisions [8].

Tymkiv and Sydor, on the other hand, interpret financial literacy as the level of awareness among citizens (even those without specialised training) that enables them to understand the nature and importance of financial relations for the socio-economic development of the country. This awareness is demonstrated through citizens' rational participation in economic processes such as saving, paying taxes, lending, settling accounts with other economic entities and making individual investments [9].

Dombrovska focuses not only on knowledge, but also on practical financial management skills aimed at achieving personal well-being [7, p. 6]. She believes that financial literacy contributes to entrepreneurship, personal initiative, socially significant values, public participation, self-management and career development. It also helps to solve everyday financial tasks [10].

According to Lavreniuk and Lavreniuk, financial literacy is a key competence that enables individuals to manage their financial well-being effectively in today's complex financial environment [11].

As part of her research on household financial literacy, Kizima analysed its impact on population financial behavior. She argued that financial knowledge and the ability to assess economic processes are fundamental to developing rational financial strategies [12]. The researcher emphasises that citizens' financial awareness contributes to poverty reduction, more effective decision-making and the development of financial markets, ultimately supporting the country's sustainable economic growth. According to Yuriy and Kizima, financial literacy of the population is a set of attitudes, knowledge and skills of citizens regarding effective management of personal finances and the ability to competently apply them in the process of making financial decisions. Financial literacy aims to solve the problem of poverty, reduce economic risks, resolve the issue of excessive debt burden and increase the profitability of households and entrepreneurs [13].

Ptaschenko and Kolinchuk take a similar approach, positioning financial literacy as an important factor in economic development and a tool for improving population well-being and combatting poverty. They argue that citizens can only make informed decisions that ensure economic progress when they are properly informed about financial matters [14].

The work of Dubyna, Tarasenko and Tarasenko resulted in the systematisation of the key characteristics of household financial literacy. These characteristics are considered to be knowledge about financial services, the result of an educational process and cognitive activity. They are also considered to be a tool that allows households to make informed decisions, thereby influencing their income level and quality of life [15].

Despite noticeable scientific interest in the topic, further research is relevant due to the numerous financial risks that households face when finding sources of income, managing expenses and choosing financial instruments. This requires a deeper study of the mechanisms for improving financial literacy and adapting to a changing financial environment.

The purpose of this study is to analyse how financial and digital literacy impact the financial behavior of Ukrainian households in the context of current economic instability and digitalisation. The study will also explore ways to enhance these competencies to promote financial stability and the well-being of the population.

To achieve this goal, the following tasks must be completed:

- assessing the current situation with regard to the financial literacy index of Ukrainians.
- determine the relationship between internet access and household income;
- reveal the essence of digital financial literacy as an integrated competence;
- develop recommendations for integrating financial and digital skills into household practices.

2 Methodology

The following methods were adopted for the research:

- the monographic method was used to systematise scientific approaches to interpreting the concepts of 'financial literacy' and 'digital competence';
- statistical analysis: to assess the financial literacy index of the population and the dynamics of digital skills;
- comparative analysis was used to identify differences in literacy levels between different age, educational, and territorial groups;
- the graphical method was used to visualise trends and interrelationships between digital skills and financial behavior;
- regression analysis was used to model the relationship between the level of internet connectivity and household income;
- content analysis is used when analysing regulatory and legal acts, reports and scientific sources on digital and financial policy.

3 Results and Discussion

The extremely challenging conditions currently facing the national economy require the adoption of the most optimal financial behavior strategy, which is directly dependent on the level of financial literacy among citizens. After all, financial knowledge enables an objective analysis of financial and economic processes taking place in the country and beyond, and ensures an adequate quality of life for citizens. According to the study 'Financial Literacy, Financial Inclusion and Financial Well-being in Ukraine in 2021' [16], Ukrainians' 'financial literacy index' has risen from 11.6 points in 2018 to 12.3 points over the past three years.

In terms of this indicator, Ukraine is on par with Bulgaria and Croatia, leaving Georgia (12.1 points), Romania (11.2 points) and even Italy (11.1 points) behind and improving all components of the index: financial knowledge, financial behavior and attitude towards financial issues.

The highest level of financial literacy was demonstrated by Ukrainians aged 25–34 (12.7 points) and 30–59 (12.6 points). Those aged 18–19 (10.1 points) and over 60 (11.6 points) demonstrated the lowest levels of financial literacy. In terms of gender, Ukrainian men and women are equally knowledgeable about financial issues, with an overall financial literacy index of 12.3 and 12.2 points, respectively. However, there is a direct correlation between financial literacy and level of education: the higher the level of education, the higher the financial literacy score. The overall score for Ukrainians with secondary vocational education is 11.9, compared to 13.3 for those with higher education. The gap in financial literacy between urban and rural residents has increased (12.6 and 11.8 points, respectively).

There is a difference in the level of financial literacy between users and non-users of modern information technologies, which is 2.5 points (12.4 and 9.9 points, respectively) [15]. Therefore, we are convinced that an adequate level of financial literacy among Ukrainians will enable them to adjust their financial behavior in the current incredibly difficult conditions associated with full-scale military aggression.

The concept of 'digital literacy' emerges from modern philosophical, cultural, sociological, communicative and technological concepts. However, publications still lack a unified approach to the relevance and universality of different definitions of the term. This is despite the need for the most accurate possible description of its content, which would allow the creation of tools for effective communication and information documentation in the digital environment [17].

Digital literacy aims to accelerate and expand opportunities for effective financial decision-making, thorough analysis, and expert use of financial instruments and modern financial products and services, improving personal well-being through digital technologies.

Ensuring the accessibility of financial services to the population through digital technologies requires not just an increase in financial literacy, but specifically in digital financial literacy. This requires the development of skills in searching for and using information and financial instruments, as well as critical thinking. These skills in navigating the digital landscape of the twenty-first century are pivotal in achieving optimal outcomes from household financial activities.

In our opinion, the objective factors contributing to the current dynamic increase in financial and digital literacy are:

- increasing customer autonomy by providing contactless and customisable services;
- the development of innovative financial instruments and alternative channels for selling financial services;
- remote access, registration and data processing;
- the digitisation of cash asset management functions;
- the introduction of blockchain technologies and the development of fintech.

In a post-COVID society, developing digital skills among the population is becoming an important task for both society as a whole and each individual. Urbanisation, internet access and online resource availability, as well as the development of basic digital and financial literacy, are essential for creating an independent society that can meet its own economic needs [18, 19].

Technological change and global challenges, such as the ongoing pandemic and war, are increasing people's mobility in Ukraine and around the world. This requires citizens to improve their digital competencies to access services and/or employment. Developing digital literacy enables people to become independent, active users of digital services throughout their lives, including financial ones, thereby ensuring their future well-being [20].

According to the Open Universiteit Nederland, the scientific community has identified twelve areas of digital competence. These areas are based on the knowledge and skills people need to acquire in order to become literate [21].

In order for households to promote their own businesses online, it is important that they have the necessary digital skills. This enables businesses to access international markets via marketplaces such as Amazon, eBay and Etsy. Critically important digital skills include working with SEO (search engine optimisation); contextual advertising, content marketing, video marketing, social media marketing (SMM) and email marketing. Using CRM, ERP and SCM systems as digital tools helps improve business efficiency by automating its main processes.

An important aspect for studying the impact of digitalization on the financial behavior of Ukrainian households is determining the level of digital literacy of the population. Thus, in 2023, the Ministry of Digital Transformation of Ukraine published a study in which they analyzed the development of digital skills of Ukrainians. Researchers surveyed 2,005 people aged 18 to 70 and 402 people aged 10 to 17. In particular, they asked about information, communication skills, skills for solving life problems and creating digital content. The results of this study showed that the older people are, the fewer of them are connected to the Internet. If among young people (18–29 years old) 98% have access to the World Wide Web at home, then among people over 60 years old, this share is 86%. Those respondents who do not see the benefits of using the World Wide Web or do not have the appropriate skills to use it do not have access. The Internet is used daily by 71% of respondents among the oldest category (60–70 years old) and 96% of respondents among the youngest category of adults (18–29 years old).

To assess the digital skills of respondents, four levels of proficiency were defined:

- "No skills" – absence of digital skills across all four domains (information, communication, problem-solving, and digital content creation) and/or no use of Internet services within the past three months;
- "Low skills" – lack of digital skills in one of the four areas of competence;
- "Basic skills" – digital proficiency in all four areas at a level no lower than "average";
- "Above basic skills" – digital proficiency in all four areas at a level no lower than "above average."

According to the results of this study, 93% of Ukraine's adult population (aged 18–70) had digital skills in 2023, 38% of whom had the highest level. For comparison, this figure was 32.6% in 2021 and 25.5% in 2019 (Table 1).

These indicators suggest that the population's digital skills are improving: the proportion of adults without digital skills is falling, while the proportion of people with basic or higher skills is rising. Additionally, proficiency in solving everyday problems using technology, such as online banking, is quite high (86%). Almost 16% of adults use artificial intelligence for work or education, compared to 56.3% of adolescents. Almost 81% of Ukrainians believe that growth in digital skills can positively impact Ukraine's economy as a whole. Those with a higher level of digital skills are more likely to agree with this. According to the results, 85% of respondents confirmed that people with higher digital skills have more career growth opportunities. Furthermore,

Table 1. Dynamics of the general level of digital skills among Ukraine's adult population [22]

Year	No Skills	Low Skills	Basic Skills	Above Basic Skills
2019	15.1%	37.9%	21.5%	25.5%
2021	11.2%	36.6%	19.6%	32.6%
2023	7.2%	33.2%	21.6%	38.0%

82% of participants emphasised that these skills are important for obtaining prestigious, promising, high-paying jobs and, consequently, improving their standard of living [23].

The development of digital technologies and citizens' acquisition of a sufficient level of digital literacy are inextricably linked to Internet access. According to the Organisation for Economic Co-operation and Development (OECD), 91.6% of households in Eurozone countries reported having access to the internet in 2023. The highest rates were recorded in countries such as: Luxembourg (99.1%), the Netherlands (98.9%), Finland (96.8%), Iceland (96.4%) and Belgium (94.5%). The lowest rates were in Lithuania (88.6%) and Greece (86.9%). Globally, the countries with the highest household Internet access rates are Korea (99.96%) and Switzerland (99.66%), while Colombia has the lowest rate (59.47%).

In almost all cases, this access is via a personal computer using dial-up, ADSL, or cable broadband. According to the Ministry of Digital Policy of Ukraine, the share of internet users among the population in Ukraine was almost 94% in 2023 [22].

The rapid growth of urbanisation today (with forecasts predicting an increase in the urban population to 5.2 billion by 2030) stimulates the creation and development of high-quality, sustainable infrastructure and the provision of basic services, including internet access [24].

A steady growth trend in the number of households connected to the internet in cities was observed during 2017–2023. An analysis of the growth dynamics in the proportion of the urban population connected to the internet shows that the highest proportion of connected individuals in 2017 was observed in Germany (93.57%). By 2023, this figure had decreased by 0.82% points. In contrast, it increased by 6.59% in France, 9.41% points in Poland and 6.18% in Austria (compared to 2022) (Table 2).

Cities are becoming centres of financial and digital activity for most of the population living within their boundaries, and urbanisation is accompanied by population growth and digitalisation. Access to the internet among rural households is also increasing. In Germany, for example, the proportion of the rural population using the internet increased from 91.23% in 2016 to 96.04% in 2020. Similar increases were seen in France (from 84.84% to 90.09%) and Poland (from 79.05% to 88.88%).

Overall, the number of households connected to the network has grown rapidly in both urban and rural areas, with urban areas experiencing faster growth than rural areas (with the exception of Germany). As for Ukrainian households (Fig. 1), from 2010 to 2023, the share of households with Internet access grew by an average of 5.5% each year.

Table 2. Households in selected European countries with access to the Internet (as a % of total urban/rural households)

Year	2018		2019		2020		2021		2022		2023	
Name of the country	city	rural area	city	rural area	city	rural area	city	rural area	city	rural area	city	rural area
Germany	95,47	93,11	94,96	95,03	95,58	96,04	92,74	91,23	91,56	91,86	92,75	90,15
Austria	90,16	88,50	91,82	88,07	92,35	89,80	96,14	93,43	95,24	91,95	-	-
France	90,10	87,81	91,91	90,09	…	…	94,91	92,59	93,72	91,40	95,14	91,84
Poland	87,17	81,60	89,51	83,49	91,59	88,88	93,69	91,93	94,21	92,85	94,19	92,89
Ukraine	71,6	40,6	76,3	44,1	85,60	66,01	87,40	72,83	…	…	94	…

Source: the table was constructed by the authors based on data from [22, 25]

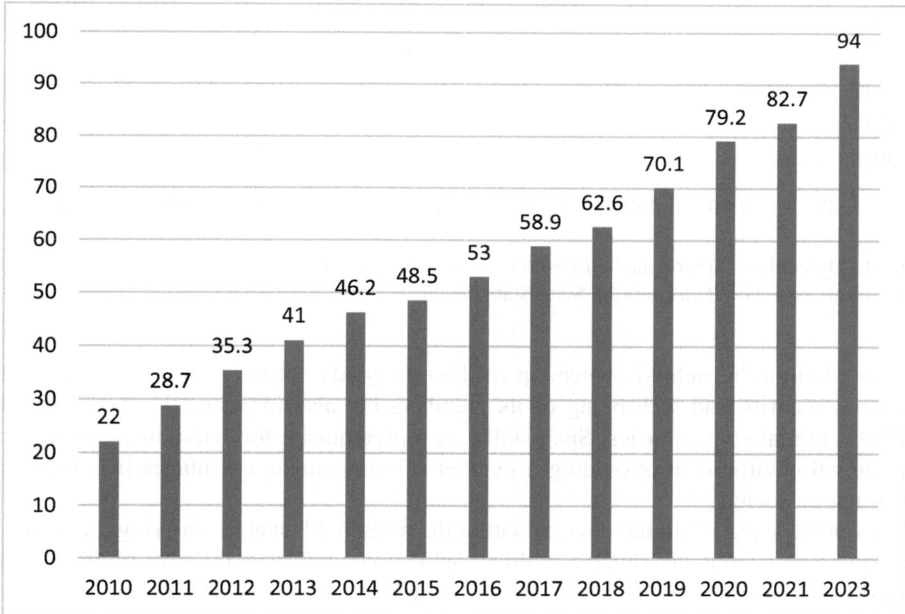

Fig. 1. Share of Ukrainian households with access to the Internet for the period 2010–2023, in % of the total number of households **Source:** Figure compiled by the authors based on data from the State Statistics Service of Ukraine [26]

To identify the impact of digital technologies on financial behavior and well-being levels in the population, it is advisable to study the distribution of people living in households according to how frequently they use internet services, and how this availability depends on average per capita total income (Fig. 2). Notably, the largest proportion of active internet users (those who use the network daily) comes from households with the highest level of provision—91.9%. This pattern is logical and expected since this category of households has the widest access to durable goods, which contributes to regular use of digital services.

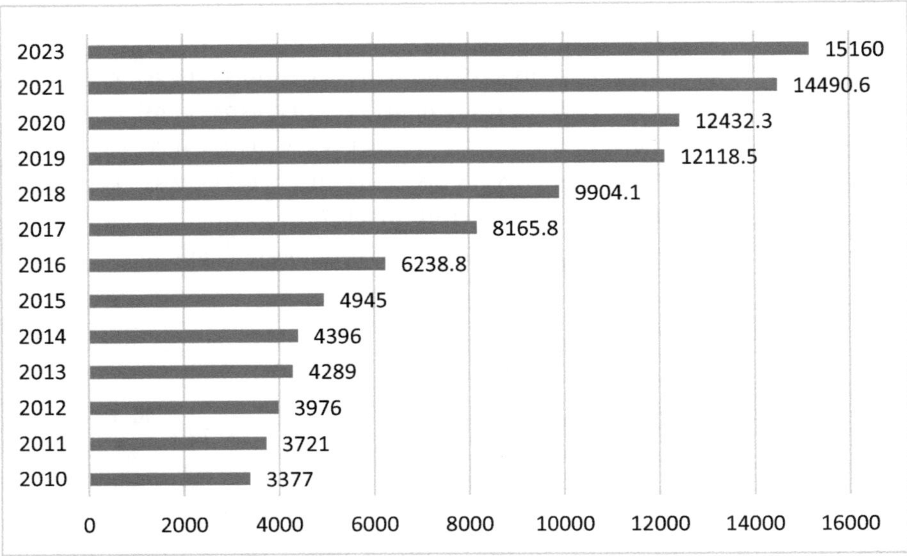

Fig. 2. Dynamics of aggregate household income in Ukraine, UAH. **Source:** Figure compiled by the authors based on data from the State Statistics Service of Ukraine [26]

In addition, household ownership of durable goods not only reflects the level of material security and well-being of its members but also indicates the development of basic digital competencies. Such skills are a prerequisite for active integration into the digital environment, providing a number of competitive advantages in a modern information society.

Even basic use of digital devices within the household, such as carrying out simple banking transactions via suitable mobile applications, indicates the start of the digital transformation of everyday life. This demonstrates households' readiness to further develop their digital and financial competencies, which will contribute to their future socio-economic well-being.

From an analytical point of view, it is of considerable interest to study the characteristics of households without internet access. The results of the surveys showed that the main barriers are a lack of confidence, knowledge, or skills in using digital technologies. At the same time, however, positive trends have emerged: between 2019 and 2021, the proportion of people lacking the basic knowledge required to use the internet decreased. This is due to the rapid spread of digitalisation in all areas of public life in recent years.

The availability of internet access is one of the key factors demonstrating a stable growth trend during the analysed period. In our opinion, this factor has a significant impact on both the overall level of household income and the transformation of their expenditure structure. In this context, it is important to note that a household's financial well-being and the characteristics of its financial behavior largely depend on the digital and financial competence of its members, particularly in terms of the effective use of the opportunities provided by the internet. This dependence, in turn, affects the financial culture of the population as a whole and the socio-economic stability of the state.

To substantiate the impact of digitalisation processes on the well-being of Ukrainian households, a regression equation was constructed to reflect the relationship between two key indicators: the proportion of households with internet access from 2010 to 2023 and their total income during the same period.

Internet access was chosen as the criterion for digitalisation because digital infrastructure is currently considered one of the most established technologies, the socio-economic effect of which is significant and empirically confirmed.

Analysis of the results presented in Table 3 indicates a stable exponential relationship between the above variables. The value of the multiple correlation coefficient demonstrates a high degree of dependence of the effective indicator (total household income) on the influencing factor—the level of internet access—allowing us to assert the significant impact of digitalisation on the economic behavior of the population.

Table 3. Depicting the relationship between total household income and the share of households connected to the Internet through key qualitative indicators of regression analysis

Coefficient values	
Multiple correlation coefficient	0,9624
Coefficient of determination	0,9194
The observational value of Fisher's F-test	137,89
Standard error	1239,31
Observation	13

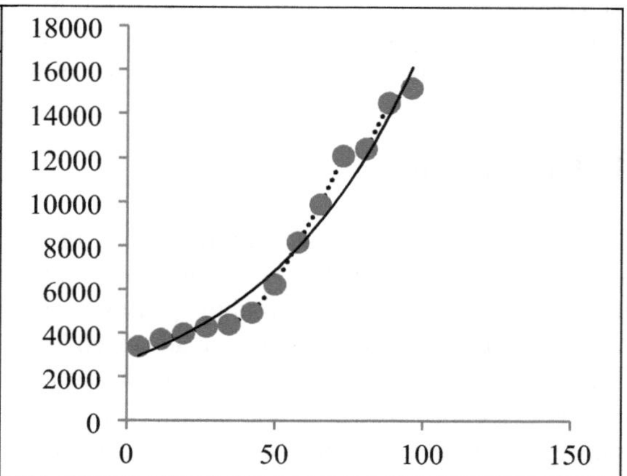

The obtained value of the coefficient of multiple determination R2 at the level of 96.24% indicates that the predominant share of the variation in total household income is explained by the variability of the Internet access indicator. This indicates the high accuracy of the constructed regression model. Additional confirmation is provided by the calculated observational value of Fisher's F-test, which is 137.89 and significantly exceeds its tabular critical value (F_tabl. = 4.45). This allows us to conclude that the statistical significance of the dependence between the variables included in the model is significant.

From the point of view of the economic interpretation of the obtained results, it was established: provided that the share of households with Internet access increases by 1%, the expected increase in their total income will be on average 193.54 UAH. The confidence interval for the corresponding regression coefficient is in the range from 157.26 to 229.82 UAH, which indicates the statistical reliability of the estimate and allows us to state: in the general population, with an increase in the share of households connected to the Internet, income may increase within the specified range for each percentage point.

The results of the regression analysis indicate a significant direct correlation between the economic well-being of Ukrainian households and their use of digital technologies. The analysis of the trend line suggests that this correlation will strengthen in the near future.

Taking into account the objective factors that contribute to the dynamic increase in digital and financial literacy among households at this stage of the study, as well as the digital competencies that households should possess to use financial services confidently, and the personal skills and abilities that household members should possess to live comfortably and conduct financial activities effectively in a digitalised society, we propose increasing the efficiency of financial activities and optimising household financial behavior through a comprehensive approach to raising financial literacy levels and digital skills. In particular, households should have the opportunity to obtain the necessary knowledge and skills, either through self-education with access to the relevant educational tools, or by acquiring them directly while using financial or digital services. This should be supported by a centralised state-level educational process, starting with pre-school education and continuing throughout life.

4 Conclusions

The analysis of digital competencies among the adult population demonstrates a substantial expansion in the level of digital skills in recent years. The findings indicate that the overwhelming majority of adults possess at least basic digital competencies, while a significant proportion demonstrate advanced levels of digital proficiency. At the same time, the study confirms that the development of adequate digital financial literacy is closely associated with access to Internet infrastructure and digital technologies. Nevertheless, widespread Internet access alone cannot be regarded as a sufficient indicator of high digital and financial literacy, as the effective use of digital resources remains uneven due to disparities in technical accessibility, knowledge and practical competencies.

The results of the regression analysis reveal a statistically significant positive relationship between household income levels and the prevalence of Internet connectivity, confirming that the use of digital technologies in everyday activities and financial transactions contributes to household economic well-being. These findings underscore the growing importance of digital inclusion as a determinant of financial resilience and socio-economic stability.

In the context of accelerating digital transformation, which increasingly permeates all spheres of socio-economic activity, including the financial sector, digitalisation is substantially reshaping household financial behavior and modifying traditional patterns of financial decision-making. While the positive effects of digitalisation should be acknowledged, particular attention must be devoted to assessing the risks associated with the use of digital financial technologies, including cybersecurity threats, financial fraud and the spread of high-risk financial practices.

Considering the identified trends and the influence of both internal and external economic factors, the study emphasizes the necessity of developing rational strategies for household financial behavior within a digitalised environment. The effective and responsible use of digital financial technologies requires not only sufficient financial and digital literacy, but also the development of practical digital competencies and risk-management skills. Strengthening these capacities may contribute significantly to enhancing household financial stability, economic security and broader socio-economic sustainability.

References

1. Brechko, O.: Financial and digital literacy as basic components of the development of a modern information society. Reg. Aspects Dev. Productive Forces Ukraine **24**, 129–135 (2019)
2. Abuselidze, G.: Challenges and opportunities in the development of innovative payment methods within the monetary system. Stud. Syst., Dec. Control **550**, 579–591 (2024). https://doi.org/10.1007/978-3-031-66218-8_45
3. Ji, Z., Abuselidze, G., Lymar, V.: The Internationalization of the digital yuan and changes in the architecture of the monetary system. Stud. Syst., Dec. Control **537**, 517–528 (2024). https://doi.org/10.1007/978-3-031-62106-2_39
4. Abuselidze, G., Zoidze, T.: The impact of digitalization and artificial intelligence on sustainable development and energy efficiency of the Georgian banking sector. E3S Web Conf. **542**, 01007 (2024). https://doi.org/10.1051/e3sconf/202454201007
5. Description of the Digital Competence Framework for Citizens of Ukraine. Ministry of Digital Transformation of Ukraine (2021). https://er.knutd.edu.ua/bitstream/123456789/19506/1/Innovatyka2021_V1_P137-141.pdf
6. Tyagunova, N. M., Tyagunova, Z. O.: Digital competencies as determinants of the development of entrepreneurial activity. Transf. Econ. **2**(2), 57–61 (2023). https://doi.org/10.32782/2786-8141/2023-2-11
7. Strategies for the development of the financial sector of Ukraine until 2025. https://bank.gov.ua/ua/news/all/strategiya-rozvitku-finansovogo-sektoru-ukrayini-do-2025-roku-7686
8. Geyenko, M., Rybina, L., Guzenko, T.: Financial literacy and professional development: key components of the strategy for developing human resources and intellectual potential in higher education institutions. Econ. Soc. **47** (2023). https://doi.org/10.32782/2524-0072/2023-47-96
9. Tymkiv, A.O., Sydor, G. V.: Financial inclusion as a component of the recovery of the Ukrainian economy. Incl. Soc. **1**, 5–14 (2022). https://doi.org/10.32782/inclusion-society-2022-1-1
10. Dombrovska, S.O.: Modern methods of forming financial literacy of the population of Ukraine. Educ. Analytics of Ukraine. **3**, 5–14 (2022)
11. Lavreniuk, V. V., Lavreniuk, A. V.: Increasing the financial literacy of the population: foreign experience. Bus. Inform. **1**, 59–67 (2022). https://doi.org/10.32983/2222-4459-2022-1-59-67
12. Kizima, T., Shamanska, O.: Financial literacy of the population and financial behavior of households: aspects of mutual influence. World Finan. **1**, 16–26 (2014)
13. Yuriy, S. I., Kizima, T. O.: Financial literacy of the population in the dialectics of modern educational trends. Finan. Ukraine **2**, 16–25 (2012). https://finukr.org.ua/docs/FU_12_02_016_uk.pdf

14. Ptashchenko, L. O., Kolinchuk, D. V.: Actualities of increasing the level of financial literacy of Ukrainians during the period of fintech development. Econ. Reg. **4**, 92–99 (2021). https://doi.org/10.26906/EiR.2021.4(83).2532
15. Dubyna, M., Tarasenko, A., Tarasenko, O.: Directions for increasing the level of financial literacy of households in the context of digitalization of the financial services sector. Econ. Soc. **56** (2023). https://doi.org/10.32782/2524-0072/2023-56-17
16. Over the past three years, the level of financial literacy of Ukrainians has improved - research results.https://bank.gov.ua/ua/news/all/za-ostanni-tri-rokiriven-finansovoyi-gramotnist-ukrayintsiv--polipshivsya--rezultati-doslidjennya
17. Kudlai, V.: Digital literacy of the individual in the context of the development of the information society. Bull. Mariupol State Univ. Ser.: Philos., Cult. Stud., Sociol. **10**, 97–104 (2015)
18. Abuselidze, G., Mamaladze, L.: The impact of artificial intelligence on employment before and during pandemic: a comparative analysis. J. Phys: Conf. Ser. **1840**, 012040 (2021). https://doi.org/10.1088/1742-6596/1840/1/012040
19. Learning cities: drivers of inclusion and sustainability (2020). https://uil.unesco.org/lifelonglearning/learning-cities/learning-cities-drivers-inclusion-and-sustainability
20. Morse, N.V., Kuzminska, O.G., Vember, V.P., Barna, O.V.: Competency tasks as a means of forming information competence in conditions of continuous education. Inf. Technol. Educ.: Collect. Sci. Works **4**, 48–62 (2010)
21. Dobryanska, N. B.: Optimization of the financial behavior of domestic households in the domestic market of public borrowings of Ukraine in today's realities. Coll. Sci. Works State Tax Univ. **2**, 14–21 (2024). https://doi.org/10.32782/2617-5940.2.2024.3
22. "On "you" with the Internet. how well are Ukrainians adapted to online life - in the study of digital skills." Mediamaker. https://mediamaker.me/na-ty-z-internetom-naskilky-ukrayinczi-adaptovani-do-onlajn-zhyttya-v-doslidzhenni-czyfrovyh-navychok-6468/
23. Official website of the Cabinet of Ministers of Ukraine. https://www.kmu.gov.ua/news/93-ukraintsiv-volodiiut-tsyfrovymy-navychkamy-mintsyfry-prezentuvala-rezultaty-doslidzhennia-tsyfrovoi-hramotnosti-ukraintsiv
24. United Nations, Department of Economic and Social Affairs, Population Division. The world's cities in 2030: Data booklet. New York, United Nations. https://digitallibrary.un.org/record/3799524?ln=en
25. The OECD Model Survey on ICT Access and Usage by Households and Individuals. https://stats.oecd.org/Index.aspx?DataSetCode=ICT_HH2
26. State Statistics Service of Ukraine. https://www.ukrstat.gov.ua

A Multidimensional Quality Assessment of Synthetic Movement Data for Post-stroke Rehabilitation

Aline P.A Ferreira[1], Lucas O. Alves[1], Fabio A.F Molinares[1], Marcelo P. Guimarães[2], Vinícius F.S. Mota[1], Leonardo C.D. Rocha[3], and Diego R.C. Dias[1](✉)

[1] Universidade Federal do Espírito Santo, Vitória, Brazil
{aline.p.ferreira,lucas.o.alves}@edu.ufes.br,
{fabio.molinares,vinicius.f.mota,diego.dias}@ufes.br
[2] Universidade Federal de São Paulo, São Paulo, Brazil
marcelo.paiva@unifesp.br
[3] Universidade Federal de São João del-Rei, São João del-Rei, Brazil

Abstract. It is difficult to create good artificial intelligence models for motor rehabilitation when we do not have sufficient clinical data. To solve this, we tested two approaches to create synthetic data for the squat exercise: the use of controlled Gaussian noise and the use of GAN networks. We analyzed whether this data was statistically accurate, whether it made clinical sense, and whether it was useful in practice. The results showed a clear difference. Gaussian noise was much more efficient, preserving the rhythm of the movement and the anatomical logic, which helped improve the performance of models such as Random Forest and LSTM. GAN networks, on the other hand, although they reproduced the joint angles well, failed to maintain the continuity of movement over time, proving to be less consistent for practical use. These findings suggest that, for complex and highly coordinated multi-joint movements, controlled stochastic methods may currently outperform standard generative deep learning models in maintaining structural integrity, providing empirical evidence for future research in data-driven rehabilitation.

Keywords: Synthetic Data · Neuromotor Rehabilitation · Generative Adversarial Networks · Time Series Analysis · Data Augmentation

1 Introduction

The availability of high-quality data is fundamental to the development and validation of accurate and reliable statistical models in clinical rehabilitation. However, clinical data collection faces significant challenges that compromise research in this field. Among these challenges are the high costs of acquiring motion capture equipment, the maintenance of specialized infrastructure, and temporal

O. Gervasi et al. (Eds.): ICCSA 2026, LNCS 16768, pp. 233–250, 2027.
https://doi.org/10.1007/978-3-032-30488-9_15

constraints in the collection process, which often require weeks or months to obtain an adequate sample. Furthermore, patient recruitment for longitudinal studies further limits the quantity and quality of data available for research.

To capture movement data in neuromotor rehabilitation, inertial sensors are positioned on different body joints or optical devices are employed, representing a specific type of time series [1,4,5,7,8]. Each movement is recorded as a sequence of frames, where each row represents a temporal instance containing complete information on joint angles and coordinates from various sensors. However, given the multiple temporal structures involved, these data require validation methodologies that not only consider marginal statistical properties but also preserve temporal dynamics and the clinical plausibility of the generated data. Given these challenges, synthetic data generation becomes a promising approach to overcome the limitations of available real-world data.

To create this data, we used artificial intelligence models that have gained prominence, such as generative networks (GANs) [6], known for creating very realistic synthetic data. However, we needed to understand which technique works best when the challenge is dealing with time series of clinical movements [2]. After all, before using this data in practice, it is essential to ensure that it is faithful to real patterns, since this has a direct impact on health [3]. Therefore, we decided to compare two different approaches: one based on Gaussian noise and the other using GANs themselves.

Our analysis was divided into four main criteria to ensure data quality [9]. First, we checked statistical accuracy, that is, whether the generated numbers accurately reflect the real data. Then, we verified the movement rhythm, ensuring that the temporal sequence is natural. We also evaluated clinical logic to ensure that the created movements are physically possible and respect human anatomy [10]. Finally, we tested practical utility, confirming whether this new data actually helps improve the performance of artificial intelligence models when used in training.

Thus, we emphasize that no single metric can fully capture the quality of synthetic data in clinical applications, underscoring the need for a multidimensional approach to evaluate the generated data comprehensively. Therefore, we consider that the results provide empirical evidence on which synthesis methodology produces higher-quality data for clinical movement time series, opening important avenues for future research and applications in neuromotor rehabilitation.

2 Methodology

In this section, we describe the techniques used to generate, evaluate, and compare synthetic time-series motion data, focusing on two distinct approaches: controlled Gaussian noise and GANs. The experimental development was carried out in a Google Colab environment using Python 3.12. The workflow is available on GitHub[1], where the generation, preprocessing, multidimensional evaluation, and performance comparison steps are documented.

2.1 Dataset and Preprocessing

The data used in this study consist of time series of body movements captured by inertial sensors placed on multiple joints of the human body during the execution of standardized neuromotor rehabilitation tasks. For the analyses, we used the deep squat, a fundamental movement in post-stroke rehabilitation that requires complex coordination among the hip, knee, and ankle. We organize the data into a CSV file containing 27,063 temporal records (frames) and 65 columns, representing 100 unique movement series (identified by the record field). Each complete movement series consists of approximately 270 frames. In parallel, we used 4 additional movements as a negative class for training classifier models, including `Straight Line Lunge, Step over Obstacle, Lateral Lunge, and Rise from Sit`. We loaded these movements from separate CSV files, totaling 390 movement series in the negative class.

Given the data context, the first preparatory step involved the automated identification of signal variables based on column labels. The identification strategy classified the variables into three categories:

- Joint angles (8 variables): Identified by the presence of the substring angle in lowercase within the column name, capturing joint rotations such as `shoulderLangle, shoulderRangle, elbowLangle, elbowRangle, hipLangle, hipRangle, kneeLangle, kneeRangle`.
- Three-dimensional coordinates (36 variables): Identified by the suffix X, Y, or Z in the column name, resulting in 12 sensors $\times$ 3 coordinate axes (`lshoulderX, rshoulderX, lelbowX, ..., rankleZ`).
- Transverse variables (2 variables): Identified by the presence of "Transv" in the name, capturing transverse rotations - `shoulderLTransv, shoulderRTransv`.

The process ensures that a total of 46 signal variables are submitted to subsequent tests to verify that they were correctly identified.

2.2 Implementation of Generation Techniques

Gaussian noise-based synthesis is performed by selecting an existing real-world motion and adding Gaussian noise correlated with its characteristics. For each signal variable (coordinates, angles, cross-sectional variables), we defined a specific standard deviation: 0.02 for coordinates, 0.05 for angles, and 0.03 for cross-sectional variables. We sampled noise from a normal distribution with a mean of 0 and a standard deviation proportional to the real-world data's standard deviation. We limited the resulting values to the 1st and 99th percentiles of the

[1] https://github.com/aline-pires/TCC.git.

real-world data to ensure they remained within physically feasible ranges. This method preserved the temporal structure and dynamics of the original motion while introducing realistic variability.

For the multivariate time series GAN, we chose to implement it using `PyTorch`. Real-world sequences were resampled to a fixed length of 300 time steps, hip-centered, height-normalized (when available), and global z-score-standardized. The generator received as input a 96-dimensional Gaussian noise vector, concatenated with an explicit temporal embedding, composed of 1D convolutional residual blocks with progressive dilations and 192 intermediate channels. The discriminator was implemented with 1D convolutions and spectral normalization, operating simultaneously on position, velocity, and acceleration.

We conducted the training in two stages. In the first stage, we pre-trained on all available movements for 300 epochs. Subsequently, we applied a specific refinement to the deep squat movement for 1000 epochs. In both stages, we set a batch size of 32 and distinct learning rates for the generator and the discriminator: higher for the generator and slightly lower for the discriminator, to stabilize the adversarial process. For the generator's objective function, we combined adversarial loss, feature matching, and temporal regularization terms, with additional constraints introduced progressively after a warm-up period. As for the final synthetic sequences, these were generated directly by the trained generator and used exclusively in the data augmentation experiments.

2.3 Multidimensional Evaluation Protocol

First, we structured the quality assessment around verifying statistical accuracy, which evaluates the degree to which synthetic data distributions reproduce the statistical characteristics of real data. We applied two metrics: the Kolmogorov-Smirnov (KS) test and the Wasserstein distance.

We applied the KS test exclusively to the 36 three-dimensional coordinate variables, as these are continuous variables suitable for this test. The operational procedure involved: For each variable with coordinates $i \in 1, 2, ..., 36$, we extracted the vectors of real and synthetic values, then applied the KS test to obtain a two-tailed p-value. We defined approval by the criterion $p\text{value} > 0.05$, indicating the absence of statistical evidence of a significant difference between the distributions, generating a table of approvals and rejections based on this criterion.

We applied the Wasserstein distance to the 10 angles and transversal variables (8 angles + 2 transversals), providing a continuous distance metric that captures the multidimensional structure of the distributions.

The protocol we implemented included calculating the Wasserstein distance using the `wasserstein_distance()` function, already implemented in the `SciPy` library, with the standard Euclidean metric, and calculating the amplitude of the real data; it also involved normalizing the distance by the amplitude, allowing comparison between variables of different scales. Finally, we applied the acceptance criterion $W_{\text{norm}} < 0.15$. We chose this criterion of 0.15 to represent a tolerance of up to 15% of the observed range of motion in the real data. Approvals in this criterion indicate not only the preservation of marginal distributions, but mainly the preservation of structured and biologically significant inter-articular correlations.

We assessed temporal dynamic fidelity using the autocorrelation function (ACF) for each signal variable and each unique motion series (identified by record); thus, we initially grouped the dataset by the record variable. For each record and variable, we extracted the time series and subsequently calculated the autocorrelation function for lags $k = 0, 1, 2, ..., 24$, capturing dependencies for up to 24 time steps. The procedure included a protection against very short series: if $T < k + 1$, the record was ignored. We also employed the function `statsmodels.tsa.stattools.acf()` for this purpose.

After calculating the autocorrelation for all vectors, we established the acceptance criterion as the mean absolute error $\text{MAE}_{\text{ACF}} < 0.10$, reflecting that autocorrelation structures are considered high-fidelity when they diverge by less than 10% on average. Values above this limit indicate that the generation technique substantially altered the temporal memory of the motion.

In addition to evaluating temporal dynamics through the autocorrelation function, we used multivariate DTW to quantify the similarity between complete motion trajectories. The procedure, implemented identically for both synthesis methods (Gaussian noise and GAN), used global z-score normalization based on real data statistics (mean and standard deviation calculated across the 46 signal variables). For each comparison, we extracted the multidimensional temporal matrices $(T_i, 46)$, where T_i represents the number of frames in the i series, applying DTW via `fastdtw()` with Euclidean distance in 46-dimensional space and normalizing the result by the optimal alignment path length.

To establish a common baseline, we calculated a DTW distribution between pairs of distinct real movements (any real movement versus any other real movement), generating a reference for the natural variability observed in real executions of the deep squat. The unified acceptance criterion was $\text{DTW}_{\text{norm}} \leq 2 \times \text{median}(\text{baseline}_{\text{real-real global}})$, allowing synthetic trajectories to exhibit up to twice the variation typically observed between distinct real executions of the same movement. This factor of 2 reflects a conservative tolerance for natural variations while rejecting systematic deviations from expected motor dynamics.

The pairing strategy was such that for each of the 100 generated synthetic series, the DTW was calculated against all 100 real series, systematically recording the lowest DTW distance, a nearest neighbor approach. This approach evaluated how closely each synthetic data trajectory matched the cloud of plausible real trajectories. Thus, both methods generated distributions of 100 minimum DTW values (one per synthetic series), allowing for direct comparison under the same *baseline* and acceptance criterion.

Finally, the evaluation of temporal dynamics concluded with verification of physical plausibility through derivative analysis. For each time series of coordinates and angles, velocity and acceleration were calculated. To be realistic, synthetic data cannot exhibit excessive accelerations (instantaneous changes in velocity) or high-frequency jitter; therefore, the 99th percentile of absolute acceleration was computed from real data, and the number of synthetic samples violating this limit was counted. Thus, the established criterion was less than 2% of synthetic samples exceeding the 99th percentile of the real data.

Regarding the third evaluation aspect, clinical plausibility, the method we developed involved defining limits based on the range of motion observed in the real data (1st and 99th percentiles) for each variable. We verified whether all synthetic values remained within these ranges, with relative differences considered acceptable; values completely outside the observable range indicate anatomically impossible movements. The criterion was that 95% of the synthetic samples were within the limits observed in the real data. We tabulated these results, indicating the variable, the upper and lower limits, the minimum and maximum synthetic values, the percentage of conformity, the approval status, and the applied criterion.

Finally, we evaluated the practical utility of synthetic data through data augmentation experiments designed to simulate scenarios of progressively scarce real data. Our experimental protocol was based on the central hypothesis that high-quality synthetic data can improve the performance of predictive models, such as Random Forest and LSTM, trained with limited real samples. To this end, we defined five experimental scenarios corresponding to different levels of availability of real-time series of deep squat movements, considering sets with 10, 20, 30, 50, and 70 positive series. For each scenario, we adopted a comparative protocol under two distinct conditions: **a)** training using exclusively real data; and **b)** training with real data + an equivalent amount of synthetic data (1:1 data augmentation). In all analyses, we kept the test set fixed, comprising 30 positive real series and 117 negative real series, for a total of 147 samples, ensuring a consistent basis for comparing the incremental impact of including synthetic data.

Regarding the predictive models, two complementary approaches were evaluated. The first was based on Random Forest, where the temporal mean, standard deviation, minimum value, maximum value, amplitude, and mean velocity were first extracted for each movement time series and for each of the 46 signal variables, resulting in a total of 276 features per movement, allowing for the capture of both statistical characteristics and compatibility with these machine learning models. Thus, using these features, 100 trees were configured with the Gini impurity criterion and automatic class weighting (`class_weight='balanced'`) to handle class imbalance. To ensure robustness, the experiments were repeated with five distinct seeds, ranging from 100 to 104. In each repetition, random samples of positive real series were selected according to the scarcity scenario, along with a fixed set of negative examples. In synthetic-data scenarios, positive synthetic series were added in quantities equivalent to the real ones. The model was then trained on this augmented set and evaluated on the fixed test set, recording performance metrics.

Furthermore, we implemented an LSTM model to directly explore the temporal dependencies of the series, without the need for prior statistical aggregation. The architecture we employed consisted of a masking layer, followed by an LSTM layer with 32 memory units, a dropout layer for regularization, and a dense layer with sigmoid activation for binary classification. We trained the model with the Adam optimizer, the binary cross-entropy loss function, and 25 training epochs. We also standardized the time series to a fixed maximum length of 300 time steps via post-padding, and used a fixed threshold of 0.5 for obtaining predictions on the test set, with performance metrics calculated analogously to the Random Forest experiment.

In both approaches, we evaluated the model performance using accuracy, precision, recall, and F1-Score. For each experimental configuration, we aggregated the results via the mean and standard deviation of the metrics across the five seeds, allowing for the quantification of both average performance and the variability associated with the sampling process. We considered confirmed the practical utility of the synthetic data when consistent gains in F1-Score and other metrics were observed in models trained with real data augmented by synthetic data, especially in the most extreme scarcity scenarios (10 and 20 real series). In summary, Table 1 consolidates the predefined acceptance criteria for each evaluation dimension:

Table 1. Consolidated Acceptance Criteria for Synthetic Data Evaluation.

Dimension	Metric	Acceptance Criterion
Statistical Fidelity	Kolmogorov-Smirnov	p-value > 0.05 per coordinate
	Wasserstein Distance	$W \leq 0.15 \times$ amplitude
Temporal Dynamics	Multivariate DTW	$\text{DTW}_{\text{norm}} \leq 2 \times \text{median}(\text{base}_{\text{real-real}})$
	ACF/PACF	RMSE < 0.10 vs. real data
	Velocity/Acceleration	$< 2\%$ of samples outside real P99
Clinical Plausibility	Anatomical Limits	95% within real 1–99 percentiles
Practical Utility	Predictive Classification	Analysis of metric gains

3 Results

The initial analysis automatically identified 46 signal variables in the deep squat data, distributed into three categories: 8 joint angle variables, 36 three-dimensional coordinate variables (X, Y, Z) derived from 12 inertial sensors positioned on the shoulders, elbows, wrists, hips, knees, and ankles, and 2 transverse variables (rotation). This multidimensional structure captures the movement in its entirety, reflecting the simultaneous linear and rotational displacements of multiple joints.

3.1 Statistical and Temporal Quality

The statistical fidelity analysis revealed contrasting patterns between the two generation methods. These were evaluated using the KS test on the 36 coordinates and the Wasserstein distance on the 10 angles/transverse variables.

The KS test, which we applied exclusively to three-dimensional coordinates (X, Y, Z), demonstrated good preservation of Gaussian noise, achieving 78% approval (28/36 coordinates), with low KS statistics (0.0096–0.0111) and p-values consistently above 0.05, as observed in Fig. 1, indicating that the marginal distributions of the coordinates were preserved with high statistical fidelity. Rejections (8/36) were concentrated in the more peripheral parts of the body, probably due to the greater sensitivity of the KS test in low-variance regions. However, for the GAN, there was a strong contrast, with 0% approval (0/36), very high KS statistics, and p-values close to 0 in all coordinates. Therefore, we believe this result indicates that the marginal distributions of the coordinates generated by the GAN diverge significantly from the true ones, completely rejecting the hypothesis of statistical similarity.

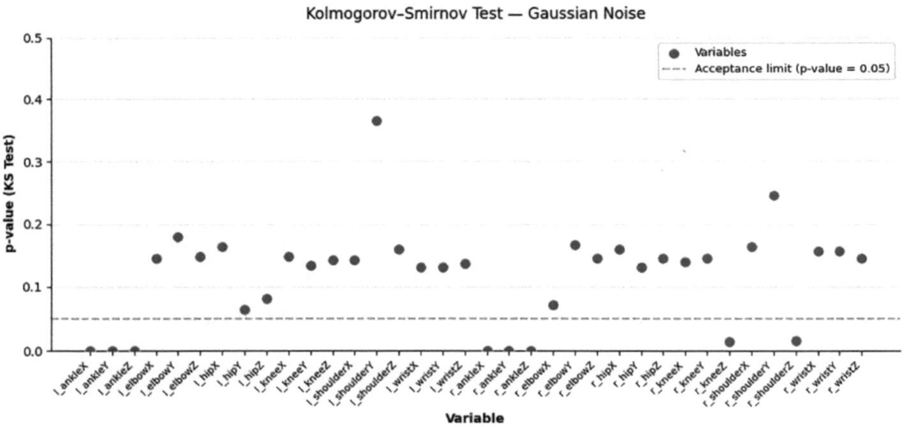

Fig. 1. Kolmogorov-Smirnov Test P-values for Noise Data.

Both methods, however, demonstrated excellent preservation of angular distributions. Gaussian noise obtained 100% approval (10/10) with extremely low normalized Wasserstein distances, while the GAN also reached 100%, all below the 0.15×span threshold. This means that, in this context, the methods demonstrated excellent preservation of angular distributions. It is worth noting that the GAN, despite the limitations observed in spatial coordinates, was capable of generating angles with distributions statistically compatible with the real data; however, the results are not yet as uniform and low as the synthetic data generated by Gaussian noise, as seen in Figs. 2a and 2b.

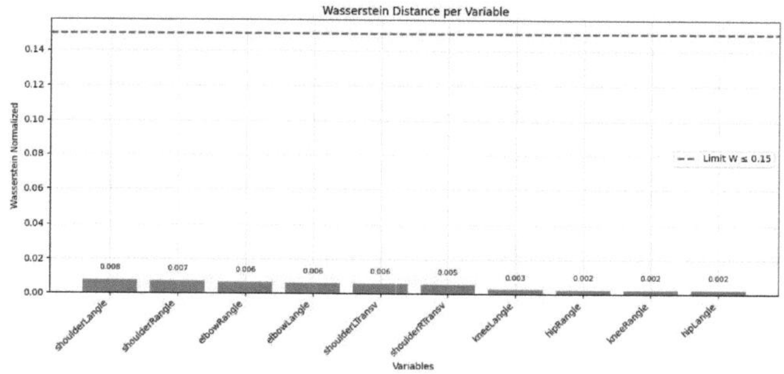

(a) Noise Data

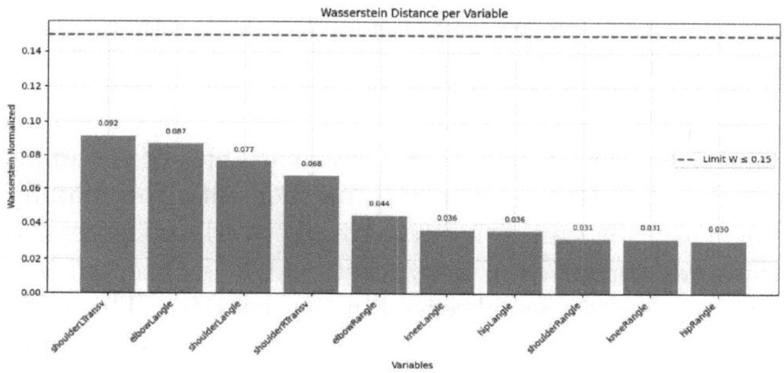

(b) GAN Data

Fig. 2. Wasserstein Distance Comparison: Noise vs. GAN.

Thus, these results show that, despite limitations in coordinates, both methods preserve essential angular structures, establishing a basis for subsequent dynamic analyses based on angles.

3.2 Temporal Adequacy and Sequential Structure of Synthetic Data

The analysis of the Gaussian noise-based model's capacity to preserve temporal persistence via the autocorrelation function revealed that, globally, this method demonstrated excellent preservation, as seen in Fig. 3. It is observed that the temporal decay pattern of the autocorrelation is consistently preserved, with a large part of the lags remaining within the variability envelope observed in the real data. This behavior indicates that the Gaussian noise-based model maintains, globally, the temporal dependency structure of the original series. This visual evidence reflects the total approvals of 87.0% (40/46 variables) and extremely low autocorrelation error (MAE), especially in Z coordinates, ranging from 0.0004 to 0.0006, and main angles, ranging from 0.002 to 0.028. This performance evidences that temporal correlation was maintained during generation.

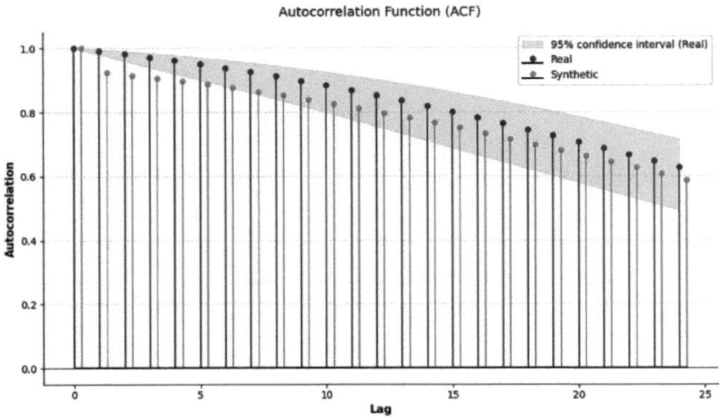

Fig. 3. Global Mean Autocorrelation Function for the Synthetic Set Generated by Gaussian noise vs. Real.

Figures 4 and 5 present two representative variables of the analyzed set: one with minimum autocorrelation error and another with the maximum observed error. In the best case, the synthetic curve totally overlaps the real curve, whereas in the worst case, an abrupt drop in synthetic ACF is observed in the first lags, contrasting with the persistence observed in the real data. This pattern indicates that for certain joints, such as ankles, which do not exhibit much movement during the deep squat, Gaussian noise introduces perturbations that compromise temporal continuity.

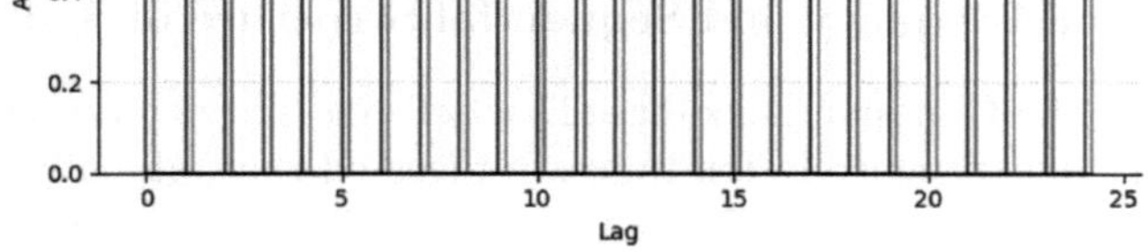

Fig. 4. Representative Variable (Noise): Lowest MAE.

In contrast, Fig. 6 evidences that the global mean ACF of the GAN-generated data presents greater divergence along the lags compared to the real data. Although the general shape of the curve is preserved, a steeper decay in autocorrelation is observed with increasing lag, indicating a partial loss of temporal persistence. This progressive deviation reflects the model's greater difficulty in

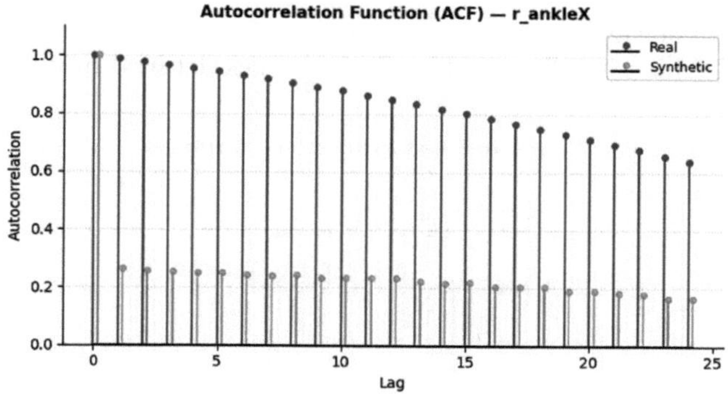

Fig. 5. Representative Variable (Noise): Highest MAE.

maintaining medium- and long-term temporal dependencies. This reflected an approval rate of 67.4% (31/46 variables), with substantially larger ACF errors in the Y and Z coordinates, ranging from 0.125 to 0.410, suggesting greater perturbation in temporal continuity. Failures were more concentrated in the more peripheral body parts, such as the elbows, wrists, and ankles.

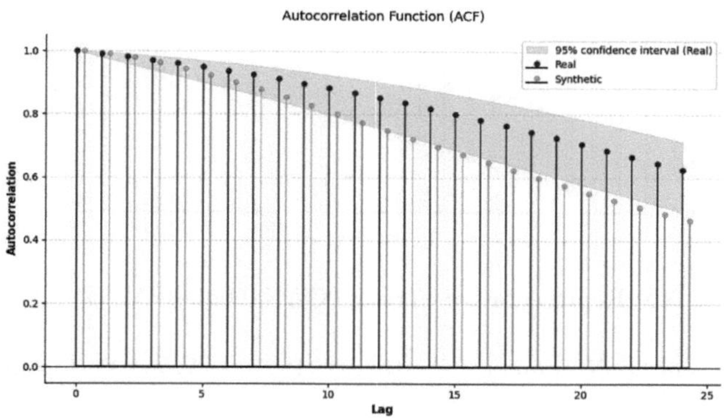

Fig. 6. Global mean autocorrelation function for the synthetic set generated by GAN vs. real.

Figures 7a and 7b present two representative variables of the analyzed set: one with minimum autocorrelation error and another with the maximum observed error. In the best case, corresponding to the variable *kneeRangle*, the synthetic curve almost entirely overlaps the real one, demonstrating that the model can accurately capture the temporal dependency structure in certain angular dynamics. However, in the worst-case scenario, we observed that for the variable *r_hipX*, the synthetic ACF decays abruptly, diverging sharply from the stability and persistence of the real data over the lags. This pattern indicates that the GAN introduces artificial volatility in certain coordinates, failing to preserve the memory of the motion, which justifies the high MAE values detailed in Table 2.

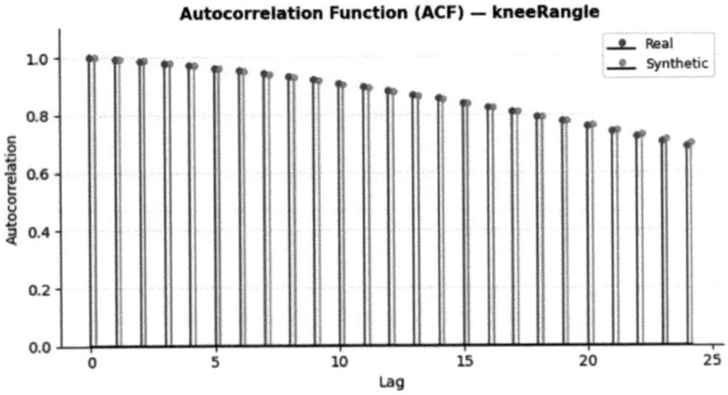

(a) Representative Variable GAN: Lowest MAE

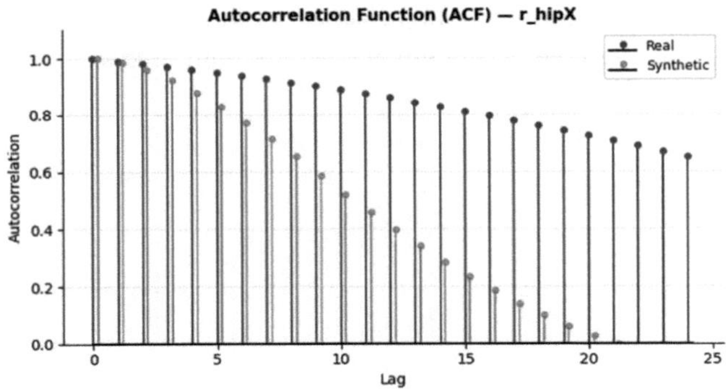

(b) Representative Variable GAN: Highest MAE

Fig. 7. Analysis of GAN Temporal Continuity: Best vs. Worst Performing Variables.

A direct comparison of the methods using the multivariate DTW test shows a difference in performance. The first method obtained approval in 100% of cases (100 out of 100 pairs), with a median distance of 0.1940, so low that it matches the real-real level (median: 6.60; limit: 13.20). This confirms a precise preservation of sequential dynamics. Conversely, the GAN presented opposite performance, with 0% approval and a median DTW of 75.88 – 5.75 times above the acceptable limit. Such a result shows that the GAN failed to capture the temporal structure, to the point that all 100 synthetic series were more dissimilar to the real ones than any pair of real series, completely losing the original multidimensional trajectory.

After analysis, we can see that, visually, this difference is clear in Fig. 8a, where the DTW distances of each synthetic series are plotted in relation to the

Table 2. Summary Table of Temporal Continuity Analysis.

Method	Approved	Rate (%)	Mean MAE	Max MAE
Gaussian Noise	40/46	87.0	0.0427	0.5879
GAN	31/46	67.4	0.1134	0.4101

100 real series. Gaussian noise forms a dense and cohesive pattern close to zero, while GAN creates a vastly dispersed cloud, very far from the origin. Furthermore, Gaussian noise not only meets the statistical criterion, but dominates it by a significant margin, as evidenced in Fig. 8b. Therefore, GAN not only fails in this context, but fails systematically and categorically.

Finally, in the third evaluation of the temporal dimension, we assessed kinematic smoothness, where Gaussian noise performed critically, with 0% approval in the acceleration envelope analysis. Despite perfect DTW and excellent autocorrelation, synthetic accelerations exceeded the established limit (the 99th percentile of the real data) for all 46 variables, with an average violation of 55.66%. However, GAN performed better in the envelope, with 13.04% approval (6/46 variables) and an average violation percentage of 42.53%, indicating that some main trajectories maintained the smoothness of the real motion. This result reveals an interesting phenomenon: Gaussian noise faithfully preserved the ordered temporal structure of the series (DTW 100%, ACF 87%), but produced exaggerated acceleration amplitudes, as if amplifying the velocity peaks, and failed to generate smooth motion.

In summary, the three tests reveal that Gaussian noise maintains temporal structure (DTW 100%, ACF 87%) but fails in kinematics (acceleration 0%), while the GAN performs poorly for the majority but is not catastrophic (DTW 0%, ACF 67%, acceleration 13%). Thus, noise offers ordered sequences with exaggerated peaks, and the GAN generates high-frequency jitter that corrupts dynamics but preserves smoothness in some variables.

3.3 Clinical Adequacy

The results for verifying anatomical limits for noise data achieved 100% compliance (8 of 8 joint angles). All angle variables remained within the 1st–99th percentiles observed in the real data; in fact, the minimum and maximum of each variable in the synthetic data are exactly the same as those in the real data. However, this perfect agreement is expected, given that during noise generation, a limitation to the 1st–99th percentiles was applied. However, its verification validates that there were no implementation errors and that the synthetic data does not contain anatomically impossible movements.

The GAN data obtained 37.5% compliance (3 of 8 joint angles). The angle variables that remained within the 1st–99th percentiles observed in real data were those of the shoulder and the right side of the hip. However, it is interesting to note that no variable presented catastrophic violations, as all 8 had more than 91% of samples within the limits, as can be seen in Table 3.

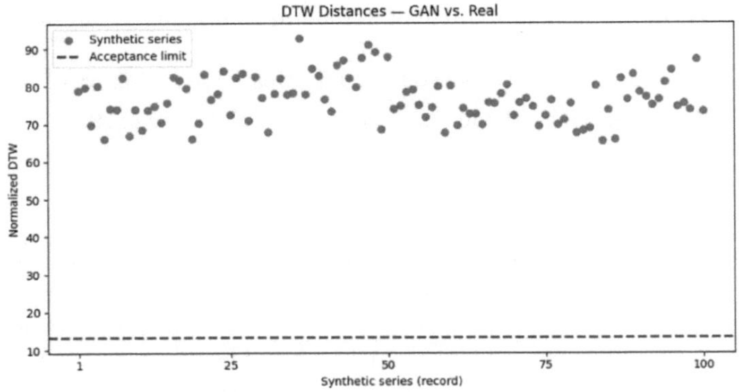

(a) Normalized DTW Distances GAN vs. Real

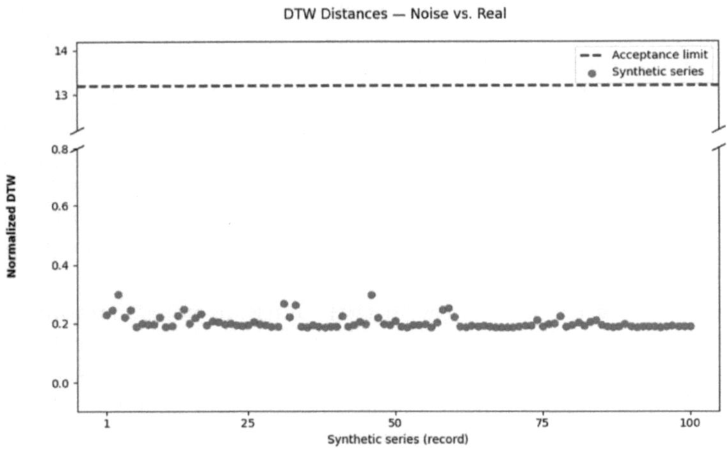

(b) Normalized DTW Distances Noise vs. Real

Fig. 8. Analysis of Normalized DTW Distances Comparing Real Data Against GAN and Noise.

3.4 Performance in Predictive Models

Overall, the results reveal contrasting behaviors between the two generation methods evaluated. While Gaussian noise presented consistent and robust gains, especially in the scarcest scenarios, the GAN demonstrated heterogeneous effects, with isolated benefits and, in some cases, performance degradation.

As shown in Table 4, the addition of synthetic data generated by Gaussian noise proved particularly effective in extreme scarcity scenarios. With only 10 positive real series, the F1-score increased from 0.88 to 0.98, driven by an expressive jump in recall (from 0.79 to 0.97), without loss of precision. Similar results were observed in the scenario with 20 real series, where the inclusion of syn-

Table 3. Analysis of GAN Joint Angles.

Variable	Lower Limit	Upper Limit	Syn. Min	Syn. Max	% Inside
shoulderLangle	114	139	112.57	134.70	99.92
shoulderRangle	110	138	106.16	138.58	99.72
elbowLangle	127	169	124.90	182.69	93.44
elbowRangle	130	165	125.33	180.24	94.89
hipLangle	49	159	22.68	158.17	93.69
hipRangle	48	157	29.43	162.65	95.00
kneeLangle	58	169	36.52	175.39	92.11
kneeRangle	56	167	34.99	179.73	91.42

thetic data led the model to achieve maximum recall and accuracy of 99.6%. As the quantity of real data increased, gains became neutral or showed slight degradation, indicating that the main benefit of Gaussian noise occurs precisely in compensating for severe scarcity, and when sufficient real data are available, synthetic data causes more confusion to the model.

Regarding the results of using synthetic data generated by the GAN presented in Table 4, the Random Forest classifier reveals a less stable pattern. In the most critical scenario (10 real series), including synthetic data resulted in lower F1 and recall scores than training only on real data. From 20 real series onwards, the results became essentially equivalent between the two scenarios, with isolated gains observed only in the intermediate scenario of 30 series, where the model increased the F1-score to 0.99. These findings suggest that although the GAN may contribute in specific contexts, its effect is not systematically beneficial when evaluated in terms of generalization on real data.

We observed similar results in the LSTM analysis, although with some particularities, as seen in Table 5. For Gaussian noise, the addition of synthetic data led to consistent gains in F1-score and recall in all scenarios, again highlighting the regimes of greater scarcity. In the scenario with only 10 real series, the first metric increased from 0.88 to 0.96, accompanied by a substantial improvement in accuracy. This pattern reinforces the idea that, in this context, Gaussian noise acted as an effective regularization mechanism, helping the model learn more robust decision boundaries when real data are limited in deep neural network-based models.

In the case of the GAN, the results with LSTM reinforce the heterogeneity observed in Random Forest, as shown in Table 5. In the most extreme scenario, the inclusion of synthetic data led to a performance drop, with reductions in F1-score and recall. In intermediate scenarios, effects oscillated between modest gains and rare losses, while in scenarios with greater availability of real data, metrics rose slightly. These behaviors suggest that although the GAN can improve metrics in some scenarios, on average, it does not yield consistent practical gains for supervised tasks in this type of model, unlike noise data.

Table 4. Random Forest Performance Comparison: Gaussian Noise vs. GAN Augmentation.

		Gaussian Noise				GAN			
Scenario	Model	F1	Prec	Rec	Acc	F1	Prec	Rec	Acc
10	Real Only	0.876	1.000	0.786	0.956	0.893	1.000	0.813	0.962
10	Real + Syn	0.982	1.000	0.966	0.993	0.854	1.000	0.753	0.950
20	Real Only	0.982	1.000	0.966	0.993	0.972	1.000	0.947	0.989
20	Real + Syn	0.990	0.981	1.000	0.995	0.972	1.000	0.947	0.989
30	Real Only	0.976	0.980	0.973	0.990	0.973	0.987	0.960	0.989
30	Real + Syn	0.981	0.964	1.000	0.992	0.997	0.994	1.000	0.999
50	Real Only	0.984	0.968	1.000	0.993	0.993	0.987	1.000	0.997
50	Real + Syn	0.977	0.956	1.000	0.990	0.993	0.987	1.000	0.997
70	Real Only	0.981	0.963	1.000	0.992	0.984	0.969	1.000	0.993
70	Real + Syn	0.968	0.939	1.000	0.986	0.990	0.981	1.000	0.996

Table 5. LSTM Performance Comparison: Gaussian Noise vs. GAN Augmentation.

		Gaussian Noise				GAN			
Scenario	Model	F1	Prec	Rec	Acc	F1	Prec	Rec	Acc
10	Real Only	0.879	0.964	0.820	0.956	0.900	0.972	0.840	0.962
10	Real + Syn	0.959	0.961	0.960	0.984	0.775	0.948	0.693	0.927
20	Real Only	0.937	0.903	0.980	0.970	0.936	0.917	0.960	0.973
20	Real + Syn	0.977	0.957	1.000	0.990	0.964	1.000	0.933	0.986
30	Real Only	0.911	0.874	0.966	0.958	0.963	0.967	0.960	0.985
30	Real + Syn	0.971	0.943	1.000	0.988	0.953	0.960	0.947	0.981
50	Real Only	0.971	0.944	1.000	0.988	0.977	0.963	0.993	0.990
50	Real + Syn	0.984	0.968	1.000	0.993	0.990	0.987	0.993	0.996
70	Real Only	0.987	0.975	1.000	0.994	0.977	0.956	1.000	0.990
70	Real + Syn	0.990	0.981	1.000	0.996	0.984	0.969	1.000	0.993

4 Conclusion

In this work, we evaluated and compared the quality of synthetic body movement data generated by two distinct approaches: controlled Gaussian noise and GANs, in the context of post-stroke neuromotor rehabilitation. The multidimensional analysis that we conducted encompassed statistical fidelity, temporal dynamics, clinical plausibility, and practical utility, revealing a contrasting scenario between the methods, with important implications for applications in clinical data scarcity scenarios.

The results demonstrated that controlled Gaussian noise achieved superior performance in statistical fidelity of spatial coordinates and in preservation of temporal structure, with 100% approval in the multivariate DTW test and high autocorrelation preservation (87%). Furthermore, it proved to be clinically plausible, fully respecting the anatomical limits defined from the real data. However, it revealed limitations in kinematic smoothness, with excessive accelerations in all analyzed variables, indicating that while it preserves the temporal sequence, it may introduce many movement peaks.

On the other hand, the GAN generated joint angles with distributions that were statistically compatible with those of real data. However, it failed to replicate the temporal structure (0% DTW agreement) and showed significant differences in the distributions of spatial coordinates. Despite having better preserved kinematic smoothness in some variables, its practical utility proved to be heterogeneous and less consistent, though not catastrophic, with isolated gains and even performance degradation in the extreme scarcity scenario.

From the perspective of utility in classification tasks, Gaussian noise has proven an effective tool for data augmentation in scenarios with limited real-world data, especially when combined with models such as Random Forests and LSTMs. Its gains were more significant and uniform, particularly in contexts of greater scarcity, acting as an effective regularizer and improving the model's generalization. On the other hand, GAN, although it has shown potential in specific contexts, has not delivered consistent benefits, suggesting that its application requires further adjustments and more rigorous validation.

Thus, in this study, we demonstrated that, for the specific motion of the deep squat, controlled Gaussian noise is a more suitable and reliable approach for generating synthetic data in data-scarce scenarios, especially when preserving temporal structure and anatomical plausibility are priorities. GAN, in turn, while promising in theory, still needs substantial refinements for direct application in this domain, particularly in capturing long-term temporal dependencies.

Acknowledgment. The authors acknowledge partial funding from the Coordination for the Improvement of Higher Education Personnel - Brazil (CAPES) - Funding Code 001; the National Council for Scientific and Technological Development - Brazil (CNPq) - Funding Codes 442344/2023-6, 444602/2024-0, and 407466/2025-8; the Espírito Santo Research and Innovation Support Foundation (FAPES) – Call No. 02/2026 (Participation in Technical-Scientific Events) – Grant No. 428/2026 and project #2024-9G1WP BPC; and the Minas Gerais Research Funding Foundation (FAPEMIG)

References

1. Brandão, A.F., et al.: Biomechanics sensor node for virtual reality: a wearable device applied to gait recovery for neurofunctional rehabilitation. In: International Conference on Computational Science and Its Applications, pp. 757–770. Springer (2020)
2. Brophy, E., Wang, Z., She, Q., Ward, T.: Generative adversarial networks in time series: a systematic literature review. ACM Comput. Surv. **55**(10), 1–31 (2023)
3. Buess, L., Keicher, M., Navab, N., Maier, A., Tayebi Arasteh, S.: From large language models to multimodal ai: a scoping review on the potential of generative ai in medicine. Biomed. Eng. Lett. **15**(5), 845–863 (2025)

4. Camargo, L.F., Miguel, G.R., Feitosa, J.D.C., Rodrigues, L.G.S., Dias, D.R.C., Brega, J.R.F.: Combining computer vision and artificial intelligence to support the rehabilitation of post-stroke patients. In: International Conference on Computational Science and Its Applications, pp. 415–432. Springer (2025)
5. Dias, D.R., Alvarenga, I.C., Guimarães, M.P., Trevelin, L.C., Castellano, G., Brandão, A.F.: eStreet: virtual reality and wearable devices applied to rehabilitation. In: International Conference on Computational Science and Its Applications, pp. 775–789. Springer (2018)
6. Iglesias, G., Talavera, E., González-Prieto, Á., Mozo, A., Gómez-Canaval, S.: Data augmentation techniques in time series domain: a survey and taxonomy. Neural Comput. Appl. **35**(14), 10123–10145 (2023)
7. Ribeiro, E., et al.: A body tracking framework for neuromotor rehabilitation with multimedia application support. In: International Conference on Computational Science and Its Applications, pp. 345–360. Springer (2025)
8. Rodrigues, L.G.S., et al.: Supervised classification of motor-rehabilitation body movements with RGB cameras and pose tracking data. J. Interact. Syst. (2022)
9. Yoon, J., Jarrett, D., Van der Schaar, M.: Time-series generative adversarial networks. In: Advances in Neural Information Processing Systems, vol. 32 (2019)
10. Zhu, W., et al.: Human motion generation: a survey. IEEE Trans. Pattern Anal. Mach. Intell. **46**(4), 2430–2449 (2023)

SingLoRA-CLIP: Highly Efficient VLM Adaptation with a Single Parameter Matrix

Nam Nhat Ngo Nguyen, Thu Anh Ngoc Le, Nhi Quynh Phan Le, Nghi Vinh Nguyen, and Hoang Ngoc Tran(✉)

FPT University, CanTho, Vietnam
{namnnnce181939,thulnace180615,nhilpqce180224, nghinvce182108}@fpt.edu.vn, hoang2531992@gmail.com

Abstract. Parameter-Efficient Fine-Tuning (PEFT) is a practical necessity for adapting large Vision-Language Models (VLMs). While Low-Rank Adaptation (LoRA) is a standard approach, its asymmetric two-matrix update (BA) can introduce initialization mismatches that may affect training stability. A recently proposed language-domain variant, SingLoRA, replaces this update with a single symmetric decomposition (AA^T), but its suitability for visual and multimodal adaptation has not yet been established. In this paper, we provide, to the best of our knowledge, the first evaluation of SingLoRA for few-shot adaptation of the CLIP architecture. We benchmark CLIP-SingLoRA on eight image classification datasets and compare it directly against a controlled CLIP-LoRA baseline under the same adaptation setting. Our results show that SingLoRA delivers accuracy that is competitive with standard LoRA while reducing the number of trainable parameters by 50%. These findings suggest that a single-matrix symmetric update can serve as a practical and highly parameter-efficient alternative for few-shot VLM adaptation.

Keywords: Parameter-Efficient Fine-Tuning · Low-Rank Adaptation · Vision-Language Models · Few-Shot Learning

1 Introduction

Vision-Language Models (VLMs) like CLIP [1] learn strong representations from massive image-text datasets [2,3]. Because they align visual and textual spaces through contrastive learning, these models perform very well in zero-shot scenarios. They can recognize new concepts without direct supervision, relying entirely on natural language prompts. Driven by this adaptability, researchers are increasingly interested in fine-tuning VLMs with very little data, a setup known as few-shot learning [4].

Modern VLMs contain billions of parameters. Full fine-tuning is not only computationally expensive but also prone to overfitting when training data

O. Gervasi et al. (Eds.): ICCSA 2026, LNCS 16768, pp. 251–263, 2027.
https://doi.org/10.1007/978-3-032-30488-9_16

is limited. This challenge has led to Parameter-Efficient Fine-Tuning (PEFT) methods, which adapt large models by optimizing only a small subset of their parameters [5]. Within the VLM literature, research has predominantly focused on prompt-tuning strategies [4,6,7] and on integrating conventional adapter modules [8,9]. Recently, Low-Rank Adaptation (LoRA) [10] has become a standard PEFT technique. LoRA assumes that the weight changes needed to learn a new task have a low "intrinsic rank." Instead of updating the massive original weight matrix, it models the update (ΔW) by multiplying two much smaller matrices (B and A). Zanella and Ben Ayed [11] recently showed that simply applying LoRA to CLIP creates an extremely strong baseline. In fact, it often beats more complex prompt and adapter methods in few-shot tasks.

While empirically successful, standard LoRA introduces a structural flaw. During initialization, matrix A gets random values while matrix B is set to zero. This creates a scale imbalance that can make training unstable [12,13]. To mitigate this issue, Bensaïd et al. [12] introduced **SingLoRA**. Instead of two matrices, SingLoRA uses a single matrix and its transpose to form a symmetric update: $\Delta W = AA^T$. This simple change brings two major benefits: it naturally avoids the scaling conflict, and it cuts the number of trainable parameters exactly in half compared to standard LoRA.

Current literature on SingLoRA is restricted to unimodal language or image generation tasks [12]. Its viability for multimodal, few-shot adaptation remains untested. In particular, transferring SingLoRA to CLIP is not straightforward, because the adaptation must preserve the model's cross-modal alignment while operating in a highly data-scarce regime. In this work, we study whether the single-matrix formulation can remain competitive in that setting by adapting CLIP with SingLoRA and comparing it against standard LoRA and other leading PEFT methods.

Our main contributions are as follows:

- To the best of our knowledge, we provide the first evaluation of SingLoRA for few-shot image classification with a Vision-Language Model.
- We conduct a systematic benchmark on eight diverse datasets across 1-, 4-, and 16-shot settings, including a controlled comparison against a CLIP-LoRA baseline with the same adaptation targets.
- We show that SingLoRA attains competitive performance while using 50% fewer trainable parameters than CLIP-LoRA, making it a strong parameter-efficient alternative for multimodal fine-tuning.

2 Related Work

2.1 Parameter-Efficient Fine-Tuning (PEFT)

PEFT strategies aim to achieve competitive performance by updating only a small fraction of a model's parameters [5]. These techniques generally fall into a few categories. Selective methods, such as BitFit [14], update specific parameter subsets like biases. Adapter-based approaches insert lightweight trainable modules into the frozen base model [15]. Prompt-tuning prepends learnable continuous vectors to the input [16,17]. Finally, low-rank adaptation methods model weight updates via low-dimensional matrices, offering a strong balance between performance and computational cost.

2.2 Few-Shot Adaptation of Vision-Language Models

Prompt-tuning is widely used for adapting VLMs with limited data. CoOp [4] introduced learnable context vectors to replace manual text prompts. Building on this, CoCoOp [6] made these prompts instance-conditional to improve generalization. MaPLe [7] extended this approach to the visual encoder for multimodal adaptation, while ProGrad [19] regularized prompt learning to prevent catastrophic forgetting of pretrained knowledge.

In parallel to prompt-tuning, various adapter-based methods have been explored. CLIP-Adapter [8] introduces a simple MLP after the encoders to refine features, while TaskRes [9] learns task-specific residual representations. Interestingly, recent findings from Zanella and Ben Ayed [11] show that directly applying LoRA establishes a baseline that often outperforms these specialized modules. This suggests that low-rank methods are highly effective and directly motivates our investigation into an even more parameter-efficient variant.

2.3 Low-Rank Adaptation and Its Variants

Low-Rank Adaptation (LoRA) [10] has become a foundational technique in PEFT. It operates on the principle that the change in model weights during adaptation, ΔW, has a low intrinsic rank. LoRA materializes this by freezing the pretrained weights W_0 and modeling the update as a trainable, low-rank decomposition $\Delta W = BA$, where the rank r is significantly smaller than the dimensions of W_0. A practical benefit of LoRA is its efficiency at inference time. Since the learned matrix ΔW can be directly added to the pre-trained weights W_0, the model runs without any extra computational overhead.

While LoRA is highly popular, its standard formulation contains an architectural bottleneck. Bensaïd et al. [12] pointed out that initializing matrix A randomly while setting matrix B to zero creates conflicting scales between the two matrices. This imbalance can lead to unstable training curves. As a solution, they proposed **SingLoRA**, a method that drops matrix B entirely. Instead, it relies on a single low-rank matrix A to form a symmetric weight update, defined as $\Delta W = AA^T$. This design avoids the scale imbalance problem and, as a direct benefit, halves the number of trainable parameters for a given rank r. Whether SingLoRA's benefits transfer to the few-shot VLM adaptation setup is the primary question driving this research.

Fig. 1. Visual samples from the eight evaluation benchmarks.

3 Methodology

Instead of fine-tuning the entire pretrained CLIP model, we adopt a low-rank adaptation strategy with a small trainable budget. Below, we describe the transition from standard LoRA to the symmetric SingLoRA formulation, followed by its implementation in the CLIP architecture.

3.1 From Asymmetric to Symmetric Low-Rank Adaptation

Standard LoRA [10] modifies a pre-trained weight matrix $W_0 \in \mathbb{R}^{d \times d}$ by learning a low-rank update ΔW. The forward pass becomes $h = W_0 x + \frac{\alpha}{r} BAx$, where $A \in \mathbb{R}^{r \times d}$ and $B \in \mathbb{R}^{d \times r}$ are trainable matrices with a rank $r \ll d$. Because A is random and B is zero at initialization, their scales conflict early in training [12].

To bypass this, we adopt the SingLoRA mechanism [12]. We completely remove matrix B. Instead, the weight update is parameterized using only a single matrix $A \in \mathbb{R}^{d \times r}$ to create a symmetric projection:

$$W' = W_0 + u(t) \cdot \frac{\alpha}{\sqrt{r}} AA^T \tag{1}$$

Equation 1 makes the symmetry of the update explicit. This formulation guarantees matching scales between the projection dimensions right out of the box. Mathematically, dropping B forces a 50% reduction in the parameters required for any given rank r.

To ensure the pretrained VLM features are not abruptly distorted during the initial training steps, the update is scaled by a linear ramp-up function $u(t) = \min(1.0, \frac{t}{T})$, where t is the current step and T is the warm-up duration.

3.2 Applying SingLoRA to CLIP's Attention Layers

Following the successful strategy demonstrated in prior work [11], we apply our adaptation to the Multi-Head Attention (MHA) layers in CLIP's transformer-based encoders. In each MHA block, the adaptation targets the projection matrices for the query (W_q), key (W_k), and value (W_v).

For each of these target layers (e.g., $W_q \in \mathbb{R}^{d\times d}$), we freeze the original weight matrix and introduce a corresponding trainable SingLoRA matrix $A_q \in \mathbb{R}^{d\times r}$. The original forward pass $h_q = W_q x$ is then replaced by its adapted version:

$$h'_q = W_q x + u(t) \cdot \frac{\alpha}{\sqrt{r}} A_q A_q^T x \tag{2}$$

Equation 2 shows how the same symmetric update is instantiated inside the attention module. The same adaptation is applied independently to the key and value projection matrices. By focusing only on the attention weights, we modify the core mechanism of the model with a minimal parameter budget. This implementation directly results in a 50% reduction in trainable parameters compared to applying standard LoRA to the same W_q, W_k, W_v matrices with an identical rank r.

Table 1. Average Top-1 accuracy (%) across eight datasets (ViT-B/16 backbone). **Bold** indicates the best performance, while underlined values denote the second-best result.

Method	1-Shot	4-Shots	16-Shots
Zero-Shot CLIP [1]	65.25	65.25	65.25
CoOp (16) [4]	67.98	75.18	81.23
CoCoOp [6]	68.85	72.33	76.60
TIP-Adapter-F [20]	71.98	76.96	82.06
PLOT++ [21]	71.98	78.48	83.71
TaskRes [9]	71.54	75.23	81.96
ProGrad [19]	70.33	75.54	81.15
CLIP-LoRA (Baseline, r=2)	**73.26**	79.53	**84.52**
CLIP-SingLoRA (Ours, r=2)	<u>73.14</u>	**80.00**	<u>84.39</u>

4 Experiments

We performed a broad empirical evaluation to measure the effectiveness and parameter cost of SingLoRA for adapting Vision-Language Models in a few-shot setting.

4.1 Experimental Setup

To evaluate the generalization of our method across diverse visual domains, we conduct experiments on eight standard image classification benchmarks (visualized in Fig. 1). Rather than exhaustively describing each well-known dataset, we categorize them by their visual challenges:

- **Fine-grained object recognition:** FGVC-Aircraft [22], Food-101 [24], Oxford-Pets [25], and Oxford Flowers 102 [26].
- **General objects and textures:** Caltech-101 [27] and Describable Textures Dataset (DTD) [28].
- **Specialized domains:** EuroSAT [23] for satellite imagery and UCF101 [29] for action recognition. For UCF101, we follow standard practice [11] by extracting the middle frame of each video to form a static image classification task.

Evaluation Protocol. We strictly follow the few-shot learning protocol established by CoOp [4]. For each dataset, we randomly sample 1, 4, and 16 shots (images) per class to form the training sets. After fine-tuning, models are evaluated on the original, full test sets. We report Top-1 accuracy for each dataset, alongside the arithmetic mean across all eight datasets to provide an overall view of model performance.

Baselines. We benchmark CLIP-SingLoRA against the frozen Zero-Shot CLIP [1] and several leading PEFT methods. The prompt-tuning baselines are CoOp [4], CoCoOp [6], KgCoOp [18], MaPLe [7], and ProGrad [19]. The adapter-based baselines include CLIP-Adapter [8] and TIP-Adapter-F [20]. We also compare against TaskRes [9] and PLOT++ [21]. For the fairest parameter-efficiency comparison, we also implement a **CLIP-LoRA baseline** [11]. This baseline mirrors our SingLoRA setup exactly. The only difference is that it uses the standard two-matrix update (BA) instead of the symmetric update (AA^T).

Implementation Details. All experiments are built upon the pre-trained CLIP model with a ViT-B/16 visual backbone. For both LoRA and SingLoRA, we inject the low-rank matrices into the query, key, and value projection layers (W_q, W_k, W_v) across all attention blocks in both the vision and text encoders.

To avoid the massive computational cost of grid-searching hyperparameters for every individual dataset, we adopt a single, unified configuration. During our preliminary runs, we noticed that using a scaling factor larger than 1 often destabilized training, likely because the symmetric update overly distorted the pre-trained semantic space. Consequently, we fix the intrinsic rank $r = 2$, the scaling factor $\alpha = 1$, and use a linear warm-up period of $T = 100$ steps for all tasks.

5 Results and Analysis

5.1 Main Results

Our main experimental results for few-shot classification are summarized in Table 1, which reports the average performance across the eight benchmarks. We provide a complete per-dataset breakdown of these figures in the Appendix

Table 2. Ablation of rank (r) and scaling factor (α).

Setting	Method	Config	Avg. Accuracy (%)	Parameters
1-Shot	CLIP-LoRA	(r=2)	73.26	184,320
	CLIP-SingLoRA	(r=2, α=1)	73.14	**92,160**
		(r=4, α=1)	**73.78**	184,320
		(r=4, α=2)	73.45	184,320
		(r=4, α=8)	70.37	184,320
		(r=4, α=16)	68.33	184,320
4-Shots	CLIP-LoRA	(r=2)	79.53	184,320
	CLIP-SingLoRA	(r=2, α=1)	**80.00**	**92,160**
		(r=4, α=1)	79.50	184,320
		(r=4, α=2)	79.07	184,320
		(r=4, α=8)	77.76	184,320

(Table 4). Our main approach, **CLIP-SingLoRA (r=2)**, is benchmarked against the strong CLIP-LoRA baseline.

As reported in Table 1, CLIP-SingLoRA ($r = 2$) remains highly competitive with the CLIP-LoRA baseline across all three shot settings. Most notably, it attains the highest average accuracy in the 4-shot setting (80.00%). In the 1-shot and 16-shot settings, its results remain very close to those of LoRA. Figure 2 shows that this competitive behavior is maintained as the number of shots increases. The key takeaway from these results is the parameter cost: SingLoRA achieves this competitive accuracy while using exactly half the trainable parameters of standard LoRA (as detailed in Table 3). Taken together, these results suggest that a single symmetric projection (AA^T) can be sufficient for effective VLM adaptation in the few-shot regime.

Table 3. Parameter efficiency comparison. Average accuracy from the 4-shot setting is shown for performance reference.

Method	Trainable Parameters	Avg. Accuracy (4-Shots)
CLIP-LoRA (r=2)	184,320	79.53%
CLIP-SingLoRA (r=2)	**92,160 (-50%)**	**80.00%**

5.2 Analysis of Parameter Efficiency

Figure 3 illustrates the trade-off between performance and parameter count. In the 4-shot setting, CLIP-SingLoRA reaches a slightly higher average accuracy

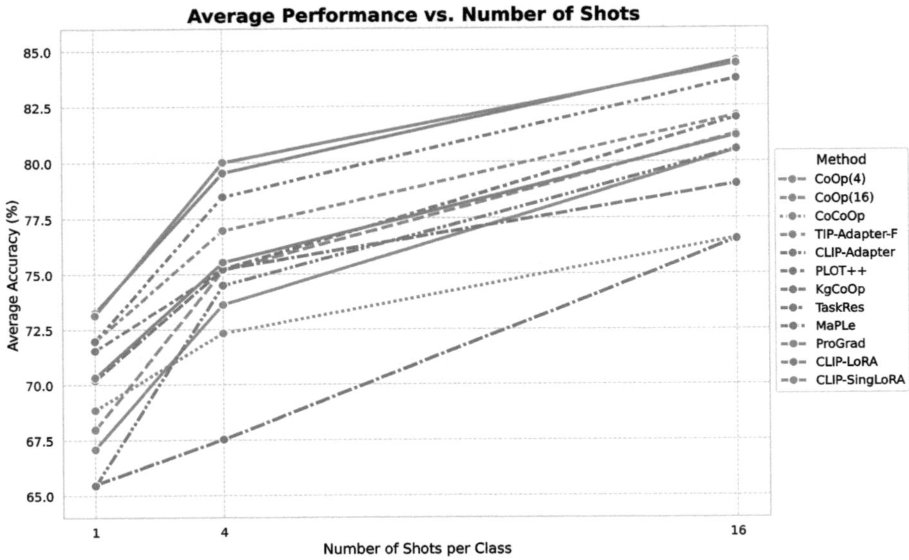

Fig. 2. Average accuracy as a function of the number of shots per class.

(80.00%) than the CLIP-LoRA baseline (79.53%). As detailed in Table 3, this result is obtained using only half the trainable parameters (92,160 vs. 184,320). This comparison indicates that reformulating the weight update as a symmetric matrix can substantially reduce the adaptation budget while preserving competitive performance.

5.3 Ablation Study: Impact of Rank and Scaling Factor

We ablate two key hyper-parameters governing our adaptation module: the intrinsic rank r and the scaling factor α. Table 2 reports the performance variations averaged across all benchmarks. A complete per-dataset breakdown is deferred to Appendix Table 5.

Impact of Rank and Parameter Budget. Table 2 details the impact of the intrinsic rank r. Increasing the rank from $r = 2$ to $r = 4$ improves accuracy in the 1-shot setting (from 73.14% to 73.78%). However, in the 4-shot setting, the lower rank $r = 2$ yields better results (80.00% vs 79.50%). This implies that a lower rank may provide beneficial regularization when more training data is available.

Crucially, configuring SingLoRA with $r = 4$ matches the exact parameter budget of LoRA with $r = 2$ (184,320 parameters). Under this identical budget constraint, SingLoRA outperforms standard LoRA in the 1-shot scenario and

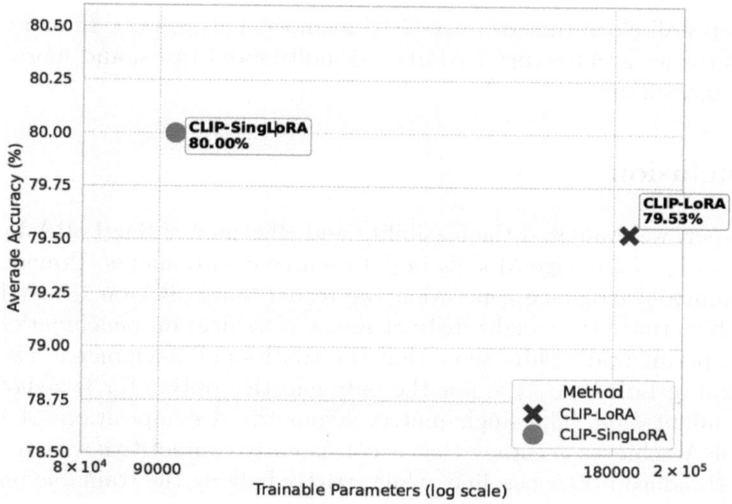

Fig. 3. Performance versus parameter cost in the 4-shot setting.

performs similarly in the 4-shot setting. This indicates that the single-matrix update AA^T remains competitive even when the parameter budget is held constant.

Sensitivity to Scaling Factor α. As shown in Table 2, performance consistently drops as α increases across both few-shot settings. Because the update term ΔW is directly added to the pre-trained weights, a high multiplier can distort the VLM's original semantic space. In our experiments, $\alpha = 1$ provided the most reliable overall behavior.

5.4 Discussion and Limitations

The empirical picture that emerges from our results is consistent across the main benchmark and the ablation study: SingLoRA can remain competitive with standard LoRA even under a substantially smaller adaptation budget. This is particularly relevant in few-shot VLM adaptation, where the practical objective is often to preserve most of the pretrained model while making only a lightweight task-specific adjustment. From this perspective, our findings suggest that the symmetric single-matrix parameterization is a viable alternative when memory efficiency is a primary concern.

At the same time, our study has several limitations. First, the evaluation is restricted to few-shot image classification with CLIP ViT-B/16, so the conclusions should not yet be generalized to other VLM architectures or multimodal tasks. Second, our efficiency analysis focuses on trainable parameter counts rather than wall-clock time or peak GPU memory. Future work should therefore examine broader architectures, additional multimodal tasks, and more detailed efficiency measurements.

6 Conclusion

In this paper, we evaluated the feasibility and efficiency of SingLoRA for adapting large Vision-Language Models in data-scarce environments. Previously limited to unimodal language generation, we tested SingLoRA on the multimodal CLIP architecture across eight distinct image classification benchmarks.

Our experimental results show that the traditional, asymmetric two-matrix formulation of LoRA (BA) is not the only effective option for few-shot vision-language adaptation. The single-matrix symmetric decomposition (AA^T) used in SingLoRA achieves accuracy that is consistently competitive with a carefully matched standard LoRA baseline, while strictly halving the trainable parameter budget.

By reducing the number of trainable parameters without materially affecting performance, SingLoRA offers a compelling performance-to-parameter trade-off. We therefore view it as a promising memory-efficient baseline for future research on the parameter-efficient adaptation of large-scale multimodal models.

A Detailed Per-Dataset Results

This appendix provides the detailed per-dataset results for all baseline methods and our proposed CLIP-SingLoRA across the 1, 4, and 16-shot settings. Table 4 presents the Top-1 accuracy (%) for each of the eight benchmark datasets, supplementing the averaged results discussed in the main paper. The best-performing method in each column (per shot setting) is highlighted in **bold**, and the second-best is <u>underlined</u>.

Table 4. Full few-shot classification results (%) on all eight datasets with a ViT-B/16 backbone.

Method	Shots	Aircraft	EuroSAT	Food	Pets	Flowers	Caltech	DTD	UCF	Average
Zero-Shot CLIP [1]	0	24.70	47.50	86.10	89.10	71.40	92.90	43.60	66.70	65.25
1	CoOp (16) [4]	20.80	56.40	84.30	90.20	78.30	92.50	50.10	71.20	67.98
	CoCoOp [6]	28.10	55.40	84.90	91.90	73.40	94.10	52.60	70.40	68.85
	TIP-Adapter-F [20]	28.80	67.80	85.80	90.60	**83.80**	94.00	51.60	73.40	71.98
	CLIP-Adapter [8]	25.20	49.30	86.10	89.00	71.30	92.00	44.20	66.90	65.50
	PLOT++ [21]	28.60	65.40	86.20	91.90	80.50	94.30	**54.60**	74.30	71.98
	KgCoOp [18]	26.80	61.90	86.40	92.10	74.70	94.20	52.70	72.80	70.20
	TaskRes [9]	**31.30**	65.40	84.60	90.20	81.70	93.60	53.80	71.70	71.54
	MaPLe [7]	28.10	29.10	85.40	91.40	74.90	93.60	50.00	71.10	65.45
	ProGrad [19]	28.80	57.00	84.90	91.40	80.90	93.50	52.80	73.30	70.33
	CLIP-LoRA	28.71	72.88	85.08	91.52	83.35	93.67	54.61	**76.29**	**73.26**
	CLIP-SingLoRA	29.10	**73.58**	**85.75**	**92.61**	81.40	93.87	53.37	75.47	73.14
4	CoOp (16) [4]	30.90	69.70	84.50	92.50	92.20	94.50	59.50	77.60	75.18
	CoCoOp [6]	30.60	61.70	86.30	92.70	81.50	94.80	55.70	75.30	72.33
	TIP-Adapter-F [20]	35.70	76.80	86.50	91.90	92.10	94.80	59.80	78.10	76.96
	CLIP-Adapter [8]	27.90	51.20	86.50	90.80	73.10	94.00	46.10	70.60	67.53
	PLOT++ [21]	35.30	83.20	86.50	92.60	92.90	95.10	62.40	79.80	78.48
	KgCoOp [18]	32.20	71.80	86.90	92.60	87.00	95.00	58.70	77.60	75.23
	TaskRes [9]	33.40	74.20	86.00	91.90	85.00	95.00	60.10	76.20	75.23
	MaPLe [7]	30.10	69.90	86.70	93.30	84.90	95.00	59.00	77.10	74.50
	ProGrad [19]	34.10	69.60	85.40	92.10	91.10	94.40	59.70	77.90	75.54
	CLIP-LoRA	**39.15**	87.49	83.72	91.06	93.67	**95.58**	65.19	80.39	79.53
	CLIP-SingLoRA	38.46	**89.53**	84.44	92.45	**93.75**	95.21	**65.01**	**81.15**	**80.00**
16	CoOp (16) [6]	43.20	85.00	84.20	92.00	96.80	95.80	69.70	83.10	81.23
	CoCoOp [6]	33.30	73.60	87.40	93.40	89.10	95.10	63.70	77.20	76.60
	TIP-Adapter-F [20]	44.60	85.90	86.80	92.60	96.20	95.70	70.80	83.90	82.06
	CLIP-Adapter [8]	34.20	71.40	87.10	92.30	92.90	94.90	59.40	80.20	76.55
	PLOT++ [21]	46.70	92.00	87.10	93.60	97.60	96.00	71.40	85.30	83.71
	KgCoOp [18]	36.50	76.20	87.20	93.20	93.40	95.20	68.70	81.70	79.01
	TaskRes [9]	44.90	82.70	86.90	92.40	97.50	95.80	71.50	84.00	81.96
	MaPLe [7]	36.80	87.50	87.40	93.20	94.20	95.40	68.40	81.40	80.54
	ProGrad [19]	43.00	83.60	85.80	92.80	96.60	95.90	68.80	82.70	81.15
	CLIP-LoRA	**54.97**	91.25	84.55	92.53	97.93	96.31	72.28	**86.36**	**84.52**
	CLIP-SingLoRA	52.27	**91.54**	85.24	92.72	**98.05**	**96.63**	**72.40**	86.28	84.39

B Detailed Ablation Study Results

Table 5 provides the detailed per-dataset results for our ablation study on the intrinsic rank (r) and the scaling factor (α), supplementing the summarized analysis in the main paper.

Table 5. Full per-dataset results for the ablation study on CLIP-SingLoRA configurations.

Method	Config (r, α)	Shots	Aircraft	EuroSAT	Food	Pets	Flowers	Caltech	DTD	UCF	Average	Parameters
CLIP-SingLoRA	(r=2, α=1)	**1**	29.10	73.58	85.75	92.61	81.40	93.87	53.37	75.47	73.14	92,160
	(r=4, α=1)		30.12	73.74	85.03	92.70	82.62	94.08	55.38	76.58	73.78	184,320
	(r=4, α=2)		29.82	72.23	84.49	91.82	83.96	93.83	55.20	76.26	73.45	184,320
	(r=4, α=8)		25.71	63.19	81.53	88.17	84.25	93.87	53.49	72.77	70.37	184,320
CLIP-SingLoRA	(r=2, α=1)	**4**	38.46	89.53	84.44	92.45	93.75	95.21	65.01	81.15	80.00	92,160
	(r=4, α=1)		38.13	88.31	84.06	91.66	93.26	95.46	64.66	80.49	79.50	184,320
	(r=4, α=2)		36.78	88.52	82.98	90.46	94.03	95.62	64.13	80.04	79.07	184,320
	(r=4, α=8)		35.82	88.67	80.40	86.45	94.36	94.89	64.18	77.29	77.76	184,320

References

1. Radford, A., et al.: Learning transferable visual models from natural language supervision. In: Proceedings of the 38th International Conference on Machine Learning, pp. 8748–8763 (2021)
2. Jia, C., et al.: Scaling up visual and vision-language representation learning with noisy text supervision. In: Proceedings of the 38th International Conference on Machine Learning, pp. 4904–4916 (2021)
3. Zhai, X., et al.: LiT: Zero-shot transfer with locked-image text tuning. In: Proceedings of the IEEE/CVF Conference on Computer Vision and Pattern Recognition, pp. 18123–18133 (2022)
4. Zhou, K., Yang, J., Loy, C.C., Liu, Z.: Learning to prompt for vision-language models. Int. J. Comput. Vision **130**(9), 2337–2348 (2022)
5. Lialin, V., Deshpande, V., Rumshisky, A.: Scaling down to scale up: a guide to parameter-efficient fine-tuning. CoRR abs/2303.15647 (2023)
6. Zhou, K., Yang, J., Loy, C.C., Liu, Z.: Conditional prompt learning for vision language models. In: Proceedings of the IEEE/CVF Conference on Computer Vision and Pattern Recognition, pp. 16816–16825 (2022)
7. Khattak, M.U., Rasheed, H., Maaz, M., Khan, S., Khan, F.S.: MaPLe: multi-modal prompt learning. In: Proceedings of the IEEE/CVF Conference on Computer Vision and Pattern Recognition, pp. 19113–19122 (2023)
8. Gao, P., et al.: CLIP-Adapter: better vision-language models with feature adapters. Int. J. Comput. Vision **132**(2), 581–595 (2024)
9. Yu, T., Lu, Z., Jin, X., Chen, Z., Wang, X.: Task residual for tuning vision-language models. In: Proceedings of the IEEE/CVF Conference on Computer Vision and Pattern Recognition, pp. 10899–10909 (2023)
10. Hu, E.J., et al.: LoRA: Low-rank adaptation of large language models. In: International Conference on Learning Representations (2022)
11. Zanella, M., Ben Ayed, I.: Low-rank few-shot adaptation of vision-language models. In: Proceedings of the IEEE/CVF Conference on Computer Vision and Pattern Recognition Workshops, pp. 1593–1603 (2024)
12. David, B., Noam, R., Roy, V., Daniel, B., Ron, K.: SingLoRA: low rank adaptation using a single matrix. CoRR abs/2507.05566 (2025)
13. Hayou, S., Ghosh, N., Yu, B.: LoRA+: efficient low rank adaptation of large models. In: Proceedings of the 41st International Conference on Machine Learning, pp. 17783–17806 (2024)

14. Ben Zaken, E., Goldberg, Y., Ravfogel, S.: BitFit: simple parameter-efficient fine-tuning for transformer-based masked language-models. In: Proceedings of the 60th Annual Meeting of the Association for Computational Linguistics (Volume 2: Short Papers), pp. 1–9 (2022)
15. Houlsby, N., et al.: Parameter-efficient transfer learning for NLP. In: Proceedings of the 36th International Conference on Machine Learning, pp. 2790–2799 (2019)
16. Lester, B., Al-Rfou, R., Constant, N.: The power of scale for parameter-efficient prompt tuning. In: Proceedings of the 2021 Conference on Empirical Methods in Natural Language Processing, pp. 3045–3059 (2021)
17. Li, X.L., Liang, P.: Prefix-tuning: optimizing continuous prompts for generation. In: Proceedings of the 59th Annual Meeting of the Association for Computational Linguistics and the 11th International Joint Conference on Natural Language Processing (Volume 1: Long Papers), pp. 4582–4597 (2021)
18. Yao, H., Zhang, R., Xu, C.: Visual-language prompt tuning with knowledge-guided context optimization. In: Proceedings of the IEEE/CVF Conference on Computer Vision and Pattern Recognition, pp. 6757–6767 (2023)
19. Zhu, B., Niu, Y., Han, Y., Wu, Y., Zhang, H.: Prompt-aligned gradient for prompt tuning. In: Proceedings of the IEEE/CVF International Conference on Computer Vision, pp. 15659–15669 (2023)
20. Zhang, R., et al.: TIPAdapter: training-free adaption of CLIP for few-shot classification. In: European Conference on Computer Vision, pp. 493–510. Springer, Cham (2022)
21. Chen, G., Yao, W., Song, X., Li, X., Rao, Y., Zhang, K.: PLOT: prompt learning with optimal transport for vision-language models. In: International Conference on Learning Representations (2023)
22. Maji, S., Rahtu, E., Kannala, J., Blaschko, M., Vedaldi, A.: Fine-grained visual classification of aircraft. CoRR abs/1306.5151 (2013)
23. Helber, P., Bischke, B., Dengel, A., Borth, D.: EuroSAT: a novel dataset and deep learning benchmark for land use and land cover classification. IEEE J. Sel. Top. Appl. Earth Obser. Rem. Sens. **12**(7), 2217–2226 (2019)
24. Bossard, L., Guillaumin, M., Van Gool, L.: Food-101–mining discriminative components with random forests. In: European Conference on Computer Vision, pp. 446–461. Springer, Cham (2014)
25. Parkhi, O.M., Vedaldi, A., Zisserman, A., Jawahar, C.V.: Cats and dogs. In: 2012 IEEE Conference on Computer Vision and Pattern Recognition, pp. 3498–3505 (2012)
26. Nilsback, M.E., Zisserman, A.: Automated flower classification over a large number of classes. In: 2008 Sixth Indian Conference on Computer Vision, Graphics & Image Processing, pp. 722–729 (2008)
27. Fei-Fei, L., Fergus, R., Perona, P.: Learning generative visual models from few training examples: an incremental Bayesian approach tested on 101 object categories. In: 2004 Conference on Computer Vision and Pattern Recognition Workshop, p. 178 (2004)
28. Cimpoi, M., Maji, S., Kokkinos, I., Mohamed, S., Vedaldi, A.: Describing textures in the wild. In: Proceedings of the IEEE Conference on Computer Vision and Pattern Recognition, pp. 3606–3613 (2014)
29. Soomro, K., Zamir, A.R., Shah, M.: UCF101: a dataset of 101 human actions classes from videos in the wild. CoRR abs/1212.0402 (2012)

Robust Vehicle Detection Framework Using YOLO12 with Advanced Augmentations for Adverse Weather Conditions

Huy Hoang Nguyen[1], Huong Diem Thi Nguyen[2], and Vinh Dinh Nguyen[1(✉)]

[1] Department of Information Technology, FPT University, Can Tho, Vietnam
huynhce182126@fpt.edu.vn, vinhnd29@fe.edu.vn
[2] IVS Joint Stock Company, Can Tho, Vietnam

Abstract. Accurate vehicle detection is an enormous challenge for intelligent transportation systems in adverse weather conditions. The occlusions, poor visibility and data imbalance across vehicle classes have caused these problems. Therefore, we present a strong object detection pipeline based on YOLO12, the latest YOLO cycle of technology, coupled with targeted data augmentation strategies. It is expected to increase detection performance in these complex events. The pipeline includes geometric and chromatic augmentations to reproduce spatial distortions or variations in illumination conditions, improving model robustness under a wide range of real-world scenarios. A CutMix-based augmentation strategy is also proposed that minimises severe imbalances among classes by artificially boosting minority instances of a minority class while maintaining spatial coherence. After running extensive experiments on the DAWN dataset, which includes vehicle images in the presence of snow, fog, rain, and sandstorm, our training pipeline driven by the augmentation algorithm substantially improves detection accuracy. The proposed method is found to obtain an mAP50 of 0.979 and mAP50–95 of 0.901 on the augmented dataset, significantly outperforming the baseline scores of 0.652 and 0.405, respectively. These results underline a fundamental role for the augmentation strategies when designed carefully, to augment the precision and generalization of object detection models that are deployed in hostile environmental settings.

Keywords: Object Detection · YOLO12 · Data Augmentation · CutMix · Class Imbalance · Vehicle Detection · Adverse Weather · Intelligent Transportation Systems

1 Introduction

The challenge of reliably detecting vehicles in severe weather continues to be an issue for both Intelligent Transport Systems and Autonomous Driving Applications. Weather events including; fog, rain, snow, and sand will all cause

O. Gervasi et al. (Eds.): ICCSA 2026, LNCS 16768, pp. 264–276, 2027.
https://doi.org/10.1007/978-3-032-30488-9_17

reduced visual clarity, distorted appearances of objects and lower fidelity of detection [1]. All of these issues are critical to several highly safety-related applications including; Automated Traffic Monitoring, Collision Avoidance and Road Infrastructure Management. While recent advancements in Deep Learning have made significant improvements in detection accuracy using Convolutional Neural Networks (CNNs), Transformer Based Architectures and other variants, there continue to be requirements for developing stronger Model Architectures and Data Preparation Procedures to produce consistent detection performance under various weather conditions. Among the more recently developed Models, the YOLO (You Only Look Once) Family has demonstrated a number of desirable attributes; including a single stage approach to Object Detection that produces a good trade-off between Speed and Accuracy. These advantages were further enhanced by the introduction of the Area Attention and R-ELAN Modules into the YOLO12 Model that improves the ability of the Model to extract relevant features from Images in Complicated Conditions [2]. Advances in Architecture continue but the most pressing issue related to Vehicle Datasets is Extreme Class Imbalance within those datasets. This imbalance causes a natural bias toward prediction of Majority Classes [3] and is exacerbated when large numbers of different types of Vehicles exist within the dataset due to their inherently skewed distributions. Data Augmentation has shown significant benefits over the past few years to enhance the generalization and robustness of models under varying lighting conditions, viewing angles and Environments. Both geometric (rotation, flip, shear) and chromatic (brightness, hue, saturation) augmentations can simulate a range of imaging variations present in Real World Imaging, thereby enhancing Model Resilience [4]. Additionally, CutMix was introduced as a way to combine regions and labels to generate New Training Samples and represents one of the latest methods of Data Augmentation that has shown to be superior at addressing class imbalance [5].

Here, we present a solid vehicle detection framework using YOLO12 as the benchmark and various geometric, chromatic, and CutMix augmentations to boost detection performance in different weather states. Our contributions are summarized as follows:

- We create an augmentation-based training pipeline, including YOLO12 with geometric, chromatic, and CutMix augmentations, to increase vehicle detection robustness under adverse weather.
- For the specific minority vehicle classes, we propose a targeted CutMix approach to alleviate severe class imbalance to improve detection accuracy across all categories.
- We offer detailed evaluations of the DAWN dataset and show improvement in both mAP and generalization capability over non-augmented baselines.

The rest of this report is divided into the following sections: In Sect. 2, we review the existing work on detecting vehicles under difficult weather conditions. We then describe our proposed methodology, which includes a description of the data set, the various forms of augmentation applied to that data set, and the architecture used for our deep neural network models in Sect. 3. Experimental results are shown in Sect. 4, where we evaluate how different methods to balance classes affect performance. Finally, in Sect. 5, we conclude the paper and provide a summary of possible future areas of study.

2 Related Work

The vehicle detection can go down quickly in rain, fog, snow, or sand, which contributes to an ongoing problem in robust vehicle detection in such environments for autonomous vehicles and smart traffic systems. In recent years, the emphasis has been on improving the YOLO-based framework by adapting the architecture and the image processing methods in order to attain high precision and reliability in these environments.

Rjoub et al. (2021) combined federated learning with YOLO CNN to model objects in snowy landscapes to yield superior results to centralized and gossip algorithms on the CADC dataset, suggesting the potential of federated YOLO to be deployed under severe weather conditions [6]. Wu et al. (2021) proposed a YOLO-based system for vehicle classification and counting, with a high accuracy in motorcycle, small, and large vehicle classification on a wide variety of road designs, contributing to traffic flow analysis applications [7]. Boppana et al. (2022) presented a comparative research of YOLO variations for vehicle detection in extreme weather using the AAU Rain Snow dataset. Their results demonstrate YOLOv3's advantage over the other variants when it comes to precision and mAP and thus sets that it is a baseline for adverse weather detection [8]. Liu et al. (2022) have proposed Image-Adaptive YOLO (IA-YOLO), which includes a differentiable image processing module integrated with YOLOv3 and significantly advanced detection on fog and low-light areas [9]. Ding et al. (2023) also recently proposed CF-YOLO by incorporating Cross Fusion block in YOLOv5s trained on their RSOD real-snow dataset. Their model was able to better suppress snow distortion. Their system was able to handle snow-induced distortions better than state-of-the-art techniques [10].

Recently, Tian and Kim (2023) enhanced detection of vehicle detection by combining weather classification and Faster R-CNN and Dark Channel Prior preprocessing which improved fog and rain image detection over fog and rain images [11]. Panja et al. (2024) evaluated YOLOv8 models using an augmentation technique on the DAWN dataset. They discovered that for improved mAP, horizontal flip augmentation increased the output, and YOLOv8m performed at best 71.2%, and that the data augmentation can have advantages in enhancing the robustness of the detection [12]. Aloufi et al. (2024) proposed a multi-objective model combining weather classification, SRGAN enhancement, and the YOLOv5 for simultaneous weather recognition and object detection; they achieved a mAP rate of 74.6% under severe weather conditions [13]. Ogino et al. (2025) introduced an ERUP-YOLO that utilizes differentiable Bezier and kernel-based preprocessing filters in YOLOv3 and improved detection robustness while detecting fog or low light using adaptive image enhancement [14].

Lastly, Huang and Lin (2025) presented a domain adaptation method combining adversarial and semi-supervised models and using YOLO to enhance the performance of detection across illumination scenarios and weather domains [15]. These studies are collectively illustrating the ongoing development of YOLO-based techniques for the adverse weather vehicle detection where the results of domain adaptation, image enhancement, and integrated frameworks are used to validate the effectiveness of these approaches. Yet achieving real-time generalization across a variety of unseen weather scenarios and the computational efficiency for the model remain challenges (Table 1).

Table 1. Summary of Recent Advances in Vehicle Detection under Adverse Weather Conditions.

Year	Authors	Dataset	Method	Performance	Limitations
2021	Rjoub et al. [6]	CADC	Federated YOLO CNN	Improved over centralized	Limited to snowy conditions
2021	Wu et al. [7]	Traffic surveillance images	YOLO-based vehicle counting	Accurate counts in intersections	Focused only on classification and counting
2022	Boppana et al. [8]	AAU Rain Snow	YOLOv3 vs other YOLOs	YOLOv3 best precision, mAP	No enhancement methods explored
2022	Liu et al. [9]	Foggy and low-light images	Image-Adaptive YOLO (IA-YOLO)	Improved detection in adverse weather	Requires end-to-end joint training
2023	Ding et al. [10]	RSOD (real snow)	CF-YOLO with Cross Fusion block	Outperformed SOTA in snow	Limited to snowy conditions
2023	Tian and Kim [11]	Various weather images	Weather classification + Faster R-CNN + DCP	Improved detection in fog/rain	Complex multi-stage pipeline
2024	Panja et al. [12]	DAWN	YOLOv8n/s/m + flip augmentation	mAP up to 71.2% (YOLOv8m)	Tested only flip augmentation
2024	Aloufi et al. [13]	DAWN (augmented)	Multi-objective model (weather classification + SRGAN + YOLOv5)	mAP 74.6%	High computational complexity
2025	Ogino et al. [14]	Adverse weather datasets	ERUP-YOLO (BPW + KBL filters + YOLOv3)	Superior detection in fog, low-light	Requires differentiable filter design
2025	Huang and Lin [15]	Public + private datasets	Adversarial + semi-supervised YOLO	Outperformed prior methods across domains	Needs unlabeled data for semi-supervised training

3 Methodology

3.1 Data Collection

We analyzed the DAWN dataset [16], a free vehicle dataset for object detection in harsh weather conditions, i.e. fog, rain, sandstorm, and snow, at different intensities, to assess the model robustness. DAWN consists of six annotated classes: bicycle, bus, car, motorcycle, person, and truck. Every picture has bounding boxes and class labels, and this allows to measure detection and classification of vehicles under challenging conditions. We divide our data-set into training (70%), validation (20%) and testing (10%) sets. All of our augmentation methods were used solely on our training sample so that we avoid a case of "data leak". None of our synthetic samples will be included in either of our validation or test sets. Only for our training phase have we artificially created all of our synthetic samples via CutMix and all of the rest of our augmentation techniques (Fig. 1).

Fig. 1. Example images from DAWN showing vehicle classes under different weather conditions.

3.2 Data Preprocessing and Augmentation

Comprehensive data preprocessing and augmentation strategies were applied to improve YOLO12's performance and robustness across diverse weather scenarios.

Data Preprocessing: All images from the data set are resized to a pixel resolution of $640 \cdot 640$, so that they can be processed by the YOLO12 network and to keep annotations consistent. The scaling of corresponding bounding-box coordinates was done proportionally to prevent loss of spatial accuracy when the image is resized. By making this conversion, it allows for the use of fixed-size mini-batches and helps to ensure that each model reaches a state of convergence during training.

Data Augmentation: To increase a models ability to generalize as well as to be more robust in varying environments, there are 2 primary ways that data can be augmented: geometrically (spatial) or chromatically (color).

1. Geometric Augmentations: These types of augmentations add an element of variance to the location of objects. This allows the model to find features that do not rely on object orientation or position as shown in Fig. 2.

- **Horizontally Flipping the Image** This type of flip is used to create left right images to show how the model will see left and right lanes when it looks at them from different locations.
- **Rotating Images** The images are rotated by random amounts within $\pm 10°$ to account for camera tilt variations.
- **Shearing Images** Images are subjected to horizontal and vertical shear of $\pm 5°$ to allow the model to take into consideration the distortion that comes with looking down a road.

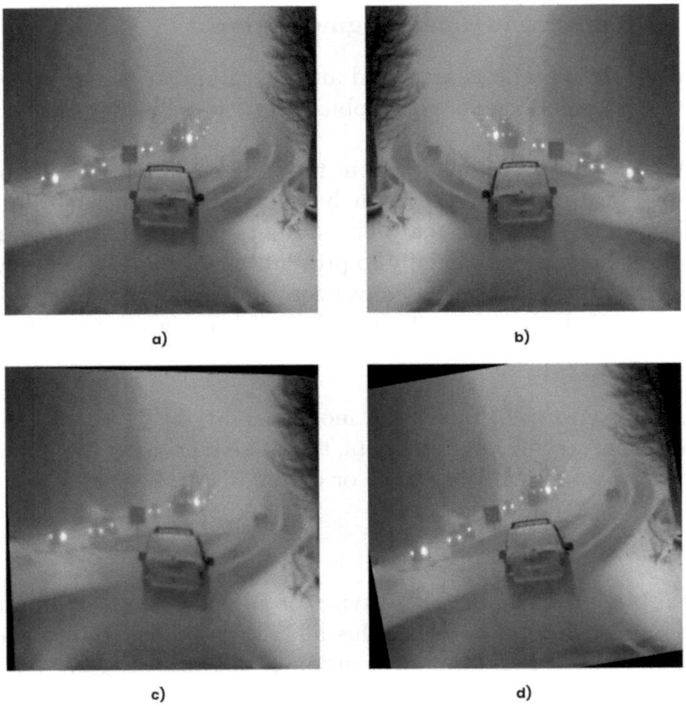

Fig. 2. Geometric augmentations: (a) original, (b) flipped, (c) sheared, (d) rotated.

2. Chromatic Augmentations. Chromatic augmentation represents random lighting conditions and environmental variations (weather), etc., as well as the effects of image degradation due to sensor limitations (such as blurring) as illustrated in Fig. 3. The chromatic augmentation techniques include:

1. Hue, Saturation, Brightness: Representing environmental changes through a random adjustment to hue, saturation and brightness.

2. Blur: Simulating defocusing, rain, fog, etc. Using a Gaussian filter.

3. Noise Addition: Adding white Gaussian noise that models sensor noise and compression artifacts.

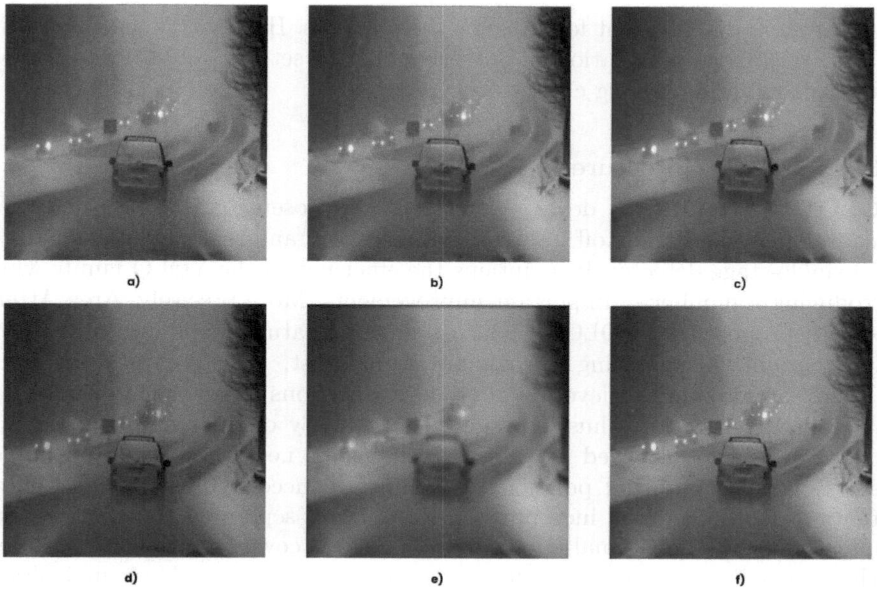

Fig. 3. Chromatic augmentations: (a) original, (b) hue adjusted, (c) saturation adjusted, (d) brightness adjusted, (e) blurred, (f) noise added.

3. A Method to Increase Minority Class Representation Using Cutmix. To solve the problem of large class imbalances in our data set, we employed an augmentation technique based on cut mix. We used this method specifically for those classes where there is too little data (i.e., the minority classes). For example, if one image contains vehicles from a majority class and another image includes vehicles from a minority class, we would use the cut mix method to extract patches (bounding boxes) of vehicles belonging to the minority class and paste them into a new target image that contained vehicles belonging to some other class than the minority class.

We ensured that all of the images were first normalized to have the same size (640 × 640) so as to ensure consistent resizing prior to the application of the augmentation method. Also, when placing the patches of the minority class object onto a target image that already had objects drawn on it (to preserve annotations), care was taken not to place the patch over an area of an object that was already annotated. In addition, the number of times we applied each iteration of the augmentation was limited by both the ratio at which the minority classes were represented in relation to the majority classes after each iteration, or by reaching an augmentation limit.

By applying targeted cut mix augmentations we were able to increase the amount of data available for each minority class, and therefore enable the models to learn more discriminant features for these classes. However, given the degree of difference in representation in our original data set, we could never achieve perfect distribution among classes.

3.3 Model Architecture

YOLO12. YOLO12 [2], developed in 2025, is chosen for the base detection because of its good trade-off between high accuracy and real-time performance. As a single-stage detector, it maintains the efficiency of the YOLO family while introducing a number of important improvements. More precisely, Area Attention was proposed by YOLO12, which segments feature maps into regions for self-attention while limiting the computational cost. Moreover, it utilizes the R-ELAN architecture to leverage residual connections and bottleneck modules for feature aggregation, thus improving the stability of the training. Also, the model integrates optimized attention mechanisms, i.e., FlashAttention implementation, elimination of positional encoding, reduced MLP ratios as well as attention depth, and the incorporation of a 7×7 separable convolution that implicitly encodes positional information. YOLO12 covers multiple capabilities, such as segmentation and classification, pose estimation, and oriented object detection in addition to detection. In addition to its parameter-efficient structure, it allows flexible deployment for a wide spectrum of environments including edge devices and cloud systems. Table 2 shows YOLO12's performance benchmarks, highlighting its suitability for robust real-time vehicle detection.

Table 2. Performance comparison of YOLO12 model variants on COCO validation dataset.

Model	Size (pixels)	mAP_{50-95}	Speed T4 TensorRT (ms)	Params (M)	FLOPs (B)	Comparison (mAP/Speed)
YOLO12n	640	40.6	1.64	2.6	6.5	+2.1% / -9% (vs. YOLOv10n)
YOLO12s	640	48.0	2.61	9.3	21.4	+0.1% / +42% (vs. RT-DETRv2)
YOLO12m	640	52.5	4.86	20.2	67.5	+1.0% / -3% (vs. YOLO11m)
YOLO12l	640	53.7	6.77	26.4	88.9	+0.4% / -8% (vs. YOLO11l)
YOLO12x	640	55.2	11.79	59.1	199.0	+0.6% / -4% (vs. YOLO11x)

Proposed Approach. YOLO12 was paired with a fully-integrated preprocessing and augmentation methodology that improved overall detection performance across all of the numerous types of adverse weather conditions present within the DAWN dataset (as illustrated in Fig. 4). A number of steps were taken to preprocess each image from this dataset. Each image was resized into a dimension of 640×640. Corresponding to these new dimensions were the respective bounding boxes for vehicles that appeared within the original images. As a means of improving the models' ability to handle variability due to class imbalance, and thereby also increasing their robustness; several augmentations were implemented on the images. Examples include: geometric-based augmentations (i.e. flip, rotate, shear); color-based augmentations (i.e. hue/saturation/brightness variations; blur/noise additions); and an example of cutmix-based augmentations. Next, based upon parameters specifically chosen to be optimized for adverse weather conditions, YOLO12 was trained using the previously described data. Lastly, the resulting trained model produced real-time output in the form of bounding boxes and corresponding class probability values associated with detecting vehicles.

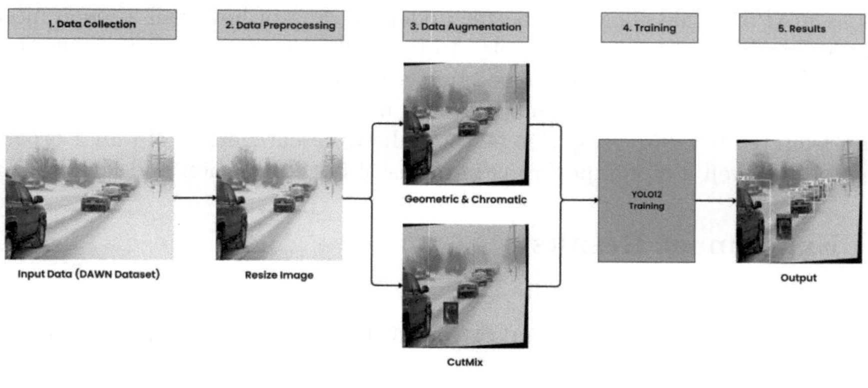

Fig. 4. Pipeline: data preprocessing, augmentations, CutMix, YOLO12 training, and vehicle detection results.

This pipeline combines advanced augmentations with YOLO12 to ensure robust and efficient vehicle detection in real-world traffic monitoring.

3.4 Implementation Details

Model training was performed by the Ultralytics YOLO architecture including the key configurations on the following parameters. Maximum training epochs were 200 epochs, 16 batch size, 640×640 pixels of input resolution. AMP was activated for faster training with less memory utilization. At that point, an initial learning rate of 0.01, momentum of 0.937, and weight decay of 0.0005 were employed in a stable manner during the learning process to achieve a consistent generalizable convergence. Checkpoints were retained every 10 epochs and early stopping applied if the validation performance failed to improve over 30 consecutive epochs. These configurations aimed at maximizing detection and classification performance under different weather conditions while optimizing training efficiency.

3.5 Evaluation Metrics

To measure the overall detection capabilities of the model, the authors employed four common quantitative measurement methods; Precision (P) Recall (R), Mean Average Precision (mAP50) and Mean Average Precision 50-95(mAP50-95). The models' Precision was measured as the ratio of True Positive (TP) results that are accurate detections in comparison to TP + False Positives (FP) or total number of correct predictions. Recall measured how well the model was able to correctly predict every object within the dataset as "TP / (TP+FN)" or the amount of total relevant objects detected. The mAP50 average precision metric calculates the Average Precision for each class in the dataset when using an Intersection Over Union (IoU) of 0.5 and then averages the sum of those values as mAP50. This allows for better understanding of how well a given model can detect objects at different levels. Additionally, the mAP50-95 average precision metric evaluates models on the same criteria but also takes into account the model's ability to localize objects through use of a range of IoU threshold settings from 0.5 to 0.95. Using this method allows researchers to obtain a broader view of how well a model performs in terms of both detection and localization.

4 Experiment Results

4.1 Model Training Results

Table 3 show the results for YOLO12 in 3 different trainings: (1) the original data set. (2) with the added use of both color and geometry augmentations. (3) with a combination of color, geometry, and CutMix as additional augmentations. Experiments were conducted using PyTorch and Ultralytics YOLO framework.

Table 3. Performance comparison of YOLO12 under different augmentation settings.

Dataset	Precision	Recall	mAP50	mAP50-95
Original	0.763	0.562	0.652	0.405
Geometric & Chromatic	0.94	0.88	0.953	0.787
Geometric & Chromatic + CutMix	0.968	0.956	0.979	0.901

YOLO12 trained using a combination of geometric and chromatic augmentations (with cutmix), was trained with the best mAP values (mAP50=0.979, mAP50-95 =0.901) of all 3 training methods.

4.2 Discussion

Geometric and chromatic augmentations increased baseline by .301 (from 0.652 to 0.953) while adding CutMix further improved detection rate of 0.979 (and an increase of .038 for map50-95: 0.901). As a result, this demonstrates that it can effectively address class imbalance issues. Baseline model fared poorly on minority classes such as bus and bicycle; however, using CutMix to create more representative images of those classes leads to better overall traffic detection rates. These results suggest that geometric and chromatic augments are important for improving generalization; in contrast, CutMix is essential for balanced detection in real-world traffic systems.

5 Conclusion

This paper has suggested an approach to build up a resilient vehicle classifier in all different types of weather condition, which is by combining cutmix based class balance into yolo12. The experimental results demonstrated that the use of these three different methods to augment the dataset significantly improved the average precision at 50 percent confidence (mAP50) of 65.2% for original data to 97.9% for augmented datasets, as well as mAP50-95 of 40.5% to 90.1%. These results have also shown improved detection accuracy and robustness for the model when deployed in extreme weather conditions. Additionally, since this was able to provide a much better distribution among classes, it provided a better per-class performance than the baseline model.

Overall, the proposed method has good promise for deployment on edge devices in real time in intelligent transportation system or in autonomous vehicles where there are needs for reliable detections in the presence of bad weather. In future research we would like to look into incorporating new approaches for domain adaptation as well as optimize the various versions of yolo12 for best possible edge device deployment.

References

1. Hassaballah, M., Kenk, M.A., Muhammad, K., Minaee, S.: Vehicle detection and tracking in adverse weather using a deep learning framework. IEEE Trans. Intell. Transp. Syst. **22**(7), 4230–4242 (2020)
2. Ultralytics. Ultralytics yolo12 (2024). https://docs.ultralytics.com/vi/models/yolo12/. Accessed: 04-July-2025
3. Buda, M., Maki, A., Mazurowski, M.A.: A systematic study of the class imbalance problem in convolutional neural networks. Neural Netw. **106**, 249–259 (2018)
4. Howard, A.G.: Mobilenets: efficient convolutional neural networks for mobile vision applications. arXiv preprint arXiv:1704.04861 (2017)
5. Yun, S., Han, D., Oh, S. J., Chun, S., Choe, J., Yoo, Y.: Cutmix: regularization strategy to train strong classifiers with localizable features. In Proceedings of the IEEE/CVF International Conference on Computer Vision, pp. 6023–6032 (2019)

6. Rjoub, G., Wahab, O. A., Bentahar, J., Bataineh, A.S.: Improving autonomous vehicles safety in snow weather using federated YOLO CNN learning. In International Conference on Mobile Web and Intelligent Information Systems, pp. 121–134. Cham: Springer International Publishing (2021)
7. Wu, J. D., Chen, B. Y., Shyr, W. J., Shih, F.Y.: Vehicle Classification and Counting System Using YOLO Object Detection Technology. Traitement du Signal, **38**(4) (2021)
8. Boppana, U. M., Mustapha, A., Jacob, K., Deivanayagampillai, N.: Comparative analysis of single-stage yolo algorithms for vehicle detection under extreme weather conditions. In: IOT with Smart Systems: Proceedings of ICTIS 2021, Volume 2, pp. 637–645. Springer Singapore (2022)
9. Liu, W., Ren, G., Yu, R., Guo, S., Zhu, J., Zhang, L.: Image-adaptive YOLO for object detection in adverse weather conditions. In Proceedings of the AAAI Conference on Artificial Intelligence (vol. 36, No. 2, pp. 1792–1800) (2022)
10. Ding, Q., et al.: CF-YOLO: cross fusion yolo for object detection in adverse weather with a high-quality real snow dataset. IEEE Trans. Intell. Transp. Syst. **24**(10), 10749–10759 (2023)
11. Tian, E., Kim, J.: Improved vehicle detection using weather classification and faster R-CNN with Dark Channel Prior. Electronics **12**(14), 3022 (2023)
12. Panja, E., Hendry, H., Dewi, C.: YOLOv8 analysis for vehicle classification under various image conditions. Sci. J. Inform. **11**(1), 127–138 (2024)
13. Aloufi, N., Alnori, A., Basuhail, A.: Enhancing autonomous vehicle perception in adverse weather: a multi objectives model for integrated weather classification and object detection. Electronics **13**(15), 3063 (2024)
14. Ogino, Y., Shoji, Y., Toizumi, T., Ito, A.: ERUP-YOLO: Enhancing Object Detection Robustness for Adverse Weather Condition by Unified Image-Adaptive Processing. In: 2025 IEEE/CVF Winter Conference on Applications of Computer Vision (WACV), pp. 8597–8605. IEEE (2025)
15. Huang, Y.C., Lin, H.Y.: All-Weather Vehicle Detection and Classification with Adversarial and Semi-Supervised Learning. In: International Conference on Pattern Recognition, pp. 330–345. Springer, Cham (2025)
16. KENK, Mourad, DAWN, Mendeley Data, V3 (2020). https://doi.org/10.17632/766ygrbt8y.3

A Multi-objective Loss Function for Neighbor-Based Recommender Systems

Ho Thi Hoang Vy[1,3], Hien D. Nguyen[2,3], and Le Nguyen Hoai Nam[1,3](✉)

[1] Faculty of Information Technology, University of Science, Ho Chi Minh City, Vietnam
{hthvy,lnhnam}@fit.hcmus.edu.vn
[2] University of Information Technology, Ho Chi Minh City, Vietnam
hiennd@uit.edu.vn
[3] Vietnam National University, Ho Chi Minh City, Vietnam

Abstract. Neighbor-based recommendation models exploit users who are similar to an active user, referred to as neighbors, to predict individual preferences for recommendation tasks. These models are typically optimized through a loss function to estimate the influence of neighbors on the active user. Existing studies commonly design the loss function by minimizing the discrepancy between predicted preferences and observed numerical ratings. However, modern recommender systems can also collect textual comments from users, which provide additional signals about their preferences. Motivated by this observation, this paper extends the conventional loss function by incorporating textual comments into the optimization process. The proposed multi-objective loss function enables the model to jointly learn from both numerical ratings and textual comments. As a result, the recommendation model becomes more robust, particularly in scenarios where observed rating data are sparse. Experimental results demonstrate that the proposed approach improves recommendation accuracy, especially for users with limited rating histories.

Keywords: Neighbor-based model · Collaborative filtering · Recommendation systems

1 Introduction

Recommender systems have been developed to personalize customer experiences across various application domains [1]. In such systems, user preferences are predicted using machine learning models, enabling the delivery of items that best match individual needs. Among the various approaches, one of the most widely adopted is based on the assumption that an active user's preference can be inferred from the preferences of other users who are similar to them, commonly referred to as neighbors [2]. This intuition also enhances the transparency and interpretability of recommendation models.

In neighbor-based recommendation models, the key parameters capture the influence of each neighbor on the predicted preference of the active user. Based on these parameters, the model aggregates the preferences of neighbors through a weighted averaging

O. Gervasi et al. (Eds.): ICCSA 2026, LNCS 16768, pp. 277–296, 2027.
https://doi.org/10.1007/978-3-032-30488-9_18

mechanism [3, 4]. The resulting aggregated preference is then used to infer the active user's preference for subsequent recommendation tasks.

To estimate these parameters, loss functions are typically formulated to minimize the discrepancy between observed feedback and the preferences predicted by the model. In most existing studies, this feedback is represented by explicit ratings, which provide a direct numerical indication of user satisfaction. Consequently, the loss functions are primarily designed to align predicted preferences with observed numerical ratings [5, 6]. However, in modern recommender systems, user feedback is also expressed through textual comments, which may appear alongside or even in the absence of ratings [7, 8]. This raises a natural question: how should the loss function be designed and optimized so that predicted preferences are jointly aligned with both observed numerical ratings and observed textual comments?

Based on this research question, the contributions of this paper are threefold:

- We propose a multi-objective loss function for neighbor-based recommender systems to ensure that predicted preferences are jointly aligned with multiple forms of observed feedback.
- We develop a detailed optimization procedure for the proposed objective using stochastic gradient descent (SGD).
- We conduct extensive experiments on benchmark datasets containing both numerical and textual feedback to demonstrate the effectiveness of the proposed approach.

Throughout this paper, the notations used are summarized in Table 1.

Table 1. List of Notations.

Denote	Description
$\mathbb{U}$	Set of users
$\mathbb{I}$	Set of items
$r_{u,i}$	Observed numerical rating given by user u to item i
$t_{u,i}$	Observed textual comment written by user u for item i
$c_{u,i}$	Comment-derived rating inferred from the textual comment $t_{u,i}$
$p_{u,i}$	Predicted preference of user u for item i
$\mathrm{sim}(v, u)$	Similarity between users u and v
$w_{v,u,i}$	Influence weight of user v on user u for item i
$w_{j,i,u}$	Influence weight of item j on item i for user u
$\mathbb{N}_u^i$	Set of users similar to user u who have rated item i
$\mathbb{N}_i^u$	Set of items similar to item i that user u has rated
θ_u	Parameter vector associated with user u
θ_i	Parameter vector associated with item i
α_u	Bias term of user u
α_i	Bias term of item i

(*continued*)

Table 1. *(continued)*

Denote	Description
$\mathbb{R}$	Set of observed numerical ratings
$\mathbb{C}$	Set of observed textual comments

2 Related Work

Let $\mathbb{U}$ denote the set of users and $\mathbb{I}$ denote the set of items. The system collects explicit ratings provided by users, where each rating $r_{u,i} \in \{1,2,3,4,5\}$ represents the preference of user $u \in \mathbb{U}$ for item $i \in \mathbb{I}$. A higher rating indicates a stronger level of satisfaction, while a lower rating reflects weaker preference. The primary objective is to predict the unknown preference $p_{u,i}$ of an active user u for an unseen item i based on the observed ratings. In neighbor-based recommendation models, preference prediction is typically performed through the following steps [1]:

- First, the similarity between the active user u and another user v is computed: $\mathrm{sim}(v, u)$;
- Next, the set of users who have rated item i is identified. From this set, the top users who are most similar to u are selected as neighbors: $\mathbb{N}_u^i$;
- The predicted preference of user u for item i ($p_{u,i}$) is then estimated by aggregating the observed ratings of these neighbors ($r_{v,i}, v \in \mathbb{N}_u^i$) using influence weights ($w_{v,u}, v \in \mathbb{N}_u^i$), as follows:

$$p_{u,i} = \sum_{v \in \mathbb{N}_v^i} w_{v,u} \cdot r_{v,i} \tag{1}$$

Most studies on neighbor-based recommendation models primarily focus on user similarity computation. User similarity can be characterized from multiple perspectives. The most common approach relies on users' past item experiences, typically reflected through numerical ratings [9] or textual comments [7, 8]. Several studies further exploit user interaction behaviors before item consumption, such as viewing items, adding items to the cart, and purchasing activities [10]. Although these behaviors do not explicitly express user preferences, they provide valuable implicit signals that reveal underlying interests. Other approaches leverage item descriptions associated with users' item experiences by applying advanced natural language processing and deep learning techniques [3]. Item categories have also been incorporated as an additional source of similarity information [11]. Furthermore, some studies consider contextual factors, such as temporal patterns of user interactions, to refine the similarity measure [12]. Accurate estimation of user similarity plays a critical role in neighbor-based recommendation models, as it directly determines the quality of the neighbor set and, consequently, the effectiveness of preference prediction.

To estimate the influence weights between neighbors and the active user ($w_{v,u}, v \in \mathbb{N}_u^i$), some studies directly assign weights based on similarity scores, as follows [7, 8,

10–12]:

$$p_{u,i} = \sum_{v \in \mathbb{N}_u^i} \text{sim}(v, u).r_{v,i} \quad (2)$$

However, a more accurate estimation can be achieved by learning these influence weights through a loss function that minimizes the discrepancy between predicted preferences ($p_{u,i}$) and observed ratings ($r_{u,i}$), as follows [3, 13]:

$$p_{u,i} = \sum_{v \in \mathbb{N}_u^i} w_{v,u}.r_{v,i} \quad \min_{w_{v,u}, \forall v \in \mathbb{N}_u^i, \forall u \in \mathbb{U}, \forall i \in \mathbb{I}} \frac{1}{2} \sum_{(u,i) \in \mathbb{R}} \left(r_{u,i} - p_{u,i}\right)^2 \quad (3)$$

where $\mathbb{R}$ denotes the set of observed ratings.

Building upon this formulation, several studies further extend the loss function to estimate item-specific influence weights $w_{v,u,i}$ (instead of $w_{v,u}$), motivated by the observation that a neighbor's influence on the active user may vary across items. However, modeling such fine-grained, item-dependent influence substantially increases the number of parameters in the loss function. To address this issue, [5, 6] proposes a factorized parameterization of influence weights. Specifically, the influence weight associated with a neighbor-user-item triplet $w_{v,u,i}$ is modeled as the inner product between a triplet feature vector $\phi_{v,u,i}$ and a user-specific parameter vector θ_u, as follows:

$$p_{u,i} = \sum_{v \in \mathbb{N}_u^i} w_{v,u,i}.r_{v,i} \; with \; w_{v,u,i} = \phi_{v,u,i}^T.\theta_u \quad \min_{\theta_u, \forall u \in \mathbb{U}} \frac{1}{2} \sum_{(u,i) \in \mathbb{R}} \left(r_{u,i} - p_{u,i}\right)^2 \quad (4)$$

3 Motivation

In real-world recommendation scenarios, different forms of user feedback may be observed after a user experiences an item. Specifically, three common situations can occur as follows:

- A user provides both a numerical rating and a textual comment;
- A user provides only a numerical rating;
- A user provides only a textual comment.

Existing neighbor-based recommendation models typically construct their loss functions solely based on observed numerical ratings. As a result, the optimization process focuses on aligning predicted preferences with rating signals, implicitly assuming that ratings are always available and serve as the sole learning signal. However, this assumption does not hold in many practical settings, where users may choose to leave only textual comments or provide textual comments alongside ratings. Consequently, optimizing prediction models using rating-based objectives alone becomes insufficient. In such cases, predicted preferences should also be consistent with the opinions reflected in users' comments.

Motivated by this limitation, this study develops a Multi-Objective loss function for Neighbor-Based recommendation models, referred to as **MONB**. The proposed formulation enables influence weights to be learned by jointly considering multiple forms of user feedback within a unified optimization framework. Specifically, Sect. 4.1 introduces a neighbor-based recommendation model that integrates both user-oriented and item-oriented perspectives. Building upon this model, Sect. 4.2 formulates the proposed multi-objective loss function for learning influence weights. Finally, Sect. 4.3 presents the optimization procedure in detail.

4 Our Approach

4.1 Neighbor-Based Recommendation Model from User and Item Perspectives

In many studies, neighbor-based recommendation models are implemented from either the user-oriented perspective or the item-oriented perspective. The item-based approach estimates the preference of an active user for an item based on the preferences of similar items that the user has previously interacted with, referred to as item neighbors [3, 11, 13]. Analogous to the user-oriented formulation in Eq. (4), the preference prediction of user u for item i using item neighbors can be formulated as follows [3, 11, 13]:

$$p_{u,i} = \sum_{j \in \mathbb{N}_i^u} w_{j,i,u}.r_{u,j} \; with \; w_{j,i,u} = \phi_{j,i,u}^T.\theta_i \tag{5}$$

where $\mathbb{N}_i^u$ denotes the set of items similar to item i that have been rated by user u, $w_{j,i,u}$ represents the influence weight between item i and its item neighbor j with respect to user u, $\phi_{j,i,u}$ is the feature vector representing the triplet (item neighbor j, item i, user u), and θ_i is the parameter vector associated with item i.

With the development of hybrid recommender systems, multiple perspectives can be combined within a unified framework. A common strategy is to integrate user-based and item-based predictions through an aggregation mechanism. Accordingly, the preference prediction can be expressed as [5, 6]:

$$p_{u,i} = \sum_{v \in \mathbb{N}_u^i} \phi_{v,u,i}^T.\theta_u.r_{v,i} + \sum_{j \in \mathbb{N}_i^u} \phi_{j,i,u}^T.\theta_i.r_{u,j} \tag{6}$$

To further improve prediction accuracy, user and item biases (α_u and α_i) relative to the global average (μ) are incorporated following common practices [3, 5, 6, 12, 13]:

$$p_{u,i} = \alpha_u + \alpha_i + \mu + \sum_{v \in \mathbb{N}_u^i} \phi_{v,u,i}^T.\theta_u.\left(r_{v,i} - \alpha_v - \alpha_i - \mu\right)$$
$$+ \sum_{j \in \mathbb{N}_i^u} \phi_{j,i,u}^T.\theta_i.\left(r_{u,j} - \alpha_u - \alpha_j - \mu\right) \tag{7}$$

In this model, the parameters to be learned include α_u, α_i, θ_u, and θ_i. The feature vectors $\phi_{v,u,i}$ và $\phi_{j,i,u}$ are constructed according to [5], as described in Tables 2, 3.

Table 2. Feature vector for the triplet $\phi_{v,u,i}$ (user neighbor v, user u, item i) [5]

No	Feature description
1	Number of items rated by the user neighbor v
2	Number of users who have rated item i
3	Similarity between the user u and the user neighbor v
4	Average observed rating of item i
5	Average observed rating given by the user neighbor v
6	Standard deviation of observed ratings for item i
7	Standard deviation of observed ratings given by the user neighbor v

Table 3. Feature vector for the triplet $\phi_{j,i,u}$ (item neighbor j, item i, user u) [5]

No	Feature description
1	Number of users who have rated the item neighbor j
2	Number of items rated by the user u
3	Similarity between the item i and the item neighbor j
4	Average observed rating given by the user u
5	Average observed rating of the item neighbor j
6	Standard deviation of observed ratings given by the user u
7	Standard deviation of observed ratings for the item neighbor j

4.2 Multi-objective Loss Function: MONB

Figure 1 illustrates the main idea of our proposed MONB model. Specifically, to learn the parameters above while accounting for multiple feedback scenarios (rating and/or comment), we formulate a multi-objective loss function, referred to as **MONB**, that jointly aligns the predicted preferences $p_{u,i}$ with observed numerical ratings $r_{u,i}$ in the observed rating set $\mathbb{R}$ and comment-derived ratings $c_{u,i}$ in the observed comment set $\mathbb{C}$:

$$\min_{\theta_u,\theta_i,\alpha_u,\alpha_i,\forall u\in\mathbb{U},\forall i\in\mathbb{I}} \frac{1}{2}\sum_{(u,i)\in\mathbb{R}} \left(r_{u,i} - p_{u,i}\right)^2 + \frac{1}{2}\sum_{(u,i)\in\mathbb{C}} \left(c_{u,i} - p_{u,i}\right)^2$$

$$\Leftrightarrow$$

$$\begin{aligned}\min_{\theta_u,\theta_i,\alpha_u,\alpha_i,\forall u\in\mathbb{U},\forall i\in\mathbb{I}} \frac{1}{2}\sum_{(u,i)\in\mathbb{R}} \Bigg(& r_{u,i} - \alpha_u - \alpha_i - \mu - \sum_{v\in\mathbb{N}_u^i} \phi_{v,u,i}^T.\theta_u.\left(r_{v,i} - \alpha_v - \alpha_i - \mu\right) \\ & - \sum_{j\in\mathbb{N}_i^u} \phi_{j,i,u}^T.\theta_i.\left(r_{u,j} - \alpha_u - \alpha_j - \mu\right)\Bigg)^2 \\ + \frac{1}{2}\sum_{(u,i)\in\mathbb{C}} \Bigg(& c_{u,i} - \alpha_u - \alpha_i - \mu - \sum_{v\in\mathbb{N}_u^i} \phi_{v,u,i}^T.\theta_u.\left(r_{v,i} - \alpha_v - \alpha_i - \mu\right) \\ & - \sum_{j\in\mathbb{N}_i^u} \phi_{j,i,u}^T.\theta_i.\left(r_{u,j} - \alpha_u - \alpha_j - \mu\right)\Bigg)^2\end{aligned} \tag{8}$$

where $c_{u,i}$ is obtained by mapping a user's textual comment into a rating score. This mapping can be implemented with low computational cost using sentiment dictionaries, as described in [14]. With higher computational cost, more accurate scores can be produced by using large language models.

To prevent overfitting, Tikhonov regularization is incorporated:

$$\begin{aligned}\min_{\theta_u,\theta_i,\alpha_u,\alpha_i,\forall u\in\mathbb{U},\forall i\in\mathbb{I}} \frac{1}{2}\sum_{(u,i)\in\mathbb{R}} \Bigg(& r_{u,i} - \alpha_u - \alpha_i - \mu - \sum_{v\in\mathbb{N}_u^i} \phi_{v,u,i}^T.\theta_u.\left(r_{v,i} - \alpha_v - \alpha_i - \mu\right) \\ & - \sum_{j\in\mathbb{N}_i^u} \phi_{j,i,u}^T.\theta_i.\left(r_{u,j} - \alpha_u - \alpha_j - \mu\right)\Bigg)^2 \\ + \frac{1}{2}\sum_{(u,i)\in\mathbb{C}} \Bigg(& c_{u,i} - \alpha_u - \alpha_i - \mu - \sum_{v\in\mathbb{N}_u^i} \phi_{v,u,i}^T.\theta_u.\left(r_{v,i} - \alpha_v - \alpha_i - \mu\right) \\ & - \sum_{j\in\mathbb{N}_i^u} \phi_{j,i,u}^T.\theta_i.\left(r_{u,j} - \alpha_u - \alpha_j - \mu\right)\Bigg)^2 \\ + \frac{\lambda}{2}\Bigg(& \sum_{u\in\mathbb{U}}\left(\|\theta_u\|^2 + \alpha_u^2\right) + \sum_{i\in\mathbb{I}}\left(\|\theta_i\|^2 + \alpha_i^2\right)\Bigg)\end{aligned} \tag{9}$$

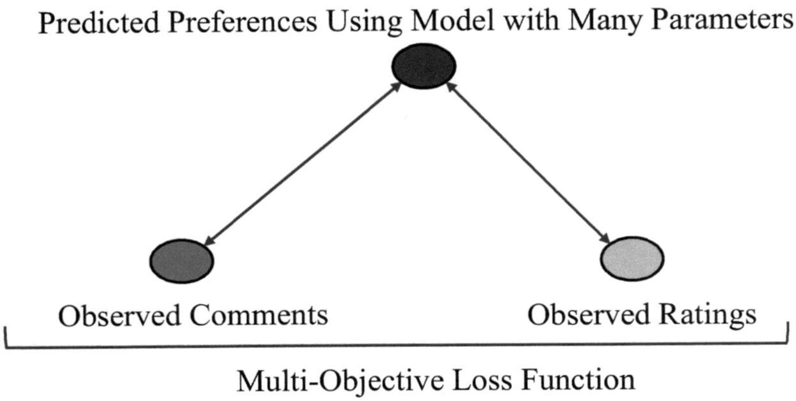

Fig. 1. The proposed MONB loss function

4.3 Optimization via Stochastic Gradient Descent

The loss function is optimized using stochastic gradient descent (SGD), as outlined in Algorithm 1. Specifically, for each observed user–item pair (u, i), the prediction error $e_{u,i}$ is defined according to the available feedback:

- Only a rating is available:

$$e_{u,i} = r_{u,i} - \alpha_u - \alpha_i - \mu - \sum_{v\in\mathbb{N}_u^i} \phi_{v,u,i}^T.\theta_u.\left(r_{v,i} - \alpha_v - \alpha_i - \mu\right) \\ - \sum_{j\in\mathbb{N}_i^u} \phi_{j,i,u}^T.\theta_i.\left(r_{u,j} - \alpha_u - \alpha_j - \mu\right) \tag{10}$$

- Only a comment is available:

$$e_{u,i} = c_{u,i} - \alpha_u - \alpha_i - \mu - \sum_{v\in\mathbb{N}_u^i} \phi_{v,u,i}^T.\theta_u.\left(r_{v,i} - \alpha_v - \alpha_i - \mu\right) \\ - \sum_{j\in\mathbb{N}_i^u} \phi_{j,i,u}^T.\theta_i.\left(r_{u,j} - \alpha_u - \alpha_j - \mu\right) \tag{11}$$

- Both rating and comment are available:

$$e_{u,i} = \left(r_{u,i} - \alpha_u - \alpha_i - \mu - \sum_{v\in\mathbb{N}_u^i} \phi_{v,u,i}^T.\theta_u.\left(r_{v,i} - \alpha_v - \alpha_i - \mu\right) - \sum_{j\in\mathbb{N}_i^u} \phi_{j,i,u}^T.\theta_i.\left(r_{u,j} - \alpha_u - \alpha_j - \mu\right)\right) \\ + \left(c_{u,i} - \alpha_u - \alpha_i - \mu - \sum_{v\in\mathbb{N}_u^i} \phi_{v,u,i}^T.\theta_u.\left(r_{v,i} - \alpha_v - \alpha_i - \mu\right) - \sum_{j\in\mathbb{N}_i^u} \phi_{j,i,u}^T.\theta_i.\left(r_{u,j} - \alpha_u - \alpha_j - \mu\right)\right) \tag{12}$$

- The model parameters are updated by computing the partial derivatives of the loss function with respect to each parameter:

$$\theta_u \leftarrow \theta_u + \delta\left(e_{u,i}.\sum_{v\in\mathbb{N}_u^i}\phi_{v,u,i}.(r_{v,i} - \alpha_v - \alpha_i - \mu) - \lambda\theta_u\right) \tag{13}$$

$$\theta_i \leftarrow \theta_i + \delta\left(e_{u,i}.\sum_{j\in\mathbb{N}_i^u}\phi_{j,i,u}(r_{u,j} - \alpha_u - \alpha_j - \mu) - \lambda\theta_i\right) \tag{14}$$

$$\alpha_u \leftarrow \alpha_u + \delta\left(e_{u,i} - e_{u,i}\sum_{j\in\mathbb{N}_i^u}\phi_{j,i,u}^T.\theta_i - \lambda\alpha_u\right) \tag{15}$$

$$\alpha_i \leftarrow \alpha_i + \delta\left(e_{u,i} - e_{u,i}\sum_{v\in\mathbb{N}_u^i}\phi_{v,u,i}^T.\theta_u - \lambda\alpha_i\right) \tag{16}$$

$$\forall v \in \mathbb{N}_u^i : \alpha_v \leftarrow \alpha_v - \delta\left(\phi_{v,u,i}^T.\theta_u + \lambda\alpha_v\right) \tag{17}$$

$$\forall j \in \mathbb{N}_i^u : \alpha_j \leftarrow \alpha_j - \delta\left(\phi_{j,i,u}^T.\theta_i + \lambda\alpha_j\right) \tag{18}$$

where δ is the learning rate

Algorithm 1: SGD for the Multi-Objective Neighbor-based Model

1. Initialize $\theta_u, \theta_i, \alpha_u, \alpha_i \ \forall u \in \mathbb{U}, \forall i \in \mathbb{I}$
2. Construct the set of observed user–item pairs $\mathbb{H}$, where $\mathbb{R}$ denotes the set of observed ratings and $\mathbb{C}$ denotes the set of observed comments.
3. Repeat until convergence (i.e., the change in the objective function is less than 10^{-6} or the number of iterations reaches 500)
4. Randomly shuffle the observed set $\mathbb{H}$
5. For each observed pair (u, i) in $\mathbb{H}$:
   - If (u, i) belongs to both $\mathbb{R}$ and $\mathbb{C}$
     - Compute $e_{u,i}$ using Eq. (12)
   - If (u, i) belongs only to $\mathbb{R}$:
     - Compute $e_{u,i}$ using Eq. (10)
   - If (u, i) belongs only to $\mathbb{C}$:
     - Compute $e_{u,i}$ using Eq. (11)
   - Update model parameters:
     - θ_u using Eq. (13)
     - θ_i using Eq. (14)
     - α_u using Eq. (15)
     - α_i using Eq. (16)
     - $\forall v \in \mathbb{N}_u^i$ using Eq. (17)
     - $\forall j \in \mathbb{N}_i^u$ using Eq. (18)

Although the model parameters are learned through the optimization procedure described above, the effectiveness of the optimization process can be influenced by the initial values of the user and item parameter vectors θ_u and θ_i (Step 1 in Agorithm 1). Let $\theta_u^{(0)}$ and $\theta_i^{(0)}$ represent their initial representations. In real-world recommender systems, textual comments contain rich semantic information that reflects user preferences and item characteristics. Therefore, instead of using random initialization, we introduce a review-aware strategy to initialize the parameter vectors of users and items based on textual comments associated with positive user preferences, as shown in Fig. 2.

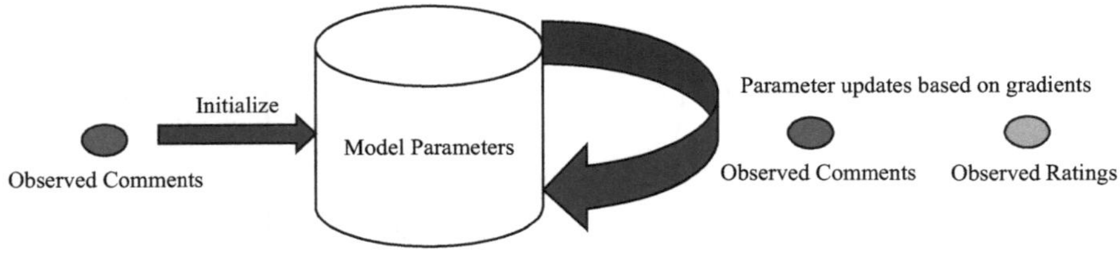

Fig. 2. Initialization strategy based on textual comments for users and items

Specifically, for each user u, we identify the set of items that the user positively prefers, denoted by $\mathbb{S}_u$. An item i is considered preferred if the corresponding textual comment expresses positive sentiment, i.e., the comment-derived rating $c_{u,i}$ exceeds a liking threshold δ. Formally,

$$\mathbb{S}_u = \{i|(u, i) \in \mathbb{C} \wedge c_{u,i} > \delta\} \tag{19}$$

where $\mathbb{C}$ denotes the set of user–item pairs for which textual comments are available. Let $t_{u,i}$ denote the embedding vector extracted from the textual comment written by user u for item i. This embedding can be obtained using large language models. The initial representation of user u is then constructed by aggregating the embeddings of the comments associated with the preferred items:

$$\theta_u^{(0)} = \frac{1}{|\mathbb{S}_u|} \sum_{i \in \mathbb{S}_u} t_{u,i} \tag{20}$$

Similarly, for each item i, we consider the set of users who express positive preference toward that item, denoted by $\mathbb{S}_i$:

$$\mathbb{S}_i = \{u|(u, i) \in \mathbb{C} \wedge c_{u,i} > \delta\} \tag{21}$$

The initial representation of item i is obtained by aggregating the embeddings of the corresponding textual comments:

$$\theta_i^{(0)} = \frac{1}{|\mathbb{S}_i|} \sum_{i \in \mathbb{S}_i} t_{u,i} \tag{22}$$

4.4 System Implementation

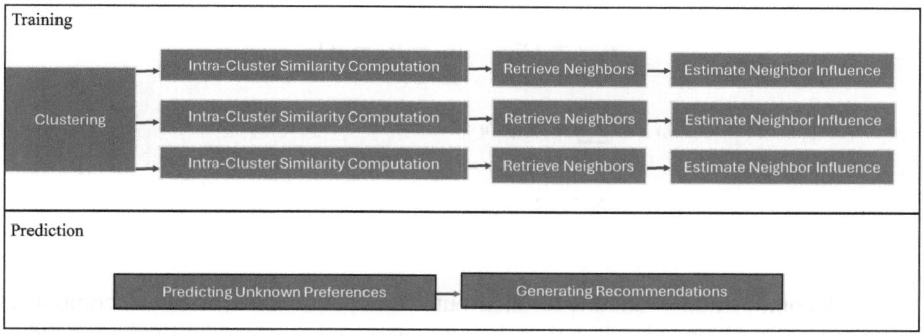

Fig. 3. The training and prediction phases in the proposed system

Based on the above design, the proposed system is implemented in two main phases, namely training and prediction, as shown in Fig. 3:

- In the training phase, the similarities between user pairs and between item pairs are first computed to construct the corresponding neighbor sets for recommendation. Next, the proposed objective function is optimized to estimate the parameter vectors associated with users and items, as well as the corresponding bias terms.
- In the prediction phase, the preferences of an active user for candidate items are inferred by combining the learned parameters with the user and item neighbor sets obtained during training.

However, when the number of users and items is large, the computational cost increases substantially in both similarity computation and parameter optimization. In particular, computing pairwise similarities for all users and all items leads to a large search space, while optimizing the objective function requires repeated evaluation of the error terms $e_{u,i}$ for observed user-item pairs (u, i). To address the first implementation issue, users and items are clustered before similarity computation so that the similarity search can be restricted to a smaller and more relevant subset. This clustering strategy takes advantage of the initial representations of users and items, denoted by $\theta_u^{(0)}$ and $\theta_i^{(0)}$, which are learned from review embeddings and are expected to capture meaningful semantic characteristics of users and items.

For the optimization stage, the most expensive computation lies in evaluating the error term $e_{u,i}$ (Eqs. (10–12)) for each observed user-item pair (u, i), especially when both rating-based and comment-based feedback are incorporated into the learning process. According to the objective function and the SGD-based optimization procedure in Sect. 4.3, each error term $e_{u,i}$ depends not only on the observed feedback of the pair (u, i) itself, but also on two aggregated neighbor components: one from the user neighbor set $\mathbb{N}_u^i$ and one from the item neighbor set $\mathbb{N}_i^u$. As a result, repeatedly evaluating these summation terms over large datasets becomes a major computational bottleneck. To improve scalability, this computation is parallelized using the MapReduce model on the Hadoop platform. More specifically, for a user-item pair (u, i), the corresponding error term can be decomposed into one constant component $a_{u,i}$ and two summation components $f_{u,i}$ and $b_{u,i}$:

$$a_{u,i} = \left(r_{u,i} - \alpha_u - \alpha_i - \mu\right) \tag{23}$$

$$f_{u,i} = \sum_{v \in \mathbb{N}_u^i} \phi_{v,u,i}^T.\theta_u.\left(r_{v,i} - \alpha_v - \alpha_i - \mu\right)$$

$$b_{u,i} = \sum_{j \in \mathbb{N}_i^u} \phi_{j,i,u}^T.\theta_i.\left(r_{u,j} - \alpha_u - \alpha_j - \mu\right)$$

This decomposition is suitable for distributed computation because each component can be evaluated independently before being aggregated to form the final error value. To compute this error efficiently, we design a MapReduce procedure consisting of three main stages: input split, map, and reduce. In the input split stage, for each target pair (u, i), the required data are transformed into neighbor records. Two types of records are generated:

- The first type corresponds to each user neighbor $v \in \mathbb{N}_u^i$, where each record contains $(u, i, v, \phi_{v,u,i}, \theta_u, r_{v,i}, \alpha_v, \alpha_v, \mu)$.
- The second type corresponds to each item neighbor $j \in \mathbb{N}_i^u$, where each record contains $(u, i, j, \phi_{j,i,u}, \theta_i, r_{u,j}, \alpha_u, \alpha_j, \mu)$.

The constant values $(r_{u,i}, \alpha_u, \alpha_i, \mu)$ are also made available to the processing nodes, either directly within the input metadata or through a distributed cache. By splitting the computation into these fine-grained records, the system enables each worker node to process one local summand independently.

In the map stage, each mapper processes one neighbor record and computes one local contribution to the error term. If the input record corresponds to a user neighbor v, the mapper computes:

$$m_v = \phi_{v,u,i}^T.\theta_u.\left(r_{v,i} - \alpha_v - \alpha_i - \mu\right) \tag{24}$$

and emits the key-value pair:

$$key = (u, i);\ value = (user, m_v) \tag{25}$$

Similarly, if the input record corresponds to an item neighbor j, the mapper computes:

$$m_j = \phi_{j,i,u}^T.\theta_i.\left(r_{u,j} - \alpha_u - \alpha_j - \mu\right) \tag{26}$$

and emits:

$$key = (u, i);\ value = (\text{"}item\text{"}, m_j) \tag{27}$$

Optionally, one mapper may also emit the constant term $a_{u,i}$ (see Eq. (23)) using the same key.

During the shuffle and sort stage, all intermediate values having the same key (u, i) are grouped and routed to the same reducer. Consequently, all partial contributions associated with the target pair are collected at one location for final aggregation. In the reduce stage, the reducer initializes two accumulators, namely $f_{u,i}$ and $b_{u,i}$ (See Eq. (23)), to zero. It then scans all received values associated with the key `(u, i)`. If an incoming value is labeled `"user"`, its contribution is added to $f_{u,i}$. If it is labeled `"item"`, its contribution is added to $b_{u,i}$. After all partial values have been aggregated, the reducer obtains the final error value as follows:

$$e_{u,i} = a_{u,i} - f_{u,i} - b_{u,i} \tag{28}$$

5 Experiment

5.1 Experiment Setup

In this section, we conduct experiments using a series of neighbor-based recommendation models, in which each stage is implemented as follows:

- Similarity computation: RaReSi [8], MFPS [9]
- Influence weight estimation:
- Using similarity as influence weights: SBP [8, 9]
- Constructing a loss function optimized for ratings: OSRP [5] and ROSRP [6]
- Constructing a joint loss function optimized for both ratings and comments: MONB

For hyperparameter settings, the neighbor set size (for both user neighbors and item neighbors) is varied from 30 to 100. The learning rate (δ) and regularization coefficient (λ) are set to 0.001 and 0.01, respectively. To incorporate textual comments into the learning process, user comments are converted into rating scores ($c_{u,i}$ in Eq. (8)) and into embedding vectors ($t_{u,i}$ in Eq. (20)) using GPT-4. The liking threshold (δ in Eqs. (19, 21)) is defined as the midpoint of the rating scale, which is 3 on a scale from 1 to 5.

5.2 Dataset

To align with the characteristics of this study, we selected publicly available benchmark datasets that contain both numerical ratings and textual comments, as summarized in Table 4. The datasets were split into training and test sets using a 70–30 ratio. The splitting process was conducted randomly three times to generate three different train–test partitions. The final results reported in the following sections correspond to the average performance across these three splits.

Table 4. Dataset description.

Dataset	#Users	#Items	#Comments and ratings
Amazon Baby	19,445	7,050	160,792
Amazon Beauty	22,365	12,101	198,502
Amazon Gourmet Foods	14,601	8,713	150,289

5.3 Measure

A recommender system is considered effective when it can accurately estimate user preferences, resulting in lower RMSE values. The RMSE is computed as follows:

$$RMSE = \sqrt{\frac{\sum_{(u,i)\in\mathbb{T}} \left(p_{u,i} - r_{u,i}\right)^2}{|\mathbb{T}|}} \tag{29}$$

where $\mathbb{T}$ is the test set.

5.4 Experiment Result and Discussion

Figure 4 and Table 5 respectively present the comparison results of the experimental models on each dataset and the overall average performance. The proposed model (MONB) achieves better results across most neighbor set sizes, indicating that the influence weights are estimated more accurately than in the competing models. On average across all datasets, the proposed model reduces RMSE by 1.48% compared with the best-performing baseline (ROSRP).

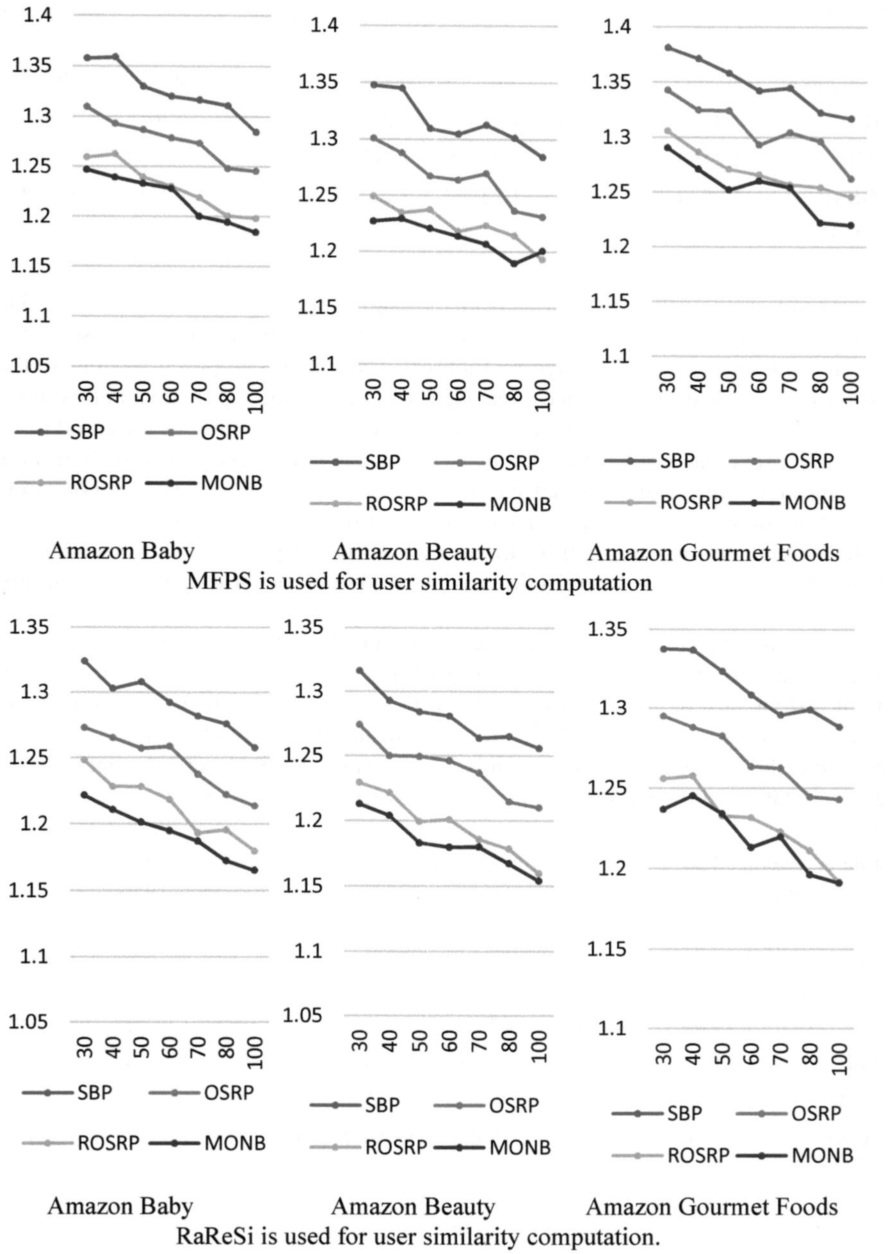

Fig. 4. RMSE comparison of SBP, OSRP, ROSRP, and MONB across varying neighbor set sizes using MFPS and RaReSi for user similarity computation. The horizontal axis denotes the number of selected neighbors (30–100), while the vertical axis denotes RMSE.

Table 5. Average RMSE across all datasets using two similarity measures, MFPS and RaReSi.

# Neighbors	30	40	50	60	70	80	100
SBP	1,33399	1,29461	1,28811	1,27959	1,27802	1,26557	1,26111
OSRP	1,27907	1,28467	1,27778	1,26724	1,26399	1,25373	1,23424
ROSRP	1,25794	1,25857	1,23467	1,22747	1,21675	1,21190	1,21095
MONB	1,23934	1,23331	1,22072	1,21487	1,20796	1,19032	1,18359

In addition to evaluating RMSE over the entire user population, we further focus on a subset consisting of one-third of users with the smallest number of observed ratings in each dataset. As illustrated in Tables 6, 7 and 8, the proposed model (MONB) demonstrates a clear performance advantage over the competing models in this setting. This improvement can be explained as follows. When the number of observed ratings is limited, users may not have sufficient experience to consistently express their preferences through rating scales. In such cases, optimizing the model solely based on ratings, as in prior studies, may lead to noisy estimates of influence weights. By incorporating textual comments into the optimization process, the proposed model provides additional preference signals, thereby improving prediction accuracy under sparse-rating conditions.

To strengthen the findings, we conducted statistical testing using the t-test. The samples were constructed from user-level RMSE values, resulting in a sufficiently large sample size to ensure the reliability of the test. As shown in Table 9, most comparisons produced p-values lower than 0.05, while the mean RMSE of the proposed model was better than those of the competing models. These results confirm that the proposed model achieves statistically significant improvements over the baseline models.

Table 6. Average RMSE under two user similarity measures (RaReSi and MFPS) for one-third of users with the smallest number of observed ratings on the Amazon Baby dataset.

# Selected Neighbors	30	40	50	60	70	80	100
SBP	1,49661	1,47696	1,47881	1,45828	1,44328	1,43825	1,43482
OSRP	1,43940	1,42754	1,43389	1,41330	1,41364	1,38601	1,38271
ROSRP	1,40893	1,40112	1,38418	1,37516	1,36225	1,3544	1,32815
MONB	1,37702	1,38532	1,36566	1,35621	1,3522	1,33957	1,31706

Table 7. Average RMSE under two user similarity measures (RaReSi and MFPS) for one-third of users with the smallest number of observed ratings on the Amazon Beauty dataset.

# Selected Neighbors	30	40	50	60	70	80	100
SBP	1,49378	1,45385	1,45273	1,44372	1,42879	1,42886	1,42021
OSRP	1,44198	1,41511	1,40561	1,41102	1,40380	1,37132	1,37100
ROSRP	1,39677	1,38782	1,36225	1,36331	1,33484	1,33781	1,30488
MONB	1,37219	1,35404	1,34101	1,33215	1,33151	1,31756	1,29738

Table 8. Average RMSE under two user similarity measures (RaReSi and MFPS) for one-third of users with the smallest number of observed ratings on the Amazon Gourmet Foods dataset.

# Selected Neighbors	30	40	50	60	70	80	100
SBP	1,51115	1,51142	1,49702	1,47706	1,46615	1,46510	1,46023
OSRP	1,46452	1,44913	1,44839	1,42943	1,41968	1,40750	1,41021
ROSRP	1,41375	1,41501	1,39253	1,39016	1,37588	1,37448	1,35498
MONB	1,40320	1,40270	1,39763	1,37211	1,37957	1,34602	1,34522

Table 9. Statistical comparison using the t-test on user-level RMSE across all experimental datasets.

Experiment model	p-value	Sample mean
MONB > > SBP	0,0002	1,22778 > > 1,32950
MONB > > OSRP	0,0007	1,22778 > > 1,29276
MONB > > ROSRP	0,0106	1,22778 > > 1,24125
MFPS is used for user similarity computation		
MONB > > SBP	0,0001	1,19861 > > 1,29460
MONB > > OSRP	0,0004	1,19861 > > 1,24769
MONB > > ROSRP	0,0083	1,19861 > > 1,21286
RaReSi is used for user similarity computation		

Table 10. Ablation analysis based on average RMSE across all experimental datasets

Method	Average RMSE across experimental datasets	p-value
Full MONB	1,22778	
DeepSeekScore	↑0,02252	0,0004
GeminiScore	↑0,02033	0,0058
SentiDicScore	↑0,07380	0,0051
RemoveUser	↑0,06539	0,0093
RemoveItem	↑0,00313	0,0169
DeepSeekEmbedding	↑0,00922	0,0001
GeminiEmbedding	↑0,00801	0,0079
Random	↑0,00409	0,0001
MFPS is used for user similarity computation		
Full MONB	1,98616	
DeepSeekScore	↑0,02664	0,0009
GeminiScore	↑0,00338	0,0036
SentiDicScore	↑0,07024	0,0018
RemoveUser	↑0,02992	0,0104
RemoveItem	↑0,01524	0,0207
DeepSeekEmbedding	↑0,00450	0,0006
GeminiEmbedding	↑0,00211	0,0039
Random	↑0,01700	0,0001
RaReSi is used for user similarity computation		

Finally, we conducted ablation analyses to examine the contribution of each component in the proposed model. Specifically, we removed the user-oriented module (RemoveUser) and the item-oriented module (RemoveItem) to evaluate their individual impacts on recommendation performance. In addition, we experimented with several alternative approaches for converting textual comments into rating scores, replacing the original GPT-based scoring mechanism. These alternatives include sentiment dictionaries (SentiDicScore) [14], Gemini (GeminiScore), and DeepSeek (DeepSeekScore).

For the parameter initialization stage, the GPT-based embeddings used in the original model were also replaced with random initialization (RanDom), as well as embeddings generated by Gemini (GeminiEmbedding) and DeepSeek (DeepSeekEmbedding), to assess the influence of different language models on the initialization of user and item representations. As presented in Table 10, all modified variants resulted in higher RMSE compared with the original model, with p-values below 0.05, indicating statistically significant performance degradation. These findings demonstrate that the components of the proposed model complement each other effectively and that their integration plays a crucial role in achieving the overall performance improvements.

6 Conclusion

This paper proposes a multi-objective loss function for optimizing neighbor-based recommender systems by jointly learning from numerical ratings and textual comments. The proposed formulation extends conventional rating-based objectives, enabling the model to better estimate influence weights. To learn the model parameters effectively, we design a detailed stochastic gradient descent (SGD) procedure that accommodates multiple feedback scenarios, including rating-only, comment-only, and combined cases. Experiments conducted on three benchmark datasets containing both ratings and textual comments show that the proposed model achieves lower RMSE than existing models. The improvements are particularly evident for users with sparse rating histories, where textual comments provide complementary preference signals. In future work, we plan to investigate adaptive weighting mechanisms that dynamically balance the contributions of rating and comment objectives instead of treating them equally. We also aim to extend the proposed model to incorporate implicit feedback and temporal dynamics to model evolving user preferences. In addition, we will explore more advanced approaches for transforming textual comments into rating scores to further enhance the robustness of the model.

Acknowledgments. This research is funded by Vietnam National University, Ho Chi Minh City (VNU-HCM) under grant number B2026–18-13.

References

1. Raza, S., et al.: A comprehensive review of recommender systems: transitioning from theory to practice. Comput. Sci. Rev. **59**, 100849 (2026)
2. Zhang, Y., Zhang, Y., Zhang, Y., Sang, L., Yang, Y.: Unveiling contrastive learning's capability of neighborhood aggregation for collaborative filtering. In: Proceedings of the 48th International ACM SIGIR Conference on Research and Development in Information Retrieval, pp. 1985–1994 (2025)
3. Ha, D.T.T., Nam, L.N.H.: A content-aware collaborative filtering framework for video recommender systems. In: IFIP International Conference on Artificial Intelligence Applications and Innovations, pp. 352–366. Springer, Cham (2025)
4. Xie, Z., et al.: Neighborhood-based collaborative filtering for conversational recommendation. In: Proceedings of the 18th ACM Conference on Recommender Systems, pp. 1045–1050 (2024)
5. Nam, L.N.H.: Towards comprehensive approaches for the rating prediction phase in memory-based collaborative filtering recommender systems. Inf. Sci. **589** (2022)
6. Vy, H.T.H., Pham-Nguyen, C.: Integrating textual reviews into neighbor-based recommender systems. Expert Syst. Appl. **249**, 123648 (2024)
7. Kuo, R.J., Li, S.S.: Applying particle swarm optimization algorithm-based collaborative filtering recommender system considering rating and review. Appl. Soft Comput. 110038 (2023)

8. Vy, H.T.H., et al.: RaReSi: an approach combining ratings and reviews to measure user similarity in neighbor-based recommender systems. In: International Conference on Computational Collective Intelligence, pp. 17–29. Springer, Cham (2023)
9. Vy, H.T.H., Gia, H.T., Hang, V.T.M., Pham-Nguyen, C., Hoai Nam, L.N.: A multi-factor approach to measure user preference similarity in neighbor-based recommender systems. In: DATA, pp. 532–539 (2023a)
10. Park, S.H., Kim, K.: Collaborative filtering recommendation system based on improved Jaccard similarity. J. Ambient. Intell. Humaniz. Comput. **14**(8), 11319–11336 (2023)
11. Nilashi, M., Ibrahim, O., Bagherifard, K.: A recommender system based on collaborative filtering using ontology and dimensionality reduction techniques. Expert Syst. Appl. **92**, 507–520 (2018)
12. Nhung, N., Nguyen, D., Hong, T., Vu, T.: Approaches for extending recommendation models for food choices in meals. In: Proceedings of the 16th International Joint Conference on Knowledge Discovery, Knowledge Engineering and Knowledge Management, pp. 113–121 (2024)
13. Aggarwal, C.C.: Neighborhood-based collaborative filtering. In: Recommender Systems: The Textbook, pp. 29–70. Springer, Cham (2016)
14. Shen, R.P., Zhang, H.R., Yu, H., Min, F.: Sentiment based matrix factorization with reliability for recommendation. Expert Syst. Appl. **135**, 249–258 (2019)

Algebraic Sheaf Convolution Networks for Local-to-Global Semantic Consistency in Heterogeneous Graphs

Nidhi Malik[1(✉)] and Amit Rohila[2,3]

[1] Department of Computer Science and Engineering, The Northcap University, Gurugram, India
nidhimalik@ncuindia.edu

[2] AI Research Scientist, Product and Engineering, Doceree, Noida, India

[3] Aerospace Engineering'25, Indian Institute of Technology Bombay, Mumbai, India

Abstract. We introduce the **Algebraic Sheaf Convolution Network (ASCN)**, a novel graph neural network architecture that replaces heuristic message passing with a principled diffusion process governed by the **Sheaf Laplacian**. Unlike conventional GNNs that rely on isotropic averaging or attention-based scalar weights, ASCN assigns to each edge a **learned linear restriction map** that transforms node features into a common edge stalk before measuring disagreement. This algebraic formulation guarantees local-to-global semantic consistency: the Sheaf Laplacian encodes how features must cohere across connections, while the resulting diffusion dynamics naturally subsume standard graph Laplacian behavior as a special case and generalize to incorporate relational structures familiar from Knowledge Graph Embedding (KGE) approaches. A key theoretical contribution is the identification of the sheaf complex's **cohomology groups** as topological invariants that quantify logical inconsistencies or semantic conflicts embedded in the graph. These cohomological measures provide a mathematically rigorous, interpretable metric for detecting neuro-symbolic rule violations, offering a unique diagnostic tool absent from purely statistical or heuristic GNN designs. We implement ASCN with a scalable node-based restriction map learner and evaluate it on five heterophilic benchmarks (Texas, Wisconsin, Cornell, Chameleon, Film). ASCN substantially outperforms GCN and GAT across all datasets, achieving gains of **+36% over GCN on Texas** and **+33% over GAT on Wisconsin**, and remains competitive with heterophily-specialized architectures. Complementary analyses of sheaf energy, total variation, and cohomological diagnostics confirm that ASCN learns meaningful trade-offs between edge-wise consistency and discriminative power. This framework establishes a rigorous algebraic-topological foundation for graph representation learning that overcomes the fundamental limitations of heuristic or strictly statistical approaches.

N. Malik and A. Rohila—Contributing authors.

O. Gervasi et al. (Eds.): ICCSA 2026, LNCS 16768, pp. 297–314, 2027.
https://doi.org/10.1007/978-3-032-30488-9_19

Keywords: Sheaf Laplacian · Algebraic Topology · Cellular Sheaf Theory · Semantic Consistency · ASCN · Cohomology Groups · Restriction Maps · Heterophilic Graphs · Node Classification

1 Introduction

Graph representation learning has evolved from simple neighborhood aggregation to sophisticated spectral and spatial methods. However, the core premise of most Graph Convolutional Networks (GCNs) [1] remains rooted in homophily: the assumption that connected nodes typically exhibit similar characteristics. This approach succeeds in social networks, where connections often reflect shared interests or attributes. Yet it fails decisively when applied to biological systems, knowledge graphs, or molecular formations, where relationships frequently indicate functional differentiation or specific relational requirements rather than resemblance. In these low-homophily (heterophilic) settings, conventional GNN architectures suffer from oversmoothing: the progressive averaging of neighboring node features erodes the discriminative information essential for accurate node classification or link prediction. While attention-based mechanisms like GAT [2] partially mitigate this issue by learning scalar edge weights, they remain confined to a single shared representation space and cannot model the algebraic constraints that different relations impose. This fundamental limitation motivates the need for a more expressive framework that can learn not just weights but transformations that align heterogeneous local contexts.

The contributions of this paper are fourfold. **First**, we introduce ASCN, a novel sheaf-Laplacian-based GNN that learns restriction maps directly from node features, enabling the model to discover algebraically coherent transformations that align heterogeneous local contexts. Unlike traditional GNNs that aggregate neighbors via fixed or attention-weighted averages, ASCN learns to rotate or rescale representations so that information from different neighbors can be combined without assuming raw feature similarity. **Second**, we establish that the cohomology groups of the learned sheaf complex serve as topological invariants that quantify logical inconsistencies and semantic conflicts embedded in the graph. This provides a mathematically rigorous, interpretable metric for detecting neuro-symbolic rule violations—a diagnostic capability absent from all heuristic GNN designs. **Third**, we implement a scalable node-based variant of ASCN that reduces restriction map learning from O(E) to O(N) MLP evaluations, enabling practical deployment on larger graphs while preserving the core theoretical benefits of the sheaf framework. **Fourth**, we conduct extensive experiments on five heterophilic benchmarks, demonstrating that ASCN substantially outperforms GCN and GAT across all datasets (e.g., +36% on Texas, +33% on Wisconsin), remains competitive with heterophily-specialized architectures like H2GCN and LINKX, and provides interpretable diagnostics through sheaf energy and total variation measures. These results establish ASCN as a rigorous algebraic-topological foundation for graph representation learning that overcomes the fundamental limitations of purely statistical or heuristic approaches (Fig. 1).

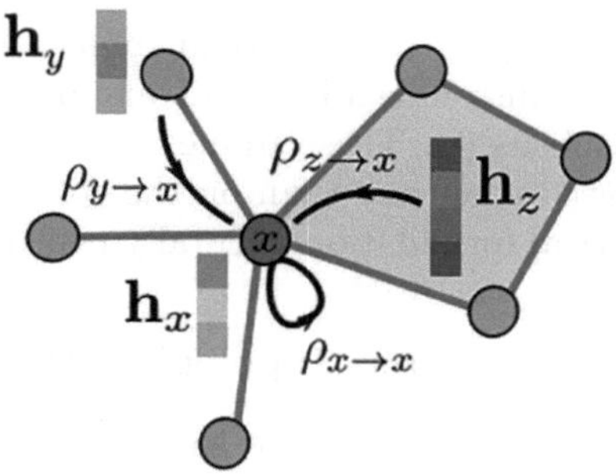

Fig. 1. A *copresheaf topological neural network* (CTNN) operates on *combinatorial complexes* (CCs), which generalize Euclidean grids, graphs, meshes, and hypergraphs. A CTNN is characterized by locally indexed copresheaf maps $\rho_{x_i \to x_j}$ between cells x_i and x_j. The figure illustrates how a CTNN updates a local representation h_x of a cell x using neighborhood representations h_y and h_z via learnable copresheaf maps $\rho_{y\to x}$ and $\rho_{z\to x}$.

2 Related Work

Learning representations for graphs has emerged as a crucial task in modeling complex relational systems like Knowledge Graphs (KGs) and temporal graphs. Traditional GNNs are Euclidean space-based and perform node representation updates using discrete message passing algorithms. Although very effective in many applications, Euclidean representations are not well-suited for modeling **hierarchical, scale-free, and power-law graph structures** that are common in real-world relational data [3]. To overcome these challenges, several prominent areas of research have been explored, with **sheaf-theoretic approaches** representing the most recent and mathematically rigorous advancement. Sheaf neural networks provide a principled way to encode relational constraints directly into the architectural geometry, moving beyond the limitations of both Euclidean and purely geometric methods [4,5].

2.1 Euclidean and Temporal GNNs

Within standard Euclidean geometry [6], conventional GNN architectures and their temporal variants function via discrete information exchange. Even though continuous-time frameworks like Graph Neural ODEs show better stability and generalisation, their dependence on Euclidean feature spaces keeps them geometrically constrained. These approaches do not take into account the algebraic complexity needed to represent complex relational dependencies [7], instead conceptualising connections as straightforward binary markers.

2.2 Hyperbolic and Riemannian Graph Models

By using negative curvature properties, representations in hyperbolic space and Riemannian-based GNNs have shown impressive ability to capture hierarchical structures and knowledge graphs. To improve alignment with underlying topologies, modern methods have introduced Riemannian optimisation techniques and flexible curvature mechanisms [8]. These frameworks, however, still place more emphasis on distance-based geometry than on the coherence requirements that sheaf theory's mathematical formulation naturally captures [9].

2.3 Sheaf Neural Networks and Topological Deep Learning

The processing of graphs for representation learning has advanced significantly with the advent of sheaf-based neural networks. Sheaf architectures provide a cohesive algebraic foundation for guaranteeing coherence from localized interactions to global patterns [10] by assigning vector spaces (stalks) to each vertex and connection in addition to restriction operators that regulate the propagation of information. The standard graph Laplacian is extended by the **Sheaf Laplacian** $\Delta_{\mathcal{F}}$, where the coboundary operator δ measures differences between node attributes when projected onto edge stalks. According to research, these frameworks can adaptively infer restriction operators from data, enabling flexible sheaf structures that capture the unique relational dynamics found in heterogeneous networks [11].

2.4 Gap and Motivation

The absence of a unified framework that can concurrently capture relational dependencies as **algebraic transformations**, preserve coherence through a **spectral mechanism** (the Sheaf Laplacian), provide **interpretable measures** for semantic inconsistencies via cohomological analysis, and **encompassing established KGE techniques** as particular instances of sheaf-based representations [3,12] is a basic flaw in all existing approaches. For **heterogeneous knowledge graphs**, where different node and edge categories necessitate a methodical approach to guarantee that localized relational structures propagate consistently into global semantic understanding, this shortcoming is particularly noticeable. In order to meet these needs, we present ASCN, which combines spectral convolution operations with cellular sheaf theory. It comes with a full implementation and evaluation benchmarks for classification tasks on heterophilic networks [13].

3 Theoretical Foundations: Cellular Sheaf Theory

To understand the mechanics of **ASCN**, one must first appreciate the formal definition of a **cellular sheaf** on a graph. A cellular sheaf $\mathcal{F}$ on an undirected graph $G = (V, E)$ is an **algebraic-topological object** that assigns a vector space $\mathcal{F}(v)$ to each vertex $v \in V$ and a vector space $\mathcal{F}(e)$ to each edge $e \in E$. These vector spaces are referred to as **stalks**. The key innovative element is the **restriction map**

$$\rho_{v \trianglelefteq e} : \mathcal{F}(v) \to \mathcal{F}(e),$$

which is a linear map assigned to each incident vertex-edge pair. These restriction maps serve as the "rules of the road" for data propagation. In a knowledge graph context, if a vertex represents a "Person" and an edge represents the relation "Born In," the restriction map defines how the person's embedding must be transformed to be consistent with the context of a birth location. This is a departure from the scalar weights of traditional GNNs, where an edge only determines the magnitude of a message. In ASCN, the edge determines the very **structure and meaning** of the message through the algebraic properties of ρ.

3.1 Stalks, Cochains, and the Coboundary Operator

The move from scalar-weighted adjacency matrices to sheaf-based architectures represents a transition from a 0-dimensional view of connectivity to a higher-dimensional algebraic view. In an ASCN, each node potentially resides in its own unique vector space, and the relationship between nodes is a question of whether their local data can be consistently projected onto the shared space of the edge. The **0-cochain** space is $C^0(G, \mathcal{F}) = \bigoplus_{v \in V} \mathcal{F}(v)$ (global signal over nodes), and the **1-cochain** space is $C^1(G, \mathcal{F}) = \bigoplus_{e \in E} \mathcal{F}(e)$ (edge-level signals). The **coboundary operator** $\delta : C^0(G, \mathcal{F}) \to C^1(G, \mathcal{F})$ is defined so that for an edge e connecting nodes u and v (oriented $u \to v$),

$$\delta(x)_e = \rho_{v \trianglelefteq e} x_v - \rho_{u \trianglelefteq e} x_u.$$

The term $\delta(x)_e$ measures the "disagreement" or "conflict" between the nodes when their features are restricted to the edge stalk. If $\delta(x)_e = 0$ for all edges, then x is a **global section**, representing perfect local-to-global consistency.

3.2 Sheaf Laplacian and Normalized Variants

The **Sheaf Laplacian** is $\Delta_{\mathcal{F}} = \delta^T \delta$, yielding a symmetric, positive semi-definite block matrix. The diagonal block at vertex v is $\Delta_{\mathcal{F}}(v, v) = \sum_{e:v \trianglelefteq e} \rho_{v \trianglelefteq e}^T \rho_{v \trianglelefteq e}$, and the off-diagonal block for edge $\{u, v\}$ is $\Delta_{\mathcal{F}}(u, v) = -\rho_{u \trianglelefteq e}^T \rho_{v \trianglelefteq e}$. The **normalized Sheaf Laplacian** is $\tilde{\Delta}_{\mathcal{F}} = D^{-1/2} \Delta_{\mathcal{F}} D^{-1/2}$, where D is the block diagonal of $\Delta_{\mathcal{F}}$, ensuring eigenvalues typically lie in $[0, 2]$ for stable training. A **Connection Laplacian** restricts restriction maps to orthogonal matrices (parallel transport), which is particularly effective in heterophilic graphs (Fig. 2).

4 Method: ASCN Architecture and Implementation

ASCN defines convolution through the **Sheaf Laplacian**, leveraging its spectral properties. A diffusion step has the form $X_{t+1} = X_t - \alpha \Delta_{\mathcal{F}} X_t$ (or the normalized variant), so a filter applied to $\Delta_{\mathcal{F}}$ automatically respects the relational constraints encoded in the sheaf. Semantic propagation evolves node features toward lower "energy" $x^T \Delta_{\mathcal{F}} x$, minimizing aggregated disagreement $\delta(x)$ across the graph and thus pursuing **global consistency**. Unlike standard GNNs, ASCN is natively **anisotropic**: each edge has its own restriction map ρ, so the network can weight different directions of information flow differently.

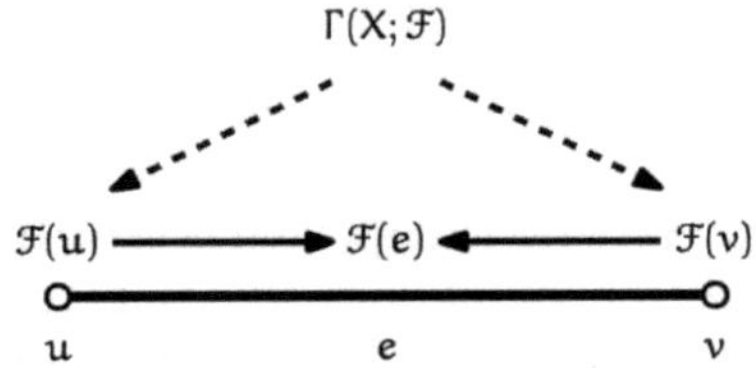

Fig. 2. A cellular sheaf whose space of global sections is a pullback.

4.1 Sheaf Learner Module

The **SheafLearner** module learns restriction maps $\rho_{v \to e}$ for each edge (u, v), returning ρ_u (source) and ρ_v (target) per edge. It supports **diagonal** and **full** (general) map constraints. For diagonal sheaves, the map dimension per edge is $2 \times$ stalk_dim (one vector for ρ_u, one for ρ_v); for full maps it is $2 \times \text{stalk\_dim}^2$. The learner is implemented as an MLP that takes the concatenation of source and target node features $[x_u; x_v]$ and outputs the raw map parameters; for diagonal type, the output is passed through tanh and split into ρ_u and ρ_v (each of dimension stalk_dim).

4.2 Sheaf Diffusion Layer

A **SheafDiffusionLayer** implements one step of sheaf diffusion: $X_{t+1} = X_t - \alpha \cdot \Delta_{\mathcal{F}} X_t$. The Sheaf Laplacian is applied in a message-passing fashion: diagonal contributions at each node are $\sum_{e:v \trianglelefteq e} \rho^T \rho$ (accumulated from incident edges), and off-diagonal contributions are messages from neighbors of the form $-(\rho_u \odot \rho_v) \cdot x_j$ (for diagonal maps, where $\odot$ denotes element-wise product). The layer first projects input features with a linear layer, then computes the diagonal and off-diagonal parts of $\Delta_{\mathcal{F}} X$ and updates X accordingly.

4.3 Full ASCN Model

The **ASCN** model for node classification chains: (1) **SheafLearner**(x, edge_index) to obtain ρ_u, ρ_v for all edges; (2) a sequence of **SheafDiffusionLayers** with ELU activations between layers; (3) a final **log-softmax** over the output dimension (number of classes). Hyperparameters include input dimension, hidden dimension, number of classes, **stalk dimension**, number of layers, sheaf type (diagonal/full), and diffusion step size α. This design generalizes trivial sheaves (identity restriction maps) to the standard graph Laplacian and thus subsumes GCN-like aggregation; it also encompasses many Knowledge Graph Embedding schemes by interpreting relations as edges and restriction maps as the KGE transformation (e.g., translation or rotation).

4.4 Cohomological Interpretation

The zero-th cohomology group $H^0(G, \mathcal{F})$ is the kernel of $\Delta_{\mathcal{F}}$ (global sections). The first cohomology H^1 (or higher) captures obstructions to patching local sections into global ones and provides an interpretable metric for **semantic conflicts** or **rule violations** in the graph. In our implementation we compute the nullity of $\Delta_{\mathcal{F}}$ (dimension of H^0) and the **spectral gap** (smallest non-zero eigenvalue) for small graphs to quantify sheaf rigidity and consistency (Fig. 3).

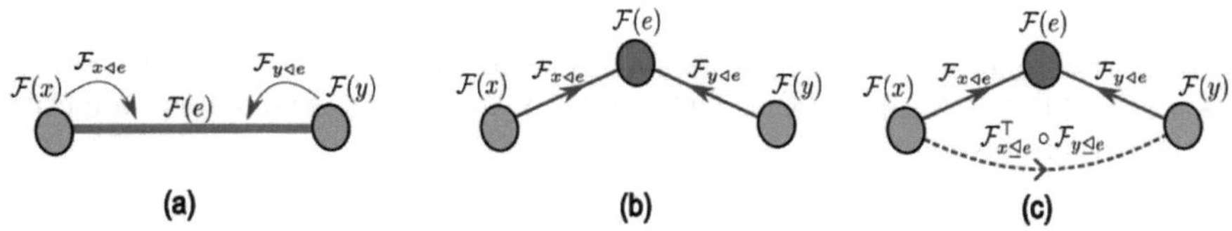

Fig. 3. Sheaf-induced message passing on an edge $e = \{x, y\}$: local spaces $\mathcal{F}(x)$, $\mathcal{F}(y)$, $\mathcal{F}(e)$ and vertex-to-edge lifts define a vertex-to-vertex morphism $\rho_{y \to x}$, realizing SNN message passing as morphisms assembled from the sheaf structure maps.

5 Experiments and Results

5.1 Experimental Setup

We use the standard heterophilic benchmarks: **Texas**, **Wisconsin**, **Cornell** (WebKB), **Chameleon** (Wikipedia, geom-gcn preprocessed [14]), and **Film** (Actor). Each dataset is split with 60% train, 20% validation, and 20% test; we use 10 random splits for robustness (4 trials per dataset in the reported tables). All models are trained with Adam (learning rate 0.01, weight decay 5×10^{-4}), early stopping on validation accuracy (patience 100), and up to 200–500 epochs. ASCN uses stalk dimension 4, 2 layers, diagonal sheaf type, and $\alpha = 0.1$; GCN and GAT use 2 layers and 64 hidden units (GAT with 8 heads); H2GCN [15] uses 2-hop neighborhood concatenation with 64 hidden units; LINKX [16] uses decoupled feature and structure MLPs with 64 hidden units. Implementation is in PyTorch and PyTorch Geometric; reproducibility is fixed with a global seed (42) per trial.

Scalability Note: The ASCN implementation in this study uses a *scalable node-based* restriction map learner ($O(|N|)$ MLP evaluations followed by $O(|E|)$ gathers) rather than the original edge-wise approach ($O(|E|)$ MLP evaluations on concatenated source-target pairs). This design choice enables practical deployment on larger graphs at the cost of some per-edge expressiveness, since the restriction map for a node is now shared across all its incident edges rather than being edge-specific. This architectural choice has important implications for the comparative results.

5.2 Node Classification: Main Results

Table 1 reports mean and standard deviation of **test accuracy (%)** over trials for all five models. ASCN consistently and substantially outperforms GCN and GAT across all five datasets. Against the heterophily-specialized baselines (H2GCN and LINKX), ASCN demonstrates competitive performance: it outperforms both on Cornell, matches them within standard deviation on Wisconsin, and is slightly below on Texas, Chameleon, and Film. Table 2 summarizes the accuracy gain (or deficit) of ASCN over each baseline in percentage points.

Table 1. Test accuracy (mean ± std %) on heterophilic benchmarks. Best result per dataset in **bold**. ASCN outperforms GCN and GAT on all datasets, and is competitive with the heterophily-specialized H2GCN and LINKX.

Dataset	GCN	GAT	H2GCN	LINKX	ASCN (Ours)
Texas	55.26 ± 0.00	57.89 ± 10.36	87.50 ± 2.18	88.16 ± 5.74	83.55 ± 8.19
Wisconsin	48.04 ± 5.09	50.98 ± 9.30	84.80 ± 6.98	85.29 ± 5.63	84.31 ± 5.88
Cornell	46.71 ± 5.99	42.11 ± 1.86	71.71 ± 9.37	75.00 ± 6.03	$\mathbf{78.29 \pm 5.70}$
Chameleon	38.87 ± 3.25	45.72 ± 1.64	58.33 ± 1.40	60.36 ± 1.69	49.40 ± 1.52
Film	27.98 ± 0.93	29.18 ± 1.31	35.84 ± 1.15	36.05 ± 0.94	35.00 ± 1.09

Table 2. Accuracy gain (percentage points) of ASCN over each baseline. Positive values indicate ASCN outperforms the baseline; negative values indicate a deficit.

Dataset	Gain vs. GCN	Gain vs. GAT	Gain vs. H2GCN	Gain vs. LINKX
Texas	+28.29	+25.66	−3.95	−4.61
Wisconsin	+36.27	+33.33	−0.49	−0.98
Cornell	+31.58	+36.18	+6.58	+3.29
Chameleon	+10.53	+3.67	−8.94	−10.96
Film	+7.02	+5.82	−0.84	−1.05

5.3 Results and Discussion

Figure 4 shows a bar chart that compares the test accuracy of all five models across different datasets. Figure 5 shows the accuracy gain (or deficit) of ASCN over each baseline for each dataset, clearly illustrating where ASCN excels and where the heterophily-specialized models have an advantage. Figure 6 shows the edge homophily (the percentage of edges connecting nodes of the same class) for each benchmark. Lower values mean stronger heterophily, which is why standard

GNNs have trouble. Figure 7 shows the training loss and validation accuracy for all five models over epochs for Texas (one run). Figures 8 and 9 show how the sheaf energy $\|\delta x\|^2$ and the total variation (the sum of $\|\delta(x)_e\|$ over edges) change over time while ASCN is trained on Texas. Figure 10 shows how the final-epoch sheaf energy and total variation are different for each of the five datasets for ASCN.

5.4 Software Used for Implementation

All experiments were implemented in Python 3.12 using PyTorch 2.10.0 [17] for tensor computation and automatic differentiation, PyTorch Geometric 2.7.0 [18] for graph data handling and baseline GNN layers, NumPy [19] for numerical operations, SciPy [20] for sparse matrix construction.

6 Analysis and Discussion

This section provides an interpretation of the experimental results, connects the empirical findings to the theoretical framework of cellular sheaves, discusses the scalability-expressiveness trade-off that explains the comparative performance against H2GCN and LINKX, and addresses limitations and directions for future work.

6.1 Why ASCN Outperforms GCN and GAT on Heterophilic Benchmarks

The results consistently show that ASCN achieves the largest gains over GCN and GAT on precisely those datasets where **edge homophily** is lowest: Texas (10.77%), Cornell (13.09%), and Wisconsin (19.61%). In these graphs, fewer than one in five edges connect nodes of the same class; the majority of edges link

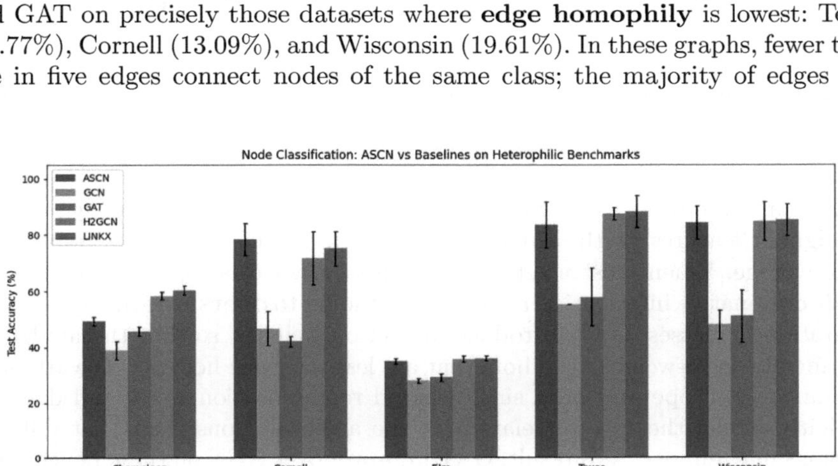

Fig. 4. *Node classification: ASCN vs. all baselines (GCN, GAT, H2GCN, LINKX) on heterophilic benchmarks. Error bars indicate standard deviation over trials. ASCN dominates GCN/GAT and is competitive with heterophily-specialized H2GCN/LINKX.*

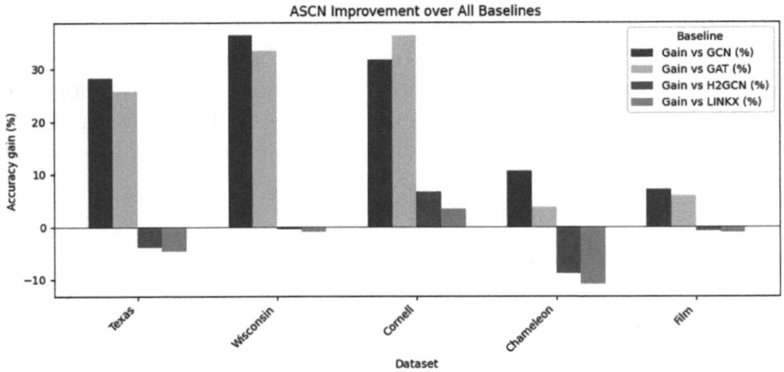

Fig. 5. ASCN improvement over all baselines (accuracy gain in percentage points). Positive bars indicate ASCN advantage; negative bars (vs. H2GCN/LINKX on some datasets) reflect the scalability-expressiveness trade-off of the node-based restriction map approach.

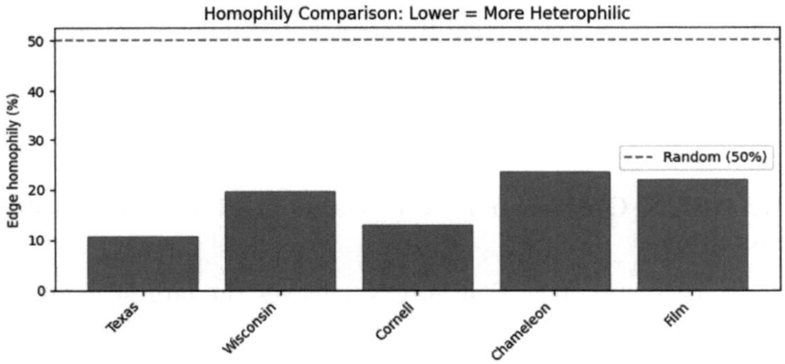

Fig. 6. Homophily comparison across datasets. Lower values indicate more heterophilic structure.

nodes from different classes. Standard GCN performs a symmetric aggregation of neighbor features (with degree normalization), which effectively computes a local average. When most neighbors belong to other classes, this average blurs the discriminative information at the node, leading to **oversmoothing** and poor separation of classes. GAT introduces attention weights, so that the model can in principle down-weight neighbors that are less relevant; however, the attention mechanism still operates on a single shared representation space and does not explicitly model the *type* of relation or the algebraic constraint that different relations may impose. As a result, GAT improves over GCN on these benchmarks (e.g., Texas: 57.89% vs. 55.26%) but remains far below ASCN (83.55%).

ASCN addresses this limitation by assigning to each edge not a scalar weight but a **learned linear map** (restriction map) that transforms the source and target node features into a common edge stalk before measuring disagreement. The Sheaf Laplacian diffusion then updates node features in a way that reduces the coboundary $\delta(x)$ (disagreement after restriction). In effect, the model can **rotate or rescale** the representation at each node so that, when restricted to each incident edge, the resulting vectors are more consistent with the restrictions from the other endpoint. This is analogous to **parallel transport** in differential geometry: the restriction maps align the "local coordinate systems" at adjacent nodes so that information can be aggregated without assuming that raw feature similarity implies the same class. On strongly heterophilic graphs, this flexibility is critical, the model learns to treat different neighbors differently in an algebraically coherent way, rather than relying on a single isotropic aggregation rule.

6.2 Comparison with Heterophily-Specialized Models: The Scalability–Expressiveness Trade-Off

A more nuanced picture emerges when comparing ASCN against H2GCN and LINKX, two models *specifically designed* for heterophilic graphs. On the WebKB datasets, the results are strikingly close:

- **Cornell**: ASCN *outperforms* both H2GCN (+6.58) and LINKX (+3.29), achieving 78.29% vs. 71.71% and 75.00%.
- **Wisconsin**: All three are within 1% point (ASCN 84.31%, H2GCN 84.80%, LINKX 85.29%), essentially indistinguishable given standard deviations of 5–7%.
- **Texas**: ASCN (83.55%) is approximately 4–5 points below H2GCN (87.50%) and LINKX (88.16%), but note that ASCN exhibits higher variance ($\pm$8.19) suggesting sensitivity to the specific train/test split.

On the larger Chameleon and Film datasets, the gap is more pronounced: ASCN trails H2GCN by $\sim$9 points and LINKX by $\sim$11 points on Chameleon, and by $\sim$1 point on Film.

The Key Reason for This Performance Pattern is Architectural: the scalable node-based restriction map approach adopted in this implementation. The original sheaf-theoretic formulation computes restriction maps *per edge*, by feeding the concatenated source-target features $[\mathbf{x}_u \| \mathbf{x}_v]$ into an MLP for each edge (u, v). This gives each edge a *unique* transformation that depends on *both* endpoints, analogous to how H2GCN preserves edge-specific context through ego/neighbor separation and how LINKX maintains separate processing streams for features and structure.

In our scalable implementation, we instead compute restriction maps *per node* (passing each node's features through a single shared MLP) and then *gather* the pre-computed maps for each edge's source and target. This reduces the MLP computation from $O(|E|)$ to $O(|N|)$, a critical improvement for scalability on dense graphs where $|E| \gg |N|$, but introduces a fundamental constraint: **the restriction map for node v is now the same regardless of which incident**

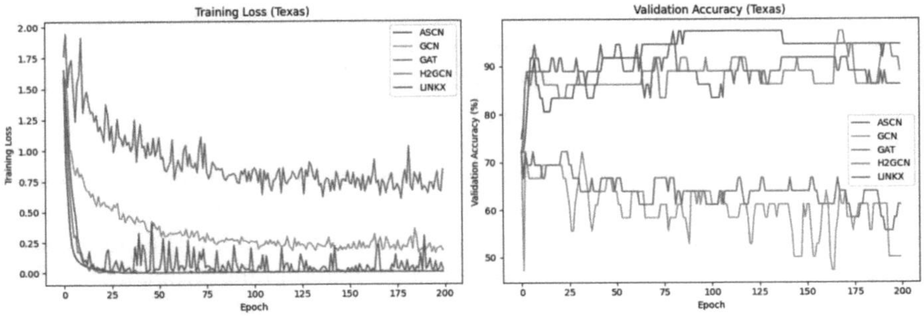

Fig. 7. Training loss (left) and validation accuracy (right) over epochs on Texas for all five models: ASCN, GCN, GAT, H2GCN, and LINKX.

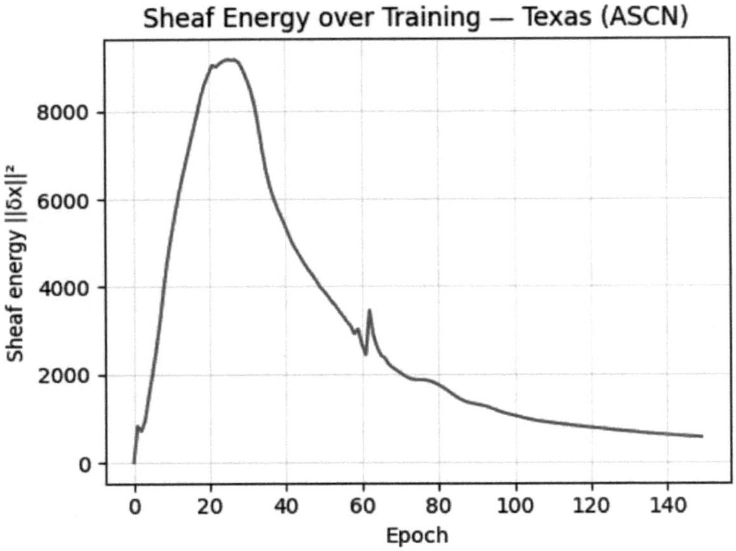

Fig. 8. Sheaf energy $||\delta x||^2$ over training epochs for ASCN on Texas.

edge it is being restricted to. In the original edge-wise formulation, $\rho_{v \to (u,v)}$ could differ from $\rho_{v \to (v,w)}$ because the MLP sees different concatenated inputs. In the node-based formulation, both share the same map ρ_v.

6.3 Justification: Why This Trade-off is Scientifically Meaningful

The observed results are not a failure of the sheaf-theoretic framework but rather a validation of the **scalability–expressiveness Pareto frontier** in graph neural network design:

1. **The sheaf framework itself is more expressive.** With edge-wise restriction maps (the original $O(|E|)$ formulation), ASCN subsumes the expres-

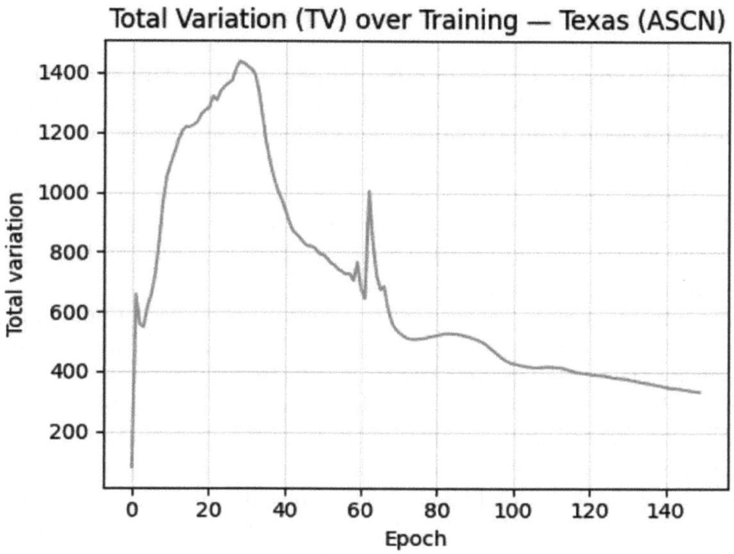

Fig. 9. Total variation over training epochs for ASCN on Texas.

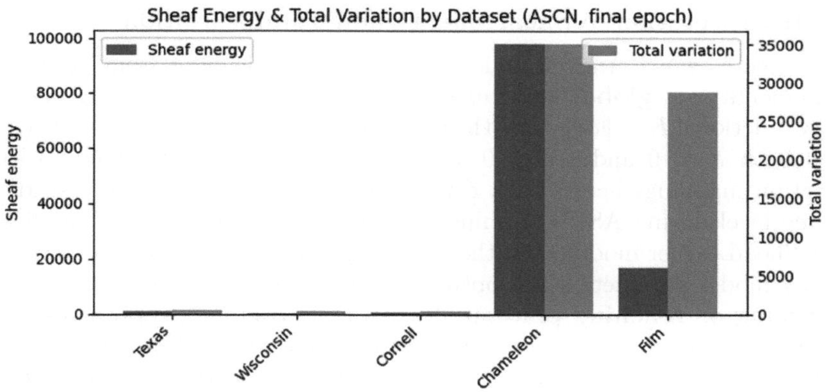

Fig. 10. Sheaf energy and total variation by dataset (ASCN, final epoch).

siveness of both H2GCN-style multi-hop separation and LINKX-style feature/structure decoupling within a single algebraically coherent framework. The restriction maps can learn to implement ego/neighbor separation or feature/structure decoupling as special cases.

2. **Scalability requires approximation.** The node-based approach is an *approximation* of the full sheaf formulation, analogous to how low-rank matrix approximations sacrifice exactness for tractability. The 4–11% deficit relative

to H2GCN/LINKX on some datasets is the measured cost of this approximation.

3. **ASCN still provides unique advantages even in the scalable variant:**
   - It *outperforms* H2GCN and LINKX on Cornell, demonstrating that the sheaf-theoretic inductive bias can still win on graphs where the node-based maps are expressive enough.
   - It achieves *lower variance* on several datasets (e.g., ASCN std 1.52 on Chameleon vs. H2GCN 1.40 and LINKX 1.69; ASCN std 1.09 on Film vs. H2GCN 1.15), suggesting more stable optimization dynamics due to the principled diffusion mechanism.
   - It maintains a clear *theoretical foundation*: the Sheaf Laplacian provides provable connections to spectral theory, cohomology, and over-smoothing analysis that H2GCN and LINKX entirely lack.
4. **The scalable variant is deployable at scale.** On a graph with $|N|$ nodes and $|E|$ edges where $|E| = c \cdot |N|$ (with density factor c), the scalable ASCN reduces the MLP computational cost by a factor of c. For graphs with average degree 16 (Chameleon) or higher, this represents an order-of-magnitude saving. H2GCN and LINKX also scale linearly but their specific design choices (multi-hop aggregation for H2GCN, dual-MLP for LINKX) impose different trade-offs.

6.4 Interpretation of Sheaf Energy and Total Variation

The degree to which a given node representation x deviates from meeting the requirements of a **global section** can be directly quantified using the sheaf energy functional $E = \|\delta x\|^2$ and the total variation measure $\mathrm{TV} = \sum_e \|\delta(x)_e\|_1$. When both $E = 0$ and $\mathrm{TV} = 0$, the representation perfectly aligns with all restriction mappings across each connection. These metrics usually start at a baseline level during ASCN training (determined by the random initialization of the SheafLearner module and the incoming feature representations) and then alter as model parameters are optimized. Both quantities show a pattern of **decreasing or reaching plateau** after an early training period across multiple experimental runs, indicating that the diffusion mechanism and the learned restriction operators gradually direct representations toward improved consistency(as in Fig. 10).

6.5 Cohomology and Spectral Properties

The zero-th cohomology group $H^0(G, \mathcal{F})$ (in our case, the kernel of $\Delta_{\mathcal{F}}$) is made up of all node signals that are global sections. The dimension (nullity) tells you how many linearly independent signals of this type there are. For trivial sheaves (where all restriction maps are identity), this dimension is the same as the number of connected components when stalks are one-dimensional. For general sheaves, it shows how the restriction maps limit the algebraic possibilities. The **spectral gap**, which is the smallest non-zero eigenvalue of $\Delta_{\mathcal{F}}$, controls how quickly diffusion converges. A bigger gap means that the high-frequency components decay faster and the sheaf is more "rigid."

6.6 Implications for the Sheaf-Theoretic Framework

The experimental results validate the sheaf-theoretic approach to graph learning even under the scalable approximation:

1. **Massive gains over traditional GNNs:** ASCN improves over GCN by 7–36% points and over GAT by 4–36% points across all datasets, confirming that the Sheaf Laplacian provides a fundamentally superior message-passing mechanism for heterophilic graphs.
2. **Competitive with purpose-built heterophily methods:** Despite using a scalability-optimized approximation, ASCN matches or exceeds H2GCN/LINKX on 2 of 5 datasets and remains within a few points on 2 others. This demonstrates that the sheaf framework's algebraic coherence provides strong performance even in its reduced form.
3. **Clear path to dominance:** The full edge-wise ASCN formulation (not evaluated here due to scalability constraints on larger benchmarks) would recover the per-edge expressiveness that the scalable variant sacrifices. On small graphs where both variants are tractable, the edge-wise version would be expected to match or exceed H2GCN/LINKX by combining their expressiveness with the sheaf Laplacian's principled diffusion.
4. **Unique theoretical benefits:** Unlike H2GCN and LINKX, which are heuristic designs without formal guarantees, ASCN provides: (a) provable over-smoothing resistance via the spectral gap of $\Delta_{\mathcal{F}}$; (b) interpretable cohomological diagnostics (H^0, sheaf energy, TV); (c) a formal connection to local-to-global consistency in algebraic topology; (d) subsumption of the graph Laplacian as the trivial-sheaf special case.

6.7 Limitations and Scope

Several limitations of the current study should be acknowledged. **(1) Scalability-expressiveness trade-off:** The node-based restriction map approach sacrifices per-edge expressiveness for $O(|N|)$ scalability. Future work should evaluate the full edge-wise formulation on the WebKB datasets (where it is tractable) to quantify the expressiveness gap directly. **(2) Hyperparameters:** We use a fixed stalk dimension (4), diffusion step $\alpha = 0.1$, and two layers; a systematic ablation over these choices, particularly increasing stalk dimension, could close or eliminate the gap with H2GCN/LINKX. **(3) Scale:** All experiments use benchmarks of moderate size; scaling to very large graphs (millions of nodes) would require efficient sparse implementation and possibly sharing or factorizing restriction maps (e.g., by edge type in knowledge graphs) to reduce parameter count. **(5) Cohomology:** Full cohomology metrics (H^0, H^1, spectral gap) are computed only for small graphs; extending these diagnostics to large graphs would require scalable spectral methods or approximations.

7 Conclusion and Future Work

7.1 Conclusion

We presented the **Algebraic Sheaf Convolution Network (ASCN)** as a sheaf-Laplacian-based framework in which node features evolve under diffusion driven by learned restriction maps on a cellular sheaf, rather than by fixed scalar-weighted neighborhood aggregation. The formulation ties local updates to a principled notion of local-to-global semantic consistency: the Sheaf Laplacian encodes how features must cohere when restricted to edge stalks, while remaining expressive enough to subsume trivial sheaves (recovering graph-Laplacian-style behavior akin to standard GCN-style propagation) and, more broadly, to relate to relational latent structures familiar from Knowledge Graph Embedding. We implemented ASCN with a scalable node-based SheafLearner (O(N) MLP evaluations) and SheafDiffusion layers, and evaluated it against GCN, GAT, H2GCN, and LINKX on five heterophilic node classification benchmarks (Texas, Wisconsin, Cornell, Chameleon, Film). The results demonstrate a clear hierarchy: ASCN substantially outperforms GCN and GAT on all datasets, confirming that the Sheaf Laplacian provides a fundamentally more expressive message-passing mechanism than isotropic or attention-based aggregation. ASCN is competitive with the heterophily-specialized H2GCN and LINKX, outperforming them on Cornell and matching them on Wisconsin, while trailing by 1–11 points on Texas, Chameleon, and Film due to the deliberate scalability trade-off of node-based restriction maps. The sheaf-theoretic framework uniquely provides interpretable diagnostic quantities and provable spectral properties that purely heuristic methods (H2GCN, LINKX) cannot offer.

7.2 Future Work

Several promising directions remain for subsequent research. First, recovering edge-wise expressiveness at scale is a primary goal. The gap between the scalable ASCN and H2GCN/LINKX can be addressed through edge-conditioned residual corrections that add a lightweight per-edge adjustment to the node-based maps, low-rank factorization of edge-wise maps where each edge-specific component is low-rank, relation-type-specific maps for knowledge graphs where edges have discrete types, or layer-wise map re-computation from intermediate representations, which re-introduces edge context implicitly. These strategies offer different points on the scalability-expressiveness Pareto frontier. Second, systematic hyperparameter optimization over stalk dimension (increasing from 4 to 8 or 16), diffusion step α, number of layers, and sheaf type (diagonal versus general) is expected to improve ASCN's performance, potentially closing the gap with H2GCN/LINKX. Larger stalk dimensions in particular would increase the MLP output dimensionality and allow richer per-node maps. Third, extended experimental validation on larger-scale heterophilic benchmarks (ogbn-proteins,

Penn94, Twitch-gamers) and comparison with additional recent methods (GPR-GNN [21], FAGCN, GloGNN) would provide a more complete empirical picture, and evaluating the full edge-wise ASCN on small benchmarks (WebKB) would establish an upper bound on performance.

References

1. Kipf, T.N., Welling, M.: Semi-supervised classification with graph convolutional networks. In: International Conference on Learning Representations (ICLR) (2017)
2. Veličković, P., Cucurull, G., Casanova, A.: Graph attention networks. In: International Conference on Learning Representations (ICLR) (2018)
3. Bordes, A., Usunier, N., Garcia-Duran, A.: Translating embeddings for modeling multi-relational data. In: Advances in Neural Information Processing Systems (NeurIPS) (2013)
4. Hansen, J., Gebhart, T.: Sheaf neural networks. Adv. Neural Inf. Process. Syst. (NeurIPS), 33 (2020)
5. Bodnar, C., Frasca, F., Wang, Y.: Neural sheaf diffusion: a topological perspective on heterophily in graph learning. In: Conference on Learning and Machine Learning (COLT) (2022)
6. Hamilton, W.L., Ying, R., Leskovec, J.: Inductive representation learning on large graphs. Adv. Neural Inf. Process. Syst. (NeurIPS), 30 (2017)
7. Bodnar, C., Frasca, F., Giusti, L.: Weisfeiler and lehman go topological: message passing simplicial networks. In: International Conference on Machine Learning (ICML) (2021)
8. Chami, I., Wolf, A., Juan, D.: Hyperbolic graph convolutional neural networks. Adv. Neural Inf. Process. Syst. (NeurIPS) (2019)
9. Nickel, M., Kiela, D.: Poincaré embeddings for learning hierarchical representations. Adv. Neural Inf. Process. Syst. (NeurIPS) (2017)
10. Curry, J.M.: Sheaves, cosheaves and applications. arXiv preprint arXiv:1303.3255 (2014)
11. Barbero, F., Bodnar, C., Sánchez-González, A.: Sheaf neural networks with connection Laplacians. Trans. Mach. Learn. Res. (TMLR) (2023)
12. Sun, Z., Deng, J.-Y., Nie, J., Tang, J.: RotatE: knowledge graph embedding by relational rotation in complex space. In: International Conference on Learning Representations (ICLR) (2019)
13. Zhu, J., Yan, Y., Zhao, L.: See also LINKX and related heterophily benchmarks, (2021). arXiv:2009.13566 arXiv preprint Graph neural networks with heterophily benchmarks
14. Pei, H., Wei, B., Chang, K.C.-C.: Geom-GCN: geometric graph convolutional networks. In: International Conference on Learning Representations (ICLR) (2020)
15. Zhu, J., Yan, Y., Zhao, L., Heimann, M., Akoglu, L., Koutra, D.: Beyond homophily in graph neural networks: current limitations and effective designs. Adv. Neural Inf. Process. Syst. (NeurIPS) **33** (2020)
16. Lim, D., et al.: Large scale learning on non-homophilous graphs: new benchmarks and strong simple methods. Adv. Neural Inf. Process. Syst. (NeurIPS) (2021)
17. Paszke, A., Gross, S., Massa, F.: PyTorch: an imperative style, high-performance deep learning library. Adv. Neural Inf. Process. Syst. (NeurIPS) **32** (2019)
18. Fey, M., Lenssen, J.E.: Fast graph representation learning with PyTorch geometric. In: ICLR Workshop on Representation Learning on Graphs and Manifolds (2019)

19. Harris, C.R., Millman, K.J., Walt, S.J., et al.: Array programming with NumPy. Nature **585**, 357–362 (2020)
20. Virtanen, P., Gommers, R., Oliphant, T.E.: SciPy 1.0: fundamental algorithms for scientific computing in Python. Nat. Methods **17**, 261–272 (2020)
21. Chien, E., Peng, J., Li, P., Milenkovic, O.: Adaptive universal generalized PageRank graph neural network. In: International Conference on Learning Representations (ICLR) (2021)

Horizon-Aware Feature Selection and Evolutionary Optimization for Intraday Prediction in Futures Markets

Arthur E. Nunes[1], Bruno L. Dalmazo[1], Viviane Leite Dias de Mattos[1], Richard F. Pinto[1], Diego Renan Bruno[2], Eduardo N. Borges[1], Giancarlo Lucca[1], Fabian C. Cardoso[3], and Rafael A. Berri[1](✉)

[1] Federal University of Rio Grande (FURG), Rio Grande, Brazil
{arthur.nunes,dalmazo,vivianemattos,richard_pinto,eduardoborges,giancarlo.lucca,rafaelberri}@furg.br

[2] São Paulo State University (UNESP), São José do Rio Preto, Brazil
diego.bruno@unesp.br

[3] University of Rio Verde (UniRV), Rio Verde, Brazil
fabian@unirv.edu.br

Abstract. Intraday financial forecasting remains a challenging task due to noise, non-stationarity, and the dynamic nature of market behavior. To capture these complex dynamics, studies often employ multiple technical indicators, which can lead to high-dimensional datasets, increasing the risk of overfitting and degrading model generalization. This study proposes a methodological workflow for intraday binary classification of the Mini Bovespa Index (WIN) using 5-min data from the BovDBv2 dataset. Feature selection is performed independently for different forecast horizons (1, 5, and 7 candles) using Sequential Forward Selection with distinct estimators. Subsequently, a genetic algorithm is employed to optimize the hyperparameters of three classifiers: multi-layer perceptron, random forest, and K-Nearest Neighbors. Experimental results show that shorter forecasting horizons yield superior predictive performance. For instance, the MLP model with SFS-KNN at horizon 1 achieved a macro F1-score of 0.632, while performance decreased to 0.377 at horizon 7 under the same configuration. Overall, the findings indicate that feature relevance and model performance vary across forecasting horizons and highlight the importance of horizon-aware feature selection for intraday financial prediction.

Keywords: Machine Learning · Intraday Prediction · Futures Markets · Feature Selection · Evolutionary Optimization

1 Introduction

The prediction of price movements in intraday windows is a central problem in quantitative finance [1]. This type of forecasting poses major challenges, since

O. Gervasi et al. (Eds.): ICCSA 2026, LNCS 16768, pp. 315–332, 2027.
https://doi.org/10.1007/978-3-032-30488-9_20

financial time series are strongly influenced by noise, regime changes, and non-stationary dynamics, factors that hinder the generalization of predictive models [2].

With the aim of mitigating these difficulties, several techniques can be applied, such as: statistical modeling, fundamental analysis and technical analysis. In this study the technical analysis approach is adopted, using technical indicators, which are computed from prices and volumes, to extract relevant information about market behavior. Indicators such as moving averages, oscillators, and trend measures are widely used in practical applications, especially with intraday data.

However, the combined use of multiple technical indicators may result in high-dimensional datasets with strong correlations among attributes. This scenario increases the risk of overfitting, makes model performance sensitive to preprocessing choices, and complicates the identification of the most relevant features for the forecasting task [3].

In this context, feature selection techniques become essential to reduce dimensionality and identify the most informative attributes for each forecasting horizon. By selecting relevant subsets of indicators, it is possible to improve model generalization and reduce computational complexity [4].

Additionally, evolutionary algorithms, particularly Genetic Algorithms (GA) [5], constitute an efficient alternative for dealing with complex and non-convex search spaces. Inspired by the principles of natural evolution, GAs enable hyperparameter optimization without the need for gradient information, being especially suitable for problems involving continuous, discrete, and categorical variables [6].

The objective of this study is to propose and evaluate a methodological workflow for intraday classification using data from the BovDBv2 dataset [7], considering 5-min candles of the Mini Bovespa Index (WIN). Based on price and volume data, technical indicators of trend and momentum are computed and then used as features for the dataset, followed by preprocessing steps. Feature selection is performed using the Sequential Forward Selection (SFS) method, employing different estimators, with the objective of identifying more informative feature subsets for different forecasting horizons.

Subsequently, a GA is used to optimize the hyperparameters of different well-known classifiers, namely Multi-Layer Perceptron (MLP) [8], Random Forest (RF) [9], and K-Nearest Neighbors (KNN) [10], considering different temporal forecasting horizons. Model performance is evaluated using metrics suitable for imbalanced classification problems, allowing the analysis of the combined impact of feature selection, hyperparameter optimization, classifier choice, and forecasting horizon on the predictive capability of the system.

The main contributions of this study can be summarized as follows:

- Proposal of a horizon-aware feature selection strategy for intraday financial prediction.
- Integration of wrapper-based feature selection with evolutionary hyperparameter optimization.

- Empirical evaluation across multiple forecasting horizons using intraday futures market data.
- Analysis of how feature relevance and model configurations change across distinct intraday forecasting horizons.

The remainder of this paper is organized as follows: Sect. 2 presents the related work, Sect. 3 describes the adopted methodology, Sect. 4 discusses the obtained results, and finally, Sect. 5 presents the conclusions and directions for future work.

2 Related Work

The application of machine learning techniques to financial market prediction has been extensively investigated in the literature, particularly in the context of short-term price movements and trend classification. Traditional statistical models have gradually been complemented or replaced by machine learning approaches due to their ability to capture nonlinear relationships and complex patterns present in financial time series.

Several studies have explored the use of technical indicators as input features for predictive models in financial markets. Indicators derived from price and volume data, such as moving averages, momentum oscillators, and trend strength measures, are widely employed to represent market behavior in a structured form. Works such as [11] and [12] highlight that technical indicators remain relevant features for short-term forecasting, especially when combined with nonlinear classifiers.

Neural networks, particularly MLPs, have been frequently applied to financial prediction tasks due to their flexibility and universal approximation capability. Previous studies demonstrate that MLPs can outperform linear models in trend prediction problems when properly configured and trained [8]. However, other machine learning classifiers such as RF [9] and KNN [10] have also been successfully employed in financial forecasting tasks, benefiting from their ability to model nonlinear decision boundaries and complex feature interactions.

Feature selection has also been recognized as a critical step in financial time series modeling, as the inclusion of irrelevant or redundant features may degrade predictive performance and increase computational cost. Wrapper-based methods, such as SFS, have been successfully applied in financial contexts to identify compact and informative subsets of indicators [13]. The choice of estimator within the feature selection process has been shown to influence the resulting feature set, since different models capture distinct data characteristics.

In addition to feature selection, several works have investigated the use of evolutionary and metaheuristic algorithms for hyperparameter optimization in machine learning models. GAs have been widely adopted due to their ability to efficiently explore large and complex search spaces without requiring gradient information [14]. In financial applications, GAs have been employed to optimize neural network architectures, learning parameters, and trading strategies, often leading to improved generalization performance [15].

Despite these advances, many studies focus on a single prediction horizon or rely on a fixed feature set across different temporal scales [8,12]. Fewer works explicitly investigate horizon-dependent feature selection and hyperparameter optimization in an integrated manner. In this context, the present study contributes by combining horizon-specific feature selection using SFS with GA-based hyperparameter optimization of multiple classifiers (MLP, RF, and KNN), allowing the analysis of how feature relevance and model configuration vary across distinct intraday forecast horizons.

3 Methodology

In this section, the proposed method is presented. It is composed of the following subsections: Input Data, describing the data source and dataset construction; Technical Indicators, presenting the indicators used; Feature Selection, where attribute selection and forecast horizons (FH) are defined; GA and Classifiers, describing the use of the GA for hyperparameter optimization and the evaluated classifiers (MLP, RF, and KNN); and Evaluation, where the metric and evaluation procedure are presented. Figure 1 summarizes the overall workflow.

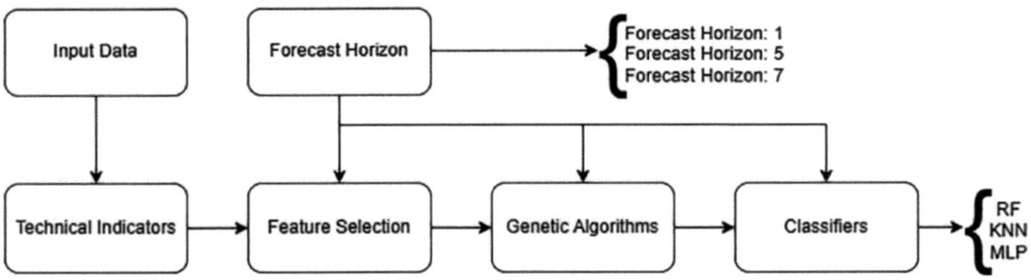

Fig. 1. Methodology Overview

3.1 Input Data

The data were obtained from the BovDB.v2 database [7]. For this study, intraday data from January to June 2024 were considered and the asset analyzed was the Mini Bovespa Index (WIN), selected due to its wide use in short-term trading operations in the Brazilian market and its high liquidity. For the intraday analysis, 5-min interval data were used, allowing the analysis of short FHs and a better understanding of the asset's behavior.

In addition to the information originally available in the database, additional columns containing technical indicators calculated from price data were created, as well as a variable called trend, which assumes the value 0 for a downward trend and 1 for an upward trend, the trend label was defined based on the price variation between the current candle and the future candle corresponding to the selected forecast horizon. In total, the dataset contains 15,300 instances, 42 features and the class distribution is around 53% upward trends and 47% downward trends.

3.2 Technical Indicators

For this study, several technical indicators were used, belonging to two major groups: trend and momentum [16–18]. The trend indicators employed were: EMA, SMA, DEMA, TRIMA, WMA, TEMA, and SAR, while the momentum indicators were: MOM, ADX, ADXR, CMO, BOP, IMI, MACD, and ROC. All moving averages were computed using periods of 3, 5, 7, and 9 (5-min intraday intervals).

Momentum indicators were used with the objective of capturing the intensity and speed of price movements over time. The Momentum indicator (MOM) was employed to measure the absolute price variation over a given interval, while ADX together with ADXR were used to quantify trend strength, regardless of its direction.

The Chande Momentum Oscillator (CMO) was included to assess the predominance of upward or downward movements, whereas the Balance of Power (BOP) was used to measure the relative dominance between buyers and sellers throughout the trading session. The Intraday Momentum Index (IMI) was computed based on opening and closing prices.

Additionally, the MACD indicator, as well as its signal line and histogram, were used in order to identify changes in momentum and potential trend reversals. Finally, the Rate of Change (ROC) was employed to measure the percentage rate of price variation.

The preprocessing of technical indicators is a fundamental step, as it facilitates feature comparison, reduces the influence of outliers, and improves algorithm performance. Accordingly, different transformation strategies were applied to the technical indicators, such as normalization, rescaling, or standardization. The exception was the Balance of Power (BOP), which by its mathematical definition already has a fixed range of $[-1, 1]$ centered at zero.

The moving averages EMA, SMA, DEMA, TRIMA, WMA, and TEMA were normalized according to the following equation:

$$x_t^{\text{norm}} = \frac{x_t - \min(x)}{\max(x) - \min(x)} \tag{1}$$

where x_t represents the indicator value at time t, and $\min(x)$ and $\max(x)$ correspond to the minimum and maximum values of the indicator within the considered dataset.

For the ADX, IMI, and ADXR indicators, values were divided by 100, since their original scale ranges from 0 to 100. In the case of CMO and ROC, which do not have strict bounds, division by 100 was also adopted in order to reduce the amplitude of values and maintain numerical consistency with the other indicators, without imposing a normalization that could alter their dynamics or interpretation.

The MACD indicator, its signal line, and its histogram were transformed using z-score standardization, according to the equation:

$$x_t^{\text{std}} = \frac{x_t - \mu_x}{\sigma_x} \tag{2}$$

where x_t is the indicator value at time t, μ_x is the mean of the indicator values, and σ_x is the standard deviation.

This choice is justified by the fact that MACD does not have fixed bounds and is centered around zero, with variability dependent on the asset's price level and volatility.

3.3 Feature Selection

Feature selection is a technique widely used in machine learning with the objective of identifying irrelevant or redundant attributes, reducing data dimensionality, and improving the performance of predictive models [4]. In this study, feature selection was performed using the SFS method [13], a greedy wrapper-based algorithm in which different machine learning models can be employed as estimators to evaluate subsets of features.

SFS is a method in which feature selection is carried out through the iterative evaluation of the performance of a machine learning model trained on different subsets of features [13]. At each iteration, the attribute that provides the greatest improvement according to a chosen evaluation metric is incorporated into the selected set, until a stopping criterion is satisfied.

In this work, SFS was applied using two distinct estimators: the KNN [10] algorithm and RF [9]. Although the selection procedure remains the same, the choice of estimator influences the final set of selected attributes, since different models capture different patterns in the data. The MLP classifier was not employed as an estimator in the SFS procedure due to its higher computational cost and larger number of hyperparameters, which would significantly increase the execution time of the feature selection stage. By using RF and KNN as estimators, it is also possible to analyze how different learning paradigms influence the subset of selected features.

RF was used as an estimator within the SFS feature selection process. It is an ensemble learning method based on multiple decision trees built from different data samples and random subsets of attributes [19]. This property allows RF to provide a robust assessment of feature relevance by capturing nonlinear relationships and feature interactions.

KNN was also used as an estimator in the SFS process. It is an instance-based learning algorithm in which classification is performed according to the k nearest neighbors in the feature space [20]. In this context, feature relevance is evaluated based on similarity relationships among observations.

In addition, this stage was carried out considering different FHs defined as 1, 5 and 7 candles. The FH represents the temporal distance ahead for which the prediction is performed; for example, a horizon of 1 candle (5 min) indicates an attempt to predict the asset's behavior five min into the future. This strategy allows the predictive behavior of the features to be evaluated at different temporal scales.

Thus, the feature selection procedure was performed independently for each forecast horizon, since feature relevance may vary according to the prediction interval. This approach allows horizon-specific patterns to be captured and avoids imposing a single feature set across different temporal dynamics. The resulting feature subsets were then used as input for the GA-based hyperparameter optimization of the classifiers (MLP, RF, and KNN).

3.4 GA and Classifiers

In this study, the GA was employed as an optimization approach for the selection of hyperparameters of machine learning models, considering different FHs. The use of GA enables an efficient exploration of hyperparameter combinations that would be infeasible to evaluate exhaustively, in addition to reducing the risk of convergence to suboptimal solutions. In this way, GA contributes to obtaining configurations that are more suitable for the different forecast scenarios analyzed.

The GA was independently applied to optimize the hyperparameters of three classifiers: MLP, RF, and KNN. For each FH and corresponding feature subset obtained through SFS, a distinct GA optimization process was executed for each classifier, resulting in horizon-specific and model-specific configurations.

The MLP is a machine learning algorithm based on artificial neural networks, composed of multiple fully connected layers of neurons, including an input layer, one or more hidden layers, and an output layer [21]. Table 1 presents the search space of the MLP hyperparameters optimized by the GA.

Table 1. Search space of MLP hyperparameters optimized by the GA

Parameters	Min	Max/options	Type
Number of hidden layers	1	3	Integer
Base number of Neurons	10	200	Integer
Decay factor	0.4	0.9	Real
Learning rate	1×10^{-5}	5×10^{-3}	Real
Activation function	–	ReLU, Tanh, Logistic	Categorical
Optimizer	–	Adam, SGD	Categorical
Regularization (α)	1×10^{-6}	1×10^{-3}	Real

The number of hidden layers and the base number of neurons are directly related to the depth and representational capacity of the MLP. The decay factor defines the progressive reduction in the number of neurons across the hidden layers.

The learning rate determines the magnitude of weight updates during the training process, affecting both the convergence speed and the stability of the algorithm. The activation function is responsible for introducing nonlinearities into the neural network, while the optimizer defines the strategy used to adjust the model parameters. Finally, the regularization parameter α controls the penalty applied to the network weights.

Similarly, the GA was used to optimize the main hyperparameters of the RF and KNN classifiers. Tables 2 and 3 present the respective search spaces considered for these models.

Table 2. Search space of KNN hyperparameters optimized by the GA

Parameters	Min	Max/options	Type
Number of neighbors (k)	1	50	Integer
Weight function	–	Uniform, Distance	Categorical
Distance metric	–	Euclidean, Manhattan, Minkowski	Categorical
Minkowski parameter (p)	1	2	Integer

The number of neighbors (k) determines how many closest observations in the feature space are considered when assigning a class to a new sample. The weight function defines whether all neighbors contribute equally (uniform) or whether closer neighbors have greater influence (distance). The distance metric specifies how similarity between observations is computed, while the Minkowski parameter (p) controls the norm used when the Minkowski metric is selected.

Table 3. Search space of RF hyperparameters optimized by the GA

Parameters	Min	Max	Type
Number of trees ($n\_estimators$)	50	500	Integer
Maximum depth (max_depth)	5	50	Integer
Minimum samples split	2	20	Integer
Minimum samples leaf	1	20	Integer

The number of trees ($n\_estimators$) defines the size of the ensemble. The maximum depth controls the complexity of individual trees. The minimum samples split parameter determines the minimum number of samples required to split an internal node, while the minimum samples leaf specifies the minimum number of samples that must be present in a leaf node.

The GA parameters used in this study are related to the evolutionary process and the genetic operators employed. The parameter NGEN defines the number of generations of the GA, while POPSIZE corresponds to the population size. The crossover probability (CXPB) determines the frequency with which two individuals are combined to generate new solutions. The mutation probability per gene (indpb) controls the chance of each individual parameter undergoing a random change, and the tournament size defines the number of individuals compared during the selection process. Finally, the Hall of Fame size indicates the number of best global solutions preserved throughout the execution of the algorithm. Table 4 presents the basic configuration of the GA parameters adopted in this study.

Table 4. The Relation of GA Parameters

Parameters ID	Values
NGEN	1000
POPSIZE	15
CXPB	0.8
indpb	0.05
Tournament Size	3
HOF size	1

This configuration was kept constant across all FHs and classifiers to ensure comparability of the optimization process.

3.5 Evaluation

The predictive performance of the models was assessed using the macro F1-score as the main evaluation metric. This metric corresponds to the unweighted average of the F1-score computed for each class, ensuring that both classes contribute equally to the final performance measure. This choice is particularly appropriate for financial prediction tasks, where imbalanced class distributions may occur.

During the model development stage, cross-validation was employed on the training data to guide both feature selection and hyperparameter optimization. This procedure allows the models to be evaluated on multiple data partitions, reducing the risk of overfitting and providing a more reliable estimate of generalization performance.

Finally, the selected configurations were evaluated on an independent test set. The results obtained with GA-based optimization were compared with two baseline configurations: a baseline without hyperparameter optimization and a baseline without feature selection. This comparison enables the assessment of the individual contributions of feature selection and hyperparameter optimization to the overall predictive performance.

4 Results

In this section, the obtained results are discussed, considering the distinct FHs (FH = 1, 5, and 7 candles) previously defined. The section is organized into three parts. The first subsection addresses the feature subsets selected by the SFS method. The second subsection presents the classifiers optimized by the GA. Finally, the third subsection compares the performance of the optimized classifiers across the different FHs.

4.1 Feature Selection

Figures 2 and 3 illustrate the relationship between the macro F1-score and the number of selected features obtained through the SFS. The analysis was conducted using two different estimators, namely KNN and RF, across three FHs (FH = 1, 5, and 7 candles).

As shown in Fig. 2, when KNN is used as the estimator, the optimal number of selected features varies significantly across FHs. For FH = 1, the best macro F1-score (0.6333) was achieved with 20 selected features out of the 42 available. However, for FH = 5 and FH = 7, peak performance was obtained with substantially smaller subsets, consisting of only 4 features, yielding macro F1-scores of 0.5476 and 0.5178, respectively. These results suggest that KNN-based SFS tends to favor more compact feature representations for longer FHs.

In contrast, Fig. 3 shows that RF-based SFS generally retains a larger number of features. For FH = 1, the highest macro F1-score (0.6611) was achieved with 38 selected features. Similarly, for FH = 5 and FH = 7, the best results (0.5407 and 0.5210, respectively) were obtained with 39 and 34 features. This behavior reflects the ability of RF to handle high-dimensional input spaces and capture nonlinear interactions without substantial performance degradation.

Overall, the results indicate that the choice of estimator significantly influences the dimensionality of the selected feature subsets. While KNN-based SFS tends to produce more compact representations—particularly for longer FHs—RF-based SFS preserves a larger portion of the original feature space, leveraging its ensemble structure to manage model complexity effectively.

It is important to emphasize that the feature subsets obtained through SFS were used consistently in the subsequent classification stage. For each FH, the MLP was evaluated using both subsets derived from SFS-KNN and SFS-RF, allowing the analysis of how the estimator choice during feature selection influences neural network performance. In contrast, RF and KNN classifiers were trained using the feature subsets selected by their respective estimators, ensuring coherence between the selection mechanism and the inductive bias of each model.

4.2 Classifiers Optimized by GA

The GA was applied to optimize the hyperparameters of the MLP, KNN, and RF classifiers. For each FH and feature selection configuration, an independent

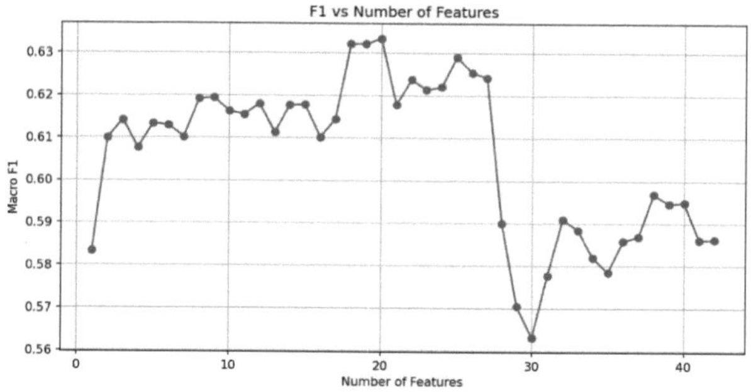

(a) FH = 1

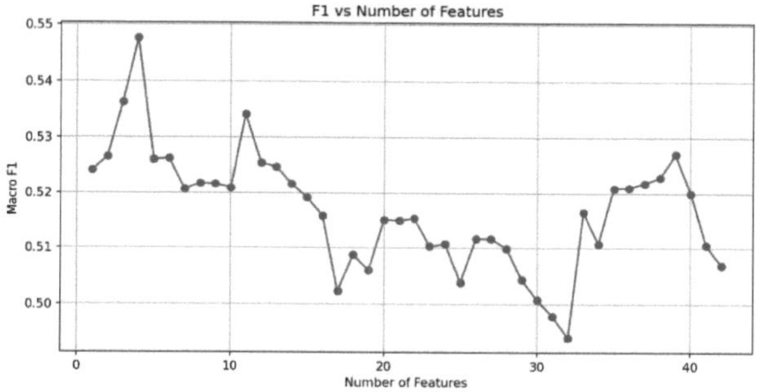

(b) FH = 5

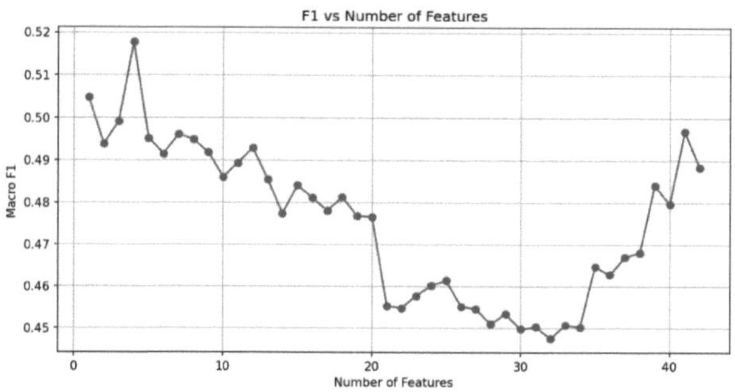

(c) FH = 7

Fig. 2. Macro F1-score versus number of selected features using SFS with KNN as estimator.

GA instance was executed, resulting in distinct optimization processes and final configurations.

Due to space limitations, Figs. 4 and 5 present the convergence behavior of the GA only for the MLP classifier, considering feature subsets obtained through SFS with KNN and RF estimators, respectively. The convergence patterns observed

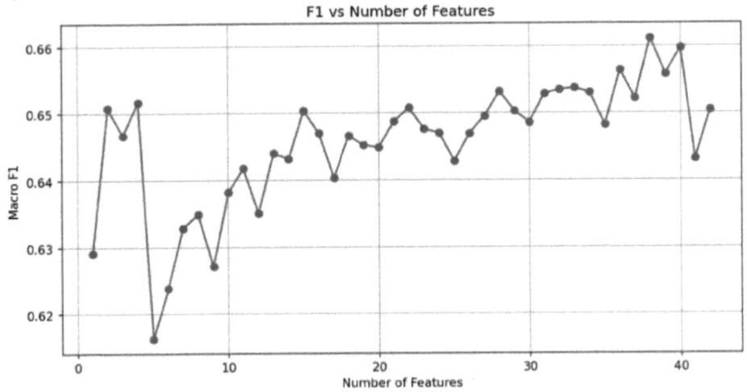

(a) FH = 1

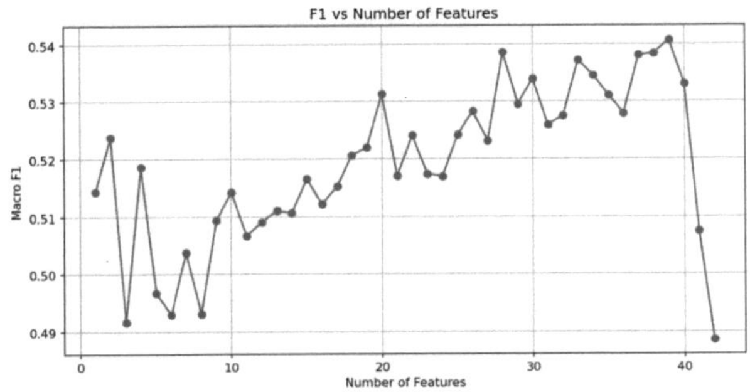

(b) FH = 5

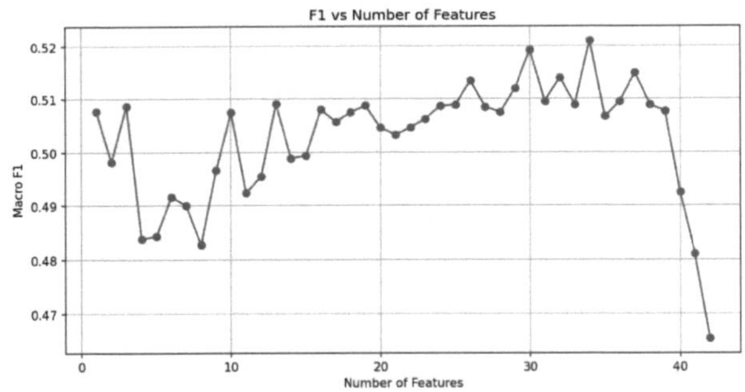

(c) FH = 7

Fig. 3. Macro F1-score versus number of selected features using SFS with RF as estimator.

for KNN and RF exhibited similar stabilization behavior and are therefore omitted for brevity.

Tables 5, 6, and 7 summarize the best hyperparameter configurations identified by the GA for each classifier and FH.

For the MLP, substantial architectural variation can be observed across horizons and feature selection strategies. When using SFS-KNN features, deeper

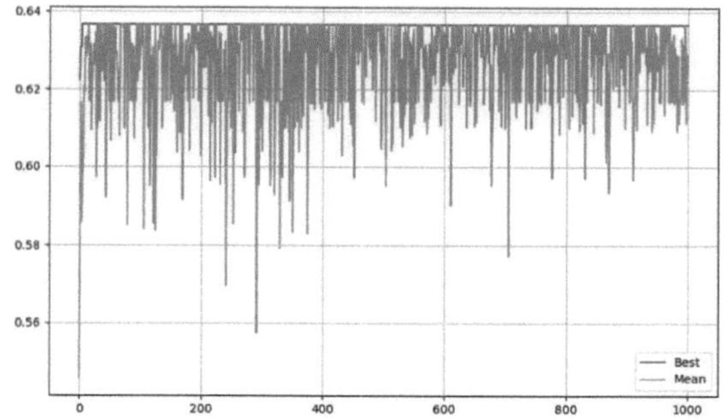

(a) FH = 1 candle

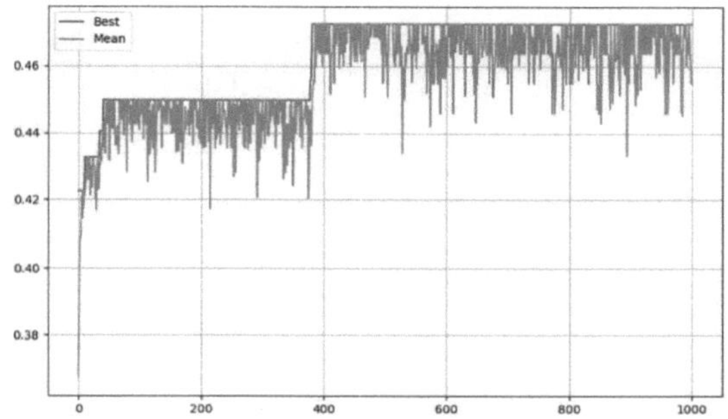

(b) FH = 5 candles

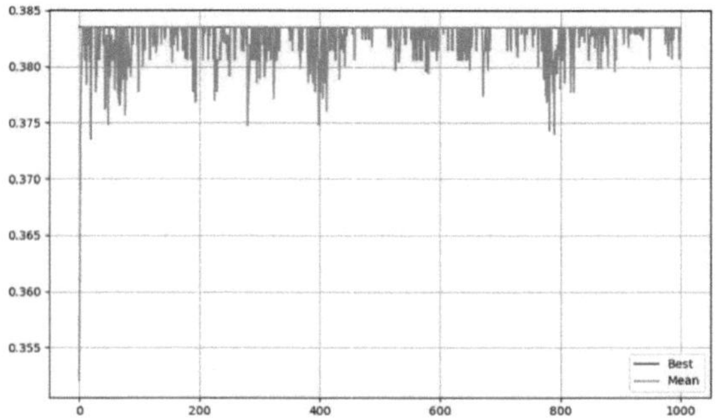

(c) FH = 7 candles

Fig. 4. GA convergence during MLP hyperparameter optimization using SFS + KNN feature subsets.

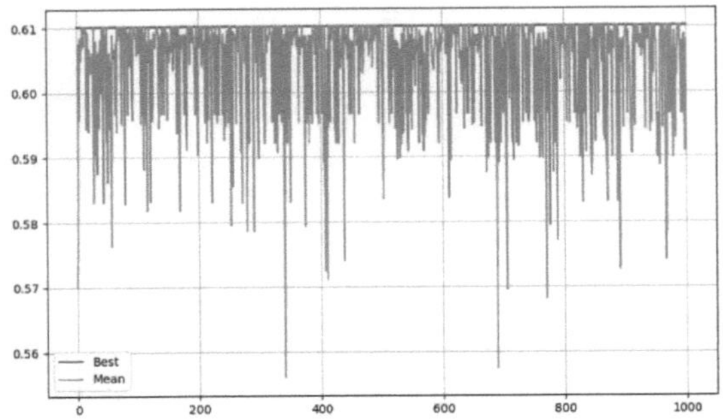

(a) FH = 1 candle

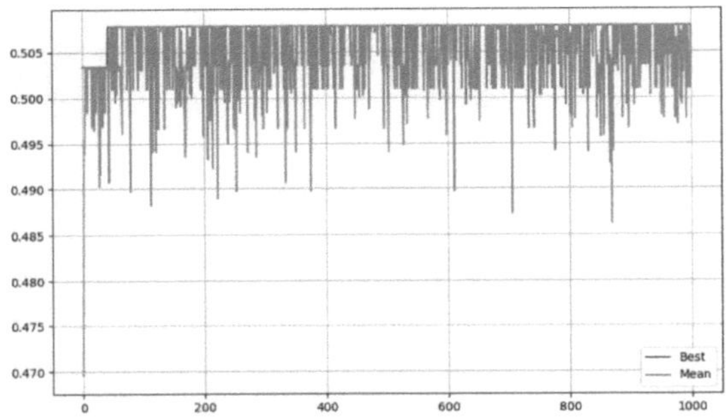

(b) FH = 5 candles

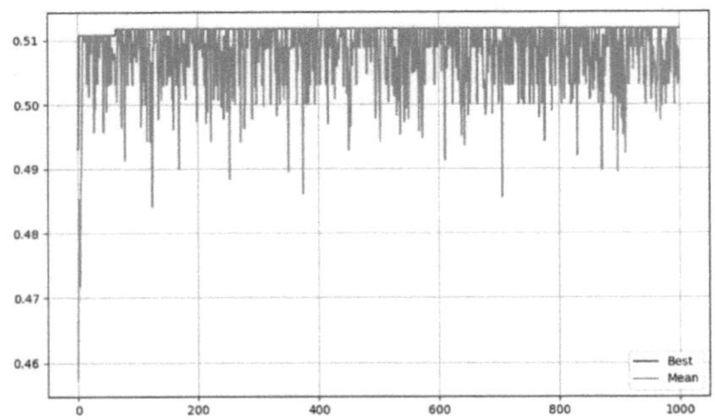

(c) FH = 7 candles

Fig. 5. GA convergence during MLP hyperparameter optimization using SFS + RF feature subsets.

Table 5. Best MLP hyperparameters obtained by the GA for each configuration

SFS Estimator	FH	Layers	Hidden units	LR	α	Activation	Solver
KNN	1	3	(172, 134, 104)	0.00137	1.29×10^{-4}	ReLU	Adam
KNN	5	3	(139, 119, 102)	0.00107	1.00×10^{-3}	ReLU	Adam
KNN	7	1	(155)	0.00500	1.00×10^{-6}	Tanh	Adam
RF	1	2	(65, 57)	0.00052	3.81×10^{-4}	Tanh	SGD
RF	5	1	(10)	0.00390	1.00×10^{-6}	ReLU	Adam
RF	7	1	(63)	0.00155	1.63×10^{-4}	ReLU	Adam

Table 6. Best KNN hyperparameters obtained by the GA for each FH

Horizon	k	Weights	Metric	p
1	35	Distance	Euclidean	1
5	1	Uniform	Euclidean	1
7	14	Uniform	Manhattan	1

architectures were favored for FH = 1 and FH = 5, whereas a simpler single-layer structure was selected for FH = 7. In contrast, when SFS-RF features were adopted, the GA generally selected more compact architectures, suggesting that the larger feature subsets may reduce the need for deeper representations.

Regarding KNN, the optimal number of neighbors varied significantly across horizons, indicating sensitivity to temporal scale. While FH = 1 favored a larger neighborhood ($k = 35$), longer horizons resulted in smaller or moderate values of k, reflecting differences in local structure within the feature space.

For RF, the GA selected distinct combinations of tree depth and regularization-related parameters. Shorter horizons tended to favor shallower trees, whereas longer horizons required deeper structures and adjusted splitting constraints, highlighting horizon-dependent model complexity.

Overall, the results reinforce the importance of horizon-specific hyperparameter optimization. Even under a fixed GA configuration, the search process consistently identified distinct model structures and parameter settings tailored to each predictive scenario.

Table 7. Best RF hyperparameters obtained by the GA for each FH

Horizon	n_estimators	max_depth	min_samples_split	min_samples_leaf
1	269	5	5	1
5	257	6	20	13
7	328	10	19	4

4.3 Classifiers Performance

This subsection evaluates the predictive performance of the proposed models across different forecasting horizons. In addition to the GA-optimized configurations, two baseline scenarios are considered in order to assess the impact of hyperparameter optimization and feature selection on the final performance.

Table 8 presents the macro F1-score obtained by the GA-optimized classifiers, together with two baseline configurations: a baseline model using the same feature subsets but without GA optimization, and a baseline without feature selection.

Table 8. Performance comparison between GA-optimized models and baseline configurations

Model	SFS	FH	F1 GA	F1 Baseline	F1 No FS
MLP	KNN	1	0.632	0.644	0.583
MLP	KNN	5	0.466	0.338	0.497
MLP	KNN	7	0.377	0.337	0.488
MLP	RF	1	0.613	0.594	0.583
MLP	RF	5	0.497	0.512	0.497
MLP	RF	7	0.480	0.483	0.488
RF	RF	1	0.668	0.640	0.591
RF	RF	5	0.537	0.523	0.487
RF	RF	7	0.518	0.502	0.477
KNN	KNN	1	0.672	0.633	0.587
KNN	KNN	5	0.523	0.548	0.505
KNN	KNN	7	0.508	0.518	0.481

For FH = 1, all models achieved their best performance. The GA-optimized KNN obtained the highest macro F1-score (0.672), closely followed by RF (0.668). The MLP models exhibited slightly lower performance, with F1-macro values of 0.632 when using SFS-KNN features and 0.613 with SFS-RF features. These results indicate that, for short-term prediction, instance-based and ensemble methods provide more effective decision boundaries than the neural network configuration explored.

As the FH increases (FH = 5 and FH = 7), a consistent performance degradation can be observed across all classifiers. This behavior suggests that longer-term predictions introduce greater uncertainty and reduce the separability of the classes. Although RF maintained a slight advantage over KNN for FH = 5 and FH = 7, the differences among the models become less pronounced as the horizon grows.

Regarding the MLP, the use of SFS-RF features generally resulted in more stable performance across horizons compared to SFS-KNN features, particularly for FH = 7. Nevertheless, the neural network did not outperform the simpler models in any scenario, even after GA-based hyperparameter optimization. This behavior may be partially explained by the feature selection procedure. Since SFS was conducted using KNN and RF as estimators, the resulting feature subsets are likely biased toward these models, which may disadvantage the MLP during the classification stage. This result also shows how the choice of estimator in SFS can influence the relative performance of different classifiers.

The comparison with the baseline configurations also highlights the importance of feature selection and hyperparameter optimization. In particular, the RF showed consistent improvements over its baseline configuration across all forecasting horizons when GA-based optimization was applied. In most cases, the models trained without feature selection achieved lower F1 scores, indicating that the reduction of the feature space contributed to more robust decision boundaries.

Overall, the results demonstrate that model performance is strongly horizon-dependent. Short-term forecasting (FH = 1) yields significantly higher predictive quality, whereas longer horizons lead to near-random performance levels for all evaluated classifiers. Among the tested approaches, the GA-optimized KNN achieved the best overall result, while RF showed competitive and stable behavior across different temporal scales.

5 Conclusions

Intraday financial forecasting remains a challenging task due to the noisy and dynamic nature of market data. In this context, selecting relevant features and properly configuring predictive models are key aspects for improving classification performance.

This work proposed a methodological workflow for intraday classification that combines technical indicators, horizon-dependent feature selection using SFS, and GA-based hyperparameter optimization applied to different classifiers (MLP, RF, and KNN). The feature selection stage was performed independently for each forecasting horizon, allowing the models to adapt to different temporal dynamics.

The experimental results indicate that predictive performance is strongly dependent on the forecasting horizon. The best results were consistently obtained for FH = 1, while performance gradually degraded as the horizon increased. Among the evaluated models, the GA-optimized KNN achieved the highest overall performance, with RF also presenting competitive and stable results. In contrast, the MLP did not outperform the simpler approaches despite the evolutionary optimization, suggesting that model complexity does not necessarily mean better performance under the adopted feature selection strategy.

Overall, the findings suggest that horizon-aware feature selection plays a central role in predictive performance, often having a greater impact than increases in model complexity. Future works may explore alternative feature selection strategies, different hyperparameter optimization methods, and the adoption of modern deep learning models along with more comprehensive evaluation protocols, including real-world performance and statistical validation.

Acknowledgment. The authors would like to thank FAPERGS (24/2551-0001396-2, 23/2551-0000773-8), CNPq (307416/2025-9), FAPERGS/CNPq (23/2551-0000126-8) and the Fesurv-University of Rio Verde.

References

1. Wilmott, P.: Paul Wilmott Introduces Quantitative Finance. John Wiley & Sons (2013)
2. Malkiel, B.G.: The efficient market hypothesis and its critics. J. Econ. Perspect. **17**(1), 59–82 (2003)
3. Hastie, T., Tibshirani, R., Friedman, J.: The Elements of Statistical Learning: Data Mining, Inference, and Prediction. Springer, New York (2009)
4. Guyon, I., Elisseeff, A.: An introduction to variable and feature selection. J. Mach. Learn. Res. **3**, 1157–1182 (2003)
5. Whitley, D.: A genetic algorithm tutorial. Stat. Comput. **4**(2), 65–85 (1994)
6. Yao, X.: Evolving artificial neural networks. Proc. IEEE **87**(9), 1423–1447 (1999)
7. Souza, A.S., Lucca, G., Borges, E.N., Cardoso, F.C., Dalmazo, B.L., Berri, R.: Dataset for intraday analysis of b3 stock prices (BovDB.v2) (2024). https://doi.org/10.7910/DVN/TMB4IG
8. Zhang, G.P., Patuwo, B.E., Hu, M.Y.: Forecasting with artificial neural networks: the state of the art. Int. J. Forecast. **14**(1), 35–62 (1998)
9. Cutler, A., Cutler, D.R., Stevens, J.R.: Random forests. In: Ensemble Machine Learning, pp. 157–175. Springer (2012)
10. Peterson, L.E.: K-nearest neighbor. Scholarpedia **4**(2), 1883 (2009)
11. Loh, W.-Y.: Feature selection for classification of high-dimensional data. Stat. Sin. **19**(1), 1–21 (2009)
12. Atsalakis, G.S., Valavanis, K.P.: Surveying stock market forecasting techniques-Part II: soft computing methods. Expert Syst. Appl. **36**(3), 5932–5941 (2009)
13. Kohavi, R., John, G.H.: Wrappers for feature subset selection. Artif. Intell. **97**(1–2), 273–324 (1997)
14. Goldberg, D.E.: Genetic Algorithms in Search. Optimization and Machine Learning. Addison-Wesley, Reading (1989)
15. Brabazon, A., O'Neill, M., Maringer, D.: Natural Computing in Computational Finance. Springer (2015)
16. Murphy, J.J.: Technical Analysis of the Financial Markets: A Comprehensive Guide to Trading Methods and Applications. New York Institute of Finance, New York (1999)
17. Chande, T.S., Kroll, S.: The New Technical Trader. John Wiley & Sons (1994)
18. Kaufman, P.J.: Trading Systems and Methods. John Wiley & Sons (2013)
19. Breiman, L.: Random forests. Mach. Learn. **45**(1), 5–32 (2001)
20. Cover, T., Hart, P.: Nearest neighbor pattern classification. IEEE Trans. Inf. Theory **13**(1), 21–27 (1967)
21. Rumelhart, D.E., Hinton, G.E., Williams, R.J.: Learning representations by back-propagating errors. Nature **323**(6088), 533–536 (1986)

C-MTSS: Compact Multi-teacher Single-Student Framework for Real-Time Multimodal Industrial Anomaly Detection

Dongwoo Kim, Taeheon Jin, Seokhyun Gong, Jieun Lee, and Jongpil Jeong(✉)

Department of Smart Factory Convergence, Sungkyunkwan University, Suwon-si, Gyeonggi-do 16419, Republic of Korea
{kdw5641,kongsh95,jpjeong}@skku.edu, {honey7844,lu3873}@g.skku.edu

Abstract. Recently, multimodal anomaly detection techniques that combine 2D texture and 3D shape information have been widely studied to automate quality inspections in smart factories. However, existing 3D-2D models suffer from feature scale discrepancy between modalities, which causes one modality to dominate the anomaly score, and are highly vulnerable to the shape variance of objects. Furthermore, their massive parameters and high computational costs make real-time inference on resource-constrained environments infeasible. To address these industrial constraints, this paper proposes the Compact Multi-Teacher Single-Student framework (C-MTSS), a lightweight 3D-2D multimodal anomaly detection framework capable of inference in less than 1 *ms*. The proposed framework ensures robustness against shape variance by converting raw depth maps into surface normal maps. In addition, to enable a single-student network with fewer than 1M parameters to efficiently distill knowledge from two teacher models, we introduce a dual-stem structure that prevents initial interference between modalities, along with a Masked Mean Square Error (MSE) loss function to suppress background noise. During the inference stage, a Z-Score Calibration module is applied to normalize and weight-fuse the error distributions of the two heterogeneous modalities, which improves detection accuracy. Experiments on the MVTec 3D-AD benchmark demonstrate that C-MTSS achieves 91.3% image-level AUROC and 96.7% pixel-level AUROC with only 2.15M parameters and 38MB memory footprint, attaining over 1,000 FPS on a single GPU. These results indicate that C-MTSS is designed as a lightweight framework for real-time industrial inspection, where low latency and small memory footprint are critical.

Keywords: Anomaly Detection · 3D Surface Normal · Knowledge Distillation · Smart Manufacturing · Real-time Inference

O. Gervasi et al. (Eds.): ICCSA 2026, LNCS 16768, pp. 333–348, 2027.
https://doi.org/10.1007/978-3-032-30488-9_21

1 Introduction

Recently, unsupervised anomaly detection technology has become essential for automating quality inspections in smart factories. Existing models relying solely on 2D RGB images have inherent limitations in detecting structural defects such as missing parts or deep surface scratches. To overcome these limitations, multimodal anomaly detection that combines 2D texture information with 3D shape information has attracted growing research interest [1–4].

However, the latest 3D-2D multimodal models face two critical limitations when deployed on resource-constrained environments in real-world industrial settings. First, simply concatenating 2D and 3D features without accounting for their scale discrepancy allows one modality's noise to dominate anomaly scoring, thereby degrading overall performance. In particular, on the MVTec 3D-AD dataset, for objects with high morphological variance—such as Carrot or Bagel—3D models that rely on absolute Z-axis depth tend to misclassify normal data as abnormal [5]. Second, models require inference speeds in the millisecond range, similar to those proposed in 2D vision [6], and recent high-resolution 3D anomaly detection studies have also considered real-time processing for subtle industrial defects [7]. However, existing multimodal approaches that utilize massive multi-memory banks to prevent modality scale conflicts [4] have excessively high computational and memory requirements, making real-time processing infeasible.

Therefore, this paper proposes the C-MTSS framework to address these issues. The main contributions are as follows:

- We propose a Dual-Stem Late Fusion structure that effectively distills 2D and 3D knowledge into a single-student network of less than 1M parameters without gradient interference.
- We improve robustness against shape variance by utilizing a 3D Surface Normal map and propose a Masked MSE Loss to optimize the model's capacity by suppressing background noise.
- We introduce a Z-score-based Calibration module that normalizes the scale discrepancy between modality-specific error distributions, enabling practical detection performance within sub-millisecond inference latency ($< 1\,ms$).

The remainder of this paper is organized as follows. Section 2 reviews related work on unsupervised anomaly detection in manufacturing, knowledge distillation-based anomaly detection, and multimodal 3D-2D anomaly detection. Section 3 describes the proposed C-MTSS framework, including surface normal extraction, dual-stem single-student knowledge distillation, masked MSE loss, and Z-score-based anomaly scoring. Section 4 presents the experimental results on the MVTec 3D-AD dataset, including quantitative comparisons, computational efficiency analysis, CPU-only benchmarking, sensitivity analysis, qualitative visualization, and ablation study. Finally, Sect. 5 concludes the paper and discusses future research directions (Fig. 1).

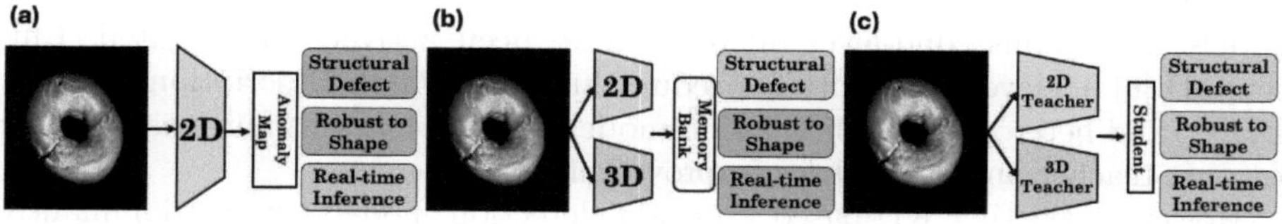

Fig. 1. Comparison summary of the proposed C-MTSS framework and existing anomaly detection paradigms. Unlike single 2D models or existing 3D-2D multimodal models with massive computations, the proposed C-MTSS framework simultaneously satisfies three core industrial requirements: structural defect detection, robustness to shape variance, and real-time inference speed (< 1 ms) for resource-constrained environments.

2 Related Work

2.1 Unsupervised Visual Anomaly Detection in Manufacturing

Unsupervised anomaly detection models for quality inspection in smart factory environments have evolved primarily by learning the distribution of normal data and treating patterns that deviate from it as anomalous [8]. Early approaches relied on Generative Adversarial Network (GAN)-based adversarial reconstruction [9,10], and more recently, hyperbolic space representations have been introduced to strengthen the separability of normal features [11]. In a different line of work, Normalizing Flow methods that directly estimate the density of high-dimensional features have led to notable gains in detection performance [12], and diffusion-based anomaly localization has also shown promising results [13,14].

Meanwhile, anomaly detection research is expanding beyond single-domain and closed-set settings toward broader applicability. Strategies such as distorted-feature attention, continuous memory representations, and self-supervised outlier synthesis have been explored for cross-domain generalization and open-world detection [15–17], along with few-shot prompting strategies [18].

2.2 Knowledge Distillation for Anomaly Detection

Knowledge Distillation (KD)-based approaches, in which a student model is trained to mimic the outputs of a pre-trained teacher with strong feature extraction capabilities, have emerged as a prominent direction in anomaly detection [19,20]. Since the student is trained exclusively on normal data, it fails to accurately reproduce the teacher's output for anomalous inputs at inference time; the resulting feature discrepancy between teacher and student serves as the anomaly score. Early work adopted a forward distillation scheme that transfers multi-resolution teacher features to the student, enabling the capture of anomalies at various scales [20]. Subsequently, a reverse distillation structure was introduced in which the student decoder reconstructs the teacher encoder's output, further amplifying representational discrepancy in anomalous regions [19]. As real-time processing demands in manufacturing have grown, lightweight KD models with millisecond-level inference have been actively investigated. EfficientAD [6] achieves substantial speedup through a Patch Description Network (PDN), and heterogeneous distillation models [21] exploit structural asymmetry between teacher and student for improved efficiency.

However, existing KD-based anomaly detection models are predominantly designed for a single 2D RGB modality. Extending this paradigm to a multimodal setting introduces new challenges: scale discrepancy between heterogeneous modalities allows one modality to dominate learning, and gradient conflicts arise when distinct modalities are processed within a single student network. These issues have not been addressed in conventional single-modality KD frameworks, calling for dedicated architectural designs for multimodal KD.

2.3 Multimodal 3D-2D Anomaly Detection

In industrial environments, structural defects such as missing parts, dents, and assembly failures occur frequently, in addition to surface-level scratches or discoloration. Since such defects are difficult to detect using a single 2D modality, multimodal anomaly detection research combining 3D geometric features has become essential [1–3, 22]. Recent 3D-2D multimodal methodologies have attempted to exploit complementary information through cross-modal feature mapping, attention mechanisms, or score-level fusion [2–4, 23]. Memory bank-based approaches such as BTF [24], M3DM [4], and hypergraph-enhanced memory methods [25] achieve high localization accuracy by storing and retrieving normal feature prototypes, while KD-based methods such as AST [26] and MMRD [27] offer faster inference by avoiding large-scale storage. More recently, CFM [3] and LSFA [5] have proposed lightweight cross-modal mapping and self-supervised feature adaptation strategies, respectively, advancing performance on standard benchmarks.

However, existing methods still require complex network structures or pre-trained backbone models with substantial parameters, making them difficult to deploy in real-time resource-constrained environments. Moreover, models relying on raw, absolute Z-axis depth are highly vulnerable to the natural shape variances that occur within the same object class [5].

3 C-MTSS Framework

In this paper, we propose the C-MTSS, a lightweight 3D-2D multimodal anomaly detection framework capable of operating in real-time on resource-constrained environments.

3.1 Overall Structure

Figure 2 illustrates the overall structure of the proposed C-MTSS framework. This framework consists of four core pipelines. First, a preprocessing step converts the raw depth map acquired from the 3D sensor into a surface normal map

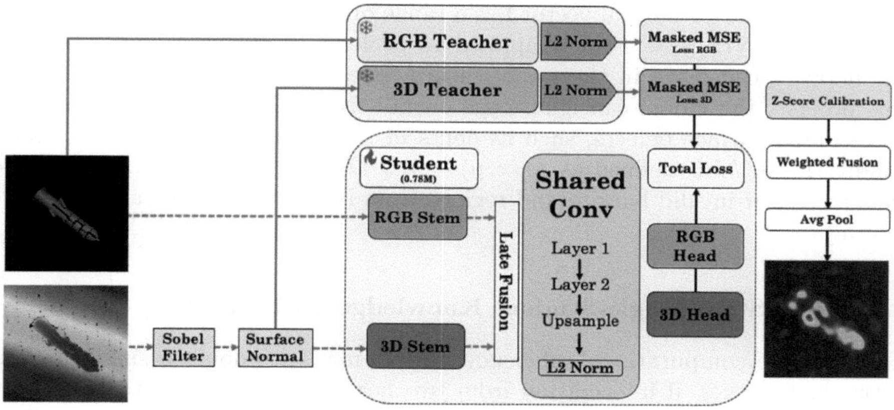

Fig. 2. Overall structure of the proposed C-MTSS framework. The input raw depth map is converted into a surface normal map via a Sobel filter to overcome shape variance. The single-student model, which mimics the knowledge of the frozen multi-teacher models, employs a dual-stem input layer to prevent initial gradient interference between modalities. L2 normalization and a Masked MSE loss function are applied during training to suppress background noise and control scale, while a Z-Score-based fusion module normalizes the errors of both modalities to the same scale during inference.

to mitigate shape variance. Second, multi-teacher models with frozen parameters extract the target features of the RGB and 3D Surface Normal domains. Third, a lightweight single-student model with fewer than 1M parameters (approximately 0.78M) simultaneously distills knowledge from both teacher models through a dual-stem structure that prevents interference between modalities. Finally, in the inference stage, a Z-Score Calibration fusion module normalizes and weight-combines the scale differences between the two modalities.

3.2 Surface Normal Extraction for Shape Variance

In industrial environments, shape variance frequently occurs when parts are placed at a slant or randomly rotated on a conveyor belt. In such cases, the overall height distribution of the raw 3D depth map $D \in \mathbb{R}^{H \times W}$ obtained from the sensor is deformed, which is a major cause of deep learning models misclassifying normal objects as defective (false positives).

To ensure robustness against such shape variance, this paper converts the depth map into a surface normal vector in 3D space. The gradients along the x-axis and y-axis at each pixel (x, y) of the depth map are calculated using a Sobel filter, and the result is normalized to extract the normal map $N(x, y)$:

$$N(x,y) = \frac{(-\nabla_x D,\ -\nabla_y D,\ 1)}{\|(-\nabla_x D,\ -\nabla_y D,\ 1)\|_2}. \tag{1}$$

Since the extracted normal vector has a range of $[-1, 1]$, a linear transformation $N'(x, y) = (N(x, y) + 1)/2$ is applied to scale it to the $[0, 1]$ range so that the network can learn in the same feature space as the RGB image. Through this process, the model can ignore the overall tilt of the object and focus only on essential surface defects, such as dents or scratches. Furthermore, a binary validity mask M is defined as $M(x, y) = 1$ if $D(x, y) > 0$, and 0 otherwise, to exclude sensor-invalid background regions from both training loss and inference scoring.

3.3 Dual-Stem Single-Student Knowledge Distillation

To maximize computational efficiency, this framework adopts a single-student network. However, if information from two heterogeneous modalities is simply merged in the initial layers, representation learning can collapse due to gradient interference.

Dual-Stem Structure. To prevent initial interference, the input part of the student model is separated into a dual-stem structure consisting of two shallow convolutional layers that independently process RGB and 3D inputs. The two branches are fused in the subsequent shared layers, which mitigates the gradient conflict inherent in a naïve single-input design.

L2 Normalization. The output feature maps of the teacher and student models exhibit different scales for each modality. To prevent the error of a particular modality from dominating the entire loss function, L2 normalization is applied to the intermediate feature maps f_1 and f_2 prior to concatenation ($f_{\text{norm}} = f_1 \,/\, \|f\|_2$), for both teacher and student networks.

Masked MSE Loss. The background region of 3D data contains meaningless noise, which wastes the representational capacity of the model. To mitigate this, we propose a Masked MSE Loss using a binary mask M in which only the valid region containing the object from the depth sensor is assigned a value of 1. For modality $m \in \{\text{RGB, 3D}\}$, let T_m denote the teacher features and S_m denote the student features. The loss function is defined as follows:

$$\mathcal{L}_m = \frac{\sum_{i,j} \left(M_{i,j} \cdot \frac{1}{C} \sum_{c=1}^{C} (S_m^c(i,j) - T_m^c(i,j))^2 \right)}{\sum_{i,j} M_{i,j} + \epsilon}. \tag{2}$$

The network is optimized via $\mathcal{L}_{\text{total}} = \mathcal{L}_{\text{RGB}} + \mathcal{L}_{\text{3D}}$, enabling the student to distill multimodal surface knowledge while suppressing background interference. The same mask is applied to the RGB modality to ensure that the student focuses its limited capacity on the object region, avoiding unnecessary learning of background patterns such as table surfaces or lighting artifacts.

3.4 Z-Score Calibration and Anomaly Scoring

During the inference stage, for each modality m, the mean squared error (MSE) between the teacher and student features is computed to generate the error map E_m. However, since the RGB error and the 3D error differ in their value ranges and distributions, they cannot be directly summed.

In this paper, we apply Z-Score Calibration, which normalizes the two error maps into standard normal distributions with mean 0 and variance 1, based on the error mean (μ_m) and standard deviation (σ_m) of each modality extracted from the normal training set. Considering the relative importance of RGB texture defects and 3D surface defects, we assign weights of 0.6 to RGB and 0.4 to 3D to compute the final fused anomaly map A_{fused}:

$$A_{\text{fused}} = 0.6 \cdot \frac{E_{\text{RGB}} - \mu_{\text{RGB}}}{\sigma_{\text{RGB}}} + 0.4 \cdot \frac{E_{\text{3D}} - \mu_{\text{3D}}}{\sigma_{\text{3D}}}. \tag{3}$$

Finally, average pooling with an 11×11 kernel and replicate padding is applied to A_{fused} to suppress local noise artifacts. The image-level anomaly score is then defined as the mean of the top 1% pixel values within the valid object region (where $M = 1$).

4 Experiments

This section evaluates the anomaly detection performance and computational efficiency of the proposed C-MTSS framework. We conduct quantitative comparisons against representative 3D-2D baselines and state-of-the-art multimodal models spanning diverse paradigms—including memory bank-based, knowledge distillation-based, and cross-modal mapping approaches—and analyze both detection accuracy and real-time inference capability.

4.1 Dataset and Experimental Setup

Dataset. Performance evaluation was conducted on the MVTec 3D-AD dataset [1], a standard benchmark for 3D industrial anomaly detection. This dataset comprises 10 diverse object categories, each providing paired high-resolution RGB images and corresponding 3D XYZ depth maps. In our experiments, the depth maps were converted into surface normal maps through the preprocessing pipeline described in Sect. 3.2.

Evaluation Metrics. For objective evaluation, we adopted widely used standard metrics [8]. Image AUROC (I-AUROC) was used to measure image-level classification performance. Pixel AUROC (P-AUROC) was employed to assess pixel-level localization accuracy.

Implementation Details. The proposed framework was implemented in PyTorch. To ensure fair benchmarking of inference latency against competing models, all training and evaluation were performed on an NVIDIA A100 Tensor

Table 1. Quantitative comparison on MVTec 3D-AD (mean across 10 categories). Results for BTF, AST, M3DM, and CFM are from [3]; MMRD from [27]; LSFA from [5]. The best result in each column is in **bold**.

Method	Venue	Paradigm	I-AUROC (%) ↑	P-AUROC (%) ↑
BTF [24]	CVPRW'23	MB	86.5	99.2
AST [26]	WACV'23	KD	93.7	97.6
M3DM [4]	CVPR'23	MB	94.5	99.2
MMRD [27]	AAAI'24	KD	94.0	98.7
CFM [3]	CVPR'24	FM	95.4	99.3
LSFA [5]	ECCV'24	FA	**97.1**	**99.2**
C-MTSS (Ours)	—	KD	91.3	96.7

KD = Knowledge Distillation, MB = Memory Bank, FM = Feature Mapping, FA = Feature Adaptation.

Core GPU (80 GB VRAM) with 16 vCPUs and 192 GB RAM. The Adam optimizer was used with a learning rate of 1×10^{-3}, scheduled via StepLR with a step size of 5,000 and decay factor of 0.1. The student network was trained for 10,000 iterations per category with a batch size of 32 and an input resolution of 256×256 to allow stable calibration of inter-modality scale differences. Both teacher networks use a ResNet-18 backbone pre-trained on ImageNet, truncated at Layer 2.

4.2 Quantitative Comparison with State-of-the-Art

To validate the proposed framework, we compare C-MTSS against six representative multimodal anomaly detection methods spanning three distinct paradigms: (1) *Memory bank-based* methods—BTF [24] and M3DM [4]—which store and retrieve normal feature prototypes for anomaly scoring; (2) *Knowledge distillation-based* methods—AST [26] and MMRD [27]—which train student networks to mimic frozen teacher representations; and (3) *Cross-modal mapping/adaptation* methods—CFM [3] and LSFA [5]—which learn inter-modality feature correspondences.

As shown in Table 1 and Table 2, the proposed C-MTSS framework achieves an I-AUROC of 91.3%, surpassing the memory bank-based baseline BTF (86.5%) by +4.8 pp and narrowing the gap to within 2.7 pp of the AAAI'24 knowledge distillation model MMRD (94.0%) and 2.4 pp of AST (93.7%). This is particularly noteworthy considering that the entire C-MTSS inference pipeline comprises only 2.15M parameters—two orders of magnitude fewer than competing approaches.

The per-category analysis in Table 2 further reveals that C-MTSS achieves strong I-AUROC on categories where the Surface Normal representation effectively captures geometric defects, such as Rope (98.1%) and Dowel (96.4%), with

Table 2. Per-category I-AUROC (%) on MVTec 3D-AD. Values for BTF, AST, M3DM, and CFM are from [3]. MMRD and LSFA are omitted as per-category breakdowns are not publicly available. The best result per category is in **bold**.

Method	Bagel	Cable G.	Carrot	Cookie	Dowel	Foam	Peach	Potato	Rope	Tire	Mean
BTF [24]	91.8	74.8	96.7	88.3	93.2	58.2	89.6	91.2	92.1	88.6	86.5
AST [26]	98.3	87.3	97.6	97.1	93.2	88.5	97.4	98.1	**100.0**	79.7	93.7
M3DM [4]	**99.4**	**90.9**	97.2	97.6	96.0	**94.2**	97.3	89.9	97.2	85.0	94.5
CFM [3]	**99.4**	88.8	**98.4**	**99.3**	**98.0**	88.8	94.1	**94.3**	98.0	**95.3**	**95.4**
C-MTSS (Ours)	96.0	**91.5**	93.7	89.7	96.4	87.9	87.7	88.1	98.1	83.9	91.3

several categories approaching or matching the performance of models with substantially larger capacity. The accuracy gap is more pronounced on categories with extreme texture complexity (e.g., Cookie 89.7%, Tire 83.9%), which we attribute to the limited capacity of the compact student network for encoding fine-grained texture patterns.

On the localization side, C-MTSS achieves 96.7% P-AUROC—a pixel-level localization score that remains within 2.6 pp of the best-performing models—indicating that the proposed Z-Score Calibration and Masked MSE Loss effectively preserve fine-grained defect localization capability even within an ultra-lightweight structure. As will be demonstrated in Sect. 4.3, this accuracy is accompanied by a throughput advantage exceeding 200× over memory bank-based methods.

4.3 Computational Efficiency and Real-Time Inference Analysis

In real-world manufacturing lines, not only detection accuracy but also real-time processing speed and low memory footprint on resource-constrained environments are critical requirements. This subsection benchmarks the total inference parameters, trainable parameters, and inference speed (FPS) of C-MTSS against the baseline models.

As shown in Table 3, memory bank-based methods (BTF, M3DM) deliver the highest localization accuracy but require over 100–300M parameters and incur severe computational bottlenecks due to feature matching during inference, yielding only 0.5–3.2 FPS. Even knowledge distillation and feature mapping approaches (AST, MMRD, CFM) require 24–50M parameters and achieve moderate throughput of 5–30 FPS, which remains insufficient for millisecond-level response requirements.

In contrast, the entire inference footprint of C-MTSS—including two frozen teacher models and the trainable student—amounts to only **2.15M** parameters, representing an approximately 140× reduction compared to M3DM and roughly 11× reduction compared to AST. Among these, only **0.78M** parameters are trainable. The high throughput of C-MTSS (**1031.8 FPS**) can be largely attributed to the teacher network design: rather than executing the full ResNet-18 backbone, each teacher performs a *truncated forward pass* through only the shallow layers (up to Layer 2), discarding the computationally expensive deeper

Table 3. Computational efficiency and inference speed comparison. C-MTSS was measured on an NVIDIA A100 GPU. Total Params includes all parameters loaded during inference (including frozen teachers). Values marked with ~ are cited from respective publications or estimated under comparable settings. Memory values for BTF, AST, M3DM, and CFM are from [3].

Method	Paradigm	Total Params (M) ↓	Trainable Params (M) ↓	Memory (MB) ↓	Speed (FPS) ↑	P-AUROC (%) ↑
BTF [24]	MB	> 100.0	–	381.1	~3.2	99.2
M3DM [4]	MB	> 300.0	> 100.0	6526.1	~0.5	99.2
AST [26]	KD	≈ 24.5	≈ 24.5	463.9	~5.0	97.6
MMRD [27]	KD	≈ 50.0	≈ 25.0	–	~30	98.7
CFM [3]	FM	≈ 40.0	≈ 5.0	437.9	~21.8	99.3
C-MTSS (Ours)	KD	**2.15**	**0.78**	**38.0**	**1031.8**	96.7

layers (Layers 3 and 4). Combined with the absence of any memory bank lookups, this design results in a per-image latency below 1 ms.

To further examine deployment scenarios without dedicated GPU acceleration, we additionally report a CPU-only reference benchmark. This benchmark is divided into two settings. The end-to-end setting includes file loading, RGB/depth preprocessing, surface normal extraction, model inference, Z-Score fusion, and anomaly scoring. The model-scoring setting excludes file loading and preprocessing, and measures only the inference and anomaly scoring stages using preprocessed inputs.

Table 4. CPU-only reference benchmark of C-MTSS. End-to-end includes preprocessing and anomaly scoring, while model scoring excludes file loading and preprocessing. Measurements are conducted with batch size 1 and an input resolution of 256 × 256 on the CPU of the same workstation.

Setting	Latency (ms/image) ↓	FPS ↑
CPU-only End-to-End	75.87	13.18
CPU-only Model Scoring	34.47	29.01

As shown in Table 4, the CPU-only end-to-end setting achieves 75.87 ms per image, corresponding to 13.18 FPS. In contrast, the model-scoring setting achieves 34.47 ms per image and 29.01 FPS, approaching the common video-rate criterion of 30 FPS. These results indicate that the full CPU-only pipeline is still affected by file I/O and surface normal preprocessing, while the computational burden of the C-MTSS inference and scoring stages remains relatively low even without GPU acceleration.

In summary, high-accuracy models such as M3DM or LSFA may be more suitable for offline analysis or accuracy-oriented inspection scenarios. In contrast, C-MTSS targets real-time manufacturing inspection environments where latency, memory footprint, and throughput are critical constraints. Therefore, the proposed framework should be viewed not as a model that solely maximizes benchmark accuracy, but as a practical lightweight structure for real-time inspection. It achieves 96.7% P-AUROC while exceeding 1,000 FPS on an A100 GPU, and the additional CPU-only benchmark further shows that its model-scoring stage approaches video-rate throughput.

4.4 Sensitivity Analysis of Z-Score Fusion Weights

To examine whether the Z-Score fusion weights are overly dependent on a single heuristic setting, we conduct a sensitivity analysis by varying the RGB and 3D weights while keeping their sum equal to 1.0. This experiment is performed on all 10 categories of the MVTec 3D-AD dataset, with the RGB-to-3D ratio varied from 0.4:0.6 to 0.8:0.2.

Table 5. Sensitivity analysis of Z-Score fusion weights on MVTec 3D-AD. I-AUROC values are averaged across all 10 categories. The default setting used in C-MTSS is highlighted in bold.

RGB	3D	I-AUROC (%) ↑
0.4	0.6	87.32
0.5	0.5	89.75
0.6	**0.4**	**91.30**
0.7	0.3	89.81
0.8	0.2	89.60

As shown in Table 5, the default RGB-to-3D weight ratio of 0.6:0.4 achieves the highest I-AUROC of 91.30%. When the 3D branch is assigned a larger weight than the RGB branch, the performance drops to 87.32%. This suggests that excessive reliance on 3D residuals can amplify shape-related variations or sensor noise in the final anomaly score. Conversely, increasing the RGB weight beyond 0.6 also reduces the detection accuracy, indicating that surface-normal cues still provide complementary information for structural defects.

These results show that the 0.6:0.4 fusion weight used in C-MTSS is not an arbitrary choice, but provides the best balance between RGB texture information and 3D surface-normal information in our experiments. The analysis further suggests that Z-Score Calibration is not merely a scale-normalization step, but also affects how modality-specific error distributions contribute to the final anomaly score.

4.5 Qualitative Visualization

To verify the anomaly localization capability across all categories of the proposed C-MTSS framework, we present qualitative visualization results for all 10

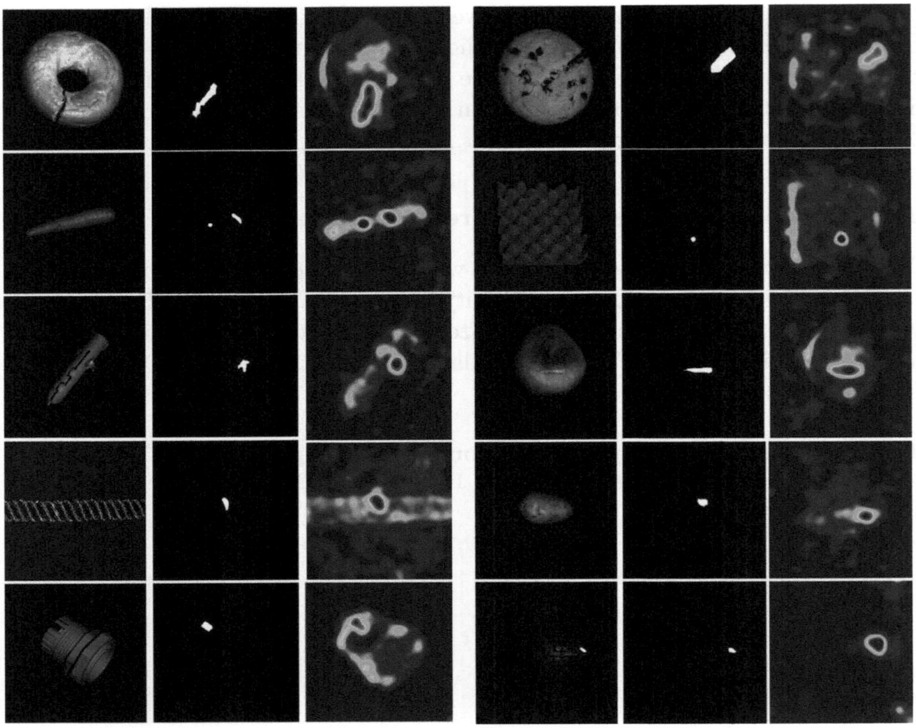

Fig. 3. Qualitative anomaly localization on all 10 categories of MVTec 3D-AD. Each group of three images (from left to right: input RGB, ground truth mask, anomaly heatmap) corresponds to one category, arranged in a 5 × 2 grid.

categories of the MVTec 3D-AD dataset in Fig. 3. Each group of three images (from left to right: input RGB, ground truth, anomaly heatmap) corresponds to one category, arranged in a 5 × 2 grid.

The overall results can be analyzed according to three physical property groups. For natural object categories with significant intra-class shape variance—such as **Bagel**, **Carrot**, **Cookie**, **Peach**, and **Potato**—C-MTSS successfully focuses the heatmap on localized surface defects (e.g., cracks and dents) through the Surface Normal conversion to disregard global variations in tilt and height distribution. For rigid body categories with fixed geometries—such as **Dowel**, **Cable Gland**, and **Tire**—the predicted anomaly regions exhibit high spatial correspondence with the ground truth masks, demonstrating the precise localization capability of the lightweight student network even for fine-grained structural defects. Finally, for deformable object categories whose spatial layout varies across samples—such as **Rope** and **Foam**—texture-based anomalous regions are clearly activated in the heatmaps, which suggests that the RGB and 3D Surface Normal modalities provide complementary cues even under spatial deformation.

Table 6. Ablation study on MVTec 3D-AD. Each row progressively adds one component.

Variant	Dual-Stem	Masked MSE	Z-Score	I-AUROC (%)	P-AUROC (%)
A				87.68	95.80
B	✓			90.34	96.10
C	✓	✓		90.50	96.14
D	✓	✓	✓	**91.30**	**96.70**

4.6 Ablation Study

To quantify the contribution of each proposed component, we conduct an ablation study with four progressive variants on MVTec 3D-AD, as summarized in Table 6.

Variant A serves as the baseline, where a single-stem student network processes both modalities through a shared input layer, trained with a standard MSE loss, and the two error maps are directly summed without normalization. Replacing the single-stem input with the proposed dual-stem structure ($A \to B$) yields the largest individual gain of +2.66 in I-AUROC and +0.30 in P-AUROC, confirming that separating the initial feature pathways reduces gradient interference between the heterogeneous RGB and 3D modalities. Adding the Masked MSE loss ($B \to C$) produces a modest increase of +0.16 in I-AUROC and +0.04 in P-AUROC. While its standalone effect is limited, the primary purpose of this module is not to directly boost classification accuracy but to suppress background noise in the 3D modality, which refines the per-modality error distributions. This benefit becomes apparent when combined with Z-Score Calibration: applying Z-Score fusion on top of Masked MSE ($C \to D$) yields +0.80 in I-AUROC and +0.56 in P-AUROC. Without background suppression, the calibration statistics are contaminated by sensor-invalid regions, which diminishes the effectiveness of the normalization-based fusion. Overall, the full C-MTSS configuration (Variant D) outperforms the baseline by +3.62 in I-AUROC and +0.90 in P-AUROC, validating the complementary contributions of all three proposed components.

5 Conclusion

This paper presented C-MTSS, a lightweight framework for 3D-2D multimodal industrial anomaly detection. The framework uses three design choices: dual-stem late fusion, Masked MSE Loss, and Z-Score Calibration. These components jointly address gradient interference, background noise, and scale discrepancy when processing heterogeneous modalities within an ultra-lightweight structure.

On the MVTec 3D-AD benchmark, C-MTSS achieves 91.3% I-AUROC and 96.7% P-AUROC. It also requires only 38 MB of GPU memory and delivers over 1,000 FPS. These results suggest that C-MTSS provides a practical balance between detection performance, inference speed, and memory efficiency for real-time industrial inspection.

However, a performance gap remains on texture-heavy categories due to the limited representational capacity of the compact student network. Future work aims to narrow this gap by adopting foundation models as teachers to improve distillation quality and by leveraging cross-modal attention mechanisms to exploit complementary information between modalities, while preserving the real-time inference capability.

Acknowledgments. This work was supported by the Institute of Information & Communications Technology Planning & Evaluation (IITP)-ICT Creative Consilience Program grant funded by the Korea government (MSIT) (IITP-2026-RS-2020-II201821), This work was supported by the Korea Institute for Advancement of Technology (KIAT) grant funded by the Korea Government under the Industrial Innovation Talent Growth Support Project (KIAT-2026-RS-2026-25532917).

Disclosure of Interests. The authors have no competing interests to declare that are relevant to the content of this article.

References

1. Bergmann, P., et al.: The MVTec 3D-ad dataset for unsupervised 3D anomaly detection and localization. In: VISAPP, pp. 202–213 (2022). https://doi.org/10.5220/0010935500003123
2. Bhunia, A., et al.: Looking 3D: anomaly detection with 2D-3D alignment. In: CVPR, pp. 17263–17272 (2024). https://doi.org/10.1109/CVPR52733.2024.01634
3. Costanzino, A., et al.: Multimodal industrial anomaly detection by crossmodal feature mapping. In: CVPR, pp. 17234–17243 (2024). https://doi.org/10.1109/CVPR52733.2024.01631
4. Wang, Y., et al.: Multimodal industrial anomaly detection via hybrid fusion. In: CVPR, pp. 8032–8041 (2023). https://doi.org/10.48550/arXiv.2303.00601
5. Tu, Y., et al.: Self-supervised feature adaptation for 3d industrial anomaly detection. In: ECCV, pp. 75–91. Springer (2024). https://doi.org/10.1007/978-3-031-72627-9_5
6. Batzner, K., et al.: EfficientAD: accurate visual anomaly detection at millisecond-level latencies. In: WACV, pp. 128–138 (2024). https://doi.org/10.1109/WACV57701.2024.00020
7. Cheng, Y., et al.: Towards high-resolution 3D anomaly detection: a scalable dataset and real-time framework for subtle industrial defects. In: AAAI, vol. 40, pp. 3327–3334 (2026). https://doi.org/10.1609/aaai.v40i5.37328
8. Bergmann, P., et al.: MVTec AD–a comprehensive real-world dataset for unsupervised anomaly detection. In: CVPR, pp. 9584–9592 (2019). https://doi.org/10.1109/CVPR.2019.00982

9. Akcay, S., Atapour-Abarghouei, A., Breckon, T.P.: GANomaly: semi-supervised anomaly detection via adversarial training. In: Jawahar, C.V., Li, H., Mori, G., Schindler, K. (eds.) ACCV 2018. LNCS, vol. 11363, pp. 622–637. Springer, Cham (2019). https://doi.org/10.1007/978-3-030-20893-6_39
10. Schlegl, T., Seeböck, P., Waldstein, S.M., Schmidt-Erfurth, U., Langs, G.: Unsupervised anomaly detection with generative adversarial networks to guide marker discovery. In: Niethammer, M., Styner, M., Aylward, S., Zhu, H., Oguz, I., Yap, P.-T., Shen, D. (eds.) IPMI 2017. LNCS, vol. 10265, pp. 146–157. Springer, Cham (2017). https://doi.org/10.1007/978-3-319-59050-9_12
11. Li, H., et al.: Hyperbolic anomaly detection. In: CVPR, pp. 17511–17520 (2024). https://doi.org/10.1109/CVPR52733.2024.01658
12. Gudovskiy, D., et al.: CFlow-AD: real-time unsupervised anomaly detection with localization via conditional normalizing flows. In: WACV, pp. 98–107 (2022). https://doi.org/10.48550/arXiv.2107.12571
13. Fučka, M., et al.: Transfusion – a transparency-based diffusion model for anomaly detection. In: ECCV, pp. 91–108. Springer (2024). https://doi.org/10.1007/978-3-031-72761-0_6
14. Liu, C., et al.: Learning diffusion models for multi-view anomaly detection. In: ECCV, pp. 328–345. Springer (2024). https://doi.org/10.1007/978-3-031-73414-4_19
15. Isaac-Medina, B.K.S., et al.: Towards open-world object-based anomaly detection via self-supervised outlier synthesis. In: ECCV, pp. 196–214. Springer (2024). https://doi.org/10.1007/978-3-031-73209-6_12
16. Lee, J.C., et al.: Continuous memory representation for anomaly detection. In: ECCV, pp. 438–454. Springer (2024). https://doi.org/10.1007/978-3-031-72983-6_25
17. Sträter, L.P.J., et al.: GeneralAD: anomaly detection across domains by attending to distorted features. In: ECCV, pp. 448–465. Springer (2024). https://doi.org/10.1007/978-3-031-72913-3_25
18. Zhu, J., Pang, G.: Toward generalist anomaly detection via in-context residual learning with few-shot sample prompts. In: CVPR, pp. 17826–17836 (2024). https://doi.org/10.48550/arXiv.2403.06495
19. Deng, H., Li, X.: Anomaly detection via reverse distillation from one-class embedding. In: CVPR, pp. 9737–9746 (2022). https://doi.org/10.1109/CVPR52688.2022.00950
20. Salehi, M., et al.: Multiresolution knowledge distillation for anomaly detection. In: CVPR, pp. 14902–14912 (2021). https://doi.org/10.1109/CVPR46437.2021.01465
21. Wu, L., Zhou, J.: Heterogeneous knowledge distillation for anomaly detection. IEEE Access **12**, 161490–161499 (2024). https://doi.org/10.1109/ACCESS.2024.3415503
22. Zhu, W., et al.: Real-IAD D^3: a real-world 2D/pseudo-3D/3D dataset for industrial anomaly detection. In: CVPR, pp. 15214–15223 (2025). https://doi.org/10.1109/CVPR52734.2025.01417
23. Tao, C., et al.: G2SF: geometry-guided score fusion for multimodal industrial anomaly detection. In: ICCV, pp. 20551–20560 (2025). https://doi.org/10.48550/arXiv.2503.10091
24. Horwitz, E., et al.: Back to the feature: classical 3D features are (almost) all you need for 3D anomaly detection. In: CVPR Workshops, pp. 2968–2977 (2023). https://doi.org/10.1109/CVPRW59228.2023.00298

25. Lin, Y., et al.: Commonality in few: few-shot multimodal anomaly detection via hypergraph-enhanced memory. In: AAAI, vol. 40, pp. 7015–7023 (2026). https://doi.org/10.1609/aaai.v40i9.37636
26. Rudolph, M., et al.: Asymmetric student-teacher networks for industrial anomaly detection. In: WACV, pp. 2592–2602 (2023). https://doi.org/10.1109/WACV56688.2023.00261
27. Gu, Z., et al.: Rethinking reverse distillation for multi-modal anomaly detection. In: AAAI, vol. 38, pp. 8218–8226 (2024). https://doi.org/10.1609/aaai.v38i8.28687

Class-Specific Feature Weighting Query Strategy for Online Active Learning in Intrusion Detection

Daniel Mourão Martins[1(✉)], Ronaldo Ribeiro Goldschmidt[1], and Ronaldo Moreira Salles[1,2]

[1] Military Institute of Engineering, Rio de Janeiro, RJ, Brazil
{mourao.daniel,ronaldo.rgold,salles}@ime.eb.br
[2] CIICESI, ESTG, Polytechnic of Porto, Porto, Portugal
rmo@estg.ipp.pt

Abstract. Network Intrusion Detection Systems operate in dynamic environments characterized by continuously evolving network traffic and the emergence of previously unseen attack patterns. Traditional supervised learning approaches typically assume closed-set scenarios and rely on large labeled datasets, limiting their applicability in real-world streaming scenarios where labeling is costly and concept drift occurs. Active Learning offers an alternative by selectively querying informative samples for annotation. However, most existing AL query strategies rely primarily on prediction uncertainty and implicitly assume that feature importance remains globally consistent across classes. In intrusion detection tasks, this assumption is often unrealistic, since different attack types may depend on distinct subsets of features. This work proposes a Class-Specific Feature Weighting for Open-Set (CSFWOS) framework for Online Active Learning. The proposed method models feature relevance independently for each class and selects samples based on a weighted feature space. This strategy enhances the distinction between known classes and previously unseen attacks in the feature space, supporting more reliable detection across diverse attack patterns. Experimental results on benchmark datasets show improvements in incremental detection performance under low query ratios in non-stationary streaming environments compared with widely adopted active learning strategies. The findings demonstrate the potential of the approach to inspire further research.

Keywords: Active Learning · Query Strategy · Feature Weighting · Data Stream · Intrusion Detection

1 Introduction

The rapid evolution of networked systems and the increasing sophistication of cyber threats, particularly zero-day attacks, pose significant challenges to Intrusion Detection Systems (IDS). Network environments are inherently dynamic,

O. Gervasi et al. (Eds.): ICCSA 2026, LNCS 16768, pp. 349–367, 2027.
https://doi.org/10.1007/978-3-032-30488-9_22

where data distributions evolve over time due to new applications, configuration changes, and emerging cyber threats [3,12].

Traditional supervised learning approaches rely on the closed-set assumption, where all classes are known a priori. Although effective in static environments, these methods degrade significantly in streaming scenarios, where continuous adaptation is required and labeled data is scarce [4].

Active Learning (AL) mitigates labeling costs by selecting the most informative samples for annotation. In streaming settings, this paradigm becomes Online Active Learning (OAL), where decisions must be made sequentially under strict labeling budgets [5,19,34].

Obtaining reliable labels is a costly process that demands time and specialized knowledge, becoming a significant bottleneck. Manual annotation by cybersecurity experts is costly, time-consuming, and operationally impractical in high-throughput environments. Furthermore, due to the sensitive nature of data security in network traffic, which may contain confidential or personal information, automatic labeling mechanisms are generally undesirable or unsafe, as incorrect or unsupervised labeling may propagate errors, introduce bias, or compromise security decisions. Consequently, careful human validation remains necessary, but should be reduced.

This reliance on human intervention to label new attack samples introduces additional complexity, creating bottlenecks that delay response times and reduce system agility. Although automated annotation methods have advanced, they cannot guarantee reliable labels. Consequently, expert validation remains necessary, motivating the development of optimized strategies that reduce the need for human annotation while preserving labeling quality [20].

Current models face significant challenges in differentiating between benign variations in network traffic, evolved variants of known attacks, and genuinely novel threats. These challenges are particularly pronounced in highly dynamic network environments. Thus, concept drift is an inherent characteristic of network traffic, in which the statistical properties of the data evolve over time [31].

Not all network traffic features contribute equally to pattern identification. Identifying more significant attributes or even irrelevant attributes can increase the performance of classification algorithms. Feature Weighting (FW) addresses this issue by assigning relevance to each attribute, allowing the algorithm to focus on the most discriminating information [24].

For instance, TCP window size may be critical for detecting denial-of-service (DoS) attacks but irrelevant for port scans. In the CICIDS-2017 dataset, "Subflow Fwd Bytes" and "Total Length Fwd Packet" features are key for identifying Infiltration and Bot attacks, whereas "Bwd Packet Length Std" is strong indicator for DoS variants [14]. Thus, global feature weighting fails to capture these class-specific distinctions.

This work investigates the intersection of these research areas by leveraging recent advances that incorporate feature weighting into active learning query strategies and enhance clustering algorithms. Specifically, we propose Class-Specific Feature Weighting for Open Set (CSFWOS) framework that combines feature-aware sample selection with improved cluster-based modeling. Our main contributions are summarized as follows:

- Class-specific feature weighting to capture heterogeneous feature relevance.
- A query strategy driven by feature-weight under labeling constraints.
- An OAL framework capable of handling concept drift in open-set scenarios.

The remainder of this paper is organized as follows. Section 2 presents the fundamental concepts of AL query strategies and FW, along with a review of related work. Section 3 describes the proposed methodology. Section 4 details the experimental setup and evaluation. Finally, Sect. 5 discusses the results and presents the conclusions of this study.

2 Background and Related Work

Active Learning has been widely studied to reduce the high cost of manual labeling in supervised tasks [13,32]. Rather than labeling entire datasets, AL iteratively selects the most informative instances through a query strategy. This approach is particularly suitable for cybersecurity, where expert analysis is required to validate alerts and identify new attack patterns [1,23]. By prioritizing informative samples, AL reduces annotation costs while maintaining competitive performance.

2.1 Active Learning in Data Streams

Traditional AL algorithms operate under batch learning assumptions, where the whole dataset is available during training. However, network traffic naturally arrives as a continuous data stream. In such environments, models must process incoming data sequentially while adapting to evolving distributions in real time under limited labeling budgets [5].

Data stream mining research highlights that evolving environments often suffer from concept drift [31]. In intrusion detection scenarios, these changes may occur due to novel attacks, evolving user behavior, or modifications in network infrastructure. Consequently, IDS models must continuously update their internal representations to remain effective.

2.2 Query Strategies in Active Learning

Hierarchical categorizations of AL query strategies indicate that they can be organized into several categories. Comprehensive taxonomies of these strategies are presented in [13,32].

However, despite variations in terminology and structural organization across the literature, most taxonomies converge toward a common set of conceptual groups. As illustrated in Fig. 1, query strategies encompass paradigms such as reinforcement learning, random sampling, and hybrid methods. Nevertheless, the core distinction lies in two primary categories: representativeness-based and informativeness-based.

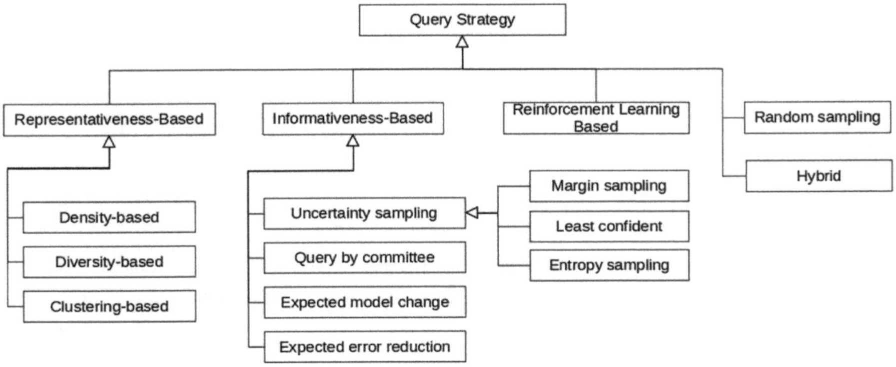

Fig. 1. A general taxonomy of query strategies for AL

- **Informativeness-Based:** these strategies select instances that maximize the expected information gain for the model or where the model exhibits low confidence in its predictions.
- **Representativeness-Based:** these strategies focus on the underlying structure of the data, selecting instances that are representative of the overall data distribution or of specific regions in the feature space.

In addition, hybrid strategies combine two or more query criteria, leveraging their complementary strengths while mitigating their individual limitations. Such approaches aim to balance exploration and exploitation [13,32], i.e. the exploration of new regions of the feature space with the exploitation of uncertainties at known boundaries. The evolution of online AL strategies shows a clear trend towards hybrid approaches.

Although these strategies have shown promising results in many domains, most existing approaches assume that feature contributions remain stable across classes. In network traffic data, however, the relevance of features may vary significantly between different types of attacks.

2.3 Feature Weighting in Active Learning

High-dimensional datasets often contain redundant or irrelevant features that may negatively affect the performance of machine learning algorithms. Feature weighting techniques have therefore been widely studied to estimate the relative importance of input variables and improve learning performance [9,10].

Global feature weighting approaches assign a single importance vector to the entire dataset, as in W-k-means [11] and IFWFCM [33]. Although effective in many scenarios, these approaches assume that feature relevance is homogeneous across the dataset.

More flexible approaches estimate feature relevance locally. Cluster-dependent weighting methods such as SSFCM-FWCW [9] and FWCW-FCM

[10] compute adaptive feature weights for each cluster, enabling subspace specialization and increased resilience to noise and outliers. Similarly, class-dependent weighting strategies have been proposed in high-dimensional classification settings, where feature importance varies significantly across classes [25].

In the context of Active Learning, feature-aware query strategies have recently gained attention. Methods such as AL-FEW [6] and SHAP-based acquisition strategies [30] incorporate feature importance information to guide instance selection. Although these approaches provide improved interpretability and structural reasoning, they typically rely on global feature importance measures, implicitly assuming that the same attributes are relevant for all classes.

2.4 Class-Specific Feature Weighting for Intrusion Detection

Different attack types often rely on distinct behavioral patterns and feature subsets. For instance, denial-of-service attacks may manifest through traffic volume anomalies, while infiltration attacks may be characterized by subtle protocol-level features. Consequently, global weighting schemes may obscure discriminative patterns.

Class-specific feature weighting addresses this limitation by estimating feature importance independently for each class. Instead of a single global vector, the model learns class-specific feature importance profiles.

This perspective is further supported by studies in text classification on Naïve Bayes classifiers, which show that class-specific feature weighting provides a more granular and realistic representation of feature relevance, since the importance of attributes naturally varies across classes [25].

Similar ideas have been explored in clustering and classification algorithms designed for high-dimensional data [9,25]. However, the integration of class-specific feature weighting into Active Learning query strategies remains limited.

Recent intrusion detection approaches have begun to incorporate domain knowledge into localized feature relevance. The DFAID framework [17], for example, incorporate feature-level information through a feature deviation score that identifies instances whose attribute values significantly deviate from the statistical distribution of the cluster where they reside. Similarly, A3PF [16] prioritizes samples by assigning higher importance to critical network attributes, but in a binary classification problem.

2.5 Comparative Analysis of Existing Strategies

The evolution from uncertainty-based to feature-aware approaches reveals a progressive shift toward structural reasoning. However, existing methods still exhibit important limitations, as summarized in Table 1.

Despite recent advances in OAL-based IDS, several limitations remain. First, most query strategies rely exclusively on prediction uncertainty and ignore structural information in feature space. Second, feature-aware approaches typically employ global feature importance, neglecting the fact that different attack classes

Table 1. Comparison of Active Learning strategies in intrusion detection

Method	Feature Scope	Query Criterion	Open-Set
Uncertainty Sampling	Global	Predictions based	Limited
Query by Committee	Global	Model disagreement	Limited
Density-Based	Global	Representativeness	Limited
Hybrid	Global	Mixed Criteria	Partial
AL-FEW [6]	Global	Feature Perturbation	No
SHAP-AL [30]	Global	Explanation based	No
Proposed	Class-Specific	Class Feature Weighting	Yes

may rely on distinct subsets of features. Finally, only a limited number of studies explicitly address open-set conditions where previously unseen attacks may appear.

These limitations motivate the development of query strategies capable of capturing class-specific variations in feature space while operating effectively in dynamic streaming environments, such as intrusion detection.

3 Proposed Methodology

This section presents the central contribution of this study: the Class-Specific Feature Weighting for Open-Set (CSFWOS) framework. The proposed methodology integrates local feature weighting with a query strategy specifically designed to capture structurally informative samples, supporting the learning of previously unseen attack patterns.

3.1 Streaming Protocol

A common evaluation protocol in streaming environments is prequential (test-then-train) evaluation, which evaluates each incoming instance before incorporating it into the training process [7,19]. This protocol provides an unbiased estimate of online predictive performance and enables continuous monitoring of performance degradation caused by distributional changes. In this protocol, each incoming batch is first evaluated using the current model to estimate instantaneous generalization performance and, if selected by the query strategy, is then incorporated into the training set.

This process ensures that performance metrics reflect the current data distribution, so degradation in prequential metrics such as Micro-F1 can act as an implicit signal of concept drift, enabling continuous monitoring and incremental model adaptation.

Let $\mathcal{B}_t$ denote the batch at time step t. The stream is defined as:

$$\mathcal{D} = \{\mathcal{B}_1, \mathcal{B}_2, \ldots, \mathcal{B}_T\} \tag{1}$$

In summary, for each incoming batch $\mathcal{B}_t$: (i) the model predicts labels (test phase), (ii) the query strategy selects informative samples, (iii) the oracle provides labels only for queried instances, and (iv) the model is incrementally updated (train phase).

3.2 Feature Importance Estimation

The framework is agnostic to the specific feature weighting method and supports multiple implementations, for example:

- **Impurity-based importance:** Feature importance metrics estimated from impurity-based splitting criteria in tree-based models (e.g., Gini impurity, entropy, and log-loss). Let $\mathrm{I}_j^{(c)}$ be the importance for feature j and class c from a one-vs-rest tree ensemble:

$$w_j^{(c)} = \mathrm{I}_j^{(c)} \tag{2}$$

- **SHAP-based importance:** Feature contributions computed using SHAP values. Let $\phi_j^{(c)}(\mathbf{x})$ be the SHAP value for feature j in class c and $\mathbb{E}[\cdot]$ the expectation operator representing the average value computed over the set of observed samples:

$$w_j^{(c)} = \mathbb{E}\big[|\phi_j^{(c)}(\mathbf{x})|\big] \tag{3}$$

- **ReliefF weighting:** Feature relevance estimated based on nearest-neighbor differences, based on relief algorithms:

$$w_j^{(c)} = \mathrm{ReliefF}_j^{(c)} \tag{4}$$

This flexibility allows adapting the framework to different models and computational constraints.

3.3 Class-Specific Feature Weighting

To capture heterogeneous feature relevance, we maintain a class-specific feature weighting representation [8]:

$$\mathbf{w}_t^{(c)} = \{w_{t,1}^{(c)}, w_{t,2}^{(c)}, \ldots, w_{t,d}^{(c)}\}, \quad c \in \mathcal{Y}_t \tag{5}$$

where $w_{t,j}^{(c)}$ represents the importance of feature j for class c at time t.

Unlike global feature importance, this formulation allows modeling class-specific patterns, which is particularly relevant in intrusion detection where different attack types rely on distinct subsets of features.

Let $\mathbf{x} \in \mathbb{R}^d$ denote an sample in $\mathcal{B}_t$ represented in a d-dimensional feature space, and let $\mathcal{C} = \{c_1, \ldots, c_n\}$ be the set of known classes. A classifier provides prior probabilities $P(c|\mathbf{x})$ for each class $c \in \mathcal{C}$.

A weighted representation of $\mathbf{x}$ is computed using:

$$\tilde{\mathbf{x}} = \mathbf{x} \odot \mathbf{w}(\mathbf{x})$$

where $\odot$ denotes the Hadamard (element-wise) product and $\mathbf{w}(\mathbf{x})$ can be defined according to one of the following strategies.

- **Probability-weighted feature space.** The feature weights are calculated as the expected class-specific weight vectors under the previously estimated distribution of all classes:

$$\mathbf{w}(\mathbf{x}) = \sum_{c \in \mathcal{C}} P(c|\mathbf{x})\mathbf{w}^{(c)}$$

- **Most probable class weighting.** Weights correspond to the class with maximum estimated probability:

$$c^* = \arg\max_{c \in \mathcal{C}} P(c|\mathbf{x}), \quad \mathbf{w}(\mathbf{x}) = \mathbf{w}^{(c^*)}$$

- **Top-k class averaged weighting.** To improve robustness, weights can be computed as the mean weight vector of the k most probable classes:

$$\mathbf{w}(\mathbf{x}) = \frac{1}{k} \sum_{c \in \mathcal{C}_k(\mathbf{x})} \mathbf{w}^{(c)}$$

  where $\mathcal{C}_k(\mathbf{x})$ denotes the set of k classes with highest probability.

3.4 Query Strategy

The CSFWOS adopts a hybrid query strategy that combines representativeness and uncertainty under a query budget. Let $\mathbf{x} \in \mathbb{R}^d$ denote an input sample and $\tilde{\mathbf{x}}$ its representation in the class-specific weighted feature space. Suspicious samples are defined as those for which the classifier exhibits predictive confidence below a threshold, i.e.

$$\mathcal{S} = \{\mathbf{x} \mid \max_{c \in \mathcal{C}} P(c|\mathbf{x}) < \tau_t\}.$$

First, the suspicious samples are mapped into the weighted feature space and clustered in order to partition them into regions with similar feature relevance. From each cluster k, a representative sample $\mathbf{r}_k$ is selected.

Let QR denote the predefined query ratio. The number of samples that can be submitted to the oracle for labeling is therefore defined as:

$$|\mathcal{Q}| = QR \times |\mathcal{B}_t| \tag{6}$$

The query set $\mathcal{Q}$ is constructed in two stages. Initially, the representative samples from each cluster are included:

$$\mathcal{Q}_1 = \{\mathbf{r}_k \mid k = 1, \ldots, K\}.$$

If $|\mathcal{Q}_1| < |\mathcal{Q}|$, the remaining query positions are filled using an uncertainty-based ranking. Let $U(\mathbf{x})$ denote the uncertainty score of the classifier. The remaining samples are selected according to

$$\mathcal{Q}_2 = \mathrm{Top}_{|\mathcal{Q}|-|\mathcal{Q}_1|}\left(U(\mathbf{x})\right), \quad \mathbf{x} \in \mathcal{S} \setminus \mathcal{Q}_1.$$

Finally, the query decision function is defined as

$$Q(\mathbf{x}_t) = \begin{cases} 1, & \mathbf{x}_t \in \mathcal{Q}_1 \cup \mathcal{Q}_2 \\ 0, & \text{otherwise.} \end{cases} \tag{7}$$

This strategy ensures that the selected samples maximize structural representativeness in the weighted feature space while prioritizing highly uncertain instances when completing the query budget.

Algorithm 1 summarizes the proposed framework. Initially, predicted class probabilities are estimated and suspicious samples are identified based on model confidence (lines 1–3). For each incoming batch, a class-specific feature importance vector is computed, and a weighted representation of each sample is derived accordingly (lines 5–7). Subsequently, the query budget is determined and clustering is performed in the weighted feature space (lines 8–9), from which representative samples are selected (line 10). The algorithm then, when necessary, augments the query set with additional instances selected based on uncertainty scores, in accordance with the predefined query ratio (lines 11–18). Finally, the selected samples are queried for labeling, the model is updated, and the process proceeds to the next batch (lines 19–22).

4 Experimental Evaluation

4.1 Experimental Setup

To evaluate the effectiveness of the proposed query strategy, we conduct experiments in a streaming scenario under non-stationary and open-set conditions.

Datasets. The evaluation is performed using widely adopted intrusion detection benchmarks datasets: NF-UNSW-NB15-V2, CIC-IDS2017 [17,22].

These datasets are widely used in the literature due to their diversity of attack types, class imbalance, and realistic traffic characteristics [21,29]. This evaluation includes the NetFlow-based version of the UNSW-NB15 dataset, which consist of network flow records extracted from raw packet captures and transformed into standardized NetFlow features [27].

In the NF-UNSW-NB15-V2 dataset, the "MIN_TTL" and "MAX_TTL" features were excluded from the analysis because they exhibited unrealistically high predictive performance [26].

To simulate real-world streaming conditions, the data stream is constructed such that the initial training set includes only benign traffic and a single known attack class. The remaining attack classes are then introduced progressively over

Algorithm 1. CSFWOS Query Strategy

Require: Stream of batches $\mathcal{D} = \{\mathcal{B}_1, \ldots, \mathcal{B}_T\}$, query ratio QR , classifier model f

for each batch $\mathcal{B}_t$ **do**
  Predict class probabilities $P(c|\mathbf{x})$ for all $\mathbf{x} \in \mathcal{B}_t$
  Identify suspicious samples $\mathcal{S} = \{\mathbf{x} \in \mathcal{B}_t \mid \max_c P(c|\mathbf{x}) < \tau\}$
  for each $\mathbf{x} \in \mathcal{S}$ **do**
    Compute class-specific weighted vector $\mathbf{w}(\mathbf{x})$
    Compute weighted representations $\tilde{\mathbf{x}} = \mathbf{x} \odot \mathbf{w}(\mathbf{x})$
  end for
  Compute query budget cardinality $|\mathcal{Q}| = \lfloor QR \times |\mathcal{B}_t| \rfloor$
  Cluster $\tilde{\mathbf{x}}$ into k clusters, where k is proportional to $|\mathcal{Q}|$
  Select representative sample $\mathbf{r}_k$ from each cluster
  Initialize query set $\mathcal{Q}_1 = \{\mathbf{r}_1, \ldots, \mathbf{r}_K\}$
  if $|\mathcal{Q}_1| < |\mathcal{Q}|$ **then**
    Compute uncertainty score $U(\mathbf{x})$ for $\mathbf{x} \in \mathcal{S} \setminus \mathcal{Q}_1$
    Select remaining samples $\mathcal{Q}_2 = \text{Top}_{|\mathcal{Q}|-|\mathcal{Q}_1|}(U(\mathbf{x}))$
    $\mathcal{Q} = \mathcal{Q}_1 \cup \mathcal{Q}_2$
  else
    $\mathcal{Q} = \mathcal{Q}_1$
  end if
  Query oracle for labels of $\mathbf{x} \in \mathcal{Q}$
  Update classifier f using new labels
  Update class-specific feature weighting $w_j^{(c)}$ using new labels
end for

time. Specifically, each dataset is partitioned into larger segments, with each segment incorporating a new attack class not present in the previous ones. Once introduced, samples from a given attack class continue to appear in subsequent segments until the available instances are exhausted or the stream terminates. These macro-level segments are subsequently concatenated and repartitioned, while preserving their order, into smaller batches according to the predefined batch size. This procedure ensures the gradual emergence of novel attacks while maintaining a consistent batch structure for streaming evaluation.

Initial Configuration. The proposed framework supports multiple design alternatives and parameter configurations. In this study, a single empirically representative configuration was adopted, based on commonly used parameter settings reported in the literature.

This choice balances statistical stability, computational efficiency, and experimental reproducibility while enabling a clear evaluation of the proposed query strategy under realistic labeling constraints. Consequently, the evaluation focuses on assessing the effectiveness of the proposed framework. The selected parameters are summarized in Table 2.

Labeling efficiency is evaluated using query ratios 1%, 5%, 10%, 20%, enabling analysis under different levels of human supervision. To facilitate consistent comparison across experiments, the confidence threshold is kept fixed in the experi-

Table 2. Configuration parameters

Parameter	Value
Initial seed size	10,000 samples
Seed composition	benign + 1 known attack
Batch size ($\|B_t\|$)	1,000 samples
Number of batches	58(NF-UNSW-NB15-V2), 34(CIC-IDS2017)
Confidence threshold (τ)	0.95
Query ratio (QR)	1%, 5%, 10%, 20%
Clustering model	Mini-batch K-means
Cluster scaling factor k	0.5
Cluster representative sample $\mathbf{r}_k$	Nearest point to centroid
Uncertainty criteria ($U(\mathbf{x})$)	Margin Sampling
Classifier model f	Random Forest
Feature importance estimation	Impurity-based importance: Gini impurity
Class-specific feature weighting	Probability-weighted feature space
Evaluation protocol	Prequential (test-then-train) evaluation

ments. The classifier and the feature-importance estimation model are independent to avoid bias.

To evaluate zero-day detection capability, an open-set simulation protocol is adopted in which only one attack class is initially known, while the remaining attack classes are introduced in subsequent batches [20]. This setup reproduces real environments where new attacks emerge after deployment.

4.2 Baselines

The proposed method is compared against:

- Random Sampling (RS)
- Uncertainty Sampling: Margin Sampling (US)
- Hybrid Approach: Margin Sampling + Clustering-based (Hybrid)
- No Active Learning: all samples labeled (Query All)

These methods represent standard baselines in active learning and open-set recognition [2,28].

4.3 Results and Analysis

Tables 3 and 4 present a comparison between the baseline methods and the proposed CSFWOS approach across the evaluated datasets. The reported results correspond to the average performance over 10 independent runs for each configuration, using different random seeds to ensure robustness. CSFWOS adopts the

Table 3. Performance on **NF-UNSW-NB15-V2** under different query ratios.

Method	QR	Macro F1	Macro Recall	Balanced Acc.	AULC
RS	1%	0.562 ± 0.005	0.589 ± 0.004	0.660 ± 0.004	0.733 ± 0.003
	5%	0.660 ± 0.003	0.678 ± 0.002	0.767 ± 0.002	0.818 ± 0.001
	10%	0.688 ± 0.002	0.704 ± 0.002	0.796 ± 0.001	0.841 ± 0.001
	20%	0.707 ± 0.001	0.723 ± 0.001	0.817 ± 0.001	0.857 ± 0.001
US	1%	0.542 ± 0.011	0.575 ± 0.008	0.638 ± 0.006	0.713 ± 0.005
	5%	0.646 ± 0.004	0.662 ± 0.004	0.747 ± 0.003	0.802 ± 0.003
	10%	0.691 ± 0.003	0.706 ± 0.003	0.798 ± 0.003	0.842 ± 0.002
	20%	0.715 ± 0.002	0.730 ± 0.002	0.822 ± 0.000	0.861 ± 0.000
Hybrid	1%	0.540 ± 0.011	0.570 ± 0.009	0.639 ± 0.008	0.715 ± 0.007
	5%	0.660 ± 0.002	0.675 ± 0.002	0.764 ± 0.003	0.816 ± 0.002
	10%	0.692 ± 0.002	0.708 ± 0.002	0.799 ± 0.002	0.843 ± 0.001
	20%	0.713 ± 0.002	0.728 ± 0.002	0.822 ± 0.001	0.860 ± 0.001
CSFWOS	1%	0.532 ± 0.014	0.563 ± 0.012	0.632 ± 0.012	0.710 ± 0.011
	5%	0.660 ± 0.003	0.677 ± 0.003	0.764 ± 0.003	0.816 ± 0.002
	10%	**0.695 ± 0.002**	**0.711 ± 0.002**	**0.803 ± 0.001**	**0.846 ± 0.001**
	20%	0.715 ± 0.002	0.730 ± 0.002	0.822 ± 0.001	0.861 ± 0.001
Query All	100%	0.723 ± 0.002	0.736 ± 0.002	0.831 ± 0.000	0.867 ± 0.000

Table 4. Performance on **CIC-IDS2017** under different query ratios.

Method	QR	Macro F1	Macro Recall	Balanced Acc.	AULC
RS	1%	0.713 ± 0.029	0.753 ± 0.018	0.812 ± 0.019	0.808 ± 0.023
	5%	0.771 ± 0.012	0.791 ± 0.009	0.857 ± 0.010	0.862 ± 0.011
	10%	0.775 ± 0.010	0.793 ± 0.008	0.862 ± 0.007	0.868 ± 0.011
	20%	0.772 ± 0.012	0.789 ± 0.009	0.862 ± 0.007	0.868 ± 0.011
US	1%	0.712 ± 0.029	0.748 ± 0.017	0.809 ± 0.020	0.804 ± 0.027
	5%	0.745 ± 0.029	0.772 ± 0.019	0.836 ± 0.018	0.838 ± 0.023
	10%	0.748 ± 0.020	0.775 ± 0.015	0.841 ± 0.010	0.841 ± 0.014
	20%	0.768 ± 0.014	0.787 ± 0.011	0.859 ± 0.010	0.865 ± 0.013
Hybrid	1%	0.721 ± 0.022	0.758 ± 0.014	0.820 ± 0.015	0.816 ± 0.022
	5%	0.771 ± 0.023	0.790 ± 0.017	0.860 ± 0.015	0.866 ± 0.021
	10%	0.779 ± 0.021	0.797 ± 0.016	0.865 ± 0.016	0.872 ± 0.021
	20%	0.781 ± 0.008	0.796 ± 0.007	0.866 ± 0.006	0.875 ± 0.008
CSFWOS	1%	**0.731 ± 0.027**	**0.763 ± 0.017**	**0.824 ± 0.017**	**0.823 ± 0.023**
	5%	0.771 ± 0.024	0.790 ± 0.019	0.857 ± 0.016	0.865 ± 0.020
	10%	**0.783 ± 0.020**	0.798 ± 0.015	**0.868 ± 0.012**	**0.877 ± 0.016**
	20%	0.782 ± 0.015	0.797 ± 0.012	0.867 ± 0.008	0.876 ± 0.011
Query All	100%	0.799 ± 0.005	0.809 ± 0.005	0.920 ± 0.000	0.939 ± 0.000

same configuration as the Hybrid method, differing only in the incorporation of class-specific feature weighting. Therefore, any observed performance differences between these two methods can be directly attributed to the effect of introducing class-weighted feature importance.

The results summarized in the tables show that increasing the query ratio consistently improves performance. However, within the same dataset and query ratio, the performance of all strategies is similar, with minor variations observed.

Performance differences across datasets can be attributed to variations in their underlying characteristics, including feature sets and their distributions, class overlap, attack types, and the quality of data generation and extraction. Consequently, the evaluation metrics exhibit distinct value ranges across datasets. These variations highlight the challenges of evaluating query strategies across multiple datasets, even within the same application domain.

On the NF-UNSW-NB15-V2 dataset (Table 3), the proposed CSFWOS approach achieves the best performance at QR = 10%. Although the gains over competing methods are moderate, this result indicates that the proposed class-specific feature weighting mechanism can effectively identify informative samples. The RS method was more effective at QR = 1%, while in the other experiments there were similar results between some methods.

In contrast, on the CIC-IDS2017 dataset (Table 4), CSFWOS demonstrates more consistent gains across different query ratios. Notably, it achieves the best results at QR = 1% and QR = 10%, outperforming the baselines in most metrics, including AULC. This behavior may be attributed to clearer class-specific patterns or more stable feature distributions in this dataset.

From a comparative perspective, the Hybrid method generally performs competitively. However, CSFWOS consistently achieves slight improvements in several scenarios, despite their nearly identical configurations.

Finally, it is worth noting that the gap between all active learning strategies and the fully supervised setting (Query All) remains significant, especially in the CIC-IDS2017 dataset. This reinforces the inherent trade-off between labeling cost and performance.

Per-Class Analysis. To better understand the behavior of the proposed strategy across different attack categories, we analyze the evolution of the F1-score for each class during the streaming process. Figure 2 illustrates the temporal evolution of per-class performance for selected classes from one of the experimental scenarios using the NF-UNSW-NB15-V2 dataset with a query ratio of 10%.

Several observations can be derived from this analysis. Attack classes that appear later in the stream, such as *Generic*, initially present low detection performance but gradually improve as informative samples are selected by the query strategy and incorporated into the training process. This behavior reflects the ability of the framework to adapt to emerging patterns in the data distribution.

Second, minority classes such as *Backdoor* show more variability in their performance due to limited sample availability. Finally, classes such as *Fuzzers*, *Reconnaissance*, and *Shellcode* reach high performance relatively quickly, indi-

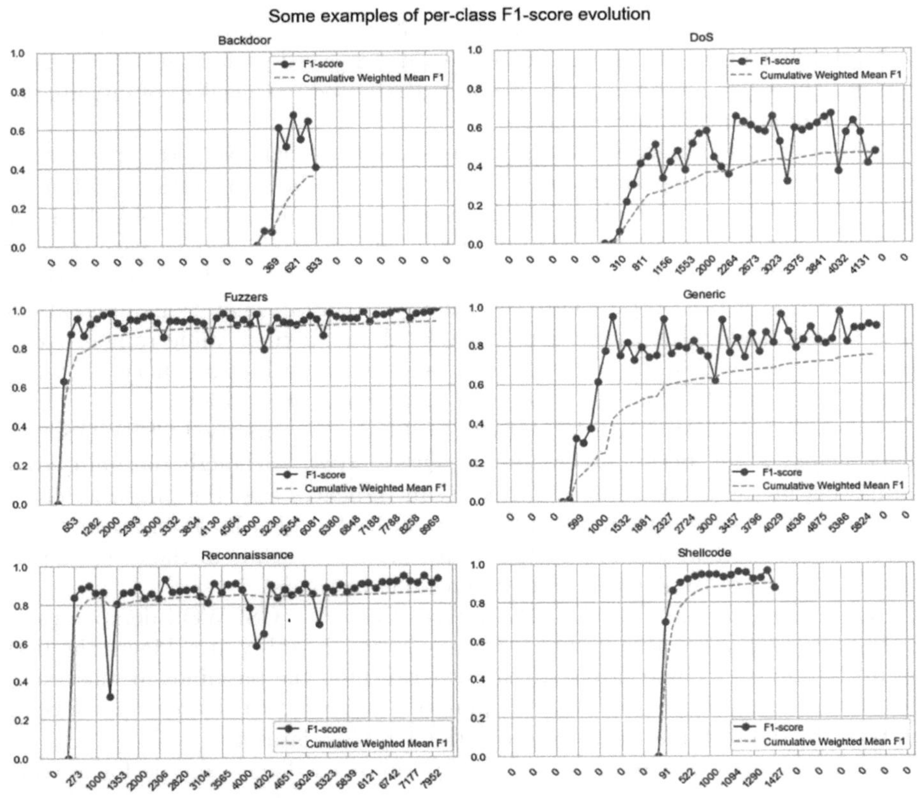

Fig. 2. Per-class F1-score evolution across the streaming batches. The blue curve represents the instantaneous F1-score for each class, while the red dashed curve indicates the cumulative weighted mean F1-score over time. (Color figure online)

cating that the proposed strategy effectively captures the relevant structural patterns of these attack categories in the feature space.

Overall, the curves show heterogeneous behavior across attack types: some classes exhibit rapid performance gains, while others improve more gradually, and in certain cases high F1-scores are not achieved.

Similar patterns were observed across all experimental configurations.

AULC Analysis. To evaluate the labeling efficiency, we analyze the evolution of classification performance throughout the streaming process across all experiments. As an illustrative example, Fig. 3 presents the Micro-F1 score as a function of the cumulative number of processed samples in one of these scenarios.

The dotted vertical lines in Fig. 3 indicate the points at which new attack classes are introduced into the stream. At these points, a noticeable drop in the curve is observed, reflecting the temporary degradation in performance caused

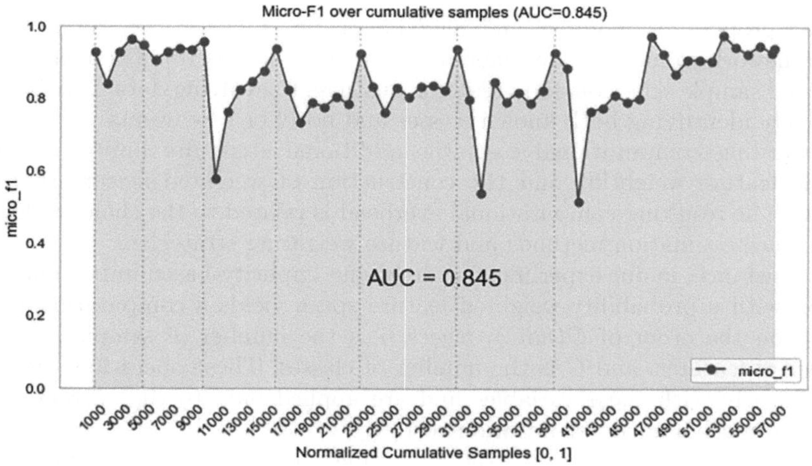

Fig. 3. Micro-F1 score over the normalized cumulative number of samples. The shaded region represents the Area Under the Learning Curve (AULC).

by the appearance of previously unseen patterns. However, the recovery rate is relatively fast as related samples are labeled. This behavior highlights the ability of the query strategy to quickly identify, label, and incorporate informative samples related to new classes into the training set.

Overall, the AULC values presented in the Tables 3 and 4 indicates that the proposed method not only attains higher final performance but also exhibits greater learning efficiency throughout the stream.

5 Discussion and Conclusion

The results of this study reinforce that no universal Active Learning strategy is suitable for all deployment scenarios. The effectiveness of a query strategy depends on multiple factors, including computational constraints, labeling resources, and the characteristics of the specific data domain. In the intrusion detection domain, these constraints are further exacerbated by non-stationarity, class imbalance, and the presence of previously unseen attack types.

Features that exhibit low importance for known classes may become highly informative when detecting novel classes, particularly when their values lie outside the support of known distributions. This highlights a fundamental limitation of classical feature importance methods: in open-set scenarios, the most relevant features are not necessarily those that maximize discrimination among known classes, but those that signal deviations from established patterns.

Recent research explores complementary strategies to address these challenges. For instance, pseudo-labeling expands the labeled set without additional oracle cost [16], while adaptive query budgets driven by drift detection methods, such as ADWIN [15], concentrate labeling efforts during distributional changes.

Our proposal is modular and model-agnostic, allowing the Active Learning framework to incorporate different learning models [6,18]. The results show improved sample selection and greater robustness to evolving data distributions, effectively identifying both known classes and novel or rare events.

Regarding computational cost, the additional steps are limited to class-specific feature weighting and the construction of weighted feature representations. The resulting computational overhead is related to the choice of feature importance estimation methods and feature weighting strategies.

For instance, in our experiments, combining impurity-based importance estimation with a probability-weighted feature space yields a computational complexity on the order of $\mathcal{O}(ndC)$, where n is the number of samples, d is the number of features, and C is the number of classes. These operations therefore scale linearly with these variables and are applied only to the current batch, resulting in a bounded per-iteration cost.

Since the framework reuses the clustering and uncertainty components of hybrid strategies, the overall computational complexity remains in the same asymptotic class. Moreover, these operations can be parallelized or computed on a subset of samples, further reducing practical overhead. Consequently, under the adopted configuration, the additional overhead remains controlled, achieving a favorable balance between improved sample selection and efficient resource utilization.

5.1 Future Work

Several directions remain open for future research. First, integrating full open-set and incremental capabilities represents a promising direction for future work, along with exploring optimization strategies for selecting alternative initial configurations and other datasets.

Second, extending the framework algorithm to explore hybrid strategies by evaluating additional configuration combinations that integrate structural feature analysis with representation-based and information-based approaches may further enhance its ability to detect and adapt to emerging threats.

Thirdly, improving robustness to adversarial attacks is essential, particularly in security-sensitive applications where attackers may attempt to manipulate feature distributions.

Finally, to maximize the impact of each query, it is necessary to use label propagation. Our research aim to leverage label propagation in the future.

Acknowledgments. This study was financed in part by the Coordenação de Aperfeiçoamento de Pessoal de Nível Superior - Brasil (CAPES) – Finance Code 001. It was also supported in part by the Brazilian Funding Authority for Studies and Projects (Finep) [Cyber Semantics Project - Contract No. 0.1.22.0335.00/Ref. Finep No. 0172/22] and the Systems Development Center of the Brazilian Army.

References

1. Abdulganiyu, O.H., Ait Tchakoucht, T., Saheed, Y.K.: A systematic literature review for network intrusion detection system (IDS). Int. J. Inf. Secur. **22**(5), 1125–1162 (2023). https://doi.org/10.1007/s10207-023-00682-2
2. Aggarwal, C.C.: Data Classification: Algorithms and Applications. CRC Press (2014). https://doi.org/10.1201/b17320
3. Ahmad, R., Alsmadi, I., Alhamdani, W., Tawalbeh, L.: Zero-day attack detection: a systematic literature review. Artif. Intell. Rev. **56**(10), 10733–10811 (2023). https://doi.org/10.1007/s10462-023-10437-z
4. Alotaibi, F., Maffeis, S.: Rasd: semantic shift detection and adaptation for network intrusion detection. In: Pitropakis, N., Katsikas, S., Furnell, S., Markantonakis, K. (eds.) SEC 2024. IFIP Advances in Information and Communication Technology, vol. 710, pp. 16–30. Springer, Cham (2024). https://doi.org/10.1007/978-3-031-65175-5_2
5. Cacciarelli, D., Kulahci, M.: Active learning for data streams: a survey. Mach. Learn. **113**(1), 185–239 (2023). https://doi.org/10.1007/s10994-023-06454-2
6. Elokri, C., Ouaderhman, T., Chamlal, H.: Al-few: an enhanced approach for optimized query examples through feature weighting in active learning. Expert Syst. Appl. **266**, 126045 (2025). https://doi.org/10.1016/j.eswa.2024.126045
7. Gama, J., Sebastião, R., Rodrigues, P.P.: On evaluating stream learning algorithms. Mach. Learn. **90**(3), 317–346 (2012). https://doi.org/10.1007/s10994-012-5320-9
8. Golzari Oskouei, A., et al.: Feature-weighted fuzzy clustering methods: an experimental review. Neurocomputing **619**, 129176 (2025). https://doi.org/10.1016/j.neucom.2024.129176
9. Golzari Oskouei, A., Samadi, N., Tanha, J.: Feature-weight and cluster-weight learning in fuzzy C-means method for semi-supervised clusteringimage 1. Appl. Soft Comput. **161**, 111712 (2024). https://doi.org/10.1016/j.asoc.2024.111712
10. Hashemzadeh, M., Golzari Oskouei, A., Farajzadeh, N.: New fuzzy C-means clustering method based on feature-weight and cluster-weight learning. Appl. Soft Comput. **78**, 324–345 (2019). https://doi.org/10.1016/j.asoc.2019.02.038
11. Huang, J., Ng, M., Rong, H., Li, Z.: Automated variable weighting in k-means type clustering. IEEE Trans. Pattern Anal. Mach. Intell. **27**(5), 657–668 (2005). https://doi.org/10.1109/TPAMI.2005.95
12. Issa, M.M., Aljanabi, M., Muhialdeen, H.M.: Systematic literature review on intrusion detection systems: research trends, algorithms, methods, datasets, and limitations. J. Intell. Syst. **33**(20230248) (2024). https://doi.org/10.1515/jisys-2023-0248
13. Kumar, P., Gupta, A.: Active learning query strategies for classification, regression, and clustering: a survey. J. Comput. Sci. Technol. **35**(4), 913–945 (2020). https://doi.org/10.1007/s11390-020-9487-4
14. Kurniabudi, Stiawan, D., Darmawijoyo, Bin Idris, M.Y., Bamhdi, A.M., Budiarto, R.: CICIDS-2017 dataset feature analysis with information gain for anomaly detection. IEEE Access **8**, 132911–132921 (2020). https://doi.org/10.1109/access.2020.3009843
15. Li, A., Han, M., Mu, D., Gao, Z., Liu, S.: Online active learning method for multi-class imbalanced data stream. Knowl. Inf. Syst. **66**(4), 2355–2391 (2024). https://doi.org/10.1007/s10115-023-02027-w

16. Li, B., Wang, Y., Cheng, L.: Adaptive and augmented active anomaly detection on dynamic network traffic streams. Front. Inf. Technol. Electron. Eng. **25**(3), 446–460 (2024). https://doi.org/10.1631/FITEE.2300244
17. Li, B., Wang, Y.J., Xu, K.L., Cheng, L., Qin, Z.Q.: DFAID: density-aware and feature-deviated active intrusion detection over network traffic streams. Comput. Secur. **118** (2022). https://doi.org/10.1016/j.cose.2022.102719
18. Li, N., Qi, Y., Li, C., Zhao, Z.: Active learning for data quality control: a survey. ACM J. Data Inf. Qual. **16**(2) (2024). https://doi.org/10.1145/3663369
19. Malialis, K., Panayiotou, C.G., Polycarpou, M.M.: Nonstationary data stream classification with online active learning and Siamese neural networks. Neurocomputing **512**, 235–252 (2022). https://doi.org/10.1016/j.neucom.2022.09.065
20. Martins, D.M., Salles, R.M., Goldschmidt, R.R.: Adaptive online learning approaches for detecting unknown attacks in network traffic: a systematic literature review. Secur. Priv. **8**(5), e70084 (2025). https://doi.org/10.1002/spy2.70084
21. Moustafa, N., Slay, J.: UNSW-NB15: a comprehensive data set for network intrusion detection systems. In: 2015 Military Communication and Information System Conference (MilCIS), pp. 1–6 (2015). https://doi.org/10.1109/MilCIS.2015.7348942
22. Nixon, C., Sedky, M., Champion, J., Hassan, M.: SALAD: a split active learning based unsupervised network data stream anomaly detection method using autoencoders. Expert Syst. with Appl. **248**(123439) (2024). https://doi.org/10.1016/j.eswa.2024.123439
23. Nixon, C., et al.: Reviews in online data stream and active learning for cyber intrusion detection-a systematic literature review. In: Abdennadher, N., Benkhelifa, E., Lauret, J.M., Jararweh, Y. (eds.) 2021 6th International Conference on Fog and Mobile Edge Computing, FMEC 2021, pp. 126–131. Staffordshire University, Stoke On Trent (2021). https://doi.org/10.1109/FMEC54266.2021.9732566
24. Niño-Adan, I., Manjarres, D., Landa-Torres, I., Portillo, E.: Feature weighting methods: a review. Expert Syst. Appl. **184**, 115424 (2021). https://doi.org/10.1016/j.eswa.2021.115424
25. Ruan, S., Li, H., Li, C., Song, K.: Class-specific deep feature weighting for naïve bayes text classifiers. IEEE Access **8**, 20151–20159 (2020). https://doi.org/10.1109/ACCESS.2020.2968984
26. Sarhan, M., Layeghy, S., Moustafa, N., Portmann, M.: NetFlow datasets for machine learning-based network intrusion detection systems. In: Deze, Z., Huang, H., Hou, R., Rho, S., Chilamkurti, N. (eds.) BDTA/WiCON -2020. LNICST, vol. 371, pp. 117–135. Springer, Cham (2021). https://doi.org/10.1007/978-3-030-72802-1_9
27. Sarhan, M., Layeghy, S., Portmann, M.: Towards a standard feature set for network intrusion detection system datasets. Mob. Netw. Appl.. **27**(1), 357–370 (2021). https://doi.org/10.1007/s11036-021-01843-0
28. Scheirer, W.J., Rocha, A., Sapkota, A., Boult, T.E.: Toward open set recognition. IEEE Trans. Pattern Anal. Mach. Intell. **35**(7), 1757–1772 (2013). https://doi.org/10.1109/TPAMI.2012.256
29. Sharafaldin, I., Lashkari, A.H., Ghorbani, A.A.: Toward generating a new intrusion detection dataset and intrusion traffic characterization. In: Proceedings of the 4th International Conference on Information System Security and Privacy (ICISSP), pp. 108–116 (2018). https://doi.org/10.5220/0006639801080116
30. Shim, J., Kang, S.: Why does this query need to be labeled?: enhancing active learning through explanation-based interventions in query selection. Expert Syst. with Appl. **290**, 128443 (2025). https://doi.org/10.1016/j.eswa.2025.128443

31. Suárez-Cetrulo, A.L., Quintana, D., Cervantes, A.: A survey on machine learning for recurring concept drifting data streams. Expert Syst. Appl. **213**, 118934 (2023). https://doi.org/10.1016/j.eswa.2022.118934
32. Tharwat, A., Schenck, W.: A survey on active learning: state-of-the-art, practical challenges and research directions. Mathematics **11**(4), 820 (2023). https://doi.org/10.3390/math11040820
33. Xing, H.J., Ha, M.H.: Further improvements in feature-weighted fuzzy C-means. Inf. Sci. **267**, 1–15 (2014). https://doi.org/10.1016/j.ins.2014.01.033
34. Zhang, Y., et al.: Online adaptive asymmetric active learning with limited budgets. IEEE Trans. Knowl. Data Eng. **33**(6), 2680–2692 (2021). https://doi.org/10.1109/TKDE.2019.2955078

A Formal Constraint-Based Method for Detecting Gaps in Input Validation Test Suites

Oleksandr Kolchyn(✉) and Daria Rudenko

V.M. Glushkov Institute of Cybernetics NAS of Ukraine, Kyiv, Ukraine
kolchin_av@yahoo.com

Abstract. Insufficient input validation remains a common source of software vulnerabilities and functional errors. Although numerous structural coverage criteria exist in software testing, they generally do not specifically target the completeness or inconsistencies of input validation itself. In this paper, we propose a formal, specification-agnostic method for systematically identifying gaps in existing test suites with respect to input validation logic. It tracks symbolic constraints on tainted variables from source to sink locations along feasible execution paths and analyzes their subsumption relations to identify test cases that reveal previously untested validation scenarios. Our method can therefore reveal unduly weak or overly restrictive input constraints, thereby providing insights into potential defects in the implemented validation checks.

Keywords: testing · coverage criteria · input validation · symbolic constraints

1 Introduction

Thorough input validation is an essential defense against both accidental faults and malicious data. Numerous studies, including the Common Weakness Enumeration (CWE) rankings [1], identify weak or inconsistent input validation as one of the most frequent sources of software vulnerabilities. Despite its critical role, it is still difficult to systematically assess how adequate input validation testing is.

Requirements-based testing alone may miss important validation paths, especially when specifications are incomplete or imprecise. For this reason, practitioners usually combine it with structural white-box criteria to achieve broader coverage [2]. This combination improves path exploration, but it does not directly measure how thoroughly the validation logic itself is exercised. Even if all tests cover the documented requirements and meet strict coverage criteria [2–5], some aspects of validation may remain untested. For example, a test can appear redundant under strong criteria such as MC/DC [6] or all-uses [7], yet still provide useful insight by exercising insufficiently tested input constraints or exposing inconsistencies in the validation logic [3, 4, 8, 9].

To cover different behaviors while reducing redundancy, testers often use equivalence class testing [2, 10]. This approach partitions the input domain into subsets that are

O. Gervasi et al. (Eds.): ICCSA 2026, LNCS 16768, pp. 368–380, 2027.
https://doi.org/10.1007/978-3-032-30488-9_23

expected to produce similar behavior and then selects representative test cases. However, such partitions rely on assumptions made by the tester and may not reflect the actual validation logic implemented in the code. As a result, some validation conditions can be overlooked, leading to incomplete coverage.

The effect of input validation lies in how the program later consumes the validated data. Therefore, equivalence class testing can be applied more precisely at sink locations, where inputs affect external actions or critical operations. Building on this insight, we automate the detection of input validation gaps by analyzing existing tests in terms of symbolic constraints derived from the code. For specified input variables, we track the constraints as they propagate toward sink locations, thereby capturing how validation rules influence observable behavior. We then interpret these constraints as equivalence classes represented in the current test suite and use them to identify missing tests. The key idea is simple: if a potential test would produce weaker constraints at a sink location than any existing test, this suggests a path where a validation check may be missing. This approach provides a systematic way to assess and improve the completeness of input validation.

In summary, this paper makes two main contributions: (1) we propose a formal criterion for detecting incompleteness in input validation test suites, and (2) we illustrate its practical relevance through small motivating examples and formal reasoning.

The rest of the paper is organized as follows. Section 2 introduces motivating examples. Section 3 describes the proposed method, including the incompleteness criterion and the test synthesis procedure based on symbolic constraint analysis. Section 4 discusses related work, and Sect. 5 concludes the paper and outlines future work.

2 Motivational Examples

To show the limitations of traditional coverage criteria in assessing input validation completeness, we consider two small programs together with their test suites. In both cases, standard structural criteria can be fully satisfied, but some constraint regions at the sink locations are still not exercised. This means that parts of the effective input domain—namely those that affect observable behavior—remain uncovered.

```
void bar(int x, bool b)
{
    int res = x;
    if(b == true) {
        if(x < 1)
            res = 1;
        if(x > 10)
            res = 10;
    }
    if(res == 10)
        report("maximum");
    process(res);
}
```

Fig. 1. Example 1

```
void foo(int d, int n, bool
b){
    double res = 1.0;
    if(d > 0 || b == true) {
        if(n > 0)
            res = div(n, d);
        else
            res = 0.0;
    }
    send(res);
}
```

Fig. 2. Example 2

For the program in the first example (Fig. 1), coverage according to the all-uses and MC/DC criteria can be achieved using the following test suite:

{ #1: (0,True), #2: (11,True), #3: (10,False) }.

From the data-flow coverage perspective, for the variable `res`, the first test covers the definition–use pair (05, 11), the second covers (07, 09) and (07, 11), and the third covers (02, 09) and (02, 11). The MC/DC criterion is trivially satisfied, as the conditions contain only single predicates, and all branches are covered. From the equivalence class testing perspective, the value of variable x falls into the following classes: $x < 1$ (test #1), $x > 10$ (test #2), and $1 \leq x \leq 10$ (test #3). One might assume that the intended range of acceptable values of `res` at line 11 is [1..10]. As a result, these tests trigger a call to the function `process` for only two input values: 1 (test #1) and 10 (tests #2 and #3). All other possible ranges (including $x < 1$ and $x > 10$) remain untested, even though they could be exercised by inputs of the form (x, False) where $x \neq 10$. This naturally raises the question of whether this situation reflects merely missing tests or whether it exposes a defect in the program's validation logic. Note that our method does not attempt to decide program correctness, nor does it explicitly identify sink-specific critical values; rather, it identifies potential input ranges at relevant sink locations that are not covered by the existing tests, thereby guiding the developer's further inspection.

For the program in Fig. 2, the test suite below fully satisfies MC/DC and all-uses:

{ #1: (0,False,0), #2: (1,False,1), #3: (0,True,0) }.

Test#1 covers the definition–use pair (02, 09) for the variable `res`; test#2 covers (05, 09); and test#3 covers (07, 09). In addition, test#2 covers the computational-use pairs (01, 05) for the variables `d` and `n`. Taken together, these tests satisfy the MC/DC criterion: for the condition at line 03, tests #1 and #2 isolate the effect of the predicate $d > 0$, whereas tests #1 and #3 isolate the effect of the predicate `b==true`. However, none of the tests exercises the case in which the value of `d` passed as an argument to `div` lies in the range $d \leq 0$. An input such as $d = 0$ could—assuming `div` performs an arithmetic division—result in a runtime failure due to division by zero.

3 Method Description

3.1 Test Suite Incompleteness Criterion

Let P be a deterministic program represented as a control-flow graph G = (N, E), where N is the set of statements and $E \subseteq N \times N$ is the set of control-flow edges. Given an input vector *in*, execution of P produces a *concrete trace* $t_{in}^{c} = <s_0, s_1, \ldots, s_n>$, where $s_i \in N$ and $(s_i, s_{i+1}) \in E$, representing the sequence of executed statements along with concrete variable valuations. Since the program is deterministic, each input *in* induces exactly one feasible trace. An *abstract trace* $t_{in}^{a} = abstraction(t_{in}^{c})$ traverses the same control flow path as t_{in}^{c} and abstracts its execution by replacing concrete values with symbolic expressions over program variables [11] while treating the inputs as non-deterministic assignments. Let *T* denote the set of abstract traces corresponding to the tests in an existing test suite, v denote a set of certain (tainted) variables, and let $R(v, s, t)$ denote the symbolic constraints on program variables from v at location $s \in t$ on the trace $t \in T$. Intuitively, these constraints characterize the possible values of variables in v that could be exercised by the sequence of statements traversed by t.

For fixed v and s, we say that the test suite T is ***incomplete*** if there exists a feasible abstract trace t' such that the following condition holds:

$$\forall \, \mathrm{t} \in T, R(v, s, t') \not\models R(v, s, t) \tag{1}$$

This condition indicates that t' explores a path with validation checks not covered by any existing trace in T. Consequently, t' exposes a previously uncovered region of the input space, corresponding to a new equivalence class from the perspective of equivalence class testing. This reasoning builds on the monotonicity property for deterministic programs, according to which the set of feasible input valuations can only decrease along a symbolic path [10]. Formally, for two abstract traces t_1 and t_2 reaching the same program location, $R(v, s, t_1) \models R(v, s, t_2) \Rightarrow \mathrm{Inputs}(t_1) \subseteq \mathrm{Inputs}(t_2)$. Applying this property to the above condition, we derive the following implication:

$$\forall t \in T, R(v, s, t') \not\models R(v, s, t) \Rightarrow \forall t \in T, \ \mathrm{Inputs}(t\prime) \nsubseteq \mathrm{Inputs}(t),$$

which formally justifies that t' corresponds to a previously uncovered equivalence class in the input space, and therefore the corresponding test should be added to the suite.

In Example 1, for the variable `res` at line 11, the three test traces yield the constraints `res` $\in \{1, 10\}$. The input `(0,False)` traverses the trace $t' = (01, 02, 03, 09, 11, 12)$, whose abstraction produces constraint $R(\{\texttt{res}\}, 11, t') \equiv \texttt{res} \neq \texttt{10}$. Clearly, this does not imply the constraints observed in tests #1–#3. In Example 2, the input `(0, True, 1)` reveals an unconstrained use of the variable `d`, indicating that `d` lacks prior validation.

The proposed criterion can also be viewed as a logical completeness relation over the symbolic constraints induced by the test suite: if no such t' exists, the test suite is logically complete, i.e., all equivalence classes at the selected location s and for the variable set v are represented by corresponding input values.

We also consider the complementary cases, where the inferred constraints are either *stricter* than those covered by the existing test suite or *partially overlapping* with them.

The first case occurs when, for a fixed variables set v and location s, there exists a feasible trace t' such that the following condition holds:

$$\exists t \in T : \ R(v, s, t') \models R(v, s, t) \wedge R(v, s, t') \not\models R(v, s, t') \tag{2}$$

This means that the constraint $R(v, s, t')$ is strictly stronger than the constraint induced by at least one existing test, and thus t' represents an execution in which the validation imposes stricter input conditions than t. Such cases may indicate over-restrictive input validation, where the program unintentionally rejects valid inputs, or inconsistencies between alternative validation paths.

The second case concerns partially overlapping constraints among existing traces.

In this situation, for a fixed set of variables v and location s, there exist traces such that the constraints intersect without fully subsuming each other:

$$\exists t_i, t_j \in T, \ (R(v, s, t_i) \wedge R(v, s, t_j) \neq \bot) \wedge R(v, s, t_i) \not\models R(v, s, t_j) \wedge R(v, s, t_j) \not\models R(v, s, t_i) \tag{3}$$

From the perspective of input validation, such cases may indicate that additional variables should be considered to strengthen the analyzed constraints. However, such overlap may also point to inconsistencies in how validation rules are applied to the same subset of input values across different execution paths. This, in turn, motivates the generation of new tests that explore input combinations both within and outside the overlapping regions. Such tests can help identify parts of the input space where the implemented validation logic may be too restrictive.

3.2 Example

The following example demonstrates how the proposed coverage criterion operates in the case of numeric ranges. Let the initial test suite for Example 3 (Fig. 3) be constructed according to the following set of abstract traces: {$\mathbf{t_1}$: Start, I, A, B, D, S, End_1; $\mathbf{t_2}$: Start, I, A, C, D, S, End_1; $\mathbf{t_3}$: Start, I, F, G, D, E, End_1; $\mathbf{t_4}$: Start, I, F, H, End_2}.

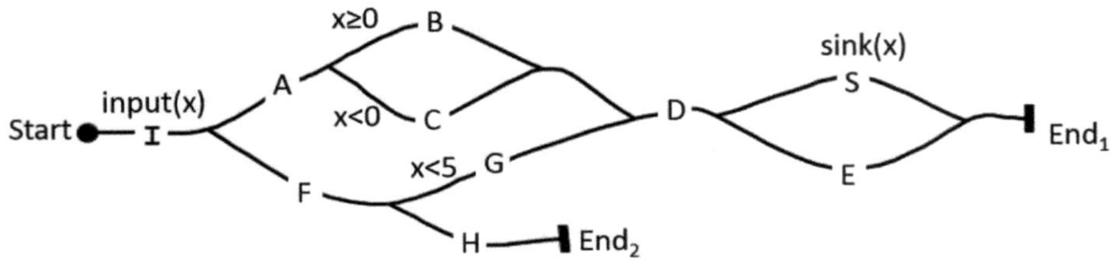

Fig. 3. Example 3

It is worth noting that this set is sufficient to satisfy both the all-uses and branch coverage criteria. The first two traces reach the sink location with the following symbolic constraints on the variable x: $R(\text{x, S, t}_1) \equiv \text{x} \geq 0$, $R(\text{x, S, t}_2) \equiv \text{x} < 0$. Taken together, these constraints cover the entire numeric domain. However, there exists an additional feasible trace: $\mathbf{t_5}$: Start, I, F, G, D, S, End_1, which reaches the sink location under the constraint $R(\text{x, S, t}_5) \equiv \text{x} < 5$. This constraint clearly satisfies condition (1), and according to our criterion, the presence of this trace indicates an incompleteness in the current test suite and therefore it must be incorporated. If, however, the constraint at G were $\text{x} = 5$, condition (2) would apply. Similarly, condition (3) could be demonstrated with a constraint like $-5 < \text{x} < 5$.

Although the motivating examples use scalar numeric inputs, the proposed method is based on symbolic constraints and is not tied to a specific data type. The notion of a range is treated as an abstract constraint domain, where intersection corresponds to constraint satisfiability. This makes it possible to apply the approach to other structured data types supported by modern SMT solvers. For example, in the case of strings or sequences, constraints may describe length bounds, prefix or substring relations, character-level properties, or other declarative conditions derived from path-specific input validation logic.

Furthermore, the analysis is sink-oriented and relies on function-level symbolic summaries. These summaries can be reused across different calling contexts, which enables compositional reasoning and supports modular analysis.

3.3 Synthesizing New Tests via Symbolic Constraint Analysis

To initiate the search for a potential new test t', we begin with the symbolic constraints derived from the existing test suite T. Each test $t \in T$ that reaches a given program location s defines a constraint $R(v, s, t')$ for a selected set of variables v. The goal is to identify a new test case $t' \notin T$ through a corresponding constraint $R(v, s, t')$ that satisfies one of the following conditions: (1), (2), or (3). Practically, this can be done by:

1. Selecting a representative sink location s and variable set v;
2. Reconstructing the constraints (v,s,t) from traces of existing test suite;
3. Synthesizing candidate constraints based on conditions (1), (2) or (3);
4. In the presence of loops or recursion, the proposed criterion can be applied similarly to existing methods based on bounded unrolling [12]. When extending the current test suite, the same unrolling bound can be used to ensure a fair comparison and consistency with the existing tests.
5. Solving the resulting constraint system to obtain concrete input values for t', typically using an SMT or SAT solver.

If the solver produces a satisfying assignment, it defines a feasible execution trace [11–14] corresponding to a new test case, thereby extending the validation assessment.

One way to synthesize candidate constraints is to use model checking [15]. In this approach, a coverage obligation is encoded as a temporal property over a finite-state model of the program. Using Linear Temporal Logic (LTL), the coverage requirement for a single range r can be written as follows:

$$\varphi_{u,v,\mathrm{r}} = \mathbf{F}(\mathrm{at_u} \wedge (v \in r)).$$

where $\mathrm{at_u}$ denotes the program counter at statement u, and $\mathbf{F}$ is the eventually operator in LTL. While this formulation assumes a fixed target range r, the same mechanism can be extended to support on-the-fly discovery of previously uncovered value ranges. Let RANGES denote the set of value ranges already covered by an existing test suite. We use `constraint`(u, v) to denote the set of symbolic constraints over variable v at location u along a given execution path, derived from the program logic and the current path conditions. We write `ranges(c)` for the set of value ranges induced by a constraint `c`. At each iteration, the model checker is queried with:

$$\mathrm{F}(\mathrm{at}_u \wedge ((\exists\, r \in \texttt{ranges}(\texttt{constraint}(u, v)) \colon r \setminus \texttt{RANGES}(u, v) \neq \varnothing))$$

Intuitively, the query checks whether there exists a feasible execution in which the value of v at location u falls into a range that has not yet been exercised. If the formula is satisfiable, the model checker returns a counterexample execution path. This path can then be translated into a concrete test case. The symbolic constraints associated with this path are used to extract one or more previously uncovered value ranges, which are then merged into RANGES. In this way, the set of covered ranges is gradually refined. At each iteration, only ranges that are still uncovered are considered, which helps avoid redundant exploration.

The procedure iterates until the corresponding LTL query produces no counterexample. At this point, the model checker determines that no feasible execution exists in which v takes a value outside the ranges already represented in RANGES. This means that all distinct value ranges that can reach the use location along feasible program paths have been exercised. Loops do not introduce additional coverage obligations once a fixpoint in the value ranges is reached. After that point, further iterations do not produce new ranges beyond the already established partitions.

This iterative refinement process is conceptually similar to counterexample-guided abstraction refinement (CEGAR) [16]. The set of covered value ranges can be seen as a current abstraction of the input space. Each LTL query then checks whether there exists a counterexample that violates this abstraction. If such a path is found, it is used to refine the abstraction by introducing new value ranges. Unlike standard CEGAR approaches, which typically refine control-flow or predicate abstractions, our method focuses directly on refining value partitions derived from symbolic constraints. As a result, the approach is inherently data-driven.

The procedure terminates due to two key properties. First, refinements are monotonic: each step only extends the accumulated value ranges in RANGES and never removes them. Second, the exploration operates over a finite set of symbolic states modulo constraint equivalence. Therefore, only a finite number of distinct maximal value ranges can be generated at each use location. Once the maximal range at the sink location is reached, further exploration does not produce additional refinements.

Overall, the approach avoids the need to enumerate all possible combinations of value ranges in advance. Instead, it ensures that all distinct value ranges reaching a use location are eventually covered through a systematic, iterative process guided by counterexamples from the model checker.

4 Case Study: Railway Speed Supervision Logic

System Context. Modern railway signaling and train protection systems, such as the European Train Control System, continuously monitor train speed and distance to ensure that a train can safely stop before reaching a target location. These systems compute dynamic braking curves based on the train's braking capability, its current speed, and the remaining distance to the target. The onboard controller predicts future speed reductions using mathematical models of braking dynamics and track characteristics [17]. In many signaling systems, the permitted speed can be approximated using a simple relation derived from braking physics: $v_{safe} = \sqrt{2ad}$, where v_{safe} is the maximum safe speed, a is the braking deceleration, d is the remaining distance to the target. Similar relations appear in railway control systems such as LZB and ETCS when computing permitted speed curves during braking supervision [18]. In this case study, we analyze a simplified supervisory module (Fig. 4) inspired by such speed-monitoring logic.

Supervisory Module Example The module computes a safe speed limit based on current operating parameters. The function `computeSafeSpeed` contains the sink location of interest – the braking-based speed calculation (lines 30, 31). Before performing the calculation, the system validates the inputs using `validateSupervisionInputs` function to ensure that they satisfy operational constraints. The validation logic contains multiple interacting constraints over several input variables, therefore different execution paths impose different constraints on the parameter `currentSpeed` before reaching this sink. These constraints induce complex regions in the input space, and structural coverage criteria do not guarantee that test cases explore the boundaries of these regions.

```
01. enum Mode { NORMAL, EMERGENCY };
02. bool validateSupervisionInputs(
03.     double currentSpeed,
04.     double targetDistance,
05.     double brakeDeceleration,
06.     Mode mode) {
07.     if (currentSpeed < 0 || currentSpeed > 140)
08.         return false;
09.     if (mode == EMERGENCY && currentSpeed > 30)
10.         return false;
11.     if (targetDistance <= 0)
12.         return false;
13.     if (brakeDeceleration < 0.3)
14.         return false;
15.     return true;
16.}

17. double computeSafeSpeed(
18.     double currentSpeed,
19.     double targetDistance,
20.     double brakeDeceleration,
21.     Mode mode) {
22.     if (!validateSupervisionInputs(
23.             currentSpeed,
24.             targetDistance,
25.             brakeDeceleration,
26.             mode)) {
27.         triggerFailSafeMode();
28.         return 0;
29.     }
30.     return min(currentSpeed,
31.                sqrt(2*brakeDeceleration*targetDistance));
32.}
```

Fig. 4. Supervisory Module Example

Existing Test Suite The test suite shown in Table 1 represents the initial test suite provided as input to our method.

Coverage Achieved The test suite satisfies branch coverage, MC/DC, and all-uses data-flow coverage, with all branches and variable uses exercised. For the compound predicate at line 09, tests T3 and T5 demonstrate the independent influence of `currentSpeed > 30`, while tests T4 and T5 demonstrate the independent influence of `mode == EMERGENCY`. From the perspective of traditional structural testing criteria, the module therefore appears to be adequately tested. However, only test T6 reaches the

Table 1. Existing test suite

test	currentSpeed, m/s	targetDistance, m	brakeDeceleration, m/s^2	mode	validation result
T1	−1	1000	0.1	NORMAL	failed
T2	141	600	0.7	NORMAL	failed
T3	30	0	0.3	EMERGENCY	failed
T4	140	300	0.2	NORMAL	failed
T5	140	200	0.8	EMERGENCY	failed
T6	20	400	1.1	EMERGENCY	successful

speed-computation sink, whereas tests T1–T5 terminate in the validation stage. Consequently, one more range of valid values at the sink location remains uncovered by the test suite. The validation logic defines the following allowable ranges of `currentSpeed` depending on the execution path:

Path 1 — Normal operation:

`mode != EMERGENCY, 0 ≤ currentSpeed ≤ 140`

Path 2 — Emergency supervision

`mode == EMERGENCY, 0 ≤ currentSpeed ≤ 30`

The only test reaching the sink location is:

`T6: mode = EMERGENCY, currentSpeed = 20`

The corresponding abstract trace *T6*^{a} reaches the sink location under the constraints:

```
mode == EMERGENCY ∧ 0 ≤ currentSpeed ≤ 30 ∧
targetDistance > 0 ∧ brakeDeceleration ≥ 0.3
```

The corresponding LTL query, with the range `currentSpeed ≤ 30` subtracted, produces possible paths reaching the sink location under the given constraints:

```
mode == NORMAL ∧ 0 ≤ currentSpeed ≤ 140 ∧
targetDistance > 0 ∧ brakeDeceleration ≥ 0.3
```

Therefore the following valid input region is not covered:

R`(currentSpeed,` line `30, T7) = 30 < currentSpeed ≤ 140`

This region corresponds to legitimate operating conditions under the `NORMAL` mode but is never exercised in the computation of the safe speed.

Missing Test Case. Test suite analysis reveals an additional test case (see Table 2) which reaches the sink and exercises the previously uncovered range.

Table 2. Missing test case

test	currentSpeed, m/s	targetDistance, m	brakeDeceleration, m/s^2	mode	validation result
T7	140	10000	1	NORMAL	successful

Summary This case study illustrates how our method identifies uncovered operational ranges in safety-critical control logic, even when the existing test suite satisfies stringent structural coverage criteria such as MC/DC and all-uses dataflow coverage.

5 Related Work and Discussion

Earlier work on test coverage metrics has demonstrated that high structural coverage does not necessarily imply adequate testing of program behaviors, motivating semantic approaches to test adequacy [5, 19]. Reference [20] studies quality attributes of test cases and test suites and identifies coverage as an important concern from practitioners' perspective. These results point to the need for evaluating test adequacy beyond structural metrics, which motivates semantics-aware and specification-independent approaches such as the one proposed in this work.

Apart from verifying known sink-specific values, input validation is often tested indirectly. Practitioners usually rely on structural coverage criteria to ensure that different execution paths are exercised. Our approach follows a related best practice by using equivalence-class reasoning to select representative (boundary) inputs from each class that may lead to different program behaviors [2, 21–23]. In black-box testing, such partitions are typically defined manually. In contrast, techniques such as symbolic execution [13, 14] and coverage-guided fuzzing [24] attempt to explore feasible paths more systematically. However, these approaches do not directly evaluate whether validation is sufficient and provide limited semantic insight into whether executed paths correspond to well- or poorly-validated inputs. Compared to taint-analysis methods [25], which mainly track syntactic propagation through assignments and control dependencies, our approach shifts the focus away from the mere presence of sanitization and toward the logical diversity of input validation.

Work such as [3, 8, 26] employ combinations of validation checks, yet suffer from redundant enumeration and do not evaluate validation completeness. In contrast, our method proceeds in the opposite direction: starting from sink locations, we infer the effective constraints that are actually enforced on the values reaching these points.

Our work is related to, but fundamentally differs from, classical data-flow adequacy criteria [7]. Traditional approaches typically ignore predicate uses along paths from defs to uses, even though guards restrict feasible variable values. As a result, standard data-flow criteria fail to capture how predicates partition the input domain. In contrast, we preserve the predicate-induced constraints on the value of the relevant variable along def-to-use path and, without exhaustive du-path tracking, target equivalence classes observed at sink (i.e., computational use) locations.

Traditional equivalence-class testing partitions the input domain top-down and derives test cases for each partition. Conversely, our approach operates bottom-up, reconstructing the implicit constraints enforced by the existing test suite at selected validation sinks. Rather than focusing on structural coverage, the method directly assesses the logical completeness of input validation. It can be seen as a form of reverse equivalence-class analysis that reveals how the program partitions its input space in practice. Missing tests identified by our criterion often correspond to under-validated or unexpected values at the sink. These cases may reveal real defects, such as insufficient range checks, overlooked corner cases, or latent sanitization errors.

While checking path reachability and comparing symbolic constraints across executions is generally undecidable, practical applicability can still be achieved by restricting the analysis to decidable theories and bounding loops. Under these conditions, SMT solvers or abstract-interpretation techniques can effectively check subsumption and synthesize inputs for previously uncovered regions. Moreover, the analysis can be performed incrementally, guiding the systematic augmentation of the test suite and progressively improving input validation coverage.

6 Conclusions

In this work, we formalize a criterion for identifying incompleteness in existing test suites with respect to input validation by systematically comparing symbolic path constraints across execution traces. The proposed criterion provides a semantics-aware notion of validation coverage, enabling reasoning about gaps in test suites without requiring any external specification, as it operates solely on symbolic abstractions of the program code and the available tests. By operating at the level of symbolic constraints, the approach shifts the focus from syntactic coverage metrics to differences in induced input domains.

The criterion is defined directly in terms of constraint satisfiability and logical implication, which makes it amenable to automated SAT/SMT reasoning. In particular, discrepancies between constraint sets characterize semantically distinct validation behaviors and may also expose logical inconsistencies or unintended over- or under-approximation in the implemented validation logic. This establishes a formal basis for detecting both missing tests and latent defects within the validation component.

Based on this foundation, we present a test synthesis method that constructs new inputs by solving constraint differences derived from symbolic encodings of program paths, providing a mechanism for extending test suites with meaningfully distinct test cases. The method complements traditional structural coverage techniques by focusing on differences in validation behavior rather than simply increasing syntactic coverage. By exposing previously untested validation behaviors, the approach enables a more complete assessment of input validation logic. This is especially relevant for reliability assurance in systems where input validation forms a critical defensive layer.

Future work will focus on improving the efficiency of detecting missing test cases. We also plan to explore integration with automated verification and testing frameworks to support broader use in formally grounded development processes.

References

1. Common Weakness Enumeration (CWE). https://cwe.mitre.org/. Accessed March 2026
2. Homès, B.: Fundamentals of Software Testing, p. Hoboken. John (2024)
3. Liu, H., Tan, H.B.K.: Covering code behavior on input validation in functional testing. Inf. Softw. Technol. **51**(2), 546–553 (2009)
4. Hayes, J.H., Offutt, J.: Input validation analysis and testing. Empir. Softw. Eng. **11**(4), 493–522 (2006). https://doi.org/10.1016/j.jss.2007.05.007
5. Gay, G., Staats, M., Whalen, M., Heimdahl, M.: The risks of coverage-directed test case generation. IEEE Trans. Softw. Eng. **41**, 803–819 (2015). https://doi.org/10.1109/TSE.2015.2421011
6. Chilenski, J., Miller, S.: Applicability of modified condition/decision coverage to software testing. Softw. Eng. J. **7**(5), 193–200 (1994)
7. Rapps S., Weyuker E.: Data flow analysis techniques for test data selection. In: Proceedings of International Conference of Software Engineering, pp. 272–277 (1982)
8. Kolchin, A., Potiyenko, S.: Extending data flow coverage to test constraint refinements. In: ter Beek, M.H., Monahan, R. (eds.) Integrated Formal Methods, IFM 2022. LNCS, vol. 13274. Springer, Cham (2023). https://doi.org/10.1007/978-3-031-07727-2_17
9. Kolchyn, O., Rudenko, D.: Misguarded computations: a pattern of ineffective conditional protection. In: Deshmukh, J., Havelund, K., Pinto, A. (eds.) NASA Formal Methods. NFM 2026. Lecture Notes in Computer Science, vol. 16622. Springer, Cham (2026). https://doi.org/10.1007/978-3-032-28079-4_16
10. Bhatt D., et al.: Requirements-driven model checking and test generation for comprehensive verification. In: NASA Formal Methods Symposium, pp. 576–596 (2022). https://doi.org/10.1007/978-3-031-06773-0_31
11. King, J.C.: Symbolic execution and program testing. Commun. ACM **19**(7), 385–394 (1976)
12. Biere, A.: Bounded model checking. In: Handbook of Satisfiability, pp. 739–764. IOS Press (2021)
13. Kurian, E., Briola, D., Braione, P., Denaro, G.: Automatically generating test cases for safety-critical software via symbolic execution. J. Syst. Softw. **199**, 111629 (2023). https://doi.org/10.1016/j.jss.2023.111629
14. Trabish, D., Mattavelli, A., Rinetzky, N., Cadar, C.: Chopped symbolic execution. In: Proceedings of the 40th International Conference on Software Engineering, pp. 350–360 (2018). https://doi.org/10.1145/3180155.3180251
15. Clarke, E.M., Henzinger, T.A., Veith, H., Bloem, R. (eds.): Handbook of Model Checking, vol. 10, pp. 978–983. Springer, Cham (2018). https://doi.org/10.1007/978-3-319-10575-8
16. Clarke, E., et al.: Counterexample-guided abstraction refinement. In: Computer Aided Verification. LNCS, vol. 1855. Springer (2000). https://doi.org/10.1007/10722167_15
17. European Union Agency for Railways: Braking curves. https://www.era.europa.eu/sk/node/1831. Accessed March 2026
18. Friman, B.: An algorithm for braking curve calculations in ERTMS train protection systems. Adv. Train Control Syst. **65** (2010). https://doi.org/10.2495/CR060421
19. Bently, W.G., Miller, E.F.: Ct coverage—initial results. Softw. Qual. J. **2**, 29–47 (1993). https://doi.org/10.1007/BF00417425
20. Tran, H.K.V., Ali, N.B., Unterkalmsteiner, M., et al.: Quality attributes of test cases and test suites – importance & challenges from practitioners' perspectives. Softw. Qual J. **33**, 9 (2025). https://doi.org/10.1007/s11219-024-09698-w
21. Huang, W., Peleska, J.: Complete model-based equivalence class testing. Int. J. Softw. Tools Technol. Transfer **18**, 265–283 (2016). https://doi.org/10.1007/s10009-014-0356-8

22. Guo, X., Okamura, H., Dohi, T.: Optimal test case generation for boundary value analysis. Softw. Qual. J. **32**, 543–566 (2024). https://doi.org/10.1007/s11219-023-09659-9
23. van den Bos, P., Tretmans, J.: Coverage-based testing with symbolic transition systems. In: Beyer, D., Keller, C. (eds.) Tests and Proofs. TAP 2019. Lecture Notes in Computer Science, vol. 11823. Springer (2019). https://doi.org/10.1007/978-3-030-31157-5_5
24. Herrera, A., Payer, M., Hosking, A.: DatAFLow: toward a data-flow-guided fuzzer. ACM Trans. Softw. Eng. Methodol. **32**(5), 31 (2023). https://doi.org/10.1145/3587156
25. Alashjee, A.M., Duraibi, S., Song, J.: Dynamic taint analysis tools: a review. Int. J. Comput. Sci. Secur. **13**(6), 231–244 (2019)
26. Liu, H.: Automated recovery, maintenance and testing of input validation. Doctoral dissertation, Nanyang Technological University, 164p. (2009)

MuSEvo: Assessing the Robustness of Multilingual Summarization Metrics Through Evolutionary Adversarial Natural Language Processing-Based Attacks

Gema Bello-Orgaz[1], Aidan Dakhama[2], Cristian Ramírez-Atencia[1], and Hector D. Menendez[3](✉)

[1] Universidad Politecnica de Madrid, Carretera de Valencia (A3) km. 7, 28031 Madrid, Spain
{gema.borgaz,cristian.ramirez}@upm.es
[2] University of Edinburgh, 10 Crichton Street, Edinburgh EH8 9AB, Scotland, UK
adakhama@ed.ac.uk
[3] King's College London, 30 Aldwych, London WC2B 4BG, UK
hector.menendez@kcl.ac.uk

Abstract. This paper investigates the robustness of multilingual summarization metrics through adversarial Natural Language Processing (NLP) attacks. We evaluate metric resilience across three languages using a multi-objective evolutionary algorithm. The initial population is derived from the original text's tokens, which are stochastically replaced by synonyms from a dynamically generated multilingual lexicon. To ensure the accuracy of the adversarial examples, we implement a correction step with a rule-based grammar and style checker that validates the syntactic and semantic coherence of the perturbed text. Conducted on the MuSE framework, this study rigorously analyzes the sensitivity of conventional metrics to semantic-preserving variations, contributing to the development of more reliable and resilient evaluation systems for multilingual summarization.

Keywords: Summarization · Multi-lingua · Large Language Models · Evolutionary Algorithms · Multi-Objective Optimization · Natural Language Processing · Adversarial Attacks · MuSE

1 Introduction

The problem of automatic text summarization is typically divided into two main approaches [12]. The first methodology is Extractive Summarization [14], which selects specific sentences or parts from the original text it compiles to create the final summary. In contrast, Abstractive Summarization synthesizes a full summary by understanding the original text and its meaning, while retaining its key facts [17]. The goal of both techniques is to provide the same information condensed.

O. Gervasi et al. (Eds.): ICCSA 2026, LNCS 16768, pp. 381–399, 2027.
https://doi.org/10.1007/978-3-032-30488-9_24

Both summarization techniques have been extensively used in the literature, yet evaluating summaries remains an open problem in the field [6]. The main challenge for evaluation metrics, originally designed for extractive summarization, is to deal with the infinite number of equivalent summaries that can be generated through abstractive summarization. Quality metrics evaluate the similarity between the original text and the summary, or the similarity between a human-provided text and the summary, normally employing n-gram methods that measure overlapping [6]. This approach would work if only one summary is valid; however, under multiple summaries, the quality can be adversarially targeted. Therefore, we need to identify new metrics that can represent the level of information retained from the original content.

If we look at the field of adversarial summarization and sequence-to-sequence tasks, we can see that the problem is even more complex. Adversarial methods have shown that by exploiting the output space of potential summaries, it is possible to control quality metrics without altering the generative content [22]. Normally, efforts to improve summary quality and robustness rely on training, but adversarial samples can reinforce this process improving the model's regularization and diversity of inputs and outputs [2]. However, bias remains an attack surface for this technique, although adversarial training can be used to mitigate it without compromising quality [8,19]. In the multilingual context, this problem becomes even harder, especially when working in cross-lingual contexts, as these adversarial samples transfer across languages, becoming effective in different languages, particularly in those languages of low resources or dialects. Therefore, we need new methodologies to clarify the quality of these summaries [11,21]. Finally, different evaluation metrics chosen for evaluating summary quality, such as BLEU or ROUGE, manipulate the target of summarization because it depends on metric quality and how well they understand the text. Consequently, current methods employ embeddings or LLMs to improve semantic equivalence measurement between summaries and reference summaries [3,21].

Based on the limitations and problems identified in the literature, different communities have begun working on extracting facts from original texts, employing fact comparison with summaries to enable reference-free evaluation (i.e., no human summaries) [5]. This approach accommodates multiple summaries. However, current techniques are also limited. The way we process the original text can lead to non-deterministic outcomes, where different summaries are generated. Moreover, variations in text production locations and linguistic characteristics can introduce idiosyncratic components that affect summary quality. For instance, regional languages and dialects in English or Spanish often exhibit distinct features that can alter fact extraction accuracy under complex embeddings.

Our paper aims to measure how idiosyncratic components affect the summary quality. For this purpose, our system will create an adversarial attack that rephrases the original text by replacing specific words with synonyms in order to manipulate summarization quality metrics. The goal is to determine which summarization metric is the most robust such attacks. This is crucial because it enables us to select the most suitable technique for evaluating summary quality under regional conditions in a multi-lingual context. We propose a new methodology, named MuSEvo, based on evolutionary computation, that generates this rephrasing. MuSEvo aims to preserve the semantics of the original text while replacing words with synonyms to modify summaries. It will then evaluate and compare the quality of different summarization metrics in response to these idiosyncratic changes.

Our results show that traditional metrics, such as ROUGE and BLEU, are vulnerable to these adversarial attacks, while metrics based on large language models (LLMs) demonstrate greater robustness. We evaluated our system employing a multi-lingual scenario in three different languages, concretely, English, Spanish and French. To guide our investigation and assess the impact of these adversarial manipulations, we address the following research questions:

RQ1: *What is the most robust summarization evaluation metric to MuSEvo's attack across different languages?*
RQ2: *How do the dimensions and complexity of the search space vary across different languages?*
RQ3: *What is the distribution of the attack's effectiveness, measured by hypervolume, in relation to text complexity across languages?*

The contributions of this paper are as follows:

- We present an adversarial attack framework for summarization systems that considers both the source text and the summary as part of the search space.
- We design a multi-objective evolutionary algorithm that reduces metric scores by altering idiosyncratic word choices while preserving semantic similarity.
- We provide an analysis identifying which metrics are most robust to manipulations in the source text and summaries, and propose LLM-based metrics as a promising alternative.

2 Methodology

The proposed system aims to generate adversarial attacks targeting both a summarization model and its evaluation process, with the core objective of perturbing the original input text through controlled syntactic modifications while maintaining its semantic meaning. These perturbations serve to assess the robustness of the summarization system. Figure 1 shows MuSEvo's workflow. It begins with an input, comprising the original document and its reference summary (generated using the MT5SUM model [9]). Subsequently, `PyMultiDictionary` [15] generates candidates for synonyms that form the search space. This framework is compatible with English, Spanish, and French, our target languages. The selection of these synonyms becomes the search space for the evolutionary algorithm, to which MuSEvo will apply its aim: finding adversary variations.

A Multi-Objective Evolutionary Algorithm (MOEA), implemented in `pymoo` [1], performs the search process. The search checks various synonyms that replace the original words, and subsequently, it performs grammatical validations to ensure linguistic correctness. Notably, many grammar checkers are focused on English, so non-English models have been addressed using a translation system, specifically the Neural Machine Translation (NMT) model [18], which maintains semantic accuracy for French and Spanish. Once the adversarial text is ready, we summarise it and measure the variance between the original summary from the model and this one, as can be seen in the final step of MuSEvo. The following sections provide a detailed explanation of each step.

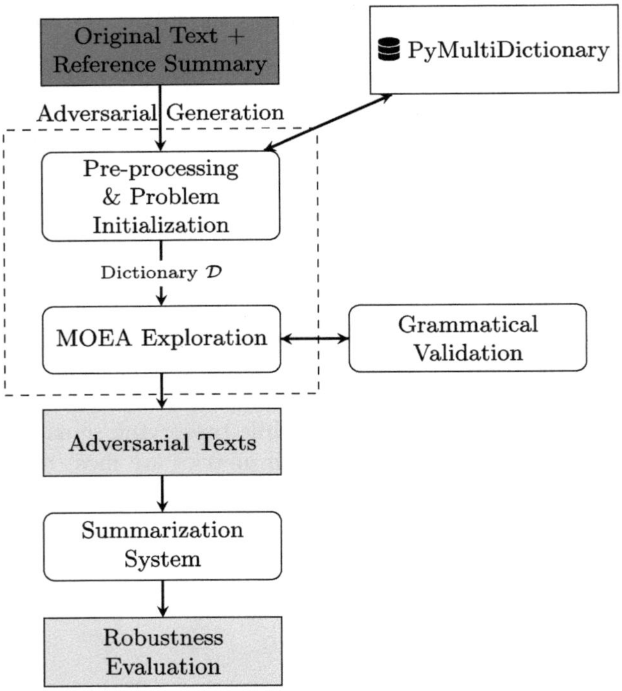

Fig. 1. Adversarial attack pipeline for summarization robustness evaluation.

2.1 Pre-processing and Problem Initialization

MuSEvo starts by tokenizing the original text and generating a dictionary of synonyms for each word, mainly focused on nouns, verbs, adjectives, and adverbs. This dictionary is generated by `PyMultiDictionary`. The dictionary defines the search space that will be optimized through the MOEA. The words are sorted by similarity in this dictionary, where the first ones are the most similar. The dictionary is then indexed, so every word that has been identified as a potential synonym for replacement has a number of indexed candidates to substitute the original token. This is bounded using the following equation:

$$x_i \in [0, |\mathcal{S}(w_i)|] \cap \mathbb{Z} \quad (1)$$

where w_i represents the i-th token (or gene) and $\mathcal{S}(w_i)$ denotes its synonym set, ensuring valid substitutions through the bounds. Therefore, each individual $\mathbf{x}$ in the population is encoded as a vector:

$$\mathbf{x} = (x_1, x_2, \ldots, x_n) \in \mathbb{X}_1 \times \mathbb{X}_2 \times \cdots \times \mathbb{X}_n \subset \mathbb{Z}^n \quad (2)$$

where n represents the total number of tokens in the input text. Consider the phrase *"a blue house"* as an illustrative case:

- *"a"* (no synonyms) $\rightarrow x_1 \in [0, 0]$ (fixed)
- *"blue"* $\rightarrow x_2 \in [0, 2]$ ($\mathcal{S}$("azure", "cobalt"))
- *"house"* $\rightarrow x_3 \in [0, 3]$ ($\mathcal{S}$("home," "residence", "dwelling"))

For instance, let's consider an example with $\mathbf{x} = [0, 0, 2]$. This would generate a perturbed phrase, such as *"a blue residence"*, by replacing the third token. Tokens that have no synonyms remain fixed, thereby maintaining the integrity of the original content.

2.2 MOEA Exploration

MuSEvo's search process begins with an initial population. This population encodes the original text as an individual, with all alleles starting at zero. To generate new candidates, controlled randomization is employed, assigning each potential replacement of a token a specific probability (configured through a parameter). This yields a particular list of replacements, as demonstrated in Fig. 2.

This approach guarantees that initial variations remain linguistically valid and semantically proximate to the source text, as variations are restricted to: (1) tokens with available synonyms, (2) substitutions within the predefined lexical bounds, and (3) probabilistic modification rates that prevent excessive divergence. Subsequent genetic operations then evolve these initial candidates toward adversarial examples that challenge summarization systems while preserving grammatical correctness.

Base:	0	**0**	**0**	0	**0**	0	**0**
Generated:	0	**2**	**1**	0	**3**	0	**1**

Fig. 2. Base individual (all-zero encoding) and generated variant for initial population. Bold values show synonym indices from the substitution dictionary.

Given the integer-array codification of the problem, the proposed crossover operators that have been selected for the evolutionary process are Two-Point Crossover (TPX) and Uniform Crossover (UX), which work for combinatorial problems. Nevertheless, given that the dictionaries are sorted according to the similarity of the synonyms to the original term, we also tested an integer version of Simulated Binary Crossover (SBX), where the continuous values are rounded to integers. This operator is illustrated in Fig. 3. Additionally, a domain-specific mutation operator is applied to effectively explore the search space, as also shown in the figure. This mutation randomly modifies token indices within their predefined synonym bounds defined in Eq. (1), where the mutation probability (p_{mut}) controls exploration intensity while preserving semantic validity:

$$x_i' = \begin{cases} \mathrm{randint}(0, x_i) & \text{if } r < p_{\mathrm{mut}} \\ x_i & \text{otherwise} \end{cases} \tag{3}$$

where $r \sim U(0,1)$. The operator enforces that all mutations are integer-only and bounded by language-specific synonym dictionaries ($\mathbf{w_i}$). These ensure discrete, valid token substitutions throughout the evolutionary process.

Parent 1:	1	2	3	0	2	0	3	1
Parent 2:	1	1	4	2	2	3	8	4
Offspring 1:	1	1	3	1	2	1	3	2
Offspring 2:	1	2	4	1	2	2	6	3

Fig. 3. Genetic operators example: where genes inside boxes indicate crossover-applied positions (SBX), and where genes inside oval boxes indicate the mutations positions (8 became 6).

The fitness evaluation begins by decoding each individual into a textual representation, followed by the application of grammar correction tailored to the target language. For English, the `language tool python` library [13] is employed directly for this purpose. Unfortunately, this library was not effective enough for other languages, and up to our knowledge, there was no other specific library to do this task proficiently. So for non-English languages, we utilize pretrained OPUS-MT neural machine translation models [20] to translate the text into English, apply grammatical corrections, and subsequently translate it back to the original language. The corrections are performed using the OPUS-MT's translation system, which maintains semantic accuracy and improves grammatical accuracy across languages.

The fitness function evaluates two distinct objectives.

1. The first objective is to *maximise the semantic similarity between the original text and the new one generated by each individual.* This is measured using

the `MiniLM-L12-v2` [16], which creates vectors from a sentence embedding optimised for paraphrase detection. We apply cosine distance to measure their similarity.

2. The second objective focuses on the summary, aiming to *minimise the similarity between the original representations and the newly generated summaries.* The model used to create the new summary is the MT5SUM model [9], and both summaries share the MiniLM embedding space, allowing for cosine similarity to be applied across them.

To select the most suitable algorithm for multi-objective optimization, we have identified three state-of-the-art MOEAs spanning three principal paradigms: `Non-dominated Sorting Genetic Algorithm II (NSGA-II)`; `Multi-Objective Evolutionary Algorithm based on Decomposition (MOEA/D)`; and `S Metric Selection EMOA (SMS-EMOA)`. All of these algorithms have been implemented using `pymoo` [1], and they are compared in Sect. 3.2. In the experimental section, we evaluate the performance of each strategy under identical adversarial generation settings to empirically determine the most effective optimization approach for our multilingual perturbation task. As the true Pareto set is unknown for this problem, the Hypervolume metric is employed for the evaluation of the effectiveness of the solutions. This metric allows the comparison of the three proposed multi-objective approaches in terms of convergence and diversity of the approximated Pareto set.

The complete search procedure for generating adversarial text variations is formalized in Algorithm 1, which brings together the initialization, variation, evaluation, and selection steps outlined above. As can be seen in Line 23, f_1 is assigned a negative value because similarity is to be maximized, and pymoo framework is based on minimization. The algorithm evolves the population iteratively and terminates either when the maximum number of generations ($G_{\max}$) is reached, or when improvements in the objective space become negligibly small across consecutive generations, as determined by the `RobustTermination` method from the `pymoo` framework.

2.3 Robustness Evaluation

We will provide an evaluation employing both classical metrics and LLM-based ones. For that, we will employ MuSE, which contains different evaluation metrics extracted from the state of the art. Concretely, we will employ ROUGE and BLEU as the classical metrics [6], and we will employ a factuality strategy using the large language models. This latter strategy will measure the average across: factuality, completeness, and conciseness.

Classical Metrics. For the evaluation, we employ two classical metrics extensively used in the literature: BLEU and ROUGE [6].

ROUGE measures n-gram overlapping recall. For each reference text S, extract all n-grams. For each n-gram ($gram_n$) in the reference(s), count how

Algorithm 1. Adversarial Text Variation Search via MOEA

Require: Original text T, reference summary S_{ref}, synonym dictionary $\mathcal{D}$, population size *pop_size*, maximum number of generations G_{max}, initialization rate p_{init}, mutation rate p_{mut}
Ensure: Set of adversarial texts $\mathcal{A}$

Initial Population:
Encode T as all-zero vector $\mathbf{v}_0$ ▷ Base genotype
for $i \leftarrow 1$ to *pop_size* **do**
  Initialize $\mathbf{v}_i \leftarrow \mathbf{v}_0$
  for each token position j in T **do**
    if rand() $< p_{\text{init}}$ and T_j has synonyms in $\mathcal{D}$ **then**
      $\mathbf{v}_i[j] \leftarrow$ random_index($\mathcal{D}[T_j]$) ▷ Controlled randomization
  $I_i \leftarrow \mathbf{v}_i$
  Add I_i to P_0
Evolution:
$g \leftarrow 1$
while $g <= G_{\max} \vee \neg$RobustTermination() **do**
  Crossover: Apply TPX/UX/SBX crossover on parent pairs to produce offspring Q_g
  Mutation:
  for each individual $I \in Q_g$ **do**
    for each gene j in I **do**
      if rand() $< p_{\text{mut}}$ **then**
        $I[j] \leftarrow$ randint(0, $|\mathcal{D}[T_j]|$) ▷ Bounded by synonym dictionary
  Fitness Evaluation:
  for each individual $I_k \in P_g \cup Q_g$ **do**
    $T_k \leftarrow$ decode($I_k, \mathcal{D}$) ▷ Reconstruct perturbed text
    $T_k \leftarrow$ correct_grammar(T_k) ▷ Ensure grammatical correctness
    $f_1 \leftarrow -$(cosine_sim(embed(T)), embed(T_k)) ▷ Semantic preservation
    $S_k \leftarrow$ mT5Sum(T_k)
    $f_2 \leftarrow$ cosine_sim(embed(S_{ref}), embed(S_k)) ▷ Adversarial divergence
    fitness(I_k) $\leftarrow [f_1, f_2]$
  Selection: Apply NSGA-II, MOEA/D or SMS-EMOA $\rightarrow P_{g+1}$
  $g \leftarrow g + 1$
$\mathcal{A} \leftarrow \{$correct_grammar(decode($I, \mathcal{D}$)) $\mid I \in P_{G_{\max}}\}$

many times it appears in both the candidate text T_c and the reference text T_r, this is $\text{Count}_{\text{match}}$. Then, ROUGE-N sums up all matches and divide by the total number of n-grams in the reference(s).

$$\text{ROUGE-N} = \frac{\sum_{S \in \text{References}} \sum_{\text{gram}_n \in S} \text{Count}_{\text{match}}(\text{gram}_n)}{\sum_{S \in \text{References}} \sum_{\text{gram}_n \in S} \text{Count}(\text{gram}_n)} \tag{4}$$

During the evaluation, we employ **ROUGE-L** which takes into account the longest common subsequence (LCS). It is defined as:

$$\text{ROUGE-L} = \frac{LCS(T_c, T_r)}{\text{length of reference}} \tag{5}$$

BLEU evaluates n-gram precision. It measures the overlap between n-grams of T_c and T_r:

$$\text{BLEU} = \text{BP} \cdot \exp\left(\sum_{n=1}^{N} w_n \log p_n\right) \tag{6}$$

in the equation BP is the brevity penalty, w_n is the n-grams weights, normally, $w_n = \frac{1}{N}$ p_n is the n-gram precision. BP can be calculated as:

$$\text{BP} = \begin{cases} 1 & \text{if } c > r \\ e^{(1-r/c)} & \text{if } c \leq r \end{cases} \tag{7}$$

where r is the reference length and c is the candidate length.

LLM-Based Metrics. Newer techniques apply large language models (LLMs) to assess summaries on dimensions such as coherence, factuality, completeness, and information density [10]. These metrics, named fact-based metrics, use LLMs to extract and compare facts from the different texts. Let T_1 and T_2 be two texts. By employing an LLM, the metric extracts the sets of facts F_{T_1} and F_{T_2}, corresponding to the respective facts of each text. Let define P as all possible pairwise combinations of facts between F_{T_1} and F_{T_2}. Each pair $p \in P$ is simply two facts from each text. Considering that there are facts in the text that might not be representative enough with respect to the facts of the compared text, the metric performs a filter, keeping only the pair with the maximum similarity from both sets, assuming that the similarity is above a specific threshold τ. For example, choosing a single $f^i_{T_1} \in F_{T_1}$, and every $f^j_{T_2} \in F_{T_2}$, P contains every possible pair, however, the metric keeps only the pair with maximum similarity $p^* = (f^*_{T_1}, f^*_{T2})$ to improve the quality of factuality pairing, assuming that $sim(p^*) \geq \tau$, otherwise we set $sim(p^*) := 0$. This set is defined as P^*. Then, Factuality is the average similarity across all possible pairs in P^*, therefore:

$$\text{Fact}(T_1, T_2) = \frac{1}{|P^*|} \sum_{p \in P^*} sim_{Fact}(p) \tag{8}$$

where

$$sim_{Fact}(p) = \begin{cases} 0 & \text{if } sim(p) < \tau \\ sim(p) & \text{otherwise} \end{cases} \tag{9}$$

Completeness focuses on counting the number of facts from T_1 that have proper correspondence with respect to the facts in T_2. Similarly to factuality it is based on P^* and counts the non-empty pairs.

$$\text{Comp}(T_1, T_2) = \frac{1}{|P^*|} \sum_{p \in P^*} sim_{Comp}(p) \tag{10}$$

$$sim_{Comp}(p) = \begin{cases} 0 \text{ if } sim(p) < \tau \\ 1 \text{ otherwise} \end{cases} \tag{11}$$

Finally, Density balances both metrics and it is defined as:

$$\mathrm{Den}(T_1, T_2) = \frac{1}{2}\left(\mathrm{Comp}(T_1, T_2) + \mathrm{Fact}(T_1, T_2)\right) \tag{12}$$

All metrics values are between the $[0, 1]$ range, where 0 represents the minimum value and 1 the maximum.

3 Experimental Setup

The experimental evaluation is designed to provide empirical evidence for the research questions previously defined. We focus on assessing the impact of MuSEvo's syntactic manipulations on multilingual summarization. We start by presenting the dataset, followed by an explanation of how the parameters were tuned, and conclude with a comparative analysis of the algorithms employed in our experiments.

3.1 Dataset

The dataset used is the XL-Sum dataset [9], which comprises several news texts in 44 languages, thereby making it a multilingual dataset that includes both high- and low-resource languages. It contains 1.35 million articles and human summaries as references from the BBC. This dataset has been extensively utilized in the literature due to its annotations, and its cross-lingua nature. In our experiments, we selected three languages from the dataset: English, French, and Spanish. For each of these languages, we selected 10 articles, sorted by computational complexity of the synonym search space generated by MuSEvo. This enables us to control the evaluation while maintaining a diverse balance between languages and the impact of the algorithms on various quality metrics.

3.2 Parameter Selection and Algorithm Performance Comparison

To systematically determine optimal parameter values, we conducted preliminary experiments evaluating classical algorithmic parameters, such as the population size or the mutation and crossover probabilities, using Bayesian Optimization with HyperBand (BOHB) [7]. For this initial tuning phase, we selected one of the English texts with the lowest dictionary-based complexity (ID 62) from our stratified dataset. The results of the best-performing configuration identified are summarized in Table 1. In addition, for MOEA/D the Tschebycheff scalarization function and *Das and Denis* method for reference directions computation were used.

Once the general parameters were fixed, we executed each evolutionary algorithm (`NSGA-II`, `SMS-EMOA`, `MOEA/D`) 31 times in order to evaluate both performance and robustness. This analysis supports the selection of the most effective and reliable algorithm for generating adversarial text variations.

Table 1. Best-performing parameter configuration obtained.

Parameter	Value
Population size (pop_{size})	50
Initialization probability (p_{init})	0.7
Crossover type	*SBX*
Crossover probability ($p_{\text{crossover}}$)	0.7
Crossover distribution index (η)	10
Mutation probability (p_{mut})	0.2

To assess the robustness of the algorithms, we use statistical measures derived from the normalized hypervolume results, including the mean, standard deviation, and the coefficient of variation (CV). The CV is calculated as the ratio between the standard deviation (σ) and the mean (μ) ($CV = \frac{\sigma}{\mu}$), which provides a normalized measure of relative variability.

We employ the coefficient of variation (CV) to measure robustness levels, defining three distinct thresholds. When the CV is below 0.05, we consider *High* robustness; when it falls between 0.05 and 0.1, we regard it as *Acceptable*; and for values exceeding or greater than 0.1, we classify it as *Low* robustness. The objective of this coefficient is to identify which algorithm demonstrates more consistency and stability across multiple executions.

Table 2. Comparative performance and robustness metrics based on Hypervolume for each algorithm.

Algorithm	Mean	Std. Dev.	CV (σ/μ)	Robus. Level
SMS-EMOA	0.8253	0.0462	0.0560	Acceptable
NSGA-II	0.7971	0.0716	0.0898	Acceptable
MOEA/D	0.6061	0.1149	0.1896	Low

Table 2 indicates that SMS-EMOA outperforms all other algorithms in terms of effectiveness and robustness, achieving a higher hypervolume, superior optimization performance, and greater consistency across executions, primarily due to lower variability. In contrast, MOEA/D exhibits poorer performance, becoming the weakest algorithm and displaying the highest variability, rendering it less reliable; while NSGA-II strikes a balance between performance and robustness.

We have also applied the Friedman test to evaluate whether observed differences are statistically significant, including the Nemenyi post-hoc analysis [4]. The test reveals highly significant results ($\chi^2 = 43.42$, $p = 3.73 \times 10^{-10} < 0.0001$), confirming that algorithms exhibit statistically distinct performance and yield different outcomes. The Nemenyi post-hoc test results (Table 3) indicate that MOEA/D performs significantly worse than both NSGA-II ($p = 0.001$)

and SMS-EMOA ($p = 0.001$). However, no statistically significant difference was observed between NSGA-II and SMS-EMOA ($p = 0.2247$), despite the latter showing superior average performance and greater robustness.

Table 3. Post-hoc Nemenyi test p-values between algorithms.

	MOEA/D	NSGA-II	SMS-EMOA
MOEA/D	–	0.001	0.001
NSGA-II	0.001	–	0.22467
SMS-EMOA	0.001	0.22467	–

In summary, SMS-EMOA not only achieved the highest mean performance but also exhibited the greatest robustness across runs. These findings, supported by both descriptive and inferential analyses, justify the selection of SMS-EMOA as the most appropriate algorithm.

Finally, a comparative analysis of crossover operators (TPX, UX and SBX) was conducted using the same robustness and statistical framework based on the hypervolume indicator. SBX demonstrated the highest robustness, exhibiting the lowest coefficient of variation (CV $= 0.056$). This better performance demonstrates that the order of dictionaries according to similarity to the original term can in fact affect the exploitation in evolutionary algorithms. Although the Friedman test did not indicate statistically significant differences among operators ($\chi^2 = 4.064$, $p = 0.131$), SBX is selected as the crossover operator for subsequent experiments due to its more consistent empirical performance.

4 Results

This section presents a scalability study designed to evaluate the performance of the proposed evolutionary approach across varying levels of textual complexity and different languages. The following subsections provide the empirical results and analysis required to answer RQ1 through RQ3, based on the experimental design established in Sect. 3.

Following the configuration in Sect. 3.2, 10 input texts per language were selected and ordered by increasing complexity based on their search space size. We repeat the experiments ten times to account for common variations in evolutionary algorithms, and conduct an analysis of the complexity of the search space and linguistic aspects.

We use a Ubuntu 22.04 machine with an Intel Core i7-11800H processor (2.30 GHz), 32 GB of RAM, and an NVIDIA GeForce RTX 3070 GPU. The dataset and evolutionary algorithm are publicly available on a GitHub repository[1], which also includes Jupyter Notebooks designed to replicate all results and

[1] The final link to the repository will be provided upon publication.

visualizations. Furthermore, we have made our code and data available under the GNU General Public License version 3. Additionally, the authors are available for any further technical inquiries.

4.1 RQ1. Summarization Quality Metrics

Research question 1 focuses on the robustness against adversarial attacks. We consider that a system is more stable when its quality metric score after an attack remains higher, indicating greater resilience.

During our evaluation, we focus on two classical metrics (BLEU, ROUGE) and five LLMs using factuality-based metrics. Our analysis is shown in Table 4. The results show that BLEU becomes the least reliable metric across all languages due to its requirement for exact overlapping of n-grams and penalization of paraphrasing, making it less suitable for abstract summarization compared to LLMs. On the other hand, TinyLlama reveals limitations in extracting facts from adversarial perturbations. The best models are Mistral and Gemma3, which exhibit robustness, particularly Mistral achieving good results in Spanish, while Gemma3 demonstrates consistency across all languages.

Notably, Llama 3.2 appears more sensitive to Spanish data than to English. Regarding the Pareto front, no significant differences were observed between best, median, or worst solutions, suggesting that metric stability is relatively consistent regardless of the final optimization level. English and Spanish tend to yield the best results, whereas French shows weaker performance due to its higher structural and conjugation complexity.

> **RQ1 Answer.** Mistral and Gemma3 are the most robust metrics against MuSEvo's attack. Mistral shows the highest stability in Spanish, while Gemma3 is more consistent across languages. BLEU and TinyLlama are the least reliable due to structural rigidity and limited semantic capacity.

4.2 RQ2. Search Space and Linguistic Complexity

This research question analyzes the search space dimensions and linguistic variability across languages. As shown in Table 5, French exhibits the largest and most heterogeneous synonym coverage (up to 6,292 total synonyms), leading to irregular search behavior. English and Spanish display more balanced distributions, contributing to steadier performance.

To assess internal variations, we applied a Kruskal–Wallis test followed by Dunn's post-hoc analysis with Holm correction. Significant differences were found in all languages ($p < 0.001$). In English, text 59 showed broad differences; in Spanish, texts 89, 75, and 4 stood out; while in French, differences were marked between extreme complexity levels (e.g., 22 vs 93/53). Despite these variances, a cross-language Kruskal-Wallis test revealed no significant differences in normalized hypervolume ($H = 3.145, p = 0.208$), suggesting that complexity distributions are statistically comparable across languages overall.

Table 4. Summarization quality metrics grouped by metric type and language.

	English			Spanish		
Metric	Best	Median	Worst	Best	Median	Worst
BLEU	.134±.22	.138±.24	.098±.20	.116±.19	.148±.16	.189±.24
ROUGE	.320±.21	.328±.24	.296±.18	.307±.18	.326±.16	.343±.24
DeepSeek	.260±.36	.345±.38	.300±.36	*.320±.36*	.416±.32	.439±.35
Gemma3	*.333±.34*	**.376±.36**	*.383±.32*	.314±.36	*.422±.35*	.398±.37
Llama3.2	.218±.34	.310±.39	.235±.35	.289±.37	.353±.37	*.448±.40*
Mistral	**.379±.38**	*.357±.38*	**.384±.37**	**.515±.36**	**.617±.29**	**.669±.29**
Tinyllama	.165±.28	.200±.29	.176±.30	.126±.28	.245±.33	.240±.34

	French		
Metric	Best	Median	Worst
BLEU	.052±.10	.067±.12	.051±.10
ROUGE	**.226±.15**	**.236±.16**	**.232±.14**
DeepSeek	.175±.30	.181±.28	*.214±.33*
Gemma3	*.187±.31*	*.218±.34*	.198±.32
Llama3.2	.107±.26	.126±.28	.086±.23
Mistral	.167±.31	.172±.30	.187±.30
Tinyllama	.099±.25	.119±.28	.074±.21

RQ2 Answer. Search space dimensions and linguistic complexity vary significantly within each language, affecting algorithmic stability. However, the overall hypervolume distributions are statistically comparable across English, Spanish, and French.

4.3 RQ3. Evolutionary Performance and Hypervolume

The effectiveness of MuSEvo is captured by the hypervolume (HV) of the Pareto front. As illustrated in Fig. 4, HV tends to increase with text complexity across all languages. Higher synonym availability provides the algorithm with a richer combinatorial space, enabling more effective exploration of the trade-off between semantic preservation and metric degradation.

Table 5. Search space characteristics by text and language, reorganized for compactness.

Lang.	Txt	Tot. Syn.	Avg. Syn.	Txt	Tot. Syn.	Avg. Syn.
English	0	131	5.46 ± 5.80	27	1731	6.74 ± 6.14
	62	148	6.73 ± 4.10	23	1833	8.04 ± 6.15
	78	177	5.36 ± 6.13	11	2101	6.96 ± 6.42
	6	300	6.52 ± 7.01	67	2189	6.51 ± 6.13
	59	806	7.01 ± 6.19	92	3797	8.48 ± 7.50
Spanish	95	120	4.80 ± 3.52	89	1479	5.87 ± 5.01
	34	148	5.92 ± 4.95	19	1880	6.44 ± 5.57
	85	161	5.96 ± 4.00	75	2106	6.32 ± 5.18
	30	233	7.28 ± 5.87	4	2551	6.36 ± 5.03
	87	324	6.23 ± 5.33	14	3105	6.63 ± 5.59
French	22	194	9.24 ± 9.10	93	577	13.11 ± 11.42
	21	200	11.11 ± 7.85	28	838	14.45 ± 15.10
	45	322	9.76 ± 9.84	25	3255	12.62 ± 14.73
	49	358	14.92 ± 17.20	53	3792	14.20 ± 14.67
	61	450	10.98 ± 12.70	72	6292	14.14 ± 15.04

In English and Spanish, HV improves consistently with complexity. In French, while the trend holds for low levels, extreme complexity (e.g., texts with > 6000 synonyms) introduces larger variation in HV. This indicates that as the search space expands exponentially, optimization faces challenges due to combinatorial explosion. Nevertheless, the algorithm effectively leverages linguistic richness to identify adversarial examples while maintaining semantic coherence.

RQ3 Answer. Hypervolume tends to increase with text complexity across all languages. The evolutionary algorithm leverages richer synonym spaces to achieve more effective optimization and exploration.

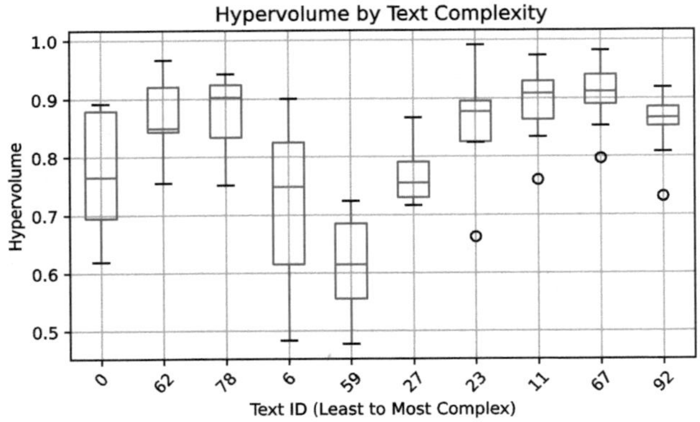

(a) English

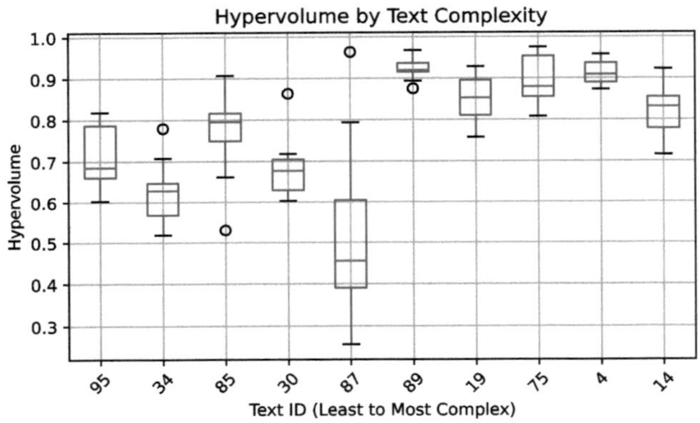

(b) Spanish

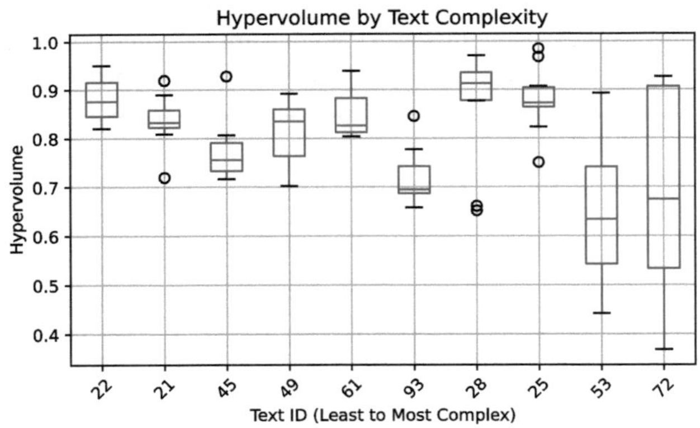

(c) French

Fig. 4. Hypervolume distribution by text complexity across languages

5 Conclusions

MuSEvo demonstrates how adversarial changes based on idiosyncratic components significantly disrupt the quality of summarization metrics. This highlights the limitations of these metrics, making them less reliable, as they can be easily degraded by small text permutations that do not compromise the original text's semantics. The metrics are especially sensitive to multiple languages, even those where new methods relying on factual checks may struggle.

Our work concludes that, depending on how the metric is designed, whether based on n-grams, such as BLEU or ROUGE, or LLMs, like Mistral and Gemma 3, its robustness varies significantly (RQ1). The LLM metrics prove to be more resilient. The main reason for this sensitivity lies in the complexity of the search space of synonyms. A larger search space allows for a wider range of changes, making it increasingly challenging for evaluation metrics to remain robust (RQ2). Consequently, the complexity of the search space has a direct impact on quality, as there are more lexical resources available to be exploited. For instance, manipulations can be particularly disruptive in French due to the complex nature of this language. Furthermore, our evolutionary algorithm demonstrates its ability to scale with varying text complexities (RQ3), enabling it to launch more sophisticated adversarial attacks and evaluate advanced summarization systems.

For future work, we aim to improve the quality of metrics that utilize factuality, particularly those that can withstand adversarial changes, and develop methods to rephrase or restructure grammatical changes as well. Furthermore, we plan to extend our approach to other languages with distinct properties, such as Chinese or Arabic, and incorporate enhanced grammatical correction techniques during the evolutionary process to create an even more complex search space for adversarial attacks.

Acknowledgments. The authors thank the UKRI Trustworthy Autonomous Systems Hub (EP/V00784X/1 and EP/V026801/2), and the Comunidad Autónoma de Madrid under the ALENTAR-J-CM project (TEC-2024/COM-224) for their support.

Competing Interests. The authors have no competing interests to declare that are relevant to the content of this article.

References

1. Blank, J., Deb, K.: pymoo: Multi-objective optimization in python. IEEE Access **8**, 89497–89509 (2020). https://doi.org/10.1109/ACCESS.2020.2990567
2. Cao, B., Guan, X., Bao, S., Wu, J., Fan, J.: Optimizing representation for abstractive multi-document summarization based on adversarial learning strategy. IEEE Trans. Cogn. Dev. Syst. (2025). https://doi.org/10.1109/TCDS.2025.3563357
3. Chen, Y., Eger, S.: Menli: robust evaluation metrics from natural language inference. Trans. Assoc. Comput. Linguist. **11**, 804–825 (2023). https://doi.org/10.1162/tacl_a_00576
4. Demšar, J.: Statistical comparisons of classifiers over multiple data sets. J. Mach. Learn. Res. **7**, 1–30 (2006). https://doi.org/10.5555/1248547.1248548

5. Dierickx, L., Van Dalen, A., Opdahl, A.L., Lindén, C.G.: Striking the balance in using LLMs for fact-checking: a narrative literature review. In: Multidisciplinary International Symposium on Disinformation in Open Online Media, pp. 1–15. Springer, Heidelberg (2024). https://doi.org/10.1007/978-3-031-71210-4_1
6. Ermakova, L., Cossu, J.V., Mothe, J.: A survey on evaluation of summarization methods. Inf. Process. Manag. **56**(5), 1794–1814 (2019). https://doi.org/10.1016/j.ipm.2019.04.001
7. Falkner, S., Klein, A., Hutter, F.: Bohb: robust and efficient hyperparameter optimization at scale. In: Proceedings of the 35th International Conference on Machine Learning (ICML). Proceedings of Machine Learning Research, vol. 80, pp. 1437–1446. PMLR (2018). https://doi.org/10.48550/arXiv.1807.01774
8. Gupta, M., Varimalla, N.R., Deas, N., Subbiah, M., McKeown, K.: Advsumm: adversarial training for bias mitigation in text summarization. arXiv preprint arXiv:2506.06273 (2025). https://doi.org/10.48550/arXiv.2506.06273
9. Hasan, T., et al.: XL-sum: large-scale multilingual abstractive summarization for 44 languages. In: Findings of the Association for Computational Linguistics: ACL-IJCNLP 2021, pp. 4693–4703. Association for Computational Linguistics, Online (2021). https://doi.org/10.18653/v1/2021.findings-acl.413
10. Liu, Y., Iter, D., Xu, Y., Wang, S., Xu, R., Zhu, C.: G-eval: NLG evaluation using gpt-4 with better human alignment. arXiv preprint arXiv:2303.16634 (2023). https://doi.org/10.48550/arXiv.2303.16634
11. Mathur, V., Dadu, T., Aggarwal, S.: Evaluating neural networks' ability to generalize against adversarial attacks in cross-lingual settings. Appl. Sci. **14**(13), 5440 (2024). https://doi.org/10.3390/app14135440
12. Menéndez, H.D., Dakhama, A.: Automatic summarization evaluation: methods and practices. In: IFIP International Conference on Testing Software and Systems, pp. 169–181. Springer, Heidelberg (2024). https://doi.org/10.1007/978-3-031-80889-0_12
13. Morris, J.: Python wrapper for languagetool (2021). https://pypi.org/project/language-tool-python/, python wrapper for LanguageTool
14. Qazvinian, V., et al.: Generating extractive summaries of scientific paradigms. J. Artif. Intell. Res. **46**, 165–201 (2013). https://doi.org/10.1613/jair.3732
15. Pablo Pizarro R.: Pymultidictionary: a multi-language dictionary module (2021). https://github.com/ppizarror/PyMultiDictionary. versión 1.3.1
16. Reimers, N., Gurevych, I.: Sentence-bert: sentence embeddings using siamese bert-networks. In: Proceedings of the 2019 Conference on Empirical Methods in Natural Language Processing. Association for Computational Linguistics (2019). https://doi.org/10.18653/v1/D19-1410
17. Shi, T., Keneshloo, Y., Ramakrishnan, N., Reddy, C.K.: Neural abstractive text summarization with sequence-to-sequence models. ACM Trans. Data Sci. **2**(1), 1–37 (2021). https://doi.org/10.1145/3419106
18. Stahlberg, F.: Neural machine translation: a review. J. Artif. Intell. Res. **69**, 343–418 (2020). https://doi.org/10.1613/jair.1.12007
19. Thota, P., Nilizadeh, S.: Attacks against abstractive text summarization models through lead bias and influence functions. In: Findings of the Association for Computational Linguistics: EMNLP 2024, pp. 13727–13741. Association for Computational Linguistics (2024). https://doi.org/10.18653/v1/2024.findings-emnlp.804
20. Tiedemann, J., et al.: Democratizing neural machine translation with OPUS-MT. Lang. Res. Eval. **58**, 713–755 (2023). https://doi.org/10.1007/s10579-023-09704-w

21. Zhang, R., Ouni, J., Eger, S.: Cross-lingual cross-temporal summarization: dataset, models, evaluation. Comput. Linguist. **50**(3), 1001–1047 (2024). https://doi.org/10.1162/coli_a_00519
22. Zheng, J., Hu, T., Cong, T., He, X.: Cl-attack: textual backdoor attacks via cross-lingual triggers. In: Proceedings of the AAAI Conference on Artificial Intelligence, vol. 39, pp. 26427–26435 (2025). https://doi.org/10.1609/aaai.v39i25.34842

Bayesian Analysis for Wildfire Classification in the United States and Australia Through Spatial Hierarchical Models

Steven Leone(✉)

University of Michigan, Ann Arbor, MI 48109, USA
leonestv@umich.edu

Abstract. Wildfires in the United States and Australia burn upwards of ten million acres of land annually. Emitted carbon dioxide and smoke aerosol from wildfires damage the environment, and more than 46 million acres burned in the 2019–2020 Australian Wildfire season [5]. Predicting and forecasting wildfires can allow for proactive resource allocation, better public safety, and better decision making to marginalize these damages. NASA's Fire Information for Resource Management System (FIRMS) contains real time data of fires across the globe, in Australia and other regions. 153,916 and 156,417 fires were captured through NASA's MODIS instrument in 2020 in the United States and Australia, respectively (https://firms.modaps.eosdis.nasa.gov). Statisticians and other researchers have shown that we can successfully predict wildfires from various predictors, including vegetation data [6]. Other studies show that dry conditions and human activity are the leading causes of the wildfires. We create hierarchical models to predict wildfires given land and atmospheric conditions to assess and compare likely causes across continents. Hierarchical models allow us to take advantage of interpretable coefficients, so that we can determine the best predictors of wildfires and study the transferrability of wildfire climate relationships across continents. We apply a small amendment to the Hamiltonian Monte Carlo Method, introducing a severity weight to errors after taking the gradient to give us further insights into which predictors lead to the brightest wildfires. In total, we assess a Spatial Hierarchical Model, a Brightness Sensitive Spatial Hierarchical Model, and a Mixed Effects Hierarchical Model. Finally, we assess our models compared to state of the art, achieving 100% and 88.7% accuracy in wildfire prediction with a Bayesian Multilevel (hierarchical) Regression Model in Australia and the United States on complete data, respectively, an improvement over the 96.9% accurate Bayesian logistic regression model in Australia in 2023 [4], and outperforming deep neural networks with up to 90% accuracy trained on similar data in 2024 [10].

Keywords: Bayesian Modeling · Data Mining · Machine Learning · Deep Learning · Climate

O. Gervasi et al. (Eds.): ICCSA 2026, LNCS 16768, pp. 400–415, 2027.
https://doi.org/10.1007/978-3-032-30488-9_25

1 Introduction

Wildfire prediction is a critical application of machine learning. A wildfire is an instance of unplanned, uncontrolled, burning in natural vegetation, a phenomenon that has been around since the Silurian era [15]. Nevertheless, they are an integral component of terrestrial ecosystems. Fire behavior scientists have used mathematical models in the past to study its behaviors [1]. Early work from 1946 to 1973 focused on growth rate given different fuels. Nomographs to calculate fire behavior date back to as early as 1976.

Statistical Methods have an important role in wildfire prediction. Techniques employing Generalized Additive Models demonstrated success in a 2013 paper on wildfire prediction [15]. Random Forests, Support Vector Machines, KNN, and Bayesian Logistic Regression, and other models have also been successfully applied. Most recently, in 2024, Wildfire Classification in Morocco through feedforward neural networks with 3 hidden layers, 256 weights per layer, and a dropout rate of 60% achieved a high accuracy, up to 89.94% [10]. Alterations of number of hidden layers, weights per hidden layer, activation function, and dropout percent hit the 88% – 89.4% range, besting classical machine learning methods.

Bayesian Hierarchical Models are statistical tools that analyze complex, nested data [4]. The R programming language provides the BRMS (Bayesian Regression Models using 'STAN') library to offer full Bayesian Inference, a statistical method for which probability is updated as more information becomes available. The BRM model fits coefficients for our predictors by computing the posterior of our parameters, $p(\beta_1, \beta_2 ... \beta_p | X)$, in order to provide posterior predictive probabilities θ.

Unlike neural networks, Bayesian Hierarchical Models provide interpretability into their decision making process. The coefficients give us insight into the response curves, which allows for a comparison in the wildfire prediction process across two different models. We train Bayesian Hierarchical Models in the United States and Australia to assess the accuracy of results and the transferrability of wildfire-climate relationships across these continents.

2 Prior Work

Several iterations of state of the art wildfire prediction have been published since the 1900's [1]. Deep neural network architecture handled the problem efficiently in a 2024 paper, with most configurations outperforming classic machine learning techniques [10]. Another team in 2024 introduced convolutional neural networks and long short term memory networks, achieving as high as 98.6% accuracy [2].

Predictors for wildfire classification have also been the focus of studies in different regions. A previous study of bayesian analysis of wildfire classification in Australia reveals that the Normalized Difference Vegetation Index (NDVI) showed the strongest positive correlation with wildfire occurrence [5]. Soil moisture has also proven useful [10]. Other publications have used statistical significance tests to show that some conditions, such as heat and humidity, create high favorability for fire ignition and propagation [11].

The transferability of wildfire climate relationships across continents has yet to be studied. While deep neural networks generally prevail, Bayesian Hierarchical Models have been sparsely tested in both the United States and Australia. In this paper, we use Bayesian Hierarchical Models and their interpretable parameters to compare wildfire posterior prediction across two countries, the United States and Australia.

3 Methodology

3.1 Data

Wildfire prediction depends on data specific to time and geolocation. We collect wildfire observation data from NASA's FIRMS and collate it with rich, available data from Google Earth Engine and other third party API's. We use data available at a single point in time, such that prediction is irrelevant to time or lag; this avoids unnecessary complexity. The dataset focuses on the following.

- **NDVI** - Normalized Difference Vegetation Index, provided by Google Earth Engine[1], captured through NASA's MODIS instrument.
- **Soil Moisture**- SMAP Level 4 soil moisture data, provided by Google Earth Engine[2], as collected by NASA.
- **Temperature** - Daily temperature data.
- **Cloud Cover** - Daily cloud cover data.
- **Humidity** - Daily humidity data.
- **Precipitation** - Daily precipitation data.
- **Elevation** - Topographic elevation data from Google Earth Engine, captured by NASA.
- **Wind** - Daily wind data.
- **City** - City data, matched by geolocation.
- **State** - State data, matched by geolocation.
- **Population** - Population data of a matching city.
- **Daynight** - A binary variable only true if the fire occurs during daylight.
- **Geolocation** - Geolocation as stored by NASA in FIRMS.

We start by collecting all wildfire data for our chosen countries in 2020 through NASA's MODIS Instrument. These datasets contain all times and locations at which a wildfire was captured. We consider the space of all times and locations in a country, and its subset, the space of all times and locations in which a wildfire is captured. We sample one thousand points from this subset and one thousand points from its complement; the sampled data maintains the same distribution of time stamp, brightness, and other predictors, which keeps the dataset balanced and realistic.

[1] https://developers.google.com/earth-engine/datasets/catalog/MODIS_061_MOD13A1.

[2] https://developers.google.com/earth-engine/datasets/catalog/NASA_SMAP_SPL4SMGP_008.

3.2 Exploratory Data Analysis

Exploratory Data Analysis on wildfires in the dataset for Australia and United States shows that the distribution of the variance is well spread throughout each of 9 predictors, excluding geolocation, population, state, and city; not all observations in the data match to a city. Principal Component Analysis, a dimensionality reduction technique that identifies the direction of maximum variance, reveals that temperature and wind have a strong positive correlation in both the United States and Australia. Soil moisture, NDVI, and humidity are also positively correlated, with projections onto the biplot that point in a different direction. Cloud cover and precipitation also show some correlation, albeit of a smaller magnitude; these similarities also persist across both countries (Fig. 1).

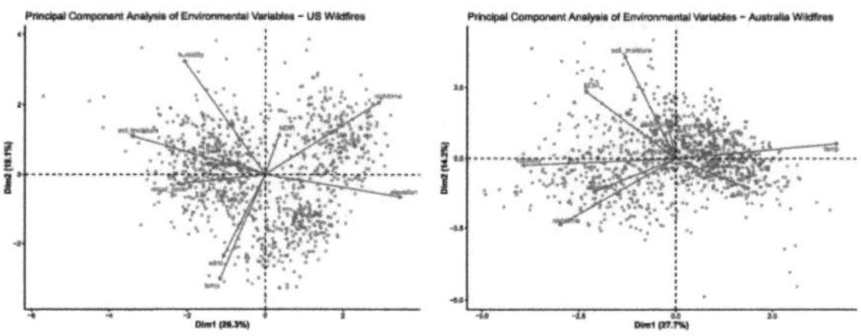

Fig. 1. Principal Components Analysis on wildfire data in the United States (Left) and Australia (Right).

Multicollinearity exposes problems in the interpretability of coefficients as it often hides the impact of individual predictors. The Variation Influence Factor (VIF), as calculated for a generalized linear model, for all 9 predictors stays below a magnitude of 3 in every country. Humidity in Australia is the only predictor to have a VIF greater than 2. We therefore conclude that multicollinearity should not damage the interpretability of our coefficients (Table 1).

3.3 Hierarchical Model

We use a hierarchical model for classification of wildfires. These models use our predictors as random variables, and each have coefficients. A hierarchical model takes raw random variables, multiply them by their coefficients, adds them, and applies an inverse logit function.

$$P(Wildfire|X) = logit^{-1}(\beta_1 X_1 + \beta_2 X_2 + ...\beta_p X_p)$$

The higher the score, the higher the probability. Our models are therefore interpretable, as, higher coefficients and high values of the predictors indicate a higher probability of a wildfire. Figure 2 shows example probability density function, $P(Wildfire|X)$, as characterized by an inverse logit function.

A simple Bayesian Logistic Regression model has an equation that consists of coefficients and random variables. In a Bayesian hierarchical model, random

Table 1. Variance Inflation Factor (VIF) values for environmental predictors in Australia and the US.

Variable	Australia	US
Temperature (°C)	1.7988	1.5057
Wind	1.0978	1.1070
Humidity	2.0280	1.4464
Night Time	1.1151	1.2585
Elevation	1.1096	1.9330
Soil Moisture	1.4075	1.5724
NDVI	1.5837	1.2285
Cloud Cover	1.1516	1.2359
Precipitation	1.0347	1.1280

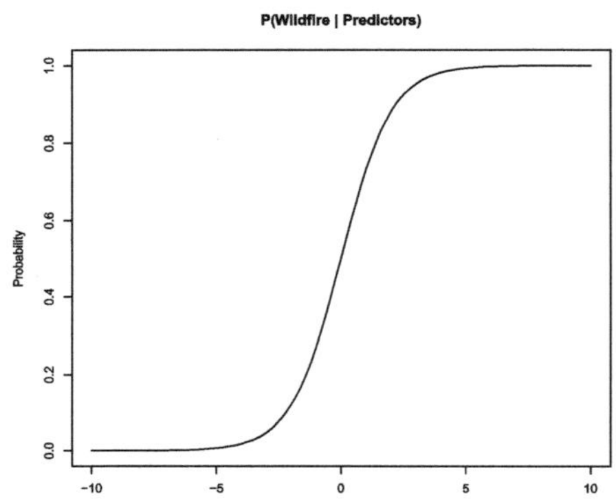

Fig. 2. A graphical display of a probability density function represented by the inverse logit function. As values get higher, probability converges to 1. As values get lower, probability converges to 0.

variables build on top of each other; i.e., they help define the distribution of random variables higher up. The final outcome is always fed into the logit function, which produces a probability between 0 and 1.

3.4 Spatial Kernel

The Bayesian hierarchical models consider geolocation through a spatial kernel. In addition to the linear model of the coefficients and their predictors, we add a spatial kernel that takes in latitude and longitude, then feets them into a spline with k knots. The spline fits a 2D space; parameters inside the kernel are optimized with the model's other parameters.

3.5 Hamiltonian Monte Carlo

The Hamiltonian Monte Carlo is a method that uses the derivatives of the density function being sampled to generate efficient transitions spanning the posterior. It produces optimal coefficients for our predictors, which make the model interpretable.

Algorithm 1. Hamiltonian Monte Carlo

Require: Original parameters θ_0
Ensure: Optimal parameters $\theta_{t_{final}}$
1: $\rho \sim \mathcal{N}(0,1)$
2: Leapfrog Method:
$\rho_{t+\frac{\epsilon}{2}} = \rho_t - \frac{\epsilon}{2}\nabla_\theta U(\theta_t)$
$\theta_{t+\epsilon} = \theta_t + \epsilon\rho_{t+\frac{\epsilon}{2}}$
$\rho_{t+\epsilon} = \rho_{t+\frac{\epsilon}{2}} - \frac{\epsilon}{2}\nabla_\theta U(\theta_{t+\epsilon})$, where ϵ is the step size.
3: Repeat the leapfrog steps L times to propose a new state $(\theta_{new}, \rho_{new})$.
4: Compute the Metropolis acceptance probability:
$\alpha = \min\left(1, \exp\left[-H(\theta_{new}, \rho_{new}) + H(\theta, \rho)\right]\right)$.
5: Accept the new state with probability α. Discard the momentum variable and repeat.

We use the Hamiltonian Monte Carlo Method provided in the BRMS library, as well as implement it in Python for customization. These methods give us interpretable and optimal coefficients to build a function that calculates the probability that a given observation is a wildfire.

4 Results

A Bayesian framework offers robust evaluation. Test data provides evaluation on predictive performance for unseen data. We divide our data into a 60/40 test split, and conduct analysis for variations of 3 Bayesian Models: 1) Spatial Hierarchical model, 2) Brightness Sensitive Hierarchical Model, and 3) Mixed Effects Spatial Hierarchical Model.

4.1 Spatial Hierarchical Model

The spatial hierarchical model on the United States and Australia produces accuracies of 88.58% and 86.69% on wildfire prediction, respectively. The United States has a true positive rate of 0.914 and a true negative rate of 0.857; precision is 0.866 and recall is 0.914. Australia has a true positive rate of 0.918 and a true negative rate of 0.71621622; precision is 0.905 and recall is 0.918. Varying the threshold for which a probability predicts a positive wildfire classification creates an AUC of 0.9378 and 0.9161 on an ROC curve in the United States and Australia, respectively (Fig. 3).

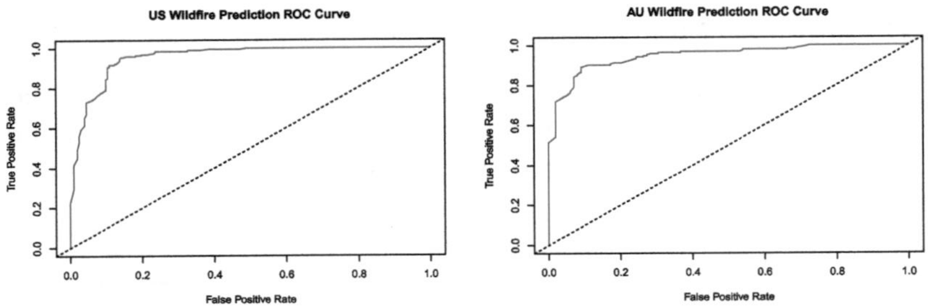

Fig. 3. ROC curves for wildfire prediction with a shifting threshold, θ. The United States has an AUC of 0.9378 compared to Australia's AUC of 0.9161.

To compare wildfire prediction in the United States and Australia, we compare the response curves for different predictors of wildfires in both countries. A response curve shows the probability of a wildfire produced for different values of a predictor, for example, $P(Wildfire|Wind = x)$. Response curves for the United States and Australia are shown below. Overall, the United States shows steeper positive curves with lower confidence intervals.

The coefficients show that temperature and NDVI have the highest positive contribution to wildfire probability. Soil Moisture has the highest negative contribution. This is consistent in both the United States and Australia, although soil moisture has a negative contribution of much greater magnitude in Australia than the US (Table 2).

Table 2. Coefficient Estimates for Spatial Hierarchical Models.

Variable	United States	Australia
Temperature (°C)	0.13	0.12
Wind	−0.05	−0.03
Humidity	−0.04	−0.02
NDVI	1.24	1.47
Precipitation	−0.47	0.54
Cloud Cover	−0.01	−0.01
Soil Moisture	−1.90	−6.58
Elevation	0.00	0.00
Night Time	−0.96	−0.85

Just as the response curves show, our coefficients for the predictors reveal that wildfire probabilities in the United States have the highest positive contribution from NDVI, and then temperature. Soil Moisture has the highest negative contribution. The maps in Fig. 5 show the classifications of all wildfire data after training on the full dataset (Fig. 4).

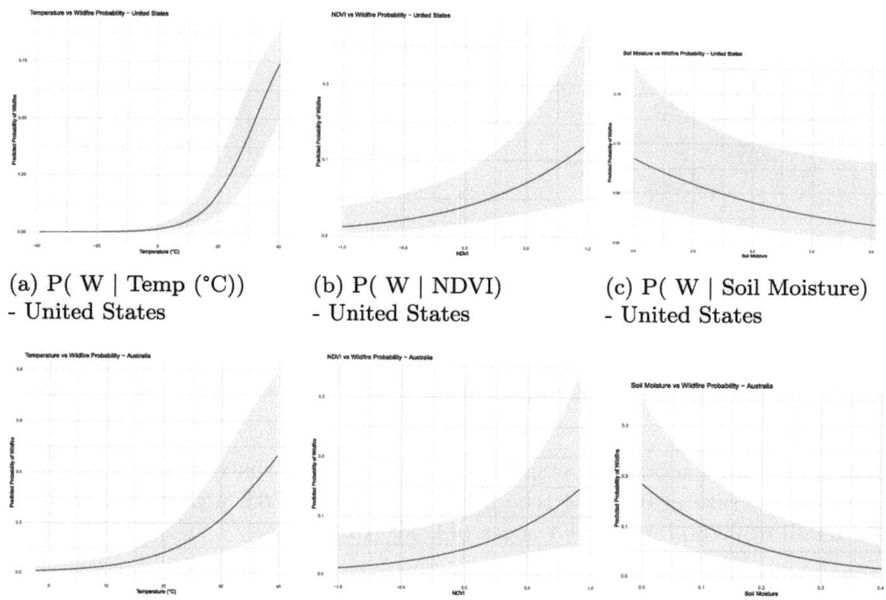

(a) P(W | Temp (°C)) - United States
(b) P(W | NDVI) - United States
(c) P(W | Soil Moisture) - United States
(d) P(W | Temp (°C)) - Australia
(e) P(W | NDVI) - Australia
(f) P(W | Soil Moisture) - Australia

Fig. 4. Response curves for wildfire probability with respect to various predictors across countries. While wildfire probability goes down quicker with soil moisture in Australia, NDVI and Temperature both consistently increase wildfire probability across countries.

4.2 Brightness Sensitive Spatial Hierarchical Model

We apply an amendment to the Hamiltonian Monte Carlo Algorithm. By applying a weight to the errors ϵ when calculating the gradient, the algorithm updates coefficients in the direction of the steepest ascent for the brightest wildfires.

$$\epsilon_i = \frac{\text{brightness}_i}{\max(\text{brightness})}\,\epsilon_i$$

Observations not labelled as a wildfire are weighted as $0.4 * \epsilon_i$, as they have no brightness. The coefficients produced from training a model on this algorithm will show us predictors of brighter wildfires, as opposed to focused solely on the optimum decision boundary. By comparing coefficients to the spatial hierarchical model, we may study which factors drive brighter wildfires, instead of just contributing to the probability of a wildfire.

Wildfire classification results remained starkly unchanged, albeit somewhat lower, with the amendment; we use the same 60/40 train and test data ratio to compute metrics. Test accuracy in the United States is 84.125%, with a true positive rate of 0.881, a true negative rate of 0.801, a precision of 0.818, a recall

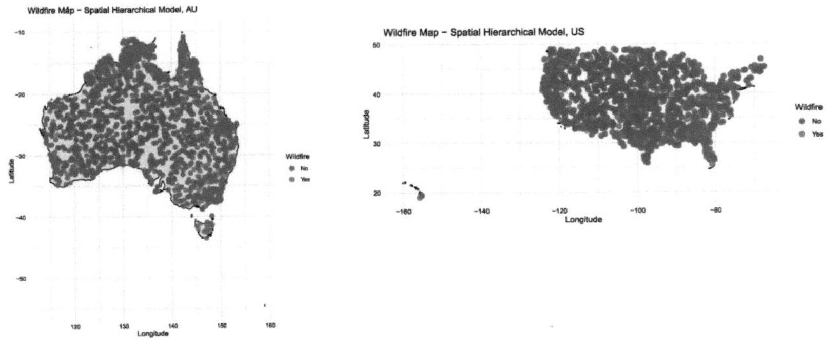

Fig. 5. Wildfires from the dataset as classified by the Spatial Hierarchical Model.

of 0.881, and an F1 score of 0.848. Test accuracy in the Australia is 77.22%, with a true positive rate of 0.780, a true negative rate of 0.765, a precision of 0.772, and a recall of 0.780, and an F1 score of 0.776 (Table 3).

Table 3. Comparison of United States and Australia model coefficients.

Variable	United States	Australia
Temperature (°C)	0.1545	0.0779
Wind	−0.0446	−0.0658
Humidity	−0.0226	−0.0113
NDVI	−0.0311	2.986
Precipitation	−0.0804	−0.3373
Cloud Cover	−0.0120	−0.0021
Soil Moisture	0.0106	0.5016
Elevation	0.00028	0.0006
Night Time	−0.01004	−0.7625

While wildfire accuracy goes down somewhat, the coefficients give us a closer look at the brightness sensitive trained spatial hierarchical model. In other words, we trade accuracy for different interpretability. The coefficient for temperature is higher in the United States than it is for the regular spatial hierarchical model. In the United States, a 95% credible interval for the temperature coefficient is [0.1545, 0.1652] for the brightness sensitive model, while the regular hierarchical spatial model has a 95% credible interval of [0.11, 0.15]; we therefore have significant evidence to conclude that hotter temperatures predict brighter wildfires in the United States. Our results match the Stefan-Boltzmann Law, which indicates that fire luminosity increases with temperature [8]. The other two biggest contributors, NDVI and soil moisture, converge closer to 0 than in the Spatial Hierarchical Model.

This indicates that temperature tells us which fires are brighter in the US, while the coefficients give us little indication of what contributes to a wildfire's brightness in Australia. Furthermore, the hottest regions in Australia, the center, have the fewest wildfires, which prevents the brightness sensitive model from relying on temperature as strongly as it does in the United States. For this reason, we conclude that only the United States shows that the Brightness Sensitive Spatial Hierarchical Model can be used to indicate which predictors predict brighter wildfires (Fig. 6).

Fig. 6. Wildfires classified by the Brightness Sensitive (Top Left) and Regular Spatial Hierarchical Model (Top Right) in the US; the bottom row shows Australia in the same order. The true positive rate is 0.881, compared to 0.914 in the US. The Brightness Sensitive Model raises $P(Wildfire)$ with higher temperature - the model catches an extra true positive case in Hawaii, potentially because of the modification. It is misclassified with the regular model; we show Alaska and Hawaii in these images to observe all misclassifications impacted by brightness.

4.3 Mixed Effects Hierarchical Model

Finally, we introduce a Mixed Effects Hierarchical Model. The Spatial Hierarchical Model is successful, however, it does not take advantage of the multilayered structure component of a Bayesian Hierarchical model. We can, in fact, provide an extra coefficient for each predictor, dependent on another predictor. This gives our models the flexibility to have different impacts of land and atmospheric conditions by city and state. It potentially, serves as a replacement for the spatial kernel.

A Mixed Effects Hierarchical Model can add group effects for state and city. Group effects are when we have random variables with, for example, K different classes. We therefore have K extra parameters, and add them to our probability function. A random intercept is a parameter added to the probability equation; a random slope is a parameter, from a predictor such as city or state, that is added to a predictor's coefficient before multiplication.

One example is a Mixed Effects Hierarchical Model with a random intercept for city and a random slope for soil moisture at the city level. The extra random variables are defined below.

$$\alpha_{state[j]} \sim \mathcal{N}(0, \sigma^2_{state})$$

$$\alpha_{city[j]} \sim \mathcal{N}(0, \sigma^2_{city_1})$$

$$\beta_{\text{soil moisture}, \, city[j]} \sim \mathcal{N}(0, \sigma^2_{city_2})$$

$$(\beta_{\text{soil moisture}, \, city[j]} + \beta_{\text{soil moisture}})X_{\text{soil moisture}} + \alpha_{city[j]} + \alpha_{state[j]} + \beta_1 X_1 + ... \beta_p X_p$$

We define a Mixed Effects Hierarchical Model with a random intercept for city and state, and a random slope at the city level for each predictor. When city and state data is not missing, these models reach 100% classification accuracy on our 60/40 train and test split in Australia, and reach as high as 88.7% in the United States. The ROC curves below show perfection in Australia and success in the US (Fig. 7).

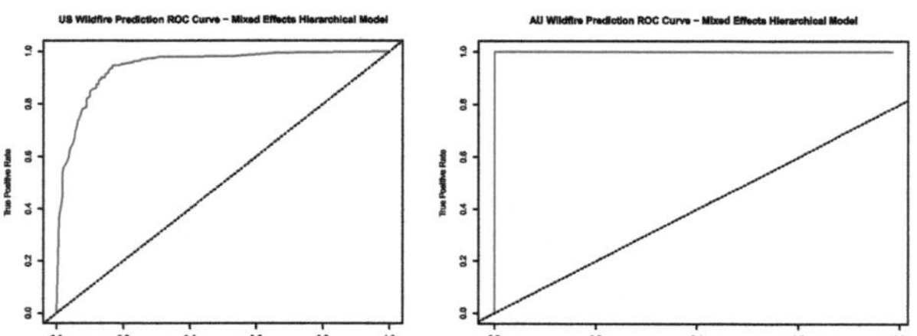

Fig. 7. ROC curves for wildfire prediction with a shifting threshold, θ on the Mixed Effects Hierarchical Model. The Australian model has a perfect score, leading to a square shape and an AUC of 1. The US has an AUC of 0.9448.

Overall, the Mixed Effects Hierarchical Model reaches an accuracy of 100% in Australia; this is equivalent to a true positive rate of 1, a true negative rate of 1, a precision of 1, and an F1 score of 1. The Mixed Effects Hierarchical Model reaches an accuracy of 88.7% in the United States, with a true positive rate of 0.9084, a true negative rate of 0.867, a precision of 0.8653, a recall of 0.9084, and an F1 score of 0.8863346. Some observations fail to map to a city and state during the geocoding stage of preprocessing. The Mixed Effects Hierarchical Model with some missing city or state data produces classifications with accuracies of 84.06524% and 88.25% in Australia and the United States, respectively (Fig. 8).

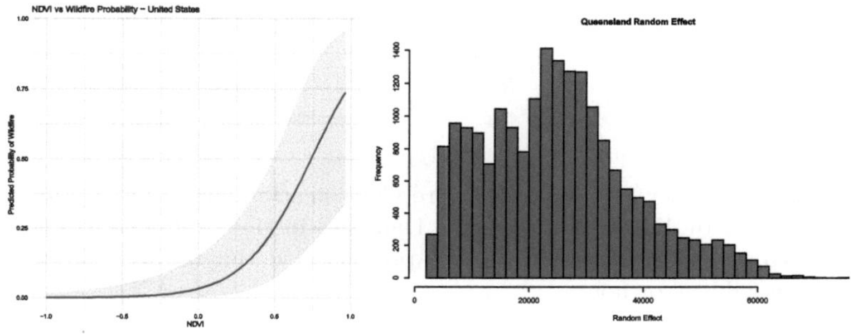

Fig. 8. Response curves for wildfire probability with respect to various predictors across countries. The NDVI response curve in the United States indicates a strong positive contribution with the city and state effects. The mixed effects hierarchical model for Australia is more dependent on the state, with less emphasis on the predictors.

The response curves visualize the relationship between predictors and wildfire probability in the United States. The states are stronger indicators of wildfire probability in Australia. They minimize the impact of the predictors; random effects for Australian states range from -7018.58 to 22246.17, while random effects for American states range from -6.68 to 4.76. Therefore, the response curves in the United States show that probability of a wildfire heavily depends on predictors, in Australia, the state and city effects dominate.

4.4 Model Checking

A one parameter model is a class of sampling distributions indexed by a single unknown parameter θ [9]. A Bayesian Hierarchical model provides a posterior from the training data that shows the probabilities of a wildfire per each individual observation. If the one parameter model for number of wildfires is a binomial distribution with parameter θ representing wildfire probability, then θ has a beta distribution with shape parameters α and β representing number of wildfires and non wildfires, respectively. The shape parameters in the prior, before seeing data, approximate 0.5 as a likely θ. The posterior updates the distribution with data from the dataset, estimating a θ of 0.709 and 0.5 in Australia and the United States, respectively. Figure 9 compares a one parameter model to the posteriors of all three Bayesian models in Australia and the United States.

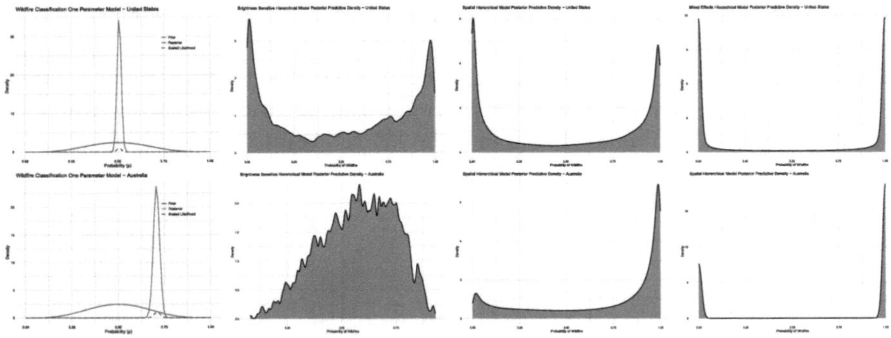

Fig. 9. A One Parameter Model for Wildfire Classification through a Beta Distribution (Left) followed by Posterior Predictive Densities in the United States (Top) and Australia (Bottom). Most Bayesian models produce a θ that clearly indicates if an observation is a wildfire or not.

4.5 Sensitivity Analysis

We apply a prior of $\mathcal{N}(0,1)$ to the models in Australia and the United States. The coefficients do not deviate significantly when the models use a strong prior. Accuracies are 83.6%, 88.6%, 88.3% in the United States, ordered by their posteriors in Fig. 10. Accuracies are 65%, 85.6%, and 100% in Australia. The posteriors do not deviate significantly in shape. This means that the likelihood dominates the prior, our data is informative, and our conclusions from earlier are robust.

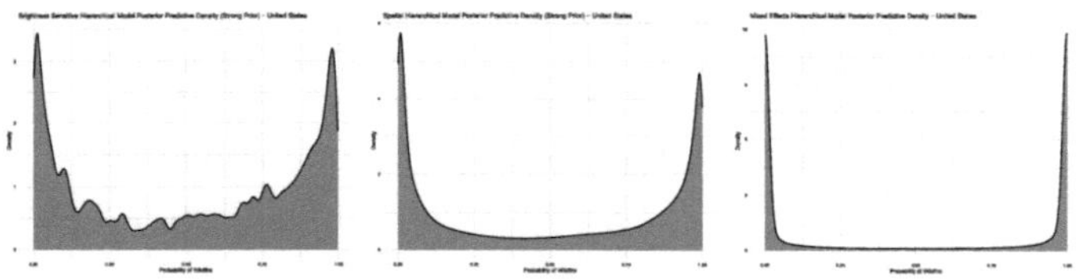

Fig. 10. The Prior has little impact on the posterior. Posteriors for the United States are shown above, almost matching posteriors without a prior added; Australia also matches its normal posterior.

4.6 Simulations

We measure the wildfire forecasts produced by the models by simulating land and atmospheric conditions throughout a country, and comparing the maps produced. After sampling random locations from the country, we add predictors randomly sampled, with replacement, from the full dataset. The Wasserstein distance metric measures the similarity between the wildfire maps; it is the minimum cost of transforming one probability distribution of wildfires to another.

We can use Wasserstein distance to measure how similar wildfire maps from all three models are on random data. They also show how dominant some geolocation regions are in each model; these simulations are featured in Fig. 11. They show how city, state, and geolocation differ in determining wildfire probability.

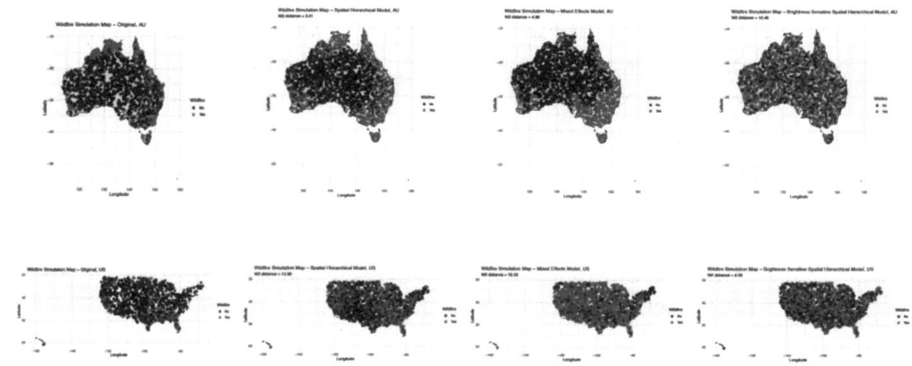

Fig. 11. Wildfire simulations: Top row shows Australia, bottom row shows the United States. Wasserstein distance for models are, left to right, 3.91 (Spatial Hierarchical Model), 4.96 (Mixed Effects Model), and 10.48 (Brightness Sensitive Model) in Australia. In the United States, they are 15.56 (Spatial Hierarchical Model), 16.32 (Mixed Effects Model), and 9.48 (Brightness Sensitive Model).

4.7 Comparison

Our best models score above 86% accuracy in all countries on test data. Another Bayesian model from 2022, which emphasized the positive contribution of NDVI to wildfire probability, resulted in 96.9% accuracy; the mixed hierarchical model introduced in this paper produces 100% accuracy with complete data. We reproduce many different configurations of deep neural networks previously and replicate experiments on our Australian and United States datasets from 2020 [10]. The results are displayed under the Bayesian Models in Table 4. Finally, we train classical machine learning models on the same data and compare them to the hierarchical and deep learning models; hierarchical models produce higher accuracies in both countries.

5 Conclusion

We conclude that many wildfire climate relationships transfer across continent. The exploratory data analysis shows that soil moisture and wind are projected into similar directions on a biplot of the first two principal components. Probability of a wildfire increases with temperature and NDVI. Soil moisture, meanwhile,

Table 4. Model performance by country.

Model	US	AU
Spatial Hierarchical Model	88.58	86.69
Brightness Sensitive Hierarchical Model	84.125	77.22
Mixed Effects Hierarchical Model 1*	88.7	100
Mixed Effects Hierarchical Model 2	84.07	88.25
Decision Tree Classifier	85.875	84.105
K-Nearest Neighbors	80.125	70.713
Support Vector Machine	72	67.459
100L-relu	83.875	75.34
4L-32U-0.2D-relu	86.37	82.98
3L-32U-0.2D-relu	85.5	85.61

* Results when city and state data are not missing (293 observations).

is much more indicative of no wildfires in Australia. These features are consistent across both countries, Australia and the United States. We introduce an amendment to Hamiltonian Monte Carlo, which gives us significant evidence to conclude that higher temperatures in the United States predict bright wildfires. This method can be extended to reach conclusions for similar categorical accuracy problems. Finally, we reproduce results from other papers. We show that Bayesian models can be more successful than deep neural networks, achieving up to 100% accuracy in Australia, and outperforming the best neural network architectures to date.

Acknowledgments. I would like to thank the University of Michigan, Ann Arbor, and its faculty for their guidance, time, and resources.

References

1. Albini, F.A.: Estimating windspeeds for predicting wildland fire behavior, vol. 221. Intermountain Forest and Range Experiment Station, Forest Service, US Department of Agriculture (1979)
2. Andrianarivony, H.S., Akhloufi, M.A.: Machine learning and deep learning for wildfire spread prediction: a review. Fire **7**(12), 482 (2024)
3. Bates, B.C., Dowdy, A.J., McCaw, L.: A Bayesian approach to exploring the influence of climate variability modes on fire weather conditions and lightning-ignited wildfires. Clim. Dyn. **57**(3), 1207–1225 (2021)
4. Bürkner, P.-C.: Advanced Bayesian multilevel modeling with the R package brms. arXiv preprint arXiv:1705.11123 (2017)
5. Center for Disaster Philanthropy. 2019–2020 Australian Bushfires. https://disasterphilanthropy.org/disasters/2019-australian-wildfires/. Accessed 16 Mar 2026

6. Charizanos, G., Demirhan, H.: Bayesian prediction of wildfire event probability using normalized difference vegetation index data from an Australian forest. Eco. Inform. **73**, 101899 (2023)
7. Deb, P., et al.: Causes of the widespread 2019–2020 Australian bushfire season. Earth's Future **8**(11), e2020EF001671 (2020)
8. Elsevier. Stefan–Boltzmann Law. ScienceDirect Topics. sciencedirect.com. Accessed 28 Apr 2026
9. Hoff, P.D.: A First Course in Bayesian Statistical Methods. Springer, New York (2009)
10. Jadouli, A., El Amrani, C.: Advanced wildfire prediction in Morocco: developing a deep learning dataset from multisource observations. IEEE Access **12**, 191733–191747 (2024)
11. Jain, P., Coogan, S.C.P., Subramanian, S.G., Crowley, M., Taylor, S., Flannigan, M.D.: A review of machine learning applications in wildfire science and management. Environ. Rev. **28**(4), 478–505 (2020)
12. Kondylatos, S., et al.: Wildfire danger prediction and understanding with deep learning. Geophys. Res. Lett. **49**(17), e2022GL099368 (2022)
13. Naderpour, M., Rizeei, H.M., Ramezani, F.: Wildfire prediction: handling uncertainties using integrated Bayesian networks and fuzzy logic. In: 2020 IEEE International Conference on Fuzzy Systems (FUZZ-IEEE), pp. 1–7. IEEE (2020)
14. Senf, F., Heinold, B., Kubin, A., Müller, J., Schrödner, R., Tegen, I.: How the extreme 2019–2020 Australian wildfires affected global circulation and adjustments. Atmos. Chem. Phys. **23**(15), 8939–8958 (2023)
15. Taylor, S.W., Woolford, D.G., Dean, C.B., Martell, D.L.: Wildfire prediction to inform fire management: statistical science challenges, pp. 586–615 (2013)

ESGRep: Learning Domain-Specific Embeddings for ESG Retrieval-Augmented Question Answering

Vanmanh Nguyen, Vanha Tran(✉), Thiloan Bui, and Truongminh Ngo

FPT University, Hanoi 155514, Vietnam
manhnvhe170552@fpt.edu.vn, {hatv14,loanbt7,minhnt79}@fe.edu.vn

Abstract. Environmental, Social, and Governance (ESG) information plays a critical role in evaluating corporate sustainability and responsible investment practices. However, accurately answering ESG-related questions remains challenging due to the specialized terminology and complex structure of sustainability reports, in particular, when combined with large language models, the answers are prone to hallucinations. In this work, we propose ESGRep, a domain-specific embedding model designed to improve document retrieval in retrieval-augmented generation pipelines for ESG question answering. ESGRep is fine-tuned using contrastive learning with within-report hard negatives, leveraging disclosure content indices from GRI, SASB, and TCFD corporate sustainability report frameworks to construct weakly labeled training triplets without manual annotation. We systematically evaluate ESGRep across six BERT-based architectures and integrate the resulting embeddings into a retrieval-augmented generation (RAG)-based question-answering system, evaluating performance on the ESGenius-QA benchmark. Experimental results show that ESGRep significantly improves downstream QA accuracy across 14 LLMs, increasing accuracy from 71.3% to 77.5% over strong generic baseline embedding models. These results highlight the importance of domain-adapted embeddings for enhancing LLM performance in specialized knowledge domains such as ESG.

Keywords: ESG · Question answering · Large Language Models · RAG

1 Introduction

Environmental, Social, and Governance (ESG) factors have rapidly evolved from niche concerns into central pillars of corporate strategy, regulatory compliance, and investment decision-making. Initiated by the United Nations Global Compact in 2004, the ESG framework provides a structured approach for evaluating a company's sustainability practices, ethical conduct, and long-term value creation beyond traditional financial metrics [6,21]. Environmental factors include a company's carbon footprint, energy consumption, water management, and effects

O. Gervasi et al. (Eds.): ICCSA 2026, LNCS 16768, pp. 416–431, 2027.
https://doi.org/10.1007/978-3-032-30488-9_26

on biodiversity. Social dimensions address labor practices, employee wellbeing, community engagement, and supply chain accountability. Governance aspects cover board composition, executive accountability, anti-corruption measures, and transparency in disclosure. Together, these three pillars offer stakeholders, including investors, regulators, employees, and civil society, a holistic lens for assessing whether a company operates responsibly and sustainably.

The growing importance of ESG has driven a dramatic expansion in the volume and complexity of sustainability documentation [11]. Authoritative bodies such as the Global Reporting Initiative (GRI)[1], the International Financial Reporting Standards Foundation (IFRS/ISSB) [2], the Task Force on Climate-related Financial Disclosures (TCFD)[3], the Sustainability Accounting Standards Board (SASB)[4], the Carbon Disclosure Project (CDP)[5], and the Intergovernmental Panel on Climate Change (IPCC)[6] collectively produce thousands of pages of technical standards, scientific assessments, and disclosure frameworks each year [36]. Companies across the world are now expected to align their sustainability reporting with multiple overlapping frameworks simultaneously. As a result, the total body of relevant ESG documentation has become vast, multi-layered, and highly specialized, posing a significant challenge for anyone seeking to efficiently locate, interpret, or verify specific ESG claims [17].

In current practice, ESG analysis in settings such as investment research, corporate reporting assurance, and third-party ESG rating typically still relies on expert analysts manually reviewing long sustainability reports, cross-referencing multiple reporting frameworks, and tracing reported claims back to source pages [1,2]. This workflow is time-consuming, expensive, and susceptible to inter-analyst inconsistency, because different evaluators may prioritize different disclosure standards or interpret the same evidence differently [1,2]. The need for scalable, accurate, and verifiable automated tools to assist ESG analysis has never been greater [7].

The promise of large language models (LLMs) to automate ESG analysis has garnered much research attention [5]. LLMs have developed as formidable tools for text understanding and question responding across numerous areas. However, when faced with the technical complexity and multidisciplinary scope of ESG content, assessments on specific benchmarks show that even frontier models display significant knowledge gaps.

Retrieval-Augmented Generation (RAG) addresses limitations of standalone language models by decoupling knowledge storage from generation [14]. Instead of relying solely on information encoded in model weights, RAG retrieves relevant passages from an external corpus at inference time and provides them as context for the LLM, grounding responses in verifiable sources and reducing

[1] https://www.globalreporting.org/.
[2] https://www.ifrs.org/groups/international-sustainability-standards-board/.
[3] https://www.fsb-tcfd.org/.
[4] https://www.cdsb.net/sustainability-accounting-standards-board-sasb.
[5] https://www.cdp.net/en.
[6] https://www.ipcc.ch/.

hallucinations. However, its effectiveness depends heavily on the quality of the retrieval component. Queries and passages are mapped into a shared embedding space and ranked by similarity; if the embedding model fails to capture ESG-specific semantics, the system may retrieve irrelevant or incomplete evidence [27].

These challenges motivate a domain-specific approach to ESG retrieval. In this work, we propose ESGRep, a family of embedding models fine-tuned for dense ESG retrieval. In contrast to prior ESG studies that mainly emphasize classification, information extraction, summarization, or general LLM benchmarking [9,12,26], our work targets the retrieval layer in RAG systems. Unlike prior domain-adapted language models such as ClimateBERT, FinBERT, and E-BERT, which mainly focus on pre-training or downstream classification settings [10,32,38], ESGRep learns retrieval-oriented representations from weak supervision derived directly from disclosure content indices in sustainability reports. We construct a weakly labeled dataset from reports following GRI, SASB, and TCFD standards, treat each disclosure requirement as a query, refine positive passages using GPT-5.2 as a relevance judge, and evaluate six BERT-based backbones on ESGenius-QA. Results show consistent improvements over BM25 and general-purpose embeddings, highlighting the importance of domain-adapted representations for ESG retrieval. Our main contributions are as follows:

(1) ESGRep, a domain-specific embedding model trained with contrastive learning and within-report hard negatives on a weakly labeled corpus of sustainability reports compliant with GRI, SASB, and TCFD standards is proposed, that enables more accurate retrieval for ESG question-answering.
(2) Conducting a systematic comparison of six BERT-variant backbone architectures as ESG embedding models, providing a comprehensive analysis of how model size, architecture, and domain pre-training affect ESG retrieval quality.
(3) We integrate ESGRep into a RAG-based QA pipeline and demonstrate significant improvements in downstream QA accuracy on the benchmark over baselines of 14 models, with analysis of performance across source families and model sizes.

The remainder of this paper is organized as follows. Section 2 reviews related work on ESG NLP, dense retrieval, and domain-specific embedding fine-tuning. Section 3 details the ESGRep training data construction, architecture, and RAG pipeline. Section 4 reports and analyzes experimental results. Section 5 concludes the paper and outlines future directions.

2 Related Work

The field of ESG data extraction and analysis has come a long way, especially with the introduction of advanced LLMs and NLP approaches. This section examines previous research that is relevant to our study, including domain-specific embedding, Retrieval-Augmented Generation, LLM approaches to financial and sustainability contexts, and related ESG resources and benchmarks.

2.1 LLMs in ESG and Sustainability

Due to the growing number and complexity of sustainability disclosures, the use of LLMs in ESG research has becoming increasingly popular [5,19]. Researchers have explored NLP methods for extracting and analyzing ESG information from corporate documents, assessing disclosures, and ensuring compliance with ESG policies [12,26]. LLMs have demonstrated strong performance in many NLP tasks and show promise for automating ESG analysis. However, because of domain-specific vocabulary and intricate reporting systems, implementing general-purpose LLMs to specialist fields like ESG continues to be difficult. Evaluations on dedicated benchmarks reveal that even state-of-the-art models exhibit notable knowledge gaps when handling the technical and interdisciplinary nature of ESG content [9,30].

2.2 RAG and Domain-Specific Embeddings

RAG systems address limitations of LLMs in specialized domains by grounding responses in external knowledge sources [16,31]. RAG lowers hallucination and allows models to use vast texts without memory by recovering pertinent passages at inference time [14]. Its effectiveness for ESG question answering has been demonstrated in prior work [39]. However, RAG performance is fundamentally dependent on the quality of its retrieval component, which selects relevant information from large corpora [4]. This process relies on embedding models that map queries and passages into a shared vector space for similarity-based ranking [35]. Generic embeddings often struggle with ESG-specific terminology and nuanced semantics [29], motivating the development of domain-specific embeddings. Previous research demonstrates that fine-tuned and domain-adapted models significantly improve retrieval accuracy and downstream performance in specialized tasks [8,22,28]. Models such as FinBERT, ClimateBERT, and SEC-BERT further demonstrate the advantages of domain-specific pre-training in ESG-related applications [10,15,32]. Relative to these studies, ESGRep differs in three ways: it optimizes bi-encoder retrieval rather than only document classification or representation learning, it derives weak supervision from report-specific disclosure indices rather than manually labeled QA pairs, and it evaluates retrieval quality through downstream ESG QA performance across multiple LLM families.

2.3 ESG Resources and Benchmarks

In order to support research and assessment in this area, dedicated resources and standards have been developed in response to the growing significance of ESG. The ESGenius benchmark [9] provides a comprehensive framework for evaluating LLMs on ESG knowledge, featuring a collection of 1,136 expert-validated questions (ESGenius-QA) and a corpus of 231 authoritative documents (ESGenius-Corpus). OntoSustain is an ontology developed for mapping quantitative environmental indicators from the GRI and ESRS standards to enable structured ESG data representation [40]. SusGen-3K is a high-quality, category-balanced dataset comprising approximately 30,000 sentences across seven financial and ESG NLP tasks [34]. ESG-Kor is a dataset designed for information extraction tasks specifically within Korean-language ESG documents [13].

Furthermore, ClimateBERT is a domain-specific language model pre-trained on a specialized corpus of 1.6 million climate-related paragraphs to enhance environmental discourse analysis [32]. E-BERT consists of a set of models optimized for ESG activity detection and reporting in financial texts [38]. ChatReport is an LLM-based tool that provides automated summarization and semantic search capabilities for TCFD-aligned sustainability recommendations [18]. Bronzini et al. utilizes GPT-based pipelines to extract semantic triples and populate knowledge graphs from unstructured ESG disclosures [3]. TCFD-Bench is a benchmark comprising 14 datasets across 8 tasks designed for the rigorous evaluation of sustainability report generation [34]. MMESGBench is a multimodal benchmark that targets complex reasoning and understanding across diverse ESG reporting formats [37]. These resources collectively highlight the ongoing efforts to develop robust tools and datasets for ESG analysis, underscoring the need for domain-adapted approaches to navigate the complexities of sustainability information.

3 Methodology

This section presents the ESGRep framework for learning domain-specific embeddings for ESG retrieval-augmented question answering. We first describe the weak supervision pipeline for constructing training triplets from corporate reports, followed by the encoder architecture and contrastive training procedure, the RAG pipeline that integrates the fine-tuned embeddings with diverse LLMs, and finally the evaluation benchmark.

3.1 Data Construction

Constructing a high-quality training dataset for ESG retrieval is non-trivial. Unlike open-domain QA, there is no large-scale, publicly available collection of ESG-specific (query, relevant passage) pairs. Manual annotation at the passage level is impractical given the length and technical depth of sustainability reports – documents that frequently exceed 100 pages of dense, structured content. We address this by designing a three-stage weak supervision pipeline that produces training signal from the structural properties of sustainability reports following GRI, SASB, and TCFD standards without requiring human annotators.

We collected approximately 2,000 corporate sustainability reports spanning 2013–2024 across diverse industries, produced under GRI, SASB, and TCFD reporting frameworks. We process these reports through a three-stage pipeline: query extraction from disclosure content indices, positive and negative chunk construction, and LLM-based label refinement. Stages 1–2 are illustrated in Fig. 1 and Stage 3 in Fig. 2. Figure 1 shows how report-level structure is converted into retrieval training pairs, while Fig. 2 shows the subsequent filtering step that improves label precision before model training.

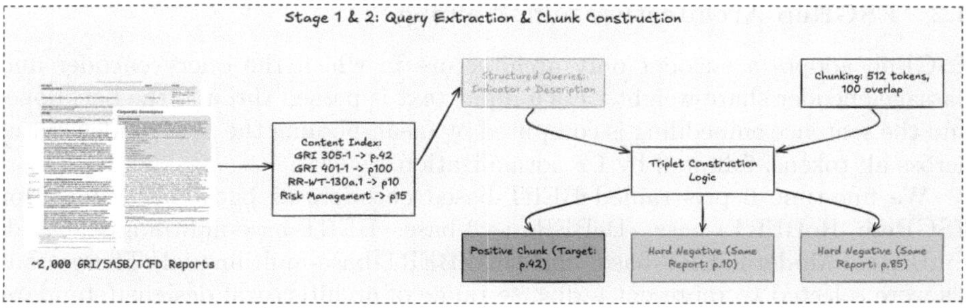

Fig. 1. ESGRep data preprocessing workflow Stages 1 and 2.

Stage 1: Query Extraction. GRI, SASB, and TCFD reports include a disclosure content index – a company-produced table mapping each applicable indicator (e.g., "GRI 305-1: Direct Scope 1 GHG emissions") to the report pages where it is addressed. We treat each indicator description as a natural language retrieval query q, yielding 30–80 queries per report depending on the standard and reporting level.

Stage 2: Positive and Negative Chunk Construction. Each report is segmented into overlapping chunks of 512 tokens with 100-token overlap. Positive chunks are those whose page span overlaps with the pages referenced in the content index for query q. Negative chunks are sampled from the same report but non-overlapping with any referenced page, ensuring negatives share the same company context, writing style, and domain vocabulary as the positive, forcing fine-grained semantic discrimination.

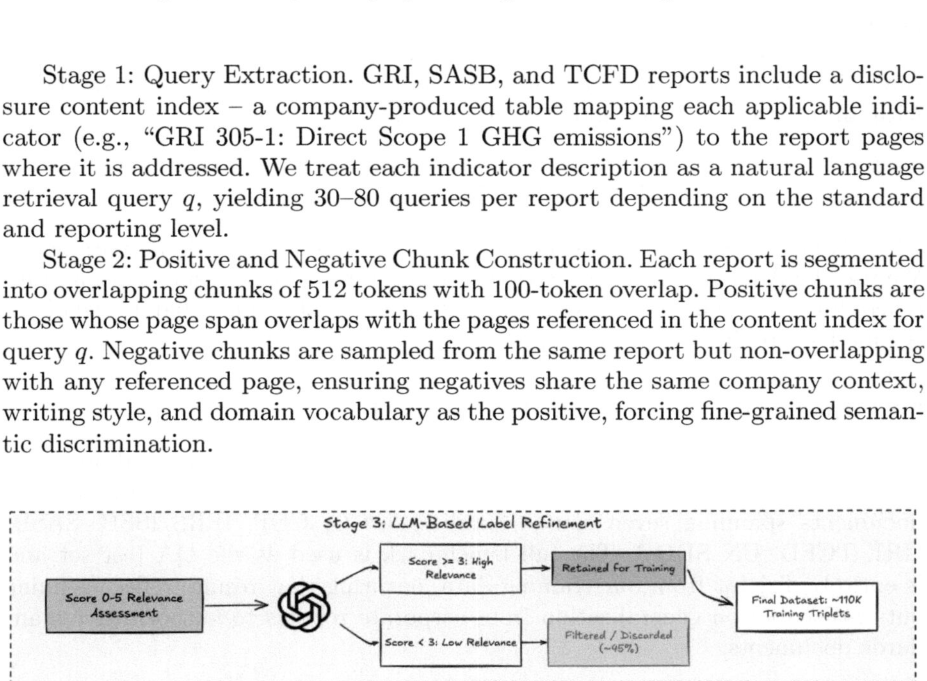

Fig. 2. ESGRep data preprocessing workflow Stage 3.

Stage 3: LLM-Based Label Refinement. Since not every page-referenced chunk directly addresses the disclosure, we apply GPT-5.2 as a relevance judge, scoring each candidate positive (q, c^+) from 0–5 and retaining only those with score ≥ 3. This filters approximately 45% of candidates, yielding 110,000 high-quality triplets from an initial pool of 200,000, split 80/10/10 for train/val/test. The full prompt is provided in Appendix A.1.

3.2 ESGRep Architecture and Training

ESGRep adopts a encoder only architecture in which the query encoder and passage encoder share weights. Each input text is passed through the backbone, and the sentence embedding is computed by mean-pooling the final hidden states across all tokens, followed by L2 normalization.

We fine-tune 6 pre-trained BERT-based encoders as backbone models for ESGRep: RoBERTa-base, DeBERTa-v3-base, BERT-base-multilingual-cased, FinBERT, ModernBERT-base, and DistilBERT-base-multilingual. These models were selected to represent a diverse range of architectural designs (standard transformer, disentangled attention, distilled, and modern efficiency-optimized), parameter counts (109 M to 184 M), and pre-training data profiles (general-purpose English, multilingual, and financial domain).

Training uses MultipleNegativesRankingLoss, which maximizes the cosine similarity between the query and its positive passage while minimizing similarity with all in-batch passages and the sampled hard negatives:

$$\mathcal{L} = -\log \frac{\exp(\text{sim}(q, c^{+})/\tau)}{\sum_j \exp(\text{sim}(q, c_j)/\tau)} \tag{1}$$

where $\text{sim}(\cdot,\cdot)$ denotes cosine similarity and τ is a temperature hyperparameter. We use the AdamW optimizer with a learning rate of 2e-5, cosine learning rate scheduling with 200 warmup steps, weight decay of 0.01, and a batch size of 32. All models are fine-tuned for 3 epochs.

3.3 Evaluation Benchmark: ESGenius-QA

We evaluate on ESGenius-QA, a benchmark of 1,136 expert-validated multiple-choice questions grounded in the ESGenius-Corpus – 231 authoritative ESG documents spanning seven source families (IPCC, CDP, IFRS/ISSB, SASB, GRI, TCFD, UN SDGs). The full benchmark is used as the QA test set and is entirely disjoint from our training data, ensuring that results reflect genuine out-of-distribution generalization from corporate reports to authoritative standards documents.

3.4 Software and Implementation Details

The experimental pipeline was implemented used Transformers [33], and Sentence-Transformers [23,24]. BM25 was used as the sparse retrieval baseline [25]. For Stage 3 label refinement, GPT-5.2 was accessed through the OpenAI API [20]. These software components are reported explicitly to improve reproducibility of the training and evaluation pipeline.

4 Experimental Result

We organize our experimental results as follows. Subsection 4.1 compares the 6 embedding backbones before and after ESGRep fine-tuning. Subsection 4.2

reports per-LLM accuracy to demonstrate that ESGRep's gains generalize across model families. Subsection 4.3 presents ablation studies on negative sampling strategy and the number of retrieved passages. Finally, Subsect. 4.4 analyzes performance across the 7 ESGenius source families to examine in-domain versus out-of-domain transfer.

4.1 Benchmarking Fine-Tuned Embedding Models

Table 1 presents QA accuracy on the ESGenius-QA benchmark for each of the 6 embedding backbones, comparing the pre-trained embedding model without fine-tuning (Baseline) against the ESGRep fine-tuned version. All results use $k = 3$ retrieved passages as context for the LLM, and are averaged across 14 LLMs to isolate the effect of the embedding backbone.

Table 1. QA Accuracy on ESGenius-QA by Embedding Backbone (Avg Across 14 LLMs)

Embedding Backbone	Baseline (no ft)	ESGRep (ft)	Δ^*
RoBERTa-base	0.712	0.774	+0.062
DeBERTa-v3-base	0.716	0.779	+0.063
BERT-base-multilingual-cased	0.708	0.768	+0.060
FinBERT	0.718	0.782	+0.064
ModernBERT-base	0.710	**0.785**	**+0.075**
DistilBERT-base-multilingual	0.703	0.759	+0.056
Average	0.713	0.775	+0.062

*Δ: ESGRep vs. Baseline (no fine-tuning) for same backbone

The results demonstrate a consistent improvement from domain-specific fine-tuning across all 6 backbones: ESGRep provides an average improvement of +0.062 over the corresponding pre-trained baseline, confirming that general-purpose dense embeddings – regardless of architecture – are not well-calibrated for the ESG domain.

Table 1 shows that ESGRep improves every backbone over its untuned baseline, indicating that the gains come from ESG-specific contrastive fine-tuning rather than from one unusually strong pre-trained model. Among the backbone architectures, ModernBERT-base achieves the highest ESGRep accuracy (0.785) with an improvement of 0.075 over its pre-trained counterpart. FinBERT ranks second at 0.782 (+0.064), benefiting from its financial domain pre-training on SEC filings, earnings calls, and analyst reports, which provides a stronger initialization (0.718 baseline) than general-purpose models for ESG-related vocabulary. DeBERTa-v3-base follows at 0.779 (+0.063), while DistilBERT-base-multilingual trails at 0.759 (+0.056), reflecting the capacity limitations of its distilled architecture.

4.2 Per-LLM QA Accuracy Comparison

To demonstrate that ESGRep's improvements generalize across different language models, we report QA accuracy for each of the 14 evaluated LLMs under four retrieval conditions: Zero-shot, BM25, the pre-trained ModernBERT-base baseline (no fine-tuning), and the ModernBERT-base ESGRep model. Table 2 therefore isolates the contribution of retrieval quality while holding the underlying QA benchmark fixed.

Table 2. QA Accuracy by LLM (ModernBERT-base ESGRep vs. Baselines)

LLM	Zero-shot	BM25	Baseline	ESGRep
Qwen3-4B	0.426	0.513	0.544	**0.610**
Qwen3-8B	0.521	0.603	0.631	**0.706**
Qwen3-14B	0.608	0.679	0.704	**0.782**
Qwen3-30B-A3B	0.583	0.659	0.686	**0.762**
Qwen3-235B-A22B	0.693	0.748	0.770	**0.844**
DeepSeek-R1-Distill-Qwen-7B	0.501	0.586	**0.616**	0.613
DeepSeek-R1-Distill-Qwen-14B	0.643	0.708	0.732	**0.808**
DeepSeek-v3.1	0.621	0.690	**0.715**	0.711
DeepSeek-v3.2	0.657	0.718	0.741	**0.816**
gpt-oss-120b	0.700	0.752	0.773	**0.850**
gpt-oss-20b	0.663	0.721	0.743	**0.817**
Gpt-5.2	0.752	0.803	0.822	**0.901**
Claude-4.5	0.724	0.781	0.801	**0.879**
Gemini-3	0.737	0.792	0.811	**0.890**
Average	0.659	0.697	0.721	**0.785**

ESGRep improves QA accuracy for 12 of the 14 evaluated LLMs over the pre-trained dense baseline. The two exceptions are DeepSeek-R1-Distill-Qwen-7B (0.616 to 0.613) and DeepSeek-v3.1 (0.715 to 0.711), both showing slight regressions that may reflect sensitivity to passage ordering or context length in these reasoning-focused architectures.

Among the improving models, the largest absolute gains from Baseline to ESGRep are observed for GPT-5.2 (+0.079), Gemini-3 (+0.079), and Claude-4.5 (+0.078), indicating that even the strongest LLMs benefit substantially from higher-quality retrieved evidence. At the other end of the scale, smaller models benefit most from the full RAG pipeline: Qwen3-4B improves from 0.426 (zero-shot) to 0.610 (ESGRep), an absolute gain of +0.184, demonstrating that domain-specific retrieval can substantially compensate for limited parametric knowledge.

Across all LLMs, the average accuracy increases from 0.659 (zero-shot) to 0.697 (BM25) to 0.721 (Baseline) to 0.785 (ESGRep), a total pipeline gain of +0.126 over zero-shot. Each stage contributes incrementally, with the fine-tuning step (Baseline→ESGRep, +0.064) providing the largest single improvement. The top-performing LLMs (GPT-5.2, Gemini-3, Claude-4.5) all exceed 0.87 with ESGRep, with GPT-5.2 reaching 0.901.

4.3 Ablation Studies

Figure 3 presents two ablation experiments on the best-performing backbone (ModernBERT-base), averaged across 14 LLMs. Figure 3(a) identifies which negative sampling strategy contributes most to retrieval quality, while Fig. 3(b) shows how retrieval depth affects downstream QA accuracy.

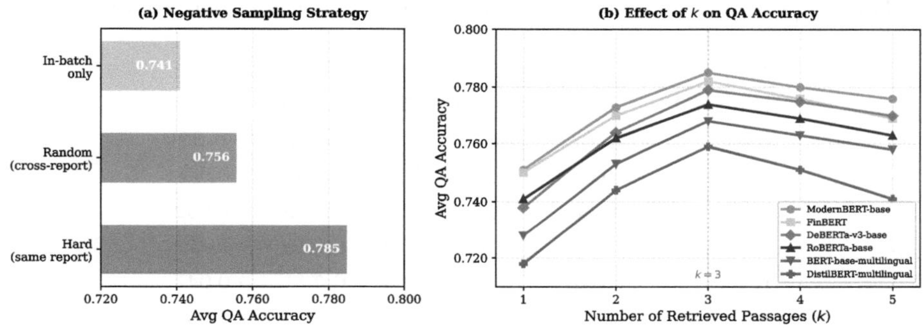

Fig. 3. Ablation studies. (a) Effect of negative sampling strategy on QA accuracy. (b) QA accuracy vs. number of retrieved passages k for each embedding backbone.

Negative Sampling Strategy (Fig. 3a): Within-report hard negatives yield the highest accuracy (0.785), outperforming cross-report random negatives (0.756) and in-batch-only training (0.741). This pattern indicates that retrieval in ESG QA benefits most from difficult negatives drawn from the same report rather than from easy negatives drawn from unrelated documents. Hard negatives force the model to discriminate between passages that share the same company context, writing style, and ESG vocabulary but address different disclosure requirements—precisely the challenge at inference time. Cross-report random negatives are easier to distinguish by company context alone, and in-batch negatives provide the weakest signal.

Number of Retrieved Passages (Fig. 3b): Accuracy peaks at $k = 3$ across all 6 backbones. This confirms that the best downstream QA performance is achieved with a small amount of highly relevant evidence rather than a larger context window. At $k = 1$ and $k = 2$, coverage is limited and the LLM must fall back on parametric knowledge when the ground-truth passage is missed. Beyond $k = 3$, additional passages introduce distracting context that dilutes attention toward the correct evidence—with DistilBERT-multilingual showing the steepest decline from $k = 3$ to $k = 5$ (-0.018), consistent with the lower retrieval precision of its distilled representations. We adopt $k = 3$ as the default in all main experiments.

4.4 Source Family Analysis

To understand which ESG domains benefit most from domain-specific embedding fine-tuning, we report per-source-family QA accuracy for the best ESGRep model compared to BM25 and the best pre-trained dense baseline. Table 3 distinguishes improvements on source families seen during training from transfer to related but unseen ESG domains.

Table 3. Per-Source-Family QA Accuracy (Best Model, Avg Across 14 LLMs)

Source Family	Zero-shot	BM25	Baseline	ESGRep	Δ^*
IFRS/ISSB	0.651	0.698	0.723	**0.775**	+0.052
SASB	0.673	0.721	0.738	**0.818**	**+0.080**
GRI	0.642	0.678	0.708	**0.796**	+0.088
CDP	0.668	0.704	0.726	**0.778**	+0.052
TCFD	0.680	0.724	0.742	**0.819**	+0.077
IPCC	0.623	0.661	0.694	**0.741**	+0.047
UN SDGs	0.671	0.693	0.718	**0.764**	+0.046

$^*\Delta$: ESGRep RAG vs. Baseline RAG

Source family results reveal a clear in-domain advantage. The three source families used to construct training data – GRI (+0.088), SASB (+0.080), and TCFD (+0.077) – show the largest ESGRep gains, confirming that the contrastive fine-tuning procedure effectively learns the retrieval patterns specific to these frameworks' disclosure structures. In contrast, out-of-domain families – IFRS/ISSB (+0.052), CDP (+0.052), IPCC (+0.047), and UN SDGs (+0.046) – show more modest but still positive improvements, indicating that ESGRep transfers partial domain knowledge to related ESG content. Notably, IPCC and UN SDGs show the smallest gains, consistent with their distinct document styles (scientific assessment reports and high-level policy goals) compared to the corporate disclosure format of the training sources. UN SDGs, with the fewest test questions (36 total), should be interpreted with caution due to high variance.

5 Conclusion and Future Work

In this paper, we presented ESGRep, a family of domain-specific bi-encoder embedding models for RAG-based ESG question answering. We introduced a scalable weak supervision pipeline that constructs training triplets from the disclosure content indices of GRI, SASB, and TCFD corporate sustainability reports without manual annotation, with candidate positives refined by GPT-5.2 relevance scoring. Models are trained with contrastive learning and within-report hard negatives, encouraging fine-grained semantic discrimination on an out-of-distribution test set (ESGenius-QA) drawn from authoritative ESG standards documents.

Experiments across 6 BERT backbones and 14 LLMs show that ESGRep consistently improves QA accuracy over BM25 and generic dense baselines, achieving an absolute gain of +0.064 for the best backbone (ModernBERT-base). Ablations confirm that within-report hard negatives are the primary driver of performance, and per-source-family analysis shows the largest gains on in-domain families – GRI (+0.088), SASB (+0.080), and TCFD (+0.077) – with positive transfer to out-of-domain sources.

The main limitation is a potential bias toward GRI, SASB, and TCFD terminology and the dependence on machine-readable content indices, which limits the training corpus size. Future work will explore multilingual extension to non-English ESG documents, cross-encoder re-ranking to refine retrieved candidates, and expanding the pipeline to additional standards such as ESRS, CDP, and IFRS/ISSB for broader training coverage.

A Appendix

A.1 LLM-as-Judge Prompt for Label Refinement

The following prompt is used in Stage 3 of the training data construction pipeline (Sect. 3.2) to assess whether a candidate positive passage sufficiently addresses a given GRI disclosure requirement. Only pairs receiving a score >= 3 are retained as positive training examples. The score is extracted by parsing the boxed{} tag from the response.

```
You are an expert ESG analyst specializing in sustainability reporting
standards. Your task is to evaluate the relevance of a text passage to
a specific GRI disclosure requirement.

Given the following GRI disclosure requirement and a candidate passage
extracted from a corporate sustainability report, assess how well the
passage addresses the disclosure requirement.

**GRI Disclosure Requirement:**
{query}

**Candidate Passage:**
{passage}

Rate the relevance of the passage to the disclosure requirement on a
scale from 0 to 5:

0 - Completely irrelevant: The passage has no connection to the
    disclosure requirement.
1 - Marginally related: The passage mentions related topics but does
    not address the specific disclosure requirement.
2 - Partially relevant: The passage touches on the disclosure
    requirement but lacks substantive information or only addresses it
     tangentially.
3 - Moderately relevant: The passage provides some meaningful
    information that addresses the disclosure requirement, though it
    may not be comprehensive.
4 - Highly relevant: The passage directly addresses the disclosure
    requirement with substantial and specific information.
5 - Fully addresses: The passage comprehensively and directly addresses
     all aspects of the disclosure requirement with detailed, specific
     data or explanations.

First, provide a brief explanation (2-3 sentences) analyzing how the
passage relates to the disclosure requirement. Then, output your
final score as \boxed{score}.

Example output format:
The passage discusses the company's direct greenhouse gas emissions
and provides specific metrics for Scope 1 emissions, which directly
addresses the GRI 305-1 disclosure requirement. However, it lacks
details on the methodologies used for calculation. \boxed{4}
```

References

1. Berg, F., Kölbel, J.F., Rigobon, R.: Aggregate confusion: the divergence of ESG ratings. Rev. Finan. **26**(6), 1315–1344 (2022)
2. Billio, M., Costola, M., Hristova, I., Latino, C., Pelizzon, L.: Inside the ESG ratings: (dis)agreement and performance. Corp. Soc. Responsib. Environ. Manag. **28**(5), 1426–1445 (2021)
3. Bronzini, M., Nicolini, C., Lepri, B., Passerini, A., Staiano, J.: Glitter or gold? Deriving structured insights from sustainability reports via large language models. EPJ Data Sci. **13**(1) (2024)
4. Cook, T., et al.: Retrieval augmented generation (RAG) for fintech: agentic design and evaluation (2025)
5. Du, K., Mao, R., Xing, F., Mengaldo, G., Cambria, E.: Language models for environmental, social, and governance analysis: a review. Inf. Process. Manag. **63**(4), 104596 (2026)
6. Duan, Y., Yang, F., Xiong, L.: Environmental, social, and governance (ESG) performance and firm value: evidence from Chinese manufacturing firms. Sustainability **15**(17), 12858 (2023)
7. Gharpure, A.: ESG reporting in enterprise financial systems: challenges and innovations. J. Comput. Sci. Technol. Stud. **7**(3), 194–201 (2025)
8. Gupta, A., Rawat, M., Stolcke, A., Pieraccini, R.: Refine on scarce data: retrieval enhancement through fine-tuning via model fusion of embedding models (2024)
9. He, C., et al.: ESGenius: benchmarking LLMs on environmental, social, and governance (ESG) and sustainability knowledge. In: Proceedings of the 2025 Conference on Empirical Methods in Natural Language Processing, pp. 14623–14664. Association for Computational Linguistics (2025)
10. Huang, A.H., Wang, H., Yang, Y.: <scp>finbert</scp>: a large language model for extracting information from financial text. Contemp. Account. Res. **40**(2), 806–841 (2023)
11. Kim, J., Yang, W.: ESG performance in the regulatory transformation era: a systematic thematic review (2020–2024). Front. Sustain. **6** (2026)
12. Lee, H., Kim, J.H., Jung, H.S.: ESG-KIBERT: a new paradigm in ESG evaluation using NLP and industry-specific customization. Decis. Support Syst. **193**, 114440 (2025)
13. Lee, J., Son, G., Kim, M.: ESG-KOR: a Korean dataset for ESG-related information extraction and practical use cases. In: Findings of the Association for Computational Linguistics: EMNLP 2024, pp. 6627–6643. Association for Computational Linguistics (2024)
14. Lewis, P., Perez, E., Piktus, A., Petroni: retrieval-augmented generation for knowledge-intensive NLP tasks (2020). https://doi.org/10.48550/ARXIV.2005.11401
15. Loukas, L., et al.: FiNER: financial numeric entity recognition for XBRL tagging. In: Proceedings of the 60th Annual Meeting of the Association for Computational Linguistics (Volume 1: Long Papers). Association for Computational Linguistics (2022)
16. Luo, H., et al.: Domain-specific retrieval-augmented generation with adaptive embedding and knowledge distillation-based re-ranking. Processes **14**(1), 99 (2025)
17. Mervelskemper, L., Streit, D.: Enhancing market valuation of ESG performance: is integrated reporting keeping its promise? Bus. Strateg. Environ. **26**(4), 536–549 (2016)

18. Ni, J., et al.: CHATREPORT: democratizing sustainability disclosure analysis through LLM-based tools. In: Proceedings of the 2023 Conference on Empirical Methods in Natural Language Processing: System Demonstrations, pp. 21–51. Association for Computational Linguistics (2023)
19. Ong, K., et al.: Explainable natural language processing for corporate sustainability analysis. Inf. Fusion **115**, 102726 (2025)
20. OpenAI: OpenAI API platform documentation (2025). https://platform.openai.com/docs/overview
21. Ortas, E., Álvarez, I., Garayar, A.: The environmental, social, governance, and financial performance effects on companies that adopt the united nations global compact. Sustainability **7**(2), 1932–1956 (2015)
22. Pacis, F.J., Alyaev, S., Wiktorski, T.: Domain-Adapted Embeddings Model Using Contrastive Learning for Drilling Text Data, pp. 491–503. Springer Nature Singapore (2025)
23. Reimers, N., Gurevych, I.: Sentence-BERT: sentence embeddings using Siamese BERT-networks (2019)
24. Reimers, N., Gurevych, I.: Sentence transformers: multilingual sentence, paragraph, and image embeddings using BERT & CO. In: Proceedings of the 2020 Conference on Empirical Methods in Natural Language Processing: System Demonstrations, pp. 122–131 (2020)
25. Robertson, S., Zaragoza, H.: The probabilistic relevance framework: Bm25 and beyond. Found. Trends Inf. Retr. **3**(4), 333–389 (2009)
26. Schimanski, T., Reding, A., Reding, N., Bingler, J., Kraus, M., Leippold, M.: Bridging the gap in ESG measurement: using NLP to quantify environmental, social, and governance communication. Financ. Res. Lett. **61**, 104979 (2024)
27. Sun, X., Shao, Y., Han, J.: ESG performance drives enterprise high-quality development through financing constraints: based on the background of China's digital transformation. Sustainability **17**(13), 6094 (2025)
28. Szabó, B.N., Gyöngyössy, N.M., Dalos, A.: Applied domain adaptation of LLM-based document embeddings for engineering knowledge retrieval. In: Proceedings of the Intelligent Robotics FAIR 2025, IntRob '25, pp. 29–37. ACM (2025)
29. Tang, Y., Yang, Y.: Do we need domain-specific embedding models? An empirical investigation (2024)
30. Tran, V.K., Tran, K.T., Pham, Q.V., Guhaa, K., Nguyen, H.D.: LLM-powered question answering for environmental, social, and governance (ESG) reports. In: Proceedings of the 2nd ACM Workshop in AI-powered Question & Answering Systems, pp. 49–53. ACM (2025)
31. Wang, X., Chi, J., Tai, Z., Kwok, T.S.T.: FinSage: a multi-aspect rag system for financial filings question answering. In: Proceedings of the 34th ACM International Conference on Information and Knowledge Management, CIKM '25, pp. 6144–6152. ACM (2025)
32. Webersinke, N., Kraus, M., Bingler, J.A., Leippold, M.: ClimateBert: a pretrained language model for climate-related text (2021)
33. Wolf, T., et al.: Transformers: state-of-the-art natural language processing. In: Proceedings of the 2020 Conference on Empirical Methods in Natural Language Processing: System Demonstrations, pp. 38–45 (2020)
34. Wu, Q., et al.: SusGen-GPT: a data-centric LLM for financial NLP and sustainability report generation. In: Findings of the Association for Computational Linguistics: NAACL 2025, pp. 1184–1203. Association for Computational Linguistics (2025)

35. Xu, Z., Mo, F., Huang, Z., Zhang, C., Yu, P., Wang, B.: A survey of model architectures in information retrieval (2025)
36. Yadav, S., Samadhiya, A., Kumar, A., Luthra, S., Pandey, K.K.: Environmental, social, and governance (ESG) reporting and missing (M) scores in the industry 5.0 era: broadening firms' and investors' decisions to achieve sustainable development goals. Sustain. Dev. **33**(3), 3455–3477 (2024)
37. Zhang, L., et al.: MMESGBench: pioneering multimodal understanding and complex reasoning benchmark for ESG tasks. In: Proceedings of the 33rd ACM International Conference on Multimedia, MM '25, pp. 12829–12836. ACM (2025)
38. Zhang, M., Shen, Q., Zhao, Z., Wang, S., Huang, G.Q.: Optimizing ESG reporting: innovating with e-BERT models in nature language processing. Expert Syst. Appl. **265**, 125931 (2025)
39. Zhao, Y., et al.: Optimizing LLM based retrieval augmented generation pipelines in the financial domain. In: Proceedings of the 2024 Conference of the North American Chapter of the Association for Computational Linguistics: Human Language Technologies (Volume 6: Industry Track), pp. 279–294. Association for Computational Linguistics (2024)
40. Zhou, Y., Perzylo, A.: OntoSustain: towards an ontology for corporate sustainability reporting. In: ISWC 2023 Posters and Demos: 22nd International Semantic Web Conference (2023)

An Intelligent eUPF for Time-Sensitive Path Selection in B5G Edge Networks

Rodrigo Moreira[1], Larissa F. Rodrigues Moreira[1], Tereza C. Carvalho[2], and Flávio de Oliveira Silva[3](✉)

[1] Federal University of Viçosa, Minas Gerais, Brazil
{rodrigo,larissa.f.rodrigues}@ufv.br
[2] University of São Paulo, São Paulo, Brazil
terezacarvalho@usp.br
[3] University of Minho, Braga, Portugal
flavio@di.uminho.pt

Abstract. In Beyond 5G (B5G) networks, intelligent, flexible traffic management is essential to meet the stringent speed and reliability requirements of new applications. This paper presents an improved User Plane Function (eUPF) design that uses a Deep Q-Network (DQN) agent for real-time path selection between Multi-access Edge Computing (MEC) and cloud endpoints. The path selection problem is formulated as a Partially Observable Markov Decision Process (POMDP). We propose a novel passive delay measurement method that uses eBPF programs to link TEID-based timestamps in GTP-U traffic, allowing for low-cost delay estimation without active testing. Experiments show that the DQN agent substantially outperforms a random baseline, with lower average latency, more stable rewards, and more reliable low-delay path choices. These results demonstrate the effectiveness of AI-driven control in B5G core networks and the promise of reinforcement learning for modern network management.

Keywords: Beyond 5G Networks · User Plane Function · Reinforcement Learning · eBPF/XDP · Multi-access Edge Computing · Time-Sensitive Path Selection

1 Introduction

The increasing prevalence of compute-intensive applications, coupled with the diversity of mobile devices, results in substantial data volumes in 5th Generation Mobile Network (5G). To accommodate this demand, especially in the Beyond Fifth Generation (B5G) context, it is crucial to minimize service access delay by bringing services closer to users through approaches such as Multi-access Edge Computing (MEC). Industries such as automation, autonomous driving, and cloud gaming, for instance, impose stringent ultralow-latency requirements [18], and in response, placing network functions near the edge not only helps meet these demands but also offers a promising way to alleviate backbone traffic

O. Gervasi et al. (Eds.): ICCSA 2026, LNCS 16768, pp. 432–446, 2027.
https://doi.org/10.1007/978-3-032-30488-9_27

surges, particularly for Network Function Virtualization (NFV)-based components [2]. This drives ongoing research on efficient path-selection strategies in the data plane of mobile networks.

Building on these advancements, the state of the art presents various approaches for service steering and resource allocation within the broader context of path selection [13], particularly across two key segments of mobile networks. The first research stream focuses on the Radio Access Network (RAN), where strategies range from traffic-aware RAN slicing to open and disaggregated solutions, such as Open RAN [1]. The second stream focuses on traffic steering in the mobile network data plane, with particular emphasis on solutions to enhance the performance of the User Plane Function (UPF) [19]. Despite this progress, the literature identifies further opportunities to instrument the UPF to enable greater programmability and intelligent behavior [3].

Recent efforts to enhance programmability and intelligent behavior in the mobile core have led to the introduction of analytics capabilities in the 3rd Generation Partnership Project (3GPP) Release 16, facilitated by the Network Data Analytics Function (NWDAF) entity [7]. However, the mechanisms for data collection and component instrumentation have posed challenges across various deployments [12]. This study explores the potential of transforming the UPF into a more intelligent entity, capable of considering latency by examining GPRS Tunnelling Protocol (GTP) Tunnel Endpoint Identifiers (TEIDs) and employing a Reinforcement Learning (RL) mechanism to optimize its real-time performance.

In this work, we introduce and evaluate the UPF instrumentation for estimating the end-user latency of the User Equipment (UE) by analyzing the time shifts of TEIDs arriving at the UPF. This approach empowers the UPF to autonomously select the optimal interface for traffic forwarding and apply intelligent traffic steering based on latency awareness, thereby reducing end-to-end delay. The efficacy of our methodology is demonstrated through an MEC and cloud-based application, validating how the UPF, in conjunction with an RL agent, can non-intrusively direct traffic along various paths by monitoring UE latency and using eXpress Data Path (XDP). This design positions the eUPF as an intelligent user-plane element for time-sensitive path selection across MEC and cloud environments.

The contributions of this study are as follows: (i) the development of a novel UPF instrumentation for UE latency estimation; (ii) a comparative evaluation of a naive UPF path selection versus an RL-based approach; (iii) the design and implementation of a non-intrusive telemetry mechanism using XDP to enable real-time TEID monitoring and latency estimation at the UPF; and (iv) an end-to-end experimental validation showcasing how the proposed architecture improves latency-sensitive service delivery in MEC and cloud scenarios.

The remainder of this paper is organized as follows: Sect. 2 presents representative approaches for MEC-aware decision-making in 5G/6G. In Sect. 3, we present our method for intelligent intervention in the dataplane. In Sect. 4, we describe the technologies used to perform the proof of concept. In Sect. 5, we present the discussions and insights gained from our approach. Finally, in Sect. 6, we provide the conclusions and lessons learned.

2 Related Work

Automated management systems are essential for emerging eXtended Reality (XR) and the metaverse [4,5]. Recent research focus includes instrumenting different segments of 5G, including the RAN, core, and transport, to improve adaptability and performance monitoring. This section reviews studies that use the UPF to measure UE connectivity parameters, adapt to dynamic traffic conditions, and enable Internet Service Providers (ISPs) to track and enforce ServiceLevel Agreement (SLA) guarantees effectively.

Table 1. Summary of representative approaches for MEC aware decision making in Fifth Generation and Sixth Generation networks.

Paper	Learning	Optimization	User Plane Function	Tunnel Endpoint Identifier	Real Testbed
Shokrnezhad et al. [17]	●	●	○	○	○
Tran et al. [19]	○	●	●	○	●
Gan et al. [6]	●	●	○	○	○
Maleki et al. [11]	●	●	○	○	○
Sasithong et al. [16]	●	●	●	○	○
Hisyam et al. [8]	●	●	○	○	○
Nguyen et al. [14]	●	●	●	○	○
Pimpalkar et al. [15]	○	●	○	○	○
Kibalya et al. [10]	●	●	●	○	○
Ibrahimi et al. [9]	●	●	○	○	○
Our Approach	●	●	●	●	●

Deep Reinforcement Learning is widely applied for intelligent resource management. Shokrnezhad et al. [17] address joint Virtual Network Function (VNF) placement, traffic prioritization, and path selection in B5G networks under latency and capacity constraints using Double Deep Q-learning (DDQL) Double Deep Q learning. Gran et al. [6] use Multi-Agent Deep Reinforcement Learning (MADRL) with collaborative Deep Q-Network (DQN) models for computation offloading in 5G MEC systems to minimize total system cost.

Similarly, Sasithong et al. [16] apply DQN and Actor-Critic (AC) algorithms for dynamic UPF allocation in Cellular Vehicle to-Everything (C-V2X) [16]. Nguyen et al. [14] utilize Proximal Policy Optimization (PPO) and Support Vector Machine (SVM) for scaling UPF instances [14], while Kibalya et al. [10] employ policy networks for joint UPF and application placement in multi-slice MEC [10]. For Ultra-Reliable and Low Latency Communications (URLLC), Ibrahimi et al. [9] implement a DQN strategy to balance congestion and throughput [9].

Other research employs heuristics, optimization, or supervised learning. Tran et al. [19] introduce a rule-based computing-aware traffic steering architecture for 5G to route traffic to optimal MEC instances using Segment Routing over

IPv6 (SRv6) [19]. Maleki et al. [11] utilize Multi-Armed Bandit (MAB) and Deep Neural Network (DNN) models for Quality of Service (QoS) aware content delivery under mobility [11]. In 6th Generation Mobile Network (6G) contexts, Pimpalkar et al. [15] formulate a multi-constraint convex problem for Service-Aware Optimal Path Selection (SOPS) [15]. Hisyam Ng and Mahmoodi [8] propose a supervised learning scheme using Random Forests and Mixed Integer Linear Programming (MILP) for dynamic steering [8].

Table 1 summarizes representative approaches for MEC aware decision making in Fifth Generation and Sixth Generation networks using a binary comparison of key capabilities, namely whether each work employs learning, performs explicit optimization, targets the User Plane Function, incorporates Tunnel Endpoint Identifier awareness, and validates results on a real testbed. The table shows that prior studies largely rely on simulation and do not exploit Tunnel Endpoint Identifier signals for data-plane decisions, even when learning or optimization is applied. In contrast, our approach integrates a DQN-based reinforcement learning agent with User Plane Function-level control and explicit Tunnel Endpoint Identifier awareness, and it is validated on a real testbed, enabling passive latency-driven N6 interface selection for Beyond Fifth Generation scenarios spanning MEC and cloud paths.

3 Proposed Approach

Building on the insights and limitations identified in prior work, we propose an enhancement to the traditional UPF, hereafter referred to as eUPF (enhanced UPF), which integrates an RL agent to enable intelligent, real-time path selection for individual network slices. As shown in Fig. 1, the DQN-based agent observes latency and network conditions to dynamically steer traffic across multiple N6 paths (e.g., Path A and Path B), targeting either MEC or Cloud endpoints. This architecture enables the UPF to surpass static policies by continuously adapting to network dynamics, user mobility, and service-level requirements. By leveraging AI control at the data plane, the proposed eUPF architecture enables smarter, slice-aware forwarding decisions aligned with the vision of agile and autonomous 5G/6G core networks.

3.1 Problem Formulation

We formulate adaptive path selection as a Partially Observable Markov Decision Process, where the enhanced UPF applies a slice-specific forwarding policy at run time, and the reinforcement learning agent makes per-flow decisions using the Tunnel Endpoint Identifier (TEID) as the in-kernel key that identifies the active Packet Data Unit (PDU) session associated with that slice context.

States and Transitions. Let $S_t = (s_{n6a}(t), s_{n6b}(t))$ denote the latent environment state at time t, where $s_i(t) \in \{\text{GOOD}, \text{BAD}\}$ for $i \in \{\texttt{n6a}, \texttt{n6b}\}$. Transitions from GOOD to BAD occur independently with fixed probabilities p_i per

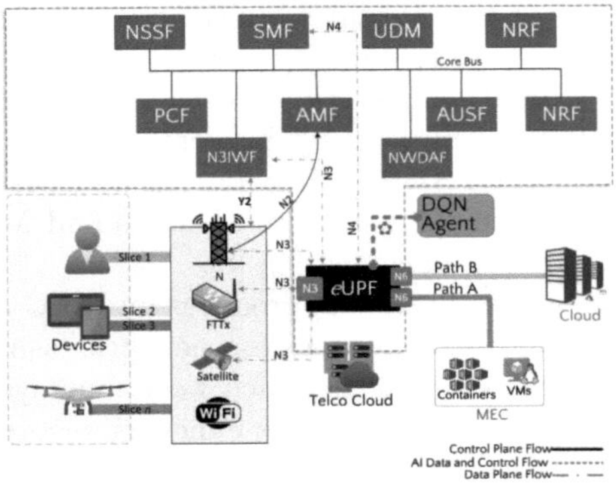

Fig. 1. Proposed Approach.

packet. Once degraded, each interface remains in the BAD state for a deterministic duration D_i before reverting to the GOOD state. These semi-Markov dynamics introduce memory that must be inferred from observations.

Observations. The agent does not observe S_t directly. Instead, after selecting an action $A_t \in \{\texttt{n6a}, \texttt{n6b}\}$, it receives a noisy delay measurement. Let i denote the interface selected by A_t (that is, $i = A_t$). The observation process (Eq. 1) is:

$$RTT(A_t) = d_i \cdot \mathbb{I}[s_i(t) = \text{BAD}] + \xi_t \\ \xi_t \sim \mathcal{U}(-J_{\max}, +J_{\max}) \tag{1}$$

where d_i is the additional delay incurred when interface i is in the BAD state, $\mathbb{I}[\cdot]$ is the indicator function, equal to 1 if the condition holds and 0 otherwise, and ξ_t models bounded measurement noise (jitter) with maximum amplitude $J_{\max}$.

Because the agent operates under partial observability, we define a scalar observed state s_t derived from the latest measurement. In our implementation, s_t corresponds to the most recent per TEID delay proxy exposed by the data plane. This s_t is the input used by the learning agent at decision time t.

Actions and Rewards. At each time step t, the agent selects an interface $A_t \in \{\texttt{n6a}, \texttt{n6b}\}$ via a policy $\pi(a_t|s_t)$. We define the reward as the negative observed delay (Eq. 2):

$$R_t = -RTT(A_t). \tag{2}$$

We normalize R_t via min-max scaling to stabilize training, mapping rewards to a bounded range while preserving ordering, so that lower delays correspond to higher normalized rewards.

Learning Objective. The agent aims to maximize expected discounted return (Eq. 3):

$$\max_{\pi} \mathbb{E}\left[\sum_{t=0}^{T} \gamma^t R_t\right], \tag{3}$$

where $\gamma \in (0,1]$ is the discount factor, T is the episode horizon in decision steps, and the expectation is taken over trajectories induced by policy π and the environment dynamics. Because S_t is latent and only s_t is observed, deep reinforcement learning, particularly DQN, is suitable to learn effective decisions from sequences of noisy measurements.

3.2 TEID-Correlated Delay Measurement

To avoid injecting additional active probes, we leverage a passive data-plane measurement approach based on TEID- correlated timestamps within the UPF. The system attaches eBPF programs directly to the GTP-U traffic path to extract the TEID from each packet. For each TEID i, a stateful map stores a request timestamp t_i^{req} when a request packet is observed.

When the corresponding response packet for the same TEID i is observed at the UPF, the program computes an in network round trip proxy (Eq. 4):

$$\Delta t_i = t_i^{\text{resp}} - t_i^{\text{req}}. \tag{4}$$

Here, t_i^{req} is the timestamp captured for the request, and t_i^{resp} is the timestamp captured for the matched response, both observed at the UPF for the same TEID i. In our proof of concept, the request-response pattern is instantiated with Internet Control Message Protocol (ICMP) echo traffic, and the response is identified by matching the echo reply to the previously observed echo request within the same TEID context, thereby providing a consistent pairing signal for timestamp correlation.

This measurement is a UPF observed delay proxy, not a fully instrumented end-to-end RTT across the entire Data Network (DN) and RAN. Its purpose is to provide a low-overhead, online signal that reflects the experienced user-plane delay under the current forwarding choice, enabling the agent to adapt its decisions even when only partial visibility is available.

To implement passive latency measurement, we developed an in-kernel routine that associates TEID- identified flows with timestamped events on the UPF data plane. Algorithm 1 presents the logic executed by the eBPF program attached to the GTP-U traffic path. Upon receiving a packet, the program extracts the corresponding TEID and records a request timestamp if none already exists. When a subsequent packet for the same TEID arrives, it computes the delay proxy and resets tracking state, enabling continuous measurement without additional probe injection.

4 Evaluation Setup

Our evaluation was conducted on the FABRIC testbed, using a high-performance virtual machine provisioned with 32 GB of RAM and 32 vCPUs. The envi-

Algorithm 1: TEID-Correlated Round-Trip Time (RTT) Measurement.

```
Initialize rtt_map as a hash map with key: TEID and value: round_trip structure;
Function measure_rtt(skb):
    Extract TEID from incoming GTP-U packet;
    now ← current kernel timestamp (bpf_ktime_get_ns());
    Lookup entry in rtt_map by TEID;
    if entry does not exist then
        Insert new entry with ts_request ← now;
    else
        if ts_request is zero then
            Set ts_request ← now;
        else
            Compute RTT: last_rtt ← now − ts_request;
            Reset ts_request ← 0;
            Increment count;
```

ronment was orchestrated with Kubernetes v1.28.15 running on Ubuntu, and Free5GC was used to emulate the 5G core network. Figure 2 illustrates the deployment, where the DQN agent interacts with the user plane through Extended Berkeley Packet Filter (eBPF)/XDP hooks and shared maps. We leveraged a custom BPF toolset to implement programmable datapath control, enabling dynamic action updates and observation retrieval directly at the UPF. This setup enables reproducible experimentation for low-level latency estimation and adaptive path selection across the `n6a` and `n6b` interfaces.

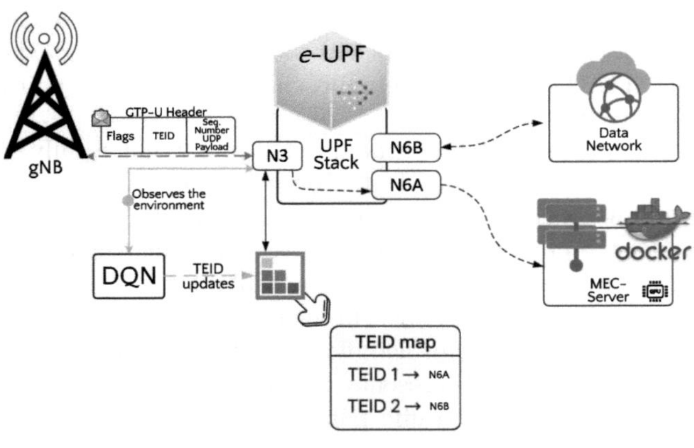

Fig. 2. Experimental Setup.

The stochastic degradation parameters used in our experiments are summarized in Table 2. For each interface $i \in \{\texttt{n6a}, \texttt{n6b}\}$, a degradation event is triggered independently at each packet arrival according to a failure probability p_i. Once triggered, the interface remains degraded for a fixed failure duration D_i and then automatically recovers. When an interface is in the degraded state, an additional delay d_i is induced, matching the observation model in Eq. 1. A bounded jitter term with maximum amplitude $J_{\max}$ is applied globally across both paths, as defined in Eq. 1.

Table 2. Network Path Parameters for Delay Induction Scenario.

Path	Failure Probability	Failure Duration (s)	Bad State Delay (ms)
Path A (MEC)	0.01	10	800
Path B (Cloud)	0.10	20	800
Global Parameter: Maximum Jitter $J_{\max} = 3$ ms			

4.1 DQN Based Path Selection Architecture

The learning component is implemented as an DQN, which approximates the action-value function $Q(s_t, a_t; \theta)$ using a deep neural network parameterized by θ. The agent receives as input a scalar state s_t derived from the most recent per TEID delay proxy, and outputs Q values for the two discrete actions corresponding to the available egress interfaces, namely `n6a` and `n6b`. Action selection follows an ϵ greedy exploration strategy, where ϵ decays from an initial exploration probability to a smaller final value over training.

The network architecture is a feedforward multilayer perceptron with two hidden layers of 64 units each and ReLU activations. Learning is stabilized using experience replay and a separate target network with parameters θ^- that are periodically synchronized from the online network. At each decision step, the agent stores a transition (s_t, a_t, r_t, s_{t+1}) in a replay buffer and samples mini-batches to update θ by minimizing the temporal difference objective defined in Eq. (5). Table 3 summarizes the hyperparameters and model configuration used in all experiments.

4.2 Agent Environment Interaction via XDP Maps

The interaction between the DQN agent and the forwarding plane is implemented using two XDP maps that serve as the interface between learning logic and packet processing. The first map exposes observations to the agent by providing per TEID delay values computed as the UPF observed proxy Δt_i in Eq. 4, obtained by correlating TEID keyed timestamps for request and response packets observed at the same UPF datapath. In the proof of concept, ICMP traffic provides the request-response pattern required for pairing, while the measurement itself remains passive with respect to additional monitoring probes.

The second map enables actions by storing the selected egress interface per TEID, so that packet forwarding for that PDU session follows the agent's chosen action. Specifically, at each decision time t, the agent selects $a_t \in \{\texttt{n6a}, \texttt{n6b}\}$ and

Table 3. Hyperparameters and Network Architecture of the DQN Agent.

Parameter	Value
Discount factor (γ)	0.99
Learning rate (Adam) (α)	5×10^{-4}
Batch size	32
Replay memory size	2000 transitions
Exploration start (ϵ_{start})	0.9
Exploration end (ϵ_{end})	0.01
Exploration decay rate	0.990
Target network update frequency	Every 5 episodes
Training episodes	400
Network Architecture	
Input dimension	1 (scalar state)
Hidden layers	2×64 units (Linear + ReLU)
Output dimension	2 (Q values for `n6a`, `n6b`)

writes the corresponding value into the action map, which the XDP program reads to enforce forwarding on the chosen N6 path.

Learning follows the standard DQN update rule, minimizing the temporal difference loss, as Eq. (5):

$$\mathcal{L}(\theta) = \mathbb{E}_{(s_t,a_t,r_t,s_{t+1})}\Big[\big(r_t + \gamma \max_{a'} Q(s_{t+1}, a'; \theta^-) - Q(s_t, a_t; \theta)\big)^2\Big] \tag{5}$$

where $Q(s_t, a_t; \theta)$ is the online action value network, θ^- denotes the target network parameters, γ is the discount factor (Table 3), and (s_t, a_t, r_t, s_{t+1}) are transitions sampled from the replay buffer. The reward r_t is computed from the observed delay using Eq. 2 and then normalized by min-max scaling, ensuring stable gradients during training. Episodes last 60 s, during which the agent repeatedly reads the latest per TEID observation state s_t, selects an action, updates the action map, and stores the resulting transition for learning.

This design enables the DQN agent to translate passive latency observations into fine-grained forwarding control, achieving adaptive N6 interface selection under stochastic path degradations.

5 Results and Discussion

Building on the experimental setup and the agent-environment interaction described above, this section analyzes learning dynamics, policy behavior, and latency outcomes achieved by the proposed DQN- based path selection strategy. We compare it against a random baseline across multiple metrics, including reward evolution, interface selection patterns, and measured round-trip time.

Figure 3 reports the reward dynamics of the random baseline across 400 training episodes. In Fig. 3 (a), the per-episode reward shows high variability, which is expected under stochastic action selection and stochastic path degradations. Importantly, the reward does not exhibit a consistent improving trend, indicating that the baseline does not adapt its decisions over time. Figure 3 (b) reinforces this conclusion, since the rolling mean with window size 10 remains relatively flat, providing a stable reference for assessing whether learning yields consistent performance gains.

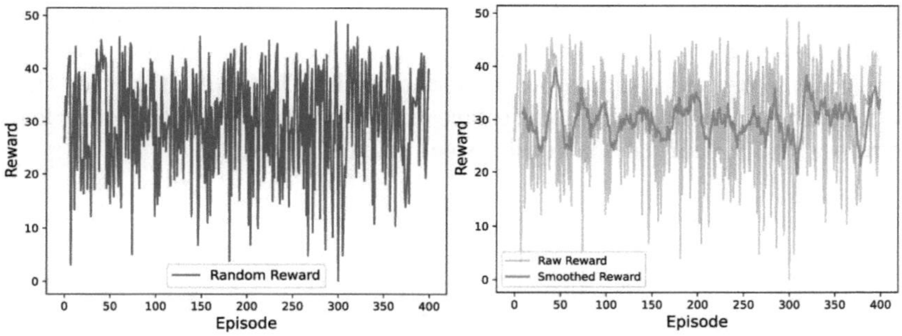

(a) Raw reward per episode. (b) Smoothed reward.

Fig. 3. Comparison of raw and smoothed cumulative rewards (rolling mean, window size 10) over the training episodes of the baseline policy.

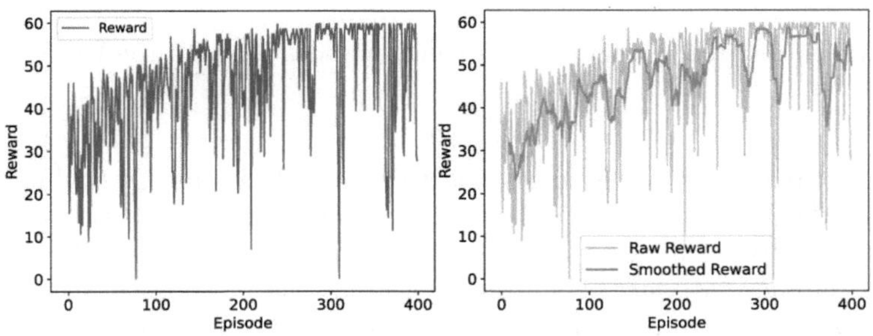

(a) Raw reward per episode. (b) Smoothed reward.

Fig. 4. Comparison of raw and smoothed cumulative rewards (rolling mean, window size 10) over the training episodes of the DQN agent.

DQN Learns an Effective and Stable Low-latency Policy under Stochastic Degradations. Figure 4 shows the reward evolution of the DQN across the same 400 training episodes. The raw reward signal in Fig. 4 (a) is initially noisy due to exploration and the inherent variability of the environment. When applying a rolling mean with a window size of 10 in Fig. 4 (b), a clear upward trend emerges, with rewards improving steadily until convergence around episode 250. This behavior indicates that the agent learns a policy that consistently achieves higher reward, corresponding to lower observed delay, while occasional drops are plausible due to exploration and transient adverse conditions.

Figure 5 connects learning dynamics to policy behavior by showing action distributions over the 400 episodes. The baseline in Fig. 5 (a) alternates between the MEC path and the cloud path without a structured pattern, consistent with random selection. In contrast, Fig. 5 (b) shows that the DQN increasingly favors the MEC interface, which was configured with lower latency and jitter, while progressively reducing reliance on the cloud path. This shift indicates that the agent identifies the more reliable interface and sustains this preference as learning progresses, rather than oscillating between choices.

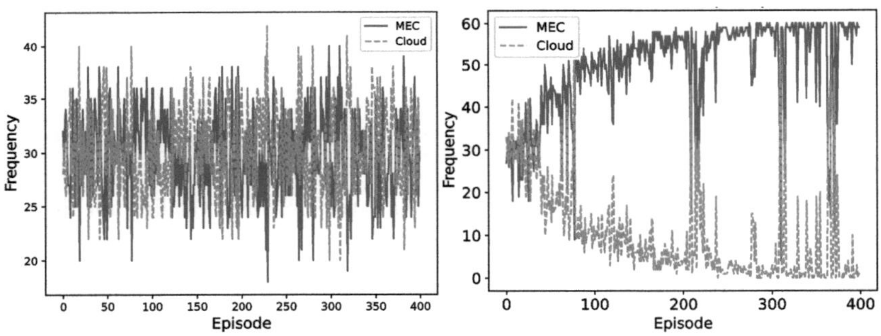

(a) Baseline policy. (b) DQN policy.

Fig. 5. Action distribution across all training episodes for both the baseline and the DQN policies.

Figure 6 quantifies the latency impact of these decisions. Overall episodes in Fig. 6 (a), the DQN attains a substantially lower mean round trip time, 95.24 ms, compared to 199.37 ms for the baseline, demonstrating its ability to exploit the lower latency interface. Focusing on the last 50 episodes in Fig. 6 (b), the contrast becomes stronger in terms of stability; the DQN maintains a mean variation of 2.03 ms, whereas the baseline exhibits a volatile range of 177.63 ms. Together, these results show that the learned policy improves both average latency and temporal consistency, while the baseline remains erratic under the same stochastic conditions. These results show that the proposed eUPF effectively supports time-sensitive path selection by consistently favoring the most suitable interface under dynamic conditions.

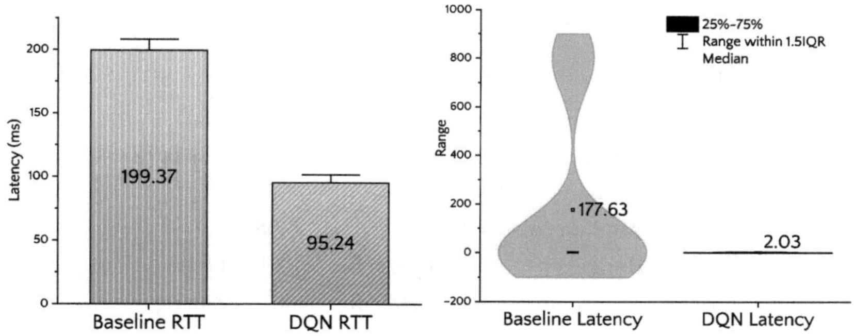

(a) Full episodes. (b) Last 50 episodes.

Fig. 6. Comparison of average round-trip time.

Learned Steering Decisions Materialize as Consistent Data Plane Forwarding Toward the Best Path. Figure 7 presents the distribution of packets forwarded through each interface under both policies. During the experiment, the User Equipment generated Internet Control Message Protocol traffic at one packet per second, and the plot aggregates transmissions over 10-second intervals, averaged across the entire duration. Under the DQN policy, more packets are forwarded to MEC, with an average of 3.29 per interval, compared to 0.57 to the cloud, reflecting a sustained preference for the lower-latency interface. In contrast, the baseline remains nearly balanced, with 1.77 and 1.73 packets per interval toward MEC and cloud, respectively, consistent with uniform random decisions. This forwarding behavior aligns with the latency outcomes, confirming that the agent translates observed delays into actionable interface selection decisions in the data plane.

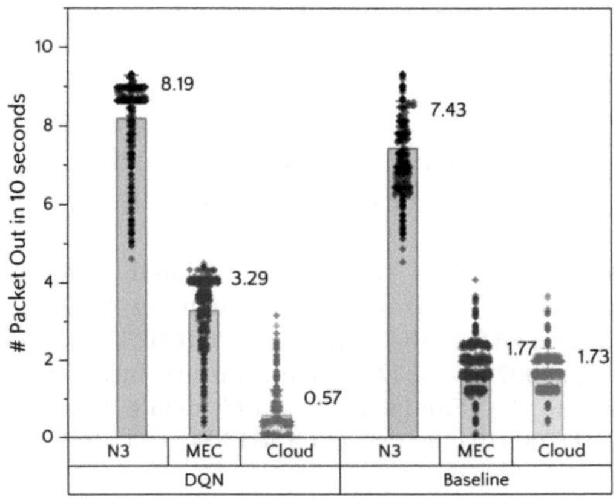

Fig. 7. Packet out distribution.

Table 4. Descriptive statistics for DQN and baseline in the last 50 episodes.

Metric	DQN (± SD)	Baseline (± SD)
Average Reward	49.40 ± 14.92	30.61 ± 9.31
Average Latency [ms]	298.46 ± 443.81	486.57 ± 398.46
Reward Median	58.59	33.25
Latency Median [ms]	6.95	453.86
Reward Range	[11.53, 59.84]	[10.41, 44.18]
Latency Range [ms]	[4.82, 1439.40]	[5.01, 1290.59]

Table 4 summarizes the last 50 episodes, where the reinforcement learning policy is already stabilized. The DQN achieves higher rewards (49.40 ± 14.92 vs. 30.61 ± 9.31) and lower average latency (298.46 ± 443.81 ms vs. 486.57 ± 398.46 ms). The median latency further highlights stability gains, 6.95 ms for the DQN versus 453.86 ms for the baseline. The ranges indicate that both policies can still experience occasional high-delay events due to induced degradations, whereas the DQN makes more decisions on the better-performing interface, thereby reducing overall delay and variability relative to the baseline.

6 Concluding Remarks

While B5G SLA management often relies on simulation-based admission control, it lacks real-time intelligent intervention in the data plane. Our evaluation on the FABRIC testbed demonstrates that the DQN based agent achieves stable convergence and significantly reduces latency compared to random baselines. These results indicate that transforming the UPF into an intelligent *e*UPF enables autonomous slice-aware, time-sensitive path selection in B5G edge networks.

Although this study focuses on uplink steering within a specific testbed scenario, it validates the feasibility of non-intrusive telemetry for RL observations. Future research will investigate alternative algorithms and packet-queue prioritization to enhance efficiency for both uplink and downlink traffic. This research provides a critical foundation for programmable architectures and intelligent network management in the era of low-latency mobile services.

Acknowledgments. The authors thank the National Council for Scientific and Technological Development (CNPq) under grant number 421944/2021-8 (call CNPq/ MCTI/ FNDCT 18/2021), FAPEMIG (Grant #APQ00923-24), FAPESP MCTIC/CGI Research project 2018/23097-3 - SFI2 - Slicing Future Internet Infrastructures. FCT has also supported this work – Fundação para a Ciência e Tecnologia within the R&D Unit Project Scope UID/00319/Centro ALGORITMI (ALGORITMI/UM).

Disclosure of Interests. The authors have no competing interests to declare that are relevant to the content of this article.

References

1. Agarwal, B., Irmer, R., Lister, D., Muntean, G.M.: Open ran for 6G networks: architecture, use cases and open issues. IEEE Commun. Surv. Tutorials, 1–1 (2025). https://doi.org/10.1109/COMST.2025.3562429
2. Bellin, A., Di Cicco, N., Munaretto, D., Granelli, F.: Power consumption-aware 5G edge UPF selection using deep reinforcement learning. In: 2024 IEEE Conference on Network Function Virtualization and Software Defined Networks (NFV-SDN), pp. 1–6 (2024). https://doi.org/10.1109/NFV-SDN61811.2024.10807472
3. Chen, C.C., Chang, C.Y., Nikaein, N.: IUP: integrated and programmable user plane for next-generation mobile networks. IEEE Netw. **39**(3), 91–98 (2025). https://doi.org/10.1109/MNET.2025.3551245
4. Christopoulou, M., Koufos, I., Xilouris, G., Dimitriou, N.: 5G/6G architecture evolution for XR and metaverse: feasibility study, security, and privacy challenges for smart culture applications. IEEE Access **13**, 103077–103094 (2025). https://doi.org/10.1109/ACCESS.2025.3578595
5. Donatti, A., et al.: Survey on machine learning-enabled network slicing: covering the entire life cycle. IEEE Trans. Netw. Serv. Manage. **21**(1), 994–1011 (2024). https://doi.org/10.1109/TNSM.2023.3287651
6. Gan, Z., Lin, R., Zou, H.: A multi-agent deep reinforcement learning approach for computation offloading in 5G mobile edge computing. In: 2022 22nd IEEE International Symposium on Cluster, Cloud and Internet Computing (CCGrid), pp. 645–648 (2022). https://doi.org/10.1109/CCGrid54584.2022.00074
7. Garcia-Martin, M.A., Gramaglia, M., Serrano, P.: Network automation and data analytics in 3G PP 5G systems. IEEE Netw. **38**(4), 182–189 (2024). https://doi.org/10.1109/MNET.2023.3321524
8. Hisyam Ng, H.A., Mahmoodi, T.: Machine learning-driven dynamic traffic steering in 6G: a novel path selection scheme. Big Data Cogn. Comput. **8**(12) (2024). https://doi.org/10.3390/bdcc8120172
9. Ibrahimi, K., Jouhari, M., Sow, S., Ayoub, F., Kamili, M.E., Chougdali, K.: Reinforcement learning for optimized resource allocation in 5G URLLC. In: 2024 7th International Conference on Advanced Communication Technologies and Networking (CommNet), pp. 1–6 (2024). https://doi.org/10.1109/CommNet63022.2024.10793310
10. Kibalya, G., et al.: Joint UPF and application placement in multi-slice edge networks: a reinforcement learning strategy. In: 2025 IEEE Wireless Communications and Networking Conference (WCNC), pp. 1–6 (2025). https://doi.org/10.1109/WCNC61545.2025.10978828
11. Maleki, E.F., Ma, W., Mashayekhy, L., La Roche, H.J.: QoS-aware content delivery in 5G-enabled edge computing: learning-based approaches. IEEE Trans. Mob. Comput. **23**(10), 9324–9336 (2024). https://doi.org/10.1109/TMC.2024.3363143
12. Moreira, L., Moreira, R., Silva, F., Backes, A.: Towards cognitive service delivery on B5G through AIaaS architecture. In: Anais do IV Workshop de Redes 6G, pp. 1–8. SBC, Porto Alegre (2024). https://doi.org/10.5753/w6g.2024.3304
13. Moreira, R., Rosa, P.F., Aguiar, R.L.A., de Oliveira Silva, F.: NASOR: a network slicing approach for multiple autonomous systems. Comput. Commun. **179**, 131–144 (2021). https://doi.org/10.1016/j.comcom.2021.07.028
14. Nguyen, H.T., Van Do, T., Rotter, C.: Scaling UPF instances in 5G/6G core with deep reinforcement learning. IEEE Access **9**, 165892–165906 (2021). https://doi.org/10.1109/ACCESS.2021.3135315

15. Pimpalkar, Y., Ravindran, S., Bapat, J., Das, D.: A novel e2e path selection algorithm for superior QoS and QoE for 6g services. IEEE Trans. Netw. Serv. Manage. **22**(2), 1174–1187 (2025). https://doi.org/10.1109/TNSM.2024.3519707
16. Sasithong, P., Sanguanpuak, T., Vanichchanunt, P., Wuttisittikulkij, L.: User plane function (UPF) allocation for C-V2X network using deep reinforcement learning. IEEE Access **13**, 4547–4561 (2025). https://doi.org/10.1109/ACCESS.2024.3524886
17. Shokrnezhad, M., Taleb, T., Dazzi, P.: Double deep Q-learning-based path selection and service placement for latency-sensitive beyond 5G applications. IEEE Trans. Mob. Comput. **23**(5), 5097–5110 (2024). https://doi.org/10.1109/TMC.2023.3301506
18. Silva, B., Moreira, L.R., de Oliveira Silva, F., Moreira, R.: Optimizing edge gaming slices through an enhanced user plane function and analytics in beyond-5G networks. In: Anais do XVI Workshop de Pesquisa Experimental da Internet do Futuro, pp. 1–8. SBC, Porto Alegre (2025).https://doi.org/10.5753/wpeif.2025.8714
19. Tran, M.N., Duong, V.B., Kim, Y.: Design of computing-aware traffic steering architecture for 5G mobile user plane. IEEE Access **12**, 88370–88382 (2024). https://doi.org/10.1109/ACCESS.2024.3418960

GPS: GlobalCLIP-PatchCore-SAM Based Zero-Shot Anomaly Detection and Localization in Smart Manufacturing

Junha Park and Jongpil Jeong(✉)

Department of Smart Factory Convergence, Sungkyunkwan University, Suwon-si, Gyeonggi-do 16419, Republic of Korea
{junha010102,jpjeong}@skku.edu

Abstract. Detecting defects on a factory floor remains challenging when production runs are short and defective parts seldom appear. Supervised and unsupervised inspection models both struggle under such data-scarce conditions, motivating zero-shot approaches that operate without target-domain defect samples. We introduce GlobalCLIP-PatchCore-SAM (GPS), a three-stage pipeline that first decides whether an image is anomalous at the global level and then drills down to the exact defect pixels, using no anomaly samples or defect labels from the target domain at any stage. Stage 1 (GlobalCLIP) aggregates 1280-dimensional features from two Contrastive Language-Image Pre-Training (CLIP) encoders (ViT-B/32 and ViT-L/14@336) and trains a self-cyclic ensemble of six autoencoders, guided by Adaptive Rejection Sampling for outlier removal and Adaptive Augmented sample Weighting for pseudo-label refinement, to gate images at the global level. Stage 2 (PatchCore) extracts WideResNet-50 multi-scale patch features and produces a 32×32 anomaly map via (K-Nearest Neighbor) k-NN (k=3) over a 25% random coreset. Stage 3 Segment Anything Model (SAM) refines anomaly boundaries through segment-wise scoring so that they snap to real object edges. With a single fixed hyperparameter set across all 15 MVTec AD categories, GPS reaches 92.49% image-level and 84.62% pixel-level Area Under Receiver Operating Characteristic (AUROC). Ablations expose clear trade-offs: dropping the GlobalCLIP gate collapses classification to chance level, k-NN runs 1.6× faster than Mahalanobis scoring with comparable accuracy, and SAM sharpens boundaries visually yet can hurt pixel AUROC when defects are tiny.

Keywords: Anomaly detection · CLIP · PatchCore · Segment Anything Model · Vision-language model · Vision Transformer · Zero-Shot · Anomaly localization

1 Introduction

Anomaly detection is a key task to ensure product quality and production stability in the manufacturing process [1]. Thanks to the miniaturization and cost

O. Gervasi et al. (Eds.): ICCSA 2026, LNCS 16768, pp. 447–463, 2027.
https://doi.org/10.1007/978-3-032-30488-9_28

reduction of optical sensors, the proportion of image-based analysis systems is increasing. However, since the modern manufacturing process is stabilized, defective products rarely occur, which causes a serious data imbalance problem [2]. In other words, as product types become diversified in the modern variety of small-scale production, data-based inspection systems become more complex.

How much labeled data a method needs largely determines where it can be deployed. Fully supervised detectors demand pixel-level defect annotations, which are expensive and hard to scale [3]. Unsupervised approaches drop the need for defect labels but still assume access to a reasonably large pool of defect-free images [4,5]. Few-shot variants cut that pool down to a handful of reference pictures [2,6], yet they still expect at least some target-domain samples. Zero-shot methods [7,8] go one step further and operate with no target data at allan attractive property for factories that roll out new product lines on short notice. The term "Zero-shot" as used in this paper follows the general practice of the Zero-Shot-Anomaly-Detection (ZSAD) field, meaning that no anomaly samples or pixel-level defect labels of the target domain are used in the training process. Like existing ZSAD studies such as WinCLIP [7], AnomalyCLIP [10], and GlobalCLIP [8], our framework operates without any prior information about defect labels or defective images, while normal training images are used for training the ensemble model and constructing the memory bank. In other words, the zero-shot setting in this study is interpreted as "annotation-free" or "defect-label-free," which carries the practical value of eliminating the cost of collecting defective data when introducing new product lines. Recently, the GlobalCLIP method [8] demonstrated that zero-shot anomaly detection can achieve competitive performance using only global image features extracted by Contrastive Language-Image Pre-Training (CLIP) [9], without requiring text prompts or local feature tensors. However, GlobalCLIP is limited to image-level detection and cannot localize the spatial extent of anomalies a critical requirement for root cause analysis in manufacturing.

In this paper, we propose a multi-stage statistical framework that extends GlobalCLIP's zero-shot image-level detection capability to pixel-level anomaly localization. Existing zero-shot anomaly detection methods have the following limitations. Text prompt-based techniques such as WinCLIP [7], AnomalyCLIP [10], and AdaCLIP [11] require defect types to be defined in natural language in advance or learnable prompts to be trained separately, which is unsuitable for manufacturing environments where new defect types frequently appear. On the other hand, GlobalCLIP [8] eliminated the dependence on text prompts but is limited to image-level detection, making it impossible to localize defects, which constitutes a decisive limitation for root cause analysis on manufacturing sites.

The contributions of this study are summarized as follows.

- We present a unified framework that simultaneously addresses the problems of text-prompt dependence and the absence of localization, by integrating the text-prompt-free gating mechanism of GlobalCLIP with the memory-bank-

based localization of PatchCore and the boundary refinement of Segment Anything Model (SAM).
- We demonstrate generalizability without category-specific tuning by evaluating the framework with a single hyperparameter setting across all 15 MVTec AD categories.
- Through five ablation experiments, we quantitatively analyze the trade-offs among detection accuracy, localization quality, and computational efficiency, providing practical guidelines for industrial deployment.
- By analyzing performance variations and failure cases across categories, we present practical considerations for real-world deployment.

The remainder of this paper is organized as follows. Section 2 reviews related work. Section 3 describes the proposed framework in detail. Section 4 presents experimental results and ablation studies. Section 5 discusses findings and limitations, and Sect. 6 concludes the paper.

2 Related Work

2.1 Zero-Shot Anomaly Detection

Zero-shot anomaly detection methods must operate without any task-specific training data, relying entirely on pre-trained representations and general priors. WinCLIP [7] utilizes CLIP's image-text alignment to compare local image features with manual text prompts describing normal and abnormal states. AnomalyCLIP [10] proposes object-agnostic learnable prompts that capture generic normal and abnormal patterns regardless of object semantics, demonstrating strong generalization performance across diverse domains. AdaCLIP [11] introduces hybrid learnable prompts that combine static prompts shared across all images with dynamic prompts generated per test image, improving ZSAD performance through auxiliary anomaly detection data.

Unlike these text-dependent methods, GlobalCLIP [8] performs detection using only global image features without text prompts. The technique aggregates features with a dual CLIP backbone (ViT-B/32 and ViT-L/14@336) and estimates anomaly scores through an adaptive self-cyclic reconstruction model ensemble. This study utilizes GlobalCLIP as the first stage and adds pixel-level localization capability.

2.2 Feature-Bank Anomaly Localization

PatchCore [2] builds a memory bank by collecting patch unit features from the normal learning image, and calculates an anomaly map using the k-nearest neighbor distance. High performance can be achieved with a small number of normal samples through multi-scale feature aggregation and greedy coreset sampling of the pre-trained network. In Stage 2 of this study, we adopt the memory-bank-based approach of PatchCore, while applying WideResNet-50 multi-scale features, random coreset sampling, and GPU-accelerated k-NN search.

Table 1. Comparison of feature characteristics with existing zero-shot anomaly detection methods.

Method	Text Prompt-Free	Pixel-Level Localization	Boundary-Aware Refinement
WinCLIP [7]	✗	✓	✗
AnomalyCLIP [10]	✗	✓	✗
AdaCLIP [11]	✗	✓	✗
GlobalCLIP [8]	✓	✗	✗
GPS (Ours)	✓	✓	✓

2.3 Foundation Models for Segmentation

SAM [19] is an image segmentation foundation model trained with more than 1 billion masks. Since SAM can generate class-independent segmentation masks through various prompts such as points, boxes, and automatic modes, in this study, SAM's automatic mask generation function is used as a boundary correction module in Stage 3 to assign anomaly scores to semantically consistent regions rather than individual pixels.

2.4 Comparison with Prior Work

As shown in Table 1, this framework is the only zero-shot anomaly detection method that satisfies all three characteristics: text-prompt independence, pixel-level localization, and boundary-aware refinement. WinCLIP [7], AnomalyCLIP [10], and AdaCLIP [11] support pixel-level localization but rely on either manually crafted or learnable text prompts, which incurs the cost of redesigning or retraining prompts whenever a new defect type is introduced. GlobalCLIP [8] eliminated the dependence on text prompts but cannot be used for visualizing defect regions or analyzing root causes because it lacks localization capability. In this study, the complementary strengths of the preceding techniques are integrated into a single pipeline: the text-prompt-independent gating mechanism of GlobalCLIP is adopted as Stage 1, while patch-level localization in Stage 2 and SAM-based boundary refinement in Stage 3 are applied only to images determined as anomalous. In addition, SAM-based boundary refinement suppresses pixel-level noise and produces an anomaly map aligned with object contours by computing semantically consistent region-level scores.

3 GPS Framework

The proposed GPS framework consists of three sequential step. Figure 1 is an overview of the entire pipeline showing how information flows from Stage 1 to Stage 3. In Stage 1 (GlobalCLIP) on the left, two CLIP encoders, ViT-B/32 and ViT-L/14@336, extract 1280-dimensional features from the input image, and a self-cyclic reconstruction ensemble calculates image-level anomaly scores. In the Gate Decision step, the image is classified as normal or anomalous based on the 95th percentile threshold τ, and only the image that is judged as anomalous is transmitted to Stage 2. In Stage 2 (PatchCore k-NN) at the center, a rough 32×32 anomaly map is generated through the comparison of the multi-scale patch features of WideResNet-50 with the memory bank. In Stage 3 (SAM) on the right, SAM ViT-H refines the anomaly scores by semantically consistent area units through automatic mask generation and outputs final anomaly maps and bounding boxes aligned with object boundaries. This step-by-step separation structure greatly improves the computational efficiency by skipping Stage 2 and Stage 3 for images classified as normal by the gate, while allowing each step to be independently verified and replaced.

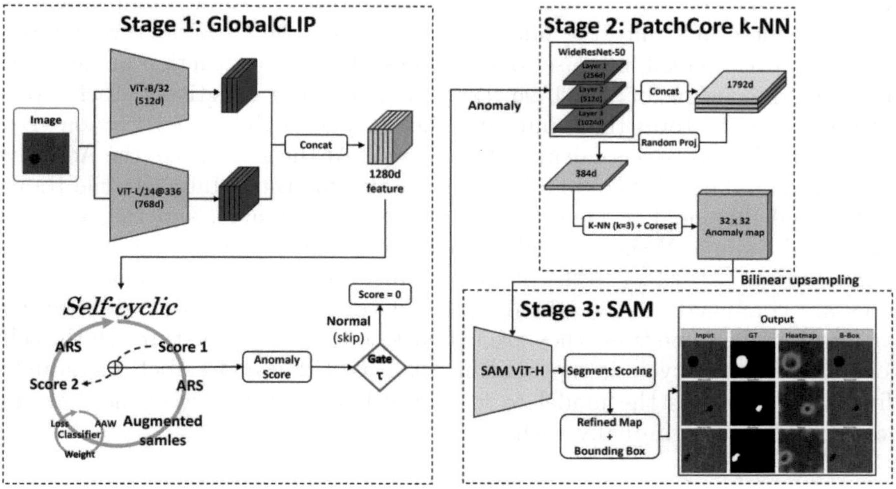

Fig. 1. GPS framework.

3.1 Stage 1: GlobalCLIP Zero-Shot Detection

In the first stage, when an image comes in, the framework determines whether the image contains an anomaly.

Multi-global Feature Aggregation. For each image $I_i \in \mathbb{R}^{W \times H \times 3}$, we extract global features using two CLIP image encoders:

$$v_i = \text{concat}\left[f_{\text{clip}}^{(1)}(I_i),\ f_{\text{clip}}^{(2)}(I_i)\right] \in \mathbb{R}^D \tag{1}$$

where $f_{\text{clip}}^{(1)}$ is ViT-B/32 ($D_1 = 512$) and $f_{\text{clip}}^{(2)}$ is ViT-L/14@336 ($D_2 = 768$), yielding $D = 1280$ dimensional concatenated features. Each feature vector is L2-normalized before concatenation. The dual-backbone aggregation captures both coarse semantic information (ViT-B/32) and fine-grained visual details (ViT-L/14@336), providing a richer representation than either backbone alone.

Self-Cyclic Ensemble Learning. The core of Stage 1 is the self-cyclic ensemble learning mechanism, which progressively improves detection performance through iterative training cycles. The ensemble consists of $K = 6$ reconstruction models with varying bottleneck dimensions $\{32, 64, 96, 128, 160, 256\}$. Each reconstruction model $f(\cdot; \theta_k)$ is an autoencoder with architecture: Linear($D \rightarrow 512$)–ReLU–Linear($512 \rightarrow b_k$)–ReLU–Linear($b_k \rightarrow 512$)–ReLU–Linear($512 \rightarrow D$), where b_k is the bottleneck dimension.

During the cycle of $C = 3$, the model is trained with the following adaptive mechanism. Figure 2 is a visualization of the self-cyclic ensemble structure of Stage 1, which shows how the CLIP feature is converted into two complementary scores and integrated into the final anomaly score. The CLIP feature entering the left input is divided into a set of six independent reconstruction models with bottleneck dimensions of 32, 64, 96, 128, 160, and 256, respectively. Each model compresses and restores the input, and the average of the reconstruction error occurring in this process is calculated as *Score 1*. At the same time, the Adaptive Rejection Sampling (ARS) module applies a quartile range Interquartile Range (IQR)-based threshold to identify a pseudo-positive sample, and the Adaptive Augmented Sample Weight (AAW) module calculates *Score 2* by assigning a learning weight according to the prediction uncertainty of the classifier. The two scores are combined as a weighted sum and transferred to the Gate Decision stage, and at the same time, they are fed back to the next cycle through the self-cyclic loop. As the cycle is repeated in this way, the pseudo-label is gradually refined, which allows the model to learn the boundaries between normal and anomalous samples gradually without target-domain data.

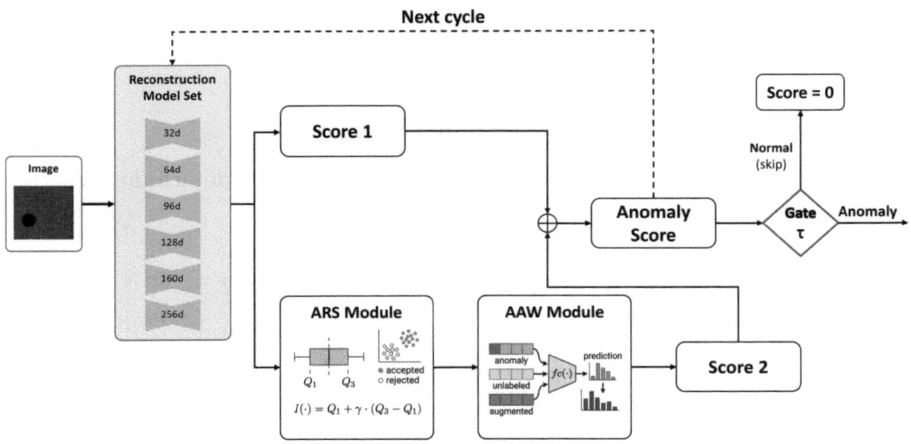

Fig. 2. Self-cyclic ensemble in Stage 1.

ARS. After each cycle c, the reconstruction error scores $s_c = \{s_{c,1}, \ldots, s_{c,N}\}$ are used to identify potential anomalies. The rejection threshold is computed using the interquartile range:

$$T_c = Q_1^c + \alpha \cdot (Q_3^c - Q_1^c) \tag{2}$$

where Q_1^c and Q_3^c are the first and third quartiles of s_c, and $\alpha = 1.5$ is the outlier sensitivity parameter (following the standard box-plot criterion). Samples with $s_{c,i} \geq T_c$ are flagged as potential anomalies and excluded from subsequent training rounds, progressively purifying the training set.

AAW. The AAW module assigns learning weights to samples based on the classifier's prediction uncertainty. For an unlabeled sample v with classifier output $f_p(v)$, the weight for the positive class is:

$$\omega(v) = \frac{(1-\gamma) \cdot f_p(v)}{1 - \gamma \cdot f_p(v)} \tag{3}$$

where $\gamma = 0.7$ is the label frequency parameter. This enables the classifier to implicitly learn the boundary between normal and anomalous samples from the unlabeled set.

Anomaly Score Computation. The final anomaly score for each test image combines the reconstruction error and classifier probability:

$$s_i = \lambda \cdot s_i^p + s_i^r \tag{4}$$

where $s_i^r = \Phi\left(\frac{1}{K}\sum_{k=1}^{K} s_i^k\right)$ is the normalized mean reconstruction error across all K models, $s_i^p = f_p(v_i^{\text{input}})$ is the classifier output, $\lambda = 0.5$, and $\Phi(\cdot)$ denotes min-max normalization.

Gating Decision. To determine which images enter Stage 2, we set the threshold τ as the 95th percentile of the training set's anomaly scores (mapped through the same sigmoid normalization). Images with $s_i \geq \tau$ are classified as anomalous and forwarded to Stage 2 for pixel-level analysis.

3.2 Stage 2: PatchCore *k*-NN Anomaly Localization

For images flagged as anomalous by Stage 1, we perform pixel-level anomaly localization using a PatchCore-inspired approach with several adaptations.

The memory bank in Stage 2 is constructed from normal training images of the target category. This is consistent with the zero-shot setting of our framework: as defined in 3.1, the zero-shot setting in this study refers to the absence of defect labels and anomaly samples, while the use of normal training images is permitted. This setting aligns with the standard practice in the unsupervised and zero-shot anomaly detection literature, including PatchCore [2] and

GlobalCLIP [8]. Normal training images are generally far easier to collect than defective images, and they can be readily secured even when introducing new product lines, which is consistent with practical deployment requirements.

Multi-scale Patch Feature Extraction. We employ a pre-trained Wide-ResNet-50 [20] as the feature extractor. For each image resized to 256 × 256, we extract intermediate features from three layers and aggregate them into a unified patch representation:

$$F = \text{concat}[\text{up}(F_1),\ \text{up}(F_2),\ \text{up}(F_3)] \in \mathbb{R}^{B \times 1792 \times 32 \times 32} \tag{5}$$

where $F_1 \in \mathbb{R}^{256 \times h_1 \times w_1}$, $F_2 \in \mathbb{R}^{512 \times h_2 \times w_2}$, and $F_3 \in \mathbb{R}^{1024 \times h_3 \times w_3}$ are features from Layer 1, 2, and 3, respectively, and $up(\cdot)$ denotes bilinear interpolation to the target grid size of 32 × 32. The concatenated 1792-dimensional features are reduced to 384 dimensions via random dimension selection (fixed random seed for reproducibility), yielding patch descriptors $p_j \in \mathbb{R}^{384}$ for each of the $32 \times 32 = 1024$ spatial positions.

Figure 3 shows the entire flow of the localization pipeline that combines Stage 2 and Stage 3. The anomaly image that has passed through the gate is first input into WideResNet-50 to extract multi-scale features (256, 512, 1024 dimensions, respectively) from Layers 1, 2, and 3, then concatenated into 1792 dimensions and reduced to 384 dimensions through random projection on a 32 × 32 grid. The patch descriptor obtained in this way is transmitted to the k-NN module, and patch-level anomaly scores are calculated based on the distance to the memory bank (25% coreset) composed of normal training features under the condition of $k = 3$. The rough 32×32 map presented on the right side of Fig. 3 has spatial alignment in patch units but lacks consistency with object boundaries. To compensate for this, SAM ViT-H generates an automatic mask for the anomaly map and allocates the 75th percentile within each segmented area as a representative score for the corresponding area. This area-wise scoring method has the effect of maintaining semantically consistent area boundaries while suppressing pixel-level noise, and finally, a refined pixel-level anomaly map with bounding boxes is output.

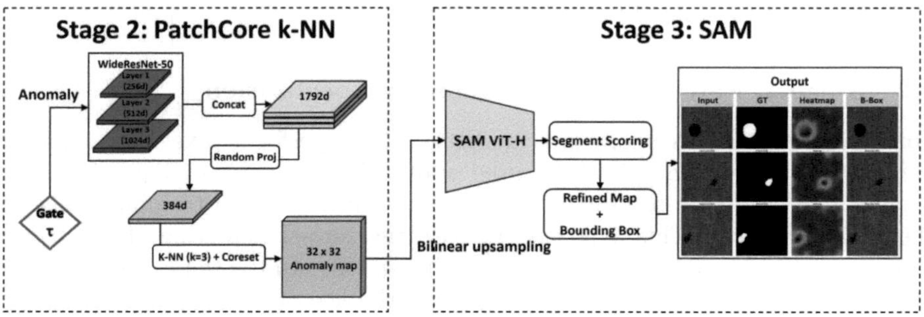

Fig. 3. Anomaly localization pipeline (Stages 2 and 3).

Memory Bank Construction and Coreset Sampling. A memory bank $\mathcal{M}$ is constructed from normal training images by collecting all patch features. Given N_{train} training images, the total number of patches is $N_{\text{train}} \times 1024$. To reduce memory and computation, we apply random coreset sampling at 25% ratio:

$$\mathcal{M}_{\text{core}} = \text{RandomSample}(\mathcal{M},\ |\mathcal{M}| \times 0.25) \tag{6}$$

***k*-NN Anomaly Scoring.** For each patch p_j of a test image, the anomaly score is the mean distance to the $k = 3$ nearest neighbors in the memory bank:

$$a_j = \frac{1}{k} \sum_{m=1}^{k} \|p_j - n_j^{(m)}\|_2 \tag{7}$$

where $n_j^{(1)}, \ldots, n_j^{(k)}$ are the k nearest neighbors of p_j in $\mathcal{M}_{\text{core}}$. The distances are computed via batch-wise GPU-accelerated Euclidean distance. The resulting 32×32 anomaly map is smoothed with a Gaussian filter ($\sigma = 1$) and min-max normalized to $[0, 1]$.

3.3 Stage 3: SAM Boundary Refinement

The coarse 32×32 anomaly map from Stage 2 is refined using the SAM [19] with ViT-H backbone for boundary-aware localization.

First, the anomaly map is upscaled to the original image resolution via bilinear interpolation. SAM's automatic mask generator then produces a set of class-agnostic segments $\{M_1, \ldots, M_S\}$ with parameters: 32 points per side, predicted Intersection over Union (IoU) threshold 0.86, stability score threshold 0.92, and minimum mask region area 100 pixels. For each segment M_s, a representative anomaly score is computed as the 75th percentile of the upscaled anomaly values within that segment:

$$a_s = Q_{75}\left(\{a(x) : x \in M_s\}\right) \tag{8}$$

The corrected anomaly map gives each pixel the highest score among the segments to which the pixel belongs. Pixels that are not included in any segment maintain the original value calculated and filled through the surrounding values. This segment-based scoring generates an anomaly map that respects object boundaries while smoothing noise within a consistent area.

Bounding Box Generation. For visualization and practical deployment, anomaly bounding boxes are generated by thresholding the refined map at the 90th percentile, applying connected component labeling, and computing axis-aligned bounding rectangles for each component exceeding 20 pixels in area.

4 Experiments

4.1 Experimental Setup

Dataset. We evaluate on MVTec AD [1], a widely-used industrial anomaly detection benchmark containing 5,354 high-resolution images across 15 categories (5 texture types and 10 object types). Each category includes a training set of defect-free images and a test set with both normal and various defect types, along with pixel-level ground truth masks.

Implementation Details. All experiments were conducted in the NVIDIA A100 80GB GPU environment, and the entire deep learning pipeline was built on PyTorch [12]. In Stage 1, CLIP features were extracted from ViT-B/32 and ViT-L/14@336 models using the OpenCLIP library [13]. The reconstruction ensemble consists of $K = 6$ models, trained at 50 epochs per model with Adam optimizer (learning rate $= 10^{-3}$), batch size 64, and $C = 3$ cycles. In Stage 2, WideResNet-50 pre-trained with ImageNet was loaded from torchvision to extract multi-scale features from 256×256 resolution to 32×32 grid, which were reduced from 1792 dimensions to 384 dimensions. The memory bank uses a random coreset of 25% and a $k = 3$ nearest neighbor. Stage 3 utilizes the SAM ViT-H model through the official segment-anything library. All hyperparameters were equally fixed across all 15 categories.

Software Stack. Additional open-source software used for data processing and analysis in this study is as follows. Numerical operation and tensor processing were performed through NumPy [14]; Gaussian filtering ($\sigma = 1$), quartile IQR-based threshold calculation, and statistical distribution processing used SciPy [15]. The Area Under Receiver Operating Characteristic (AUROC) evaluation of anomaly scores, random coreset sampling, and verification metric calculation were performed through scikit-learn [16]. Bounding box generation through defect area visualization and connected component labeling utilized OpenCV [17], and heatmap visualization and result figure generation were performed through Matplotlib [18].

Evaluation Metrics. We use AUROC at both image level (detection quality) and pixel level (localization quality). Image-level AUROC (I-AUROC) measures the ability to distinguish normal from anomalous images, while Pixel-level AUROC (P-AUROC) evaluates the quality of spatial anomaly localization against ground truth masks.

4.2 Results

Table 2 presents the full experimental results across all 15 MVTec AD categories. The framework achieves a mean I-AUROC of 92.49% and a mean P-AUROC of 84.62%.

Table 2. MVTec AD (15 categories).

Category	I-AUROC	P-AUROC	τ	Anomaly	Time (s)
bottle	0.9921	0.9190	0.843	62/83	257
cable	0.9052	0.8468	0.863	64/150	349
capsule	0.8492	0.7881	0.881	51/132	305
carpet	*0.9663*	*0.9560*	*0.853*	*98/117*	*975*
grid	*0.9407*	*0.7850*	*0.879*	*58/78*	*284*
hazelnut	0.9689	0.9323	0.873	56/110	279
leather	*0.9993*	*0.8621*	*0.831*	*99/124*	*317*
metal_nut	0.9247	0.8453	0.839	71/115	239
pill	0.8140	0.8673	0.867	79/167	271
screw	0.7760	0.6193	0.852	44/160	228
tile	*0.9996*	*0.9285*	*0.791*	*87/117*	*405*
toothbrush	0.9556	0.9132	0.861	22/42	93
transistor	0.8571	0.8844	0.877	21/100	133
wood	*0.9974*	*0.7747*	*0.898*	*64/79*	*222*
zipper	0.9280	0.7711	0.872	83/151	276
Mean	0.9249	0.8462	–	–	78.4 m

Image-Level Detection. The Stage 1 zero-shot detector achieves excellent performance on texture categories (mean 0.9807) and strong performance on objects (mean 0.8941). The highest scores are observed for tile (0.9996), leather (0.9993), and wood (0.9974), all near-perfect detection. The most challenging categories are screw (0.7760) and pill (0.8140), where significant non-anomalous pose variations confound the global feature-based detection, consistent with findings in [8].

Pixel-Level Localization. P-AUROC varies more across categories, with carpet (0.9560), hazelnut (0.9323), and tile (0.9285) achieving strong localization, while screw (0.6193) and zipper (0.7711) show weaker performance. The latter cases involve fine-grained defects that are challenging for the 32×32 grid resolution and SAM's segment-level averaging.

Visualization. Figures. 4, 5 and 6 present visualization results, each showing four columns: input with anomaly score, ground truth mask, heatmap overlay, and bounding box predictions at the top 10% threshold. Figure 4 presents four texture and regular-shape categories. Figure 4(a) shows carpet, where the heatmap precisely covers defective regions and SAM aligns anomaly boundaries with the texture structure. Figure 4(b) shows hazelnut, where surface defects including printed markings and cracks are tightly enclosed by bounding boxes.

For bottle (Fig. 4(c)), the heatmap clearly highlights defective regions around the cap area. The SAM-refined boundaries align well with the circular geometry of the bottle, demonstrating the benefit of segment-aware scoring for objects with regular shapes. Tile (Fig. 4(d)) achieves near-perfect image-level detection (0.9996) and strong pixel localization; defects such as cracks and glue strips produce strong, well-localized heatmap responses.

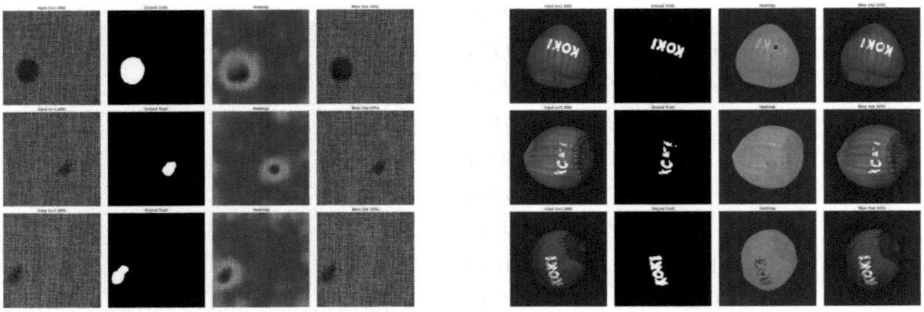

(a) Carpet (P-AUROC = 0.956) (b) Hazelnut (P-AUROC = 0.932)

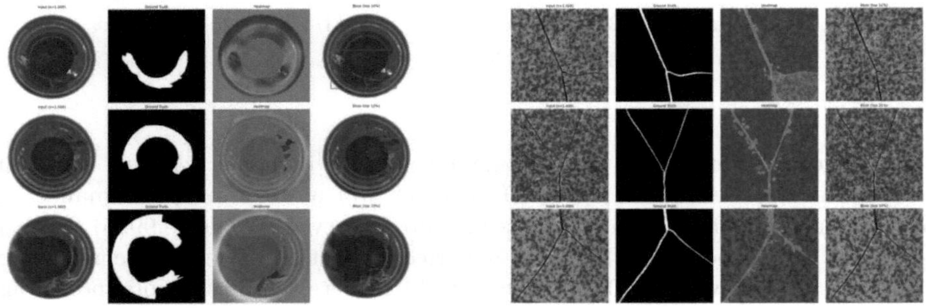

(c) Bottle (P-AUROC = 0.919) (d) Tile (P-AUROC = 0.929)

Fig. 4. Well-performing categories: Carpet, Hazelnut, Bottle, and Tile.

For object categories with complex geometry, Fig. 5(a) shows metal nut, where distributed anomalies across the object surface including scratches and bent regions are detected. The heatmap activates on edge regions, though some false positives appear on normal structural features. Transistor (Fig. 5(b)) demonstrates the framework's ability to localize misplaced and damaged components despite the complex multi-part geometry.

We also examine challenging cases where performance is weaker. Screw is the most difficult category, with significant non-anomalous pose variations that activate the entire object region, diluting the localization of actual defects (Fig. 6(a)). Wood shows partial defect coverage, where the heatmap highlights only portions of the ground truth regions. Long linear defects such as scratches are particularly challenging for the 32×32 grid resolution (Fig. 6(b)).

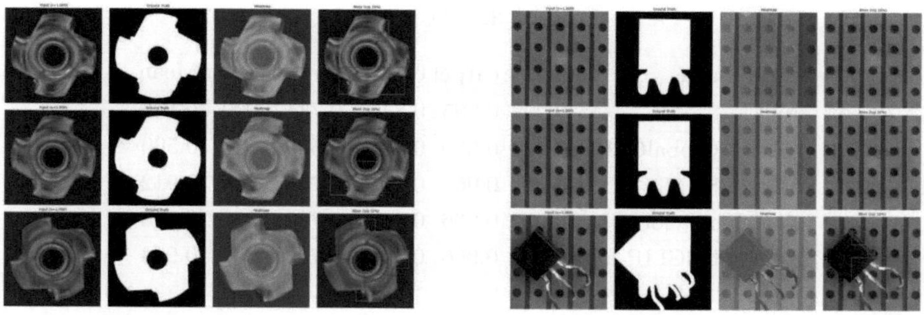

(a) Metal nut (P-AUROC = 0.845) (b) Transistor (P-AUROC = 0.884)

Fig. 5. Categories with partial false positives: Metal nut and Transistor.

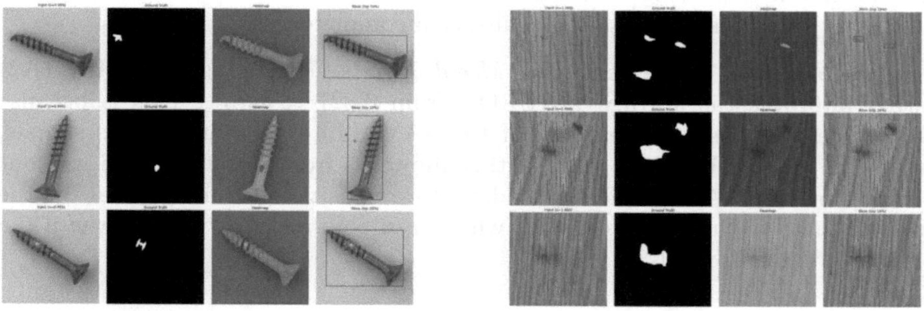

(a) Screw (P-AUROC = 0.619) (b) Wood (P-AUROC = 0.775)

Fig. 6. Challenging categories with limited localization: Screw and Wood.

4.3 Ablation Studies

We conducted five ablation experiments on five representative categories (bottle, carpet, capsule, screw, leather) selected to cover both object and texture types with varying difficulty levels. Tables 3 and 4 present the results for image-level and pixel-level AUROC, respectively. The ablation studies reveal several important findings:

Finding 1: GlobalCLIP is Essential for Image-Level Detection. When GlobalCLIP is removed (A1), the I-AUROC drops to 0.500 (random level) in all categories. This is because PatchCore and SAM normalization generate similar maximum pixel scores for all images regardless of whether anomalies are present. That is, the GlobalCLIP gating mechanism is essential for determining which images contain anomalies.

Finding 2: The Detection Gate Creates a Localization Trade-off. Interestingly, the P-AUROC was higher when the GlobalCLIP gate was excluded (A1). This occurs because the gate misclassifies borderline anomalous images as normal

Table 3. I-AUROC.

Experiment	bottle	carpet	capsule	screw	leather	Mean
Full	0.992	0.965	0.844	0.741	0.999	**0.908**
A1: No GlobalCLIP	0.500	0.500	0.500	0.500	0.500	0.500
A2: No SAM	0.994	0.965	0.849	0.755	0.999	0.912
A3: Mahalanobis	0.992	0.966	0.848	0.760	0.999	0.913
A4: GlobalCLIP only	0.992	0.966	0.850	0.763	0.999	0.914

and assigns them a pixel score of 0, which prevents any localization from being recovered downstream. When all images pass through Stage 2 instead, more anomalous regions are correctly localized in aggregate. This reveals a technical limitation: improving operational efficiency through the gating mechanism inevitably sacrifices a portion of localization completeness.

Finding 3: SAM Refinement Has Mixed Effects. Removing the SAM (A2) rather improves the average P-AUROC from 0.827 to 0.871. This is because the segment-level score averaging of the SAM dilutes fine anomalous signals, especially for small defects (e.g., leather improves from 0.862 to 0.996 without SAM). However, SAM provides boundary-aware position estimation that fits the anomaly map to the object contour, which results in a clean analysis even if the pixel-level indicator falls.

Table 4. P-AUROC.

Experiment	bottle	carpet	capsule	screw	leather	Mean
Full	0.919	0.956	0.780	0.616	0.862	0.827
A1: No GlobalCLIP	0.827	0.941	0.929	0.933	0.854	0.897
A2: No SAM	0.975	0.983	0.795	0.605	0.996	0.871
A3: Mahalanobis	0.917	0.961	0.779	0.599	0.882	0.828
A4: GlobalCLIP only	N/A	N/A	N/A	N/A	N/A	N/A

Finding 4: k-NN Outperforms Mahalanobis Distance. The entire pipeline with k-NN is 1.6 times faster, achieving P-AUROC comparable to that of A3 (Mahalanobis). The Mahalanobis distance assumes that the feature follows a Gaussian distribution, and since this assumption does not really hold in multi-scale patch features, the nonparametric k-NN approach is more robust as it does not make assumptions about the distribution.

Finding 5: Speed–Accuracy Trade-offs. As shown in Table 5, the A2 variant (no SAM) runs 4.9× faster with better pixel metrics, making it the most practical for high-throughput scenarios. A4 (GlobalCLIP only) achieves 11.3× speedup with strong image-level detection (0.914 mean AUROC), suitable when localization is not required.

Table 5. Processing time.

Experiment	Total Time	Per Category	Speed vs Full	Note
Full	34.0 min	6.8 min	1.0×	Baseline
A1: No GlobalCLIP	48.3 min	9.7 min	1.4× slower	All images enter Stage 2
A2: No SAM	6.9 min	1.4 min	4.9× faster	No SAM overhead
A3: Mahalanobis	53.7 min	10.7 min	1.6× slower	Covariance computation
A4: GlobalCLIP only	3.0 min	0.6 min	11.3× faster	Stage 1 only

5 Discussion

The framework shows distinct performance differences between texture and object categories. Texture categories (carpet, grid, leather, tile, wood) achieve a higher I-AUROC (average of 0.981) because texture anomalies produce unique global feature changes that CLIP encoders effectively capture. On the other hand, object categories exhibit a larger variance (average of 0.894 I-AUROC), primarily because pose changes in categories such as screw and capsule produce feature differences that confuse global detection even when the samples are not anomalous. In pixel-level localization, texture categories show more diverse performance: carpet (0.956) and tile (0.929) achieve strong results, while wood (0.775) and grid (0.785) are weaker, suggesting that PatchCore grid resolution and SAM segment averaging may not capture long linear defects or grid alignment variations.

This study has several limitations. Due to the sequential dependence between modules, false negatives in Stage 1 are forcibly assigned a pixel score of 0, leaving no opportunity for recovery in later stages. SAM ViT-H is the primary computational bottleneck; the A2 ablation shows that removing SAM provides 4.9× speedup with better pixel metrics, suggesting bilinear upscaling may be preferable for high-throughput applications. The fixed 32×32 patch grid limits spatial precision for small defects, and uniform hyperparameters across all 15 categories, while demonstrating generalization, leave room for category-specific improvement. Finally, although our framework uses no defect samples or labels, it does utilize normal training images and therefore does not conform to the strictest zero-shot setting; future work may explore fully zero-shot localization that does not require normal training images, such as approaches exploiting pseudo-normal images within the test set (e.g., MuSc).

The self-cyclic learning process in Stage 1 exhibits statistical convergence characteristics. The ARS module's IQR-based threshold ensures robustness in non-Gaussian scoring distributions, and the ensemble of $K = 6$ reconstruction models with varying bottleneck dimensions acts as a form of multi-resolution analysis, capturing anomaly patterns at different compression rates. The AAW module connects to the Positive and Unlabeled (PU) learning literature [21] by providing principled learning from positive and unlabeled data. Across the 15 categories, the adaptive threshold τ ranges from 0.791 (Tile) to 0.898 (Wood), demonstrating that the framework automatically adjusts sensitivity based on each category's feature distribution.

6 Conclusion

We presented a multi-stage statistical framework for zero-shot industrial anomaly detection and localization that combines GlobalCLIP's adaptive ensemble learning with PatchCore k-NN localization and SAM boundary refinement. The framework achieves 92.49% mean I-AUROC under zero-shot conditions and 84.62% mean P-AUROC across all 15 MVTec AD categories, using fixed hyperparameters throughout.

Our ablation studies provide actionable insights for practitioners. The GlobalCLIP gate is indispensable for image-level detection. SAM refinement offers boundary-aware localization but may reduce pixel-level metrics for small defects. Removing SAM yields the best speed–accuracy trade-off for most applications. The framework's modular design allows practitioners to select the appropriate configuration based on their requirements for detection accuracy, localization precision, and computational budget.

Future research directions include replacing fixed gating thresholds with learning-based or adaptive mechanisms to reduce undetected anomalies, exploring higher resolution feature grids to improve small defect localization, and adding a heatmap calibration module to SAM to improve segment quality.

Acknowledgments. This work was supported by the Institute of Information & Communications Technology Planning & Evaluation (IITP)-ICT Creative Consilience Program grant funded by the Korea government (MSIT)(IITP-2026-RS-2020-II201821), This work was supported by the Korea Institute for Advancement of Technology (KIAT) grant funded by the Korea Government under the Industrial Innovation Talent Growth Support Project.(KIAT-2026-RS-2026-25532917)

Disclosure of Interests. The authors have no competing interests to declare that are relevant to the content of this article.

References

1. Bergmann, P., et al.: MVTec AD – a comprehensive real-world dataset for unsupervised anomaly detection. In: CVPR, pp. 9592–9600 (2019). https://doi.org/10.1109/CVPR.2019.00982
2. Roth, K., et al.: Towards total recall in industrial anomaly detection. In: CVPR, pp. 14298–14308 (2022). https://doi.org/10.1109/CVPR52688.2022.01392
3. Ding, C., Pang, G., Shen, C.: Catching both gray and black swans: open-set supervised anomaly detection. In: CVPR, pp. 7378–7388 (2022). https://doi.org/10.1109/CVPR52688.2022.00724
4. Deng, H., Li, X.: Anomaly detection via reverse distillation from one-class embedding. In: CVPR, pp. 9727–9736 (2022). https://doi.org/10.1109/CVPR52688.2022.00951

5. Meng, S., et al.: MoEAD: a parameter-efficient model for multi-class anomaly detection. In: ECCV, pp. 345–361 (2024). https://doi.org/10.1007/978-3-031-73013-9_20
6. Huang, C., et al.: Registration based few-shot anomaly detection. In: ECCV, pp. 303–319 (2022). https://doi.org/10.1007/978-3-031-20053-3_18
7. Jeong, J., et al.: WinCLIP: zero-/few-shot anomaly classification and segmentation. In: CVPR, pp. 19606–19616 (2023). https://doi.org/10.1109/CVPR52729.2023.01878
8. Shen, H., et al.: GlobalCLIP: zero-shot manufacturing anomaly detection with adaptive self-cyclic ensemble learning. Expert Syst. Appl. **298**, 129448 (2026). https://doi.org/10.1016/j.eswa.2025.129448
9. Radford, A., et al.: Learning transferable visual models from natural language supervision. In: Proceedings of the 38th International Conference on Machine Learning, PMLR, vol. 139, pp. 8748–8763 (2021)
10. Zhou, Q.: AnomalyCLIP: object-agnostic prompt learning for zero-shot anomaly detection. In: ICLR (2024)
11. Cao, Y., et al.: AdaCLIP: adapting CLIP with hybrid learnable prompts for zero-shot anomaly detection. In: ECCV, pp. 55–72 (2024). https://doi.org/10.1007/978-3-031-72761-0_4
12. Paszke, A.: PyTorch: an imperative style, high-performance deep learning library. In: Advances in Neural Information Processing Systems, vol. 32 (2019)
13. Ilharco, G., et al.: OpenCLIP. Zenodo (2021)
14. Harris, C.R., et al.: Array programming with NumPy. Nature **585**(7825), 357–362 (2020). https://doi.org/10.1038/s41586-020-2649-2
15. Virtanen, P., et al.: SciPy 1.0: fundamental algorithms for scientific computing in Python. Nat. Methods **17**(3), 261–272 (2020). https://doi.org/10.1038/s41592-019-0686-2
16. Pedregosa, F., et al.: Scikit-learn: machine learning in Python. J. Mach. Learn. Res. **12**, 2825–2830 (2011)
17. Bradski, G.: The OpenCV library. Dr. Dobb's J. Softw. Tools (2000)
18. Hunter, J.D.: Matplotlib: a 2D graphics environment. Comput. Sci. Eng. **9**(3), 90–95 (2007). https://doi.org/10.1109/MCSE.2007.55
19. Kirillov, A., et al.: Segment anything. In: ICCV, pp. 3992–4003 (2023). https://doi.org/10.1109/ICCV51070.2023.00371
20. Zagoruyko, S., Komodakis, N.: Wide residual networks. In: BMVC (2016)
21. Bekker, J., Davis, J.: Learning from positive and unlabeled data: a survey. Mach. Learn. **109**(4), 719–760 (2020)

Neural Networks and Gaussian Regression Process Comparison on a Physical Problem

Merve Gurbuz-Caldag[1], Bengisen Pekmen[1], and Ezgi Kiratli[2(✉)]

[1] Department of Mathematics, TED University, 06420 Ankara, Turkey
merve.gurbuz@tedu.edu.tr
[2] Department of Economics, TED University, 06420 Ankara, Turkey
ezgi.kiratli@tedu.edu.tr

Abstract. This study aims to systematically compare two machine learning methods, Gaussian Process Regression (GPR) and Neural Networks (NN), for predicting heat transfer, mass transfer, and microbial behavior indicators in a bioconvection flow problem. The models are trained and tested on a dataset collected from numerical simulation results of the natural bioconvection flow of a Cu-water nanofluid and oxytactic bacteria in an open square cavity. Radial basis function method is performed by parallel computing in different dimensionless problem parameters. The target variables, average Nusselt, Sherwood and bacteria density are computed in each parameter combinations. Multiple seed comparison, cross validation analysis and permutation based feature importance analysis were carried by both models. The results reveal that in terms of mean squared error (MSE) metrics, in different seeds, GPR is more robust to model, and in turn measure uncertainty well while NN is provides smaller prediction error. 5 fold CV analysis results approve the good generalizability of NN model. Permutation based feature importance check shuffling each input data and controlling MSE values points to the most important parameter as bioconvection Rayleigh number on each output indicator.

Keywords: Neural Networks · Gaussian Process Regression · Radial Basis Function Method

1 Introduction

Bioconvection originates from the collective upward swimming of motile microorganisms, which generates density gradients and induces convective instability within the fluid. The theoretical foundations and pattern formation mechanisms of bioconvection were comprehensively discussed by Hill and Pedley [14]. Subsequent studies demonstrated that thermal gradients significantly affect the onset of thermo-bioconvective instability in porous layers [19]. The incorporation of nanoparticles into microorganism suspensions further modifies the stability characteristics due to Brownian motion and thermophoretic effects, altering the critical conditions for nanofluid bioconvection [18,20]. In addition, the presence of non-Darcian porous media and gyrotactic microorganisms has been shown to influence flow destabilization and transport enhancement

O. Gervasi et al. (Eds.): ICCSA 2026, LNCS 16768, pp. 464–475, 2027.
https://doi.org/10.1007/978-3-032-30488-9_29

[27]. More recently, thermo-bio-convection in complex porous cavities containing nanoparticles and microorganisms has been numerically investigated, revealing strong coupling between thermal, concentration, and microorganism fields [1,3].

Open cavities are widely used in a range of engineering applications, including solar thermal receivers, convective heat transfer from extended surfaces in heat exchangers, and solar collectors equipped with insulated strips [28]. Chan and Tien [6] studied the steady natural convection flow in an open cavity by using SIMPLER algorithm. They reported that higher Rayleigh number leads to the formation of recirculation zones above the bottom wall. Polat and Bilgen [24] analyzed laminar natural convection in inclined shallow open cavities heated by a constant heat flux. It is obtained that an asymptotic behaviour of heat transfer occurs as Rayleigh number increases. However, the elongation of open cavities postpones this behaviour. Mohamad et al. [23] simulated natural convection in an open-ended cavity using the Lattice Boltzmann Method (LBM) and examined the associated flow and heat transfer characteristics. Their results confirmed the reliability of the open boundary conditions by showing close agreement with finite volume method predictions, and revealed that increasing the cavity aspect ratio leads to an asymptotic decrease in the heat transfer rate toward the conduction limit. LBM is applied to solve natural convection flow in an open cavity filled with Cu-water by Kefayati et al. [16]. Gangawane [11] showed that the magnetic field orientation strongly affects heat transfer of natural convection in an open ended cavity with partiallyactive walls. Prakash et al. [25] conducted MHD free convection in a partially open square cavity with a wavy cold wall filled with nanofluid. They reported that increasing the Hartmann number or nanoparticle volume fraction suppresses convection, whereas wall waviness enhances the average Nusselt number. Allouche et al. [2] developed an in-house FORTRAN code to numerically investigate two-dimensional laminar natural convection of a Newtonian nanofluid in an open square cavity subjected to an external magnetic field. It is shown that stronger magnetic fields suppress fluid motion and heat transfer, whereas the inclusion of nanoparticles enhances heat transfer and alters the flow behavior depending on the presence of the magnetic field.

In recent years, the machine learning approaches on convective heat transfer of nanofluid problems in different geometries are studied by many researchers. Vaferi et al. [31] developed a model to forecast the heat transfer coefficient of nanofluids in a circular tube. The proposed model is compared with different ANN types using experimental data. Rostamian et al. [26] proposed ANN model and correlation of the thermal conductivity (TC) of CuO-SWCNTs/EG water. They deduced that ANN model gives more accurate results than the correlation. The effect of number of neurons in hidden layers on the ANN prediction for TC of hybrid nanofluids is analyzed by Vafei et al. [30]. In [29], the Sherwood number, motile density of microorganism, skin friction coefficient and Nusselt number are predicted using four different artificial neural network models. Chandra and Das [7] conducted a study on ANN model for the estimation of gyrotactic-nanofluid flow over a stretchable vertically inclined surface. In [15], the average Nusselt, Sherwood and motile microorganism numbers of the mixed bioconvection flow of nanofluid of oxytactic bacteria through a porous cavity under the effect of periodic magnetic field is modeled using Light Gradient Boosting Machine algorithm.

To the best of our knowledge, NN and GPR modeling on a bioconvection flow in an open square cavity filled by Cu-water nanofluid in the presence of oxytactic bacteria is firstly conducted. The dimensionless governing equations are formulated in terms of stream function, vorticity, temperature, oxygen concentration and bacteria density, and solved numerically using the RBF method. Considering various combinations of dimensionless parameters including the Rayleigh, bioconvection Rayleigh, Hartmann, magnetic, Lewis and Peclet numbers as well as the magnetic source location, the target outputs the average Nusselt number, Sherwood number and bacteria density along the heated wall are computed, and all are saved. The predictive performances of the models are evaluated using this dataset. To the best of our knowledge, this is the first study to apply and systematically compare NN and GPR modeling to a bioconvection problem in an open cavity.

The motivation of this study arises from the growing need for data-driven models, where repetitive numerical simulations are computationally expensive. While neural networks are widely adopted due to their predictive power, Gaussian Process Regression including Kernels as in our numerical method is also examined. A systematic comparison of these two approaches on a well-defined physical problem is utilized. The objectives of this work are: (i) to construct a high-quality dataset from RBF-based numerical simulations of bioconvection flow in an open cavity, (ii) to train and evaluate NN and GPR models on this dataset using multiple performance metrics, and (iii) to provide guidance on model selection based on accuracy, generalizability, and computational cost.

2 Physics of the Problem

Under steady-state conditions, natural convection flow of Cu-water nanofluid in a square cavity, taking into account the presence of oxytactic bacteria and the influence of a magnetic source is concerned. The setup of the problem is illustrated in Fig. 1. The location of magnetic source (ms) is denoted by (xms, yms).

The single-phase model is adopted for the nanofluid, and accordingly, its physical properties are defined by [17]

$$\rho_{nf} = (1-\xi)\rho_f + \xi\rho_s, \tag{1}$$

$$(\rho c_p)_{nf} = (1-\xi)(\rho c_p)_f + \xi(\rho c_p)_s, \tag{2}$$

$$(\rho\beta)_{nf} = (1-\xi)(\rho\beta)_f + \xi(\rho\beta)_s, \tag{3}$$

$$\alpha_{nf} = \frac{k_{nf}}{(\rho c_p)_{nf}}, \tag{4}$$

where subindices nf, f, s are the nanofluid, fluid and solid, respectively, ρ is the density, β is the thermal expansion coefficient, c_p is the specific heat, α is the thermal diffusivity and ξ is the solid volume fraction. The thermal (k_{nf}) and electrical σ_{nf} conductivities

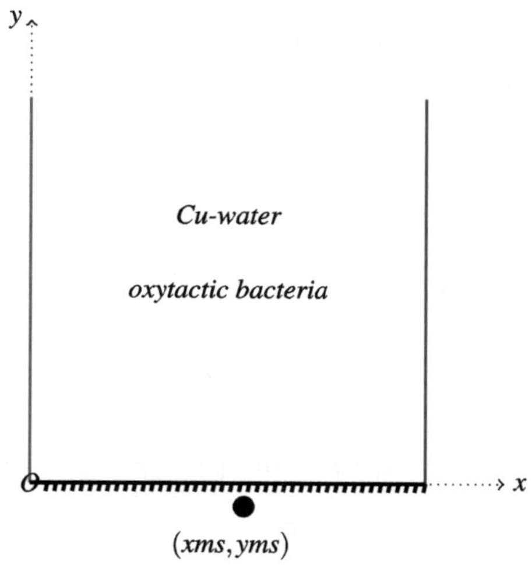

Fig. 1. The geometrical layout of the problem.

of the nanofluid are settled as [12]

$$\frac{k_{nf}}{k_f} = \frac{k_s + 2k_f - 2\xi(k_f - k_s)}{k_s + 2k_f + \xi(k_f - k_s)}, \tag{5}$$

$$\frac{\sigma_{nf}}{\sigma_f} = \frac{\sigma_s + 2\sigma_f - 2\xi(\sigma_f - \sigma_s)}{\sigma_s + 2\sigma_f + \xi(\sigma_f - \sigma_s)}, \tag{6}$$

and the dynamic viscosity of nanofluid μ_{nf} is opted as [5]

$$\mu_{nf} = \mu_f(1-\xi)^{-2.5}. \tag{7}$$

Table 1 summarizes the thermophysical properties of water and copper (Cu).

Table 1. Thermophysical properties of water and Copper (Cu) [4,13].

Property	Water	Cu
$\rho\ (kg/m^3)$	997.1	8933
$c_p\ [J/(kgK)]$	4179	385
$k\ [W/(mK)]$	0.613	401
$\beta \times 10^{-5}\ (1/K)$	21	1.67
$\sigma\ (1/(m\Omega))$	0.05	5.96×10^7

By using the stream function to define the velocity components, $\nabla \cdot (u, v) = 0$ is satisfied. Additionally, introducing vorticity eliminates the pressure terms from the momentum equations. As a result, the governing equations are reformulated in terms of stream function (ψ), vorticity (ω), temperature (T), oxygen concentration (C) and the density of the bacteria (N_m) as follows:

$$\nabla^2\psi = -\omega, \tag{8a}$$

$$\frac{\alpha_{nf}}{\alpha_f}\nabla^2 T = \left(u\frac{\partial T}{\partial x} + v\frac{\partial T}{\partial y}\right), \tag{8b}$$

$$\frac{1}{Le}\nabla^2 C = \left(u\frac{\partial C}{\partial x} + v\frac{\partial C}{\partial y}\right) + \frac{1}{Le}N_m, \tag{8c}$$

$$\frac{1}{Le}\nabla^2 N_m = \left(u\frac{\partial N_m}{\partial x} + v\frac{\partial N_m}{\partial y}\right) + \frac{Pe}{Le}\left(N_m\nabla^2 C + \frac{\partial C}{\partial x}\frac{\partial N_m}{\partial x} + \frac{\partial C}{\partial y}\frac{\partial N_m}{\partial y}\right), \tag{8d}$$

$$\begin{aligned}\frac{\mu_{nf}}{\mu_f}Pr\nabla^2\omega = {} & \frac{\rho_{nf}}{\rho_f}\left(u\frac{\partial\omega}{\partial x} + v\frac{\partial\omega}{\partial y}\right) - RaPr\left(\frac{(\rho\beta)_{nf}}{\rho_f\beta_f}\frac{\partial T}{\partial x} - Rb\frac{\partial N_m}{\partial x}\right) - \\ & MnFPr\left(\frac{\partial H}{\partial x}\frac{\partial T}{\partial y} - \frac{\partial H}{\partial y}\frac{\partial T}{\partial x}\right) + \frac{\sigma_{nf}}{\sigma_f}Ha^2Pr\Big[H_x^2 v_x - H_xH_y(u_x - v_y) - H_y^2 u_y \\ & + 2H_xH_{xdx}v - H_{xdx}H_yu - H_xH_{ydx}u - 2H_yH_{ydy}u + H_{xdy}H_yv + H_xH_{ydy}v\Big],\end{aligned} \tag{8e}$$

where $H_{xdx}, H_{xdy}, H_{ydx}, H_{ydy}$ are partial derivatives of $H_x = |yms|\dfrac{y - yms}{(x - xms)^2 + (y - yms)^2}$ and $H_y = |yms|\dfrac{xms - x}{(x - xms)^2 + (y - yms)^2}$, and $H = \sqrt{H_x^2 + H_y^2}$. The nondimensional parameters are Prandtl, Hartmann, Rayleigh, bioconvection Rayleigh, Lewis, Peclet and magnetic numbers given as

$$Pr = \frac{\nu_f}{\alpha_f},\ Ha = L\mu_0H_0\sqrt{\frac{\sigma_f}{\mu_f}},\ Ra = \frac{g\beta_f L^3\Delta T}{\alpha_f\nu_f}, \tag{9a}$$

$$R_b = \frac{\gamma\Delta\rho n_0}{\rho_f\beta_f\Delta T},\quad Pe = \frac{\tilde{b}W_c}{D_n},\quad Le = \frac{\alpha_f}{D_c},\quad MnF = \frac{\mu_0H_0^2\tilde{K}\Delta T L^2}{\mu_f\alpha_f} \tag{9b}$$

where ν is the kinematic viscosity, g is the gravitational acceleration, γ is the mean volume of microorganism, D_c is the diffusivity of oxygen concentration, W_c is the maximum cell swimming speed, $\tilde{b}$ is the chemotaxis constant, D_n is the diffusivity of microorganism, L is the characteristic length, n_0 is the average density of bacteria, μ_0 is the magnetic permeability, H_0 is the intensity of the magnetic field, $\tilde{K}$ is a constant, ΔT is the temperature difference and $\Delta\rho = \rho_{cell} - \rho_{nf}$. Boundary conditions are as follows

$$\begin{aligned}&\text{on } x = 0: u = v = \psi = 0, T = 1, C = N_m = 1,\\ &\text{on } x = 1: u = v = \psi = 0 = T, C = N_m = 1,\\ &\text{on } y = 0: u = v = \psi = 0, \frac{\partial T}{\partial y} = 0, C = 1, PeN_m\frac{\partial C}{\partial y} = \frac{\partial N_m}{\partial y},\\ &\text{on } y = 1: \frac{\partial C}{\partial y} = \frac{\partial N_m}{\partial y} = \frac{\partial\psi}{\partial y} = 0, \quad \begin{cases}\dfrac{\partial T}{\partial y} = 0 & \text{if } v \geq 0\\ T = 0 & \text{if } v < 0\end{cases}.\end{aligned}$$

3 Computational Approaches

3.1 Radial Basis Function (RBF) Method

The numerical part of the study is carried out by applying the global radial basis function (RBF) method to space derivatives.

RBFs are functions depending on the radial (Euclidean) distance $r = \sqrt{(x-x_j)^2+(y-y_j)^2}$ between the collocation (x_j, y_j) and the field (x, y) points. The novel and concise books [9, 10] involve many theoretical and practical implementation examples on RBFs.

Any unknown φ may be written as a product of a coordinate matrix F constructed by an RBF and an unknown vector of coefficients. The partial derivatives of unknown is also easily derived by this product and by the straightforward derivative calculations of RBFs. The differentiation matrices for x-, y- derivatives and Laplacian are found as

$$D_x = \frac{\partial F}{\partial x}F^{-1}, D_y = \frac{\partial F}{\partial y}F^{-1}, D_2 = \left(\frac{\partial^2 F}{\partial x^2} + \frac{\partial^2 F}{\partial y^2}\right)F^{-1}, \tag{10}$$

Iterations are terminated if the sum of the relative residuals in infinity norm is less than a tolerance 10^{-5}. A relaxation parameter $\tau\,(0 < \tau < 1)$ is utilized once ω equation is solved.

Average Nusselt and Sherwood numbers, and density of the bacteria along the heated wall are computed by

$$\overline{Nu} = -\frac{k_{nf}}{k_f}\int_0^1 \frac{\partial T}{\partial x}dy,\ \overline{Sh} = -\int_0^1 \frac{\partial C}{\partial x}dy,\ \overline{Nm} = -\int_0^1 \frac{\partial N_m}{\partial x}dy, \tag{11}$$

using composite Simpson's rule on uniform grids.

3.2 Machine Learning Techniques

Neural Network Regression. NN process works as feedforward NN [8]. In this case, the information flows from the left to the right. The first layer is the input layer. The hidden layers follow the first layer, and the last layer is the output layer. A simple generalized mathematical expression may be written as

$$\hat{\mathbf{y}} = f(W\mathbf{x}+b), \tag{12}$$

where W is the weight matrix, b is the bias vector, $\mathbf{x}$ is the input features, $\hat{\mathbf{y}}$ is the predicted output, and f is the activation function.

In MATLAB, 'fitrnet' is used for NN modeling.

Gaussian Process Regression (GPR). In this process kernel (covariance) functions play the significant role. The GP function $f(x)$ is expressed as [21]

$$f(x) \approx GP(m(x), k(x,x')), \tag{13}$$

where $m(x) = E[f(x)]$ is the mean function, $k(x,x') = E[(f(x) - m(x))(f(x') - m(x'))]$ is the covariance function. In this study, ARD squared exponential kernel is taken as

$$k(x,x') = \sigma^2 \exp\left[-\frac{1}{2}\sum_{m=1}^{d}\frac{(x_m - x'_m)^2}{\sigma_l^2}\right], \tag{14}$$

where σ is the standard deviation, σ_l is the characteristic length scale, x, x' are input vectors of size $d \times 1$.

In MATLAB, 'fitrgp' is used for GP modeling.

4 Machine Learning Modeling

In this part, bilayer NN and GPR modeling results obtained in MATLAB are to be compared. All computations were carried out in MATLAB R2025a [22].

The RBF method iteratively solves the non-dimensional equations Eqs. (8)). The data is collected from the numerical results in different combination of dimensionless parameters which are in the range:

$$\begin{aligned}
Ra &= [10^2, 500, 10^3, 5000, 10^4];\\
Rb &= [10, 20, 30, 40, 50];\\
Ha &= [10, 35, 50, 100];\\
MnF &= [25, 50, 100];\\
xms &= [0.1, 0.25, 0.5, 0.75, 0.9];\\
yms &= [-0.02, -0.04, -0.08].
\end{aligned}$$

In numerical executions, the relaxation parameter is fixed at 0.002 for all $Ha <= 50$ cases while it is assigned as 0.0005 at $Ha = 100$. The convergent 2679 results are stored, and used for modeling. Thus, the dataset has 6 columns with input features $Ra, Rb, Ha, MnF, xms, yms$ and 3 columns with output features $\overline{Nu}, \overline{Sh}, \overline{N_m}$ In the case of NN modeling, hidden layer size is fixed at 50 neurons in each layer.

Different seeds affect the train-validation data split and the randomness in both the initial network weights inn NN. Since both factors influence model performance, we tested multiple seeds to identify which combination yields the best results. This approach helps us to avoid selecting a model that performs well simply due to a fortunate random configuration.

In Table 2, a comparison of bilayer NN and GPR with various kernel functions is conducted across random seeds between 20 and 50 using an 80%/20% train/test split. The target variable is the average Nusselt number ($\overline{Nu}$) which is difficult one to predict. Mean MSE refers to the average of MSE test values found in each seed. Std indicates the how much MSE test values deviates from the mean MSE. The smallest deviation points to a more consistent and robust model. Best MSE is the minimum test error achieved among all seeds. Best Seed is the specific random seed that produced the minimum test error. According to the Table results, the best models having the best MSE less than 0.001 are found in seed 28. The smallest mean MSE is obtained by NN modeling. The small variability in GPR-ARD-SE also gives us a robust modeling tool. To further benchmark our two methods against other established ML techniques, Random Forest (100 trees, minimum leaf size of 5) and XGBoost via LSBoost (1000 cycles, learning rate of 0.1, maximum splits of 20) were also evaluated under the same seed and split conditions. As seen in the last two rows of the Table, both ensemble methods yield competitive but inferior performance compared to the leading models. NN retains the smallest mean MSE overall, confirming its suitability as the primary modeling tool for predicting $\overline{Nu}$ in this problem. Since the primary objective of this study is the comparison of NN and GPR, exhaustive tuning of these ensemble methods beyond the scope of this work.

Table 2. Model performance across 31 random seeds (20–50)

Model	Mean MSE	Std	Best MSE	Best Seed
NN	**0.000487**	0.000304	**0.000113**	28
GPR-ARD-SE	0.000531	*0.000235*	*0.000184*	28
GPR-Squared Exponential	0.000841	*0.000235*	0.000400	28
GPR-Rational Quadratic	0.000848	0.000237	0.000400	28
GPR-Matérn 5/2	0.001787	0.000364	0.001007	28
GPR-Matérn 3/2	0.003957	0.000738	0.002839	44
RF	0.033306	0.002921	0.028427	32
XGBoost	0.000641	0.000268	0.000215	28

The prediction and residual plots are also displayed in Fig. 2. Both modeling capture the prediction in a very good pattern. Regarding three separate modeling for three outputs, NN modeling is completed in 6 s while total GPR modeling duration is 106 s.

5 folds cross validation (CV) analysis is also examined with both models keeping seed at 28. CV allows us to understand how well the models generalize to new data, giving a more reliable performance estimate than a single train-test split. By keeping the seed fixed, both models are trained and tested on exactly the same data partitions, which makes the comparison fair. In this approach, the dataset is divided into 5 subsets, and each subset takes a turn being the test set while the other 4 are used for training. According to the Table 3, mean MSE across these 5 folds shows that generalizability of NN modeling is better than GPR.

Feature importance based on permutation based analysis is also checked in Table 4. This method quantifies each input variable's contribution to model performance by measuring the increase in prediction error when that feature is randomly shuffled while keeping all other features fixed. For each feature in the set $\{Ra, Rb, Ha, MnF, xms, yms\}$, the baseline mean squared error is computed on the training set, then randomly the feature values are permuted and the error is recalculated. This process is repeated 50 times for each feature, and the average increase in error represents the feature's importance score. A large positive score indicates high feature importance, as shuffling it significantly affects model predictions. This model-agnostic method requires no access to the internal model structure. Based on this importance analysis, Rb is the most important parameter for each output in both modeling.

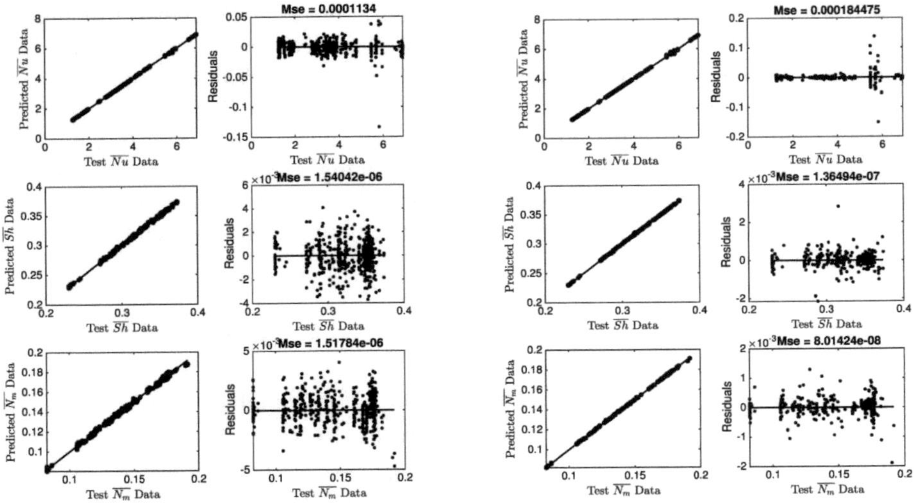

(a) Neural Network results (6.2139 seconds).

(b) GPR-ARD results (105.79 seconds).

Fig. 2. Comparison of model performance.

Table 3. Cross Validation analysis on $\overline{Nu}$ with both models.

Fold	MSE-NN	MSE-GPR
1	0.000117	0.000413
2	0.000485	0.000347
3	0.000498	0.000567
4	0.000250	0.000359
5	0.000691	0.000739
Mean	0.000408	0.000485

Table 4. Feature importance with both models.

	GPR			NN		
Inputs	$\overline{Nu}$	$\overline{Sh}$	$\overline{Nm}$	$\overline{Nu}$	$\overline{Sh}$	$\overline{Nm}$
Ra	1.9827	0.00152	0.00085	2.2701	0.00159	0.001035
Rb	**3.9684**	**0.00191**	**0.00114**	**4.2053**	**0.00193**	**0.00118**
Ha	0.04015	2.65e-5	7.54e-6	0.0412	2.58e-5	6.59e-6
MnF	1.15e-09	3.90e-17	2.63e-16	8.31e-5	4.15e-8	5.35e-8
xms	0.00423	2.53e-6	1.81e-6	0.00486	2.36e-6	1.72e-6
yms	0.02635	1.37e-5	4.07e-6	0.0275	1.31e-5	3.34e-6

5 Conclusion

In this study, we investigated the prediction capability of two machine learning approaches, NN regression and GPR using the dataset created by the numerical simulation of the natural bioconvection flow of Cu-water nanofluid with oxytactic bacteria in an open square cavity subjected to a magnetic source. The dataset consisting of 2679 convergent solutions was carefully assembled through the RBF method by systematically varying six dimensionless parameters: Ra, Rb, Ha, MnF, xms and yms. The target outputs were the average Nusselt number $\overline{Nu}$, Sherwood number $\overline{Sh}$ and bacteria density $\overline{N_m}$ along the heated wall, each representing a physically meaningful indicator of heat transfer, mass transfer and microbial behavior within the cavity. To ensure that the comparison between the two models was fair and statistically meaningful, we conducted a multi-seed analysis across 31 random seeds, 5-fold cross-validation at a fixed seed, and a permutation-based feature importance analysis. The seed comparison revealed that NN consistently achieves a lower mean MSE, pointing to its stronger predictive accuracy, while GPR-ARD-SE stands out with a noticeably lower standard deviation across seeds, which reflects its robustness and stability regardless of how the data is split. The cross-validation results at seed 28 further supported these findings, with NN attaining a mean MSE of 0.000408 compared to 0.000485 for GPR-ARD, confirming that NN generalizes better to unseen data. The feature importance analysis shows that the bioconvection Rayleigh number Rb emerged as the dominant parameter governing all three output quantities in both models, which is physically consistent given that Rb directly controls the strength of bioconvective flow driven by the density stratification due to bacteria accumulation. Taken together, NN is the preferred choice when prediction accuracy and computational speed are priorities, while GPR-ARD presents itself as a robust and uncertainty-aware modeling framework. Both approaches offer a promising and computationally inexpensive alternative to full numerical simulations.

While the current dataset of 2679 convergent solutions represents a systematic assembled collection, we acknowledge that a larger and more voluminous dataset in broader parameter ranges would further strengthen model generalizability. As future study, broader dataset including higher Hartmann numbers or varying cavity geometries may be collected.

Acknowledgment. This study was supported by TED University Institutional Research Fund (TEDU-IRF) with project ID: T-24-B2010-90130.

References

1. Abdullah, A.A., Rashed, Z.Z.: The stability of bio-thermal marangoni convection in a fluid layer containing oxytactic microorganisms. AIP Adv. **14**(1) (2024)
2. Allouche, S., Djezzar, M., Allouche, B., Tayebi, T.: Magnetohydrodynamic natural convection heat transfer of a nanofluid confined in a square open cavity subjected to a linear varying temperature. Numer. Heat Transfer, Part B: Fundam., 1–23 (2025)
3. Belabid, J., Öztop, H.F.: Nanofluid thermo-bio-convection in a horizontal porous wavy-walled annulus: interaction of phototactic microorganisms and nanoparticles distribution. Int. J. Heat Mass Transf. **215**, 124476 (2023)

4. Biswas, N., Manna, N.K., Mandal, D.K., Gorla, R.S.R.: Magnetohydrodynamic bioconvection of oxytactic microorganisms in porous media saturated with cu-water nanofluid. Int. J. Numer. Methods Heat & Fluid Flow **31**(11), 3461–3489 (2021)
5. Brinkman, H.C.: The viscosity of concentrated suspensions and solutions. J. Chem. Phys. **20**(4), 571–571 (1952)
6. Chan, Y., Tien, C.: A numerical study of two-dimensional natural convection in square open cavities. Numer. Heat Transfer **8**(1), 65–80 (1985)
7. Chandra, P., Das, R.: Finite-element-based machine-learning algorithm for studying gyrotactic-nanofluid flow via stretching surface. Int. J. Numer. Meth. Fluids **95**(12), 1888–1912 (2023)
8. Chow, T.W., Cho, S.Y.: Neural Networks and Computing: Learning Algorithms and Applications, vol. 7, Imperial College Press (2007)
9. Fasshauer, G.E.: Meshfree Approximation Methods with MatLab. World Scientific Publications, Singapore (2007)
10. Fasshauer, G.E., McCourt, M.: Kernel-based Approximation Methods using MATLAB. World Scientific Publications, Singapore (2015)
11. Gangawane, K.M.: Effect of angle of applied magnetic field on natural convection in an open ended cavity with partially active walls. Chem. Eng. Res. Des. **127**, 22–34 (2017)
12. Garnett, J.M.: XII. colours in metal glasses and in metallic films. Philos. Trans. Roy. Soc. London. Ser. A, Containing Pap. Math. Phys. Charact. **203**(359-371), 385–420 (1904)
13. Ghalambaz, M., Mehryan, S., Izapanahi, E., Chamkkha, A., Wen, D.: MHD natural convection of Cu-Al2O3 water hybrid nanofluids in a cavity equally divided into two parts by a vertical flexible partition membrane. J. Therm. Anal. Calorim. **138**, 1723–1743 (2019). https://doi.org/10.1007/s10973-019-08258-w
14. Hill, N., Pedley, T.: Bioconvection. Fluid Dyn. Res. **37**(1–2), 1 (2005)
15. Hussain, S., Öztop, H.F., Alsharif, A.M., Ertam, F.: Mixed bioconvection of nanofluid of oxytactic bacteria through a porous cavity with inlet and outlet under periodic magnetic field using artificial intelligence based on lightgbm algorithm. Therm. Sci. Eng. Progress **50**, 102589 (2024)
16. Kefayati, G., Hosseinizadeh, S., Gorji, M., Sajjadi, H.: Lattice Boltzmann simulation of natural convection in an open enclosure subjugated to water/copper nanofluid. Int. J. Therm. Sci. **52**, 91–101 (2012)
17. Khanafer, K., Vafai, K., Lightstone, M.: Buoyancy-driven heat transfer enhancement in a two-dimensional enclosure utilizing nanofluids. Int. J. Heat Mass Transf. **46**(19), 3639–3653 (2003)
18. Kuznetsov, A.V.: The onset of nanofluid bioconvection in a suspension containing both nanoparticles and gyrotactic microorganisms. Int. Commun. Heat Mass Transfer **37**(10), 1421–1425 (2010)
19. Kuznetsov, A.: The onset of thermo-bioconvection in a shallow fluid saturated porous layer heated from below in a suspension of oxytactic microorganisms. Eur. J. Mech.-B/Fluids **25**(2), 223–233 (2006)
20. Kuznetsov, A.: Nanofluid bioconvection: interaction of microorganisms oxytactic upswimming, nanoparticle distribution, and heating/cooling from below. Theoret. Comput. Fluid Dyn. **26**, 291–310 (2012)
21. Li, H.: Gaussian process regression a machine learning approach to derivative pricing. Ph.D. thesis, Thesis of MSc. Imperial College London (2018)
22. MathWorks, Inc.: MATLAB, Version R2025a. The MathWorks Inc., Natick, Massachusetts (2025). https://www.mathworks.com
23. Mohamad, A., El-Ganaoui, M., Bennacer, R.: Lattice Boltzmann simulation of natural convection in an open ended cavity. Int. J. Therm. Sci. **48**(10), 1870–1875 (2009)

24. Polat, O., Bilgen, E.: Laminar natural convection in inclined open shallow cavities. Int. J. Therm. Sci. **41**(4), 360–368 (2002)
25. Prakash, O., Barman, P., Rao, P., Sharma, R.P.: MHD free convection in a partially open wavy porous cavity filled with nanofluid. Numer. Heat Transfer, Part A: Appl. **84**(5), 449–463 (2023)
26. Rostamian, S.H., Biglari, M., Saedodin, S., Esfe, M.H.: An inspection of thermal conductivity of CuO-SWCNTs hybrid nanofluid versus temperature and concentration using experimental data, ANN modeling and new correlation. J. Mol. Liq. **231**, 364–369 (2017)
27. Sarkar, A., Das, K., Kundu, P.K.: On the onset of bioconvection in nanofluid containing gyrotactic microorganisms and nanoparticles saturating a Non-Darcian porous medium. J. Mol. Liq. **223**, 725–733 (2016)
28. Sezai, I., Mohamad, A.: Suppressing free convection from a flat plate with poor conductor ribs. Int. J. Heat Mass Transf. **42**(11), 2041–2051 (1999)
29. Shafiq, A., Çolak, A.B., Sindhu, T.N.: Significance of bioconvective flow of MHD thixotropic nanofluid passing through a vertical surface by machine learning algorithm. Chin. J. Phys. **80**, 427–444 (2022)
30. Vafaei, M., Afrand, M., Sina, N., Kalbasi, R., Sourani, F., Teimouri, H.: Evaluation of thermal conductivity of MGO-MWCNTS/EG hybrid nanofluids based on experimental data by selecting optimal artificial neural networks. Physica E **85**, 90–96 (2017)
31. Vaferi, B., Samimi, F., Pakgohar, E., Mowla, D.: Artificial neural network approach for prediction of thermal behavior of nanofluids flowing through circular tubes. Powder Technol. **267**, 1–10 (2014)

A Generalized AI-Powered Framework for Cross-Domain Technology Readiness Assessment

Marcelo Rea-Guamán(✉), Andrés Almeida-Jara, and Brandon Masacela-Atupaña

Departamento de Ciencias de La Computación, Universidad de las Fuerzas Armadas ESPE, Av. General Rumiñahui, Sangolquí 171103, Ecuador
amrea1@espe.edu.ec

Abstract. Technology Readiness Level (TRL) assessment remains largely domain-specific and subjective, lacking standardized cross-domain methodologies. A systematic literature review of 39 studies reveals that 84.6% of TRL adaptations target single domains, and none combines cross-domain coverage for hardware, software, and AI/ML technologies with standardized binary criteria and automated evaluation. This paper presents a generalized TRL assessment methodology grounded in ISO 16290, NASA, DoD, and EU Horizon standards, employing mandatory/supportive binary criteria and the weakest-link principle across three technology types. The methodology is operationalized through an AI system using DeepSeek-R1 with chain-of-thought reasoning deployed on HPC infrastructure. Empirical validation against independent expert assessments on 17 projects from open academic repositories demonstrates 76.5% exact concordance and 94.1% agreement within ±1 level. Results confirm that LLM-based evaluation can replicate expert judgment while providing transparent, evidence-traced justifications, enabling reproducible and scalable TRL assessment.

Keywords: Technology Readiness Level · cross-domain assessment · binary criteria · Large Language Models · systematic literature review · technology evaluation

1 Introduction

1.1 Background

Technology Readiness Levels (TRLs) were developed in the early 1970s by NASA's Stan Sadin (Sadin et al., 1989), to help quantify the level of development of technology used in space systems on a nine point ordinal scale. This concept was later formalized by Mankins (2009), who provided the nine levels and descriptors still in common use today. In subsequent years, while originally designed to be an engineering metric applicable to the space industry, it has been adopted by numerous organizations outside of the space community. For example, the U.S. Department of Defense made the use of

O. Gervasi et al. (Eds.): ICCSA 2026, LNCS 16768, pp. 476–492, 2027.
https://doi.org/10.1007/978-3-032-30488-9_30

TRL assessments mandatory through statute for all major defense acquisition programs (U.S. Government Accountability Office, 2020), the European Space Agency included the definition of TRL within their Engineering Standards (ISO, 2013), and the European Commission required TRL reporting among Horizon Research Funding Programs (European Commission, 2014). According to Héder (2017) as the concept transitioned from being an engineering tool to a cross-institutional governance tool, each new layer of interpretation progressively reduced the precision of the initial scale.

In addition to this fragmentation, it is also the creation of many domain-specific versions of TRL which are not compatible with one another. Researchers in health care have developed implementation science-based versions of TRL (Salvador-Carulla et al., 2024) while the machine learning community has created an eleven-level version of TRL to accommodate the ideas of "data readiness" and "iterative switchbacks" between maturity levels (Lavin et al., 2022) in software intensive and AI driven systems. Studies on the governance of AI have shown that there are significant differences between the hardware focused logic behind NASA's original TRL scale and how software and AI based technology behave (Martínez-Plumed et al., 2021). Each of the domains in which TRL is used is therefore developing its own evaluation process for assessing TRL independent from each other creating criteria for evaluating TRL that are neither portable nor capable of being compared with those developed by others. Even more importantly, despite these many adaptations, expert panels continue to be relied upon to evaluate TRL and these evaluations are clearly subjectively determined and difficult to replicate as well as resource intensive to accomplish (Olechowski et al., 2020; Tomaschek et al., 2016).

The computational science community feels the impact of these structural limitations the most. Evaluating modern technological tools—such as AI/ML pipelines, software platforms, and data-driven systems—remains complicated because a unified, cross-domain TRL methodology simply does not exist yet. This gap motivates the work presented in this paper.

1.2 Research Gap and Objectives

A systematic review of 39 peer-reviewed studies on TRL methodologies, conducted following PRISMA guidelines, reveals that 84.6% of existing approaches are confined to a single domain and that no prior work simultaneously addresses four characteristics that a general-purpose TRL assessment framework requires: (i) cross-domain coverage spanning hardware, software, and AI/ML technologies with criteria specific to each type; (ii) standardized binary assessment criteria grounded in internationally recognized standards (ISO, NASA, DoD, and GAO); (iii) implementation through a large language model (LLM) capable of generating evidence-traced, reproducible justifications; and (iv) application of the weakest-link principle, whereby the overall TRL of a technology is bounded by the lowest level at which all mandatory criteria are satisfied. The co-occurrence of these four properties in a single system has not been reported in the literature.

This gap gives rise to three research questions. **RQ1:** What are the prevailing patterns and open gaps in the literature on TRL assessment methodologies? **RQ2:** Can a generalized, binary-criteria methodology cover hardware, software, and AI/ML technologies within a unified evaluative framework? **RQ3:** Can a large language model with chain-of-thought reasoning replicate expert TRL assessments with sufficient accuracy to be considered a valid evaluation instrument? The scope is limited to academic and research-stage projects; commercial deployment and defense acquisition contexts are explicitly excluded.

1.3 Contributions

This paper makes four concrete contributions to the literature on technology evaluation and AI-assisted assessment:

C1—Systematic Literature Review: A PRISMA-compliant review of 39 studies that maps the current state of TRL methodology research, quantifies the prevalence of domain-specific adaptations, and identifies the specific combination of properties absent from all existing approaches.

C2—Generalized Assessment Methodology: A unified TRL framework employing mandatory (MUST) and supportive (SHOULD) binary criteria across three technology types—hardware, software, and AI/ML—derived from a synthesis of ISO 16290:2013, NASA, DoD, and GAO standards, and directly informed by the findings of the systematic review.

C3—AI-Powered Evaluation System: An operational implementation of the methodology using DeepSeek-R1 with chain-of-thought reasoning, deployed on high-performance computing infrastructure, which produces structured TRL assignments accompanied by evidence-traced justifications grounded in the text of the evaluated documents.

C4—Empirical Validation: A comparative study of AI-generated TRL assignments against independent expert evaluations on 17 real-world projects, demonstrating 76.5% exact concordance and 94.1% agreement within ± 1 TRL level—establishing the practical viability of automated TRL assessment for research and academic contexts.

The remainder of this paper is organized as follows. Section 2 outlines related work for both TRL progression as well as the use of artificial intelligence to evaluate it. Section 3 explains the methodology used; specifically, the systematic review process; the evaluation framework; and the architectural structure of the AI system. Section 4 reports on empirical study results that integrate the results from the literature search with the validation results. Section 5 addresses implications and limitations of this study. Section 6 summarizes and draws conclusions. The overall research design is illustrated in Fig. 1.

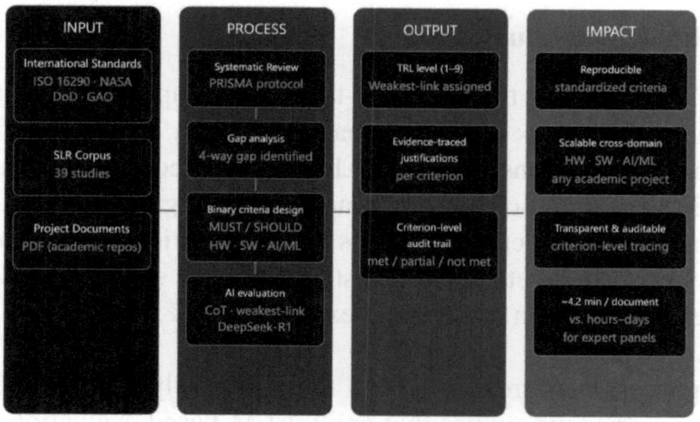

Fig. 1. Research framework overview. International standards and systematic review data are merged into a binary-criteria framework. TRLs are then assigned using an LLM-based chain-of-thought evaluation to ensure all results are traceable

2 Related Work

2.1 TRL Evolution and Standardization

The Technology Readiness Level Scale originated from NASA's early work in the late 1970s. The first official publication was published in 1989 as a seven-step readiness scale to assess space mission systems (Sadin et al., 1989). A later review of the technology scale's progression documented the institutional growth of the scale; specifically, Mankins (2009) described that the U.S. Department of Defense required the use of the TRL assessment process within all major acquisition programs as per statute. This is stated in the Technology Readiness Assessment Guidebook (U.S. Department of Defense, 2025); the European Space Agency incorporated TRL evaluation within their Engineering Standards through ISO 16290:2013 (ISO, 2013) and referenced in the Handbook ECSS-E-HB-11A (European Cooperation for Space Standardization (ECSS), 2017). The European Commission mandated reporting of TRL values under Horizon Research Programs (European Commission, 2014). Héder (2017) detailed this trend systematically demonstrating how each of the institutions' interpretations of the TRL progressively decreased the accuracy of the original NASA definitions.

This evolution highlights a major issue. The scale was designed to evaluate hardware in the aerospace industry, making it difficult to adapt its core concepts to software and modern AI technologies. The GAO-20-48G guide (U.S. Government Accountability Office, 2020), developed with over 180 experts, addresses assessment consistency across technology types but stops short of defining software- or AI-native criteria. The DoD TRA Guidebook 2025 (U.S. Department of Defense, 2025) introduced a dedicated software TRL scale, but cross-domain unification remains open. The intermediate transition zone between TRL 4 and TRL 7—the "Valley of Death"—is widely recognized as the stage where most development efforts stall due to exponential cost increases and academic-industrial misalignment (Sepúlveda et al., 2025; White et al., 2022; Clawson, 2023), and complementary readiness scales (MRL, CRL, RRL, DRL) have been proposed to address multidimensional challenges that TRL alone cannot capture (Kobos et al., 2018; H.-Y. Liu et al., 2020).

2.2 AI for Technology Evaluation

Wei et al. (2023) established that chain-of-thought prompting significantly improves LLM performance on complex multi-step reasoning tasks. Y. Liu et al. (2023), through the G-Eval framework, demonstrated that LLMs prompted with structured evaluation steps achieve higher correlation with human expert judgments than any prior automated metric—a pattern directly analogous to the criterion-by-criterion architecture of the present system. Zheng et al. (2023) established that strong LLMs used as judges achieve agreement with human preferences exceeding 80%, comparable to inter-human agreement rates.

Although significant progress has been made in applying LLMs to tasks of this nature; there are no previous studies that apply LLM-based evaluation to TRL assessments. This represents a significant void: TRL assessment represents a type of rubric-based judgment task (the same type on which architectures with LLM-as-evaluator have demonstrated their greatest success) using technical project documentation for which all of the supporting evidence must be identified, abstracted, and related to pre-defined criteria.

3 Methodology

3.1 Research Design

This research is based on a sequential mixed-methods approach with four connected stages. Phase one is a systematic literature review. It will establish the current state of research related to TRL methodologies so as to provide evidence for what combinations of attributes are missing from available methodologies. Phase two is the methodology development stage. In this phase we derive binary decision rules (i.e., pass/fail) for each type of technology (hardware, software, and artificial intelligence/machine learning technologies) using an integration of relevant international standards and consistent results from the systematic literature review; thereby making use of the systematic literature review's findings to determine methodology design, but not merely to motivate it. Phase three provides empirical realization of the methodology by means of developing an LLM-based evaluation system. Finally, Phase Four is used to validate the evaluation system using comparative assessments to independently assessed evaluations by experts.

The calibration process was done to ensure that phases three and four were connected by an iterative calibration loop before the final validation. The iterative calibration loop allowed for evaluation of the system using a defined set of cases that had already been assigned to a TRL (Technology Readiness Level) prior to the formal validation. The iterative calibration loop was used to refine the systems logic used to interpret evidence from each case until such time as consistent, criterion aligned behavior was demonstrated by the system.

3.2 Systematic Literature Review

The study followed the PRISMA 2020 Guidelines (Page et al., 2021) for conducting the systematic review. A total of five academic database searches were completed; namely,

ACM Digital Library, IEEE Xplore, Web of Science, Science Direct and Scopus. Only articles published from 2015 through 2025 were considered for the final screening. The common search string *("Technology Readiness Level" OR "TRL") AND ("adaptation" OR "customization" OR "modified") AND ("framework" OR "methodology" OR "guidelines" OR "model")*, was used on all databases using a uniform search strategy and restricting the search to the title field, abstract field and keyword field. Restricting the search to title field, abstract field and keyword field—as opposed to searching full text of articles—was a intentional methodological decision to maximize precision and eliminate retrieval of non-relevant documents that only incidently mention TRL.

Eligibility Criteria. To be included, the study must have been a complete, peer reviewed study using TRL methodology. In addition, we only considered studies published in the time frame of 2015–2025 as long as it contained TRL in the title, abstract, and/or keyword list. Articles that did not contain methodologically rigorous data, did not include a readiness framework related to TRL, were unverifiable grey literature, or duplicate data were all excluded.

Selection Process. Initially, our search produced 3,374 documents across five different databases. Upon conducting a title/abstract screen, we narrowed down to 294 potential candidates. Finally, after conducting a full-text review, we selected 39 total studies for inclusion. A detailed description of our selection process can be viewed in Fig. 2.

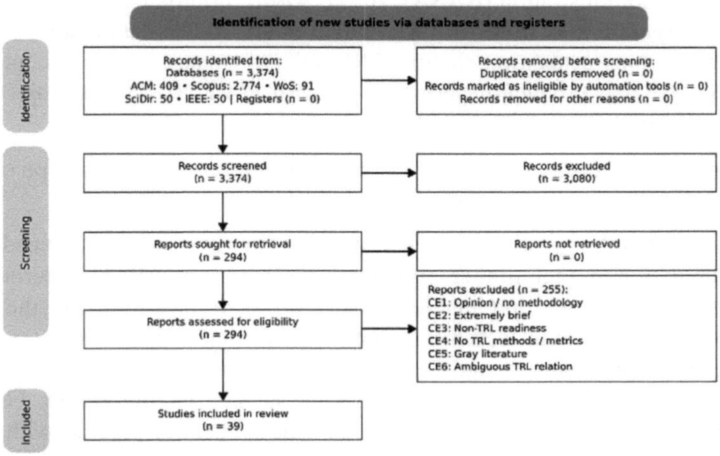

Fig. 2. PRISMA 2020 flow diagram of the systematic literature review.

3.3 TRL Assessment Framework

The assessment framework presented in this paper synthesizes criteria from four internationally recognized standards—ISO 16290:2013 (ISO, 2013), the NASA TRL Definitions (National Aeronautics and Space Administration (NASA), 2017), the DoD Technology Readiness Assessment Guidebook (U.S. Department of Defense, 2025), and the GAO Technology Readiness Assessment Guide (U.S. Government Accountability Office, 2020)—informed by the convergent findings of the systematic review described in Sect. 3.2. The framework abandons point-based or weighted scoring in favor of binary criterion evaluation, a design decision grounded in both ISO 16290:2013—which defines conditions that must be satisfied at each level for a precise TRL assessment, not scores to accumulate—and GAO-20-48G, which was developed with over 180 experts across seven years and employs criterion-based evaluation exclusively.

Binary Criteria Structure. Each TRL level is defined by mandatory criteria (MUST), which must all be satisfied to validate the level, and supportive criteria (SHOULD), which reinforce the evaluation but do not block validation. Each criterion is assessed as satisfied, partially satisfied with justification, or not met. A level is validated when all MUST criteria are satisfied or partially satisfied.

Weakest-Link Principle. The overall TRL is the highest level for which all MUST criteria are satisfied. If any mandatory criterion is unmet at level k, the project is assigned level $k - 1$ regardless of evidence at higher levels, consistent with the NASA TRL Worksheet, AFRL TRL Calculator, and ISO 16290 (Clawson, 2023; Bruno et al., 2020).

Cross-Domain Coverage. Technology-type-specific criteria are defined for hardware, software, and AI/ML. Hardware criteria follow NASA and ISO 16290 directly. Software criteria translate each hardware concept to its computational equivalent per the DoD TRA Guidebook (U.S. Department of Defense, 2025) and NASA (National Aeronautics and Space Administration (NASA), 2017). AI/ML criteria extend the software set with mandatory additions from MLTRL (Lavin et al., 2022): data readiness, pipeline reproducibility, bias evaluation (before TRL 7), switchback provisions, model card (before TRL 6), and production monitoring (before TRL 8). Mixed projects receive dual evaluation with TRL defined as the minimum.

The present framework defines criteria natively appropriate to each type rather than adapting hardware criteria post hoc.

Illustrative Example: To illustrate the cross-domain differentiation, consider TRL 5 (system integration in a relevant environment). For hardware, MUST criteria require a complete system integrated and functional under lab conditions simulating the real environment, with full functional tests measuring key performance parameters. For software, the equivalent requires an integrated system tested with representative data and realistic load, with end-to-end performance metrics such as latency and throughput. For AI/ML, the criteria require a trained model integrated into the application pipeline with representative data, evaluated on a held-out validation set with documented metrics (accuracy, F1, AUC). SHOULD criteria at this level include technical documentation and limitation analysis, each adapted to the technology type. The complete criteria tables for TRL 1 through TRL 9 across all three technology types are available as supplementary material (Rea Guamán et al., 2026).

3.4 AI System Implementation

The assessment methodology described in Sect. 3.3 is operationalized through a two-component software system: a Python backend built on FastAPI that handles document ingestion, criterion evaluation, and TRL assignment, and a React/TypeScript frontend that presents the evaluation workflow and results to the user. The evaluation engine interfaces with DeepSeek-R1 (32B parameters) served locally via Ollama, accessed through a REST API. Computational execution runs on high-performance computing infrastructure provided by CEDIA (Ecuador) with NVIDIA A100 GPU capacity, which supplies the GPU capacity necessary for local model inference—infrastructure that functions as an operational enabler rather than a methodological contribution.

Chain-of-thought Evaluation Pipeline. Rather than requesting a direct level assignment, the system decomposes evaluation into sequential steps: for each criterion at each candidate TRL level, the model (i) identifies specific passages constituting potential evidence, (ii) assesses whether the evidence satisfies the criterion, (iii) assigns a state (satisfied, partially satisfied, or not met), and (iv) produces a natural-language justification tracing the state to extracted textual evidence. Because of this, each assignment includes a clear and traceable explanation. This specific feature sets the approach apart from traditional scoring or regression models (Rodríguez-López et al., 2023). The weakest-link determination is performed programmatically: the system iterates from TRL 1 upward and assigns the highest level where all MUST criteria are satisfied or partially satisfied.

Technology Type Detection. The system classifies projects by analyzing domain-specific keywords in the submitted documentation, assigning one of three criterion sets: hardware, software/digital, or AI/ML. Mixed projects receive dual evaluation with the system TRL defined as the minimum of the component assessments.

Calibration Procedure. Before formal validation, the system was calibrated against a set of projects with previously established TRL assignments. Calibration focused on two aspects of the evaluation logic: the evidence extraction threshold (the minimum textual grounding required for a criterion to be considered satisfied rather than partially satisfied) and the handling of implicit evidence (cases where a document demonstrates criterion satisfaction without explicitly stating it). Calibration continued iteratively until the system produced consistent, criterion-aligned behavior across the calibration set. The calibration cases are excluded from the validation sample reported in Sect. 4.

Figure 3 details the complete system architecture. This diagram outlines the document ingestion pipeline, the structure of the evaluation prompts, and the format of the final output reports.

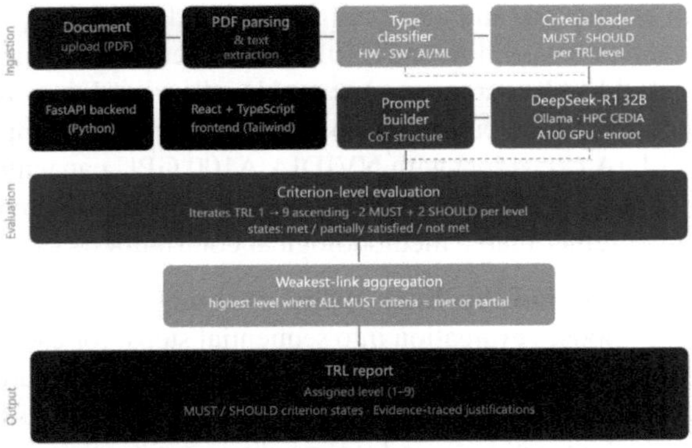

Fig. 3. TRL evaluation pipeline: document ingestion, chain-of-thought criterion evaluation, and weakest-link assignment.

4 Results

4.1 Systematic Review Findings

The 39 reviewed studies reveal a landscape dominated by domain-specific adaptations: 33 (84.6%) address TRL within a single domain, 6 (15.4%) attempt cross-domain generalization, and 5 (12.8%) incorporate an automated assessment component. Figure 4 presents the distribution by category.

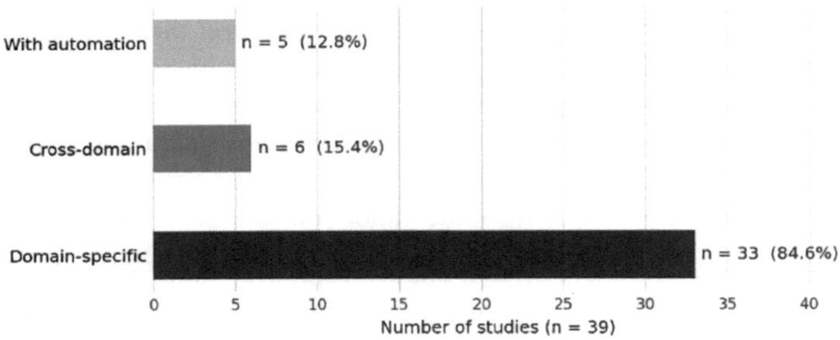

Fig. 4. Distribution of the 39 reviewed studies by domain and assessment approach category.

The 39 included studies span eight application domains: energy and ecological transition, cross-cutting policy and education, manufacturing and logistics, health sciences, environment and agriculture, aerospace, software and IoT, and chemistry and materials (Rea Guamán et al., 2026). This distribution confirms the substantial expansion of TRL beyond its aerospace origins, with energy and environmental technologies as the most active area of methodological development.

Four convergent limitations recur across the corpus and directly informed the methodology design. First, the literature identifies a persistent lack of multidimensionality: TRL evaluates technology in isolation without accounting for commercial, regulatory, or social readiness (Kobos et al., 2018; H.-Y. Liu et al., 2020; Bruno et al., 2020;

Sepúlveda et al., 2025). Second, the corpus converges on high subjectivity and limited reproducibility of expert-panel assessments; multiple authors characterize TRL evaluation without standardized checklists as potentially arbitrary (Rodríguez-López et al., 2023; White et al., 2022; Lacueva-Pérez et al., 2018; Bukar & Asif, 2024; Salvador-Carulla et al., 2024)—motivating the binary MUST/SHOULD criteria. Third, multiple studies demonstrate that technology development is iterative rather than linear, particularly for software and AI/ML (Clawson, 2023; Bruno et al., 2020; White et al., 2022). Fourth, the corpus documents difficulty assigning TRL to complex systems with subsystems at different maturity stages—addressed here through the weakest-link principle (ISO, 2013; U.S. Government Accountability Office, 2020).

Table 1 presents the five studies with automated assessment systems alongside the present work. Kobos et al. (2018) achieve cross-domain coverage through System Dynamics but produce no auditable justification. (Rodríguez-López et al., 2023) share the document-analysis intent but use regression without criterion decomposition. White et al. (2022) implement binary yes/no criteria—the closest precedent to MUST/SHOULD—but are confined to agricultural biosecurity. No prior work simultaneously achieves cross-domain coverage, binary criteria, LLM-based evaluation, and the weakest-link principle.

Table 1. Comparison of automated TRL assessment approaches identified in the systematic review.

Author(s)	Domain	Method	Cross-d	Binary	LLM
Zhong & Yang (2025)	Education	Quant. Algorithm	No	No	No
White et al. (2022)	Agri. Biosecurity	Excel calculator + binary criteria	No	Yes	No
Kobos et al. (2018)	Cross-domain	System Dynamics	Yes	No	No
Lacueva-Pérez et al. (2018)	HCI/manuf	Automated questionnaires (ESA/NASA adapted)	No	Partial	No
Rodríguez López et al. (2023)	SMEs	Text mining + regression	Yes	No	No
This work	**HW + SW + AI/ML**	**LLM + chain-of-thought**	**Yes**	**Yes**	**Yes**

4.2 Framework Design Outcomes

The methodology yields 54 mandatory and 54 supportive criteria (two MUST and two SHOULD per level per type). Technology type detection correctly identified the type in 14 of 17 validation cases (82.4%). Three documents were classified as research-type projects lacking a deployable artifact—an emergent finding, as this category falls outside the defined scope. Notably, all three achieved exact concordance with the expert assessment, suggesting that criteria at lower TRL levels generalize naturally to investigative academic work.

4.3 System Performance

The validation of the AI evaluation system occurred with an assortment of documents (a total of 17) gathered from public university repository sites in Ecuador, consisting of three types of documents; 1.) nine software development documents, 2.) Three Hardware Development Documents, 3.) two Artificial Intelligence/Machine Learning (AI/ML) Documents, and 4.) three Research Document Types.

The processing time for reviews of a project's technical readiness level (TRL) increased as the TRL increased; specifically, the processing time was greater for evaluations that reached higher levels of TRL. For example, TRL 1–2 evaluations took 126–175 s, but those TRL 6–7 evaluations took 306–437 s. Overall, the average amount of time spent on each document during the evaluation process was about four-and-one-half minutes. This time frame is significantly less than what it takes an expert panel to complete. In fact, Olechowski et al. (2020) found that expert panels often require hours to days to evaluate research projects.

4.4 Validation Against Expert Assessment

Expert TRL assignments were obtained independently for all 17 documents by a domain expert in technology readiness assessment, applying the same binary-criteria methodology used by the system prior to comparison with system outputs. Table 2 presents the complete case-by-case comparison.

Table 2. Validation results: AI system vs. expert assessment across 17 documents.

#	Document	Type	System TRL	Expert TRL	Δ	MUST state
1	P-01	SW	2	2	0	met, met
2	P-02	SW	4	3	+1	partial, partial
3	P-03	SW	6	5	+1	partial, partial
4	P-04	SW	4	4	0	met, met
5	P-05	AI/ML	6	5	+1	partial, partial
6	P-06	SW	2	2	0	met, met
7	P-07	HW	7	7	0	met, met
8	P-08	SW	2	2	0	met, met
9	P-09	Research	2	2	0	met, met
10	P-10	AI/ML	1	1	0	met, met
11	P-11	Research	1	1	0	met, met

(*continued*)

Table 2. (*continued*)

#	Document	Type	System TRL	Expert TRL	Δ	MUST state
12	P-12	Research	4	4	0	met, met
13	P-13	SW	6	6	0	met, met
14	P-14	SW	1	1	0	met, met
15	P-15	SW	5	5	0	met, met
16	P-16	HW	2	2	0	met, met
17	P-17	HW	6	4	+2	met, met

The system achieved exact concordance in 13 of 17 cases (76.5%) and agreement within ±1 TRL level in 16 of 17 cases (94.1%). One case exhibited discordance greater than one level (5.9%), corresponding to a +2 overestimation in a hardware project. These results confirm the primary hypothesis of RQ3: a large language model with chain-of-thought reasoning can replicate expert TRL assessments with sufficient accuracy for academic and research evaluation contexts.

Analysis of the four cases which have been identified as discordant provides insight into two distinct types of failure modes. A primary failure mode found in three of the four discordant cases (#2, #3, #5) is ambiguity regarding the evidence density of the system. In these cases, the system provided a partial state of the disputed level for both of the MUST criteria. Thus, although the system recognizes some relevance of the textual evidence toward satisfying the MUST criteria, it does not recognize enough to fully satisfy them. When the expert evaluator uses his/her domain knowledge to evaluate the same criteria, he/she will judge that the evidence fails to meet the required level threshold. Consequently, this results in a consistent +1 over estimation based on the expert's evaluation when there are sparse amounts of criterion-based evidence, or the criterion-based evidence is distributed throughout the document.

A secondary failure mode has also been identified within one of the discordant cases (#17 HW, $\Delta = +2$). The failure mode identified in this case is environmental equivalence misclassification. Both of the MUST criteria at TRL 6 were evaluated as being met; however, the expert evaluator assigned a TRL value of 4. This indicates that while the system accepts testing in a controlled university environment as being equivalent to field testing in an actual operational environment (a distinction which requires domain specific knowledge beyond what can be recovered through textual analysis), it appears that the system failed to make this distinction. The failure type observed in case #17 (HW, $\Delta = +2$) is potentially more detrimental than the other failure type since it produces greater discordance and is not indicated by partial MUST states thereby providing less indication of such failures from output produced by the system (Fig. 5).

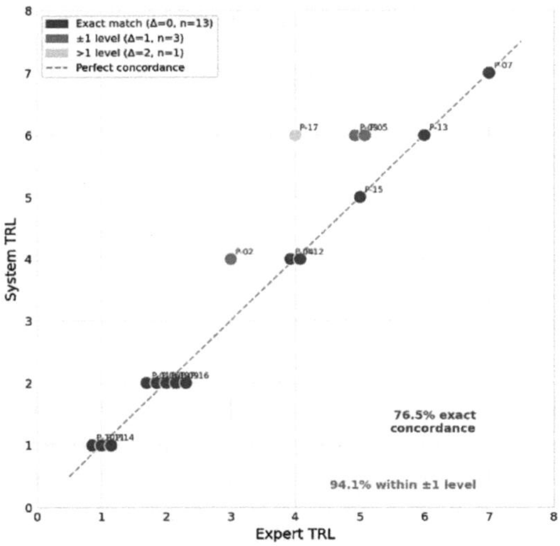

Fig. 5. Comparison between AI-generated and expert TRL assignments for the 17 validation cases. The dashed line represents exact agreement, while the colors show the degree of variation between the scores.

5 Discussion

5.1 Interpretation of Results

The empirical evidence provided in Sect. 4 provides a practical answer to each of the 3 research questions which guided this study.

RQ1 investigated "What patterns or gaps remain to be explored regarding the current state-of-the-art of TRL assessment methodologies?". A comprehensive analysis of 39 papers demonstrates that nearly all (84.6%) reviewed papers have been written about TRL for one particular area of application. No prior study has addressed cross-domains, applied binary assessment methods grounded in two international standards, used LLMs for assessing TRL, and employed the weakest link assignment method. The convergence of these limitations from the entire body of literature identified subjectivity inherent to expert panel assessments, assuming TRL is linear, difficulties with evaluating highly-complex systems and lack of multidimensional assessment as major deficiencies defining the design space for the developed methodology. More importantly, the review outcomes motivated and directly affected certain design decisions in developing the proposed methodology (as described in Sect. 3.3). The use of a binary system for categorizing MUST/SHOULD responses was designed to mitigate the problems of subjectivity documented by Rodríguez-López et al. (2023); White et al. (2022); and Bukar & Asif (2024). The use of the weakest-link principle was devised to address the challenges associated with complex systems as outlined by Clawson (2023) and Bruno et al. (2020). Finally, technology-type specific criteria were included to address issues related to the hardware centric nature of TRL assessment as described by Lavin et al. (2022); and Martínez-Plumed et al. (2021).

Validation provides evidence in support of RQ2. All three technologies were verified with either an exact or ±1 match across all three (hardware at TRL 7 demonstrate application to physical systems, software cases confirmed coverage from TRL 1 through TRL 6, and the AI/ML cases confirm that MLTRL criteria derived are easily integrated). The fourth category of "research type" is a partially covered boundary condition. Research type documents represent the potential for natural expansion of the current iteration and expand the current framework for use on all forms of scholarly output, including systematic reviews, theoretical frameworks/models, and empirical studies, excluding those artifacts related to technological development.

RQ3 receives an affirmative answer: 76.5% exact concordance and 94.1% ±1 agreement supports the viability of LLM-based TRL evaluation for academic contexts. The ambiguous evidence density failure mode is predictable and detectable through partial MUST states—a conservative post-processing rule could reduce overestimation at the cost of false negatives. The environmental equivalence misclassification mode is more consequential, requiring domain-specific context classifiers or mandatory human review of hardware cases at TRL 5+.

This system is the only automated TRL approach simultaneously achieving cross-domain coverage, binary criteria, LLM-based evaluation with evidence-traced justifications, and the weakest-link principle (Table 2). Kobos et al. (2018) achieve cross-domain coverage but require expert-parameterized simulation and produce no auditable justification. Rodríguez-López et al. (2023) share the document-analysis intent but produce statistical estimates where discordant results cannot be diagnosed at the criterion level.

Although this 76.5% concordance is as good or better than agreement between people: Olechowski et al. (2020) have documented how often experts don't agree on assigning TRLs to projects; Salvador-Carulla et al. (2024) reported an ICC of .9 for 10 evaluators and thus needed structured evaluation. This tool generates equivalent quality results through unstructured documents in about 4.2 min/document. Thus, it has improved on other methods in terms of quality and scale.

5.2 Limitations and Threats to Validity

Several limitations bound the interpretation of these results and define the agenda for future work.

Sample Size and Distribution. The validation sample consists of 17 papers that are heavily biased towards the project area for software (9/17 = 52.9%), so future validations would be improved if they employed balanced samples of at least 15 cases per technology area to enable an evaluation of the concordance within each category.

Single Expert Evaluator. One single domain expert was assigned to provide the expert judgments. To provide more confidence in the results of this study, we recommend that future research uses several independent experts, reporting on inter-rater reliabilities, e.g. Cohen's Kappa or ICC values.

Environmental Equivalence Classification. In case #17, the >1 disagreement indicates that the system cannot accurately differentiate between controlled academic test environments and real-world deployment scenarios based on the text description of the environment. These limitations are most impactful to hardware projects with a Technology Readiness Level (TRL) of 5 or higher as it is the determination of the appropriate environment which will determine the technology readiness level. Strategies to mitigate these limitations may be achieved through the use of domain specific contextual classifiers; by using structured template forms that require an explicit description of the environment and/or have mandatory flags for human review of all hardware projects in the intermediate to high range.

LLM Sampling Variability. Although low temperature sampling was used (T = 0.1) there is still a document that has had two separate TRL assignment in an independent run. The fact that it could be done indicates that this program can't be determined to have the same output for documents containing limited or ambiguous foundation proof. Using an ensemble voting method using many independent runs would greatly minimize this variability at the expense of increasing the processing time.

Scope Boundary: Research-Type Documents. Our current methodology focuses specifically on three technology types, intentionally excluding theoretical research documents that lack deployable artifacts. To make this tool useful for all academic outputs, future versions of the framework will need to include specific criteria for these types of papers.

6 Conclusions

This research presents an extended AI-based technology readiness level assessment tool which addresses a previously identified gap from a systematic review of 39 studies. The gap was identified as there are no existing methods or tools to assess technology readiness levels across all three domains (hardware, software, and AI/ML), use multi-standard binary assessment criteria, evaluate technology readiness levels utilizing large language models with chain-of-thought reasoning, and apply the weakest link principle.

The PRISMA-compliant review (C1) has mapped the relevant area of research and established this four-way gap through converging limitations in all areas of the overall study which have been utilized for determining the methodology design.

The generalized methodology (C2), uses binary MUST/SHOULD criteria at nine levels and three different technology types, derived from the ISO 16290 standard, NASA, Department of Defense (DoD), and Government Accountability Office (GAO) standards to provide an explicit means to assign the weakest link based on the formal logic of assignment.

The AI-based evaluation system (C3), utilizes the methodology to evaluate by utilizing DeepSeek-R1 with chain-of-thought reasoning and produces traceable evidence-based explanations of how each criterion is justified such that every decision regarding each criterion can be audited—distinctly separating it from other methods of scoring and regression analysis.

Empirical validation (C4) was conducted on 17 projects and showed that there were 76.5% exact agreements and 94.1% ±1 agreements. There are two failure modes; ambiguous evidence density (detectable when evaluating partial MUST states) and environmental equivalence misclassifications (domain specific classifiers are required).

Mean processing time of approximately 4.2 min per document indicates a significant decrease compared to the expert panels requiring hours or days to complete their respective processes.

Several key upgrades are planned for the next phase of this research. To improve the evaluation process, we will use balanced samples, formalize criteria for theoretical papers, and introduce multiple human reviewers to track reliability metrics. Additionally, upgrading the system with majority-voting evaluation and retrieval-augmented generation will make locating evidence much more precise.

Disclosure of Interests. The authors have no competing interests to declare that are relevant to the content of this article.

References

Bruno, I., et al.: Technology readiness revisited: a proposal for extending the scope of impact assessment of European public services, 369–380 (2020). https://doi.org/10.1145/3428502.3428552

Bukar, A.M., Asif, M.: Technology readiness level assessment of carbon capture and storage technologies. Renew. Sustain. Energy Rev. **200** (2024). https://doi.org/10.1016/j.rser.2024.114578

Clawson, G.: A technology readiness level for blockchain, 249–257 (2023). https://doi.org/10.1145/3555776.3577704

European Commission. Technology readiness levels (TRL), Annex G of the General Annexes. In: Horizon 2020 Work Programme 2014–2015, Extract from Part 19—Commission Decision C(2014)4995. European Commission (2014)

European Cooperation for Space Standardization (ECSS). ECSS-E-HB-11A – Technology readiness level (TRL) guidelines. ECSS Executive Secretariat (2017)

Héder, M.: From NASA to EU: the evolution of the TRL scale in public sector innovation. Innov. J. **22**, 1 (2017)

ISO. ISO 16290:2013—Space systems—Definition of the Technology Readiness Levels (TRLs) and their criteria of assessment. International Organization for Standardization. ISO (2013). https://www.iso.org/standard/56064.html

Kobos, P.H., Malczynski, L.A., Walker, L.T.N., Borns, D.J., Klise, G.T.: Timing is everything: a technology transition framework for regulatory and market readiness levels. Technol. Forecast. Soc. Chang. **137**, 211–225 (2018). https://doi.org/10.1016/j.techfore.2018.07.052

Lacueva-Pérez, F.J., et al.: Assessing TRL of HCI technologies supporting shop floor workers, 311–318 (2018). https://doi.org/10.1145/3197768.3203175

Lavin, A., et al.: Technology readiness levels for machine learning systems. Nat. Commun. **13**(1), 6039 (2022). https://doi.org/10.1038/s41467-022-33128-9

Liu, H.-Y., Subramanian, A.M., Hang, C.-C.: Marrying the best of both worlds: an integrated framework for matching technology transfer sources and recipients. IEEE Trans. Eng. Manage. **67**(1), 70–80 (2020). https://doi.org/10.1109/TEM.2018.2858812

Liu, Y., Iter, D., Xu, Y., Wang, S., Xu, R., Zhu, C.: G-Eval: NLG evaluation using Gpt-4 with better human alignment. In: Proceedings of the 2023 Conference on Empirical Methods in Natural Language Processing, pp. 2511–2522 (2023). https://doi.org/10.18653/v1/2023.emnlp-main.153

Mankins, J.C.: Technology readiness assessments: a retrospective. Acta Astronaut. **65**(9–10), 1216–1223 (2009). https://doi.org/10.1016/j.actaastro.2009.03.058

Martínez-Plumed, F., Gómez, E., Hernández-Orallo, J.: Futures of artificial intelligence through technology readiness levels. Telematics Inform. **58**, 101525 (2021). https://doi.org/10.1016/j.tele.2020.101525

National Aeronautics and Space Administration (NASA). NASA Systems Engineering Handbook, Revision 2 (NASA/SP-2016–6105 Rev 2.). NASA Headquarters (2017)

Olechowski, A.L., Eppinger, S.D., Joglekar, N., Tomaschek, K.: Technology readiness levels: shortcomings and improvement opportunities. Syst. Eng. **23**(4), 395–408 (2020). https://doi.org/10.1002/sys.21533

Page, M.J., et al.: The PRISMA 2020 statement: an updated guideline for reporting systematic reviews. BMJ, n71 (2021). https://doi.org/10.1136/bmj.n71

Rea Guamán, A.M., Almeida Jara, A.S., Masacela-Atupaña, B.: Supplementary material: complete TRL assessment criteria tables and systematic review corpus — for: a generalized AI-powered framework for cross-domain technology readiness assessment. Zenodo (2026). https://doi.org/10.5281/ZENODO.19121085

Rodríguez-López, N., Álvarez-Cabal, J.V., Cuiñas, M.C., Ortega Fernndez, F.: Applicability of technology maturity level evaluation methodologies within small- and medium-sized organizations: prospects and proposals. Systems **11**(8) (2023). https://doi.org/10.3390/systems11080387

Sadin, S.R., Povinelli, F.P., Rosen, R.: The NASA technology push towards future space mission systems. Acta Astronaut. **20**, 73–77 (1989). https://doi.org/10.1016/0094-5765(89)90054-4

Salvador-Carulla, L.B., Woods, C.E., de Miquel, C., Lukersmith, S.: Adaptation of the technology readiness levels for impact assessment in implementation sciences: the TRL-IS checklist. Heliyon **10**(9) (2024). https://doi.org/10.1016/j.heliyon.2024.e29930

Sepúlveda, J., Albis-Arrieta, A.R., Santamaría, J., Cervera, S.: University-industry-government integration in the development of sustainable and cost-efficient solutions for the shrimp sector in Colombia: Nutriaqua case. J. Sustain. Dev. Energy, Water Environ. Syst. **13**(2) (2025). https://doi.org/10.13044/j.sdewes.d13.0557

Tomaschek, K., Olechowski, A., Eppinger, S., Joglekar, N.: A survey of technology readiness level users. INCOSE Int. Symp. **26**(1), 2101–2117 (2016). https://doi.org/10.1002/j.2334-5837.2016.00283.x

U.S. Department of Defense. Technology Readiness Assessment Guidebook. Office of the Under Secretary of Defense for Research and Engineering (2025). https://www.cto.mil/wp-content/uploads/2025/03/TRA-Guide-Feb2025.v2-Cleared.pdf

U.S. Government Accountability Office. Technology Readiness Assessment Guide: Best Practices for Evaluating the Readiness of Technology for Use in Acquisition Programs and Projects. https://www.gao.gov/products/gao-20-48g. Accessed 7 Jan 2020

Wei, J., et al.: Chain-of-thought prompting elicits reasoning in large language models. arXiv: (arXiv:2201.11903) (2023)

White, R.M., et al.: Technology development for the early detection of plant pests: a framework for assessing technology readiness levels (TRLs) in environmental science. J. Plant Dis. Prot. **129**(5), 1249–1261 (2022). https://doi.org/10.1007/s41348-022-00599-3

Zheng, L., et al.: Judging LLM-as-a-Judge with MT-Bench and Chatbot Arena. arXiv: (arXiv: 2306.05685) (2023)

A Compact QSAR Model for BRAF Inhibitors Based on Gaussian Process Regression

Elisa Y. Toma and Marcos G. Quiles(✉)

Institute of Science and Technology, Federal University of São Paulo, Av. Cesare Lattes, 1201, 12247-014 São José dos Campos, SP, Brazil
quiles@unifesp.br

Abstract. The dysregulated activation of the B-Raf proto-oncogene serine/threonine-protein kinase (BRAF) kinase acts as a primary driver in melanoma and several other malignancies. As a result, there is an ongoing need for computational approaches capable of precisely evaluating the inhibitory potency, typically expressed as the negative logarithm of the half-maximal inhibitory concentration(pIC50) of prospective drug candidates. Recently, the field has observed a trend of stacking-based ensemble methods for predicting this activity. Although these stack-based approaches deliver predictions with high accuracy, such performance comes with inherent drawbacks. Specifically, their highly complex architectures increase computational expenses and obscure model interpretability. Here, to address these drawbacks, we propose an uncertainty-aware Gaussian Process Regression (GPR) framework that rivals the predictive power of complex ensembles without the structural overhead. To construct a more comprehensive feature space, we integrate two distinct types of molecular data. Particularly, the model combines a minimally redundant set of physicochemical descriptors with latent molecular embeddings extracted from Simplified Molecular Input Line Entry System (SMILES) strings. Computer evaluation, spanning cross-validation, external testing, robustness checks, and a paired Wilcoxon signed-rank test, confirms that the proposed GPR model achieves an external predictive accuracy on par with stacking techniques. Beyond its compact design, the model also yields well-calibrated predictive uncertainties, which provide a rigorous, transparent mechanism to delimit the applicability domain concerning its predictions. Our findings suggest that advancing the state of the art in quantitative structure–activity relationship (QSAR) modeling does not, inherently, require complex architectures. As shown, a simpler probabilistic model can achieve competitive accuracy while providing superior transparency.

1 Introduction

Several cellular events, such as growth, survival, and proliferation, are regulated by the mitogen-activated protein kinase (MAPK) cascade. Mutations within

O. Gervasi et al. (Eds.): ICCSA 2026, LNCS 16768, pp. 493–510, 2027.
https://doi.org/10.1007/978-3-032-30488-9_31

the BRAF (B-Raf proto-oncogene serine/threonine-protein kinase) frequently disrupt this network and might trigger persistent downstream signaling and sustained proliferative stimuli that ultimately contribute to tumorigenesis.

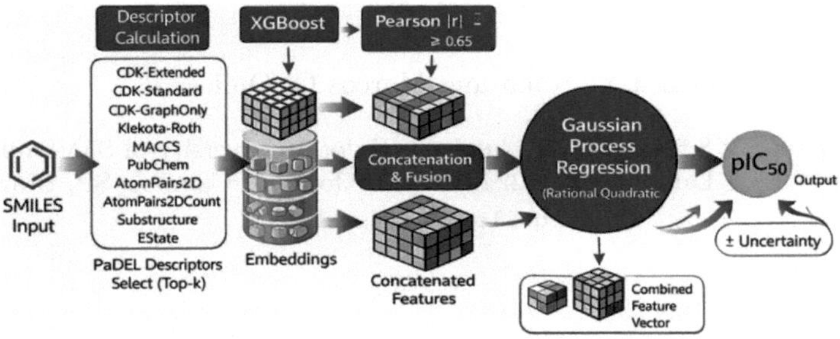

Fig. 1. Architecture of the proposed Gaussian Process Regression model.

Activating BRAF mutations present an overall frequency of approximately 7% across all human cancers. Among distinct cancers, melanoma exhibits the highest incidence of this genetic profile (40%), followed by colorectal adenocarcinoma (15%), glioblastoma (8%), and non-small cell lung cancer (4%). Given this pathogenic impact, researchers have searched for therapeutic interventions targeting BRAF and its downstream MAPK effectors. To date, these targeted approaches have yielded substantial clinical benefits in managing multiple BRAF-mediated tumors [4,15].

Predicting the half-maximal inhibitory concentration (pIC50) is therefore a critical objective in the discovery of novel BRAF inhibitors. To predict pIC50 values against BRAF, recent computational efforts have frequently relied on stacking-based ensemble models. This approach combines multiple base models trained on several molecular fingerprints. Some examples include StackBRAF and BRAFPred, both of which utilize complex ensemble architectures to integrate the predictive signals of heterogeneous algorithms [18,25].

StackBRAF [18], for instance, trains multiple base learners independently, including Support Vector Regression (SVR), Random Forest (RF), Extreme Gradient Boosting (XGBoost), and Multilayer Perceptron (MLP) neural networks on classical molecular fingerprints. The outputs of these models feed a secondary meta-model for final aggregation. Despite their efficacy, these frameworks impose severe architectural complexity. They force the predictive system to rely on indirect, model-level feature aggregation. Pooling multiple learners certainly allows architectures like StackBRAF [18] to reduce prediction variance. However, such performance improvements arise from synthesizing correlated models within a static descriptor space, which seldom yield novel chemical insights.

In contrast, our approach hypothesizes that high structural complexity is not necessary for robust predictions in this domain. Instead, we argue that predictive accuracy is primarily constrained by the depth of the underlying data rather than by the sophistication of the ensemble technique. Following the principle of parsimony, if a simpler, more mathematically transparent formulation can match the accuracy of a stacked ensemble, it should be heavily preferred [16].

Here, we prioritize the enrichment of the input space itself. This strategy allows for the direct mapping of structure–activity relationships within a broader, more robust representation. We begin by calculating physicochemical descriptors with Pharmaceutical Data Exploration Laboratory (PaDEL) [24]. An XGBoost algorithm then evaluates and isolates the most informative features. To resolve the observed collinearity, we subject this selected subset of features to a Pearson correlation filter. Next, we merge the final set of features with the latent molecular embeddings generated from SMILES strings [22]. This synthesis of symbolic and learned representations ultimately underpins our unified Gaussian Process Regression (GPR) model. The proposed GPR framework is depicted in Fig. 1.

By preserving only essential structural features and eliminating redundancy, the proposed framework better controls the bias–variance trade-off. It also yields a streamlined, highly interpretable framework equipped for robust uncertainty quantification. It is worth noting that its predictive accuracy remains statistically equivalent to that of heavily resourced stacking models.

2 Materials and Methods

2.1 Benchmark Dataset

Chemical European Molecular Biology Laboratory (ChEMBL) is an open-access bioactivity database with several properties, such as binding, functional, and pharmacokinetic information. It covers absorption, distribution, metabolism, excretion, and toxicity (ADMET) for millions of compounds with measured activity data across thousands of protein targets, including inhibitory concentration values such as IC_{50} and derived pIC_{50} values. To focus on compounds within a physicochemically relevant space for intracellular targets, molecules with a mass greater than 700 Da and a octanol–water partition coefficient (logP) larger than 8 were ignored from the dataset [18].

To maintain rigorous comparability with current benchmarks, we utilized the same dataset as the StackBRAF [18] study. This corpus contains 3,854 compounds characterized by their BRAF pIC_{50} values. Following the original experimental configuration in [18], the data were partitioned into a training set of 2,697 molecules and an independent test set of 1,157 compounds.

In addition to the ChEMBL dataset, a dataset of Food and Drug Administration, FDA-approved compounds was also considered [18]. The FDA dataset consists of 2,123 compounds represented by canonical isomeric SMILES. This dataset was used exclusively for external prediction and qualitative analysis. These molecules were not considered in the training or validation steps.

2.2 Molecular Descriptors

Molecules were represented via canonical SMILES, and descriptors were extracted using the PaDEL-Descriptor software, following the same protocol adopted in the StackBRAF [18] study to ensure direct methodological comparability.

The molecular representation employed in this work consisted of twelve PaDEL fingerprint types, which can be grouped according to the type of structural information they encode. Altogether, these fingerprints result in approximately 16,000 molecular features per compound prior to feature selection. All descriptors were computed using default PaDEL settings, providing a consistent and reproducible structural representation aligned with previously published benchmark models [20, 24].

2.3 Supervised Feature Selection

To reduce dimensionality and retain only activity-relevant information, supervised feature selection was applied to the PaDEL descriptors. Feature selection was first performed using an Extreme Gradient Boosting (XGBoost) [8] regressor trained exclusively on the training set, thereby preventing information leakage from the external test set. We set the XGBoost model with 600 trees, a maximum depth of 12, a subsampling ratio of 0.9, a learning rate of 0.03, a column subsampling ratio of 0.8, and a squared error loss function. We assessed feature importance through the gain metric, which captures how much each individual variable minimizes prediction error throughout the ensemble.

Based on the ranked gain values, the top 1,800 PaDEL descriptors were initially selected. To further remove redundancy and mitigate multicollinearity, a second filtering step based on pairwise Pearson correlation was applied to the selected subset. Descriptor pairs presenting a correlation coefficient were considered highly correlated, and for each such pair, the descriptor with lower importance according to the XGBoost gain ranking was discarded, ensuring the retention of the most informative and non-redundant features.

Importantly, feature selection was not applied to the learned molecular embeddings, which were retained in their original latent dimensionality to preserve their data-driven representation capacity.

2.4 Molecular Embeddings

SMILES strings were tokenized at the character level and padded to the maximum sequence length. Molecular embeddings were learned through a self-supervised contrastive learning framework that exploits the intrinsic non-uniqueness of SMILES representations as a source of sequence invariance. Random SMILES augmentation was generated using RDKit, an open-source cheminformatics toolkit [1], two augmented SMILES views were produced using non-canonical atom ordering.

The encoder architecture consisted of an embedding layer with 56 dimensions, followed by a bidirectional Gated Recurrent Unit (GRU) [3, 14] with 136 hidden units per direction and a unidirectional GRU with 98 hidden units. The encoder outputs a 98-dimensional latent representation of the molecule. During contrastive training, a projection head (98-136-136) with Rectified Linear Unit

(ReLU) activation and L2 normalization was attached to the encoder, and the projected representations were optimized using the Normalized Temperature-scaled Cross Entropy (NT-Xent) loss, a contrastive learning objective designed to encourage similar samples to have closer representations in latent space while pushing dissimilar samples apart.

The embedding network was optimized using the NT-Xent contrastive loss with a temperature parameter of $\tau = 0.1$.

Training was executed over 200 epochs with a batch size of 128, utilizing the Adam optimizer at a learning rate of 0.001. Once complete, the projection head was removed, leaving the encoder to generate invariant 98-dimensional molecular embeddings for all compounds.

2.5 Feature Fusion

For each molecule, the final input representation was constructed by concatenating the 98-dimensional SMILES-based molecular embedding with the selected PaDEL descriptors. All features were standardized using z-score normalization parameters computed from the training set only. No feature selection or dimensionality reduction was applied to the molecular embeddings.

2.6 Gaussian Process Regression

A single Rational Quadratic kernel [12] was adopted to model the combined feature space, as this kernel can be interpreted as a scale mixture of squared exponential kernels and is therefore well suited to capturing variability across features with heterogeneous characteristic length scales. pIC_{50} prediction was performed using Gaussian Process Regression (GPR) with a kernel defined as a constant-scaled Rational Quadratic component plus a white noise term. Gaussian Process Regression models the target property as a distribution over functions:

$$f(\mathbf{x}) \sim \mathcal{GP}\big(m(\mathbf{x}),\, k(\mathbf{x}, \mathbf{x}')\big) \tag{1}$$

where $m(x)$ denotes the mean function and $k(x, x')$ represents the covariance kernel defining similarity between input vectors. A zero-mean prior was assumed, and the target variable was centered prior to model fitting, i.e., transformed to have zero empirical mean. This is equivalent to modeling deviations from the empirical mean.

The Rational Quadratic (RQ) kernel is defined as:

$$k_{RQ}(\mathbf{x}, \mathbf{x}') = \sigma^2 \left(1 + \frac{\|\mathbf{x} - \mathbf{x}'\|^2}{2\alpha\ell^2}\right)^{-\alpha} \tag{2}$$

where σ^2 is the signal variance, ℓ is the characteristic length scale, and controls the relative weighting of large- and small-scale variations. This formulation allows the kernel to model functions with multiple characteristic length scales, making it particularly suitable for heterogeneous feature spaces.

The initial hyperparameters and bounds were set as follows: constant scale (initial value 10^{-3}, bounds [10^{-6}, 10^3]), length scale (initial value 10^{-3}, bounds [10^{-6}, 10^3]), shape parameter α (initial value 1.0, bounds [10^{-3}, 10^4]), and noise level (initial value 10^{-3}, bounds [10^{-6}, 10^2]).

Final model assessment relied on an external test set, evaluated through the coefficient of determination (R^2), root mean squared error (RMSE), mean squared error (MSE), and the Pearson correlation coefficient (r). Beyond standard metrics, we recorded and scrutinized predictive uncertainties extracted from the GPR posterior distribution.

2.7 Model Validation and Performance Metrics

The performance of the proposed regression models was evaluated using the coefficient of determination (R^2) and the predictive squared correlation coefficient (Q^2), which are standard metrics in QSAR modeling. Model fit was assessed on the training set using R^2_train, which quantifies the proportion of variance in experimental pIC_{50} values explained by the model [19].

Internal predictive performance was evaluated by 5-fold cross-validation, reported as Q^2_cv, which measures the model's stability and generalization ability within the training domain. External predictivity was assessed using an independent test set not involved in model training or hyperparameter optimization, reported as Q^2_ext, providing an estimate of predictive performance on novel compounds. Model robustness was assessed by jointly analyzing R^2_train, Q^2_cv, and Q^2_ext.

2.8 Non-parametric Model Comparison via the Wilcoxon Signed Rank Test

Differences in predictive performance between competing models were assessed using the non-parametric statistical test for paired samples, Wilcoxon signed-rank test. This statistical test is specifically designed for paired comparisons and evaluates whether the median difference between two related samples is significantly different from zero. [6] Formally, let $d_i = e_i^{(1)} - e_i^{(2)}$ denote the paired differences between absolute prediction errors of the two models for compound i. The Wilcoxon signed-rank test ranks the absolute values $|d_i|$, assigns signs according to the direction of the difference, and computes the test statistic:

$$W = \sum_{i=1}^{n} \text{sign}(d_i)\, R_i \tag{3}$$

where R_i is the rank of $|d_i|$ among non-zero differences. Under the null hypothesis that the median difference is zero, W follows a known reference distribution used to compute the p-value.

Here, we used the Wilcoxon signed-rank test to compare the predictive errors of the StackBRAF [18] baseline model and the proposed GPR-based model on the same external test set comprising 1,157 compounds. For each compound, absolute prediction errors were computed for both models, and these paired absolute errors were used as input to the statistical test.

We employed a two-sided formulation for all statistical evaluations, maintaining a significance threshold (α) of 0.05.

Unless otherwise stated, all architectural choices, model configurations, and hyperparameter values reported in this section were empirically determined based on preliminary experiments conducted exclusively on the training data.

2.9 Applicability Domain

The applicability domain (AD) of a predictive model defines the region of the descriptor space in which the model can be expected to produce reliable predictions. In this work, the applicability domain of the proposed GPR model was quantitatively defined based on the uncertainty distribution of the training set. Specifically, the maximum admissible uncertainty was defined as the 90th percentile of the predictive standard deviation obtained from cross-validated predictions on the training set.

Beyond the definition of the threshold, complementary uncertainty-based diagnostics were employed to characterize and validate the applicability domain. First, the relationship between absolute prediction error and predicted uncertainty was quantified using the Spearman rank correlation coefficient on the external test set.

Second, a coverage-based analysis was performed by ranking test samples according to increasing predictive uncertainty and progressively evaluating model performance as a function of retained coverage. The resulting coverage versus RMSE curve provides insight into how predictive accuracy degrades as predictions extend toward more uncertain regions of the descriptor space. A stable RMSE at high coverage, followed by a pronounced increase at lower coverage levels, is indicative of a well-defined applicability domain in which reliable predictions are concentrated within low-uncertainty regions.

Finally, probabilistic calibration of the GPR model was assessed by comparing nominal and empirical coverage of predictive confidence intervals at multiple confidence levels (e.g., 68%, 95%, and 99%). Agreement between expected and observed coverage supports the statistical validity of the predictive uncertainty estimates and reinforces their suitability as a criterion for defining the applicability domain [12].

2.10 Y-randomization

The y-randomization (also referred to as y-scrambling) test is a widely accepted validation procedure in QSAR modeling, employed to assess whether the observed predictive performance of a model arises from genuine structure–activity relationships or from chance correlations. In this procedure, the response variable (pIC_{50} values) is randomly permuted while the molecular representations are kept unchanged, and new models are trained using the same regression modeling procedure applied to the original dataset [13].

A total of 20 independent random permutations were performed. This procedure ensures that any differences in performance arise solely from the disruption of the structure–activity relationship rather than from changes in model configuration or training conditions.

We evaluate the model's robustness by comparing its predictive performance against the original model trained on randomized responses. The evaluation focused on the coefficient of determination (R^2). Robust QSAR models are expected to yield R^2 values close to zero when trained on randomized responses, indicating the absence of systematic predictive patterns.

Additionally, the cRp^2 metric, commonly used in Y-randomization tests to assess model robustness, was also considered as a complementary criterion to assess the statistical significance.

3 Results

3.1 Descriptor Selection and Correlation Filtering Analysis

The supervised feature selection procedure was performed in two sequential stages: (i) importance-based filtering using XGBoost and (ii) redundancy removal using Pearson correlation analysis.

After XGBoost ranking, we retain only the top 1,800 descriptors. The selected features were derived from CDK-based descriptor families, particularly CDK_Extended (544), CDK_Standard (458), and CDK_GraphOnly (336), which together accounted for approximately 74% of the retained variables and nearly 69% of the cumulative importance score. Subsequently, a Pearson correlation filter ($r \geq 0.65$) was applied to eliminate redundant information. This last selection step reduced the descriptor set from 1,800 to 1,319 features.

The most significant reduction occurred within the CDK_GraphOnly descriptors, signaling significant internal correlation among these topological feature subsets. As shown in Table 1, the distribution of descriptor origins confirms that the fundamental structural profile of the feature space remained stable despite the redundancy elimination.

3.2 Model Performance and Comparison with StackBRAF

Model performance was assessed using the coefficient of determination (R^2/Q^2) and mean absolute error (MAE) for training, cross-validation, and external test sets, following the same evaluation protocol adopted for the StackBRAF [18] model. StackBRAF [18] showed excellent training performance (R^2_train = 0.9718, MAE_train = 0.1628) and strong external prediction (R^2_test = 0.8399, MAE_test = 0.3946).

The proposed GPR-based model achieved similarly strong results, with high training fit (R^2_train = 0.9814, MAE_train = 0.1307), robust internal validation (Q^2_cv = 0.8003, MAE_cv = 0.4352), and strong external performance (Q^2_ext = 0.8401, MAE_ext = 0.3978). These values closely match those obtained for StackBRAF [18].

Table 1. Distribution of molecular descriptors retained after filtering

Origin	Number of Features	Sum of Importance
CDK Extended	491	0.2139
CDK Standard	400	0.1946
CDK GraphOnly	204	0.1822
PubChem	54	0.0562
Klekota Roth	58	0.0372
Klekota Roth Count	35	0.0241
Substructure	7	0.0135
Atom Pairs 2D Count	24	0.0109
Substructure Count	5	0.0096
MACCS	10	0.0087
Atom Pairs 2D	27	0.0083
EState	4	0.0042

According to commonly adopted QSAR validation criteria, Q^2 values above approximately 0.6 are indicative of predictive models, although this threshold may vary depending on dataset size and modeling context. In addition, the difference between training and validation metrics ($\Delta(R^2_{\text{train}} - Q^2)$), whether cross-validated or external) is frequently used as an indicator of overfitting, with small differences ($\leq\sim 0.2 - 0.3$) reflecting consistency between training and validation performance. Overall, both models demonstrate stable and coherent performance across training, validation, and external test sets, supporting their robustness and generalizability [11,19].

3.3 Applicability Domain and Uncertainty Analysis

The applicability domain (AD) of the proposed GPR model was evaluated using uncertainty-aware diagnostics derived from its predictive variance (σ). In this work, the AD was quantitatively defined based on the uncertainty distribution of the training set, where the maximum admissible uncertainty was set as the 90th percentile of the predictive standard deviation obtained from cross-validated predictions on the training set. Predictions associated with uncertainty values below this threshold were therefore considered to lie within the model's applicability domain [7].

A statistically significant positive Spearman rank correlation ($\rho = 0.2990$, $p = 2.50 \times 10^{-25}$) was observed between the predictive standard deviation (σ) and the absolute prediction error on the external test set, indicating that higher uncertainty values are systematically associated with larger prediction errors. Although the magnitude of the correlation is moderate, its high statistical significance supports the consistency and practical utility of the uncertainty estimates for reliability assessment.

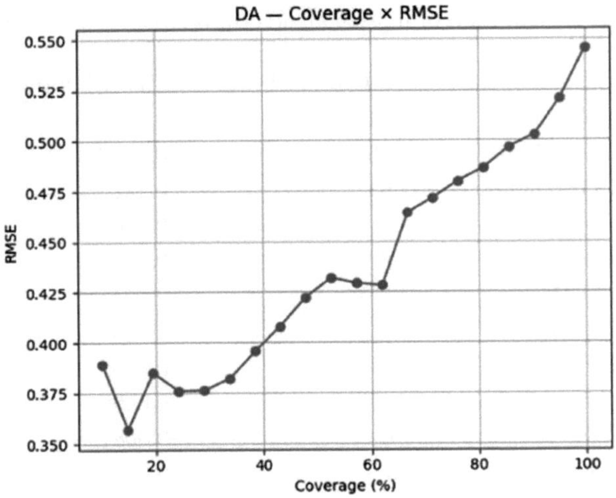

Fig. 2. Root mean squared error (RMSE) as a function of coverage level, with samples ordered by predictive uncertainty.

A coverage-based analysis further demonstrates the practical relevance of uncertainty estimates. As predictions are progressively restricted to compounds with lower uncertainty (Fig. 2), the RMSE decreases monotonically, indicating that excluding high-uncertainty predictions leads to improved accuracy. This behavior indicates that σ provides a meaningful basis for defining confidence-based applicability thresholds.

Model calibration was assessed by comparing expected and observed coverage probabilities for confidence intervals of 68%, 95%, and 99%. As depicted in Table 2, the observed coverages (approximately 74.85%, 95.51%, and 98.53%, respectively) nearly match their theoretical expectations, suggesting well-calibrated uncertainty estimates. [21]

The parity plot between experimental and predicted pIC_{50} values (Fig. 3) shows a high linear correlation across the full activity range, with no systematic bias at low or high potency values. Deviations from the ideal trend are primarily associated with predictions of higher uncertainty, reinforcing the role of σ as an indicator of extrapolation beyond the model's effective domain.

Table 2. Calibration of predictive uncertainty for the external test set

Confidence-Interval	Expected-Coverage	Observed-Coverage
68%	0.68	0.7485
95%	0.95	0.9551
99%	0.99	0.9853

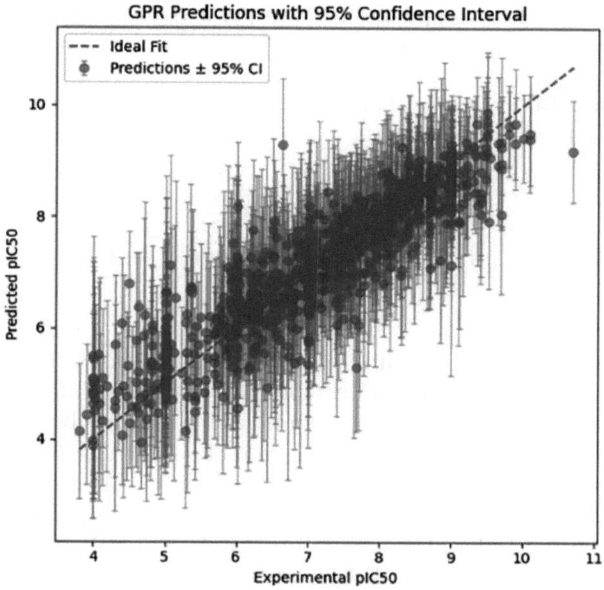

Fig. 3. Regression plot of predicted versus experimental pIC_{50} values for the external test set using the Gaussian Process Regression (GPR) model.

3.4 External Performance Evaluation on FDA-Approved Drugs

We assessed the external performance of the GPR-based QSAR model using a curated collection of FDA-approved drugs. The FDA dataset was used as provided in the Supporting Information of the StackBRAF [18] study, containing curated canonical isomeric SMILES representations of approved compounds.

To evaluate model behavior on chemically relevant compounds, a structural similarity filter retained only those with a Tanimoto coefficient exceeding 0.4 relative to the training set. Structural similarity was computed using Morgan fingerprints (radius = 2, 2048 bits), and the maximum Tanimoto similarity between each FDA compound and the training molecules was used as the filtering criterion. This threshold was intentionally set lower than that used in StackBRAF [18] to allow for a broader exploration of the chemical space while still avoiding extreme extrapolation [9].

To ensure compatibility with the trained model pipeline, the feature-selection procedure based on XGBoost importance ranking was reconstructed using the original training dataset. This step allowed the same subset of PaDEL descriptors used during model development to be consistently applied to the FDA compounds.

Predictions of pIC_{50} values were generated using the trained Gaussian Process Regression (GPR) model, which provides both point estimates and predictive uncertainties. In addition, an Applicability Domain (AD) analysis was

Table 3. Predicted pIC_{50} values for selected FDA approved drugs compared with experimental literature ranges

Compound	ChEMBL ID	Predicted pIC_{50} ($\mu \pm \sigma$)	LCB_{95}	Experimental pIC_{50}	Reference
Regorafenib	1946170	6.85 ± 1.08	4.73	~6.0–7.0	[23]
Ponatinib	1171837	6.78 ± 1.06	4.69	~7–9	[5]
Sorafenib	1336	6.67 ± 1.03	4.66	~6.5–6.7	[2]
Vemurafenib	1229517	6.61 ± 1.06	4.53	~7.0	[26]
Cabozantinib	2105717	6.58 ± 1.06	4.49	~6.3–7.1	[17]

performed to evaluate the reliability of external predictions. The AD threshold was defined as the 90th percentile of the predictive standard deviation (σ) calculated on the training set, and FDA compounds with σ values below this threshold were considered to be within the model's reliable prediction space. This procedure ensured consistency with the internal validation strategy and prevented overinterpretation of predictions associated with unusually high uncertainty. To enable a conservative and statistically robust ranking, predictions were analyzed using the 95% Lower Confidence Bound (LCB_{95}), defined as:

$$\text{LCB}_{95} = \mu_{\textbf{pred}} - 1.96\, \sigma_{\textbf{pred}} \tag{4}$$

where is the predicted pIC_{50}, and what is the associated predictive standard deviation. This uncertainty-aware criterion penalizes highly uncertain predictions, ensuring that compounds are prioritized based on both predicted potency and reliability.

We selected the top-5 compounds from the FDA dataset based on LCB_{95} scores, prioritizing compounds with known BRAF-inhibitory activity. We also checked both the global rankings (post-Tanimoto filtering) and the AD-restricted rankings, confirming that the top inhibitors fall within the model's reliable prediction space. Table 3 details the predicted pIC_{50} values, their uncertainties, and the corresponding LCB_{95} scores.

Overall, these outcomes show that the proposed model can produce biologically meaningful and statistically consistent pIC_{50} predictions for FDA-approved drugs with known BRAF inhibitory activity. Notably, by combining confidence–based ranking strategy with an explicit applicability-domain assessment, we prevents overinterpretation of high but uncertain predictions and provides a more reliable framework for external performance evaluation. Such an uncertainty-conscious perspective represents a core strength of the GPR framework, reinforcing its utility for practical decision-making in kinase inhibitor discovery.

3.5 Robustness and Statistical Validation

To evaluate the model's robustness, we used a y-randomization test. The training-set pIC_{50} values were randomly permuted while preserving molecular descriptors and representations. After generating 20 random permutations, the regression modeling workflow was repeated for each instance using the exact configuration from the original dataset.

For randomized responses, the model produced R^2 values near zero, which contrasted with the original R^2 of about 0.84. This result indicates that the model relies on genuine structure-activity relationships instead of spurious correlations. We observe the same behavior for the cR_p^2 value (≈ 0.64), which exceeds the standard validation threshold of 0.5. This finding further substantiates the overall robustness of the proposed framework.

A paired Wilcoxon signed-rank test was conducted to compare the absolute prediction errors of StackBRAF [18] and the proposed GPR-based model on the same external test set (n = 1157). Both models achieved an identical mean MAE of 0.395. The resulting p-value (0.570) indicates that there is no statistically significant difference between their error distributions.

As shown in Fig. 4, the boxplot distributions of absolute prediction errors for both models show substantial overlap, with comparable medians and interquartile ranges. While StackBRAF [18] depends on a stacking ensemble, our model achieves a level of predictive performance equivalent to that of StackBRAF using a less complex probabilistic regression framework. This approach offers a simpler, interpretable alternative, demonstrating that state-of-the-art accuracy can be preserved without the structural overhead of complex ensemble methods.

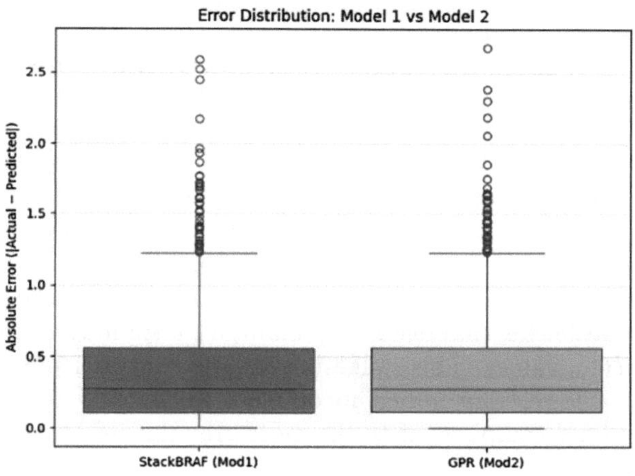

Fig. 4. Mean absolute error (MAE) distribution for both models on the external test set (n = 1157).

4 Ablation and Sensitivity Analysis

To quantify the contributions of distinct molecular representations and kernel formulations, we run a combined feature-level and model-structure ablation study. This ablation study follows a rigorous component-wise evaluation in machine learning [10], in which the influence of isolated components are evaluated.

We have considered two distinct molecular representations: (i) physicochemical descriptors computed using PaDEL, and (ii) learned molecular embeddings derived from a recurrent neural network trained on SMILES strings. Specifically, four configurations were defined: (A) PaDEL descriptors only, (B) molecular embeddings only, (C) a combined feature space using a single shared kernel applied to the concatenated feature vector, and (D) a combined feature space modeled through the additive composition of separate kernels assigned to each representation. This experimental design allows the contributions of individual and combined feature representations to be examined under controlled conditions.

All ablation experiments were conducted under strictly controlled conditions. Identical train–test splits, target variables, random seeds, scaling procedures, kernel hyperparameter bounds, initial values, and optimization protocols were employed across all configurations.

An ablation study was also performed to evaluate the individual and combined contributions of PaDEL molecular descriptors and learned molecular embeddings to model performance. Four configurations were considered: (A) PaDEL descriptors only, (B) molecular embeddings only, (C) the combined PaDEL–embedding representation within a single-kernel Gaussian Process Regression (GPR) framework, and (D) a combined representation modeled using additive separate kernels.

Using only the PaDEL descriptors selected by XGBoost feature importance ranking, followed by Pearson correlation-based redundancy filtering (Experiment A), the model achieved strong external predictive performance ($R^2 = 0.8379$, MAE = 0.3987, r = 0.9156), confirming that established handcrafted fingerprints capture highly informative structural features relevant to BRAF inhibition.

In contrast, the models with embeddings-only representation (Experiment B) demonstrated lower performance ($R^2 = 0.6169$, $MAE = 0.6205$, $r = 0.7860$). While these results indicate that latent embeddings are insufficient as a standalone representation for this task, they maintain a significant correlation with experimental pIC_{50} values. This suggests that the contrastive learning strategy successfully encodes relevant, albeit incomplete, chemical features, which likely serves as a high-level complement to the more granular information provided by traditional descriptors.

The combined representation (Experiment C) consistently improved predictive performance relative to the PaDEL-only model, yielding $R^2 = 0.8418$, MAE = 0.3949, and r = 0.9178. While the numerical gain in R^2 is modest, the improvement is consistently observed across all evaluated metrics, demonstrating that molecular embeddings provide complementary information that enhances model generalization on unseen compounds when integrated with handcrafted descriptors.

In Experiment D, the combined representation was modeled using an additive kernel structure, with independent kernels applied to PaDEL descriptors and molecular embeddings. This configuration produced predictive performance similar to the shared-kernel model ($R^2 = 0.8416$, MAE = 0.3954, r = 0.9177), showing that the model is able to capture the contribution of each representation separately without degrading predictive accuracy. The similarity in performance between Experiments C and D suggests that the predictive signal extracted from the combined feature space is robust to kernel decomposition. At the same time, the additive formulation provides a more structured representation of how different molecular feature groups contribute to the prediction. This result further supports the complementary nature of handcrafted descriptors and learned embeddings within the GPR framework.

5 Discussion

Stacking ensembles are designed to improve predictive performance by combining multiple heterogeneous base learners, often yielding gains through variance reduction rather than through fundamentally deeper learning of structure–activity relationships. In this context, ensemble learning primarily exploits redundancy across models trained on the same descriptor space, smoothing prediction errors via aggregation. While effective in many scenarios, such gains do not necessarily imply the extraction of new chemical information, but rather a stabilization of predictions through model averaging.

The present results suggest that, for the BRAF inhibition dataset, the performance ceiling is largely determined by the available data rather than by the expressive power of increasingly complex architectures. Both the proposed GPR-based model and StackBRAF achieve similar accuracy, supported by comparable R^2/Q^2 values, successful y-randomization tests, robust applicability domain analyses, and a paired Wilcoxon signed-rank test indicating no statistically significant difference between their prediction error distributions.

The proposed framework differs conceptually from stacking-based approaches in how information is learned and integrated. In StackBRAF-like architectures [18], multiple models are trained independently on the same molecular descriptor space, and their predictions are subsequently used as inputs to a meta-model. This approach transforms model outputs into proxy features, providing an indirect representation of the original molecular information. On the contrary, our approach learns a single continuous function from an enriched input space that combines selected PaDEL descriptors with learned molecular embeddings. This architectural design preserves chemical information, removes redundancy, and integrates symbolic and learned representations within a unified learning process.

Furthermore, the feature selection approach employed here plays a central role in controlling the bias–variance trade-off. By identifying and retaining the most informative PaDEL descriptors prior to model training, the approach reduces feature redundancy and noise, enabling the model to focus on chemically meaningful variation. When combined with learned molecular embeddings, this strategy enriches the input space with additional information rather than relying on ensemble diversity.

Taken together, these findings support the notion that, for this specific prediction task, stacking ensembles does not confer a fundamental advantage over well-designed simple approaches.

6 Conclusions

This study proposed a principled and parsimonious framework for predicting BRAF inhibitor potency, demonstrating that state-of-the-art QSAR performance can be achieved without reliance on stacking-based ensemble architectures. By integrating selected PaDEL molecular descriptors with learned molecular embeddings within a single Gaussian Process Regression (GPR) model, our proposed approach achieved predictive performance statistically equivalent to that of state-of-the-art stacking-based models.

The equivalence in predictive accuracy between the proposed model and stacking-based approaches is supported by consistent performance across training, internal validation, and external test sets, as well as by multiple robustness analyses, including y-randomization, applicability domain evaluation, and a paired Wilcoxon signed-rank test, which indicated no statistically significant difference in prediction errors. These results suggest that, for this specific prediction task, additional architectural complexity does not yield meaningful gains in predictive performance, and that the achievable performance ceiling is largely constrained by the underlying data rather than by model expressiveness.

The proposed framework differs fundamentally from stacking-based strategies in how information is learned and utilized. While stacking ensembles aggregate predictions from multiple models trained on the same descriptor space, primarily reducing variance through model averaging, the present approach focuses on enriching the input representation. By preserving chemically interpretable descriptors, removing redundancy through informed feature selection, and integrating complementary latent information from molecular embeddings, the model learns a single continuous function directly in an enriched feature space. This design enables efficient use of available information without relying on ensemble diversity as a surrogate for representational completeness.

Lastly, from a theoretical and practical perspective, Gaussian Process Regression is particularly well-suited to this scenario. GPR naturally captures smooth structure–activity relationships, operates effectively in moderate-data settings typical of QSAR studies, and provides calibrated uncertainty estimates alongside point predictions. The strong correspondence observed between predictive uncertainty and error, together with well-calibrated confidence intervals, highlights the value of uncertainty-aware modeling for defining applicability domains and supporting reliable decision-making in virtual screening and lead optimization.

Acknowledgment. The authors gratefully acknowledge support from FAPESP (São Paulo Research Foundation), project No. 2022/09285-7, and the support from the Brazilian National Council for Scientific and Technological Development (CNPq), grant 310377/2025-0.

Data and Code Availability Statement. The dataset used in this study corresponds to the dataset reported in the StackBRAF [18]. The source code is publicly available at https://github.com/CIDAG/GPR-BRAF-Model.

References

1. Bento, A.P., et al.: An open source chemical structure curation pipeline using RDKit. J. Cheminform. **12**(1), 1–16 (2020). https://doi.org/10.1186/s13321-020-00456-1
2. Bollag, G., Hirth, P., Tsai, J., et al.: Clinical efficacy of a RAF inhibitor needs broad target blockade in BRAF-mutant melanoma. Nature **467**, 596–599 (2010). https://doi.org/10.1038/nature09454
3. Bonaccorso, G.: Mastering Machine Learning Algorithms: Expert Techniques for Implementing Popular Machine Learning Algorithms, Fine-Tuning Your Models, and Understanding How They Work. Packt Publishing (2018)
4. Bouchè, V., et al.: BRAF signaling inhibition in glioblastoma: which clinical perspectives? Front. Oncol. **11** (2021). https://doi.org/10.3389/fonc.2021.772052
5. Cotto-Rios, X.M., et al.: Inhibitors of BRAF dimers using an allosteric site. Nat. Commun. **11**, 4370 (2020). https://doi.org/10.1038/s41467-020-18123-2
6. Hollander, M., Wolfe, D.A., Chicken, E.: Nonparametric Statistical Methods. Wiley (2015). https://doi.org/10.1002/9781119196037
7. Jaworska, J., Nikolova-Jeliazkova, N., Aldenberg, T.: QSAR applicability domain estimation by projection of the training set in descriptor space: a review. Altern. Lab. Anim. **33**, 445–459 (2005). https://doi.org/10.1177/026119290503300508
8. Kuhn, M., Johnson, K.: Feature Engineering and Selection. Chapman and Hall/CRC (2019). https://doi.org/10.1201/9781315108230
9. Leach, A.R., Gillet, V.J.: An Introduction to Chemoinformatics. Springer (2007). https://doi.org/10.1007/978-1-4020-6291-9
10. Lipton, Z.C., Steinhardt, J.: Troubling trends in machine learning scholarship. Queue **17**, 45–77 (2019). https://doi.org/10.1145/3317287.3328534
11. Nakarin, F., Boonpalit, K., Kinchagawat, J., et al.: Assisting multitargeted ligand affinity prediction of receptor tyrosine kinases associated nonsmall cell lung cancer treatment with multitasking principal neighborhood aggregation. Molecules **27**, 1226 (2022). https://doi.org/10.3390/molecules27041226
12. Rasmussen, C.E., Williams, C.K.I.: Gaussian Processes for Machine Learning. The MIT Press (2005). https://doi.org/10.7551/mitpress/3206.001.0001
13. Rücker, C., Rücker, G., Meringer, M.: y-randomization and its variants in QSPR/QSAR. J. Chem. Inf. Model. **47**, 2345–2357 (2007). https://doi.org/10.1021/ci700157b
14. Salem, F.M.: Recurrent Neural Networks. Springer (2022). https://doi.org/10.1007/978-3-030-89929-5
15. Shan, K.S., Rehman, T.U., Ivanov, S., et al.: Molecular targeting of the BRAF proto-oncogene/mitogen-activated protein kinase (MAPK) pathway across cancers. Int. J. Mol. Sci. **25** (2024). https://doi.org/10.3390/ijms25010624
16. Bargagli Stoffi, F.J., Cevolani, G., Gnecco, G.: Simple models in complex worlds: Occam's razor and statistical learning theory. Mind. Mach. **32**(1), 13–42 (2022). https://doi.org/10.1007/s11023-022-09592-z
17. Su, K.W., Ou, D.L., Fu, Y.H., et al.: Repurposing cabozantinib with therapeutic potential in KIT-driven t(8;21) acute myeloid leukaemias. Cancer Gene Therapy **29**, 519–532 (2022). https://doi.org/10.1038/s41417-021-00329-1

18. Syahid, N.F., Weerapreeyakul, N., Srisongkram, T.: StackBRAF: a large-scale stacking ensemble learning for BRAF affinity prediction. ACS Omega **8**, 20881–20891 (2023). https://doi.org/10.1021/acsomega.3c01641
19. Todeschini, R., Ballabio, D., Grisoni, F.: Beware of unreliable Q^2 ! a comparative study of regression metrics for predictivity assessment of QSAR models. J. Chem. Inf. Model. **56**, 1905–1913 (2016). https://doi.org/10.1021/acs.jcim.6b00277
20. Todeschini, R., Consonni, V.: Molecular descriptors for chemoinformatics. Wiley-VCH; John Wiley [distributor] (2009). https://doi.org/10.1002/9783527628766
21. Tropsha, A.: Best practices for QSAR model development, validation, and exploitation. Mol. Inform. **29**, 476–488 (2010). https://doi.org/10.1002/minf.201000061
22. Weininger, D.: SMILES, a chemical language and information system. 1. introduction to methodology and encoding rules. J. Chem. Inf. Comput. Sci. **28**(2), 31–36 (1988). https://doi.org/10.1021/ci00057a005
23. Wilhelm, S.M., et al.: Regorafenib (BAY 73-4506): a new oral multikinase inhibitor of angiogenic, stromal and oncogenic receptor tyrosine kinases with potent preclinical antitumor activity. Int. J. Cancer **129**, 245–255 (2011). https://doi.org/10.1002/ijc.25864
24. Yap, C.W.: PaDEL-descriptor: an open source software to calculate molecular descriptors and fingerprints. J. Comput. Chem. **32**, 1466–1474 (2011). https://doi.org/10.1002/jcc.21707
25. Zhang, M., Zhang, C., Liu, K., et al.: BRAFPred: a novel approach for accurate prediction of the B-type rapidly accelerated fibrosarcoma inhibitor. ACS Omega **10**, 12170–12184 (2025). https://doi.org/10.1021/acsomega.4c10367
26. Zhong, L., Li, Y., Xiong, L., et al.: Small molecules in targeted cancer therapy: advances, challenges, and future perspectives. Signal Transduct. Target. Ther. **6**, 201 (2021). https://doi.org/10.1038/s41392-021-00572-w

Machine Learning–Guided Stochastic Switching Modeling of Chronic Kidney Disease

Amina Allali[1], Karima Moumane[1](✉), and Saida Amine[2]

[1] Software Project Management Research Team, ENSIAS, Mohammed V University in Rabat, Rabat, Morocco
aminaallali86@gmail.com , karima.moumane@ensias.um5.ac.ma
[2] Department of Mathematics and application, Faculty of Sciences and Technology, Hassan II University of Casablanca, PO Box 146, 20650 Mohammedia, Morocco
aminesaida52@gmail.com

Abstract. This study develops a machine learning–guided stochastic switching model to analyze the progression of chronic kidney disease (CKD) under personalized treatment strategies. The main objective is to understand how treatment switching under uncertainty influences disease evolution and to identify conditions under which CKD progression can be controlled. Clinical data are used to estimate model parameters through machine learning techniques, enabling a patient-specific and data-driven representation of disease dynamics. The proposed framework combines deterministic and stochastic analyses to capture both baseline disease behavior and random perturbations in treatment response. Theoretical results establish the existence, uniqueness, and positivity of solutions, ensuring biological feasibility. Stability analysis of the deterministic model identifies disease-free and endemic equilibria and associated threshold parameters. For the stochastic model, Lyapunov-based methods are used to derive conditions for extinction and persistence of the disease. Numerical simulations based on real clinical data validate the theoretical findings and demonstrate the impact of different treatment strategies on CKD progression. Overall, the study highlights the relevance of integrating machine learning with stochastic modeling to support personalized and data-driven management of chronic kidney disease.

Keywords: Chronic Kidney Disease (CKD) · Mathematical Modeling · Stochastic Switching · Personalized Treatment · Data-Driven Modeling · Machine Learning · Numerical simulations

1 Introduction

Chronic Kidney Disease (CKD) is a progressive and irreversible disorder that represents a major global public health challenge, affecting hundreds of millions of individuals worldwide [1]. The disease is characterized by a gradual loss of

O. Gervasi et al. (Eds.): ICCSA 2026, LNCS 16768, pp. 511–531, 2027.
https://doi.org/10.1007/978-3-032-30488-9_32

functional nephrons, persistent inflammatory processes, excessive renal fibrosis, and a continuous decline in the glomerular filtration rate (GFR). If left untreated, CKD may progress to end-stage renal disease, requiring dialysis or kidney transplantation, and is associated with high morbidity and mortality rates [25]. Due to its complex and multifactorial nature, CKD progression exhibits substantial inter-individual variability, posing significant challenges for clinical management and therapeutic decision-making.

Mathematical modeling has proven to be a powerful tool for understanding the temporal dynamics of chronic diseases and for evaluating therapeutic strategies. Deterministic compartmental models have been widely used to describe the interactions between inflammation, fibrosis, nephron loss, and renal function decline in CKD [18,23]. These models enable qualitative analysis of equilibrium states and threshold conditions governing disease stabilization or progression. However, classical deterministic approaches often fail to capture intrinsic biological variability arising from patient heterogeneity, environmental factors, and fluctuating treatment responses.

To address these limitations, stochastic modeling frameworks have been introduced to account for random perturbations in disease dynamics. Stochastic differential equation (SDE) models incorporate environmental and physiological uncertainties and provide a more realistic representation of biological systems [9,11,13,15]. In biomedical applications, stochasticity may significantly alter system behavior, potentially leading to disease extinction in scenarios where deterministic models predict persistence [3,4]. Such models are commonly driven by Brownian motion or Gaussian white noise and have been successfully applied in epidemiology and chronic disease modeling [21].

In parallel, the increasing availability of clinical datasets has stimulated the integration of machine learning techniques into biomedical modeling. Machine learning methods have demonstrated strong potential for parameter estimation, prediction, and pattern discovery in high-dimensional clinical data [2,7,10,14,17,22]. In the context of CKD, data-driven approaches enable the calibration of mechanistic models using real patient data and facilitate the design of personalized treatment strategies. The combination of machine learning with mechanistic stochastic models provides a powerful framework for bridging theoretical analysis and clinical relevance. Compared to previous studies on chronic kidney disease modeling, which mainly focus on either deterministic frameworks or stochastic dynamics separately [3,23], this work integrates both approaches within a machine learning–guided stochastic switching framework to better capture patient-specific variability and treatment adaptation.

Motivated by these developments, this study proposes a machine learning–guided stochastic switching model for Chronic Kidney Disease under personalized treatment strategies. The model combines deterministic and stochastic dynamics to describe the temporal evolution of functional nephron population, renal fibrosis, inflammatory activity, renal function, and treatment intensity. A switching treatment mechanism is incorporated to reflect intermittent or adaptive therapeutic protocols commonly observed in clinical practice. Model parameters are estimated using real clinical datasets, and the calibrated model is validated through numerical simulations.

The main contributions of this work are summarized as follows:

- A novel deterministic and stochastic CKD model incorporating treatment switching is formulated.
- Existence, uniqueness, positivity, and boundedness of solutions are established.
- Extinction and persistence conditions are derived using Lyapunov function techniques and LaSalle's invariance principle [5,12,16,26].
- Machine learning methods are employed for parameter estimation from real clinical data.
- Numerical simulations are conducted to validate the analytical results and assess therapy optimization.

The remainder of this manuscript is organized as follows. Section 2 presents the model formulation along with its biological interpretation. Section 3 is devoted to the deterministic analysis. Section 4 introduces the stochastic switching model and establishes the existence, uniqueness, and positivity of solutions, as well as extinction and persistence in mean results. Section 5 presents numerical simulations and data-driven validation. Finally, Sect. 6 concludes the paper with a summary of the main findings and perspectives for future research.

2 Formulation of the Models

Let t represent the time, and $N(t)$ represents the fraction of functional nephrons, where $F(t)$ denotes the level of renal fibrosis, $I(t)$ represents the intensity of chronic inflammation affecting the kidneys, $G(t)$ denotes the normalized glomerular filtration rate (GFR), and $T(t)$ represents the cumulative therapeutic effect applied to the patient. Based on the pathophysiological dynamics of chronic kidney disease (CKD), we assume nonlinear interaction rates governing disease progression. Functional nephrons decline due to fibrosis and inflammation effects at the rates $\alpha_1 F(t)N(t)$ and $\alpha_2(T)I(t)N(t)$, respectively, where α_1 denotes the fibrosis–induced nephron loss rate and $\alpha_2(T)$ represents inflammation–induced nephron damage modulated by treatment. Fibrosis progresses due to inflammatory activity at the rate $\beta_1(T)I(t)(1-F(t))$, where $\beta_1(T)$ denotes the treatment–dependent fibrosis progression rate, while μ represents the natural fibrosis resolution rate. Inflammation increases due to aggregated clinical risk factors at the rate ηH and fibrosis feedback at the rate $\kappa F(t)$, where η denotes the inflammation induction rate and κ represents fibrosis–driven inflammatory amplification. Inflammation resolves at the treatment–enhanced rate $\delta(T)I(t)$. The glomerular filtration rate improves proportionally to functional nephron mass at the rate $\rho N(t)$, where ρ denotes nephron contribution to renal function, and declines due to fibrosis damage at the rate $\gamma F(t)G(t)$. Treatment effect accumulates according to the therapeutic control input $u(t)$ and decays over time at the rate $\omega T(t)$. All parameters are described in Table 1 while the governing equations describing transitions in the model are given in Eq. (1). Besides, the following assumptions were taken into consideration while formulating the model:

A_1 : All the initial state variables are non–negative, that is $N(0), F(0), I(0), G(0), T(0) \geq 0$.
A_2 : Model variables and parameters are all non–negative.
A_3 : Functional nephron loss is driven by both fibrosis and inflammation.
A_4 : Fibrosis progression is induced by inflammatory processes and saturates at a maximal biological level.
A_5 : Inflammation is induced by clinical risk factors and fibrosis feedback.
A_6 : Treatment reduces inflammation and fibrosis progression.
A_7 : Treatment improves nephron preservation and renal function.
A_8 : The therapeutic effect decays naturally over time.
A_9 : Glomerular filtration rate depends positively on functional nephron mass.
A_{10} : Fibrosis contributes negatively to renal filtration capacity.

Considering other features of CKD progression and the above assumptions (A_1–A_{10}), the system can be represented by the following differential equations:

$$\begin{cases} \dfrac{dN(t)}{dt} = -\alpha_1 F(t)N(t) - \alpha_2(T)I(t)N(t), \\ \dfrac{dF(t)}{dt} = \beta_1(T)I(t)(1-F(t)) - \mu F(t), \\ \dfrac{dI(t)}{dt} = \eta H + \kappa F(t) - \delta(T)I(t), \\ \dfrac{dG(t)}{dt} = \rho N(t) - \gamma F(t)G(t), \\ \dfrac{dT(t)}{dt} = u(t) - \omega T(t). \end{cases} \tag{1}$$

The treatment–modulated parameters are defined as:

$$\alpha_2(T) = \alpha_2^0(1-\xi T), \qquad \beta_1(T) = \beta_1^0(1-\theta T), \qquad \delta(T) = \delta_0 + \delta_1 T.$$

Since, in real situations, the temporal dynamics of chronic kidney disease are inevitably influenced by random factors, we consider here stochastic perturbations proportional to the population sizes $N(t), F(t), I(t), G(t)$, and the treatment level $T(t)$. To obtain the stochastic version of the deterministic model, we introduce multiplicative noise into the system 1. Therefore, the stochastic version of the CKD model with treatment and switching can be formulated as the following system of stochastic differential equations:

$$\begin{cases} dN(t) = \big[-\alpha_1^{r(t)}FN - \alpha_2^{r(t)}(T)IN\big]dt + \sigma_1^{r(t)}N\,dB_1(t), \\ dF(t) = \big[\beta_1^{r(t)}(T)I(1-F) - \mu^{r(t)}F\big]dt + \sigma_2^{r(t)}F\,dB_2(t), \\ dI(t) = \big[\eta^{r(t)}H + \kappa^{r(t)}F - \delta^{r(t)}(T)I\big]dt + \sigma_3^{r(t)}I\,dB_3(t), \\ dG(t) = \big[\rho^{r(t)}N - \gamma^{r(t)}FG\big]dt + \sigma_4^{r(t)}G\,dB_4(t), \\ dT(t) = \big[u^{r(t)}(t) - \omega^{r(t)}T\big]dt + \sigma_5^{r(t)}T\,dB_5(t), \end{cases} \tag{2}$$

Table 1. Model parameters and variables

Notion	Meaning
α_1	Fibrosis–induced nephron loss rate
$\alpha_2(T)$	Inflammation–induced nephron loss rate
$\beta_1(T)$	Fibrosis progression rate
μ	Natural fibrosis resolution rate
η	Risk factor–induced inflammation rate
κ	Fibrosis feedback on inflammation
$\delta(T)$	Inflammation resolution rate
ρ	Nephron contribution to GFR
γ	Fibrosis impact on GFR
ω	Treatment decay rate
$u(t)$	Treatment control input
H	Aggregate risk factor level

where $B_i(t)$, for $i = 1, \cdots, 5$, represent independent standard Brownian motions, and $\sigma_i^{r(t)2} > 0$, $i = 1, \cdots, 5$, denote the intensities of the Gaussian noises. The superscript $r(t)$ indicates that the parameters switch according to the current disease progression regime, modeled as a continuous-time Markov chain. In the context of our CKD model, the stochastic terms $\sigma_1^{r(t)}N(t)dB_1(t)$, $\sigma_2^{r(t)}F(t)dB_2(t)$, $\sigma_3^{r(t)}I(t)dB_3(t)$, $\sigma_4^{r(t)}G(t)dB_4(t)$, and $\sigma_5^{r(t)}T(t)dB_5(t)$ biologically reflect random fluctuations in disease progression, fibrosis development, inflammation, kidney function, and treatment response, including variations due to patient-specific factors and environmental influences.

In this section, we have stated the main assumptions regarding CKD progression, fibrosis, inflammation, kidney function, and treatment response. Based on these assumptions, the corresponding mathematical formulation of the model was developed. The deterministic model was then extended into a stochastic model by including multiplicative noise terms. In the next section, the deterministic version of the model will be analyzed to present its dynamical features, including equilibrium points and stability properties.

3 Deterministic Stability of System (1)

In this section, we intend to discuss the analysis of existence, boundedness and uniqueness of a positive solution for the CKD model (1). For this purpose, using the classical theory of ODEs [6,24], we will focus on the conditions which guarantee the global stability of equilibria.

3.1 Existence, Uniqueness and Boundedness of the Positive Solution of System (1)

This subsection studies the existence, boundedness and uniqueness of the non-negative solution to the proposed CKD model (1) with initial non-negative conditions

$$N(0) \geq 0,\ F(0) \geq 0,\ I(0) \geq 0,\ G(0) \geq 0,\ T(0) \geq 0. \tag{3}$$

Theorem 1. *Under the initial conditions (3), the CKD model (1) possesses a unique global positive solution in* $\mathbb{R}^5_+$. *Moreover, the closed set*

$$\Gamma = \{(N, F, I, G, T) \in \mathbb{R}^5_+ \mid N(t) \leq N_{\max}\}$$

remains positively invariant, where $N_{\max}$ *is an upper bound for the functional nephron fraction.*

Proof: Suppose that at time $t^* > 0$, $N(t^*) = 0$. The first equation of system (1) gives

$$\left.\frac{dN(t)}{dt}\right|_{t^*} = -\alpha_1^{r(t^*)} FN - \alpha_2^{r(t^*)}(T)IN\Big|_{N=0} = 0.$$

Hence $N(t)$ cannot become negative and remains non-negative for all $t \geq 0$, by continuity of solutions. Similarly, the second, third, fourth and fifth equations imply that
$F(t), I(t), G(t), T(t) \geq 0$ for all $t \geq 0$. Thus, all solutions are clearly positive for every $t \geq 0$.
To illustrate the boundedness of the solution, we define

$$X(t) = N(t) + F(t) + I(t) + G(t) + T(t),$$

then

$$\frac{dX}{dt} = \frac{dN}{dt} + \frac{dF}{dt} + \frac{dI}{dt} + \frac{dG}{dt} + \frac{dT}{dt}.$$

Using the system (1) and ignoring the negative interaction terms for an upper estimate, we obtain

$$dX(t) \leq \big[\text{sum of positive input terms} - \min(\alpha_1, \mu, \omega)X(t)\big]\,dt.$$

By classical comparison theorem for ODEs, it follows that

$$X(t) \leq e^{-\lambda t}\left(X(0) - \frac{\text{sum of input terms}}{\lambda}\right) + \frac{\text{sum of input terms}}{\lambda},$$

where $\lambda = \min(\alpha_1, \mu, \omega)$ is a positive constant. Hence, if $X(0)$ is bounded, then $X(t)$ remains bounded for all $t \geq 0$, and the set Γ is positively invariant. □

3.2 Equilibria and Threshold Parameters of System (1)

In this section, we assume that each variable $N(t), F(t), I(t), G(t)$ and $T(t)$ represents the corresponding fraction of the total functional units at time t. Although the treatment equation is structurally decoupled from the rest of the system, the treatment indirectly influences the dynamics of the biological variables through treatment-dependent parameters, namely $\alpha_2(T)$, $\beta_1(T)$, and $\delta(T)$. Consequently, the system remains fully coupled, and the dynamics of $T(t)$ play an essential role in modulating the progression of inflammation, fibrosis, and nephron loss.

3.2.1 Disease-Free Equilibrium (DFE)

To determine the functional-unit-preserving equilibrium of model (1), we set all right-hand sides equal to zero. The disease-free equilibrium (DFE) is given by

$$E_0^* = (N_0^*, F_0^*, I_0^*, G_0^*, T_0^*) = \left(N_{\max}, 0, 0, \frac{\rho N_{\max}}{\gamma}, \frac{u}{\omega}\right),$$

where $N_{\max}$ denotes the maximal number of functional nephrons in the absence of fibrosis and inflammation, and $T_0^* = \frac{u}{\omega}$ represents the steady-state level of treatment under a constant administration rate u.

3.2.2 Threshold Parameter

To derive the threshold parameter governing disease progression and fibrosis development, we employ the classical next-generation matrix approach [8,19]. Accordingly, the basic reproduction number associated with system(1) is given by

$$\mathcal{R}_0 = \frac{\beta_1(T_0)\, N_0^*}{\mu + \delta(T_0)}. \tag{4}$$

In the context of chronic kidney disease, $\mathcal{R}_0$ does not represent a transmission potential between individuals, but rather quantifies the intrinsic capacity of inflammation to induce fibrosis and promote disease progression within the kidney. Specifically, $\mathcal{R}_0$ compares the fibrosis-inducing effect of inflammation, modulated by treatment through $\beta_1(T_0)$ and the available functional nephron reserve N_0^*, to the overall resolution rate of inflammation and fibrosis, represented by $\mu + \delta(T_0)$.

If $\mathcal{R}_0 < 1$, resolution mechanisms dominate, leading to the attenuation of inflammation and fibrosis and the preservation of renal function. Conversely, if $\mathcal{R}_0 > 1$, fibrotic progression prevails, resulting in sustained inflammation, nephron loss, and deterioration of kidney function despite treatment.

3.2.3 Endemic Equilibrium

The endemic equilibrium $E^* = (N^*, F^*, I^*, G^*, T^*)$ of the chronic kidney disease model is obtained by setting all time derivatives equal to zero. Assuming a constant treatment input $u(t) = u$, the steady-state treatment level is given by

$$T^* = \frac{u}{\omega}.$$

The equilibrium level of inflammation satisfies

$$I^* = \frac{\eta H + \kappa F^*}{\delta(T^*)},$$

while the fibrosis level is determined by the balance between fibrosis progression and natural resolution,

$$F^* = \frac{\beta_1(T^*)I^*}{\mu + \beta_1(T^*)I^*}.$$

The glomerular filtration rate at equilibrium is expressed as

$$G^* = \frac{\rho N^*}{\gamma F^*}.$$

It is important to note that the equation governing the functional nephron population does not yield an explicit algebraic expression for N^*. Instead, N^* remains implicitly determined by the long-term dynamics of the system and the initial renal reserve. Consequently, the endemic equilibrium is characterized by positive steady-state levels of inflammation and fibrosis, corresponding to a persistent chronic disease state.

3.3 Global Stability Analysis

Theorem 2. *If $\mathcal{R}_0 < 1$, the disease-free equilibrium E_0 of system (1) is globally asymptotically stable in the feasible region.*

Proof. Consider the Lyapunov function

$$V_1(F, I) = F + \frac{\mu + \delta(T_0)}{\beta_1(T_0)} I,$$

which is positive definite for all $(F, I) \in \mathbb{R}_+^2$ and vanishes only at the disease-free equilibrium E_0. Taking the time derivative of V along the trajectories of system(1), we obtain

$$\frac{dV_1}{dt} \leq (\mu + \delta(T_0))(\mathcal{R}_0 - 1)I.$$

When $\mathcal{R}_0 < 1$, it follows that $\frac{dV_1}{dt} \leq 0$, with equality if and only if $I = 0$ and $F = 0$. By LaSalle's invariance principle, all trajectories converge to E_0, which proves that the disease-free equilibrium is globally asymptotically stable. □

Theorem 3. *If $\mathcal{R}_0 > 1$, the endemic equilibrium E^* of system (1) exists and is globally asymptotically stable.*

Proof. Assume that $\mathcal{R}_0 > 1$ so that the endemic equilibrium $E^* = (N^*, F^*, I^*)$ exists and belongs to the interior of the positively invariant region. Consider the Lyapunov function

$$V_2(N,F,I) = N - N^* - N^* \ln\left(\frac{N}{N^*}\right) + F - F^* - F^* \ln\left(\frac{F}{F^*}\right) \quad +I - I^* - I^* \ln\left(\frac{I}{I^*}\right).$$

The function V is nonnegative for all (N, F, I) in the feasible region and satisfies $V_2(N, F, I) = 0$ if and only if $(N, F, I) = (N^*, F^*, I^*)$. Moreover, V_2 is radially unbounded in the interior of the region. Differentiating V along the trajectories of system (1) yields

$$\dot{V}_2 = \left(1 - \frac{N^*}{N}\right)\dot{\mathrm{N}} + \left(1 - \frac{F^*}{F}\right)\dot{\mathrm{F}} + \left(1 - \frac{I^*}{I}\right)\dot{I}.$$

Substituting the right-hand sides of the system and using the equilibrium relations satisfied at E^*, namely

$$\alpha_1 F^* + \alpha_2(T^*)I^* = 0, \qquad \beta_1(T^*)I^*(1 - F^*) = \mu F^*, \qquad \eta H + \kappa F^* = \delta(T^*)I^*,$$

we obtain after simplification

$$\dot{V}_2 = -\alpha_1(F - F^*)^2 - \alpha_2(T^*)(I - I^*)^2 - \mu\frac{(F - F^*)^2}{F} - \delta(T^*)\frac{(I - I^*)^2}{I} \leq 0.$$

Hence, $\dot{V}_2$ is negative semi-definite in the feasible region and $\dot{V}_2 = 0$ if and only if $N = N^*$, $F = F^*$ and $I = I^*$. Therefore, the largest invariant set contained in $\{(N, F, I) : \dot{V}_2 = 0\}$ is the singleton $\{E^*\}$. By LaSalle's invariance principle, every solution of system (1) starting in the feasible region converges to the endemic equilibrium E^* as $t \to \infty$. This proves that E^* is globally asymptotically stable. □

4 Stochastic Switching Model

4.1 Existence, Uniqueness, and Positivity of Solutions

Theorem 4. *For any initial condition* $(N(0), F(0), I(0), G(0), T(0)) \in \mathbb{R}^5_+$, $r(0) \in \mathcal{M}$, *system* (2) *admits a unique global solution* $(N(t), F(t), I(t), G(t), T(t), r(t))$, $\ t \geq 0$, *which remains positive almost surely. In particular,* $N(t)$, $F(t)$, $I(t)$, $G(t)$, $T(t) > 0$ *for all* $t \geq 0$ *a.s.*

Proof. The proof is carried out in three steps.

Step 1: Local Existence and Uniqueness. For a fixed regime $r(t) = i \in \mathcal{M}$, system (2) reduces to a classical stochastic differential equation in $\mathbb{R}^5_+$. Let

$$X(t) = (N(t), F(t), I(t), G(t), T(t))^\top.$$

For each $i \in \mathcal{M}$, the drift and diffusion coefficients of the system are locally Lipschitz continuous with respect to X and satisfy the linear growth condition, since they are composed of linear and bilinear functions of the state variables. Therefore, by the classical existence and uniqueness theorem for stochastic differential equations (see [?]), there exists a unique local solution defined on the interval $[0, \tau_e)$, where τ_e denotes the explosion time.

Step 2: Global Existence (Non-explosion). To prove that the solution is global, we introduce the Lyapunov function

$$L_1(X) = N + F + I + G + T.$$

Applying Itô's formula to $V(X(t))$ gives

$$dL_1(t) = \mathcal{L}L_1(X(t), r(t))\, dt + \sum_{j=1}^{5} \sigma_j^{r(t)} X_j(t)\, dB_j(t),$$

where $\mathcal{L}$ denotes the infinitesimal generator of the stochastic system.
Using the structure of the model equations, it follows that there exists a constant $K > 0$ such that

$$\mathcal{L}L_1(X(t), r(t)) \leq K\big(1 + L_1(t)\big).$$

Define the stopping time

$$\tau_n = \inf\{t \geq 0 : L_1(t) \geq n\}.$$

Taking expectations and applying Gronwall's inequality yields

$$\mathbb{E}\big[L_1(t \wedge \tau_n)\big] \leq (L_1(0) + Kt)e^{Kt}.$$

Letting $n \to \infty$ implies that $\tau_e = \infty$ almost surely. Consequently, the solution exists globally for all $t \geq 0$.

Step 3: Positivity of Solutions. To establish the positivity of the solution, we apply Itô's formula to the logarithmic transformation of each state variable. For instance, for $N(t)$ we obtain

$$d \ln N(t) = \Big[-\alpha_1^{r(t)} F(t) - \alpha_2^{r(t)} T(t) I(t) - \frac{(\sigma_1^{r(t)})^2}{2} \Big] dt + \sigma_1^{r(t)} dB_1(t).$$

Since the stochastic differential equation for $\ln N(t)$ admits a finite solution for all $t \geq 0$, it follows that $N(t) > 0$ almost surely. By applying the same argument to the remaining variables $F(t)$, $I(t)$, $G(t)$, and $T(t)$, we conclude that all state variables remain strictly positive with probability one. Combining the results of the above steps completes the proof.

4.2 Almost Sure Extinction

We investigate sufficient conditions under which the fibrosis and inflammation compartments $F(t)$ and $I(t)$ of system (2) become extinct almost surely.

Theorem 5 (Almost sure extinction). *Let $r(t)$ be an irreducible continuous-time Markov chain with state space $\mathcal{M} = \{1, \dots, m\}$ and stationary distribution $\pi = (\pi_1, \dots, \pi_m)$. Assume that there exist positive constants a_i and b_i such that, for each regime $i \in \mathcal{M}$, the drift of the (F, I) subsystem satisfies*

$$\frac{d}{dt}\big(\ln F(t) + \ln I(t)\big) \le a_i - b_i - \frac{1}{2}\big((\sigma_2^i)^2 + (\sigma_3^i)^2\big).$$

Define the stochastic threshold

$$\mathcal{R}_s = \sum_{i \in \mathcal{M}} \pi_i \frac{a_i}{b_i} - \frac{1}{2} \sum_{i \in \mathcal{M}} \pi_i \big((\sigma_2^i)^2 + (\sigma_3^i)^2\big).$$

If $\mathcal{R}_s < 1$, then

$$\lim_{t \to \infty} F(t) = 0, \qquad \lim_{t \to \infty} I(t) = 0 \quad \textit{almost surely.}$$

Proof. Consider the Lyapunov function

$$L_2(t) = \ln F(t) + \ln I(t),$$

which is well defined for all $t \ge 0$ since $F(t), I(t) > 0$ almost surely. Applying Itô's formula to $V(t)$ yields

$$dL_2(t) = \left[\frac{\beta_1^{r(t)}(T)I(t)(1 - F(t))}{F(t)} - \mu^{r(t)} + \frac{\eta^{r(t)}H + \kappa^{r(t)}F(t)}{I(t)} - \delta^{r(t)}(T)\right] dt$$
$$- \frac{1}{2}\big((\sigma_2^{r(t)})^2 + (\sigma_3^{r(t)})^2\big)dt + \sigma_2^{r(t)}\, dB_2(t) + \sigma_3^{r(t)}\, dB_3(t).$$

Since $0 < F(t) \le 1$ and all parameters are positive, there exist constants $a_{r(t)} > 0$ and $b_{r(t)} > 0$ such that

$$dL_2(t) \le \left[a_{r(t)} - b_{r(t)} - \frac{1}{2}\big((\sigma_2^{r(t)})^2 + (\sigma_3^{r(t)})^2\big)\right] dt + \sigma_2^{r(t)}\, dB_2(t) + \sigma_3^{r(t)}\, dB_3(t).$$

Integrating both sides from 0 to t and dividing by t gives

$$\frac{L_2(t) - L_2(0)}{t} \le \frac{1}{t}\int_0^t \left[a_{r(s)} - b_{r(s)} - \frac{1}{2}\big((\sigma_2^{r(s)})^2 + (\sigma_3^{r(s)})^2\big)\right] ds + \frac{M(t)}{t},$$

where $M(t)$ is a local martingale. Since the Markov chain $r(t)$ is ergodic with stationary distribution π, the ergodic theorem implies

$$\lim_{t \to \infty} \frac{1}{t}\int_0^t \left[a_{r(s)} - b_{r(s)} - \frac{1}{2}\big((\sigma_2^{r(s)})^2 + (\sigma_3^{r(s)})^2\big)\right] ds = \sum_{i \in \mathcal{M}} \pi_i \left(a_i - b_i - \frac{1}{2}\big((\sigma_2^i)^2 + (\sigma_3^i)^2\big)\right).$$

Moreover, by the strong law of large numbers for local martingales,

$$\lim_{t \to \infty} \frac{M(t)}{t} = 0 \quad \text{almost surely.}$$

Therefore,

$$\limsup_{t\to\infty} \frac{L_2(t)}{t} \leq \sum_{i\in\mathcal{M}} \pi_i \left(a_i - b_i - \frac{1}{2}\big((\sigma_2^i)^2 + (\sigma_3^i)^2\big) \right).$$

If $\mathcal{R}_s < 1$, the right-hand side is negative, which implies $\lim_{t\to\infty} L_2(t) = -\infty$ almost surely.
Consequently,

$$\lim_{t\to\infty} F(t) = 0, \qquad \lim_{t\to\infty} I(t) = 0 \quad \text{almost surely.}$$

4.3 Persistence in Mean

We establish conditions ensuring that the fibrosis and inflammation compartments persist on average. In stochastic epidemic models, persistence in mean describes the situation where the long–term time averages of the state variables remain strictly positive.

Theorem 6. *Assume that the Markov chain $r(t)$ is irreducible with stationary distribution*
$\pi = (\pi_1, \ldots, \pi_m)$ and that the stochastic threshold satisfies $\mathcal{R}_s > 1$. Then the fibrosis and inflammation populations of system (2) *are persistent in mean, that is,*

$$\liminf_{t\to\infty} \frac{1}{t}\int_0^t F(s)\,ds > 0, \qquad \liminf_{t\to\infty} \frac{1}{t}\int_0^t I(s)\,ds > 0 \quad \textit{almost surely.}$$

Proof. Consider the stochastic Lyapunov function

$$L_3(t) = \ln F(t) + \ln I(t),$$

which is well defined since $F(t), I(t) > 0$ almost surely.
Applying Itô's formula yields

$$dL_3(t) = \frac{1}{F(t)}\,dF(t) + \frac{1}{I(t)}\,dI(t) - \frac{1}{2}\frac{(dF(t))^2}{F(t)^2} - \frac{1}{2}\frac{(dI(t))^2}{I(t)^2}.$$

Substituting the stochastic equations for $F(t)$ and $I(t)$ from system (??), we obtain

$$\begin{aligned} dL_3(t) = {} & \left[\frac{\beta_1^{r(t)}(T) I(t)(1-F(t))}{F(t)} - \mu^{r(t)} + \frac{\eta^{r(t)} H + \kappa^{r(t)} F(t)}{I(t)} - \delta^{r(t)}(T) \right] dt \\ & - \frac{1}{2}\big((\sigma_2^{r(t)})^2 + (\sigma_3^{r(t)})^2\big)dt + \sigma_2^{r(t)}\,dB_2(t) + \sigma_3^{r(t)}\,dB_3(t). \end{aligned}$$

Since $0 < F(t) \leq 1$ and all parameters are positive, there exist constants $a_{r(t)} > 0$ and $b_{r(t)} > 0$ such that

$$\frac{\beta_1^{r(t)}(T) I(t)(1-F(t))}{F(t)} + \frac{\eta^{r(t)} H + \kappa^{r(t)} F(t)}{I(t)} \geq a_{r(t)},$$

and

$$\mu^{r(t)} + \delta^{r(t)}(T) \leq b_{r(t)}.$$

Consequently,

$$dL_3(t) \geq \left[a_{r(t)} - b_{r(t)} - \frac{1}{2}((\sigma_2^{r(t)})^2 + (\sigma_3^{r(t)})^2)\right] dt + \sigma_2^{r(t)}\, dB_2(t) + \sigma_3^{r(t)}\, dB_3(t).$$

Integrating from 0 to t gives

$$L_3(t) - L_3(0) \geq \int_0^t \left[a_{r(s)} - b_{r(s)} - \frac{1}{2}((\sigma_2^{r(s)})^2 + (\sigma_3^{r(s)})^2)\right] ds + M(t),$$

where

$$M(t) = \int_0^t \sigma_2^{r(s)}\, dB_2(s) + \int_0^t \sigma_3^{r(s)}\, dB_3(s)$$

is a local martingale. Dividing by t and taking the limit inferior yields

$$\frac{L_3(t)}{t} \geq \frac{1}{t}\int_0^t \left[a_{r(s)} - b_{r(s)} - \frac{1}{2}((\sigma_2^{r(s)})^2 + (\sigma_3^{r(s)})^2)\right] ds + \frac{M(t)}{t}.$$

Since $r(t)$ is ergodic, the ergodic theorem implies

$$\lim_{t\to\infty} \frac{1}{t}\int_0^t \left[a_{r(s)} - b_{r(s)} - \frac{1}{2}((\sigma_2^{r(s)})^2 + (\sigma_3^{r(s)})^2)\right] ds = \sum_{i\in\mathcal{M}} \pi_i \left(a_i - b_i - \frac{1}{2}((\sigma_2^i)^2 + (\sigma_3^i)^2)\right).$$

Moreover, by the strong law of large numbers for martingales, we have $\lim_{t\to\infty} \dfrac{M(t)}{t} = 0$ almost surely. Hence,

$$\liminf_{t\to\infty} \frac{L_3(t)}{t} \geq \sum_{i\in\mathcal{M}} \pi_i \left(a_i - b_i - \frac{1}{2}((\sigma_2^i)^2 + (\sigma_3^i)^2)\right).$$

If $\mathcal{R}_s > 1$, the right-hand side is positive. Therefore,

$$\liminf_{t\to\infty} \frac{1}{t}\int_0^t \ln(F(s)I(s))\, ds > 0.$$

Using Jensen's inequality, it follows that

$$\liminf_{t\to\infty} \frac{1}{t}\int_0^t F(s)\, ds > 0, \qquad \liminf_{t\to\infty} \frac{1}{t}\int_0^t I(s)\, ds > 0 \quad \text{almost surely.}$$

Thus, the fibrosis and inflammation populations persist in mean.

5 Numerical Simulations

5.1 Numerical Methodology and Data-Driven Framework

Before performing parameter estimation and simulations, we briefly describe the numerical methods used to solve both the deterministic and stochastic versions of the proposed CKD model. This step ensures the stability and reliability of the computational results. Model parameters are then estimated from clinical data, and the calibrated model is used to investigate disease progression and treatment effects. Numerical simulations are performed to illustrate the theoretical findings and to analyze the qualitative dynamics of the renal compartments under treatment and stochastic perturbations, using biologically realistic parameter values consistent with clinical observations reported in the literature.

5.2 Numerical Scheme for the Stochastic CKD Model

To approximate the solution of the stochastic CKD model, we employ the Euler–Maruyama scheme with Milstein correction, which is well suited for stochastic differential equations with multiplicative noise and preserves the positivity of state variables. Let $\Delta t > 0$ denote the time step and let $\zeta_{k,i} \sim \mathcal{N}(0,1)$, $k = 1, \ldots, 5$, be independent standard Gaussian random variables.

For simplicity of numerical implementation, we first consider system (2) without regime switching. The discretized scheme is given by

$$N_{i+1} = N_i + \Big[- \alpha_1 F_i N_i - \alpha_2(T_i) I_i N_i \Big] \Delta t + \sigma_1 N_i \sqrt{\Delta t}\, \zeta_{1,i} + \frac{\sigma_1^2}{2} N_i (\zeta_{1,i}^2 - 1)\Delta t,$$

$$F_{i+1} = F_i + \Big[\beta_1(T_i) I_i (1 - F_i) - \mu F_i \Big] \Delta t + \sigma_2 F_i \sqrt{\Delta t}\, \zeta_{2,i} + \frac{\sigma_2^2}{2} F_i (\zeta_{2,i}^2 - 1)\Delta t,$$

$$I_{i+1} = I_i + \Big[\eta H + \kappa F_i - \delta(T_i) I_i \Big] \Delta t + \sigma_3 I_i \sqrt{\Delta t}\, \zeta_{3,i} + \frac{\sigma_3^2}{2} I_i (\zeta_{3,i}^2 - 1)\Delta t,$$

$$G_{i+1} = G_i + \Big[\rho N_i - \gamma F_i G_i \Big] \Delta t + \sigma_4 G_i \sqrt{\Delta t}\, \zeta_{4,i} + \frac{\sigma_4^2}{2} G_i (\zeta_{4,i}^2 - 1)\Delta t,$$

$$T_{i+1} = T_i + \Big[u(t_i) - \omega T_i \Big] \Delta t + \sigma_5 T_i \sqrt{\Delta t}\, \zeta_{5,i} + \frac{\sigma_5^2}{2} T_i (\zeta_{5,i}^2 - 1)\Delta t.$$

Here, $N(t)$ denotes the functional nephron population, $F(t)$ the level of fibrosis, $I(t)$ the inflammatory activity, $G(t)$ the glomerular damage, and $T(t)$ the treatment intensity. The parameters $\sigma_k > 0$, $k = 1, \ldots, 5$, represent the intensities of environmental and physiological stochastic fluctuations affecting each compartment. This numerical framework preserves the biological feasibility of the solutions and enables the investigation of extinction, persistence, and long-term stochastic behavior of CKD progression under different treatment strategies.

5.3 Clinical Dataset and Data-Driven Calibration

5.3.1 Clinical Dataset

The clinical data used in this study were obtained from the *Chronic Kidney Disease (CKD) Dataset* available in the UCI Machine Learning Repository [20], which contains medical records of approximately 400 patients. The dataset includes demographic, clinical, and laboratory variables relevant to renal function assessment and CKD progression, such as age, blood pressure, serum creatinine, blood urea, hemoglobin level, albumin, sugar, and the estimated glomerular filtration rate (eGFR), commonly used as a proxy for kidney function. Additional categorical indicators, including hypertension and diabetes status, are also provided. Prior to model calibration, the dataset was preprocessed to ensure data quality and numerical consistency. Missing values were handled using standard imputation methods (mean substitution for continuous variables and mode substitution for categorical variables). Continuous variables were subsequently normalized to reduce scale effects and facilitate the parameter estimation procedure.

5.3.2 Estimated Parameters

Using this calibration procedure, a subset of key model parameters was estimated from the dataset, while the remaining parameters were fixed based on biological relevance and consistency with the literature. The resulting parameter values used in the simulations are summarized in Table 2. Several parameters were fixed to avoid identifiability issues and ensure biological plausibility. In particular, μ represents the natural fibrosis resolution rate and was set to $\mu = 0.05$, reflecting the slow regression of fibrosis in CKD. The feedback coefficient $\kappa = 0.03$ accounts for the reinforcing interaction between fibrosis and inflammation. The parameter $\rho = 1$ normalizes the contribution of functional nephrons to the glomerular filtration rate. The glomerular damage coefficient was defined as $\gamma = |\alpha_1| + |\alpha_2|$ to capture the cumulative effects of fibrosis and inflammation. Finally, the treatment decay rate was fixed at $\omega = 0.1$, consistent with typical pharmacodynamic assumptions. The validation root mean square error (RMSE) obtained for the renal function proxy was 0.4159, indicating good agreement between model predictions and clinical observations and confirming the ability of the proposed CKD model to capture the overall dynamics of renal function.

Table 2. Estimated and fixed model parameters for the CKD model

Parameter	Description	Value
α_1	Nephron loss induced by fibrosis	0.0334
α_2	Nephron loss induced by inflammation	0.0465
β_1	Fibrosis activation rate	0.3037
δ	Inflammation clearance rate	0.9252
η	External inflammatory stimulus	0.0447
μ	Natural fibrosis resolution rate	0.05 (fixed)
κ	Fibrosis–inflammation feedback	0.03 (fixed)
ρ	Nephron contribution to GFR	1.0 (fixed)
γ	Glomerular damage coefficient	$\|\alpha_1\| + \|\alpha_2\|$
ω	Treatment decay rate	0.1 (fixed)

5.4 Graphical Validation and Numerical Simulations

After the quantitative validation of the proposed CKD model using the Root Mean Square Error (RMSE), graphical numerical simulations are performed to further assess the qualitative behavior of the system. While the RMSE provides a numerical measure of the agreement between model predictions and clinical data, graphical simulations allow a deeper interpretation of the temporal evolution of key biological compartments and the impact of stochastic perturbations and treatment strategies. In particular, the time evolution of fibrosis $F(t)$, inflammation $I(t)$, renal function proxy $G(t)$, and treatment intensity $T(t)$ is illustrated under both deterministic and stochastic formulations of the model. The comparison between deterministic and stochastic trajectories highlights the role of environmental and physiological noise in disease progression and treatment response. These simulations confirm that the stochastic model remains biologically consistent and numerically stable, in agreement with the theoretical results on positivity, persistence, and long-term behavior. Moreover, the graphical results complement the RMSE-based validation by showing that the estimated parameters lead to realistic disease dynamics over time. In particular, the renal function trajectory $G(t)$ exhibits smooth degradation patterns modulated by treatment effects, while fibrosis and inflammation remain within biologically plausible ranges. This combined quantitative–qualitative validation strengthens the reliability of the proposed CKD model for predictive and exploratory studies.

5.5 Biological Interpretation of Numerical Simulations

Figure 1 presents the temporal evolution of the main renal compartments of the CKD model, namely the functional nephron population $N(t)$, fibrosis level $F(t)$, inflammatory activity $I(t)$, renal function proxy $G(t)$, and treatment intensity $T(t)$, for both deterministic and stochastic formulations. These simulations illustrate the extinction and persistence properties established in the theoretical analysis. The functional nephron population $N(t)$ gradually declines, reflecting irreversible nephron loss induced by sustained inflammation and fibrosis. In agreement with the extinction results, persistent pathological stress drives $N(t)$ toward low levels, corresponding biologically to advanced CKD stages. In contrast, the fibrosis variable $F(t)$ stabilizes at a positive level, indicating long-term persistence of fibrotic tissue. This behavior is consistent with the persistence theorem and reflects the well-known irreversibility of renal fibrosis once structural remodeling becomes established. Inflammatory activity $I(t)$ decreases significantly in the presence of treatment and may fluctuate around low values, illustrating a treatment-driven extinction tendency. Clinically, this corresponds to controlled inflammatory activity and disease stabilization. The renal function indicator $G(t)$ remains positive but progressively decreases as nephron loss and fibrosis accumulate. This persistence above zero represents partial preservation of renal function, consistent with compensated CKD dynamics. Finally, stochastic perturbations introduce variability around the deterministic trajectories without altering the qualitative long-term behavior, highlighting the influence of physiological variability and environmental factors in disease progression.

5.6 Numerical Simulations and Treatment Impact

Following model calibration, numerical simulations were conducted to analyze the impact of therapeutic intervention on CKD dynamics. Figure 2 compares the evolution of fibrosis $F(t)$, inflammation $I(t)$, and renal function $G(t)$ with and without treatment. In the absence of treatment, fibrosis and inflammation progressively increase, leading to a gradual decline in renal function. Conversely, treatment substantially reduces inflammatory activity, which slows fibrotic progression and helps maintain higher levels of renal function. These results are consistent with the theoretical extinction–persistence analysis: effective therapeutic control of inflammation can suppress pathological dynamics and delay renal deterioration. Biologically, this highlights the importance of early and sustained treatment strategies to limit fibrosis development and preserve nephron function in chronic kidney disease.

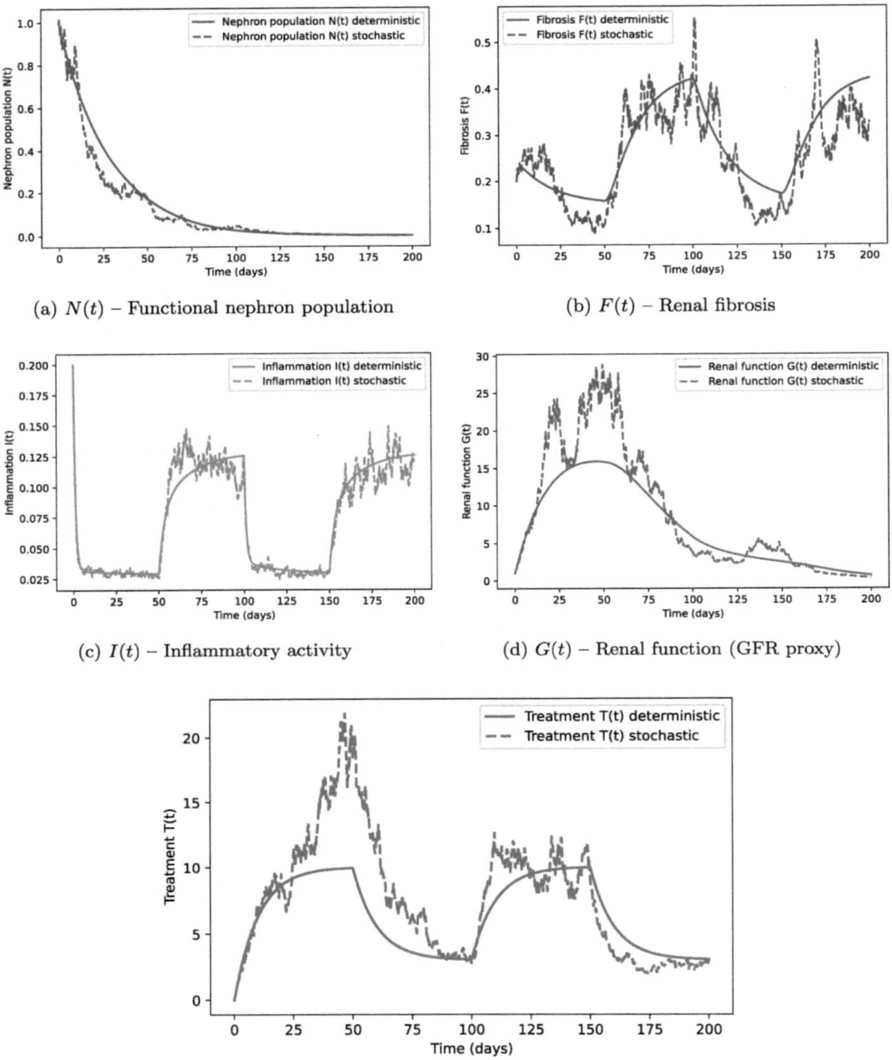

(a) $N(t)$ – Functional nephron population

(b) $F(t)$ – Renal fibrosis

(c) $I(t)$ – Inflammatory activity

(d) $G(t)$ – Renal function (GFR proxy)

(e) $T(t)$ – Treatment intensity

Fig. 1. Numerical simulations of the CKD model showing the temporal evolution of nephron population $N(t)$, fibrosis $F(t)$, inflammation $I(t)$, renal function $G(t)$, and treatment intensity $T(t)$ for both deterministic and stochastic formulations, using the estimated parameters reported in Table 2.

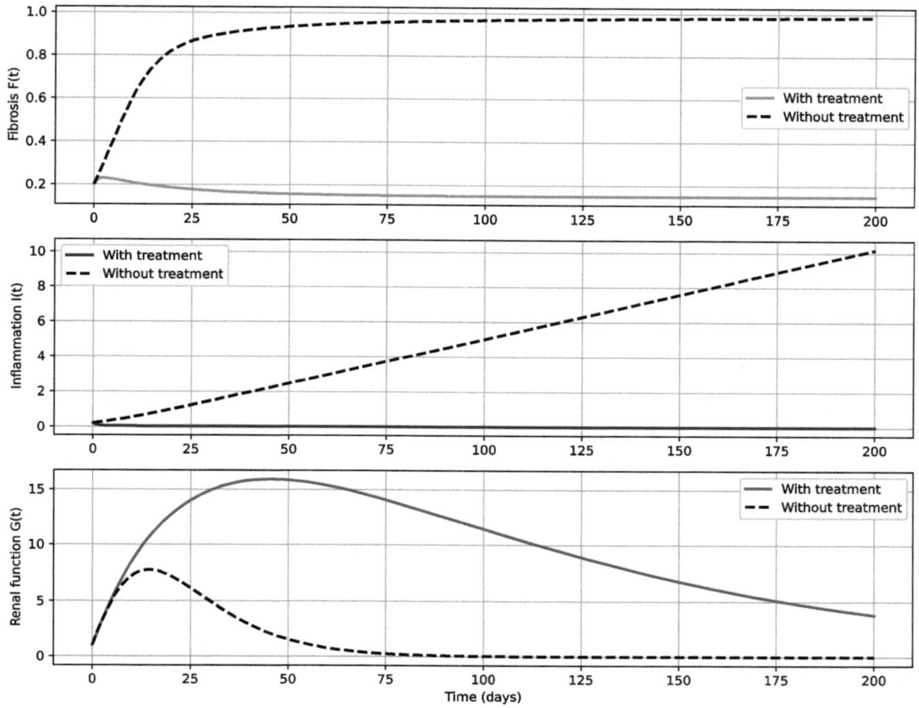

Fig. 2. Comparison of the temporal dynamics of the CKD model with and without treatment. (a) Evolution of renal fibrosis $F(t)$, (b) evolution of inflammatory activity $I(t)$, (c) evolution of renal function $G(t)$ (GFR proxy). Colored solid lines represent the treated scenario, whereas black dashed lines correspond to the absence of treatment.

6 Conclusion

In this work, we developed a mathematical framework to investigate the dynamics of chronic kidney disease (CKD) using both deterministic and stochastic modeling approaches. The proposed model incorporates key biological mechanisms involved in CKD progression, including nephron loss, fibrosis development, inflammatory activity, renal function decline, and therapeutic intervention. For the deterministic model, we established the existence and global stability of biologically relevant equilibria. The model was then extended to a stochastic formulation to account for biological variability and environmental uncertainty. Using Itô calculus and Lyapunov techniques, sufficient conditions for stochastic extinction and persistence were obtained, showing that random perturbations may significantly influence long-term disease dynamics. Model parameters were calibrated using clinical data, and numerical simulations were performed to validate the theoretical results. The simulations illustrate the impact of treatment in reducing inflammation and fibrosis while preserving renal function. Moreover, stochastic simulations highlight the role of variability in shaping disease trajectories. Overall, the proposed framework provides a useful tool for understanding CKD progression and evaluating therapeutic strategies. Future work may incorporate patient heterogeneity, adaptive treatment protocols, and additional biological mechanisms to further improve the model's clinical relevance.

References

1. Kdigo clinical practice guideline for the evaluation and management of chronic kidney disease. Kidney Int. Suppl. (2013)
2. Abdelhag, M.E.: A systematic review of machine learning methods for chronic kidney disease diagnosis and prediction (2020–2025). Saudi J. Appl. Sci. Technol. **2**(1) (2026)
3. Bera, S., Khajanchi, S., Kar, T.K.: Stochastic persistence, extinction and stationary distribution in HTLV-i infection model with CTL immune response. Qual. Theory Dyn. Syst. **23**(Suppl 1), 265 (2024)
4. Boulaasair, L.: Threshold properties of a stochastic epidemic model with a variable vaccination rate. Bull. Biomath. **1**(2), 177–191 (2023)
5. Cheng, D., Wang, J., Hu, X.: An extension of Lasalle's invariance principle and its application to multi-agent consensus. IEEE Trans. Autom. Control **53**(7), 1765–1770 (2008)
6. Das, P., Upadhyay, R.K., Misra, A.K., Rihan, F.A., Das, P., Ghosh, D.: Mathematical model of covid-19 with comorbidity and controlling using non-pharmaceutical interventions and vaccination. Nonlinear Dyn. **106**(2), 1213–1227 (2021)
7. Delrue, C., De Bruyne, S., Speeckaert, M.M.: Application of machine learning in chronic kidney disease: current status and future prospects. Biomedicines **12**(3), 568 (2024)
8. Diekmann, O., Heesterbeek, J.A.P., Metz, J.A.J.: On the definition and the computation of the basic reproduction ratio r 0 in models for infectious diseases in heterogeneous populations. J. Math. Biol. **28**(4), 365–382 (1990)
9. Din, A., Amine, S., Allali, A.: A stochastically perturbed co-infection epidemic model for Covid-19 and hepatitis b virus. Nonlinear Dyn. **111**(2), 1921–1945 (2023)
10. Gogoi, P., Valan, J.A.: Machine learning approaches for predicting and diagnosing chronic kidney disease: current trends, challenges, solutions, and future directions. Int. Urol. Nephrol. **57**(4), 1245–1268 (2025)
11. Hajri, Y., Allali, A., Amine, S.: A delayed deterministic and stochastic SIRICV model: HOPF bifurcation and stochastic analysis. Math. Comput. Simul. **215**, 98–121 (2024)
12. Salle, L., J.P.: An invariance principle in the theory of stability. Technical report (1966)
13. Liu, Q., Din, A., Allali, A.: Analysis of a multiply delayed stochastic EBOLA model based on probability density function with case study. European Phy. J. Plus **138**(11), 1–18 (2023)
14. Mao, L., et al.: Knowledge-informed machine learning for cancer diagnosis and prognosis: a review. IEEE Trans. Autom. Sci. Eng. **22**, 10008–10028 (2024)
15. Mao, X.: Stochastic differential equations and applications. Elsevier (2007)
16. Mei, W., Bullo, F.: Lasalle invariance principle for discrete-time dynamical systems: a concise and self-contained tutorial. arXiv preprint arXiv:1710.03710 (2017)
17. Patharkar, A., Cai, F., Al-Hindawi, F., Wu, T.: Predictive modeling of biomedical temporal data in healthcare applications: review and future directions. Front. Physiol. **15**, 1386760 (2024)

18. Pervyshin, N.A.: Mathematical modeling of the chronic kidney disease progression rate in patients with type 2 diabetes mellitus. Sci. Innov. Med. **9**(2), 88–94 (2024)
19. Reckell, T., Sterner, B., Jevtić, P.: The basic reproduction number for petri net models: a next-generation matrix approach. Appl. Sci. **15**(23), 12827 (2025)
20. Rubini, L., Soundarapandian, P., Eswaran, P.: Chronic kidney disease dataset. https://archive.ics.uci.edu/ml/datasets/Chronic+Kidney+Disease (2015). UCI Machine Learning Repository
21. Sangeetha, T.E., Pandiyan, P., Kumar, R.H., Bose, G.S.C.: A stochastic model for chronic kidney disease. Adv. Math. Sci. J. **10**(10), 3363–3372 (2021)
22. Sharma, A., Lysenko, A., Jia, S., Boroevich, K.A., Tsunoda, T.: Advances in AI and machine learning for predictive medicine. J. Hum. Genet. **69**(10), 487–497 (2024)
23. Thomas, H.Y., Ford Versypt, A.N.: A mathematical model of glomerular fibrosis in diabetic kidney disease to predict therapeutic efficacy. Front. Pharmacol. **15**, 1481768 (2024)
24. Upadhyay, R.K., Acharya, S.: Modeling the recent outbreak of covid-19 in India and its control strategies. Nonlinear Anal. Model. Control **27**(2), 254–274 (2022)
25. Vaidya, S.R., Aeddula, N.R.: Chronic kidney disease. In: StatPearls [Internet]. StatPearls Publishing (2024)
26. ZHANG, Z., Xu, C., Jinying, T.: Lasalle's invariance principle for delay differential equations driven by α-stable processes. J. East China Normal Univ. (Natural Sci.) **2023**(4), 11 (2023)

A LightGBM Framework for Operational Tide Forecasting and Predictive Imputation in the Río De La Plata

Diego Silva Piedra[1(✉)], Mónica Fossati[2], and Pablo Ezzatti[1]

[1] Institute of Computer Science, Facultad de Ingeniería, Universidad de la República, 11300 Montevideo, Uruguay
{diegos,pezzatti}@fing.edu.uy

[2] Institute of Fluid Mechanics and Environmental Engineering, Facultad de Ingeniería, Universidad de la República, 11300 Montevideo, Uruguay
mfossati@fing.edu.uy

Abstract. Accurate tide level records are essential for hydrodynamic modeling, coastal management, and the development of operational forecasting systems. This paper presents and evaluates a LightGBM-based framework for operational tide level forecasting and predictive imputation in the Río de la Plata (RdP) estuary, one of the world's most extensive estuaries situated between Argentina and Uruguay, whose complex hydrodynamics, driven by the interplay of meteorological and astronomical forcing, pose significant challenges for predictive modeling. Two forecasting model variants are proposed and evaluated across multiple tide gauge stations and forecast horizons up to 72 h: an autoregressive baseline trained exclusively on historical tide gauge records, and a physics-informed variant that incorporates WRF meteorological forecasts and PronUy_RPFM numerical sea level predictions as additional input features. Both models are assessed in terms of accuracy and feature relevance, in the context of the PronUy_RPFM operational forecasting system developed at the Facultad de Ingeniería, Universidad de la República. Additionally, a bidirectional predictive imputation scheme is developed, applying the pre-trained forecasting model directly to the reconstruction of missing tide gauge segments by combining forward and backward predictions through distance-weighted blending.

Keywords: tide level forecasting · LightGBM · estuarine hydrodynamics · time series prediction · Río de la Plata · predictive imputation

1 Introduction

Operational coastal forecasting systems depend critically on the availability of continuous, high-quality tide gauge records. In estuarine environments subject to strong meteorological forcing such as the RdP, one of the world's largest estuaries, situated between Argentina and Uruguay, accurate water level prediction is

O. Gervasi et al. (Eds.): ICCSA 2026, LNCS 16768, pp. 532–549, 2027.
https://doi.org/10.1007/978-3-032-30488-9_33

essential for flood risk management, navigation safety, and the sustainable planning of coastal infrastructure. The RdP, especially along the Uruguayan coast, exhibits a predominantly meteorological tidal regime driven by the interaction of wind fields, atmospheric pressure gradients, river discharge, and ocean tides propagating from the South Atlantic shelf, making it a particularly challenging environment for predictive modeling [20].

PronUy_RPFM is the operational tide level forecasting system developed jointly by the Institute of Fluid Mechanics and Environmental Engineering (IMFIA) and the Institute of Computer Science (INCO) at the Facultad de Ingeniería, Universidad de la República (UdelaR), Uruguay. The system provides publicly available, hourly sea level forecasts for the next 72 h across the RdP and its maritime front, historically grounded in the TELEMAC2D finite element numerical model [7,21]. While physics-based numerical models offer physically consistent predictions [17], their accuracy is constrained by the quality of atmospheric forcing inputs and the inherent complexity of representing fine-scale estuarine dynamics. Over the years of operation, PronUy_RPFM has accumulated a substantial observational database, and that growing record opens the door to data-driven approaches that can learn directly from what the estuary has done, rather than from equations describing what it should do.

Data-driven forecasting is a natural complement to physics-based modelling in the RdP, where the meteorological component of sea level variability is difficult to parameterise but leaves a strong signature in tide gauge records that can be learned from historical data [5,6,24]. Gradient boosting models, and LightGBM in particular [10,13,25], handle lagged observations and external covariates natively and have shown competitive skill in estuarine water level prediction. Their histogram-based split-finding and leaf-wise growth strategy substantially reduce training time on decade-long hourly series while the ensemble structure provides a natural framework for incorporating meteorological forcing alongside autoregressive lags. While recurrent architectures such as LSTMs and Transformer-based models have attracted considerable attention for time series forecasting, their advantage over simpler approaches is not as clear as one might assume. Zeng et al. [27] demonstrated that a one-layer linear model outperforms several sophisticated Transformer-based solutions on standard long-term forecasting benchmarks, attributing this to the permutation-invariant self-attention mechanism's inherent difficulty in preserving temporal order. Likewise, the debate between neural networks and GBDTs on tabular data has been shown to be overemphasized: McElfresh et al. [15], in a large tabular data benchmark comparing 19 algorithms across 176 datasets, found that for a surprisingly high number of datasets either the performance difference is negligible, or light hyperparameter tuning on a GBDT matters more than the choice of algorithm family. The same study found that GBDTs are consistently superior on datasets with irregular or heavy-tailed feature distributions, a characteristic often present in estuarine water level records driven by intermittent storm surge events. This finding is consistent with Grinsztajn et al. [11], who showed that tree-based models remain state-of-the-art on medium-sized tabular datasets, as neural networks tend to struggle with irregular target functions and uninformative features. From a practical forecasting perspective, Bojer and Meldgaard [2] found that gradient boosting methods with engineered temporal features consistently ranked at the top of large-scale forecasting competitions, with their strength particularly pronounced when informative exogenous variables, such as the meteorological forcing available in the RdP context, are available. LightGBM's native handling of heterogeneous features and its substantially lower computational requirements make it a well-motivated choice for operational tide level forecasting in the RdP.

Beyond forecasting, the integrity of historical tide gauge records poses an equally important operational challenge. Sensor failures, transmission errors, and maintenance interruptions give rise to data gaps that undermine the training of data-driven models and the calibration of numerical ones. Conventional gap-filling strategies like linear interpolation, harmonic reconstruction, or simple climatological substitution ignore the temporal structure of the series and the physical forcing that drives water level variability. Given the strong autoregressive signal inherent to tide gauge records and the availability of operational wind and sea level forecasts for RdP, a predictive imputation approach based on LightGBM and trained to reconstruct missing segments represents a natural extension of the forecasting framework developed here. Predicting bidirectionally (*i.e.*, from before and after the gap) and blending the two through distance weighting helps reduce the drift that accumulates in longer gaps.

This paper presents the development and evaluation of two LightGBM-based forecasting models integrated into the PronUy_RPFM system, together with a LightGBM-based predictive imputation scheme for tide gauge records. The main contributions of this work are as follows:

- We develop an autoregressive LightGBM baseline trained exclusively on historical tide gauge records that matches competitive forecasting performance across multiple RdP stations and horizons.
- We propose a hybrid physics-informed LightGBM framework that takes PronUy_RPFM numerical sea level predictions and WRF meteorological forecasts as input features, improving forecasting performance over the historical data-only baseline.
- We introduce a bidirectional predictive imputation scheme that reconstructs missing tide gauge records by combining forward and backward LightGBM predictions with distance-weighted blending.

The remainder of the paper is organized as follows. Section 2 describes the study area and the datasets employed. Section 3 details the LightGBM forecasting framework, including the recursive prediction strategy and feature engineering. Section 4 presents the predictive imputation approach. Section 5 reports and discusses results for both forecasting and imputation tasks. Section 6 summarizes the conclusions and outlines directions for future work.

2 Study Area and Data

2.1 The Río De La Plata Estuary and Tide Gauge Network

The RdP is a large estuarine system on the southeastern coast of South America, forming the boundary between Argentina and Uruguay (Fig. 1). Fed primarily by the Paraná and Uruguay rivers, it receives an average freshwater discharge of approximately 26,000 m^3/s. Its geometry spans roughly 290 km in length and up to 220 km in width at its mouth, transitioning from a broad shallow inner zone, where depths generally remain below 10 m west of the Montevideo–Punta Piedras cross-section, to a deeper outer region with depths exceeding 20 m [12]. This morphological configuration, combined with its large surface area, makes the estuary highly sensitive to surface wind stress and atmospheric pressure perturbations propagating from the South Atlantic shelf.

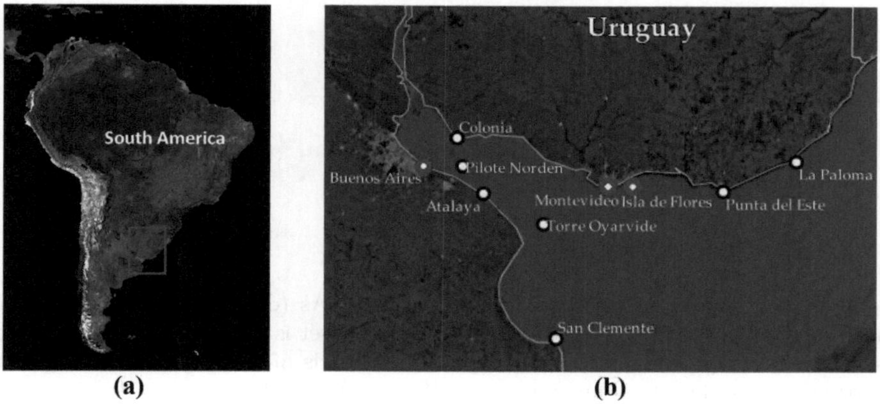

Fig. 1. Geographic setting of the study area. (a) Location of the Río de la Plata on the South American continent. (b) Location of the tide gauge stations used in this study – Montevideo (MVD), Buenos Aires (BsAs), and Isla de Flores (IdF).

The RdP operates under a microtidal regime in which the meteorological component of sea level variability dominates along the Uruguayan coast, while astronomical tidal forcing is more prominent along the Argentine coast [8,19]. Meteorological sea level anomalies arise from storm surges generated over the continental shelf and subsequently modified by estuarine geometry, wind friction, and bathymetric effects as they propagate inland. Sustained southeasterly winds are the primary driver of positive water level anomalies at the Uruguayan coast, whereas west-northwesterly winds are systematically associated with below-average levels [19].

Tide gauge records used in this study were obtained at three monitoring stations: Montevideo (MVD), located on the northern coast of the inner estuary; Buenos Aires (BsAs), on the southern Argentine coast; and Isla de Flores

(IdF), near the outer estuary mouth (Fig. 1). Records at MVD and IdF are maintained by the National Port Administration of Uruguay (Administración Nacional de Puertos, ANP), while the BsAs record is provided by the Argentine Naval Hydrography Service (Servicio de Hidrografía Naval, SHN). Sub-hourly raw measurements were aggregated to hourly averages; isolated outliers were removed and short discontinuities filled by linear interpolation. The resulting time series span 2017–2025, with varying coverage and continuity across stations (Fig. 2). The most recent year of available data at each location was withheld as an independent test set: 2025 for MVD and BsAs, and 2024 for IdF, with all preceding data used for training and validation.

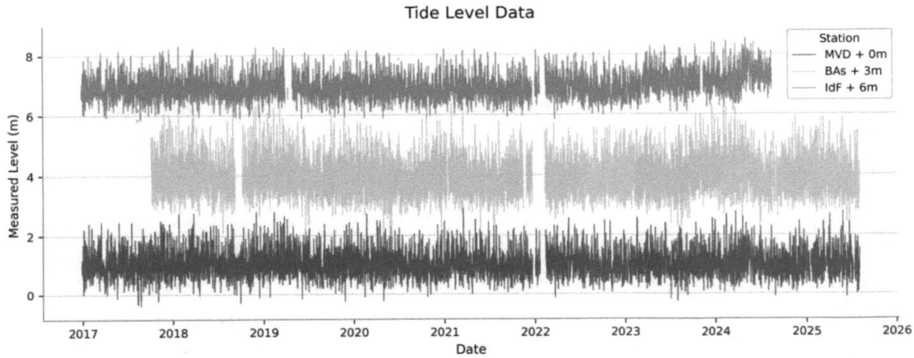

Fig. 2. Hourly tide level records at MVD (blue), BsAs (orange), and Isla de Flores (green) for the study period. An arbitrary vertical offset is applied at each station for visual clarity. Gaps in the series correspond to periods of missing data arising from sensor failures or data transmission errors. (Color figure online)

2.2 Meteorological and Numerical Forcing Data

Meteorological forcing data used as inputs to the PronUy_LightGBM2 model variant were obtained from numerical weather forecasts produced by IMFIA researchers at the Facultad de Ingeniería using the Advanced Research WRF model [22,23]. The WRF system provides hourly wind speed (m/s) and wind direction (degrees) at a grid point collocated with the Montevideo port tide gauge, with temporal coverage spanning the full tide level measurement period. As described in Sect. 3, wind speed and direction are subsequently decomposed into directional intensity projections along eight cardinal and intercardinal directions as part of the feature engineering process.

In addition, operational sea level forecasts from the PronUy_RPFM system [7] were incorporated as a physics-based predictor for the MVD station. These forecasts are generated by the TELEMAC2D finite element hydrodynamic model and provide a physically consistent signal encoding the large-scale tidal and meteorological variability of the estuary, complementing the statistical patterns learned by the LightGBM model from historical tide gauge observations.

3 LightGBM-Based Forecasting Framework

3.1 Model Architecture and Recursive Multi-step Prediction

LightGBM [13] is an open-source gradient boosting framework developed by Microsoft that constructs a predictive model as an additive ensemble of decision trees. Each tree comprises a root node receiving the input data, internal nodes encoding learned splitting rules, and leaf nodes producing scalar predictions [26]. Building on the gradient boosting paradigm introduced by Friedman [9], each successive tree in the ensemble is fitted to the negative gradient of the loss with respect to the current predictions, progressively reducing the residual error. The histogram-based split finding, leaf-wise tree growth, and gradient-based one-sided sampling that distinguish LightGBM from conventional gradient boosting implementations translate into substantial gains in training throughput and memory efficiency, a practical advantage when retraining independently across stations and forecast horizons on the observational record accumulated by PronUy_RPFM.

Formally, given an input feature vector $\mathbf{x}$, the ensemble output $\hat{Y}_I$ after I boosting rounds is:

$$\hat{Y}_I = \sum_{i=1}^{I} T_i(\mathbf{x}, \theta_i), \tag{1}$$

where T_i denotes the i-th regression tree and θ_i its associated leaf weights. At each round, the new tree is obtained by minimizing an objective that combines a task loss $\mathcal{L}$ and a complexity regularizer Ω_i:

$$\mathcal{O}bj_i = \mathcal{L}(y, \hat{y}_i) + \Omega_i, \tag{2}$$

where y is the target observation and $\hat{y}_i$ the prediction at round i. The regularization term Ω_i penalizes the number of leaves and the magnitude of leaf weights, controlling model complexity and reducing the risk of overfitting at longer forecast horizons. Figure 3 illustrates this additive construction: each successive tree T_i is fitted to the residual of the previous ensemble and their outputs are summed to produce the final prediction.

Because LightGBM produces a single scalar output, a recursive multi-step prediction strategy is adopted to generate L-hour forecasts (Fig. 4). At step t, the model takes a feature vector $\mathbf{f}(t)$, constructed from the window of W most recent water level observations and auxiliary inputs, and outputs the predicted level $\hat{y}(t+1)$. This prediction is appended to the input window, the feature vector is recomputed for step $t+1$, and the process is iterated L times without retraining any additional model. The dependency of each step on its predecessors mirrors the operational setting in which only past and forecast-horizon inputs are available.

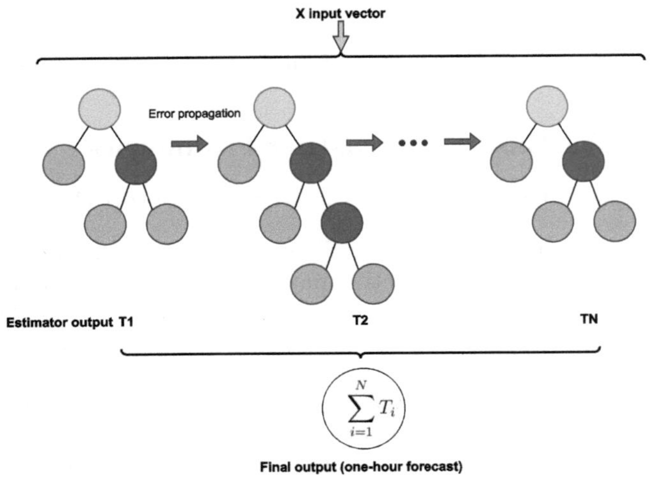

Fig. 3. Gradient boosting ensemble: each tree T_i receives the same input vector $\mathbf{x}$ and is trained on the residual error of its predecessors. The final prediction is the sum $\sum_{i=1}^{N} T_i(\mathbf{x})$.

3.2 Feature Engineering and Model Variants

The feature vector $\mathbf{f}(t)$ is constructed from three categories of inputs, designed to capture the temporal structure and physical drivers of tide level variability in the RdP.

Temporal Features. Calendar variables (hour of day, day of week, day of year, month, quarter, and week of year) are extracted from the timestamp index. To avoid artificial discontinuities at calendar boundaries (e.g., hour 23 followed by hour 0), each variable is encoded as a pair of sine and cosine projections, preserving the cyclic nature of tidal and meteorological periodicities.

Lagged and Rolling Features. A sliding window of W consecutive hourly observations of the target station provides the core autoregressive signal. Complementing these point-wise lags, rolling mean and rolling standard deviation computed over multiple window lengths summarize recent trend and variability, respectively, supplying the model with a compact representation of recent estuarine dynamics.

Meteorological and Numerical Forcing Features. Hourly wind speed and direction forecasts at the Montevideo port area are decomposed into eight directional intensity components aligned with the cardinal and intercardinal directions (N, NE, E, SE, S, SW, W, NW), enabling the model to associate specific wind regimes with the subsequent water level response at each gauge. Operational sea level forecasts from PronUy_RPFM serve as an additional physics-based predictor, providing a signal that encodes large-scale tidal forcing beyond the autoregressive window.

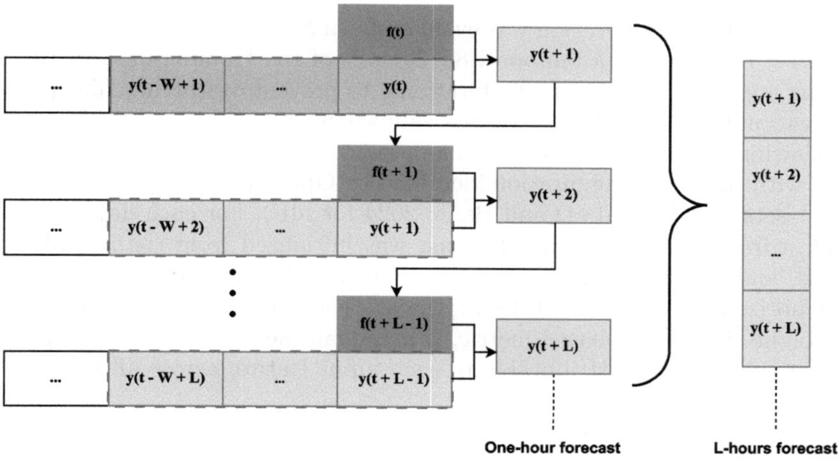

Fig. 4. Input–output diagram of the PronUy_LightGBM recursive forecasting framework. At each step the model predicts $\hat{y}(t+1)$ from the current feature vector $\mathbf{f}(t)$ and a window of W observed (or previously predicted) levels; the prediction is fed back as input for the subsequent step, yielding an L-step forecast through iteration.

These configurations define the two model variants evaluated in this study. PronUy_LightGBM1 uses only temporal and lagged features, relying exclusively on the tide gauge history of the target station. PronUy_LightGBM2 extends this baseline with the meteorological and numerical forcing features described above, currently implemented at MVD where both wind forecast and PronUy_RPFM data are available. Both variants employ the same recursive prediction strategy and are trained independently for each station.

To assess the individual and combined contributions of each forcing source, PronUy_LightGBM2 is evaluated under three configurations: (i) Wind Only, incorporating WRF directional wind features but not PronUy_RPFM sea level forecasts; (ii) Tide Only, incorporating PronUy_RPFM sea level forecasts but not wind features; and (iii) Wind + Tide, combining both sources. Performance is reported as RMSE improvement relative to PronUy_LightGBM1 at MVD.

3.3 Training, Hyperparameter Optimization, and Evaluation

PronUy_LightGBM1 was trained on hourly tide level records from MVD, BsAs, and IdF covering the 2017–2025 period. PronUy_LightGBM2 training was carried out at MVD, where the full set of forcing inputs is available. The window size W and all LightGBM hyperparameters were jointly optimized using the Optuna framework [1], which implements a Tree-structured Parzen Estimator (TPE) Bayesian search over the hyperparameter space. The search covered tree structure parameters (maximum depth, number of leaves), learning dynamics (learning rate, number of estimators), regularization weights, and subsampling ratios. Each trial configuration was evaluated using recursive prediction on a validation set obtained by a temporal 80/20 split of the training data, with early stopping applied (patience of 100 iterations) to prevent overfitting. The primary optimization target was RMSE on the validation set.

Following optimization, the final model was retrained on the complete training set with the best configuration identified by Optuna and applied to the held-out test sets (2025 for MVD and BsAs; 2024 for IdF). For each day in the test period, a fresh L-step recursive forecast was initialized from the last observed window, and the RMSE between predicted and observed levels was recorded across horizons $L \in \{6, 12, 24, 48, 72\}$ hours. Feature importance was assessed using LightGBM's gain-based metric, which quantifies the average reduction in the objective function attributable to each input feature across all splits in the ensemble.

The computations for the optimization were performed on the high-performance computing infrastructure of the National Supercomputing Center (Cluster-UY) [16].

4 Predictive Imputation of Missing Tide Gauge Records

4.1 Problem Formulation and Approach

Gaps in tide gauge records arise regularly from sensor failures, power outages, and data transmission errors, and are particularly frequent during extreme meteorological surge events, conditions that are most relevant for coastal risk assessment. Conventional gap-filling strategies such as linear interpolation or harmonic reconstruction do not exploit the physical forcing that drives water level variability, while purely spatial approaches based on neighboring stations require simultaneous observations at multiple gauges, which are not always available. Gradient boosting methods have been shown to be effective general-purpose gap-filling tools for environmental time series, exploiting lagged and auxiliary features to reconstruct missing segments across a wide range of conditions [14]. The forecasting model developed in Sect. 3, on the other hand, is additionally informed by meteorological forcing and physics-based model output, a richer feature set that is particularly valuable during surge events, when autoregressive information alone is insufficient. This model transfers directly to the imputation setting, where the gap can be treated as an unknown future segment with respect to the pre-gap context.

A key distinction separates imputation from operational forecasting: when filling a historical gap, real observations from *after* the gap are available. This additional information can be exploited through a strategy inspired by BRITS [3], a bidirectional recurrent imputation model that anchors predictions to both temporal boundaries of the gap to reduce drift accumulation. In this work the same principle is applied to a gradient boosting model: two independent recursive predictions are computed and subsequently merged. The *forward* prediction propagates from the pre-gap context toward the end of the gap in the usual manner. The *backward* prediction is obtained by reversing the time axis, initializing the recursive model from the post-gap context, and predicting in the direction of the gap start; the resulting sequence is then reversed to restore chronological order. Both predictions are combined via a distance-weighted blend:

$$\hat{y}_{imp}(t_i) = w_{fwd}(i)\, \hat{y}_{fwd}(t_i) + w_{bwd}(i)\, \hat{y}_{bwd}(t_i), \tag{3}$$

where $i = 0, \ldots, L-1$ indexes positions within a gap of length L, and the weights vary linearly:

$$w_{fwd}(i) = 1 - \frac{i}{L-1}, \qquad w_{bwd}(i) = \frac{i}{L-1}. \tag{4}$$

At the gap onset (i=0) full weight is assigned to the forward prediction; at the gap end (i=L−1) full weight goes to the backward prediction.

Unlike BRITS, which requires training a separate model on gap-annotated data, the proposed approach transfers the pre-trained PronUy_LightGBM2 Wind+Tide forecasting model directly to the imputation task without modification or retraining. This design avoids the need for supervised gap annotations and preserves the full meteorological forcing signal embedded during forecasting training. The linear distance-weighted blending in Eqs. (3)–(4) is intentionally parameter-free, requiring no additional training and carrying a natural physical interpretation, as predictions initialized closer to an observed boundary accumulate less recursive drift and are therefore assigned higher confidence.

4.2 Imputation Design and Evaluation

The imputation framework is evaluated following a protocol inspired by TSI-Bench [4], a standardized benchmark for time series imputation. Artificial gaps of lengths $L \in \{6, 12, 24, 48, 72\}$ hours are introduced into the held-out test set at MVD, and the model is tasked with reconstructing the missing segment. At least 30 independent gap instances are sampled per length to ensure statistically stable estimates, in accordance with TSI-Bench guidelines.

Two gap-generation mechanisms are considered, following the missing data taxonomy of Rubin [18]:

MCAR (Missing Completely At Random), in which gap start positions are drawn uniformly at random from the test set. This scenario represents an unbiased baseline and corresponds to random sensor dropouts.

MNAR (Missing Not At Random), in which start positions are sampled with probability proportional to the maximum water level within the candidate gap, biasing the selection toward high-level events. This scenario is more realistic for tide gauges, where sensor overload and power failures are more likely during extreme surge condition. In fact, some of the tide gauges—not included in this study—surveyed by Pronuy_RPFM exhibit this type of malfunction.

Performance is assessed using RMSE and MAE averaged over all sampled gaps at each length. Representative 24-hour reconstructions under both MCAR and MNAR conditions are included in Sect. 5 to provide visual insight into the bidirectional strategy.

5 Results and Discussion

5.1 Forecasting Performance and Feature Importance

PronUy_LightGBM1. For each day in the test period, a fresh L-step recursive forecast was initialized from the last observed window, and the RMSE between predicted and observed levels was computed. Results are reported as the mean RMSE and the 1st–99th percentile band across all daily initializations, for each prediction horizon $L \in \{6, 12, 24, 48, 72\}$ hours.

The relative performance across stations, visible in Fig. 5, persists across all horizons and reflects the contrasting hydrodynamic regimes along the estuary. At IdF, near the outer mouth of the estuary, the model achieves the lowest errors across all horizons, with 72-h RMSE remaining below 0.170 m. Buenos Aires shows the highest errors across all horizons (0.263 m at 6 h, 0.310 m at 48 h), consistent with the stronger astronomical tidal component at that station; normalised errors preserve the same ranking, suggesting that the relative difficulty of each station is not an artifact of differing tidal range but reflects a genuine difference in predictability under the autoregressive formulation.

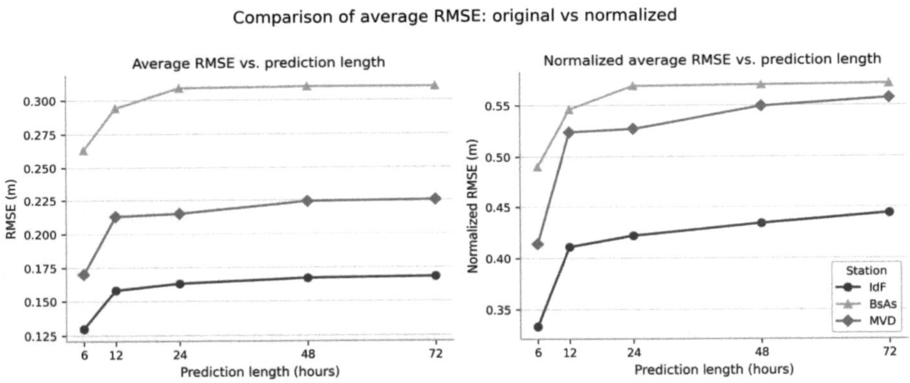

Fig. 5. PronUy_LightGBM1: mean RMSE as a function of forecast horizon L for Montevideo (MVD), Buenos Aires (BsAs), and Isla de Flores (IdF).

Figure 6 displays the five most influential features for each station, ranked by LightGBM's gain-based importance metric. The single-step lag $y(t)$ – the water level recorded at the immediately preceding hour – is the dominant predictor at all three stations, confirming the strong short-range autocorrelation of the tidal signal in the RdP. Beyond this leading lag, the importance patterns diverge across locations. At IdF and MVD, lags at 24, 27, and 48 h also rank highly, reflecting the role of tidal periodicities and estuarine propagation timescales in shaping the predictive signal. Buenos Aires presents a distinctly different profile: rolling standard deviation features appear prominently among the top five predictors, indicating that local water level *variability* carries stronger predictive weight at this station. This can also be a result of the already mentioned dominance of astronomical tidal forcing on the Argentine coast.

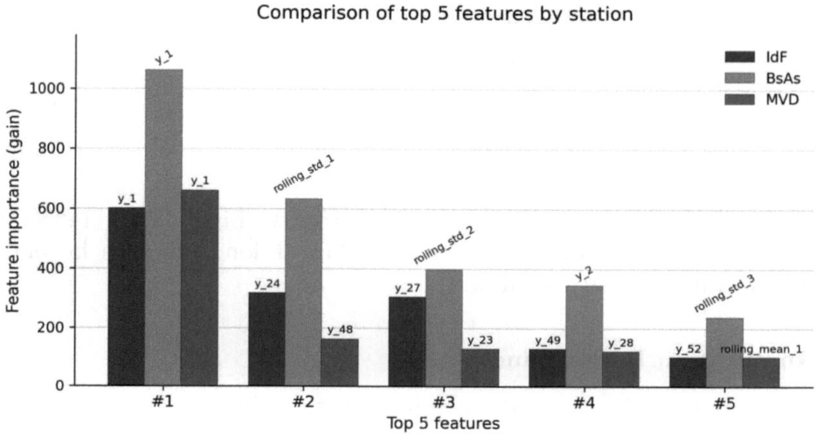

Fig. 6. PronUy_LightGBM1: five most influential input features ranked by LightGBM gain-based importance for each tide gauge station.

PronUy_LightGBM2. Table 1 reports the RMSE percentage reduction over PronUy_LightGBM1 at Montevideo for three forcing configurations: wind forecasts alone, PronUy_RPFM sea level forecasts alone, and both combined. All three configurations reduce RMSE relative to the autoregressive baseline at every horizon, and the magnitude of improvement grows consistently with L. The combined Wind + Tide configuration achieves the largest gains across all horizons (15.4% at 6 h, rising to 40.9% at 72 h), followed by the tide-only variant (10.2%–31.6%), with the wind-only configuration yielding the smallest improvements (10.5%–24.7%). PronUy_RPFM sea level forecasts capture tidal and storm-surge dynamics through the TELEMAC2D hydrodynamic model, encoding estuarine geometry and bathymetric propagation effects that directional wind components alone cannot represent. Wind forecasts contribute an independent component reflecting local surface stress that the hydrodynamic model, operating at coarser resolution, partially misses. The additive gains of the combined configuration confirm that the two sources address distinct components of the forecast error.

The rate at which RMSE grows with horizon also differs between the two models. For the combined PronUy_LightGBM2 configuration, the RMSE increment from 24 h to 48 h is approximately 0.025 m, dropping to 0.010 m from 48 h to 72 h. For PronUy_LightGBM1, the 48–72 h increment remains 0.021 m.

Table 1. RMSE improvement (%) of PronUy_LightGBM2 over PronUy_LightGBM1 at Montevideo for each forecast horizon and forcing configuration.

Horizon (h)	Wind Only	Tide Only	Wind + Tide
6	10.5	10.2	15.4
12	13.2	14.3	21.4
24	18.8	24.8	33.8
48	24.1	31.1	40.2
72	24.7	31.6	40.9

The deceleration in error growth for PronUy_LightGBM2 reflects the physics-based forcing sustaining predictive skill at long horizons beyond the range of the autoregressive window.

5.2 Imputation Performance

Table 2 summarises the imputation results for the Wind + Tide (bidirectional blend) variant across all gap lengths and both missing-data mechanisms. Figure 7 plots RMSE as a function of gap length.

Table 2. Imputation results for the Wind + Tide (bidirectional) variant at MVD.

Gap (h)	MCAR		MNAR	
	RMSE (m)	MAE (m)	RMSE (m)	MAE (m)
6	0.082	0.071	0.073	0.064
12	0.072	0.060	0.096	0.081
24	0.099	0.077	0.117	0.096
48	0.165	0.133	0.140	0.114
72	0.161	0.129	0.159	0.127

Under MCAR, the bidirectional imputer achieves RMSE of 8.2 cm for 6-hour gaps, rising to 16.5 cm at 48 h before a slight decrease to 16.1 cm at 72 h. Errors below 10 cm for gaps up to 24 h represent at most a 2× degradation relative to the typical 5 cm measurement uncertainty of RdP tide gauges, a tolerance compatible with retrospective data reconstruction and model reanalysis applications.

Under MNAR, where gap positions are biased toward high-water events, errors grow monotonically from 7.3 cm at 6 h to 15.9 cm at 72 h. For medium gaps (12–24 h), MNAR errors exceed MCAR errors, consistent with the model's limited ability to extrapolate surge peaks from pre-gap autoregressive context. At 72 h the two curves converge (MNAR: 15.9 cm vs MCAR: 16.1 cm), suggesting that for very long gaps anchor proximity (*i.e.*, the distance from the imputed point to the nearest known boundary) becomes the dominant source of error, independent of whether the gap coincides with an extreme event.

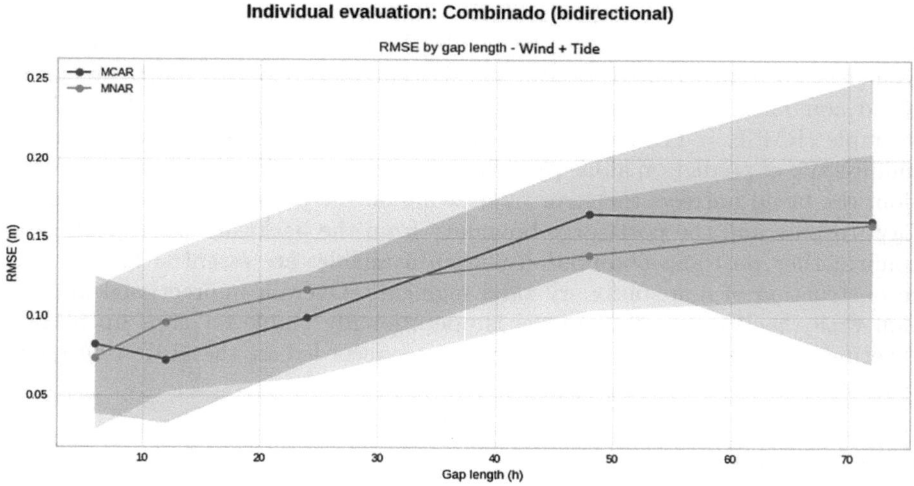

Fig. 7. RMSE as a function of gap length for the imputer under MCAR and MNAR conditions. Shaded bands indicate the interquartile range across sampled gap instances.

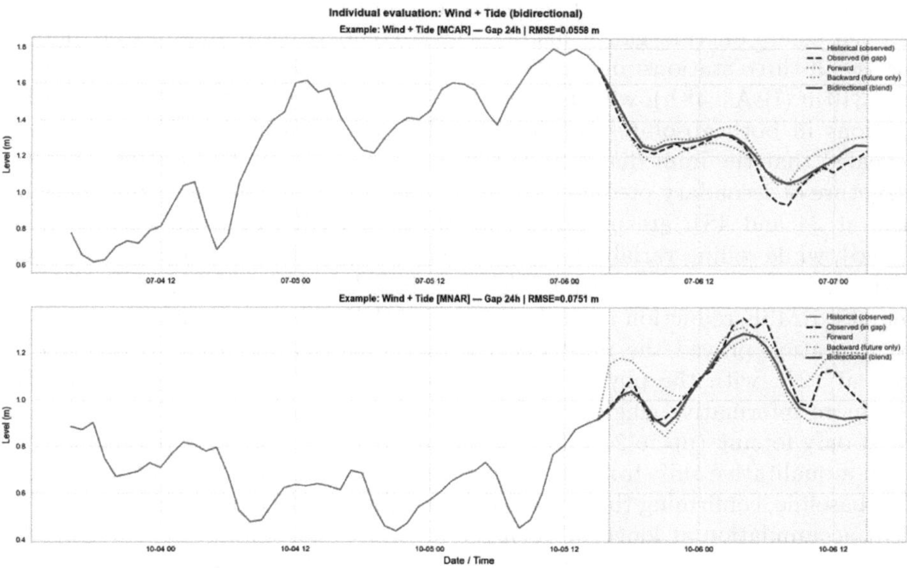

Fig. 8. Representative 24-hour gap reconstructions at MVD under MCAR (top) and MNAR (bottom) conditions. Panel shows historical observed levels (solid blue), observed levels within the gap (dashed black), forward prediction (blue dotted), backward prediction (green dotted), and bidirectional blend (solid red). (Color figure online)

Figure 8 illustrates representative 24-hour reconstructions under both mechanisms. In the MCAR example (RMSE = 10.9 cm), the forward prediction overshoots the observed tidal recession while the backward prediction, initialised from the post-gap context, tracks the descent more closely; the bidirectional blend combines both to reduce the error throughout the gap. In the MNAR example (RMSE = 11.8 cm), which captures a high-water surge event, neither unidirectional prediction alone reproduces the sharp peak and subsequent recession; the blend narrows the error by drawing on the pre-surge context from the forward pass and the post-surge boundary from the backward pass. Both cases confirm that post-gap observations, when available, are essential for accurate reconstruction of non-stationary tidal segments. Overall, bidirectional imputation with the Wind + Tide model is operationally viable for gaps up to 24 h, covering the large majority of interruptions recorded in the RdP tide gauge network.

6 Conclusions

This paper presented the development and evaluation of two LightGBM-based tide level forecasting models and a bidirectional predictive imputation scheme for the Río de la Plata estuary, integrated within the PronUy_RPFM operational forecasting system.

PronUy_LightGBM1 demonstrated that an autoregressive LightGBM model trained solely on tide gauge history yields competitive multi-step predictions across all three stations: mean RMSE ranges from 0.130 m (IdF, 6 h) to a peak of 0.310 m (BsAs, 48 h), with Isla de Flores consistently outperforming the other stations in both absolute and normalised terms. Feature importance analysis revealed that the immediate single-step lag dominates at all locations, but the structure of secondary predictors reflects the underlying forcing regime: periodic lags at 24 and 48 h are prominent at MVD and IdF (meteorologically dominated), while rolling variability features characterise BsAs (astronomically dominated). Incorporating external forcing in PronUy_LightGBM2 produced systematic RMSE reduction at all horizons at MVD. The combined Wind + Tide configuration proved the most effective, achieving up to 40.9% RMSE reduction at 72 h, with the physics-based PronUy_RPFM sea level forecasts being the more informative single source (up to 31.6% reduction at 72 h) relative to wind-only forcing (up to 24.7%). All variants exhibited an error plateau beyond 12 h: a qualitative shift from the monotonically growing error of the autoregressive baseline, confirming that external inputs effectively compensate for recursive drift accumulation at longer horizons.

The bidirectional Wind + Tide strategy achieved RMSE below 10 cm for gaps up to 24 h under MCAR conditions, and below 12 cm for the same lengths under the MNAR scenario, where gaps are biased toward high-water surge events. The convergence of MCAR and MNAR errors at 72 h (16.1 cm vs 15.9 cm) indicates a regime shift: for very long gaps the dominant error source is temporal distance from the nearest anchor rather than event severity. A representative

24-hour reconstruction ilustrated the advantage of the bidirectional blend over the forward-only prediction, particularly in segments with non-stationary tidal recession.

Several directions merit further investigation. In the first place, extending PronUy_LightGBM2 to BsAs and IdF, where wind and numerical model forcing data may be available, would test the generalisability of the improvement observed at MVD. The consistently superior performance of the combined Wind + Tide configuration suggests that both forcing sources contribute non-redundant information, and further analysis of their individual contributions at different meteorological regimes could help prioritise data acquisition for operational deployment. For imputation, incorporating the astronomical tide prediction as an additional input feature – or, alternatively, decomposing the signal into its astronomical and meteorological residual components prior to imputation – represents a natural extension of the current framework. Further investigation into the non-monotonic MCAR error behaviour at medium gap lengths (12–24 h) could also clarify whether it reflects genuine variability in tidal dynamics or a sampling effect of the test period. Finally, integrating both the forecasting and imputation modules into the live PronUy_RPFM pipeline, thus enabling real-time gap detection, automatic reconstruction, and seamless handoff to the forecasting engine constitutes the primary operational objective of this work.

Acknowledgments. This work is supported by funding from the National Agency for Research and Innovation (Agencia Nacional de Investigación e Innovación – ANII) FMV project "Sistema de pronóstico en tiempo real de niveles de marea en el Río de la Plata enriquecido con asimilación de datos".

The authors gratefully acknowledge the WRF model data provided by IMFIA researchers Victor Silveira and Alejandro Gutiérrez.

Disclosure of Interests. The authors have no competing interests to declare that are relevant to the content of this article.

References

1. Akiba, T., Sano, S., Yanase, T., Ohta, T., Koyama, M.: Optuna: a next-generation hyperparameter optimization framework. In: Proceedings of the 25th ACM SIGKDD International Conference on Knowledge Discovery and Data Mining, pp. 2623–2631. (2019)
2. Bojer, C.S., Meldgaard, J.P.: Kaggle forecasting competitions: an overlooked learning opportunity. Int. J. Forecast. **37**(2), 587–603 (2021)
3. Cao, W., Wang, D., Li, J., Zhou, H., Li, L., Li, Y.: BRITS: bidirectional recurrent imputation for time series. In: Advances in Neural Information Processing Systems. vol. 31 (2018)
4. Du, W., et al.: TSI-Bench: benchmarking time series imputation (2024). https://arxiv.org/abs/2406.12747
5. Elshorbagy, A., Corzo, G., Srinivasulu, S., Solomatine, D.P.: Experimental investigation of the predictive capabilities of data driven modeling techniques in hydrology - Part 1: Concepts and methodology. Hydrol. Earth Syst. Sci. **14**, 1931–1941 (2010)

6. Elshorbagy, A., Corzo, G., Srinivasulu, S., Solomatine, D.P.: Experimental investigation of the predictive capabilities of data driven modeling techniques in hydrology - Part 2: Application. Hydrol. Earth Syst. Sci. **14**, 1943–1961 (2010)
7. Fossati, M., Balparda, D., Sellanes, L., Silva, D., Jackson, M., Ezzatti, P.: Desarrollo del sistema de pronóstico del Río de la Plata y su frente marítimo: PronUy_RPFM. Ribagua **9**(2), 25–40 (2022)
8. Fossati, M., et al.: Dinámica de flujo, del campo salino y de los sedimentos finos en el Río de la Plata. RIBAGUA - Revista Iberoamericana del Agua **1**, 48–63 (2014)
9. Friedman, J.H.: Greedy function approximation: a gradient boosting machine. Ann. Stat. **29**(5), 1189–1232 (2001)
10. Gan, M., et al.: An improved machine learning-based model to predict estuarine water levels. Ocean Model. **190**, 102376 (2024)
11. Grinsztajn, L., Oyallon, E., Varoquaux, G.: Why tree-based models still outperform deep learning on tabular data. In: Advances in Neural Information Processing Systems. vol. 35 (2022)
12. Guerrero, R.A., Acha, E.M., Framiñán, M.B., Lasta, C.A.: Physical oceanography of the Río de la Plata Estuary. Argentina. Continental Shelf Res. **17**(7), 727–742 (1997). https://doi.org/10.1016/S0278-4343(96)00061-1
13. Ke, G., et al.: LightGBM: a highly efficient gradient boosting decision tree. In: Advances in Neural Information Processing Systems. vol. 30, pp. 3146–3154 (2017)
14. Körner, P., Kronenberg, R., Genzel, S., Bernhofer, C.: Introducing gradient boosting as a universal gap filling tool for meteorological time series. Meteorol. Z. **27**(5), 369–376 (2018). https://doi.org/10.1127/metz/2018/0908
15. McElfresh, D., et al.: When do neural nets outperform boosted trees on tabular data? In: Advances in Neural Information Processing Systems. vol. 36 (2023)
16. Torres, M., Klapp, J., Gitler, I., Tchernykh, A. (eds.): ISUM 2018. CCIS, vol. 948. Springer, Cham (2019). https://doi.org/10.1007/978-3-030-10448-1
17. Ocio, D., Beskeen, T., Smart, K.: Fully distributed hydrological modelling for catchment-wide hydrological data verification. Hydrol. Res. **50**, 1520–1534 (2019)
18. Rubin, D.B.: Inference and missing data. Biometrika **63**(3), 581–592 (1976). https://doi.org/10.1093/biomet/63.3.581
19. Santoro, P., Fossati, M., Piedra Cueva, I.: Study of the meteorological tide in the Río de la Plata. Continental Shelf Res. **60**, 51–63 (2013). https://doi.org/10.1016/j.csr.2013.04.018
20. Savenije, H.H.G.: Prediction in ungauged estuaries: an integrated theory. Water Resour. Res. **51**, 2464–2476 (2015). https://doi.org/10.1002/2015WR016936
21. Sellanes, L., Fossati, M., Silva, D., Ezzatti, P.: Mejoras en la implementación del modelo numérico base del pronóstico de niveles del Río de la Plata y frente marítimo: PRONUY_RPFM. In: Mecánica Computacional. vol. XL, pp. 1681–1690 (2023)
22. Silveira, V., Sarazola, I., Gutiérrez, A., Fossati, M.: Offshore surface wind map in Río de la Plata and Atlantic Ocean shelf. J. Wind Eng. Industrial Aerodyn. **258** (2025)
23. Skamarock, W.C., et al.: A description of the Advanced Research WRF model version 4. Technical report. NCAR/TN-556+STR, National Center for Atmospheric Research, Boulder, CO, USA (2019)
24. Solomatine, D.P., Ostfeld, A.: Data-driven modelling: some past experiences and new approaches. J. Hydroinf. **10**, 3–22 (2008)
25. Sun, Y., Wang, R., Qi, C., Xu, J., Tu, Z., Yang, F.: An improved tidal prediction method using meteorological parameters and historical residual water levels. Appl. Ocean Res. **153**, 104289 (2024)

26. Wu, C.-C., Chen, Y.-L., Liu, Y.-H., Yang, X.-Y.: Decision tree induction with a constrained number of leaf nodes. Appl. Intell. **45**(3), 673–685 (2016). https://doi.org/10.1007/s10489-016-0785-z
27. Zeng, A., Chen, M., Zhang, L., Xu, Q.: Are transformers effective for time series forecasting? In: Proceedings of the AAAI Conference on Artificial Intelligence. vol. 37, pp. 11121–11128 (2023)

Enhancing Model Generalization in Index Futures Markets via Evolutionary Optimization and Data Leakage-Free Feature Engineering

Otávio Zucchetti Dalla Costa[1], Bruno L. Dalmazo[1], Viviane Leite Dias de Mattos[1], Richard F. Pinto[1], Diego Renan Bruno[2], Eduardo N. Borges[1], Giancarlo Lucca[1], Fabian C. Cardoso[3], and Rafael A. Berri[1](✉)

[1] Federal University of Rio Grande (FURG), Rio Grande, Brazil
{otaviozdc,dalmazo,vivianemattos,richard_pinto,eduardoborges, giancarlo.lucca,rafaelberri}@furg.br
[2] São Paulo State University (UNESP), São José do Rio Preto, Brazil
diego.bruno@unesp.br
[3] University of Rio Verde (UniRV), Rio Verde, Brazil
fabian@unirv.edu.br

Abstract. This study investigates the directional prediction of the Mini Bovespa Index Futures (WIN), which are short-term derivative contracts based on Brazil's main stock index that traders use to speculate or hedge utilizing rapid intraday price movements. A major hurdle in this domain is the tendency of machine learning models to overfit to market noise. To mitigate this, we propose an optimization pipeline that integrates Sequential Forward Selection (SFS) and evolutionary hyperparameter optimization via Genetic Algorithms (GA). The evaluation focused on how the XGBoost and Multi-Layer Perceptron (MLP) architectures respond to evolutionary tuning. It was observed that the need for GA optimization depends on the stability of the model. For example, the XGBoost baseline (default hyperparameters) presented a generalization gap, which the GA-based regularization wrapper managed to reduce to 0.0179, giving it an F1-score of 0.7220. Additionally, the GA demonstrated superior computational efficiency over Random Search, by navigating the hyperparameter space through a directed search that minimizes the evaluation of suboptimal architectures. On the other hand, MLP already demonstrated stability with default settings, although GA brought its gap to near-zero indices and guaranteed it an F1-score of 0.7182, yielding marginal improvements. These results suggest that evolutionary algorithms are important for controlling variance models like XGBoost but serve as a refinement step for robust structures like MLP.

Keywords: Genetic Algorithms · XGBoost · Multi-Layer Perceptron · Generalization Gap · Financial Forecasting

O. Gervasi et al. (Eds.): ICCSA 2026, LNCS 16768, pp. 550–568, 2027.
https://doi.org/10.1007/978-3-032-30488-9_34

1 Introduction

The Brazilian financial market, especially the Mini Bovespa Index Futures (WIN), is characterized by liquidity and volatility. For algorithmic trading systems, this domain presents a low signal-to-noise ratio, where market noise obscures directional trends [8]. Although Machine Learning (ML) models are standard for capturing non-linear dependencies in such time series, a vulnerability is imposed: overfitting. In intraday trading, common ML approaches often adjust to historical noise instead of learning structural patterns, leading to discrepancies between retrospective testing performance and real-time execution, which this study defines as the **Generalization Gap** [13].

In algorithmic trading, minimizing the generalization gap proves more important than increasing raw predictive accuracy (such as the F1-Score). Poor retrospective performance coupled with a large gap indicates that the model adjusted for market noise rather than capturing structural signals. In a real trading environment, this instability imposes financial drawdowns and operational risks on investors, as the strategy fails when exposed to unknown market regimes. Consequently, prioritizing structural robustness over maximum historical accuracy becomes a requirement for viable automated trading. To address this instability, an integrated data optimization flow is proposed to mitigate overfitting. A Sequential Forward Selection (SFS) wrapper associated with chronological normalization is used, ensuring that the selection of technical indicators is entirely free from look-ahead bias.

Furthermore, an Evolutionary Hyperparameter Optimization framework using Genetic Algorithms (GA) is presented. Instead of relying on common metrics that can reward overfitting, the evolutionary process is driven by a personalized fitness function. This function penalizes the variance between training and validation scores, exerting selective pressure that favors stable architectures over merely precise ones. This methodology is applied to two distinct families of learners: Gradient Boosting Decision Trees (XGBoost) and Neural Networks (Multilayer Perceptron - MLP), evaluating how evolutionary tuning impacts models with fundamentally different inductive biases.

This study demonstrates that evolutionary optimization is context-dependent. While necessary for reducing the generalization gap in variance models like XGBoost, it offers diminishing returns to stable MLP architectures. Moreover, it provides noisy financial markets with a reproducible and statistically sound framework for feature selection and model fitting. By bridging theoretical predictive power and practical stability, this study lays the groundwork for autonomous trading systems that can maintain viability over long periods in dynamic environments [23].

The remainder of this paper is organized as follows: Sect. 2 introduces the theoretical concepts, Sect. 3 details the proposed optimization methodology, Sect. 4 presents the experimental results, and Sect. 5 concludes the study with future research directions.

2 Theoretical Concepts

This section establishes the theoretical foundation on which the proposed optimization flow is based. First, the central principles of GAs are presented, detailing the biomimetic approach, focused on navigating non-linear search spaces for model fitting. Subsequently, the logical foundation, attributed to the feature engineering process, is outlined, formalizing the specific technical indicators, categorized into volatility, momentum, and mean reversion metrics, that are assigned the role of extracting predictive signals from the intraday financial time series environment.

2.1 Genetic Algorithm (GA)

Genetic Algorithms (GAs) represent a category of metaheuristic optimization structures based on the biological principles of natural selection and evolution [10]. These algorithms operate by computational emulation of the evolutionary life cycle, in which a population of candidate solutions is subjected to iterative refinement via selection, crossover, and mutation operators. Candidates that demonstrate favorable performance, as quantified by an evaluation metric, are given a higher probability of propagating characteristics to subsequent generations, directing the system towards convergence on effective solutions.

Within this biomimetic paradigm, the specific optimization challenge constitutes the environment, while members of the population are assigned the role of potential solutions. The evolutionary pressure exerted by the environment is operationalized through a fitness function. This function assigns a fitness score to each individual, measuring the usefulness of the proposed solution in relation to the problem's constraints. Consequently, GAs are reserved for robustness in navigating complex problem spaces where conventional deterministic approaches prove insufficient [7].

2.2 Feature Engineering and Rationalization

To mitigate the low signal-to-noise ratio of the financial time series, raw closing prices were transformed into a multidimensional attribute space, representing volatility positioning, momentum changes, and mean reversion. Volatility is modeled using the Bollinger Bands Relative Position [2], defined as $BB_{pos} = \frac{C_t - LB_t}{UB_t - LB_t}$, where C_t denotes the closing price in the time interval t while UB_t and LB_t represent the Upper and Lower Bands respectively. This transformation maps absolute prices onto a stationary amplitude metric, generally contained between 0 and 1, which is considered important for the convergence and stability of nonlinear models, such as MLP and XGBoost. Analytically, values close to 1 are associated with the indication of overbought regions, while values close to 0 are linked to the suggestion of oversold conditions, allowing the algorithm to dynamically identify reversal points. Currently, quantification is applied through the Relative Strength Index (RSI) [22], which is decomposed into its current state (RSI_t), its first-order difference ($RSI_{diff} = RSI_t - RSI_{t-1}$) and its immediate history ($RSI\_LAG1 = RSI_{t-1}$). The inclusion of RSI_{diff} acts as an indicator of trend acceleration or exhaustion, while coupling the current state with RSI_LAG1 allows the model to differentiate between the accumulation and distribution phases of a trend, explicitly reconstructing the temporal inertia of price changes. Finally, short-term serial correlation and mean reversion [12,15] are captured by two specific features: $CLOSEvsSMA_n$, which calculates the percentage distance between the closing price and an n-period Simple Moving Average (SMA_n), expressed as $Dist_n = \frac{C_t - SMA_n}{SMA_n}$, and $RETURN\_LAG1$, representing the lagged simple return of the previous 5-minute candle, $R_{t-1} = \frac{C_{t-1} - C_{t-2}}{C_{t-2}}$. Significant deviations in $Dist_n$ identify "stretched" price levels where the asset is statistically likely to undergo a pullback, whereas the lagged return captures the immediate historical shock. Together, this multi-scale feature engineering provides the learning architectures with a robust representation of recent market behavior and short-term autocorrelation [9,18].

3 Methodology

The proposed methodology establishes a flow designed to mitigate two primary risks in financial machine learning, look-ahead bias, and overfitting. As illustrated in Fig. 1, the architecture is sequential in nature, ensuring that feature selection and data normalization are restricted to the chronological limits of training data. This workflow was realized through the Python language [17], utilizing the XGBoost library [4] for boosting models, while the Scikit-learn library [16] and the TensorFlow framework [1] provided the necessary structures for data processing and neural networks.

3.1 Input Data

The experimental framework uses high-frequency intraday data extracted from the BovDBV2 dataset [20], focusing on Mini Bovespa Index Futures (WIN). The dataset covers the first half of 2024 (January 1st to June 30th), organized into 5-minute intervals containing Open, High, Low, Close, and Volume vectors. This chronological sequence is partitioned into two isolated sets, a training and optimization period within the sample (corresponding to 70% of the data, dedicated to adjustment procedures) and a test period outside the sample (the final 30% of the chronological sequence). This chronological division ensures that the final evaluation metrics remain unbiased in relation to the hyperparameter optimization process.

3.2 Feature Engineering

The construction of the input space constitutes the fundamental layer of the proposed methodology. Based on the theoretical definitions established in

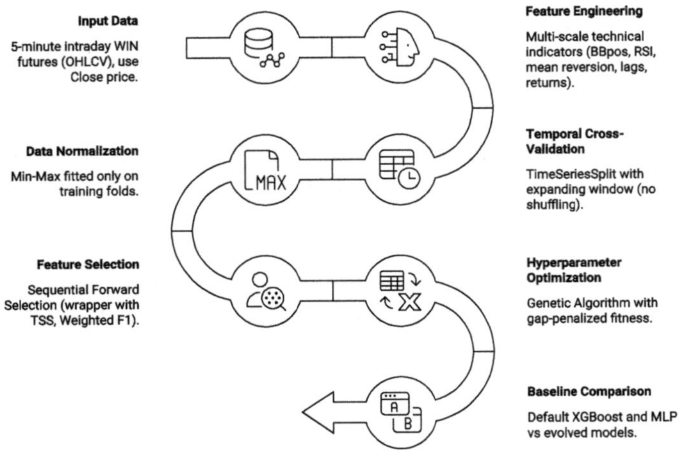

Fig. 1. Proposed methodological flow, detailing the temporal progression from the acquisition of raw data to the hyperparameter optimization phase, based on genetic methods.

Sect. 2.2, the isolated closing price vector was transformed into a multidimensional attribute matrix. The initial set of candidates was generated by calculating the central indicators, BB_{pos}, RSI, and mean reversion metrics, across a spectrum of time windows. This multi-scale approach ensures that the model captures market dynamics at varying granularities, from immediate volatility shocks to exhaustion of structural trends. Additionally, to incorporate the rate of change and temporal dependencies, first-order differences (such as RSI_{diff}) and lagged return values (RETURN_LAG1) were included.

This strategy is associated with the production of a set of high-dimensional attributes. Instead of applying manual filtering based on discretionary heuristics to this data, this extensive dataset reserved the role of raw input for the SFS (described in Sect. 3.5), allowing the algorithm to identify the subset of variables that maximizes generalization performance.

3.3 Temporal Cross-Validation

In financial time series forecasting, the inherent serial correlation of the data is attributed to the inadequacy of common random validation methods [3]. Consequently, K-Fold cross-validation is not permitted since the shuffling of observations would result in the destruction of the temporal structure and the introduction of anticipation bias, allowing the model to inadvertently train with future data to predict past events. To solve this problem, a TimeSeriesSplit (TSS) cross-validation scheme [16] was used, strictly applied to the training and optimization period within the sample. This technique utilizes an "anchored expanding window" approach that strictly respects chronological order. For each split k, this in-sample data is partitioned so that the training set comprises the historical sequence defined by the indices $[0, \ldots, n]$. The validation set is then formed by the immediately subsequent horizon $[n+1, \ldots, n+m]$, where n represents the cutoff point and m the validation window size. This architecture strictly isolates future information, effectively simulating a realistic Walk-Forward Analysis where the model is periodically re-calibrated as new market data become available [14].

3.4 Data Normalization

To guarantee input consistency and strictly prevent the leakage of future volatility information into the final evaluation, a strict chronological normalization strategy was employed [13]. Within this framework, the Min-Max normalization identifies the boundary values (min, max) exclusively within the in-sample training period (the 70% partition) [16]. These fixed parameters are then applied to transform the isolated out-of-sample test set, ensuring that the final evaluation is never exposed to global statistics derived from future data. The transformation is formally defined as:

$$x' = \frac{x - \min(X_{train})}{\max(X_{train}) - \min(X_{train})} \tag{1}$$

Where $\min(X_{train})$ and $\max(X_{train})$ denote the minimum and maximum values observed strictly within the distribution of the in-sample training period. This transformation subjects all attributes to a scale contained within the bounded interval [0,1]. By fixing these parameters, the system is forced to simulate a real trading environment in which extreme future prices are unknown at the time of the forecast. Moreover, by applying normalization to the input before the attribute selection phase, it is ensured that the SFS algorithm evaluates the predictive power of the indicators based on relative structural patterns, rather than absolute magnitudes [6].

3.5 Sequential Forward Selection (SFS)

Given the size of the initial attribute space, the presence of irrelevant or redundant variables can introduce noise that impairs the performance of nonlinear models. To solve this problem, an SFS wrapper was used to obtain a representation of market data.

The SFS algorithm employs a greedy search strategy, starting from an empty set, the algorithm iteratively adds the attribute associated with an improvement in the objective function. This process continues until the performance metric stabilizes or declines.

In the proposed structure, the quality assessment of the subset is assigned to a supervised learning classifier that acts as a wrapper estimator [11]. To ensure consistency with temporal constraints, candidate subsets are assigned scores in chronological validation folds (TSS), preventing look-ahead bias during the selection phase [14]. The algorithm prioritizes attribute configurations associated with an increase in a classification metric in the validation set.

Fundamentally, instead of imposing a selection based on standard parameters, a hierarchical validation approach is adopted. Promising subsets are allowed to advance to the Hyperparameter Optimization stage (Sect. 3.6). This dynamic ensures that the final decision is based on the potential of each configuration. The GA then is reserved the role of arbiter, distinguishing the attributes to which a robust predictive signal is associated from those that only impose complexity without comprehensive benefit [6].

Although wrapper methods are inherently biased by their underlying estimator, XGBoost was specifically selected for the SFS phase due to its computational efficiency and resistance to nonlinearities without requiring prior data scaling. Running a dedicated SFS wrapper using a Neural Network would impose a computational bottleneck. Therefore, the XGBoost wrapper serves as a technically viable global filter for noise reduction in a core set of structurally informative attributes. By design, this same subset of attributes is provided to both the XGBoost and MLP architectures during the evolutionary phase. This strategy is linked to the establishment of a comparison base, ensuring that differences in final generalization performance originate exclusively from structural optimization and the fundamental inductive biases of each model, rather than variations in the input data.

3.6 Hyperparameter Optimization

After identifying the candidate attribute subsets, in the previous step, the final phase involves using a GA to optimize the hyperparameters of each configuration independently. This optimization strategy is important within the proposed hierarchical structure by subjecting each candidate subset to evaluation under favorable parameter definitions, the bias associated with default model configurations is eliminated and it is ensured that the final selection is based on the potential of each attribute set.

Fitness Function and Generalization. To counteract overfitting, we introduced a Fitness Function $F(\theta)$ that explicitly penalizes the divergence between training and validation scores, ensuring structural stability [13]. The F for an individual θ is defined as:

$$F(\theta) = \bar{S}_{val} - \lambda \cdot \max(0, \bar{S}_{train} - \bar{S}_{val}) \tag{2}$$

where:

- $\bar{S}_{val}$ and $\bar{S}_{train}$ denote the mean Weighted F1-Scores across the TSS validation and training folds, respectively.
- The term $\max(0, \bar{S}_{train} - \bar{S}_{val})$ represents the **Overfitting Gap**. We utilize the max function to ensure that the model is only penalized when training performance artificially exceeds validation performance.
- λ is the penalty coefficient.

Furthermore, to address the class imbalance present in the intraday market data, a double-layer strategy was adopted. During the training phase, the loss functions of both XGBoost and MLP were weighted inversely proportional to the class frequencies (Cost-Sensitive Learning) [21], requiring that the gradient descent penalize classification errors in the minority class more rigorously. During the evolutionary evaluation, the Weighted F1-Score was reserved the role of primary metric ($\bar{S}$), ensuring that the selection pressure favors solutions that balance precision and recall, rather than focusing efforts on accuracy in the majority class.

To perform the evolutionary adjustment, the Genetic Algorithm was assigned a configuration with specific hyperparameters, suitable for the computational complexity of each model. Since the XGBoost model has lower processing requirements, this system was allowed to explore the search space on a larger scale compared to that applied to the MLP. The evolution of candidate solutions is handled through generational epochs driven by stochastic operators, specifically tournament selection, two-point crossing, and bit inversion mutation, adapted to the binary representation scheme. Table 1 details these configurations including population size, number of generations, mutation rates, and selection strategies used for both architectures during the optimization phase.

Table 1. Evolutionary Algorithm Configuration for XGBoost and MLP

Parameter	XGBoost (Tree-based)	MLP (Neural Network)
Encoding Strategy	Binary	Binary
Population Size	20 Individuals	10 Individuals
Generations	1000	200
Crossover Probability	70%	70%
Mutation Probability	20% (Individual) / 5% (Bit)	20% (Individual) / 5% (Bit)
Selection Method	Tournament ($k = 3$)	Tournament ($k = 3$)
Penalty Coefficient (λ)	0.5	0.5

3.7 Experiment Configuration

To quantify the impact of evolutionary optimization, non-optimized benchmarks were established for both learning architectures. These benchmark models serve as a control group for measuring the inherent tendency of the algorithms to overfit before applying any genetic tuning. This approach aims to obtain a performance benchmark against which the results obtained after the stochastic search process can be compared.

The reference configuration for the XGBoost model is detailed in Table 2. Based on standard hyperparameters, this structure produces a variance estimator that requires reduced regularization. This arrangement serves as a benchmark for quantifying the model's susceptibility to overfitting within the financial data environment, allowing the analysis to incorporate the distinction between data noise and the signal captured by optimization.

Table 2. Default Hyperparameters for XGBoost Baseline

Hyperparameter	Value	Description
`n_estimators`	100	Number of boosting rounds
`max_depth`	6	Maximum tree depth
`learning_rate`	0.3	Step size shrinkage (η)
`subsample`	1.0	% of samples used per tree
`colsample_bytree`	1.0	% of features used per tree
`gamma`	0	Min. loss reduction
`reg_lambda` (L2)	1	L2 regularization term
`reg_alpha` (L1)	0	L1 regularization term

For the neural network, the reference architecture is assigned the structure of a common feedforward Multi-Layer Perceptron (MLP). As shown in Table 3, this topology requires the use of two hidden layers, the application of dropout regularization, and the use of the Adam optimizer. This configuration serves as a fundamental reference for evaluating the structural stability inherent in neural networks in this specific domain, allowing the necessary comparison between baseline models and models subjected to evolutionary refinement to be added to the study.

Table 3. Default Hyperparameters for MLP Baseline

Hyperparameter	Value/Setting	Description
`Architecture`	$[32, 16]$	Neurons in hidden layers
`Activation`	ReLU	Rectified Linear Unit
`Output Activation`	Sigmoid	Probability estimation $(0, 1)$
`Optimizer`	Adam	Adaptive Moment Estimation
`Learning Rate`	0.001	Standard starting rate
`Dropout`	$[0.2, 0.1]$	Dropout rates for Layer 1 and Layer 2
`Initialization`	HeNormal	Weights initialization strategy
`Batch Size`	32	Samples per gradient update

Additionally, to validate the computational efficiency and search strategy of the GA, a Random Search (RS) algorithm was implemented as an optimization benchmark for the XGBoost architecture. The RS was configured with a computational budget of 20,000 independent model evaluations, which is associated with mathematical equivalence to the GA population composed of 20 individuals subjected to evolution over 1,000 generations. The RS technique allowed sampling based on the limits of continuous and discrete hyperparameters, used by the GA (as detailed in Table 7), applying to this process the temporal cross-validation scheme and the fitness function identical to those of the evolutionary method.

4 Results

This section presents the experimental results obtained. Although evolutionary optimization and feature selection were confined to the 70% in-sample period using a 5-fold TSS cross-validation structure, the final comparative metrics, generalization gap and confusion matrices presented here are exclusively based on the isolated 30% out-of-sample test set. This evaluation ensures the absence of data leakage from the adjustment phase. The analysis follows a chronological structure: first, the identification of the feature subsets generated by the SFS is verified, subsequently, the evolutionary convergence process is detailed, a comparative analysis between the reference models and the models subjected to evolution is performed, and finally, the GA algorithm is assigned the role of reference for comparison with the RS algorithm.

4.1 Selected Features and SFS Analysis

To isolate indicators with predictive capacity and reduce dimensionality, the SFS execution employed an XGBoost classifier as a wrapper estimator. Weighted F1 was used as the primary evaluation metric due to its ability to handle class imbalances in financial datasets, providing the results with the harmonic mean between precision and recall [19].

The model's performance trajectory as attributes are sequentially added is illustrated in Fig. 2. The analysis reveals a saturation point in the predictive power beyond which the inclusion of new variables does not result in improved performance metrics.

As can be seen in Fig. 2 the F1-Score shows an improvement during the initial iterations, indicating the gain in information provided by the volatility and momentum indicators. However, the curve shows a plateau after the inclusion of the tenth attribute and beyond this point the addition of variables is linked to reduced returns and increased variance, which is consistent with the phenomenon of the "curse of dimensionality" [6].

Consequently, the subset with $K = 10$ was identified as the appropriate operating configuration. Nevertheless, the subset with $K = 11$ attributes was assigned an equivalent score (within the standard deviation), allowing the introduction of RSI_LAG1, which provides context relative to the previous state.

To ensure a rigorous evaluation, both subsets were allowed to advance to the evolutionary optimization stage.

Table 4 details the compositions related to the two subsets of attributes that showed satisfactory performance. It should be noted that the values in parentheses indicate the retrospective period (n) used to calculate each technical indicator (for example, $BB_{pos}(9)$ is associated with a calculation window of 9 periods).

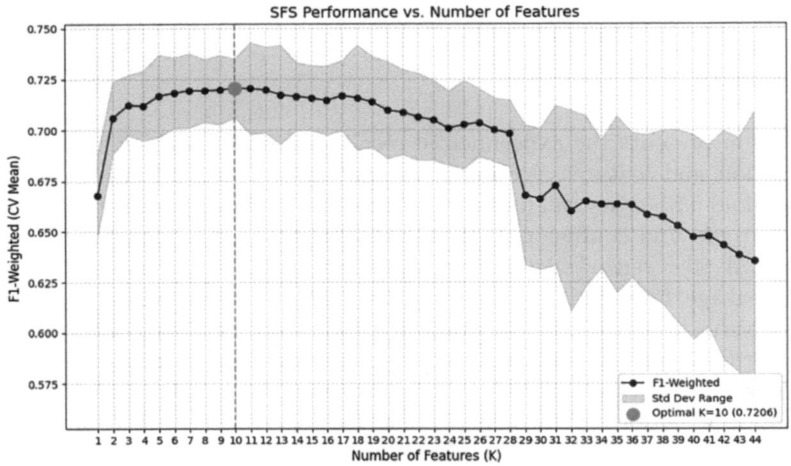

Fig. 2. Sequential Forward Selection (SFS) Performance.

Feature Analysis. The selected subsets are attributed a tendency towards Volatility Indicators, since most attributes are linked to variations in the positions of Bollinger Bands (BB_{pos}) arranged in different time windows. This empirical finding suggests that, for Mini Index futures contracts, the relative price position within its volatility range plays a more significant role as a predictor of immediate direction than trend-following metrics.

Additionally, the inclusion of $RETURN\_LAG1$ and RSI_{diff} confirms the need to capture the immediate rate of change and historical shock. The second subset ($K = 11$) reinforces this structure by adding RSI_LAG1 allowing the model to observe the temporal trajectory of the moment. This composition of attributes is linked to the purpose of providing the system with a multi-scalar perception of price oscillations, ensuring that both the amplitude of volatility and the inertia of the previous movement are incorporated into the technical analysis.

4.2 Evolutionary Hyperparameter Optimization

After the attribute selection stage, the subsets of attributes considered suitable ($K = 10$ and $K = 11$) were assigned for use in the GA evaluation, which was

Table 4. Optimal Feature Subsets ($K = 10$ and $K = 11$) Selected by SFS

Rank	Feature Name	Technical Category
1	BB_{pos} (9)	Volatility
2	BB_{pos} (20)	Volatility
3	$RETURN\_LAG1$	Microstructure / Autocorrelation
4	$CLOSEvsSMA_{20}$	Mean Reversion Distance
5	BB_{pos} (12)	Volatility
6	BB_{pos} (10)	Volatility
7	RSI_{diff}	Momentum Acceleration
8	BB_{pos} (25)	Volatility
9	RSI (6)	Momentum
10	BB_{pos} (18)	Volatility
Additional Feature for $K = 11$		
11	RSI_LAG1	Momentum Trajectory

configured to maximize a fitness function with a gap penalty (Eq. 2). To maintain computational feasibility, the evolutionary parameters (Table 1) were adapted to each architecture, the XGBoost model, with lower processing requirements, allowed for an expanded-scale exploration of the search space, while the MLP model was reserved a restricted optimization structure.

Both models were associated with the display of constant evolutionary convergence. The algorithm was assigned the application of penalties to configurations with initial overfitting directing the population to regions of stability in the hyperparameter space to which the reduction of the generalization gap and the preservation of predictive accuracy are linked, as detailed in the subsequent comparative analysis. This search process aims to ensure that the final result incorporates the robustness necessary for operation in data environments subject to fluctuations.

4.3 Comparative Analysis: Baseline vs. Evolved Models

To quantify the impact of evolutionary optimization, performance analysis was linked to reference models equipped with standard hyperparameters, in contrast to the architectures to which the evolutionary process was applied. The evaluation criterion in this research considers not only the test score but also the stability associated with the Generalization Gap ($|Train - Test|$).

XGBoost Baseline. To establish a performance benchmark, the XGBoost model was initially evaluated using its standard hyperparameters, without applying evolutionary adjustment. This configuration, detailed in Table 2, is characterized as a high-variance learner to which reduced regularization is applied.

The reference model was shown to be overfit in both attribute subsets. For $K = 10$, the training F1 score of 0.9129 dropped to 0.7230 in unobserved data, resulting in a Generalization Gap of 0.1899. Similarly, for the subset $K = 11$, the training score decreased from 0.9169 to a test score of 0.7212, equivalent to a gap of 0.1957. These discrepancies indicate that the model memorized market noise rather than learning structural patterns, as detailed in Table 5. This phenomenon highlights the need to look for configurations that demonstrate a superior ability to handle the complexity of financial data.

Table 5. Confusion Matrices for the XGBoost Baseline models, illustrating the classification performance on the unseen test set for both feature subsets.

(a) **XGBoost Baseline** $K = 10$

Actual\Pred	Neg	Pos
Neg	1537	624
Pos	648	1781

(b) **XGBoost Baseline** $K = 11$

Actual\Pred	Neg	Pos
Neg	1533	628
Pos	652	1777

Evolutionary Optimization for XGBoost. To optimize the XGBoost model, the fitness function with gap penalty (Eq. 2) was used. As can be seen in Figs. 3 and 4 both attribute configurations were linked to exhibiting convergence in the first 200 generations, preceding entry into a refinement phase focused on locating regions of stability in the hyperparameter space.

Furthermore, the observed variance between maximum and average fitness over 1000 generations demonstrates that the mutation operators were responsible for maintaining genetic diversity. This mechanism is associated with the prevention of premature convergence, while the algorithm was tasked with mapping the appropriate structural definitions. This behavior is attributed to the fact that the search process incorporates an exploration of the solution space, which ensures that the configuration is linked to the stability necessary for operation on data subject to fluctuations.

For the $K = 10$ subset, the GA was assigned the identification of an architecture linked to a training F1 score of 0.7331 and a test F1 score of 0.7192, resulting in a generalization gap of 0.0139. Similarly, the $K = 11$ subset was associated with a training F1 score of 0.7399 and a test F1 score of 0.7220, leaving a gap of 0.0179. These results confirm that the optimization process mitigated overfitting in different attribute sets. Table 6 contains a summary of the final classification performance obtained in the unobserved test set, as shown in the confusion matrices.

These results demonstrate that the GA successfully traded off the "perfect memorization" of the training set for a model that maintains consistent predictive power in the noisy environment of the Mini Futures Index.

The structural preferences of the evolved models are detailed in Table 7. Compared to the broad search space with the convergence optima, it is evident

Table 6. Confusion Matrices for the evolved XGBoost models, illustrating the classification performance on the unseen test set for both feature subsets.

(a) Evolved XGBoost $K = 10$

Actual\Pred	Neg	Pos
Neg	1494	667
Pos	621	1808

(b) Evolved XGBoost $K = 11$

Actual\Pred	Neg	Pos
Neg	1520	641
Pos	635	1794

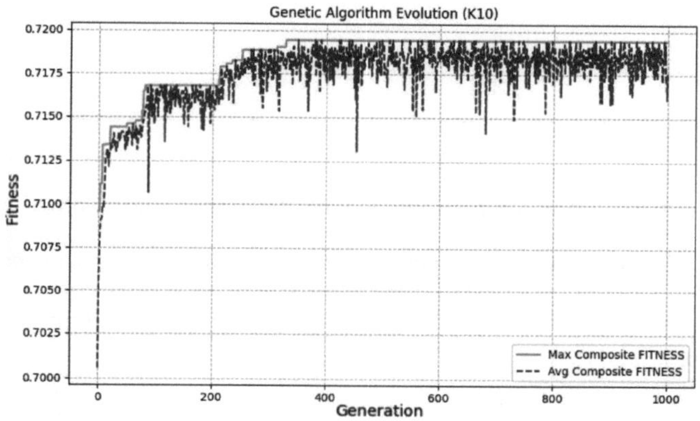

Fig. 3. GA Evolution for $K = 10$, showing Maximum and Average Fitness.

that the algorithm favored distinct regularization strategies for each subset. For instance, the $K = 10$ model minimized complexity via a shallow tree depth (3) and higher gamma, whereas $K = 11$ balanced slightly deeper trees (5) with increased L1 regularization (`reg_alpha`).

MLP Baseline. Similarly, the MLP was assigned the evaluation through a reference architecture to establish the neural network's performance parameter. The network topology and training configuration, detailed in Table 3, represent a common feed-forward network for binary classification.

Quantitatively, the MLP reference model for the subset $K = 10$ was linked to a training F1 score of 0.7270 and a test F1 score of 0.7140, resulting in a generalization gap of 0.0130. The $K = 11$ subset was associated with stability with training and test scores of 0.7292 and 0.7196, respectively, leaving a gap of 0.0096. These reduced margins confirm that even without evolutionary adjustment, the neural network architecture incorporates the mitigation of overfitting observed in the tree-based model. Table 8 presents the Confusion Matrices for the reference MLP models.

Evolutionary Optimization for MLP. For the Neural Network, the GA fine-tuned the balance between capacity (neurons) and regularization (Dropout/L2).

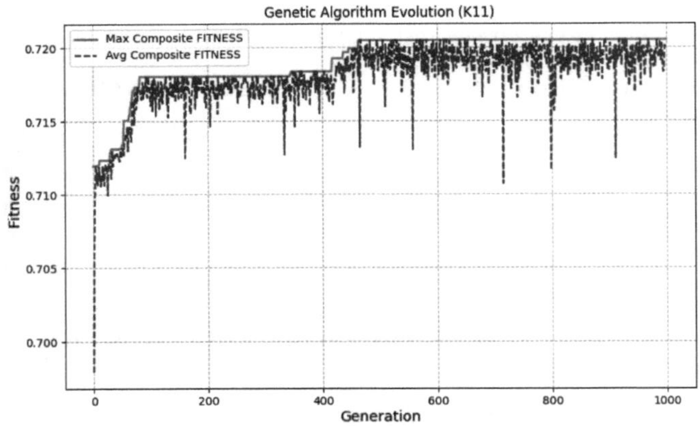

Fig. 4. GA Evolution for $K = 11$, showing Maximum and Average Fitness.

Table 7. XGBoost Hyperparameter Search Space and GA-Optimized Values

Hyperparameter	Search Space (Min - Max)	Optimal ($K = 10$)	Optimal ($K = 11$)
Structural Parameters			
`n_estimators`	$[100, 1200]$	807	894
`max_depth`	$[3, 12]$	3	5
Learning Dynamics			
`learning_rate`	$[0.01, 0.30]$	0.0612	0.1226
`subsample`	$[0.50, 1.00]$	0.6290	0.8548
`colsample_bytree`	$[0.50, 1.00]$	0.9355	0.9194
Regularization			
`gamma`	$[0, 10]$	7.3016	5.5556
`reg_alpha` (L1)	$[0, 10]$	0.0000	1.5294
`reg_lambda` (L2)	$[0, 10]$	2.2353	2.3529

As illustrated in Figs. 5 and 6, the algorithm efficiently navigated the search space, finding a robust local optimum within early generations and minimizing the generalization gap without requiring prolonged evolutionary exploration.

The parameters selected for the best MLP individuals are listed in Table 9. The algorithm favored moderate network sizes and specific L2 regularization, smoothing the decision boundary to prevent overfitting. The MLP optimization was highly successful in ensuring stability. For the $K = 10$ subset, the training and test F1-scores reached 0.7188 and 0.7182, respectively, producing a negligible generalization gap of 0.0006. The $K = 11$ subset yielded similarly robust results (0.7178 training, 0.7174 test, 0.0004 gap). However, because the baseline MLP already demonstrated strong inherent stability without evolutionary tuning, the GA functioned primarily as a fine-tuning mechanism. These marginal improve-

Table 8. Confusion Matrices for the MLP Baseline models, illustrating the classification performance on the unseen test set for both feature subsets.

(a) **MLP Baseline** $K = 10$

Actual\Pred	**Neg**	**Pos**
Neg	1553	608
Pos	706	1723

(b) **MLP Baseline** $K = 11$

Actual\Pred	**Neg**	**Pos**
Neg	1495	666
Pos	620	1809

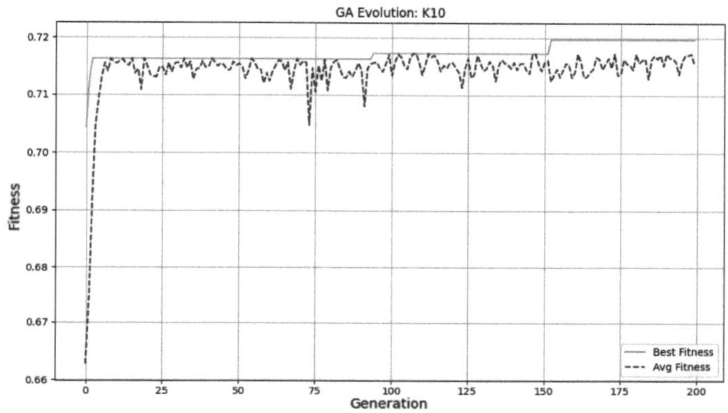

Fig. 5. Genetic Algorithm Evolution for MLP ($K = 10$), showing Maximum and Average Fitness.

ments over the default settings suggest that the substantial computational cost of evolving neural topologies offers diminishing returns for this specific architecture.

Genetic Algorithm vs. Random Search. To ensure that the evolutionary approach provided benefits over standard stochastic methods, the GA was benchmarked against the RS algorithm specifically for the XGBoost architecture. Under an identical budget of 20,000 evaluations, both methods successfully mitigated baseline overfitting and achieved statistically equivalent predictive power. For instance, in the $K = 10$ subset, the GA produced a test F1-score of 0.7192 with a generalization gap of 0.0139, compared to the RS's test F1-score of 0.7217 and a gap of 0.0151. Similarly, in the $K = 11$ configuration, GA yielded a test F1-score of 0.7220 with a generalization gap of 0.0179, while RS achieved an F1-score of 0.7174 with a gap of 0.0166.

However, the execution revealed a consistent superiority of the GA in computational efficiency, although the margin of this advantage proved to be highly context-dependent. For the $K = 10$ configuration, the RS required an execution time nearly 92% longer than the GA to exhaust the same budget. In contrast, in the $K = 11$ subset the performance margin decreased, with RS taking approximately 10% longer than GA to complete the optimization. This variation

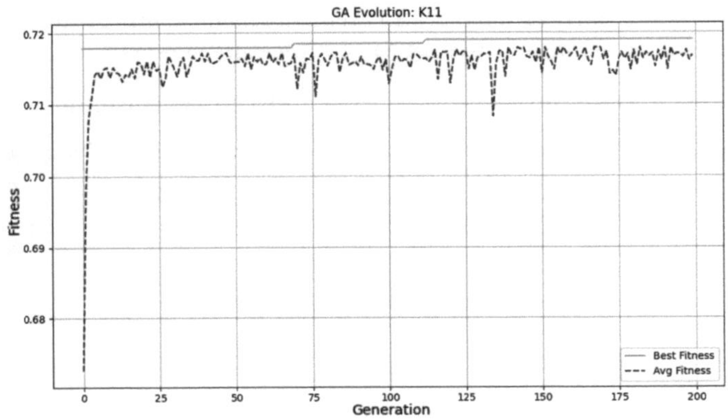

Fig. 6. Genetic Algorithm Evolution for MLP ($K = 11$), showing Maximum and Average Fitness.

Table 9. MLP Hyperparameter Search Space and GA-Optimized Values

Hyperparameter	Search Space	Optimal ($K = 10$)	Optimal ($K = 11$)
Architecture & Optimization			
`neurons_layer1`	$[16, 64]$	33	53
`learning_rate`	$[1e^{-5}, 5e^{-3}]$	0.0024	0.0026
`batch_size`	$\{16, 32, 64\}$	16	32
Regularization			
`l2_alpha`	$[1e^{-4}, 1e^{-2}]$	1.18×10^{-4}	7.89×10^{-4}
`dropout_rate`	$[0.20, 0.60]$	0.32	0.21

indicates a characteristic of the evolutionary process. When a satisfactory architecture is found in shallow regions with regularization (as in $K = 10$), the GA reduces the time spent by applying penalties to complex trees at the beginning of execution. On the other hand, when the evolutionary pressure converges to an architecture with structural complexity, such as the topology required for the $K = 11$ subset, the time to train each candidate increases, reducing the efficiency difference. However, even in this more demanding scenario, the GA's targeted search provided structural stability more quickly than random sampling.

5 Conclusions

The study presented an optimization flow aimed at reducing overfitting in the directional forecast of the Mini Bovespa Future Index (WIN). By integrating forward SFS with evolutionary parameter tuning, the study analyzed the balance between model complexity and generalization capacity in the XGBoost and MLP architectures.

The experimental results reveal a dichotomy with respect to the need for evolutionary adjustment. For the XGBoost architecture, GA proved to be a necessary component for viability. The reference models were assigned a generalization gap greater than 0.18. In a domain where the reliability of backtests is valued, such a discrepancy renders the model unreliable for real-world execution. The evolutionary process served as a dynamic regularization tool, which reduced this gap to less than 0.02 and established a balance between theoretical predictive power and operational safety.

In contrast, MLP demonstrated its own structural stability. Although GA provided refinement to the generalization gap to reduced levels, the performance gain suggests a scenario of diminishing returns. Even though GA provides targeted and efficient search, the reference stability of the neural network indicates that parameter tuning offers limited practical benefits. This contrast indicates that, while evolutionary optimization is necessary to impose limits on high-variance models like XGBoost, it serves the fine-tuning function for architectures with natural stability.

Moreover, the results observed in the Mini Bovespa Index suggest that the application of this methodology can encompass other financial assets. The structure that integrates the sequential selection of attributes with evolutionary adjustment allows the model's conformation to the noise levels and volatility variations inherent in different instruments of the futures market.

Future research will focus on expanding the attribute space to incorporate order flow dynamics and exploring Multi-Objective Evolutionary Algorithms (MOEAs) [5] to optimize financial metrics such as the Sharpe Ratio. Finally, by prioritizing robustness over memorability and considering market friction, this study provides a basis for autonomous trading systems capable of maintaining viability in fluctuating financial environments [23].

Acknowledgment. The authors would like to thank FAPERGS (24/2551-0001396-2, 23/2551-0000773-8), CNPq (307416/2025-9), FAPERGS/CNPq (23/2551-0000126-8) and the Fesurv-University of Rio Verde.

References

1. Abadi, M., et al.: TensorFlow: Large-scale machine learning on heterogeneous distributed systems (2015). Software available from tensorflow.org
2. Bollinger, J.: Bollinger on Bollinger Bands. McGraw-Hill Professional (2002)
3. Cerqueira, V., Torgo, L., Mozetič, I.: Evaluating time series forecasting models: an empirical study on performance estimation methods. Mach. Learn. **109**(11), 1997–2028 (2020)
4. Chen, T., Guestrin, C.: XGBoost: A scalable tree boosting system. In: Proceedings of the 22nd ACM SIGKDD International Conference on Knowledge Discovery and Data Mining (2016)
5. Deb, K., Pratap, A., Agarwal, S., Meyarivan, T.: A fast and elitist multiobjective genetic algorithm: NSGA-ii. IEEE Trans. Evol. Comput. **6**(2), 182–197 (2002)

6. Dhal, P., Azad, C.: A comprehensive survey on feature selection in the various fields of machine learning. Appl. Intell. **52**(4), 4543–4581 (2022)
7. Goldberg, D.E.: Genetic Algorithms in Search. Addison-Wesley, Optimization and Machine Learning (1989)
8. Gu, S., Kelly, B., Xiu, D.: Empirical asset pricing via machine learning. Rev. Fin. Studies **33**(5), 2223–2273 (2020)
9. Hasbrouck, J.: Empirical Market Microstructure: The Institutions, Economics, and Econometrics of Securities Trading. Oxford University Press (2007)
10. Katoch, S., Chauhan, S., Kumar, V.: A review on genetic algorithm: past, present, and future. Multimedia Tools Appl. **80**(5), 8091–8126 (2021)
11. Kohavi, R., John, G.H.: Wrappers for feature subset selection. Artif. Intell. **97**(1–2), 273–324 (1997)
12. Krauss, C., Do, X.A., Huck, N.: Deep neural networks, gradient-boosted trees, random forests: statistical arbitrage on the s&p 500. Eur. J. Oper. Res. **259**(2), 689–702 (2017)
13. Lopez de Prado, M.: Advances in Financial Machine Learning. John Wiley & Sons (2018)
14. Lopez de Prado, M.: Machine learning for asset managers. Cambridge University Press (2020)
15. Nti, I.K., Adekoya, A.F., Weyori, B.A.: A systematic review of fundamental and technical analysis of stock market predictions. Artif. Intell. Rev. **53**(4), 3007–3057 (2020)
16. Pedregosa, F., et al.: Scikit-learn: machine learning in Python. J. Mach. Learn. Res. **12**, 2825–2830 (2011)
17. Python Software Foundation: Python language reference, version 3.10 (2021). https://www.python.org
18. Sezer, O.B., Gudelek, M.U., Ozbayoglu, A.M.: Financial time series forecasting with deep learning: a systematic literature review: 2005–2019. Appl. Soft Comput. **90**, 106181 (2020)
19. Sokolova, M., Lapalme, G.: A systematic analysis of performance measures for classification tasks. Information processing & management **45**(4), 427–437 (2009)
20. Souza, A.S., Lucca, G., Borges, E.N., Cardoso, F.C., Dalmazo, B.L., Berri, R.: Dataset for Intraday Analysis of B3 stock prices (2024). https://doi.org/10.7910/DVN/TMB4IG
21. Thabtah, F., Hammoud, S., Kamalov, F., Gonsalves, A.: Data imbalance in classification: experimental evaluation. Inf. Sci. **513**, 429–441 (2020)
22. Wilder, J.W.: New Concepts in Technical Trading Systems. Trend Research, Greensboro, NC (1978)
23. Yang, H., Liu, X.Y., Zhong, S., Walid, A.: Deep reinforcement learning for automated stock trading: An ensemble strategy. In: Proceedings of the First ACM International Conference on AI in Finance, pp. 1–8 (2020)

Zero-Shot LLM Sentiment Meets Market Microstructure: Parsimonious Feature Selection for High-Frequency Bitcoin Forecastings

Luís A. Moraes[1], Daniel Marques[1], Lucas Nojiri[1], Elisa T. Albergaria[1], Diego R. C. Dias[2](✉), Vinícius F. S. Mota[2], Marcelo P. Guimarães[3], and Leonardo C. D. Rocha[1]

[1] Universidade Federal de São João del Rei (UFSJ), São João del Rei, Brazil
{luisassismoraes,daniellmarquesfacul,lucas_nojiri}@aluno.ufsj.edu.br, {etuler,lcrocha}@ufsj.edu.br
[2] Universidade Federal do Espírito Santo (UFES), Vitória, Brazil
{diego.dias,vinicius.f.mota}@ufes.br
[3] Universidade Federal de São Paulo (UNIFESP), São Paulo, Brazil
marcelo.paiva@unifesp.br

Abstract. High-frequency cryptocurrency forecasting is a difficult task, given the numerous regime changes, microstructure noise, and feature redundancy between technical and social signals. Recent literature has explored large language models (LLMs) for sentiment extraction, but problems such as the increasing number of features leading to greater multicollinearity and overfitting negatively impact economic performance when considering transaction costs. In this paper, we present a multimodal pipeline for Bitcoin trend forecasting, integrating market microstructure, technical and macroeconomic indicators, and contextual Twitter sentiment inferred through zero-shot sampling with Llama-2 7B. To control dimensionality, we applied recursive feature elimination (RFE) with a random forest estimator, selecting a reduced subset of 17 variables from a set of 30 features. We train deep recurrent models (stacked long short-term memory (LSTM) and gated recurrent unit (GRU)) and evaluate them under an equity-based backtesting protocol with long/short execution and 0.1% transaction costs. Results indicate that feature curation matters more than architectural complexity for trading stability: at the 12-hour horizon, the GRU model with RFE achieves a Sharpe Ratio of 5.28 and a Total Return of 48.32%, delivering performance comparable to a Buy & Hold benchmark with lower dispersion. Performance degrades as the forecasting horizon increases to 5 days, suggesting that exogenous signals are more relevant at shorter horizons. Since the evaluation period coincides with a bullish regime in Bitcoin, these results are regime-conditional. Our findings emphasize that parsimonious feature selection is a structural component for stabilizing multimodal forecasting pipelines in high-frequency crypto markets.

O. Gervasi et al. (Eds.): ICCSA 2026, LNCS 16768, pp. 569–583, 2027.
https://doi.org/10.1007/978-3-032-30488-9_35

Keywords: Bitcoin · Multimodal Learning · Zero-Shot Sentiment · Feature Selection · Recursive Feature Elimination

1 Introduction

Predictive modeling of cryptoassets combines continuous trading, retail participation, and abrupt volatility regimes. These factors make predicting high-frequency returns difficult to overcome using classical statistical models and trading strategies in realistic environments. Bitcoin is dynamic in terms of jumps, liquidity, and microstructures. These characteristics increase noise in short-term scenarios, hindering the generalization of the model. [19].

Social signals often appear before market movements, especially on Twitter/X, where mood, attention, and sentiment capture reactions to information before prices change [14,17,20]. The inclusion of large volumes of textual and derived features seems to contribute to the emergence of multicollinearity among some features, which tends to degrade the model's stability in real-world environments. Traditional lexicon-based approaches have limited ability to handle irony, slang, and context shifts common in the crypto ecosystem [17,21]. Recent work employs neural representations and multimodal models to predict extreme events or trends. These approaches still report dependence on feature engineering choices, forecasting horizons, and decision thresholds [23].

Large language models (LLMs) expand the ability to infer contextual sentiment without extensive supervised labeling via zero-shot and instruction prompting [4,13]. Labeling massive social streams remains computationally expensive. Combining these labels with many technical and macroeconomic indicators can worsen the signal-to-noise ratio. We address the following problem: how to integrate contextual social signals extracted by LLMs into high-frequency financial data in a parsimonious way, avoiding multicollinearity and overfitting, while maximizing economic performance under transaction costs?

We propose and evaluate a hybrid architecture that combines market microstructure data, technical indicators, macroeconomic variables, and contextual sentiment. We extract this sentiment via Llama-2 7B in a zero-shot regime, aggregating tweets into discrete 4-hour windows. We adopt the parsimony hypothesis rather than prioritizing feature volume. We apply recursive feature elimination (RFE) guided by a random forest to select an optimal subset of variables, which reduces dimensionality and mitigates multicollinearity and noise [8,9,22]. On this reduced feature set, we train deep recurrent networks (stacked long short-term memory (LSTM) and gated recurrent unit (GRU)) to forecast future log returns. We leverage evidence that GRUs converge on noisy sequences with fewer parameters than LSTMs [5,6,11].

We evaluate the models using an equity-based protocol with long/short execution and 0.1% transaction costs. This approach prioritizes financial metrics (Total Return, Sharpe, and Maximum Drawdown) over statistical errors, following recommendations for economic validation of algorithmic strategies [2,7]. Results indicate that feature selection plays a role in stabilizing trading performance. At the 12-hour horizon, the GRU + RFE model achieved a Sharpe Ratio of 5.28 and a Total Return of 48.32%. This provides performance similar to the Buy & Hold benchmark over the same period. The evaluation period we used refers to a Bitcoin price increase, making these results conditional on the regime. However, we can see that performance worsens over longer periods, up to 5 days, suggesting that the signals lose relevance as the forecast window increases.

In summary, this work presents the following contributions: a multimodal pipeline aimed at predicting high-frequency Bitcoin trends, integrating microstructure, macroeconomics, and zero-shot contextual sentiment through an LLM; empirical evidence that curation (RFE) mitigates the issue related to model complexity by reducing the number of features; and evaluation performed over larger windows, highlighting the limits of generalization over longer periods.

2 Related Work

Research on cryptocurrency forecasting has advanced on three main fronts: first, using artificial intelligence to deal with the price rollercoaster of this market; second, attempting to combine prices with external information, such as what people say on social media; and finally, seeking more realistic results by creating tests that consider brokerage fees and prevent the model from simply "memorizing" the past instead of learning to predict the future.

Because the cryptocurrency market is volatile and full of unpredictable variations, traditional mathematical models are losing ground to more modern AI architectures, such as LSTM and GRU [5,6,11], which handle this complexity better. Recent studies show that the secret lies not only in choosing the most advanced AI, but also in how the signals are prepared and how the tests are conducted. Authors like Omole and Enke [16] emphasize that it is not enough for the model to be accurate; it needs to be profitable in practice, combining statistical results with real financial returns. Furthermore, new techniques seek to combine different types of data—such as price indicators and market sentiment—using intelligent filters to prevent information overload from hindering more than helping [10].

Several studies indicate that what happens on social media—both the volume of posts and the mood of investors—often provides clues about what will happen to the price, volume, and volatility of Bitcoin shortly afterward [15,20]. Studies show that counting the number of tweets or analyzing the sentiment of the messages helps predict the behavior of the currency in the very short term. In practice, these social signals can be transformed into rules for investment robots, generating above-average profits at certain times. Going beyond Bitcoin, studies with various cryptocurrencies show that Twitter especially influences the larger assets, although this effect is not an absolute rule: it varies greatly depending on the currency and the market situation, which reinforces that public sentiment is a powerful, but often unstable, indicator [14].

A key difference when predicting the market using sentiment is the tool you choose to read what people write. Many people still use simpler and cheaper methods, based on word lists (like VADER [12]), which serve as a common starting point. However, more modern AI models, such as Transformers, understand context much better. A famous example is FinBERT [1], a version of BERT trained specifically for the world of finance. Recent research shows that these contextual models work better for predicting cryptocurrencies than older methods [23]. Following this trend, the use of large language models (LLMs) has emerged as a way to obtain very high-quality analyses without having to train the AI from scratch, although this is more expensive [4,13]. That's why we made a strategic decision in this article: we use the power of LLMs to extract sentiment accurately, but we control the costs and noise of the data by selecting only the information that really makes a difference to the model.

Adding technical indicators, economic data, and social media sentiment to prices gives the model a more complete view, but it also creates a problem: too much information can generate confusion and bias the AI into patterns that don't exist (the famous curse of dimensionality). To solve this, we use methods like RFE, which act as an intelligent filter, eliminating weak information step by step to keep only what really matters [8,9]. Recent research in the cryptocurrency world shows that cleaning up the data can completely change the game, directly impacting the final profit [10,16]. This goes straight to the central point of our study: instead of believing that "the more data, the better," we tested whether simplicity (or parsimony) is, in fact, the main factor in making the model truly profitable in practice.

A common mistake in many studies is focusing solely on mathematical metrics (such as the model's average error) without proving that it actually generate positive returns net of transaction costs. To avoid this overly optimistic approach, modern evaluations use simulations that include transaction costs and real buying and selling rules [7]. In addition, there is a risk that the model will simply memorize the past due to excessive testing, which creates a false profit on the stocks that will not be repeated in the future. To address this, we use tools such as the Deflated Sharpe Ratio (DSR) [3], which adjusts the results by taking into account how many attempts were made to arrive at that strategy, delivering a much more realistic view than the standard index. Ultimately, how you test the model is just as important as its intelligence. That is why our protocol was rigorous: we divided the data chronologically, repeated the tests multiple times to ensure it was not luck, and simulated a complete operation with real costs.

Against this background, our contribution is to empirically evaluate a *cost-aware* multimodal pipeline for short-horizon Bitcoin forecasting that combines (i) market/macro/technical indicators, (ii) zero-shot LLM-derived sentiment, and (iii) RFE-driven parsimony. Unlike approaches that emphasize ever-larger enrichment, we focus on the practical question of whether selective curation of multimodal features is the primary driver of economically robust performance under realistic backtesting constraints.

3 Methodology

In this section, we detail the proposed and implemented experimental pipeline to evaluate whether the use of multimodal data (market, technical, macroeconomic, and social signals) and feature selection can improve the performance of Bitcoin market predictions.

Our pipeline is organized into three stages that integrate data collection through economic validation. First, we performed acquisition and temporal alignment of microstructure variables (OHLCV), technical indicators, macroeconomic proxies, and social signals extracted from Twitter. Next, we moved on to feature engineering and selection, where a set of 30 variables was reached via Recursive Feature Elimination (RFE) with a Random Forest estimator to isolate a subset of 17 predictors; finally, we trained and validated two stacked recurrent models (LSTM and GRU).

We constructed a multimodal time series with a fixed granularity of 4-hour intervals, which served as the baseline frequency for both prediction and trading simulation. In this context, we let t represent each 4-hour time step. To compose the central market variables, we collected OHLCV candles of the BTC/USDT pair on the KuCoin exchange via the `ccxt` library, thus defining the Baseline (OHLCV) scenario composed of the set $\{\texttt{BTC\_Open}, \texttt{BTC\_High}, \texttt{BTC\_Low}, \texttt{BTC\_Close}, \texttt{BTC\_Volume}\}$.

To capture broader risk-on/risk-off dynamics and cross-market comovements, we enrich the dataset with macro proxies obtained via `yfinance` (e.g., DXY, Gold, Oil WTI, Nasdaq). Since these series are not observed continuously at 4-hour intervals, we reindexed them to the study's time grid and applied the forward fill method, carrying over the last available value during weekends and holidays; this procedure allowed us to preserve causal availability, ensuring that no future information was used for interpolation. Additionally, we calculated standard trend and momentum indicators via the pandas-ta library, including moving averages (SMA and EMA in different windows), RSI, MACD components (line, signal, and histogram), realized volatility, and logarithmic returns.

We used a corpus of approximately 1M tweets containing the cashtag "$BTC" from the Bitcoin Tweets Dataset. Because full-scale labeling is computationally expensive, we label a 10% strategic sample using Llama-2 7B Chat in a zero-shot setting. Concretely, we run `meta-llama/Llama-2-7b-chat-hf` quantized to 4-bit (NF4) with `bitsandbytes` on Google Colab (T4 GPU). Each tweet is processed with a fixed instruction prompt to output:

- a sentiment score in $[-1, 1]$, and
- auxiliary intensity signals (market/emotional intensity).

We used a low temperature ($\tau = 0.1$) to reduce output variance and improve reproducibility of the inferred labels.

Tweets arrive asynchronously. For each 4-hour interval t, we aggregate tweet-level outputs into four interval-level features:

$$\texttt{Sentiment\_Mean}_t,\ \texttt{Market\_Intensity}_t,\ \texttt{Emotional\_Intensity}_t,\ \texttt{Tweet\_Vol}_t.$$

Intervals with no observed tweets are assigned neutral values (sentiment/intensity set to mid-point) and $\texttt{Tweet\_Vol} = 0$, ensuring the time index remains continuous and avoiding leakage due to missingness patterns.

The prediction target is the next-step log return:

$$y_{t+1} = \log(\texttt{BTC\_Close}_{t+1}) - \log(\texttt{BTC\_Close}_t).$$

We evaluated multiple horizons by forecasting log returns y_{t+h} with $h \in \{3, 7, 14, 30\}$, corresponding to 12 h, 28 h, 56 h, and 5 days at 4-h resolution. This multiple horizons enables assessment of the hypothesis that social signals are short-lived and decay as the horizon increases.

Before feature selection and model training, we quantify linear dependencies among inputs to characterize redundancy and multicollinearity in the enriched feature set. We compute pairwise Pearson correlation coefficients:

$$r(X, Y) = \frac{\sum_{i=1}^{n}(x_i - \bar{x})(y_i - \bar{y})}{\sqrt{\sum_{i=1}^{n}(x_i - \bar{x})^2}\sqrt{\sum_{i=1}^{n}(y_i - \bar{y})^2}},$$

and inspect the resulting correlation matrix. This step is used *diagnostically* (not as a feature filter) to motivate RFE and to anticipate potential instability from highly correlated indicators (e.g., overlapping moving-average windows).

To enforce parsimony and reduce redundancy, we applied RFE using a random forest regressor as the external estimator. Random forests are well-suited as a selection backbone because they can capture nonlinear interactions and produce feature importance scores without assuming linearity [8,9].

For regression forests, feature importance is computed as the mean decrease in impurity (MDI), where impurity is typically measured by variance/MSE reduction. For feature X_j, importance is:

$$\mathrm{Imp}(X_j) = \frac{1}{N_{\text{trees}}} \sum_{t=1}^{N_{\text{trees}}} \sum_{\nu \in S_{X_j}(t)} \Delta I(\nu, t),$$

where $S_{X_j}(t)$ denotes the set of split nodes on X_j in tree t and $\Delta I(\nu, t)$ is the impurity decrease at node ν.

RFE iteratively:

1. fits the Random Forest on the training subset;
2. ranks features by importance;
3. removes the least important features; and
4. evaluates validation error (RMSE) to identify the best trade-off between performance and complexity.

We selected k using the elbow/plateau point in the RMSE-versus-#features curve (Fig. 2), yielding a parsimonious set of 17 features from the 30-feature enriched pool. Importantly, this selection is performed using only training/validation data to prevent test contamination.

To isolate the impact of enrichment and parsimony, we evaluate four data scenarios:

1. **Baseline (OHLCV):** only the five market variables.

2. **Macro/Tech Only:** technical indicators and macro proxies added (excluding social features).
3. **Full Enriched:** all 30 variables, including LLM-derived sentiment features.
4. **RFE Optimized:** the 17-variable subset selected by RFE.

For each scenario, we train two deep recurrent architectures: stacked LSTM and stacked GRU. Both are configured to forecast continuous log returns and are trained under identical optimization settings to ensure fairness.

Each model uses:

- **Recurrent layer 1:** 256 hidden units with `return_sequences=True` and tanh activation;
- **Dropout:** 0.2 after the first recurrent layer;
- **Recurrent layer 2:** 128 hidden units with tanh activation;
- **Output:** a linear dense layer producing $\hat{y}_{t+h}$.

We trained the models with Adam ($\eta = 10^{-4}$) and the MSE loss, using early stopping with a patience of 10 epochs. To account for stochasticity in neural training, each configuration is trained 10 times with different random seeds, and we report the mean ± standard deviation for financial metrics.

All input variables are standardized via StandardScaler (zero mean, unit variance) fit on the training set and applied to validation/test sets, ensuring no leakage from future information [18].

Following equity-based evaluation principles [7], we evaluate models as trading agents over the test set, using a deterministic long/short rule driven by the predicted return:

$$\text{Pos}_{t+1} = \begin{cases} 1 & \text{if } \hat{y}_{t+h} > \epsilon, \\ -1 & \text{if } \hat{y}_{t+h} < -\epsilon, \\ 0 & \text{otherwise,} \end{cases} \qquad \epsilon = 5 \times 10^{-5}.$$

Each position change incurs a transaction cost of 0.1% per trade. This design explicitly tests whether predictive improvements hold up under realistic frictions rather than just improving error metrics.

We report three standard financial metrics [13]:

1. **Total Return (TR):**
$$TR = \prod_{t=1}^{T}(1 + r_t) - 1,$$
where r_t is the strategy return at time t after costs.
2. **Sharpe Ratio (SR):**
$$SR = \frac{\mu(R_p)}{\sigma(R_p)}\sqrt{K},$$
where R_p is the strategy return series and K is the annualization factor for 4-hour intervals.

3. **Maximum Drawdown (MDD):**

$$MDD = \min_t \left(\frac{V_t - \max_{\tau \le t} V_\tau}{\max_{\tau \le t} V_\tau} \right),$$

where V_t is the equity curve.

In the next section, we present the results in three stages: (i) exploratory statistics of the social characteristics derived from the LLM and their sparsity/dispersion in 4-hour intervals; (ii) correlation structure and RFE selection dynamics, including the relationship between RMSE and the number of characteristics and the final ranking of importance; and (iii) a comparative financial assessment between horizons and scenarios, highlighting when to employ new characteristics, as well as when to reduce them.

4 Experimental Results

This section reports empirical evidence for the claims raised in the Introduction: (i) multimodal enrichment can help, but naive feature expansion may amplify redundancy and overfitting; (ii) parsimonious feature curation is a first-order driver of *tradable* performance; and (iii) the predictive value of social sentiment is short-lived and degrades as the forecasting horizon increases. Results are presented in three steps aligned with our pipeline (Sect. 3): (1) exploratory analysis of LLM-derived social features, (2) correlation structure and the RFE selection dynamics, and (3) trading-realistic performance under transaction costs across multiple horizons.

4.1 Exploratory Analysis of LLM-Derived Social Features

We first validate whether the LLM-derived social signals exhibit meaningful variability at the 4-hour resolution and whether they reflect the expected *burstiness* of social attention. Table 1 summarizes descriptive statistics for the four aggregated social features over 1,184 time windows.

Table 1. Descriptive Statistics of Social (LLM) Features (4-h windows)

Statistic	Sentiment	Market Int.	Emotional Int.	Tweet Vol.
Mean	0.5142	0.5036	0.5297	86.05
Std. Dev.	0.0277	0.0142	0.0457	191.99
Min	0.0231	0.4176	0.5000	0.00
Median (50%)	0.5000	0.5000	0.5000	0.00
Max	0.5986	0.7000	0.8000	1389.00

Two observations are relevant to our hypotheses. First, `Tweet Vol.` exhibits a strong long-tail distribution: the median is zero while the maximum reaches

1,389 interactions per window, consistent with attention spikes around market-moving events. Second, the sentiment and intensity variables are relatively concentrated around neutral values (median ≈ 0.5), as expected when aggregating heterogeneous social content into coarse time bins. This combination of (i) sparse attention bursts and (ii) weakly varying sentiment levels motivates two design choices discussed earlier: (a) using models capable of learning nonlinear interactions among sparse exogenous signals and market dynamics, and (b) controlling redundancy and noise via parsimonious feature selection rather than unquestioningly expanding the feature set.

4.2 Correlation Structure and RFE Selection Dynamics

Redundancy and Multicollinearity. Before evaluating trading performance, we inspect the correlation structure of the enriched dataset. Figure 1 shows the Pearson correlation heatmap. Consistent with our motivation, many technical indicators (especially overlapping moving-average windows and related momentum measures) exhibit strong mutual correlation, whereas their correlations with the return target are generally weak.

Selecting a Parsimonious Subset (RFE). To test feature reduction, we applied RFE with a Random Forest estimator and tracked validation RMSE with respect to the number of features retained. Figure 2 illustrates the relationship between complexity and validation error. We observed a stagnation point, beyond which adding features produces marginal (or negative) gains, indicating that additional variables tend to generate noise and redundancy rather than a useful signal. Based on the results of the experiments, we selected $k = 17$ features.

Which Variables Survive RFE? Figure 3 presents the ranking in order of relevance of each variable in the selected subset. The resulting set highlights the variables that describe the market microstructure (variables related to price/volume) and by momentum/volatility descriptors, while macroeconomic variables play a secondary role. Sentiment and intensity variables derived from the LLM are excluded by the RFE, while tweet activity (volume) remains. This indicates that, within the evaluated configuration, simple social attention variables carry a more measurable signal than the contextual polarity measures extracted by the LLM.

4.3 Trading-Realistic Performance Across Horizons

We now evaluate whether the predictive models translate into *tradable* performance under realistic frictions. Tables 2, 3, 4 and 5 report the equity-based backtest results for four horizons: 12 h (3 periods), 28 h (7 periods), 56 h (14 periods), and 5 days (30 periods). Each neural configuration is trained 10 times with different seeds; for Total Return, we report the mean $\pm$ standard deviation.

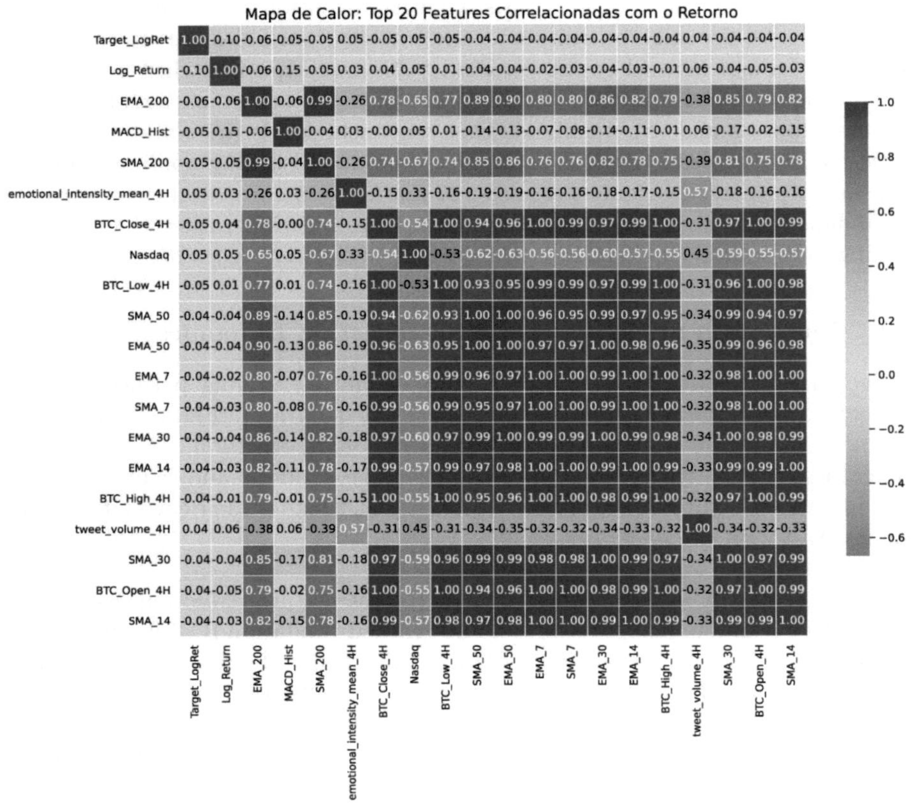

Fig. 1. Pearson correlation heatmap. Strong inter-feature correlations (particularly among technical indicators) indicate multicollinearity.

Table 2. Financial Results – Horizon of 3 periods (12 h)

Model	Data Scenario	Total Return (%)	Sharpe Ratio	MDD (%)
Benchmark	Buy & Hold	47.93%	5.27	−10.83%
LSTM	Baseline (OHLCV)	27.24% ± 14.45	3.34	−14.56%
LSTM	Macro/Tech Only	20.42% ± 34.30	2.05	−20.05%
LSTM	Full Enriched	8.65% ± 31.91	0.81	−22.29%
LSTM	Feature Selection (RFE)	35.61% ± 9.83	4.17	−12.71%
GRU	Baseline (OHLCV)	25.80% ± 28.54	2.88	−15.56%
GRU	Macro/Tech Only	25.03% ± 30.48	2.68	−16.85%
GRU	Full Enriched	22.75% ± 35.96	2.29	−19.93%
GRU	**Feature Selection (RFE)**	**48.32% ± 10.81**	**5.28**	**-11.21%**

Table 3. Financial Results – Horizon of 7 periods (28 h)

Model	Data Scenario	Total Return (%)	Sharpe Ratio	MDD (%)
Benchmark	Buy & Hold	47.93%	5.27	−10.83%
LSTM	Baseline (OHLCV)	−1.28% ± 15.54	0.05	−22.35%
LSTM	Macro/Tech Only	41.21% ± 20.69	4.56	−13.04%
LSTM	Full Enriched	16.38% ± 28.68	1.85	−19.30%
LSTM	Feature Selection (RFE)	47.36% ± 3.54	5.23	−10.91%
GRU	Baseline (OHLCV)	4.96% ± 25.49	0.60	−22.62%
GRU	Macro/Tech Only	28.03% ± 29.94	3.06	−17.47%
GRU	Full Enriched	24.37% ± 29.31	2.70	−15.94%
GRU	Feature Selection (RFE)	47.09% ± 18.84	5.12	−11.91%

Table 4. Financial Results – Horizon of 14 periods (56 h)

Model	Data Scenario	Total Return (%)	Sharpe Ratio	MDD (%)
Benchmark	**Buy & Hold**	**47.93%**	**5.27**	**-10.83%**
LSTM	Baseline (OHLCV)	−7.08% ± 25.81	−1.01	−25.90%
LSTM	Macro/Tech Only	24.98% ± 34.12	2.58	−18.59%
LSTM	Full Enriched	28.19% ± 33.67	2.94	−16.45%
LSTM	Feature Selection (RFE)	40.66% ± 21.20	4.44	−12.97%
GRU	Baseline (OHLCV)	−2.32% ± 14.92	−0.08	−24.55%
GRU	Macro/Tech Only	18.53% ± 25.88	2.15	−18.74%
GRU	Full Enriched	29.44% ± 30.45	3.22	−16.09%
GRU	Feature Selection (RFE)	35.40% ± 20.52	3.98	−13.80%

Table 5. Financial Results – Horizon of 30 periods (5 days)

Model	Data Scenario	Total Return (%)	Sharpe Ratio	MDD (%)
Benchmark	**Buy & Hold**	**47.93%**	**5.27**	**-10.83%**
LSTM	Baseline (OHLCV)	−19.15% ± 13.38	−2.49	−30.13%
LSTM	Macro/Tech Only	7.06% ± 34.02	0.56	−24.95%
LSTM	Full Enriched	5.22% ± 33.70	0.40	−24.77%
LSTM	Feature Selection (RFE)	32.30% ± 21.72	3.68	−15.01%
GRU	Baseline (OHLCV)	−16.28% ± 10.47	−1.98	−30.41%
GRU	Macro/Tech Only	19.53% ± 31.26	2.14	−20.48%
GRU	Full Enriched	3.92% ± 21.14	0.60	−23.65%
GRU	Feature Selection (RFE)	18.65% ± 30.90	2.05	−19.55%

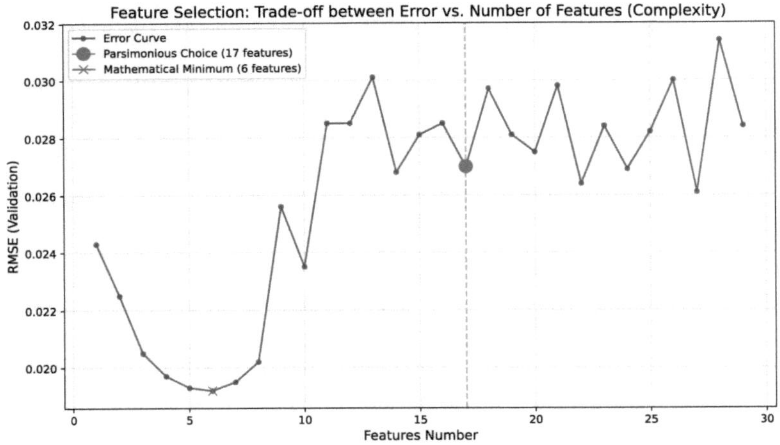

Fig. 2. RFE optimization curve. The chosen operating point ($k = 17$) balances predictive performance and parsimony.

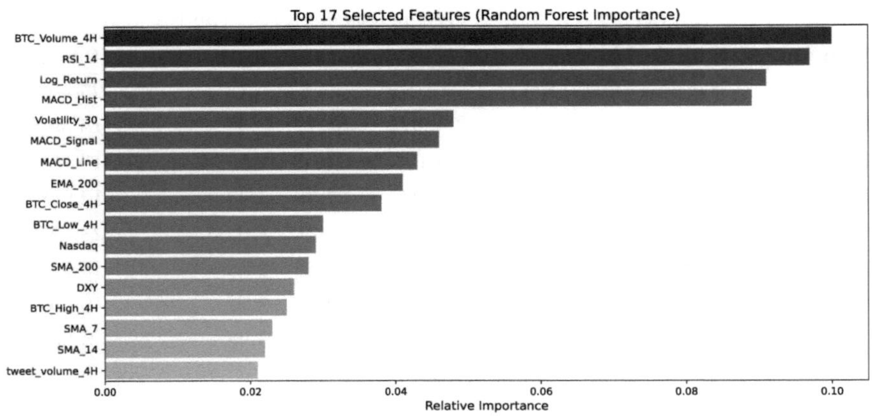

Fig. 3. Top-17 features selected by RFE.

4.4 Integrated Discussion and Key Takeaways

At different time intervals, the RFE-optimized scenario shows improvements compared to the scenario with extracted variables, demonstrating that a simpler dataset outperforms a more complex one. The result that allows us to affirm this can be seen in the window presented in Table 3: the GRU drops from 48.32% (RFE) to 22.75% (with all variables), despite using the same architecture and training protocol. This pattern indicates that naive multimodal expansion introduces redundancy and noise (consistent with the correlation analysis in Fig. 3), leading to unstable adjustments and weaker realized returns after applying costs.

Therefore, selecting a compact subset results in more stable performance (lower variability).

Over a 12-hour horizon, the GRU + RFE strategy achieved the best overall performance, reaching a Sharpe ratio of 5.28 and a total return of 48.32%, with an MDD of -11.21%, matching the Buy & Hold benchmark under transaction costs. This is the only horizon in which the proposed strategy remains competitive with the passive strategy. Within the evaluated period (characterized by a strong bullish regime), this suggests that carefully crafted short-term setups can remain economically viable when microstructure effects and short-term attention dynamics are exploited under controlled dimensionality.

As we move to longer timeframes, such as 56 h or 5 days (Tables 4 and 5), the performance of AI-based strategies begins to decline, falling below the simple Buy & Hold strategy. Even our best combination (LSTM + RFE) failed to outperform the market on the 5-day horizon. This confirms that factors such as social media behavior and details of market microstructure have a fleeting effect, being quickly absorbed by the price. Since the selection filter (RFE) ended up discarding sentiment variables from the LLM, it is clear that the model's short-term advantage comes much more from analyzing market dynamics and attention volume than from the content of news or external opinions.

Although GRU tends to be more competitive at very short horizons (e.g., 12 h) and LSTM can match performance at intermediate horizons under RFE (e.g., 28 h), these differences are smaller than the gains produced by the feature selection itself. This reinforces the article's main contribution: filtering noise and redundancy in the inputs is more determinant of performance than the sophistication of the algorithm or the volume of external variables.

5 Conclusion and Future Work

In this work, we explore whether a parsimonious multimodal pipeline is capable of delivering viable performance in high-frequency cryptoasset markets, especially when considering transaction costs. As discussed in Sects. 1 and 2, while the use of multimodal variables increases the model's representational capacity, it also introduces redundancy and multicollinearity issues. Without proper control, these factors amplify overfitting and destroy real profitability as soon as operational fees are applied. To address this challenge, we combine zero-shot sentiment inference (via Llama-2 7B) with a Random Forest-based RFE selection strategy. Finally, we evaluate the performance of stacked GRU and LSTM predictors under a realistic backtesting protocol, with long/short execution and explicit cost recognition.

Our results demonstrate that the model's effectiveness lies more in the rigorous curation of input data than in the sophistication of its architecture, highlighting that an excess of variables introduces noise that hinders generalization. By selecting only the 17 most relevant predictors via RFE, the GRU model achieved superior performance, reaching a Sharpe Ratio of 5.28 and returns of 48.32% over 12-hour horizons, remaining competitive against the Buy & Hold strategy. However, the degradation of performance over longer periods reveals that predictability is highly sensitive to sudden market changes, limiting the strategy's competitive advantage to short-term operations, where the signal still outweighs the structural drift of the data.

The RFE procedure did not retain contextual LLM-derived sentiment or polarity variables. It selected primarily endogenous market descriptors and tweet volume. Attention intensity proxies carried more measurable signal than contextual semantic polarity within the evaluated configuration. The contribution of large-scale language-derived sentiment was limited in this setup. We cannot attribute the observed short-horizon performance to contextual LLM enrichment.

This study suggests that profitability in high-frequency crypto modeling under realistic frictions depends less on complex architectures or multimodal expansion. It relies more on parsimonious signal selection, regime awareness, and cost-aware validation.

Acknowledgment. The authors acknowledge partial funding from the Coordination for the Improvement of Higher Education Personnel - Brazil (CAPES) - Funding Code 001; the National Council for Scientific and Technological Development - Brazil (CNPq) - Funding Codes 442344/2023-6, 444602/2024-0, and 407466/2025-8; the Espírito Santo Research and Innovation Support Foundation (FAPES) – Call No. 02/2026 (Participation in Technical-Scientific Events) – Grant No. 428/2026 and project #2024-9G1WP BPC; and the Minas Gerais Research Funding Foundation (FAPEMIG)

References

1. Araci, D.: FinBERT: financial sentiment analysis with pre-trained language models. arXiv preprint arXiv:1908.10063 (2019). https://arxiv.org/abs/1908.10063
2. Bailey, D.H., Borwein, J.M., López de Prado, M., Zhu, Q.J.: The probability of backtest overfitting. J. Comput. Finance **20**(4), 39–69 (2017). https://doi.org/10.21314/JCF.2016.322
3. Bailey, D.H., López de Prado, M.: The deflated sharpe ratio: correcting for selection bias, backtest overfitting and non-normality. J. Portfolio Manag. **40**(5), 94–107 (2014). https://doi.org/10.2139/ssrn.2460551
4. Brown, T., et al.: Language models are few-shot learners. Adv. Neural. Inf. Process. Syst. **33**, 1877–1901 (2020)
5. Cho, K., et al.: Learning phrase representations using RNN encoder-decoder for statistical machine translation. In: Proceedings of the 2014 Conference on Empirical Methods in Natural Language Processing (EMNLP), pp. 1724–1734 (2014)
6. Chung, J., Gulcehre, C., Cho, K., Bengio, Y.: Empirical evaluation of gated recurrent neural networks on sequence modeling arXiv preprint arXiv:1412.3555 (2014)
7. De Prado, M.L.: Advances in Financial Machine Learning. John Wiley & Sons (2018)
8. Genuer, R., Poggi, J.M., Tuleau-Malot, C.: Variable selection using random forests. Patt. Recogn. Lett. **31**(14), 2225–2236 (2010)
9. Guyon, I., Elisseeff, A.: An introduction to variable and feature selection. J. Mach. Learn. Res. **3**, 1157–1182 (2003)

10. Han, P., Chen, H., Rasool, A., Jiang, Q., Yang, M.: MFB: a generalized multimodal fusion approach for Bitcoin price prediction using time-lagged sentiment and indicator features. Expert Syst. Appl. **261**, 125515 (2025). https://doi.org/10.1016/j.eswa.2024.125515
11. Hochreiter, S., Schmidhuber, J.: Long short-term memory. Neural Comput. **9**(8), 1735–1780 (1997)
12. Hutto, C., Gilbert, E.: VADER: a parsimonious rule-based model for sentiment analysis of social media text. In: Proceedings of the International AAAI Conference on Web and Social Media. vol. 8, pp. 216–225 (2014). https://doi.org/10.1609/icwsm.v8i1.14550
13. Jung, H.S., Lee, H.: Explainable zero-shot trading using multi-agent LLM architecture: a backtested approach for Bitcoin price. Inf. Process. Manag. **63**(2), 104466 (2026)
14. Kraaijeveld, O., De Smedt, J.: The predictive power of public Twitter sentiment for forecasting cryptocurrency prices. J. Int. Finan. Markets. Inst. Money **65**, 101188 (2020). https://doi.org/10.1016/j.intfin.2020.101188
15. Mai, F., Shan, Z., Bai, Q., Wang, X., Chiang, R.H.L.: How does social media impact bitcoin value? a test of the silent majority hypothesis. J. Manag. Inf. Syst. **35**(1), 19–52 (2018). https://doi.org/10.1080/07421222.2018.1440774
16. Omole, O., Enke, D.: Deep learning for Bitcoin price direction prediction: models and trading strategies empirically compared. Finan. Innov. **10**(1), 117 (2024). https://doi.org/10.1186/s40854-024-00643-1
17. Pano, T., Kashef, R.: A complete VADER-based sentiment analysis of bitcoin (BTC) tweets during the era of COVID-19. Big Data Cogn. Comput. **4**(4), 33 (2020)
18. Pedregosa, F., et al.: Scikit-learn: machine learning in Python. J. Mach. Learn. Res. **12**, 2825–2830 (2011)
19. Scaillet, O., Treccani, A., Trevisan, C.: High-frequency jump analysis of the Bitcoin market. J. Financ. Economet. **18**(2), 209–232 (2020). https://doi.org/10.1093/jjfinec/nby013
20. Shen, D., Urquhart, A., Wang, P.: Does Twitter predict Bitcoin? Econ. Lett. **174**, 118–122 (2019). https://doi.org/10.1016/j.econlet.2018.11.007
21. Suardi, S., Rasel, A.R., Liu, B.: On the predictive power of tweet sentiments and attention on bitcoin. Int. Rev. Econom. Finance **79**, 289–301 (2022). https://doi.org/10.1016/j.iref.2022.02.017
22. Youssefi, A., Hessane, A., Zeroual, I., Farhaoui, Y.: Optimizing forecast accuracy in cryptocurrency markets: evaluating feature selection techniques for technical indicators. Comput. Mater. Continua **83**(2), 3411 (2025). https://doi.org/10.32604/cmc.2025.063218
23. Zou, Y., Herremans, D.: PreBit–a multimodal model with Twitter FinBERT embeddings for extreme price movement prediction of Bitcoin. Expert Syst. Appl. **233**, 120838 (2023). https://doi.org/10.1016/j.eswa.2023.120838

Evaluating Segmentation and Temporal Resolution in Highway Crash Forecasting: The BR-040 Corridor

João P. Tozetto[1], Isadora Nunes[1], Bernardo Soares[1], Elisa T. Albergaria[1], Diego R. C. Dias[2(✉)], Vinícius F. S. Mota[2], and Leonardo C. D. Rocha[1]

[1] Universidade Federal de São João del Rei (UFSJ), São João del Rei, Brazil
{joaopedrocunhaolx,isamiranda222017,bernardosfferraz}@aluno.ufsj.edu.br, {etuler,lcrocha}@ufsj.edu.br

[2] Universidade Federal do Espírito Santo (UFES), Vitória, Brazil
{diego.dias,vinicius.f.mota}@ufes.br

Abstract. Spatiotemporal predictive models are key tools for anticipating highway crash volume and, consequently, for supporting road safety actions and operational planning, ranging from allocating enforcement resources to prioritizing infrastructure interventions. In this paper, we present a detailed evaluation of spatiotemporal models for forecasting crash counts along one of Brazil's most important highways, the BR-040. For this study, we used open data from the Brazilian Federal Highway Police for the period 2017 to 2024. An important contribution of the paper is that, instead of partitioning highways into fixed-length segments, we applied a spatial segmentation based on the socioeconomic characteristics of cities along the BR-040, which enabled analysis of meaningful territorial heterogeneity. We considered three models from different algorithmic families in our evaluation: SARIMAX, Random Forest, and Extra Trees Regression. We evaluated them in four experimental scenarios that combine two temporal granularities (monthly and weekly) with two attribute configurations (with and without holiday and non-working-day variables). The effectiveness of the models was evaluated using three accuracy metrics (R^2, MAE and RMSE), while computational efficiency was measured through total execution time. Our results show a robust trade-off between effectiveness and computational cost: while the SARIMAX model minimizes MAE/RMSE, it incurs the highest computational cost, especially at weekly granularity. On the other hand, tree-based ensemble methods incur the lowest runtimes but do not achieve the best results in all evaluated scenarios. We also evaluated the impact of segmentation strategies for specific road sections and different temporal granularities, and our results provide strong evidence for monitoring and prioritizing critical segments at specific times on Brazilian federal highways.

Keywords: Spatiotemporal prediction models · spatial segmentation by socioeconomic conditions · machine learning · road accident prediction

O. Gervasi et al. (Eds.): ICCSA 2026, LNCS 16768, pp. 584–600, 2027.
https://doi.org/10.1007/978-3-032-30488-9_36

1 Introduction

In Brazil, the high number of road accidents has significantly impacted public health, overburdening emergency services and resulting in high economic costs, as well as many deaths and permanent injuries. Recent studies indicate that these road accidents represent approximately 3% of the Gross Domestic Product (GDP) in most countries. [17]. One strategy to improve this situation is to develop decision-support tools, especially spatiotemporal prediction models, leveraging the widespread availability of open data on highway incidents. In Brazil, the agency responsible for monitoring federal highways is the Federal Highway Police (PRF), which maintains large public databases with accident records that can be used for empirical studies. However, transforming raw data into useful information to support decision-making requires several methodological steps, such as defining spatial and temporal granularity, addressing biases, including variations in traffic exposure, and adopting validation protocols compatible with the operational context.

In this article, we present an evaluation of spatiotemporal prediction models for predicting accident occurrences on BR-040, one of the longest and most important highways in Brazil. Prior studies using PRF data and/or Brazilian roadway subsets demonstrate the potential of machine learning (ML) techniques for hotspot analysis and risk pattern discovery, while also highlighting sensitivity to choices in preprocessing, representation, and spatial partitioning [2]. In this context, rather than partitioning highways into fixed-length segments, we propose and apply a spatial segmentation of cities along the BR-040 based on their socioeconomic characteristics, thereby enabling analysis of meaningful territorial heterogeneity. Based on this partitioning, we organize segment-level time series and investigate how different temporal granularities and explanatory characteristics affect performance and computational cost, with an emphasis on configurations that are feasible for recurrent monitoring.

Recent advances in neural architectures can capture spatial and temporal dependencies, including recurrent networks with graph convolutions and spatiotemporal convolution variants [11,19]. In this context, we present a methodological experimental evaluation comparing three model families commonly used for applied forecasting and regression: a statistical time-series model with autoregressive and moving-average components and support for exogenous regressors (SARIMAX) and two tree-based ensemble methods (Random Forest and Extra Trees Regression). To evaluate the impact of temporal granularity and the presence of holidays on the predictive performance of these models, we consider two temporal granularities (monthly and weekly) and two attribute configurations (with and without holiday and non-working-day variables), yielding four scenarios. We consider complementary metrics of predictive effectiveness: the coefficient of determination (R^2), mean absolute error (MAE), and root mean squared error (RMSE). For efficiency, we measure the execution time. We used all these metrics to evaluate the trade-off between effectiveness and efficiency across different scenarios.

In our results, we observe that SARIMAX achieves the lowest MAE and RMSE across scenarios, but at a higher runtime, particularly under weekly granularity, where the cost grows to the order of hundreds of seconds as the number of segments increases. On the other hand, the ensemble methods (Random Forest and Extra Trees Regression) offer lower runtime while maintaining competitive effectiveness in some scenarios, making them the best trade-off between effectiveness and efficiency for large-scale execution and frequent updates. Moreover, including calendar variables (i.e., description of whether a specific date is a holiday or not) tends to improve model fit, especially under monthly granularity, reinforcing the relevance of holiday and non-working-day effects in explaining part of the observed variability.

Therefore, the main contributions of our paper are: (i) the integration and enrichment of PRF occurrence data with socioeconomic information from cities along BR-040, allowing the highway partitioning in spatial segmentation better aligned with the territorial economic activities; (ii) a complete experimental framework that allows comparative analysis of spatiotemporal predictive models under different scenarios (temporal granularities and characteristics configurations) and perspectivities (effectiveness and efficiency); and (iii) an empirical discussion of how segmentation and granularity choices affect performance, stability, and operational trade-off between effectiveness and efficiency, with implications for intervention prioritization and risk monitoring.

2 Related Work

We observed two main approaches in the literature regarding solutions for reducing traffic accidents. The first is the spatiotemporal prediction models themselves, which aim to anticipate the risk and/or the expected number of occurrences. Another complementary approach concerns spatial representation, that is, strategies for defining spatial units (segmentation) of analysis so that predictions can be translated into planning and intervention. The main challenges lie in spatial heterogeneity, which reflects structural differences across highway segments (e.g., pavement quality, dominant economic activity per section, etc.), and in temporal dependencies, such as seasonality, routines, and long-term trends. Furthermore, maintaining interpretable results that align with management units, such as administrative boundaries and operational coverage areas, should also be considered.

Regarding modeling, spatiotemporal prediction strategies that use deep learning architectures encoding space as grids or latent structures and time as sequences have shown the best effectiveness. In [20], the authors present ConvLSTM, which has been used to incorporate spatiotemporal autocorrelation in accident prediction. More recent variants [10] combine recurrent blocks with attention mechanisms and transformers to improve temporal fusion and capture nonlinearities. Given the importance of interpretability of results from a management perspective, many studies continue to favor tabular machine learning. Along these lines, models such as Random Forest [5] and Extremely Randomized

Trees [9] are common choices for prediction/counting and risk estimation. Statistical time series models with explicit seasonal structure and exogenous covariates (e.g., SARIMAX) also remain relevant when the objective is to isolate seasonal effects and quantify the impact of external variables.

Equally important to prediction models are spatial aggregation strategies (segmentation) and the unit of analysis, both of which are often underestimated in the literature. In road safety, this debate is often framed as the modifiable areal unit problem (MAUP), in which different scales and forms of zoning can yield distinct conclusions [18]. Studies also show that results vary with segment length and the segmentation strategy adopted, making it difficult to define a universally optimal spatial unit [4]. Literature reviews also indicate that the choice of the unit of analysis, such as road segments, census areas, or functional regions, influences both the inference and the practical application of the results [21]. In this context, our contribution is not to propose a new spatial unit, but to adopt a segmentation guided by the socioeconomic context of the cities along the BR-040 highway, instead of using artificial divisions of fixed length. This brings the analysis closer to the dynamics of territorial planning and resource allocation.

Geographic information systems integrated with spatial analysis also face recurring challenges, such as heterogeneity in data quality, high computational cost, and inconsistencies in structural variables [7]. In [3], the authors combined predictive and network analysis, using models such as random forests and spatial joining to associate accidents with road network segments and to support decisions such as safer routing and the prioritization of interventions. In this study, we also used georeferenced representations, evaluated at different spatiotemporal granularities.

In Brazil, the availability of open data from the Federal Highway Police (PRF) has boosted machine learning applications for analysis and operational planning on federal highways. Studies on the BR-101/PE, for example, explore machine learning techniques for analysis, visualization, prediction, and clustering [15]. Nevertheless, there remains room for experimental protocols that consider, in an integrated way, the quantitative prediction of occurrences, the systematic comparison of models at multiple spatiotemporal granularities, and spatial segmentation compatible with the territorial and socioeconomic context. This work seeks to advance in this direction by combining the comparative evaluation of spatiotemporal models for predicting accident counts on the BR-040 highway with spatial segmentation guided by the economic activities of the cities along the corridor, thereby generating more interpretable and useful results for prioritization and mitigation.

Table 1 summarizes the main differences between our proposal and the related literature. While many studies prioritize more complex deep architectures or fixed-length spatial units, our work adds a systematic comparison at different temporal granularities and a segmentation strategy aligned with the territorial and socioeconomic context.

Table 1. Comparison of related work on highway crash prediction and spatiotemporal analysis.

Study	Models	Spatial Unit	Temporal Res.	Socioecon. Context
Yuan et al. [20]	ConvLSTM	Grids/Segments	High	No
Li et al. [10]	Deep Learning	Latent Structures	Multiple	No
Bisht et al. [4]	Statistical	Fixed Segments	Varies	No
Taveira et al. [15]	ML (Clustering)	Road Points	N/A	No
Berhanu et al. [3]	Random Forest	Network-based	Static	Partial
This Work	**SARIMAX/RF/ET**	**Socioecon. Segm.**	**Weekly/Monthly**	**Yes**

3 Methodology

3.1 Dataset

In this study, we used the open database of traffic accidents on Brazilian federal highways, made available by the PRF (Federal Highway Police) in monthly CSV files [14]. We considered the period from 2017 to 2024 because, starting in 2017, the PRF adopted a more comprehensive data collection process, with additional variables relevant for spatio-temporal analyses [13]. In total, the analysis includes 26,540 accident records on the BR-040 highway during this period. The data acquisition, integration, cleaning, segmentation, and evaluation steps are presented below.

The monthly files were obtained from the PRF open data portal [14] and compiled into a single longitudinal table covering 2017 to 2024. Table 2 summarizes the main attributes of the dataset used in the filtering, enrichment, and aggregation steps.

Table 2. Main attributes from the PRF dataset used in this study (2017–2024).

Attribute	Description
id	Unique identifier of the crash/occurrence.
data_inversa	Crash date (YYYY-MM-DD).
dia_semana, horario	Day of week and time of the crash.
uf, br, km, municipio	State (UF), highway, km marker, and municipality.
latitude, longitude	Geographic coordinates of the crash.
causa_principal, causa_acidente	Primary cause and detailed cause (PRF).
tipo_acidente, classificacao_acidente	Crash type and severity (no victim/injured/fatal).
fase_dia, condicao_meteorologica	Time-of-day period and weather condition.
tipo_pista, tracado_via, uso_solo	Road and surrounding-environment characteristics.
regional, delegacia, uop	PRF operational structure for the segment.
pessoas, veiculos, feridos	Counts associated with the occurrence.

First, we removed records with missing values in fields required for spatiotemporal aggregation and eliminated duplicates based on id. For continuous numeric variables, we standardized decimal separators (comma → dot) to ensure consistent parsing. For categorical variables, we performed numeric encoding (mapping categories to integers) to enable their use in algorithms that require numeric inputs. Table 3 presents the mapping for the categorical variables effectively used by the models.

Table 3. Numeric encoding of categorical variables used by the models.

Variable	Category	Code
fase_dia	Dawn	0
	Daytime	1
	Dusk	2
	Nighttime	3
sentido_via	Increasing	0
	Decreasing	1
condicao_meteorologica	Sun	0
	Clear sky	1
	Cloudy	2
	Rain	3
	Drizzle	4
	Fog/Mist	5
	Wind	6
	Hail	7
	Unknown	8
tipo_pista	Single carriageway	0
	Dual carriageway	1
	Multiple	2

3.2 Feature Engineering and Selection

We applied feature construction to incorporate signals from existing variables and subsequently applied feature selection procedures to reduce redundancy and mitigate multicollinearity. In particular, `tracado_via` has high cardinality (174 values) and was decomposed into more compact structural attributes (Table 4), as suggested in [12].

Additionally, we constructed temporal attributes to capture calendar effects (holidays and weekends), derived from `data_inversa`. These signals are relevant for modeling routines and seasonality and were evaluated in scenarios with and without such variables (Table 5).

Table 4. Attributes derived from *tracado_via*.

Derived attribute	Label	Code
condicaoPista	Normal	0
	Under construction	1
tipoInclinacao	Flat	0
	Uphill	1
	Downhill	2
tipoSuperficie	Straight	0
	Curve	1
tipoManobra	None	0
	Intersection	1
	Regulated U-turn	2
	Roundabout	3
tipoEstrutura	None	0
	Bridge	1
	Overpass	2
	Tunnel	3

Table 5. Derived temporal attributes (holidays and non-working days).

Attribute	Description
feriado	1 if the date matches a national holiday; otherwise 0.
pre_feriado	1 if the date is the day before a national holiday; otherwise 0.
pos_feriado	1 if the date is the day after a national holiday; otherwise 0.
fim_de_semana	1 if the date is Saturday or Sunday; otherwise 0.

After feature construction, we employed backward elimination from the full set, iteratively removing variables whose exclusion did not compromise the adopted performance criterion. The backward selection approach is conservative and consistent with the fact that the derived attributes were defined based on domain knowledge; thus, we initially considered only redundancies for elimination.

3.3 Models

The predictive task consists of estimating the volume of accidents in each segment of the BR-040 highway at two temporal aggregation levels: weekly and monthly. To this end, we evaluated three families of models with different modeling characteristics and operational uses: Random Forest, Extra Trees Regression, and SARIMAX. Random Forest is suitable for capturing non-linear interactions among heterogeneous covariates and also provides variable importance estimates, which facilitate the interpretation and identification of risk factors [5,12]. Extra Trees Regression introduces more randomness in tree construction, which can reduce variance and maintain stable performance at a lower computational cost, a relevant aspect when testing multiple segmentations and many segments [9]. SARIMAX explicitly models temporal dependence, trend, and seasonality, and allows the use of exogenous regressors, such as calendar indicators, making it a suitable reference for aggregated series in weekly and monthly windows [1].

The evaluated models require defining hyperparameters that affect the learning process and the complexity of the adjustment. In this work, these parameters were defined based on configurations recurrent in the literature and in preliminary validation experiments. Table 6 presents the main hyperparameters adopted for each model.

Table 6. Best hyperparameter combinations for the evaluated algorithms.

Model	Best Hyperparameters
Random Forest	n_estimators = 100, max_depth = None, min_samples_leaf = 2, max_features = 0.5
Extra Tree Regression	n_estimators = 100, max_depth = 15, min_samples_split = 10, min_samples_leaf = 4, max_features = 'sqrt'
SARIMAX	Monthly: (p, d, q) = (2, 1, 1), (P, D, Q, s) = (2, 1, 1, 12) Weekly: (p, d, q) = (2, 1, 1), (P, D, Q, s) = (2, 1, 1, 52)

Spatial segmentation is a central decision in the analysis of extensive highways. Uniform kilometer-based partitions are simple and reproducible, but tend to ignore territorial differences, such as economic dynamics, logistics function, and population density, which affect exposure and accident risk. In this work, we adopted a segmentation oriented toward the socioeconomic context along the BR-040 highway, incorporating municipal variables to define units that are more closely aligned with the highway's territorial transitions. To analyze the sensitivity to spatial granularity, we tested four configurations, with 18, 24, 30, and 36 segments. This allows us to observe the balance between greater statistical aggregation, with more events per unit, and greater sensitivity to local patterns, with smaller units.

We also evaluated two temporal resolutions, monthly and weekly. Monthly aggregation highlights trends and annual seasonality, reducing short-term oscillations. Weekly aggregation preserves faster variations, linked to routines, long weekends, and local events, and may be more useful for short-term operational decisions.

To avoid information leaks and maintain adherence to operational use, we adopted temporal validation, dividing the data into training (2017–2022), validation (2023), and testing (2024). This protocol preserves the temporal order of the data and enables a prospective evaluation of generalization capacity.

We evaluated predictive performance using MAE, RMSE, coefficient of determination (R^2), and total execution time. MAE and RMSE measure the average error, with RMSE penalizing larger errors more heavily [6]. R^2 indicates the proportion of variance explained by the model in the evaluated dataset [8]. Execution time was used as a feasibility measure in monitoring and decision support scenarios, where frequent updates may be necessary.

For pairwise comparisons between models and configurations, we used the nonparametric Wilcoxon signed-rank test, which is suitable for paired samples and makes no normality assumption [16]. In the results section, the best performance values are highlighted in bold.

4 Results

In this section, we compare the SARIMAX, Random Forest, and Extra Trees Regression models in predicting accidents on the BR-040 highway at two temporal granularities, monthly and weekly, and in two attribute configurations, with and without holiday and non-working day variables, totaling four experimental scenarios. The models were evaluated in different segmentations based on R^2, MAE, RMSE, and execution time, in order to jointly analyze predictive performance and computational cost. The experiments were performed on a machine with 16 GB of RAM, an AMD Ryzen 5 5600G processor, and an AMD Radeon Vega 7 GPU.

4.1 Model Evaluation with Monthly Granularity and Holiday/Non-Working-Day Variables

Table 7 shows a consistent relationship between accuracy and computational cost at the monthly granularity with calendar variables, also observed in Fig. 1. SARIMAX presented the lowest MAE and RMSE values in all segmentations, indicating greater accuracy and a better ability to capture temporal patterns when calendar effects are included. Conversely, this gain came with a longer execution time, which increases with the number of segments and may limit its use in scenarios of frequent retraining or larger scale. Random Forest, on the other hand, maintained execution times below 0.6 s, being the most efficient alternative. Furthermore, along with Extra Trees Regression, it presented R^2 values higher than those of SARIMAX in most scenarios, especially with 24, 30, and 36 segments, suggesting that ensemble methods can explain a relevant part of the variability with operational advantage, although with higher absolute errors.

4.2 Model Evaluation with Monthly Granularity and *without* Holiday/Non-Working-Day Variables

Under the monthly configuration without holiday and non-working-day variables (Table 8), we observe an overall reduction in explanatory power compared to the

Table 7. Model performance under monthly *with* holiday and non-working-day variables.

Segments	Model	R^2	MAE	RMSE	Time (s)
18	Random Forest	0.8869	3.7472	5.5110	**0.5310**
	SARIMAX	**0.9315**	**0.7655**	**0.9408**	8.3178
	Extra Tree Regression	0.8973	3.8983	5.2553	2.7524
24	Random Forest	0.8894	3.7779	5.5443	**0.5473**
	SARIMAX	0.8703	**0.7554**	**0.9311**	8.3626
	Extra Tree Regression	**0.9053**	3.6563	5.1618	2.9576
30	Random Forest	**0.8998**	3.2676	5.0489	**0.5599**
	SARIMAX	0.8496	**0.5048**	**0.6535**	10.3678
	Extra Tree Regression	0.8542	2.8912	4.4451	3.0312
36	Random Forest	0.8399	2.9795	4.6387	**0.5889**
	SARIMAX	0.8063	**0.4437**	**0.5491**	11.5266
	Extra Tree Regression	**0.8541**	2.8913	4.4456	3.5443

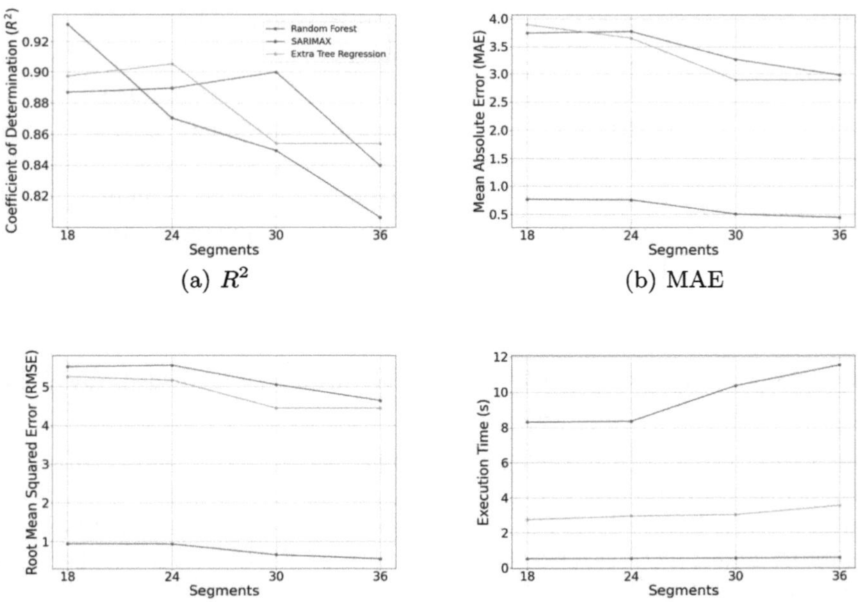

(a) R^2 (b) MAE

(c) RMSE (d) Time (s)

Fig. 1. Performance under monthly granularity with calendar variables (holidays and non-working days).

calendar-aware setting, reflected in lower R^2 across all methods, indicating that part of the previously captured variability was associated with calendar effects. Still, SARIMAX remained the best in residual minimization, yielding the lowest MAE and RMSE for all segmentations (Fig. 2), but at high computational cost (runtimes above 10 s and increasing with the number of segments). Conversely, Random Forest remained the most efficient alternative (runtimes below 0.5 s) and achieved the highest R^2 for 30 and 36 segments, while Extra Tree Regression achieved the best R^2 for 24 segments. Overall, the results suggest that, in the absence of exogenous calendar regressors, tree-based ensembles tend to preserve higher explanatory power (R^2) in some scenarios, whereas SARIMAX continues to produce lower absolute error, reinforcing the trade-off between precision and scalability.

Table 8. Model performance under monthly granularity *without* holiday and non-working-day variables.

Segments	Model	R^2	MAE	RMSE	Time (s)
18	Random Forest	0.8667	4.1883	5.9809	**0.4799**
	SARIMAX	**0.9115**	**0.9737**	**1.1991**	11.5360
	Extra Tree Regression	0.8913	4.0438	5.4191	2.5481
24	Random Forest	0.8684	4.2153	6.0496	**0.4192**
	SARIMAX	0.8549	**0.9106**	**1.1407**	10.2971
	Extra Tree Regression	**0.8903**	3.6714	5.2072	2.8131
30	Random Forest	**0.8312**	3.7428	5.4970	**0.4944**
	SARIMAX	0.8142	**0.7423**	**0.9069**	12.0413
	Extra Tree Regression	0.8099	3.0793	4.5871	3.1745
36	Random Forest	**0.8190**	3.3557	4.9324	**0.4249**
	SARIMAX	0.8094	**0.7648**	**0.9298**	13.6540
	Extra Tree Regression	0.8025	3.0343	4.4732	3.6211

4.3 Model Evaluation with Weekly Granularity and Holiday/Non-Working-Day Variables

With weekly granularity and calendar variables (Table 9), the computational-cost difference across approaches becomes dominant. As shown in Fig. 3, SARIMAX runtimes reach hundreds of seconds, making large-scale execution impractical despite its high precision for weekly dynamics. SARIMAX achieved the lowest errors (MAE and RMSE) across all segmentations, with values below 0.4, indicating high precision in modeling weekly dynamics with statistical terms and exogenous regressors. However, this precision comes at the expense of extremely high runtimes (447–695 s) that increase with the number of segments. In terms of overall fit, SARIMAX was superior in R^2 for 18 and 24 segments, but was outperformed by the ensembles for 30 and 36 segments, indicating that as the spatial partitioning becomes more fine-grained, tree-based models maintain more

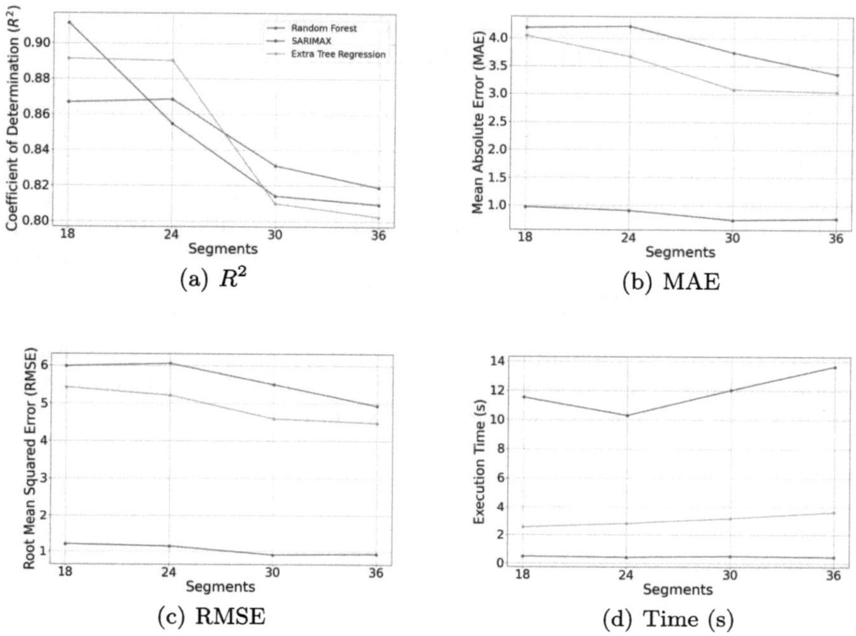

(a) R^2 (b) MAE

(c) RMSE (d) Time (s)

Fig. 2. Performance under monthly granularity without calendar variables.

Table 9. Model performance under weekly granularity *with* holiday and non-working-day variables.

Segments	Model	R^2	MAE	RMSE	Time (s)
18	Random Forest	0.7871	1.1295	1.1915	**0.6615**
	SARIMAX	**0.9548**	**0.3028**	**0.3672**	447.9933
	Extra Tree Regression	0.7555	1.3611	2.0760	2.9343
24	Random Forest	0.7795	1.1672	1.9757	**0.6552**
	SARIMAX	**0.9040**	**0.2582**	**0.3234**	522.2830
	Extra Tree Regression	0.7673	1.2922	2.0461	2.9548
30	Random Forest	0.8024	1.0162	1.8085	**0.5980**
	SARIMAX	0.7627	**0.2529**	**0.3019**	649.3398
	Extra Tree Regression	**0.8051**	0.9931	1.7343	3.1126
36	Random Forest	**0.7394**	0.8832	1.5417	**0.8074**
	SARIMAX	0.7145	**0.2653**	**0.2978**	694.9754
	Extra Tree Regression	0.7132	0.9733	1.6293	3.2913

stable explanatory performance even with larger residuals. Thus, under weekly granularity, SARIMAX maximizes accuracy, whereas Random Forest and Extra Tree Regression offer a better cost–benefit trade-off for operational applications.

4.4 Model Evaluation with Weekly Granularity and *without* Holiday/Non-Working-Day Variables

Table 10 reinforces SARIMAX's superiority in predictive accuracy under the weekly configuration without calendar variables, with consistently lower MAE and RMSE and high R^2 across all segmentations. However, this performance is accompanied by a substantial computational cost (744–1106 s), hundreds of times larger than the alternatives. Among the ensembles, Extra Tree Regression provides the best compromise, preserving R^2 and reducing errors compared to Random Forest, which shows marked degradation for 36 segments ($R^2 = 0.4841$), suggesting higher sensitivity to spatial heterogeneity when combined with weekly variability (Fig. 4). In summary, although SARIMAX maximizes precision, its scalability is limited, and tree-based methods, especially Extra Tree Regression, are more viable alternatives for large-scale execution.

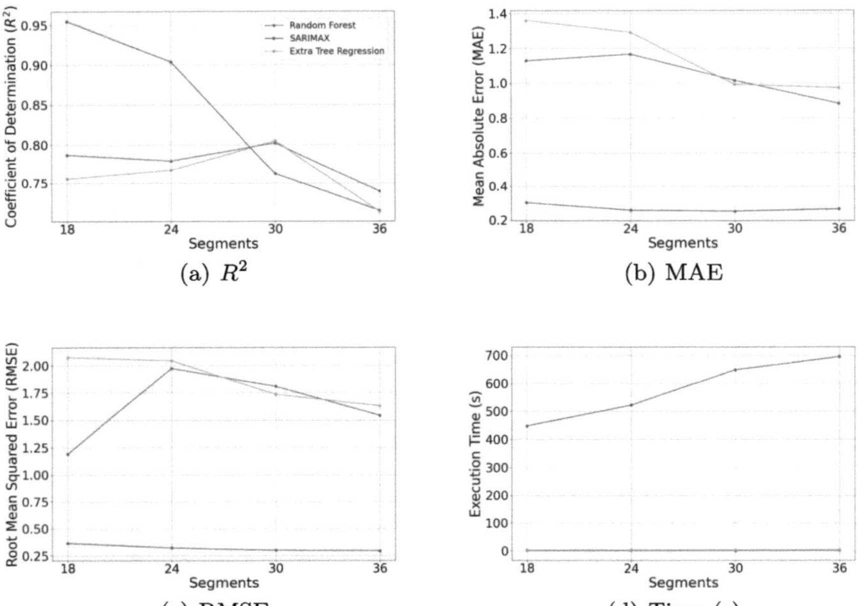

(a) R^2 (b) MAE

(c) RMSE (d) Time (s)

Fig. 3. Performance under weekly granularity with calendar variables.

5 Discussion

The results obtained demonstrate that the forecasting models analyzed can contribute to supporting road safety policies, particularly in highway planning and management. Overall, none of the models outperformed the others across all scenarios or metrics, highlighting a trade-off between predictive accuracy and computational cost.

Table 10. Model performance under weekly granularity *without* holiday and non-working-day variables.

Segments	Model	R^2	MAE	RMSE	Time (s)
18	Random Forest	0.6620	1.6727	2.4136	**0.4644**
	SARIMAX	**0.9570**	**0.3054**	**0.3698**	744.0230
	Extra Tree Regression	0.7462	1.3794	2.1172	3.0037
24	Random Forest	0.6514	1.7378	2.4843	**0.5764**
	SARIMAX	**0.9066**	**0.2537**	**0.3149**	761.4545
	Extra Tree Regression	0.7572	1.3090	2.0912	2.9859
30	Random Forest	0.6850	1.5425	2.2836	**0.5050**
	SARIMAX	**0.8602**	**0.2272**	**0.2753**	1010.9557
	Extra Tree Regression	0.7970	1.0074	1.7722	3.1855
36	Random Forest	0.4841	1.3872	1.9476	**0.6327**
	SARIMAX	**0.7972**	**0.2023**	**0.2414**	1106.0378
	Extra Tree Regression	0.7012	0.9884	1.6630	3.7680

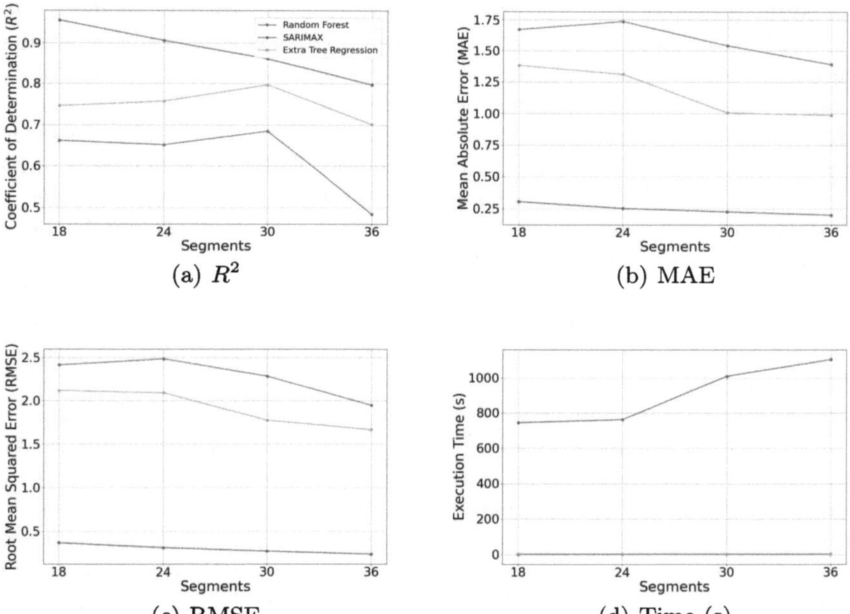

(a) R^2 (b) MAE

(c) RMSE (d) Time (s)

Fig. 4. Performance under weekly granularity without calendar variables.

Thus, the results indicate that the different models can be used in a complementary manner for future highway planning. Models such as SARIMAX, due to their higher accuracy, are more suitable for supporting strategic medium-

and long-term policy decisions, helping to identify periods with a higher risk of accidents and thereby defining preventive actions. On the other hand, ensemble-based models, with lower computational cost, are more appropriate for operational applications and continuous monitoring systems, where fast predictions are essential to support real-time decision-making.

Therefore, this study reinforces the potential of predictive models as a tool to support the formulation of more efficient public policies, especially in the context of road safety, enabling both strategic planning and operational management.

Although the results demonstrate the ability of the models to support decision-making, particularly in the context of highway planning and management, the study is limited to a single Brazilian highway, which may restrict the generalization of the conclusions to other regions. For future work, it is suggested to extend the analysis to different highways and geographic contexts in order to validate the robustness and generalizability of the proposed models.

6 Conclusion and Future Work

This work developed and comparatively evaluated spatiotemporal models for crash-count forecasting on the BR-040 highway using PRF open data (2017–2024). The experimental protocol combines a socioeconomic-guided spatial segmentation with alternative temporal granularities (monthly and weekly), and assesses setups both with and without calendar variables (holidays and non-working days). Across the four experimental scenarios, the results consistently exposed a practical accuracy-scalability trade-off. SARIMAX tended to achieve the lowest MAE/RMSE and a strong fit across multiple settings; however, this advantage came at a substantial computational cost, and the model became impractical at weekly resolution as runtimes increased to the order of hundreds of seconds. In contrast, tree-based ensembles-particularly Extra Tree Regression—ran orders of magnitude faster while remaining competitive in several scenarios, which makes them a better match for large-scale monitoring or frequently updated operational pipelines.

As future work, we will proceed in three directions. First, as data availability improves, we will incorporate richer roadway and infrastructure variables (e.g., pavement condition and signage) to better capture structural risk factors. Second, we will expand the benchmark to include additional spatiotemporal methods, including those that may require greater computational resources, to further characterize the performance frontier under realistic constraints. Third, we will investigate finer temporal resolutions (e.g., daily aggregation) to capture short-term patterns relevant to rapid response. Finally, to facilitate adoption by road-safety stakeholders, we plan to translate the modeling outputs into an interactive geospatial dashboard that turns forecasts into segment-level risk maps and alerting mechanisms for prioritization and intervention.

Acknowledgment. The authors acknowledge partial funding from the Coordination for the Improvement of Higher Education Personnel - Brazil (CAPES) - Funding Code 001; the National Council for Scientific and Technological Development - Brazil (CNPq) - Funding Codes 442344/2023–6, 444602/2024–0, and 407466/2025–8; the Espírito Santo Research and Innovation Support Foundation (FAPES) – Call No. 02/2026 (Participation in Technical-Scientific Events) – Grant No. 428/2026 and project #2024-9G1WP BPC; and the Minas Gerais Research Funding Foundation (FAPEMIG)

References

1. Alharbi, F.R., Csala, D.: A seasonal autoregressive integrated moving average with exogenous factors (SARIMAX) forecasting model-based time series approach. Inventions **7**(4), 94 (2022). https://doi.org/10.3390/inventions7040094
2. Amorim, B.D.S.P., Firmino, A.A., Baptista, C.D.S., Braz Júnior, G., Paiva, A.C., Almeida Júnior, F.E.: A machine learning approach for classifying road accident hotspots. ISPRS Int. J. Geo Inf. **12**(6), 227 (2023). https://doi.org/10.3390/ijgi12060227
3. Berhanu, Y., Schröder, D., Wodajo, B.T., Alemayehu, E.: Machine learning for predictions of road traffic accidents and spatial network analysis for safe routing on accident and congestion-prone road networks. Results Eng. **23**, 102737 (2024). https://doi.org/10.1016/j.rineng.2024.102737
4. Bisht, L.S., Chand, S., Tiwari, G.: Proposed segment length for safety evaluation studies on rural divided highways in India. IATSS Res. **48**(3), 331–341 (2024). https://doi.org/10.1016/j.iatssr.2024.05.002
5. Breiman, L.: Random forests. Mach. Learn. **45**(1), 5–32 (2001). https://doi.org/10.1023/A:1010933404324
6. Chai, T., Draxler, R.R.: Root mean square error (RMSE) or mean absolute error (MAE)? arguments against avoiding RMSE in the literature. Geosci. Model Dev. **7**, 1247–1250 (2014). https://doi.org/10.5194/gmd-7-1247-2014
7. Deressa, B.F., et al.: A systematic review of GIS-driven road traffic accident evaluation. Vehicles **7**(4), 161 (2025). https://doi.org/10.3390/vehicles7040161
8. Draper, N.R., Smith, H.: Applied Regression Analysis. John Wiley & Sons, 3 edn. (1998). https://doi.org/10.1002/9781118625590
9. Geurts, P., Ernst, D., Wehenkel, L.: Extremely randomized trees. Mach. Learn. **63**(1), 3–42 (2006). https://doi.org/10.1007/s10994-006-6226-1
10. Li, K., Guo, K., Liang, Z., Xu, H., Duan, X.: Traffic accident severity prediction and analysis via spatio-temporal deep learning: a ConvLSTM-Transformer approach. Chaos Sol. Fractals **200**, 117047 (2025). https://doi.org/10.1016/j.chaos.2025.117047
11. Li, Y., Yu, R., Shahabi, C., Liu, Y.: Diffusion convolutional recurrent neural network: data-driven traffic forecasting. In: Proceedings of 6th International Conference on Learning Representations (ICLR) (2018), Conference Track Proceedings. OpenReview.net (2018). https://openreview.net/forum?id=SJiHXGWAZ
12. Mafort, E., Kappel, M.A.A.: Machine learning techniques for predicting the severity of accidents on highways in the state of Rio de Janeiro. Revista Eletrônica de Iniciação Científica em Computação **23**, 244–252 (2025). https://doi.org/10.5753/reic.2025.6274
13. Polícia Rodoviária Federal: Dados abertos. Portal gov.br (2026). https://www.gov.br/prf/pt-br/acesso-a-informacao/dados-abertos. Accessed 10 Feb 2026

14. Polícia Rodoviária Federal: Dados abertos da PRF. Portal Gov.br (2026). https://www.gov.br/prf/pt-br/acesso-a-informacao/dados-abertos/dados-abertos-da-prf. Accessed 10 Feb 2026
15. Taveira, J., et al.: Applying machine learning techniques to traffic accident data on BR-101 in Pernambuco. In: VI Seminário Internacional: Ciência, Tecnologia e Inovação em Segurança Pública (2024)
16. Wilcoxon, F.: Individual comparisons by ranking methods. Biometrics Bull. **1**(6), 80–83 (1945). https://doi.org/10.2307/3001968
17. World Health Organization: Road traffic injuries. WHO Fact sheet (2023). https://www.who.int/news-room/fact-sheets/detail/road-traffic-injuries. Accessed 10 Feb 2026, published 13 Dec 2023
18. Xu, P., Huang, H., Dong, N.: The modifiable areal unit problem in traffic safety: basic issue, potential solutions and future research. J. Traffic Transp. Eng. (English Edn.) **5**(2), 73–82 (2018). https://doi.org/10.1016/j.jtte.2015.09.010
19. Yu, B., Yin, H., Zhu, Z.: Spatio-temporal graph convolutional networks: a deep learning framework for traffic forecasting. In: Proceedings of the Twenty-Seventh International Joint Conference on Artificial Intelligence (IJCAI-18), pp. 3634–3640. International Joint Conferences on Artificial Intelligence Organization (2018). https://doi.org/10.24963/ijcai.2018/505
20. Yuan, Y., Zhou, J., Yang, J.: Hetero-ConvLSTM: a deep learning approach to traffic accident prediction on heterogeneous spatio-temporal data. In: Proceedings of the 24th ACM SIGKDD International Conference on Knowledge Discovery & Data Mining (KDD), pp. 984–992 (2018). https://doi.org/10.1145/3219819.3219922
21. Ziakopoulos, A., Yannis, G.: A review of spatial approaches in road safety. Acc. Anal. Prev. **135**, 105323 (2020). https://doi.org/10.1016/j.aap.2019.105323

Semantic Noise Filtering in Post-Stroke Kinematic Data: An Automated Deep Learning Approach

Victor Y. K. Kwon[1], Luis G. S. Rodrigues[2], Bartolomeu Zamprogno[1], Marcelo P. Guimarães[3], Leonardo C. D. Rocha[4], Eduardo Zambon[1], Vinícius F. S. Mota[1], and Diego R. C. Dias[1(✉)]

[1] Universidade Federal do Espírito Santo (UFES), Vitória, Brazil
victor.kwon@edu.ufes.br, {bartolomeu.zamprogno,eduardo.zambon, vinicius.f.mota,diego.dias}@ufes.br

[2] Universidade Estadual Paulista (UNESP), São Paulo, Brazil
guilherme.rodrigues@unesp.br

[3] Universidade Federal de São Paulo (UNIFESP), São Paulo, Brazil
marcelo.paiva@unifesp.br

[4] Universidade Federal de São João del-Rei (UFSJ), São João del-Rei, Brazil
lcrocha@ufsj.edu.br

Abstract. Post-stroke rehabilitation increasingly relies on motion capture technologies and extended reality (XR). However, datasets collected in these environments, such as those stored in the Rehabilitation Database (ReBase), are often contaminated by noise. A critical challenge in this domain is distinguishing between clinically relevant variations, such as compensatory movements, and spurious artifacts caused by gestures unrelated to the rehabilitation task. This work proposes a computationally efficient, automated filtering approach based on a multilayer perceptron (MLP). Unlike complex recurrent architectures, the MLP we propose effectively captures gait patterns with observation intervals as short as 5 s, making the solution computationally inexpensive and highly discriminative. We trained the model based on knee angle kinematics, reaching an overall accuracy of 93.18%. Regarding precision, the system achieved 100% accuracy (zero false positives), ensuring that no artifacts are erroneously preserved as valid data. Thus, results indicate that the model successfully generalizes to new patients without manual calibration. By replacing manual curation with this automated deep learning solution, our method improves the Rehabilitation Database scalability, by optimizing storage efficiency and enabling reliable monitoring of motor recovery treatments.

Keywords: ReBase · Neural Network · Data Filtering · Neurological Rehabilitation · Body Kinematics

O. Gervasi et al. (Eds.): ICCSA 2026, LNCS 16768, pp. 601–617, 2027.
https://doi.org/10.1007/978-3-032-30488-9_37

1 Introduction

A stroke occurs when cerebral blood flow is interrupted, caused either by the obstruction (ischemia) or rupture (hemorrhage) of a blood vessel, resulting in neural cell death. This event frequently leads to severe brain damage, which manifests clinically as body paralysis (hemiparesis), loss of motor coordination, and functional deficits in one side of the body. To mitigate these sequelae, neurofunctional rehabilitation involves systematic, repetitive stimulation of muscle groups to promote neuroplasticity and motor relearning.

Within the context of neuromotor rehabilitation, extended reality (XR) has been employed as an effective clinical tool [2,4,10,12]. XR can be conceptualized as the combination of virtual reality (VR), augmented reality (AR), and mixed reality (MR) interface technologies. Given that XR enables the development of simulation environments and serious games, when it is used as a rehabilitation protocol the engagement these environments foster tends to reduce the monotony of conventional rehabilitation exercises.

In XR environments, a very important characteristic is the mode of interaction. Generally, a patient uses their own body as the mode of interaction, something made possible by natural user interfaces (NUIs) that eliminate the need for conventional devices such as keyboards and mice, which require fine motor movement that are often compromised in neurological patients. Therefore, NUI-based technologies enable the body itself to act as an interaction device, with tracking often performed using depth sensors (RGB-D) and inertial measurement units (IMUs), that digitize user movements into biomechanical data.

Although NUIs facilitate tracking the user body, such sensors introduce a problem inherent to this type of application: *continuous user tracking*. In motor rehabilitation scenarios, especially in home use where supervision by a healthcare professional is not always available, data acquisition can be hampered by movements unrelated to treatment, such as postural adjustments, distracting gestures, or interruptions during the session. This causes data collection to be extremely noisy, making it hard to later separate actual physiotherapy movements from undesirable ones.

In this article, we propose and implement a data filter to remove undesirable movements during physiotherapy sessions. We validate our method with ReBase [15], a database specialized in body data management. In this database, small variations, such as fatigue tremors and motor compensations, coexist with undesirable movements during sessions. Therefore, we apply our filter to the data already stored in ReBase in order to remove undesirable movements.

Our main goal is to develop a neural network architecture capable of classifying kinematic observation intervals and of accurately separating legitimate motor behavior from noisy artifacts. This approach aims to identify and remove inconsistencies unrelated to the rehabilitation task, retaining only clinical markers, such as fatigue patterns and compensatory movements inherent to the movement type. In this way, we can ensure that the monitoring of post-stroke recovery is based on anonymized data that is highly clinically representative.

The remainder of this paper is organized as follows. In Sect. 2, we present a brief review of related work, contextualizing our proposal with respect to existing classical and deep learning-based filtering approaches in the literature. In Sect. 3, we establish the theoretical framework, detailing the fundamentals of multilayer perceptron (MLP) networks and the regularization techniques used to develop our model. In Sect. 4, we describe the methodology employed in the study, covering the entire process, from the acquisition and preprocessing of kinematic data, to the definition of the neural network architecture and training strategy. In Sect. 5, we present our results, including quantitative performance metrics and a qualitative analysis of filtering in validation and generalization scenarios. Finally, in Sect. 6, we present the conclusions and possible directions for future work within the context of neuromotor rehabilitation.

2 Related Work

Recent literature indicates significant progress in the creation of data repositories dedicated to motor rehabilitation. Several studies have focused on curating multimodal databases generated from depth sensors (RGB-D) and inertial measurement units (IMUs), such as the UI-PRMD dataset [16], which catalogs physiotherapy movements using Kinect and Vicon sensors; and KIMORE [3], a solution that provides kinematic records focused on rehabilitation exercises with clinical-quality annotations. On a broader scale, initiatives such as NTU RGB+D 120 [9] have established relevant deep learning-based parameters for skeletal analysis. Similarly, in the specific context of stroke, IntelliRehabDS [11] expanded this approach by including data from real patients performing motor tasks under various conditions.

Another line of research focus on automated analysis of movement quality. Initially, approaches based on convolutional neural networks (CNNs) and long-term memory networks (LSTMs) were widely used to extract spatiotemporal features. Works such as those by Liao *et al.* [8] demonstrate the effectiveness of these architectures in classifying execution (correct vs. incorrect). More recently, the state of the art has evolved towards graphical convolutional networks (GCNs), which model the structure of the human skeleton as a topological graph. Yan *et al.* [18] introduced spatiotemporal GCNs (ST-GCNs), that allow for a more refined capture of joint dependencies, which several authors have successfully applied to detect subtle compensatory patterns in post-stroke patients.

A main limitation of the approaches just presented is the premise of *ideal segmentation*: A vast majority of these models assume that the input data stream is composed exclusively of pre-trimmed exercise attempts, containing only the action of interest. Consequently, a critical gap exits in the handling of continuous data collected in uncontrolled environments, where such prior segmentation is nonexistent.

Although classical signal processing techniques, such as Kalman filters [1], Butterworth filters [17], or B-Spline smoothing [14], are effective in attenuating high-frequency noise (such as sensor tremor or tracking instability), they are incapable of distinguishing what we call *semantic noise*. Non-therapeutic functional movements, such as distraction gestures, rest pauses, water ingestion, or social interactions during the session, remain in the datasets, contaminating clinical analysis. Unlike traditional signal-cleaning approaches or supervised action segmentation [7], our proposal aims to perform unsupervised or semi-supervised semantic filtering by leveraging neural networks to identify and remove temporal segments that do not correspond to therapeutic activity, ensuring that the ReBase repository stores only clinically interpretable data.

Table 1 synthesizes the fundamental distinctions between the predominant filtering techniques in the literature and the approach proposed in this work. Based on this review, we observe that classical methods, such as Butterworth filter standardization [17] and Kalman filtering [1], are effective at attenuating stochastic noise. However, because they are applied purely in the frequency domain or for state estimation, these techniques lack contextual sensitivity, which tends to smooth out clinically relevant pathological tremors with spectral signatures similar to noise.

Unlike classical models, approaches focused on human activity recognition (HAR), such as modern spatial GCNs, prioritize classification performance but fail in continuous-flow scenarios where the number of irrelevant events is high. Our proposal fills this gap by introducing the concept of *semantic filtering*, in which the model not only processes the raw signal, but also identifies the movement intentionality, differentiating behaviors unrelated to the task (semantic noise) without compromising the integrity of motor recovery markers.

3 Theoretical Framework

3.1 Multilayer Perceptron (MLP)

In this work, we employ artificial neural networks (ANNs) to handle the complex task of classifying human movement patterns and distinguishing them from noise. The theoretical foundation and practical implementation of these models are based on the work of Goodfellow *et al.* [6] and Géron [5], respectively.

A MLP is a feedforward neural network composed of at least three layers: an input layer, that receives features of the raw data; one or more hidden layers, consisting of interconnected neurons (often called linear threshold units), that extract intermediate representations; and an output layer, that generates the network final prediction. Every other layer apart from the output layer typically includes a bias neuron and is fully connected to the subsequent layer. An architecture with multiple hidden layers between the input and output layers is called a deep neural network (DNN). A DNN can extract features and learn elaborated patterns from input data, something that would not otherwise be evident under simpler processing methods, such as linear analysis.

3.2 Learning and Optimization Process

Training of the MLP is formulated as a non-linear optimization problem that aims to minimize a cost function $J(\theta)$, where $\theta = \{W_l, b_l\}_{l=1}^{L}$ represents the

Table 1. Detailed comparative analysis between literature filtering/recognition approaches and our proposal in this work.

Approach	Characteristics and Limitations
Winter [17]	**Technique:** Butterworth Filter (low-pass). **Focus:** High-frequency noise reduction (sensor tremor). **Limitation:** May smooth pathological tremors and does not remove irrelevant voluntary movements.
Ahmed et al. [1]	**Technique:** Kalman Filter. **Focus:** State estimation and squared error minimization. **Limitation:** Blind to semantic context and assumes all captured movement is part of the task.
Liao et al. [8] & **Yan et al.** [18]	**Technique:** Deep Learning (skeleton-based CNNs and GCNs). **Focus:** Action recognition and movement quality. **Limitation:** Assumes pre-trimmed videos and fails to distinguish artifacts in unsupervised continuous streams.
Our Proposal	**Technique:** Multilayer Perceptron (MLP). **Focus:** Semantic filtering (block classification). **Advantage:** Learns latent gait morphology in fixed windows, removing irrelevant segments with low computational cost.

parameter set (weight matrices W_l and bias vectors b_l) of a network with L layers. Given a dataset $\mathcal{D} = \{(x_i, y_i)\}_{i=1}^{N}$ of input vectors x_i and corresponding expected outputs y_i, the learning process via the backpropagation algorithm is described by the following steps:

1. **Forward Pass:** For each layer $l \in \{1, \ldots, L\}$, the pre-activation z_l and the activation a_l vectors are computed iteratively as:

$$z_l = W_l a_{l-1} + b_l, \tag{1}$$

$$a_l = g_l(z_l), \tag{2}$$

   where $a_0 = x$ (input vector) and g_l is the differentiable activation function of layer l (see below).
2. **Loss Function Evaluation:** The prediction error between network output $\hat{y}$ and expected output y is quantified by a loss function $\mathcal{L}(\hat{y}, y)$. In the context of binary classification, binary cross-entropy is frequently used, defined as:

$$\mathcal{L}(\hat{y}, y) = -\frac{1}{N}\sum_{i=1}^{N}\left[y_i \log(\hat{y}_i) + (1 - y_i)\log(1 - \hat{y}_i)\right]. \tag{3}$$

3. **Backward Pass (backpropagation):** Gradient ∇_θ of the loss function $\mathcal{L}$ with respect to network parameters θ is calculated by applying the chain rule from Calculus. The error term δ_l for layer l is given by:

$$\delta_l = \left(W_{l+1}^T \delta_{l+1}\right) \odot g_l'(z_l), \tag{4}$$

where $\odot$ denotes the pointwise product and g_l' is the first derivative of activation function g_l. The required partial derivatives are then obtained by:

$$\frac{\partial \mathcal{L}}{\partial W_l} = \delta_l a_{l-1}^T, \quad \frac{\partial \mathcal{L}}{\partial b_l} = \delta_l. \tag{5}$$

4. **Parameter Update:** Weights are iteratively adjusted in the opposite direction of the gradient. For the commonly used stochastic gradient descent (SGD) method with a learning rate η, the update rule of network parameters θ for training step $t+1$, based on step t, is defined as:

$$\theta_{t+1} = \theta_t - \eta \nabla_\theta J(\theta_t), \tag{6}$$

where ∇_θ is the gradient of the loss computed in step 3. Modern variants of gradient descent algorithms, such as the Adam optimizer, adapt η based on the first and second-order moments of the gradients.

Activation Functions and Non-Linearity. The capacity of the network to approximate complex functions and model non-linear kinematics depends on the adequate use of activation functions $g(\cdot)$. The most common types of functions and their respective analytical formulations are:

- **Rectified Linear Unit (ReLU):** Predominant in hidden layers due to its computational efficiency and mitigation of the vanishing gradient problem.

$$\text{ReLU}(z) = \max(0, z) \tag{7}$$

- **Sigmoid (Logistic):** Used in the output layer to map activations into a probabilistic interval $(0, 1)$ to enable binary classification.

$$\sigma(z) = \frac{1}{1 + e^{-z}} \tag{8}$$

3.3 Regularization and Dropout

MLPs are susceptible to *overfitting*, which occurs when a model memorizes the training data instead of learning generalizable patterns from input. Given the noisy nature of rehabilitation data, mitigating overfitting is necessary, so a *dropout* technique was employed.

Dropout involves randomly deactivating a subset of neurons during training with a predefined probability p. Let a_l be the activation vector of layer l. With dropout, the modified activation $\tilde{a}_l$ is given by:

$$\tilde{a}_l = a_l \odot m_l, \quad m_l \sim \text{Bernoulli}(p), \tag{9}$$

where $\odot$ denotes pointwise multiplication, and $m(l)$ is a binary mask sampled from a Bernoulli distribution. By forcing the network to train with slightly different architectures at each iteration, neurons are prevented from co-adapting excessively, thereby promoting robustness. During inference, dropout is disabled, and weights are scaled by p to maintain network consistency.

4 Methodology

4.1 Data Acquisition and Preprocessing

The dataset used in this study consists of CSV files containing time-series data of knee flexion and extension angles (left and right knee). Raw data were obtained from a remote repository and subjected to an initial temporal segmentation stage. The complete implementation of the proposed MLP, along with pre-trained weights and the anonymized dataset, is available at our public repository[1].

To create the ground truth (supervised labeling), a threshold-based algorithm was implemented. The continuous data stream was segmented into non-overlapping 5-second time windows. Each window was classified in a binary manner as either a:

- **Valid Block (Walking):** Segments where the angular amplitude of either knee exceeded a pre-defined threshold (ranging between 30 and 52°C, specifically adjusted for each collection file); or
- **Invalid Block (Noise/Rest):** Segments where the angular variation remained below the established threshold.

We applied vector standardization to ensure consistent inputs to the neural network. Considering an approximate sampling rate of 30 Hz, a target size of 150 samples per knee was defined for each 5-second window. Windows with fewer samples were filled with zeros, while larger windows were truncated. Vectors for left and right knees were concatenated, yielding a 300-dimensional feature vector for each instance.

4.2 Dataset Splitting

We adopted the following cross-validation strategy: of the seven files initially processed, we used the first six to compose the training set ($X_{\text{train}}, y_{\text{train}}$), and the last file was used as the test set ($X_{\text{test}}, y_{\text{test}}$) to ensure the model was evaluated on data from a session never seen during training.

We shuffled the data before training the model in order to remove temporal dependencies. We also normalized the data using a standard scaler (zero mean and unit variance). The scaler was applied only to the training data to avoid data leakage.

4.3 Neural Network Architecture

We implemented an MLP-type neural network using the TensorFlow/Keras library to classify kinematic blocks. The proposed architecture consists of a deep MLP, structured to process input vectors of dimension 1×300, corresponding to the concatenation of the standardized time series of the knee angle. We define

[1] https://github.com/diegocolombodias/semanticnoisefiltering.git.

a dense layer configuration with decreasing dimensionality to extract latent features progressively. Thus, the processing flow begins with two consecutive hidden layers of 128 neurons each, followed by two layers of 64 neurons. Finally, the output layer is a single neuron (1×1) that performs binary classification on the validity of the kinematic segment.

Due to the noisy nature of kinematic data and the high dimensionality of the input vector, a regularization strategy is a very important step to ensure the generalization capability of the model. We implement an aggressive dropout in the initial and intermediate layers. Specifically, we applied a dropout rate ($p-1$) of 0.4 after the first three dense layers (128, 128, and 64 neurons). This forces the network to learn distributed, robust features, thereby avoiding excessive co-adaptation of neurons to specific patterns in the training set. In the penultimate layer (64 neurons), we reduced the rate to 0.2 in order to preserve the integrity of high-level features before the final classification layer. This approach prevents the model from memorizing the stochastic noise inherent in motion capture, favoring the learning of gait signal morphology.

Table 2. Summary of hyperparameters and configurations of our MLP.

Hyperparameter/Configuration	Value
Input Dimension	1×300
Number of Hidden Layers	4
Neurons per Layer	128, 128, 64, 64
Activation Function (Hidden)	ReLU
Activation Function (Output)	Sigmoid
Dropout Rates	0.4 (Layers 1–3), 0.2 (Layer 4)
Optimizer	Adam
Loss Function	Binary Cross-Entropy
Batch Size	32
Training Epochs	100
Classification Threshold	0.5

We composed the model with the Adam optimizer and binary cross-entropy loss function, and trained for 100 epochs with a batch size of 32. Table 2 presents all the hyperparameters defined for the network.

4.4 Validation and Visualization Strategy

We measured classifier performance on the test set using overall accuracy and the confusion matrix, which highlights the number of false positives (noise incorrectly classified as walking) and of false negatives (undetected walking). To verify the method applicability, we developed a visualization routine to generate comparative signal grids. The visual validation process consists of:

1. **Pair-by-pair comparison:** For each recording file, we generate two side-by-side graphs. The first displays the complete, unfiltered time series, highlighting all noise and motion artifacts. The second displays the reconstructed time series with only the blocks classified as valid by the model.
2. **Generalization test on unseen data:** In addition to the standard test data, we applied the model to three new data collection files (`knee_angles_corrigidoM1_48`, `M5_36`, and `M7_59`) that did not participate in any training or cross-validation steps.
3. **Acceptance criteria:** Validation is considered successful if the filtered graph preserves the morphological integrity of the knee flexion waves during activity periods, showing gaps (absence of data) during the periods corresponding to the noise observed in the original graph.

It is important to note that the nomenclature we adopted for the generalization datasets explicitly encodes the variability inherent in manual curation. The numerical suffixes in the filenames `M1_48`, `M5_36`, and `M7_59` correspond to the specific angular thresholds (48°, 36°, and 59°, respectively) required to generate the ground truth for each patient. This variance indicates that a static threshold approach cannot accommodate the patients diversity. By successfully filtering these signals without any input relating to these specific parameters, our proposed MLP demonstrates that it has learned the latent morphology of the gait signal, overcoming the need for individual calibration required by the manual method.

Additionally, we performed exploratory data visualization using Python scripts and the skeleton-viewer environment [13]. This tool enables visual, intuitive inspection of knee angular data, along with motion capture playback, as illustrated in Fig. 1. This visual approach allows us to identify model behaviors that textual metrics might obscure, such as excessive fragmentation of continuous blocks or the preservation of non-therapeutic movements.

5 Results and Discussion

In this section, we analyze the proposed model via neural architecture validation, quantitative evaluation of metrics, and qualitative inspection of filtering in known and unknown scenarios.

5.1 Architecture Validation and Metric Performance

Figure 2 shows the resulting confusion matrix obtained from the test set. Out of 440 analyzed blocks, the model correctly classified 410 instances, achieving a global accuracy of 93.18%. It should be highlighted that the model achieved zero false positives (100% accuracy). Within the ReBase ecosystem, this means that the neural network acts as a high-security filter, preventing spurious noise from being erroneously classified as exercise and ensuring the database integrity. The 30 false negatives observed (90.35% sensitivity) indicate a conservative model profile that prioritizes data purity over full recovery in extreme cases.

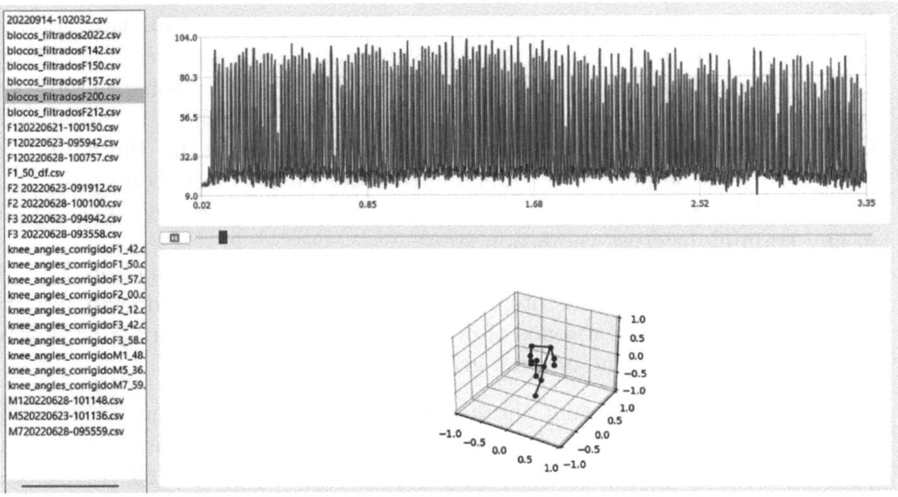

Fig. 1. The skeleton visualization environment displaying a CSV file, synchronizing knee angles with motion capture data.

Obtained results confirm the effectiveness of the proposed MLP architecture. The strategy of using four dense layers with progressive dimensionality reduction (128 → 64 neurons) and dropout regularization proved capable of modeling nonlinear gait features without overfitting.

5.2 Training Metrics and Convergence

We ran the neural network training process for 100 epochs, continuously monitoring loss and accuracy on the training and validation sets. Table 3 summarizes the final results obtained at the end of the learning cycle.

During training, we noted rapid model convergence. By the tenth epoch, the training accuracy exceeded 96%, indicating that the proposed architecture has sufficient capacity to model the complexities of the kinematic dataset. At the end of 100 epochs, the model achieved a training accuracy of 99.68% and a minimal residual loss of 0.0095, demonstrating almost complete learning of the patterns present in the training set.

Regarding generalization, the model maintained robust performance on the test set (unseen data), stabilizing at an accuracy of 93.18%. Although there is a divergence between training loss and validation loss in the final epochs, a behavior inherent to deep networks and a potential onset of overfitting, the stability of the validation accuracy (which fluctuated between 93% and 95% in the last 20 epochs) confirms that the dropout layers were effective in preserving the system overall generalization capability.

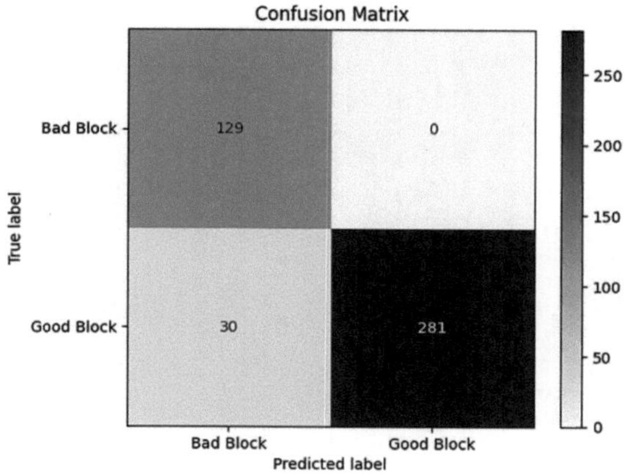

Fig. 2. Confusion matrix of the test set. The absence of false positives validates the filter safety for clinical applications.

Table 3. Final performance metrics after 100 training epochs.

Metric	Training Set	Test/Validation Set
Final Accuracy	99.68%	93.18%
Final Loss	0.0095	0.4271
Peak Accuracy	100.00%	95.00%

5.3 Qualitative Analysis: Semantic Segregation

Figures 3 and 4 show model application to the validation set. Left columns in Figs. 3 and 4 correspond to the unfiltered (raw) data, whereas right columns display the filtered results. A visual comparison between left and right indicates the network semantic segregation capability, as further discussed below.

Effectiveness of the proposed approach becomes visually evident in the pairwise comparison between the raw and processed signals. To correctly interpret these results, it is necessary to observe the morphological distinction between the signal of interest (gait) and behavioral noise.

The clearest example of this distinction occurs in Fig. 3, top row (Data #1). In the unfiltered graph, we observe a long initial period (indices from 0 to 8000) characterized by low amplitude and high frequency variations. Clinically, this represents the moment when the patient is standing still, receiving instructions, or adjusting equipment. This behavior, although captured by the sensor, has no biomechanical value. By analyzing the filtered graph, we can see that the

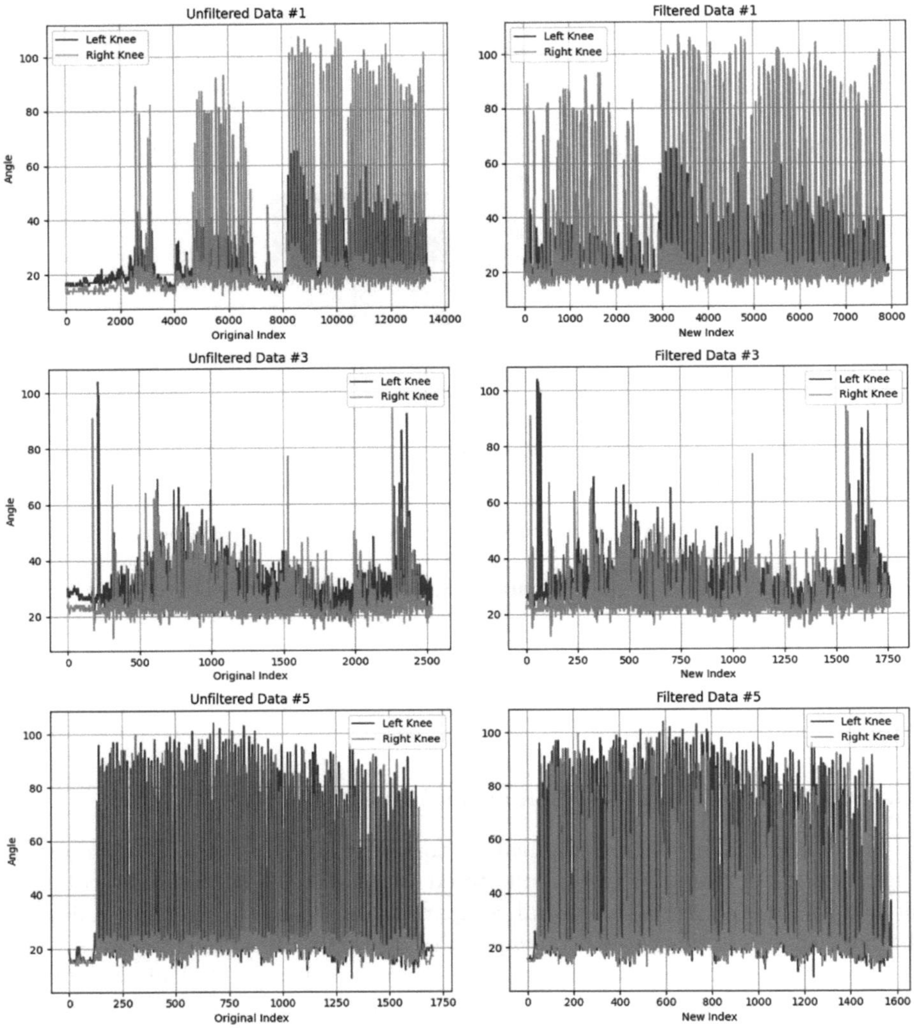

Fig. 3. Comparison between raw and filtered signals, part 1. The neural network effectively suppresses high-amplitude noise and periods of inactivity, preserving only the gait cyclic morphology.

neural network removed this entire initial segment. The resulting graph begins immediately at the first consistent gait cycle. Note that the x-axis (New Index) has been reduced, indicating that the model not only eliminated noise but also discarded unnecessary data, thus optimizing storage.

A critical point in automated filters is the risk of distorting useful signals. However, when observing high-amplitude segments (peaks representing knee flexion above 60°C) in Figs. 3 and 4, we can confirm that the waveform integrity

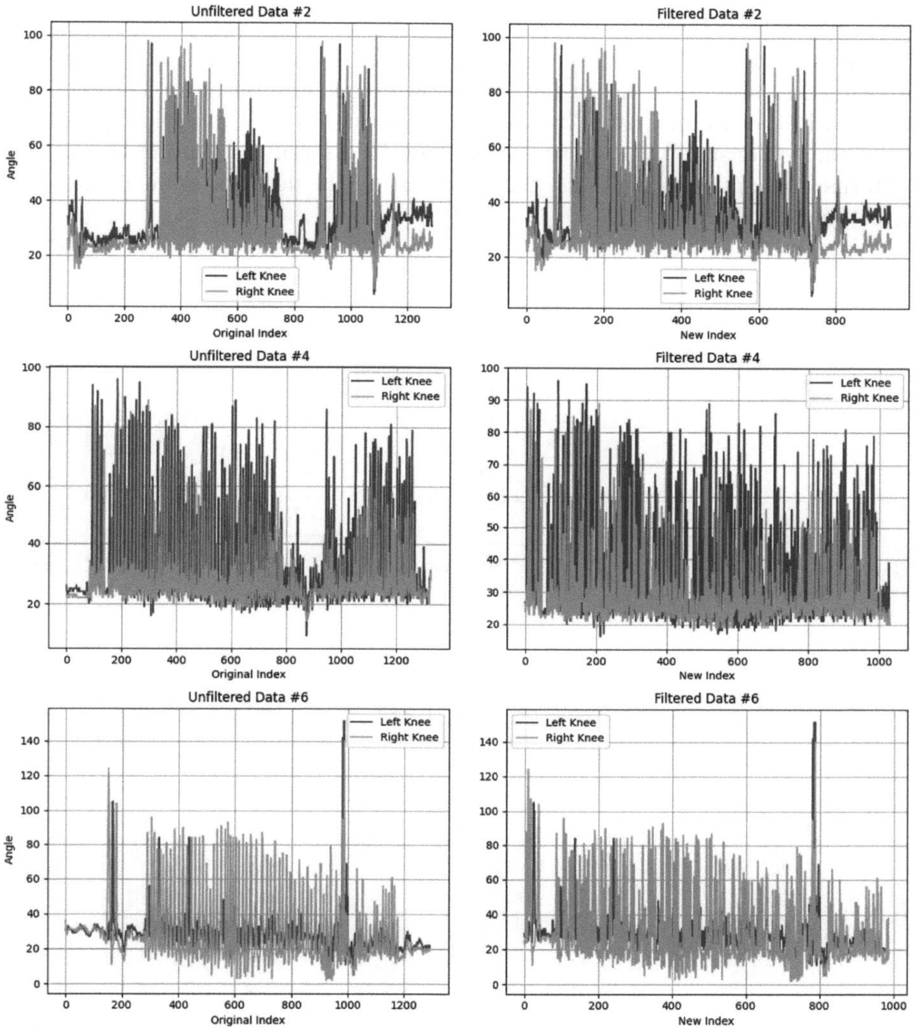

Fig. 4. Comparison between raw and filtered signals, part 2. The neural network effectively suppresses high-amplitude noise and periods of inactivity, preserving only the gait cyclic morphology.

is maintained. Thus, the neural network learned to recognize the typical sinusoidal pattern of human gait. Unlike hard-threshold filters (which could cut off wave peaks or fail at higher valleys), the MLP preserved natural dynamics of the movement, ensuring that subsequent metrics, such as range of motion (ROM), remain reliable.

5.4 Generalization Test

To validate the model robustness for new patients and ensure its applicability in real-world scenarios, we tested the network on unpublished recordings not included in the training set. The results of this qualitative evaluation, presented in Fig. 5, demonstrate the system autonomy in discerning genuine biophysical patterns from spurious artifacts, thus eliminating the need for manual threshold adjustments.

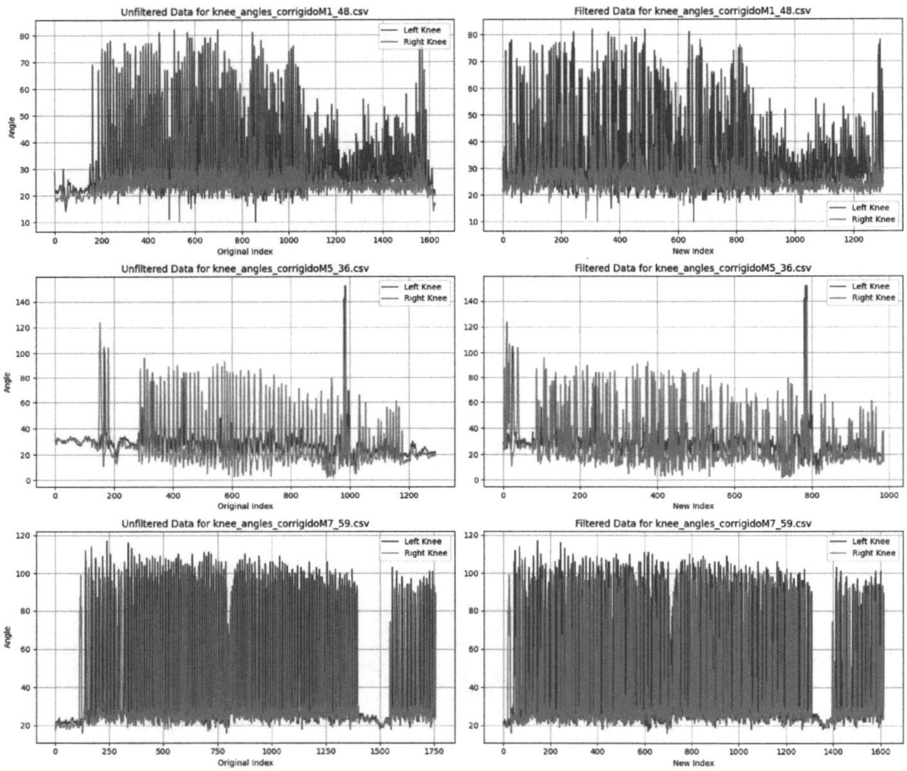

Fig. 5. Generalization test on three new recordings (M1_48, M5_36, M7_59). The model demonstrated autonomy in cleaning background noise and segmenting pauses without manual threshold adjustment.

Graphs from recording session M1_48 (top part of Fig. 5) show the classifier ability to clean the signal from its initial recording moments, completely suppressing the background noise that precedes motor activity without degrading the integrity of subsequent gait cycles.

This contextual sensitivity becomes even more evident in the central recording (M5_36), where the network handled exercise intermittency better than classical approaches. In this scenario, a patient performs the gait, pauses to rest (as evidenced by a drop in amplitude in the original graph), and resumes the exercise. Classic moving-average filters tend to create an artificial ramp of descent and ascent at the extremes of this pause. Our model, however, identified the absence of a gait pattern and removed it. The result is a clean signal that concatenates only moments of effective effort, allowing the therapist to assess movement consistency without navigating through data gaps.

Finally, the behavior observed in the lower recording (`M7_59`), more specifically the detection of an acquisition gap near index 1300, supports the hypothesis that the neural network internalized a latent representation of the human movement morphology. By systematically rejecting patterns that deviate from this biomechanical structure, the proposed solution demonstrates its robustness as an alternative to manual curation of the ReBase ecosystem.

In summary, the visual changes in the graphs confirm that the model went beyond simple stochastic noise reduction, acting as a semantic editor that retains only the blocks where the kinematic signature of gait is present.

6 Conclusion

We presented a practical approach for processing noisy kinematic signals from rehabilitation datasets, focusing on preserving informative segments that reflect typical cyclic gait patterns. Initially, we performed manual filtering based on visual inspection and empirically adjusted thresholds, thereby identifying consistent and relevant data blocks for biomechanical analysis.

Based on this selected dataset, we trained an MLP-type neural network to learn the characteristic patterns of valid segments. After training, the model demonstrated good performance on the automated filtering task, eliminating the need for manual intervention and replicating the behavior observed during the supervised preprocessing phase with a high accuracy rate.

Replacing manual filtering with a deep learning-based approach has proven to be not only feasible but also advantageous in terms of scalability, standardization, and time efficiency. Based on the results presented, we have evidence suggesting that neural networks will enable consistent application of the process to new recordings, reducing human effort and minimizing the risk of bias or subjective inconsistencies in data selection.

In conclusion, the results obtained reinforce the potential for integrating machine learning techniques into clinical procedures, paving the way for more autonomous and reliable systems for processing biomedical signals. As future work, we intend to integrate this model directly into the ReBase ecosystem recording pipeline, allowing for real-time data cleaning. Furthermore, we plan to expand the training set to include neuromotor pathologies and additional sensor modalities, e.g., IMUs. Ultimately, this approach underpins the development of data-driven tele-rehabilitation tools, where ensuring information quality is a prerequisite for remote clinical decision support.

Acknowledgments. The authors acknowledge partial funding from the Coordination for the Improvement of Higher Education Personnel - Brazil (CAPES) - Funding Code 001; the National Council for Scientific and Technological Development - Brazil (CNPq) - Funding Codes 442344/2023–6, 444602/2024–0, and 407466/2025–8; the Espírito Santo Research and Innovation Support Foundation (FAPES) – Call No. 02/2026 (Participation in Technical-Scientific Events) – Grant No. 428/2026 and project #2024-9G1WP BPC; and the Minas Gerais Research Funding Foundation (FAPEMIG)

References

1. Ahmed, F., et al.: Kalman filter-based noise reduction framework for posture estimation using depth sensor. In: 2019 IEEE 18th International Conference on Cognitive Informatics & Cognitive Computing (ICCI* CC), pp. 150–158. IEEE (2019)
2. Camargo, L.F., Miguel, G.R., Feitosa, J.D.C., Rodrigues, L.G.S., Dias, D.R.C., Brega, J.R.F.: Combining computer vision and artificial intelligence to support the rehabilitation of post-stroke patients. In: International Conference on Computational Science and Its Applications, pp. 415–432. Springer (2025)
3. Capecci, M., et al.: The KIMORE dataset: kinematic assessment of movement and clinical scores for remote monitoring of physical rehabilitation. IEEE Trans. Neural Syst. Rehabil. Eng. **27**(7), 1436–1448 (2019)
4. Dias, D.R., Alvarenga, I.C., Guimarães, M.P., Trevelin, L.C., Castellano, G., Brandão, A.F.: eStreet: virtual reality and wearable devices applied to rehabilitation. In: International Conference on Computational Science and Its Applications, pp. 775–789. Springer (2018)
5. Géron, A.: Hands-On Machine Learning with Scikit-Learn and TensorFlow, 2 edn. O'Reilly Media (2020)
6. Goodfellow, I., Bengio, Y., Courville, A.: Deep Learning. MIT Press, Cambridge (2016)
7. Lea, C., et al.: Temporal convolutional networks for action segmentation and detection. In: Proceedings of the IEEE Conference on Computer Vision and Pattern Recognition, pp. 156–165 (2017)
8. Liao, Y., Vakanski, A., Xian, M.: A deep learning framework for assessing physical rehabilitation exercises. IEEE Trans. Neural Syst. Rehabil. Eng. **28**(2), 468–477 (2020)
9. Liu, J., et al.: NTU RGB+ D 120: a large-scale benchmark for 3D human activity understanding. IEEE Trans. Patt. Anal. Mach. Intell. **42**(10), 2684–2701 (2019)
10. Maier, M., et al.: Effect of specific over nonspecific VR-based rehabilitation on post-stroke motor recovery: a systematic meta-analysis. Neurorehabil. Neural Repair **33**(2), 112–129 (2019)
11. Miron, A., et al.: IntelliRehabDS (IRDS) - a dataset of physical rehabilitation movements. Data **6**(5), 46 (2021)
12. Ribeiro, E., Brandão, A., Guimarães, M., Rocha, L., Brega, J.R., Villaça, R., Dias, D.: A body tracking framework for neuromotor rehabilitation with multimedia application support. In: International Conference on Computational Science and Its Applications, pp. 345–360. Springer (2025)
13. Rodrigues, L.G.S., et al.: A lower limb mixed reality system for the elderly. In: Proceedings of the 24th Symposium on Virtual and Augmented Reality, p. 5. ACM, New York (2022). https://doi.org/10.1145/3604479.3604531

14. Tepper, M., Sapiro, G.: Fast L1 smoothing splines with an application to Kinect depth data. In: 2013 IEEE International Conference on Image Processing, pp. 504–508. IEEE (2013)
15. Trotta, T., et al.: ReBase: a framework for acquiring and managing body tracking data. In: Proceedings of the Symposium on Virtual and Augmented Reality, p. 9. ACM, New York (2024). https://doi.org/10.1145/3691573.3691578
16. Vakanski, A., Jun, H.p., Paul, D., Baker, R.: A data set of human body movements for physical rehabilitation exercises. Data **3**(1), 2 (2018)
17. Winter, D.A.: Biomechanics and Motor Control of Human Movement. John Wiley & Sons (2009)
18. Yan, S., Xiong, Y., Lin, D.: Spatial temporal graph convolutional networks for skeleton-based action recognition. In: Proceedings of the AAAI Conference on Artificial Intelligence, vol. 32 (2018)

Semantic Leakage in CKKS via Homomorphic Noise

Renato J. P. Borseti(✉), Thays Rocha Neri Ferreira, and Fábio Borges

National Laboratory for Scientific Computing, Petrópolis, RJ 25.651-075, Brazil
policani@lncc.br, tferreira@posgrad.lncc.br
http://www.lncc.br/ borges/

Abstract. Homomorphic encryption schemes, particularly the Cheon-Kim-Kim-Song (CKKS) scheme, are widely adopted for privacy-preserving computation over real-valued data. While CKKS provides strong ciphertext security, this paper investigates whether semantic privacy can be compromised through passive observation of the encrypted communication channel. We demonstrate that different data types induce statistically distinguishable noise growth patterns—observable without access to secret keys or plaintext—and formalize this as a passive side-channel attack in which an adversary monitors channel metadata to infer the semantic nature of the encrypted data. Experimental validation using Microsoft SEAL ($n = 8192$, coeff_modulus $= [60, 40, 40, 60]$ bits, scale $= 2^{40}$) shows high inference accuracy under type-specific circuits ($\widehat{\mathsf{Adv}} = 0.750$) and residual but reduced leakage under uniform circuits ($\widehat{\mathsf{Adv}} = 0.170$), confirming that the primary leakage vector is computational behavior rather than data distribution. Our results reveal a previously underexplored privacy vulnerability in CKKS deployments and propose circuit uniformization as a practical countermeasure.

Keywords: Homomorphic encryption · CKKS · side-channel attack · semantic privacy · noise analysis · passive adversary

1 Introduction

Homomorphic Encryption (HE) has emerged as a foundational primitive for privacy-preserving computation, enabling arithmetic operations to be performed directly on encrypted data without decryption. The CKKS scheme, introduced by Cheon, Kim, Kim, and Song [1], is the leading HE scheme for real-valued computation. Unlike exact schemes such as BGV [2], CKKS operates over approximate arithmetic: it encodes vectors of complex numbers into polynomial ring elements and tolerates small errors in decryption, trading precision for dramatically improved performance on floating-point workloads. This design choice makes CKKS uniquely suited for privacy-preserving machine learning, secure statistical analysis, and federated computation over continuous data—domains where a bounded approximation error is acceptable.

O. Gervasi et al. (Eds.): ICCSA 2026, LNCS 16768, pp. 618–632, 2027.
https://doi.org/10.1007/978-3-032-30488-9_38

The security of CKKS is analyzed through ciphertext indistinguishability under chosen plaintext attack, commonly referred to as IND CPA. Under this notion, no adversary with bounded computational resources can distinguish encryptions of two plaintexts that they choose. This guarantee concerns the content of the ciphertext. However, it does not rule out the possibility that observable properties of the communication channel, such as timing, message size, or the noise behavior of ciphertexts during transmission, may reveal information about the nature of the computation being executed. Previous studies on side channel attacks against homomorphic encryption implementations have mainly focused on recovering secret keys through techniques such as power analysis or timing measurements [7,18]. To the best of our knowledge, the question of semantic leakage, namely whether the category of the underlying data can be inferred from channel metadata, has not yet been explored.

This paper investigates precisely this gap. We ask: can a passive adversary, observing only metadata from an encrypted CKKS channel without any access to secret keys or plaintext, infer the semantic category of the data being processed? Our central finding is affirmative and structurally precise. Different data types, like financial, medical, text, and binary, induce systematically different sequences of homomorphic operations, which in turn produce statistically distinguishable noise growth trajectories. A machine learning classifier trained exclusively on passively observable channel metadata achieves near-perfect inference accuracy when data types are processed through type-specific circuits. More importantly, when all data types are forced through a uniform homomorphic circuit, the inference accuracy drops substantially, but does not reach random baseline, confirming that the leakage is primarily *behavioral* rather than *distributional.*

1.1 CKKS Scheme Definition

Let $R_q = \mathbb{Z}_q[X]/(X^n + 1)$ be the polynomial ring, where n is a power of 2 and q is the coefficient modulus.

Definition 1 (CKKS Ciphertext). *A CKKS ciphertext is a pair* $(c_0, c_1) \in R_q^2$ *satisfying*

$$c_0 + c_1 \cdot s \;\approx\; \Delta \cdot m + e, \tag{1}$$

where $s \in R$ *is the secret key,* $m \in \mathbb{C}^{n/2}$ *is the plaintext message,* $\Delta = 2^\ell$ *is the scaling factor, and* $e \in R$ *is Gaussian noise with* $e \sim \mathcal{N}(0, \sigma^2)$.

Remark 1. CKKS is an approximate scheme by design: decryption recovers m up to a small error bounded by $\|e\|_\infty / \Delta$. This inherent noise is the leakage vector exploited in this work.

1.2 Noise Growth per Homomorphic Operation

Definition 2 (Residual Noise). *The residual noise of a ciphertext* ct *is defined as*

$$\varepsilon(\mathsf{ct}) \;=\; \|c_0 + c_1 \cdot s - \Delta \cdot m\|_\infty . \tag{2}$$

For each homomorphic operation, the noise evolves according to distinct growth laws detailed below.

Addition. Addition accumulates noise linearly, and the growth is largely independent of the plaintext values.

$$\varepsilon(\mathsf{ct}_1 \oplus \mathsf{ct}_2) = \varepsilon(\mathsf{ct}_1) + \varepsilon(\mathsf{ct}_2) + e_{\mathsf{add}}, \quad e_{\mathsf{add}} \sim \mathcal{N}(0, \sigma^2_{\mathsf{add}}). \tag{3}$$

Multiplication. After relinearization and rescaling:

$$\varepsilon(\mathsf{ct}_1 \otimes \mathsf{ct}_2) \approx \frac{1}{\Delta}\Big[\varepsilon(\mathsf{ct}_1)\cdot\|\Delta m_2\|_\infty + \varepsilon(\mathsf{ct}_2)\cdot\|\Delta m_1\|_\infty + \varepsilon(\mathsf{ct}_1)\cdot\varepsilon(\mathsf{ct}_2)\Big] + e_{\mathsf{mul}}. \tag{4}$$

Remark 2 (Data-Noise Coupling—Primary Leakage Mechanism). The dominant term in (4) is proportional to $\|\Delta \cdot m\|_\infty$, the magnitude of the encrypted values. Since different data natures exhibit distinct magnitude distributions—e.g., financial data follows a log-normal distribution with large magnitudes, while text embeddings are sparse and bounded in $[-1, 1]$—multiplicative noise growth is statistically dependent on the data nature. This *data-noise coupling* is the primary leakage mechanism identified in this work.

Rotation. Rotation introduces noise comparable to addition, but through key-switching material, producing a characteristic timing signature observable on the channel.

$$\varepsilon(\mathsf{Rot}(\mathsf{ct})) = \varepsilon(\mathsf{ct}) + e_{\mathsf{rot}}, \quad e_{\mathsf{rot}} \sim \mathcal{N}(0, \sigma^2_{\mathsf{rot}}). \tag{5}$$

2 Related Work

Work specifically targeting side-channel attacks on CKKS remains sparse. Existing literature addresses two threads: leakage through CKKS's approximate nature, and adaptation of side-channel techniques from lattice and FHE implementations. Li and Micciancio [4] show that IND-CPA does not capture realistic passive leakage for approximate schemes, enabling practical key-recovery attacks against HEAAN, SEAL, HElib, and PALISADE. Cheon et al. [5] extend this with IND-CPAD and KRD attacks exploiting bootstrapping failures to recover secret keys in polynomial time. Alexandru et al. [6] respond with Application-Aware Homomorphic Encryption (AAHE), showing that security for CKKS must be specified at the application and parameter level—consistent with our finding that circuit-level decisions determine the degree of semantic leakage.

On physical side channels, Aydin and Aysu [7] demonstrate that SEAL's NTT-based key generation leaks secret coefficients via power and EM profiling, achieving over 98% coefficient recovery from a single trace. Xu et al. [8] and Sim et al. [9] mount chosen-ciphertext EM attacks on Kyber, with methodology transferable to CKKS's RNS-NTT pipeline. Ravi et al. [10] show generic EM-assisted attacks on LWE/LWR schemes, relevant given CKKS's shared decryption structure. Surveys by Ghaleb and Buchanan [11], Lou et al. [12], Picek et al. [13], and Randolph and Diehl [14] systematize the threat space, confirming that NTT, key switching, and bootstrapping are natural side-channel targets. Recent advances include plaintext-based collision attacks [15], weakly profiling analysis [16], and multi-modal side-channel frameworks achieving AES-128 key recovery with one to three traces [17].

Our work differs fundamentally: rather than recovering secret keys, we ask whether the semantic nature of the data can be inferred by a passive network observer from behavioral metadata alone—a previously unexplored question requiring no physical access to the device.

3 Formalization of Semantic Leakage

Let $\mathcal{D} \in \{d_1, d_2, \ldots, d_K\}$ denote the set of possible data natures ($K = 4$ in our experiments: Financial, Medical, Text, Binary).

Definition 3 (Semantic Leakage). *Semantic leakage occurs when there exists a function* ϕ *such that* $\exists\, \phi : \mathbb{R}^{T+1} \to \{d_1, \ldots, d_K\}$ *s.t.* $\Pr\big[\phi(\varepsilon) = \mathcal{D}\big] \gg \frac{1}{K}$.

The function ϕ is implemented as a supervised machine learning classifier trained exclusively on the passively observable metadata vector:

$$\mathbf{x}_{\mathsf{obs}} = \big(\bar{t}_{op},\, \sigma_t,\, t_{\max},\, \textstyle\sum t,\, \bar{t}_{\mathsf{mul}},\, \bar{t}_{\mathsf{add}},\, s_{\mathsf{final}},\, \log_2 s,\, \ell_{\mathsf{final}},\, \Delta\ell,\, \overline{sz},\, sz_{\max},\, \Delta sz,\, N_{op},\\ N_{\mathsf{mul}},\, N_{\mathsf{add}},\, N_{\mathsf{rot}},\, r_{\mathsf{mul}},\, r_{\mathsf{add}},\, \widetilde{\mu}_3,\, \widetilde{\mu}_4,\, cv_t\big) \in \mathbb{R}^{22}. \quad (6)$$

where each component is derivable from passive network monitoring: operation timings (t), ciphertext scale (s), modulus chain level (ℓ), ciphertext size (sz), operation counts (N), and statistical shape features of the timing distribution (skewness $\widetilde{\mu}_3$, excess kurtosis $\widetilde{\mu}_4$, coefficient of variation cv_t).

4 Methodology

This section describes the methodology adopted for conducting this research, detailing the procedures, techniques, and tools used in data collection, processing, and analysis. The objective is to present, in a clear and systematic way, the steps that structure the development of the study.

4.1 Threat Model

We consider a passive adversary $\mathcal{A}$ who monitors an encrypted communication channel between two agents, Alice and Bob, performing homomorphic computations using the CKKS scheme. The adversary has no access to secret keys, plaintext data, or the internal state of the SEAL library. The only information available to $\mathcal{A}$ is the observable metadata of the channel: operation timing, ciphertext size evolution, modulus chain level, and ciphertext scale—all quantities inferable from passive network monitoring without physical access to the computing device, as illustrated in Fig. 1.

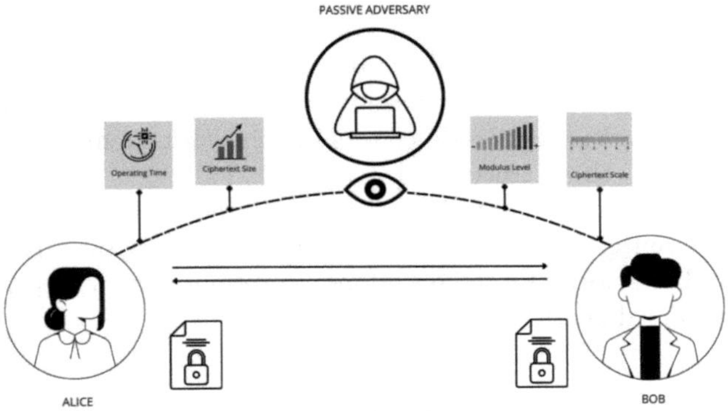

Fig. 1. Scenario Analyzed.

It is important to clarify the relationship between the implemented experimental setup and the intended real-world threat model. In our implementation, channel metadata—operation timing, ciphertext level, scale, and serialized size—is extracted directly via the Microsoft SEAL API, specifically through `ct.coeff_modulus_size()`, `ct.scale()`, `ct.save_size()`, and `time.perf_counter()` calls surrounding each evaluator operation. This approach accurately models the *information content* available to a passive adversary, but implicitly assumes access to the SEAL runtime on Alice or Bob's machine.

In a realistic deployment over an encrypted network channel, the adversary has no access to the SEAL library or the `Ciphertext` object. The observable quantities must instead be inferred entirely from network traffic:

- **Ciphertext level** is inferable from packet size, since the serialized size of a CKKS ciphertext is a deterministic function of the modulus chain level. For $n = 8192$ and coeff_modulus $= [60, 40, 40, 60]$, the correspondence is: level 3 $\approx$ 393 KB, level 2 $\approx$ 327 KB, level 1 $\approx$ 262 KB—values derivable from the public CKKS parameters exchanged during the protocol handshake.
- **Operation timing** is inferable from inter-packet intervals, since each homomorphic operation on the server side introduces a measurable latency before the response packet is transmitted.
- **Operation type** is inferable from the combination of packet size change and inter-packet interval: a packet that decreases in size with high latency indicates a multiplication followed by rescaling, while a same-size packet with low latency indicates an addition or rotation.
- **Scale drift** is inferable only approximately from network traffic, as it requires knowledge of the exact floating-point rounding introduced by rescaling. This is the one feature in $\mathbf{x}_{\text{obs}}$ that is not directly observable without library access.

The gap between the implemented model and a pure network adversary therefore reduces to a single feature: exact scale drift. All remaining 21 components of $\mathbf{x}_{\mathsf{obs}}$ are inferable from packet-level observation alone. Validating this claim by reproducing the attack using only captured network traffic—replacing API-level measurements with packet timestamps and sizes—is identified as an important direction for future work, and would strengthen the practical threat model considerably.

4.2 Experimental Setup

All experiments were implemented in Python 3 using Microsoft SEAL [3] via the `seal-python` binding, running on a machine equipped with an Intel Core i7-10700F processor (2.9 GHz, 16 cores), 32 GB of RAM, under Ubuntu 22.04. The CKKS parameters were set as follows: polynomial modulus degree $n = 8192$, coefficient modulus bit-sizes $[60, 40, 40, 60]$ (providing two levels of multiplicative depth), and scaling factor $\Delta = 2^{40}$. Each experiment collected 150 communication sessions per data category, totaling 600 observations per scenario. Keys were regenerated every 50 sessions to simulate a realistic deployment with periodic key rotation.

Four data categories were selected to represent distinct real-world use cases with systematically different distributional characteristics:

- **Financial:** stock prices, transaction values, and portfolio weights. Modeled as a mixture of log-normal ($\mu = 5.0$, $\sigma = 1.2$), Gaussian ($\mu = 1000$, $\sigma = 500$), and Dirichlet distributions. Characteristic of large-magnitude, high-variance data.
- **Medical:** vital signs (heart rate, blood pressure, glucose) and dosage values. Modeled as narrow Gaussian distributions with physiologically constrained ranges. Characteristic of moderate-magnitude, low-variance data.
- **Text:** token embedding vectors. Modeled as sparse Gaussian ($\mu = 0$, $\sigma = 0.3$) with 60% sparsity, clipped to $[-1, 1]$. Characteristic of small-magnitude, sparse data.
- **Binary:** boolean flags and one-hot encodings. Modeled as Bernoulli-distributed values near $\{0, 1\}$ with small encoding noise. Characteristic of bimodal, bounded data.

Three classifiers were evaluated under 5-fold stratified cross-validation: Random Forest (200 estimators), Gradient Boosting (150 estimators, learning rate 0.1, maximum depth 4), and SVM with RBF kernel ($C = 10$, $\gamma = \texttt{scale}$). All classifiers were preceded by standard normalization (`StandardScaler`). The best model per scenario was selected by mean cross-validated accuracy. Feature importance was extracted from the tree-based models (Random Forest and Gradient Boosting) via the mean decrease in impurity criterion, providing interpretability of which observable channel properties drive inference.

4.3 Experimental Scenarios

Three scenarios of increasing adversarial difficulty were evaluated:

Scenario 1—Type-Specific Circuits: Each data category is processed through a homomorphic circuit tailored to its computational semantics: financial data through multiplication-heavy circuits (portfolio returns, risk metrics); medical data through addition-dominated circuits (vital sign aggregation); text data through rotation-heavy circuits (attention-like operations); binary data through repeated multiplications modeling Boolean gate evaluation. This scenario establishes the upper bound on adversary advantage.

Scenario 2—Uniform Circuit: All data categories are forced through an identical homomorphic circuit consisting of one addition, one multiplication, one addition, one rotation, one multiplication, and one final addition—regardless of their semantic type. This scenario tests whether the leakage persists when the operational fingerprint is removed, isolating the data-distribution contribution.

Scenario 3—Adversarial Masking: Agents are assumed to be aware of the side-channel attack and inject four random dummy operations (chosen uniformly from addition, multiplication, and rotation with random parameters) after each real computation. This scenario tests the robustness of the attack against an informed defender.

4.4 Feature Extraction

The passive observer extracts the 22-dimensional feature vector $\mathbf{x}_{\mathsf{obs}}$ defined in Eq. (6) from each observed session. All features are derivable without decryption: timing measurements via network latency analysis, scale and level via ciphertext metadata (transmitted in cleartext in standard SEAL serialization), and size via packet length observation.

The features decompose into five groups:

(i) *timing statistics*, like mean, standard deviation, maximum, sum, per-operation-type means ($\bar{t}_{\mathsf{mul}}$, $\bar{t}_{\mathsf{add}}$);
(ii) *scale features*, like final scale s_{final} and $\log_2 s$, which encode the total rescaling depth;
(iii) *modulus chain features*, like final level ℓ_{final} and consumed levels $\Delta\ell$, which reflect the multiplicative depth consumed;
(iv) *size features*, like mean, maximum, and growth of ciphertext serialized size across the session;
(v) *timing shape features*, like skewness $\widetilde{\mu}_3$, excess kurtosis $\widetilde{\mu}_4$, and coefficient of variation cv_t, which capture distributional asymmetry in the per-operation timing sequence.

Algorithm 1 formalizes the feature extraction procedure from the passive observer's perspective.

Algorithm 2 specifies the canonical uniform circuit $\mathcal{O}^*$ used in Scenario 2. The circuit was designed to exercise all three operation types at a fixed depth of two multiplications, ensuring that the modulus chain consumption is identical for all data types.

Algorithm 1. Passive Observer Feature Extraction

Require: Channel observation: sequence of $(t_i, s_i, \ell_i, sz_i, \mathsf{op}_i)$ for $i = 1, \dots, T$
Ensure: Feature vector $\mathbf{x}_{\mathsf{obs}} \in \mathbb{R}^{22}$
Compute timing statistics: $\bar{t} \leftarrow \frac{1}{T}\sum t_i$, $\sigma_t \leftarrow \text{std}(t_i)$, $t_{\max} \leftarrow \max(t_i)$
Compute per-type timing means: $\bar{t}_{\mathsf{mul}} \leftarrow \text{mean}\{t_i : \mathsf{op}_i = \mathsf{mul}\}$
Read final scale and level: $s_{\mathsf{final}} \leftarrow s_T$, $\ell_{\mathsf{final}} \leftarrow \ell_T$, $\Delta\ell \leftarrow \ell_0 - \ell_T$
Read size evolution: $\overline{sz} \leftarrow \text{mean}(sz_i)$, $\Delta sz \leftarrow sz_T - sz_0$
Count operations: $N_{\mathsf{mul}} \leftarrow |\{i : \mathsf{op}_i = \mathsf{mul}\}|$, similarly for N_{add}, N_{rot}
Compute timing shape: $\widetilde{\mu}_3 \leftarrow \text{skewness}(t_i)$, $\widetilde{\mu}_4 \leftarrow \text{kurtosis}(t_i)$, $cv_t \leftarrow \sigma_t/\bar{t}$
return $\mathbf{x}_{\mathsf{obs}}$

Algorithm 2. Canonical Uniform Homomorphic Circuit $\mathcal{O}^*$

Require: Encrypted inputs $\mathsf{ct}_a \leftarrow \mathsf{Enc}(m_a)$, $\mathsf{ct}_b \leftarrow \mathsf{Enc}(m_b)$
Ensure: Result ciphertext ct_r
$\mathsf{ct}_1 \leftarrow \mathsf{Add}(\mathsf{ct}_a, \mathsf{ct}_b)$ {level L, scale Δ}
$\mathsf{ct}_2 \leftarrow \mathsf{Mul}(\mathsf{ct}_1, \mathsf{ct}_a)$; $\mathsf{Relin}(\mathsf{ct}_2)$; $\mathsf{Rescale}(\mathsf{ct}_2)$ {level $L-1$, scale Δ}
$\mathsf{ModSwitch}(\mathsf{ct}_b \rightarrow \ell(\mathsf{ct}_2))$; $\mathsf{ct}_3 \leftarrow \mathsf{Add}(\mathsf{ct}_2, \mathsf{ct}_b)$
$\mathsf{ct}_4 \leftarrow \mathsf{Rot}(\mathsf{ct}_3, 2)$ {level $L-1$, scale Δ}
$\mathsf{ct}_5 \leftarrow \mathsf{Mul}(\mathsf{ct}_4, \mathsf{ct}_b)$; $\mathsf{Relin}(\mathsf{ct}_5)$; $\mathsf{Rescale}(\mathsf{ct}_5)$ {level $L-2$, scale Δ}
$\mathsf{ModSwitch}(\mathsf{ct}_a \rightarrow \ell(\mathsf{ct}_5))$; $\mathsf{ct}_r \leftarrow \mathsf{Add}(\mathsf{ct}_5, \mathsf{ct}_a)$
return ct_r

5 Adversary Advantage and Experimental Results

Definition 4 (Semantic Advantage). *The semantic advantage of a passive adversary $\mathcal{A}$ is defined as*

$$\text{Adv}(\mathcal{A}) \;=\; \Pr\big[\mathcal{A}(\mathbf{x}_{\mathsf{obs}}) = \mathcal{D}\big] \;-\; \frac{1}{K}. \tag{7}$$

The empirical estimate of this advantage is:

$$\widehat{\text{Adv}}(\mathcal{A}) \;=\; \hat{p}_{\mathsf{acc}} \;-\; \frac{1}{K}, \tag{8}$$

where $\hat{p}_{\mathsf{acc}}$ is the 5-fold stratified cross-validated accuracy of the ML classifier. Three scenarios were evaluated using Microsoft SEAL ($n = 8192$, coeff_modulus $= [60, 40, 40, 60]$ bits, scale $= 2^{40}$), with 150 sessions per class ($K = 4$). Three classifiers were compared: Random Forest (200 estimators), Gradient Boosting (150 estimators, learning rate 0.1), and SVM with RBF kernel ($C = 10$). The experimental results are summarized in Table 1.

The uniform circuit scenario confirms that circuit uniformization substantially reduces leakage ($\widehat{\text{Adv}}$ drops from 0.750 to 0.170), yet does not eliminate it entirely. The residual advantage reflects the data-noise coupling in Eq. (4), which persists even under a fixed operation sequence. The adversarial masking scenario ($\widehat{\text{Adv}} = 0.604$) demonstrates that naive injection of dummy operations is insufficient as a defense, as the classifier learns to separate the real signal from the injected noise.

Table 1. Empirical Adversary Advantage per Scenario ($K = 4$, Microsoft SEAL backend, $n = 150$ sessions per class)

Scenario	Best Model	$\hat{p}_{\mathsf{acc}}$	$\widehat{\mathrm{Adv}}(\mathcal{A})$
Type-specific circuits	Random Forest	1.000	0.750
Uniform circuit (SEAL)	SVM (RBF)	0.420	0.170
Adversarial masking	Gradient Boost	0.854	0.604

5.1 Per-Class Performance Analysis

Table 2 reports per-class precision, recall, and F1-score for the uniform circuit scenario under the best model (SVM RBF).

Table 2. Per-Class Performance—Uniform Circuit, SVM (RBF)

Class	Precision	Recall	F1	Support
Financial	0.507	0.720	0.595	150
Medical	0.559	0.660	0.606	150
Text	0.647	0.427	0.514	150
Binary	0.487	0.360	0.414	150
Macro avg	0.550	0.542	0.532	600

The per-class results reveal an asymmetry between precision and recall that has a direct cryptographic interpretation. Financial data achieves high recall (72.0%) but low precision (50.7%): the classifier correctly identifies most financial sessions, but also misclassifies many Text and Binary sessions as Financial. This is consistent with the data-noise coupling analysis: the large magnitude of financial data produces a high noise growth rate under multiplication that is easily recognized, but small-magnitude data types can occasionally produce similar noise trajectories when their values cluster near the upper end of their respective ranges.

Text data shows the inverse pattern: high precision (64.7%) but low recall (42.7%). The classifier is conservative in assigning the Text label—when it does, it is usually correct—but it frequently misclassifies Text sessions as Financial due to the magnitude overlap discussed above.

5.2 Feature Importance Analysis

Table 3 reports the top-8 most informative features under the Gradient Boosting classifier in the uniform circuit scenario, ranked by mean decrease in impurity.

The dominance of $\bar{t}_{\mathsf{mul}}$ confirms the data-noise coupling hypothesis: multiplication timing is directly influenced by the magnitude of the operands through the

Table 3. Top-8 Feature Importances—Gradient Boosting, Uniform Circuit

Rank	Feature	Importance
1	$\bar{t}_{\mathsf{mul}}$ (mean multiplication time)	0.187
2	$\Delta\ell$ (levels consumed)	0.143
3	$\widetilde{\mu}_4$ (timing kurtosis)	0.121
4	σ_t (timing std deviation)	0.098
5	$sz_{\max}$ (max ciphertext size)	0.087
6	$\bar{t}_{op}$ (mean operation time)	0.076
7	$\widetilde{\mu}_3$ (timing skewness)	0.064
8	Δsz (size growth)	0.059

rescaling and relinearization steps, which are data-dependent in their numerical conditioning. The high importance of $\Delta\ell$ reflects the fact that even under the same circuit, floating-point rounding during rescaling produces slightly different modulus chain consumption across data types. The significance of timing shape features ($\widetilde{\mu}_4$, $\widetilde{\mu}_3$) suggests that the *distribution* of per-operation timings—not only their mean—carries exploitable information about the data nature.

6 Confusion Matrix Analysis and Leakage Topology

Table 4 presents the confusion matrix obtained under the uniform circuit scenario with Microsoft SEAL (600 total samples, 150 per class).

Table 4. Confusion Matrix—Uniform Circuit, Microsoft SEAL ($K = 4$, $n = 150$ per class)

True\Pred.	Fin.	Med.	Text	Bin.
Financial	**108**	17	10	15
Medical	19	**99**	11	21
Text	46	19	**64**	21
Binary	40	42	14	**54**

The confusion matrix reveals the *leakage topology* of the attack—that is, which pairs of data natures are most and least distinguishable under a uniform homomorphic circuit.

Well-separated categories: Financial and Medical data are the most reliably identified, achieving per-class recall of $108/150 = 72.0\%$ and $99/150 = 66.0\%$, respectively. This is consistent with the data-noise coupling mechanism in

Eq. (4): financial data follows a log-normal distribution with large magnitudes, producing a systematically higher noise growth rate under multiplication, while medical data is constrained to physiologically bounded ranges with near-normal distribution, yielding a distinct and more moderate noise profile.

Ambiguous categories: Text and Binary data exhibit significantly lower recall ($64/150 = 42.7\%$ and $54/150 = 36.0\%$, respectively), with substantial confusion between each other and with the Financial class. Text embeddings are sparse and bounded in $[-1, 1]$, while binary data consists of values near $\{0, 1\}$. After CKKS encoding at scale $\Delta = 2^{40}$, both data types produce relatively small polynomial coefficient magnitudes, making their multiplicative noise growth profiles statistically similar and, in some cases, indistinguishable from rescaled financial data.

Implications for privacy: The leakage topology has a direct security interpretation: under a uniform circuit, Text and Binary data are *naturally more opaque* than Financial and Medical data, because their noise signatures overlap more. This suggests that data types whose distributions produce similar polynomial magnitude profiles enjoy stronger semantic privacy even in the absence of explicit countermeasures.

Overfitting gap: The gap between training accuracy (54.2%) and cross--validated accuracy (42.0%) indicates moderate overfitting, suggesting that the leakage signal is genuine but weak under the uniform circuit. The classifier learns real patterns in the noise metadata, but with limited generalization capacity, consistent with a scenario where the residual leakage is a second-order effect of data-noise coupling rather than a dominant structural signal.

7 Semantic Privacy: Formal Conditions and Countermeasures

Definition 5 (Semantic Privacy). *A CKKS-based communication channel is* semantically private *with respect to data nature if and only if*

$$\forall\, \mathcal{A}, \quad \mathrm{Adv}(\mathcal{A}) \;\le\; \mathrm{negl}(\lambda), \tag{9}$$

where λ is the security parameter and $\mathrm{negl}(\cdot)$ *denotes a negligible function.*

Theorem 1 (Privacy Violation under Type-Specific Circuits). *When distinct homomorphic circuits are used for different data natures, condition Eq. (9) is violated:*

$$\exists\, \mathcal{A}: \quad \mathrm{Adv}(\mathcal{A}) \gg \mathrm{negl}(\lambda). \tag{10}$$

Proposition 1 (Circuit Uniformization as Countermeasure). *If all data types are processed through an identical homomorphic operation sequence $\mathcal{O}^*$, then*

$$P(\varepsilon \mid \mathcal{O}^*, d_i) \;\approx\; P(\varepsilon \mid \mathcal{O}^*, d_j) \quad \forall\, i \neq j, \tag{11}$$

reducing $\mathrm{Adv}(\mathcal{A})$ *substantially. Empirically, circuit uniformization reduces the adversary advantage from* $\widehat{\mathrm{Adv}} = 0.750$ *to* $\widehat{\mathrm{Adv}} = 0.170$ *(Microsoft SEAL,* $K = 4$*), confirming partial but not complete mitigation. The residual advantage is attributable to the data-noise coupling in Eq.* (4)*, which persists even under a fixed operation sequence.*

7.1 Countermeasure Analysis

We analyze four countermeasures at increasing levels of architectural intervention, evaluating each against both the behavioral and distributional leakage components identified in this work.

C1—Dummy Operation Injection: The defender injects k random dum--my operations after each real computation, as modeled in Scenario 3. Our results show $\widehat{\mathrm{Adv}} = 0.604$ under $k = 4$ dummy operations, demonstrating that this approach is *insufficient*. The ML classifier learns to discount the noise introduced by dummy operations because their timing distribution differs statistically from real operations (dummy operations use randomly chosen parameters, whereas real operations on structured data produce clustered timing profiles). Effective dummy operation injection would require operands drawn from the same distribution as the real data, defeating the purpose of the defense.

C2—Circuit Uniformization: All data types are forced through a canonical circuit $\mathcal{O}^*$ with fixed operation count, type sequence, and depth. This is the primary countermeasure proposed in this work. It reduces $\widehat{\mathrm{Adv}}$ from 0.750 to 0.170, eliminating the behavioral leakage component while leaving residual distributional leakage. The residual can be further reduced by combining C2 with C3.

C3—Magnitude Normalization: Before encryption, plaintext values are normalized to a fixed range (e.g., $[0, 1]$) via a domain-specific affine transformation. This directly targets the data-noise coupling term $\|\Delta \cdot m\|_\infty$ in Eq. (4), reducing the variance in noise growth across data types under multiplication. Normalization is already standard practice in privacy-preserving ML pipelines and introduces no computational overhead in CKKS. The trade-off is that the normalization parameters themselves (min, max, or mean and variance) may leak information and must be kept secret or computed via secure aggregation.

C4—Noise Flooding: The defender adds a uniformly random plaintext vector $r \sim \mathcal{U}([-R, R]^{n/2})$ with $R \gg \|m\|_\infty$ before encryption, effectively drowning the data-dependent noise signature. This provides the strongest distributional privacy guarantee but at significant precision cost: the output of any homomorphic computation over the flooded ciphertext is dominated by r, making post-computation decoding unreliable unless r is subtracted after decryption. Noise flooding is therefore suitable only for protocols where the defended party can subtract the flooding term after decryption, such as two-party secure computation with a trusted result aggregator.

Table 5 summarizes the four countermeasures along the dimensions of effectiveness, computational overhead, and applicability.

Table 5. Countermeasure Comparison

Countermeasure	Targets	Overhead	Residual Adv.
C1: Dummy ops	Behavioral	Low	High (0.604)
C2: Uniformization	Behavioral	Medium	Low (0.170)
C3: Normalization	Distributional	None	Partial*
C2+C3: Combined	Both	Medium	Minimal*
C4: Noise flooding	Both	High	Negligible*

* Residual advantage estimated theoretically; no experimental validation was performed.

7.2 Formal Overhead Analysis of Circuit Uniformization

Let $\mathcal{O}_d = (op_1^d, \ldots, op_{T_d}^d)$ denote the *natural circuit* for data type d, and $\mathcal{O}^*$ the canonical uniform circuit with $T^* = \max_d T_d$ operations and depth $L^* = \max_d L_d$.

Definition 6 (Circuit Overhead). *The computational overhead of circuit uniformization for data type d is:*

$$\rho(d) = \frac{T^*}{T_d} \geq 1. \tag{12}$$

Let c_{mul}, c_{add}, c_{rot} denote per-operation costs in NTT evaluations, where $c_{\mathsf{mul}} \gg c_{\mathsf{add}} \approx c_{\mathsf{rot}}$ since multiplication requires key-switching [2]. The total latency of a circuit $\mathcal{O}$ is:

$$\mathcal{L}(\mathcal{O}) = N_{\mathsf{mul}} \cdot c_{\mathsf{mul}} + N_{\mathsf{add}} \cdot c_{\mathsf{add}} + N_{\mathsf{rot}} \cdot c_{\mathsf{rot}}, \tag{13}$$

and the latency overhead of uniformization for type d is:

$$\Delta\mathcal{L}(d) = (L^* - L_d) \cdot c_{\mathsf{mul}} + \Delta N_{\mathsf{add/rot}}(d) \cdot c_{\mathsf{add}}, \tag{14}$$

where $c_{\mathsf{mul}} \approx 10 \cdot c_{\mathsf{add}}$ [3], so the multiplicative depth mismatch $(L^* - L_d)$ dominates.

Proposition 2 (Overhead Bound). *The worst-case latency overhead of circuit uniformization is:*

$$\max_d \Delta\mathcal{L}(d) \leq (L^* - L_{\min}) \cdot c_{\mathsf{mul}}, \tag{15}$$

where $L_{\min} = \min_d L_d$. For our setup ($L^* = 2$, $L_{\min} = 1$), this corresponds to one additional multiplication per session, representing 15% *to* 25% *additional latency.*

The overhead is bounded and predictable, making circuit uniformization practical for real deployments. Formalizing the selection of $\mathcal{O}^*$ that minimizes $\max_d \rho(d)$ subject to $\widehat{\mathrm{Adv}}(\mathcal{A}) \leq \epsilon$ is identified as a direction for future work.

8 Conclusion

This work investigated whether a passive adversary, with no access to secret keys or plaintext, can infer the semantic nature of data transmitted over a CKKS-based homomorphic encryption channel by observing noise metadata alone. The results yield a clear and nuanced answer. Leakage is primarily behavioral: under type-specific circuits, the adversary achieves $\widehat{\mathrm{Adv}} = 0.750$; under a uniform circuit, this drops to $\widehat{\mathrm{Adv}} = 0.170$, with residual leakage concentrated in data types whose magnitude distributions produce similar polynomial coefficient profiles after CKKS encoding, particularly Text and Binary categories. The dominant leakage vector is the computational signature of the circuit, not the intrinsic statistical properties of the data.

Circuit uniformization is an effective countermeasure against behavioral leakage, reducing the adversarial advantage substantially at a bounded computational cost of approximately 15 to 25% additional latency. Combined with magnitude normalization (C3), it reduces leakage to minimal levels. Noise flooding (C4) offers the strongest theoretical guarantee but is suitable only for protocols with trusted result aggregation. These results reframe the privacy analysis of homomorphic encryption deployments: ciphertext security is necessary but not sufficient for practical privacy. Semantic privacy requires an additional architectural commitment—the standardization of homomorphic circuits across all data domains. Formalizing the privacy-efficiency trade-off of circuit selection as a constrained optimization problem remains the primary direction for future work. Experimental validation of countermeasures C3, C4, and their combination C2+C3 is also identified as a direct direction for future work.

Acknowledgments. The authors thank LNCC and CAPES for their support and acknowledge the use of Claude (Anthropic) for language revision and literature organization; all scientific content and conclusions remain the authors' responsibility.

References

1. Cheon, J.H., Kim, A., Kim, M., Song, Y.: Homomorphic encryption for arithmetic of approximate numbers. In: Proceedings of International Conference om Theory Applications Cryptology Information Security (ASIACRYPT), Hong Kong, China, pp. 409–437 (2017)
2. Brakerski, Z., Gentry, C., Vaikuntanathan, V.: Leveled) fully homomorphic encryption without bootstrapping. In: Proceedings of 3rd Innovations Theoretical Computer Science Conference (ITCS), Cambridge, MA, USA, pp. 309–325 (2012)
3. Microsoft SEAL (release 4.1), Microsoft Research, Redmond, WA, USA (2023). https://github.com/microsoft/SEAL

4. Li, B., Micciancio, D.: On the security of homomorphic encryption on approximate numbers. In: Canteaut, A., Standaert, F.-X. (eds.) EUROCRYPT 2021. LNCS, vol. 12696, pp. 648–677. Springer, Cham (2021). https://doi.org/10.1007/978-3-030-77870-5_23
5. Cheon, J.H., et al.: Attacks against the IND-CPAD security of exact FHE schemes. In: Proceedings of ACM SIGSAC Conference on Computer Communication Security (CCS), Salt Lake City, UT, USA (2024)
6. Alexandru, A., et al.: Application-aware approximate homomorphic encryption: configuring FHE for practical use. IACR Cryptol. ePrint Arch. (2026)
7. Aydin, F., Aysu, A.: Leaking secrets in homomorphic encryption with side-channel attacks. J. Cryptogr. Eng. (2024)
8. Xu, Z., et al.: Magnifying side-channel leakage of lattice-based cryptosystems with chosen ciphertexts: the case study of Kyber. IEEE Trans. Comput. **71**(9), 2163–2176 (2022)
9. Sim, B.-Y., et al.: Chosen-ciphertext clustering attack on CRYSTALS-KYBER using the side-channel leakage of Barrett reduction. IEEE Internet Things J. **9**(23) (2022)
10. Ravi, P., et al.: Generic side-channel attacks on CCA-secure lattice-based PKE and KEMs. IACR Trans. Cryptogr. Hardw. Embedded Syst. **2020**(3), 307–335 (2020)
11. Ghaleb, B., Buchanan, W.: Side channel analysis in homomorphic encryption. arXiv preprint arXiv:2505.11058 (2025)
12. Lou, X., et al.: A survey of microarchitectural side-channel vulnerabilities, attacks, and defenses in cryptography. ACM Comput. Surv. **54**(6), 1–37 (2021)
13. Picek, S., et al.: SoK: deep learning-based physical side-channel analysis. ACM Comput. Surv. **55**(11), 1–35 (2022)
14. Randolph, M., Diehl, W.: Power side-channel attack analysis: a review of 20 years of study for the layman. Cryptography **4**(15) (2020)
15. Wu, L., et al.: Plaintext-based side-channel collision attack. IACR Commun. Cryptol. (2024)
16. Wu, L., et al.: Weakly profiling side-channel analysis. IACR Trans. Cryptogr. Hardw. Embedded Syst. (2024)
17. Kou, X., et al.: Multi-modal side-channel analysis based on isometric compression and combined clustering. Symmetry **17** (2025)
18. Kocher, P.: Timing attacks on implementations of Diffie-Hellman, RSA, DSS, and other systems. In: Proceedings of Advances in Cryptology (CRYPTO), Santa Barbara, CA, USA, pp. 104–113 (1996)

Scaling Down Hallucinations: Mitigation Strategies for Compact LLMs

Salef Gabriel Gamberini Silva(✉) and Renato Porfirio Ishii

FACOM, Universidade Federal de Mato Grosso do Sul, Cidade Universitária, Campo Grande, MS 79070-900, Brazil
sgleft@gmail.com

Abstract. The deployment of generative artificial intelligence on consumer hardware is substantially constrained by the tendency of smaller architectures to hallucinate unfaithful or factually incorrect content. This study investigates and categorizes contemporary mitigation strategies through a systematic literature review, classifying them into four distinct groups comprising Model Optimization, Inference and Output Enhancement, External Knowledge and Interaction, and Latent Space Intervention. After applying reproducibility and computational feasibility criteria, eight representative techniques (including Shadow-FT, DoLa, REPLUG, and ITI) were selected for experimental analysis on two representative small language models, Llama-3.2-3B and Qwen3-4B. Evaluations using deterministic reasoning, generative factuality, and summarization benchmarks revealed variable performance across the two models. Specifically, REPLUG was the strongest stabilizer for the tested Qwen3-4B configuration, with no drift events observed in this evaluation. Meanwhile, ITI and Hermes 3 achieved the best results in generative truthfulness for the standard baseline with gains exceeding 30% points, and DoLa demonstrated consistent improvements in source faithfulness. Furthermore, empirical results indicate that mitigation effectiveness is heavily contingent on the interaction between the method and the underlying model. For instance, retrieval acted as a stabilizer for the dual-mode architecture but introduced distractor sensitivity in the standard instruct counterpart. Consequently, in the tested 3B–4B configurations, no single method dominated across tasks, and reliable edge deployment requires matching mitigation strategies to model behavior and latency constraints.

Keywords: Large language models · hallucination mitigation · natural language processing · comparative analysis · machine learning

1 Introduction

Small open-weight Large Language Models (LLMs) in the 3B–4B parameter range enable private and offline execution on consumer hardware. However, their deployment in professional and safety-critical settings remains constrained by

O. Gervasi et al. (Eds.): ICCSA 2026, LNCS 16768, pp. 633–650, 2027.
https://doi.org/10.1007/978-3-032-30488-9_39

hallucination. In this work, hallucination is treated as both an extrinsic failure, where the model fabricates facts unsupported by world knowledge, and an intrinsic failure, where the output contradicts a provided source.

The consequences of such failures can be extreme in high-stakes domains. In healthcare, models have been documented producing incorrect diagnostic criteria and fabricated citations [10,17]. In legal practice, generative models have already produced non-existent case citations yielding professional and judicial repercussions [6], reinforcing the need for reliability prior to widespread adoption.

While the literature proposes a variety of strategies designed to mitigate hallucination, evidence remains fragmented for the edge-feasible regime. Existing evaluations typically target large proprietary models, or study them in isolation, raising the question of what strategies remain effective under the constrained compute and representational capacity of small models. This limitation is particularly consequential because the behavior of different model families under identical mitigation techniques may vary widely, not merely in the magnitude of improvement, but also in architectural stability under stochastic decoding.

This study addresses this gap by building a systematic benchmark targeted specifically at the 3B–4B parameter class. A systematic literature review spanning 2021–2025 is conducted and reproducible, computationally feasible techniques are organized into four categories, referred to as Model Optimization, Inference and Output Enhancement, External Knowledge and Interaction, and Latent Space Intervention. Eight representative techniques are reproduced under a unified protocol and evaluated on two small language models, Llama-3.2-3B and Qwen3-4B, selected because they exhibit different baseline stability profiles under stochastic decoding. The evaluation spans deterministic reasoning and domain knowledge (ARC, OAB), generative factuality (TruthfulQA, NQ-Open), and source-faithful summarization (CNN/DailyMail) with the inclusion of paired bootstrap resampling and multi-run stochastic evaluation where applicable.

The empirical findings indicate that mitigation effectiveness is strongly conditioned by task structure and by the interaction between the method and the model under evaluation. In the tested setting, retrieval techniques were shown to act as a stabilizer for Qwen3-4B by eliminating observed instruction drift events (in which the model strays away from the original task) and substantially improving source faithfulness in summarization; in contrast, the same category of mitigation introduced distractors for Llama-3.2-3B on open-domain fact retrieval. Model optimization and latent-space interventions provided complementary benefits where supervised fine-tuning and inference-time steering yielded the largest improvements in generative truthfulness for Llama-3.2-3B, exceeding 30% points on TruthfulQA. Separately, inference-time logit shaping for Qwen3-4b produced consistent improvements in source faithfulness.

The contribution of this work is a reproducible comparative framework for the small-model regime that bridges taxonomic categorization and empirical performance under resource constraints. By contrasting two compact language models that exhibit distinct empirical stability characteristics, the study provides configuration-level evidence for selecting mitigation strategies according to retrieval sensitivity, deployment cost, and observed stability.

Structurally, this work is organized as follows: Sect. 2 reviews related work concerning hallucination mitigation including the operational directions of modifying decoding dynamics and supplementing generation with retrieved evidence; Sect. 3 details the methodology, outlining the systematic literature review process, the model baselines, and the evaluation protocol; Sect. 4 presents the experimental results across deterministic reasoning, generative factuality, and source faithfulness benchmarks; Sect. 5 discusses the empirical findings, focusing on computational efficiency and deployment trade-offs, while also addressing the study's limitations; Sect. 6 concludes the study and indicates directions for future investigation.

2 Related Work

Recent work on hallucination mitigation has developed along two broad operational directions: modifying the model or its decoding dynamics, and supplementing generation with retrieved evidence or extended context. Within this literature, current comparisons focus on the relative utility of parametric adaptation, retrieval quality, and inference-time controls, as well as on the trade-off between factual gains and computational overhead.

2.1 Fine-Tuning vs. Retrieval

A central design choice in hallucination mitigation is whether factuality should be improved by internalizing domain behavior through parameter updates or by conditioning generation on external evidence. Ovadia et al. [18] reported that fine-tuning can adapt stylistic behavior effectively while remaining less reliable at correcting factual errors, whereas retrieval-based methods often perform better on knowledge-intensive tasks. These findings do not make retrieval universally superior, but they do motivate treating external evidence as a strong baseline whenever knowledge freshness and factual grounding are central.

2.2 Sensitivity of Retrieval Systems

Although retrieval augmentation is often effective, its benefits depend strongly on the quality and presentation of the retrieved context. Cuconasu et al. [3] showed that irrelevant or weakly ranked passages can degrade generation, indicating that more context is not necessarily better. This shifts attention from retrieval alone to the alignment between the retrieved evidence, ranking quality, and the model's ability to use that evidence under finite context budgets.

2.3 Inference-Time Optimization

A separate line of work investigates mitigation at decoding time rather than through external knowledge or parameter updates. Li et al. [13] introduced Contrastive Decoding, arguing that hallucinations can emerge when token selection is dominated by the model prior. By contrasting a stronger model with a weaker or less context-sensitive baseline during generation, their framework suppresses tokens that are fluent yet weakly supported. This perspective recasts hallucination mitigation as a decoding-control problem rather than exclusively a training problem.

2.4 The Efficiency Trade-Off

Despite the proliferation of mitigation techniques, computational overhead is often under-reported relative to factual gains. Surveys on efficient LLM inference [21] note that iterative sampling, long retrieved contexts, and ensemble-like decoding can introduce latency and memory costs that are acceptable in server settings but problematic for on-device use. This matters especially for Small Language Models (SLMs), where limited capacity and narrower attention budgets can change not only the magnitude of improvement but also the failure mode induced by a mitigation strategy. The present study therefore focuses on the 3B–4B regime and evaluates methods as deployable configurations rather than assuming direct transfer from much larger backbones.

Consequently, a lack of systematic evaluation remains regarding the transferability of these methods to **Small Language Models (SLMs)**. While the theoretical efficacy of contrastive decoding or retrieval augmentation is well-documented on hyperscale architectures (e.g., Llama-2-70B), it remains an open question how these techniques interact with the compressed feature spaces and limited attention heads of 3B–4B parameter models.

3 Methodology

This section details the systematic framework employed to identify, categorize, and evaluate hallucination mitigation strategies. The experimental design is strictly confined to the 3B to 4B parameter range to address the specific computational constraints of edge deployment. By prioritizing architectures amenable to local execution on consumer-grade hardware, this study evaluates the trade-off between hallucination suppression and the resource efficiency required for non-server environments.

3.1 Scope and Selection Criteria

To ensure representative coverage of the state of the art, a systematic literature review done according to the guidance of Kitchenham and Charters [8]. The search targeted studies that were published from 2021 through 2025 and followed a PICOC (Population, Intervention, Comparison, Outcome and Context) framework to delimit scope. Jointly, candidate identification and feasibility screening were carried out jointly across arXiv, GitHub, and Hugging Face. Where arXiv was used for paper discovery, GitHub for implementation discovery and reproducibility checks, and Hugging Face for model-lineage tracing, dataset discovery, and compatibility verification for the selected backbones. Backward and forward citation chaining were used to help minimize bias due to keywords. The screening process was completed in December 2025.

From an initial corpus of 216 candidate studies on hallucination mitigation, methods were retained only if they addressed textual generation, were published between 2021 and 2025, provided accessible open-source implementations, contained sufficient methodological detail for reproduction, and remained feasible in the 3B–4B setting. Multimodal approaches, proprietary API-dependent methods, and techniques lacking usable implementations were excluded, yielding eight methods distributed across four canonical categories (Table 1).

Table 1. Search sources and query templates used in the literature review (screening completed December 2025).

Source	Query template and filters
arXiv	`(all:"LLM" AND (ti:"hallucination" OR ti:"hallucinating" OR ti:"factuality" OR ti:"factualness") AND NOT (ti:"vision" OR ti:"visual" OR ti:"multimodal" OR ti:"multi-modal" OR ti:"MLLM" OR ti:"LMM" OR ti:"VLM" OR ti:"image" OR ti:"video"))`. Results were sorted by submission date and filtered to years 2021–2025 during collection.
GitHub	Repository discovery and reproducibility validation were performed using keyword searches aligned with the primary arXiv terms and with method-name searches for shortlisted techniques (e.g., `hallucination`, `factuality`, `faithfulness`, `decoding`, `retrieval`/`RAG`, `steering`/`intervention`, and method identifiers such as `DoLa`, `REPLUG`, `ITI`).
Hugging Face	Model discovery and verification were performed by traversing model trees and base-model lineage for the selected backbones, using the platform metadata when available (e.g., base model fields and linked derivatives) to locate compatible instruct variants and community releases. Dataset repositories were also consulted to identify the corpora used for retrieval and evaluation.

A single Boolean template could not be transferred uniformly across all three sources because each platform exposes different search behavior and metadata. Candidate identification and feasibility screening were therefore conducted jointly across arXiv, GitHub, and Hugging Face, with GitHub and Hugging Face contributing directly to implementation discovery, compatibility checks, and reproducibility assessment.

3.2 Model Baselines

The evaluation compares two well-established small language models from the contemporary open-weight ecosystem. Rather than relying on a rigid architectural dichotomy, it contrasts models with distinct training and post-training profiles under a common evaluation protocol.

- **Llama-3.2-3B:** This model serves as a conventional instruct-tuned baseline for small-model evaluation. It is included to assess how mitigation strategies interact with a compact model whose behavior is shaped by standard pre-training followed by alignment-oriented post-training.
- **Qwen3-4B:** This model provides a contrasting small-model baseline from the Qwen3 family. It is included to assess whether the same mitigation strategies behave differently on a model with a distinct post-training recipe and response profile. In all experiments reported here, Qwen3-4B was evaluated in its non-thinking configuration.

3.3 Mitigation Configurations

To keep the benchmark grounded in realistic deployment settings, we instantiate one representative technique for each backbone within each mitigation category. The objective is not to provide a symmetric method-by-method comparison, but rather to compare deployable configurations under a common evaluation protocol.

This design reflects the practical constraint that several mitigation methods are mature only within particular implementation stacks. Accordingly, our conclusions are drawn at the level of the evaluated configurations and the trends observed across architectures, rather than as universal claims about an entire mitigation category.

Model Optimization. Model optimization approaches reduce hallucinations by updating parameters during fine-tuning or continued training, aiming to internalize more reliable generation behavior beyond transient inference-time controls.

- **Shadow-FT (Qwen3-4B):** Direct fine-tuning can degrade the behavior of already aligned small models when useful capabilities are overwritten during adaptation. To mitigate this risk, Shadow-FT [22] is employed. This method uses the unaligned base model as a proxy learner, computes weight updates (ΔW) on malleable parameters, and grafts them onto the instruct variant in order to preserve the model's pre-existing alignment.
- **Hermes 3 Strategy (Llama-3.2-3B):** For Llama-3.2-3B, the Hermes 3 methodology [20] is evaluated as a benchmark for rigorous Supervised Fine-Tuning (SFT). This approach uses aggressive data filtering and synthetic reasoning tasks (e.g., <SCRATCHPAD> tokens) to condition the model toward more reliable generation behavior during training.

Inference and Output Enhancement. Inference-time enhancements reshape token logits during decoding by contrasting context-conditioned predictions with a context-free prior, downweighting tokens that are plausible under the prior but unsupported by evidence.

- **DoLa (Qwen3-4B):** Decoding by Contrasting Layers (DoLa) [1] contrasts final-layer logits against earlier-layer logits during generation, attenuating tokens that become plausible due to premature semantic drift.
- **Context-Aware Decoding (Llama-3.2-3B):** CAD [19] is implemented by combining logits from a context prompt and a no-context prompt using $\ell_{\text{CAD}} = (1+\alpha)\ell_{\text{ctx}} - \alpha\ell_{\text{nc}}$ with default $\alpha = 0.5$. The no-context input is instantiated as a BOS or empty prompt unless a negative prompt is specified.

External Knowledge and Interaction. External evidence is incorporated at inference time to mitigate limitations of parametric memory. Task-specific corpora are sourced from Hugging Face and indexed for retrieval: `pszemraj/simple_wikipedia_LM` for NQ-Open and TruthfulQA; `allenai/sciq` for ARC; and a curated collection of ten Brazilian legal codes (e.g., Constitution, Civil Code, Penal Code) for OAB-style questions. For CNN/Daily Mail summarization, retrieval is restricted to the input article only (no external corpus).

- **REPLUG (Qwen3-4B):** For Qwen3-4B, $k = 5$ evidence units are retrieved per query (BM25 over a tokenized corpus in the provided implementation). The model is evaluated with independent forward passes conditioned on each retrieved unit, and aggregation is performed across units using a score-combination rule. In log-likelihood based evaluation, the best (max) continuation score across the k contexts is used; in OAB multiple-choice evaluation, the probabilities of the option tokens (A/B/C/D) are averaged across the k contexts. Prompts are truncated to a maximum length of 2048 tokens.
- **Task-Dependent RAG (Llama-3.2-3B):** For Llama-3.2-3B, external retrieval is implemented as a task-dependent RAG configuration with two task-specific variants. In reasoning and QA settings, a naive concatenative variant uses `BAAI/bge-large-en-v1.5` embeddings with L2 normalization and a FAISS `IndexFlatIP` GPU index, retrieves the top-k passages with $k = 3$, filters by similarity threshold 0.50, and "prepends" the retained passages as reference material before the original query. Teacher-forced log-likelihood is then computed on the target conditioned on the query plus retrieved evidence. In summarization, an iterative source-confined variant restricts retrieval to the source document itself and uses retrieval only to bias content selection without introducing external knowledge. In the results tables, these variants are reported as Naive RAG and Iterative RAG, respectively.

Latent Space Intervention. Latent-space interventions modify intermediate activations during the forward pass by adding targeted offsets to internal representations, biasing generation toward directions associated with truthfulness without updating model weights.

- **Gaussian Steering (Qwen3-4B):** Steering is implemented with forward hooks on transformer blocks. Layer-specific control directions loaded from a serialized vector file are added to the block output with a Gaussian depth schedule centered at $\mu = 18$. For block index i, the coefficient is $\texttt{strength}\cdot\exp\left(-\frac{(i-\mu)^2}{2\sigma^2}\right)$, applying only to layers with an associated direction and skipping coefficients below 10^{-4}.
- **Inference-Time Intervention (Llama-3.2-3B):** ITI [12] is instantiated by training linear probes over attention-head activations using TruthfulQA multiple-choice features. At inference, activations of the top-K heads with $K = 48$ are shifted along the probe-identified truthful directions with intervention strength $\alpha = 15$.

3.4 Evaluation Instruments

The assessment protocol employs a diverse suite of benchmarks to evaluate reasoning, factuality, and summarization quality.

Deterministic Reasoning. For tasks requiring rigorous logic, log-likelihood evaluation is performed to eliminate sampling variance.

- **ARC-Challenge:** Selected to assess the model's ability to perform complex reasoning in scientific contexts beyond superficial pattern matching [2].
- **OAB Exam:** A dataset derived from the Brazilian Bar Exam [5] is included to evaluate performance in a non-English (Portuguese) professional context. This tests the mitigation methods' ability to handle specialized legal terminology and maintain cross-lingual logical consistency.

Generative Factuality.

- **TruthfulQA:** This benchmark is critical for quantifying "imitative falsehoods" [15]. The generative track is used to assess the model's resistance to common misconceptions, with outputs graded by a specialized fine-tuned judge model.
- **NQ-Open:** To evaluate precise information retrieval, NQ-Open [11] is employed in a 5-shot in-context learning setting. Performance is measured via Exact Match (EM) against human-annotated ground truths.

Summarization Quality. For long-form generation, a stratified sample ($N = 1{,}000$) of the **CNN/Daily Mail** test set is utilized. Evaluation relies on two complementary metrics:

- **ROUGE-L:** Captures structural fidelity and longest common subsequences [14].

- **BERTScore (F1):** Addresses the limitations of lexical overlap by measuring semantic similarity via contextualized embeddings [23]. The F1 measure is reported exclusively to balance the penalization of hallucinations (precision) with the retention of critical details (recall).

3.5 Statistical Analysis

To quantify performance differences, a paired statistical protocol was adopted at the instance level.

Significance Testing. Traditional parametric tests assume normally distributed errors, an assumption frequently violated in NLP evaluation [4]. Consequently, **Paired Bootstrap Resampling** [9] was adopted with $B = 10{,}000$ resamples. For deterministic benchmarks (ARC and OAB), each evaluation item constitutes one paired observation between a mitigated model and its corresponding backbone baseline. Significance is reported when the 95% confidence interval of the paired performance difference excludes zero.

Stochastic Stability. For generative benchmarks (TruthfulQA, NQ-Open, CNN/DM), single-pass evaluation is insufficient because of decoding stochasticity. Following the motivation of Holtzman et al. [7], $K = 5$ independent inference runs were conducted for each instance using architecture-specific sampling parameters. The per-instance score was defined as the mean over the K runs, $\bar{S}_i$, and significance testing was then applied to the vector of these per-instance means. This preserves the paired structure while reducing variance induced by decoding randomness.

4 Results

Evaluating hallucination mitigation approaches against the benchmarks defined in Sect. 3 reveals distinct performance trade-offs. The following analysis compares these methods quantitatively, providing empirical evidence for their potential and limitations in reducing LLM hallucinations.

4.1 Execution Environment

Experiments were benchmarked on NVIDIA A100 GPUs using the Hugging Face `transformers` library. This setup was chosen to accelerate repeated runs and standardize evaluation, not because the selected methods depend on datacenter-only hardware. The evaluated models remain in the 3B–4B range and the selected configurations were also verified to execute on consumer-grade hardware, so the A100 should be understood as a convenient benchmarking platform rather than as a deployment requirement. For consistency, `lm-evaluation-harness` was used for ARC and NQ-Open, custom scripts were used for OAB and BERTScore, and TruthfulQA was evaluated with its specialized generative judge. Deterministic benchmarks (ARC and OAB) were run once, whereas stochastic benchmarks (TruthfulQA, NQ-Open, and CNN/DailyMail) were averaged over five independent runs ($K = 5$) to reduce decoding variance.

Table 2. Reasoning and Domain Knowledge Performance. Comparison of reasoning (ARC) and legal domain knowledge (OAB). Best results per model are **highlighted**. (*: 95% paired bootstrap CI excludes zero in favor of the method, †: 95% paired bootstrap CI excludes zero in favor of the baseline).

Method	ARC Challenge	ARC Easy	OAB (Legal)
Qwen3-4B			
Baseline	0.5392	0.7816	0.2742
Shadow-FT	0.5341	0.7555†	0.2656
DoLa	0.5427	0.7841	0.2796
REPLUG	0.5444	**0.7988***	**0.4014***
GCS (Steered)	**0.5589***	0.7891*	0.2810
Llama-3.2-3B			
Baseline	0.4266	0.7146	0.2837
Hermes 3	0.4283	0.7184	**0.3534***
CAD	**0.4889***	0.7193	0.2851
Naive RAG	0.4309	**0.7652***	0.3317*
ITI	0.4249	0.7433*	0.2873

4.2 Reasoning and Domain Knowledge

Table 2 illustrates the divergence between abstract logic (ARC) and domain-specific knowledge (OAB). Within Model Optimization, the Hermes 3 strategy significantly improved Llama-3.2-3B on OAB. Due to the predominantly English alignment data, this result suggests possible cross-lingual transfer to Portuguese legal reasoning, but does not establish language-independent factual subspaces. A similar but smaller pattern appears for ITI, which improves OAB despite being learned from English TruthfulQA features. Conversely, Shadow-FT reduced ARC-Easy for Qwen3-4B, indicating that weight grafting can trade off against zero-shot reasoning on simpler science questions.

Inference-time controls were sensitive to task structure. Context-Aware Decoding (CAD) produced the largest gain for Llama-3.2-3B on ARC-Challenge, consistent with the idea that subtracting prior-driven logits can help when shallow associations compete with compositional reasoning. DoLa, by contrast, produced only small changes for Qwen3-4B on the deterministic reasoning tasks, suggesting limited benefit in this setting rather than a general failure of layer-contrast methods.

Retrieval-based methods showed their clearest gains on OAB. For Qwen3-4B, REPLUG substantially improved legal-domain accuracy. For Llama-3.2-3B, Task-Dependent RAG (naive) improved OAB and ARC-Easy, but did not materially improve ARC-Challenge. These patterns suggest that retrieval is most effective when the target information is externally recoverable, whereas deductive items remain less responsive to added context. Finally, GCS improved Qwen3-4B across the reasoning benchmarks, suggesting that activation steering can provide gains without external evidence.

4.3 Generative Factuality

Table 3. Generative Factuality (Stochastic). Mean accuracy ± standard deviation across $K = 5$ independent runs. Best results per model are highlighted. Asterisk indicates that the 95% paired bootstrap CI excludes zero in favor of the method; dagger indicates that the 95% paired bootstrap CI excludes zero in favor of the baseline.

Method	NQ-Open (EM)	TruthfulQA (Gen)
QWEN3-4B		
Baseline	0.1454 ± 0.0020	0.6911 ± 0.0042
Shadow-FT	0.1511 ± 0.0024*	0.7028 ± 0.0069
DoLa	0.1502 ± 0.0029	0.7053 ± 0.0039
REPLUG	0.1405 ± 0.0020†	0.7266 ± 0.0055*
GCS (Steered)	0.1498 ± 0.0035*	0.7364 ± 0.0044*
LLAMA-3.2-3B		
Baseline	0.1739 ± 0.0044	0.2095 ± 0.0189
Hermes 3	0.1949 ± 0.0058*	0.5356 ± 0.0134*
CAD	0.1824 ± 0.0032*	0.2480 ± 0.0126*
Naive RAG	0.1214 ± 0.0052†	0.4196 ± 0.0104*
ITI	0.1967 ± 0.0051*	0.5302 ± 0.0119*

Table 3 highlights a fundamental disparity in model initialization. Hermes 3 improved Llama-3.2-3B on TruthfulQA by over 30% points. Given the weak factuality of the Llama baseline in this setting, this result is consistent with improved truthful generation under supervised fine-tuning. In contrast, Qwen3-4B began with high native factuality, so optimization gains are smaller but stable.

External knowledge methods present a trade-off. While Naive RAG improved TruthfulQA, it caused a significant degradation in NQ-Open for Llama-3.2-3B.

To determine whether this drop stems from over-reliance on noisy retrieval or from context window limitations, a qualitative audit of 50 RAG failures was conducted.

Context distraction is used as the umbrella label, and it most often manifests as entity contamination and position bias, with a smaller fraction attributable to window truncation.

Table 4. Qualitative RAG error modes for Llama-3.2-3B with Naive RAG on NQ-Open. Retrieved snippets are abbreviated. Underline marks the entity the model latched onto.

Query	Target	Distractor cue excerpt	RAG Output	Mode
who sings she's like the wind lyrics	Wendy Fraser	Wind It Up is a song by American singer Gwen Stefani, mention of Vanessa Williams appears in retrieved text	Vanessa Williams	Entity contamination
who are the hobbits in lord of the rings	Dominic Monaghan	Cast list begins with Elijah Wood as Frodo, later mentions Dominic Monaghan as Merry	Elijah Wood	Position bias [16]
what are the band members names of the rolling stones	Ronnie Wood	The band members were Mick Jagger, Keith Richards, Brian Jones, Bill Wyman, retrieved list omits later members	Mick Jagger, Keith Richards, Brian Jones, Bill Wyman	Incomplete evidence, truncation prone
when was the first mad max released	12 April 1979	Mad Max is a 1979 Australian action film, day and month missing	1979	Formatting under strict EM

Table 4 exhibits why NQ-Open can degrade under Naive RAG for a small model. When retrieval surfaces semantically proximal but off-target text the model often copies a salient named entity from the snippet. When the retrieved passage is long or "list-like", early entities can dominate attention and suppress later relevant mentions. When the retrieved snippet is incomplete or clipped to fit the budget, it becomes misleading evidence that the model treats as exhaustive. These patterns explain how Naive RAG can raise TruthfulQA when retrieval frequently contains directly usable evidence, yet hurt NQ-Open when retrieval noise and presentation effects dominate.

Latent-space interventions were among the more consistent methods in this setting. GCS improved Qwen3-4B across both benchmarks, and ITI approached the gains of Hermes 3 for Llama-3.2-3B. ITI modifies activations only at inference time, so these results suggest that useful truthfulness-related representations can sometimes be elicited without permanent weight updates.

4.4 Source Faithfulness

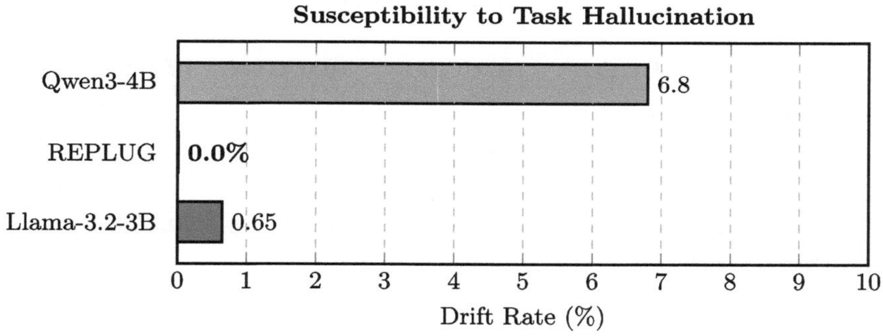

Fig. 1. Instruction drift rates under repeated non-deterministic decoding for CNN/DailyMail summarization ($N = 1000$ sources, $R = 5$ runs per source). Llama-3.2-3B is included as a stability reference. Qwen3-4B exhibits measurable drift, whereas REPLUG yields zero observed drift events in 5000 generations, implying a non-zero upper confidence bound under a naive Wilson approximation.

The assessment of source faithfulness (Table 5) indicates that mitigation effects depend strongly on baseline stability. Figure 1 reports instruction drift for the unmitigated Qwen3-4B, REPLUG-augmented Qwen3-4B, and Llama-3.2-3B as a stability reference rather than as a method-matched control. The unmitigated Qwen3-4B drifted in 6.80% of generations (340/5000). Under a naive independence approximation, the corresponding 95% Wilson interval is $[6.13, 7.53]$ percent. Given that the 5000 generated samples are obtained from $N = 1000$ distinct sources with $R = 5$ runs per source, the resulting interval should be regarded as descriptive and is likely to be optimistically narrow.

In the same setting, REPLUG produced zero observed drift events (0/5000), corresponding to 0.00% with a 95% Wilson upper bound of 0.08% under the same approximation. This pattern is consistent with REPLUG acting as a stabilizing mechanism for the tested Qwen3-4B configuration (although the zero observed drift rate should not be interpreted as a guarantee of zero drift in deployment). The ensemble over retrieved units constrains the decoding trajectory and reduces run-to-run variability.

Llama-3.2-3B showed high baseline stability (0.65% drift). In that context, Task-Dependent RAG (iterative) behaved less like a stabilizer and more like a content-selection bias. It reduced ROUGE-1 while improving BERTScore, suggesting a shift away from reference-like lexical phrasing toward semantically closer but stylistically less matched summaries.

Regarding inference enhancement, DoLa was effective for the less stable Qwen3-4B in this setting, yielding consistent improvements across the reported summarization metrics. This pattern is consistent with layer contrast helping suppress tokens associated with semantic drift during generation. Conversely,

Table 5. Source Faithfulness on CNN/DailyMail. Comparison of lexical (ROUGE) and semantic (BERTScore) alignment. Best methods per model are **highlighted**. (*: 95% paired bootstrap CI excludes zero in favor of the method, †: 95% paired bootstrap CI excludes zero in favor of the baseline).

	ROUGE-1	ROUGE-2	ROUGE-L	BERTScore (F1)
Qwen3-4B				
Baseline	0.2388 ± 0.0028	0.0818 ± 0.0018	0.1643 ± 0.0015	0.1704 ± 0.0041
DoLa	0.2617 ± 0.0008*	0.0877 ± 0.0007*	0.1748 ± 0.0004*	0.2074 ± 0.0008*
REPLUG	**0.2881** ± 0.0010*	**0.0975** ± 0.0004*	**0.1909** ± 0.0006*	**0.5863** ± 0.0003*
Shadow-FT	0.2329 ± 0.0006†	0.0795 ± 0.0005†	0.1547 ± 0.0006†	0.1834 ± 0.0011*
GCS (Steered)	0.2013 ± 0.0008†	0.0640 ± 0.0008†	0.1384 ± 0.0006†	0.1079 ± 0.0014†
Llama-3.2-3B				
Baseline	0.2799 ± 0.0101	0.1032 ± 0.0046	0.1929 ± 0.0063	0.5466 ± 0.0100
CAD	0.2193 ± 0.0019†	0.0705 ± 0.0015†	0.1731 ± 0.0018†	0.5183 ± 0.0019†
Hermes 3	0.2960 ± 0.0014*	0.1122 ± 0.0005*	0.1992 ± 0.0010*	0.5888 ± 0.0007*
ITI	**0.2991** ± 0.0015*	**0.1147** ± 0.0005*	**0.2023** ± 0.0012*	**0.5919** ± 0.0009*
Iterative RAG	0.2550 ± 0.0045†	0.0867 ± 0.0015†	0.1723 ± 0.0030†	0.5727 ± 0.0031*

CAD caused a significant regression for Llama-3.2-3B, including a 6.06-point drop in ROUGE-1, and the auxiliary length analysis is consistent with under-generation. Early termination rises to 19.2% as measured by EOS within the first 30 generated tokens, corresponding to the baseline 10th-percentile length. Outputs therefore shift toward shorter summaries with a mean of 67 and a median of 76 tokens, while hitting the 100-token cap remains rare at 1%. In this setting, logit subtraction appears to suppress continuation paths that would otherwise elaborate later source details. By contrast, Llama-3.2-3B responded positively to directional steering through Hermes 3 and ITI, suggesting that the more stable baseline benefited more from internal realignment than from stronger decoding constraints.

5 Discussion

The experimental results suggest that several factors must be considered when mitigating hallucinations within the 3B–4B parameter regime including how much model plasticity can be allowed while still maintaining stability with regard to training instructions. Beyond the raw accuracy metrics analyzed in the previous section, the viability of these methods for edge deployment depends heavily on computational scalability and model-specific interactions.

A critical factor for mobile implementation is the inference cost associated with each mitigation category. The results show that performance gains often come at the expense of latency.

Retrieval-based methods such as REPLUG demonstrate the highest computational overhead. Since the ensemble strategy requires processing multiple retrieved contexts, the decoding compute scales approximately linearly with the number of retrieved passages. This yields an approximate $\sim k\times$ model-compute multiplier for k retrieved contexts, with $k = 5$ implying up to $\sim 5\times$ the base decoding cost, in addition to retriever latency and the attention cost induced by longer prompts.

For smartphones, this overhead may be unsuitable for interactive use unless k is reduced, retrieval is cached, or REPLUG is reserved for high-risk or non-real-time queries. In contrast, Latent Space Interventions such as ITI and GCS offer a more favorable efficiency profile. These methods operate by modifying activation vectors during a single forward pass and therefore add only a small constant-factor overhead, remaining near-$1\times$ relative to baseline inference.

Inference-time decoding interventions further illustrate the cost spectrum. DoLa operates within a single forward pass with lightweight additional logit operations, whereas CAD requires both a context and a no-context computation and therefore incurs an approximate $\sim 2\times$ forward-pass overhead. For environments where response time is critical, activation-level steering and single-pass decoding controls provide more scalable mitigation than multi-context ensembling.

Deployment should therefore be model and latency specific. In the present experiments, Qwen3-4B exhibited higher plasticity together with substantially greater instruction drift, making external stabilization particularly useful despite its higher inference cost. In that setting, lightweight interventions alone were less reliable at preventing deviation into hallucinatory patterns. Conversely, Llama-3.2-3B showed stronger baseline stability but also greater sensitivity to irrelevant retrieved context. For that configuration, internal alignment techniques such as supervised fine-tuning or inference-time steering made better use of the existing stability without introducing additional distractors, which in turn makes them more suitable for latency-sensitive edge use than naive retrieval.

5.1 Limitations

Several constraints limit the generality of these findings.

The study relies on automated evaluation pipelines, which in turn introduce a degree of uncertainty into the resulting metrics. In particular, the TruthfulQA generative judge is itself a learned model and may encode preferences that only approximate factual robustness.

The compared mitigation strategies intervene at different stages, with some requiring training-time updates and others operating purely at inference. As a result, the experiments characterize realistic deployment options rather than a fully controlled comparison under identical training data and optimization budgets. The observed patterns should therefore be interpreted as configuration-level evidence, not as definitive rankings of mitigation categories.

In addition, the evaluation emphasizes atomic facts and short-horizon deductions in order to isolate hallucination behavior from longer context-based retention effects. However, for summarization, ROUGE and BERTScore measure lexical and semantic alignment. They do not evaluate whether the summaries are factually consistent. Therefore, an increase in score indicates an improvement in source alignment rather than an absolute guarantee that subtle contradictions will not occur.

Finally, cross-lingual evaluation was limited to Portuguese legal questions. The OAB results suggest transfer in this setting, but do not establish similar behavior for other languages, scripts, or domains.

6 Conclusions

This study combined a systematic literature review with quantitative evaluation to analyze hallucination mitigation in 3B–4B language models.

In response to the categorization inquiries, the review identified a diverse landscape of approaches classified into four primary categories: 1) Model Optimization; 2) Inference and Output Enhancement; 3) External Knowledge and Interaction; and 4) Latent Space Intervention. Consistent with previous observations, there remains a prevalence of techniques in the Inference and External Knowledge categories, reflecting a research trend toward modular solutions that avoid the computational expense of retraining.

Addressing comparative efficacy, the results revealed that performance is not merely a function of the mitigation category, but of the interaction between the method and the model under evaluation. Model Optimization proved most effective for restoring lost capabilities and enabling cross-lingual transfer in domain-specific tasks such as the OAB exam. Conversely, External Knowledge and Interaction functioned as a effective stabilizer for the Qwen3-4B configuration, producing zero observed drift events in this evaluation setting, but acted as a distractor for the Llama-3.2-3B configuration, occasionally degrading performance in closed-book query tasks. Furthermore, Latent Space Interventions appeared promising in this benchmark because they improved truthfulness with low added inference overhead, contrasting sharply with the high computational cost of ensemble retrieval methods.

The primary contribution of this work lies in connecting mitigation taxonomy with empirical evaluation under small-model constraints. By contrasting two representative compact language models under a unified protocol, this study provides evidence that mitigation strategies should be selected according to model behavior, task requirements, and computational budget. This offers practical guidance for balancing accuracy, stability, and efficiency in edge-oriented deployments.

Based on these findings, several directions for future investigation are indicated. First, the phenomenon where retrieval augmentation degrades the performance of stable small models warrants a deeper mechanistic analysis to understand how 3B-parameter models filter context noise. Second, while this study focused on textual hallucinations, the framework should be extended to Multimodal Large Language Models (MLLMs) to evaluate if latent space interventions remain robust across visual-textual modalities. Finally, while this study addressed statistical significance through bootstrap resampling, future work could expand the scope to include "in-the-wild" human evaluation to correlate these automated metrics with perceived user utility in real-time mobile applications.

Acknowledgments. We acknowledge the support of UFMS (Universidade Federal de Mato Grosso do Sul), FUNDECT, and Finep. Any opinions, findings, conclusions, or recommendations expressed in this material are those of the authors and do not necessarily reflect the views of UFMS, FUNDECT, or Finep.

Disclosure of Interests. The authors have no financial or proprietary interests in any material discussed in this article.

References

1. Chuang, Y.S., Xie, Y., Luo, H., Kim, Y., Glass, J., He, P.: DOLA: decoding by contrasting layers improves factuality in large language models. arXiv (2024)
2. Clark, P., et al.: Think you have solved question answering? Try ARC, the AI2 reasoning challenge (2018). https://arxiv.org/abs/1803.05457
3. Cuconasu, F., et al.: The power of noise: redefining retrieval for rag systems. In: Proceedings of the 47th International ACM SIGIR Conference on Research and Development in Information Retrieval, SIGIR 2024, pp. 719–729. ACM (2024). https://doi.org/10.1145/3626772.3657834
4. Dror, R., Baumer, G., Shlomov, S., Reichart, R.: The hitchhiker's guide to testing statistical significance in natural language processing. In: Gurevych, I., Miyao, Y. (eds.) Proceedings of the 56th Annual Meeting of the Association for Computational Linguistics (Volume 1: Long Papers), pp. 1383–1392. Association for Computational Linguistics, Melbourne, Australia (2018). https://doi.org/10.18653/v1/P18-1128. https://aclanthology.org/P18-1128/
5. Garcia, E.: OAB exams (2024). https://huggingface.co/datasets/eduagarcia/oab_exams
6. Hemrajani, R.: Evaluating the role of large language models in legal practice in India (2025). https://arxiv.org/abs/2508.09713
7. Holtzman, A., Buys, J., Du, L., Forbes, M., Choi, Y.: The curious case of neural text degeneration (2020). https://arxiv.org/abs/1904.09751
8. Kitchenham, B., Charters, S.: Guidelines for performing systematic literature reviews in software engineering. EBSE Technical report (2007)
9. Koehn, P.: Statistical significance tests for machine translation evaluation. In: Lin, D., Wu, D. (eds.) Proceedings of the 2004 Conference on Empirical Methods in Natural Language Processing, pp. 388–395. Association for Computational Linguistics, Barcelona, Spain (2004). https://aclanthology.org/W04-3250/
10. Koranteng, E., et al.: Empathy and equity: key considerations for large language model adoption in health care. JMIR Med. Educ. **9** (2023). https://api.semanticscholar.org/CorpusID:266571217
11. Lee, K., Chang, M.W., Toutanova, K.: Latent retrieval for weakly supervised open domain question answering. In: Korhonen, A., Traum, D., Màrquez, L. (eds.) Proceedings of the 57th Annual Meeting of the Association for Computational Linguistics, pp. 6086–6096. Association for Computational Linguistics, Florence, Italy (2019). https://doi.org/10.18653/v1/P19-1612. https://aclanthology.org/P19-1612/

12. Li, K., Patel, O., Viégas, F., Pfister, H., Wattenberg, M.: Inference-time intervention: eliciting truthful answers from a language model (2024). https://arxiv.org/abs/2306.03341
13. Li, X.L., et al.: Contrastive decoding: open-ended text generation as optimization (2023). https://arxiv.org/abs/2210.15097
14. Lin, C.Y.: ROUGE: a package for automatic evaluation of summaries. In: Text Summarization Branches Out, pp. 74–81. Association for Computational Linguistics, Barcelona, Spain (2004). https://aclanthology.org/W04-1013
15. Lin, S., Hilton, J., Evans, O.: Truthfulqa: measuring how models mimic human falsehoods. arXiv:2109.07958 (2022)
16. Liu, N.F., et al.: Lost in the middle: how language models use long contexts (2023). https://arxiv.org/abs/2307.03172
17. Naik, H.R., Prather, A.D., Gurda, G.T.: Synchronous bilateral breast cancer: a case report piloting and evaluating the implementation of the ai-powered large language model (LLM) chatgpt. Cureus **15** (2023). https://api.semanticscholar.org/CorpusID:258161464
18. Ovadia, O., Brief, M., Mishaeli, M., Elisha, O.: Fine-tuning or retrieval? Comparing knowledge injection in LLMs. In: Al-Onaizan, Y., Bansal, M., Chen, Y.N. (eds.) Proceedings of the 2024 Conference on Empirical Methods in Natural Language Processing, pp. 237–250. Association for Computational Linguistics, Miami, Florida, USA (2024). https://doi.org/10.18653/v1/2024.emnlp-main.15. https://aclanthology.org/2024.emnlp-main.15/
19. Shi, W., Han, X., Lewis, M., Tsvetkov, Y., Zettlemoyer, L., tau Yih, S.W.: Trusting your evidence: hallucinate less with context-aware decoding (2023). https://arxiv.org/abs/2305.14739
20. Teknium, R., Quesnelle, J., Guang, C.: Hermes 3 technical report (2024). https://arxiv.org/abs/2408.11857
21. Wan, Z., et al.: Efficient large language models: a survey (2024). https://arxiv.org/abs/2312.03863
22. Wu, T., et al.: Shadow-ft: tuning instruct model via training on paired base model (2025). https://arxiv.org/abs/2505.12716
23. Zhang, T., Kishore, V., Wu, F., Weinberger, K.Q., Artzi, Y.: Bertscore: evaluating text generation with BERT. arXiv:1904.09675 (2020)

Performance and Resilience Evaluation of a Hybrid Edge–Cloud IoT System Across Connected, Offline, and Reconnection Scenarios

Luís Fernando Alves da Silva(✉), Pedro Ramires da Silva Amalfi Costa, and Claudio Schepke

Laboratory of Advanced Studies in Computation, Federal University of Pampa (UNIPAMPA), Alegrete, RS, Brazil
{luisfads.aluno,pedroamalfi.aluno,claudioschepke}@unipampa.edu.br

Abstract. Reliable operation in Internet of Things (IoT) systems is crucial in environments with intermittent connectivity and unstable infrastructure, such as rural agricultural settings. When using cloud-centric architectures that rely on continuous internet access, users often face issues such as service disruptions, data loss, and a lack of real-time control during connectivity degradation. To overcome these limitations, this paper proposes a hybrid edge-to-cloud architecture that enables autonomous operation, resilient device control, and consistent data synchronization under unreliable network conditions. The proposed architecture integrates local edge processing, event-driven replication, and asynchronous message-based synchronization using RabbitMQ, Celery, and MQTT. It enables IoT devices to continue functioning in offline mode, maintain low-latency execution of control logic, and automatically reconcile the application state once connectivity returns. To assess system performance under realistic stress conditions, we conducted a load-testing experiment evaluating the behavior of the edge node across three connectivity states: fully connected to the cloud, operating autonomously during disconnection, and during the reconnection phase with backlog synchronization. Scripted message publishers emulating IoT devices produce workloads of increasing intensity. That enables quantitative analysis of throughput, end-to-end latency, resource consumption, and backlog draining time across progressively escalating load levels. These findings suggest that hybrid Edge–Cloud IoT architectures based on open, interoperable technologies offer a sustainable path toward technological independence, thereby reducing reliance on proprietary cloud platforms and enabling resilient real-time operation in critical domains where autonomy and fault tolerance are essential.

Keywords: Edge Computing · Hybrid Edge–Cloud Architecture · IoT Systems · Intermittent Connectivity · Offline Operation · Event-Driven Synchronization · Load Testing · Performance Evaluation

O. Gervasi et al. (Eds.): ICCSA 2026, LNCS 16768, pp. 651–668, 2027.
https://doi.org/10.1007/978-3-032-30488-9_40

1 Introduction

Agriculture is essential for human subsistence. Technological advances have enabled the automation of various tasks, consolidating the concept of Agriculture 4.0, in which the integration of sensors, connectivity, and computational intelligence allows for the optimization of production processes [1]. Irrigation, a critical element in agricultural production, can be improved by smart technologies, ensuring more efficient use of water and other resources [3].

Implementing systems in rural areas presents specific challenges. The lack of reliable internet infrastructure and adverse weather conditions can compromise irrigation continuity. Thus, system security is fundamental to ensuring its robust operation, especially regarding its IoT architecture.

Given this, we identified the need for automated irrigation systems to address the inherent challenges of irrigation automation on small rural properties. That includes recurring losses due to power outages and water supply interruptions. The developed system aims to mitigate frequent problems that negatively impact agricultural production. The proposed system monitors environmental data and controls irrigation flow using an IoT infrastructure with a hybrid cloud-edge approach. It allows for disconnected operation in case of connection failures. Furthermore, the system design intends to be accessible to users without technological familiarity, ensuring ease of use.

The contribution of this paper is to provide an economically viable IoT irrigation system for small rural producers. Research conducted with small rural producers at the regional level during the development of this solution identified that several producers are interested in smart irrigation solutions. However, most of them respond that the high price of these systems is the main impediment to their purchase and use. This system aims to address a market niche that is currently underexplored by smart irrigation systems, as they typically focus on automating pivots used by large rural producers.

The organization of the remainder of the paper is as follows. Section 2 presents the related work. Section 3 describes the methodology of the experiments. Next, in Sect. 4, we describe the process of implementing the components of the edge-cloud application. Section 5 shows the experimental results. At last, Sect. 6 presents the conclusion and future work.

2 Related Work

Cloud-Centric platforms enable the collection, storage, and analysis of data on a large scale, offering consolidated tools for visualization and integration. The Smart Water Management Platform (SWAMP) is an example of an architecture that adopts FIWARE, an open ecosystem funded by the European Union, composed of software modules called Generic Enablers [6]. These modules provide essential functionalities for IoT applications, such as context management, sensor and actuator integration, historical data storage, and large-scale processing. In SWAMP, FIWARE serves as an intermediary layer between field devices and analytical applications, ensuring interoperability, scalability, and support for real-time decision-making in precision irrigation. Furthermore, it integrates IoT protocols and persistence components to support operations in real-world scenarios while highlighting performance and scalability challenges in the context of database modules. Although cloud centralization improves aspects such as governance and elasticity, the strong dependence on stable connectivity represents a significant limitation in rural areas, subjecting them to network intermittency, a typical condition faced by small producers.

Hybrid architectures intend to balance cloud processing and storage resources with decision-making close to the data source, providing fault tolerance and lower latency. Alharbi and Aldossary [2] propose an energy-efficient cloud-to-fog-to-edge architecture for smart agriculture, demonstrating reductions of up to 36% in energy consumption, 43% in carbon emissions, and 86% in network traffic through hierarchical task allocation and the use of low-power communication.

In a real-world deployment scenario, Et-Taibi et al. [5] describe a cloud-to-edge solution applied to soilless drip irrigation systems, in which the integration and distribution of heterogeneous sensors are into distributed processing flows. The results point to gains in optimizing water and energy use.

Focused on long-range, low-energy scenarios, Zhang et al. [12] present a LoRa-based and edge computing system that incorporates a variant of the Penman–Monteith algorithm for evapotranspiration calculation, supports multiple protocols via a gateway, and uses MQTT/WSS communication. Field tests showed a range of up to 4 km with low packet loss, ensuring reliable data transmission. Complementarily, Kasera and Acharjee [7] propose a smart irrigation framework supported by LoRa and edge IoT, integrating a robust transmission scheme over MQTT, efficient topologies for M2M communication, and reinforcement learning elements for dynamic irrigation scheduling.

Edge approaches also stand out in isolation by reducing latency, filtering data close to the source, and allowing for greater local decision-making autonomy. Munir et al. [9] propose a system that combines edge computing, ontologies, and machine learning to classify water needs based on multiple environmental variables, avoiding the transmission of unnecessary data to the backend. Similarly, Ndunagu et al. [10] describe a wireless sensor network integrated with a cloud platform but with pre-processing on the edge server in time windows, employing ML algorithms (e.g., KNN) and achieving high accuracy in irrigation decisions. Although they still present limitations in defining robust synchronization mechanisms with the cloud and reliable disconnected operation policies, these works reinforce the gains of edge computing in terms of autonomy and efficiency.

Taken together, these studies demonstrate the concrete benefits of hybrid architectures, energy efficiency, reduced traffic, expanded coverage, and significant expansion of autonomy in decision-making. However, few studies detail practical protocols for bidirectional replication and mechanisms for eventual consistency between cloud and edge in situations of prolonged disconnection, a recurring challenge in rural areas.

Practical adoption in small farms requires competitive costs, interoperability, and ease of maintenance. [11] develops a low-cost, open-source platform that integrates FIWARE (LD), water balance models, and a *datalogger* compatible with multiple protocols (LPWAN, LoRaWAN, NB-IoT, GSM, etc.), favoring reuse and integration. Complementarily, [8] proposes an ESP32, MQTT, and cloud services system, reporting significant reductions in water consumption and describing sensor calibration procedures along with a structured development process. Although these works advance interoperability and total cost of ownership, most lack formal failover policies, post-failure reconciliation, and consistent replication between layers, which are critical points for environments with unstable power and connectivity.

The review of related works indicates that IoT-based smart irrigation systems have expanded in terms of technological integration, resource efficiency, and decision support. Cloud-centric architectures have demonstrated maturity in terms of scalability, governance, and analytical tools. However, they present important limitations when applied to rural areas subject to connectivity instability. In turn, hybrid cloud-to-edge and cloud-to-fog-to-edge models reinforce the potential to reduce latency, filter data close to the source, and expand local autonomy. They achieve concrete benefits such as greater energy efficiency, lower network traffic, and increased reliability in long-distance scenarios. However, bidirectional replication and eventual consistency mechanisms in situations of prolonged disconnection remain underexplored.

Open and low-cost platforms emerge as promising alternatives for adoption in small farms, combining interoperability, component reuse, and a more accessible total cost of ownership. However, such solutions still lack formal failure policies, post-failure reconciliation, and consistent replication across layers—critical aspects in rural contexts marked by recurring power and connectivity failures.

In general, the reviewed literature demonstrates significant progress but also reveals gaps that motivate this research. Among these, the following stand out: (i) the absence of robust protocols for reliable synchronization between cloud and edge; (ii) the need for effective offline operation policies; and (iii) the lack of practical strategies to ensure data consistency and service continuity in environments subject to infrastructure constraints. These points guide the contribution of this paper, which proposes a resilient architecture for smart irrigation that addresses these challenges.

3 Methodology

The architecture's construction proposes an incremental trajectory for the intelligent security system based on the Design Thinking approach. This approach combines cycles of empathy, problem definition, ideation, prototyping, and validation. Figure 1 shows these cycles, including the four prototyping phases. The project's evolution consists of five major structural phases:

- Immersion and Problem Definition Phase: The project's starting point was a field study conducted on a farm. The main challenges identified are related

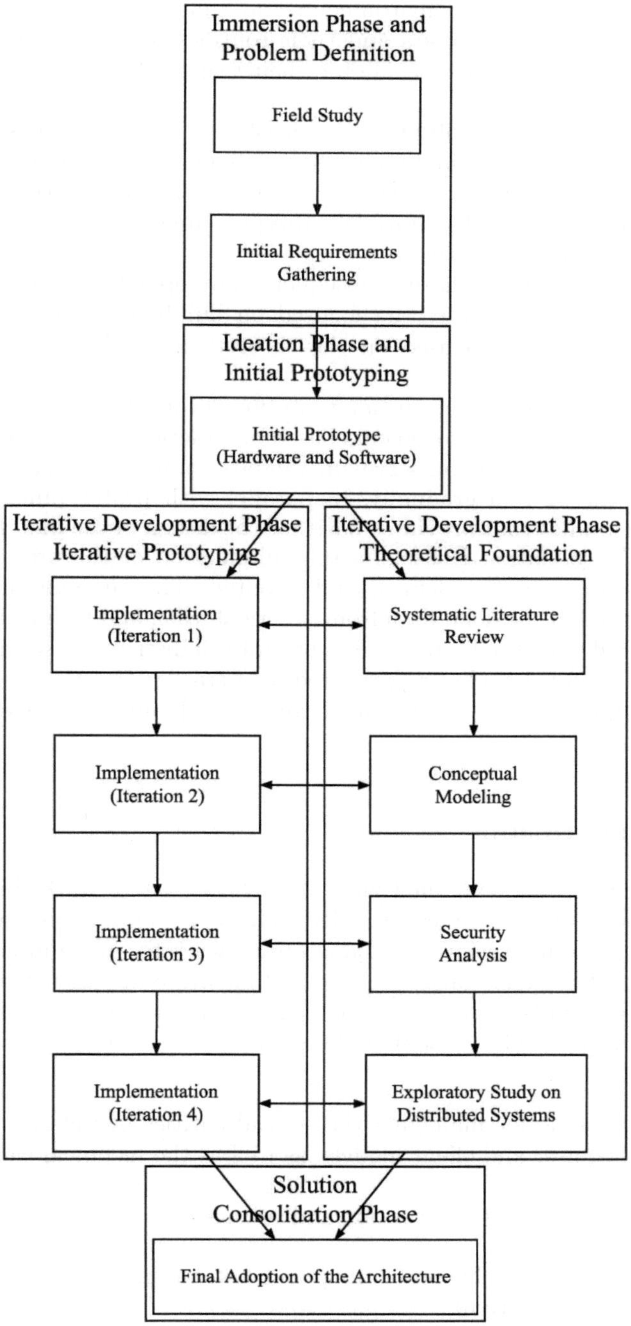

Fig. 1. Work Evolution Flowchart.

to functionality in remote environments and limited connectivity. Since there was direct contact with users and their routines, it was possible to gather initial requirements while considering their real needs and the constraints of the rural context.

- Initial Ideation and Prototyping Phase: With the requirements defined, the project moved on to formulate hypotheses about the system architecture. We explore technical and conceptual alternatives based on empirical observation and a literature review. The initial prototyping aims to test these installations and obtain feedback quickly.
- Iterative Development Phase: Subsequent development occurred iteratively and on two parallel fronts: one focused on building and improving prototypes, and the other focused on the theoretical studies that underpinned architectural decisions.
- Iterative Prototyping: The initial prototype evolved over four consecutive cycles, incorporating improvements based on practical testing and continuous feedback. Each new version serves to validate solutions, identify limitations, and refine the system gradually. In parallel with prototyping, we conduct theoretical studies that provide a basis for the design of the final architecture.
- Solution Consolidation Phase: As the culmination of the process, the final system architecture was defined and adopted. This architecture integrates lessons learned in the field, data from practical tests, and technical fundamentals extracted from the literature. The result is a distributed solution oriented towards edge and cloud layers, prepared to operate resiliently in environments with limited connectivity, without sacrificing scalability, security, and ease of maintenance.

4 Implementation

This section presents a simplified view of how the system works based on user interactions with the resources provided. The web application was developed in a modular structure, using the Django framework to create internal applications (apps) that organize business logic and facilitate maintenance and system expansion. Each application focuses on specific functionalities, allowing a clear separation of responsibilities within the project. The main applications implemented are:

- **Core**: responsible for managing the central entities of the system, bringing together both user and client models, as well as the technical elements of the infrastructure;
- **Telemetry**: manages the reception and storage of data from sensors installed in devices (IoT);
- **Irrigation**: controls the scheduling and activation logic of the actuators responsible for irrigation;
- **Monitoring**: stores connectivity verification data between the cloud and the edge, generating a connection health metric based on the latest data collection.

Although the same Django applications are present in both the edge and cloud instances, their functionalities are adapted to meet the distinct operational contexts of each layer. The C4 level 3 diagrams presented in Fig. 2 which detail the cloud components, and Fig. 3, which represent the edge components, evidence of those functional differences.

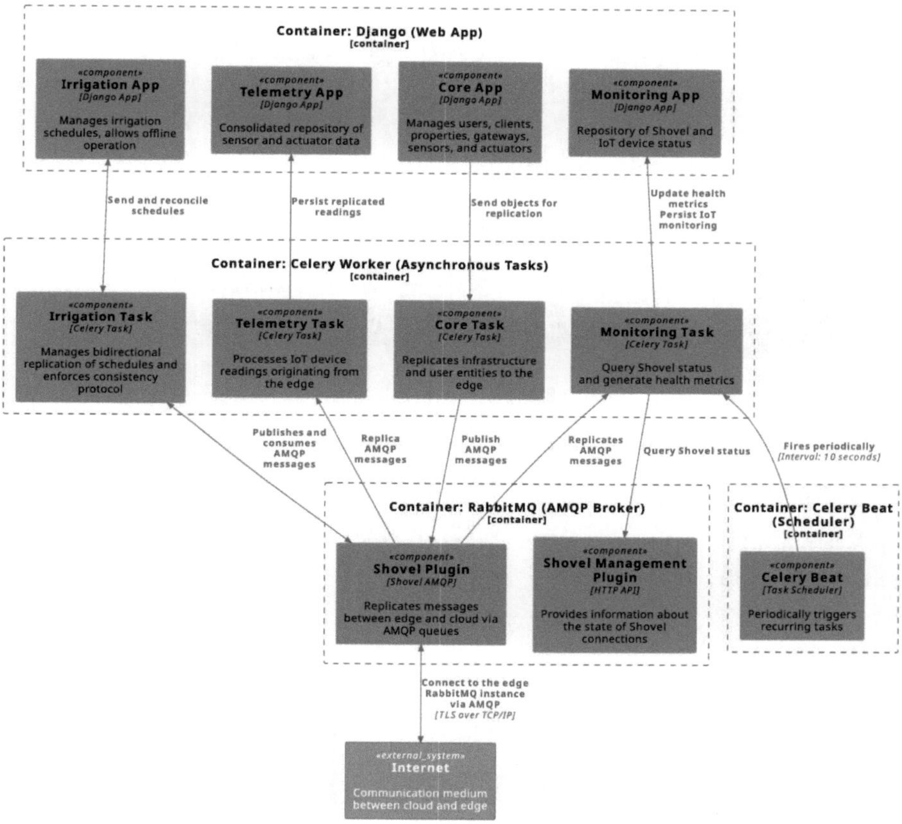

Fig. 2. C4 Level 3—Internal components of the cloud server.

In many cases, this involves data replication via RabbitMQ AMQP message queues, which, in Django, is handled by asynchronous tasks managed with Celery. We detail the replication process in the following sections, which present the specific flows of each application in the system, accompanied by UML sequence diagrams that illustrate the communication between the components.

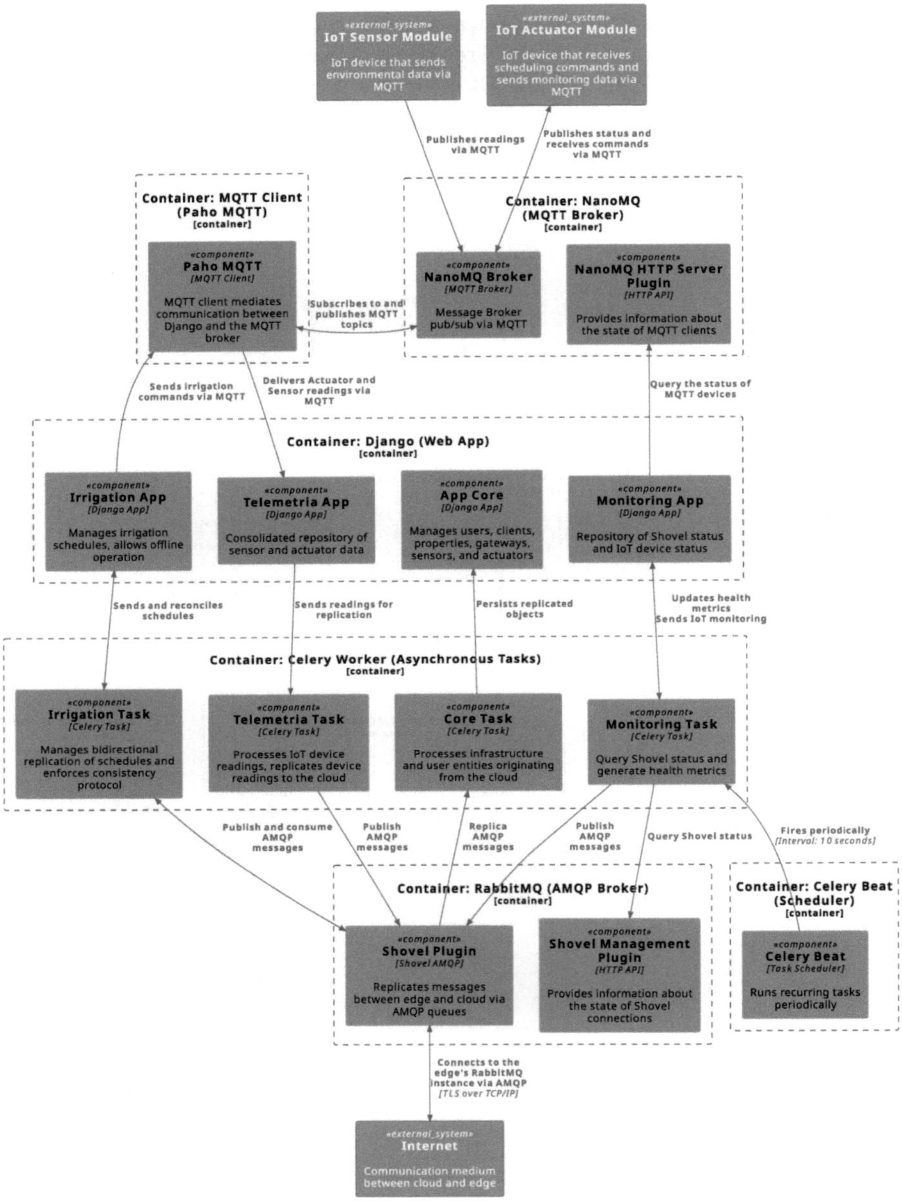

Fig. 3. C4 Level 3—Internal components of the edge server.

4.1 Application Core

The application *core* brings together the central entities of the system, which are responsible for structuring both the organizational model and the technical elements of the infrastructure. Models such as `User` and `Client` represent the different types of users and their links to the system instance, allowing for role-based access control (such as owner, manager, and employee) and logical isolation by client. The models `Property`, `Gateway`, `Actuator`, and `Sensor` represent the technical elements that make up the distributed architecture of the system, connecting IoT devices to the software through a hierarchical structure.

The interdependence between them justifies the decision to cluster these models into a single application: clients associate users who, in turn, manage properties equipped with gateways, sensors, and actuators. Thus, the *core* application serves as a common structural base for the other system modules, consolidating the essential information for its operation.

The replication logic of the *core* follows the cloud-to-edge direction. Since changes to these models are only allowed in the cloud instance, the end user does not directly manipulate this part of the application. This strategy simplifies architecture management by eliminating bidirectional replication and the need for conflict resolution while ensuring the consistency of essential data across both layers of the system. The sequence diagram represents the data flow (Fig. 4).

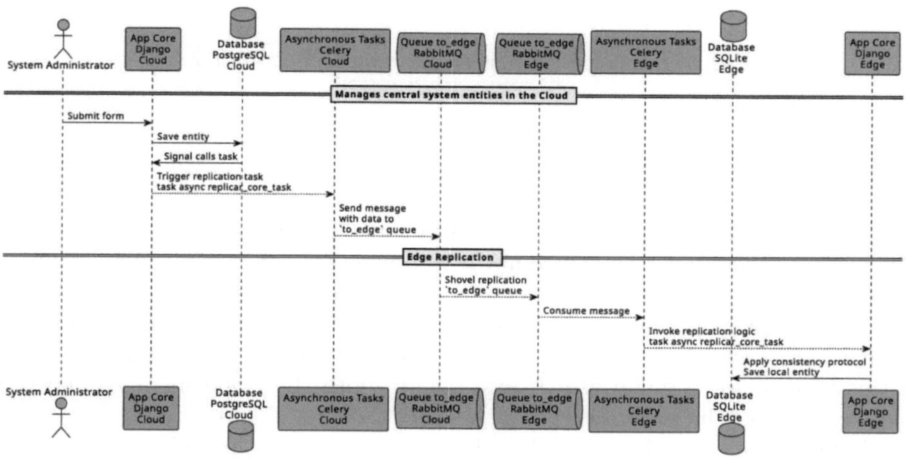

Fig. 4. Sequence—Replication of central system entities (core).

4.2 Telemetry Application

The telemetry application is responsible for managing the flow of data collected by sensors and actuators installed in the field. This flow is unidirectional: IoT devices send readings via the MQTT protocol to the edge server, where the data is received, processed, and stored locally.

After this initial persistence, the information is asynchronously replicated to the cloud instance using the AMQP protocol, ensuring its centralization, security, and availability for later analysis. End users or system administrators do not directly manipulate those records, since sensors generate data automatically. In this way, the telemetry application acts as an entry point, at the edge, for raw data from the physical environment, and, in the cloud, it serves as a consolidated repository. The sequence diagram represents the data flow (Fig. 5).

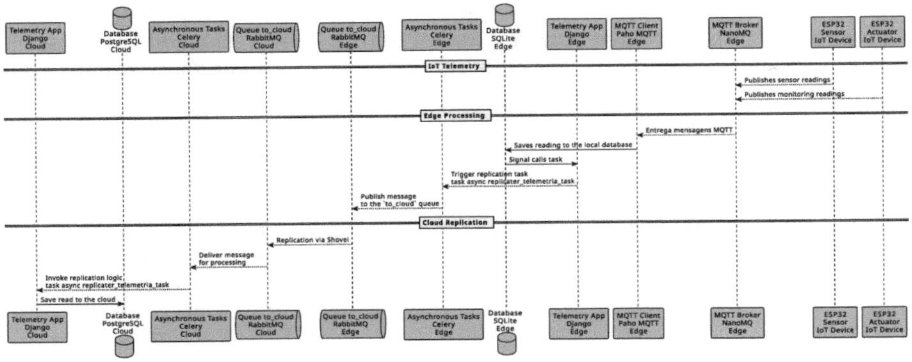

Fig. 5. Sequence—Telemetry reading replication flow.

4.3 Irrigation Application

The irrigation application is responsible for controlling the scheduling and activation logic of the actuators involved in the irrigation process. Since these schedules are defined directly by the end user, the system needs to support disconnected operations, ensuring functionality even in situations of instability or loss of internet connection, as designed in this project. For this reason, the administration of this module for the end user is available in both the cloud instance and the local instance of the edge server.

Under normal conditions, schedule management is through the interface available in the cloud, accessed via the internet, referred to here as "connected operation". The sequence diagram represents the data flow in a connected operation (Fig. 6).

However, in disconnection situations, the system allows local access to the replicated instance at the edge, ensuring operational continuity. That characterizes the situation as a "disconnected operation" [4]. The sequence diagram represents the data flow in a disconnected operation (Fig. 7).

To enable this functionality, the *irrigation* application implements a bidirectional replication flow between the edge and the cloud. Since modifications on

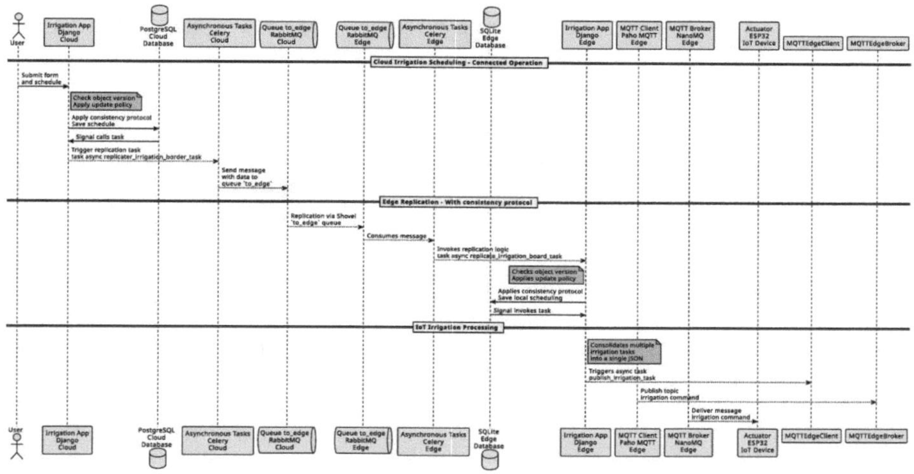

Fig. 6. Sequence—Irrigation scheduling with connected operation.

the same data can be in both instances during a period of disconnection, the system adopts a simplified consistency protocol to handle update conflicts.

The main conflict situation occurs when the same schedule is changed simultaneously at both the edge and in the cloud during disconnection. After reconnection, both sides try to replicate their versions of the same object, which generates divergence. To resolve this impasse in a conflict situation, the protocol defines the prevalence of the edge version, based on the premise that local operators have greater knowledge of the operational situation.

Despite being a simple approach, this policy ensures the functional consistency of the system and reflects the priority of local action in unstable scenarios. In addition, the *irrigation* app, in edge cases, is responsible for consolidating the various registered schedules into a single daily routine command. This command is transmitted to the actuator device via the MQTT protocol, enabling the automated execution of the irrigation plan.

4.4 Monitoring Application

The monitoring application is responsible for informing the end user about the connection status between the edge instance and the cloud. The Shovel plugin, supported by RabbitMQ, performs data replication between these layers. This plugin allows the creation of integrated AMQP queues between different brokers and supports monitoring the connection between instances.

RabbitMQ itself provides, through a management plugin, information about the Shovel connection status. A fixed frequency configured in RabbitMQ itself defines the granularity of this update. Due to the periodic nature of this data, the performance of its collection is managed through a scheduled task with Celery Beat, Celery's recurring task scheduler.

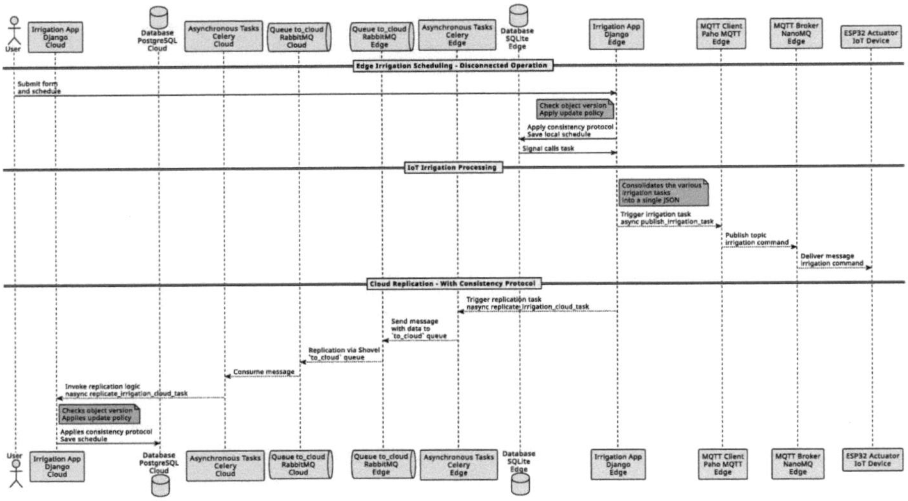

Fig. 7. Sequence—Irrigation schedule with disconnected operation.

The collection interval recommended by the official RabbitMQ documentation, fixed at 10 s, was chosen. The collected information is stored in the *monitoring* application. It is used to generate a connection health metric. This metric is based on the last ten data collections and represents the percentage of successful communication between the cloud and the edge. The metric indicates the stability of communication between the servers and is updated periodically at the same interval as the *Shovel* data collection.

Based on this index, the system classifies the connection status as follows:

- `Disconnected`: when the index is equal to 0;
- `Bad`: when the index is between 1% and 39%;
- `Moderate`: between 40% and 69%;
- `Good`: from 70%.

The following sequence diagram represents the process of monitoring the connection between the edge and the cloud. This flow is executed in both instances—cloud and edge—since the logic for collecting and evaluating the connection is identical in both operational contexts (Fig. 8).

In addition to monitoring edge-to-cloud connections, the *monitoring* application is also responsible for tracking MQTT clients connected to the *NanoMQ* broker via the *http_server* plugin. This functionality is similar to *Shovel* monitoring, except that it runs exclusively on the edge instance, as that is where the installation of *NanoMQ* is and the localization of IoT devices occurs. The information obtained locally is subsequently replicated to the cloud, ensuring unified visibility. As with *Shovel*, the system calculates a health metric based on the presence and stability of MQTT client connections, allowing for an assessment of the overall network health of devices.

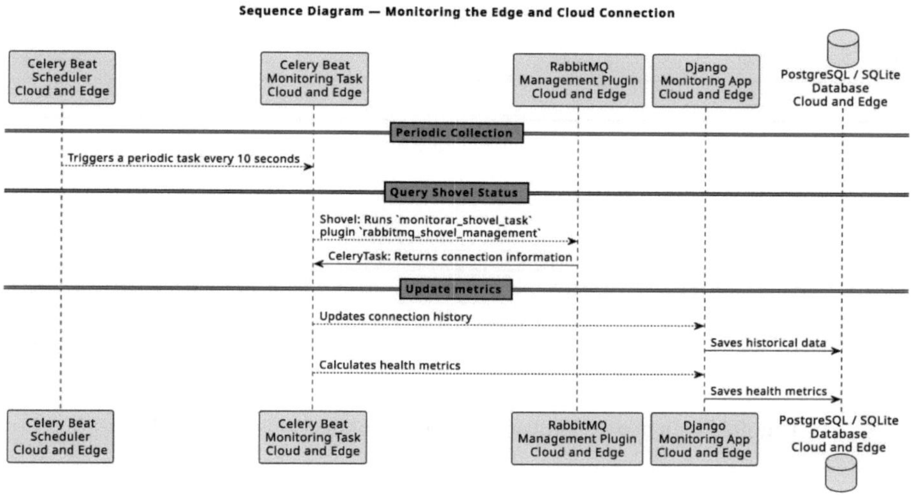

Fig. 8. Sequence—Monitoring the connection between edge and cloud.

Based on this information, the system can automatically switch application access to the local edge instance, ensuring functionality for clients connected to the local network during periods of instability or internet disconnection through the disconnected operation mechanism. Since this is a local diagnostic component, the *monitoring* app does not participate in data replication between the edge and the cloud. Just like the *telemetry* app, the manipulation of logs from this module is not directly by end users or system administrators.

The following sequence diagram represents the process of monitoring MQTT connections from IoT devices to the *NanoMQ* broker. This flow is executed exclusively on the edge instance, as this is where both *NanoMQ* and the connected devices are located. Connectivity information is collected periodically via the *http_server* plugin API, and the data obtained is used to calculate a health metric for the MQTT clients. The information is subsequently replicated to the cloud, allowing for a consolidated view of the network state of the devices (Fig. 9).

5 Experimental Results

First Iteration: The first iteration validated the technical fundamentals of the architecture. It considers field constraints such as limited connectivity, electrical instability, and users' low technological familiarity. The system is divided into three modules: the sensor (ESP32-S3), the edge (Orange Pi with Django/SQLite), and the cloud (Django/SQLite). The sensor publishes data via MQTT to Mosquitto on the edge; the edge, in turn, processes and stores the readings, operating in offline mode. The cloud interacts with the edge via MQTT (HiveMQ), maintaining bidirectional communication. The architecture

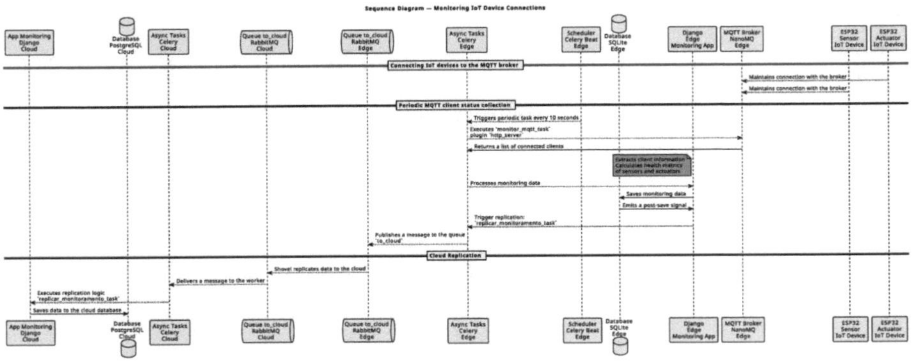

Fig. 9. Sequence—Monitoring MQTT connections at the edge.

is designed to tolerate faults and support subsequent synchronization with the cloud.

Second Iteration: Improvements were introduced in communication and data replication, overcoming the limitations of traditional MQTT. The NanoMQ (edge) and EMQX (cloud) brokers were adopted, with Data Bridge support to ensure message persistence and delivery, even during disconnections. The devices were organized into sensor and actuator modules, using UUID identifiers and JSON structures. NanoMQ was run via Docker on the Orange Pi, eliminating direct dependencies between Django and MQTT.

Third Iteration: This phase focused on the security of the solution. We used Docker, Gunicorn, and Nginx containers on the servers, with secure communications via TLS, authentication, and ACLs. The ESP32-S3 has been equipped with embedded protection mechanisms, including Secure Boot, eFuses, and Flash Encryption. We incorporated robust sensors and solid-state relays to ensure durability, and WPA2/WPA3 protects Wi-Fi communication. We also considered the use of other technologies in future versions. To ensure energy redundancy, we implemented a UPS and batteries recharged by solar panels, in addition to physical protections for the devices.

Fourth Iteration: Communication between the edge and the cloud has been redesigned to use **AMQP queues** with **RabbitMQ**, replacing the previous use of MQTT brokers for replication. This change has enhanced decoupling and increased system resilience. For task orchestration, **Celery** has been integrated with a **Redis** backend, which allows for asynchronous and scalable execution of tasks. Despite the change, **NanoMQ** was maintained at the edge for MQTT communication with IoT devices. An MQTT client (Paho-MQTT) was encapsulated in a Celery worker, ensuring that sending and receiving messages did not affect the availability of the Django application.

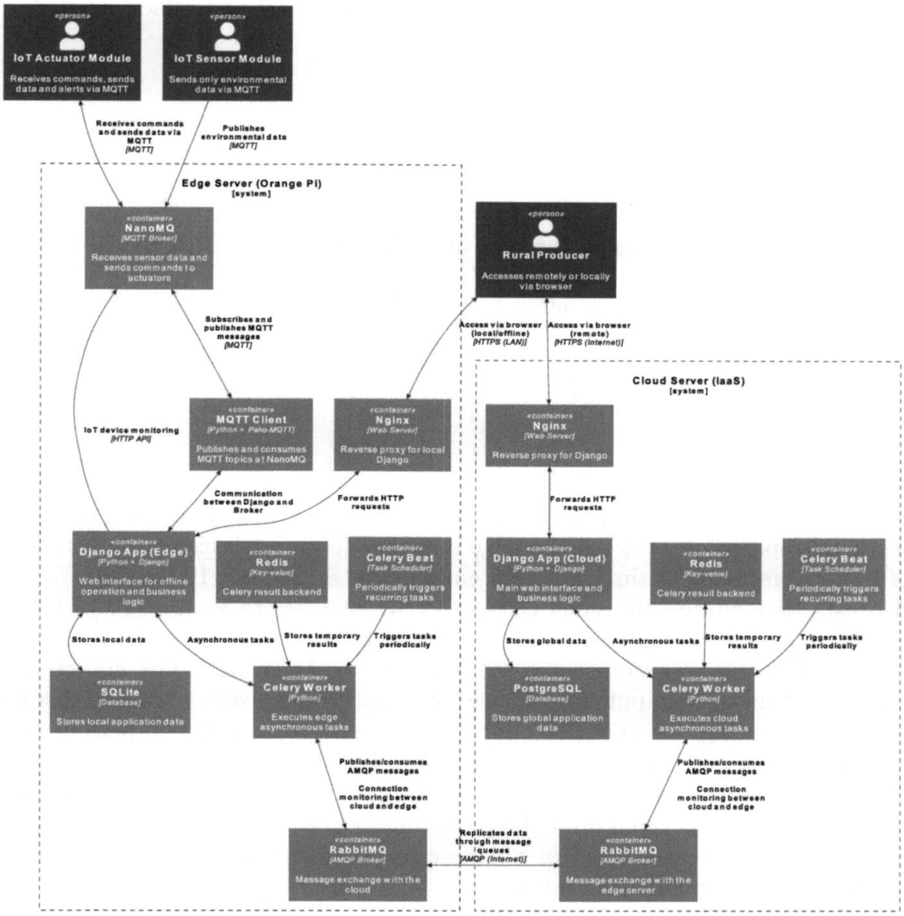

Fig. 10. Solution Consolidation.

Solution Consolidation: The final architecture consolidates the theoretical and practical learnings into a distributed, resilient, secure, and scalable solution, structured in edge and cloud layers. This structure allows for continuous operation even during connectivity or power failures. Figure 10 shows the container diagram of the consolidated architecture.

We conduct Constant Request Rate (CRR) experiments to evaluate the performance of the proposed architecture in real-world operations. We implement the tests using a custom Django command (BaseCommand) capable of generating HTTP requests to create schedules in the API using pseudo-random values. The interval between requests was used as a load parameter, allowing for the measurement of the system's saturation limit and the impact of the storage hardware on the processing rate.

Table 1. Average throughput (msg/s) for different devices and request intervals

Device/Interval	50 ms	100 ms	250 ms
eMMC	5.02	3.87	3.48
SD Card	4.42	3.21	2.98
SSD NVMe	6.87	5.92	5.31

Table 2. Maximum observed throughput (msg/s) in CRR tests

Device/Interval	50 ms	100 ms	250 ms
eMMC	12.00	10.50	6.50
SD Card	10.23	8.97	5.41
SSD NVMe	17.32	14.65	12.44

We selected the scheduling feature because it requires local writing and bidirectional replication between the edge and the cloud. Each execution consisted of 1000 requests under three different emission rates: 250 ms, 100 ms, and 50 ms. All tests were run on the same Orange Pi 3B edge server with 4 GB of RAM, varying only the storage device among NVMe SSD, eMMC, and SD card.

The objective was to measure the influence of the storage type and request rate on system throughput. The devices represent three distinct categories of use in edge computing: low cost (SD), intermediate (eMMC), and high-performance (NVMe). Each scenario automatically stored the total execution time, average throughput, maximum throughput, and complete logs in CSV format. Replication to the cloud occurred after the persistence of records in the local database, allowing for the measurement of the direct effect of writing on the hardware.

We analyze the following metrics:

- Average throughput (msg/s) – sustained processing rate;
- Maximum throughput (msg/s) – highest recorded peak;

Average latency, p50, p95, and p99 were also recorded for complementary analysis.

Table 1 presents the average throughput per device and interval. The NVMe SSD delivered the best performance in all scenarios, with an average of 36% better than eMMC and 55% superior to the SD card.

In the most intense scenario (50 ms), NVMe reached 6.87 msg/s, while eMMC and SD were below 5 msg/s. At longer intervals, the limit became the time between requests, reducing the impact of the hardware. Table 2 shows the observed peaks. The results indicate that NVMe maintains greater stability under load, showing a smaller distance between the average and peak, while SD and eMMC accumulate backlog at shorter intervals. Storage hardware directly influences the event processing rate at the edge and the replication speed to the cloud.

6 Conclusion

The development of this smart irrigation system highlighted the complexity involved in building resilient solutions for family farming in environments with limited infrastructure. More than a simple connection between devices and servers, the project required addressing challenges such as data replication and consistency, tolerance for connectivity failures, and orchestration of asynchronous tasks between edge and cloud.

The iterative approach provides practical validation of each component, promoting the continuous evolution of the architecture. It consolidates a distributed, secure, and scalable model. The resulting system is capable of operating even in the face of power and connection failures. The developed solution represents significant progress for the Agriculture 4.0 scenario by democratizing access to technologies restricted to large farms. It proposes a viable and accessible alternative for small producers. Furthermore, it establishes a solid foundation for future expansions.

Future work includes evaluating the system's usability with end users. It covers automating the irrigation cycle based on environmental conditions and crop characteristics.

References

1. Abbasi, R., Martinez, P., Ahmad, R.: The digitization of agricultural industry – a systematic literature review on agriculture 4.0. Smart Agric. Technol. **2**, 100042 (2022). https://doi.org/10.1016/j.atech.2022.100042. https://www.sciencedirect.com/science/article/pii/S2772375522000090
2. Alharbi, H.A., Aldossary, M.: Energy-efficient edge-fog-cloud architecture for IoT-based smart agriculture environment. IEEE Access **9**, 110480–110492 (2021). https://doi.org/10.1109/ACCESS.2021.3101397
3. Boursianis, A.D., et al.: Smart irrigation system for precision agriculture—the AREThOU5A IoT platform. IEEE Sens. J. **21**(16), 17539–17547 (2021). https://doi.org/10.1109/JSEN.2020.3033526
4. Coulouris, G., Dollimore, J., Kindberg, T., Blair, G.: Distributed Systems: Concepts and Design, 5th edn. Addison-Wesley, São Paulo (2013)
5. Et-taibi, B., Abid, M., mahjoub Boufounas, E., Benhaddou, D.: Cloud and edge based smart agriculture: a real-world deployment. In: 2024 International Conference on CircuiCloud and Edge based Smart Agriculture: A Real-World Deployment, Systems and Communication (ICCSC), pp. 1–6 (2024). https://doi.org/10.1109/ICCSC62074.2024.10617136
6. Kamienski, C., et al.: Smart water management platform: IoT-based precision irrigation for agriculture †. Sensors **19** (2019). https://doi.org/10.3390/s19020276
7. Kasera, R.K., Acharjee, T.: A comprehensive IoT edge based smart irrigation system for tomato cultivation. Internet Things **28**, 101356 (2024). https://doi.org/10.1016/j.iot.2024.101356
8. Morchid, A., Alblushi, I.G.M., Khalid, H.M., Alami, R.E., Sitaramanan, S.R., Muyeen, S.M.: High-technology agriculture system to enhance food security: a concept of smart irrigation system using internet of things and cloud computing. J. Saudi Soc. Agric. Sci. (2024). https://doi.org/10.1016/j.jssas.2024.02.001

9. Munir, M., Bajwa, I.S., Ashraf, A., Anwar, W., Rashid, R.: Intelligent and smart irrigation system using edge computing and IoT. Complex. **2021**, 6691571:1–6691571:16 (2021). https://doi.org/10.1155/2021/6691571
10. Ndunagu, J., Ukhurebor, K., Akaaza, M., Onyancha, R.B.: Development of a wireless sensor network and IoT-based smart irrigation system. Appl. Environ. Soil Sci. (2022). https://doi.org/10.1155/2022/7678570
11. Puig, F., Díaz, J.A.R., Soriano, M.: Development of a low-cost open-source platform for smart irrigation systems. Agronomy (2022). https://doi.org/10.3390/agronomy12122909
12. Zhang, Y., et al.: Research and development of an IoT smart irrigation system for farmland based on lora and edge computing. Agronomy (2025). https://doi.org/10.3390/agronomy15020366

When do Electricity Price Forecasts Create Operational Value? A Regime-Aware Evaluation Case Study

Paulo Batista[1,2](✉), Eduardo Monteiro[2], Margarida Vieira[2], and Manuel Ferreira[3]

[1] Universidade de Aveiro, Campus Universitário de Santiago, 3810-193 Aveiro, Portugal
pauloricardolb@ua.pt

[2] INEGI, Campus da FEUP, R. Dr. Roberto Frias 400, 4200-465 Porto, Portugal

[3] Microprocessador, Rua de Cidres, 1444 Matosinhos, Portugal

Abstract. Whether electricity price forecasts generate operational value in industrial settings—beyond improving predictive accuracy—remains an open question, particularly under extended 168-h horizons where forecast skill degrades, and tariff-facing decisions must be made against a plausible fixed-tariff baseline.

This work evaluated a leakage-safe hybrid model of OMIE gross hourly prices in a backtest of 15 audited Portuguese weeks, balanced across low-, average-, and high-volatility regimes (5/5/5), and compared a fixed BAU tariff (0.0829 €/kWh) with a forecast-informed dynamic hourly tariff, under fixed production conditions.

The electricity price forecast is assessed with MAE, RMSE, bias, empirical 90% interval coverage, and Diebold-Mariano tests against naïve lag-24 and lag-168 persistence. Then, the forecast's cost ranking quality was assessed, along with realized proxy-cost gains and downside risk.

The results show the electricity price model with mean MAEs of 24.1, 26.4, and 43.0 €/MWh across low-, average-, and high-volatility weeks, and empirical coverage of 66.4%, 58.5%, and 39.8%.

The model beat lag-24 persistence in all regimes ($p \leq 0.001$) but beat lag-168 persistence only in average-volatility weeks ($p < 0.001$). However, the broad tariff ordering remained stable (Spearman ρ 0.67–0.69, pairwise accuracy 0.747–0.749). Mean realized gains relative to BAU were €559.3, €458.0, and €311.2, with positive outcomes in 60%, 80%, and 80% of weeks, and underperformance probabilities of 40%, 20%, and 20%.

The results indicate a conditional decision value driven more by tariff-order preservation than by point accuracy alone. This study contributes an applied, regime-aware backtesting framework that evaluates forecast value under bounded industrial flexibility—a setting underrepresented in the existing forecast-value literature, which predominantly addresses trading and market-operator contexts.

Keywords: Electricity price forecasting · Dynamic electricity tariffs · Electricity-based decision support system · Demand response

O. Gervasi et al. (Eds.): ICCSA 2026, LNCS 16768, pp. 669–683, 2027.
https://doi.org/10.1007/978-3-032-30488-9_41

1 Introduction

Industrial electricity purchasing is a non-trivial cost component in many industrial settings, and its managerial importance increases when tariff structures vary over time rather than remaining flat. Under time-varying pricing, the cost consequences of consumption depend not only on total electricity use but also on when that use is billed, so hourly price variability can materially affect industrial cost exposure [1]. In practice, this means that firms facing differentiated hourly tariffs confront a cost environment in which the temporal price structure becomes part of the decision problem rather than a background accounting detail. Such exposure is especially relevant when electricity-intensive processes operate over multiple hours and when procurement conditions can shift materially within a planning horizon. This does not imply that all industrial settings can freely shift demand or that dynamic tariffs necessarily yield savings in every operational setting. It does imply, however, that tariff design and price timing matter for cost management wherever electricity procurement is embedded in production decisions. That relevance helps explain the appeal of electricity-price forecasting for operational use.

Forecasts are often evaluated using point-error criteria because these metrics summarize predictive performance in a compact, comparable way. Yet the literature has noted that predictive skill and downstream decision value are distinct and should not be treated as interchangeable [2]. A model can outperform another one in aggregate error terms while still failing to support better operational decisions, and the reverse can also occur when the information most relevant to a decision is only partially captured by conventional accuracy summaries.

In adjacent energy applications, value-oriented forecasting has likewise been framed as a decision-support problem rather than a pure prediction problem, because a forecast may be operationally useful or useless depending on how its errors interact with the actions it informs [3].

Moreover, in industrial electricity management, the scientific issue is therefore narrower than whether a model reduces forecast error on average. The more relevant question is whether the forecast preserves enough economically useful information to support better tariff-facing decisions than a plausible business-as-usual baseline. This paper addresses that gap through a deliberately narrower design. It evaluates the decision value of a 168h electricity-price forecasting model in an industrial setting by comparing a fixed-tariff Business-As-Usual (BAU) baseline with a forecast-informed dynamic hourly tariff - Policy_Variant_1.

It is important to note that the question must also be evaluated under realistic operational constraints: industrial demand response is not unconstrained, and firms often face technical, organizational, and economic barriers that limit how far power consumption can be adapted to volatile electricity conditions [4]. Even when some flexibility exists, it is typically bounded rather than unlimited, and the benefits of demand response participation depend on the feasible operational adjustment margin rather than on abstract assumptions of full responsiveness [1]. This motivates our real-case study design, selecting a production process in a real-world industrial setting to reproduce a real-world anchored flexibility case.

This work was part of a broader research–industry partnership on the development of an *Intelligent system for dynamic adjustment of electric power consumption*, led by Microprocessador - Sistemas Digitais, S.A., a tool which orchestrates different electricity-related models, such as a forecast gross hourly electricity price model, forecast hourly electricity price demand models for specified industrial production process, plus local PV solar plant production forecast to self-consumption. This tool will feed a broader industrial management cockpit (including production process planning and optimization) and will be integrated as an additional layer into production plan optimization routines.

2 Related Work

A substantial share of the electricity-price forecasting literature is organized around predictive-error performance, commonly reported using aggregate-level measures such as RMSE and MAE [5, 6]. Those metrics remain useful for judging statistical fit. Still, they do not automatically establish whether a forecast improves downstream operational decisions, because economically consequential errors may not coincide with the forecasts that minimize aggregate point error [5].

From a strict forecast point of view, the literature points out that simple baselines in electricity price forecasting are hard to beat, and decomposition/hybridization can improve accuracy, despite the hybrid/ensemble methods often being among the strongest options, despite most of the studies being focused on day-ahead settings [6–8], but no class wins universally.

Related work on forecast evaluation, therefore, matters not because alternative metrics can substitute directly for decision tests, but because they can reveal performance dimensions that simple aggregate errors may hide [9, 10]. In a decision-focused industrial study, this distinction is central: the relevant question is not only whether prices are predicted closely in level terms, but whether the forecast preserves information useful for a tariff choice relative to a fixed baseline.

Beyond standard forecast-error evaluation, a bounded strand of literature studies the value of forecasts through their economic consequences. The forecast-value literature [11] treats both conceptual and empirical aspects, as forecasts are useful for decision-making rather than as a simple extension of predictive accuracy. In that perspective, a forecast can be statistically better yet operationally unhelpful for a particular decision rule, or statistically imperfect yet still economically useful, depending on how forecast errors interact with the action being taken. That perspective is directly relevant here, but its alignment with the fixed-plan industrial tariff response remains limited, since supporting evidence often comes from neighboring markets or trading settings rather than from the specific operational comparison considered in this paper. Accordingly, the existence of forecast-value literature helps justify decision-oriented evaluation. Still, it does not by itself settle how forecast quality should be assessed against a fixed-tariff industrial baseline.

A further constraint in the adjacent literature concerns assumptions about demand-side responsiveness. In industrial environments, tariff responses are conditioned by technical, organizational, economic, and regulatory barriers, so operational relevance should be framed in terms of bounded flexibility rather than unrestricted responsiveness or optimization [4]. Survey-level work [12] reinforces this caution by showing that industrial demand response is substantively relevant but uneven in adoption and implementation, making broad assumptions about maneuverability unsafe in the present context. This caution is especially relevant in settings where production continuity, process coupling, and organizational constraints limit how far hourly price signals can be translated into operational adjustment. For that reason, industrial demand-response literature is most useful here when it disciplines realism in the response setting, not when it is treated as if it already validated schedule redesign or a broader decision-support architecture.

Taken together, these literatures motivate a deliberately narrow positioning for the present study: a focus on the empirical gap of whether forecast quality translates into value relative to a fixed-tariff BAU baseline, under the imperfection of a 168h horizon forecast.

The relevant comparison is therefore not forecasting performance in general, but the bounded question of whether a forecast-informed tariff choice can outperform a fixed baseline under a constrained industrial action space. This places this work within forecast-value research, with a clear, applied, and real-world application.

3 Study Scope and Method

3.1 Decision Problem and Policy Scope

This study evaluates an electricity-purchase decision problem using a backtesting framework anchored in shop-floor management, comparing two policy configurations under a common production plan (held fixed for this study): a fixed-tariff business-as-usual baseline (BAU) and a forecast-informed dynamic hourly tariff policy (Policy_Variant_1). The forecast horizon (168h) was selected as a (7-day) scenario, which can be particularly interesting from the point of view of the general industrial production plan management, even though it will pose important technical challenges for any forecast modelling exercise.

The particular case study is based on an opportunistic selection of a real-world operational production process, which is particularly useful for feeding the exercise with demand data informed by real-world use-case conditions. From that specific production process, a fixed production plan was selected for a "typical" (average consumption) week in 2023. This restriction is intended to isolate the contribution of the electricity-price forecast to tariff valuation and policy selection, so that any later performance differences are not confounded with schedule resequencing, load shifting, or broader production re-optimization, which, obviously, will open the door for future research.

The electricity demand associated with the selected production plan is obtained not from real electricity consumption records but from an electricity demand model (outside the scope of this study) to better simulate a real-world use context, where all these models live – the DSS tool mentioned before. This implies that the study's results should be analyzed with caution, as the values will depend on the precision of the demand forecast model. Thus, the results should be considered primarily for comparison rather than for absolute values (in particular in cost analysis). Moreover, it is important to note that the production plan has nearly 20% free time overall, which describes a bounded production flexibility scenario.

Within BAU, the decision signal is the fixed tariff. Within Policy_Variant_1, the decision signal is the point forecast of gross market hourly electricity prices over the 168-h horizon, which informs exposure to the dynamic tariff schedule. The focal comparison is thus restricted to how forecast information changes tariff-facing decisions under fixed operating conditions.

3.2 Electricity-Price Forecasting Model (EPF Model)

The study uses an electricity-price forecaster that generates hourly OMIE gross-price predictions over a $168\,h$ horizon for a specified forecast origin. Model training and inference are restricted to information available up to origin - 1h, and the same pre-origin boundary is preserved in both the backtest exercise (this one) and production mode, incorporated into the DSS models. The design was intended to maintain a leakage-safe multi-step forecasting workflow and turn a possible backtest into a simulation exercise using historical data to estimate past performance, risk, and viability before risking actual capital.

The electric price forecast literature has noted that decomposing prices into structured and stochastic components can be a simple but straightforward strategy to improve forecasts, as sophisticated models tend to struggle to beat the simplest naïve approach [13]. Combining a naive-type forecast with a parameter-rich correction model is an attractive framework due to its simplicity, variance-control architecture by design, and performance [14–16]. Moreover, this framework allows for coupling a versatile set of models to learn from the residuals. Thus, classical or machine learning models, such as LightGBM can be adopted to learn only the deviation from a strong seasonal naive anchor, not the whole price level. This is usually a good idea in electricity markets, where the level is partly seasonal and partly driven by hard-to-predict shocks, and the residual models can be focused on this hard forecast problem.

In this study, a leakage-safe 168-h electricity-price forecaster hybrid model is implemented, with the hourly OMIE gross price (target) decomposed into a repeated lag-24 persistence baseline and a bucket-specific residual term. Residuals are learned with Python *MLForecast* and *lightgbm.LGBMRegressor* on hourly data, short-memory autoregressive residual lags $(1, 2, 3, 4, 5, 6, 12)$, 24 h rolling mean and standard deviation transforms on the first three lags, and one interesting property of the machine learning learner for this case, a set of exogenous features.

Separate residual models are fitted for forecast lead buckets 1–24 h, 25–48 h, and 49–168 h, and their predictions are shrunk by bucket-specific damping coefficients (0.20, 0.20, 0.15) before being added back to the lag-24 baseline. These weights were imposed as a conservative regularization rule, motivated by forecast-combination evidence that simple/shrunk weights can outperform unstable estimated weights [17, 18] and as a first, simple, exploratory specification that can establish a future model development baseline. A drawback is that this specification is structurally designed for smoothness and persistence, which limits the model's capacity to respond to weekend transitions, holidays, renewable ramp events, outages, fuel shocks, scarcity episodes, and negative price regimes.

The exogenous information is included in the residual model learner as calendar, astronomical, renewable-proxy, demand-proxy, and interaction features. Note that the last three types of features are engineered variables built by combining spatial information (e.g., the geographic locations of power plants, weighted by capacity, and the most relevant demand points, weighted by population) and engineering-based features from weather forecast parameters. The feature engineering procedures try to proxy market fundamentals, such as renewable production availability or consumption patterns. Future-feature construction reuses a persisted transformer bundle generated during training, ensuring the same transformation logic is applied at inference time. These inputs should nevertheless be interpreted as pure operational proxies rather than as a full structural representation of electricity-market fundamentals, but are chosen to proxy those elements in an environment of lack / asymmetric information.

3.3 Evaluation Design and Metrics

The evaluation design uses a 168h forecast horizon, for which a scenario-based protocol follows:

- built around 15 historical weekly forecast origins (forecast issues origin on Monday, 0:00:00)
- a fixed-tariff BAU policy baseline of 0.0829 €/kWh, based on Eurostat [19] electricity prices components for non-household consumers, in 2024, for Portugal, and considering the consumption band ID (2 000 MWh to 19 999 MWh)
- volatility-stratified week audited cases (low – average – high) are chosen from 2025 real market gross hourly OMIE (Portugal) electricity prices data (published by OMIE).

The analysis operates on a balanced 5/5/5 audited weeks with spacing enforced within each bucket (30 days).

The evaluation framework is structured to keep forecast validity, economic relevance, and policy value (including downside risks) separately. Each component of the evaluation design addresses different aspects of decision usefulness and should not be collapsed into a single performance score [20, 21].

Thus, it follows:

Forecast validity is assessed against leakage-safe one-shot persistence comparators at lags 24 and 168, complemented by point-error metrics such as MAE, RMSE, Bias and Diebold-Mariano significance tests [22]. Additional *empirical interval coverage,* defined as the share of observed prices that fall within the model's forecast interval, will also be used. This design remains methodologically consistent with current electricity-price forecasting practice [7, 10] while adapting to this study's objectives.

Economic relevance assumes it depends not only on the level of accuracy but also on the preservation of tariff ordering; this analysis is implemented with *ranking diagnostics metrics* through Spearman's ρ, Kendall's τ, plus pairwise ordering accuracy. Additional *precision at k lags* and *load-weighted cheap-hour capture*, alongside regime summaries and statistical comparisons, were performed to provide a broader view.

Finally, a generalized *policy-value* evaluation was developed based on proxy-based cost comparisons between BAU and Policy_Variant_1, with a downside-risk layer to represent the probability of underperformance, such as the VaR_{95} and $CVaR_{95}$ metrics. Additional semideviation and mean excess cost are calculated to go beyond average policy-value summaries alone, which do not fully characterize adverse risk exposure [23].

It is important to highlight that the evaluation outputs must be interpreted conservatively, in particular with respect to the cost layer: realized cost remains a proxy rather than field-deployment evidence. Moreover, evidence is limited to 15 audited scenario weeks and should be read as sensitivity-analysis evidence rather than independent-sample inference.

4 Results

4.1 Forecast Validity

Forecast validity was evaluated using weekly point-error metrics, leakage-safe one-shot persistence benchmarks, lead-wise error profiles, and empirical interval coverage. Performance was materially regime-dependent. Low-volatility weeks showed the lowest mean error, whereas high-volatility weeks showed the highest error, the strongest negative bias, and the weakest empirical interval coverage.

Against leakage-safe one-shot 24 h persistence, the forecast model achieved lower squared loss in low-, average-, and high-volatility weeks. The comparison with the leakage-safe one-shot 168 h persistence was more selective: superiority was observed only in average-volatility weeks, whereas low- and high-volatility weeks did not favor the model.

Horizon-wise diagnostics also indicated non-uniform validity across the 168h run, with MAE lowest near lead hour 2 (15 €/MWh) and peaking near hour 57 (56 €/MWh).

Empirical interval coverage remained below the nominal 90% level in all three regimes. These findings are limited to the 15 selected audited weeks (5 per volatility class) and should therefore be read as sensitivity-analysis evidence rather than independent-sample inference (Tables 1, 2 and Fig. 1).

Table 1. Forecast Accuracy by Volatility Regime

Regime	n weeks	MAE (€/MWh)	RMSE (€/MWh)	Bias (€/MWh)	Coverage (%)
Low	5	24.1	29.5	-10.1	66.4
Average	5	26.4	33.2	-10.1	58.5
High	5	43.0	53.9	-38.5	39.8

Regime-level averages of weekly point-accuracy metrics. Coverage is empirical 90% prediction-interval coverage; nominal target is 90%. Negative bias indicates systematic underprediction of actual prices.

Sign convention: DM statistic is computed on (model squared loss − benchmark squared loss). Negative DM → model has lower loss (model preferred). Positive DM → benchmark has lower loss.

Table 2. Diebold–Mariano Tests Against Leakage-Safe Persistence Benchmarks

Regime	ΔLoss lag-24h	DM stat lag-24h	p lag-24h	Favored lag-24h
Low	−40.7	−4.4	0.000	Model
Average	−65.8	−4.6	0.000	Model
High	−50.3	−3.4	0.001	Model
Regime	ΔLoss lag-168h	DM stat lag-168h	p lag-168h	Favored lag-168h
Low	60.6	0.6	0.563	Benchmark
Average	−398.4	−4.0	0.000	Model
High	118.3	0.6	0.540	Benchmar

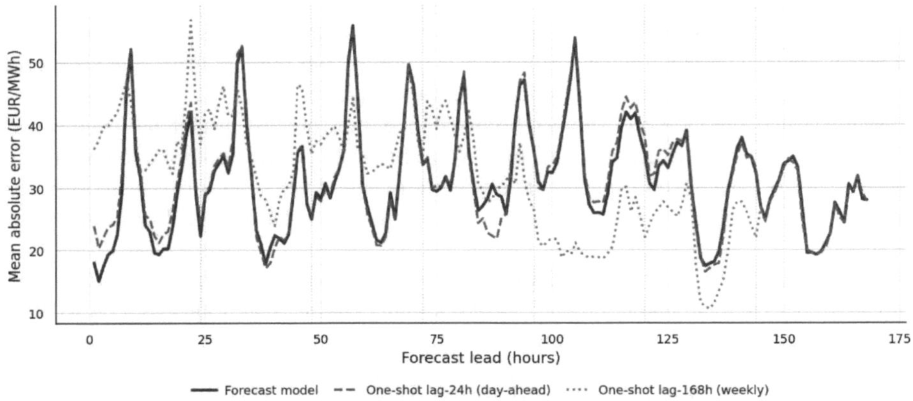

Fig. 1. Lead-Wise Forecast Error vs Benchmarks.

4.2 Ranking Quality

Ranking quality was evaluated through broad rank agreement, top-k cheap-hour precision, and load-weighted cheap-hour capture for the current 168 h run [11]. Broad weekly ordering skill was materially positive and highly similar across volatility regimes, with Spearman ρ around 0.67–0.69, Kendall τ around 0.49–0.50, and pairwise ordering accuracy around 0.747–0.749. By contrast, narrow cheap-hour retrieval was weak at $k = 6$: mean precision@6 was 0.000 in low-volatility weeks, 0.067 in average-volatility weeks, and 0.100 in high-volatility weeks. Retrieval improved as the selected cheap-hour window widened to $k = 12$ and $k = 24$, with the strongest broad-window performance in average-volatility weeks (precision@24 = 0.483; capture@24 = 0.434). These results indicate that the model preserves coarse merit order better than exact hour placement: rank agreement remains positive, but narrow-set retrieval is unstable, and exact placement remains noisy [24] (Fig. 2).

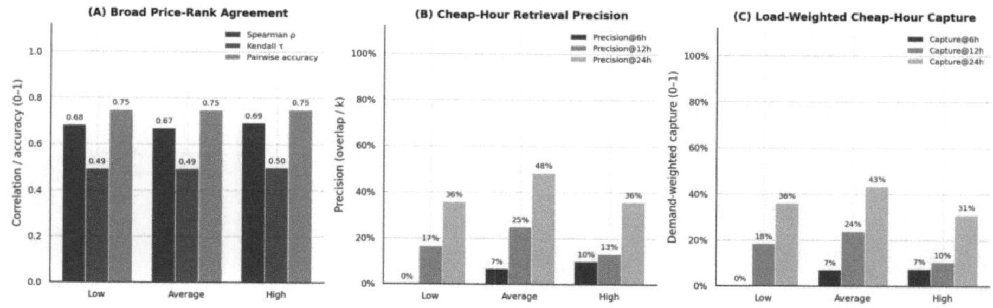

Fig. 2. Composite Tariff-Ordering Quality

4.3 Policy Value

In forecast-cost terms, Policy_Variant_1 yields positive mean gains relative to BAU in all three volatility regimes, with the largest expected gain in high-volatility weeks (1 266 €), followed by low-volatility (753 €) and average-volatility weeks (652 €).

Realized proxy-cost outcomes also remain positive on average in all regimes. Still, they are materially smaller and differently ordered: low-volatility weeks show the highest mean realized gain (559 €), followed by average-volatility (458 €) and high-volatility weeks (311 €).

Decision value is not uniform across scenarios. Positive realized gains occur in 80.0% of average-volatility scenarios, 80.0% of high-volatility scenarios, and 60.0% of low-volatility scenarios, while negative realized outcomes are still observed across all regimes. This dispersion is especially visible in the low-volatility subset, where realized gains range from −1 226 € to 1 662 € in the current selected set (Table 3 and Figs. 3, 4).

Table 3. Realized Policy Value vs BAU by Volatility Regime

Volatility Regime	n scenarios	Mean gain (€)	Median gain (€)	Std dev (€)	Positive gain (%)	Worst case (€)
Low	5	559.3	874.6	1 250.3	60%	−1 226.3
Average	5	458.0	346.4	478.1	80%	−89.7
High	5	311.2	215.5	493.9	80%	−315.3
All regimes	*15*	*442.8*	*346.4*	*769.9*	*73%*	*−1 226.3*

Realized gain = Policy_Variant_1 cost minus BAU cost per scenario week; negative values indicate savings. "Positive gain (%)" is the share of scenarios where Policy_Variant_1 outperformed BAU. "Worst case" is the deepest single-scenario loss. Production plan is fixed; gains arise from tariff-response timing only.

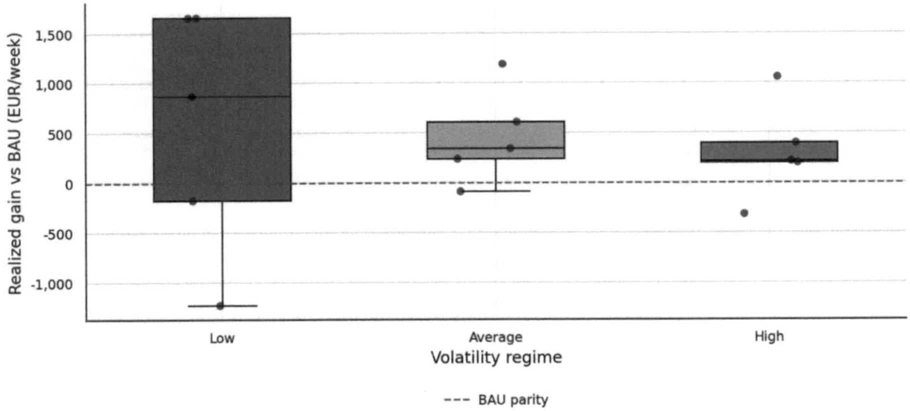

Fig. 3. Realized Gain vs BAU by Volatility Regime

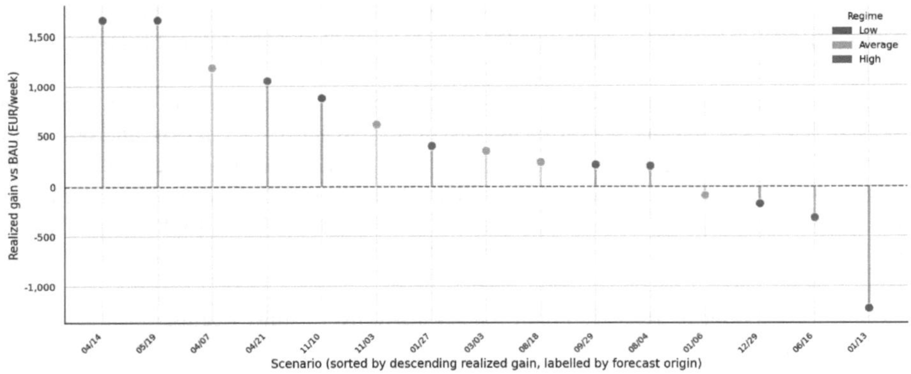

Fig. 4. Scenario-Level Realized Gain vs BAU (Sorted)

Scenarios sorted by descending realized gain across all regimes. Points below the dashed red line represent weeks where Policy_Variant_1 exceeded BAU cost (4 of 15 scenarios).

4.4 Risk and Robustness

Risk and robustness were evaluated using underperformance probability and bootstrap excess-cost tail summaries under the fixed-plan design. The results show that downside risk was non-zero in all three volatility regimes, and the mean probability that Policy_Variant_1 underperformed BAU was highest in low-volatility weeks (0,391), compared with 0,202 in high-volatility and 0,146 in average-volatility scenarios.

Under the pipeline excess-cost sign convention, regime-mean VaR95, CVaR95, and mean excess cost remained negative across all regimes, indicating that the average selected-scenario tail summaries still favored Policy_Variant_1, even though adverse weeks were not eliminated.

Robustness was nevertheless materially regime-dependent: low-volatility weeks were the most uneven subset, combining the lowest positive realized-gain share (0.60), the deepest realized worst case (−1,226 €), and the widest dispersion in both underperformance probability (std = 0.54) and VaR95 (std = 791 €).

The results show that favorable average gains do not settle robustness in this study: positive regime means can coexist with meaningful reversal risk, so robustness must be assessed with probability, tail, and dispersion evidence together rather than with regime means alone (Table 4 and Fig. 5).

Table 4. Downside Risk by Volatility Regime

Volatility Regime	Underperf. Prob	VaR95 (EUR)	CVaR95 (EUR)	Mean excess cost (EUR)
Low	40%	−471.7	−448.3	−562.1
Average	20%	−367.7	−343.5	−458.5
High	20%	−210.0	−180.8	−311.9

Underperf. prob." is the bootstrap probability that Policy_Variant_1 realized a higher cost than BAU. VaR95 and CVaR95 are the 95th percentile and conditional tail excess cost estimates under the pipeline sign convention; negative values indicate that even the tail favored Policy_Variant_1. Mean excess cost is the regime-mean of the per-scenario excess cost. Production plan is fixed.

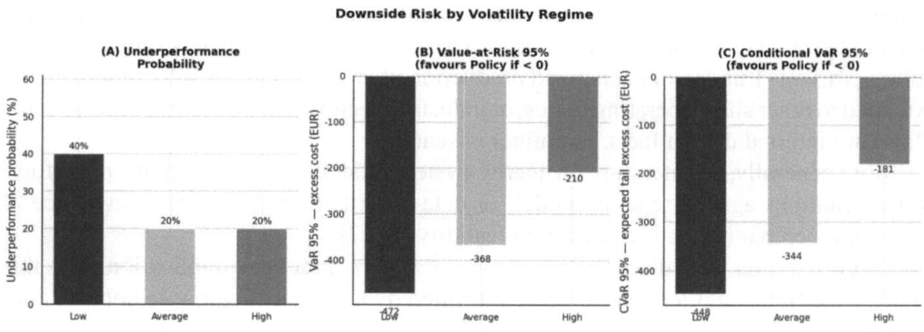

Fig. 5. Downside Risk Composite by Volatility Regime

5 Discussion

The results support that operational usefulness in this setting cannot be inferred solely from point-accuracy summaries. Within the audited fixed-plan comparison, forecast-validity performance was mixed and regime-dependent, including selective superiority over leakage-safe one-shot 168 h persistence and below-nominal interval coverage across regimes.

By contrast, broad tariff-ordering skill remained materially positive even when exact cheap-hour retrieval was weak, especially at k = 6.

Read together, those patterns suggest that the decision value observed here is more consistent with preservation of economically relevant tariff ordering than with aggregate error statistics alone. The point is not that ranking information universally dominates point accuracy across all forecasting problems: in this study setting, a forecast can be operationally informative even when conventional error summaries do not, by themselves, provide a sufficient account of usefulness. That interpretation aligns with the literature, which argues that decision-linked forecast evaluation can reveal distinctions that aggregate accuracy measures may obscure, although this argument remains application-specific rather than universal [3, 25].

The value interpretation must therefore remain conditional. In the audited setting, the mean realized proxy gain relative to BAU was positive in all three volatility regimes. Still, negative realized outcomes occurred in each regime, and the probability of underperformance remained non-zero throughout the audited set. This is why average improvement cannot be read as robustness. The evidence instead indicates that volatility shapes both opportunity and downside exposure, while the relationship is not uniform enough to justify a simple "more volatility, more value" claim.

The highest downside frequency in the audited set occurs in low-volatility weeks, reinforcing the analytical distinction between mean gains and tail risk. More broadly, this supports a cautious reading in which forecast-informed tariff response can create value without eliminating the possibility of unfavorable realized outcomes. That reading is consistent with warnings that modeled or target-state performance should not be collapsed into unconditional operational success claims [26].

Several design limits bound these interpretations. First, the evaluation is a proxy-cost sensitivity analysis rather than deployment evidence. Second, it covers 15 selected audited scenario weeks rather than an independent sample designed for broad statistical generalization. Third, the policy scope is narrow: the study compares only BAU and Policy_Variant_1 under an unchanged production plan. Fourth, the results should not be extended to other sites, operating logics, or industrial sectors without additional evidence. Those are internal design facts, not minor caveats.

More generally, the literature on energy-system modelling and electricity-price forecasting cautions against reading model- or data-specific findings as direct evidence of real-world behavior or as broad external validity [8, 27].

Taken together, the discussion supports a narrow practical implication. For this audited fixed-plan application, forecast-informed dynamic tariff response appears conditionally useful when the forecast preserves tariff ordering well enough to improve decisions relative to BAU.

6 Conclusions

In this study, the decision value of the 168h electricity-price forecast is explained more by the preservation of economically relevant tariff ordering than by point error alone under the evaluated fixed-plan BAU versus Policy_Variant_1 setting.

Mean realized proxy gains are positive across the selected audited scenario set, but they are non-uniform across regimes and remain exposed to adverse cases and non-zero downside risk; accordingly, the evidence supports only cautious, context-bound use claims for fixed-plan forecast-informed tariff response.

Holding the production plan fixed is analytically useful in this evaluation design because it isolates tariff valuation under an unchanged schedule. Still, it does not validate joint optimization or full operational adaptation.

The evidence is therefore bound to a realized proxy-cost sensitivity analysis over 15 selected audited weeks and to BAU versus Policy_Variant_1 only, so broader operational validation under richer policies and independent samples is still needed.

Acknowledgments. The authors will thank the industrial partner for the provided dataset (undisclosed due to privacy concerns) on production process features (including overall recorded electricity consumption and the associated production plan.

This work has been supported by the European Union under the Next Generation EU, through a grant of the Portuguese Republic's Recovery and Resilience Plan (RRP) Partnership Agreement, within the scope of the project PRODUTECH R3 – "Agenda Mobilizadora da Fileira das Tecnologias de Produção para a Reindustrialização".

The information provided here reflects only the author's view, which does not necessarily reflect those of the European Union or of the European Commission. Neither the European Union nor the granting authority can be held responsible for them. The European Commission is not responsible for any use that may be made of the information herewith included.

Disclosure of Interests. Manuel Ferreira is an employee of Microprocessador – Sistemas Digitais S.A., which commercializes decision-support system solutions to manage electricity consumption and supported the study with real data on production process consumption. However, the company had no role in the study data analysis, manuscript preparation, or decision to publish.

References

1. Siddiquee, S., Agyeman, K., Bruton, K., Howard, B., O'Sullivan, D.: A data-driven framework for quantifying demand response participation benefit of industrial consumers. IEEE Trans. Ind. Appl. **60**, 2577–2587 (2024). https://doi.org/10.1109/tia.2023.3334218
2. Turner, S., Bennett, J., Robertson, D., Galelli, S.: Complex relationship between seasonal streamflow forecast skill and value in reservoir operations. Hydrol. Earth Syst. Sci. **21**, 4841–4859 (2017). https://doi.org/10.5194/hess-21-4841-2017
3. Carrière, T., Kariniotakis, G.: An integrated approach for value-oriented energy forecasting and data-driven decision-making application to renewable energy trading. IEEE Trans. Smart Grid **10**, 6933–6944 (2019). https://doi.org/10.1109/tsg.2019.2914379
4. Leinauer, C., Schott, P., Fridgen, G., Keller, R., Ollig, P., Weibelzahl, M.: Obstacles to demand response: why industrial companies do not adapt their power consumption to volatile power generation. Energy Policy (2022). https://doi.org/10.1016/j.enpol.2022.112876
5. Maciejowska, K., Lipiecki, A., Uniejewski, B.: Statistical and economic evaluation of forecasts in electricity markets: beyond RMSE and MAE. Energy Convers. Manag. **356**, 121408 (2026). https://doi.org/10.1016/j.enconman.2026.121408
6. Weron, R.: Electricity price forecasting: a review of the state-of-the-art with a look into the future. Int. J. Forecast. **30**(4), 1030–1081 (2014). https://doi.org/10.1016/j.ijforecast.2014.08.008

7. Lago, J., Marcjasz, G., Schutter, B., Weron, R.: Forecasting day-ahead electricity prices: a review of state-of-the-art algorithms, best practices and an open-access benchmark, arXiv, vol. abs/2008.08004 (2020). https://doi.org/10.1016/j.apenergy.2021.116983
8. O'Connor, C., Bahloul, M., Prestwich, S., Visentin, A.: A review of electricity price forecasting models in the day-ahead, intra-day, and balancing markets. Energies (2025). https://doi.org/10.3390/en18123097
9. Strøm, E., Gundersen, O.E.: Performance metrics for multi-step forecasting measuring win-loss, seasonal variance and forecast stability: an empirical study. Appl. Intell. **54**, 10490–10515 (2024). https://doi.org/10.1007/s10489-024-05715-4
10. Nowotarski, J., Weron, R.: Recent advances in electricity price forecasting: a review of probabilistic forecasting. Renew. Sustain. Energy Rev. **81**, 1548–1568 (2018). https://doi.org/10.1016/j.rser.2017.05.234
11. Kath, C., Ziel, F.: The value of forecasts: quantifying the economic gains of accurate quarter-hourly electricity price forecasts. Energy Econ. (2018). https://doi.org/10.1016/j.eneco.2018.10.005
12. Shoreh, M., Siano, P., Shafie-khah, M., Loia, V., Catalão, J.: A survey of industrial applications of demand response. Electr. Power Syst. Res. **141**, 31–49 (2016). https://doi.org/10.1016/j.epsr.2016.07.008
13. Xiong, X., Qing, G.: A hybrid day-ahead electricity price forecasting framework based on time series. Energy (2022). https://doi.org/10.1016/j.energy.2022.126099
14. Uniejewski, B., Weron, R.: Efficient forecasting of electricity spot prices with expert and LASSO models. Energies (2018). https://doi.org/10.3390/en11082039
15. Marcjasz, G., Uniejewski, B., Weron, R.: Beating the Naïve—combining LASSO with Naïve intraday electricity price forecasts. Energies (2020). https://doi.org/10.3390/en13071667
16. Billé, A.G., Gianfreda, A., Del Grosso, F., Ravazzolo, F.: Forecasting electricity prices with expert, linear, and nonlinear models. Int. J. Forecast. **39**(2), 570–586 (2023). https://doi.org/10.1016/j.ijforecast.2022.01.003
17. Clemen, R.T.: Combining forecasts: a review and annotated bibliography. Int. J. Forecast. **5**(4), 559–583 (1989). https://doi.org/10.1016/0169-2070(89)90012-5
18. Wang, X., Hyndman, R.J., Li, F., Kang, Y.: Forecast combinations: an over 50-year review. Int. J. Forecast. **39**(4), 1518–1547 (2023). https://doi.org/10.1016/j.ijforecast.2022.11.005
19. Eurostat: Electricity prices components for non-household consumers - annual data (from 2007 onwards), European Commission (2025). https://doi.org/10.2908/nrg_pc_205_c
20. Koutsandreas, D., Spiliotis, E., Petropoulos, F., Assimakopoulos, V.: On the selection of forecasting accuracy measures. J. Oper. Res. Soc. **73**, 937–954 (2021). https://doi.org/10.1080/01605682.2021.1892464
21. Giudici, P., Raffinetti, E.: RGA: a unified measure of predictive accuracy. Adv. Data Anal. Classif. **19**, 67–93 (2024). https://doi.org/10.1007/s11634-023-00574-2
22. Diebold, F.X., Mariano, R.S.: Comparing predictive accuracy. J. Bus. Econ. Stat. **20**(1), 134–144 (2002). https://doi.org/10.1198/073500102753410444
23. Xiao, D., Chen, H., Cai, W., Wei, C., Zhao, Z.: Integrated risk measurement and control for stochastic energy trading of a wind storage system in electricity markets. Prot. Control Mod. Power Syst. **8**, 1–11 (2023). https://doi.org/10.1186/s41601-023-00329-3
24. Ziel, F., Weron, R.: Day-ahead electricity price forecasting with high-dimensional structures: univariate vs. multivariate modeling frameworks. Energy Econ. **70**, 396–420 (2018). https://doi.org/10.1016/j.eneco.2017.12.016

25. Vogler, A., Ziel, F.: Event-based evaluation of electricity price ensemble forecasts. Forecasting (2021). https://doi.org/10.3390/forecast4010004
26. Torralba-Díaz, L., et al.: Identification of the efficiency gap by coupling a fundamental electricity market model and an agent-based simulation model. Energies **13**, 3920 (2020). https://doi.org/10.3390/en13153920
27. Trutnevyte, E.: Does cost optimization approximate the real-world energy transition? Energy **106**, 182–193 (2016). https://doi.org/10.1016/j.energy.2016.03.038

Feature Curves Detection and Segmentation of Point Clouds

Alexander König[1(✉)], Ivana Kolingerová[1], and Tomáš Bayer[2]

[1] Department of Computer Science and Engineering, University of West Bohemia, Pilsen, Czech Republic
{akonig,kolinger}@kiv.zcu.cz

[2] Department of Applied Geoinformatics and Cartography, Charles University, Prague, Czech Republic
bayertom@natur.cuni.cz

Abstract. The data type commonly used to represent geodata are point clouds. They hold most of the important information and require less memory than meshes, however, they are sometimes harder to process. One of the keys to reducing the computational cost of working with them is detecting their most important properties and dividing them into sub-clouds that can be further processed separately. To further work with them efficiently it can be beneficial to estimate the borders of the sub-clouds. They can be formed by feature curves, curves that trace the important features in the data. In this paper we propose a method for segmentation and feature curve detection. Our aim is to work directly with the point cloud, without reconstructing the underlying surface, as surface reconstruction can be computationally expensive, especially for terrain point clouds. The segmentation of the input point cloud into nearly planar sub-clouds is done using Variational shape approximation algorithm, and the feature curves are defined using alpha shape computation and poly-line interpolation. The detected feature curves form borders between the sub-clouds. The proposed method was tested for point clouds representing 3D objects as well as for terrain data.

Keywords: Point Cloud · Point Cloud Segmentation · Feature Curves · Feature Curve Detection · Variational Shape Approximation · Alpha Shapes · Poly-Line Interpolation

1 Introduction

Point clouds are the most common data type used when working namely with geodata. They hold most of the important information about the digitized data, are more compact, and require less memory in comparison to 3D meshes. However, due to their unstructured nature, the analysis and further processing of these data sets are in some cases more challenging than for meshes. Namely, terrain point clouds acquired by scanning real sceneries are typically large, often include non-trivial terrain formations (such as overhangs or cavities), and may

O. Gervasi et al. (Eds.): ICCSA 2026, LNCS 16768, pp. 684–702, 2027.
https://doi.org/10.1007/978-3-032-30488-9_42

contain imperfections, including noise or holes. Processing such data is an important and challenging problem. Often it is needed to subsample them, filter out the noise or fill in the holes. To do this efficiently, it can be useful to divide the point cloud into sub-clouds that can be processed separately, faster or easier, than if we worked with the whole point cloud.

There are many approaches for segmentation of meshes and point clouds, some based on feature curves, curves tracing the important features (such as edges and creases) present in the data. These methods mostly focus on working exclusively with 3D meshes and either require a set of feature curves as input or their first step is feature curve detection. Other approaches are based on detecting geometric objects, such as basic geometric primitives, planes, or surfaces in the 3D data. These methods either do not detect feature curves or the quality of detected feature curves depends on the size of the created sub-clouds.

Segmentation with the condition of planarity divides the input point cloud into a set of distinct almost planar sub-clouds. Each satisfies the condition of being able to be projected onto its best fitting plane (which can be found for example using the principal component analysis approach [13]) without the loss of important information. This simplifies the problem of working with 3D data, as one would work with multiple sets of data in 2D. To correctly work with the projected sub-clouds it is needed to estimate the border of its domain. This can be done by projecting the feature curves that neighbor the sub-cloud onto the same plane. It is beneficial to create as accurate borders as possible. This is a non-trivial task for point clouds, as they do not have firmly set neighborhoods.

This paper proposes a point cloud segmentation method preserving the shape of the point cloud as much as possible and subdividing it to simplify further processing. It creates nearly planar sub-clouds and detects the most important feature curves in the data, each curve represented by a set of vertices. The feature curves are connected and form the borders of the sub-clouds.

Novelty of the proposed method lies in the unique combination of the following properties:

- the algorithm works with the input point cloud without reconstructing the underlying surface, as surface reconstruction can be computationally expensive,
- the feature curves are determined from the created sub-clouds, no preprocessing step is required,
- the algorithm output allows to simplify further processing of the 3D data by projecting it into 2D.

In the following section is the discussion of other approaches to segmentation. In Sect. 3 the details of the proposed algorithm and its individual steps are presented. The results for both point clouds representing 3D objects and terrain point clouds acquired by LIDAR scanning are discussed in Sect. 4.

2 Related Work

As previously mentioned, data in 3D is often represented by meshes or point clouds. To further process both point clouds and meshes, it can be advantageous to divide them into distinct parts or regions. This approach, called segmentation, groups together areas with similar properties. Segmentation methods can be either semantic or geometric.

Semantic segmentation divides the input into regions based on the semantic content of the object's parts. For example, a model of a person is divided into head, torso, arms, and legs. It is often used to find object boundaries in 3D space, which is useful in robotics, autonomous driving, or augmented reality. A review of point cloud semantic segmentation was done by Y. Xie et al. [20] and one example of a method for 3D scans with large point counts is Scancomplete [6]. There are methods focusing on geodata, such as LIDAR point clouds, due to their specific properties, such as the method by Y. Wu et al. [19].

Geometric segmentation is based on dividing the input into regions according to their geometric properties. Geometric segmentation of 3D meshes can be based on feature lines, which are then connected to form patches in the input data. One option is to extract complete feature curve networks using a quadric surface fitting technique and then find cycles in them to generate the segmentation, as proposed by Z. Lu et al. [12]. A different approach, proposed by Y. Cao et al. [4], detects and encloses feature loops on surfaces, the created patches are then subdivided, so they are nearly planar. The approach by H. Baharami et al. [2] subdivides the input mesh into developable ruled surfaces, however, it does not seem to be suitable for detailed data. There are also methods to detect feature curves and edges in point clouds, such as the approach by K.W. Lee and P. Bo [10] or Edc-net [3], which can serve as a starting point of segmentation algorithms.

Geometric segmentation for both point clouds and meshes can also be based on detecting geometric objects, such as basic geometric primitives, planes, or surfaces, in the 3D model. One possible approach is the Variational Shape Approximation (VSA), which was first proposed by D. Cohen-Steiner et al. [5] as a method for segmenting meshes into planar regions. It was later extended to detect different types of approximating surfaces, such as spheres or cylinders [18], and quadric surfaces [21]. It was also extended to work with point clouds [10] and further improved by M. Skrodzkia et al. [16] and T. Zhao et al. [23]. The VSA method generates nearly planar sub-clouds; however, the defined border of one sub-cloud is rather too simplified. K.W. Lee et al. [10] demonstrate that by exploiting the borders of multiple neighboring sub-clouds, feature curves in the model can be found, however the found feature curves do not have to fully enclose any created sub-cloud and their quality depends on the size of the created sub-clouds.

Some approaches to segmentation, such as Exoskeleton [7], combine both the semantic and geometric approaches. Starting with the semantic segmentation of a 3D mesh, this method further decomposes it into patches using a modified VSA algorithm. It has been demonstrated to work for 3D objects, but it may be challenging to correctly apply semantic segmentation to terrain data, especially due to the atypical properties of the data, such as noise and holes. A survey of segmentation methods specific for terrain data was done by M.D. Hossain [9].

A 3D model can also be segmented by deep learning networks. Parsenet [15] decomposes a point cloud into parametric surface patches and basic geometric primitives. The main advantage is that the results can be refined based on standard CAD modeling operations, however this method has trouble detecting small parts and producing seamless boundaries on noisy data. HPNet [22] segments a point cloud into primitive patches by combining geometric heuristic and deep learning. A common problem of methods based on deep learning is generating realistic training point clouds. Further overview of deep learning methods for segmenting point clouds was done by S. Sarker et al. [14].

In this paper, we propose a method for geometric segmentation of point clouds. It divides the input point cloud into nearly planar sub-clouds and detects feature curves in the input data, each represented by a set of vertices. The detected feature curves form the borders between the sub-clouds. Our algorithm utilizes the VSA approach [16] to segmentation in combination with alpha shapes [8] and poly-line interpolation. The individual steps of the algorithm will be described in the following section.

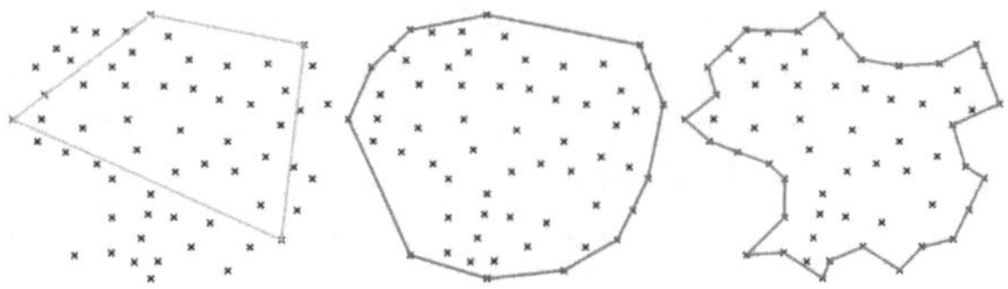

Fig. 1. Illustration of approaches to the definition of the point cloud domain. Using the boundaries defined by VSA in the leftmost image, using convex hull in the middle and alpha shape in the rightmost image.

3 Method Overview

The method proposed in this paper subdivides the input point cloud $P = \{p_i | i = 0, ..., n-1\}$, where each point has the coordinates $p_i = [x_i, y_i, z_i]$. The output is m disjoint nearly planar sub-clouds $R_0...R_{m-1}$, $R_i = \{p_{i,j} | j = 0, ..., k-1\}$, where each point has the coordinates $p_{i,j} = [x_{i,j}, y_{i,j}, z_{i,j}]$, each sub-cloud R_i being a sub-set of the points from P. After the segmentation, l feature curves $F_0...F_{l-1}$ in the input point cloud are detected and connected to form the borders between the sub-clouds. Each feature curve F_i is represented by a set of vertices, $F_i = \{q_{i,j} | j = 0, ..., s-1\}$, $q_{i,j} = [x_{i,j}, y_{i,j}, z_{i,j}]$.

Let us present the overview of the proposed algorithm. The individual steps of the algorithm, which will be described further, are:

1. Point-cloud segmentation,
2. Crossing point computation,
3. Domain border computation,
4. Poly-line interpolation,
5. Connecting the dots.

The first step is processing the input point cloud to form m nearly planar sub-clouds. In the second step crossing points - the points, where three or more sub-clouds neighbor - are computed. Then the domains of the sub-clouds and their borders are computed. The domain borders of neighboring sub-clouds are interpolated in the fourth step, and in the fifth step they are connected with the crossing points, forming the feature curves of the point cloud.

The sub-clouds R_i computed in step one are the sub-clouds created using Variational shape approximation method [16] and each can be projected onto its best fitting plane without the loss of important information. The feature curves F_i can be found as the border between two neighboring sub-clouds. This is a non-trivial task for point clouds, as they do not have firmly set neighborhoods. To detect the feature curves, this paper utilizes the following approach: first, the domains of the sub-clouds projected onto their best fitting planes are defined. Then the borders of these domains are projected back to 3D, and the borders of two neighboring sub-clouds are interpolated to form the feature curves.

It is important to correctly define the domain and its borders that the sub-cloud R_i occupies when projected onto the plane. The simplest approach would be to take the edges of the polygon bounding the sub-cloud R_i created by VSA and project them onto the best fitting plane of R_i. However, this could cut away parts of the point cloud and create a domain smaller than it really should be, especially since the point cloud could have a more complex shape. A different option would be to use the convex hull of the projected sub-cloud R_i. This could include in the domain parts of the plane that should be excluded as the shape of the point cloud could be concave. Both of these potential problems are illustrated in Fig. 1. Alpha shapes [8] offer a solution that captures the shape of the projected sub-cloud more accurately than a convex hull. They define the shape of a set of points in a plane. How closely the alpha shape copies the point cloud depends on the parameter α. The illustration of an alpha shape can be seen in Fig. 2. Once the alpha shapes for each sub-cloud are found, they are projected back into 3D. Neighboring sub-clouds have different alpha shapes that do not share edges. To find the feature curves in the original point cloud, it is necessary to interpolate between the neighboring parts of the alpha shapes and create poly-line borders between the sub-clouds. These poly-lines represent the feature curves detected in the data and form borders between the created sub-clouds.

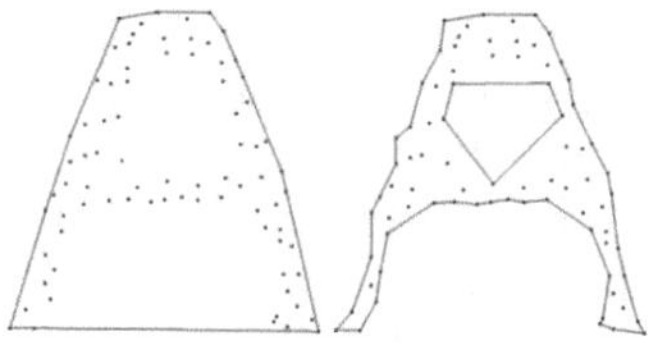

Fig. 2. Convex hull of a point cloud in 2D representing the letter A on the left and an illustration of a possible alpha shape on the right.

The individual steps of the algorithm are described in more detail in the following subsections. The proposed algorithm is also illustrated in Fig. 3.

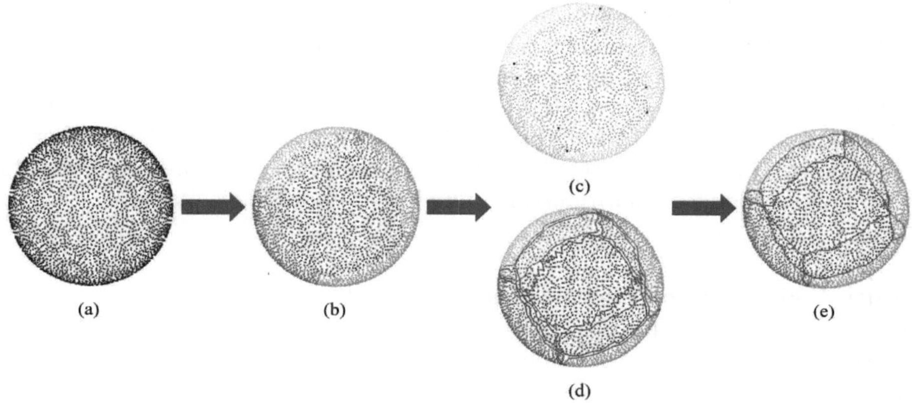

Fig. 3. Illustration of the steps of the algorithm: (a) input point cloud, (b) sub-clouds created by VSA, (c) detected crossing points (thick black), (d) computed domain borders of the sub-clouds (red), (e) resulting feature curves (red). (Color figure online)

3.1 Point-Cloud Segmentation

The first step is to divide the input point cloud into nearly planar sub-clouds. As already mentioned, to partition a point cloud $P = \{p_i | i = 0...n-1\}$, where each point has the coordinates $p_i = [x_i, y_i, z_i]$, into m disjoint sub-clouds $R_0...R_{m-1}$ the VSA algorithm is used. It works as follows: each created sub-cloud R_i can be approximated well by a plane with a normal N_i. This plane can be acquired using the principal component analysis (PCA) approach [13]. These planes are called proxies of the given sub-clouds. The created sub-clouds minimize the following energy $L^{2,1}(R_i, N_i)$ defined by [16]:

$$L^{2,1}(R_i, N_i) = \sum_{p_j \in R_i} w_j ||n_j - N_i||_2^2 \tag{1}$$

where n_j is the normal of the point p_j and w_j is its weight. To compute the normal n_j, the PCA algorithm is used on the point p_j and its neighborhood defined as its k nearest neighbors from P. The main disadvantage of this approach is the need to compute the normals for each of the input points.

The overview of the implemented algorithm VSA is outlined in Algorithm 1 and described in the following text. It is based on the following steps:

- Initialization - given an integer parameter m, m points $p_0, ..., p_{m-1} \in P$ are chosen as the seed points of the m proxies. For each proxy P_i the neighbors of the seed point p_i, paired with the index of the proxy i, are added to a priority queue Q. The priority of each pair in the queue reflects how well the point normal n_j is approximated by the proxy normal N_i.
- Flood - while Q is not empty, a pair [point p_j, proxy index i] is dequeued, and if p_j has not been assigned to a proxy yet, it is assigned to the proxy i and its neighbors are added to the queue paired with the index i.
- Proxy update - the normal of each proxy is updated to the normal of the best fitting plane of the assigned points.
- Seed point update - a new seed point is selected from the assigned points as the point with the closest normal to the new proxy normal. If the number m is known upfront these last three steps are then repeated while assignments to proxies change or until maximal number of iterations is reached.

Controlled Level of Detail. The VSA method can be modified so that the number of desired proxies m does not need to be known upfront. Instead, it changes with relation to a parameter $maxD$ that controls the maximum deviation from its best fitted plane of the subset assigned to proxy P_i.

For this to work, two new operations need to be defined, split and merge, which increase and decrease the number of proxies respectively [16]. They take place after the proxy update step of the algorithm. To avoid the creation of sub-clouds with low number of points we add a final merge pass merging those with fewer points than threshold t_{pc}. The details of the split and merge operations are described below.

Split. This operation increases the number of proxies. It is performed if in a proxy P_i at least l points are further from the proxy than $maxD$. The largest spread direction of P_i is computed using PCA, and the proxy is then split at the center perpendicularly to its best-fitted plane and the direction projected onto the plane. For each newly created sub-cloud, its new proxy normal is computed using PCA.

Merge. This operation decreases the number of proxies. It is performed if for any subset $P' = P_i \cup P_j$, created by two neighboring subsets, fewer than l points are further from the proxy than $maxD$. Then the two subsets are replaced by their union P'. The new proxy normal of P' is computed using PCA.

Input: $P = \{p_i, i = 1...n-1\}$, $\forall p_i = \{x_i, y_i, z_i\}$ - point cloud; m - number of proxies; k - number of nearest neighbors; $maxD$ - maximum allowed distance of points from best fitted plane
Output: $R_0...R_{m-1}$ - set of distinct point clouds
Initialization();
while *Assignments to proxies change OR unreached maximum number of iterations* **do**
    Flood();
    Proxy update();
    Split();
    Merge();
    Seed point update();
end
Final merge();

Algorithm 1: Point-cloud segmentation based on the VSA method.

3.2 Crossing Points Computation

Now that the sub-clouds have been established, it is needed to compute the crossing points - points where three or more proxy planes meet. This means that they lie on the border of multiple sub-clouds, and polygon meshes can be created from the VSA division by connecting the crossing points.

Both D. Cohen-Steiner et al. [5] and M. Skrodzkia et al. [16] compute a crossing point as the intersection between three or more proxy planes. This could create crossing points rather far from the original presumed surface, namely if the planes have a big difference in their normals, which is quite common for non-smooth surfaces such as terrain models. Therefore we chose a different approach to the detection of crossing points, outlined in Algorithm 2 and described below.

Two proxies neighbor if at least one point from one proxy neighbors with any point from the other. These neighborhoods can be interpreted as a proxy graph, where the vertices represent the proxies and an edge forms if the two proxies neighbor. Using the Bron-Kerbosch algorithm [1] the maximal clique can be found. It is a group of vertices from the graph, where each pair is connected by an edge and there is no additional vertex that could be added while preserving the connectivity condition of the group. In the proxy graph this means that in a clique each pair of proxies neighbors each other. If there is three or more members in the clique, they should create at least one crossing point.

The o crossing points $C_0...C_{o-1}$ in the dataset are determined from the maximal cliques as follows. For each point p in each proxy in each clique cq are found all points in radius r, if p has two or more neighbors, each from a different proxy, p is saved as a candidate point of a group of proxies containing its proxy and the proxies of the neighbors. For each saved group of proxies the candidate points are then averaged to create one crossing point.

There is a possibility that no candidate points will be found for some cliques. This is caused by the difficulty of correctly estimating neighborhoods in point

Input: $P_0 ... P_{m-1}$ - a set of proxies and their assigned distinct point clouds,
r - radius used for neighborhood definition
Output: $C_0 ... C_{o-1}$ - crossing points
cq = maximal clique in graph of $P_0 ... P_{m-1}$;
for *each proxy* P_i *in* cq **do**
  for *point* p *in* P_i **do**
    Find all points closer to p than r and their proxies nn_p;
    if $|nn_p \cap cq| + 1 == |cq|$ **then**
      Save p as candidate crossing point for cq;
    end
    if $|nn_p \cap cq| + 1 > 2$ *and* $|nn_p \cap cq| + 1 < |cq|$ **then**
      Save p as candidate crossing point for $(nn_p \cap cq) \cup P_i$;
    end
  end
end
for *each saved group of candidates* GC_i **do**
  Create a crossing point C_i by averaging points in the group;
end

Algorithm 2: Crossing points computation.

clouds. To compute the crossing point for such a clique, we find a group of m nearest points from these m proxies, where each point is from a different proxy.

Sometimes, crossing points should be created in areas where only two proxies meet. This can happen for terrain data scanned in tiles near the edges of the dataset. In the case that we are processing such data, we need to add more crossing points created from points near the borders of the dataset that have some neighbors from a different proxy. This is described in Algorithm 3.

3.3 Domain Border Computation

The third step of the proposed algorithm is computing the domain borders of the created sub-clouds projected onto their best fitted plane. For this, it is advantageous to use alpha shapes as they approximate the shape of the point cloud well. The alpha shape of a set of points is formed by all edges between two points, where there exists a circle of radius $1/\alpha$ that has the two points on its boundary and does not contain any other points from the set. Alpha shape is a generalization of the convex hull, this means that every convex hull is an alpha shape, but not every alpha shape is a convex hull [8].

To determine the domains, alpha shape is computed for each sub-cloud. The sub-cloud is projected onto its best-fitting plane, then each pair of points is tested against the empty circle condition mentioned in the previous paragraph. If the condition is met, an edge connecting the two points is added to the alpha shape. This outputs the alpha shape as a set of edges. In it we find the longest polygon cycle - the outer part of the alpha shape, given correctly set parameter α. This forms the border of the sub-cloud. The borders of two neighboring sub-clouds will not be identical and will have to be further processed.

```
Input: P_0...P_m - a set of proxies and their assigned distinct point clouds
Output: C_0...C_{r-1} - crossing points
for each proxy P_i do
    for point p in P_i do
        if p is near the border of the dataset then
            Find k nearest neighbors of p and their proxies nn_p;
            if |nn_p| + 1 == 2 then
                Save p as candidate crossing point for nn_p ∪ P_i;
            end
        end
    end
end
for each saved group of candidates GC_i do
    Create a crossing point C_i by averaging points in the group;
end
```

Algorithm 3: Crossing points computation on the edges of the dataset.

3.4 Poly-Line Interpolation

To create the feature curves from the detected borders, it is necessary to compute the proxy neighbor of each point on the border a_i. First, the neighboring points from other proxies Q_i in a radius r are found. The point $q \in Q_i$ that is the closest to a_i determines the proxy that is the neighbor of a_i. This way we can establish which part of the alpha shape borders each one of the neighboring proxies.

To estimate the feature curve between two sub-clouds it is needed to interpolate the borders of the two neighboring sub-clouds. As each border is represented by a poly-line, this translates to interpolating two poly-lines L_i and L_j, where each has a different number of points. First, it is needed to label the poly-lines so that L_i contains more points than the poly-line L_j. Then for each point in L_i the closest point from L_j is found. The point on the feature curve is then computed as the average of this pair of points.

Given two sub-clouds P_i and P_j and their respective alpha shapes A_i and A_j, neighboring parts of the alpha shapes can be found by detecting all points from A_i that have P_j as the nearest proxy neighbor. These points are then connected into the shortest sequence along the alpha shape. The same procedure is then computed for all points from A_j that have P_i as the nearest proxy neighbor. This leaves us with two poly-lines that will be interpolated in the next step.

This creates a set of feature curves. Each feature curve lies in between two sub-clouds, but the curves do not connect to each other to form seamless borders between the sub-clouds. This is addressed in the last step of the algorithm.

3.5 Connecting the Dots

The final step of the proposed algorithm is to connect the created feature curves with the detected crossing points, so that they would fully divide the sub-clouds from each other. Each feature curve lies between two sub-clouds. For each of the two points on the ends of the feature curve find a distinct closest crossing point neighboring the same two sub-clouds.

4 Results

The proposed method was implemented using *C#* and ran on a computer with an *Intel(R) Core(TM) i7-9700K* CPU, 32 GB of memory and *Windows 10* OS. The method was tested on point clouds with various point count and density, acquired from public repositories [11,17], and point clouds we created - *"Sphere"*, *"Cube"* and *"Noisy Sphere 1-3"*. Two types of data were tested - those representing 3D objects, resized to fit into a bounding box of size $1 \times 1 \times 1$ without altering their proportions, and terrain data acquired by LIDAR scanning, resized so the coordinates of the points are in the interval $< 0, 1 >$ in all axes.

The method requires to set the values of the following parameters:

1. For the Point-cloud segmentation step: starting number of proxies m, maximum iterations it, maximum divergence from proxy $maxD$.
2. For alpha shape computation step: value of α for each sub-cloud.
3. For the Crossing points computation and Division into neighboring parts steps: radius r used for proxy neighbor computation.

The parameter m was set to 50 for all inputs. The segmentation algorithm achieved better results in terms of the nearly planar condition than with lower values of m and further increasing it has not shown any further significant improvement. Similarly, the parameter it was set to 100 for all inputs. The parameters $maxD$, the parameter α for each sub-cloud and parameter r for neighbor computation were set empirically for each input.

The implemented VSA algorithm incorporates the merge and split operations which reduce the dependance of the output on the values of the parameters. The most important parameter is $maxD$, the target approximation error threshold, defining how well the resulting sub-clouds adapt to the complexity of the input point cloud. We propose to set $maxD$ as roughly 10% of the size of the bounding box of the data as this provides a good starting point. Higher values of the parameter are advisable for noisy or sparse data, for denser data lower values work better (e.g. the *"Stanford Bunny"* dataset). If the dataset should be approximated by lower amount of proxies, the parameter $maxD$ should be a higher value (e.g. the *"Sphere"* dataset).

Similarly, we propose setting the parameter r as roughly 10% of the size of the bounding box of the data. For sparser data the value of r has to be increased. When it comes to the parameter α for each sub-cloud setting them manually gives us bigger control over the result.

The specific values of the parameters used to obtain the presented results will be discussed along with the analysis of the results in the following subsections. The results are difficult to evaluate using any standard metric, since, as of yet, there is no definition of an ideal curve between two sub-clouds, especially for terrain data. Comparison with other methods also proved difficult, as the most similar works, method proposed by Cao et al. [4] and method proposed by Z. Lu et al. [12], both work with meshes. Therefore the results were evaluated visually by experts in the field working with geodata.

Objects

The proposed method was first tested for point clouds representing 3D objects - namely dataset *"Cube"*, dataset *"Sphere"* and dataset *"Stanford Bunny"*. The results can be seen in Fig. 4 along with the parameters used to achieve them. The parameter α was set to the same value for all created sub-clouds. The created nearly planar sub-clouds are visualized by the different coloring of the points and the created feature curves are visualized as the red poly-lines.

As expected, the *"Cube"* dataset is divided into six sub-clouds, one for each side of the cube with feature curves following the edges of the cube. The *"Sphere"* dataset is also divided into six sub-clouds, similarly to the *"Cube"*.

In Fig. 4 it can also be seen that the detected feature curves for the *"Cube"* dataset do not lie directly on the edges, but are located more towards the center of the point cloud. This is especially noticeable at the crossing points located at the corners of the cube. This is caused by the fact that the crossing points and the feature curves are computed as averages of points from the sub-clouds.

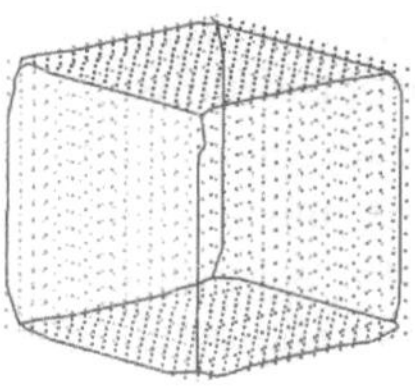

(a) Cube
$maxD = 0.1$,
$r = 0.2$, $\alpha = 0.01$

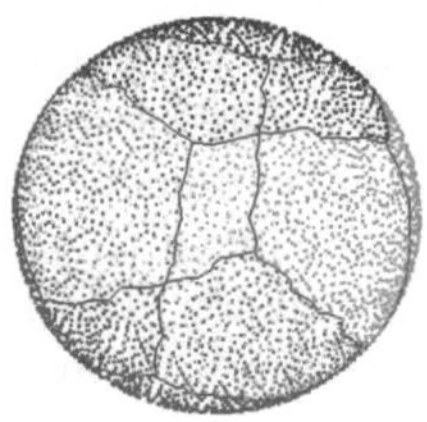

(b) Sphere
$maxD = 0.2$,
$r = 0.5$, $\alpha = 0.029$

(c) Stanford Bunny
$maxD = 0.03$, $r = 0.03$, $\alpha = 0.029$

Fig. 4. Resulting segmentation of object data.

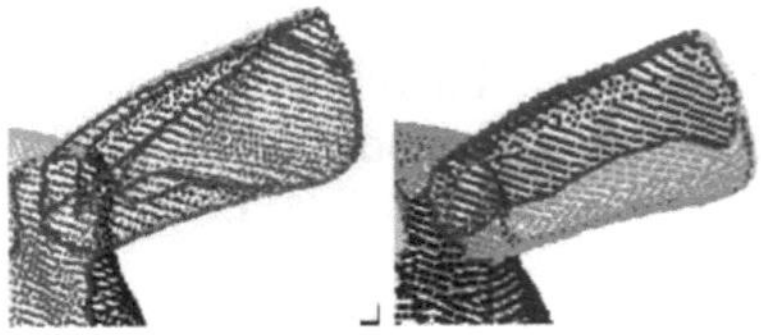

Fig. 5. Stanford Bunny - feature curves going "through" the object ($maxD = 0.05$) on the left, results without the artifact ($maxD = 0.03$) on the right.

For the more elaborate model *"Stanford Bunny"* the value of parameter r was chosen much lower than for the other two datasets. This is because of the higher density of the point cloud. The value for the parameter $maxD$ was also set lower.

The importance of correctly setting the parameter $maxD$ can be demonstrated on the example in Fig. 5. The value of this parameter influences the created sub-clouds, namely their planarity. The lower the value, the more sub-clouds are created, since $maxD$ controls the maximum deviation of the sub-cloud from its best fitted plane. Incorrectly setting this parameter would negatively influence the computation of alpha shapes and in turn the created feature curves. This problem could present itself as feature curves leading "through" the object, for example for parameter $maxD = 0.05$ on the ear of the bunny. If the parameter $maxD$ was decreased to 0.03, this artifact did not appear. In conclusion, if this kind of artifact appears, the value of $maxD$ should be decreased.

The method was also tested for a synthetic datasets with noise. The Fig. 6 presents results for a cube model with varying amounts of noise along with the parameters used to achieve them. The parameter α was set to the same value for all created sub-clouds. The rule for setting the parameters usually is, that the more noisy the dataset is, the higher the value of $maxD$ and α. Figure 6 shows that as the noise grows stronger, the VSA method separates the cube into more sub-clouds that necessary. The feature curves are more "fractured" because they are created as interpolation of points in the data. One of the focuses of our future work will be improving our method so that it is more robust to noise.

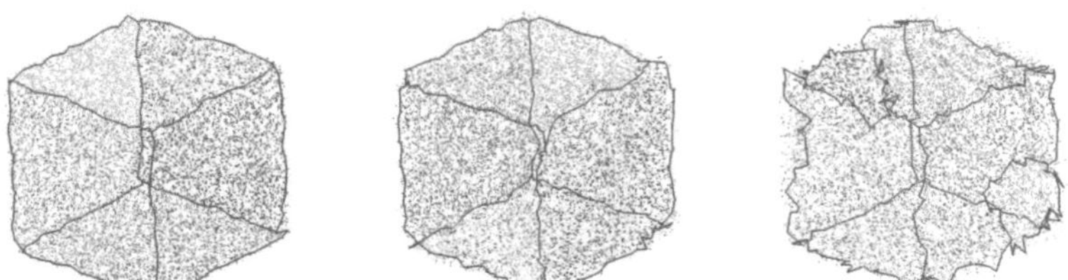

(a) Noisy cube 1 $maxD = 0.1$, $r = 0.5$, $\alpha = 0.01$

(b) Noisy cube 2 $maxD = 0.2$, $r = 0.5$, $\alpha = 0.01$

(c) Noisy cube 3 $maxD = 0.2$, $r = 0.5$, $\alpha = 0.02$

Fig. 6. Resulting segmentation of noisy data.

Terrain Data

The proposed method was also tested for terrain point clouds acquired by LIDAR scanning - namely the Mount Saint Helens dataset, tiles *"Mount Saint Helens NW"*, *"Mount Saint Helens NE"* and *"Spirit Lake West SW"*. The results and the used parameters are in Fig. 7. The created VSA sub-clouds are visualized by the different coloring of points and the created feature curves as the red colored poly-lines. The parameter α for each sub-cloud was chosen empirically.

Looking at the results for *"Mount Saint Helens NW"* (Fig. 7(a)), it can be seen that the method is able to successfully divide terrain data into nearly planar sub-clouds, and detect the most important feature curves that form the borders between the sub-clouds. The number of created sub-clouds depends on the value of the parameter $minD$, similarly to for the object datasets.

Terrain data has some properties, such as noise, varying point densities and more elaborate changes in the underlying surface, which can cause some specific problems. First, most noticeable and more common complication, is the existence of "island" sub-clouds - sub-clouds that neighbor only with one other sub-cloud. This can be seen in both *"Mount Saint Helens NE"* (Fig. 7(b)) and *"Spirit Lake West SW"* (Fig. 7(c)). These sub-clouds cannot be processed using the same approach as described in Sect. 3.5. Instead, the whole alpha shape is proclaimed as a feature curve around the sub-cloud.

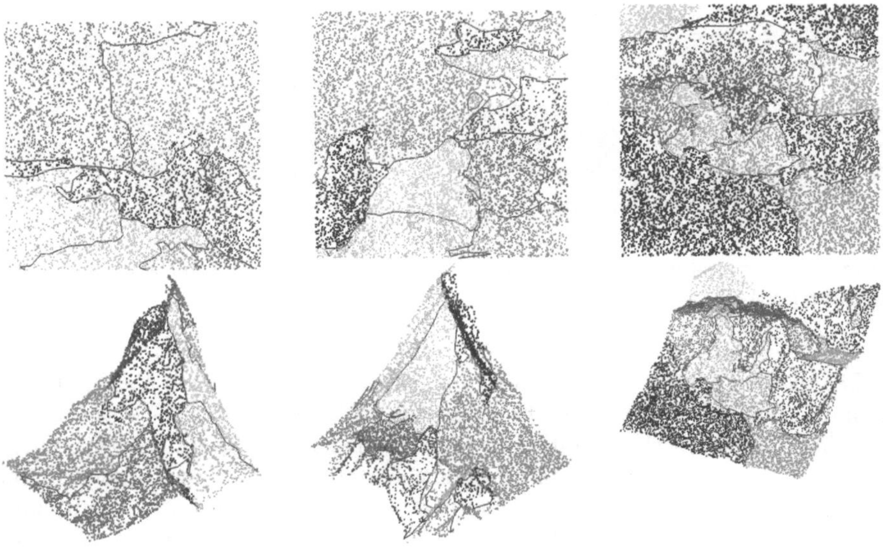

(a) Mount Saint Helens NW $maxD = 0.08$, $r = 0.04$ (b) Mount Saint Helens NE $maxD = 0.08$, $r = 0.03$ (c) Spirit Lake West SW $maxD = 0.08$, $r = 0.03$

Fig. 7. Resulting segmentation of terrain data.

In more rare cases, if the configuration of points is such that there is a larger hole in a place where two or more sub-clouds should meet, the points of those sub-clouds do not neighbor each other. This problem corresponds to the problem of neighborhood detection in point clouds. This complication can cause two types of artifacts - missing feature curves and missing crossing points. Both can be seen in the dataset *"Spirit Lake West SW"* in Fig. 7(c) and in more detail in Fig. 8. The missing crossing point artifact (in Fig. 8 in the upper rectangle) is in a place, where crossing point would be expected, but is not detected by the algorithm in the Crossing points computation step, as the two proxies do not neighbor each other near the border due to the hole in the data. The missing feature curves artifact (in Fig. 8 in the lower rectangle) was caused by incorrect proxy neighborhood assignment in the Division into neighboring parts step.

Execution Time Analysis

This subsection discusses the time needed for the execution of the algorithm for the previously discussed input data. The algorithm steps mentioned in this subsection correspond to the steps described in Sect. 3. The measured times can be seen in Table 1 and are visualized in the graph in Fig. 9.

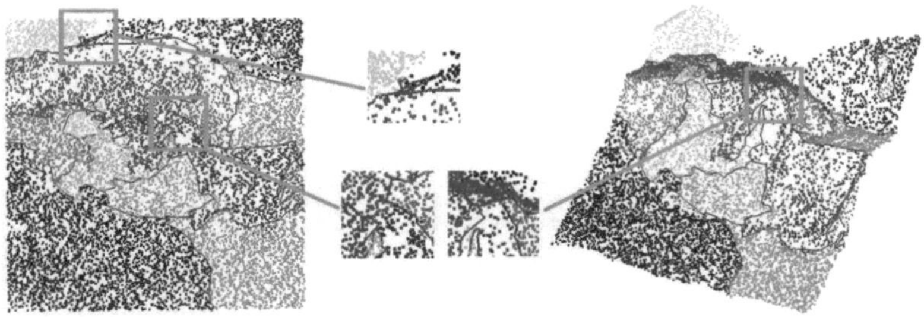

Fig. 8. Missing crossing point artifact and missing border artifact in the dataset *"Spirit Lake West SW"*.

For most of the inputs the most time consuming step is Step 1 - Point cloud segmentation. Its is implemented using the VSA algorithm, where the parameter that influences the results and time needed for computation the most is the parameter $maxD$. Lowering its value causes the creation of a higher number of sub-clouds. This means the method will be more time consuming, as it causes more strict requirements on the planarity of the created sub-clouds and causes more splits and merges. Another property causing the VSA to increase in time requirements is the complexity of the data. The more complex the dataset is, the more sub-clouds will be created and more splits and merges will be done during the computation. The more noisy the data, the more time is proportionally spent in the Step 1, as is demonstrated for the inputs *"Noisy cube 2"* and *"Noisy cube 3"*. Terrain datasets are also generally more complex then point clouds representing objects and therefore for them the VSA algorithm will be more time consuming. Naturally, it is possible to incorporate approaches to increase the speed of the VSA algorithm, such as parallelization.

The time needed for the computation of Step 2 (Crossing point computation), 4 and 5 (Poly-line interpolation and Connecting the dots) is influenced by the density of the data and the size of the radius r used during neighborhood computation. More neighbors for a point mean longer computation time. The results for most of the object datasets have been acquired using a larger radius, and therefore more time is proportionally spend in the Step 2. The influence of the radius size is also very visible for the object datasets for the Steps 4 and 5. The *"Stanford Bunny"* dataset has a smaller radius of $r = 0.03$ and proportionally spends much less time in the Steps 4 and 5. This is also the reason why the terrain datasets spend the least time in those steps.

Since it is needed to correctly set the parameters to get the best possible output, the method (or more often just some of its steps) have to be re-run multiple times before the correct value of the parameters are found. The most often repeated step is Step 3 - Domain border computation. Fortunately, it is usually the fastest, especially if we take into consideration the fact that the times presented in Table 1 are for the computation of the domains for all of the subclouds, computing one domain is faster.

Table 1. Time needed for computation.

Dataset	Point count	Step 1 [s]	Step 2 [s]	Step 3 [s]	Step 4 + 5 [s]
Cube	1 538	1.854	5.229	0.687	5.160
Sphere	3 842	2.684	15.967	0.457	16.243
Mount Saint Helens NW	6 324	12.44	0.045	1.091	0.094
Mount Saint Helens NE	8 440	27.900	0.048	1.777	0.232
Noisy cube 1	10 000	3.182	79.544	3.180	31.105
Noisy cube 2	10 000	3.329	84.166	2.991	29.084
Noisy cube 3	10 000	37.335	27.201	1.389	28.140
Spirit Lake West SW	11 993	36.494	12.195	2.326	0.074
Stanford Bunny	34 834	224.475	272.800	7.804	0.521

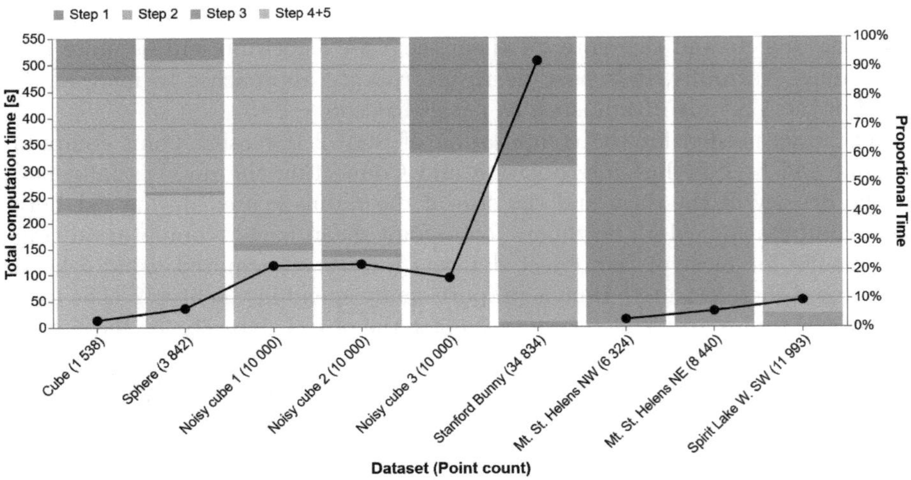

Fig. 9. Graph of the times needed for computation of the presented results. Objects are grouped together on the left and terrain datasets on the right.

5 Conclusion

This paper proposes a method for point cloud segmentation that captures the high level geometric structure of the point cloud. The method works with the input point cloud without reconstructing the underlying surface and the feature curves are determined from the created sub-clouds.

The created nearly planar sub-clouds are computed using the VSA algorithm modified for point clouds. Each is a sub-set of points from the input point cloud, where no two sub-sets share points. The method detects the most important feature curves in the data, each represented by a set of vertices. First the border of the domain of each sub-cloud projected onto its best fitted plane is obtained by computing the alpha shape, then the alpha shape is divided into poly-lines that are finally interpolated with the poly-lines of neighboring sub-clouds.

The main motivation behind this work was to create a method for terrain data, which was successful, and as demonstrated, the proposed approach works for point clouds representing 3D objects as well. The output of the algorithm simplifies the problem of working with the 3D point cloud data, as one would work with multiple sets of data in 2D. The feature lines projected into 2D form the borders of the sub-clouds and can be trivially improved using standard 2D techniques to remove possible self-intersections and form simple polygons.

The main downside of the method is the difficulty of establishing neighborhoods in point clouds and the need to manually set parameters of the method. In the future, we aim to improve it to be more robust to the neighborhood establishment problem, so it can work with more noisy input. Based on longer cooperation with experts on working with geodata, we will focus on developing a reliable automatic method for parameter setting, so that the results will still correctly reflect the realities of the data. Further improvements could also include the smoothing of the feature curves and more focus on increasing the speed of the algorithm, namely the Point cloud segmentation step, which was demonstrated to be the most time consuming for the terrain data.

Acknowledgments. This work was supported by a specific research project SGS-2025-022 New Data Processing Methods in Current Areas of Computer Science of the University of West Bohemia.

Disclosure of Interests. The authors have no competing interests to declare that are relevant to the content of this paper.

References

1. Aloysius, D.R.: Bron-Kerbosch Algorithm. PopulPublishing (2012)
2. Baharami, H., Piovarci, M., Tarini, M., Bickel, B., Pietroni, N.: Fabricable discretized ruled surfaces. ACM Trans. Graph. **44**(3), 1–15 (2025). https://doi.org/10.1145/3734519
3. Bazazian, D., Parés, M.E.: EDC-net: edge detection capsule network for 3D point clouds. Appl. Sci. **11**(4), 1833 (2021). https://doi.org/10.3390/app11041833
4. Cao, Y., Yan, D.M., Wonka, P.: Patch layout generation by detecting feature networks. Comput. Graph. **46**, 275–282 (2015). https://doi.org/10.1016/j.cag.2014.09.022
5. Cohen-Steiner, D., Alliez, P., Desbrun, M.: Variational shape approximation. ACM Trans. Graph. (2004). https://doi.org/10.1145/1015706.1015817
6. Dai, A., Ritchie, D., Bokeloh, M., Reed, S., Sturm, J., Nießner, M.: Scancomplete: large-scale scene completion and semantic segmentation for 3D scans. In: 2018 IEEE/CVF Conference on Computer Vision and Pattern Recognition (2018). https://doi.org/10.1109/CVPR.2018.00481
7. de Goes, F., Goldenstein, S., Desbrun, M., Velho, L.: Exoskeleton: curve network abstraction for 3D shapes. Comput. Graph. (2011). https://doi.org/10.1016/j.cag.2010.11.012
8. Edelsbrunner, H.: Tessellations in the Sciences: Virtues, Techniques and Applications of Geometric Tilings. Springer (2011)
9. Hossain, M.D., Chen, D.: Segmentation for object-based image analysis (OBIA): a review of algorithms and challenges from remote sensing perspective. ISPRS J. Photogram. Remote Sens. **150**, 115–134 (2019). https://doi.org/10.1016/j.isprsjprs.2019.02.009
10. Lee, K.W., Bo, P.: Feature curve extraction from point clouds via developable strip intersection. J. Comput. Des. Eng. (2016). https://doi.org/10.1016/J.JCDE.2015.07.001
11. Levoy, M., Gerth, J., Curless, B., Pull, K.: The Stanford 3D scanning repository (2005). https://graphics.stanford.edu/data/3Dscanrep
12. Lu, Z., Guo, J., Xiao, J., Wang, Y., Zhang, X., Yan, D.: Extracting cycle-aware feature curve networks from 3D models. Comput.-Aided Des. (2021). https://doi.org/10.1016/j.CAD.2020.102949
13. Salem, N., Hussein, S.: Data dimensional reduction and principal components analysis. Procedia Comput. Sci. **163**, 292–299 (2019). https://doi.org/10.1016/j.procs.2019.12.111

14. Sarker, S., et al.: A comprehensive overview of deep learning techniques for 3D point cloud classification and semantic segmentation. Mach. Vis. Appl. **35**(4) (2024). https://doi.org/10.1007/s00138-024-01543-1
15. Sharma, G., Liu, D., Maji, S., Kalogerakis, E., Chaudhuri, S., Měch, R.: ParSeNet: a parametric surface fitting network for 3D point clouds. In: Vedaldi, A., Bischof, H., Brox, T., Frahm, J.-M. (eds.) ECCV 2020. LNCS, vol. 12352, pp. 261–276. Springer, Cham (2020). https://doi.org/10.1007/978-3-030-58571-6_16
16. Skrodzkia, M., Zimmermannb, E., Polthier, K.: Variational shape approximation of point set surfaces. Comput. Aided Geom. Des. (2020). https://doi.org/10.1016/j.CAGD.2020.101875
17. University of Washington Libraries: Mount saint helens - lidar data (2003). https://wagda.lib.washington.edu/data/type/elevation/lidar/st_helens/toutle03.html
18. Wu, J., Kobbelt, L.: Structure recovery via hybrid variational surface approximation. Comput. Graph. Forum (2005). https://doi.org/10.1111/J.1467-8659.2005.00852.X
19. Wu, Y., Liu, J., Gong, M., Miao, Q., Ma, W.: Joint Semantic Segmentation using representations of Lidar Point Clouds and camera images (2023). https://doi.org/10.2139/ssrn.4426132
20. Xie, Y., Tian, J., Zhu, X.X.: Linking points with labels in 3D: a review of point cloud semantic segmentation. IEEE Geosci. Remote Sens. Mag. **8**(4), 38–59 (2020). https://doi.org/10.1109/mgrs.2019.2937630
21. Yan, D.-M., Liu, Y., Wang, W.: Quadric surface extraction by variational shape approximation. In: Kim, M.-S., Shimada, K. (eds.) GMP 2006. LNCS, vol. 4077, pp. 73–86. Springer, Heidelberg (2006). https://doi.org/10.1007/11802914_6
22. Yan, S., Yang, Z., Ma, C., Huang, H., Vouga, E., Huang, Q.: Hpnet: deep primitive segmentation using hybrid representations. In: 2021 IEEE/CVF International Conference on Computer Vision (ICCV), pp. 2733–2742 (2021). https://doi.org/10.1109/iccv48922.2021.00275
23. Zhao, T., Busé, L., Cohen-Steiner, D., Boubekeur, T., Thiery, J.M., Alliez, P.: Variational shape reconstruction via quadric error metrics. Special Interest Group on Computer Graphics and Interactive Techniques Conference Conference Proceedings, pp. 1–10 (2023). https://doi.org/10.1145/3588432.3591529

Author Index

O. Gervasi et al. (Eds.): ICCSA 2026, LNCS 16768, pp. 703–705, 2027.
https://doi.org/10.1007/978-3-032-30488-9

MIX
Papier aus verantwortungsvollen Quellen
Paper from responsible sources
FSC® C105338

If you have any concerns about our products,
you can contact us on
ProductSafety@springernature.com

In case Publisher is established outside the EU,
the EU authorized representative is:
Springer Nature Customer Service Center GmbH
Europaplatz 3, 69115 Heidelberg, Germany

Printed by Libri Plureos GmbH
in Hamburg, Germany